Wine behind the label

2004 edition

Philip Williamson & David Moore

Williamson Moore Publishing Limited

First published in 2003 by Williamson Moore
34 Ivy Close Winchester Hampshire SO22 4QR United Kingdom
Tel/Fax +44 (0)1962 865 693
E-mail: info@williamson-moore.co.uk

A catalogue record for this book is available from the British Library.

ISBN 0-9544097-1-X

Designed by Nucleus
Editor: Janey Gilbert
Editorial assistance from Bill Evans and Ed Francis

Printed and bound in Great Britain by Biddles Limited
Guildford & King's Lynn

Whilst every care has been taken in the preparation of this guide,
the publishers and authors cannot accept responsibility of any kind for
consequences arising from reliance upon information contained in it.

Contents

Introduction   5

About the authors   7

How to use this guide   9

EUROPE

   FRANCE

   Bordeaux   11

   Médoc, Graves & Sauternes   19

   St Emilion, Pomerol & other Bordeaux   45

   Burgundy   66

   Chablis & Yonne   78

   Côte d'Or & Côte Chalonnaise   89

   Mâconnais & Beaujolais   142

   Alsace   153

   Champagne   165

   Loire Valley   179

   Rhône Valley   198

   Northern Rhône   205

   Southern Rhône   221

   Languedoc-Roussillon & Provence   246

   Regional France   276

   ITALY

   Piedmont & North-West Italy   285

   Tuscany   327

   North-East Italy   375

   Central Italy   398

   Southern Italy & Islands   411

   SPAIN (incl. Sherry)   430

   PORTUGAL (incl. Port & Madeira)   451

   GERMANY   480

   AUSTRIA & SWITZERLAND   508

   OTHER EUROPE & MIDDLE EAST   520

NORTH AMERICA

California North Coast	**524**
Napa & Carneros	**544**
California Central Coast	**574**
Oregon & Washington	**591**
Rest of North America	**603**

SOUTH AMERICA   **606**

AUSTRALASIA

AUSTRALIA

South Australia	**619**
Victoria & Tasmania	**660**
New South Wales & Queensland	**683**
Western Australia	**691**

NEW ZEALAND   **702**

AFRICA

SOUTH AFRICA   **719**

Grape Glossary	**729**
Glossary	**740**
Agent codes	**749**
Index	**770**

Our concept

When we finalised the concept of this guide nearly two years prior to releasing the 2003 edition, we were aware of the frustration of wine drinkers at the lack of a single authoritative guide that could provide both depth and criticism about quality wines whatever their provenance. In an age of 'dumbing down' we opted instead for 'wising up' yet endeavoured to produce a reference that is accessible to the novice and learned alike. Even more important than providing a critical assessment of a producer's wine we are trying to provide more pertinent information about as many quality wine producers as possible. It is a guide for enthusiasts or would-be enthusiasts, not for those who can't detect any differences or don't care too. Those producers profiled with their own entry are a selection of the best established producers and some of the new and upcoming stars. In this, the 2004 edition, we have added a significant number of new producers of quality wine yet it is still far from exhaustive. The very best of those listed at the end of each section and other emerging stars will be profiled in future editions.

Our philosophy

The industrial mentality which has given us brilliant cars and computers doesn't have a place in high quality wine (or food) production. An essential difference between a high production brand and one produced on a more human scale is the personal effort and commitment that the family or individuals who make it have put into it. We have tried to bring the producer a little closer to whoever is drinking their wine so that some inkling of their philosophy and effort might enrich the enjoyment the wine brings. It is our intention to give strong support both to small producers and talented winemakers but every quality wine is considered on it merits. A small producer, no matter how earnest or sincere, will not make good wine if he or she doesn't manage the vineyards well and employ sound winemaking practice. Equally, spending exorbitant sums on PR and marketing doesn't always mean the wine in the bottle is poor – though it is likely given the money spent that it could be better value. More and more of the world's finest wines are hard to get hold of but in many instances there is a first point of contact that will sell direct by mail-order or over the Internet. (see also Buying Guide under Agent codes). Browsing a section will also highlight alternatives.

Winemaking ethics

Specifically bringing to account those involved in bad or unethical production is not within the scope of this book. However we do want to encourage producers to be open in providing as much information as possible about what they are producing and what techniques are employed in the wine-making. Rather than making judgements about new technologies we'd simply like to give the reader a clearer idea of to what extent their wine has been processed (including the use of additives and the extent of fining and/or filtration). We want, too, to pass on information about whether the wines are produced according to organic or biodynamic principles. The current trend to giving more detail about a wine's provenance we'd also like to encourage. Even if a wine is sourced from numerous small parcels and these change from year to year, any single vintage of a wine has to be sourced from a definable area or areas. It is not an argument about the quality of single vineyard wines versus blends as the latter may often be superior. It is a case of providing more information and allowing the consumer to learn something of the individual parcel or parcels that play a part in the wine's character. It is also of course a way of keeping tabs on the biggest premium brands. Some famous names have for instance, lost some of the finest vineyard sources which contributed to their early quality and fame. It is also our hope that more producers will also provide information concerning the total production of a given vintage, yield per ha, density of vines per hectare and most importantly average yield per vine.

Help

This guide does contain a lot of information about producers and their wines. This year we have added two new features we hope will help you find the information you need more quickly. The lists of producers by appellation or region at the end of each section's introduction should make it clearer as to who is covered, and from where. We also appreciate that most readers probably only have the time to dip in and out of the book and to this end have added an 'Author's Choice' at the end of each section. These contain a selection of some of the best and most interesting wines though are necessarily more limited in their usefulness in the regions with the most extensive coverage. It is hoped that they will serve as an alternative starting point to discovering new producers.

The response to our first edition 2003 has been fantastic and for 2005 we want to do still more. Single page map inserts as a quick reference is one suggestion but we'd like as much input as possible and will encourage this through our website as we develop it further. Alternatively please write to, or email, us with your constructive criticisms.

Tasting, ratings, and assessing producers

Our ratings as explained in the How to Use section more fully reflect a wine's true quality as they are almost always based on a minimum of two vintages. These are recent vintages as we give short shrift to the one vintage wonders or those where the quality has fallen away. Wine shows and competitions encourage the production of wines of flattering first impressions but don't always reward those that show at their best with age. Nor do they address the implications of the vintage characteristics. Rather than a snapshot, consensual tasting mentality we believe in tasting wines again and again (both blind and non-blind) in order to gain a better understanding of a wine's style and when it should be drunk. This we have endeavoured to pass on in individual producer entries. A rating combined with an understanding of the style is the key to discovering the best wines. A higher rating doesn't necessarily reflect a better wine but one that may develop more complexity, have the structure for greater longevity or simply show greater intensity or persistence in the mouth.

We have focussed less on whether a wine tastes of this or that and more on whether it brings enjoyment. The question should always be which wine works best now, reflects my mood, personality or whatever ? What flavours do I want? How much flavour? Whether the wine is drunk immediately or cellared. If it is kept the character of different vintages of the same wine can be contrasted. Alternatively from a case of the same wine the gradual development and increasing maturity of a specific vintage can be assessed over a decade or more.

Conclusion

Think of this book as a catalogue to a vast array of vinous riches. Choose with the certainty of trying wines of dependable quality that our labours and experience provide through our rating system. If you haven't tasted Austrian Grüner Veltliner or Californian Syrah then try a three star example from at least two or three profiled producers. Buy the best new reds from the Languedoc-Roussillon or Portugal's Douro, try old-vine Barossa Shiraz or a Barolo of certifiable class. Alternatively seek out new names from Burgundy, Bordeaux or the Rhône. Most of all we implore you to taste more widely.

Philip Williamson

I only took a serious interest in wine in my mid-twenties having rarely drunk it before then, well save a nasty bottle or two at University. After entrying the wine trade in 1987 I have spent more than half the subsequent 16 years devoted solely to assessing wine quality and writing about it. My greatest inspiration has been great bottles of wine and some of the wonderful individuals who have created them; propelled on by special moments whether a sip of Domaine Leflaive whites or tasting with Aldo Conterno in Piedmont.

I've also enjoyed working with Oz Clarke and share his enthusiasm for every new bottle opened that represents human effort and skill. I feel fortunate to have immersed myself in wine during an era of its production that continually provides ever more stimulating and exciting finds. My taste is eclectic and extends from the old classics of Port, Sherry and Madeira, to relatively modern styles such as Barossa Shiraz, Priorat reds or Wachau Riesling even if I'm most passionate about Burgundy and Italy. My considerable experience as both an editor and specialist contributor to leading wine books I believe formed an important part of my apprenticeship prior to undertaking this joint collaboration with my friend, colleague and expert wine taster, David Moore.

Despite a perception of glamour, tasting professionally is often arduous, requiring a disciplined and analytical approach to wine assessment. Yet for me, the most exciting wines continue to provoke an emotional response. Writing about wine also means taking a more detached, considered view – understanding the global picture while being uncompromising in the support of local traditions and diversity. The integrity and honesty I see in the best producers I want to reflect in taking a serious approach to writing about their wines. I want to convey quality and style in such a way as to encourage its wider appreciation including by those normally intimidated by the complexity of the subject. I care most that wine is drunk and enjoyed, a magic drink that should be accessible to all, yet not trivialised or abused; rather a source of pleasure, fun and stimulation – both sensual and cerebral.

Philip Williamson

David Moore

Like many people I became interested in wine quite by chance. In my case it was a trip to the Loire Valley in 1988 and the lure of the trade quickly followed. Since then I've sold and bought wine before teaching, lecturing and for over six years writing about and tasting wine critically. In between I've managed to fit in six months getting my hands dirty in wineries in Australia. This as much as anything has taught me what is involved in producing wines of real quality. I've had the good fortune to witness first hand that wine at its best, is about both the land and people. I'm at my happiest listening to a winemaker in their cellar enthusing about what they do. What I hope we achieve in this book is to guide you to those characters and give a real indication of what they do in making their wines and how they seek to achieve it. Sometimes the results are great and sometimes not.

In the seven or eight years that we've been throwing ideas about and researching this book what continues to intrigue and fascinate me is the sheer diversity that wine has to offer. I'm always at a loss when someone asks me what my favourite wine or region is. Its almost impossible to say. The most important thing is individuality. Really pleasurable drinking can be had when you find wine that truly displays its character and it doesn't have to be expensive. Philip and I have both been judges for a series of themed tastings for the New York Times for wine regions right across the globe. What never ceases to amaze me, even tasting through 120 wines in a day from the same region, is the sheer range of flavours, styles and quality differences often within a single appellation.

What are my dislikes in wine? I feel it should always be enjoyed and not speculated on, the thought of cases of fine claret tucked away in bonded warehouses never likely to see the light of day is a thoroughly depressing one. I also dislike the intellectualising of wine, there is no good reason why people should be made to feel intimidated by the subject. I hope we will go some way in these pages to telling you how it is but lending some interest and understanding to what you're drinking and buying. My greatest hobby is riding a motorcycle at weekends for fun. Not the most conformist of activities but I always feel the greatest wines are made by characters who are just that and their wines always excite me most. Hopefully you'll get some inspiration from these pages and discover some of these gems as well.

David S. Moor

Within each section you will find an introduction including, where possible, vintage information. In this edition we have also added a list of the producers, either by region or appellation, that have been profiled within the A-Z that makes up the bulk of the section. At the end of the A-Z of producers, is a list of other wines of note from that region. Many are of high quality or produce at least one good wine. The best of these are likely to be added to the guide in future editions after further assessment. Some in these lists also produce more quality wines than are indicated as we have included only those we have tasted at least once. At the very end of each section under Author's Choice we have added lists of wines that are a personal selection but are also often themed by a shared style or grape variety and so should aid navigation. For individual A-Z entries we have provided the winery addresses and wherever possible we have also provided website addresses. In some instances we have provided email addresses where there is no website. The use of CAPS (eg Louis JADOT) indicates the existence of a cross-referenced entry that can be found from the Index.

Vintages Charts:

In those sections where vintages have the greatest significance, Vintage Charts are also provided (as is text on individual years for the classic wines of Bordeaux, Burgundy, Piedmont, Tuscany and Port). Specific styles of wine are given an overall vintage rating between one and five stars for individual years. In some instances it is not possible to provide a balanced judgement on the vintage until nearer the wines' release (with Brunello di Montalcino for example). These have been designated NYR (not yet rated). When to drink the wines of a given vintage is a largely subjective, personal judgement and can depend as much on mood or context but the letter (A-D) following the ratings gives a general indication of their likely development:

A - wines to Anticipate, not ready for drinking

B - wines that can be Broached, but with much more to give

C - wines to Consume, at or near their best

D - wines likely to be in Decline, past their best

A-Z Order:

The order of the A-Z entries is based on the name they are most commonly referred to and they appear as they are written but with priority to surnames. 'Domaine' is ignored but 'Château', 'Castello', 'Quinta' etc are respected as is the definite article when implicitly part of the name (eg Il Poggione appears under 'I'). The only exception to these principles is in Bordeaux where the name of the château or estate takes precedent.

A: (Agent code)

'A' in A-Z producer entries indicates the existence of a UK agent or stockists of a given producer's wines. Details of these codes can be found under the Agent Codes section. Also given here is general information on buying wine and additional comments on purchasing wines from Bordeaux – where the complexities of sale and distribution preclude the inclusion of codes. Though not all agents can sell direct to consumers they will at least be able to give details of where the wines can be bought.

Ownership:

Ownership is also given throughout and wherever this appears in *bold* it refers to a corporate owner rather than an individual or individuals. Obviously contact with a corporate owner shouldn't be assumed to be possible via the winery's address that follows it.

How to use this guide

Symbols:

● red wine

O white wine

◉ rosé wine

Ratings:

★   a wine of good quality, not just sound but of good fruit and with some character.

★★   a wine with more depth, interest and concentration, usually with some aging potential

★★★   a very good, even fine, wine. In the case of many reds repaying lengthy cellaring.

★★★★   a wine of very high quality, among the very best even in a top appellation or region.

★★★★★   outstanding quality, potentially a classic.

✪✪✪✪✪   super 5 stars, restricted to the true classics, out-and-out world class.

We have rated as many of a producer's wines as possible, but in some instances the wines are too new or, too scarce to have yet received a rating. Such wines are covered in the text only.

Tasting notes and scores:

It is not in the style of this guide to provide tasting notes for individual vintages along with their scores. However this information will be provided by our website over the coming year and we intend to give readers the opportunity to receive the scores for currently available vintages by electronic means. Given that scores are vintage specific, they sometimes exceed or fall short of the rating that is based on repeated tastings. (also see 'Tasting, Ratings, and assessing producers' in the Introduction)

Prices:

Prices are per bottle but are only an estimation of current retail or market value (particularly as some wines are not imported into the UK or only available through brokers or auction houses). A standard 75cl bottle size is assumed so price codes for those produced only in 1.5 litre (magnums), 50 cl (half litre) or 37.5 cl (half bottle) formats have been given 75cl equivalents. A half bottle costing £8.95 for instance will have a price code of £D.

A: less than £5:00	E: £20 - 30
B: £ 5 - 10	F: £30 - 50
C: £10 - 15	G: £50 - 75
D: £15 - 20	H: £75 or more

To most people Bordeaux is probably the most well-known of France's great wine regions. In recent years it has enjoyed bountiful harvests, the maintenance of quality – and many improvements too – and until the last couple of years a remarkably buoyant market for its premium wines. The last few years have also seen dynamic changes on the Right Bank of the Gironde in Saint-Émilion with major investment in established properties and the creation of a number of exciting new labels. The development of the so-called garagiste wines, produced in tiny quantities all over the Saint-Émilion appellation, has been welcome in instances where exotic and fine and ageworthy blends have been produced from first class isolated terroirs. However, where these wines are sourced from lesser sites, they tend to be simply over-extracted, lacking in class but nevertheless still marketed and sold at very high prices. Perhaps if the current trend towards more realistic pricing in general continues there may be a much-needed reality check. The lesser areas like Fronsac and particularly the Côtes de Castillon continue to forge ahead with exciting developments at prices that mere mortals can afford. It is also important not to lose sight of the fact that there are properties, particularly on the Left Bank in the Médoc, which have consistently been producing some of the world's greatest wines for decades and continue to do so.

Geography

The Bordeaux region can effectively be looked at in three parts. There are the appellations surrounding Bordeaux itself and stretching to both the north and south. These vineyards are all located on the western side of the Gironde estuary and further south the river Garonne. This is often referred to as the Left Bank. The Right Bank comprises the vineyard areas east of the Gironde and the river Dordogne, particularly the appellations of Saint-Émilion and Pomerol near Libourne. There is another vast tract of vineyard land between the Dordogne and the Garonne. This is neither Left nor Right Bank and is largely dry white wine territory, including the large Entre-Deux-Mers AC. The vast bulk of Bordeaux's commercial wine trade emanates from the city itself. Libourne, though, is also important commercially, with a number of its own *négociants*.

Generic Bordeaux

AC **Bordeaux**, the bottle you're most likely to come across, can be sourced anywhere within the large Bordeaux region, which includes the areas mentioned above and other outlying appellations. The total production is mind-boggling. Some 5.5 to 6 million hectolitres of red and nearly another million of white are produced every year. Around two-thirds of this is generic Bordeaux. This would not be such a huge problem in itself but most of the red is vinified from Merlot, the workhorse grape of the region and often grown in heavy and productive soils. This allied to over-ambitious yields is always going to present a challenge to fully ripening the crop. So much generic Bordeaux not only tastes dilute but can also have a green, vegetal component. Ripening the white grapes here tends to be less of a problem and these wines can often be better bets.

Médoc, Graves and Sauternes

Some of the world's greatest and noblest red wines are produced here as well as benchmark sweet whites and a very small amount of immensely stylish dry white. The **Médoc** AC itself, rather than the area of the Médoc which runs from Bordeaux north to Soulac at the mouth of the Gironde, is centred around the small town of Lesparre-Médoc and is the northernmost of the Left Bank ACs. There is a higher proportion of clay in the soil rather than the fabled gravel and the wines are generally soft and forward, with a few better examples. The **Haut-Médoc** encompasses all four of the great communal appellations close to the Gironde (Saint-Estèphe, Pauillac, Saint-Julien and Margaux) as well as Listrac and Moulis. There can be a wide variation in quality in the Haut-Medoc AC but a few properties are very serious indeed, producing classic, long-lived cedary reds. Both **Listrac-Médoc** and **Moulis** are located just to the north-west of Margaux. Listrac seems to offer less potential but there are attempts here to fashion some modern *garagiste*-style wines and make the best of the fruit available. Moulis has greater potential, with a number of very good properties.

The northernmost of the great red wine appellations of the Médoc is **Saint-Estèphe**. There are five Classed Growths and the wines are generally the densest, sturdiest examples of the area. Modern winemaking has gone some way to address those firm youthful tannins and the wines are more approachable than they were even a decade ago and are very impressive at their best. **Pauillac** is synonymous with some of the greatest wines of the region. Châteaux Latour, Lafite-Rothschild and Mouton-Rothschild are all here. The deep gravel vineyards provide an ideal base for these strikingly rich styles laden with cassis and spice. The top wines need considerable age. To the south, the wines of **Saint-Julien** are less opulent than Pauillac, more perfumed and with intense cigar box and cedar notes. There are eleven Classed Growths and the extraordinarily refined Léoville-Las-Cases should be a First Growth in many people's books. **Margaux** is just to the north of Bordeaux and contains 21 Classed Growths. At their best these are are the most elegant and refined wines of the Médoc. For a long time Margaux has been an underperforming appellation but change is happening aplenty – new investment, a renewed commitment to quality and, in Marojallia and Clos du Jaugueyron, the first serious *garagiste* wines on the Left Bank. Marojallia is vinified by Jean-Luc Thunevin, owner of Valandraud, one of the first *garagiste* wines in Saint-Émilion.

Immediately south of Bordeaux, indeed part of the AC is in the outer suburbs of the city, are the vineyards of **Pessac-Léognan**. Originally part of the larger **Graves** appellation it was granted its own appellation status in 1987 in recognition of the superior quality of its sites. The soil is finely drained deep gravel and all of the properties in the 1959 Classification of the Graves are to be found here. Only Haut-Brion, with its First Growth status in the 1855 Classification, was absent from the list. Some splendid reds are produced here as well as a small number of dry whites. At their best these are rich, complex and very ageworthy and rival the great whites of the Côte de Beaune (see Burgundy). White winemaking in general throughout the Graves has improved immeasurably in recent years. The rest of the region stretches to the east and some way south of the Garonne. It is never as good as Pessac-Léognan but some good red and dry white are regularly produced. There are also a few sweet wines under the **Graves Supérieures** AC, but these are largely pretty dull.

Just north-west of the town of Langon are the great sweet wine appellations of Sauternes and Barsac. A third sweet wine appellation, **Cérons**, is immediately to the north but does not benefit to the same degree as the other two AC's from the remarkable geographical influence of the tiny Ciron river, which creates the conditions for the development of noble rot. Cérons and also the sweet wines from immediately across the Garonne in **Sainte-Croix-du-Mont** and **Loupiac** can be impressive but they never achieve the same intense botrytis quality as **Sauternes**. **Barsac** is one of the five communes of Sauternes and properties here may chose to label their wines Sauternes or Barsac. After a run of very successful vintages in the 1980s these wines are now fetching the kinds of prices that make their production economic and indeed profitable. Fifteen to 20 years ago it was nigh-on impossible for producers to achieve a commercial return. Harvesting is incredibly labour-intensive, with multiple *tris* (passes through the vineyard), and the yield is necessarily tiny. However, major investment has dramatically changed the area. Many wines of truly magnificent concentration and intensity are now being made. In the lesser years cryo-extraction has been used by a number of châteaux to improve quality.

Saint-Émilion, Pomerol and the Rest of Bordeaux

Saint-Émilion and Pomerol are the two great names associated with the Right Bank but there are an increasing number of well-priced, exciting wines emerging from the other ACs here. It is also interesting to note that these are all red wine appellations. **Saint-Émilion** itself is the driving force in terms of volume and accounts for some 40 per cent of all wines produced here. As a result it's not surprising that there is a wide variation in quality and very diverse *terroirs*, some exceptional and some, particularly in the southern plains of the AC, distinctly ordinary, with heavy productive soils. Many of Bordeaux's major developments in vinification techniques and the influence of consultant winemakers have their origins in Saint-Émilion. Pre-fermentation cold soaking (or maceration), malolactic fermentation in barrel and micro-oxygenation are now practised all over the world.

Saint-Émilion's Classification was last revised in 1996 and will be again in 2006. There are 14 Premiers Grands Crus Classés with two A-rated properties, Ausone and Cheval-Blanc, as well as 51 properties rated Grand Cru Classé. There have been major investments in recent years in both vineyards and cellars, resulting in some highly priced wines made in very limited quantities. The most notable of these has been La Mondotte, produced at Canon-La-Gaffelière. Many other tiny-production wines or *vins des garagistes* have also emerged. Some have been very impressive, but many are over-extracted and all are expensive.

Pomerol, in contrast, continues to provide some impressive and startlingly opulent wines, full of dark and spicy fruit, generally supple and more approachable than many of the other top wines in Bordeaux. Inevitably there are exceptions to the rule and these tend to occur where there is a higher proportion of Cabernet Franc or Cabernet Sauvignon planted or the soil has more gravel. Pomerol's clay soils suit Merlot very well and provide this uniquely exotic style. Pomerol's wines can also be some of the priciest anywhere on the globe. There has been investment and development here but not on the scale of Saint-Émilion's. The lower tier of the appellation, though, can disappoint. The odd wine of distinction is also beginning to emerge from the lesser Saint-Émilion satellite ACs, **Lussac-Saint-Émilion, Montagne-Saint-Émilion, Puisseguin-Saint-Émilion** and **Saint-Georges-Saint-Émilion,** as well as **Lalande-de-Pomerol**.

To the north-west of Libourne are the areas of **Côtes de Bourg** and **Côtes de Blaye**. The former produces reds, some decent and some very impressive while dry whites are produced in the latter. To the immediate west of Libourne are **Fronsac** and **Canon-Fronsac**. Good, stylish, well-made dark fruited styles have been produced here for a decade or so. To the east of Saint-Émilion are the **Côtes de Castillon** and **Bordeaux-Côtes de Francs**. Again these are areas of great potential and the best wines are still well-priced, if becoming less so.

Between the Dordogne and Garonne rivers is a substantial vineyard area comprising some nine appellations. Geographically and physically by far the most important is the **Entre-Deux-Mers,** an appellation devoted to dry whites. A number of properties here are also producing good AC Bordeaux red. The appellation is all about maximising modern white winemaking with some good results, using pre-fermentation skin contact, ageing on lees and, in the more expensive wines, limited barrel fermentation and ageing with new wood as well. Some well-priced wines have been available for some time now. Vibrant red and rosé is made in the **Premières Côtes de Bordeaux,** just to the east across the Garonne from the city of Bordeaux, and there are good sweet wines on the eastern bank of the river at **Cadillac, Loupiac** and **Sainte-Croix-du-Mont**. In the far east is **Saint-Foy-de-Bordeaux,** where there are reds as well as dry and sweet whites.

A-Z Producers by appellation/region

Médoc, Graves & Sauternes

Barsac
CH. CLIMENS
CH. COUTET
CH. DOISY-DAËNE
CH. DOISY-VÉDRINES
CH. NAIRAC

Graves
CH. DE CHANTEGRIVE
CLOS FLORIDÈNE
CH. VILLA BEL AIR

Haut-Médoc
CH. D'AGASSAC
CH. BELGRAVE
CH. CAMENSAC
CH. CANTEMERLE
CH. CHARMAIL
CH. CISSAC
CH. LA LAGUNE
CH. LANESSAN
MA VÉRITÉ
CH. SOCIANDO-MALLET
CH. LA TOUR CARNET

Listrac-Médoc
CH. CLARKE

Margaux
CH. D'ANGLUDET
CH. BEL AIR MARQUIS D'ALIGRE
CH. BOYD-CANTENAC
CH. BRANE-CANTENAC
CH. CANTENAC-BROWN
CH. DAUZAC
CH. FERRIÈRE
CH. D'ISSAN
CH. KIRWAN
CH. MALESCOT-SAINT-EXUPÉRY
CH. MARGAUX
CH. PALMER
CH. PRIEURÉ-LICHINE
CH. RAUZAN-SÉGLA

Médoc
CH. POTENSAC
CH. ROLLAN-DE-BY

Moulis
CH. CHASSE-SPLEEN
CH. POUJEAUX

Pauillac
CH. D'ARMAILLAC
CH. BATAILLEY
CH. CLERC-MILON
CH. DUHART-MILON
CH. GRAND-PUY-LACOSTE
CH. HAUT-BATAILLEY
CH. LAFITE-ROTHSCHILD
CH. LATOUR
CH. LYNCH-BAGES
CH. MOUTON-ROTHSCHILD
CH. PICHON-LONGUEVILLE
CH. PICHON-LONGUEVILLE-LALANDE
CH. PONTET-CANET

Pessac-Léognan
CH. CARBONNIEUX
CH. LES CARMES HAUT-BRION
DOM. DE CHEVALIER
CH. COUHINS-LURTON
CH. DE FIEUZAL
CH. HAUT-BAILLY
CH. HAUT-BRION
CH. LARRIVET HAUT-BRION
LA SERÉNITÉ
CH. LATOUR MARTILLAC
CH LAVILLE HAUT-BRION
CH. LA LOUVIÈRE
CH. MALARTIC-LAGRAVIÈRE
CH LA MISSION HAUT-BRION
CH. PAPE-CLÉMENT
CH. SMITH-HAUT-LAFITTE
CH. LA TOUR HAUT-BRION

Saint-Estèphe
CH. CALON-SÉGUR
CH. COS D'ESTOURNEL
CH. COS LABORY
CH. HAUT-MARBUZET
CH. LAFON-ROCHET
CH. MONTROSE

Saint-Julien
CH. BEYCHEVELLE
CH. BRANAIRE
CH. DUCRU-BEAUCAILLOU
CH. GLORIA
CH. GRUAUD-LAROSE
CH. LAGRANGE
CH. LANGOA-BARTON
CH LÉOVILLE-BARTON
CH. LÉOVILLE-LAS-CASES
CH. LÉOVILLE-POYFERRÉ
CH. SAINT-PIERRE
CH. TALBOT

Sauternes
CH. D'ARCHE
CH. BASTOR-LAMONTAGNE
CH. CAILLOU
CH. CLOS HAUT-PEYRAGUEY
CH. GUIRAUD
CH. LAFAURIE-PEYRAGUEY
CH. LAMOTHE-GUIGNARD
CH. DE MALLE
CH. RABAUD-PROMIS
CH. RAYMOND-LAFON
CH. DE RAYNE-VIGNEAU
CH. RIEUSSEC
CH. SIGALAS-RABAUD
CH. SUDUIRAUT
CH. LA TOUR BLANCHE
CH. D'YQUEM

Saint-Emilion, Pomerol & other Bordeaux

Bordeaux
CH. THIEULEY
EXCELLENCE DE BOIS PERTUIS

Bordeaux Cotes de Francs
CH. PUYGUERAUD

Bordeaux Supérieur
CH. REIGNAC

Canon-Fronsac
CH. CANON-DE-BREM
CH. MOULIN-PEY-LABRIE

Côtes de Bourg
CH. ROC DE CAMBES

Côtes de Castillon
DOM. DE L'A
CH. D'AIGUILHE
CLOS PUY ARNAUD

Entre-Deux-Mers
CH. BONNET

Fronsac
CH. FONTENIL
CH. MOULIN-HAUT-LAROQUE
CH DE LA RIVIÈRE
CH. LA VIEILLE-CURE

Lussac-Saint-Émilion
LA CROIX DE PEYROLIE

Pomerol
CH. BEAUREGARD
CH LE BON PASTEUR
CH. CERTAN-DE-MAY
CH. CLINET
CLOS L'ÉGLISE
CH. LA CONSEILLANTE
CH. LA CROIX-DE-GAY
CH. L'ÉGLISE-CLINET
CH. L'ÉVANGILE
CH. LA FLEUR-PÉTRUS
CH. GAZIN
CH. LAFLEUR
CH. LATOUR-À-POMEROL
CH. PETIT-VILLAGE
CH. PÉTRUS
CH. LE PIN
CH. TROTANOY
VIEUX-CHÂTEAU-CERTAN

Premières Côtes de Blaye
PASSION DU PRIEURÉ MALESAN

Premières Côtes de Bordeaux
CH. CARSIN
CH. REYNON

Saint-Émilion Grand Cru
CH. LA BIENFAISANCE
CH. FAUGÈRES
CH. FOMBRAUGE
LA MONDOTTE
LE DÔME
CH. MONBOUSQUET
CH. MOULIN SAINT-GEORGES
CH. QUINAULT
CH. TERTRE-RÔTEBOEUF
CH. TEYSSIER
CH. DE VALANDRAUD

Saint-Émilion Grand Cru Classé
CH. ANGÉLUS
CH. L'ARROSÉE
CH. AUSONE
CH. BEAU-SÉJOR-BÉCOT
CH. BEAUSÉJOUR
CH. CANON
CH. CANON-LA-GAFFELIÈRE
CH. CHAUVIN
CH. CHEVAL-BLANC
CH. LA CLOTTE
CH. LA COUSPAUDE
CH. LA DOMINIQUE
CH. FIGEAC
CLOS FOURTET
CH. LA GAFFELIÈRE
CH. GRAND-MAYNE
CH. GRAND-PONTET
CH. MAGDELAINE
CLOS DE L'ORATOIRE
CH. PAVIE
CH. PAVIE-DECESSE
CH. PAVIE MACQUIN
CH. TROPLONG-MONDOT

Bordeaux Vintages

As in other parts of France Bordeaux has been generally very lucky with vintages during the last six or seven years. There hasn't been the uniformly excellent run as there has been, say, in the Rhône Valley from 1998 but after the disappointments of the early 1990s things have been decidedly better. Winemaking has evolved here and generally for the better. With the top reds, particularly, it is worth bearing in mind if you are purchasing from a fine current vintage like 2000 that the approach in the cellar is different to that of 20 years ago. The wines are suppler and more approachable but it remains to be seen whether they will be as long-lived as some of their predecessors.

2002: This looks likely to be a good rather than spectacular vintage for reds. It is also the smallest crop since 1991. However so far this has not had any effect on prices with the recent depressed world economy and global political position dampening consumer enthusiasm. The 2002s are very reasonably priced and maybe this will spin off elsewhere in the wine world. The year has turned out to be more successful in the Medoc, particularly Saint-Julien and to the north. It is predominantly a Cabernet Sauvignon year. Earlier ripening Merlot was most hit by late September rains. Some very good whites were produced and this will be a good year too for Sauternes.

2001: After the magnificent 2000 red vintage this is a good, sometimes very good year for reds with once again an abundant crop. The style is sturdy, dense and with firm tannins and notable but not excessive acidity. These are classically structured wines rather than particularly ripe or opulent ones. Look for good wines on both the Left and Right Banks, including some fine examples from the lesser appellations. Sauternes and sweet wines in general look to be very impressive indeed. This could be the best vintage for botrytised wines since 1990. The dry whites were also close to exceptional.

2000: Quite simply a magnificent year for red Bordeaux. The crop was bountiful and the quality exceptional. The combination of a hot dry August followed by a long even and balmy ripening period throughout September provided the châteaux with perfect late-harvesting conditions. Grapes were picked full of deep colour, super-ripe, fine, supple tannins and intense and heady flavour. This is the best vintage since 1990 for reds throughout Bordeaux. While dry whites enjoyed conditions nearly as good, this was a disappointing year for Sauternes, with minimal quantities and low levels of botrytis, the warm weather paradoxically having a negative effect.

1999: A generally impressive year throughout the region for all wine styles with an impressively large crop, indeed the largest overall during the late 1990s. The summer was good, with warm consistent weather, however early rains in September meant that there was some variation. Those châteaux who went for maximum ripeness and harvested late did well. Whites have generally been good and were harvested before the rain, whereas Sauternes had a successful late harvest and some splendid wines have been produced.

1998: There was a lot of late September rain in the Médoc and quality is variable. Many wines just lack an extra dimension as well as displaying some angular and at times hard tannins. To the south Graves fared a little better but it was mainly earlier-ripening Merlot on the Right Bank that did best, producing wines with suppler and riper tannins. Dry whites were good and generally harvested in ideal weather. Sauternes was also very good although the crop was tiny.

1997: A generally trying year, the one exception being Sauternes, which produced its best vintage since 1990. Quantities, though, were small, which kept upward pressure on prices. Indeed, considering the overall quality of the vintage it was surprising that the Bordelais managed to get away with hyping prices as much as they did. The greatest problem with reds was uneven ripening. The top châteaux, who were rigorous in their selection, produced the best results. The dry whites were generally average to good but some properties harvested grapes lacking in full flavour development and many of these wines should now be drunk.

1996: This was another year when the Bordeaux money men should have been singing the praises of the gods. It was the second very large harvest in a row, a trend that was to continue through to the millennium. It was also a year of great wines in the Médoc, particularly in the northern appellations. The Right Bank fared less well, being hit by rain just as the Merlot ripened. Late-harvested Cabernet Sauvignon was consistently more successful. Very good dry whites were produced and the best wines are drinking well now. Sauternes had its best year since 1990. The wines are rich, heady and very intense.

1995: A good, indeed very good year for both Left and Right Bank. The harvest was reasonably consistent and although there was some rain during Setember it was not heavy enough to cause real problems with ripening. The results were very good in Pauillac and Saint-Julien and the wines are not only classically structured but have rich ripe fruit as well. The lesser reds are now beginning to drink well, the top wines need more time. There were some good dry whites and these are now drinking well. However Sauternes was generally disappointing.

1994: After a warm and at times hot, dry summer had promised much, September turned out to be a great disappointment, with persistent rain. Careful control during selection and throughout vinification produced generally agreeable reds on both Right and Left Banks. Many top wines are now beginning to drink well. It was a good year for dry whites and the top wines will still be showing well. Lesser white Pessac-Léognan should now be drunk. This was a dismal year in Sauternes.

1993: This was a disappointing vintage throughout the region with a wet harvest for all styles. The odd decent result emerged on both Banks and these wines should now be drunk. Sauternes was disastrous.

1992: A very disappointing year in the Médoc, while slightly better on the Right Bank.

1991: Much of France was hit by severe spring frosts and Bordeaux was no exception. The yield was poor and the resulting wines lacked substance.

1990: The finest red wine vintage since 1982. Also impressively good for dry whites, some of the very best are still drinking well now. It was exceptional for Sauternes. The weather was remarkably even up to and throughout the harvest and the wines consequently had exceptional balance. Most reds, apart from the very top growths, are drinking now but will continue to develop.

1989: This was generally a very good year, producing excellent reds on both banks, the only question mark being excessive ripeness. The summer and early part of September were very hot and the harvest was early. The wines turned out to have considerable extract and fruit but not entirely perfect balance. Sweet wines were very good and many are now drinking well.

1988: A good rather than great year. The top wines turned out well. The reds are classically structured and restrained and in general will continue to drink well for at least another decade. Excellent Sauternes, which is drinking and will continue to develop harmoniously.

1986: A great vintage in the Médoc with many harmonious long-lived wines. More patchy on the Right Bank though. A very fine year for Sauternes as well.

1985: Good for both Left and Right Banks but exceeded by the quality of the 1986s.

1982: This was a classic year with many superb reds being made. The Médocs look to have turned out better than those from the Right Bank.

For older vintages great Médocs from 1978 and 1970 are superb, the best will evolve further. A handful of 1975s have turned out very well. 1966 was good in the Médoc. 1964 might be worth a look for top Saint-Émilion or Pomerol. 1961 was a classic and many wines are still excellent. You could also consider 1959, 55, 49, 47, 45 and if you're exceptionally adventurous 35 or 28. Bear in mind that the provenance of the wine is as important as anything if you are acquiring very old vintages.

Bordeaux vintages

	Northern Médoc inc Saint-Èstephe, Paulliac, Saint-Julien	Southern Médoc inc Margaux	Red Graves	White Graves
2002	★★★★ A	★★★/★★★★ A	★★★★ A	★★★★ A
2001	★★★/★★★★ A	★★★/★★★★ A	★★★/★★★★ A	★★★★/★★★★★ A
2000	★★★★★ A	★★★★★ A	★★★★★ A	★★★★ A
1999	★★★/★★★★ A	★★★/★★★★ A	★★★/★★★★ A	★★★★ B
1998	★★★/★★★★ A	★★★/★★★★ A	★★★★ A	★★★★/★★★★★ B
1997	★★★ B	★★★ B	★★★ B	★★★★ C
1996	★★★★/★★★★★ A	★★★★ A	★★★★ B	★★★★ C
1995	★★★★ A	★★★★ B	★★★★ B	★★★/★★★★ C
1990	★★★★★ B	★★★★★ B	★★★★ C	★★★★/★★★★★ C
1989	★★★★ C	★★★★ C	★★★★ C	★★★/★★★★ C
1988	★★★★ B	★★★/★★★★ C	★★★★ C	★★★★ D
1986	★★★★/★★★★★ C	★★★★ C	★★★★ C	★★★ D
1985	★★★★ C	★★★★ C	★★★★ C	-
1983	★★★★ C	★★★★/★★★★★ C	★★★★ C	-
1982	★★★★★ C	★★★★/★★★★★ C	★★★★★ C	-

	Saint-Émilion	Pomerol	Sauternes
2002	★★★/★★★★ A	★★★/★★★★ A	★★★★/★★★★★ A
2001	★★★★ A	★★★★ A	★★★★/★★★★★ A
2000	★★★★★ A	★★★★★ A	★★ A
1999	★★★/★★★★ A	★★★/★★★★ A	★★★★ A
1998	★★★★ A	★★★★/★★★★★ A	★★★★ A
1997	★★★ B	★★★ B	★★★★ A
1996	★★★/★★★★ B	★★★/★★★★ B	★★★★/★★★★★ B
1995	★★★★ B	★★★★ B	★★★/★★★★ B
1990	★★★★★ B	★★★★★ B	★★★★ C
1989	★★★★/★★★★★ C	★★★★/★★★★★ C	★★★★ C
1988	★★★★ C	★★★★ C	★★★★★ C
1986	★★★/★★★★ C	★★★/★★★★ C	★★★★/★★★★★ C
1985	★★★★ C	★★★★ C	★★★★ C
1983	★★★/★★★★ C	★★★/★★★★ C	★★★★/★★★★★ C
1982	★★★★★ C	★★★★★ C	★★★ D

Médoc, Graves & Sauternes

CH. D'AGASSAC   Haut-Médoc   www.agassac.com

Owner: Groupama   33290 Ludon-Médoc
Things are taking a turn for better at this medium-sized operation based in the southern part of the Haut-Médoc and owned by the insurance company Groupama. The wine is now showing good depth and some attractive dark fruit notes and harmonious tannins. A medium-weight style, better with five or six years' ageing. Good in 2000 and 1999, a little less impressive in 98. (DM)
● **Château d'Agassac** Haut-Médoc★★ £C

CH. D'ANGLUDET   Margaux   www.chateau-dangludet.fr

Owner: Sichel family   33460 Cantenac
Well-established Cru Bourgeois with 25-year-old vineyards planted to Cabernet Sauvignon, Merlot and Petit Verdot, which comes from the oldest parcel of vines and adds extra character. The emphasis at the property is to achieve a natural balance in the vineyard and this shows through in the quality of the wine which is medium-weight with refinement and finesse. There is a second label, La Ferme d'Angludet, and a rosé, Clairet d'Angludet. Impressive in 2001 and 2000 but the wines have generally shown more class in the late 1990's. (DM)
● **Château d'Angludet** Margaux★★★ £D

CH. D'ARCHE   Sauternes 2ème CC

Owner: Pierre Perromat   33210 Sauternes
Small production (only around 5,000 cases a year) of reasonably impressive, full and concentrated Sauternes with a generally good performance in the most favourable vintages over the two decades since the involvement of Pierre Perromat. Harvesting is as selective as necessary, and a portion of new oak is used to age the wine. Good rather than spectacular in 2001. 2000, 98 and 97 are all worth seeking out. (DM)
O **Château d'Arche** Sauternes★★★ £E

CH. D'ARMAILHAC   Pauillac 5ème CC   www.bpdr.com

Owner: Baron Philippe de Rothschild SA   33250 Pauillac
Like its prestigious neighbour MOUTON ROTHSCHILD this château is also owned by Baronne Philippine de Rothschild. At its best, in years like 2000, 99, 98 and 95, this medium-sized property is undoubtedly producing three-star Pauillac. When conditions are less favourable, though, the wine struggles a little to achieve those heights. Grown in relatively light soils the wine is structured but not overly so, retaining some of the marked cassis and cedar notes of its big brother, and will provide good drinking at six or seven years. (DM)
● **Château d'Armailhac** Pauillac★★★ £D

CH. BASTOR-LAMONTAGNE   Sauternes   www.bastor-lamontagne.com

Owner: Michel Garat   33210 Preignac
A consistently fine, small to medium-sized operation which has performed admirably over a long period, providing the essence of Sauternes at an affordable price. As well as Sémillon and Sauvignon

Blanc, Michel Garat has just a small amount of Muscadelle to add aroma. The wine is barrel-fermented for an extended three to four weeks with around 15 per cent new oak to lend structure and shows classic honeyed, peachy botrytis character even in lesser years. Look out for 1998, 97 and 96. 2001 also looks very promising. The second wine produced from young vines is Les Remparts de Bastor. (DM)

● **Château Bastor-Lamontagne** Sauternes★★★ £E

CH. BATAILLEY   Pauillac 5ème CC

Owner: Héritiers Castéja   33250 Pauillac
A consistently reasonably priced Fifth Growth, Batailly is a wine that has performed reliably throughout the 1990s but never more than that. Good classic blackcurrant and cedar notes can be found, and the wine has sufficient oak with creamy vanilla notes and a supple texture aided by malolactic in barrel. Good without great depth or real complexity. (DM)

● **Château Batailley** Pauillac★★ £D

CH. BEL AIR MARQUIS D'ALIGRE   Margaux

Owner: Jean-Pierre Boyer   33460 Soussans
Cru Bourgeois property that has been performing impressively in recent years. Small to medium-sized, the château produces around 14–15,000 cases a year from meticulously tended vineyards. The resulting wine is a refined medium-weight style, very Margaux with a real fruit intensity and stylish perfume. Very good in 1998, 96, 95 and in the great 1990 vintage. (DM)

● **Château Bel Air Marquis d'Aligre** Margaux★★★ £D

CH. BELGRAVE   Haut-Médoc 5ème CC

Owner: Vignobles Dourthe   33112 Saint-Laurent-de-Médoc
Purchased by Vignobles Dourthe in 1980, it was only with the 1998 vintage that the quality really began to forge ahead. During the past two decades the vineyard has been replanted. Cabernet Sauvignon dominates the blend, with a tiny amount of Petit Verdot. Now that the vines are maturing, the wine is evolving from a straightforward, essentially fruit-driven style in the early to mid-1990s, to one where there is real depth and refinement. It represents particularly good value for money. (DM)

● **Château Belgrave** Haut-Médoc★★★ £D

CH. BEYCHEVELLE   Saint-Julien 4ème CC   www.beychevelle.com

Owner: SC Grands Millésimes de France   33250 Saint-Julien-Beychevelle
Beychevelle is a sizeable property with 90 ha of vineyards planted to Cabernet Sauvignon, Merlot, Cabernet Franc and a little Petit Verdot. It is a Classed Growth with a reasonable, rather than spectacular, track record over recent years. At its best the wine shows real finesse, splendid purity of fruit and very subtle oak, not full and powerful but more refined and elegant. Choose your vintage with a bit of caution and avoid lesser years. Amiral de Beychevelle, the second wine, is entitled to the Saint-Julien AC, while Les Brulières-de-Beychevelle is from vineyards in the Haut-Médoc. (DM)

● **Château Beychevelle** Saint-Julien★★★ £E

CH. BOYD-CANTENAC Margaux 3ème CC www.boyd-cantenac.fr

Owner: Lucien Guillemet 33460 Margaux
Despite its Third Growth status this property has spent decades in the doldrums and would not have been on anyone's shopping list until recent vintages, which have shown a marked turn for the better. An increasing use of new oak – up to 60 per cent – and, since 1997, no filtration has contributed to this improvement. The wine is fragrant and supple with attractive dark berry fruit and an increasing richness. (DM)

● **Château Boyd-Cantenac** Margaux★★ £E

CH. BRANAIRE Saint-Julien 4ème CC www.branaire.com

Owner: Patrick Maroteaux 33250 Saint-Julien
For a long time this was, a seriously underachieving property. However there has been a significant turn-around here during the last six or seven years. Investment in the cellar, along with a commitment to quality that avoids filtration and employs only limited egg-white fining and racking by gravity, is undoubtedly paying off. The style has moved from light to much fuller and richer. The Cabernet Sauvignon component now really shows and the wines are sturdier and denser with much greater depth and power. Almost all the vintages since 1994 have impressed. 1995, 96, 98 and 99 are all on the cusp of four stars. (DM)

● **Château Branaire** Saint-Julien★★★ £F

CH. BRANE-CANTENAC Margaux 2ème CC www.lucienlurton.com

*Owner: **Domaines Lucien Lurton & Fils** 33460 Margaux*
Since the late 1990s Brane-Cantenac has been showing real evidence of its status as a Second Growth. After 1996 the only vintage which has disappointed has been the 97. The wine is a classic blend of Cabernet Sauvignon, Merlot and Cabernet Franc with intense, cedary Margaux perfume, subtle oak and sheer class and intensity. Domaines Lucien Lurton also own a number of other important châteaux, among them CLIMENS in Barsac, DURFORT-VIVENS in Margaux and BOUSCAUT in Pessac-Léognan. 1999 is clearly four-star quality here. The second wine, Baron de Brane, is of decent quality. (DM)

● **Château Branaire** Margaux★★★ £F ● **Baron de Brane**★★ £D

CH. CAILLOU Sauternes 2ème CC www.chateaucaillou.fr

Owner: Michel & Marie-Josée Pierre 33720 Barsac
This is one of those confusingly labelled properties which takes the Sauternes AC although it is located in Barsac. There are two *cuvées* of the principal wine, the regular Caillou and a barrel selection, La Private Cuvée, produced in top years such as 1995, 97 and 99. Fermentation is in a mix of new oak and *inox* and ageing is between 18 and 24 months with a marked new oak component. This is an intense and heady sweet white but inevitably the regular Caillou suffers in those vintages when La Private Cuvée is released. A second wine, Château Haut-Mayne, is also produced. (DM)

O **Château Caillou** Sauternes★★★ £E

CH. CALON-SÉGUR Saint-Estèphe 2ème CC

Owner: Denise Capbern-Gasqueton 33180 Saint-Estèphe
Like many Bordeaux properties Calon-Ségur has shown a marked upturn in quality during the late

1990s. As well as a more meticulous approach in the vineyard, which has resulted in a reduced crop, the objective in the winemaking has been to produce an altogether suppler, more harmonious style. The wine achieves this and is both opulent and modern with weight, concentration and power. It has a much more velvety texture than of old. Very good since 1996, although below par in 97. (DM)

● **Château Calon-Ségur** Saint-Estèphe★★★★ £F

CH. CAMENSAC   Haut-Médoc 5ème CC   www.chateaucamensac.com

Owner: Forner family   Route de Saint-Julien, 33112 Saint-Laurent-de-Médoc
The quality of this property during the tenure of the Forner family has gradually improved since it was acquired in 1964. Much of the vineyard has been replanted and there is now a relatively high proportion of Merlot (25 per cent) contributing to the style, which is round, forward and accessible. The wine drinks well at five years or so. Just a notch up in 1999 and 2000. (DM)

● **Château Camensac** Haut-Médoc★★ £D

CH. CANTEMERLE   Haut-Médoc 5ème CC   www.chateau-cantemerle.com

Owner: Philippe Dambrine   33460 Macau
The 87 ha at Cantemerle are planted to a mix of 50 per cent Cabernet Sauvignon and, unusually for the Left Bank, a whopping 40 per cent Merlot, with the remaining 10 per cent divided evenly between Cabernet Franc and Petit Verdot. Production is sizeable, with 50,000 cases produced annually. After significant replanting two decades ago the vine age is beginning to show and this together with the high proportion of Merlot provides a rich, vibrantly dark-fruited Médoc at its best. The very latest vintages are promising and 1998 and 96 are good. It has to be said, though, that the wine has not performed well in lesser years, particularly in the early 1990s. (DM)

● **Château Cantemerle** Haut-Médoc★★ £E

CH. CANTENAC-BROWN   Margaux 5ème CC   www.cantenacbrown.com

Owner: AXA Millésimes   33460 Cantenac
Purchased in 1987 by AXA Millésimes, who also own a number of other prestigious Bordeaux properties including PICHON-LONGUEVILLE and SUDUIRAUT in Sauternes. Quality has been disappointing throughout the 1970s, 80s and, with the exception of 1990, the 90s prior to 96. The rating is for its current performance rather than earlier vintages and, given the performance of other châteaux within the AXA group, one would expect things here to continue to improve. (DM)

● **Château Cantenac-Brown** Margaux★★★ £E

CH. CARBONNIEUX   Pessac-Léognan CC   www.chateaucarbonnieux.com

Owner: Antony Perrin   33850 Léognan
Good rather than memorable red and white Pessac-Léognans. Production is substantial for the appellation at over 30,000 cases a year. The white is good and has performed well through-out the 1990s. Some skin contact is allowed before fermentation in barrel, around half of which is new, and ageing is on lees. The red doesn't quite reach the same level but has also been consistent over recent vintages. Sound, well-crafted and approachable, it is lighter than other Pessac-Léognan reds but displays attractive berry fruit and a fine mineral undercurrent. Both white and red will benefit from five years' bottle-ageing. Château Haut-Vigneau is another solid property producing decent red under the AC and there is a second wine, La Tour Léognan,

produced in both red and white. The latter can often impress. (DM)

● **Château Carbonnieux** Pessac-Léognan★★ £E   ● **Château Haut-Vigneau** Pessac-Léognan★ £D
O **Château Carbonnieux** Pessac-Léognan★★★ £E

CH. LES CARMES HAUT-BRION   Pessac-Léognan   www.les-carmes-haut-brion.com

Owner: Chantecaille-Furt family   197 Avenue Jean Cordier33600 Pessac
This a tiny property and, like HAUT-BRION, located amongst the suburbs of Bordeaux. Just 4.5 ha
are under vine, with an unusually high proportion of 50 per cent Merlot, along with 40 per cent
Cabernet Sauvignon amd 10 per cent Cabernet Franc. Dedication to quality has delivered
impressive results in the late 1990s. Vinification in small vats enables plots within the vineyard to be
fermented separately. Malolactic takes place in barrel and around one-third new wood is used. The
wine is supple and rich, with firm but nicely rounded tannins. (DM)

● **Château les Carmes Haut-Brion** Pessac-Léognan★★★ £E

CH. DE CHANTEGRIVE   Graves   www.chateau-chantegrive.com

Owner: Henri Lévèque   33720 Podensac
This property consists of 50 ha of red varieties and 38 ha of white, with production now quite
substantial at over 40,000 cases a year. Four wines are produced. A good red with a fine balance of dark
fruit, cedar and subtle oak is joined by a regular white Graves, an easy, fruit-driven style fermented at
low temperatures. There is also the limited production Cuvée Caroline, barrel-fermented in a portion
of new oak with regular use of *bâtonnage* to add weight and a rich, creamy texture. The sweet Cérons
is a full, fat style with good depth and some honeyed complexity. (DM)

● **Château de Chantegrive** Graves★★ £C
O **Château de Chantegrive** Graves★ £B Cuvée Caroline★★★ £C
O **Château de Chantegrive** Cérons★★ £C

CH. CHARMAIL   Haut-Médoc

Owner: Olivier Seze   33180 Saint-Seurin-de-Cadourne
A consistent performer during the last five or six vintages, located just to the north of Saint-Estèphe.
The wine, which has a high proportion of Merlot (55 per cent of the vineyard) is modern and stylish.
Neither fined nor filtered, it is marked by supple tannin and attractive, forward, dark berry fruit and
hints of cassis, not least as a result of a touch of pre-fermentation maceration. There are none of the
often green and herbaceous notes found in some lesser Bordeaux reds dominated by the variety. (DM)

● **Château Charmail** Haut-Médoc★★★ £D

CH. CHASSE-SPLEEN   Moulis   www.chasse-spleen.com

Owner: Céline Villars-Foubet   33480 Moulis-en-Médoc
Chasse-Spleen, along with POUJEAUX and MAUCAILLOU, is one of the only wines in the Moulis
AC really to perform with any consistent class. The property is sizeable, with just under 85 ha under vine.
The wine is a blend of Cabernet Sauvignon, Merlot and Petit Verdot. With the odd exceptions (1997, 94
and 91) this property has fashioned a rich, concentrated and harmonious red. The 2001, 00 and 99
are noteworthy. It's a shame there aren't more properties turning out wines of this class in the
appellation. The second wine, L'Ermitage de Chasse-Spleen, can be better than most. (DM)

● **Château Chasse-Spleen** Moulis★★★ £E

DOM. DE CHEVALIER Pessac-Léognan CC   www.domainedechevalier.com

Owner: Olivier Bernard   102 Chemin de Mignoy, 33850 Léognan

An important and sizeable producer, noted particularly for its splendid white. The production of this is very low, with just 4.5 of the 37.5 ha vineyard planted to Sauvignon Blanc and Sémillon. There is a high proportion of Sauvignon (70 per cent) in the blend. Barrel-fermented and aged it is a remarkably fine and elegant white capable of considerable age. The red has been less impressive than the white in recent years but since 1996 there has been a fair step up in quality and the wine has regularly been approaching four stars. In short, solid and ageworthy. (DM)

● **Domaine de Chevalier** Pessac-Léognan★★★ £E
O **Domaine de Chevalier** Pessac-Léognan✪✪✪✪✪ £F

CH. CISSAC Haut-Médoc www.chateau-cissac.com

Owner: Danielle Viallard   33250 Cissac-Médoc

Cissac is still made in a traditional, firm Médoc style but it is very fairly priced and generally well-crafted. But, although structured and austere when very young, it is increasingly rounder and suppler than of old with a little age. Wooden as well as stainless steel vats are used for fermentation and an increasing amount of new wood (30 to 40 per cent) is used to age the wine. From the best vintages the wine is undoubtedly complex and harmonious but really needs cellaring for eight to ten years to show at its best. (DM)

● **Château Cissac** Haut-Médoc★★★ £C

CH. CLARKE Listrac-Médoc chateau.clarke@wanadoo.fr

Owner: Baron Benjamin de Rothschild   33480 Listrac

Listrac, like Moulis, is quite a long way inland from the Gironde and the soil here has even less gravel than it does nearer the estuary, which will always hinder the admirable efforts made here. This property with increasingly old vines outclasses almost all of its neighbours but there remains a slightly coarse note. However, since 1995 the wine is more concentrated and harmonious, while retaining its soft and supple, earthy, dark fruit character. (DM)

● **Château Clarke** Listrac-Médoc★★ £C

CH. CLERC-MILON Pauillac 5ème CC   www.bpdr.com

Owner: Baron Philippe de Rothschild SA   33250 Pauillac

Moderate-sized property, with some 30 ha of vineyards and production running at just under 15,000 cases a year. The Cabernet Sauvignon component is quite low at less than 50 per cent and 35 per cent of the vineyard is planted to Merlot. As a result the style is very rounded and surprisingly approachable for Pauillac. While overshadowed by its sister château and neighbour MOUTON-ROTHSCHILD, Clerc-Milon is nevertheless an excellent, stylish source of the appellation, with a harmonious mix of dark fruits and cedar, all of which is nicely underpinned by its ripe and plummy Merlot component. At its current level since 1995.

● **Château Clerc-Milon** Pauillac★★★★ £F

CH. CLIMENS Barsac ler CC www.chateau-climens.fr

Owner: Bérénice Lurton 33720 Barsac

Climens is an exceptional sweet wine and the leading property in the Barsac commune. It is outclassed only by Château d'YQUEM amongst the great botrytised wines of the Sauternes. Production is low at just over 3,000 cases a year and the vineyard, which is just 29 ha, is planted solely to Sémillon. Despite the absence of Sauvignon Blanc the wine possesses not only intense and very concentrated honeyed fruit but a marvellously fresh acid balance as well. Best to age it for at least five years and it will be better with twice that time in the cellar. The wine was truly great in 1998, 96, 90, 88 and 86. A few hundred cases are also produced under the Doisy-Dubroca label. (DM)

● **Château Climens** Barsac✪✪✪✪ £G

CLOS FLORIDÈNE Graves www.denisdubourdieu.com

Owner: Denis & Florence Dubourdieu 21 Route de Cardan, 33410 Beguey

The main focus is on white wine, with 13 ha planted as opposed to 5.5 ha for red varieties. The white is a particularly impressive example and puts many more exalted Pessac-Léognans to shame. It is barrel-fermented and aged with *bâtonnage* to add richness but it is the citrus and mineral quality of the fruit that really marks it out. It will evolve nicely over the short to medium term. The red is sound and well-crafted but lacks the same excitement. Denis Dubourdieu also produces the wines of Château REYNON. (DM)

● **Clos Floridène** Graves★ £C
O **Clos Floridène** Graves★★★ £C

CH. CLOS HAUT-PEYRAGUEY Sauternes ler CC

Owner: J & J. Pauly 33210 Bommes

Very small Sauternes property. There are just 12 ha of vineyards, 90 per cent of which are Sémillon, the balance Sauvignon Blanc. Quality is good to very good but the wine just lacks the depth and intensity of the best of the other First Growths of the appellation. The style is more one of finesse and elegance than sheer weight and concentration. Very good in 1998, 97, 90 and 88, while other years are not quite of the same order. The second wine is Château Haut Bommes. (DM)

● **Château Clos Haut-Peyraguey** Sauternes★★★ £E

CH. COS D'ESTOURNEL Saint-Estèphe 2ème CC www.estournel.com

Owner: Taillan group 33180 Saint-Estèphe

One of the greatest wines of the Médoc and the premier château in Saint-Estèphe. Purchased from Bruno Prats by the Taillan Group, who also own GRUAUD-LAROSE, in 1998. Jean-Guillaume Prats remains in charge of running and directing the property. It is to be hoped that the Prats family's exceptional standards here throughout the 1970s, 80s and 90s will be maintained. The vintages of the late 1990s and 2000 have not reached the usual exemplary standards. Using sophisticated vinification including must concentration, malolactic in barrel and new oak for ageing, the wine is very powerful as well as opulent. It should, however, show remarkable depth and harmony with a decade or more in the cellar. The second wine was originally called MARBUZET, which is itself a Cru Bourgeois, but is now labelled Les Pagodes de Cos. The former has regularly been at one to two stars throughout the 1990s. (DM)

● **Château Cos d'Estournel** Saint-Estèphe✪✪✪✪ £G

CH. COS LABORY Saint-Estèphe 5ème CC cos-labory@wanadoo.fr

Owner: Bernard Audoy 33180 Saint-Estèphe
Although overshadowed by its famous neighbour COS D'ESTOURNEL, this property improved greatly in the late 1980s and some of the vintages since have been impressive. 1996, 95, 90 and 88 were all a notch up on what has generally been achieved here over the last 12-15 years. The late 1990s have somewhat disappointingly not maintained this level. At its best the wine is full, marked by impressive blackcurrant fruit and underpinned by a firm, rounded, tannic structure. (DM)
● **Château Cos Labory** Saint-Estèphe★★ £E

CH. COUHINS-LURTON Pessac-Léognan CC ww.andrelurton.com

Owner: Les Vignobles André Lurton 33420 Grézillac
André Lurton is now a major proprietor in the Graves, Entre-Deux-Mers and Margaux. At this tiny 5.5-ha Pessac property he produces less than 2,000 cases of very stylish white a year from Sauvignon Blanc. No Sémillon is planted here but the wine is barrel-fermented in 50 per cent new wood and aged with *bâtonnage* and has the structure and density to age well in bottle. Both 1999 and 2000 were particularly good examples. (DM)
O **Château Couhins-Lurton** Pessac-Léognan★★★ £E

CH. COUTET Barsac 1er CC

Owner: Baly family 33720 Barsac
Very good property and near neighbour of CLIMENS, although the wine here doesn't quite reach the same heights. As well as Sémillon, which accounts for 75 per cent of the blend, and Sauvignon Blanc, there is a little Muscadelle, just 3 per cent. There is no doubt that there is a marked aromatic character in the wine in addition to its classic rich vanilla and peach notes. In exceptional years a special super-concentrated Cuvée Madame is released. This is certainly of super-five quality. (DM)
O **Château Coutet** Barsac★★★★ £F

CH. DAUZAC Margaux 5ème CC www.andrelurton.com

Owner: Les Vignobles André Lurton 33460 Labarde
Another André Lurton-controlled property. There are 46 ha under vine here and production is just shy of 25,000 cases, so it is a sizeable operation. The style is supple and rich with an emphasis on approachable dark fruit and well-judged oak. The wine is only kept in barrel for 12 months but 50–80 per cent is new. Quality has improved dramatically since the 1990s. (DM)
● **Château Dauzac** Margaux★★★ £E

CH. DOISY-DAËNE Barsac 2ème CC www.denisdubourdieu.com

Owner: Pierre & Denis Dubourdieu 33720 Barsac
This is a Barsac marked by its elegance rather than its sheer weight or richness. It can be piercingly aromatic, though, and very intense. Of a completely different order – richer and fuller – is an occasional very limited *cuvée* called L'Extravagance. It is only produced in exceptional vintages, including 2001, 97 and 96. As well as the sweet wines a good dry Bordeaux Blanc is rich and fruity. (DM)
O **Château Doisy-Daëne** Barsac★★★ £E O **Bordeaux**★★ £C

CH. DOISY-VÉDRINES   Barsac 2ème CC

Owner: Pierre Castéja   1 Rue Védrines, 33720 Barsac
This is the biggest of the three Doisy properties with 27 ha. In contrast to DOISY-DAENE and most other fine Barsacs, this property tends to produce wine with more overt luscious honeyed fruit. It is very impressive, though retaining an elegant finesse in lighter years when the wine carries less sheer weight. There is 5 per cent Muscadelle planted here, which helps in providing an aromatic undercurrent in the wine. (DM)
● **Château Doisy-Védrines** Sauternes★★★★ £E

CH. DUCRU-BEAUCAILLOU   Saint-Julien 2ème CC   www.chateau-ducru-beaucaillou.com

Owner: Borie family   33250 Saint-Julien-Beychevelle
One of the greatest wines of Saint-Julien. The 50 ha of Ducru based in the south of the appellation are planted to a mix of Cabernet Sauvignon (65 per cent), Merlot (25 per cent), and an equal portion of Cabernet Franc and Petit Verdot. It is a very impressive, classically structured example of the appellation. Always elegant, very intense, with subtle cedar and dark fruit underpinned by finely integrated oak; requiring patience and cellaring. From the current crop of excellent vintages 1998, 96 and 95 were exemplary but 97 was somewhat of a disappointment. (DM)
● **Château Ducru-Beaucaillou** Saint-Julien❂❂❂❂❂ £H

CH. DUHART-MILON   Pauillac 4ème CC   www.lafite.com

Owner: Domaines Barons de Rothschild/Chalone Wine Group   33250 Pauillac
Intriguingly, this Rothschild property is also part-owned by the Chalone Wine Group from the USA, who established their reputation with the CHALONE winery in Monterey, California. There is no doubt that the 50 ha of vineyards have benefited greatly from the Lafite input since the property was purchased in 1962. Fermentation is modern in stainless steel and ageing taking place in barrels, 50 per cent new, that are coopered at Lafite-Rothschild. 1999, 98 and 96 were all nudging four-star quality. (DM)
● **Château Duhart-Milon** Pauillac★★★ £E

CH. FERRIÈRE   Margaux 3ème CC   www.ferriere.com

Owner: Merlaut family   33460 Margaux
Small Classed Growth which has improved dramatically during the 1990s. Production is barely more than 4,000 cases a year and the dedicated commitment to quality here by Claire Villars (aided by the Merlaut family who run the Taillan group, owners of COS D'ESTOURNEL and GRUAUD-LAROSE) has ensured that this is one of the best properties in the Margaux appellation. The wine is rich, intense and concentrated and now shows great harmony and refinement. There is minimal processing with egg-white fining and malolactic in barrel. The wine comfortably absorbs the impact of 60 per cent new oak. (DM)
● **Château Ferrière** Margaux★★★★ £E

CH. DE FIEUZAL   Pessac-Léognan CC   www.fieuzal.com

Owner: Lachlann Quinn   124 Avenue de Mont-de-Marsan, 33850 Léognan
The style here, particularly with the red, is to produce opulent, richly textured, forward, modern and

approachable wines, accessible very shortly after release. The white, which unlike the red is not in fact a Cru Classé, also shows rich, forward, honeyed fruit with a solid dose of new oak but with a depth and structure that ensures good, medium-term cellaring and is the more impressive of the two. The wines, particularly the whites, offer very good value. (DM)

● **Château de Fieuzal** Pessac-Leognan★★★ £E
O **Château de Fieuzal** Pessac-Leognan★★★★ £E

CH. GLORIA   Saint-Julien

Owner: Triaud family   33250 Saint-Julien-Beychevelle
A consistently good and impressive Cru Bourgeois, Gloria has performed admirably throughout the 1970s, 80s and 90s. It is a sizeable property, with some 47 ha under vine producing around 25,000 cases a year. The wine is not immensely complex or long-lived but is full of vibrant, dark, brambly blackcurrant fruit, nicely judged oak and an elegant hint of cedar in the background. (DM)

● **Château Gloria** Saint-Julien★★ £E

CH. GRAND-PUY-LACOSTE   Pauillac 5ème CC

Owner: Borie family   33250 Pauillac
Under the same ownership as DUCRU-BEAUCAILLOU, this has been an admirable and classic red Bordeaux for the past three decades and there have been many admirable vintages since World War II. This is the quintessential example of what you expect from fine Pauillac, a wine loaded with cassis and cedar, refined and elegant but with real power and density. 1990, and more recently 95 and 96, are wines of significant class and 2000 looks very much of the same order. (DM)

● **Château Grand-Puy-Lacoste** Pauillac★★★★ £F

CH. GRUAUD-LAROSE   Saint-Julien 2ème CC

Owner: Taillan group   33250 Saint-Julien-Beychevelle
Large Saint-Julien property with production approaching 40,000 cases a year, responsible for some formidable and massively structured wines during the 1980s. 1982 and 86 were without a doubt of super-five star quality, with a number of others on the cusp. Quality generally has remained impressive throughout the 1990s but not at quite the same level. These are powerful, dense and tannic reds in need of at least eight to ten years' cellaring. The second wine, Sarget de Gruaud-Larose, can be good, particularly in better years. (DM)

● **Château Gruaud-Larose** Saint-Julien★★★★ £F

CH. GUIRAUD   Sauternes 1er CC   www.chateauguiraud.fr

Owner: Narby family   33210 Sauternes
Xavier Planty, in charge of production here, has been turning out impressive Sauternes in the top vintages of the 1990s. A consistent replanting process has much improved the ratio of Sémillon to Sauvignon Blanc and plantings of the former now account for 70 per cent of the vineyard. The result is wines of sometimes blockbuster proportions, rich, very honeyed and peachy, with spice and vanilla from new oak. It is not to all tastes, and on occasion more refinement would help. (DM)

O **Château Guiraud** Sauternes★★★★ £F

CH. HAUT-BAILLY Pessac-Léognan CC www.chateau-haut-bailly.com

Owner: Robert J Wilmers Route de Cadaujac, 33850 Léognan
A supple, elegant and consistently well-crafted red which is both approachable and refined. Unlike most of its neighbours, no white is made here. Haut-Bailly was purchased by Robert Wilmers, an American banker, in 1998 but the original proprietors, the Sanders family, are still involved in the direction and management of the property. Consistent throughout the mid- to late 1990s. The wine ages very well indeed. (DM)
● **Château Haut-Bailly** Pessac-Léognan★★★★ £E

CH. HAUT-BATAILLEY Pauillac 5ème CC je-borie@je-borie-sa.com

Owner: Borie family 33250 Saint-Julien-Beychevelle
Under the same ownership as DUCRU-BEAUCAILLOU and GRAND-PUY-LACOSTE. Quality here was somewhat variable and lesser vintages were light and lacking in substance as well as possessing a hard, at times austerely firm edge. This was surprising given the quality of the other properties owned by the Borie family but the mid-1990s saw an improvement and change in style. The wine is now less aggressive and raw and possesses a fine, more supple and even texture. It is altogether more accessible and harmonious. Significantly more impressive in 1995 and 96 and 2000 also looks very promising. (DM)
● **Château Haut-Batailley** Pauillac★★ £E

CH. HAUT-BRION Pessac-Léognan 1er CC www.haut-brion.com

Owner: Domaine Clarence Dillon 33608 Pessac Cedex
One of the four original properties classified as a First Growth in the 1855 Classification of the red Bordeaux wines. The vineyards are planted in superbly drained gravel soils that provide an almost ideal supply of moisture to optimise fruit ripening. Reds grapes occupy 43 ha, while less than 3 ha provides a tiny amount of exquisite, subtly barrel-fermented white from Sémillon and Sauvignon Blanc. The property, now surrounded by the ever-encroaching suburbs of Bordeaux, is small in comparison to the other First Growths, producing a total of some 12,500 cases a year, most of it red. Both red and white have been magnificent through the late 1990s, only the 1997 and 91 red dipping a little. Great older vintages include 1990, 89, 86, 82, 75 and the astonishing 61. The second wine, Le Bahans, can also be very impressive. (DM)
● **Château Haut-Brion** Pessac-Léognan✪✪✪✪✪ £H   ● **Le Bahans Haut Brion**★★★ £E
○ **Château Haut-Brion** Pessac-Léognan✪✪✪✪✪ £G

CH. HAUT-MARBUZET Saint-Estèphe

Owner: Henri Duboscq 33180 Saint-Estèphe
Henri Duboscq produces a massive, powerful, very rich Saint-Estèphe marked by well integrated new oak. Not only is this an outstanding Cru Bourgeois but it is only surpassed within the appellation by COS D'ESTOURNEL and MONTROSE. Production is not inconsiderable at close to 30,000 cases a year. The wine has been impressive in recent vintages, performing comfortably out of its class, and offers very good value. (DM)
● **Château Haut-Marbuzet** Saint-Estèphe★★★★ £D

CH. D'ISSAN   Margaux 3ème CC   www.chateau-issan.com

Owner: Cruse family   33460 Cantenac

This property was often disappointing in the late 1980s and early 90s. However since 1995 things have been looking decidedly better and the wine is once more in the elegant, cedary and perfumed style that represents fine Margaux. Major investment in both vineyard and cellars and input on the winemaking from Jacques Boissenet (one of a number of high-profile Bordeaux consultants, who also advises André Lurton as well as the Napa Valley QUINTESSA operation) are clearly having a positive effect. (DM)

● **Château d'Issan** Margaux★★★ £E

CH. KIRWAN   Margaux 3ème CC   www.chateau-kirwan.com

Owner: Schÿler family   33460 Cantenac

The Schÿler family, who also run the Schroder and Schÿler *negociant* operation in Bordeaux, had sold their interest in this small to medium-sized property in the early 1990s but promptly bought it back again a couple of years later. The result has been a real boost for the fortunes of the property and in particular the quality of the wine. Michel Rolland has provided guidance on the winemaking front and quality has been consistently good since 1996, if a touch overextracted in 98. (DM)

● **Château Kirwan** Margaux★★★ £E

CH. LAFAURIE-PEYRAGUEY   Sauternes 1er CC

*Owner: **Domaines Cordier**   33210 Bommes*

From 40 ha under vine in the commune of Bommes, with a grape mix of Sémillon (90 per cent), Sauvignon Blanc (8 per cent) and Muscadelle (just 2 per cent), some of the finest Sauternes is now being made at this property. This has only been the case for the last 15 years or so. The 1970s were a disappointment but the wines are now quite exemplary. They combine the intense richness and honeyed concentration of the finest Sauternes with something of the elegance found in CLIMENS. The wines are very stylish and long-lived. The 1999, 98 and 97 are all extraordinarily fine super-fives and 2001 may have the potential to be exquisite. (DM)

● **Château Lafaurie-Peyraguey** Sauternes★★★★★ £F

CH. LAFITE-ROTHSCHILD   Pauillac 1er CC   www.lafite.com

*Owner: **Domaines Barons de Rothschild**   33250 Pauillac*

One of the world's great wines and a consistent and superlative performer throughout the mid- to late 1990s. The 1998 and 96 are exceptional wines and 2000 shows similar promise, which is not surprising considering the quality of the vintage. However, all has not always been rosy here and 20 or so years ago the quality was much more uneven. The vineyard is planted to some 100 ha of Cabernet Sauvignon (75 per cent), Merlot (20 per cent), Cabernet Franc (4 per cent) and Petit Verdot (a mere 1 per cent). Time, a minimum of 15 to 20 years, is really required to achieve a harmony between the formidable, powerful tannins and the intense and fragrantly rich cedar and cassis fruit. 1982 marked a real turning point in the quality of the wine and other years of particular note are 1986, 88 and 90. The 53 and 59 were both superb but surprisingly 61 failed to achieve the high quality of that year. The second wine, Les Carruades de Lafite-Rothschild, is very impressive for a second label. (DM)

● **Château Lafite-Rothschild** Pauillac✪✪✪✪✪ £H   ● **Les Carruades de Lafite-Rothschild**★★★★ £F

CH. LAFON-ROCHET   Saint-Estèphe 4ème CC

Owner: Tesseron family   33180 Saint-Estèphe
Under the same ownership as PONTET-CANET, Lafon-Rochet has performed well, sometimes very well throughout the mid- to late 1990s. The vintages of the early 1990s did not achieve the same level but that is unsurprising given the difficult conditions of those years. The wine is a great deal more supple and approachable than it used to be and much of the reason has been a progressive replanting of the vineyard with a higher proportion of Merlot, now some 40 per cent. 1998, 96 and 95 stand out. (DM)
● **Château Lafon-Rochet** Saint-Estèphe★★★ £E

CH. LAGRANGE   Saint-Julien 3ème CC   www.chateau-lagrange.com

*Owner: **Suntory**   33250 Saint-Julien-Beychevelle*
The Japanese-owned Suntory company has pushed wine quality at this property forward dramatically since its purchase in the early 1980s and Lagrange is now very well run by Marcel Ducasse. Lagrange is very large, even by the standards of the Médoc, with over 110 ha under vine. The wine is rich and concentrated, but in an approachable style, with supple, well-rounded tannin. Consistently good over the last five or six years, it just needs that extra dimension to take it into the top division. (DM)
● **Château Lagrange** Saint-Julien★★★ £F

CH. LA LAGUNE   Haut-Médoc 3ème CC

Owner: Ducellier Family   33290 Ludon-Médoc
Some great reds were made at this property during the 1970s and 80s but more recently this sizeable 77 ha estate has been through a period producing some less exciting wines. The vineyard is mainly Cabernet Sauvignon (60 per cent), Merlot (20 per cent) and the balance Cabernet Franc and Petit Verdot. Under the current ownerhip things appear to be taking a turn for the better. Some medium weight elegant and cedary claret is being made using stainless steel, temperature controlled tanks for vinification and ageing in an increasing amount of new oak. (DM)
● **Château La Lagune** Haut-Médoc★★ £F

CH. LAMOTHE-GUIGNARD   Sauternes 2ème CC

Owner: Philippe & Jacques Guignard   33210 Sauternes
This is the larger of the two Lamothe properties in Sauternes. The other LAMOTHE, owned by Guy Despujols, does not quite reach the same heights. 90 per cent of the vineyard is planted to Sémillon along with 5 per cent Muscadelle and 5 per cent Sauvignon Blanc. The style is increasingly elegant with luscious botrytis character showing through in the best years. (DM)
O **Château Lamothe-Guignard** Sauternes★★★ £E

CH. LANESSAN   Haut-Médoc

*Owner: **SCEA Delbos Bouteiller**   33460 Cussac-Fort-Médoc*
This is a somewhat old-fashioned style of Médoc located close to Saint-Julien. Medium- rather than full-bodied or super-rich, the wine can be long-lived, elegant and intense, particularly in the best vintages when it shows at its best and most importantly can really ripen its at times angular tannins. With time, complex cedar and elegant, evolved tertiary characters emerge. It was particularly good

in 1996 and 2000 shows real promise also. (DM)

● **Château Lanessan** Haut-Médoc★★ £D

CH. LANGOA-BARTON   Saint-Julien 3ème CC

Owner: Anthony Barton   33250 Saint-Julien-Beychevelle

Sister property to LÉOVILLE-BARTON and in the Barton family for nearly two centuries. This has always been a consistent performer, producing consistent and elegant Saint-Julien, but inevitably it is overshadowed by its sibling château, being a mere Third Growth. Both wines are in fact vinified at Langoa as Léoville has no winery. Both share the same label for the second wine, Réserve de Léoville-Barton, which can be good. 1998 stands out among recent vintages. (DM)

● **Château Langoa-Barton** Saint-Julien★★★ £E

CH. LARRIVET HAUT-BRION   Pessac-Léognan

Owner: Société Andros   84 Route de Cadaujac, 33850 Léognan

There are 52 ha of vines planted here, 43 ha of which account for an even split of Cabernet Sauvignon and Merlot. The white varieties are also evenly split, between Sémillon and Sauvignon Blanc. Both wines are impressive and consultancy input on the winemaking is provided by Michel Rolland. The property is worthy of being upgraded to Cru Classé status. Both 1998 and 99 are very good and the potential for 2000 and 01 looks very good also. The red, particularly, is nudging four-star quality. It is stylish, refined and approachable at a few years, while the white is an elegant and notably piercing barrel-fermented style with a harmonious mix of fresh green and citrus fruits and subtle oak. (DM)

● **Château Larrivet Haut-Brion** Pessac-Léognan★★★ £E
O **Château Larrivet Haut-Brion** Pessac-Léognan★★★ £E

LA SÉRÉNITÉ   Pessac-Léognan

Owner: Bernard Magrez   7. Rue du Professeur-Bernard, 33170 Gradignan

This is a special *garagiste* style label produced at Château POUMEY. Proprietor Bernard Magrez has also released a number of other similarly styled wines from small low yielding properties throughout the region. The wines are marketed as Terroirs d'Exception and have been sourced from a number high quality vineyard sites owned by both Bernard Magrez and film actors Gérard Depardieu and Carole Bouquet; not only in Bordeaux but also in the Midi, as well as Italy and in Morocco and Algeria. Further wines are planned from Argentina, Uruguay and Chile. La Serénité is a very full, rich and extracted style. Produced from an almost equal blend of Merlot and Cabernet Sauvignon, it is vinified and aged in wood and everything in the cellars is handled by gravity. (DM)

● **La Serénité** Pessac-Léognan★★★ £E

CH. LATOUR   Pauillac Ier CC   www.chateau-latour.com

Owner: François Pinault   Saint-Lambert, 33250 Pauillac

To many this is the greatest of all the great wines of the Médoc and to some the greatest in the entire region. There is no doubt that it is one of the world's most remarkable reds, which at its magnificent best is both massive and concentrated but at the same time harmonious and very refined. It requires cellaring and you should allow one or preferably two decades. While the wine performs consistently at a very high level now, a number of vintages in the early to mid-1980s were less impressive, nowhere near its current super-five ranking. Fortunately, with a production of over 30,000 cases a year, the wine is not impossible to find – unlike a number of new 'super' wines being made elsewhere around the world. Recent vintages of particular note include 1999, 96, 95 and 90. Among the great earlier years 82, 71, 66, 61, 59 and 49 are all legendary. Les Forts de Latour is a very impressive second wine. (DM)

● **Château Latour** Pauillac✪✪✪✪✪ £H ● **Les Forts de Latour**★★★★ £F

CH. LA TOUR CARNET Haut-Médoc

Owner: Bernard Magrez 33112 Saint-Laurent-Médoc
A rich, fleshy style of Médoc which is produced from Cabernet Sauvignon (52 per cent), Merlot (42 per cent) and a little Cabernet Franc and Petit Verdot. Michel Rolland consults over the winemaking for which fermentation is carried out in wooden vats and malolactic typically carried out in barrique. 70 per cent new oak is used and all operations are now carried out by gravity. Ripe and reasonably forward, four to five years are required to integrate the fruit and youthfully dominant oak. (DM)

● **Château La Tour Carnet** Haut-Médoc★★★ £C

CH. LATOUR-MARTILLAC Pessac-Léognan CC www.latour-martillac.com

Owner: Kressmann family 33650 Martillac
Good to very good white and red Pessac is produced at this property, with around three-quarters of the output red. Maturing vines is one of the reasons why quality has surged forward during the 1990s. The red varieties now average 30 years and the whites a full 40 years. The red is an approachable, supple wine with refined tannins and nicely judged oak that varies between 30 and 50 per cent depending on the year. The white is rich and honeyed, with a real toasty, creamy character from barrel-fermentation and *bâttonage* and underlying all this is loads of character and style. Both offer good value for money. (DM)

● **Château Latour-Martillac** Pessac-Léognan★★★ £D
O **Château Latour-Martillac** Pessac-Léognan★★★ £D

CH. LAVILLE HAUT-BRION Pessac-Léognan CC www.haut-brion.com

Owner: Domaine Clarence Dillon 33608 Pessac
Like HAUT-BRION this property is owned by the Domaine Clarence Dillon. The wine, a blend of Sémillon (70 per cent), Sauvignon Blanc (27 per cent) and just a hint of Muscadelle (at 3 per cent), is produced at LA MISSION HAUT-BRION, as is LA TOUR HAUT-BRION, although all three are from separate and distinct vineyard plots. Laville is one of the great Pessac whites, powerfully structured and developing intense honeyed, mineral notes with age. It is barrel-fermented and aged mostly in new oak and requires considerable cellaring to show all its magic – at least seven or eight years. (DM)

O **Château Laville Haut-Brion** Pessac-Léognan✪✪✪✪ £G

CH. LÉOVILLE-BARTON Saint-Julien 2ème CC

Owner: Anthony Barton 33250 Saint-Julien-Beychevelle
This marvellously consistent red has long been one of Bordeaux's great-value wines. It is produced from 48 ha of vineyards planted to a mix of Cabernet Sauvignon (70 per cent), Merlot (22 per cent) and Cabernet Franc (8 per cent). It is vinified at its sister property LANGOA-BARTON as there is no winemaking facility on the Léoville property. The wine is a stylish, cedary, medium-full claret with well-judged oak and a supple but youthfully firm texture that requires time to achieve balance and harmony. It is no blockbuster but very good and long-lived nonetheless. It was seriously nudging

super-five in 1996 and potentially 2000 as well. The 89, 86 and 82 were also very fine. (DM)

● **Château Léoville-Barton** Saint-Julien★★★★★ £F

CH. LÉOVILLE-LAS-CASES Saint-Julien 2ème CC

Owner: Delon family 33250 Saint-Julien-Beychevelle

Almost universally regarded now as the finest of the super-seconds, on many occasions this magnificent property outclasses the First Growths. Not surprisingly the wine carries a price to match this performance and has in a number of vintages held up extraordinarily well on auction markets. This is also a fairly significant château, with 97 ha under vine. The high standards in place here ensure that a significant amount of the Grand Vin is declassified as Clos du Marquis, which is one of the very best of the Médoc's second labels. The quality was top-notch throughout the 1990s – only 1992 and 91 saw some ground lost, and the wine was a testament to the trying conditions of those years. Recent benchmarks are 96, 95 and 90, while 86 and 82 are also legendary. (DM)

● **Château Léoville-las-Cases** Saint-Julien✪✪✪✪✪ £H   ● **Clos du Marquis**★★★ £E

CH. LÉOVILLE-POYFERRÉ Saint-Julien 2ème CC www.leoville-poyferre.fr

Owner: Cuvelier family 33250 Saint-Julien-Beychevelle

The third among the great Léoville super-seconds. This was originally regarded as the first among equals and today, after a period of relative decline in the 1960s and 70s, it is once more challenging the other two Léoville properties. Poyferré, while a serious, dense and powerfully structured wine, is more approachable than the other two. It has a more vibrant, upfront, dark blackcurrant and mulberry fruit character and is an altogether more opulent style, partly achieved through a portion of the wine being put through malolactic in barrel. Nevertheless it remains very refined and elegant, an excellent expression of its *terroir*. 1996 and 90 were both extremely fine examples, of five-star quality. The second wine, Moulin Riche, is good to very good on occasion. (DM)

● **Château Léoville-Poyferré** Saint-Julien★★★★ £F

CH. LA LOUVIÈRE Pessac-Léognan www.andrelurton.com

*Owner: **Les Vignobles André Lurton** 33890 Léognan*

This is another property in the André Lurton Graves empire. As well as the wines of La Louvière, two other labels are vinified here: Château de CRUZEAU and Château ROCHEMORIN. The La Louvière vineyard comprises some 48 ha, of which 33 ha are planted to Cabernet Sauvignon and Merlot. The smaller white vineyard holding is dominated by Sauvignon Blanc, which accounts for around 85 per cent, the balance being Sémillon. Both wines are approachable and forward in style but will also age well in the medium term. The red is supple, with refined, nicely rounded tannin and the white ripe and full of citrus and subtle toasted oak. (DM)

● **Château la Louvière** Pessac-Léognan★★★ £E
O **Château la Louvière** Pessac-Léognan★★★ £E

CH. LYNCH-BAGES Pauillac 5ème CC www.lynchbages.com

Owner: Jean-Michel Cazes 33250 Pauillac

Regarded rightly during the 1980s as one of the great super-seconds despite its lower official classification. Talented Jean-Michel Cazes unquestionably had a vast influence on quality here during that period. During the late 1990s he has lost just a touch of the sheen. The wine at its best is still very fine, full of dark cassis and ripe stylish tannin, and is surprisingly approachable. A good straightforward lightly oaked Bordeaux Blanc is also produced, along with the second wine, Haut-Bages-Avérous. Among recent vintages both the 1996 and 95 Grand Vin were very impressive. Among earlier years the trio of 88, 89 and 90 were very fine, as were 85, 82 and 70. (DM)

● **Château Lynch-Bages** Pauillac★★★★★ £F
O **Château Lynch-Bages** Bordeaux★★ £D

CH. MALARTIC-LAGRAVIÈRE   Pessac-Léognan CC   www.malartic-lagraviere.com

Owner: Alfred-Alexandre Bonnie   43 Avenue de Mont-de-Marsan, 33850 Léognan
This property was sold by Champagne house LAURENT-PERRIER to the Bonnie family in 1997and since then there has been significant investment with a dramatic raising of standards. Quality since the 1997 vintage has been very good. Prior to this the whites had shown class on occasion but the red was generally a disappointment. The vineyard is now tended organically with reduced yields and a massive renovation of the cellars now means that winery operations are handled where possible by gravity. Denis Dubourdieu consults for the whites and Michel Rolland for the reds. With 20 per cent Sémillon added to the white it offers a ripe and opulent, lightly oaked style with none of the sulphur of old, while the red is rich, ripe and approachable. Both will develop well over the medium term. The second label for both red and white, Le Sillage de Malartic, now offers reliable drinking. (DM)

● **Château Malartic-Lagravière** Pessac-Léognan★★★ £E
O **Château Malartic-Lagravière** Pessac-Léognan★★★★ £E

CH. MALESCOT-SAINT-EXUPÉRY   Margaux 3ème CC

Owner: Zuger family   33460 Margaux
During the 1980s and early 90s this was a reliable if somewhat unexciting Margaux, but reasonably priced. Quality has taken a significant step up in recent vintages and the price has risen but not excessively so. As is so often the case, a new generation has meant progressive moves forward. The wine is now riper and fuller but not at all extracted, retaining a typically elegant, perfumed Margaux character. With the exception of 1997, which was a touch below par, every recent vintage looks pretty good. (DM)

● **Château Malescot-Saint-Exupéry** Margaux★★★ £F

CH. DE MALLE   Sauternes 2ème CC

Owner: Comtesse de Bournazel   33210 Preignac
The Comtesse de Bournazel has been producing consistently fine and elegant Sauternes since the late 1980s. The château itself is registered as a national monument and open to the public. The wine increasingly shows a rich opulent character as well as an intense fragrance. It perfectly balances weight and finesse. It was very good in 1997 and 98 was of undoubted four star quality. 2001 looks equally promising. A decent white Graves, M de Malle, is also made as well as a red, Château de Cardaillan. (DM)

● **Château de Malle** Sauternes★★★ £E

CH. MARGAUX   Margaux 1er CC   www.chateau-margaux.com

Owner: Agnelli & Mentzelopoulos families   33460 Margaux

Corinne Mentzelopoulos and general manager Paul Pontallier have crafted truly great red Bordeaux now for upwards of two decades. The wine is not only remarkably elegant, with the unmistakably intense perfume of the appellation, but also enormously rich. Loaded with dense but supple tannins, Margaux is remarkably powerful and needs a minimum of 10–12 years' ageing to begin to reveal itself. Meticulous care in the vineyard and at harvest, along with traditional vinification in wooden fermenters, defines the style and quality. The second label, Pavillon Rouge, ensures the integrity of the Grand Vin but is itself regularly very impressive. As well as the 78 ha of red varieties planted there are some 12 ha of Sauvignon Blanc, which produce an intense floral, grassy and complex white sold under the humble Bordeaux AC. Among the great years are 1999, 96, 95, 90, 86, 83, 82, 79 and 78. It was very uneven prior to this and the Mentzelopoulos family involvement. 1961, good for most other top Bordeaux châteaux, was disappointing. (DM)

● **Château Margaux** Margaux✪✪✪✪✪ £H   ● **Pavillon Rouge de Château Margaux**★★★★ £F
○ **Pavillon Blanc de Château Margaux** Bordeaux★★★★★ £F

MA VÉRITÉ   Haut-Médoc

Owner: Gérard Depardieu   c/o Terroirs d'Exception, 33330 Saint-Christophe des Bardes

Produced from a tiny 2 ha vineyard, this is marketed along with a number of other properties throughout the region including LA SERÉNITÉ, PASSION DU PRIEURÉ MALESAN and LA CROIX DE PEYROLIE as part of the Terroirs d'Exception range by Bernard Magrez. The clay and limestone soils are planted to a mix of 55 per cent Cabernet Sauvignon, 40 per cent Merlot and the balance Cabernet Franc and Petit Verdot. Yields are kept very low at less than 20 hl/ha and leaf plucking and *vendange vert* are practiced in the vineyard. Richly textured, with considerable extract the wine nevertheless possesses an elegant cedary character as well as offering copious quantities of ripe cassis and spicy new oak. It will benefit from five or six years ageing. (DM)

● **Ma Vérité** Haut-Médoc★★★★ £F

CH. LA MISSION HAUT-BRION   Pessac-Léognan CC   www.haut-brion.com

*Owner: **Domaine Clarence Dillon**   33608 Pessac*

Like HAUT-BRION, LAVILLE HAUT-BRION and LA TOUR-HAUT-BRION this property is owned by the Domaine Clarence Dillon. La Tour-Haut-Brion used to be the second wine at La Mission but is now handled as its own separate vineyard and property. La Mission is only surpassed among Graves reds by Haut-Brion itself. This is a massive, dense and powerful red. Dark, mineral and black fruits are underpinned by cedar and oak. While the wine perhaps lacks the absolute refinement of its illustrious stablemate, it hasn't fallen far short and is on occasion the more impressive of the two. 1998 and 95 are recent benchmarks and 90, 89, 82, 78 and 75 were all of legendary quality. The second wine, La Chapelle de la Mission Haut-Brion, is a four-star wine in the ripest years. (DM)

● **Château la Mission Haut-Brion** Pessac-Léognan✪✪✪✪✪ £H

CH. MONTROSE   Saint-Estèphe 2ème CC

Owner: Charmolüe family   33180 Saint-Estèphe

This 68-ha property produces around 28,000 cases of exceptional Saint-Estèphe a year. The property is second only behind fellow Second Growth COS D'ESTOURNEL in the appellation hierarchy. These are massive, powerful, brooding wines – dense, tannic and long-lived. Sometimes the fruit struggles to emerge through the iron fist in which it is enveloped. Generally though, in the last decade the wine has become suppler and possesses greater harmony and it was consistently good through the 1990s. 1990 and 95 suggest super-five quality and 2000 may well turn out the same. La Dame de Montrose is an impressive second wine. (DM)

● **Château Montrose** Saint-Estèphe★★★★★ £F   La Dame de Montrose★★★ £E

CH. MOUTON-ROTHSCHILD   Pauillac 1er CC   www.bpdr.com

Owner: Baron Philippe de Rothschild SA   33250 Pauillac
Unique among the First Growths of Bordeaux in that the wine was elevated to its current classification only in 1973, after the successful lobbying of Baron Philippe de Rothschild. The wine is the most opulent and approachable of the top growths, full of dark cassis and cigar box aromas, supported by powerful, supple tannin. Stunning wine was produced in 1982 and 86 but there was some loss of form in the late 80s and early 90s. However, 1996, 98 and 99 have all been back among the very best. The second wine is Le Petit Mouton, and a small amount of a premium white Aile d'Argent is also produced. There is a sizeable merchant business owned by Baronne Philippine de Rothschild, producing a range of pretty ordinary generic AC labels along with the dreary Mouton Cadet. Of greater interest are the two premium partnerships of OPUS ONE with ROBERT MONDAVI in California and ALMAVIVA with CONCHA Y TORO in Chile. (DM)

● **Château Mouton-Rothschild** Pauillac✪✪✪✪✪ £H

CH. NAIRAC   Barsac 2ème CC

Owner: Nicolas Tari-Heeter   33720 Barsac
A small property of just some 17 ha with annual production of barely more than 1,000 cases. The wine often outperforms its Second Growth status. Always picked very ripe, it gains real structure from a high proportion of new oak used for ageing. At times this can seem almost overpowering in its youth but given patience the wine can show a marvellous balance of intense, peachy botrytised fruit and almost sweet vanilla oak. Definitely cellar for six or seven years. (DM)

● **Château Nairac** Barsac★★★★ £E

CH. PALMER   Margaux 3ème CC   www.chateau-palmer.com

Owner: Mahler Besse/Sichel Families   Cantenac, 33460 Margaux
This marvellous property is often thought of as a Second Growth and for a period before the Mentzelopoulos years at Château MARGAUX it was also the benchmark for the AC. At its best the wine displays not only the perfume of the appellation but ripe, powerful, almost sumptuous dark fruit. In part this must be down to the very high proportion of Merlot planted, at 47 per cent the same as Cabernet Sauvignon. The second wine, Alter Ego de Palmer, tends to have an even higher proportion of Merlot in the final blend. 1995, 96 and 98 Palmer were of a very high standard and the most recent vintages have similar promise. Of the great years here, 89 and 83 also stand out as do the earlier years of 70, 66 and 61. (DM)

● **Château Palmer** Margaux★★★★ £G

CH. PAPE-CLÉMENT   Pessac-Léognan CC   www.pape-clement .com

Owner: Léo Montagne/Bernard Magrez   216 Avenue du Docteur-Nancel-Pénard, 33650 Martillac
Excellent 32.5-ha property dominated by red vine plantings and like Haut-Brion engulfed by the

suburbs of Bordeaux. The white varieties account for a mere 2.5 ha with 10 per cent of this being Muscadelle. Both wines are rich and powerful and the red has real density and power but is still approachable and harmonious. The tiny production of white has an elegant, intense mineral and citrus streak adding to its complexity and all nicely supported by sufficient creamy new oak. Generally very good throughout the 1990s and particularly after 1995. The red in 98 and 99 was worth a five-star rating. (DM)

● **Château Pape-Clément** Pessac-Léognan★★★★ £E
O **Château Pape-Clément** Pessac-Léognan★★★★ £E

CH. PICHON-LONGUEVILLE   Pauillac 2ème CC   www.chateaupichonlongueville.com

Owner: AXA Millésimes   33250 Pauillac
Sizeable Second Growth with some 73 ha under vine, bought in 1987 by AXA Millésimes – the fine wine arm of the AXA insurance company. Jean-Michel Cazes, who owns Château LYNCH-BAGES, took over the management of the Bordeaux AXA operation and quality quickly improved with very successful vintages in 1989 and 90. These are world-class, super-five wines: deep, dark, powerful Pauillac but very finely balanced. Quality since then has not been at quite the same heady heights; very good certainly but not quite of the same order. (DM)

● **Château Pichon-Longueville** Pauillac★★★★ £F

CH. PICHON-LONGUEVILLE-LALANDE   Pauillac 2ème CC   www.pichon-lalande.com

Owner: Lencquesaing family   33250 Pauillac
A property marked by its rich, elegant, almost sumptuous style of wine. It is no surprise that there are considerable plantings of Merlot (35 per cent). The balance is Cabernet Sauvignon (45 per cent), Cabernet Franc (12 per cent) and a relatively whopping 8 per cent of very old Petit Verdot. The vineyards border Saint-Julien and this also helps contribute to the wine's intense, fragrant and complex style. However, there have been some strange variations in quality over the last couple of decades. Vintages of the late 1990s have been strangely disappointing, whereas 1995 and 96 were magnificent, clear super-five wines. Other exceptional years have included 86, 83 and, of course, the legendary 82. Réserve de la Comtesse is the second wine. (DM)

● **Château Pichon-Longueville-Lalande** Pauillac★★★★★ £G   ● **Réserve de la Comtesse**★★ £E

CH. PONTET-CANET   Pauillac 5ème CC   www.pontet-canet.com

Owner: Tesseron Family   33250 Pauillac
This property has been in the ownership of the Tesseron Family, who also own Château LAFON-ROCHET, for over two decades. They have been responsible for bringing it up to its current level, where it has generally justified its Fifth Growth status. Produced from vineyards planted on some of the best gravel soils of the appellation, at its peak it is exactly what you think of as quintessential Pauillac – big, powerful and dense with supple, well-rounded tannin and an intense fragrance of cassis and cedar. 1989 saw a significant upturn in quality. After the generally poor years between 91 and 93, really only 97 has been lighter and less impressive, indeed 99 clearly rated four stars. (DM)

● **Château Pontet-Canet** Pauillac★★★ £F

CH. POTENSAC   Médoc   www.chateau-potensac.com

Owner: Delon family   33340 Ordonnac
Under the same ownership as LÉOVILLE-LAS-CASES, this is without doubt the finest property sold as Médoc AC. The now very old vines are planted on a mix of alluvial gravel and clay soils. The wine is consistently excellent, ripe but sufficiently firm, with a hint of new wood (about 20 per cent) providing additional depth. Bottled without filtration it is better with five years' cellaring. The 1996 is particularly impressive. All in all this is a very good-value claret. (DM)
● **Château Potensac** Médoc★★★ £D

CH. POUJEAUX   Moulis   www.chateaupoujeaux.com

Owner: Theil family   33480 Moulis-en-Médoc
Along with CHASSE-SPLEEN, this is one of the two best wines in the Moulis AC, performing with an impressive consistency throughout the last ten years and more. There are 53 ha under vine here, with Cabernet Sauvignon accounting for slightly more of the vineyard than Merlot. Like most quality-conscious wine producers, there is a dedication in the vineyard and cellar which contributes to the final wine. The style is rich and sumptuous with a hint of vanilla from its twelve months of oak-ageing. Handling is kept to a minimum with just egg-white fining and no filtration. A further notch up from 1996, including 97. (DM)
● **Château Poujeaux** Moulis★★★ £E

CH. PRIEURÉ-LICHINE   Margaux 4ème CC   prieure.lichine@wanadoo.fr

Owner: Ballande family   34 Avenue de la Cinquième République, 33460 Cantenac
The Ballandes, who run the *négociant* operation the Ballande group, purchased this property from the Lichine family in 1999. Unusually there are parcels of vineyard spread throughout the appellation. There has been consultancy input from Michel Rolland as well as the talented young enologist Stéphane Derenoncourt. The wine is increasingly sumptuous and supple. This is an ambitious operation and it will be interesting to see how quality develops over the next five years or so. The wine showed good potential in 1996 and 98 and this standard looks like being maintained. (DM)
● **Château Prieuré-Lichine** Margaux★★★ £E

CH. RABAUD-PROMIS   Sauternes 1er CC

Owner: Philippe Dejean   33210 Bommes
After a long period in the doldrums, this 33-ha property has now been making impressive Sauternes for well more than a decade. This is a full, rich and honeyed wine with not only impressive depth, concentration and the structure to age very well but also real balance and harmony. It can be very intense and stylish, particularly in top years. Very impressive since 1994 and prior to that 90, 89 and 88 are very good indeed. (DM)
O **Château Rabaud-Promis** Sauternes★★★★ £F

CH. RAUZAN-SÉGLA   Margaux 2ème CC

Owner: Wertheimer family   33460 Margaux
This château was acquired by the Wertheimers, who own the Chanel perfume business, in 1994 and a large amount of investment has been put into the property since then. They also now own Château CANON in Saint-Émilion. Prior to the change of ownership the property performed remarkably well

in the run of vintages from 1988 to 90 but this wasn't always so. Vinification is now very modern, using temperature-controlled stainless steel, and ageing is in 60 per cent new oak for 18 months. The wine has a fine, elegant texture and displays a complex array of dark fruits and cedar. There is surprising tannin here, though, and the wine will improve with at least five or six years' cellaring. It has been very consistent since 1995, with the exception of 97 which was a disappointment. (DM)

● **Château Rauzan-Ségla** Margaux ★★★★ £F

CH. RAYMOND-LAFON   Sauternes   www.chateau-raymond-lafon.fr

Owner: Meslier family   33210 Sauternes
The production is tiny at just over 1,600 cases a year from the 18 ha of vineyard. The blend is 80 per cent Sémillon with the balance Sauvignon Blanc and no Muscadelle. Not a Classed Growth, Raymond-Lafon is located right next to Yquem and has consistently produced wines in the great years of the last two decades which rival all but the absolute best in Sauternes. This has been achieved through a dedicated approach in the vineyard, tiny yields of just 8.5 hl/ha, careful and repeatedly selective harvesting (*tris*) and extensive use of new oak in the cellar. The wine is barrel-fermented and aged for up to three years in wood. (DM)

O **Château Raymond-Lafon** Sauternes★★★★★ £F

CH. DE RAYNE-VIGNEAU   Sauternes 1er CC

Owner: SC Ch. de Rayne-Vigneau   La Croix Bacalan, 109. Rue Achard, BP 154, 33042 Bordeaux
Relatively sizeable, this property has some 80 ha of vineyards. It is under the same ownership as Château GRAND-PUY-DUCASSE in Pauillac. The gravel soils here suggest a real potential to the *terroir* that has not yet fully been realised. However, like so many Sauternes châteaux, its reputation has improved over the last two decades. The wine is characterised by its elegant and complex botrytised fruit, with a tight, restrained structure. These are not overfull, super-weighty wines but at their best are impressively refined and intense. (DM)

O **Château de Rayne-Vigneau** Sauternes★★★ £E

CH. RIEUSSEC   Sauternes 1er CC   www.lafite.com

Owner: Domaines Baron de Rothschild   33210 Fargues-de-Langon
Under the same ownership as LAFITE-ROTHSCHILD, this Sauternes is generally regarded as being second only in weight and power to YQUEM. It has generally performed at that level since 1995 and particularly during the trio of great Sauternes years from 88 to 90. Aged in a high proportion of new oak it is almost always a powerful, very rich, opulent but classically structured wine in need of eight to ten years' ageing, often longer in truly great vintages. (DM)

O **Château Rieussec** Sauternes✪✪✪✪✪ £F

CH. ROLLAN-DE-BY   Médoc   www.rollandeby.com

Owner: Jean Guyon   7 Route Rollan-de-By, 33340 Bégadan
This 37-ha property has performed with distinction throughout the past decade and is a shining light for other producers in the outlying areas of the Médoc. The vineyard is planted with a sizeable 70 per cent Merlot and this, allied to the judicious use of new oak, accounts for the ripe, almost lush, plump and approachable fruit style. Haut-Condissas is a premium label with more Cabernet Sauvignon in the blend. (DM)

● **Château Rollan-de-By** Médoc★★ £D   Haut-Condissas ★★★ £E

CH. SAINT-PIERRE Saint-Julien 2ème CC

Owner: Triaud family 33250 Saint-Julien-Beychevelle
This property was purchased in 1981 by the late Henri Martin (the former owner of GLORIA) and is now run by his daughter, Françoise Triaud. Although the wine has been consistently good throughout the last ten years, it has never quite achieved the potential that its classification suggests. The approach to vinification is always meticulous, with a rigorous selection pre-fermentation and judicious use of new oak. The wine was certainly above average in 1990 and may well achieve similar heights again with the fine 2000 vintage. (DM)
● **Château Saint-Pierre** Saint-Julien★★★ £E

CH. SIGALAS-RABAUD Sauternes 1er CC

Owner: Lambert des Granges family 33210 Bommes
This is the smaller part of the original Château Rabaud, which was divided nearly a century ago. The other half is RABAUD-PROMIS and both are Sauternes First Growths. The wine is very rich and gloriously honeyed and can show very marked botrytis but it is still refined and very elegant. Indeed the wine has been impressive for years and was one of the few properties to perform well in the 1960s and 70s, a period of recession in the appellation. The great vintages in these decades can at least be approached with some optimism. More recently 1999, 98, 97and 96 were all on top form and are nudging five stars, as are the great trio of 88, 89 and 90. (DM)
O **Château Sigalas-Rabaud** Sauternes★★★★ £F

CH. SMITH HAUT LAFITTE Pessac-Léognan CC   www.smith-haut-lafitte.com

Owner: Daniel & Florence Cathiard 33650 Martillac
The wines here under the current ownership are now very good. Around 80 per cent of the production is red, with a mix of 55 per cent Cabernet Sauvignon, 35 per cent Merlot and the balance Cabernet Franc. The white is dominated by Sauvignon Blanc but there is a sprinkling of Sémillon and more unusually Sauvignon Gris (similar in flavour to Sauvignon Blanc but with a slight pink tinge to its skin). The red is lighter in style than some of its neighbours but now possesses impressive depth. The white is fermented relatively cool to retain a marked floral, herbal core and is aged in 50 per cent new oak. Neither wine is filtered and both have performed admirably since 1995, 97 being a touch weak for the red, but 2000 was on the cusp of five stars for both red and white. (DM)
● **Château Smith Haut Lafitte** Pessac-Léognan★★★★ £F
O **Château Smith Haut Lafitte** Pessac-Léognan★★★★ £F

CH. SOCIANDO-MALLET Haut-Médoc

Owner: Jean Gautreau 33180 Saint-Seurin-de-Cadourne
This is now undoubtedly the most impressive estate in the Haut-Médoc, a title at one stage that would almost invariably have been given to La LAGUNE. Quality here since 1995 has been good to very good. Perhaps in 97 and 98 it did not quite rate four stars but the wines are impressive dark, powerful and very ageworthy all the same. The style is of a true *vin de garde*, in part due to the well-drained gravel soils, which produce supple but youthfully firm, powerful tannins. Impressive earlier vintages include 1990, 89 and the classic 82. The second wine is Demoiselle, which can be good. (DM)
● **Château Sociando-Mallet** Haut-Médoc★★★★ £E

CH. SUDUIRAUT Sauternes 1er CC www.suduiraut.com

Owner: AXA Millésimes 33210 Preignac

Purchased by the current owners in 1992 and more care is now taken with harvesting at this property which neighbours YQUEM. The fruit is now picked more selectively and late enough to maximise the effect of noble rot. As a result the wine has become increasingly full and rich. It is aged for 18 to 24 months in barrel, adding to its impressive depth and concentration as well. It was very good in 1989 and 90 as well as more recently in 95, 96 and 97. 2001 also looks extremely promising. The second wine, Castelnau de Suduiraut, can be of sound quality and ensures the integrity of the Grand Vin. (DM)

O **Château Suduiraut** Sauternes★★★★★ £F

CH. TALBOT Saint-Julien 2ème CC www.chateau-talbot.com

Owner: Lorraine Rustmann/Nancy Bignon 33250 Saint-Julien-Beychevelle

Originally a Cordier *négociant* property, Talbot has been retained by members of the family and the quality of the Grand Vin has remained reasonably consistent, particularly after 1995. It is now very international in styled and quite different to some of the very firm earlier examples under Cordier ownership. 1998 and 2000 were both very good and 01 looks to be similarly promising. The second wine, Connetable Talbot, has been good in the better years and there is a small amount of a white, Caillou Blanc, produced under the Bordeaux AC. This used to be variable with marked sulphur but a more modern approach to its vinification is now undertaken with better results. (DM)

● **Château Talbot** Saint-Julien★★★ £F

CH. LA TOUR BLANCHE Sauternes 1er CC

Owner: Ministère de l'Agriculture 33210 Bommes

There are a total of some 40 ha under vine at this property run by the Ministry of Agriculture and although this is also an agricultural school very high standards are maintained. The vineyards are particularly well sited and result in a big, full-bodied Sauternes produced with marked botrytis and well-judged new oak. The wines have real intensity and power. 1998, 97 and 96 have all been good and the trio of 88, 89 and 90 were also excellent.

O **Château la Tour Blanche** Sauternes★★★★ £F

CH. LA TOUR HAUT-BRION Pessac-Léognan CC www.haut-brion.com

Owner: Domaine Clarence Dillon 33608 Pessac

Originally the second wine at LA MISSION HAUT-BRION, this property stands alone with its own identity now that the vineyard is ageing. It neighbours its former big brother and, although the wines are still overshadowed by the powerful dense style of La Mission, they are becoming increasingly impressive in their own right. Eighty per cent of the vineyard is planted to Cabernet Sauvignon and Cabernet Franc, resulting in a very srurdy style in the wine's youth. 1995 and 98 were both very impressive and 2000 looks to have equal potential. (DM)

● **Château la Tour Haut-Brion** Pessac-Léognan★★★ £E

CH. VILLA BEL AIR   Graves   www.villabelair.com

Owner: Jean-Michel Cazes   33650 Saint-Morillon
Reliable Graves property producing around 12,000 cases each of red and white Graves. The property was taken over by Jean-Michel Cazes in 1990 and the cellars modernised and the winemaking brought up to speed. Barrel-fermentation for the white and a red which emphasises attractive dark, black fruit in a supple, approachable style are the keys here. Generally good in 2000, 1999 and 98 although prices do seem to be creeping up as well. (DM)

● **Château Villa Bel Air** Graves★★ £C
O **Château Villa Bel Air** Graves★★ £C

CH. D'YQUEM   Sauternes 1er GCC

Owner: LVMH   33210 Sauternes
Arguably the greatest sweet wine in the world. Owned by the Lur Saluces family for more than two centuries it was purchased by LVMH in 1999. Alexandre de Lur Saluces continues to make the wine. There are 103 ha under vine but the vineyards have a superb exposure in the centre of the appellation and enjoy an ideal mix of morning mist and warm sunshine. With a sizeable production of around 8,000 cases a year it is certain that, while occasional TBAs from Germany or SGNs from Alsace might rival it for sheer depth, dimension and fruit intensity, they never will at the volume produced at Yquem. The same remarkable level of attention is spent producing the wine, with harvesting not so much by *tris* but more berry by berry and at a microscopic yield. New oak is used throughout and the wine is bottled without filtration after spending more than three years in cask. These are wines of supreme quality that will last for half a century or more, always outstanding in top years. (DM)

O **Château d'Yquem** Sauternes✪✪✪✪✪ £H

MÉDOC, GRAVES & SAUTERNES/OTHER WINES OF NOTE

CH. BEL-AIR ● **Saint-Estèphe** £C
CH. BELLE VUE ● **Haut-Médoc** £C
CH. BISTON-BRILLETTE ● **Moulis** £C
CH. BROWN ● **Pessac-Léognan** £D
CH. BERNADOTTE ● **Haut-Médoc** £C
CH. BOUSCAUT O **Pessac-Léognan** £D
CH. CITRAN ● **Haut-Médoc** £C
CLOS DU JAUGEYRON ● **Haut-Médoc** £C   ● **Margaux** £F
CH. COUFRAN ● **Haut-Médoc** £C
CRU BARRÉJATS O **Sauternes** £F
CH. DE CRUZEAU ● **Pessac-Léognan** £D   O **Pessac-Léognan** £D
CH. DESMIRAIL ● **Margaux** £E
CH. DURFORT-VIVENS ● **Margaux** £E
CH. DES EYRINS ● **Margaux** £C
CH. DE FARGUES O **Sauternes** £F
CH. FILHOT O **Sauternes** £E
CH. FONBADET ● **Pauillac** £D
CH. LA GARDE ● **Pessac-Léognan** £D
CH. GILETTE O **Sauternes** £G
CH. GISCOURS ● **Margaux** £D

CH. GRAND-PUY-DUCASSE ● Pauillac £E
CH. LES GRANDS CHÊNES ● Médoc £D Prestige £D
CH. GREYSAC ● Médoc £C
CH. HAUT-BAGES-LIBÉRAL ● Pauillac £D
CH. HAUT-BERGEY ● Pessac-Léognan £E O Pessac-Léognan £E
CH. HAUT-GARDÈRE ● Pessac-Léognan £D
CH. HAUT-BERGERON O Sauternes £E
CH. LES JUSTICES O Sauternes £E
CH. LABÉGORCE-ZÉDÉ ● Margaux £E
CH. LAFON ● Médoc £C
CH. LAMOTHE O Sauternes £E
CH. LASCOMBES ● Margaux £E
CH. LILIAN-LADOUYS ● Saint-Estèphe £D
CH. LIOT O Barsac £D
CH. LYNCH-MOUSSAS ● Pauillac £E
MAGREZ TIVOLI ● Haut-Médoc £F
CH. MARBUZET ● Saint-Estèphe £C
MAROJALLIA ● Margaux £H
CH. MARQUIS-DE-TERME ● Margaux £D
CH. MAUCAILLOU ● Moulis £C
CH. MEYNEY ● Saint-Estèphe £D
CH. MILLE-ROSES ● Haut-Médoc £C
CH. MONBRISON ● Margaux £D
CH. DU MOULIN ROUGE ● Haut-Médoc £C
CH. OLIVIER ● Pessac-Léognan £D O Pessac-Léognan £D
CH. LES ORMES-DE-PEZ ● Saint-Estèphe £D
CH. LES ORMES-SORBET ● Médoc £D
CH. DE PEZ ● Saint-Estèphe £D
CH. PEYRABON ● Haut-Médoc £D
CH. PHÉLAN-SÉGUR ● Saint-Estephe £D
CH. PIBRAN ● Pauillac £E
CH. POUMEY ● Pessac-Léognan £D
CH. RAHOUL ● Graves £C O Graves £C
CH. RAMAGE-LA-BATISSE ● Haut-Médoc £C
CH. RAUZAN-GASSIES ● Margaux £E
CH. RESPIDE-MÉDEVILLE ● Graves £D O Graves £D
CH. DE ROCHEMORIN O Pessac-Léognan £E
CH. ROMER-DU-HAYOT O Sauternes £D
CH. SÉNÉJAC ● Haut-Médoc £C Cuvée Karolus £D
CH. SIRAN ● Margaux £E
CH. SOUDARS ● Haut-Médoc £C
CH. SUAU O Barsac £E
CH. DU TERTRE ● Margaux £D
CH. TOUR-HAUT-CAUSSAN ● Médoc £C
CH. TOUR DU HAUT-MOULIN ● Haut-Médoc £C
CH. VERDIGNAN ● Haut-Médoc £C
VIEUX CHÂTEAU GAUBERT ● Graves £C O Graves £C
VIEUX CHÂTEAU-LANDON ● Médoc £C
CH. VIEUX ROBIN ● Médoc £C

Author's choice (DM)

MÉDOC, GRAVES & SAUTERNES

Great cellarworthy Left Bank reds
CH. COS D'ESTOURNEL ● Saint-Estèphe 2ème CC
CH. DUCRU-BEAUCAILLOU ● Saint-Julien 2ème CC
CH. HAUT-BRION ● Pessac-Léognan I er CC
CH. LAFITE-ROTHSCHILD ● Pauillac I er CC
CH. LATOUR ● Pauillac I er CC
CH. LÉOVILLE-LAS-CASES ● Saint-Julien 2ème CC
CH. MARGAUX ● Margaux I er CC
CH. LA MISSION-HAUT-BRION ● Pessac-Léognan CC
CH. MOUTON-ROTHSCHILD ● Pauillac I er CC
CH. PICHON-LONGUEVILLE-LALANDE ● Pauillac 2ème CC

The best of Sauternes and Barsac
CH. CLIMENS O Barsac I er CC
CH. COUTET O Barsac I er CC
CH. GUIRAUD O Sauternes I er CC
CH. LAFAURIE-PEYRAGUEY O Sauternes I er CC
CH. RABAUD-PROMIS O Sauternes I er CC
CH. RAYMOND-LAFON O Sauternes
CH. RIEUSSEC O Sauternes I er CC
CH. SIGALAS-RABAUD O Sauternes I er CC
CH. SUDUIRAUT O Sauternes I er CC
CH. D'YQUEM O Sauternes I er GCC

Classic dry whites
CH. CARBONNIEUX O Pessac-Léognan CC
DOM. DE CHEVALIER O Pessac-Léognan CC
CLOS FLORIDÈNE O Graves
CH. DE FIEUZAL O Pessac-Léognan
CH. HAUT-BRION O Pessac-Léognan
CH. LAVILLE-HAUT-BRION O Pessac-Léognan CC
CH. LA LOUVIÈRE O Pessac-Léognan
CH. PAPE-CLÉMENT O Pessac-Léognan
PAVILLON BLANC DE MARGAUX O Bordeaux
CH. SMITH-HAUT-LAFITTE O Pessac-Léognan

Saint-Emilion, Pomerol & other Bordeaux

DOM. DE L'A   Côtes de Castillon

Owner: Stéphane Derenoncourt   Pavie Nord, 33330 Saint-Émilion
This is the tiny 4-ha home property of winemaking guru Stéphane Derenoncourt. It is planted to old vine Merlot, Cabernet Franc and a little Cabernet Sauvignon and is farmed biodynamically. The result is remarkably dense and powerful wine from this outlying Bordeaux appellation. The wine is fermented in wood, aged on lees to add weight and texture and afterwards bottled without fining or filtration. Along with a number of other small impressive properties, this is a model for producers from the region's lesser ACs. (DM)
● **Domaine de l'A** Côtes de Castillon★★★ £E

CH. D'AIGUILHE Côtes de Castillon www.neipperg.com

Owner: Comte Stephan von Neipperg 33350 Saint-Philippe-d'Aiguilhe
This very fine Castillon property is part of the same ownership as CANON LA GAFFELIÈRE and LA MONDOTTE. The property consists of 65 ha of which 42 are planted to vines on the upper slopes which not only have an excellent southerly exposure but also very well drained clay/limestone soils. The wine is blended from Merlot 80 per cent and the balance Cabernet Franc. Fermentation is in oak vats but with temperature control and the wine is aged in a very high proportion (80 per cent) of new oak on its lees. It is neither fined nor filtered. Lushly textured, concentrated and impressively complex there is a fine, youthfully firm structure to the tannin which needs a good five or six years' ageing. (DM)
● **Château d'Aiguilhe** Cotes de Castillon★★★★ £E

CH. ANGÉLUS Saint-Émilion 1er GCC www.angelus.com

Owner: Bouard de la Forest et Fils 33330 Saint-Émilion
This has consistently been one of the top-performing Saint-Émilion Grands Crus Classés over the last 10–15 years. In 1996 the property was upgraded to Premier Grand Cru Classé. These are deeply coloured, concentrated wines, extracted with deep, and dark blackcurrant and plum fruit. They are always produced with well-judged oak treatment but very finely balanced as well. 1995 and 2000 have both been outstanding vintages. (DM)
● **Château Angélus** Saint-Émilion Grand Cru Classé★★★★★ £H

CH. L'ARROSÉE Saint-Émilion GCC

Owner: François Rodhain 33330 Saint-Émilion
Solidly impressive Grand Cru Classé producing ripe, moderately dense and powerful wines. They tend to be marked by their lush and velvety texture and can be broached at around five years or so, despite having around 40 per cent Cabernet Sauvignon in the blend. At present this is a good, rather than great, property. (DM)
● **Château l'Arrosée** Saint-Émilion Grand Cru Classé★★ £F

CH. AUSONE Saint Émilion 1er GCC

Owner: Alain Vauthier 33330 Saint-Émilion
One of the great wines of the Right Bank. Ausone, along with CHEVAL-BLANC, has always been considered to stand out and the two are classified Premiers Grands Crus Classés A-grade properties. The wine has been consistently impressive since the late 1980s and in the last half a dozen years has been produced in a rich, supple and immensely velvety style. Very fine and complex it is now increasingly rich and oaky. Alain Vauthier has gained valuable input on the winemaking approach from Michel Rolland. The blend comprises a roughly equal proportion of Merlot and Cabernet Franc. It has been absolutely top-flight since 1995 with the exception of 97. Approachable at five or six years, the wine benefits from twice that time. (DM)
● **Château Ausone** Saint Émilion Grand Cru Classé✪✪✪✪✪ £H

CH. BEAU-SÉJOUR BÉCOT   Saint-Émilion 1er GCC   www.beausejour-becot.com

Owner: Gérard & Dominique Bécot   33330, Saint-Émilion
This 16.5-ha property was reintroduced to the ranks of the Premiers Grands Crus Classés in 1996. The style is one of considerable extraction and the Bécot brothers seek to produce an opulent, rich, heavily oaked red with sumptuous, plummy fruit. In general they succeed very well. They also make a *garagiste*-style *cuvée* called La Gomerie. Less than a thousand cases of this Merlot aged in 100 per cent new oak are produced. It is sourced from a tiny 2.5-ha plot which is itself unclassified. Both wines need five or six years to shed the hard edge of their tannins. (DM)
● **Château Beau-Séjour Bécot** Saint-Émilion Grand Cru Classé★★★★ £G
● **La Gomerie** Saint-Émilion Grand Cru★★★★★ £H

CH. BEAUREGARD   Pomerol

Owner: Vincent Priou   33500 Pomerol
One of Pomerol's lesser-known châteaux, this 17.5-ha property has an unusually high proportion of Cabernet Franc planted, around 30 per cent. This is in part because of a high gravel component in the soil. The wine is ripe and forward, with attractively brambly fruit and a hint of oak spice, but with less overtly fleshy, plummy Merlot fruit than some others in the appellation. Very good in 1998, of four-star quality, tight, intense and composed. It is approachable and supple at four or five years. (DM)
● **Château Beauregard** Pomerol★★★ £E

CH. BEAUSÉJOUR   Saint-Émilion 1er GCC   www.premiers-saint-emilion.com

Owner: Héritiers Duffau-Lagarrosse   33330 Saint-Émilion
Prior to 1985 this property was a notable underperformer among the Premier Grands Crus Classés. Since then the wine has been altogether more impressive. The style is medium to full with a marked black fruit opulence but sufficiently firm tannins to provide the structure needed for real cellaring. 1990 was truly impressive and the property has been consistent throughout the 1990s with 2000 again looking like providing that additional dimension. (DM)
● **Château Beauséjour** Saint-Émilion Grand Cru Classé★★★ £G

CH. LA BIENFAISANCE   Saint-Émilion GC   www.labienfaisance.com

Owner: Duval-Fleury family   33330 Saint-Christophe-des-Bardes
Good small property located on the northern plateau of Saint-Émilion with a total of 16 ha planted in limestone, sand and clay/limestone soils across three parcels. Merlot dominates plantings at around 80% with 15% Cabernet Franc, along with a smattering of Cabernet Sauvignon. Vinification for La Bienfaisance is traditional with fermentation in cement and ageing in a small proportion of new oak. A richer and more opulent garage style wine is also produced. Sanctus is aged in 100 per cent new oak. Produced with consultation from Stéphane Derenoncourt, it is less extracted and better balanced than many of its peers. The 2002 was right on the cusp of four stars. (DM)
● **Château La Bienfaisance** Saint-Émilion Grand Cru ★★ £D
● **Sanctus** Saint-Émilion Grand Cru ★★★ £E

CH. LE BON PASTEUR   Pomerol

Owner: Michel Rolland   33500 Pomerol
Small Pomerol property owned by roving wine consultant Michel Rolland. The vineyards are rigorously maintained and yields tightly harnessed. The wine is inevitably fleshy, rich and characteristic of the Rolland style with malolactic fermentation instigated in barrel. While structured and ageworthy the wine is supple, rounded and approachable with just a few years' cellaring. (DM)
● **Château le Bon Pasteur** Pomerol★★★★ £F

CH. BONNET   Entre-Deux-Mers   www.andrelurton.com

Owner: André Lurton   33420 Grézillac
This now very substantial operation is owned by André Lurton who produces first-class results with a number of Châteaux in the Graves and Pessac-Léognan appellations, including Château LA LOUVIÈRE. Production is around 125,000 cases a year and the property has some 122 ha of red and 103 ha of white varieties under vine. Red, white and a Bordeaux *clairet* – a lightly coloured style of rosé – are all produced. The reds take the Bordeaux appellation and include a Réserve aged partly in new wood. The dry whites, a tank-fermented Classique and barrel fermented Réserve, are sold as Entre-Deux-Mers. A new prestige red *cuvée,* Divinus, has been added to the range. (DM)
● **Château Bonnet** Bordeaux Réserve★★ £B

CH. CANON   Saint-Émilion 1er GCC   contact@chateau-canon.com

Owner: Wertheimer family   33330 Saint-Émilion
Now under the same ownership as Château RAUZAN-SEGLA. Historically a very significant property and one that is now making a welcome return to the top division of Saint-Émilion estates. The vineyard has recently been extended with the purchase of Château Curé-Bon, which has been incorporated into Canon. The cellars have also been cleaned up and modernised after taint problems. The 1998 was a clear step-up in quality and recent vintages have maintained this trend. Prior to this you should tread with caution. At its best this is a taut, restrained style with finely structured tannin. It is elegant, medium weight and once more very ageworthy. (DM)
● **Château Canon** Saint-Émilion Grand Cru Classé★★★ £F

CH. CANON-DE-BREM   Canon-Fronsac

Owner: Carrefour   33500 Libourne
Impressive property formerly owned by the Moueix family's *négociant* arm and now by Carrefour. Performance here was somewhat erratic during the early 1990s but has shown a significant improvement of late. The style is purposefully structured and the tannin can be almost austere when the wine is young. Additional refinement is achieved through limited use of new oak and from 1998 the wine has shown an impressive level of ripe, dark plummy fruit and a fleshy, if gripping texture. Better with five years' ageing. (DM)
● **Château Canon-de-Brem** Canon-Fronsac★★ £C

CH. CANON-LA-GAFFELIÈRE   Saint Émilion GCC   www.neipperg.com

Owner: Vignobles von Neipperg   33330 Saint-Émilion
Canon-la-Gaffelière is now one of a number of striking labels and properties run by Stéphan von

Neipperg, who owns the CLOS DE L'ORATOIRE, also in Saint-Émilion, and the outperforming Château D'AIGUILHE in the Côtes de Castillon. The style here, as with all the von Neipperg wines, is opulent, rich and supple, with finely integrated oak and soft, velvety tannin. Canon-la-Gaffelière is itself surprisingly approachable at three or four years. The property is located on the lower-lying limestone slopes below the town of Saint-Émilion. Dominated by old vine Cabernet Franc, it has been consistently good over the last six or seven vintages. The *super-cuvée* LA MONDOTTE is also now made here. (DM)

● **Château Canon-la-Gaffelière** Saint Émilion Grand Cru Classé★★★★£G

CH. CARSIN   Premières Côtes de Bordeaux   www.carsin.com

Owner: Julia Berglund   33410 Rions
A good example of what many properties are now beginning to achieve in the less fashionable outlying appellations of Bordeaux. It is based in the Premières Côtes de Bordeaux and the reds are labelled as such, the whites as Bordeaux AC. The regular bottlings are sound and attractive enough, with nicely developed forward fruit, but it is the white Cuvée Prestige and red Cuvée Noire that particularly stand out here. The white has a touch of barrel-fermentation and is ripe and lightly tropical, with well-judged oak. The red is supple, soft and approachable, with just a hint of vanilla oak underpinning it. Signature l'Etiquette Gris is a limited-production white from Sauvignon Gris and there is also a sweet, moderately intense Cadillac. (DM)

● **Château Carsin** Premières Côtes de Bordeaux Cuvée Noire★★£C
O **Château Carsin** Bordeaux Cuvée Prestige★★£B

CH. CERTAN-DE-MAY   Pomerol

Owner: Mme Barreau-Badar   33500 Pomerol
Very good, stylish and elegant Pomerol from a tiny holding of vineyards close to PÉTRUS. This is more classically structured than many of its peers and is tight and almost austere when young. Cabernet Franc accounts for 25 per cent of the vineyard, along with a little Cabernet Sauvignon that lends tannin and grip. The wine becomes very harmonious with up to a decade's age. (DM)

● **Château Certan-de-May** Pomerol★★★★£H

CH. CHAUVIN   Saint-Émilion GCC   www.chateauchauvin.com

Owner: Marie-France Février et Beatrice Ondet   1 Cabanne Nord, 33330 Saint-Émilion
This property has been a consistent performer through most of the mid- to late 1990s. Consultancy input has been provided by Michel Rolland and the style is full, rich and fleshy, with supple, well-rounded tannin and real complexity in 1998 and 99. A special bottling, Vieux Château Chauvin, has so far only been produced in 1998. (DM)

● **Château Chauvin Saint-Émilion** Grand Cru Classé★★★£E

CH. CHEVAL BLANC   Saint-Émilion 1er GCC   www.chateau-cheval-blanc.com

Owner: Bernard Arnault & Albert Frère   33330 Saint-Émilion
One of the two great wines of Saint-Émilion and produced in much greater quantity than AUSONE, some 12,500 cases a year as against barely 2,000. It has also regularly performed at the very highest level throughout the last two decades. Cheval Blanc is located close to the appellation boundary with Pomerol. There is a high proportion of Cabernet Franc in the vineyard (over 50 per cent), which makes the wine quite different to its near neighbours. Bernault Arnault and Albert Frère purchased

the property in the late 1990s and no expense will be spared in attempting to establish Cheval Blanc as the greatest property on Bordeaux's Right Bank. The style is rich, concentrated and opulent, with intensely complex, dark berry fruit and spice all underpinned by a structured velvety texture. To fully appreciate it in all its glory, 10 years or more of ageing is required. A wine of truly legendary proportions in 1990, 83 and 82 and 2000 may yet reach similar heights. (DM)

● **Château Cheval Blanc** Saint-Émilion Grand Cru Classé✪✪✪✪✪ £H

CH. CLINET Pomerol www.wines-uponatime.com

Owner: Jean-Louis Laborde 3 Rue Fénelon, 33000 Bordeaux

Michel Rolland has provided consultancy input at this property for over 10 years, first to the late Jean-Michel Arcaute and now to Jean-Louis Laborde. The style has remained consistent throughout the period. Ripe to very ripe, full, rich and almost opulent with a supple silky texure, the wine is always bottled with neither fining nor filtration and is aged in 100 per cent new oak. Don't be fooled, though, as there is both depth and a firm tannic structure to the young wine. Best with at least five years of ageing. (DM)

● **Château Clinet** Pomerol★★★★ £G

CLOS L'ÉGLISE Pomerol

Owner: Sylvain Garcin-Cathiard 33500 Pomerol

There are just 6-ha of vines producing this fine and impressively dense and powerful Pomerol. The wine is lent considerable structure by the inclusion of up to 40 per cent Cabernet Franc. It was very stylish in 1998 and 99 and will cellar well for up to a decade. There is also a good second wine, L'Esprit de l'Église. (DM)

● **Clos l'Église** Pomerol★★★★ £G

CH. LA CLOTTE Saint-Émilion GCC

Owner: SCEA du Château la Clotte 33330 Saint-Émilion

The quality here was good prior to 1997 but really no more. Things are taking a turn for the better, though. Consultancy is provided by Stéphane Derenoncourt and the style is now more opulent and concentrated with harmonious, well-judged oak and sufficient depth and firm, structured tannin to develop well in bottle over five years or so. A property to watch. (DM)

● **Château La Clotte** Saint-Émilion Grand Cru Classé★★ £E

CH. LA CONSEILLANTE Pomerol chateau.la.conseillante@wanadoo.fr

Owner: Nicolas family 33500 Pomerol

One of the great Pomerol names, La Conseillante has an excellent vineyard aspect and is located close to L'ÉVANGILE and CHEVAL BLANC across the appellation boundary. With some Cabernet Franc (20 per cent) as well as Merlot (80 per cent) planted in gravel soils, the wine is both rich, fleshy and full of dark fruit but also firmly structured. The best years show a remarkably complex array of dark fruits and oriental spices. The wine benefits from six to seven years' ageing at least. 2000 could well be exceptional and of a similar order to the great 89 and 90. Earlier classics were 85 and 82. (DM)

● **Château La Conseillante** Pomerol★★★★★ £G

CH. LA COUSPAUDE St-Émilion GCC www.la-couspaude.fr

Owner: Vignobles Aubert 33330 Saint-Émilion
This is now a very impressive property located to the east of the appellation and planted with Merlot and 15 per cent each of Cabernet Sauvignon and Cabernet Franc in limestone soils. The property is another of many benefiting from Michel Rolland's consultancy and the style is characteristically sumptuous and fleshy, with supple, velvety tannin and a complex, dark fruited character with abundant oak spice. Half a decade or so of ageing is needed to throw off the initially firm tannic grip. (DM)
● **Château La Couspaude** Saint-Émilion Grand Cru Classé★★★ £F

CH. LA CROIX-DE-GAY Pomerol

Owner: Chantal Lebreton & Alain Raynaud 33500 Pomerol
This is a good middle-ranking Pomerol with an attractive plump, plummy Merlot character after three or fours years of bottle-age but without any great depth or complexity. There are 10 ha planted, 90 per cent of it Merlot. What marks the property out is the quality of a superior selection called la Fleur-de-Gay. Produced from 100 per cent Merlot, this is dense, opulent, rich and oaky. Not surprisingly it is fairly pricey. (DM)
● **Château La Croix-de-Gay** Pomerol★★ £E
● **La Fleur-de-Gay** Pomerol★★★★ £H
● **Château La Dominique** Saint-Émilion Grand Cru Classé★★★★ £G

CH. LA DOMINIQUE Saint-Émilion GCC

Owner: Clément Fayat 33330 Saint-Émilion
This property, ideally situated in very close proximity to CHEVAL BLANC, has been a reasonably consistent performer since the late 1980s. The wine is vinified with consultancy input from Michel Rolland. The style is not only opulent and fleshy with marked new oak and rich, concentrated, spicy, dark fruit but there is an underlying finesse and quality here. Supple but well-structured and very ageworthy. 1998 was very good and 2000 looks set to be in the same mould. A small volume garage wine Saint Dominique is also made from an adjacent parcel to the property.(DM)
● **Château La Dominique** Saint-Émilion Grand Cru Classé★★★★ £G

CH. L'ÉGLISE-CLINET Pomerol

Owner: Denis Durantou 33500 Pomerol
Magnificent small Pomerol property with a holding of just 5.5 ha of Merlot and Cabernet Franc. The vineyard is very old, with some of the vines nearing 100 years. The style bears little comparison with those neighbours who opt for modern extracted wines and dollops of new oak. L'Église-Clinet is structured, dense and backward when young. Given six or seven years the result is an elegant velvety and classically proportioned example of the appellation. Very impressive in 1998, 97, 96 and 95. 2000 should be every bit as good. (DM)
● **Château L'Église-Clinet** Pomerol✪✪✪✪✪ £H

CH. L'ÉVANGILE Pomerol www.lafite.com

*Owner: **Domaines Barons de Rothschild** 33500 Pomerol*
This is an impressively deep, structured and powerful example of Pomerol. Like L'ÉGLISE-CLINET,

markedly different to many of its supple, rounded, softly structured neighbours. Owned since 1990 by the Rothschilds, the wine is traditionally vinified and possesses sturdy, dense firm tannin when young, along with formidably concentrated levels of complex, dark, spicy fruit. There is oak evident here but its very harmoniously integrated. It was remarkably good in the best years in the last decade or so; 1990 was of legendary quality – super-five stars – and 2000 may well end up of a similar stature. (DM)

● **Château l'Évangile** Pomerol★★★★★ £H

EXCELLENCE DE BOIS PERTUIS   Bordeaux

Owner: Bernard Magrez   c/o Terroirs d'Exception, 33330 Saint-Christophe des Bardes
Although merely a humble AC Bordeaux this is one of a number of wines Bernard Magrez is releasing under his Terroir d'Exception label. Others include LA SERÉNITÉ in Pessac Leognan as well as Gérard Depardieu's property MA VERITÉ in the Haut-Médoc. The 2 ha vineyard is planted solely to Merlot which is now 25 years old. Yields are kept very low at just over 20 hl/ha and crop thinning is practiced. The wine is fermented in wooden vats and ageing is in new wood. It is rich, dense and opulently plummy and with marked extract. The youthfully firm tannin needs three or four years to subside. (DM)

● **Excellence de Bois Pertuis** Bordeaux★★★ £D

CH. FAUGÈRES   Saint-Émilion GC   www.chateau-faugères.com

Owner: Corinne Guisez   Saint-Étienne-de-Lisse, 33330 Saint-Émilion
Major investment in both the vineyard and cellars under the current ownership has wrought major change and delivered increasingly impressive wines. The Château Faugères regular Saint-Émilion is a dense, richly concentrated and spicy Grand Cru which is aged in 100 per cent new oak and has the depth and structure to develop well over a decade or more. Since 1998 a super-rich special *cuvée*, Château Péby Faugères, has been produced which is both sumptuously fleshy and very powerful. The Cap de Faugères is a supple, rounded and forward style produced from vineyards owned in the Côtes de Castillon. (DM)

● **Château Faugères** Saint-Émilion Grand Cru★★★ £E

CH. FIGEAC   Saint-Émilion 1er GCC   www.chateau-figeac.com

Owner: Thierry Manoncourt & Eric d'Aramon   33330 Saint-Émilion
The traditional qualities of this Premier Grand Cru Classé – namely refinement, elegance and a harmonious balance of subtle, dark, spicy fruit and lightly smoky oak – have been apparent in a number of recent vintages but strangely absent in others when one would expect the property to have performed well. The vineyard has an unusually high proportion of Cabernet Sauvignon and Cabernet Franc for Saint-Émilion, mainly because of the marked gravel component of the soil, with just one-third planted to Merlot. The resulting wines are inevitably powerful and structured when at their best and long-lived. Recent vintages look very good, four stars at least, but 1996 and 97 were strangely disappointing. (DM)

● **Château Figeac** Saint-Émilion Grand Cru Classé★★★ £G

CH. LA FLEUR-PÉTRUS   Pomerol

Owner: Moueix family   33500 Pomerol
Like PÉTRUS itself this property is owned by the Moueix family. The vineyards have a higher

proportion of gravel than is commonly found here and the wine is less opulent and rich than many of its neighbours. It is refined, medium- rather than full-bodied and tightly structured and restrained in its youth. With age it will become very fine and complex and is extraordinarily long-lived. 1975 still seems youthful. Somewhat erratic in the 1980s, the wine has been a model of consistency in the mid- to late 90s. (DM)

● **Château la Fleur-Pétrus** Pomerol★★★★ £G

CH. FOMBRAUGE   St-Émilion GC   www.fombrauge.com

Owner: Bernard Magrez   33330 Saint-Christophe des Bardes

Bernard Magrez, owner of PAPE-CLEMENT in Pessac-Léognan, purchased Fombrauge in 1999. While Fombrauge has been going from strength to strength, particularly throughout the late 1990s, it has achieved new heights under the current ownership. With over 50 ha of vineyards and located to the north-east of the appellation, away from the established grandee properties, Fombrauge is proving as elsewhere that the less-fancied plots in this sizeable appellation can provide impressive wines. A limited-production, highly priced special *cuvée,* Magrez-Fombrauge, has also now been released. Massively powerful and extracted, it remains to be seen how this wine will develop, as with other *super-cuvées* from lesser plots, but it has considerable promise. Bernard Magrez has also produced a number of small-scale *garagiste*-style wines of great potential from a number of properties throughout the region and has provided input to actor Gérard Depardieu and actress Carole Bouquet in similar properties in both Bordeaux and the Midi and most excitingly Morocco and Algeria. (DM)

● **Château Fombrauge** Saint-Émilion Grand Cru★★★ £D
● **Magrez-Fombrauge** Saint-Émilion Grand Cru★★★★★ £G

CH. FONTENIL   Fronsac   www.expressions-de-fronsac.com

Owner: Michel & Dany Rolland   33141 Saillans

This small Fronsac property is owned by Michel and Dany Rolland. The wine is lushly textured, rich and supple and full of opulence, with just a hint of cassis adding depth and weight to the bramble and dark berry fruit. The new oak so apparent when the wine is young, will become more balanced and harmonious with time. One of the better examples of this lesser appellation. (DM)

● **Château Fontenil** Fronsac★★★ £C

CLOS FOURTET   St-Émilion 1er GCC   www.premiers-saint-emilion.com

Owner: Philippe Cuvelier   3330 Saint-Émilion

Under new ownership since 2001. There are 20 ha of vineyards planted to a mix of Merlot (80 per cent), Cabernet Sauvignon (12 per cent) and the balance Cabernet Franc. The resulting wines have generally been big, full and sturdy, particularly during the last decade, which has seen a consistent raising of standards. The wine is densely extracted and sees a high proportion of new oak. Recent vintages have been refined and classy. This trend is likely to continue and the property should move towards greater things. (DM)

● **Clos Fourtet St-Émilion** Grand Cru Classé★★★ £F

CH. LA GAFFELIÈRE   Saint-Émilion 1er GCC   www.chateau-la-gaffeliere.com

Owner: Comte de Malet Roquefort   33330 Saint-Émilion

After a period when this 22 ha property was relatively disappointing in the early to mid-1990s the wines appear to be consistently improving. There has been no new ownership or marked change in the style, just, it would appear, a general sharpening of the act. This is very much a classically structured Saint-Émilion, stylish medium-rather than full-bodied with a restrained mineral character as well as subtle, smoky, dark fruit. It will add weight with five years cellaring. (DM)

● **Château la Gaffelière** Saint-Émilion Grand Cru Classé★★★ £G

CH. GAZIN   Pomerol   www.gazin.com

Owner: Balliencourt family   Le Gazin, 33500 Pomerol
This is among Pomerol's larger properties, with over 30 ha under vine, the vast majority being Merlot. The wines were generally disappointing a decade ago but the 1990s have seen a transformation, with better management and control in both vineyard and cellar. The style is rich, forward and opulent with ripe and plummy dark fruit and an increasing amount of new oak used. (DM)

● **Château Gazin** Pomerol★★★ £G

CH. GRAND-MAYNE   Saint-Émilion GCC   www.grand-mayne.com

Owner: Nony family   33330 Saint-Émilion
Grand-Mayne produces impressively dark, dense and well-structured Saint-Émilions. There are some 17 ha under vine and the estate is located towards the western side of the appellation. Quality has much improved in recent vintages and the wine is suppler and has better fruit quality than of old. An increasing use of new oak is helping to underpin the character of the château. While firmly structured when young, the wine avoids austerity. (DM)

● **Château Grand-Mayne** Saint-Émilion Grand Cru Classé★★★★ £F

CH. GRAND-PONTET   Saint-Émilion GCC   chateau.grand.pontet@wanadoo.fr

Owner: Pourquet-Bécot family   33330 Saint-Émilion
There are 14 ha of vines mainly Merlot with a reasonably high proportion of Cabernet Franc (15 per cent) and Cabernet Sauvignon (10 per cent). The clay-rich soils provide a subtle and elegant style. The wine has been at least good throughout the mid- to late 1990s, with greater fruit ripeness and suppler tannins. (DM)

● **Château Grand-Pontet** Saint-Émilion Grand Cru Classé★★★ £D

LA CROIX DE PEYROLIE   Lussac-Saint-Émilion

Owner: Carole Bouquet   c/o Terroirs d'Exception, 33330 Saint-Christophe des Bardes
Owned by French film actress Carole Bouquet, a former Bond girl, La Croix de Peyrolie is marketed under the Terroirs d'Exception label by Bernard Magrez, owner of Fombrauge. The vineyard is tiny at just 1.3 hectares and yields a mere 12.5 hl/ha, very much a garage style operation. Vinification is in wooden barrels, with manual *pigeage* and malolactic is instigated in new oak, where the wine spends 20 months. Rich and very concentrated, with a fine and firmly tannic youthful structure it will benefit from five or six years ageing. You feel, as in a number of Magrez wines that there can be just a touch too much extract in a lesser year like 2002. Very impressive nonetheless. (DM)

● **La Croix de Peyrolie** Lussac-Saint-Émilion★★★★ £F

CH. LAFLEUR   Pomerol

Owner: Marie Robin   Grand Village, 33240 Mouillac

Tiny Pomerol property consisting of a mere 4.5 ha of vines, half surprisingly planted to Cabernet Franc. This component helps provide the considerable structure which will enable the wine to age gracefully for two decades and more. In recent vintages an increasing amount of new oak has been used and the wine possesses not just a finely structured, almost mineral core but a rich, concentrated, black-fruited opulence also. It was remarkably consistent throughout the 1990s and outperformed in the difficult years early in the decade. (DM)

● **Château Lafleur** Pomerol✪✪✪✪✪ £H

LA MONDOTTE   Saint-Émilion   www.neipperg.com

Owner: Comte Stephan von Neipperg   33330 Saint-Émilion

Along with LE DÔME, this is one of the two great garage wines to emerge in the last half decade. Produced at CANON-LA-GAFFELIÈRE, the vineyard consists of 4.5 ha planted on clay/silt soils over a rocky subsoil. It is superbly drained with an unusually steep south facing aspect. It is this *terroir* with low yields that produces a wine of remarkable depth and concentration. Blended from 80 per cent Merlot and 20 per cent Cabernet Franc it offers a truly opulent exotic array of dark fruits and oriental spices. Produced in the classic Derenoncourt style with ageing on lees in new oak for a year and a half. It is bottled unfiltered. (DM)

● **La Mondotte** Saint-Émilion Grand Cru★★★★★ £H

CH. LATOUR-À-POMEROL   Pomerol

Owner: Mme Lacoste-Loubat/Moueix Family   33500 Pomerol

This is another property under the Moueix family umbrella. These are supple, ripe and at their best richly plummy examples of Pomerol, produced to showcase the more opulent character of the appellation. The wine has generally performed well during the period from 1994 onwards, with just the odd hint of aggressive tannin sometimes marring the style. It develops well with six or seven years' age. (DM)

● **Château Latour-à-Pomerol**★★★ £H

LE DÔME   Saint-Émilion   info@teyssier.fr

Owner: Jonathan Maltus   33330 Vignonnet

This vies with LA MONDOTTE to be first among the garage wines of Saint-Émilion. It is produced by Jonathan Malthus at his property Château TEYSSIER, from a single parcel of 2.85 ha which neighbours Château ANGELUS. Cabernet Franc is the main component at 70 per cent, with the balance Merlot. The wine is modern in style with a pre-fermentation maceration and both *pigeage* and pumping over are employed during fermentation. Malolactic is conducted in barrel and then 50 per cent is drawn off and aged in a second series of brand new oak. Despite this, while deep and very concentrated the wine's fine mineral structure provides exemplary balance. It will require seven or eight years patience to show at its peak. (DM)

● **Le Dôme** Saint-Émilion Grand Cru Classé★★★★ £G

CH. MAGDELAINE   Saint-Émilion 1er GCC   www.premiers-saint-emilion.com

Owner: Moueix family   33330 Saint-Émilion

Another Moueix family property. This is an opulent, richly plummy Merlot-dominated wine crafted from older vines than usual for the region. Supple and approachable but nevertheless possessing a fine, well-structured mineral backbone, the wine can be enjoyable with as little as five years' cellaring and will keep for much longer. (DM)

● **Château Magdelaine** Saint-Émilion Grand Cru Classé★★★★ £D

CH. MONBOUSQUET   Saint-Émilion GC   www.chateaupavie.com

*Owner: **Vignobles Perse**   33330 Saint-Émilion*

Another fine example of modern extractive winemaking producing a typically ripe and bold style of Saint-Émilion. Michel Rolland is the winemaking consultant and his techniques of ripe, late-harvested fruit, deep colour and malolactic in barrel are all on show here. The driving force behind the renaissance of this once mediocre property is Gérard Perse, who also owns PAVIE and PAVIE-DECESSE. Expect the wines to develop well in the medium term. (DM)

● **Château Monbousquet** Saint-Émilion Grand Cru★★★★ £F

CH. MOULIN HAUT-LAROQUE   Fronsac   www.moulinhautlaroque.fr.st

Owner: Jean-Noël Hervé   Le Moulin, 33141 Saillans

This is one of the more impressive properties in the increasingly fashionable Fronsac appellation. The 15 ha are mainly Merlot but there is a significant amount of old-vine Cabernet Franc, along with Cabernet Sauvignon and Malbec. The style is ripe and full with an element of new oak showing through and a supple, velvety structure. Better with four to five years' age. (DM)

● **Château Moulin Haut-Laroque** Fronsac★★ £C

CH. MOULIN PEY-LABRIE   Canon-Fronsac

Owner: Bénédicte & Gregoire Hubau   33126 Fronsac

Small property of some 6.5 ha producing modern, stylish and ripe reds with a high proportion of Merlot and increasing use of new oak. The approach mirrors that of other quality-minded properties from lesser Bordeaux appellations in emphasising forward, dark and richly plummy fruit in a soft, fleshy, textured style. The rounded, velvety tannin is assisted by completion of the malolactic fermentation in barrel. (DM)

● **Château Moulin Pey-Labrie** Canon-Fronsac★★★ £D

CH. MOULIN SAINT-GEORGES   Saint-Émilion GC

Owner: Vauthier Family   33330 Saint-Émilion

Located in close proximity to AUSONE and in fact owned by the same family. Quality here has been consistently improving in recent vintages. The 8-ha Merlot-dominated vineyard is meticulously managed and careful vinification produces richly fruity and fleshy wines with marked new oak. They will be all the better for four or five years' ageing. (DM)

● **Château Moulin Saint-Georges** Saint-Émilion Grand Cru★★★ £E

CLOS DE L'ORATOIRE   Saint-Émilion GCC   info@neipperg.com

Owner: Vignobles von Neipperg   33330 Saint-Émilion
Under the same ownership as CANON-LA-GAFFELIÈRE and the *super-cuvée* LA MONDOTTE. As at Stéphan von Neipperg's other properties, the style here is modern and approachable but the wine is neither overripe nor excessively extracted. There is an underlying refinement and elegance which hallmarks the wine. The finely crafted tannins need five or six years to achieve real harmony. Classy and ageworthy. (DM)

● **Clos de l'Oratoire Saint-Émilion** Grand Cru Classé★★★★£G

PASSION DU PRIEURÉ MALESAN   Premières Côtes de Blaye

Owner: Bernard Magrez   c/o Terroirs d'Exception, 33330 Saint-Christophe des Bardes
This, (it is just one of a number of other wines Bernard Magrez is now marketing as Terroirs d'Exception), is a tiny production garage style wine from one of Bordeaux's humbler appellations. Magrez also works with French film actor and vineyard owner Gerard Depardieu in this project. Similarly impressive reds have been made in the Roussillon along with Depardieu's north African Domaine SAINT AUGUSTIN and LUMIÈRE wines. Passion du Prieuré Malesan is produced from mainly Merlot but also a little Cabernet Franc, the vineyard yields a miserly 20 hl/ha or less. The result is a wine which is deeply extracted, rich and concentrated with very evident new oak. It will benefit from three or four years' ageing. (DM)

● **Passion du Prieure Malesan** Premières Côtes de Blaye★★★£D

CH. PAVIE   Saint-Émilion 1er GCC   www.chateaupavie.com

Owner: Vignobles Perse   33330 Saint-Émilion
This property was purchased in 1998 by Gérard Perse who also owns PAVIE-DECESSE, MONBOUS-QUET and PETIT-VILLAGE. The formerly variable quality here will undoubtedly continue to improve after substantial investment in the cellars. With state-of-the-art winery equipment, a modern approach to vinification with minimal handling and a commitment to quality in the vineyard, the style is now both refined and very opulent, producing wines which are concentrated, harmonious and elegant, with the hallmark of greatness. Prior to 1998 the wines were adequate at best with only the earlier vintages of 1990, 89, 86 and 82 being of real note. (DM)

● **Château Pavie** Saint-Émilion Grand Cru Classé★★★★ £H

CH. PAVIE-DECESSE   Saint-Émilion GCC   www.chateaupavie.com

Owner: Vignobles Perse   33330 Saint-Émilion
Like PAVIE, owned by Gérard Perse and now producing wines of greater density and finesse than a few years back. The style, as at Pavie, is for rich and opulent reds but there has always been a tighter, leaner edge to Decesse when compared with its larger, more illustrious neighbour. The wine is nevertheless very elegant and harmonious with well-judged use of oak and since 1997 of impressive quality. It will age very well. (DM)

● **Château Pavie-Decesse** Saint-Émilion Grand Cru Classé★★★★£G

CH. PAVIE-MACQUIN   Saint-Émilion GCC   pavie.macquin@wanadoo.fr

Owner: Corre-Macquin family   33330 Saint-Émilion
Consultancy input here comes from Stéphane Derenoncourt and the property is farmed biodynamically. It shares the same limestone plateau as PAVIE-DECESSE and possesses a similarly hard, tight and structured mineral edge to its character. In the cellar minimal handling is the order of the day and the results are enormously impressive. The wines are dense, powerful and structured, with seamlessly integrated dark, spicy fruit and oak. They age very well. Only 1992 looks really disappointing. The wines of the late 1990s show a serious hike in quality. (DM)
● **Château Pavie-Macquin** Saint-Émilion Grand Cru Classé★★★★★ £F

CH. PETIT-VILLAGE   Pomerol

*Owner: **Vignobles Perse**   33500 Pomerol*
Once part of AXA Millésimes, this property used to be under the same ownership as PICHON-LONGUEVILLE in Pauillac. It has now been purchased by Gérard Perse, who owns the revitalised PAVIE and PAVIE-DECESSE. The style here has been for fairly sturdy, structured wines without necessarily the refinement and depth one might wish for. There has, however, been a step up here since the property changed hands in 1998 and the Perse influence will no doubt ensure this continues. (DM)
● **Château Petit-Village** Pomerol★★★ £G

CH. PÉTRUS   Pomerol

Owner: Moueix family   1 Rue Petrus-Arnaud, 33500 Pomerol
One of the most expensive wines in the world, it used to be the most expensive by a long way but has been challenged in recent years not only by near neighbours but also by limited-production special *cuvées* in California. Much depends on the trends and vagaries of the international auction markets. There is no doubt, though, that Petrus is one of Bordeaux's truly great reds. A very high proportion of Merlot (95 per cent), with the balance Cabernet Franc, are planted in vineyards that sit upon a plateau of remarkably well-drained clay soils and provide a unique *terroir*. Extraordinary care is taken in both the vineyard and cellars in producing a wine that is immensely rich and concentrated with a bewildering array of dark fruits, oriental spices and seamlessly integrated oak, all supported by very fine supple tannins. It is consistently great and perhaps only struggles very slightly in lesser years, but then so does every other property in the region. (DM)
● **Château Pétrus** Pomerol✪✪✪✪✪ £H

CH. LE PIN   Pomerol

Owner: Jacques Thienpont   Les Grands Champs, 33500 Pomerol
Production here is tiny at only around 700 cases a year and two decades ago the wine was just a hobby of owner Jacques Thienpont. However, it has become an auction favourite and, partly because of its scarcity, has on occasion fetched higher prices than PÉTRUS. The style is for ripe, opulent and approachable wines rather than ones that are overstructured and austere and the vinification reflects this approach. Malolactic is carried out in barrel and the wine sees 100 per cent new oak which is seamlessly integrated. Undoubtedly a very fine and richly opulent example of Pomerol. (DM)
● **Château le Pin** Pomerol✪✪✪✪✪ £H

CLOS PUY ARNAUD   Côtes de Castillon

Owner: Thierry Valette   7 Puy Arnaud, 33350 Belvès de Castillon

This is one of a handful of really impressive properties from this now excellent satellite appellation. Unlike neighbouring Château d'AIGUILHE, the vineyard area here is small at a mere 7 ha. Planted to a mix of 70 per cent Merlot, 20 per cent Cabernet Franc and the balance Cabernet Sauvignon, its aspect is excellent with south facing slopes while the limestone based soils provide excellent drainage. The vines are also now farmed biodynamically. Clos Puy Arnaud is dense and richly concentrated with dark berry fruit, spicy oak and supple firmly structured tannin all in evidence. Consultant Stéphane Derenoncourt uses all his techniques during vinification, pre-fermentation maceration, malolactic in barrel and ageing on lees in 50 per cent new oak. The wine is consistently right on the cusp of four stars, 2000 was undoubtedly so. Pervenche Puy Arnaud is a very decent second wine. (DM)

● **Clos Puy Arnaud** Côtes de Castillon★★★ £D
● **Château Pervenche Puy Arnaud** Côtes de Castillon★ £B

CH. PUYGUERAUD   Bordeaux-Côtes de Francs

Owner: Nicolas Thienpont   33570 Saint-Cibard

There are a number of impressive producers in this small appellation north-east of Saint-Émilion but Puygueraud particularly stands out. The wine is both refined and surprisingly structured for a lesser appellation and displays an impressive array of cedar, dark fruit and oriental spices, all tightly gripped by firm youthful tannin. The wine will benefit from a few years in the cellar. A special limited production wine, Cuvée Georges, was produced in 2000. (DM)

● **Château Puygueraud** Bordeaux-Côtes de Francs★★★ £C

CH. QUINAULT   Saint-Émilion GC   www.chateau-quinault.fr

Owner: Alain Raynaud   30 Chemin Videlot, 33500 Libourne

Alain Raynaud produces around 5,000 cases a year, mainly from some very old Merlot and Cabernet Franc. There are a total of 12 ha; Merlot accounts for 65 per cent and Cabernet Sauvignon and Malbec just 15 per cent between them, with the balance Cabernet Franc. Despite being only a regular Saint-Emilion Grand Cru, this is a serious enterprise and the wine bears little resemblance to many of the *garagiste* operations who produce barely more than a few hundred cases a year. The style is rich, supple and opulent and is best with eight to ten years' age. (DM)

● **Château Quinault L'Enclos** Saint-Émilion Grand Cru★★★★ £F

CH. REIGNAC   Bordeaux-Supérieur   chateau.reignac@wanadoo.fr

Owner: Vatelot family   33450 Saint-Loubès

Stéphanie and Yves Vatelot produce one of the very best examples of this lesser appellation and it should be a benchmark for others. They have a sizeable holding of some 76 ha of which just 2 ha are devoted to whites. The red blend has a slightly higher proportion of Merlot than Cabernet Sauvignon and the wine is dense, dark and structured. It should develop very well in the medium term. There is also a special limited-release Cuvée Spéciale. (DM)

● **Château Reignac** Bordeaux Supérieur★★★ £B

CH. REYNON   Premières Côtes de Bordeaux   www.denisdubourdieu.com

Owner: Denis & Florence Dubourdieu   21 Route de Cardan, 33410 Beguey
Denis Dubourdieu, the owner of CLOS FLORIDÈNE in the Graves, is an extremely well known and respected professor of enology in the region. At Château Reynon, he makes some very good dry white and red, along with a little sweet Cadillac from a total of some 57 ha of vineyards. The red is good and stylish in a medium-weight style, the regular white crisp and fresh, the Vieilles Vignes classier and subtly barrel-fermented. Both the Vieilles Vignes white and the red will evolve nicely in the short term. (DM)

● **Château Reynon** Premières Côtes de Bordeaux★★ £C
O **Bordeaux** Vieilles Vignes★★ £B

CH. DE LA RIVIÈRE   Fronsac   www.chateau-de-la-riviere.com

Owner: Jean & Jeanne Le Prince   33126 La Rivière
A decade ago this substantial Fronsac property was producing wines of somewhat variable quality. There are 59 ha under vine, mainly Merlot with Cabernet Sauvignon, Cabernet Franc and a few hectares of Malbec. During the late 1990s some of the quality achieved during the mid-1980s has been replicated, although the wines are now modern and produced in an attractively ripe, dark berry-fruit style with soft velvety tannins. A special bottling Aria is very good but pricey and a *clairet* is also made. The reds will benefit from four or five years' aging. (DM)

● **Château la Rivière** Fronsac★★ £D

CH. ROC DE CAMBES   Côtes de Bourg

Owner: François Mitjaville   33330 Saint-Laurent-des-Combes
This property is not only a serious benchmark for the Côtes de Bourg but also for all the lesser Right Bank appellations. The property is relatively small at 10 ha and Merlot dominates the plantings, accounting for 60 per cent of the vineyard. Always harvested as late as possible and from very low yields, the wine is typically rich and ripe, always displaying dense, dark, spicy berry fruit and a hefty dollop of well-integrated oak. It is long, complex, powerful and ageworthy. Minimal cellar handling helps to ensure consistently impressive results. 2000, 99 and 98 were all very impressive. (DM)

● **Château Roc de Cambes** Côtes de Bourg★★★★ £F

CH. TERTRE-RÔTEBOEUF   Saint-Émilion GC

Owner: François Mitjaville   33330, Saint-Laurent-des-Combes
Although this remarkable Saint-Émilion has not been elevated to Grand Cru Classé status, the property enjoys a highly propitious site for fine winemaking. Low yields, meticulous care in the vineyard and ageing in new oak for a year and a half all contribute to the very high quality of the wine, which has been exemplary for the last 15 years. It is immensely complex with a myriad of dark and spicy fruits and stylish oak. It will age gracefully and requires six or seven years' patience. (DM)

● **Château Tertre-Rôteboeuf** Saint-Émilion Grand Cru★★★★★ £H

CH. TEYSSIER   Saint-Émilion GC

Owner: Maltus family   33330 Saint-Émilion
Englishman Jonathan Maltus purchased this property in 1994 and since then has added a number

of other more impressively sited vineyard holdings. Teyssier itself is a soft and attractive, relatively forward, spicy Saint-Émilion full of fleshy, dark, plummy fruit. It is sourced from the low-lying vineyards in the south of the appellation and is a testament to what can be achieved from these lesser sites. Vinification is modern, as with all the wines here, with pre-fermentation maceration, malolactic in barrel and ageing on lees for added richness. Château Laforge is produced from a number of superior Grand Cru sites, including the Le Chatelot vineyard purchased from Château CANON in 2000. The wine is rich and supple, finely structured and with impressive depth and concentration. The high Merlot content (92 per cent) of the blend accounts for its opulent, exotic style. LE DÔME is the top red label and comes from a single parcel neighbouring Château ANGELUS. There is also an excellent barrel-fermented white, Clos Nardian, which blends all three white Bordeaux varieties. The Muscadelle comes from vines planted in the mid-1930s. Sourced from three tiny, ideally exposed parcels in limestone soils just across the river Dordogne south of the Saint-Émilion AC, this is a rich and complex, subtly oaked white. Maltus also produces a good red and white Bordeaux, Château LACROIX, both of which are vinified at Teyssier. (DM)

● **Château Teyssier** Saint-Émilion Grand Cru★★★ £D
● **Château Laforge** Saint-Émilion Grand Cru★★★★ £F
O **Clos Nardian** Bordeaux★★★★ £F

CH. THIEULEY Bordeaux

Owner: Francis Courselle   La Sauve, 33670 Créon

This is an excellent example of what can be achieved under the humble Bordeaux AC but so very rarely is. Francis Courselle now has some 80 ha of vineyard, 45 ha of which are planted to red varieties. These go towards the crafting of stylish, straightforward, berry-fruited AC Bordeaux, impressively dense, structured Supérieur Réserve and attractively fruity *clairet*. A Premières Côtes de Bordeaux, Clos Sainte-Anne, is also now produced. The regular white is crisp and fresh and full of grassy green apple fruit, whereas the Cuvée Francis Courselle, which is barrel-fermented and aged with *bâtonnage,* is elegantly toasty and oaky. (DM)

● **Château Thieuley** Bordeaux★ £B Bordeaux Supérieur Francis Courselle Réserve★★ £C
O **Château Thieuley** Bordeaux★ £B Bordeaux Cuvée Francis Courselle★★ £C

CH. TROPLONG-MONDOT Saint-Émilion GCC chateautroplongmondot@wanadoo.fr

Owner: Valette family   33330 Saint-Émilion

This has been a consistently excellent source of top Saint-Émilion over the past decade and longer and is unquestionably a serious candidate for elevation to Premier Grand Cru Classé status. There are some 30 ha of vines, the bulk of which are Merlot. This high percentage is reflected in the wine, which is full, rich, plump and fleshy with marked new oak and considerable refinement. The initial firm tannic structure means the wine needs six or seven years' cellaring. Very long and impressive and top-notch in recent vintages. The 2000 was of five-star quality. (DM)

● **Château Troplong-Mondot** Saint-Émilion Grand Cru Classé★★★★ £G

CH. TROTANOY Pomerol

Owner: Moueix family   33500 Pomerol

Typically small Pomerol property of 7 ha, which, like PÉTRUS, is owned by the Moueix family. The wine is dense and very seriously structured, with considerable grip and tannin when young. Seven or eight years' cellaring will see the evolution of all sorts of opulent black fruit characters and oriental spices all effortlessly wrapped up in very classy new wood. On top form since 1997, although there were a number of disappointing vintages in the 1980s. (DM)

● **Château Trotanoy** Pomerol★★★★★ £H

CH. DE VALANDRAUD   Saint-Émilion GC   www.thunevin.com

Owner: Jean-Luc Thunevin   6 Rue Guadet, 33330 Saint-Émilion

This is really the original *garagiste* wine, first made in 1991. Like most of its kind it was originally produced in limited volume, although that is increasing following vineyard acquisitions. The property consists of various plots, some of them on the lowe- lying plain below the town of Saint-Émilion. New plots have been added in 1998 and 99 and there are now two second labels, Clos Badon and Belair, which will help in ensuring the integrity of Valandraud. Yields are resticted and the harvest is carefully sorted prior to vinification. The winemaking is modern, with a pre-fermentation cold soak and malolactic in barrel. The wine is neither fined nor filtered and, while dense, fleshy and extracted, tends to lack the outright refinement of the best of the appellation. Although the style is forward and accessible, there is impressive grip and structure. Jean-Luc Thunevin is involved with the production of a number of other small-scale projects, among them GRACIA and Andréas in Saint-Emilion, Griffe de Cap d'Or in Saint-Geoges-Saint-Emilion and the micro-vinification MAROJALLIA in Margaux. (DM)

● **Château de Valandraud** Saint-Émilion Grand Cru★★★★ £F

CH. LA VIEILLE CURE   Fronsac   www.expressions-de-fronsac.com

Owner: Colin Ferenbach   Coutreau, 33141 Saillans

This is yet another of a number of outperformers in Bordeaux's lesser appellations and money has been pumped into the property to improve quality over the last 15 years. There are 18 ha under vine, 75 per cent of it Merlot. Michel Rolland has provided consultancy input and the wine is typically extracted, ripe and seductive in style. Only the slightest hard edge can occasionally drift into the equation. The wine is a good medium-term ageing prospect. It has been good to very good since the late 1990s. There is also now an impressive second wine, Sacristie de La Vieille Cure, which other more esteemed properties from grander appellations would struggle to emulate. (DM)

● **Château La Vieille Cure** Fronsac★★★ £D

VIEUX-CHÂTEAU-CERTAN   Pomerol   www.vieuxchateaucertan.com

Owner: Thienpont family   33500 Pomerol

Cabernet Franc and Cabernet Sauvignon account for forty per cent of the 14 ha of vineyard here and this is in part the reason for the surprisingly dense and powerful structure of the wine. The tannin can be very firm in the wine's youth and it really needs a decade to begin to show its true class, when it becomes very refined and harmonious with time. Excellent from 1998 on – five stars. 1995 and 90 were also very good here. (DM)

● **Vieux-Château-Certan** Pomerol★★★★ £H

SAINT-ÉMILION, POMEROL & OTHER BORDEAUX/OTHER WINES OF NOTE

CH. BALESTARD-LA-TONNELLE ● **Saint-Émilion** Grand Cru Classé £E
CH. BARDE-HAUT ● **Saint-Émilion** Grand Cru £E
CH. BARRABAQUE ● **Canon-Fronsac** Cuvée Prestige £C
CH. BAUDUC O **Bordeaux** Les Trois Hectares £C
CH. BEAULIEU ● **Bordeaux** £C

CH. BEAU-SOLEIL ● Pomerol £E

CH. BEL AIR LA ROYÈRE ● Premières Côtes de Blaye £D

CH. BELLEFONT-BELCIER ● Saint-Émilion Grand Cru £D

CH. BELLEVUE ● Saint-Émilion Grand Cru £D

CH. BERLIQUET ● Saint-Émilion Grand Cru Classé £E

CH. BONALGUE ● Pomerol ● Pomerol £E

CH. BRÛLESÉCAILLE ● Côtes de Bourg £B

CH. BRUN DESPAGNE ● Bordeaux Supérieur £B

CH. CADET BON ● Saint-Émilion Grand Cru Classé £E

CH. CANON ● Canon-Fronsac £C

CH. CANTELAUZE ● Pomerol £F

CH. CAP DE MOURLIN ● Saint Émilion Grand Cru Classé £D

CH. CARIGNAN ● Premières Côtes de Bordeaux £D

CH. CASSAGNE HAUT-CANON ● Canon-Fronsac £B Truffière £C

CH. DE CÉRONS O Cérons £B

CH. DU CHAMP DES TREILLES ● Bordeaux Supérieur La Chapelle d'Aliénor £C

CLOS DU CLOCHER ● Pomerol £E

CH. CLOS DES JACOBINS ● Saint-Émilion Grand Cru Classé £E

CONFIANCE ● Premières Côtes de Blaye £E

CH. CÔTE MONPEZAT ● £B

DOMAINE DE COURTEILLAC ● Bordeaux Supérieur £B O Bordeaux Supérieur £B

LA CROIX CANON ● Canon-Fronsac £C

CROIX DE LABRIE ● Saint Émilion £G

CH. DU CROS O Loupiac £C

CH. DALEM ● Fronsac £D

CH. DASSAULT ● Saint-Émilion Grand Cru Classé £E

CH. DE LA DAUPHINE ● Fronsac £B

CH. DESTIEUX ● Saint-Émilion Grand Cru £E

CH. FAIZEAU ● Montagne Saint-Émilion £C

CH. FALFAS ● Côtes de Bourg £B

CH. FEYTIT-CLINET ● Pomerol £E

CH. FLEUR CARDINALE ● Saint-Émilion Grand Cru £D

LA FLEUR DU BOÙARD ● Lalande-de-Pomerol £E

CH. FONROQUE ● Saint-Émilion Grand Cru Classé £E

CH. DE FRANC MAYNE ● Saint-Émilion Grand Cru £F

CH. DE FRANCS ● Bordeaux-Côtes de Francs £B

CH. LE GAY ● Pomerol £E

GRACIA ● Saint-Émilion Grand Cru £F

CH. GRAND RENOUIL ● Canon-Fronsac £C

CH. LA GRAVE ● Fronsac £B

CH. LA GRAVE ● Pomerol £E

CH. HAUT-BERTINERIE O Premières Côtes de Blaye £C ● Premières Côtes de Blaye £C

CH. HAUT-CARLES ● Fronsac £D

CH. HAUT-CHAIGNEAU ● Lalande-de-Pomerol £B

CH. HAUT-CORBIN ● Saint-Émilion Grand Cru Classé £E

CH. HAUT-SEGOTTES ● Saint-Émilion Grand Cru £D

CH. HAUT-TROPCHAUD ● Pomerol £E

HOMMAGE DE MALESAN ● Bordeaux £D

CH. HOSANNA ● Pomerol £F

CH. LES JONQUEYRES ● Premières Côtes de Blaye £B

CH. LAFLEUR-GAZIN ● Pomerol £E

CH. LAGRANGE ● Pomerol £E

CH. LARMANDE ● Saint-Émilion Grand Cru Classé £E

CH. LARCIS-DUCASSE ● Saint-Émilion Grand Cru Classé £D

CH. LOUBENS O Sainte-Croix-du-Mont £C

CH. DU LYONNAT ● Lussac-Saint-Émilion £C
CH. MARSAU ● Bordeaux-Côtes de Francs £C
CH. MONGIRON ● Bordeaux La Fleur Mongiron £C
CH. MONTVIEL ● Pomerol £F
CH. PENIN ● Bordeaux Supérieur Grande Sélection £B
CH. LE PIN BEAUSOLEIL ● Bordeaux Supérieur £C
CH. LA POINTE ● Pomerol £D
CH. PRESSAC ● Saint-Émilion Grand Cru £D
CH. LA RAME ○ Sainte-Croix-du-Mont Tradition £C Réserve £E
CH. RAUZAN DESPAGNE ○ Bordeaux Blanc Cuvée Passion £C
CH. ROCHER BELLEVUE FIGEAC ● Saint-Émilion Grand Cru £D
CH. ROL VALENTIN ● Saint-Émilion £F
CH. ROUGET ● Pomerol £E
CH. DE SALES ● Pomerol £D
CH.SANSONNET ● Saint-Émilion Grand Cru £F
CH. SEGONZAC ● Premières Côtes de Blaye £B
CH DE SEGUIN ● Bordeaux Supérieur £B Prestige £C
CH. LA SERGUE ● Lalande-de-Pomerol £E
CH. TAILLEFER ● Pomerol £E
CH. TAYAC ● Côtes de Bourg Cuvée Prestige £C Cuvée Reservée £C
CH. TERTRE-DAUGAY ● Saint-Émilion Grand Cru Classé £E
CH. LA TOUR FIGEAC ● Saint-Émilion Grand Cru Classé £E
CH. TOUR DE MIRAMBEAU ● Bordeaux Cuvée Passion £C
CH. LA TOUR-DU-PIN-FIGEAC ● Saint-Émilion Grand Cru Classé £E
CH. TROTTEVIEILLE ● Saint-Émilion 1er Grand Cru Classé £F
CH. VILLARS ● Fronsac £B
CH. VILLEMAURINE ● Saint-Émilion Grand Cru Classé £D
CH. YON FIGEAC ● Saint-Émilion Grand Cru Classé £E

Author's choice (DM)

SAINT-ÉMILION, POMEROL & OTHER BORDEAUX

Great cellarworthy Right Bank reds
CH. AUSONE ● Saint-Émilion 1 er Grand Cru Classé
CH. CHEVAL-BLANC ● Saint-Émilion 1 er Grand Cru Classé
CH. LA CONSEILLANT ● Pomerol
CH. L'ÉVANGILE ● Pomerol
CH. LAFLEUR ● Pomerol
CH. PAVIE-MACQUIN ● Saint-Émilion Grand Cru Classé
CH. PÉTRUS ● Pomerol
CH. LE PIN ● Pomerol
CH. TERTRE-RÔTEBOEUF ● Saint-Émilion Grand Cru
CH. TROPLONG-MONDOT ● Saint-Émilion Grand Cru Classé

New Right Bank classics
CH. BEAU-SÉJOUR BÉCOT ● Saint-Émilion La Gomerie Grand Cru
CH. LA BIENFAISANCE ● Saint-Émilion Sanctus Grand Cru
LE DÔME ● Saint-Émilion Grand Cru
CH. FAUGÈRES ● Saint-Émilion Péby-Faugères Grand Cru
LA FLEUR DU BOÙARD ● Lalande-de-Pomerol
CH. FOMBRAUGE ● Saint-Émilion Magrez-Fombrauge Grand Cru

LA MONDOTTE ● Saint-Émilion Grand Cru

CH. PAVIE ● Saint-Émilion Grand Cru Classé

CH. QUINAULT ● Saint-Émilion Quinault l'Enclos Grand Cru

CH. DE VALANDRAUD ● Saint-Émilion Grand Cru

Emerging reds from the satellites

DOM. DE L'A ● Côtes de Castillon

CH. D'AIGUIHE ● Côtes de Castillon

LA CROIX DE PEYROLIE ● Lussac-Saint-Émilion

CH. FONTENIL ● Fronsac

CH. MOULIN PEY-LABRIE ● Canon-Fronsac

CLOS PUY ARNAUD ● Côtes de Castillon

CH. PUYGUERAUD ● Bordeaux-Côtes des Francs

CH. DE LA RIVIÈRE ● Fronsac

CH. ROC DE CAMBES ● Côtes de Bourg

CH. LA VIEILLE CURE ● Fronsac

France/Burgundy

What a difference a new generation and a responsive market can make. Younger, highly-trained and talented winemakers have played their part in transforming quality in this the most complex and magical of France's wine regions. No stronger argument can be made for the validity of terroir than in Burgundy, where subtle differences of climate, soil composition and aspect identified over the course of centuries and expressed in individual climats make this region so complex and fascinating. Red Burgundy should enthrall with its perfume, complexity, finesse and textural qualities rather than power, oak and out-and-out concentration. White Burgundy should express complexity in both aroma and flavour, be it more minerally or buttery and nutty, and have a depth, structure and balance proportionate to its origins. Both should be more than just the most noble expression of two grapes, now familiar the world over, Pinot Noir and Chardonnay.

A change of direction

In the Côte d'Or, Burgundy's heart, the fragmentation of the vineyard area is extreme, and a complete contrast to Bordeaux's more coherent, larger patchwork. With a few rows here and a few there and the difficulties of vinifying such small quantities of grapes, it made sense to sell to a *négociant* as almost all growers did in the early 20th century. The cost in terms of quality has been well documented but through buying, trading and marriage a host of new independent growers have formed an important part of the new desire for quality.

Yet as recently as 20 years ago Burgundy was in dire straits. Excessive use of potassium and other chemicals on the soils (especially in the Côte de Nuits) led to reduced natural acidity levels and the dependence on pesticides, in turn leading to generally debilitated vineyard health. The resulting grapes were low in both sugar and acidity. Many producers considered it necessary to both over- chaptalize and acidify, a dual-pronged desperation made illegal in 1987. Whilst one practice or the other may be employed within strict limits there is little doubt that some producers still continue to do both despite some high-profile prosecutions by the authorities. Others, though, have sought to restore the health of their vineyards and obtain grapes of high quality and a new order of producers has emerged, better qualified but more often than not getting back to basics. They have improved the soil and plant health and consequently that of the grapes and wines . A movement towards organic and biodynamic viticulture has been stronger here than probably anywhere else in the wine-producing world. Currently many top estates take the advice of soil scientist Claude Bourguignon to enhance further the quality of their soils. Another consequence of the Burgundy's weak constitution was a tendency towards excessive fining and filtration in order to ensure the wine's stability. Better fruit quality as well as widely expressed criticism of heavy reliance on these practices, mean this trend has been reversed. Much too is made of lower yields, but there is still plenty of argument about how this is best achieved – whether through winter pruning, increasing vine densities, the use of different rootstocks or the use of green harvesting.

The best wines are now cleaner, riper and much more consistent even in more difficult years – though in the 1990s nature seems to have rewarded the many varied efforts – yet the wines are far from standardised. And even though there has been a general trend to ever bigger, oakier and more concentrated wines, at least some succeed admirably in retaining balance without losing the stamp of *terroir*. Where there were pockets of quality and occasional bright spots in some of the larger appellations now there are many producers turning out consistently high-quality wines. Yet from too many of the big merchants or *négociants* the wines continue to be very mediocre and it is why so many of them are missing from the following producer profiles. The ones included are the exception and in some instances are very good indeed. Much of the best wine comes from the smaller growers but an increasing number now also buy in some grapes.

Chablis & Yonne:

Chablis is one of the great white wines of the world, even though the marginal cultivation of the Chardonnay grape is fraught with annual battles against frost and rain and demands constant diligence. The importance of fully ripe fruit cannot be understated. The wines should be vigorous, fresh but with generosity and length of flavour without the greeness, harshness or indeed sulphur that some disciples have been duped into believing was authentic Chablis character. A fine, subtle gun-flint, smoke or mineral character and greengage, plum aromas are typical – but these must be ripe plums. Some wines are more floral or peachy but there should still be an unmistakable minerally, steely character and marvellous depth, with a toasty, nutty (or honeyed) complexity with age. The vintage matters greatly; while the longevity of Chablis should never be underestimated, most wines from a weaker vintage will evolve quite quickly and the leaness, often greeness on the palate will never disappear.

Two major areas of debate in the past two decades have been the extension of the *premier cru* vineyard area and the use of new oak but as important to quality are the issues of yield (often too high) and mechanical harvesting, which is widespread. The Union des Grands Crus in Chablis recently banned mechanical harvesting but many *premiers crus* are harvested in this way, in part due to the greater ease of using this method here in contrast to the Côte d'Or, where difficulties are posed by the more fragmented ownership of vineyards. Much of the argument over expansion of the *vignoble* concerns soil types and whether Portlandian and other limestones are capable of the same quality as fossilised Kimmeridgian limestone found in the established *grands* and *premiers crus*. The second area of debate is whether to oak or not to oak. There are now many good exponents of both schools of thought, though the style of each varies significantly. A *grand cru* from Domaine François Raveneau (aged in used oak) is a benchmark but most of the new oak versions from Drouhin or Verget are also of very high quality and have as much validity, as those from the unoaked camp. Quality is the key, the question of style is more subjective and, unless the oak overwhelms the wine it is down to personal choice. That said, Chablis should always taste of its origins and not be mistaken for something from the Côte de Beaune or further afield.

Understanding the Chablis classification is straightforward. There are four levels: **Chablis Grand Cru**, **Chablis Premier Cru**, **Chablis** and **Petit Chablis**. The seven *grands crus* that total 106 ha of vineyards are Blanchot, Bougros, Les Clos, Grenouilles, Preuses, Valmur and Vaudésir. Arguably the most consistent class comes from Les Clos, Valmur and Vaudésir but the producer is more important and their best *premiers crus* easily outperform weaker *grand cru* efforts. There is seven times the area designated Chablis Premier Cru, encompassing forty names. Less than half of these are in common usage as the main *premier cru* name is usually taken. This unfortunately causes confusion and better definition of these large vineyard areas might make for easier quality identification. Those *premiers crus* with the greatest potential to be fine are Fourchaume, Montée de Tonnerre and Mont de Milieu, all lying on the same side (northern, right bank) of the river Serein as the *grand crus* and with similar exposures. But poorer examples of these will be surpassed easily by the best versions of *premiers crus* from the other side of the Serein (left bank), especially Montmains, Vaillons and Vau de Vey. The quality of regular Chablis is very much dependent on the producer whilst Petit Chablis is, for the most part, best avoided. Most of the wines made in the area surrounding Chablis are prefixed Bourgogne and are made from Chardonnay, Pinot Noir or Aligoté. Sauvignon de Saint-Bris, though recently promoted to appellation status, is only rarely exciting.

Côte d'Or & Côte Chalonnaise:

The basic hierarchy in the Côte d'Or is of *grands crus* at the top, followed by *premier crus* – always associated with one of 25 villages (*premiers crus* are often blended together due to fragmentation, so labelled simply Premier Cru) – then the level of the village itself (e.g. Gevrey-Chambertin) before the sub-regional appellations (such as Côte de Nuits-Villages) and finally the regional generics: **Bourgogne Rouge** (Pinot Noir), **Bourgogne Blanc** (Chardonnay) and **Bourgogne Aligoté**. The lowest level is not necessarily the humblest, however, as wine from any level may be sold as a generic (for instance, recently replanted vines that have only just come into production or vines that lie just outside a classified area). It is also worth noting that *premier cru* wine may also be included in part of a village-level bottling. This may be due to insufficient quantities for a separate bottling or a grower's decision not to compromise the integrity of his *premier cru* when faced with unsatisfactory quality in a difficult vintage. Also important to understanding the appellation system in Burgundy is the concept of *climat* or individual vineyard areas. Occasionally only part of a named area may be designated *premier cru* (e.g Chambolle-Musigny la Combe d'Orveaux) while within the unclassified village areas (which may be large, as in Meursault) the named vineyards (*lieux-dits*) may be added to the label (e.g. Meursault Tillets). The best of these will be close to *premier cru* level, just as several *premiers crus* are comparable to some of the less well-defined *grands crus*. Note too that the spelling of a particular vineyard can vary slightly from one producer to another. What follows is a brief breakdown of the most important villages and their most important *crus*.

Production from the more northerly Côte de Nuits is almost exclusively red. **Marsannay** and **Fixin** at the north end of the Côte de Nuits, begin the band of mostly east-facing hills that stretches, with twists and breaks, until Santenay and Maranges in the tail of the Côte de Beaune. Marsannay tends to be light but scented and produces, unusually for the Côte de Nuits, a significant amount of rosé and white. Fixin in contrast, produces quite forceful, earthy Burgundy, including some powerful reds from *premiers crus* on slopes above the village. The wine, like that from the southern end of the Côte de Nuits, can be sold as **Côte de Nuits-Villages**. After the briefest of interludes (around Brochon) begins Burgundy's great rich seam of red.

Gevrey-Chambertin has 26 *premiers crus* including the outstanding Clos Saint-Jacques (*grand cru* in all but name) and Les Cazetiers at the centre of an arc of *premiers crus* on slopes to the east of the town. South of the village itself begins the great chain of *grands crus* that run almost to the southern edge of Vosne-Romanée. Of the nine in Gevrey, the 12.9 ha **Chambertin** and 15 ha **Clos-de-Bèze** are easily the most important. Seven others all append the name Chambertin: **Mazis-Chambertin** and **Ruchottes-Chambertin** are arguably the next best in potential; **Griottes-Chambertin**, **Charmes-Chambertin** (under which much of **Mazoyères-Chambertin** is sold) and **Chapelle-Chambertin** are also capable of greatness; the last, **Latricières-Chambertin**, rarely reaches the quality of the best *premiers crus*. Gevrey at any level should be distinguished by its greater power, concentration and structure than its neighbouring communes. Despite a radical improvement, too much of it remains pretty poor. **Morey-Saint-Denis** undeservedly lacks the lustre of Gevrey and Chambolle, but can combine the muscle of the former with the elegance of the latter, though which prevails to the greater degree depends as much on the grower as the on vineyard site. A tiny amount of white is made here too. While significantly smaller than Gevrey, it still boasts 20 *premiers crus* and four *grands crus* – **Clos de la Roche** (17 ha), **Clos Saint-Denis** (6.6 ha), **Clos des Lambrays** (8.8 ha) and **Clos de Tart** (7.5 ha) – as well as a thin slice of the 15 ha **Bonnes Mares** which falls mostly in **Chambolle-Musigny**. Bonnes Mares, with its mixed soils, is of variable style but is usually sturdier when sourced from the Morey end of the vineyards. Then the chain of *grands crus* is broken, before continuing with **Le Musigny** (10.7 ha) at the southern end of the commune. Some fine *premier cru* vineyards lie between the two, including Cras, Fuées and Baudes, but closest in style and proximity to Musigny are the often superb Amoureuses and Charmes. Musigny, like no other *cru*, can express the sumptuous elegant beauty of red Burgundy.

The commune of **Vougeot** is dominated by the massive 50-ha *grand cru* of **Clos Vougeot**. Though continuous and walled-in, in its lower flatter reaches it juts deep into what corresponds to only village-quality land in neighbouring Vosne-Romanée. Arguably it ought to be partitioned into three different levels. Without due care you may find you have paid a *grand cru* price for what is, in effect, only village-level wine, although your choice of grower among the 80 owners of the vineyard counts for as much as the position of the vines. At its highest it adjoins both Musigny and Grands Echezeaux and at its best is full, rich and complex if less aristocratic than the former. Both of the *grands crus* **Echezeaux** and **Grands Echezeaux** (with 32 ha and 9 respectively in production) fall in the commune of Flagey-Echezeaux. At their best both produce sturdy, characterful Burgundy, though much of Echezeaux lacks the class expected in a *grand cru*. Neighbouring **Vosne-Romanée** is a commune like no other in the Côte de Nuits. Behind the village lie the great vineyards that produce Burgundy's most expensive and sought-after wines. At the heart of 27 ha of *grands crus* are **La Romanée** (0.85 ha) and **Romanée-Conti** (1.8 ha) with **Richebourg** (8 ha) to the north, **Romanée-Saint-Vivant** (9.4 ha) closer to the village, and **La Grande Rue** (1.65 ha) and **La Tache** (6.1 ha) to the south. These in turn are flanked by some marvellous *premiers crus* including Malconsorts, Chaumes and Clos des Réas on the southern edge of the commune with Nuits-Saint-Georges; with Brûlées, Suchots and Beaux Monts on the northern side, the latter two pressing up against Echezeaux. The best of these are rich, intense and concentrated but with varying degrees of finesse, opulence or silkiness, dependent as much on producer as location. Village-level Vosne comes from east of the village.

The last major village in the Côtes de Nuits is **Nuits-Saint-Georges** though vineyards continue on south to Comblanchien. Here, the best wines offer power and intensity as well as a degree of finesse in the best of 38 *premiers crus* (which extend into the more southerly commune of Prémeaux). Damodes, Boudots and Murgers are some of the best between Nuits-Saint-Georges (the town) and Vosne-Romanée; Vaucrains, Pruliers and Les Saint-Georges are the most notable to the south of Nuits. There are no *grand crus*. Lesser wine can be flavoursome if chunky but the worst is rough and dilute. The cooler hinterland of the Côte de Nuits contains pockets of vineyards in favourable sites which constitute the **Hautes-Côtes de Nuits**. South of the town of Beaune is the equivalent **Hautes-Côtes de Beaune**. A significant amount of the wine is made by the co-op Les Caves des Hautes-Côtes; these wines or an example from a top grower can be good in an exceptional vintage.

The Côte de Beaune's reputation is more for white than red yet the majority of wines are in fact red. From here south the gradients are lower and the swathe of vineyards wider, occasionally receding into the hills behind the main slopes. It begins in a cluster of villages around the famous hill of Corton. The humble AC of **Ladoix** (with seven *premiers crus*) is not widely seen and some of the wine is sold under the sub-regional appellation of **Côte de Beaune-Villages**. Wine for the latter can also come from another 15 villages, making it much more important than the Nuits equivalent. **Aloxe-Corton** at the foot of the Corton hill includes the famous appellations of Corton and Corton-Charlemagne, though vineyards spill into adjoining Ladoix and Pernand-Vergelesses. Most of the white from Burgundy's largest *grand cru* is sold as **Corton-Charlemagne** (51 ha) and most of the red as **Corton** (98ha), though there is a little white Corton too (2.5 ha). The trend to planting Chardonnay begun in the mid-19th century continues, the paler soils at the top of the hill being the best site. Great Corton-Charlemagne is full-bodied but slow-developing due to a powerful structure and requires patience. Red Corton (which oftens attaches one of several *lieu-dit* names) can be similarly austere when young but develops a richness and a distinctive minerally elegance with age. Aloxe-Corton AC, almost entirely red, includes 13 *premiers crus* which lie directly below the red Corton vineyards. To the west of the Aloxe-Corton commune lies **Pernand-Vergelesses**, some of it tucked into the folds in the hills. Increasingly good red and white is made under the AC. The best *premier cru*, Ile de Vergelesses favours reds of finesse rather than power but they add weight with age. To the south, it adjoins **Savigny-lès-Beaune**, which extends east up a little valley to the village itself. The best vineyards lie on both sides, the more northern band of *premiers crus* (including Guettes, Serpentières and Lavières) are more elegant than those from the southern band (including Dominodes, Marconnets, Narbantons and Peuillets), which tend to be fuller and firmer. Importantly, this is a reasonably plentiful source of good-value Burgundy. Rarely exciting is wine from **Chorey-lès-Beaune**, from flat land to the east of the Savigny AC.

Beaune, historically and commercially, is the heart of Burgundy but it is also one of the three leading

Côte de Beaune red wine villages and includes some excellent *premiers crus* from the gentle slopes west of the town. Due to diverse soil types, leading *premiers crus* vary from the full and firm to softer, more elegant wines. Marconnets, Fèves and Bressandes are of the first category, Grèves and Teurons are richer and softer, Clos des Mouches full but elegant too. Important vineyard owners such as Jadot, Albert Morot, Bouchard Père and Drouhin all provide the opportunity to compare and contrast some of the best *crus* from a single source. Another major vineyard owner, and one of the most important in the Côte de Beaune, is the Hospices de Beaune, their many (often oaky) *cuvées* (unique blends of predominantly *premiers crus* named for their benefactor) are sold at the famous auction in November. The wines are then 'finished' by the purchasing *négociant*, a factor that has a further bearing on their (variable) quality. The rarely seen **Côte de Beaune** AC is for a few vineyards in the hills behind Beaune AC. **Pommard** is a continuation of Beaune and its reputation for sturdy, full-bodied reds is in part due to more clayey, often iron-rich, soils than its neighbours. Grands Epenots and Rugiens Bas are the finest *premiers crus*. In **Volnay** the soils are lighter and poorer, contributing to the wine's refinement and elegance. Most of the best *premiers crus* come from south of the village, including Taillepieds, Clos des Chênes, Caillerets Dessus and Santenots. Santenots actually lies within the adjacent Meursault but is generally sold as Volnay when made from Pinot Noir, and as Meursault if from Chardonnay. South and west of Volnay an ascending flank of vineyards extends into the hills and includes the villages of **Monthelie**, **Auxey-Duresses** and **Saint-Romain**. The first two can provide excellent reds from several *premiers crus* but also a little good village white, especially in Auxey-Duresses. Good Saint-Romain white can be better than its position in the Hautes-Côtes de Beaune hills might suggest.

Meursault is one of the three biggest communes in the Côte d'Or and is the most important white wine village. But as with Beaune or Gevrey-Chambertin, with size comes variability. At its worst it is heavy and characterless but good examples are full, ripe and fruit-rich. The finest are intense, stylish and in the case of the would-be *grand cru*, Perrières, minerally and refined. There are no *grands crus* but other fine *premiers crus* include the best examples of Genevrières, Charmes, Poruzots and Goutte d'Or. Village *lieux-dits* names of note include Chevalières, Grands Charrons, Narvaux, Tessons and Tillets. **Blagny** is a small red wine outpost nestled against Meursault and **Puligny-Montrachet**. 'Puligny' and 'world's best' often share the same sentence and with good reason. The village includes the *grands crus* **Chevalier-Montrachet** (7.36 ha), **Bienvenues-Bâtard-Montrachet** (3.69 ha) and half of the 8 ha **Le Montrachet** and 6 ha of the 11.87 ha **Bâtard-Montrachet**. Le Montrachet is the greatest, and most expensive, of all but is a wine capable of marvellous concentration, sublime proportions and exquisite complexity. Chevalier-Montrachet, from thinner soils above, is potentially the closest in quality but Bâtard-Montrachet, from flatter vineyards, can offer superb richness and intensity too. There are many outstanding *premiers crus* which also command high prices. Caillerets (including Les Demoiselles) and Pucelles, adjoining the *grands crus*, will surpass any *grand cru* not at its full potential. Clavoillon and Folatières and the more elevated Champ Gain and La Garenne can highlight the Puligny finesse and intensity as can Champ-Canet, Combettes and Referts which extend as far as Meursault's Perrières and Charmes. As well as the continuation of *grands crus* Le Montrachet and Bâtard-Montrachet, the village of **Chassagne-Montrachet** adds the tiny 1.57-ha *grand cru* of Criots-Bâtard-Montrachet. The wines sold under the Chassagne AC were once predominantly red but its reputation is now emphatically white. Leading *premiers crus* include Caillerets, Champs Gains, Embrazées, Morgeots, La Romanée and Ruchottes – mostly confined to lighter-coloured soils on the higher slopes. Reds vary from the thin and unripe to full and fleshy and can be a source of good value (they only command around half the price of a white from the same vineyard, thus the trend to white continues). La Boudriotte, Clos Saint-Jean, La Maltroie, Morgeots and Chenevottes are the most noted red *premiers crus*. Behind Chassagne and Puligny lies the commune of **Saint-Aubin**. Some remarkably good white is produced by the best growers from the most worthy *premier cru* vineyards: La Chatenière and those that adjoin Chassagne (Le Charmois) and Puligny (En Remilly and Murgers des Dents de Chien – backing on to the Mont Rachet hill). Reds tend to be relatively light and slightly earthy.

Santenay is the Côte de Beaune's last significant commune for quality as the tail of the vineyard area swings west. From south-facing vineyards red wines dominate, the best of these are both full and stylish. These are likely to come from the *premiers crus* Gravières, La Comme and Clos des Tavannes that extend to the edge of Chassagne. One or two excellent whites are also being produced. While a fast improving AC with some excellent-value wines, Santenay is not so good from a weaker vintage or from a mediocre producer when the wine may be lean and stalky. To the west the vineyards adjoin **Maranges**, more earthy and robust than the best Santenay, though exceptions exist.

As a source of quality and value the best Côte Chalonnaise growers provide a real alternative to the lesser villages of the Côte d'Or. To the east of the Santenay and Maranges vineyards, and south of the town of Chagny, lie those of **Bouzeron**, the first of five separate appellations within the Côte Chalonnaise region. This is not a continuation of the Côte d'Or but an area of less sheltered rolling hills where the grapes ripen later and the wines are lighter. Bouzeron is classified for Aligoté only, its Pinot Noir and Chardonnay sold as **Bourgogne Côte Chalonnaise**. **Rully** lies east and south of Bouzeron and makes more white than red – both of which can reveal ripe, attractive fruit in a top example. Less ripe Chardonnay is likely to be made into **Crémant de Bourgogne**. South of Rully is **Mercurey**, the most important Chalonnaise appellation. Most of the wine is a quite structured red, surprisingly rich and intense from a combination of a top year and producer, but often hard and lean when not. A little good white is also produced. Slightly more supple yet stylish reds are produced in **Givry**, where the balance of red and white is similar to that of Mercurey. The southernmost appellation is **Montagny**, where exclusively white wine is made. The wines can be fuller if sometimes less distinguished than those from Rully. The reputable Buxy co-op, La Cave des Vignerons de Buxy, is based here.

Mâconnais & Beaujolais:

The Mâconnais produces as much wine as the Côte d'Or and Côte Chalonnaise combined, though much of it is pretty ordinary. Red under the **Mâcon** and **Mâcon Supérieur** ACs is usually poor and Gamay-based, any better reds are likely to be sold as Bourgogne Rouge. Limestone soils are important to the increasing percentage of Chardonnay planted in the region and much of what is produced is sold as **Mâcon-Villages** or hyphenated with the name of the individual village (such as La Roche Vineuse). From a reputable grower this is a good source of inexpensive white Burgundy. Since 1998, **Viré-Clessé** has been a separate appellation for wines from Viré and Clessé.

The real excitement, however, is centred around four communes in the very south of the Mâconnais. Chaintré, Fuissé, Solutré and Vergisson comprise **Pouilly-Fuissé**, the latter two famous for the rock bluffs that proved useful in prehistoric times for herding and killing wild animals. Now the slopes that run down from the foot of the cliff are some of the best in the region for producing rich, ripe, full-bodied whites. The potential for heavy, alcoholic whites exists but radical improvement over the last ten years in particular has seen the emergence of wines to rival all but the most elegant, refined and complete Côte de Beaunes, surpassed only by the top *premiers* and *grands crus*. The top wines impress particularly for their richness but as well as displaying increasing balance and harmony there is definite refinement and elegance from the top sites. At a lower level the wines are more immediate and obvious than something from the Côte de Beaune but are more likely to be fully ripe. Attached to the southern end and east of Pouilly-Fuissé, above Chaintré, are the separate villages of **Pouilly-Loché** and **Pouilly-Vinzelles** which, though small, are at last showing considerable potential in the right hands. **Saint-Véran** encompasses Chardonnay vineyards from villages to the north and south of Pouilly-Fuissé. Its quality is very producer-dependent, ranging from moderate Mâcon-Villages quality to a fine Pouilly-Fuissé substitute at considerably lower prices. More potential is also beginning to be exploited from other sites further along a north-west axis from Pouilly-Fuissé, such as by Verget at Sologny.

The Mâconnais melts into Beaujolais where a few Chardonnay vines qualify to be sold as Beaujolais Blanc. But the real story concerns the Gamay grape and its predisposition for a radically different growing environment as granite soils take over from the limestone-based soils of Burgundy proper. In these soils old vines seem to count for more than low yields and grapes must be hand-picked as they are subject (in most instances) to a vinification that involves semi-carbonic maceration of whole un-destemmed bunches of grapes. The quality of the fruit can leave much to be desired and too much Beaujolais finishes abruptly with a hard, green edge. Better examples are richly fruity but relatively short-lived with little real structure but easy drinkability. Different interpretations of style do exist however, and some producers get more structure into the wines without losing too much of their charm and quaffability. Jadot and one or two others make the wines in the style of red Burgundy with a similar vinification and oak-ageing as for Pinot Noir-based reds. Though it may not seem worth the effort the difference a dedicated progressive grower can make to the quality of Beaujolais can be a revelation.

The best Beaujolais comes from the northern or Haut-Beaujolais, with purer soils and better slopes. It is sold as **Beaujolais-Villages** or better still as one of ten recognised *crus* from within this area. There is a trend to increasing identification of individual *climats* within the *crus*. The vineyards of **Saint-Amour**, where Beaujolais takes over from Mâconnais, are on rather mixed soils and are generally a little unexciting. **Juliénas** in contrast, from well-positioned slopes, is a consistent provider of wines with better depth and intensity than most. Lighter **Chénas** occupies higher ground than the adjoining **Moulin-à-Vent** and it is the latter that has the most strength, structure and longevity of all the *crus*. It prices are only matched by **Fleurie**, the best examples of which are perfumed but also often unequalled for their density of fruit and lush texture. **Chiroubles** has some of the most elevated vineyards in the region; the best wines are light but as refined as they get. At the heart of **Morgon** is the Côte de Py with its distinctive *roches pourries* soils of friable schist, the wines are dense and intensely cherryish. **Regnié** is the most recent *cru* and rarely exciting. The large **Brouilly** *cru* surrounds the hill of Mont Brouilly whose slopes provide **Côte de Brouilly**. The best Brouilly can have attractive fruit but much of it is poor, while Côte de Brouilly is usually marginally better.

A-Z Producers by appellation/region

Chablis & Yonne

Chablis
JEAN-CLAUDE BESSIN
BILLAUD-SIMON
DOM. DE BOIS D'YVER
JEAN-MARC BROCARD
LA CHABLISIENNE
DOM. DE CHANTEMERLE
DANIEL DAMPT
RENÉ ET VINCENT DAUVISSAT
DANIEL-ÉTIENNE DEFAIX
JEAN-PAUL DROIN
JOSEPH DROUHIN
GÉRARD DUPLESSIS
JEAN DURUP ET FILS
WILLIAM FÈVRE
JEAN-PIERRE GROSSOT/CORINNE PERCHAUD
DOM. LAROCHE

BERNARD LEGLAND/DES MARRONNIERS
LONG-DEPAQUIT
DOM. DES MALANDES
DOM. LOUIS MICHEL ET FILS
DOM. LOUIS MOREAU
GILBERT PICQ ET SES FILS
DOM. LOUIS PINSON
DENIS POMMIER
LAURENCE ET DENIS RACE
DOM. FRANÇOIS RAVENEAU
DOM. DE VAUROUX
DOM. VOCORET

Irancy
ANITA ET JEAN-PIERRE COLINOT

Saint-Bris
GHISLAINE ET JEAN-HUGUES GOISOT

Côte d'Or & Côte Chalonnaise
(from north to south)

Marsannay
BRUNO CLAIR

Gevrey-Chambertin
DENIS BACHELET
LUCIEN BOILLOT ET FILS
ALAIN BURGUET
PHILIPPE CHARLOPIN
DOM. PIERRE DAMOY
CLAUDE DUGAT
BERNARD DUGAT-PY
FRÉDÉRIC ESMONIN
SYLVIE ESMONIN
DOM. FOURRIER
GEANTET-PANSIOT
DENIS MORTET
DOM. ARMAND ROUSSEAU
CHRISTIAN SÉRAFIN
DOM. TRAPET PÈRE ET FILS

Morey-Saint-Denis
CLOS DE TART
DOM. DUJAC
ROBERT GROFFIER
DOM. DES LAMBRAYS
HUBERT LIGNIER
DOM. MICHEL MAGNIEN ET FILS
PERROT-MINOT
DOM. PONSOT

Chambolle-Musigny
AMIOT-SERVELLE
GHISLAINE BARTHOD
HUDELOT-NOËLLAT
JACQUES-FRÉDÉRIC MUGNIER
DOM. ROUMIER
DOM. COMTES GEORGES DE VOGÜÉ

Vosne-Romanée
DOM. ROBERT ARNOUX
SYLVAIN CATHIARD
BRUNO CLAVELIER
DOM. CONFURON-COTÉTIDOT
DOM. RENÉ ENGEL
DOM. JEAN GRIVOT
ANNE GROS
MICHEL GROS
FRANÇOIS LAMARCHE
MÉO-CAMUZET
MUGNERET-GIBOURG/GEORGES MUGNERET
DOM. DE LA ROMANÉE-CONTI
EMMANUEL ROUGET

Nuits-Saint-Georges
BERTRAND AMBROISE
DOM. DE L'ARLOT
ROBERT CHEVILLON
DOM. JEAN-JACQUES CONFURON
DOM. FAIVELEY
DOM. HENRI GOUGES
DOMINIQUE LAURENT
NICOLAS POTEL
DOM. DANIEL RION ET FILS
PATRICE & MICHÈLE RION
DOM. CHARLES THOMAS
DOM. DE LA VOUGERAIE

Aloxe-Corton
COMTE SENARD

Corton-Charlemagne
DOM. BONNEAU DU MARTRAY

Pernand-Vergelesses
DOM. RAPET PÈRE ET FILS

Savigny-lès-Beaune
DOM. SIMON BIZE ET FILS
CHANDON DE BRIAILLES
DOM. ANTONIN GUYON
JEAN-MARC PAVELOT

Chorey-lès-Beaune
DOM. DU CH. DE CHOREY
TOLLOT-BEAUT

Beaune
BOUCHARD PÈRE ET FILS
MAISON CHAMPY
JOSEPH DROUHIN
A F GROS & FRANÇOIS PARENT
LOUIS JADOT
LOUIS LATOUR
DOM. ALBERT MOROT

Pommard
COMTE ARMAND
JEAN-MARC BOILLOT
DOM. DE COURCEL

Volnay
MARQUIS D'ANGERVILLE
DOM. JEAN BOILLOT ET FILS
MICHEL LAFARGE
HUBERT DE MONTILLE

Monthelie
DARVIOT-PERRIN

Auxey-Duresses
DOM. LEROY
Saint-Romain
DOM. D'AUVENAY

Meursault
MICHEL BOUZEREAU ET FILS
BOYER-MARTENOT
JEAN-FRANÇOIS COCHE-DURY

ARNAUD ENTE
JEAN-PHILIPPE FICHET
DOM. HENRI GERMAIN ET FILS
PATRICK JAVILLIER
FRANÇOIS JOBARD
RÉMI JOBARD
DOM. DES COMTES LAFON
LATOUR-GIRAUD
DOM. MATROT
FRANÇOIS MIKULSKI
PIERRE MOREY/MOREY BLANC
DOM. ROULOT

Puligny-Montrachet
LOUIS CARILLON ET FILS
GÉRARD CHAVY ET FILS
OLIVIER LEFLAIVE
DOM. LEFLAIVE
DOM. PAUL PERNOT ET FILS
ÉTIENNE SAUZET

Chassagne-Montrachet
DOM. GUY AMIOT ET FILS
BLAIN-GAGNARD
MICHEL COLIN-DELÉGER ET FILS
RICHARD FONTAINE-GAGNARD
JEAN-NOËL GAGNARD
BERNARD MOREY
DOM. MARC MOREY
MICHEL NIELLON
JEAN PILLOT ET FILS
RAMONET

Saint-Aubin
DOM. MARC COLIN ET FILS
HUBERT ET OLIVIER LAMY

Santenay
ROGER BELLAND
VINCENT GIRARDIN

Bouzeron
AUBERT ET PAMÉLA DE VILLAINE

Rully
DOM. VINCENT DUREUIL-JANTHIAL
HENRI ET PAUL JACQUESON

Mercurey
DOM. BRINTET
DOM. MICHEL JUILLOT
ANTONIN RODET

Givry
FRANÇOIS LUMPP

Other
VERGET

Mâconnais & Beaujolais

Mâcon-Villages
DOM. GUFFENS-HEYNEN
MERLIN
JEAN THÉVENET

Pouilly-Fuissé
DANIEL ET MARTINE BARRAUD
CH. DE FUISSÉ
CH. DES RONTETS
DOM. CORDIER PÈRE ET FILS
CORSIN
DOM. J A FERRET
DOM. ROGER LASSARAT
DOM. ROBERT-DENOGENT
SAUMAIZE-MICHELIN
DOM. THIBERT PÈRE ET FILS
DOM. VALETTE

Pouilly-Vinzelles
DOM. LA SOUFRANDIÈRE

Saint-Véran
DOM. DES DEUX ROCHES

Viré-Clessé
ANDRÉ BONHOMME
DOM. RIJCKAERT

Beaujolais
GEORGES DUBOEUF
HENRY FESSY

Moulin-à-Vent
CH. DES JACQUES
DOM. PAUL ET ERIC JANIN

Fleurie
CLOS DE LA ROILETTE/COUDERT

Morgon
DOM. F & J CALOT
DOM. LOUIS-CLAUDE DESVIGNES
JEAN FOILLARD

Côte de Brouilly
CH. THIVIN

Chablis, Côte d'Or & Côte Chalonnaise vintages

In general terms red Burgundy doesn't offer the same potential longevity as do Bordeaux or other great Cabernet-based wines. Exceptional wines can, however, be very long-lived, though often the top whites will outlast the best reds. Ageing potential also depends as much on the style favoured by the particular producer or on the origin of the wines. Therefore comments about the character of the vintage made here should be considered against remarks made in the individual producer profiles. The very best estates, aided by a generally fine run of vintages in the past decade or so, now produce consistently high quality. Yet away from the top names and most famous sites the choice of vintage remains crucial, especially at a lower level, given the struggle for ripeness in Burgundy's many more marginal vineyard sites.

2002: This looks to be a very exciting red wine vintage in Burgundy despite a spell of warm but wet weather in early September. Yields were low, the grapes small but high in sugar, with good colour and acidity that should ensure intense, ripe and ageworthy wines throughout the Côte d'Or. Whites are very promising too, from Chablis to the Mâconnais. The first wines promise concentration, structure, perfectly ripe fruit and good balance that should match the high quality from 99 and 2000.

2001: A repeat of 2000 in the sense that the more northerly Côte de Nuits looks better than the Côte de Beaune (with reduced quantities in Volnay and Pommard due to hail). A wet year but with a mostly fine finish, this is likely to be one where only the best-managed vineyards produce ripe, concentrated grapes with good acidities. The difficult weather has made for variable white wines; some have both good acidity and concentration but others lack ripeness. A good producer will be essential. Reasonable promise in Chablis, less so in the Côte Chalonnaise.

2000: In red this was a much better vintage in the Côte de Nuits than the Côte de Beaune. Santenay was particularly badly affected by rain. Not one to cellar but fine quality further up the hierarchy. Generally a very good vintage for whites if slightly less consistent than 1999. Opinions are divided amongst growers as to the better of the two years for white; some have better ripeness, concentration and acidity in the latter, some in the former. Fine Chablis, too and decent quality in the Côte Chalonnaise.

1999: A generally excellent large vintage for reds with remarkable colour, good acidity and ripe tannins. The size of the crop encouraged growers to be more rigorous in removing the less promising bunches. These reds, particularly good in the Côte de Beaune, are vigorous and intense and only the generic or more humble village appellations be should be drunk now. Whites were plentiful too, and, though more variable than the reds, also fine. There are generally outstanding whites at the top estates and some very good Chablis, though some growers here were affected by rains at the end of harvest. An excellent vintage in the Côte Chalonnaise in both colours.

1998: A problematic growing season lowered expectations but this has turned out to be a vintage with more potential than 1997 thanks to better acidity and more stuffing. Quantities were down due to severe Easter frosts. Though generally very good, quality is much more irregular at a lower level, with a lack of full ripeness in the tannins due in part to some very hot August days. Isolated hail hit the volume of whites, especially in Meursault, and quality is variable; some wines lack concentration and others will evolve quite quickly. The best, though, will not disappoint. Less good in Chablis.

1997: A much smaller vintage of more forward reds than 1996 but very attractive and one that has already given much pleasure. The wines have lowish acidities but it is a good vintage for drinking now if not for keeping. Whites can have lowish acidities too but there is no lack of richness or intensity in the top wines. The best in both colours will still keep. Chablis shows very attractive fruit but the structures were compromised by a very hot August followed by September rain before a fine harvest. Nonetheless, after 1995 and 96, the third good Chablis vintage in a row.

1996: One of the finest red wine vintages of the 1990s, with both quantity and quality at the top level. There is excellent fruit intensity and ripeness in the tannins allied to good acidity that will repay further keeping. The best have closed up but more humble appellations from a good grower can be drunk now. A similar picture in white, including Chablis, with excellent concentration and structure in the best wines. Also a vintage in which the very best reds and whites from the Côte Chalonnaise might still be considered.

1995: Not a vintage of great richness in the reds but fine nonetheless. The best have added weight with age, are ripe and structured and will still improve. An excellent vintage for whites; good examples can be drunk now but will continue to improve. Chablis had its best vintage for many years and these now have the development to show what a well-sourced *premier cru* (or *grand cru*) tastes like with age.

1994: Arguably the weakest red wine vintage in the last 15 years but there is not much between this and 1992 in quality. A better bet in the Côte de Nuits than the Côte de Beaune. Whites are merely attractive when from a good producer, others are best left for the unwary. If 1994 is the only choice of Chablis available make sure it's from a top producer.

1993: A very fine red wine vintage with great vigour, structure and intensity. Good village-level examples or those from lesser *climats* should be drunk now but the best will still improve. Much weaker in the whites, though some have both concentration and structure and provide rich, mature drinking now. Only the very best will still improve. Chablis tends to lack ripeness and concentration with few exceptions.

1992: A large red harvest, though not as much as 1990, and some of it full and charming though missing the extra concentration or structure of a really good vintage. Producers noted for their low yields are a safer bet though generally there is a lack of intensity and definition. Whites showed some delicious fruit but only in the top examples can this still be enjoyed. Corton-Charlemagne Bonneau du Martray shows what was possible. Only a relatively small number of Chablis are fine.

1991: Many rich, concentrated and structured reds. The best still have plenty of life but some lack harmony and fully ripe tannins. Find a good bottle, though, and it's likely to be much cheaper than the 1990 of the same wine. Good drinking now, though a handful might keep a bit longer. Whites were mostly ordinary at best and should only be bought with extreme care.

1990: A superlative vintage for red wines and unequalled in recent decades for the overall quality of the vintage, though due to vinicultural improvements many individual producers have made wines of higher quality since. A very good vintage for whites too, including Chablis. Many fine bottles, including those from some of the lesser *climats*, and these will last for many years to come.

1989: A warm, plentiful vintage with relatively low acidity in the reds, though it is still good at top level. Whites had particularly good structure and have proved more long-lived than 1988, 90 or 92.

1988: A rather firm, austere vintage with high acidity and tannins in the reds. It has taken a long time to come into its own but the best examples are only now revealing the underlying refinement. Whites are less good though some have lasted; Chablis is the best bet – the very best of which will still keep.

Earlier Years

At the top level 1985 can still provide good drinking, though whites are a safer bet as the once rich, ripe reds are mostly past their best due to low acidity levels. A few of the structured reds from the 1983 vintage can still be vigorous where rot was avoided. Even older vintages might only be considered for an outstanding *cru* from an impeccable source. Vintages from the 1970s include 78, 76 and 71 while the more successful 1960s include 69, 66, 64, 62 and 61. For these and wines from any older vintages, however, consider the advice of a trusted merchant or friend who still has other bottles of the same wine, or consult Michael Broadbent's *Vintage Wine*.

Burgundy vintages

	Côte de Nuits Red	Côte de Beaune Red	Côte Chalonnaise Red	Beaujolais
2002	★★★★/★★★★★ A	★★★★/★★★★★ A	★★★★A	★★/★★★B
2001	★★/★★★ A	★★ A	★★ B	★★ B
2000	★★★ A	★★ A	★★ B	★★★★★ B
1999	★★★★ A	★★★★/★★★★★ A	★★★★/★★★★★ B	★★★★/★★★★★ C
1998	★★★/★★★★ B	★★★ B	★★★ C	★★/★★★ C
1997	★★★B	★★/★★★ C	★★/★★★ C	★★★C
1996	★★★★/★★★★★ A	★★★★/★★★★★ B	★★★★ C	★★/★★★ D
1995	★★★★ B	★★★★ C	★★★/★★★★ C	★★★★ C
1994	★/★★ C	★/★★ C	★★ D	★★★ D
1993	★★★★ B	★★★★C	★★★ D	★★/★★★ D
1992	★★ C	★★ C	★★ D	★★ D
1991	★★★/★★★★ C	★★★/★★★★ C	★★★/★★★★ D	★★★★/★★★★★D
1990	★★★★★ B	★★★★★ C	★★★★/★★★★★ C	★★★ D
1989	★★★★ C	★★★★ C	★★★★ D	★★★/★★★★ D
1988	★★★★ B	★★★★ C	★★★ D	★★★★ D

	Chablis	Côte de Beaune White	Pouilly-Fuissé
2002	★★★★ A	★★★★/★★★★★ A	★★★★/★★★★★ A
2001	★★★ A	★★★ A	★★★ B
2000	★★★★ A	★★★★/★★★★★ A	★★★★/★★★★★ B
1999	★★★★ B	★★★★/★★★★★ B	★★★★ C
1998	★★★ B	★★/★★★ B	★★★/★★★★ C
1997	★★★★ B	★★★/★★★★ B	★★★★ C
1996	★★★★★ B	★★★★/★★★★★ B	★★★★ C
1995	★★★★ C	★★★★/★★★★★ B	★★★★ C
1994	★★/★★★ C	★★★ C	★★/★★★ D
1993	★/★★ C	★★ C	★★/★★★ D
1992	★★★ C	★★★★ C	★★★★ C
1991	★★/★★★ D	★★/★★★ D	★★/★★★ D
1990	★★★★/★★★★★ C	★★★/★★★★C	★★★/★★★★ D
1989	★★★★/★★★★★ C	★★★★/★★★★★ C	★★★★/★★★★★ C
1988	★★★★ C	★★★/★★★★ D	★★★★D

Chablis & Yonne

JEAN-CLAUDE BESSIN
A: M&V

Owner: Jean-Claude Bessin   3 Rue de la Planchotte, 89800 Chablis
One of Chablis' best small domaines. Former architects Jean-Claude Bessin and his wife had the good fortune to inherit (from her family) prime Chablis vineyards. Seven of their 12 ha are located in three leading *crus*, the *premiers crus* Montmains and Fourchaume, and *grand cru* Valmur; the Fourchaume in particular contains a wealth of fine old vines. Bessin has only been bottling his own wine since 1992 but has already produced plenty of rich, fruit-intense, unoaked Chablis notable for its ripeness. Oak is now employed for the Valmur but doesn't overwhelm its concentrated fruit, instead adding structure that should enhance its longevity. The regular Chablis can be drunk quite young, but the *crus* drink well with three years' age or more. (PW)
O **Chablis Grand Cru** Valmur★★★ £D
O **Chablis Premier Cru** Montmains★★ £C Fourchaume★★★ £C O **Chablis**★★ £B

BILLAUD-SIMON
A: BBR, CTy, L&W, HHB, WSc

Owner: Billaud-Simon family   Quai de Reugny, BP 46, 89800 Chablis
A family domaine dating from 1815 making brilliant, predominantly unoaked Chablis under the winemaking direction of Samuel Billaud. Together with his uncle Bernard Billaud, they have considerably advanced the quality level over the past decade. The estate's 20 ha include a little of three *grands crus* (Les Clos, Preuses and Vaudésir) and a tiny bit of Blanchots, as well as significant vineyards in the *premiers crus* of Mont de Milieu, Montée de Tonnerre and Vaillons, and a little Fourchaume. Except for Fourchaume, there is a high proportion of old vines – the Mont de Milieu is also made in a Vieilles Vignes bottling. This contributes to the depth and concentration of the wines, which have a distinctive minerally, occasionally smoky, ripe fruit character and great definition and structure. A carefully temperature-controlled vinification in stainless steel is followed by a lengthy low-temperature *débourbage*. Barrel-fermentation and ageing are only employed exceptionally, as in the case of the Les Clos (from 55-year-old vines), where it enhances the structure but takes nothing from the wine's purity. In short, these are quite delicious, graceful, stylish Chablis with extra distinction and depth at the *premier cru* level and wonderful dimension and complexity at the *grand cru* level. If the prices are edging upwards they still represent marvellous value vis-à-vis similar quality from the Côte de Beaune. Even the Petit Chablis is worth considering here. (PW)
O **Chablis Grand Cru** Preuses★★★★ £E Vaudésir★★★★★ £E Les Clos★★★★★ £E
O **Chablis Grand Cru** Blanchots Vieilles Vignes★★★★★ £F
O **Chablis Premier Cru** Vaillons★★★★ £C Mont de Milieu★★★★ £C Montée de Tonnerre★★★★ £C
O **Chablis Premier Cru** Fourchaume★★★ £D
O **Chablis**★★ £B Tête d'Or★★★ £C O **Petit Chablis**★ £B

DOMAINE DE BOIS D'YVER
A: JNi, CPp

Owner: Georges Pico & Eleana Puentes   Grande Rue Nicolas Droin, Courgis, 89800 Chablis
This 22-ha estate at Courgis makes a sound range of Chablis both from its own vineyards and from grapes bought in from another grower. The wines show something of a leesy influence, though this is more pronounced at the lower levels, with added minerality and fruit depth in the Vaillons and Montmains *premiers crus*. Though for the most part machine-harvested, they usually show good ripeness, a certain elegance and good balance. Used oak is employed for ageing the Blanchots, which shows a *grand cru*-like complexity, though wants for greater fruit intensity on the finish for a higher

rating. Those from bought-in grapes, which includes the Blanchots, are labelled only as 'mis en bouteille par Domaine de Bois d'Yver'. (PW)

O **Chablis Grand Cru** Blanchots★★★ £E
O **Chablis Premier Cru** Beauregard★★ £C Vaillons★★★ £C Montmains★★★ £C
O **Chablis**★★ £B

JEAN-MARC BROCARD www.domaine-brocard.fr A: JBa, Adm, BWC, J&B, Odd

Owner: Jean-Marc Brocard 3 Route de Chablis, Préhy, 89800 Chablis

Thirty years ago Jean-Marc Brocard had a single hectare of vines, now he has 96 ha and climbing (though not all of it in the Chablis AC). Based at Préhy, on the edge of the Chablis region, he has turned out consistent, lively, assertive Chablis since the early 1980s. The emphasis is on producing 'typical' Chablis that is minerally and elegant. Though, for the most part, from mechanically harvested grapes, these stainless steel-vinified Chablis usually deliver adequate fruit and structure, particularly with a couple of years' bottle-age, though they can sometimes be a bit lean and underripe. The most interest and character is to be found among the *premiers* and *grands crus*, which though not first rate can offer decent value for money. They should, however, not be drunk too young (four years is a minimum). A series of Bourgogne Blancs are also produced to differentiate between different soil types in the Chablis region (not unlike the different terroirs exploited by SIEUR D'ARQUES in a series of different Toques et Clochers Chardonnay *cuvées* in the Languedoc-Roussillon). (PW)

O **Chablis Grand Cru** Bougros★★ £D Vaudésir★★ £D Les Clos★★★ £E
O **Chablis Premier Cru** Beauregard★★ £C Vaucoupin★★ £C Côte de Jouan★★ £C
O **Chablis Premier Cru** Montée de Tonnerre★★ £C
O **Chablis**★ £B Vieilles Vignes★ £B
O **Bourgogne Blanc** Jurassique★ £B Kimméridgien★ £B Portlandien★ £B
O **Bourgogne Aligoté**★ £B

LA CHABLISIENNE www.chablisienne.com A: SsG, Cib, E&T, Maj, WSc

Owner: 'Cooperative' 8 Boulevard Pasteur, BP 14, 89800 Chablis

The La Chablisienne co-op draws on a massive chunk of the Chablis *vignoble*, producing a third of all Chablis made. Much of what appears under the labels of the large Beaune *négociants* is sourced from here. The operation is very competently run by Hervé Tucki and considerable sums are spent on renewing a battery of oak barrels. At the village level or lower (Petit Chablis) the wines can be lean and dilute, while some of the *premiers crus* and *grands crus* are excessively oaked despite the intention to bring out the *terroir*. In poor vintages at least, there just doesn't seem to be the fruit of sufficient quality to achieve this. That said, and while a bad bottle can put you off, *premiers crus* like Vaulorent, Montmains and Montée de Tonnerre can be really good and the Vieilles Vignes with some oak influence is typically concentrated with good balance. The most prized wine is that bottled from the best part of 6 ha of Grenouilles as Château Grenouilles, though sadly the oak can be a bit overdone. Most significantly, quality and style depend to a large degree on the requirements of the customer, be it a *négociant* or supermarket chain. If its standards are high then expect a decent Chablis. While a Chablis from a good small grower is still likely to be a better bet, nonetheless there are some fine bottles that may be encountered in top restaurants and elsewhere. Unfortunately, while a co-op can mean great value, prices for Chablisienne-labelled wines are near the top of the hierarchy for their respective appellations. Listed below are some of the most consistent of the leading crus. (PW)

O **Chablis Grand Cru** Blanchots★★★ £E Grenouilles★★★ £E Preuses★★★ £E Château Grenouilles★★ £F
O **Chablis Premier Cru** Montmains★★ £D Montée de Tonnerre★★ £D Vaulorent★★ £D
O **Chablis** Vieilles Vignes★★ £C

DOM. DE CHANTEMERLE

A: L&S, Maj

Owner: Adhémar & Francis Boudin   27 Rue de Serein, La Chapelle Vaupelteigne, 89800 Chablis

Also known as Domaine Adhémar et Francis Boudin, this is an exciting small domaine based in the village of La Chapelle Vaupelteigne, producing ripe, characterful Chablis from 15 ha of vineyards close by. Low yields, manual harvesting and vinification in inert vats contribute to a rich, ripe almost buttery style (yet minerally too) but without any oak influence. Particularly worth seeking out is L'Homme Mort, bottled separately from the rest of Fourchaume – not perhaps an inspired choice of name but the resulting wine has great vitality and individuality. All the wines can be drunk quite young but if you think their immediacy suggests they won't keep, you are wrong. The depth, structure and concentration of fruit means they'll keep for a decade and that often includes the regular Chablis. (PW)

O **Chablis Premier Cru** Fourchaume★★★ £C   L'Homme Mort★★★ £D   O **Chablis**★★ £B

ANITA ET JEAN-PIERRE COLINOT   Irancy

Owner: Anita et Jean-Pierre Colinot   1 Rue des Chariats, 89290 Irancy

If the pure, pristine, cherry-scented character of very cool-climate Pinot drives you to distraction then this is the place to come. One or two others in Irancy can also make enticing red but their wines are let down more often by a lack of complete ripeness. From 10 ha (which, typically for this Auxerrois region, includes a little César), Jean-Pierre Colinot and his wife make light but very elegant wines with a gentle charm and good intensity of flavour and length. Of the various *cuvées*, the Côte du Moutier has perhaps the most structure, Palotte slightly more obvious fruit. As well as those below, wines from other parcels of vines, including Les Mazelots, are also made. Unfortunately the wines have a certain following in France and can be difficult to find but it's worth the effort, particularly from a good vintage. Though light in body, the wines are not fragile and will keep well for five years. For another intriguing Auxerrois red see Ghislaine et Jean-Hugues GOISOT. (PW)

● **Irancy** Vieilles Vignes★★ £B   Palotte★★ £B   Côte du Moutier★★ £B

DANIEL DAMPT   www.dampt-defaix.com

A: Bal, HHC, NYg

Owner: Dampt family   1 Rue des Violettes, Milly, 89800 Chablis

Daniel Dampt married the daughter of Jean Defaix, a respected *vigneron* who little by little reclaimed vineyards abandoned following phylloxera in the late 19th century. The Dampts now make very good Chablis from 26 ha of vineyards, including 13 ha of *premiers crus* (predominantly Côte de Léchet and Vaillons). The wines are vinified in stainless steel, with the emphasis on a ripe fruit and floral character but retaining firm acidity and a minerally influence. The pride of the domaine are the Côte de Léchet vineyards, which lie close to the winery and produce arguably the most classic, minerally wine, but there is good quality in all the *premiers crus*. If not amongst the top names this is nonetheless a good inexpensive source of Chablis that drinks well with three or four years' age but will keep for longer in the case of the *premiers crus*. (PW)

O **Chablis Premier Cru** Beauroy★★★ £C   Vaillons★★ £C   Fourchaume★★★ £C   Côte de Léchet★★★ £C
O **Chablis**★★ £B

RENÉ ET VINCENT DAUVISSAT

A: DDr, HHB, J&B, L&S, Tan

Owner: René & Vincent Dauvissat   8 Rue Émile Zola, 89800 Chablis

The Dauvissats have deep roots in the region going back centuries. Vincent's grandfather started domaine bottling in the 1930s and his father René built up and maintains a rich viticultural resource;

almost all of the 11 ha are either *premier* or *grand cru*. In the vineyard, a uniform high average vine age is maintained as old or weak vines are replaced individually, grafted from the best existing vines (*sélection massale*). In addition, all the grapes are manually picked, not just the leading *crus* – a relatively rare occurrence in Chablis. Vincent uses oak, used not new, to ferment and age most of the wines. The resulting Chablis are simply marvellous, characterised by their depth, breadth and body, filled with a gently honeyed ripeness and stylish minerality. All are fine, even the Petit Chablis, but the distinctive minerally yet contrasting *premiers crus* Vaillons and Forest are surpassed by the bigger, more concentrated *grands crus* Preuses and Les Clos. The latter need six or seven years' ageing, *premiers crus* four or five, and even the regular Chablis three or four. The wines can be in short supply, having long been favoured by top Parisian restaurants. (PW)

O **Chablis Grand Cru** Preuses★★★★★ £F Les Clos✪✪✪✪✪ £F
O **Chablis Premier Cru** Séchet★★★★ £E Forest★★★★ £E Vaillons★★★★ £E
O **Chablis**★★★ £C O **Petit Chablis**★★ £B

DANIEL-ÉTIENNE DEFAIX

A: GFy, BBR, L&W, Tan

Owner: Daniel Defaix & family 23 Rue de Champlain, Milly, 89800 Chablis
The Defaix lineage goes back centuries in the Chablis region. Even recent history relating to the domaine goes back to the 18th century. The domaine's reputation rests with three *premiers crus* of 4 ha each, almost half the estate's total of 25 ha. Viticulture is effectively organic, though not certified as such, vine age is high and grape selection rigorous. A sustained fermentation and long lees contact also contribute to the character of these wines. There is less of the floral, mineral and pure fruit character of other good producers but there is depth, intensity and complexity. The Les Lys has more mineral, citrus character plus honey with age; in Côte de Léchet and Vaillons there is more of a leesy influence but a little more structure too, particularly in the latter. Rarely seen is a little Bourgogne Rouge from very old vines, successful in the best vintages. A tiny amount of Grand Cru Blanchots is also made. Most of the wines can be drunk soon after their delayed release but will keep for longer. (PW)

O **Chablis Premier Cru** Côte de Léchet★★★ £D Les Lys★★★ £D Vaillons★★★ £D
O **Chablis** Vieilles Vignes★★ £C

JEAN-PAUL DROIN   www.jeanpaul-droin.fr

A: RsW, DDr, BBR, Bib, A&B

Owner: Jean-Paul Droin 14 bis Rue Jean Jaurès, 89800 Chablis
Jean-Paul Droin and his son Benoît draw from 20 ha of vines spread over five *grands crus* (with around 1 ha each of Vaudésir, Valmur and Les Clos) and seven *premiers crus*. The range is generally of high quality. At the *premiers* and *grands crus* level the wines are (to a greater or lesser degree) fermented and aged in oak of varying age and provenance, resulting in rich, ripe (occasionally too ripe), full wines. The use of oak has become gradually more refined over the past decade and, though there are still some oak flavours, these now rarely overwhelm the ripe, minerally fruit. Nearly all the wines can be drunk with just three or four years' ageing, but will improve for as long again. Try the *crus*, particularly the Montée de Tonnerre, Vaudésir and Les Clos; the regular Chablis and Petit Chablis are more variable. In addition to those below, a little *grand cru* Blanchots and *premiers crus* Côte de Lechet and Vaucoupin are also made. (PW)

O **Chablis Grand Cru** Valmur★★★ £E Grenouilles★★★★ £E Vaudésir★★★★ £E Les Clos★★★★ £E
O **Chablis Premier Cru** Vaillons★★★ £C Montmains★★★ £C Montée de Tonnerre★★★★ £C
O **Chablis Premier Cru** Fourchaume★★★ £C Vosgros★★★ £C

JOSEPH DROUHIN (CHABLIS) www.drouhin.com   A: DAy

Owner: Drouhin family   Moulin de Vaudon, Chichée, 89800 Chablis

Under Robert Drouhin, the house of Joseph DROUHIN, an important high-quality Beaune *négociant*, added Chablis vineyards to its holdings in the Côte d'Or in the late 1960s. Though the grapes are vinified at the company's headquarters in Beaune, the grapes from more than 40 ha are pressed locally. The estate includes 3 ha of *grand cru* vineyards spread over four *climats,* mostly Vaudésir and Les Clos but a little Bougros and Preuses too. Low yields contribute to ripe, concentrated fruit and, though oak is important to the style, it is only used in the top wines and there is usually a good minerally aspect to their character. As well as *premiers crus* Vaillons and Sécher, some Montmains and a regular Chablis Premier Cru from a blend of other sites are bottled separately. (PW)

O **Chablis Grand Cru** Preuses★★★ £F Vaudésir★★★★ £F Les Clos★★★★★ £F
O **Chablis Premier Cru** Sécher★★★ £E Vaillons★★★ £E
O **Chablis★** £B Domaine de Vaudon★★ £C

GÉRARD DUPLESSIS   A: RsW, A&B, Rae

Owner: Gérard Duplessis   5 Quai de Reugny, 89800 Chablis

This excellent small grower's 7 ha of vineyards are mostly in four of the very best *premiers crus*. Gérard Duplessis vinifies in stainless steel and matures in old wood for classic Chablis flavours. The wines can start out a little austere but there is that wonderful Chablis combination of underlying richness and a steely, minerally character that can provide wonderful drinking with five years' ageing, and is even better with another five or ten if produced in a top vintage. (PW)

O **Chablis Grand Cru** Les Clos★★★★ £E
O **Chablis Premier Cru** Fourchaume★★★ £D Montée de Tonnerre★★★ £D Montmains★★★ £D
O **Chablis Premier Cru** Vaillons★★ £D   O **Chablis★★** £C

JEAN DURUP ET FILS www.durup-chablis.com   A: ABy, DDr, THt, HRp, Tan

Owner: Jean Durup   4 Grande Rue, Maligny, 89800 Chablis

Jean Durup led the movement for expansion of the Chablis *vignoble* in direct opposition to WILLIAM FÈVRE in the 1970s and 80s. His estate, partly as a consequence of the authorised expansion, is the largest in the region (much of it regular Chablis but there are also substantial holdings of *premiers crus*). It is very competently run and is increasingly directed by Jean Durup's son, Jean-Paul. While derided by some at the time, Jean has gradually earned greater respect for the quality of his wines. He has also been a leading advocate of unoaked Chablis, and the wines are generally well-balanced, with adequate richness if sometimes lacking a little character and extra flair. Most of the wines drink well with two or three years' ageing but the *premiers crus* from a good vintage can improve for the best part of a decade. While the most important labels are Jean Durup, Domaine de l'Eglantière and Château de Maligny, the same wines are also bottled under the Domaine de la Paulière and Domaine des Valéry labels for specific overseas clients. Some *grand cru* Vaudésir has been made in the most recent vintages. (PW)

O **Chablis Premier Cru** Fourchaume★★ £C Montée de Tonnerre★★ £C L'Homme Mort★★★ £C
O **Chablis Premier Cru** Vau-de-Vey★★ £C
O **Chablis★** £B Vieilles Vignes★★ £B Vigne de la Reine★★ £C Carré de César★★ £C

WILLIAM FÈVRE
A: HBJ, JEF, BBR, WSc

Owner: Joseph Henriot (Champagne)   21 Avenue d'Oberwesel, 89800 Chablis
The Domaine de la Maladière comprises 47 ha and includes an unrivalled collection of *premiers* and *grands crus*. Almost 16 ha are *grand cru* and include six of the seven *climats*. William Fèvre was the staunchest and most vocal of those opposed to the expansion of the Chablis vineyards. The use of new oak became an increasing theme too, to the point of compromising the inherent fruit character of Chablis, but the domaine's reputation has been rapidly restored since its takeover by Joseph Henriot (who have also worked wonders at BOUCHARD PÈRE in the Côte d'Or). Under the direction of Didier Seguier, there has been a return to manual harvesting and much more rigorous grape selection. New oak is still used but the wines are bottled later and there is better concentration and something more of each wine's origin is captured and enhanced rather than compromised by the oak. Though most of the wines are domaine-sourced, some also are made from bought-in grapes. Wines appear also under the Domaine de la Maladière label and the names Ancien Domaine Auffray and Jeanne-Paule Filipi have also been used. Vintages since 1998 and older vintages are highly recommended, but ones in the mid-1990s are more variable in quality. (PW)

Domaine wines:
O **Chablis Grand Cru** Preuses★★★★ £F Les Clos★★★★★ £F Valmur★★★★★ £F Vaudésir★★★★★ £F
O **Chablis Grand Cru** Bougros Côte de Bougerots★★★★ £F Grenouilles★★★★ £F
O **Chablis Premier Cru** Fourchaume Côte de Vaulorent★★★★ £E Montée de Tonnerre★★★★ £D
O **Chablis Premier Cru** Montmains★★★ £D Butteaux★★★ £D Vaillons★★★ £D
O **Chablis Premier Cru** Forêts★★ £D Beauroy★★ £D O **Chablis**★★ £C

GHISLAINE ET JEAN-HUGUES GOISOT
A: DDr, HHB

Owner: Ghislaine & Jean-Hugues Goisot   30 Rue Bienvenu Martin, 89530 Saint-Bris-le-Vineux
The Goisots' vineyards lie outside the Chablis appellation in the less than glamorous Saint-Bris, which promotes Sauvignon rather than Chardonnay. But both Sauvignon and Chardonnay are produced here (an extremely rare occurrence in France, in contrast to much of the New World) along with Aligoté and Pinot Noir from a total of 27 ha of vineyards. Through meticulous and dedicated winemaking, all the wines are of extremely high quality yet don't command high prices thanks to their lowly appellations. The pure-fruited Chardonnay is sold as Bourgogne Côtes d'Auxerre and the pungent green-pepper Sauvignon will now appear under the newly promoted Saint-Bris AC, while the Aligoté and Pinot Noir are sold as humble Bourgogne. The wines are ripe, concentrated and aromatic, with lovely definition and length, and under the Corps de Garde label are worth keeping for two or three years. (PW)
O **Bourgogne Côtes d'Auxerre**★ £B Corps de Garde★★ £C
O **Sauvignon de Saint-Bris** ★★ £B Corps de Garde★★ £B
O **Bourgogne Aligoté**★ £B ● **Bourgogne** Rouge★ £B Corps de Garde★★ £C

JEAN-PIERRE GROSSOT & CORINNE PERCHAUD
A: L&W, Lib, OWL, Eno

Owner: Jean-Pierre Grossot & Corinne Perchaud   4 Route de Mont de Milieu, Fleys, 89800 Chablis
This is a great source for Chablis whether labelled Grossot or sold under the label established by his wife, Corinne Perchaud. If initially a little austere, the wines are intensely fruity, with excellent definition, weight and fine perfumes. Though there are no *grands crus*, the 18 ha includes some excellent *premiers crus*. Stainless steel dominates their production but some oak is used for the Fourneaux and Mont de Milieu *premiers crus* and the village *cuvée*, 'Grossot' or Fûts de Chênes. Only the latter is obviously oaky, the others properly racy and minerally. While the wines are delicious with

three or four years' ageing, they will keep. Prices are very reasonable here too. (PW)

O **Chablis Premier Cru** Fourneaux★★ £C Vaucoupin★★ £C Fourchaume★★★ £C Mont de Milieu★★★ £C
O **Chablis**★ £B Fûts de Chênes★ £B La Part des Anges★★ £C

DOM. LAROCHE www.michellaroche.com A: Bib, NYg

Owner: Michel Laroche L'Obédiencerie, 22 Rue Louis Bro, 89800 Chablis

Michel Laroche is one of Chablis' major players and has recently become almost as well-known for wines made in the South of France (he also has a joint venture with Jorge Coderch in Chile) as for his many prestigious Chablis *crus*. The estate's offices are based in the Obédiencerie in the heart of Chablis, originally a monastery dating back to the ninth century. The Saint-Martin monks here established Chablis' first vines. Though the Laroche domaine dates from the mid-19th century, its major expansion has been only recently, under Michel and his father Henri, and it now covers 100 ha of vines. Most of the the wine is exported around the globe. There are 6 ha of *grands crus*, mostly Blanchots but also some Les Clos and a little Bouguerots (Bougros), and 29 ha of *premiers crus* centred on Fourchaume, Vaillons and Vau de Vey. Lesser wines can be a bit light, but can show typical minerally fruit. In the top wines the style is more unusual, with marked oak influence and sometimes a discernible lactic character in the top *crus*. The wines are supple and gently creamy, without the austerity more characteristic of young Chablis but still retaining a mineral stamp. *Grand crus* can be very good; a small portion of the Blanchots is set apart for the top wine, Réserve de l'Obédience, while the Fourchaumes and Vaillons are labelled Vieilles Vignes for their old vine fruit. Good as the wines can be, the price-for-quality ratio is less convincing. (PW)

O **Chablis Grand Cru** Les Clos★★★★ £F Blanchots★★★ £E Blanchots Réserve de l'Obédience★★★★ £F
O **Chablis Premier Cru** Vaillons Vieilles Vignes★★★ £D Fourchaumes Vieilles Vignes★★★ £D
O **Chablis Premier Cru** Beauroy★★ £D Montmains★★ £D Vau de Vey★★★ £C
O **Chablis** Saint-Martin★ £B

BERNARD LEGLAND/DOM. DES MARRONNIERS A: Bib, GWW

Owner: Bernard Legland Rue de Chablis, Préhy, 89800 Chablis

This is a good source of attractive, well-made and relatively inexpensive Chablis. Bernard Legland's 18 ha doesn't include much in the way of prime vineyards; 2.5 ha of Montmains is the most prized possession. The domaine was established in 1976 and has adhered to a principle of unoaked Chablis. Previously the *premiers crus* (there is also a little Côte de Jouan) were made from relatively young vines but these are now more than 20 years old and consequently the wines show added richness and depth. (PW)

O **Chablis Premier Cru** Côte de Jouan★★ £C Montmains★★★ £C
O **Chablis**★ £B

LONG-DEPAQUIT A: All, Bal, BBR, Wav

Owner: Maison Albert Bichot 45 Rue Auxerroise, 89800 Chablis

This historic estate dates from the time of the French Revolution. There are now 65 ha but much of it has been acquired in the last 30 years or so. As well as a sprinkling of wines from *premier* and *grand cru* vineyards, the wine of the famous La Moutonne vineyard is made here. Acquired in 1791 by Simon Depaquy, it is a *monopole* of 2.35 ha that straddles part of *grands crus* Vaudésir and Preuses that belonged originally to the monks of the Abbey of Pontigny. Though most of the wines are both vinified and aged in stainless steel in order not to compromise the classic, flinty, minerally Chablis style, the *grands crus* see varying percentages of oak. Quality can be a bit uneven but at their best they have intensity, style and finesse; the top wines, especially La Moutonne, develop a gentle honeyed richness with age. The selected *crus* below are the most consistently fine and ageworthy, lesser wines are more of a gamble but can also be good. Prices are on the high side for the quality level. (PW)

O **Chablis Grand Cru** Blanchots★★★ £E Vaudésir★★★ £E Les Clos★★★ £E La Moutonne★★★★ £F

O **Chablis Premier Cru** Vaucoupin★★ £C Vaillons★★ £C Montée de Tonnerre★★★ £D

DOM. DES MALANDES   www.domainedesmalandes.com   A: CHk, H&B, N&P, WSc

Owner: Jean-Bernard et Lyne Marchive   63 Rue Auxerroise, 89800 Chablis
Established in 1986 from the family inheritance of Lyne Marchive (*née* Tremblay), this 25-ha estate has a good following for unoaked Chablis. The reputation has been built on producing wines from low yields and fully ripe fruit and a non-interventionist winemaking philosophy. The wines are ripe, more floral and fruit-driven in the lesser *cuvées* but with more minerally intensity and complexity, as well as concentration, in the *grands crus*. Fourchaume and Montmains are the pick of the *premiers crus* and both the *grands crus* reflect their respective terroir. Though all can be drunk fairly young, these are the wines to keep. Attractive, ripe and intense as the wines are, they lack a little extra depth and structure that would put them among the top names. (PW)

O **Chablis Grand Cru** Vaudésir★★★★ £D Les Clos★★★★ £D

O **Chablis Premier Cru** Côte de Léchet★★ £C Montmains★★★ £C Fourchaume★★★ £C

O **Chablis Premier Cru** Vau de Vey★★ £C

O **Chablis★** £B Vieilles Vignes Tour du Roy★★ £B

DOM. LOUIS MICHEL ET FILS   A: OWL, DAy, BBR, Eno, Odd, WSc

Owner: Jean-Loup Michel   9-11 Boulevard de Ferrières, 89800 Chablis
Fifth-generation Jean-Loup Michel has made the wines here in recent years but the 23-ha estate's international reputation was established by his father, Louis Michel, who died in 1999. Much of the production is now exported and widely available but remarkably without the high prices and compromised quality of some exporters. For its unoaked style of Chablis this is perhaps the most lauded producer in the English-speaking press. The wines spend an extended period of time in stainless steel before a relatively late bottling. Austere but with an underlying minerally fruit richness when young, the *premiers crus* are always better with three to five years' ageing, the *grands crus* with five or more. At their best these are excellent Chablis with fine *terroir* definition and real elegance and length on the palate if not the texture or dimension of the very best. Though generally very consistent, a cool or wet vintage (such as 1993) can reveal some shortcomings, with a lack of full ripeness and a tendency to age more rapidly than usual. Chablis and Petit Chablis are usually a good bet, too. (PW)

O **Chablis Grand Cru** Grenouilles★★★ £D Vaudésir★★★ £D Les Clos★★★★ £E

O **Chablis Premier Cru** Fourchaume★★★ £C Montmains★★★ £C Vaillons★★★ £C

O **Chablis Premier Cru** Montée de Tonnerre★★★ £C

O **Chablis★★** £B O **Petit Chablis★** £B

DOM. LOUIS MOREAU   www.domaine-louismoreau.com   A: Eur, Vin

Owner: Louis Moreau   10 Grande Rue, Beines, 89800 Chablis
Louis and Anne Moreau control 120 ha comprising mostly village Chablis and including the separate estates of Domaine de Biéville and Domaine du Cèdre Doré. The wines should not be confused with those of the *négociant* house, Moreau. Vinified in stainless steel, without recourse to any wood, the wines are quite racy and austere when young but have great reserves of fruit underneath, particularly in the two *premiers crus*, Vaulignot (Vau Ligneau) and Fourneaux. Some top *grands crus*, previously

leased out, have been produced from the 2002 vintage. These see a little new oak and though only moderately concentrated should add richness with age. Led by a classy Vaudésir, they also include Valmur, Les Clos and, from a plot of vines within Les Clos, Clos des Hospices. (PW)

O **Chablis Premier Cru** Fourneaux★★★ £C Vaulignot★★★ £C
O **Chablis**★ £B Domaine du Cèdre Doré★★ £B Domaine de Biéville★★ £B

GILBERT PICQ & SES FILS
A: M&V, MCI, NYg

Owner: Didier & Pascal Picq 3 Route de Chablis, Chichée, 89800 Chablis
The small village of Chichée lies some 3km south-east of the town of Chablis. Here the Picqs have 13 ha, including a little of Chichée's two *premiers crus*. The *fils* are brothers Didier, who is responsible for the winemaking, and Pascal, who maximises grape quality. The grapes are picked as late as possible and both fermentation and ageing are in stainless steel. The wines are crisp and fresh, quite floral and fruity in style but with good intensity in the Vieilles Vignes and extra character and concentration in the *premiers crus*. From most vintages the Vieilles Vignes should be drunk with at least three years' ageing, the *premiers crus* with five or more. (PW)

O **Chablis Premier Cru** Vaucoupin★★★ £C Vosgros★★★ £C
O **Chablis**★★ £B Vieilles Vignes★★ £B

DOM. LOUIS PINSON   www.domaine-pinson.com
A: A&B, CPp, L&W, Maj

Owner: Laurent & Christophe Pinson 5 Quai Voltaire, 89800 Chablis
Perpetually rustic would perhaps best describe the atmosphere *chez* Pinson as almost anyone who has visited the estate over the past couple of decades I'm sure would endorse. But brothers Laurent and Christophe, the current generation in charge of this small 11-ha estate, seem set on a new image while continuing to make Chablis of real depth and character. The parcels of vines are all of the first order, including 2.5 ha of Les Clos and nearly 5 ha of Mont de Milieu. Used oak is employed in their ageing (only the regular Chablis is unoaked), which contributes to their excellent texture and breadth but only subtly influences flavour, though it is sometimes more apparent on the Montmain. The wines have been a little uneven in terms of their ability to age but quality is often remarkably high. All the wines are better with five years' ageing or more, the Les Clos often with ten or more. A little of the *premiers crus* Vaillons and Vaugiraut are also made. (PW)

O **Chablis Grand Cru** Les Clos★★★★ £D
O **Chablis Premier Cru** La Forêt★★★ £C Mont de Milieu★★★ £C Montmain★★★ £C
O **Chablis**★★ £B

DENIS POMMIER
A: L&S

Owner: Denis Pommier 31 Rue Poinchy, Poinchy, 89800 Chablis
Denis Pommier now has 10 ha but started out with just 2.5 ha in 1990. He is already forging a reputation as a young *vigneron* of some talent. Though he has started fermenting and ageing his *premiers crus* in barrel, apart from the Beauroy, only part of the wine gets this treatment and then only a small percentage of the oak is new. Certainly the the quality of the grapes is very good and the wines show concentrated ripe fruit; the mineral and citrus intensity set against a spicy oak character and a gently buttery texture in the most recent vintages of the Côte de Léchet. The overall balance and oak influence in the Beauroy is less convincing but it will be interesting to see how the style evolves here. At present the small production quickly sells out. The Vieilles Vignes also shows some oak influence but the regular version sees no oak whatsoever. A very small amount of Fourchaume is also made from relatively young vines. (PW)

O **Chablis Premier Cru** Côte de Léchet★★★ £C   Beauroy★★ £C
O **Chablis**★★ £B   Vieilles Vignes★★ £B

LAURENCE ET DENIS RACE   www.chablisrace.com   A: M&V, Mar, PWa

Owner: Laurence & Denis Race   5a Rue de Chichée, 89800 Chablis
Denis Race is another exponent of unoaked Chablis. He and his wife have 15 ha of vines including 5.5 ha of *premier cru* Montmains. There is careful attention to the grapes prior to harvesting (and what is left ready for picking) – the key to quality when the grapes are machine-harvested as so much in Chablis now is. The Montmains appears in two bottlings, the Vieilles Vignes version from vines that are 65 years old. Sometimes in Chablis this designation is applied even though there isn't that much really old-vine fruit either in the blend or apparent in the resulting wine, but there is a marked difference in depth and concentration in the Races' wines. All the wines show good *terroir* definition. A steely, minerally Mont de Milieu contrasts with a softer, more elegant Vaillon. A little *grand cru* Blanchots is also made. (PW)
O **Chablis Premier Cru** Montmains Vieilles Vignes★★★ £D   Montmains★★ £C
O **Chablis Premier Cru** Mont de Milieu★★ £C Vaillon★★
O **Chablis**★ £B

DOM. FRANÇOIS RAVENEAU   A: JAr, HHC, Sec, Blx

Owner: Jean-Marie & Bernard Raveneau   9 Rue de Chichée, 89800 Chablis
If I had to chose one source of Chablis above all others this would be it. Continuing the work of their father, François Raveneau, brothers Jean-Marie and Bernard Raveneau make superb Chablis from just 7.5 ha of *premier* and *grand cru* sites. Unquestionably the grape quality is paramount, all are hand-picked and from low-yielding vines, but if anyone makes the case for the use of oak and how it should be used, surely this is the model to emulate. The wines have fabulous structure yet never taste as if they have seen the inside of a barrel. Typically pure minerally, citrusy, greengage notes prevail on the nose, if occasionally more floral or with a hint of smoke, while the palate is taut, intense and steely when young but with wonderful dimension, underlying concentration and depth that builds in richness and complexity over a decade or longer. No two wines are quite the same but there is fine quality here even in weaker vintages. The domaine also has small plots in Chapelot, Forest (Forêt) and Montmains. Prices are surprisingly reasonable unless you buy them second- or third-hand. (PW)
O **Chablis Grand Cru** Blanchots★★★★★ £E   Valmur★★★★★ £E   Les Clos❂❂❂❂❂ £E
O **Chablis Premier Cru** Butteaux★★★★ £E   Vaillons★★★★ £E   Montée de Tonnerre★★★★ £E

DOM. DE VAUROUX   www.domaine-de-vauroux.com   A: L&W, Con, Eno

Owner: Claude & Olivier Tricon   Route d'Avallon, 89800 Chablis
Oliver Tricon has taken full responsibility for the running of this estate from his uncle only since 1999 but is already a very experienced winemaker and *négociant*. A thoroughly modern operation, the domaine has 30 ha of vines, mostly village Chablis but with a little *grand cru* Bougros and a reasonable quantity of *premiers crus* Montmains and Montée de Tonnerre. The style is for stainless steel-vinified and aged Chablis and the resulting wines are clean and flinty, with good concentration and fruit. The wines are given some bottle-ageing before release. As well as the Vauroux wines, estate wines have also been made under the Domaine Olivier Tricon label, while *négociant* wines appear as Maison Olivier Tricon. Prices are reasonable for the quality. (PW)
Domaine de Vauroux:
O **Chablis Grand Cru** Bougros★★★ £E

○ **Chablis Premier Cru** Montmains★★ £C   Montée de Tonnerre★★★ £C
○ **Chablis★** £B   Vieilles Vignes★★ £C

DOM. VOCORET   www.vocoret.com   A: HHB, Maj

Owner: Patrice & Jérôme Vocoret   40 Route d'Auxerre, 89800 Chablis
This family domaine of 40 ha includes around 4 ha of *grands crus* (mostly Blanchots and Les Clos) and more than 15 ha of *premiers crus* (especially Vaillons and La Forêt). Third-generation Jérôme makes the wines while his uncle Patrice manages the vineyards. Though much of the fruit is mechanically harvested, the fruit is generally ripe and concentrated. Vinification is in stainless steel but the *crus* are aged in large used oak. Quality is generally very good with an intense, vibrant fruit character and reasonable depth, though the wines can miss a little extra concentration in more difficult vintages. In addition to those below, small quantities of the *grands crus* Valmur and Vaudésir, and *premier cru* Mont de Milieu, are also made. (PW)

○ **Chablis Grand Cru** Blanchot★★★ £D   Les Clos★★★ £D
○ **Chablis Premier Cru** Côte de Léchet★★ £C   La Forêt★★ £C   Montmains★★ £C
○ **Chablis Premier Cru** Montée de Tonnerre★★ £C   Vaillons★★ £C
○ **Chablis★** £B

Also see the following Burgundy *négociants* with an entry in the section *Côte D'Or & Côte Chalonnaise:*

OLIVIER LEFLAIVE FRÈRES
VERGET

CHABLIS & YONNE/OTHER WINES OF NOTE

CHRISTAN ADINE/DOM. DE LA CONCIÈRGERIE ○ **Chablis Premier Cru** Montmains £C
DOM. BARAT ○ **Chablis Premier Cru** Côte de Léchet £C   Fourneaux £C   Vaillons £C
DOM. BERSAN ○ **Chablis Premier Cru** Montmains £C
PASCAL BOUCHARD ○ **Chablis Grand Cru** Les Clos £E   Vaudésir £E
○ **Chablis Premier Cru** Fourchaumes Vieilles Vignes £D
DOM. DU CHARDONNAY ○ **Chablis Premier Cru** Montée de Tonnerre £C   Montmains £C
○ **Chablis Premier Cru** Vaillons £C
DOM. JEAN COLLET ET FILS ○ **Chablis Premier Cru** Vaillons £C   ○ **Chablis** £B
DOM. D'ÉLISE ○ **Chablis** £B
DOM. ALAIN GEOFFREY ○ **Chablis Premier Cru** Beauroy £C
THIERRY HAMELIN ○ **Chablis Premier Cru** Beauroy £C   Vau Ligneau £C   ○ **Chablis** Vieilles Vignes £B
SYLVAIN MOSNIER ○ **Chablis Premier Cru** Beauroy £C   Côte de Léchet £C
○ **Chablis** £B   Vieilles Vignes £B
FRANCINE ET OLIVIER SAVARY ○ **Chablis** Vieilles Vignes £B
DOM. SERVIN ○ **Chablis Premier Cru** Montée de Tonnerre £C   Vaillons £C
PHILIPPE TESTUT ○ **Chablis Premier Cru** Montée de Tonnerre £D   ○ **Chablis** £B
GÉRARD TREMBLAY ○ **Chablis Grand Cru** Vaudésir £E   ○ **Chablis Premier Cru** Côte de Léchet £C
○ **Chablis Premier Cru** Fourchaume £C
DOM. LAURENT TRIBUT ○ **Chablis Premier Cru** Beauroy £C   Côte de Léchet £C   ○ **Chablis** £B

Author's Choice for Chablis & Yonne (PW)

15 'true' Chablis

JEAN-CLAUDE BESSIN O Chablis
BILLAUD-SIMON O Chablis Premier Cru Vaillons
DOM. DE CHANTEMERLE O Chablis Premier Cru L'Homme Mort
DANIEL DAMPT O Chablis Premier Cru Côte de Léchet
RENÉ ET VINCENT DAUVISSAT O Chablis
JEAN-PAUL DROIN O Chablis Premier Cru Montée de Tonnerre
JOSEPH DROUHIN O Chablis Grand Cru Les Clos
WILLIAM FEVRE O Chablis Grand Cru Valmur
JEAN-PIERRE GROSSOT O Chablis Premier Cru Mont de Milieu
DOM. LAROCHE O Chablis Grand Cru Blanchots Réserve de l'Obédience
DOM. DES MALANDES O Chablis Premier Cru Fourchaume
DOM. LOUIS MICHEL O Chablis
GILBERT PICQ ET SES FILS O Chablis Vieilles Vignes
DOM. LOUIS PINSON O Chablis Premier Cru Mont de Milieu
DOM. FRANÇOIS RAVENEAU O Chablis Grand Cru Blanchots

Côte d'Or & Côte Chalonnaise

BERTRAND AMBROISE Nuits-Saint-Georges www.ambroise.com A: Bal, BBR, CTy, Win

Owner: Bertrand Ambroise Rue de l'Église, Prémeaux-Prissey, 21700 Nuits-Saint-Georges

Ambroise's red Burgundies are at one extreme of the Burgundian spectrum of wine styles. Their colour and strength are virtually unmatched in the Côte d'Or. The biggest reds are bold, oaky and tannic when young but the depth and concentration ensure that both something of the wine's origin and a certain finesse come with age. Of some 20 ha of vineyards spread over several communes in the centre of the Côte d'Or, around a quarter is for whites, with some notable Saint-Aubin and Corton-Charlemagne. Whites are rich and not excessively oaky and show a structure and depth worthy of their appellations, often with a real succulence that encourages early drinking. If not to everyone's taste, the wines are consistent and well-priced. Lesser reds (Bourgogne Rouge and Bourgogne Rouge Vieilles Vignes) and whites (Bourgogne Chardonnay and Hautes-Côtes de Nuits) can seem a little coarse but don't lack for fruit or flavour. (PW)

● **Corton Le Rognet**★★★ £F ● **Clos de Vougeot**★★★ £F
● **Nuits-Saint-Georges**★★ £D Vieilles Vignes★★★ £D 1er Cru Rue de Chaux★★★ £E
● **Nuits-Saint-Georges** 1er Cru Clos des Argillières★★★ £E 1er Cru Les Vaucrains★★★ £E
● **Côte de Nuits-Villages**★ £C ● **Vougeot** 1er Cru Les Cras★★ £D
O **Chassagne-Montrachet** 1er Cru Maltroie★★★ £E O **Corton-Charlemagne**★★★ £F
O **Saint-Romain**★ £C O **Saint-Aubin** 1er Cru Murgers Dents de Chien★★ £C

DOM. GUY AMIOT ET FILS Chassagne-Montrachet A: Bal, Bib, HHB, HRp, L&S

Owner: Guy & Thierry Amiot 13 Rue de Grand-Puits, 21190 Chassagne-Montrachet

Guy Amiot and his son Thierry make a string of white Chassagne-Montrachet *crus*, which have shown increasing refinement and complexity in the most recent vintages. The wines are now bottled later than previously but perhaps more importantly Thierry has made changes in the vineyard resulting in richer, riper fruit from vines with an increasingly high average age (especially Vergers and Caillerets). At least as interesting if not at the same quality level are the red wines, which have very good richness for southern Côte de Beaune reds, with added length and style in the Clos Saint-Jean bottling. All the better reds deserve at least three or four years' age. Only a very little Puligny-Montrachet Premier Cru Les Demoiselles and Montrachet are made. Lesser whites can be drunk young but the best need at least three or four years' ageing. (PW)

O **Chassagne-Montrachet** 1er Cru Les Caillerets★★★★ £E   1er Cru Les Vergers★★★ £E
O **Chassagne-Montrachet**★★ £D   1er Cru Les Baudines★★★ £E   1er Cru Les Macharelles★★★★ £E
O **Chassagne-Montrachet** 1er Cru Clos Saint-Jean★★★ £E   1er Cru Champgains★★★ £E
O **Puligny-Montrachet** 1er Cru Les Demoiselles★★★★★ £E   O **Saint-Aubin** 1er Cru En Remilly★★★ £E
● **Chassagne-Montrachet** 1er Cru Clos Saint-Jean★★★ £E   1er Cru La Maltroie★★ £E
● **Chassagne-Montrachet**★ £C   Les Chaumes★★ £C   ● **Santenay** La Comme Dessus★ £C

AMIOT-SERVELLE   Chambolle-Musigny   www.amiot-servelle.com   A: Dec, CTy

Owner: Christian & Elizabeth Amiot   21220 Chambolle-Musigny
Christian and Elizabeth Amiot farm almost 7 ha of vines. The wines are sturdy, and can at times be a little too structured to let the fruit sing through. However, when it does, the wines are rich and plump as in 1995, 96 and 97. The 98s and 99s are firmer, more robust and in their youth seem rather hard, extracted and lacking in generosity. Nevertheless these are fine, often from old vines and will always offer more with a few years' bottle-age. As well as a concentrated Chambolle-Musigny Amoureuses, the little known *premier cru* Derrière la Grange (which lies below Les Fuées) can show lots of style and there's some well-sited Clos de Vougeot. Bourgogne Rouge and a little Aligoté and Chardonnay are also made. (PW)

● **Clos de Vougeot**★★★ £E
● **Chambolle-Musigny**★ £D   1er Cru Derrière la Grange★★ £E   1er Cru Les Charmes★★ £E
● **Chambolle-Musigny** 1er Cru Les Amoureuses★★★ £F

MARQUIS D'ANGERVILLE   Volnay   A: C&B, CTy, JAr, OWL

Owner: D'Angerville family   Volnay, 21190 Meursault
The greatly respected Jacques d'Angerville died in July 2003 but the legacy of his estate and wines seems certain to continue. These marvellous expressions of Volnay are taut and structured when tasted very young but are classy and refined with concentrated, intense fruit underneath. Production from 13 ha is dominated by four *premiers crus*, including the prize 2.4 ha *monopole* Clos des Ducs. Low yields, with rigorous selection and full destemming are part of the formula and the red-fruits inten-sity is always well integrated with subdued oak. The wines have been on very good form since the late 1980s. Through a string of very different vintages in the late 90s the wines are wonderfully consistent but in every vintage deserve to be drunk with at least five or six years' age. All *crus* show the elegance and refinement of Volnay. Of the four most important *crus*, the elegant, stylish Frémiets is complemented by a medium-full, fragrant yet quite powerful Champans. Taillepieds combines great refinement and fullness while Clos des Ducs reveals a marvellous structure and superb length and class. Meursault Santenots is also made. (PW)

● **Volnay** 1er Cru Clos des Ducs★★★★ £F   1er Cru Champans★★★★ £E   1er Cru Taillepieds★★★★ £E
● **Volnay** 1er Cru Caillerets★★★ £E   1er Cru Frémiets★★★ £E

DOM. DE L'ARLOT   Nuits-Saint-Georges   A: ABy, JAr, L&W, HRp, WSc

Owner: Jean-Pierre de Smet   RN74 Prémeaux-Prissey, 21700 Nuits-Saint-Georges
This worthy estate, created in 1987 after the purchase of an existing domain by French insurance giant AXA Millésimes, has now had 15 years of steady direction under Jean-Pierre de Smet. Some 14 ha includes 2 ha of white grapes and two substantial Nuits-Saint-Georges *monopoles*, the 7-ha Clos

des Fôrets-Saint-Georges and 3-ha Clos de l'Arlot. Great care is taken in the vineyards and there is minimal interference in the vinification and only a moderate use of new oak. The whites are more consistent than the reds as they do not tend to show the leanness encountered in lighter vintages for reds. Due at least partly to a policy of not destemming, there can be a lack of both flesh and depth to the reds and at times a stemmy quality (as some of the stalks included must still retain a green aspect, despite careful selection). However, in the ripest vintages this is rarely a problem and elegance and class shine through. The wines will always put on weight with age too, losing any sturdiness of youth to become very refined and harmonious. Recent vintages have been better, though even the best 1997s and 2000s do not compare with the superior 98s and 99s. A regular Nuits-Saint-Georges made from young vines in the Clos des Fôrets has been redesignated *premier cru* from 2000. (PW)

- ● **Romanée-Saint-Vivant★★★★** £G ● **Vosne-Romanée** 1er Cru Les Suchots★★★ £E
- ● **Nuits-Saint-Georges★★** £D 1er Cru Clos de l'Arlot★★ £E
- ● **Nuits-Saint-Georges** 1er Cru Clos des Fôrets-Saint-Georges★★★ £E
- ● **Côtes de Nuits-Villages** Clos du Chapeau★ £C
- O **Nuits-Saint-Georges★★** £E 1er Cru Clos de l'Arlot★★★ £F

COMTE ARMAND   Pommard   www.domaine-des-epeneaux.com   A: HRp, L&S, L&W,M&V

Owner: Comte Armand   Place de l'Église, 21630 Pommard

The Comte Armand's Domaine des Epeneaux for long produced just one wine, the famous Pommard Clos des Epeneaux from a 5-ha vineyard that forms part of the *premier cru* Les Grands Epenots. Since 1995 red and white Auxey-Duresses have been added, as has a very good Volnay Frémiets. Yields are low and the reds are notable for their colour, structure and depth. In 1999 Benjamin Leroux took over making the wines from Pascal Marchand, who had firmly established a quality regime here from the mid-1980s. Pascal's minimal use of chemicals has been taken a stage further with biodynamic practices now in place. The Clos continues to be made from three separately vinified parcels of vines differentiated by their age. The wine is always full-bodied and powerful but balanced and complex. Village Pommard is produced from some of the younger-vine fruit not used in the Clos. A little Meursault, Meix-Chavaux has also been produced. (PW)

- ● **Pommard★★★** £D 1er Cru Clos des Epeneaux★★★★ £E
- ● **Volnay** Frémiets★★★ £E ● **Auxey Duresses** 1er Cru★★ £C O **Auxey-Duresses★** £C

DOM. ROBERT ARNOUX   Vosne-Romanée   A: A&B, BWC, Eno, CTy, HRp, Res, JAr

Owner: Arnoux family   RN3 21700 Vosne-Romanée

Pascal Lachaux is the son-in-law of the late Robert Arnoux and he has been making better and better wines here over the past decade. The top wines, of which there are several, receive 100 per cent new oak treatment but rarely is this obvious. The wines are sturdy, structured with at times almost overwhelming intensity and power. In vintages like 1996 and 99 the Suchots and the *grands crus* are outstanding but they are very good in other recent vintages too. (PW)

- ● **Romanée-Saint-Vivant⊙⊙⊙⊙⊙** £H ● **Clos de Vougeot★★★★** £F ● **Echezeaux★★★★** £F
- ● **Vosne-Romanée★★★** £D Les Hautes-Maizières★★★ £E 1er Cru Les Chaumes★★★ £E
- ● **Vosne-Romanée** 1er Cru Aux Reignots★★★★ £F 1er Cru Les Suchots★★★★ £F
- ● **Nuits-Saint-Georges★★★** £D Les Poisets★★★ £E 1er Cru Les Procès★★★ £E
- ● **Nuits-Saint-Georges** 1er Cru Les Corvées Pagets★★★ £E

DOM. D'AUVENAY   Saint-Romain   A: Far, J&B, HRp

Owner: Lalou Bize-Leroy   Domaine d'Auvenay, 21190 Meursault

This is the private estate of Madame Lalou Bize and is quite distinct from both the considerably larger

Domaine LEROY and the Leroy *négociant* business. Though there are just 3.9 ha (farmed biodynamically) there are several exquisite small *crus* which are made to the same exacting standards as Domaine Leroy. While reds dominate the production of Domaine Leroy, apart from a little *grand cru* Bonnes-Mares and Mazis-Chambertin, here it is white magic that prevails. The wines are rich, pure and concentrated – even at the level of Auxey-Duresses or Bourgogne Aligoté. Prices are astoundingly high and though the same general ratings apply, (five stars for the *grands crus*, four for the *premier crus* and three for the other wines) I'd find the individuality and grandeur of the Domaine Leroy reds a greater temptation if I had the money to spend. The wines to look out for are: Chevalier-Montrachet, Criots-Bâtard-Montrachet, Puligny-Montrachet (La Richarde, 1er Cru Folatières), Meursault (Narvaux, 1er Cru Goutte d'Or), Auxey-Duresses (Boutonniers, Les Clous) and some Bourgogne Aligoté. A straight village Meursault is sometimes bottled separately as Chaumes de Perrières and Pré de Manche. (PW)

DENIS BACHELET   Gevrey-Chambertin   A: HRp, M&V

Owner: Denis Bachelet   54 Route de Beaune, 21220 Gevrey-Chambertin
Denis Bachelet's wines are not that widely seen, such are the small quantities he produces, but they are wines of great finesse and class with lovely fruit intensity and harmony. In fact they might almost be considered atypical for an appellation that delivers up powerful, meaty, sometimes tannic, examples of Pinot. If the rich, intense *premier cru* Les Corbeaux and complex and classy *grand cru* Charmes-Chambertin are hard to find, the village Gevrey-Chambertin Vieilles Vignes is a super example at this level; all three are made from old vines. There's also reasonable quantities of a Côte de Nuits-Villages and a Bourgogne Rouge that make delicious red Burgundy seem almost affordable. (PW)
- **Charmes-Chambertin**★★★★ £F
- **Gevrey-Chambertin** Vieilles Vignes★★★ £D   1er Cru Les Corbeaux★★★ £E
- **Côte de Nuits-Villages**★★ £C   ● **Bourgogne Rouge**★★ £B

GHISLAINE BARTHOD   Chambolle-Musigny   A: BBR, Rae, RsW, Tan

Owner: Barthod-Noëllat family   Rue du Lavoir, 21220 Chambolle-Musigny
This small family domaine has just 6.5 ha of vineyards but all lie within this pretty commune that epitomises finesse in the Côte de Nuits. Seven small plots of *premiers crus* can all be measured in ares rather than hectares, such is their size. Ghislaine Barthod's wines have grace, finesse and succulence, there is nothing brash or harsh yet they have very good structure and personality. Beaux-Bruns, Cras and Charmes are probably the pick though the Véroilles (only the family's holding is of *premier cru* status) is also consistently fine. Cras is the most structured and profound, Charmes is concentrated and classy but there are no weak wines here, as even the village Chambolle-Musigny is always a good example and the Bourgogne Rouge is attractive, fruity and delicious. (PW)
- **Chambolle-Musigny** 1er Cru Les Chatelots★★★ £E   1er Cru Les Charmes★★★★ £E
- **Chambolle-Musigny** 1er Cru Les Cras★★★★ £E   1er Cru Les Véroilles★★★ £E
- **Chambolle-Musigny** 1er Cru Les Beaux Bruns★★★ £E   1er Cru Les Fuées★★★ £E
- **Chambolle-Musigny**★★ £D   1er Cru Les Baudes★★★ £E   ● **Bourgogne Rouge**★★ £B

ROGER BELLAND   Santenay   www.domaine-belland-roger.com   A: Lib, BBR

Owner: Roger Belland   3 Rue de la Chapelle, B P 13, 21590 Santenay
This is now an excellent source of top white Burgundy. Roger Belland is based in Santenay but a little over 4 ha of a total of 23 ha of vineyards include fine Chassagne-Montrachet (Morgeot Clos Pitois, a *monopole*), some Puligny and even some of the tiny Criots-Bâtard-Montrachet *grand cru*. In common

with many of the great domaines, Belland is a dedicated viticulturalist and goes to great lengths in the vineyard to maximise the quality of the fruit. Whites see new oak – 100 per cent for the *grand cru* Criots – but the intensity and depth of the fruit are only enhanced by it. Red Santenay includes the leading *premiers crus* at the northern end of this sizeable appellation; these are very good examples, full of ripe berry fruits but with good structure and length too. (PW)

O **Criots-Bâtard-Montrachet**★★★★ £H   O **Chassagne-Montrachet** 1er Cru Morgeot Clos Pitois★★★ £E
O **Puligny-Montrachet** 1er Cru Les Champs Gains★★★ £F
● **Chassagne-Montrachet** 1er Cru Morgeot Clos Pitois★★ £D
● **Santenay** Charmes★ £C   1er Cru Commes★★ £C   1er Cru Beauregard★★ £C   1er Cru Gravières★★ £C
● **Pommard** Les Cras★★ £E   ● **Volnay** 1er Cru Santenots★★ £E

DOM. SIMON BIZE ET FILS Savigny-lès-Beaune   A: HRp, JAr, L&W, OWL

Owner: Patrick Bize   12 Rue du Chanoine-Donin, 21420 Savigny-lès-Beaune
This serious and expanding operation, now with 22 ha, is one of the leading exponents of Savigny-lès-Beaune. The wines have greatly improved since 1999 after some rather flat and slightly over-extracted wines in the mid- to late 1990s contrasted starkly with the refinement and class of the likes of Jean-Marc PAVELOT. Long *cuvaison* times and only partial destemming contribute to a bold, sturdy and sometimes gamy style. Yet despite a tendency to rusticity at the bottom of the range, the best wines show increasing refinement and composure with bottle-age and there is enough fruit and structure for them to improve well beyond five years. Best are the *premiers crus*, with good weight and richness in the Marconnets (an extension of Beaune Marconnets) and the most elegance and refinement in Les Vergelesses. Whites are very good, with plenty of fruit and good structure in both versions of Savigny and additional style in Corton-Charlemagne. Basic Bourgogne Rouge and Blanc are made from Les Champlins and Les Perrières vineyards. A little Latricières-Chambertin is also made. (PW)

● **Savigny-lès-Beaune** 1er Cru Aux Vergelesses★★ £D   1er Cru Marconnets★★ £D
● **Savigny-lès-Beaune** 1er Cru Aux Serpentières★★ £D   1er Cru Aux Guettes★★ £D
● **Savigny-lès-Beaune** 1er Cru Aux Fourneaux★ £D   Aux Grands Liards★ £C   Les Bourgeots★ £C
● **Aloxe-Corton** Le Suchot★ £D
O **Corton-Charlemagne**★★★ £F   O **Savigny-lès-Beaune**★ £C   Aux Vergelesses★★ £D

BLAIN-GAGNARD Chassagne-Montrachet   A: JAr, HHC, Maj

Owner: Jean-Marc et Claudine Blain-Gagnard   15 Route de Santenay, 21190 Chassagne-Montrachet
Jean-Marc and his wife Claudine (whose father is Jacques Gagnard) have a small selection of precious sites, thanks largely to her family. The wines are handled carefully with restrained oak and not over-worked, resulting in wines of good richness and structure that remain true to their origins. A ripe, minerally and well-structured regular Chassagne develops nicely with three to four years' age. The *premiers crus* add more depth and richness and, although they can be drunk fairly young, deserve four or five years' age. Considerably more expensive but a big step up in quality is a Bâtard-Montrachet made in reasonable quantities. This has the characteristic Bâtard power and terrific dimension on the palate, becoming marvellously complex with even a little age. A little Criots-Bâtard-Montrachet is also made and a tiny amount of Le Montrachet (from Jacques Gagnard) has also recently been added. Basic Chassagne red is reasonably elegant if sometimes lean, while Clos Saint-Jean adds a little more depth. Both, as with all the whites, are reasonably priced. Gagnard-Delagrange is Jacques Gagnard's label, which includes three-star La Boudriotte and Morgeots and outstanding, super-five Bâtard-Montrachet and Montrachet. Though the vineyards have been gradually relinquished to the next generation some of the wines have continued to be made in recent vintages. (PW)

O **Bâtard-Montrachet**★★★★ £F
O **Chassagne-Montrachet**★★ £D   1er Cru Clos Saint-Jean★★★ £E   1er Cru La Boudriotte★★★ £E

○ **Chassagne-Montrachet** I er Cru Caillerets★★★ £E   I er Cru Morgeots★★★ £E
● **Chassagne-Montrachet** I er Cru Clos Saint-Jean★ £C   ● **Volnay** I er Cru Champans★ £D

DOM. JEAN BOILLOT ET FILS   Volnay   A: Eno, CCC, CTy, L&S

Owner: Jean Boillot   Rue des Angles, 21190 Volnay
Henri Boillot, brother of Jean-Marc BOILLOT, is now making the wines on his father's domaine as
well as running an expanding *négociant* business, Maison Henri Boillot. Though the domaine is based
in Volnay, there's a decent parcel of Puligny vines, including a substantial wholly owned *lieu-dit* within
Perrières, Clos de la Mouchère, as well as one or two other choice *crus*. The fruit is picked very late,
the reds 100 per cent destemmed and both reds and whites see a lot of new oak. The wines are rich,
even opulent and consequently can be drunk quite young, though the Volnays, particularly the
excellent Caillerets, deserve at least four or five years' aging. The pick of the whites, Les Pucelles,
which reflects the class and finesse of that wonderful site, also demands a little patience. The
négociant Henri Boillot wines includes some top-notch *crus*, and can be very good indeed if slightly
less consistent. (PW)

Domaine Jean Boillot:
● **Volnay** I er Cru Frémiets★★★ £E   I er Cru Chevrets★★★ £E   I er Cru Caillerets★★★★ £F
● **Beaune** I er Cru Clos du Roi★★★ £E   I er Cru Epenottes★★★ £E
● **Savigny-lès-Beaune** I er Cru Les Lavières★★ £D
○ **Puligny-Montrachet**★★★ £E   I er Cru Les Perrières★★★★ £E   I er Cru Clos de la Mouchère★★★★ £E
○ **Puligny-Montrachet** I er Cru Les Pucelles★★★★ £F
○ **Meursault** I er Cru Les Genevrières★★★★ £F   ○ **Savigny-lès-Beaune** I er Cru Les Vergelesses★★★ £D

JEAN-MARC BOILLOT   Pommard   A: BBR, DDr, L&S, Rae, RsW

Owner: Jean-Marc Boillot   La Pommardière, 21630 Pommard
Jean-Marc Boillot seems equally at ease making both red or white, as indeed he needs to be with half
of his 10 ha planted to Chardonnay. The wines have a fruit richness and depth to marry with the oak
input. The reds range from a full Beaune to more structured Pommards, including a tiny amount of
superb rich Rugiens, and a Volnay-like Jarolières (contiguous with Volnay Frémiets) to stylish,
perfumed Volnays. Even the village examples are very good. The whites if anything are even better. A
string of Puligny *premiers crus* (the SAUZET inheritance) all have an intense pure fruit and great class,
nowhere better expressed than in Les Combettes. Some Rully and Puligny-Montrachet Les Pucelles
have recently been made from bought-in fruit. Jean-Marc Boillot is now also making wine in the
Coteaux du Languedoc (see Languedoc-Roussillon). (PW)

● **Pommard**★★★ £D   I er Cru Jarolières★★★ £E   I er Cru Rugiens★★★★ £F
● **Volnay**★★★ £E   I er Cru Carelle-sous-Chapelle★★★ £E   I er Cru Pitures★★★ £E
● **Volnay** I er Cru Le Ronceret★★★ £E   ● **Beaune** I er Cru Montrevenots★★ £D
○ **Puligny-Montrachet** I er Cru Champ Canet★★★★ £F   I er Cru Les Combettes★★★★ £F
○ **Puligny-Montrachet** I er Cru Les Referts★★★★ £F   I er Cru La Truffière★★★ £F
○ **Puligny-Montrachet**★★★ £E   I er Cru La Garenne★★★ £F

LUCIEN BOILLOT ET FILS   Gevrey-Chambertin   A: BBR, CTy, Eno, WSc

Owner: Lucien, Louis & Pierre Boillot   1 Rue Docteur Magnon Pujo, 21220 Gevrey-Chambertin
Though Gevrey-based, this domaine draws half of its grapes from original family vineyards in Volnay
and Pommard. Lucien's sons Louis and Pierre haven't quite the sites or wines of other Boillot
domaines (see Jean BOILLOT and Jean-Marc BOILLOT) but nonetheless have a diverse and interesting
resource with which to work. The grapes are only partially destemmed and an extended maceration

is favoured, resulting in wines with structure, breadth and flavour intensity, though not always with the concentration or fullness to match. A lack of ripeness and finesse in the tannins can also detract. Though reasonably priced, the wines can be disappointing, missing the fruit depth and richness in lighter years and some of the vintages of the late 1990s. (PW)

● **Gevrey-Chambertin** Evocelles★★ £D 1er Cru Les Cherbaudes★★ £D 1er Cru Les Corbeaux★★★ £E
● **Nuits-Saint-Georges** 1er Cru Les Pruliers★★★ £D ● **Beaune** Epenottes★ £C
● **Pommard**★ £C 1er Cru Les Croix Noires★★ £D 1er Cru Fremiers★★★ £D
● **Volnay**★ £C 1er Cru Angles★★ £D 1er Cru Brouillards★★ £D 1er Cru Caillerets★★ £D

DOM. BONNEAU DU MARTRAY Corton-Charlemagne A: HHC, L&W, HRp, L&S, JAr

Owner: Jean-Charles Le Bault de la Morinière 21420 Pernand-Vergelesses
An outstanding 11-ha domaine producing just two wines. The white Corton-Charlemagne comes from 9.5 ha of the best-sited part of the famous vineyard. The red comes from 1.5 ha at the base of the Corton hill. As good as the wines are now, the reputation of this domaine has only been fully re-established by Jean-Charles Le Bault de la Morinière, who has made tremendous progress since taking over from his father. The red, in particular, has improved; since 1995 a previously rather dilute, insubstantial wine has taken on greater flesh and extract without sacrificing its finesse. The white has long been a wine of tremendous richness and great depth and character that will keep for many years from the best vintages. It is also one of the few wines made from this large vineyard to show true *grand cru* class. (PW)

O **Corton-Charlemagne** ✪✪✪✪✪ £F ● **Corton**★★★★ £F

BOUCHARD PÈRE ET FILS Beaune www.bouchard-pereetfils.com A: JEF, F&R

Owner: Joseph Henriot 15 Rue du Château, 21200 Beaune
This merchant is one of the best-known names in Burgundy, thanks in part to its substantial holdings. Domaine vineyards total 130 ha, including 12 ha of *grands crus* and 74 ha of *premiers crus* and two-thirds of the vineyards are planted to Pinot Noir. Its decline under family ownership and the scandal of its conviction for flouting legal winemaking practices have been well-documented. Yet from the time of the purchase by the much respected Champenois Joseph Henriot (see HENRIOT) in 1995, quality has dramatically improved. Despite the poor health of the vineyards, almost immediately the reds showed greater richness and better structure and more recently have added more expression and individuality. The ongoing investment in both people and winemaking facilities is backed by a determination to maximise quality and consistency. In more difficult vintages, such as 2000 for red, Bouchard was prepared to sell off a large quantity of wine in order to maintain the progress made in re-establishing the integrity of its label. The best whites show superb fruit combined with excellent structure and concentration and are particularly fine in 2000. As with other leading *négociants* the range is quite vast. While we have included only the best of the 'domaine' bottlings below, there are many other worthy wines. Chambertin Clos-de-Bèze and Latricières-Chambertin are two very fine examples produced from bought-in grapes. Others include good Puligny-Montrachet (Chalumeaux, Champs Gain and others), Santenay (such as Grand Clos Rousseau) and several Chablis. (PW)

All Domaine Wines:
● **La Romanée**✪✪✪✪✪ £H ● **Chambertin**★★★★ £H ● **Bonnes Mares**★★★★ £G
● **Clos de Vougeot**★★★ £G ● **Echezeaux**★★★ £G ● **Chambolle-Musigny**★★★ £E
● **Gevrey-Chambertin** 1er Cru Les Cazetiers★★★ £F ● **Vosne-Romanée** 1er Cru Aux Reignots★★★ £G
● **Nuits Saint-Georges** 1er Cru Clos des Argillières★★ £E 1er Cru Les Cailles★★★ £E
● **Nuits Saint-Georges** 1er Cru Clos Saint-Marc★★ £E
● **Beaune** 1er Cru★★ £D 1er Cru Clos de la Mousse★★ £E
● **Beaune** 1er Cru Grèves Vigne de L'Enfant Jésus★★★ £E

● **Volnay** ler Cru★★ £D   ler Cru Caillerets★★★ £E   ler Cru Clos des Chênes★★★ £E
● **Volnay** ler Cru Fremiets Clos de la Rougeotte★★★ £E   ler Cru Taillepieds★★★ £E
● **Pommard** ler Cru★★ £D   ler Cru Les Chanlins★★★ £E   ler Cru Pezerolles★★★ £E
● **Pommard** ler Cru Rugiens★★★ £E   ● **Savigny-lès-Beaune**★ £C   ler Cru Les Lavières★★ £C
● **Monthelie**★ £C   ler Cru Les Duresses★★ £D   ler Cru Clos des Champs Fuillot★★★ £D
O **Le Montrachet**✪✪✪✪✪ £H   O **Bâtard-Montrachet** ★★★★ £H
O **Corton-Charlemagne**★★★★ £F   O **Chevalier-Montrachet** ★★★★   £H
O **Meursault** ler Cru Genevrières★★★★ £F   ler Cru Perrières★★★★ £F   ler Cru Le Poruzot★★★ £E
O **Meursault**★★ £E   ler Cru Charmes★★★ £E   ler Cru Les Gouttes d'Or★★★ £E
O **Beaune** ler Cru★ £C   ler Cru Clos Saint-Landry★ £C   ler Cru Sur Les Grèves★★ £C

MICHEL BOUZEREAU ET FILS   Meursault   A: BBR, CTy, M&V

Owner: Michel & Jean-Baptiste Bouzereau 3 Rue de la Planche-Meunière, 21190 Meursault
Devotees of white Burgundy will recognise a Michel Bouzereau label as a good bet for ripe, full yet elegant Meursault and as Michel's son Jean-Baptiste assumes responsibility it seems certain to remain that way. The domaine comprises 12 ha, more than three-quarters of it white. Stylish and pure, the whites show good definition with subtle differences between the various *crus*. Meursault Blagny is the most austere and minerally, Genevrières has lovely depth and real class yet there is plenty of style and fruit in the humbler village-level Limouzin and Les Tessons too. A super Caillerets is much the better of the two Pulignys but this is reflected in the price difference. There's only a little red and if it's not at the same level as the whites it is at least reasonably priced for the quality. Good value, too, are the basic Bourgogne Aligoté and Bourgogne Chardonnay. (PW)
O **Meursault** ler Cru Blagny★★★ £E   ler Cru Charmes★★★ £E   ler Cru Genevrières★★★★ £E
O **Meursault** Grands Charrons★★ £D   Limouzin★★ £D   Les Tessons★★★ £D
O **Puligny-Montrachet** ler Cru Champ Gain★★★ £E   ler Cru Cailllerets★★★★ £F
O **Bourgogne Aligoté**★ £B, Chardonnay★ £B
● **Beaune** Epenottes★ £C   ler Cru Vignes Franches★★ £D

BOYER-MARTENOT   Meursault   A: BBR, CTy, For

Owner: Yves Boyer 17 Place de l'Europe, 21190 Meursault
Yves Boyer makes classic rich, plump and full-flavoured Meursault, traditional in the best sense but with plenty of oak in the top *cuvées*. A high average vine age continues to be maintained as is apparent in wines with plenty of personality and depth but that are also well-balanced with good definition. Perrières is arguably the best Meursault, with a little extra breadth and complexity characteristic of the vineyard, but the top wine is the more intense, refined and classy Puligny-Montrachet Le Cailleret. All the better *crus* will keep for six to eight years but can readily be drunk with just two or three. Good Bourgogne Chardonnay can show good fruit and flavour, too, if in a simpler fashion. (PW)
O **Meursault** ler Cru Charmes★★★ £F   ler Cru Genevrières★★★ £F   ler Cru Perrières★★★ £F
O **Meursault** En L'Ormeau★★ £D   Narvaux★★ £E   Tillets★★★ £E
O **Puligny-Montrachet** Le Cailleret★★★★ £F   O **Bourgogne** Chardonnay★ £B

DOM. BRINTET   Mercurey   www.domaine-brintet.com   A: OWL, Ear, Gel, GWW

Owner: Luc & Véronique Brintet Grande Rue, 71640 Mercurey
Luc Brintet's 13 ha are mostly red as would be expected in Mercurey but he makes a little white that is every bit as good. Reds are rigorously sorted and totally destemmed and a long *cuvaison* is sought with an extended period of pre-fermentation maceration. Both reds and whites are oakier than some but have ripe succulent fruit underneath and good structure and definition. The *premiers crus* are a

definite notch up in quality and are among the best in the appellation. Whites are better with two or three years' age, reds with three to five. (PW)

● **Mercurey** 1er Cru Crêts★★ £C   1er Cru Vasées★★ £C   1er Cru Levrières★★★ £C
● **Mercurey**★ £B   Charmée★ £B   Perrières★ £B   Vieilles Vignes★★ £C
O **Mercurey**★ £B   Vieilles Vignes★★ £C   1er Cru Crêts★★★ £C

ALAIN BURGUET   Gevrey-Chambertin   A: HRp

Owner: Alain Burguet   18 Rue de l'Église, 21220 Gevrey-Chambertin
Already experienced, Alain Burguet first got a foothold of his own in Gevrey back in 1974 and has now progressed to 6 ha. His reputation is for being tough and intransigent both in personality and in his approach to winemaking. Yet there is clearly a mellowing of sorts as he has modified and refined his vinification and ageing methods in the 1990s, including complete destemming and longer oak ageing. It has taken a couple of vintages to perfect but since 1998 the wines have been more stylish and complete though still with good richness and power. If most of the wines are only village level (there is now a little *premier cru* Champeaux), a Vieilles Vignes bottling (now labelled Mes Favorites), of great depth and richness, is consistently of comparable quality to some of the best Gevrey made. All the wines show good classic Gevrey spice, strength and red and black fruit intensity. Older vintages can be slightly tougher, more rustic but can mellow and soften with age, too and are unlikely to disappoint from a good vintage. (PW)

● **Gevrey-Chambertin** Vieilles Vignes Mes Favorites★★★★ £E   1er Cru Champeaux★★★ £E
● **Gevrey-Chambertin** Tradition★★ £D   Billard★★★ £D   Reniard★★★ £D   ● **Bourgogne Rouge**★ £B

LOUIS CARILLON ET FILS   Puligny-Montrachet   A: BBR, CTy, Fie, L&W, JNi

Owner: Carillon family   21190 Puligny-Montrachet
The wines of Louis Carillon et Fils are widely distributed and with good reason. This is a star Puligny domaine that has been making excellent wines for decades, with a lineage that goes back several centuries. The whites have great vibrancy, expressive fruit and in a way are more direct and easier to appreciate than others of comparable quality – but are not lesser wines for that. Out of a total of 12 ha, 3.5 ha are planted to Pinot Noir but the fuss is rightly about the Puligny *premiers crus*. Central to the style are low yields and minimal manipulation during both vinification and ageing. Champ Canet is the most elegant and approachable when quite young; Combettes is seductive and more immediate than the bigger, more structured Perrières; the citrusy, minerally Referts fattens up with age and like Perrières will benefit from extra bottle age. The *grand cru* Bienvenues is the most complex and refined of all, and while deserving of the most patience, shows great power and intensity when young. To an extent the prices reflect the high regard in which the wines are held, though the sound reds are much more affordable. (PW)

O **Bienvenues-Bâtard-Montrachet**★★★★ £H
O **Puligny-Montrachet** 1er Cru Perrières★★★★ £F   1er Cru Referts★★★ £E
O **Puligny-Montrachet**★★★ £E   1er Cru Champ Canet★★★ £F   1er Cru Combettes★★★ £F
● **Puligny-Montrachet**★ £C   ● **Saint-Aubin** 1er Cru Pitangerets★ £C

SYLVAIN CATHIARD   Vosne-Romanée   A: OWL, Res, BBR, HHC

Owner: Sylvain Cathiard   20 Rue de la Goillotte, 21700 Vosne-Romanée
Sylvain Cathiard makes very refined, subtle but harmonious wines. In the past some of the lesser wines have been lean and struggling for full ripeness but the best Vosne wines have plenty of substance and are ripe with increasing intensity and length of flavour, culminating in an inspired

grand cru Romanée-Saint-Vivant. Of the Vosne *premiers crus*, En Orveau (nearest to Chambolle-Musigny) and the recently replanted Aux Reignots are lighter, though the latter can be expected to add more weight and substance from 2000 onwards. The purity of Suchots contrasts with the richer, more structured Malconsorts. A sophisticated Bourgogne Rouge and elegant Chambolle-Musigny apart, all the wines deserve to be kept for at least five or six years from the vintage date. (PW)

● **Romanée-Saint-Vivant**✪✪✪✪✪ £H
● **Vosne-Romanée** 1er Cru Aux Reignots★★★ £F   1er Cru Les Malconsorts★★★★ £F
● **Vosne-Romanée**★★★ £E   1er Cru En Orveau★★★ £F 1er Cru Les Suchots★★★★ £F
● **Chambolle-Musigny** Clos de L'Orme★★★ £E
● **Nuits-Saint-Georges** 1er Cru Aux Murgers★★★ £E   ● **Bourgogne Rouge**★★ £C

MAISON CHAMPY   Beaune   www.champy.com   A: HHC, Pol

Owner: Meurgey family   5 Rue Grenier à Sel, 21202 Beaune
This 280-year-old *négociant* house, the oldest in Burgundy, has been in the hands of the Meurgey family for a little over a decade, but how its fortunes have been revived. Quality has been good since the mid-1990s but the hiring of Dimitri Bazas is providing a further boost. As well as bought-in grapes, around 13 ha are now owned. The winemaking hand is light, allowing the individual *terroirs* to shine through. Among the many reds, Vosne-Romanée Les Suchots, from a well-established vineyard (35–40 years), always stands out with fine fruit, lots of class and great length; a Bonnes-Mares is more classy and complex again, as is the Romanée-Saint-Vivant. At a lower level, Beaune Champs Pimont is a consistently plump and approachable red full of raspberry fruit. The 2000 whites are the best yet and if not yet the equal of the top growers, are well-made and reasonably priced, particularly regular Savigny-lès-Beaune and Pernand-Vergelesses. Puligny Enseignères has nice richness for a village-level example, while Corton-Charlemagne adds more breadth; both can be drunk fairly young but will develop further with age. All in all this is a increasingly good, reliable source of Burgundy. Listed are most of the best wines that are regularly made. Other good examples may be encountered, though the basic generics are of more modest quality. (PW)

● **Bonnes Mares**★★★★ £G   ● **Romanée-Saint-Vivant**★★★★ £G   ● **Clos de Vougeot**★★★ £F
● **Vosne-Romanée** 1er Cru Les Beaumonts★★★ £F   1er Cru Les Suchots★★★★ £F
● **Gevrey-Chambertin** 1er Cru Les Cazetiers★★★ £E   ● **Nuits-Saint-Georges** 1er Cru Les Argilières★★ £E
● **Aloxe-Corton** 1er Cru Les Vercots★★ £D   ● **Volnay** 1er Cru Les Caillerets★★★ £E
● **Beaune** Vieilles Vignes★★ £D   1er Cru Les Champs Pimont★★ £D   1er Cru Les Grèves★★ £D
● **Savigny-lès-Beaune** Aux Fourches★ £C   1er Cru Les Peuillets★★ £C   1er Cru Les Vergelesses★★ £C
○ **Corton-Charlemagne**★★★ £F
○ **Puligny-Montrachet** Les Enseignères★★★ £E   1er Cru Les Chalumeaux★★★ £E
○ **Meursault** Grand Charrons★★★ £E   1er Cru Genevrières★★★ £E   ○ **Pernand-Vergelesses**★★ £C
○ **Savigny-lès-Beaune**★★ £C   ○ **Saint-Aubin** 1er Cru Murgers Dents de Chien★ £C

CHANDON DE BRIAILLES   Savigny-lès-Beaune   A: HHC, L&S, Tan

Owner: De Nicolay family   Rue Soeur Goby, 21420 Savigny-lès-Beaune
A popular and fine domaine and a leading proponent of Savigny-lès-Beaune, Pernand-Vergelesses and Corton. François de Nicolay and his sister Claude Drouhin work with their mother to produce wines from low yields that favour elegance over power. Corton Clos du Roi is the top red, the most structured and profound. Corton-Bressandes has better dimension, weight and length than Les Maréchaudes, though the latter almost matches it for finesse and style. The Pernand-Vergelesses are only medium-bodied, though the racy, slender but classy Île des Vergelesses adds a little more weight with age. Both Savigny wines can be good value, though Les Lavières has been a bit lean in recent vintages – as were the 2000 reds generally, if still with the characteristic intensity and style. This was also the first

vintage of a Volnay Caillerets. Whites are very good too, tight and minerally when very young but with real intensity and length, becoming quite rich with a little age. The Corton becomes fuller and broader than a deeper, more minerally Corton-Charlemagne. François de Nicolay also owns a vineyard in his own right, producing an aromatic, plump white Savigny. (PW)

● **Corton** Clos du Roi★★★★ £F   ● **Corton** Bressandes★★★★ £E   ● **Corton** Les Maréchaudes★★★ £E
● **Pernand-Vergelesses** 1er Cru Les Vergelesses★★ £D   1er Cru Île des Vergelesses★★★ £D
● **Savigny-lès-Beaune** 1er Cru Aux Fourneaux★ £C   1er Cru Les Lavières★ £D
○ **Corton-Charlemagne**★★★★ £F   ○ **Corton** Blanc★★★★ £F
○ **Pernand-Vergelesses** 1er Cru Île des Vergelesses★★★ £D
○ **Savigny-lès-Beaune** 1er Cru Aux Vergelesses★★ £C (François de Nicolay)

PHILIPPE CHARLOPIN   Gevrey-Chambertin   A: IVV

Owner: Philippe Charlopin   18 Route de Dijon, 21220 Gevrey-Chambertin
Starting from a meagre 1.8 ha of family vineyards in 1976, Philippe Charlopin's holdings have mushroomed to 15 ha in 2002. To the more humble village parcels have been added small segments of several *grands crus*. Harvesting often very late for Burgundy, Philippe subjects his very ripe grapes to a rigorous selection. Vinification involves a long maceration followed by minimal racking (sometimes leading to a measure of reduction in the wines) and quite liberal helpings of new oak; 100 per cent new oak in the case of the Vieilles Vignes Gevrey-Chambertin and the seven *grands crus*. They are also unfined and unfiltered. The result is richly textured, chewy, sometimes tannic wines, more to the so-called American taste than those from most of his neighbours. This beefy style does, however, work for the most part, and the wines still reflect the general style of their appellations. The regular village wines have plenty of immediate appeal and are for relatively early drinking. The top wines will keep for at least a decade should you decide to resist the power and hedonism of youth. Of the simpler reds, the Marsannay and Bourgogne Rouge can be good value while the whites, too, can offer ample fruit and character. The newest of the *grands crus*, Bonnes Mares, Clos de Vougeot and Echezeaux, have not been rated. (PW)

● **Chambertin**★★★★ £G   ● **Charmes-Chambertin**★★★★ £F   ● **Mazis-Chambertin**★★★★ £F
● **Clos Saint-Denis**★★★★ £F   ● **Morey-Saint-Denis**★★ £D
● **Gevrey-Chambertin** La Justice★★ £D   Vieilles Vignes★★★ £E
● **Chambolle-Musigny**★★ £D   Vosne-Romanée★★ £D   ● **Fixin** Clos de Fixey★ £C
● **Marsannay** En Montchenevoy★★ £C   ● **Bourgogne Rouge**★ £C
○ **Fixin** Blanc★★ £C   ○ **Marsannay** Blanc★ £C

GÉRARD CHAVY ET FILS   Puligny-Montrachet   A: BBR, CTy, Eno, HRp, M&V

Owner: Chavy family   12 Rue de Château, 21190 Puligny-Montrachet
Alain and Jean-Louis, sons of Gérard, have made many changes at their family's small domaine, with the result that this is now one of the emerging stars of the appellation. Typical of small, well-run family domaines, there are no short cuts taken and every wine is given the same measure of respect, so the humbler wines rarely disappoint. Bourgogne Chardonnay tastes like a mini-Puligny, the regular example of Puligny has some substance and style, and a good example of Saint-Aubin is made too. But it is the *premiers crus* that are forging the reputation, including a very minerally, full Perrières and an elegant Clavoillons that contrasts with the firmer, more structured Folatières. Given the excellent quality here, the prices are really smart too. (PW)

○ **Puligny-Montrachet** 1er Cru Perrières★★★★ £E
○ **Puligny-Montrachet**★★ £D   1er Cru Folatières★★★★ £E   Charmes★★ £D   1er Cru Clavoillons★★★ £E
○ **Bourgogne Blanc**★ £B

ROBERT CHEVILLON Nuits-Saint-Georges   A: F&R, J&B, Sec, WTs

Owner: Chevillon family   68 Rue Félix Tisserand, 21700 Nuits-Saint-Georges
Robert Chevillon is one of the celebrated names of this appellation at the southern end of the Côte de Nuits, a village that is synonymous with red Burgundy. Robert is making way for his sons and Bertrand Chevillon now makes the wines from the vines tended by his older brother, Denis. There are no less than eight different *premiers crus* (six of them in the central section of Nuits, which has a higher clay content and is south of the town itself), all with a high average vine age. No two taste quite the same, each giving a different expression of its individual *terroir*. With relatively high fermentation temperatures and a small percentage of stems retained, the wines are fairly full-bodied and tannic but with the flesh, depth and fruit intensity to be very rich and satisfying with eight to ten years' age. The regular Nuits, Bousselots and to a lesser extent Chaignots (the Chevillons' two *crus* north of Nuits) can be a bit light in lesser vintages but the others regularly deliver the fruit to match their robust structures. The fullest and most structured are the Les Saint-Georges and Vaucrains, followed by Les Cailles. Also made is a little white Nuits-Saint-Georges with a very good reputation and some Bourgogne Rouge. (PW)

- **Nuits-Saint-Georges** 1er Cru Les Vaucrains★★★★ £E   1er Cru Les Saint-Georges★★★★ £E
- **Nuits-Saint-Georges** 1er Cru Les Perrières★★★ £E   1er Cru Les Pruliers★★★ £E
- **Nuits-Saint-Georges** 1er Cru Les Roncières★★★ £E   1er Cru Les Chaignots★★★ £E
- **Nuits-Saint-Georges** 1er Cru Les Cailles★★★ £E
- **Nuits-Saint-Georges** Vieilles Vignes★★ £D   1er Cru Les Bousselots★★ £D

DOM. DU CH. DE CHOREY Chorey-lès-Beaune   www.chateau-de-chorey.com   A: DDr

Owner: Germain family   Château de Chorey-lès-Beaune, 21220 Beaune
The fine château of this domaine provides accomodation for those who have come in search of good red and white Burgundy. Formerly called Domaine Germain Père et Fils, the wines of the 17 ha estate have, over the last decade, increasingly been made by François Germain's son, Benoît, who now runs the estate with his sister, Aude. The wines are good rather than great, with full-flavoured, balanced white Pernand-Vergelesses and fairly full, sturdy yet not inelegant reds. The latter are completely destemmed and subject to a pre-fermentation maceration. Ratings apply to the best and most recent vintages. Occasionally in the past some of the reds have been a little too extracted and lacked fully ripe tannins, as is evident with the uneven 98s. As well as those listed, two other red *premiers crus* Beaunes (Boucherottes and Cent Vignes) and a little white (Sur les Grèves) are also made. A village Meursault, Les Pellans, has been made since 1999. (PW)

- **Beaune** 1er Cru Vignes Franches★★ £E   1er Cru Cras★★ £E   1er Cru Teurons★★ £E
- **Chorey-lès-Beaune★** £C   **O Pernand-Vergelesses★★** £C

BRUNO CLAIR Marsannay   A: J&B, Tan, WSc

Owner: Bruno Clair   5 Rue du Vieux Collège, BP 22, 21160 Marsannay-la-Côte
Bruno Clair has been a style leader for a couple of decades, producing the mostly northern Nuits reds of great balance, harmony and elegance. One of the beneficiaries of the noted Clair-Daü estate (many of the prime vineyards went to Louis JADOT), he now commands 23 ha, nearly 5 ha of which are planted to Chardonnay. The classics are his Gevrey *premiers crus* Clos Saint-Jacques and Cazetiers, and the *grand cru* Chambertin Clos de Bèze. These are wines with great purity, elegance and with exceptional length of flavour. Not to be overlooked are the *monopole* Clos du Fonteny, a gutsy, meaty Savigny, La Dominode, and an increasingly classy Corton-Charlemagne. The best value lies in the three Marsannay reds (though a white can be good too), with the

floral, intense Longeroies usually vying with the slightly darker-fruited Grasses Têtes as the best of these. While the reds have been generally less impressive in lighter vintages such as 1997, there are excellent 96s, 98s and 99s, and the 2000s look promising. All the reds can seem a little firm and austere when young and shouldn't be drunk with less than three or four years' age; seven or eight for the top examples. A rare Morey-Saint-Denis white is made from the same vineyard as the red, while a white Pernand-Vergelesses is a recent addition. (PW)

● **Chambertin Clos de Bèze**★★★★ £G
● **Gevrey-Chambertin** 1er Cru Clos Saint-Jacques★★★★ £G 1er Cru Les Cazetiers★★★★ £F
● **Gevrey-Chambertin** 1er Cru Petite Chapelle★★ £E 1er Cru Clos du Fonteny★★★ £F
● **Morey-Saint-Denis** En La Rue de Vergy★ £E ● **Chambolle-Musigny** Véroilles★ £D
● **Vosne-Romanée** Champs-Perdrix★★ £E ● **Savigny-lès-Beaune** 1er Cru La Dominode★★★ £E
● **Marsannay** Grasses Têtes★★ £C Longeroies★★ £C Vaudenelles★ £C
O **Corton-Charlemagne**★★★ £G O **Marsannay** Blanc★ £C

BRUNO CLAVELIER Vosne-Romanée   A: Dec, HRp, OWL, Res

Owner: Bruno Clavelier 6 Route Nationale 74, 21700 Vosne-Romanée
Bruno Clavelier is a relatively new star who took over his grandfather's vines in 1987 and started bottling wine previously sold in bulk. He has since expanded into other Côte de Nuits communes. The domaine is now fully biodynamic and there has been a steady refinement in the wines while adding greater richness and expression, particularly in the most recent vintages. The amount of new oak used is low and the average vine age very high (most are either 50 or 65 years old), giving wines with delicious fruit, ample concentration and a real sense *terroir*. Of the *premiers crus*, Vosne-Romanée Beaux-Monts has the greater structure, Aux Brulées a touch more refinement. The Nuits-Saint-Georges, lying close to Vosne-Romanée, tastes like a cross between the two appellations. The Chambolle-Musigny is even better, combining grace with richness. From 2000 the regular Vosne-Romanée, from some of the highest slopes in the commune, has been bottled as La Combe Brulée and Les Hauts de Beaux Monts. A third of an hectare of Corton Rognets was purchased in 1999 and is also from old vines and promises to be the best wine of the lot, while Bruno's old-vine Aligoté is just about as good as it gets. (PW)

● **Vosne-Romanée** Les Hauts Maizières★★★ £E 1er Cru Les Beaux Monts★★★★ £F Aux Brulées★★★★ £F
● **Vosne-Romanée** La Montagne★★★ £E ● **Gevrey-Chambertin** 1er Cru Les Corbeaux★★★ £E
● **Chambolle-Musigny** 1er Cru Combe d'Orveau★★★★ £F
● **Nuits-Saint-Georges** 1er Cru Aux Cras★★★ £E

CLOS DE TART Clos de Tart   A: Cas, F&R, HRp, Res, WSc

Owner: Mommessin family 21220 Morey-Saint-Denis
Winemaker Sylvain Pitiot has made this 7.53 ha *grand cru monopole* great again. Lying between Bonnes Mares and Clos des Lambrays, Clos de Tart has remained intact since being named by Benedictine monks in the late 12th century. The wine is increasingly adding some of the succulence of Clos des Lambrays to the power and sturdiness of Bonnes Mares. There is greater depth and concentration than previously, together with the complexity, class and elegance of a *grand cru*. Yields are low, the vine age high and being such a large site, different parcels are vinified separately. Spice, red and black cherries are the predominant flavours if drunk fairly young but wait 10 years from a top vintage. While there are many good earlier vintages, buy to cellar from 1996 or later. (PW)

● **Clos de Tart**✪✪✪✪✪ £G

JEAN-FRANÇOIS COCHE-DURY Meursault   A: BBR, Far, Res

Owner: Jean-François Coche-Dury 9 Rue Charles Giraud, 21190 Meursault

An outstanding domaine. Jean-François's Meursaults are rivalled only by those from LAFON and perhaps one or two others. Yet apart from from a little *grand cru* Corton-Charlemagne and *premier cru* Perrières, his reputation has been established with village-level wines, an indication of his talent and dedication. There is great attention to detail in the vineyard and as at many top-quality estates vines are replaced one at time when necessary and from the best existing plant material. The approach to vinification is flexible to maximise the potential of each vintage and long fermentations are also favoured. What makes the wines so special? Well, a grace, subtlety and purity allied to a remarkably well-delineated complexity. The depth, length, structure and concentration are givens. The floral, fruit and mineral components, as well as a fine grilled nuts character that comes with age, give the wines extra finesse over most other examples. Of 11 ha, almost 2.5 are planted to Pinot Noir and a chance to try the Volnay Premier Cru shouldn't be passed up. A little red Auxey-Duresses and Monthelie are also made. The Meursault Vireuils is now being bottled separately as Vireuils Dessous and Vireuils Dessus. Nearly all the whites deserve five years' age but will keep for 10 or more. Due to the demand, finding any of the wines at reasonable prices would be a minor miracle. (PW)

O **Corton-Charlemagne**✪✪✪✪✪ £H   O **Meursault** 1er Cru Perrières✪✪✪✪✪ £H Rougeots★★★★ £F
O **Meursault** Luchets★★★ £F Vireuils★★★ £F Narvaux★★★★ £F Caillerets★★★★ £G Chevalières★★★★ £F
O **Puligny-Montrachet** Les Enseignières★★★ £F
● **Volnay** 1er Cru★★★ £F   ● **Bourgogne Pinot Noir**★ £C
O **Bourgogne Aligoté**★ £C   ● **Bourgogne Chardonnay**★★ £D

DOM. MARC COLIN ET FILS Saint-Aubin   A: CCC, RsW, F&R

Owner: Colin family Gamay, 21190 Saint-Aubin

Marc Colin and his sons, Joseph, Pierre-Yves and Damien manage 20 ha and the domaine's reputation is built on its finest whites. These are rich, ripe wines with good complexity and a distinct and attractive minerality in the best examples. Several Chassagne-Montrachets, led by an intense, minerally Caillerets, are made to a high standard and there is a galaxy of really fine Saint-Aubin in both colours (more than a third of the estate is planted to Pinot Noir). A very minerally, stylish En Remilly vies with a slightly more structured La Chatenière as the best Saint-Aubin white. For red, the Santenay Vieilles Vignes shows what is possible from that appellation, particularly when from an excellent vintage such as 1999. New are further bottlings of Saint-Aubin whites (including a very promising *premier cru* Sentier du Clou) and Puligny-Montrachet. This still-expanding domaine also produces some *négociant* wines, including a Bâtard-Montrachet. (PW)

O **Montrachet**★★★★ £H   O **Chassagne-Montrachet** 1er Cru Caillerets★★★ £F
O **Chassagne-Montrachet**★★ £E   1er Cru Champ Gain★★★ £E   1er Cru Vide Bourse★★★ £E
O **Puligny-Montrachet** 1er Cru Garennes★★★ £E
O **Saint-Aubin** 1er Cru Les Cortons★★ £D 1er Cru La Chatenière★★★ £D 1er Cru En Remilly★★★ £D
O **Saint-Aubin** 1er Cru Les Charmois★★ £D 1er Cru Les Combes★★ £D 1er Cru En Montceau★★ £D
O **Saint-Aubin** Fontenotte★★ £C 1er Cru Pitangerets★★ £D
● **Chassagne-Montrachet**★★ £D   ● **Santenay** Vieilles Vignes★★★ £D
● **Saint-Aubin**★ £C 1er Cru★★ £C 1er Cru Frionnes★★ £D

MICHEL COLIN-DELÉGER ET FILS Chassagne-Montrachet A: BWC, BBR, MCW, HRp

Owner: Colin-Deléger family 3 Impasse des Crêts, 21190 Chassagne-Montrachet

As much of the wine here is red as white but, as so often with Chassagne producers, the attention they receive is based almost solely on the quality of the whites. The standard here is very high, with intense, concentrated but beautifully balanced wines produced from low-yielding vines. En Remilly heads a raft of fine Chassagne-Montrachet *premiers crus*. The reds used to be a little tough but are now richer with riper tannins, especially from a good red wine vintage. Santenay Gravières and Chassagne-Montrachet Morgeots both stand out; Michel Colin is unusual in producing a fine example of both red and white Morgeots. The best reds, like the whites, will benefit from five or six years' age, sometimes more. Of a range of very fine Puligny-Montrachet *premiers crus* made in small quantities, Les Demoiselles is tucked up against a tiny amount of *grand cru* Chevalier-Montrachet. Other attractive whites are made on a *négociant* basis. (PW)

O **Chassagne-Montrachet** 1er Cru Morgeots★★★ £F 1er Cru Vergers★★★★ £F 1er Cru En Remilly★★★★£F
O **Chassagne-Montrachet**★★★ £E 1er Cru Les Chaumées★★★ £F 1er Cru Chevenottes★★★ £F
O **Chassagne-Montrachet** 1er Cru La Maltroie★★★ £F
O **Puligny-Montrachet**★★★ £E 1er Cru Les Demoiselles★★★★ £G 1er Cru La Truffière★★★★ £G
O **Saint-Aubin** 1er Cru Les Charmois★★ £C
● **Chassagne-Montrachet**★ £C Vieilles Vignes★★ £C Morgeots★★★ £D ● **Santenay**★ £B
● **Santenay**★ £B 1er Cru Gravières★★ £C

DOM. JEAN-JACQUES CONFURON   Nuits-Saint-Georges   A: Bal, OWL, Eno

Owner: Alain & Sophie Meunier   Prémeaux-Prissey, 21700 Nuits-Saint-Georges
Alain Meunier and his wife make increasingly good wines from 7 ha of their own vineyards in the heart of the Côte de Nuits. By following organic principles, much has been done to restore the health of the vineyard and yields are low. A cold pre-fermentation maceration is employed, with moderately high temperatures, and a lot of new oak is used in ageing the wines. Quite dense and concentrated when young, the powerful fruit unfurls with five to ten years' age. The results can be a little uneven and the wines can suffer from a little reduction and sometimes excessive oakiness. But if patience is needed there's great intensity and length of flavour, particularly in the *premiers* and *grands crus*. Alain Meunier also oversees production for the part-domaine, part-*négociant* Domaine Féry/Féry-Meunier label. (PW)

● **Romanée-Saint-Vivant**★★★★ £G ● **Clos Vougeot**★★★★ £G
● **Vosne-Romanée** 1er Cru Beaux Monts★★★ £E ● **Chambolle-Musigny**★★ £D 1er Cru★★★ £E
● **Nuits-Saint-Georges** Fleurières★★ £D Chaboeufs★★★ £E 1er Cru Boudots★★★ £E
● **Côte de Nuits-Villages** Les Vignottes★★ £C

DOM. CONFURON-COTÉTIDOT   Vosne-Romanée   A: HHB, L&S, OWL

Owner: Jacky Confuron-Cotétidot   10 Rue de la Fontaine, 21700 Vosne-Romanée
The Confuron domaine was one of the original private estates in the Côtes de Nuits and Yves Confuron now maintains this fine 11-ha property, further building on his father's considerable achievements. Jacky Confuron's dedication and skill as a *vigneron* has produced healthy vines of a high average age with really low yields. A so-called traditional approach has long been adhered to in the winemaking. There is no destemming (requiring ripe stalks as well as fruit), a long pre-fermentation maceration and lengthy *cuvaison*, while the subsequent ageing utilises a relatively low percentage of new oak, though this has recently been increased. This usually results in intense, deep and, at times, tannic Burgundies but there is more refinement in the latest releases. Across a range of appellations with good *terroir*, the wines show varied character but almost always good colour, body and ripe fruit. While not every wine in every vintage always achieves its full potential, each does require attention on the part of the drinker. These are wines that require assessment and often, patience; wines to devote cellar space to so they can be revisited over a period of years. A tiny amount of Mazis-Chambertin and only a little Clos de Vougeot are also made. Yves also makes some excellent Pommard at the De COURCEL estate. (PW)

● **Charmes-Chambertin**★★★★ £F ● **Echezeaux**★★★★ £F ● **Vosne-Romanée**★★★ £E

- **Vosne-Romanée**★★★ £E 1er Cru Suchots★★★★ £F
- **Gevrey-Chambertin**★★★ £E 1er Cru Petite Chapelle★★★ £F 1er Cru Lavaux-Saint-Jacques★★★★ £F
- **Chambolle-Musigny**★★★ £E ● **Nuits-Saint-Georges**★★★ £E 1er Cru★★★ £F

DOM. DE COURCEL Pommard   A: HRp, OWL, L&S, Res, C&C

Owner: De Courcel family Place de l'Église, 21630 Pommard
As at his family's domaine, CONFURON-COTÉTIDOT, winemaker Yves Confuron favours whole-bunch fermentation after having harvested late for fully ripe grapes. Yields are low and the percentage of wine bottled by the domaine has gone from around half to the lion's share of what it grows. At the heart of the estate's 8 ha is 5 ha of Grand Epenots, supplemented by sometimes brilliant Rugiens and another classy *premier cru*, Fremiers. There were some fine wines made prior to Yves's arrival but the standard is even higher now. Recent vintages have been vigorous, sturdy, concentrated, more oaky than previously and capable of ageing for a decade; the Grand Clos des Epenots and the Rugiens need almost that long before they've even started to open up. The elegance and complexity of the Rugiens is only fully apparent with age. Consistently excellent Bourgogne Rouge deserves a couple of years' bottle-age, too. The wines make for an interesting comparison with those from Comte ARMAND and Jean-Marc BOILLOT. Another fine village Pommard, Vaumuriens, has been made since 1999. (PW)

- **Pommard** 1er Cru Rugiens★★★★ £F 1er Cru Grand Clos des Epenots★★★★ £F
- **Pommard** Croix Noires★★★ £E 1er Cru Fremiers★★★ £E ● **Bourgogne Rouge**★★ £C

DOM. PIERRE DAMOY www.domaine-pierre-damoy.com A: Las, L&W, OWL, Res, Dec, JNi

Owner: Damoy family 11 Rue du Maréchal de Lattre de Tassigny, 21220 Gevrey-Chambertin
Under the direction of the young Pierre Damoy (the current generation Damoy who shares the domaine's name), this important 11-ha estate only started to realise its potential in the 1990s. A remarkable 5.3 ha are in Chambertin Clos-de-Bèze but as well as a decent chunk (2.2 ha) of Chapelle-Chambertin there's some Chambertin and a solely-owned village *lieu-dit*, Clos Tamisot. The wines are harvested late and the yields are now low, considerably reduced from what they were prior to Pierre's stewardship. The wines are lush, powerful and concentrated, with good breadth and length, but are also oaky with a lot of tannin, particularly in a heavily structured and more austere Chambertin. There has been a lack of consistency, too, in recent years other than 1999, which worked more in favour of the style of wines here. Extra harmony and class is required before the top wines rival the best in their respective *grands crus* but a degree or two of fine-tuning will make this a sought-after name. Ripe, fruity Bourgogne Blanc and a lightish Bourgogne Rouge are also made. (PW)

- **Chambertin Clos-de-Bèze**★★★★ £G ● **Chambertin**★★★ £G ● **Chapelle-Chambertin**★★★ £G
- **Gevrey-Chambertin**★★ £E Clos Tamisot★★★ £E

DARVIOT-PERRIN Monthelie   A: A&B, JAr, Dec, L&W, May, HRp

Owner: Darviot-Perrin family Grande Rue, 21190 Monthelie
Didier Darviot's cellar is in the quiet pretty village of Monthelie but his 9.5 ha estate includes Volnay, Meursault and Chassagne-Montrachet, much of it inherited by his wife. The wines are elegant and racy with fine pure fruit, and are increasingly generous and complex with five years' age. *Premiers crus* Charmes and Perrières are excellent examples of their noble *terroirs*. Dark, deep and intense Volnay with classic perfumes and really delicious fruit show similarly sophisticated winemaking. Though not quite at the same level, this is, in fact, a very credible alternative if superstars like COCHE-DURY or COMTES LAFON remain out of reach due to the demand-inflated prices. Village-level Meursaults Clos de la Velle and Tessons have only been produced separately from 2000 and new from 2001 is

some Meursault Premier Cru Genevrières. A little red Monthelie and Pommard are also made. (PW)

○ **Chassagne-Montrachet** La Bergerie★★ £E   1er Cru Blanchots-Dessus★★★★ £F

○ **Meursault** Clos de la Velle★ £D   Tessons★★★ £E   1er Cru Charmes★★★★ £E   1er Cru Perrières★★★★£F

● **Volnay** Les Blanches★★★ £D   1er Cru La Gigotte★★★ £E   1er Cru Santenots★★★★ £E

● **Chassagne-Montrachet** 1er Cru Les Bondues★★ £D

JOSEPH DROUHIN   Beaune   www.drouhin.com   A: DAy, OWL, C&R, L&W, MCW

Owner: Drouhin family   7 Rue d'Enfer, 21200 Beaune

An excellent high-profile domaine (owning over 60 ha) and *négociant* that combines integrity and know-how. Equally adept at producing red as white, Drouhin delivers good quality wine at every level. As celebrated as any of the Drouhin wines are the red and white from the Beaune *premier cru* Clos des Mouches. While the red can be good, it can be surpassed by a Grèves bottling, but the white can be superb, with its delicate spice, flavour complexity, real presence on the palate and considerable elegance. Generally the wines are not big or overly powerful yet show good expression and are subtle and elegant. Occasionally wines miss a little extra concentration but it is important not to expect immediate gratification. The wines add weight and their centres usually fill in with the requisite bottle-age. Of the reds, the attractive Côte de Beaune (a Beaune appellation but usually including young-vine Clos des Mouches) and similarly-priced examples usually need three years' ageing; Vosne, Chambolle and other village-level wines and the Beaune *premiers crus* around six; the top *crus* eight to ten years. Not all the *grands crus* are of the same standard but Drouhin's versions of Griotte-Chambertin and Grands-Echezeaux, where good examples can be hard to find, are usually excellent. In Chablis, where Drouhin is an important vineyard owner (see Joseph DROUHIN CHABLIS), there are facilities to press the grapes, though vinification takes place in Beaune. Drouhin also make the wines for the Marquis de Laguiche including the brilliant Montrachet, which comes from the appellation's largest single parcel. DOMAINE DROUHIN is the company's quality outpost in Oregon, run by Veronique, daughter of Robert Drouhin. As well as those listed, a little of the *grands crus* Chambertin, Chambertin Clos de Bèze, Charmes-Chambertin, Clos Saint-Denis, Clos de la Roche, Romanée-Saint-Vivant, Corton and Bâtard-Montrachet are also made, as are generic examples of leading village appellations. (PW)

● **Musigny**✪✪✪✪ £H   ● **Griotte-Chambertin**★★★★ £G   ● **Grands-Echezeaux**★★★★ £G

● **Bonnes Mares**★★★★ £G   ● **Clos de Vougeot**★★★ £F   ● **Echezeaux**★★★ £F

● **Corton** Bressandes★★★ £F

● **Chambolle-Musigny**★★ £E   1er Cru★★★ £E   1er Cru Amoureuses★★★★ £F

● **Morey-Saint-Denis** 1er Cru Clos Sorbé★★★ £E

● **Vosne-Romanée**★★★ £E   1er Cru Petits Monts★★★ £F

● **Beaune** 1er Cru Clos des Mouches★★★ £E   1er Cru Grèves★★★ £E

● **Volnay**★★ £D   1er Cru Chevret★★ £E   1er Cru Clos des Chênes★★★ £E

● **Côte de Beaune**★★ £D   ● **Côte de Beaune-Villages**★ £C

● **Savigny-lès-Beaune**★ £C   1er Cru Serpentières★★ £D   ● **Chorey-lès-Beaune**★ £C   ● **Rully**★ £B

○ **Montrachet** Marquis de Laguiche✪✪✪✪ £H   ○ **Corton-Charlemagne**★★★★ £G

○ **Beaune** 1er Cru Clos des Mouches★★★★ £F   ○ **Chassagne-Montrachet** Marquis de Laguiche★★★ £F

○ **Puligny-Montrachet** 1er Cru Folatières★★★ £F   ○ **Meursault**★★★ £E   ○ **Côte de Beaune**★★ £D

○ **Saint-Aubin**★ £D   ○ **Saint-Romain**★ £C   ○ **Rully**★ £B

CLAUDE DUGAT   Gevrey-Chambertin   A: Eno, HRp

Owner: Claude Dugat   1 Place de l'église, 21220 Gevrey-Chambertin

There are similarities between Claude Dugat and his cousin Bernard (Bernard DUGAT-PY). Both have small holdings (Claude has just 4 ha) and both make very rich, concentrated wines swaddled in, but not swamped by, new oak. In addition, yields are low, occasionally very low, and there is an intuitive feel for the vine that runs back a generation or two. Unsurprisingly perhaps, Claude Dugat's wines have gone down a treat in the US and their prices have soared (at first filling the pockets of the middlemen). The wines are rich with, in some instances, old-vine succulence as well as balancing fine ripe tannins and good acidities but how many of these wines get the six to ten years' ageing they deserve, and occasionally need, I wouldn't hazard a guess at. As well as the *premiers crus* and *grands crus* there's very good if no longer inexpensive village-level Gevrey and Bourgogne Rouge. Oh, and both cousins have beautiful, restored medieval cellars. (PW)

● **Charmes-Chambertin**✪✪✪✪✪ £H ● **Griottes-Chambertin**✪✪✪✪✪ £H
● **Gevrey-Chambertin**★★★ £F 1er Cru★★★★ £G 1er Cru Lavaux-Saint-Jacques★★★★ £G
● **Bourgogne Rouge**★★ £D

BERNARD DUGAT-PY Gevrey-Chambertin www.dugat-py.com A: THt, BBR, Blx, Sec, JNi

Owner: Bernard Dugat Rue de Planteligone, BP 31, 21220 Gevrey-Chambertin
Bernard Dugat has been making wine since 1975 but only bottling his own since 1989. His 7.2 ha are planted exclusively to Pinot Noir. The concentration and richness of fruit, lush oak, silky textures and fine tannins make the wines irresistible. Nearly all the wines see 100 per cent new oak but only rarely does this or the amount of extract or tannin seem overdone. These are big, dense wines but in the best sense. The Lavaux-Saint-Jacques and the *grands crus* have extra class and dimension as well as concentration. The Chambertin is distinguished by very, very concentrated black fruits that make the structure difficult to assess, a testament to very low-yielding and very old, very densely planted vines. A new Vosne-Romanée (from 70-year-old vines) has only been made since 1999 and a special *cuvée* of Bourgogne Rouge, Cuvée Halinard, since 2000. Only tiny amounts of Mazis-Chambertin and Chambertin are made. (PW)

● **Chambertin**✪✪✪✪✪ £H ● **Mazis-Chambertin**✪✪✪✪✪ £H
● **Charmes-Chambertin**✪✪✪✪✪ £H ● **Gevrey-Chambertin** 1er Cru Petite Chapelle★★★★ £G
● **Gevrey-Chambertin** 1er Cru★★★★ £G 1er Cru Lavaux-Saint-Jacques★★★★ £G
● **Gevrey-Chambertin** Vieilles-Vignes★★★ £F Coeur de Roy★★★ £F Évocelles★★★ £F

DOM. DUJAC Morey-Saint-Denis www.dujac.com A: OWL, L&W, HRp, WSc, ABy, T&W

Owner: Jacques Seysses 7 Rue de la Bussière, 21220 Morey-Saint-Denis
Jacques Seysses is one of the best-known and most respected winemakers in Burgundy. His openness and generosity have helped many a fellow Burgundian and more than a few New World Pinot-phile winemakers along their way. Perhaps unsurprisingly the winemaking reflects modern influences as well as Burgundian traditions. There is great attention to detail, scrupulous hygiene and new oak is favoured for the top wines. A preference for clonal selection and cultured yeasts is offset by a desire for whole-bunch fermentation (no destemming). As a consequence the wines are never that deeply coloured but are intense, clean, elegant and perfumed. Now that Seysses is assisted by his son Jeremy, past criticisms of a lack of weight and occasionally too much oak have been countered with a slightly more flexible approach in recent vintages. At any rate the wines gain in richness and harmony with age, becoming ever more expressive of their *terroir*. Of the five *grands crus*, the Bonnes Mares is arguably the best, with remarkable breadth, power and flavour profile. An intense, vigorous Echezeaux and an expansive Clos de Roche are stylish examples of their respective appellations but all are fine and individual, as are the Chambolle and Gevrey *premiers crus*. The splendid regular Morey-Saint-Denis *premier cru* comes from Ruchots and some younger vines in Clos de la Roche. Some Vosne-Romanée Premier Cru Les Beaumonts is also made on a sharecropping basis. A little of the estate's 12-odd ha is planted to Chardonnay for some white Morey-Saint-Denis, including some Monts Luisants from 2000. (PW)

● **Bonnes Mares**✪✪✪✪✪ £H ● **Clos de la Roche**★★★★★ £H ● **Echezeaux**★★★★ £H
● **Clos Saint-Denis**★★★★★ £G ● **Charmes-Chambertin**★★★★ £G

- **Gevrey-Chambertin** 1er Cru Les Combottes★★★★ £G
- **Chambolle-Musigny**★★★ £E 1er Cru Les Gruenchers★★★ £G
- **Morey-Saint-Denis**★★★ £E 1er Cru★★★★ £F O **Morey-Saint-Denis**★ £E

DOM. VINCENT DUREUIL-JANTHIAL   Rully   A: THt, CdP, OWL, Rae, CPp

Owner: Vincent Dureuil 10 Rue de la Buisserolle, 71150 Rully
Vincent Dureuil's 7-ha estate is planted to more red than white but the whites are the better suit and
among the best made by a local grower. Having established his own domaine he is able to add to it
bit by bit with plots inherited from his father, Raymond, who also makes attractive red and white
Rully, albeit in a slightly less modern style. Greater use of new oak is apparent but whites have a depth
and fullish fruit character as well as decent acidity to drink well with two or three years' ageing. The
stars are *premiers crus* that come from low-yielding old vines. A departure is a little Nuits-Saint-
Georges Clos des Argillières, first made in 1999. (PW)
O **Rully**★ £B 1er Cru Margotée★★ £C 1er Cru Le Meix Cadot★★ £C
- **Rully** Vieilles Vignes★ £C ● **Mercurey**★ £C

DOM. RENÉ ENGEL www.domaine-engel.com   A: Con, Gau, HHB, HRp, M&V

Owner: Philippe Engel 3 Place de la Mairie, 21700 Vosne-Romanée
Over the past two decades Philippe Engel has steadily revived the estate established by his industrious
and learned grandfather René. All 7 ha are in the commune of Vosne and neighbouring Flagey and
Vougeot. The style is one of power, structure and richness and is achieved in part through destemming,
high fermentation temperatures, long *cuvaisons* and a moderately high percentage of new oak. The
wines are typically deep coloured, full and structured with a dark fruit richness and impressive depth
and length. Older vintages had a tendency to be a bit too brutal but in the 1990s the wines gained
better balance and now show more of their intrinsic quality and class, while retaining their muscular,
concentrated stamp. Ever richer and more luscious with age, the village Vosne-Romanée needs five
years' ageing; the others are better with 10 years. (PW)
- **Grands-Echezeaux**✪✪✪✪✪ £G ● **Clos de Vougeot**★★★★ £F ● **Echezeaux**★★★★ £F
- **Vosne-Romanée**★★★ £E 1er Cru Les Brulées★★★★ £E

ARNAUD ENTE Meursault   A: M&V

Owner: Arnaud Ente 12 Rue de Mazeray, 21190 Meursault
Arnaud Ente is a young grower able to make only a relatively small amount of wine but a lot of effort
goes into each one. Yields are kept low and there is a good smattering of old vines. The wines are ripe,
concentrated but not overdone with fine structures and good flavour intensity and depth. Of the two
superior Meursaults, the Goutte d'Or has a more floral, exotic character in contrast to a citrusy but
very concentrated Vieilles Vignes. The Puligny has a spicy intensity but less depth. Decent Bourgogne
Blanc and Bourgogne Aligoté usually show good fruit too. (PW)
O **Puligny-Montrachet** 1er Cru Les Referts★★★ £F
O **Meursault**★★★ £E Vieilles Vignes★★★★ £F 1er Cru Goutte d'Or★★★ £F

FRÉDÉRIC ESMONIN Gevrey-Chambertin   A: JAr, HRp

Owner: Frédéric Esmonin 1 Rue de Curley, 21220 Gevrey-Chambertin
This small estate only started bottling its own wines in the late 1980s after Frédéric's father, André,
had established a reputation as a top grower. Most of the wines here are made from leased vineyards

on a sharecropping basis; in addition some of the top *crus* are from bought-in grapes as this estate has also established a separate small *négociant* operation. Most significant is 1 ha of the prized small *premier cru* Estournelles; the wine's concentration, depth and refinement do justice to the *cru*'s caché. The other estate wines show fine fruit and depth too. An intense, meaty, structured Ruchottes-Chambertin is rivalled by a very powerful, black-fruited and classy Mazis-Chambertin, made from the Esmonin's share of that which they cultivate for the Hospices de Beaune. A fine example of another *grand cru*, Griottes-Chambertin was made here until 1999. Wines made to a high standard from purchased grapes (or wine) include Clos de Vougeot, Chambertin and Chambertin Clos-de-Bèze. Prices are very reasonable across the range. (PW)

● **Mazis-Chambertin**★★★★ £F ● **Ruchottes-Chambertin**★★★★ £F
● **Gevrey-Chambertin** 1er Cru Lavaux Saint-Jacques★★★ £E 1er Cru Estournelles★★★★ £E
● **Gevrey-Chambertin** Clos Prieur★★★ £D

SYLVIE ESMONIN Gevrey-Chambertin   A: M&V, HHB

Owner: Sylvie Esmonin Clos Saint-Jacques, 1 Rue Neuve, 21220 Gevrey-Chambertin
This small 7-ha domaine, previously called Domaine Michel Esmonin et Fille (after Sylvie's father) makes some splendid Gevrey-Chambertin. Prior to 1987 most of the wine was sold to *négociants* but the highly trained Sylvie Esmonin has worked with her father for more than a decade and after making an immediate impact has continued to improve the wines. There is an extra vigour and concentration in the most recent vintages but this has been added whilst retaining their silky elegance. The wines can be drunk reasonably young but the 1999s, in particular, need more time. (PW)

● **Gevrey-Chambertin**★★ £E Vieilles Vignes★★★ £E 1er Cru Clos Saint-Jacques★★★★ £F
● **Volnay** Santenots★★★ £E ● **Côte de Nuits-Villages**★★ £C ● **Bourgogne Rouge**★ £C

DOM. FAIVELEY Nuit-Saint-Georges   A: MMD, BBR, HHC, HRp, JAr, L&W

Owner: Faiveley 8 Rue de Tribourg, 21701 Nuits-Saint-Georges
Faiveley command 120 ha of vines in the Côte d'Or and Côte Chalonnaise. Nearly all the wines of an extensive high-quality range come from their own vineyards, either owned or leased, and quality is closely supervised by François Faiveley. A long *cuvaison* is favoured and temperatures are kept well below the average for the red wine fermentation. The wines typically show fine perfumes combined with lots of depth and dimension on the palate. They also add richness with age and are proven keepers at every level. The character varies enormously from appellation to appellation, from intense, raspberryish Mercureys to burly, meaty Nuits-Saint-Georges Clos de la Maréchale to deep, stylish Gevrey Cazetiers to splendid, classy Clos des Cortons. The wines can be a little slight in lighter years such as 1997 or 2000, though they will still keep well. They are superb in the best years, as the 1999 is showing. The Clos des Cortons and most of the Mercureys are *monopoles*. All the leading domaine wines are listed below but there are others. (PW)

● **Chambertin Clos-de-Bèze**✪✪✪✪✪ £H ● **Corton** Clos des Cortons✪✪✪✪✪ £G
● **Mazis-Chambertin**★★★★ £G ● **Latricières-Chambertin**★★★ £G
● **Clos de Vougeot**★★★ £G ● **Echezeaux**★★★ £G
● **Gevrey-Chambertin** Les Marchais★★ £E 1er Cru Combe aux Moines★★★ £F 1er Cru Cazetiers★★★★£F
● **Chambolle-Musigny** 1er Cru La Combe d'Orveau★★★ £F 1er Cru Les Fuées★★★ £F
● **Nuits-Saint-Georges** 1er Cru Aux Chaignots★★★ £E 1er Cru Damodes★★★ £E
● **Nuits-Saint-Georges** 1er Cru Les Saint-Georges★★★ £F
● **Nuits-Saint-Georges** 1er Cru Porets Saint-Georges★★ £E 1er Cru Vignerondes★★ £E
● **Nuits-Saint-Georges** 1er Cru Lavières★ £E 1er Cru Clos de la Maréchale★★ £E
● **Mercurey** Clos des Myglands★★ £C Clos du Roy★★ £C La Framboisière★★ £C
● **Mercurey** Domaine de la Croix Jacquelet★ £C Les Mauvarennes★ £C
○ **Corton-Charlemagne**★★★★ £H ○ **Mercurey** Les Mauvarennes★ £C Clos Rochette★ £C

JEAN-PHILIPPE FICHET Meursault

A: M&V, Bal, HHB, Goe, WSc

Owner: Jean-Philippe Fichet 21190 Meursault

Jean-Philippe Fichet produces ever better white wines from a range of different *climats* in the Côte de Beaune. Most come from vineyards managed on a sharecropping basis but he is able to supplement his production by buying back the vineyard owners' share of the crop. Though most of the Meursault is village-level wine, individual *lieux-dits* are bottled separately and show definite stylistic differences from a ripe, typical Meursault Gruyaches through minerally Chevalières to a structured, classy Tessons that needs the greatest amount of time to show all its qualities. All contrast with a Puligny of real vigour and intensity. Without a superstar tag his wines are reasonably priced if made in fairly modest quantities. A little red wine is also made. (PW)

O **Meursault** Meix sous le Château★★★ £E Gruyaches★★★ £E Chevalières★★★ £E Tessons★★★★ £E
O **Meursault**★★★ £D Criots★★★ £E O **Puligny-Montrachet** 1er Cru Les Referts★★★★ £F
O **Bourgogne Blanc**★★ £B O **Auxey-Duresses**★★ £B

RICHARD FONTAINE-GAGNARD Chassagne-Montrachet

A: JAr, Dec, Maj

Owner: Richard Fontaine 19 Route de Santenay, 21190 Chassagne-Montrachet

Richard Fontaine married one of Jacques Gagnard's daughters, Jean-Marc Blain the other (see BLAIN-GAGNARD). Both make fine wines. There are three *grands crus* and a host of Chassagne *premiers crus* made to increasingly high standards from a 9-ha estate. The wines are full and ripe, with lots of fruit, good breadth and balanced acidities, not heavy or overoaked. All the *premiers crus* show fine citrus and mineral intensity when young but generally drink best with between four and eight years' age. The *grands crus* add more weight, breadth and class: the Criots has more finesse but the Bâtard more richness, while the Montrachet has both and then some. In addition to those listed, other fine *premier cru* Chassagne-Montrachet whites include La Grande Montagne, Les Murées, Chevenottes and Morgeots. Some Pommard Rugiens is also made. (PW)

O **Montrachet**❂❂❂❂❂ £H O **Bâtard-Montrachet**★★★★ £G O **Criots-Bâtard-Montrachet**★★★★ £G
O **Chassagne-Montrachet** 1er Cru La Boudriotte★★★★ £E 1er Cru La Maltroie★★★★ £E
O **Chassagne-Montrachet** 1er Cru Caillerets★★★★ £F
O **Chassagne-Montrachet**★★★ £E 1er Cru La Romanée★★★★ £E 1er Cru Vergers★★★★ £E
● **Volnay** 1er Cru Clos des Chênes★★★ £E
● **Chassagne-Montrachet**★ £C 1er Cru Clos Saint-Jean★★ £D 1er Cru Morgeots★★ £D

DOM. FOURRIER Gevrey-Chambertin

A: THt, JAr, Ben, Gau, Goe, HRp

Owner: Jean-Claude Fourrier 7 Route de Dijon, 21220 Gevrey-Chambertin

Since assuming control from his father in the mid-1990s, Jean-Marie Fourrier has determinedly pursued quality. Yields are kept low and while there is nothing unusual in a cold pre-fermentation maceration, minimal or no sulphur is utilised. A steady and gentle fermentation is sought in the pursuit of finer structures that allow the fruit to shine. To the same end, a relatively low percentage of new oak is used. He certainly has a good smattering of diverse *crus* from which subtle differences of *terroir* may be unearthed. All the wines are deep and ripe, with increasing concentration and complexity in the top wines. There is an excellent example of the would-be *grand cru*, Cru Clos Saint-Jacques (five stars on the most recent form), and very good Combe aux Moines too. Saint-Denis is also made as is a little Griottes-Chambertin. (PW)

● **Gevrey-Chambertin** 1er Cru Clos Saint-Jacques★★★★ £F 1er Cru Combe aux Moines★★★★ £E
● **Gevrey-Chambertin** 1er Cru Cherbaudes★★★★ £E 1er Cru Champeaux★★★★ £E
● **Gevrey-Chambertin**★★★ £D Aux Echezeaux★★★ £D 1er Cru Goulots★★★ £E
● **Chambolle-Musigny**★★★ £E 1er Cru Les Gruenchers★★★★ £E

JEAN-NOËL GAGNARD   Chassagne-Montrachet   A: GBa, Far, J&B, WSc

Owner: Jean-Noël Gagnard and family   21190 Chassagne-Montrachet
Caroline Lestimé has taken over the running of this domaine, one of the leading Chassagne estates, from her father, Jean-Noël Gagnard (whose brother is Jacques Gagnard – see BLAIN-GAGNARD). With half a dozen or so vintages to her credit, the wines have gained in both richness and finesse. As well as a fine village example, Les Masures, there are several *premiers crus*, from the lighter but elegant and more forward Chevenottes, through fuller Champgains, to rich, concentrated Blanchot-Dessus and Caillerets that need at least five or six years to reveal their full glory. The Bâtard-Montrachet adds more again but can usually be drunk from a similar age. The reds, including some Santenay Clos des Tavannes and Chassagnes Clos Saint-Jean and Morgeots, can be attractive but lack richness and depth, even in better years. In addition to those listed some Chaumées, Morgeots and La Maltroie white Chassagne *premiers crus* are made. (PW)

O **Bâtard-Montrachet**★★★★ £H   O **Chassagne-Montrachet** 1er Cru Caillerets★★★★ £F
O **Chassagne-Montrachet** 1er Cru Champgains★★★ £F   1er Cru Blanchots-Dessus★★★★ £F
O **Chassagne-Montrachet** Les Masures★★★ £E   1er Cru Chevenottes★★★ £E   Clos de la Maltroye★★★ £F

GEANTET-PANSIOT   Gevrey-Chambertin   www.geantet-pansiot.com   A: DDr, HRp, EoR

Owner: Vincent Geantet   3 Route de Beaune, 21220 Gevrey-Chambertin
This 13-ha estate is a fine source for intense, concentrated and well-balanced northern Côte de Nuits reds. Vincent Geantet employs long macerations, but at a low temperature, prior to fermentation and has gone to great lengths to reduce yields and ensure optimum ripeness in his grapes. The very high average vine age shows in the wines, adding a succulence and intensity to the fruit. There are no poor wines here and they increasingly show well in lighter vintages as well the best years. The Charmes-Chambertin (from almost half a hectare) is a really fine example of how good this *grand cru* can be. Since taking full control in 1989, Vincent Geantet has steadily built up the estate and from 1999 has had a new cellar and some new wines following the sale of the Vachet-Rousseau domaine. New village Gevrey-Chambertins (from 2000) include En Champ, from a small parcel of extremely old vines, and Les Croisettes, while some *premier cru* Petite Chapelle is promised. There's good value here, too. (PW)

● **Charmes-Chambertin**★★★★ £F
● **Gevrey-Chambertin** Jeunes Rois★★★ £D   Vieilles Vignes★★★ £D   1er Cru Le Poissenot★★★ £E
● **Chambolle-Musigny** Vieilles Vignes★★★ £E   1er Cru★★★★ £E
● **Marsannay** Champ-Perdrix★★ £C   ● **Bourgogne Rouge**★ £C

DOM. HENRI GERMAIN ET FILS   Meursault   A: L&S, Tan, Adm, HRp

Owner: Henri Germain   4 Rue des Forges, 21190 Meursault
Henri Germain possess just 5 ha, two of Pinot Noir and three of Chardonnay, but his son Jean-François continues the habit of making fine wines. Even the village Meursault is of good quality and exemplifies the efforts that go into every wine; its weight, structure and balance is particularly impressive so that it tastes attractive when fairly young, with pronounced citrus, spice and floral aspects, but it also has the capacity to keep far longer than average. Much is made of the importance of a cold cellar for the *élevage* and this does seem to be borne out here. The wines' slow development makes for late bottling. Reds are subject to both a cold maceration and long *cuvaisons,* evident in both the fine, complex, sappy but ripe, cherry, berry aromas and the real intensity and breadth on the palate. Both reds and whites are better with a little age and promise much more with six years or so. Some red Chassagne-Montrachet is also made, while more Meursault will be added as the estate expands a little. (PW)

O **Meursault**★★★ £D   Limozin★★★ £E   Chevalières★★★ £E   1er Cru Charmes★★★★ £E

O **Chassagne-Montrachet** Ier Cru Morgeot★★★★ £E   O **Bourgogne Blanc**★★ £B
● **Beaune** Ier Cru Bressandes★★★ £D

VINCENT GIRARDIN   Santenay   A: THt, CTy, OWL, BWC, HRp, Tan, JNi, WSc

Owner: Vincent Girardin   4 Route de Chassagne-Montrachet, 21590 Santenay
This dynamic Santenay-based grower acquired a *négociant's* licence only in the mid-1990s but has
rapidly expanded, requiring a second move to larger winemaking premises in 2002. From his own
14-ha estate (half red, half white) he has made some brilliant affordable red and white Santenay. The
wines are modern, fruit-rich and clean with a healthy but rarely excessive dose of new oak. There is
an energy and zip about most of the wines, a certain style and precision, yet they are still indicative
of their respective appellations. In his *négociant* role, only grapes (rather than wine) are bought in, for
while the sources are good this allows for further sorting for quality. Girardin vinifies both red and
white with equal ease and is as sucessful in producing both more humble village wines as *grands crus*,
though some of the top wines fail to match the very best made. There is real consistency too, important
in an extensive and growing range of wines. Despite the number of wines, most are made in relatively
small quantities and Girardin's total production is dwarfed by the likes of JADOT or Louis LATOUR.
Those wines that are regularly made are listed below, new is a little Chambertin Clos-de-Bèze and
Bonnes Mares. (PW)

O **Bâtard-Montrachet**★★★★ £H   O **Corton-Charlemagne**★★★★ £F
O **Puligny-Montrachet** Ier Cru Champs Gain★★★ £E   Ier Cru Folatières★★★ £E
O **Chassagne-Montrachet** Ier Cru Le Cailleret★★★ £E   Ier Cru Morgeot★★★ £E
O **Meursault** Narvaux★★ £D   Ier Cru Poruzots★★ £E   Ier Cru Charmes★★★ £E
O **Santenay** Ier Cru Beaurepaire★★ £C   Ier Cru Clos du Beauregard★★ £C
● **Charmes-Chambertin**★★★★ £G   ● **Clos de la Roche**★★★★ £G
● **Corton** Renardes★★★★ £F   ● **Gevrey-Chambertin** Lavaux Saint-Jacques★★★★ £F
● **Pommard** Ier Cru Grands Epenots★★★ £E   Ier Cru Rugiens★★★ £E
● **Beaune** Ier Cru Clos des Vignes Franches★★ £C
● **Volnay** Ier Cru Santenots★★★★ £F   ● **Chassagne-Montrachet** Ier Cru Clos de la Boudriotte★★★ £D
● **Santenay** Ier Cru Gravières Vieilles Vignes★★★ £C   ● **Maranges** Clos des Loyères★★ £C

DOM. HENRI GOUGES   Nuit-Saint-Georges   www.gouges.com   A:CTy OWL, Res, NYg, Sec

Owner: Gouges family   7 Rue du Moulin, 21700 Nuits-Saint-Georges
This famous 14.5-ha estate is run by two cousins. Pierre takes care of the vines, Christian the winemaking, but it was their grandfather, Henri, who first established the domaine and was one of the
pioneers of domaine bottling in Burgundy. He amassed a full hand of some of Nuits' best *crus*, including
Les Saint-Georges, Vaucrains and Pruliers as well as the 3.5-ha *monopole* of Clos des Porrets-Saint-
Georges. The use of grasses to counter erosion has also made it possible to move slowly towards an
essentially organic operation. The grapes are fully destemmed but the use of new oak is minimal (a
maximum of 20 per cent). Christian makes powerful, structured wines with excellent definition but
most of all with an intensity and a quality to the fruit (particularly in the Vaucrains and the Les Saint-
Georges) that sets them apart from most other Nuits. This core of quality is evident even when young
and relatively tannic. Lush, soft and easy thankfully they are not; all the wines deserve (demand) at
least six to eight years' ageing. A further *premier cru*, Les Chaînes Carteaux is also made. The Nuits
white (from a Pinot Noir mutation) is a treat with its spice, mineral and unusual exotic flavour
intensity but benefits from a little age too. Prices are very good for the quality. (PW)

● **Nuits-Saint-Georges** Ier Cru Les Vaucrains★★★★ £E   Ier Cru Les Saint-Georges★★★★ £F
● **Nuits-Saint-Georges** Ier Cru Les Pruliers★★★ £E   Les Chaignots★★★ £E
● **Nuits-Saint-Georges**★★ £D   Ier Cru Clos des Porrets-Saint-Georges★★★ £E
● **Bourgogne Rouge**★ £C   O **Nuits-Saint-Georges** Ier Cru La Perrière★★★ £E

DOM. JEAN GRIVOT Vosne-Romanée www.grivot.com A: Bal, BBR, HRp, RsW, Sec

Owner: Grivot family 6 Rue de la Croix Rameau, 21700 Vosne-Romanée
A brilliant 15-ha estate whose wines are much sought after. In 1987 Étienne took over the already successful family domaine built up by his grandfather, Gaston Grivot, in the first half of the 20th century. He immediately embraced some of the principles of the controversial consultant enologist Guy Accad. After a period of adjustment, the wines since the mid-1990s have been better than ever. The use of a cold pre-fermentation maceration seems to have been the main legacy of Accad's input but much thought and precision goes into every aspect of both viticulture and vinification. The wines are marvellous, combining great richness and concentration, and despite their size avoid any heaviness, with an excellent balance of acidity and fine tannins. The wines can sometimes show a reductive quality when tasted young but this doesn't persist. They all need at least five years' age and will be better with 10 or more. The top Vosnes and *grands crus* are an excellent cellaring prospect if you can afford them. Tiny amounts of Vosne *premiers crus* Les Chaumes and Les Reignots are also made to a very high standard. (PW)

- **Richebourg**✪✪✪✪✪ £H ● **Echezeaux**✪✪✪✪✪ £G ● **Clos de Vougeot**★★★★ £F
- **Vosne-Romanée** 1er Cru Les Beaux Monts✪✪✪✪✪ £F 1er Cru Les Suchots✪✪✪✪✪ £F
- **Vosne-Romanée**★★★ £D Bossières★★★ £E 1er Cru Les Rouges★★★ £E 1er Cru Aux Brulées★★★★ £F
- **Nuits-Saint-Georges** 1er Cru Les Boudots★★★★ £F 1er Cru Les Pruliers★★★ £F
- **Nuits-Saint-Georges** Les Charmois★★★ £E Les Lavières★★★ £E 1er Cru Les Roncières★★★ £E
- **Chambolle-Musigny** La Combe d'Orveaux★★★ £E

ROBERT GROFFIER Morey-Saint-Denis A: A&B, Blx, Lay

Owner: Robert Groffier 35 Route des Grands Crus, 21220 Morey-Saint-Denis
Since the late 1990s the wines have become very rich and concentrated, adding to their already intense and classy character. With 8 ha, Robert and his son Serge make a little wine across several different appellations. Most stunning are the *grands crus*; a small amount of Clos-de-Bèze and almost a hectare of Bonnes Mares are owned. There is also slightly over 1 ha (the largest holding) of the excellent *premier cru* Les Amoureuses from Chambolle-Musigny. While new oak contributes to the wines' lush texture, low yields of first-rate fruit is the underlying reason behind the quality. The whole range is impressive and only rarely is the oak excessive, with real charm and style in the Hauts Doix and Les Sentiers and greater richness, dimension and complexity in the top trio. The wines can be drunk fairly young but bring further rewards to the patient; wait eight years for the best. (PW)

- **Chambertin Clos-de-Bèze**✪✪✪✪✪ £H ● **Bonnes Mares**✪✪✪✪✪ £G
- **Chambolle-Musigny** 1er Cru Les Amoureuses★★★★ £G
- **Chambolle-Musigny** 1er Cru Les Hauts Doix★★★ £F 1er Cru Les Sentiers★★★ £F
- **Gevrey-Chambertin**★★★ £E ● **Bourgogne Rouge**★★ £C

A F GROS & FRANÇOIS PARENT Beaune A: BSh, Dec, HHC, Res

Owner: Anne-Françoise Gros La Garelle, 21630 Pommard
Anne-Françoise Gros is one of many family members involved in wine. Like brother Michel GROS she also includes some Vosne-Romanée in her range of wines. The wines are made by Anne-Françoise's husband, François Parent and share the same cellar space as his wines, in Beaune. While the wines have very good depth and breadth, they had a tendency to be somewhat alike and in distinguishable. However, since 1999 there has been more finesse and flair, with particularly successful 2000s. The Vosne-Romanée *lieux-dits* are reasonably priced, the Echezeaux rich and concentrated and the Richebourg really profound, intense and very powerful and long. François Parent, in addition to existing Beaune and Pommard vineyards, has recently acquired a further 12 ha from Pommard-based Raymond

Launay. Some fine solid Beaune and Pommard are made under his label. (PW)

A.F Gros:

● **Richebourg✪✪✪✪✪** £H   ● **Echezeaux★★★★** £F
● **Vosne-Romanée** Clos de la Fontaine★★ £D Aux Maizières★★★ £D Aux Réas★★★ £D
● **Chambolle-Musigny★★** £D   ● **Savigny-lès-Beaune** 1er Cru Clos des Guettes★★ £D
● **Bourgogne-Hautes Côtes de Nuits★** £B

F Parent:

● **Beaune** 1er Cru Les Boucherottes★★ £D   ● **Pommard** 1er Cru Les Arvelets★★★ £E

ANNE GROS   Vosne-Romanée   www.anne-gros.fr   A: Adm, Lay, L&W, HRp

Owner: Anne Gros   11 Rue des Communes, 21700 Vosne-Romanée

Anne's 6.5 ha is the smallest of the various Gros estates but the wines are the most complete and refined of all. From Bourgogne Rouge to Richebourg, though deeply coloured with plenty of extract, there is a harmony and fruit quality that set the wines apart. A new cellar contains vats that can be adjusted in size according to the amount of wine to be vinified. Though only village-level, Chambolle-Musigny and Vosne-Romanée are lovely examples of their respective appellations. The outstanding Clos de Vougeot and Richebourg absorb the high percentage of new oak used and both have a wonderful, silky texture that belies an excellent structure. Not surprisingly the small quantities of wine are keenly sought after. In addition to some Bourgogne Blanc, a little Bourgogne-Hautes Côtes de Nuits Blanc has been made from 2000. Older wines will be labelled Domaine Anne et François Gros. (PW)

● **Richebourg✪✪✪✪✪** £H   ● **Clos de Vougeot** Le Grand Maupertui★★★★ £F
● **Vosne-Romanée** Les Barreaux★★★ £E   ● **Chambolle-Musigny** La Combe d'Orveau★★★ £E
● **Bourgogne Rouge★★** £C   ● **Bourgogne Hautes-Côtes de Nuits★** £C
○ **Bougogne Blanc★★** £C   ○ **Bourgogne Hautes-Côtes de Nuits★★** £C

MICHEL GROS   Vosne-Romanée   www.domaine-michel-gros.com   A: THt, ABy, Tan, Res,

Owner: Michel Gros & Jean Gros family   7 Rue des Communes, 21700 Vosne-Romanée

For a time Michel Gros made wines both under his own name and those of his family's domain (Domaine Jean Gros). Now the estate of Michel Gros is, like those of his brother Bernard (Gros Frère et Soeur) and sister Anne-Françoise (A F GROS), a distinct entity. Michel has nearly 18 ha but much of it lies in the Hautes-Côtes de Nuits and only a little in the top sites. The real exception is the 2.12 ha *monopole* Clos des Réas, a Vosne-Romanée *premier cru*. A dedicated and skilled *vigneron*, Michel avoids green-harvesting by careful pruning earlier in the growing season. Quite a lot of new oak is used, with 100 per cent in the Clos de Vougeot. These are intense, elegant, very stylish wines, structured but not big or overpowering. Some Richebourg used to be made but this has now been relinquished. New is a Morey-Saint-Denis produced from young vines in En La Rue de Vergy. The Hautes Côtes de Nuits is a consistently good example. (PW)

● **Clos de Vougeot★★★★** £F
● **Vosne-Romanée** 1er Cru Brulées★★★★ £F 1er Cru Clos des Réas★★★ £F
● **Nuits-Saint-Georges★★★** £E Chaliots★★★ £E 1er Cru★★★ £F   ● **Chambolle-Musigny★★★** £E
● **Bourgogne Hautes-Côtes de Nuits★** £C

DOM. ANTONIN GUYON   Savigny-lès-Beaune   www.guyon-bourgogne.com   A: Frw

Owner: Michel & Dominique Guyon   2 Rue de Chorey, 21420 Savigny-lès-Beaune

Two brothers, Michel and Dominique Guyon oversee this relatively large (48 ha), predominantly red wine domaine that has only recently moved up an extra notch or two in quality. They are now producing rich, clean, concentrated wines with an immediate appeal that is only partly due to a measure of new oak. While yields are high, many of the wines of the late 1990s have shown an extra depth and intensity. The cellars are in Savigny but the extensive range of wines includes some of the best sites from the surrounding appellations, in some instances from old vines. If not of the very highest order, there are some very good medium-term reds and delicious whites. A little Corton Renardes is also made, as is some Gevrey-Chambertin and Chambolle-Musigny. (PW)

● **Corton** Bressandes★★★ £F   ● **Corton** Clos du Roy★★★★ £F   ● **Volnay** Clos des Chênes★★★ £E
● **Pernand-Vergelesses** 1er Cru Fichots★★ £D   1er Cru Vergelesses★★ £D
● **Aloxe-Corton** 1er Cru Fournières★★ £E   1er Cru Vercots★★★ £E   ● **Savigny-lès-Beaune**★★ £D
● **Bourgogne Hautes-Côtes de Nuits** Dames de Vergy★ £C
○ **Corton-Charlemagne**★★★★ £G   ○ **Meursault** 1er Cru Charmes Dessus★★★ £F
○ **Pernand-Vergelesses** 1er Cru Sous Frétille★★ £C

HUDELOT-NOËLLAT   Chambolle-Musigny   A: Dec, JAr, Res, HRp, Col

Owner: Alain Hudelot-Noëllat   Ancienne Route Nationale, 21220 Chambolle-Musigny
Greater consistency has been a feature of this domaine in the 1990s and the latest vintages continue to endorse this view. The estate's 10 ha is planted entirely to Pinot Noir and the constancy of the landholding makes it possible to track older vintages of many of the wines. The vines are more productive than some but there is good balance in the vineyard, with relatively little interference with the vines during the growing season. A light but responsive hand can be seen in the winemaking, along with an adeptness at bringing out the best in the grapes. A small proportion of the stems are usually retained and 100 per cent new oak is used in the top wines. Some of the wines have a certain rigour and austerity when young but become supple, opulent, stylish wines with great depth and expression with the appropriate age; about eight years for the Vosne *premiers crus* and the *grands crus* but closer to five for the other wines. Only a little Richebourg (the top wine) and Vosne Malconsorts is made. Village wines and *premiers crus* are remarkably good value. (PW)

● **Romanée-Saint-Vivant**★★★★ £H   ● **Clos de Vougeot**★★★ £F
● **Vosne-Romanée** 1er Cru Malconsorts★★★★ £E
● **Vosne-Romanée**★★★ £D   1er Cru Beaux-Monts★★★ £E   1er Cru Suchots★★★ £E
● **Chambolle-Musigny**★★ £D   1er Cru Charmes★★★ £E   ● **Vougeot** 1er Cru★★★ £D
● **Nuits-Saint-Georges** 1er Cru Murgers★★★ £E

HENRI ET PAUL JACQUESON   Rully   A: THt, BWC, L&S, JNi, HHB

Owner: Henri & Paul Jacqueson   5-7 Rue de Chèvremont, 71150 Rully
This small domaine run by Paul Jacqueson (son of Henri) makes superb Rully in both colours. The 9 ha of vineyards are planted mostly to Pinot Noir and Chardonnay but also include a little Aligoté and Gamay. The wines are natural, pure and expressive, with delicious fruit. Of the whites a Pucelle is full and stylish, with a slightly floral, exotic character, while the Grésigny is more structured and minerally. Red Chaponnières has an enticing perfume and good depth but not the extra weight or class of Les Cloux. These delightful but not simple wines are also affordable, though due to a long-established reputation are not always that easy to find. Another white Rully, Raclot, is now also made, as is a rare, decent example of Bourgogne Passetoutgrains. (PW)

○ **Rully** 1er Cru Grésigny★★ £C   1er Cru La Pucelle★★★ £C   ○ **Bourgogne** Aligoté★ £B
● **Rully** Chaponnières★★ £C   1er Cru Les Cloux★★ £C
● **Mercurey** 1er Cru Les Naugues★★ £C

LOUIS JADOT   Beaune   www.louisjadot.com   A: HMA

Owner: Kopf family   21 Rue Eugène Spuller, BP 117, 21203 Beaune

Under the direction of André Gagey, and more recently his son Pierre-Henry, and the winemaking mastery of Jacques Lardière, this giant (by Burgundian, not international standards) has made Burgundy of the highest order. Around half of the 144 ha is in the Côte d'Or, the rest in Beaujolais (see CHÂTEAU DES JACQUES). As well as a string of *grands crus*, there are many of the leading *premiers crus* and most of the top wines come from their own vineyards, comprising five separate domaines. The Domaine des Héritiers Louis Jadot provides Corton, Corton-Charlemagne and Chevalier-Montrachet *grands crus* and other important Côte de Beaune *premiers crus*. Domaine Louis Jadot includes the superb Côte de Nuits *grands crus* and *premiers crus*, much of it from the original Clair-Däu domaine. Domaines André Gagey, Robert Tourlière and Duc de Magenta add further riches. The key is the know-how that ensures the highest possible quality from a diverse range of sources (including every village in the Côte d'Or) in every vintage, and the expert organisation of logistics. Destemming, a pre-fermentation maceration, high fermentation temperatures and long *cuvaisons* are important features of the red wine vinification. New oak, where it is used (up to 30 per cent), never takes on more than a supporting role. A flexibile, responsive but generally non-interventionist approach can similarly seen in the white winemaking. Reds nearly always have good colour, excellent breadth and depth and plenty of structure but also marvellous concentration, complexity and class in the top wines. Not every bottle is a great one but most will provide a very good example of its appellation and if your only experience of Jadot is one of the humble generics then try one of the many fine domaine wines listed below. There are also several other outstanding wines, including red *grands crus* Romanée-Saint-Vivant, Clos de la Roche and white Bâtard-Montrachet, Bienvenues-Bâtard-Montrachet and Le Montrachet. (PW)

- ● **Musigny**❂❂❂❂❂ £H   ● **Bonnes Mares**❂❂❂❂❂ £H   ● **Chambertin Clos de Bèze**❂❂❂❂❂ £H
- ● **Clos Saint-Denis**★★★★ £G   ● **Chapelle-Chambertin**★★★★ £G
- ● **Clos de Vougeot**★★★★ £G   ● **Echezeaux**★★★★ £H
- ● **Gevrey-Chambertin** 1er Cru Estournelles-Saint-Jacques★★★★ £F   1er Cru Clos Saint-Jacques❂❂❂❂❂£F
- ● **Gevrey-Chambertin** 1er Cru Cazetiers★★★★ £F   1er Cru Lavaux-Saint-Jacques★★★★ £F
- ● **Chambolle-Musigny** 1er Cru Les Baudes★★★ £F   1er Cru Les Amoureuses★★★★ £F
- ● **Nuits-Saint-Georges** 1er Cru Boudots★★★★ £F   ● **Corton** Pougets★★★★ £F
- ● **Beaune** 1er Cru Clos de Couchereaux★★★ £E   1er Cru Clos des Ursules★★★ £E
- ● **Beaune** 1er Cru Cent Vignes★★★ £E   ● **Beaune** 1er Cru Teurons★★★ £E
- ● **Beaune** 1er Cru Avaux★★★ £E   1er Cru Bressandes★★★ £E   1er Cru Grèves★★★ £E
- ● **Savigny-lès-Beaune** 1er Cru La Dominode★★★ £D   ● **Santenay** Clos de Malte★★ £D
- ● **Marsannay**★★ £C
- ○ **Chevalier-Montrachet** Les Demoiselles❂❂❂❂❂ £H   **Corton-Charlemagne**❂❂❂❂❂ £G
- ○ **Puligny-Montrachet** 1er Cru Champ Gain★★★ £G   1er Cru Les Folatières★★★★ £G
- ○ **Beaune** Grèves★★ £E   ○ **Santenay** Clos de la Malte★★ £D   ○ **Marsannay**★ £C

Duc de Magenta:

- ○ **Puligny-Montrachet** 1er Cru Clos de la Garenne★★★★ £G
- ○ **Chassagne-Montrachet** Morgeots Clos de la Chapelle★★★★ £G

PATRICK JAVILLIER   Meursault   A: ACh, BBR, L&W, Lib, OWL

Owner: Patrick Javillier   7 Impasse des Acacias, 21190 Meursault

Patrick Javillier produces a range of fine village Meursaults and bottles individually several different *lieux-dits*. The best of these actually taste like *premiers crus* and certainly offer better value than a top site from an underperforming producer. The wines are rich and ripe, with surprising class and depth for their origins. Though they can occasionally tend to be a bit too broad and slightly clumsy, Les Clous, Les Tillets and Les Narvaux always show a little more verve and racy minerality. Tête de

Murgers is the richest, deepest and most complex of all. Two Bourgogne Blancs are also treated like Meursault – which the richer, more structured of the two, Cuvée Oligocène, effectively is. A village-level Puligny-Montrachet, in contrast, shows more of a Puligny style, with more finesse and delineation, if less character, than the Meursaults. There's good white Savigny-lès-Beaune, too. All the whites are now being vinified in two different ways before being blended back together prior to bottling. A little *grand cru* Corton-Charlemagne has been made since the 1999 vintage and a tiny amount of *premier cru* Meursault Charmes might also be found. An increasing amount of red is also being produced; Savigny-lès-Beaune Grand Liards and *premier cru* Serpentières are reasonable examples of their appellation. (PW)

O **Meursault** Tête de Murgers★★★★ £F Les Tillets★★★ £E
O **Meursault** Clos du Cromin★★ £E Les Clous★★★ £E Les Narvaux★★★ £E
O **Puligny-Montrachet** Levrons★★★ £E O **Savigny-lès-Beaune** Montchevenoy★★ £D
O **Bourgogne Blanc** Cuvée des Forges★ £C Cuvée Oligocène★★ £C

FRANÇOIS JOBARD   Meursault   A: RsW, A&B, Rae, Sec

Owner: François Jobard   2 Rue de Leignon, 21190 Meursault
François Jobard makes somewhat tighter, more traditional wines than his nephew, Rémi JOBARD. Low yields are achieved through rigorous pruning, while vinification is a relatively hands-off affair. While favouring long oak-ageing with extended lees contact, the percentage of new wood is kept low. A rather old-fashioned, heavy sulphur treatment can show in the wines when tasted young but they are meant to be aged. More austere and minerally but with underlying intensity when young, a deep, ripe, leesy nuttiness and flavour complexity develops with extended cellaring. In general the Blagny is usually deep and minerally, Poruzots is also minerally but peachier, Genevrières the more honeyed and the Charmes the most refined. The Meursaults, particularly the *premiers crus,* deserve at least five years' ageing but even the Bourgogne Blanc needs three or more. A little Puligny-Montrachet and some red Blagny is also made. (PW)

O **Meursault** 1er Cru Charmes★★★ £F 1er Cru Genevrières★★★ £F 1er Cru Poruzots★★★ £F
O **Meursault** En la Barre★★ £E 1er Cru Blagny★★★ £F O **Bourgogne Blanc**★★ £C

RÉMI JOBARD   Meursault   A: L&S

Owner: Rémi Jobard   12 Rue Sudot, 21190 Meursault
Rémi Jobard has assumed the responsibility of running this 8-ha estate from his father, Charles (brother of François JOBARD). These are rich, ripe concentrated Meursaults with good depth and balance. The three *premiers crus* show more class and length but there is good style, too, in the village bottlings, even if the Sous la Velle and Chevalière tend to be broader and slightly heavy in warm years. The Charmes is consistently the finest Meursault with superb fruit, excellent balance and a long, intense finish. The most recent vintages, benefitting from later bottling after being refreshed in tank, show increasing finesse. Despite having so many different *cuvées* of Meursault, only around half the estate is planted to Chardonnay. Inexpensive Bourgogne Aligoté is regularly made and from 2.5 ha of Pinot Noir there is good Bourgogne Rouge and some Monthelie and Volnay Santenots. (PW)

O **Meursault** 1er Cru Charmes★★★★ £F 1er Cru Genevrières★★★ £F 1er Cru Poruzots-Dessus★★★ £F
O **Meursault** Sous la Velle★★ £D Chevalière★★★ £E En Luraule★★★ £E O **Bourgogne Blanc**★ £C

DOM. MICHEL JUILLOT   Mercurey   www.domaine-michel-juillot.fr   A: DDr, HHB

Owner: Juillot family   59 Grande Rue, BP 10, 71640 Mercurey
The Juillot vineyards comprise 21 ha of Pinot Noir and 9 ha of Chardonnay. Laurent Juillot has taken over from his father and there are some very attractive whites and excellent reds, including four *premiers*

crus culminating in the well-sited Clos des Barraults. The latter is the most forbidding and structured red but all reveal good depth and richness with three years' age or more. Both pumping over and punching down are employed, no doubt contributing to some youthful austerity. As well as the reds listed below, some Combins and a few magnums of the highly regarded Clos du Roi (both *premiers crus*) are also made. Other than Mercurey, a little of the *grands crus* Corton Perrières (red) and Corton-Charlemagne together with some village-level Aloxe-Corton are produced. (PW)

● **Mercurey** Ier Cru Clos des Barraults★★ £D Ier Cru Champs-Martin★★ £D
● **Mercurey★** £B Ier Cru Clos Tonnerre★★ £C ○ **Mercurey** Ier Cru Clos des Barraults★★ £D
○ **Mercurey** Ier Cru Clos des Barraults★★ £D Ier Cru Champs-Martin★★ £D
○ **Mercurey★** £B Ier Cru En Sazenay★ £C

MICHEL LAFARGE Volnay   A: BBR GFy, Gau, HRp, Sec

Owner: Lafarge family   Domaine Michel Lafarge, 21190 Volnay

Michel and and his son Frédéric have an excellent and deserved reputation for Volnay and are as good a source of fine Côte de Beaune reds as anybody. The domaine is now farmed biodynamically and relatively old vines that give lowish yields are picked at full physiological ripeness to provide the fine raw materials, while care and consideration is evident at every step of the winemaking process. There is much experience to draw on in order to adapt to the particular conditions of each vintage. The wines are elegant and sophisticated, with magical aromas and superb fruit together with good structure and concentration; and vintages like 1993, 96 or 99 show added intensity and concentration. Most of the wines can be drunk fairly young but will only really start to open out after five years or more; in the case of the Clos des Chênes this is a minimum. Otherwise some of the class and complexity is tantalising but remains partially hidden. A Lafarge bottle always delivers fine quality wine that is balanced and complete and a lovely expression of where it comes from. Only 8 ha of a total of 10 is planted to Pinot Noir and some Meursault is made. There's also a little Pommard Premier Cru Pézerolles. New is a small amount of Volnay Premier Cru Caillerets, which was purchased by Frédéric and will appear under his own label from the 2000 vintage. Bourgogne Rouge is always a fine example. (PW)

● **Volnay** Ier Cru★★★ £F Ier Cru Clos du Château des Ducs★★★ £F Ier Cru Clos des Chênes★★★★ £F
● **Volnay★★★** £E Vendange Sélectionée★★★ £E ● **Beaune** Ier Cru Grèves★★★ £F
● **Côte de Beaune-Villages★★** £C ● **Bourgogne Rouge★★** £C

DOM. DES COMTES LAFON Meursault   A: M&V, BBR

Owner: Lafon family   Clos de la Barre, 21190 Meursault

The finest domaine in Meursault and one of the very best in the Côte d'Or, with some excellent Volnay as well as outstanding Meursault. Dominique Lafon has had the mastery of this 14-ha estate for two decades now and in recent years has converted its viticulture to a biodynamic regime. In the Meursault *premiers crus* the fruit is intense, rich and pure and encased in a precise but seamless structure. An opulent Gouttes d'Or, wonderfully expressive Charmes and remarkably profound Genevrières are only surpassed by a peerless Perrières. Yet even the village wines, such as the Clos de la Barre, show good dimension and a touch of class. The fine Volnays are crowned by a rich Santenots du Milieu, with great finesse and length. The acclaim for these wines adds a premium and they need to be bought before changing hands too many times if prices are to be remotely proportionate to their quality. Most expensive, from just a few barrels, is a Montrachet of exalted reputation. A little Puligny-Montrachet Premier Cru Champ Gain is also made and some very good wines are now being produced in the Mâconnais Domaine des HERITIERS COMTES LAFON. (PW)

○ **Meursault** Ier Cru Perrières✪✪✪✪✪ £G Ier Cru Goutte d'Or★★★★ £G Ier Cru Charmes★★★★★ £G
○ **Meursault★★★** £E Désirée★★★ £F Clos de la Barre★★★ £F Ier Cru Genevrières★★★★★ £G

● **Volnay** Ier Cru Clos des Chênes★★★ £E Ier Cru Santenots du Milieu★★★★ £F
● **Volnay**★★ £E Ier Cru Champans £E ● **Monthelie** Ier Cru Duresses★★ £D

FRANÇOIS LAMARCHE www.domaine-lamarche.com A: Col, Rae, RsW ,Sec

Owner: Lamarche family 9 Rue des Communes, 21700 Vosne-Romanée
Only recently much improved, this estate has some prized possessions in its patchwork of 10 ha, including all 1.65 ha of that wedge of *grand cru*, La Grande Rue, lying between La Tâche and La Romanée-Conti. The wines previously showed a certain finesse but missed their real potential but have become more concentrated and classy under François's direction. Yields have been reduced, the grapes are now fully destemmed and up to 60 per cent new oak is used but the wines still start out quite tight and tannic and this noble but at times slightly austere style demands patience. Deep and intense, La Croix Rameau and Malconsorts are arguably the finest Vosne *premiers crus*, which is reflected in their marginally higher prices. Yet there are currently even better examples of most of the *crus* to be had from other producers. La Grande Rue however, is not only unique but very fine indeed. In addition to the three other *grands crus*, a small amount of Grands-Echezeaux is made. Only the most recent vintages should be bought for cellaring. A decent example of inexpensive Hautes-Côtes de Nuits red can be found here too. (PW)

● **La Grande Rue**❶❶❶❶❶ £G ● **Echezeaux**★★★★ £F ● **Clos de Vougeot**★★★ £F
● **Vosne-Romanée** Ier Cru Chaumes★★★ £E Ier Cru Malconsorts★★★★ £F
● **Vosne-Romanée**★★ £E Ier Cru La Croix Rameau★★★★ £E Ier Cru Les Suchots★★★★ £E

DOM. DES LAMBRAYS Morey-Saint-Denis A: BBR, HHC, HRp, OWL, Res

Owner: Freund family 31 Rue Basse, 21220 Morey-Saint-Denis
The historic 8.8-ha Clos des Lambrays is almost entirely owned by Gunter Freund and, though relatively small, it is certainly a big chunk of *grand cru* under single ownership. After years of neglect, the Clos was partially replanted in 1981 and around the same time upgraded from *premier cru* to *grand cru*. Much effort and expense was poured into the estate under the guidance of winemaker Thierry Brouin, whose efforts have only really paid full dividends since 1996, coinciding with the most recent change of ownership. The wine is seductively plump and silky but with terrific class and complexity too, softer than adjoining Clos de Tart or indeed Bonnes Mares or Chambertin yet of true *grand cru* status. Morey-Saint-Denis (both in a village-level and a *premier cru* bottling) shares the delicious fruit and superfine tannins if missing the depth and dimension of the *grand cru*. Small quantities of two very exciting whites are made from a few rows in top Puligny *premiers crus*. They have a depth, weight and structure allied to class, particularly the Clos du Cailleret (behind Les Pucelles and the northern extension of Le Montrachet). Unfortunately they have high prices to match. (PW)

● **Clos des Lambrays**★★★★★ £F ● **Morey-Saint-Denis**★★★ £E Ier Cru★★★★ £E
O **Puligny-Montrachet** Ier Cru Clos du Cailleret★★★★ £F Ier Cru Les Folatières★★★ £F

HUBERT ET OLIVIER LAMY Saint-Aubin A: BBR, DDr, HHB, L&S, L&W

Owner: Lamy family Le Paradis, 21190 Saint-Aubin
This is another estate where the input of a new generation has had a positive impact on quality. Already good Saint-Aubin whites have been honed into ripe, rich and stylish examples under the winemaking expertise of Hubert Lamy's son, Olivier. Only 5 of the 16.5 ha of vineyard are planted to Pinot Noir but the reds are increasingly ripe and concentrated too, especially from a good year like 1999. This is a good source of both red and white Burgundy without silly prices. The bottling of Puligny, Les Tremblots, for instance, could pass for a *premier cru* wine. A very small amount of Criots-Bâtard-Montrachet is also made. (PW)

○ **Chassagne-Montrachet** 1er Cru Macherelles★★★ £F ○ **Puligny-Montrachet** Les Tremblots★★★ £E
○ **Saint-Aubin** 1er Cru En Remilly★★★ £D 1er Cru Murgers Dents de Chien★★★ £D
○ **Saint-Aubin** Princée★★ £C 1er Cru Les Frionnes★★★ £C 1er Cru Clos de la Chatenière★★★ £D
● **Saint-Aubin** 1er Cru Les Castets ★★ £C 1er Cru Derrière Chez Edouard★★★ £C
● **Chassagne-Montrachet** Goujonne Vieilles Vignes★★ £C

LOUIS LATOUR www.louislatour.com　　　　　A: LLt, Hay, BBR, C&R, MCW

Owner: Latour family 18 Rue des Tonneliers, 21200 Beaune
With an annual production of 5.5 million bottles, this historic Burgundy house (and domaine of 50
ha) is one of the most widely seen labels outside of France. Not only are wines made from Chablis
down through the Côte d'Or to the Chalonnaise, Mâconnais and Beaujolais, but beyond into the
Ardèche and the Var. The continued use of flash-pasteurisation for the red wines (in order to kill bacteria) and filtration remain the most controversial aspects of their production. In addition a short
cuvaison (eight to ten days) has long been favoured – in search of greater finesse it is argued – but too
often the reds lack vigour, depth and vibrancy as well as the flavour amplitude they surely
otherwise have the potential for. White grapes are harvested late for optimum ripeness, yields are low
and plenty of new oak is used in their *élevage*. While generally better quality and value can be found
elsewhere, some of the top *crus* (including all six white *grands crus*) can be astonishingly good, with
great concentration, complexity and power. A selection of the best white wines is listed below. Of the
reds, Corton-Grancey and Beaune Vignes Franches are two tasted that are rather better than some
further down the pecking order. (PW)
○ **Bâtard-Montrachet★★★★** £H ○ **Chevalier-Montrachet** Demoiselles★★★★ £H
○ **Corton-Charlemagne★★★★** £G
○ **Meursault** 1er Cru Château de Blagny★★★ £E 1er Cru Goutte d'Or★★★ £E
○ **Puligny-Montrachet** 1er Cru Folatières★★ £E 1er Cru Truffières★★★ £E
○ **Chassagne-Montrachet** 1er Cru Morgeot★★ £E

LATOUR-GIRAUD Meursault　　　　　　　　　　A: Bib, THt

Owner: Jean-Pierre Latour 21190 Meursault
This previously underperforming domaine is now making whites of a quality expected of its impressive
holdings. Of 10 ha, eight planted to Chardonnay, arguably the most prized is that of a large, 2.4 ha
section of Genevrières. Recent vintages show great class and an elegant and intense expression that is
true to its origins. Both this and the tiny production of a minerally Perrières shouldn't be rushed; the
depth and intensity will slowly unfurl with up to 10 years' ageing. As well as some fine Charmes, two
other *premiers crus*, Bouchères and Poruzots, are also made but there's also fine quality in Le Limozin
and Cuvée Charles Maxine, which both give classic Meursault style and richness with less age and at
a more affordable price. Besides a little Puligny some red is made, mostly from Maranges. (PW)
○ **Meursault** 1er Cru Genevrières★★★★ £F 1er Cru Perrières★★★★ £F
○ **Meursault** 1er Cru Charmes★★★★ £F Charles Maxime★★★ £E Le Limozin★★★ £E
○ **Puligny-Montrachet** Champs Canet★★★★ £F

DOMINIQUE LAURENT Nuits-Saint-Georges　　　　A: Vig, Far, HBJ, N&P, HRp

Owner: Dominique Laurent 2 Rue Jacques-Duret, 21700 Nuits-Saint-Georges
Ex-pastry chef Dominique Laurent buys only the best small lots of young red wine made from old
low-yielding vines, ages them himself, then sells the many individual *cuvées* for very high prices. His

considerable following in both France and other premium wine markets stems in part from the support of Michel Bettane and *La Revue du Vin de France*. The wines are typically big, powerful and very concentrated, with lots of extract and tannin. Oak, and lots of it, was an early theme, resulting in some excessively oaky wines, though this is much less common in more recent releases. Now, in the same way that pastries can be butter-rich, many of the wines can be oak-rich (but without compromising the wine's structure with excessive oak tannins as is typical in a badly wooded wine) with the requisite balance of fruit richness and extract that is enriched and enhanced by the oak, resulting in a succulent creaminess. Quality is generally very high indeed but rare lapses can result in rather tough chewy wines. Thanks, though, to the high prices obtained for other wines, even these can be declassified. Though all the wines are bought in, many of the exact same parcels can be acquired year after year. Some of the wines made fairly regularly include: (*grands crus*) Chambertin Clos de Bèze, Mazis-Chambertin, Le Musigny, Bonnes Mares, Clos de la Roche and Clos de Vougeot; (*premiers crus*) Vosne-Romanée Beaux Monts and Suchots, Chambolle-Musigny Charmes, Gevrey-Chambertin Clos Saint-Jacques, Nuits-Saint-Georges Les Saint-Georges, Vaucrains and Richemone, Volnay Clos des Chênes, Pommard Epenots, Beaune 1er Cru and Grèves as well as some excellent village examples designated Vieilles Vignes. If you like vibrant, rich, oaky Burgundy with often remarkable depth, length and intensity, never turn down the chance to taste any of the many varied offerings. Dominique applies some of the same methods in both the northern and southern Rhône (and beyond) where with Michel Tardieu he turns out small volume, high-priced *cuvées* under the TARDIEU-LAURENT label. (PW)

OLIVIER LEFLAIVE Puligny-Montrachet www.olivier-leflaive.com A: **C&B, HHC, L&W, WSc**

Owner: Olivier Leflaive (& others)   Place du Monument 21190 Puligny-Montrachet

Olivier Leflaive set up this merchant house in 1984 and continued to co-manage the family domaine (Domaine Leflaive) until 1994. The company now has a small 12-ha domaine of its own, though the lion's share of production (three-quarters of a million bottles) is made from bought-in grapes. Franck Grux, the winemaker for more than a decade, has provided a largely consistent and sometimes enviable range of white Burgundy. Leading *premiers crus* from Puligny-Montrachet, Chassagne-Montrachet and Meursault can be good if a little variable. In addition, examples of all six Côte de Beaune *grands crus* are made, including very fine Criots-Bâtard-Montrachet and Le Montrachet. If at a lower level the wines can be a little dull, occasionally even dilute in a lesser vintage, the Côte Chalonnaise whites, Rully and Montagny, can be also be very good. A increasing amount of fine Chablis is being made, including a range of fine *premiers crus*. While more than 90 per cent of production is white, a relatively small range of reds is also made. The best, mostly Pommard and Volnays, are quite structured, with appreciable oak, but have the depth and richness to be very satisfying with five years' age or more. Bourgogne Blanc Les Sétilles is usually a good example of everyday white Burgundy. Listed are only some of the best wines that are regularly made. Franck Grux also makes some good Meursault Meix Chavaux under his own label. (PW)

O **Montrachet❂❂❂❂❂** £H   O **Criots-Bâtard-Montrachet★★★★** £G
O **Puligny-Montrachet** 1er Cru Champ Canet★★★ £F 1er Cru Pucelles★★★ £F
O **Puligny-Montrachet** 1er Cru Champs Gain★★ £F 1er Cru Les Referts★★★ £F
O **Puligny-Montrachet** 1er Cru Les Chalumeaux★★ £E
O **Chassagne-Montrachet** 1er Cru Les Chaumées★★★ £E 1er Cru Abbaye de Morgeot★★★ £F
O **Meursault** Narvaux★★ £E 1er Cru Poruzots★★★ £F 1er Cru Perrières★★★★ £F
O **Chablis Premier Cru** Fourchaumes★★★ £D Montée de Tonnerre★★★ £D Vaillons★★★ £D
O **Saint-Aubin** 1er Cru Les Perrières★ £C 1er Cru En Remilly★★ £D
O **Rully** 1er Cru★ £C 1er Cru Les Clous★★ £C 1er Cru Rabourcé★★ £C
O **Montagny** 1er Cru★ £B 1er Cru Bonneveaux★ £C
● **Volnay★★** £D 1er Cru Clos des Angles★★★ £E 1er Cru Champans★★★ £E

● **Pommard**★★ £D 1er Cru Charmots★★★ £E 1er Cru Rugiens★★★ £E
● **Aloxe-Corton**★ £D ● **Santenay**★ £C

DOM. LEFLAIVE Puligny-Montrachet www.leflaive.fr A: JAr, BBR, Goe, L&W, HRp, Tan

Owner: Leflaive family Place des Marronniers, 21190 Puligny-Montrachet
Under the direction of Vincent Leflaive this estate gained a fabulous reputation during the 1960s and 70s, so much so that the wines have been both sought-after and very expensive for as long as many wine enthusiasts can remember. Under the direction of his daughter Anne-Claude, who initially worked with her cousin Olivier (dedicated to his own business OLIVIER LEFLAIVE since 1994), the unsurpassed holding of prime white Burgundy vineyard has become progressively biodynamic, totally so since 1998. Of the 23.5 ha, 11.5 ha are of *premiers crus*, 5 ha of *grands crus*, including nearly 2 ha each of Chevalier-Montrachet and Bâtard-Montrachet. Pierre Morey has made the wines in recent years and brought to an end some of the criticism directed at wines from vintages between the mid-1980s and early 90s, when yields were high and the wines' considerable reputation for ageing was tarnished. With the balance and the health of the vineyards now paramount, wines from recent vintages look set to rival past glories. No end of descriptions of flavour nuances can do them justice. The wines have wonderful purity and clarity, great concentration and intensity but almost perfect precision and poise, together with compelling complexity, dimension and length in the *grands crus*. (PW)
O **Le Montrachet**✪✪✪✪✪ £H O **Chevalier-Montrachet**✪✪✪✪✪£H
O **Bienvenues-Bâtard-Montrachet**✪✪✪✪✪ £H O **Bâtard-Montrachet**✪✪✪✪✪ £H
O **Puligny-Montrachet** 1er Cru Les Pucelles★★★★★ £G 1er Cru Les Combottes★★★★ £G
O **Puligny-Montrachet**★★★ £F 1er Cru Clavoillon★★★★ £F 1er Cru Les Folatières★★★★ £G
O **Bourgogne** Blanc★★ £D

DOM. LEROY www.domaineleroy.com A: JAr, BBR, C&R, Far, HRp, Sec

Owner: Leroy and Bize families Rue du Pont-Boillot, 21190 Auxey-Duresses
Madame Lalou Bize-Leroy, one of the most formidable and dynamic wine personalities on the planet, directs one of Burgundy's most prestigious domaines. Built around the former Domaine Charles Noëllat (Vosne-Romanée) purchased in 1988, it now boasts 22 ha of some of the finest *crus* in the Côte d'Or. Lalou Bize has championed the cause of biodynamic viticulture and has built a domaine to rival the Domaine de la ROMANÉE-CONTI, which she co-managed until 1993. In terms of out and out quality there is arguably no finer estate. Yields are tiny (20–24 hl/ha is typical), and in common with Romanée-Conti there is no destemming, long *cuvaisons* and more than enough new oak to keep the *tonnelier* (barrelmaking) firms happy. The wines are distinguished by quite staggering concentration and richness, in some instances with almost overwhelming extract and structure, as well as great intensity, depth and length. Every wine needs the best part of a decade's age and they usually have the balance to keep for much longer. Due to insufficient repeated tastings of the wines they have not been rated individually but as an indication of their likely ratings (which will be added in future editions), generally the *grands crus* (eight red and one white) are five stars, leading *premiers crus* four stars, and others at least three stars. Reds include: (*grands crus*) Chambertin, Latricières-Chambertin, Clos de la Roche, Musigny, Clos de Vougeot, Richebourg, Romanée-Saint-Vivant and Corton Renardes; (*premiers crus*) Gevrey-Chambertin Combottes, Chambolle-Musigny Charmes, Vosne-Romanée Aux Brulées and Beaux Monts, Nuits-Saint-Georges Boudots and Vignerondes, Volnay Santenots and Savigny-lès-Beaune Narbantons; (village-level) Chambolle-Musigny Frémières, Vosne-Romanée Genevrières, Nuits-Saint-Georges Au Bas du Combe, Aux Allots and Lavières and Pommard Les Vignots. The only white is some Corton-Charlemagne. Bize-Leroy's own domaine is Domaine D'AUVENAY, while Leroy SA is the *négociant* and distribution operation. (PW)

HUBERT LIGNIER   Morey-Saint-Denis   A: RRI, Eno, C&R, Far

Owner: Hubert Lignier   45 Grande Rue, 21220 Morey-Saint-Denis
Romain Lignier, Hubert's son, has gradually honed the quality of his family's wines over the last decade. Almost 8 ha include a decent amount of Clos de la Roche and five *premier cru* bottlings. There is also a tiny amount of Charmes Chambertin. Moderately low yields are maintained and good extraction is favoured; Romain aids the *pigéage* by entering the vats himself and physically agitating the grapes and pulp in what seems to be a family proclivity. The wines can start off quite tight but have real depth and intensity that more than covers their fine but abundant tannin. The wines don't lack for oak, particularly the Combottes, but this is generally better integrated than previously. The *premiers crus* are markedly more expensive than the village wines but this is where the real quality kicks in. The excellent Morey-Saint-Denis Premier Cru Vieilles Vignes combines the *crus* of Faconnières and Chenevery and is a little bolder and deeper than the other two Morey *premiers crus*. Chambolle-Musigny is the best of the three village-level wines. (PW)

● **Clos de la Roche**✪✪✪✪✪ £H
● **Morey-Saint-Denis** 1er Cru La Riotte★★★ £F   1er Cru Vieilles Vignes★★★★ £F
● **Morey-Saint-Denis**★ £E   1er Cru Les Chaffots★★★ £F 1er Cru Vieilles Vignes★★★★ £F
● **Gevrey-Chambertin**★ £E   1er Cru Les Combottes★★★ £G
● **Chambolle-Musigny**★★ £E   1er Cru Les Baudes★★★ £F

FRANÇOIS LUMPP   Givry   A: THt, L&S, N&P, JNi

Owner: Isabelle & François Lumpp   Le Pied du Clou, 36 Avenue de Mortières, 71640 Givry
One of the best Givry producers (others include Joblot, René Bourgeon and Clos Salomon) with wines to match the best from the other Côte Chalonnaise appellations, too. From just 6.5 ha (5 Pinot Noir) François Lumpp keeps yields low and shows a light hand in the winemaking that results in supple, harmonious and balanced reds, especially with a couple of years' bottle-age. The red from Crausot is particularly impressive. Whites are fine, too, ripe but not overripe, with good intensity and balanced acidities and an elegant minerality in the Petite Marole. (PW)

O **Givry** 1er Cru Petit Marole★★ £C   Clos des Vignes Rondes★★ £C   1er Cru Crausot★★ £C
● **Givry** 1er Cru Clos du Gras Long★★ £C   1er Cru Clos Jus★★ £C   1er Cru Crausot★★★ £C
● **Givry** Pied du Clou★ £C   1er Cru Petite Marole★★ £C

DOM. MICHEL MAGNIEN ET FILS   Morey-Saint-Denis   A: Las, JAr

Owner: Michel & Frédéric Magnien   4 Rue Ribordot, 21200 Morey-Saint-Denis
Frédéric Magnien works with his father to make the wines on the family domaine but also makes a large number of *négociant* wines under his own label. The 11-ha domaine includes some excellent sites, mostly in the communes of Morey-Saint-Denis and Gevrey-Chambertin but they have only been bottling all of their production since 1994. The Magnien style is for richness and extract combined with lots of new oak. The wines are succulent, fleshy and richly fruity, with fine ripe tannins, at least in the best years. A lighter hand is needed in merely good years to avoid overly tannic, structured wines. The 1997s and 98s are not likely to be encountered due to their withdrawal following a bacterial contamination in the new cellars. With their own premises sealed off, Frédéric was fortunate to be offered winemaking facilities *chez* DUJAC in 1999. The resulting wines show a lot of new oak but have the fruit to match. While the top reds will keep, the hedonistic pleasure that just five or six years' age brings, will sway many wine drinkers. The balance in the 2000s and 2001s is less satisfactory and shows a marked contrast. A little Charmes-Chambertin and other Morey-Saint-Denis are also made. (PW)

Domaine Michel Magnien et Fils:

- **Clos de la Roche**★★★ £F ● **Clos Saint-Denis**★★★★ £G
- **Gevrey-Chambertin** Seuvrées★★★ £D Aux Echezeaux★★★ £D 1er Cru Les Cazetiers★★★ £F
- **Morey-Saint-Denis** 1er Cru Aux Charmes★★★ £E 1er Cru Les Milandes★★★ £E Les Chaffots★★★ £E
- **Chambolle-Musigny** Les Fremières★★ £D

DOM. MATROT Meursault   A: C&B, BBR, Gau, GFy, MCW

Owner: Matrot family   12 Rue de Matray, 21190 Meursault

The shape of this domaine will evolve as another Matrot estate, that of Thierry's sister, comes into existence. Currently the wines may appear under any of three labels (Thierry, Pierre or Joseph Matrot). Thierry is a devoted *vigneron*, bestowing great care on his vines, ensuring low yields and harvesting as late as possible. He is not a huge fan of new oak and is not an advocate of *bâtonnage* but produces rich, powerful and structured whites, sometimes with more than a hint of sulphur when young. The wines can seem a little awkward at first, but all the *premiers crus* should have a minimum of five years' age before they are ready. Amongst the reds, both Volnay Santenots and Blagny are ripe, long and quite classy. (PW)

- O **Meursault** 1er Cru Perrières★★★★ £F 1er Cru Blagny★★★ £E 1er Cru Charmes★★★ £F
- O **Meursault**★★ £E Chevalière★★ £E
- O **Puligny-Montrachet** 1er Cru Les Chalumeaux★★★ £F 1er Cru Les Combettes★★★★ £F
- **Blagny** 1er Cru La Pièce sous le Bois★★★ £E Volnay Santenots★★★ £E

MÉO-CAMUZET Vosne-Romanée www.meo-camuzet.com   A: BBR, Fie, RsW,Sec

Owner: Jean Méo   11 Rue des Grands Crus, 21700 Vosne-Romanée

One of Burgundy's great 20th-century winemakers, Henri Jayer, made the wines from this Domaine between 1945 and 1988. The rich legacy of prime vineyards that belonged to Étienne Camuzet provided Jayer with the opportunity to make some magnificient wines both for himself and others. The Méo-Camuzet label has only been around since the 1980s but most of that Camuzet legacy is now in the hands of the current generation, who have built up the holdings to 15 ha. Jean-Nicolas Méo, son of Jean Méo, continues with the Jayer method, including total destemming, cold pre-fermentation maceration and an extended *cuvaison* and 100 per cent new oak. The new oak is nearly always in evidence but there is a polish and a completeness that is the hallmark of these wines. At a lower level there is not the purity or intensity of others, especially at comparable prices, but the Cros Parentoux and Richebourg and increasingly the Corton and Echezeaux are very classy, very exciting wines. They have always been expensive and as good as some of them are, there's better value to be had. (PW)

- **Richebourg**✪✪✪✪✪ £H ● **Clos de Vougeot**★★★ £H ● **Echezeaux**★★★★ £H
- **Corton**★★★★ £H ● **Vosne-Romanée** 1er Cru Cros Parentoux★★★★ £H
- **Vosne-Romanée**★★★ £F 1er Cru Les Chaumes★★★ £G 1er Cru Aux Brulées★★★★ £H
- **Nuits-Saint-Georges**★★★ £F 1er Cru Aux Boudots★★★ £G 1er Cru Aux Murgers★★★★ £G

FRANÇOIS MIKULSKI Meursault   A: Eno, GFy, Han, N&P, Sec, Blx

Owner: François Mikulski   5 Rue de Leignon, 21190 Meursault

François is one of the newest stars of the Côte de Beaune and makes the sort of wines that get noticed. He has 7 ha and concentrates on Meursault. The wines are ripe and full-bodied and develop a creamy, honeyed richness with even a little age. Most convincing and complete of three *premiers crus* is the Genevrières, which has the structure to match the concentration. Yet a deeply flavoured, citrusy Poruzots and a floral, exotic old-vine Charmes are in much the same style. A regular Meursault is rich and ripe too but if you find the Meursaults out of reach then there's ripe, fruity Bourgogne Blanc and Aligoté that don't lack for flavour or character. Two reds, a Meursault and a Volnay, are also made but these don't as yet show the flair of the whites. (PW)

O **Meursault**★★ £E 1er Charmes★★★ £F 1er Cru Genevrières★★★★ £F 1er Cru Poruzots★★★ £F
O **Bourgogne Blanc**★★ £B O **Bourgogne Aligoté**★ £B

HUBERT DE MONTILLE Volnay   A: HHB, OWL, HRp, CTy, GFy

Owner: Hubert et Étienne de Montille Rue de Pied de la Vallée, 21190 Volnay
One of the leading producers of both Volnay and Pommard, Hubert de Montille was well-known for
his dislike of high alcohol wines and has always kept chaptalisation to an absolute minimum. He also
favoured fermentation at high temperatures and an extended *cuvaison* followed by a low percentage of
new oak. The wines? They showed great dimension and depth but also tended to have a lot of extract
and tannin, only opening out with 10 years' age, but vintages since 1998 have been made by Hubert's
son Étienne. The wines are now a little less formidable, with finer tannin yet without sacrificing their
elegance and individuality. Of the Pommards, the Rugiens is that little bit more intense and classy but
all three are full and stylish. The Volnays can be a little lighter, though are full and concentrated in a
year like 1999; the Taillepieds reveals great length and finesse. An extremely good Puligny Cailleret,
made initially by Jean-Marc ROULOT, is now also made by Étienne. (PW)

● **Pommard** 1er Cru Rugiens★★★★ £F 1er Cru Grands Epenots★★★ £F 1er Cru Pézerolles★★★ £F
● **Volnay** 1er Cru★★★ £E 1er Cru Champans★★★ £F 1er Cru Mitans★★★ £F 1er Cru Taillepieds★★★★ £F
O **Puligny-Montrachet** 1er Cru Cailleret★★★★ £F

BERNARD MOREY Chassagne-Montrachet   A: BWC, A&B, Las, DDr, HHB, CTy

Owner: Bernard Morey 21190 Chassagne-Montrachet
Bernard Morey is a true *vigneron* and takes great pride in his vineyards. Vines are replaced individually
and propagated from the best old vines rather than bought-in clones. As a result the average vine age
is increasingly high as is the health and balance in the vineyards. He also favours late picking and
produces ripe, ample and flavoursome whites with well-integrated oak. Of the consistently fine
Chassagne-Montrachet, the Vieilles Vignes come from almost 80-year-old vines as does the Vide
Bourse and both show very ripe fruit, with lots of depth and richness if not the definition and structure of the Caillerets or Morgeots. A rich powerful, minerally but stylish Puligny La Truffière can be
even better. Several other Chassagne-Montrachets (including a very good *premier cru* Les Macharelles)
are made from grapes purchased as part of the *négociant* side of the business. A little Bâtard-
Montrachet is also made. The reds, particularly both Chassagnes, can be good but suffered a little at
the hands of the elements in 2000 and 2001. (PW)

O **Chassagne-Montrachet** 1er Cru Caillerets★★★★ £E 1er Cru Morgeot★★★★ £E
O **Chassagne-Montrachet** 1er Cru Embrazées★★★ £E 1er Cru Vide Bourse★★★ £E
O **Chassagne-Montrachet** Vieilles Vignes★★★ £E 1er Cru Baudines★★★ £E
O **Puligny-Montrachet** 1er Cru La Truffière★★★★ £F O **Saint-Aubin** 1er Cru Charmois★★ £C
O **Santenay** 1er Cru Passetemps★★ £D
● **Chassagne-Montrachet** Vieilles Vignes★ £C 1er Cru Clos Saint-Jean★★ £D
● **Santenay** Vieilles Vignes★ £C 1er Cru Passetemps★ £D Grand Clos Rousseau★ £D
● **Beaune** 1er Cru Grèves★★ £E   ● **Maranges** 1er Cru La Fuissière★ £C

DOM. MARC MOREY Chassagne-Montrachet   A: Gau, HHC, JAr

Owner: Bernard Mollard 3 Rue Charles Paquelin, 21190 Chassagne-Montrachet
Bernard Mollard now makes outstanding whites from a small 9.5-ha domaine that has improved
year-on-year under his direction. All the vineyards lie within or close to Chassagne-Montrachet. An
excellent, minerally village-level example is structured, with good citrus intensity and can be drunk

young or kept for three or four years. The *premiers crus* are all classy, with depth, intensity and fine structure. Les Vergers is tight and minerally in contrast to a more forward, fatter, more obvious Virondot. Cailleret and Morgeot are both rich and concentrated. The top wine is a powerful, classy and complex Bâtard-Montrachet. A very respectable Bourgogne Blanc is always attractive and fruity with decent acidity. Some Saint-Aubin comes from the Les Charmois *premier cru* adjacent to Chassagne-Montrachet, while some Puligny Les Pucelles is currently out of production. Prices are reasonable for the quality, with excellent 2000s but generally very good since 1998. A significant amount of red is made too. These are slightly austere when young but, while the regular version can lack for ripeness, Morgeot has attractive red fruit and good breadth. (PW)

O **Bâtard-Montrachet**✪✪✪✪✪ £G
O **Chassagne-Montrachet** 1er Cru Morgeot★★★★ £E 1er Cru Cailleret★★★★ £E
O **Chassagne-Montrachet** 1er Cru En Virondot★★★ £E 1er Cru Les Vergers★★★★ £E
O **Chassagne-Montrachet**★★ £D 1er Cru Les Chenevottes★★★ £E
O **Bourgogne Blanc**★ £B ● **Chassagne-Montrachet** 1er Cru Morgeot★★ £C

PIERRE MOREY/MOREY BLANC Meursault   A: HRp, L&W, MCW, Res, Tan

Owner: Pierre Morey 13 Rue Pierre Mouchoux, 21190 Meursault
Pierre Morey is one of Burgundy's most highly regarded white winemakers, making the wines for Domaine Leflaive as well as those of his own. He has nearly 3 ha of Pinot Noir as well as 6 for whites, (predominantly Chardonnay but some Aligoté too). The wines build great richness and opulence with age, becoming nutty, buttery and peachy. Of his own estate wines there's intense minerally depth in the Meursault Perrières and indisputable class and complexity in the Bâtard-Montrachet. The wines can have quite a lot of sulphur and are generally quite closed when young. Buy these wines to cellar and give them at least five to six years from a good vintage. Good Bourgogne Blanc and Aligoté are usually better with a couple of years too. Reds include good Pommard Epenots. Morey Blanc is the label for the *négociant* wines, made to the same high standards but from bought-in grapes. (PW)

Pierre Morey:

O **Bâtard-Montrachet**✪✪✪✪✪ £H
O **Meursault**★★ £E Tessons★★★ £F 1er Cru Perrières★★★★ £F
O **Bourgogne Blanc**★ £B O **Bourgogne Aligoté** £B
Morey Blanc:
O **Meursault**★★ £E Navaux★★★ £E 1er Cru Genevrières★★★ £E O **Saint-Aubin** 1er Cru Combes★★ £C

DOM. ALBERT MOROT Beaune   A: Hal, N&P, Res

Owner: Choppin family Avenue Charles Jaffelin, 21200 Beaune
This 7-ha domaine, based on vineyards acquired in the 1890s, has until very recently been run by Mademoiselle Choppin, whose grandfather Albert Morot ran a *négociant* business. From the beginnning of the new millennium her nephew, Geoffroy Choppin de Janvry, has been in charge. The domaine is unusual in that it produces almost exclusively *premier cru* Beaune from the heart of the richest vein of *crus* on the slopes behind the town. The only exception is a sturdy but concentrated *premier cru* Savigny, with impressive depth and length for the appellation. All the wines see a percentage of new oak after an extended maceration, resulting in wines that can be quite robust and meaty when young but with a great propensity to age, especially in top vintages. All of the wines are of a high standard and all deserve at least five years' cellaring; a rich, concentrated and classy Teurons can be the most satisfying but is at least matched for complexity by an old-vine Bressandes. As well as three other *premiers crus*, a miniscule amount of Grèves is also made. New with the 2001 vintage is some Beaune Les Aigrots, sited closer to Pommard than the existing *premiers crus*. (PW)

- **Beaune** ler Cru Bressandes★★★★ £E ler Cru Teurons★★★★ £E
- **Beaune** ler Cru Cent Vignes★★★ £E ler Cru Marconnets★★★ £E ler Cru Toussaints★★★ £E
- **Savigny-lès-Beaune** ler Cru Bataillère aux Vergelesses★★★ £E

DENIS MORTET   Gevrey-Chambertin   A: BBR, DDr, Sec, WSc, HHB

Owner: Denis Mortet   22 Rue de l'Église, 21220 Gevrey-Chambertin
One of the truly outstanding Gevrey estates, with 11 ha of fine *premiers crus* and some of the best village *lieux-dits*. Denis Mortet's first vintage under his own name was as recent as 1992, after he and his brother Thierry (who also makes fine Gevrey and Chambolle-Musigny) split up the former Domaine Charles Mortet. After a flying start the wines have continued to improve. As with all the best *vignerons*, there is attention to each and every vine. What matters is the yield and health of each individual plant rather than an average low yield, which may disguise overbearing vines offset by poorly specimens. Rigorous selection, total destemming, a pre-fermentation maceration and a long *cuvaison* are important to the style, while the type and percentage of new oak is carefully adapted to each different *cuvée*. These are marvellously complete wines, full, ripe and rich and with everything in balance. The one criticism, that the oak and extraction were slightly overdone, has been countered in the most recent vintages, which show still greater refinement and harmony. Apart from the regular Gevrey-Chambertin and the Marsannay, all the wines should be drunk with five years' ageing or more, and closer to 10 from a vintage like 1999. New are a village Gevrey-Chambertin En Derée from very old vines and a straight Gevrey-Chambetin Premier Cru, a blend of several lesser known *premiers crus*. A touch of reduction can be a problem if the reds are drunk very young. A little Aligoté and Bourgogne Blanc are also made. (PW)

- **Chambertin✪✪✪✪** £H ● **Clos de Vougeot**★★★★ £G
- **Gevrey-Chambertin** ler Cru En Champeaux★★★★ £F ler Cru Lavaux Saint-Jacques★★★★ £F
- **Gevrey-Chambertin** Au Vellé★★★ £E En Champs★★★ £E En Motrot★★★ £E
- **Gevrey-Chambertin**★★★ £E La Combe de Dessus★★★ £E
- **Chambolle-Musigny** ler Cru Beaux Bruns★★★★ £F ● **Marsannay** Les Longeroies★★ £D
- **Bourgogne Rouge**★★ £C

MUGNERET-GIBOURG/GEORGES MUGNERET   Vosne-Romanée A: HRp, L&S, OWL

Owner: Mugneret family   5 Rue des Communes, 21700 Vosne-Romanée
Sisters Marie-Christine and Marie-Andrée, assisted by their mother, make consistently refined wines from this 8.8-ha estate. The original vineyards of the property are sold under the Mugneret-Gibourg label while those acquired by their widely respected late father, Dr Georges Mugneret, are sold under his name. Most of the vineyards are taken care of by others on a sharecropping basis. The grapes are now fully destemmed and the wine is given a maceration on the skins both before and after a fermentation at relatively high temperatures. Up to 80 per cent new oak is used for the *grands crus*, each one being made in small quantities, but all the wines show a measure of oak. They also have a lovely ripe pure Pinot fruit within a firm structure and there is real class, style and definition to each. The village wines and the elegant, seductive Chambolle-Musigny need five years, the complex, refined Chaignots and the *grands crus* eight or more. (PW)

- **Clos de Vougeot**★★★★ £F ● **Ruchottes-Chambertin**★★★★ £F ● **Echezeaux**★★★★ £F
- **Chambolle-Musigny** ler Cru Les Feusselottes★★★★ £E ● **Vosne-Romanée**★★★ £D
- **Nuits-Saint-Georges**★★★ £D ler Cru Les Chaignots★★★ £E ● **Bourgogne Rouge**★ £C

JACQUES-FRÉDÉRIC MUGNIER Chambolle-Musigny www.mugnier.fr A: HHB, HRp, Sec

Owner: Jacques-Frédéric Mugnier   Château de Chambolle-Musigny, 21220 Chambolle-Musigny
The early 18th-century Château de Chambolle-Musigny is rather at odds with the style of the wines here. For me, the architecture of the building pales beside the elegance, finesse even grandeur of these, at times, sublime wines. Since taking charge in 1984, Frédéric Mugnier has not only refined the practices on this small 4-ha estate (grape quality and selection are paramount and high fermentation temperatures are a feature of the vinification) but he has also pursued his passion for flying as a commercial airline pilot (as an aerial photo on the website shows). Don't come looking for powerful blockbusters; not even the more robust Bonnes Mares, the most sturdy of these wines, offers that. And if it's masses of oak, extract and flesh you want in your glass, then again look elsewhere. Building in richness and complexity with age, these are beautiful wines true to their appellations and with wonderful finesse and harmony. The regular Chambolle-Musigny can be a little slight but there's a hint of nobility even here. (PW)

● **Musigny**✪✪✪✪✪ £H ● **Bonnes Mares**★★★★ £G
● **Chambolle-Musigny**★★★ £E 1er Cru Les Fuées★★★ £F 1er Cru Les Amoureuses★★★★★ £G

MICHEL NIELLON Chassagne-Montrachet   A: OWL, BBR, RRI

Owner: Niellon family   1 Rue du Nord, 21190 Chassagne-Montrachet
This domaine is remarkably small considering some of the plaudits it has received. The wines are made in quite a reductive manner (with minimal aeration), the oak is restrained and the wines tight and intense when young. The *grands crus* are usually brilliant but the *premiers crus*, while often very good, do not approach the same level in the way that that they do at other estates. At their best there is depth, fine fruit concentration and good style. When tasted young the wines can be a bit reduced but will usually come round with aeration. At any rate all the wines deserve at least five to six years' age. Some Chassagne-Montrachet Premier Cru Vergers used to be made but is currently being replanted. The *grands crus* are very expensive due to their scarcity and reputation; the *premiers crus* can be bought for prices more in line with their quality but don't offer better value than other examples. (PW)

○ **Chevalier-Montrachet**✪✪✪✪✪ £H   ○ **Bâtard-Montrachet**✪✪✪✪✪ £H
○ **Chassagne-Montrachet** 1er Cru Les Chaumées★★★ £F 1er Cru Clos de la Maltroie★★★ £F
○ **Chassagne-Montrachet**★★ £E 1er Cru Champs Gain★★★ £F 1er Cru Clos Saint-Jean★★★ £F

JEAN-MARC PAVELOT Savigny-lès-Beaune   A: JTD, DDr, Res

Owner: Pavelot family   1 Chemin des Guettottes, 21420 Savigny-lès-Beaune
A superior domaine in an appellation with a reputation for providing wines with plenty of fruit and body, though they can also be a bit coarse and simple too. Not so here. Jean-Marc Pavelot has *premiers crus* from Savigny's more northern band, where the wines are generally lighter and more elegant, but also in the southern group of *premiers crus* (nearer Beaune), where the wines are fuller but firmer yet all his wines have a grace and charm that sets them apart. From the northern band both a vigorous Guettes and a seductive Aux Gravains reveal delicious fruit and a stylish complexity with a little age; Narbantons and Peuillets from closer to Beaune are fuller, meatier but less stylish. La Dominode comes from very old vines and is the richest and most complete Savigny. Regular red and white Savigny have ample fruit and good structure and are great drinking with a little bottle-age. The *premiers crus* are capable of ageing for at least eight to ten years, though I doubt many are kept that long. Jean-Marc's son, Hughes, is now taking over the winemaking responsibility. (PW)

● **Savigny-lès-Beaune** 1er Cru La Dominode★★★ £D
● **Savigny-lès-Beaune** 1er Cru Aux Gravains★★★ £D 1er Cru Narbantons★★★ £D

● **Savigny-lès-Beaune**★★ £C I er Cru Peuillets★★ £D I er Cru Guettes★★ £C
● **Pernand-Vergelesses** I er Cru Les Vergelesses★★ £C O **Savigny-lès-Beaune**★★ £C

DOM. PAUL PERNOT ET FILS Puligny-Montrachet A: JAr, Bal, L&S, HRp, Las, BWC

Owner: Pernot family 7 Place du Monument, 21190 Puligny-Montrachet

The owners of this relatively large estate of 19 ha only bottle a portion of the grapes they grow, but it is very good. The remainder must be gratefully received by the merchants. Paul Pernot is assisted by two of his sons and makes concentrated, powerful whites that become increasingly rich and honeyed with age. There's arguably not the definition or poise of a Domaine Leflaive equivalent but there is wonderful proportion and balance despite the wines' size, and real finesse as well as great complexity in the *premiers* and *grands crus*. Several Côte de Beaune reds are also made, including a Volnay Premier Cru Les Carelles. The *grands crus*, though hardly cheap, are better priced than most others and the village Puligny-Montrachet is remarkably good value. (PW)

O **Bâtard-Montrachet**✪✪✪✪✪ £G O **Bienvenues-Bâtard-Montrachet**✪✪✪✪✪ £G
O **Puligny-Montrachet**★★★ £E I er Cru Folatières★★★★ £F I er Cru Les Pucelles★★★★ £F
O **Bourgogne Blanc**★ £C ● **Beaune** I er Cru Teurons★★ £D ● **Pommard** Noizons★★ £D

PERROT-MINOT Morey-Saint-Denis www.perrot-minot.com A: Bal, Blx, F&R, HHB

Owner: Henri Perrot-Minot 54 Route des Grands Crus, 21220 Morey-Saint-Denis

Christophe Perrot works with his father to produce wines less extracted than previously but still with impressive power and intensity. The wines can still be quite austere and firm when young but nearly always have the fruit richness underneath to reveal great style and individuality with seven or eight years' age or more. Though all the wines are true to the general style, they are also true to their appellations and individual *terroirs*. The Chambolle-Musigny Premier Cru La Combe d'Orveau, adjacent to Le Musigny, is arguably the most classy and complex wine of all, though the *grands crus*, particularly the Chambertin, contrast with greater power and structure. The standard of the range is consistently high, with good Bourgogne Rouge at a lower level. The purchase of the Pernin-Rossin domaine in Vosne-Romanée has enlarged the family's holdings to 14 ha. These exciting new wines include some old-vine Nuits-Saint-Georges La Richemone and some Vosne-Romanée Les Beaux-Monts. The first releases would seem to have already obtained the same balance, intensity and combination of elegance and vigour seen in the existing wines. (PW)

● **Chambertin**★★★★ £G ● **Charmes-Chambertin**★★★★ £F ● **Mazoyères-Chambertin**★★★★ £F
● **Chambolle-Musigny** I er Cru La Combe d'Orveau★★★★ £F
● **Chambolle-Musigny** Vieilles Vignes★★★ £E I er Cru Les Fuées★★★ £F
● **Morey-Saint-Denis** En la Rue de Vergy★★★ £E I er Cru La Riotte Vieilles Vignes★★★ £F
● **Gevrey-Chambertin**★★★ £E ● **Bourgogne Rouge**★★ £B

JEAN PILLOT ET FILS Chassagne-Montrachet A: C&C, Eno, BBR, Res, CTy, JNi

Owner: Pillot family Rue Combard, 21190 Chassagne-Montrachet

Jean-Marc Pillot runs this family domaine of 10 ha. The estate's reputation, like that of the commune (albeit only in modern times), is for whites, yet half the vines are Pinot Noir and this is an increasingly good source of red Chassagne. The whites have long been good but have become more consistent and richer, riper and oakier under Jean-Marc's hand. There is now marvellous concentration, breadth and depth in the top *premiers crus*. A bottle from a fine vintage is particularly rewarding. The reds show proper ripeness and richness too; a particularly oaky version (labelled L'Exception) of the otherwise very good Morgeots was made in 1999. The range is continuing to expand and, as well as very good estate wines, some very fine Puligny-Montrachet Premier Cru Les Caillerets and Chevalier-Montrachet is made from bought-in wine. Good Saint-Romain white, red Santenay and Bourgogne red and white are made in most vintages too. The wines have been labelled both as Jean Pillot et Fils and Jean-Marc Pillot. (PW)

O **Chassagne-Montrachet** 1er Cru Les Chevenottes★★★★ £E   1er Cru Caillerets★★★★ £E
O **Chassagne-Montrachet** 1er Cru Morgeots★★★★ £E 1er Cru Les Vergers★★★ £E
O **Chassagne-Montrachet**★★ £D   1er Cru Les Macherelles★★★ £E   1er Cru Les Champs Gain★★★ £E
O **Puligny-Montrachet**★★★ £D
● **Chassagne-Montrachet**★ £C 1er Cru Les Macherelles★★ £D 1er Cru Morgeots★★★ £D

DOM. PONSOT   Morey-Saint-Denis   www.domaine-ponsot.com   A: M&V, Bal, Goe, L&W

Owner: Ponsot family   17-21 Rue de la Montagne, 21220 Morey-Saint-Denis
This is a very serious traditional and historic family estate that places huge importance on *terroir* and respect for the soil and the natural order. Laurent Ponsot has gradually assumed control from his father, Jean-Marie over the past decade or so. Several decades of expertise and refinement can be seen in the wines. The Ponsots undertake to pick the grapes as late as possible from vines with an average age of 40 years, though some individual parcels are as much as twice that age. Yields are very low, and naturally so without any green harvesting, which is abhorred. The Ponsots do not have a high tolerance for new oak or sulphur either and their use is kept to a minimum. No two wines are quite alike but there is a strength underpinning the truly marvellous expression and fine, silky textures that can be spellbinding. Though a charge of inconsistency has often been levelled at the domaine's wines, there seems little evidence of this in recent vintages, particularly since the atypically good 1997s. The Morey-Saint-Denis white, made mostly from Aligoté in recent vintages, is very full and ripe but structured too, not remotely like most Aligoté. A very small amount of Chambertin is also made. Village Gevrey and Morey can be superb value. (PW)

● **Clos de la Roche** Vieilles Vignes✪✪✪✪✪ £H   ● **Clos Saint-Denis** Vieilles Vignes✪✪✪✪✪ £H
● **Griotte-Chambertin**✪✪✪✪✪ £G   ● **Chapelle-Chambertin**★★★★ £G
● **Morey-Saint-Denis** Cuvée des Grives★★★ £E   1er Cru Alouettes★★★★ £E
● **Gevrey-Chambertin** Cuvée de l'Abeille★★★ £D   ● **Chambolle-Musigny** 1er Cru Les Charmes★★★ £F
O **Morey-Saint-Denis** Clos des Mont-Luisants★★★ £E

NICOLAS POTEL   Nuits-Saint-Georges   A: GFy, Bib, BBR, L&W, Tan, JNi, WSc

Owner: Nicolas Potel   21 Rue Thurot, 21700 Nuits-Saint-Georges
Nicolas Potel is the hottest new *négociant* in town. He fashioned some seriously good reds with his late father at the Domaine de la Pousse d'Or until 1997 and since then has been employing his talents on an extensive range of bought-in wines. Volnay is still a strength but now he makes a host of others to a generally high standard, though there is some variability, more perhaps as a result of the disparate sources than anything else. Already well-established are some stylish, fragrant Volnays, concentrated Pommards and full, quite classy Nuits-Saint-Georges. His Clos de Vougeot is a marvellous example of this frustratingly uneven *grand cru*. Though there is now a very extensive range only a relative handful have a sufficient track record to include here. It is to be hoped that the best sources become long-standing. Echezeaux, Grands Echezeaux, Bonnes Mares, Romanée Saint-Vivant and Vosne-Romanée *premiers crus* are also made and still newer wines include Charmes-Chambertin, Chambertin-Clos de Bèze and other northern Côte de Nuits *premiers* and *grands crus*. (PW)

● **Clos de Vougeot**★★★★ £F
● **Nuits-Saint-Georges** 1er Cru Les Saint-Georges★★★ £E   1er Cru Roncières★★★ £E
● **Nuits-Saint-Georges** 1er Cru Vaucrains★★★ £E   ● **Volnay** 1er Cru Santenots★★★ £E
● **Volnay** Vieilles Vignes★★ £D   1er Cru Champans★★★ £E   1er Cru Pitures★★★ £E
● **Pommard** 1er Cru Epenots★★★ £E   1er Cru Rugiens★★★ £E

● **Beaune** 1er Cru Epenottes ★★ £D   1er Cru Grèves★★ £D
● **Savigny-lès-Beaune**★★ £C   ● **Bourgogne Rouge** Maison Dieu Vieilles Vignes★★ £B

RAMONET   Chassagne-Montrachet   A: C&B, Far, OWL, Res, HRp

Owner: Ramonet family   21190 Chassagne-Montrachet
Ramonet is another of the great white Burgundy estates. There is a division of responsibilities between brothers Jean-Claude and Noël Ramonet but it is Noël who makes the wines. There are 17 ha of mostly first-rate Chassagne-Montrachet vineyard plus a little of three *grands crus* in Puligny, which makes for a fantastic array of wines. The winemaking is somewhat intuitive and responsive to the vintage conditions but usually results in wines that have an explosive concentration and breadth within a powerful structure. Only occasionally has anything less than very good wine been produced in the last couple of decades but there is some variability, with a tendency to be almost too structured and slightly hard in some instances. Others have lacked balance, with excess alcohol for the fruit concentration, and there can be a reductive quality in others. However these are the exceptions and can be avoided by taking the precaution of tasting and/or comparing notes of a specific wine and vintage before adding one or more of these great wines to a cellar (an approach advisable not just here but anywhere that involves the kind of sums the world's best wines now command). Reds play second fiddle to the whites but have been very good in recent good vintages including some Chassagne-Montrachet Premier Cru La Boudriotte (owned by Noël Ramonet and sold under his own label). A little Montrachet is made, as is some Puligny-Montrachet Premier Cru Champ Canet, while some Chevalier-Montrachet is produced from bought-in wine. (PW)

O **Bâtard-Montrachet**✪✪✪✪✪ £H   O **Bienvenues-Bâtard-Montrachet**★★★★ £H
O **Chassagne-Montrachet** 1er Cru Caillerets★★★★ £F   1er Cru Grandes Ruchottes★★★★ £F
O **Chassagne-Montrachet**1er Cru Boudriottes★★★ £F   1er Cru Morgeots★★★ £F
O **Chassagne-Montrachet**★★ £E   1er Cru Les Chaumées★★★ £F   1er Cru Les Vergers★★★ £F
O **Saint-Aubin** 1er Cru Le Charmois★★ £D   O **Bourgogne Aligoté**★ £B
● **Chassagne-Montrachet**★ £D   1er Cru Clos Saint-Jean★★ £E   1er Cru Morgeots★★ £E
● **Chassagne-Montrachet** 1er Cru Clos de la Boudriotte★★★ £E

DOM. RAPET PÈRE ET FILS   Pernand-Vergelesses   A: Anl, Goe, Res, HRp

Owner: Rapet family   Rue des Paulands, 21420 Pernand-Vergelesses
The input of Vincent Rapet over recent vintages has given a considerable boost to this long-established domaine. Though some two-thirds of the 18 ha are planted to Pinot Noir, the reputation rests as much with the whites as reds. The core of the production is very good Pernand-Vergelesses but fine examples of Corton and Corton-Charlemagne are also made. There is now better grape selection, the whites have longer lees-contact than previously and show good depth, richness and restrained oak. Reds can be sturdy, occasionally with slightly coarse tannins, but generally show more refinement and depth in the most recent vintages, particularly in the very stylish Pernand-Vergelesses. All the better reds should be drunk with five years' or more, but whites can be drunk younger. New from 1999 is a second Beaune *premier cru*, Grèves. From the 2000 vintage white Pernand-Vergelesses is now being bottled as separate specified *premiers crus* (including Le Clos du Village, En Caradeux and Sous Frétille) following the recent promotion of some village land. (PW)

● **Corton**★★★★ £E   ● **Corton** Pougets★★★★ £E
● **Pernand-Vergelesses** 1er Cru Les Vergelesses★★ £D   1er Cru Île de Vergelesses★★★ £E
● **Beaune** 1er Cru Clos du Roi★★★ £D   ● **Aloxe-Corton**★★ £D
O **Corton-Charlemagne**★★★★ £F   O **Pernand-Vergelesses** En Caradeux★★ £D

PATRICE & MICHÈLE RION Nuits-Saint-Georges   A: M&V, NYg, UnC

Owner: Rion family 21700 Prémeaux-Prissey

Some very good wine was made by Patrice Rion for his own label even before he handed over the winemaking reins at the family domaine (Daniel RION ET FILS) to his two brothers. From 2000 the range here has been greatly expanded to include bought-in wines but these are labelled as simply Patrice Rion. Given an insistence on high-quality fruit, this promises to be a good quality range of *négociant* wines. Selected *cuvées* that appear on a regular basis will be rated in the future but will include both village examples and *premiers crus* from Nuits, Vosne and Gevrey. (PW)

Patrice & Michèle Rion:

● **Chambolle-Musigny** Les Cras★★★ £E ● **Bourgogne Rouge** Bons Batons★★ £D

DOM. DANIEL RION ET FILS Nuits-Saint-Georges   A: M&V, N&P, JNi, WSc

Owner: Rion family 21700 Prémeaux-Prissey

Christophe and Olivier are now making the wines here on their own after the departure of their brother, Patrice (Patrice & Michèle RION), following the 2000 vintage. Over the course of two decades Patrice had established a solid reputation for this estate created by his father. The 19 ha is based primarily on Nuits-Saint-Georges and Vosne vineyards and includes some Chardonnay and Aligoté as well as Pinot Noir. The wines have long been characterised by their strength and a certain firmness allied to depth and intensity. In recent years there has been a gradual shift to finer tannins and more immediate richness and the wines are particularly successful in the best years, if sometimes a little harsh or tough in lighter vintages. New with the 1998 vintage was some Echezeaux as well as some Clos de Vougeot from a different source to that previously made. (PW)

● **Clos de Vougeot**★★★★ £F
● **Vosne-Romanée**★★ £D 1er Cru Chaumes★★★ £E 1er Cru Beaux-Monts★★★ £E
● **Nuits-Saint-Georges** 1er Cru Clos des Argillières★★★ £E 1er Cru Hauts-Pruliers★★★ £E
● **Nuits-Saint-Georges** 1er Cru Vignes Rondes★★★ £E Vieilles Vignes★★★ £E
● **Nuits-Saint-Georges** Lavières★★ £D Grandes Vignes★★ £D
● **Chambolle-Musigny** 1er Cru Charmes★★★ £E ● **Côte de Nuits-Villages**★ £C

ANTONIN RODET Mercurey www.rodet.com   A: Par, C&R, MCW

Owner: Worms & Cie Antonin Rodet, 71640 Mercurey

Directed by Bertrand Devillard, this is a *négociant* house with substantial holdings in both the Côte d'Or and Côte Chalonnaise. The following estates are all either owned, partly owned or made and distributed by Antonin Rodet: Château de Rully (Rully), Château de Mercey (Maranges-based for Hautes Côtes de Beaune red and white, and Mercurey), Château de Chamirey (Mercurey), Domaine des Perdrix (Bertrand Devillard's own 12-ha property in Nuits-Saint-Georges) and the Meursault-based Domaine Jacques Prieur. The later is run in conjunction with co-owner Martin Prieur and its previously flagging reputation has been at least partly restored in recent years by Rodet's winemaker, Nadine Gublin. The Jacques Prieur whites are rich, ripe and powerful though sometimes at the expense of expression and finesse and include *grands crus* Le Montrachet, Chevalier-Montrachet and Corton-Charlemagne. Reds include *grands crus* Musigny, Echezeaux, Chambertin, Clos de Vougeot and Corton Bressandes; and *premiers crus* from Volnay (Santenots and *monopole* Clos des Santenots) and Beaune (Grèves and *monopole* Clos de la Féguine). Though the reds are richer, fresher with better depth and length than previously, there's not yet the quality or consistency of the top Rodet or Perdrix wines and for this reason they have not yet been rated. The best wines under the Antonin Rodet label (many of them designated Cave Privée) are consistently very good indeed, at times quite oaky but rich and ripe, with great depth and complexity. Those listed include some of the best wines made on a regular basis. At a humbler level there are some remarkably good Côte Chalonnaise wines under the respective estate labels. In addition, as well as a range of Vin de Pays d'Oc varietals Antonin Rodet also owns the Domaine de l'AIGLE in Limoux, Languedoc-Roussillon. (PW)

Antonin Rodet
- **Charmes-Chambertin★★★★** £G ● **Clos de Vougeot★★★★** £G
- **Gevrey-Chambertin** 1er Cru Estournelles★★★★ £F
- **Nuits-Saint-Georges** 1er Cru Les Saint-Georges★★★ £F 1er Cru Porêts-Saint-Georges★★★★ £F
- O **Meursault** 1er Cru Perrières★★★★ £F O **Bourgogne Blanc** Vieilles Vignes★★ £C

Domaine des Perdrix
- **Echezeaux★★★★** £G ● **Vosne-Romanée★★★** £E
- **Nuits-Saint-Georges★★★** £E 1er Cru Aux Perdrix★★★★ £F

Château de Chamirey
- O **Mercurey★** £C 1er Cru La Mission★★ £D ● **Mercurey★★** £C 1er Cru Les Ruelles★★★ £D

Château de Mercey
- O **Bourgogne Hautes-Côtes de Beaune★** £B O **Mercurey★** £C
- **Bourgogne Hautes-Côtes de Beaune★** £B ● **Mercurey** 1er Cru En Sazenay ★★ £C

Château de Rully
- O **Rully★★** £C ● **Rully★** £C

DOM. DE LA ROMANÉE-CONTI Vosne-Romanée　　　　　　A: C&B, BBR, F&R

Owner: de Vilaine and Leroy/Bize/Roch families 1 Rue Derrière le Four, 21700 Vosne-Romanée
DRC, as it referred to by both devotees and novices alike, is considered by many to be Burgundy's greatest domaine. The history and nobility of these famous *grand cru* vineyards make this a difficult assertion to refute, though over the past decade this domaine has been seriously challenged by part-owner Lalou Bize-Leroy's own estate, Domaine LEROY. Any serious text on Burgundy will provide background on both the estate and individual wines. Currently yields are lower than previously, the average vine age is now high across all the wines and the viticulture is now essentially biodynamic (in practice if not in name), making for healthier soils than previously. The most distinctive features of the vinification are that there is little or no destemming and automatic punching down is carried out. All the wines see 100 per cent new oak. Individual wines seem to have had slight ups and downs and my own experience of both recent and older vintages is not sufficient in order to be able assert whether all the wines do indeed rate five stars, although there seems little doubt that all have the potential. Montrachet apart, all are made in decent quantities by Burgundian standards, assuming, that is, you can afford them. The holdings are: La Romanée Conti (1.81 ha), La Tâche (6.06 ha), Richebourg (3.51 ha), Romanée-Saint-Vivant (5.28 ha), Echezeaux (4.67 ha), Grands-Echezeaux (3.53 ha) and the solitary white, Le Montrachet (0.68 ha). All the wines are £H. The first two are *monopoles* and are considered the brightest stars in the firmament, while the other reds account for a substantial proportion of the vineyard area of their respective appellations. (PW)

EMMANUEL ROUGET Vosne-Romanée　　　　　　A: J&B, RsW, BBR, Blx, Sec

Owner: Emmanuel Rouget Flagey-Echezeaux, 21700 Vosne-Romanée
Emmanuel Rouget is the nephew of Henri Jayer and has retained a portion of the vineyards that Jayer, one of the great 20th-century figures in Burgundy, made famous. Jayer's use of a cold pre-fermentation maceration, 100 per cent destemming, plenty of new oak, no filtration and rigorous attention to hygiene transformed the face of Burgundy as many others followed in his footsteps. Rouget's early efforts looked promising but some of the wines from vintages in the late 1990s seem to have lost a

bit of the vigour of old, though no there is no lack of style or class. Prices are very high. (PW)

● **Echezeaux**★★★★ £H
● **Vosne-Romanée**★★ £G   1er Cru Les Beaumonts★★★ £H   1er Cru Cros Parentoux★★★★ £H
● **Nuits-Saint-Georges**★★ £F   ● **Bourgogne Rouge**★ £C

DOM. ROULOT   Meursault   www.domaineroulot.com   A: DDr, HHC, JAr, BWC

Owner: Roulot family   1 Rue Charles Giraud, 21190 Meursault
Since 1989 Jean-Marc Roulot has run this highly respected domaine with a hatful of Meursault *crus*,
built up by his father Guy some 30 years earlier. The wines show something of a leesy character and
and some new oak influence but neither dominate and the percentage of new oak is sometimes less
than 20 per cent. The *premiers crus* Charmes, Perrières (and more recently, Bouchères) are the top
wines, the Perrières easily the most complex and complete of the three, but this is reflected in their
prices. The most significant proportion of the estate's 12 ha comes from vineyards lying on higher
slopes running towards Auxey-Duresses. Les Tessons and Les Tillets (from vines with a high average
age) are arguably the pick of these and offer relatively good value for Meursault. Though majoring on
Meursault, Roulot also produces an intense, vibrant, minerally Monthelie *premier cru* that adds
richness with two or three years' age. Bourgogne Aligoté and a flavoursome, scented Bourgogne Blanc
are more than dependable. (PW)

O **Meursault** 1er Cru Bouchères★★★ £F   1er Cru Charmes★★★ £F   1er Cru Perrières★★★★ £F
O **Meursault** Meix Chavaux★★ £D   Les Luchets★★★ £D   Les Tessons★★★ £D   Les Tillets★★★ £D
O **Meursault** Les Vireuils★★★ £D
O **Monthelie** 1er Cru Champs Fulliot★★ £C   O **Bourgogne Blanc**★ £B

DOM. ROUMIER   Chambolle-Musigny   www.roumier.com   A: JAr, HHC, HRp, M&V, Tan, Res

Owner: Christophe Roumier   Rue de Vergy, 21220 Chambolle-Musigny
A fabulous domaine whose wines express the essence of Chambolle-Musigny. Christophe Roumier
has now had two decades of input, achieving ever better balance in his vineyards and maximising the
potential of each site. The vines are of a high average age and low-yielding, but naturally so without
the need for the excessive pruning or green harvesting required elsewhere. Quality is consistently high
but that is not to say the wines are the same year in, year out; rather each expresses something of the
vintage without its defects. What is most impressive is the structure of the wines; always there's a
dimension and depth without a trace of hardness, allied to harmony and persistence. The
Chambolles, in particular, are fragrant and elegant with more power, depth and concentration in the
premiers crus. In the *grands crus* the power and elegance of Le Musigny contrasts with the muscle,
intensity and grip of Bonnes Mares. From outside Chambolle-Musigny, the 2.5-ha *monopole* Clos de
la Bussière in Morey-Saint-Denis produces a firmer, tighter wine, now showing more refinement and
class than previously, and it can be very good value (as with the four-star 1998). Tiny amounts of very
high quality Ruchottes-Chambertin and Charmes-Chambertin are also made, as is a little Corton-
Charlemagne. (PW)

● **Le Musigny**✪✪✪✪✪ £H   ● **Bonnes Mares**✪✪✪✪✪ £H
● **Chambolle-Musigny**★★★ £D   1er Cru Les Cras★★★★ £F   1er Cru Les Amoureuses✪✪✪✪✪ £G
● **Morey-Saint-Denis** 1er Cru Clos de la Bussière★★★ £E   ● **Bourgogne Rouge**★ £B

DOM. ARMAND ROUSSEAU   www.domaine-rousseau.com   A: HRp, BBR, HBJ, OWL, Res

Owner: Charles Rousseau   1 Rue de l'Aumônerie, 21220 Gevrey-Chambertin
Eric Rousseau and his sister, Corinne are gradually assuming control of this the most famous Gevrey-

Chambertin domaine that has been directed by their father, Charles Rousseau, for more than 40 years. The estate was built up in the early part of the 20th century by their grandfather Armand but was further enlarged by Charles. A remarkable 8 ha of the 14 ha planted exclusively to Pinot Noir are *grands crus*. The top wines, Chambertin and Chambertin Clos-de-Bèze, show all the class and breed of great *grand cru* Burgundy, with a breadth and presence in the mouth that even the very best *premiers crus* lack. These and the Clos Saint-Jacques receive 100 per cent new oak but the oak treatment is rarely, if ever, excessive, though shows more in the Clos-de-Bèze than the Chambertin. Other *crus* receive at most 30 per cent new oak. In the Charmes-Chambertin and Mazy-Chambertin finesse and elegance are emphasised yet there is a vigour and intensity about all the wines. The textures of all the Rousseau wines are very impressive too, even if other wines may provide greater richness and extract. Only a small percentage of the stems are retained to assist a moderately long vinification complete with automatic *pigeage*. All the wines need five years, the top wines 10 or more. The *premier cru* Lavaux Saint-Jacques, normally part of the regular Gevrey, was bottled separately in 1999 and 2000. (PW)

● **Chambertin✪✪✪✪** £H ● **Chambertin Clos-de-Bèze✪✪✪✪** £H
● **Charmes-Chambertin★★★★** £F ● **Clos de la Roche★★★** £F
● **Mazy-Chambertin★★★★** £F ● **Ruchottes-Chambertin** Clos des Ruchottes★★★★★ £F
● **Gevrey-Chambertin★★★** £E 1er Cru Les Cazetiers★★★★ £F 1er Cru Clos Saint-Jacques★★★★★ £G

ETIENNE SAUZET www.etienne-sauzet.com A: HHC, OWL, BBR, Res, Tan, JAr, WSc

Owner: Gérard & Jeanine Boudot 11 Rue de Poiseul, 21190 Puligny-Montrachet
This estate has a fabulous reputation and highly respected winemaker in Gérard Boudot. However it is now significantly smaller than it once was. Gérard's wife, Jeanine Boudot, grand daughter of Étienne Sauzet, has retained only a third of the vines, though their company has another third under contract for some time to come (the rest of the legacy has gone to brother Jean-Marc BOILLOT). There are now 8 ha (but much boosted by bought-in grapes) with small amounts of four *grands crus* (Bâtard-Montrachet, Bienvenues-Bâtard-Montrachet, Le Montrachet and Chevalier-Montrachet) and more significant amounts of some of Puligny's best *premiers crus*. Yet form in the 1990s has been irregular and despite good richness in most of the 98s, and some of the 99s, the 2000s seem a notch or two lower again. Some of the class and finesse for which they are famous remains but they are also leaner and less than should be expected of their respective appellations. Nor have some of the wines aged as well as previously. High demand has of course contributed to high prices but despite a recent drop the wines are currently overpriced for the quality. Whether *grand cru*, *premier cru*, village level or Bourgogne Blanc there are better and less expensive examples from other producers. Given the current lapse in quality the *grands crus* (all £H) have not been rated. (PW)

O **Puligny-Montrachet★★** £E 1er Cru Les Folatières★★ £F 1er Cru La Garenne★★★ £F
O **Puligny-Montrachet** 1er Cru Les Combettes★★★★ £F 1er Cru Les Referts★★★ £F
O **Puligny-Montrachet** 1er Cru Champ-Canet★★★ £F 1er Cru Les Perrières★★★ £F

COMTE SENARD Aloxe-Corton A: AnI, F&R

Owner: Senard family 21420 Aloxe-Corton
Philippe Senard was one of those to work with the controversial consultant Guy Accad in the early 1990s, aiming for more colour and greater aroma and fruit intensity, in part from an extended cold maceration on skins prior to fermentation. Like other producers advised by Accad, he has gradually incorporated the best of his advice to make stylish, aromatic and intensely fruity red Burgundies. Some of the lesser wines can struggle for full ripeness but typically there is a cool, pure vibrant fruit intensity to which is added more breadth, length and elegance in the various Cortons. This is a good cellar from which to compare several different Cortons. Bressandes and Clos du Roi show lots of

intensity and depth, En Charlemagne a cool, classy fruit and good dimension. All deserve at least five years' age. Good whites are also made, including an Aloxe-Corton from old-vine Pinot Gris, but the vines are still young for the Corton and Corton-Charlemagne. Other reds include a Chorey-lès-Beaune and a *premier cru* Beaune. (PW)

● **Corton** Bressandes★★★ £F ● **Corton** Clos du Roi★★★ £F ● **Corton** Clos de Meix★★★ £F
● **Corton** En Charlemagne★★★ £F
● **Aloxe-Corton**★★ £D   1er Cru Les Valozières★★ £E
○ **Corton** Blanc★★ £F ○ **Corton-Charlemagne**★★ £F ○ **Aloxe-Corton**★★ £D

CHRISTIAN SÉRAFIN   Gevrey-Chambertin   A: Eno, Goe, BBR, IGH

Owner: Christian Sérafin   7 Place du Château, 21220 Gevrey-Chambertin
Christian Sérafin has been quietly working away on his family's small 5-ha estate, gradually refining his winemaking practices and producing ever more satisfying and consistently good wines. His signature is the power that might be expected from Gevrey together with plenty of oak and spice that embellish wines that are lush and fruit-rich, with lots of obvious appeal. The top *crus* add more class and breadth. The best wine made in any real quantity is the Vieilles Vignes bottling, which is meaty and full of ripe fruit, with plenty of depth. All the wines show very well with just five years' age. A tiny amount of top-quality Charmes-Chambertin is also made but is likely to be hard to find. (PW)

● **Gevrey-Chambertin** 1er Cru Les Cazetiers★★★★ £F 1er Cru Les Corbeaux★★★ £F
● **Gevrey-Chambertin**★★ £E Vieilles Vignes★★★ £E 1er Cru Fontenys★★★ £F
● **Chambolle-Musigny** 1er Cru Les Baudes★★★ £F ● **Morey-Saint-Denis** 1er Cru Les Milandes★★★ £F

DOM. CHARLES THOMAS   Nuits-Saint-Georges   A: CRs

Owner: Thomas family   2 Rue François Mignotte, 21700 Nuits-Saint-Georges
This is the domaine of the Thomas family previously known as Domaine Thomas-Moillard. The *négociant* arm, Moillard-Grivot, is run separately. Although a lot of generic Bourgogne is made, almost half of the 50 ha is of Côte-de-Nuits *crus*, including several *grands crus*. At the core of the domaine are some sizeable plots of Vosne-Romanée and Nuits-Saint-Georges, with two *monopoles* (Clos de Thorey and Clos des Grandes Vignes) in the latter. Some of the vines are under a share-cropping arrangement with leading growers but the growers' half is bought back too. The grapes are fully destemmed and most wines are vinified in special stainless steel vats with rotating arms. The resulting wines are usually deep in colour, firm and sturdy in their youth, with marked tannin and extract. The *monopoles* are particularly robust, but becoming full and meaty, with good depth and complexity in the best examples, after a minimum of five to eight years' ageing. Top *premiers* and *grands crus* (made in traditional vats) see plenty of new oak but also show the expected class and character. Good Beaune, Pommard and Volnay are also made from the recently acquired Domaine des Obiers. Lesser reds are more inconsistent and most whites lack sophistication. The Moillard-Grivot (Thomas Frères) wines have tended to be softer, simpler and rarely exciting. (PW)

● **Romanée-Saint-Vivant**★★★★ £G ● **Bonnes Mares**★★★★ £G ● **Chambertin Clos-de-Bèze**★★★ £G
● **Corton** Clos du Roi★★★ £G ● **Clos de Vougeot**★★★ £G
● **Vosne-Romanée** 1er Cru Les Beaumonts★★★ £F 1er Cru Les Malconsorts★★★ £F
● **Nuits-Saint-Georges** 1er Cru Clos de Thorey★★ £E 1er Cru Clos des Grandes Vignes★★ £E
● **Nuits-Saint-Georges**★ £D Les Porets-Saint-Georges★★ £E Les Richmones★★ £E
● **Beaune** Grèves★★ £D ● **Savigny-lès-Beaune**★ £C

TOLLOT-BEAUT   Chorey-lès-Beaune   A: DDr, L&W, OWL, Tan, HHB

Owner: Tollot families   Rue Alexandre Tollot, 21200 Chorey-lès-Beaune

Tollot-Beaut's 24-ha estate includes some of the northern Côte de Beaune's lesser but better-value appellations. With lots of new oak and ripe, forward fruit, the wines have had plenty of appeal in the past but also a tendency to lack a little structure despite some firm tannins and some have aged quite quickly. However since 1999 the wines have shown better definition and balance and, if less upfront, will have much more to offer with four or five years' age than previously. It has always been a team effort but the current members in charge, Nathalie, Jean-Paul and Olivier, look set to make better wines than ever before. Yields have been lowered, though they were never high. The Chorey-lès-Beaune is a very attractive, relatively inexpensive red Burgundy. Only a little white is made but includes some Corton-Charlemagne. There are new labels but prices remain much the same. Ratings apply to the most recent vintages only. (PW)

● **Corton**★★★ £F ● **Corton** Bressandes★★★★ £F
● **Aloxe-Corton**★★ £D 1er Cru Vercots★★ £E 1er Cru Fournières★★★ £E
● **Beaune** 1er Cru Clos du Roi★★★ £E 1er Cru Grèves★★★ £E ● **Chorey-lès-Beaune**★★ £C
● **Savigny-lès-Beaune** 1er Cru Champs Chevrey★★ £D 1er Cru Lavières★★ £D

DOM. TRAPET PÈRE ET FILS   www.domaine-trapet.com   A: C&B, C&C, Res

Owner: Jean et Jean-Louis Trapet   53 Route de Beaune, 21220 Gevrey-Chambertin

The original Domaine Louis Trapet (source of some famous bottles from the 1950s and 60s) was built up from the late 19th century before being divided in 1990 between Jean and his sister (Rossignol-Trapet). Jean's son, Jean-Louis, has revived their venerable vineyards, which include nearly 2 ha of Chambertin and decent segments of Chapelle-Chambertin and Latricières-Chambertin. The raw material is now of much higher quality than previously, with reduced yields from higher than typical vine densities under a regime that has become progressively more biodynamic in the late 1990s. The 13 ha also includes some excellent *premier cru* Petite Chapelle and Clos Prieur as well as village Gevrey-Chambertin and Marsannay. There is a measured use of new oak but the accent is on the quality of the fruit and producing wines of finesse and real class. From relatively limited tastings it is apparent that there is a particular strength and definition characteristic to the wines, which require patience. Five years' is needed for Gevrey, five to 10 for the *premiers crus*, and a minimum of 10 for Chambertin. Given time these wines are some of the best from Gevrey and are reasonably priced in that context. (PW)

● **Chambertin**★★★★★ £G
● **Gevrey-Chambertin**★★★ £D 1er Cru Petite Chapelle★★★★ £F 1er Cru Clos Prieur★★★★ £F
● **Marsannay**★★ £C

VERGET   A: Far, L&S, L&W, BBR

Owner: Jean-Marie Guffens-Heynen & others   71960 Sologny

In just over a decade Jean-Marie Guffens has constructed a merchant house of remarkable constitution. It is not built around the great *crus* of the Côte de Beaune, though there are some of those, but rather the less hallowed vineyards of the Mâconnais and increasingly Chablis, where a new winemaking base has been established in conjunction with Olivier LEFLAIVE for their joint but independent use. The Maconnais wines (including Pouilly-Fuissé, Saint-Veran and various Mâcon-Villages) are covered, together with the wines of his own private estate, GUFFENS-HEYNEN in the Mâconnais and Beaujolais section. The wines from the Côte d'Or are true to the Verget style, which is one of great extract, concentration and richness, made from fully ripe grapes sourced from low-yielding vineyards. The wines from Chablis are also deep and concentrated but a little tighter, cooler and more minerally than his other wines (particularly in contrast to the Mâconnais wines). Largely eschewing the use of oak here, the wines are riper and fuller, if slightly less steely, than examples from other producers but nevertheless archetypal Chablis and very fine. Almost all of the Verget wines can be broached fairly young but should keep for a decade. (PW)

O **Bâtard-Montrachet★★★★** £H   O **Corton-Charlemagne★★★★** £E
O **Meursault** Tillets★★★★ £E   Rougeots★★★ £E   O **Chassagne-Montrachet** Franchemont★★★ £E
O **Puligny-Montrachet** Enseignières★★★ £F   1er Cru Sous le Puits★★★ £F
O **Chablis Grand Cru** Bougros Côte de Bougueyraud★★★★ £F
O **Chablis Premier Cru** Les Forêts★★★ £D   Montée de Tonnerre★★★ £E   Vaillons★★★★ £D

AUBERT ET PAMÉLA DE VILLAINE   Bouzeron   A: C&B

Owner: Aubert et Paméla de Villaine   2 Rue de la Fontaine, 71150 Bouzeron
It still seems remarkable that the co-director of the Côte d'Or's most prestigious estate (Domaine de la ROMANÉE-CONTI) should choose to make wine in the Côte Chalonnaise but Aubert de Villaine and his wife Paméla have done so to great acclaim. More than half of 21 ha is planted to Aligoté (the grape which dominates the appellation) and a fine characterful example is produced as well as some red Mercurey and white Rully. The wines are elegant and harmonious with real depth and intensity in the Mercurey Montots. All are better with two or three years' age, even the Aligoté. (PW)

● **Mercurey** Montots★★ £C   ● **Bourgogne Pinot Noir** La Digoine★★ £C
O **Rully** Saint-Jacques★★ £C   O **Bouzeron Aligoté★★** £B

DOM. COMTE GEORGES DE VOGÜÉ   Musigny   A: Men, DWS, JAr, BBR, Blx, Far, Sec

Owner: Ladoucette family   Rue Sainte Barbe, 21220 Chambolle-Musigny
This estate is known for one of the single greatest red Burgundies made. The Musigny has an exalted reputation based in part on the on-going quality of the wine but also on some legendary old vintages (including 1945, 47, 59, 69 and 72). The domaine owns 7.2 ha of the 10.7 ha *grand cru*, though this includes 0.5 ha of Musigny Blanc (recently sold as Bourgogne Blanc), the only place in the commune of Chambolle-Musigny where Chardonnay is permitted to be grown. François Millet has made the wines here since the Comte died in 1986 and his daughter took over the running of the estate. Vine age is high and yields vary but are kept low; adjustments are made where necessary in response to vintage conditions. The approach to vinification is also vintage-responsive, with individual parcels of vineyard treated in different ways, though a long *cuvaison* is favoured. Since 1990 few if any expert tasters have been left in any doubt about the true greatness of the Musigny Vieilles Vignes after some leaner offerings in the 1970s and 80s. The wine is now more deeply coloured than previously and its extraordinary aromatics, with preserved fruits and floral notes, precede a considerable structure that underpins the silky texture, wonderful definition and mouthfilling dimension on the palate that becomes increasingly opulent with age, the intense flavours being sustained long on the finish. Its remarkable longevity from top vintages make it a cellaring must for the few who can afford it. There is wonderful class, intensity and concentration in the Amoureuses too; and a rich, sturdy, darker fruit density to the Bonnes Mares. (PW)

● **Musigny** Vieilles Vignes❁❁❁❁❁ £H   ● **Bonnes Mares★★★★** £H
● **Chambolle-Musigny★★★** £F   1er Cru Les Amoureuses★★★★ £H

DOM. DE LA VOUGERAIE www.domainedelavougeraie.com A: Hay, M&V, L&W, BWC

Owner: Boisset Rue de l'Église, 21700 Premeaux-Prissey

This newcomer is a southern Côte de Nuits-based estate that comprises all of Boisset's (Burgundy's single biggest producer) own vineyards. Boisset recruited Pascal Marchand, the very highly regarded winemaker of the Clos des Epeneaux (Comte ARMAND) in Pommard, to direct operations. He made the wines in 1999 but has only assumed full responsibility for both viticulture and winemaking from 2000. The vineyards total an impressive 37 ha, which are certified organic and now treated biodynamically, predominantly planted to Pinot Noir and much of it in the Côte de Nuits. Yields are low (less than 30 hl/ha in the reds), which is immediately apparent in wines of richness, depth and class. Gevrey-Chambertin and Nuits-Saint-Georges feature, including some *premier cru* sites, while *grands crus* run to Corton Clos du Roi, Clos de Vougeot, Bonnes Mares, Charmes-Chambertin and a third of a hectare of Musigny. It is early yet to assess more than a few of the wines but nearly all promise to be, at the very least, good examples of their respective appellations. Corton-Charlemagne and the solely-owned Vougeot *cru* are already very good whites. (PW)

- ● **Clos de Vougeot★★★★** £F ● **Charmes-Chambertin★★★★** £F
- ● **Vougeot** 1er Cru Les Cras★★★ £F ● **Vougeot** Clos du Prieuré★★★ £E
- ● **Gevrey-Chambertin** 1er Cru Les Evocelles★★★★ £F ● **Bourgogne Rouge★★** £B
- ○ **Vougeot** 1er Cru Clos Blanc de Vougeot★★★★ £F
- ○ **Corton-Charlemagne★★★★** £F

CÔTE D'OR & CÔTE CHALONNAISE/OTHER WINES OF NOTE

This list includes notable wines from a range of producers but is not intended to be a comprehensive list of a given producer's wines; just those that we have encountered. In some instances there may be several more good wines.

STÉPHANE ALADAME ○ **Montagny** 1er Cru £C 1er Cru Cuvée Selection £C 1er Cru Les Coères £C
FRANÇOIS D'ALLAINES ○ **Montagny** £C ○ **Rully** Saint-Jacques £C
○ **Saint-Aubin** 1er Cru En Remilly £D
ROBERT AMPEAU ○ **Puligny-Montrachet** 1er Cru Combettes £F
○ **Meursault** £E 1er Cru Pièce sous le Bois £F 1er Cru Perrières £F
○ **Auxey-Duresses** 1er Cru Ecusseaux £D ● **Volnay** 1er Cru Santenots £F
● **Savigny-lès-Beaune** 1er Cru Lavières £D
HERVÉ ET CYPRIEN ARLAUD ● **Charmes-Chambertin** £F
● **Morey-Saint-Denis** £E 1er Cru Ruchots £F
ARNOUX PÈRE ET FILS ● **Beaune** 1er Cru Cent Vignes £D ● **Savigny-lès-Beaune** £C
● **Savigny-lès-Beaune** 1er Cru Vergelesses £D ● **Chorey-lès-Beaune** Confrelins £C
JEAN-CLAUDE BACHELET ○ **Saint-Aubin** 1er Cru Les Champlots £C
○ **Puligny-Montrachet** £E 1er Cru Sous le Puits £E
BACHELET-RAMONET ○ **Chassagne-Montrachet** £D 1er Cru Caillerets £E 1er Cru Grde Montagne £E
● **Chassagne-Montrachet** 1er Cru Clos Saint-Jean £D
DOM. BERTAGNA ● **Vougeot** 1er Cru Petits Vougeots £F 1er Cru Clos de la Perrière £F
PIERRE BERTHEAU ● **Chambolle-Musigny** 1er Cru £E 1er Cru Charmes £F
BILLARD-GONNET ● **Pommard** £D 1er Cru Chaponnières £E 1er Cru Pezerolles £E
● **Pommard** 1er Cru Rugiens £F
VINCENT BITOUZET-PRIEUR ○ **Meursault** Clos du Cromin £E 1er Cru Perrières £F
● **Volnay** £D 1er Cru Pitures £E
JEAN-MARC BOULEY ● **Volnay** £ D 1er Cru Clos de la Cave £D 1er Cru Caillerets £D
● **Pommard** 1er Cru Frémiers £E 1er Cru Rugiens £E
RENÉ BOURGEON ● **Givry** £B Baraude £C ○ **Givry** Clos de la Brulée £B

DOM. RENÉ BOUVIER ○ **Marsannay** Vieilles Vignes £C Le Clos £C ● **Fixin** Crais de Chêne £C
● **Marsannay** Longeroies £C En Ouzeloy £C Clos du Roy £C Champs Salomon £C
● **Morey-Saint-Denis** 1er Cru Genevrières £E ● **Gevrey-Chambertin** Jeunes Rois £D
● **Gevrey-Chambertin** Racines du Temps Très VV £E 1er Cru Petite Chapelle £F 1er Cru Les Cazetiers £F
● **Chambolle-Musigny** 1er Cru Les Noirots £F ● **Clos Saint-Denis** £G
JEAN-CLAUDE BRELIÈRE ○ **Rully** 1er Cru Margotée £C
● **Rully** 1er Cru Préaux £C 1er Cru Montpalais £C
DOM. MICHEL BRIDAY ○ **Rully** Bergerie £B 1er Cru Grésigny £C
● **Rully** Quatre Vignes £B 1er Cru Champs-Cloux £C
CAVE DES VIGNERONS DE BUXY ● **Montagny** Domaine des Pierres Blanches £C
○ **Montagny** 1er Cru Cuvée Speciale £C 1er Cru Chaignots £C
DOM. CAILLOT ○ **Meursault** £D Limozin £E ○ **Bourgogne Blanc** £B
LUCIEN CAMUS-BRUCHON ● **Savigny-lès-Beaune** Liards Vieilles Vignes £C 1er Cru Lavières £D
● **Beaune** 1er Cru Clos du Roi £D ● **Pommard** 1er Cru Arvelets £E
○ **Savigny-lès-Beaune** Goudelettes £D
DOM. CARRÉ-COURBIN ● **Pommard** £D 1er Cru Grands Epenots
● **Volnay** £D Vieilles Vignes £E 1er Cru Les Lurets £E 1er Cru Robardelle £E
● **Volnay** 1er Cru Clos de la Cave des Ducs £E 1er Cru Taillepieds £E
CHANSON PÈRE ET FILS ○ **Beaune** Clos des Mouches £F ○ **Pernand-Vergelesses** Caradeux £E
● **Beaune** 1er Cru Grèves £E 1er Cru Clos des Fèves £F ● **Côte de Beaune-Villages** £C
CHARTRON & TRÉBUCHET ○ **Puligny-Montrachet** 1er Cru Clos des Caillerets £F
○ **Saint-Aubin** 1er Cru Châtenière £D ○ **Bourgogne Chardonnay** Jean Chartron Vieilles Vignes £C
CHÂTEAU DE LA SAULE ○ **Montagny** 1er Cru £C 1er Cru Vignes sur les Cloux £C
JEAN CHAUVENET ● **Nuits-Saint-Georges** £D 1er Cru Bousselots £E 1er Cru Damodes £E
● **Nuits-Saint-Georges** 1er Cru Vaucrains £F
HUBERT CHAUVENET-CHOPIN ● **Nuits-Saint-Georges** £C 1er Cru Murgers £D
● **Côte de Nuits-Villages** £B
CHOFFLET-VALDENAIRE ● **Givry** £B 1er Cru Clos de Choué £C 1er Cru Clos Jus £C
○ **Givry** Galaffres £B
DENIS ET FRANÇOISE CLAIR ● **Santenay** Clos Genet £C 1er Cru Clos de la Comme £C
● **Santenay** 1er Cru Clos des Tavannes £C
CLOS SALOMON ● **Givry** 1er Cru £C
DOM. ALAIN COCHE-BIZOUARD ○ **Meursault** Luchets £D 1er Cru Charmes £E
○ **Meursault** 1er Cru Gouttes d'Or £E ○ **Bourgogne Blanc** £B
VINCENT DANCER ○ **Meursault** Grands Charrons £E 1er Cru Perrières £F
○ **Chassagne-Montrachet** 1er Cru Romanée £F
JEAN-YVES DEVEVEY/DOM. DU BOIS GUILLAUME ● **Beaune** 1er Cru Pertuisots £D
○ **Hautes-Côtes de Beaune** Les Champs Perdrix £B
JEAN-PIERRE DICONNE ● **Auxey-Duresses** 1er Cru Duresses £C ○ **Auxey-Duresses** £C
DIGIOIA-ROYER ● **Chambolle-Musigny** Vieilles Vignes £E 1er Cru Groseilles £E 1er Cru Gruenchers £E
DAVID DUBAND ● **Nuits-Saint-Georges** £D 1er Cru Procès £E 1er Cru Pruliers £E
● **Bourgogne-Hautes Côtes de Nuits** £B
MAURICE ECARD ET FILS ● **Savigny-lès-Beaune** 1er Cru Narbantons £D 1er Cru Jarrons £D
● **Savigny-lès-Beaune** 1er Cru Serpentières £D
DOM. FOREY PÈRE ET FILS ● **Echezeaux** £F ● **Vosne-Romanée** 1er Cru Gaudichots £F
FOUGERAY DE BEAUCLAIR ● **Fixin** Clos Marion £D ● **Marsannay** Saint Jacques £C
DOMINIQUE GALLOIS ● **Gevrey-Chambertin** 1er Cru Combe aux Moines £E
PAUL GARAUDET ● **Monthelie** £C 1er Cru Clos Gauthey £C 1er Cru Duresses £D ● **Volnay** £D
JEAN-MICHEL GAUNOUX ○ **Meursault** £D 1er Cru Gouttes d'Or £E 1er Cru Perrières £E
GÉNOT-BOULANGER ○ **Chassagne-Montrachet** 1er Cru Chevenottes £E 1er Cru Vergers £E
JEAN-JACQUES GIRARD ● **Savigny-lès-Beaune** 1er Cru Lavières £C 1er Cru Peuillets £D
● **Savigny-lès-Beaune** 1er Cru Serpentières £D ○ **Savigny-lès-Beaune** £C
○ **Pernand-Vergelesses** Belles Filles £C
CAMILLE GIROUD ● **Beaune** 1er Cru Avaux £D 1er Cru Cras £D
● **Volnay** Clos des Chênes £E 1er Cru Carelles £E

ALBERT GRIVAULT ○ **Meursault** £D 1er Cru Perrières £E

GROS FRÈRE ET SOEUR ● **Clos de Vougeot** Musigni £F ● **Bourgogne-Hautes Côtes de Nuits** £B

HERESZTYN ● **Gevrey-Chambertin** £D 1er Cru Champonnets £E ● **Chambolle-Musigny** £D
● **Morey-Saint-Denis** 1er Cru Milandes £E

HUMBERT FRÈRES ● **Gevrey-Chambertin** £D 1er Cru Poissenots £E

DOM. LUCIEN JACOB ● **Savigny-lès-Beaune** £C ○ **Savigny-lès-Beaune** £C

DOM. JAYER-GILLES ● **Echezeaux** £H ● **Hautes Côtes de Nuits** £D
○ **Bourgogne-Hautes Côtes de Nuits** £D

DOM. JEANNIN-NALTET ● **Mercurey** Clos des Grands Voyens £C

DOM. JOBLOT ● **Givry** Pied de Chaume £C 1er Cru Servoisine £C
○ **Givry** Pied de Chaume £C ○ **Givry** 1er Cru Servoisine £C

VINCENT ET FRANÇOIS JOUARD ○ **Chassagne-Montrachet** 1er Cru Champ Gain £E
○ **Chassagne-Montrachet** 1er Cru Chaumées £E 1er Cru Maltroie £E 1er Cru Morgeot Fairendes £E

DOM. ÉMILE JUILLOT ● **Mercurey** £B 1er Cru Cailloute £C 1er Cru Croichots £C
● **Mercurey** 1er Cru Combins £C ○ **Mercurey** £B 1er Cru Cailloute £C

RENÉ LAMY-PILLOT ○ **Chassagne-Montrachet** £D, 1er Cru Morgeots £E;
● **Chassagne-Montrachet** 1er Cru Clos Saint-Jean £E 1er Cru Morgeots £E

DOM. LARUE ○ **Saint-Aubin** 1er Cru En Remilly £D 1er Cru Murgers des Dents de Chien £D
○ **Chassagne-Montrachet** £E

DOM. ALETH LE ROYER-GIRARDIN ● **Pommard** £D 1er Cru Charmots £E
● **Beaune** Clos des Mouches £D

DOM. LECHENAUT ● **Nuits-Saint-Georges** £D 1er Cru Cailles £F ● **Morey-Saint-Denis** £D
● **Vosne-Romanée** £E

DOM. LORENZON ● **Mercurey** £C 1er Cru Champs-Martin £C
○ **Mercurey** 1er Cru Croichots £C 1er Cru Champs Martin £C

JEAN-PAUL MAGNIEN ● **Morey-Saint-Denis** 1er Cru Faconnières £D ● **Chambolle-Musigny** £D

CHÂTEAU DE LA MALTROYE ○ **Chassagne-Montrachet** 1er Cru Clos du Château de Maltroye £E
● **Chassagne-Montrachet** 1er Cru Clos du Château de Maltroye £E ● **Santenay** 1er Cru Comme £D

JEAN-PHILIPPE MARCHAND ● **Gevrey-Chambertin** Vieilles Vignes £D
● **Gevrey-Chambertin** 1er Cru Lavaux Saint-Jacques £E

MAROSLAVAC-LEGER ○ **Puligny-Montrachet** 1er Cru Combettes £E 1er Cru Champgains £E

BERTRAND MAUME ● **Gevrey-Chambertin** 1er Cru £D 1er Cru Champeaux £D
● **Gevrey-Chambertin** 1er Cru Lavaux Saint-Jacques £E

ALAIN MICHELOT ● **Nuits-Saint-Georges** 1er Cru Chaignots £E 1er Cru Vaucrains £E
● **Morey-Saint-Denis** 1er Cru Charrières £E

JEAN-MARC MILLOT ● **Echezeaux** £F ● **Vosne-Romanée** £D

DOM. BERNARD MOREAU ET FILS ○ **Chassagne-Montrachet** 1er Cru Chevenottes £E
○ **Chassagne-Montrachet** 1er Cru Maltroie £E

DOM. MICHEL MOREY-COFFINET ○ **Chassagne-Montrachet** £D 1er Cru En Remilly £E
○ **Chassagne-Montrachet** 1er Cru Fairendes £E 1er Cru Romanée £E

THIERRY MORTET ● **Gevrey Chambertin** £D 1er Cru Clos Prieur £E
● **Chambolle-Musigny** £D 1er Cru Beaux Bruns £E

GÉRARD MOUTON ● **Givry** 1er Cru Clos Jus £C

GÉRARD MUGNERET ● **Vosne-Romanée** £D ● **Nuits-Saint-Georges** 1er Cru Boudots £E
● **Bourgogne Rouge** £B

DOM. LUCIEN MUZARD ET FILS ● **Santenay** 1er Cru Beauregard £C 1er Cru Clos Faubard £C
● **Santenay** 1er Cru Clos des Tavannes £C

PHILIPPE NADDEF ● **Gevrey-Chambertin** Vieilles Vignes £D 1er Cru Cazetiers £E

DOMAINE JEAN ET ANNICK PARENT ● **Monthelie** 1er Cru Duresses £C
● **Pommard** 1er Cru Rugiens £E

DOM. PARIZE PÈRE ET FILS ● **Givry** Champ Nalot £B 1er Cru Grandes Vignes £C
○ **Givry** 1er Cru Grandes Vignes £C

DOM. JEAN PASCAL ET FILS ○ **Puligny-Montrachet** 1er Cru Hameau de Blagny £E

FERNAND & LAURENT PILLOT ○ **Chassagne-Montrachet** 1er Cru Vergers £E 1er Cru Morgeots £E
○ **Chassagne-Montrachet** 1er Cru Vide Bourse £E 1er Cru Grande Ruchottes £E

O **Meursault** 1er Cru Caillerets £E ● **Pommard** 1er Cru Rugiens Peregrinus £F

PAUL PILLOT O **Chassagne-Montrachet** 1er Cru Caillerets £F O **Saint-Aubin** 1er Cru Charmois £D

HENRI PRUDHON O **Puligny-Montrachet** Les Enseignières £E

● **Saint-Aubin** Les Argillers £C 1er Cru Sentier du Clou £C

MICHEL PRUNIER O **Auxey-Duresses** Vieilles Vignes £C

DOM. RAGOT ● **Givry** 1er Cru Grande Berge £C

FRANÇOIS RAQUILLET ● **Mercurey** Vieilles Vignes £C 1er Cru Vasées £C 1er Cru Veleys £C

● **Mercurey** 1er Cru Puillets £C 1er Cru Naugues £C O **Mercurey** 1er Cru Veleys £C

HENRI ET GILLES REMORIQUET ● **Nuits-Saint-Georges** Allots £D 1er Cru Damodes £E

● **Nuits-Saint-Georges** 1er Cru Les Saint-Georges £E

ROBLET-MONNOT ● **Volnay** 1er Cru Brouillards £E 1er Cru Taillepieds £E

JOSEPH ROTY ● **Charmes-Chambertin** Tres Vieilles Vignes £G

● **Gevrey-Chambertin** 1er Cru Fontenys £F

DOM. MICHEL SARRAZIN ET FILS ● **Givry** Clos de la Putin £C 1er Cru Grands Pretants £C

O **Givry** Grognots £C

DOM. DE SUREMAIN ● **Monthelie** Château de Monthelie £C 1er Cru Sur La Velle £E

O **Rully** 1er Cru £C

H ET Y DE SUREMAIN ● **Mercurey** 1er Cru En Sazenay £C

JEAN TARDY ● **Clos de Vougeot** £G ● **Vosne-Romanée** Chaumes £F

JOSEPH VOILLOT ● **Volnay** £D ● **Pommard** £D

Author's Choice for Côte d'Or & Côte Chalonnaise (PW)

30 classic red Burgundies

MARQUIS D'ANGERVILLE ● **Volnay** 1er Cru Clos des Ducs

DOM. DE L'ARLOT ● **Nuits-Saint-Georges** 1er Cru Clos des Forêts-Saint-Georges

COMTE ARMAND ● **Pommard** 1er Cru Clos des Epeneaux

DOM. ROBERT ARNOUX ● **Vosne-Romanée** 1er Cru Les Suchots

GHISLAINE BARTHOD ● **Chambolle-Musigny** 1er Cru Les Charmes

BOUCHARD PÈRE ET FILS ● **Pommard** 1er Cru Rugiens

SYLVAIN CATHIARD ● **Romanée-Saint-Vivant**

ROBERT CHEVILLON ● **Nuits-Saint-Georges** 1er Cru Les Saint-Georges

BRUNO CLAIR ● **Gevrey-Chambertin** 1er Cru Les Cazetiers

CLOS DE TART ● **Clos de Tart**

DOM. DE COURCEL ● **Pommard** 1er Cru Grand Clos des Epenots

DOM. DUJAC ● **Clos de la Roche**

DOM. RENÉ ENGEL ● **Clos de Vougeot**

DOM. FAIVELEY ● **Chambertin Clos-de-Bèze**

GEANTET-PANSIOT ● **Charmes-Chambertin**

DOM. HENRI GOUGES ● **Nuits-Saint-Georges** 1er Cru Les Vaucrains

DOM. JEAN GRIVOT ● **Vosne-Romanée** 1er Cru Les Beaux Monts

ANNE GROS ● **Richebourg**

LOUIS JADOT ● **Gevrey-Chambertin** 1er Cru Clos Saint-Jacques

MICHEL LAFARGE ● **Volnay** 1er Cru Clos des Chênes

DOM. DES LAMBRAYS ● **Clos des Lambrays**

MÉO-CAMUZET ● **Vosne-Romanée** 1er Cru Cros Parentoux

HUBERT DE MONTILLE ● **Volnay** 1er Cru Taillepieds

DENIS MORTET ● **Gevrey-Chambertin** 1er Cru Lavaux Saint-Jacques

JACQUES-FRÉDÉRIC MUGNIER ● **Musigny**

DOM. PONSOT ● **Griotte-Chambertin**

DOM. ROUMIER ● **Bonnes Mares**

DOM. ARMAND ROUSSEAU ● **Chambertin**

DOM. TRAPET PÈRE ET FILS ● **Gevrey-Chambertin** 1er Cru Petite Chapelle

DOM. COMTES GEORGES DE VOGÜÉ ● **Musigny** Vieilles Vignes

15 consistently fine Côte de Beaune whites

DOM. GUY AMIOT ET FILS O Chassagne-Montrachet 1er Cru Les Caillerets
ROGER BELLAND O Chassagne-Montrachet 1er Cru Morgeot Clos Pitois
DOM. BONNEAU DU MARTRAY O Corton-Charlemagne
MICHEL BOUZEREAU ET FILS O Meursault 1er Cru Genevrières
LOUIS CARILLON O Puligny-Montrachet 1er Cru Perrières
GÉRARD CHAVY ET FILS O Puligny-Montrachet 1er Cru Folatières
JEAN-FRANÇOIS COCHE-DURY O Meursault 1er Cru Perrières
MICHEL COLIN-DELÉGER ET FILS O Puligny-Montrachet 1er Cru Les Demoiselles
JEAN-PHILIPPE FICHET O Meursault Tessons
VINCENT GIRARDIN O Chassagne-Montrachet 1er Cru Morgeot
PATRICK JAVILLIER O Meursault Les Tillets
DOM. DES COMTES LAFON O Meursault 1er Cru Charmes
DOM. LEFLAIVE O Puligny-Montrachet 1er Cru Les Pucelles
BERNARD MOREY O Chassagne-Montrachet 1er Cru Caillerets
DOM. ROULOT O Meursault 1er Cru Perrières

Mâconnais & Beaujolais

DANIEL ET MARTINE BARRAUD Pouilly-Fuissé   A: L&S, NYg

Owner: Daniel et Martine Barraud Le Bourg, 71960 Vergisson
This couple are leaders in differentiating and better defining the different terroirs of Pouilly-Fuissé. This large appellation has a little over twice the vineyard area of Meursault and there are considerable differences in both quality and style across the four communes it covers. Most of the Barrauds' 7 ha of vines are on the higher slopes of Vergisson, beneath the dramatic rock itself, where the grapes generally ripen a little later than in lower-lying vineyards. While new oak is employed, its use is generally well-judged. Wines from vineyards with an average vine age in excess of 40 years are designated Vieilles Vignes. The En Buland is the richest, most full-bodied of the various *cuvées*, though the Les Crays shows great concentration and intensity and a mineral influence, and La Roche more of a piercing mineral elegance. Of two Saint-Vérans, the lighter En Crèches shows more style than a fatter, more four-square Les Pommards. The Mâcon-Vergisson also comes from Vergisson vineyards but from just outside the Pouilly-Fuissé boundaries. The 2000s are particularly rich and powerful but with the fruit and structure to keep the best part of a decade (in the top *cuvées*). The wines remain reasonably priced for their quality. (PW)
O **Pouilly-Fuissé** La Roche★★★ £C Les Crays Vieilles Vignes★★★ £C En Bulands Vieilles Vignes★★★★ £D
O **Pouilly-Fuissé** En France★★ £C La Verchère Vieilles Vignes★★ £C
O **Saint-Véran** En Crèches★★ £B Les Pommards★★ £C
O **Mâcon-Vergisson** La Roche ★★ £B

ANDRÉ BONHOMME Viré-Clessé   A: DDr, WSc

Owner: André Bonhomme 71260 Viré
Bottling longer than anyone else in the Mâcon-Villages area (since 1957), in an attempt to be profitable rather than just accepting what the *négociants* were prepared to pay, André Bonhomme has a reputation as a reliable source for fine inexpensive white Burgundy. His 9 ha are manually harvested and there has always been a willingness to wait until the grapes are fully ripe. The wines are now made by André's son, Pascal, but this domaine has been the one of the few steady alternatives to the lean, acidic wines that are still too prevalent in the Mâconnais. The regular *cuvée* is vinified solely in vats but oak is used in part for the Cuvée Speciale and Vieilles Vignes, around a quarter new for the latter. Older wines, (they can

keep for up to five years), made before the new Viré-Clessé appellation came into being, are labelled as Mâcon-Viré. (PW)

O **Viré-Clessé**★ £B Cuvée Spéciale★★ £B Vieilles Vignes★★ £C

DOM. F ET J CALOT Morgon   A: HHB

Owner: François et Jean Calot   Le Bourg, 69910 Villié-Morgon

This 11.5-ha estate has long been an excellent source of ripe, concentrated and characterful Morgon. There are several *cuvées*, from a supple, fruity regular Cuvée Tradition to a deep, intense Vieilles Vignes that needs three years or so in order to soften a little. Vinification is traditional and not the semi-carbonic maceration favoured by most. An old-fashioned vertical press is employed and both small and large oak are used for ageing. A small amount of Tête de Cuvée and Cuvée Jeanne have also been made in recent vintages. All are very reasonably and honestly priced for the quality – there has been no attempt to sell any of the wines at a premium to enhance their status or cash flow as some growers in the region have done. (PW)

● **Morgon** Tradition★★ £B Vieilles Vignes★★ £B Tête de Cuvée★★ £B Cuvée Jeanne★★ £B

CH. DE FUISSÉ Pouilly-Fuissé www.chateau-fuisse.fr   A: ABy, BBR, Res

Owner: Vincent family   Château de Fuissé, 71960 Fuissé

Arguably Pouilly-Fuissé's most famous estate, it has been in the Vincent family since 1852 but has come to prominence under Jean-Jacques Vincent since he assumed control of the domaine in 1966. There are now 30 ha, mostly in the commune of Fuissé from which a number of different Pouilly-Fuissé *cuvées* are made, including three separate *climats* (Le Clos, Les Brûles, Les Combettes). All are vinified in oak followed by nine months' ageing in barrel. Saint-Véran, Mâcon-Villages and Mâcon-Fuissé are also made under the Château-Fuissé label. At their best, the top wines combine a ripe fruit intensity with excellent structure and depth. The wines can sometimes be a little reduced when young but usually come into their own with at least five years' age, which is what they deserve. A second range of wines is made under the Vincent label, in part from family domaines and in part from bought-in grapes. These include Pouilly-Fuissé, Saint-Véran (Domaine des Morats), Mâcon-Villages, Mâcon-Fuissé and two Beaujolais, Morgon Les Charmes and Juliénas Domaine le Cotoyon. (PW)

Château-Fuissé:
O **Pouilly-Fuissé**★★★ £D Les Combettes★★★ £D Le Clos★★★★ £E Vieilles Vignes★★★★ £E
O **Saint-Véran**★ £C

Vincent:
O **Pouilly-Fuissé**★★ £C   O Saint-Véran Domaine des Morats★★ £C

CH. DES JACQUES Moulin-à-Vent www.louis-jadot.com   A: HMA

*Owner: **Louis Jadot**   Château des Jacques, 71570 Romanèche-Thorins*

Long before its recent purchase by Louis JADOT, this was the leading estate in the Beaujolais region. Singular in its approach to vinification, with a Pinot-like destemming followed by fermentation in open tanks and *pigeage*, the wines have been richer, fuller and with none of the woodiness or greeness that the whole-bunch fermentation practised by others can bring. Following the arrival of Jadot's Jacques Lardière, maceration times have been extended and there is some use of automatic *pigeage*. In addition, five separate sites have been isolated from within the estate's 27 ha of Gamay vines and each of these is aged in new oak (Clos du Grand Carquelin, Clos de Rochegrès, Champ de Cour, La Roche and Les Thorins). So the Côte d'Or has come to Beaujolais and with some clout, in order to promote further efforts towards higher quality (and higher prices). It is too early to rate these wines and, though they show a previously unseen sumptuous, velvety quality, it remains to be seen just how much complexity and nobility of structure is possible from these terroirs and the Gamay grape. There are also 9 ha of Chardonnay from which the white Beaujolais (stainless steel-vinified) and Bourgogne Blanc (barrel-fermented and aged) are made. Combe aux Jacques doesn't come from this winery but is a separate facility dedicated to producing high-quality Beaujolais-Villages in conjunction with local growers. In 2001 Jadot added Château Bellevue, one of Morgon's most prized estates, where a similar prestigious string of *crus* is being made along the same lines as at Château des Jacques. (PW)

Château des Jacques:
● **Moulin-à-Vent**★★ £C
O **Beaujolais-Villages** Chardonnay★★ £B   O **Bourgogne Blanc** Clos de Loyse★★ £B

CH. DES RONTETS   Pouilly-Fuissé   A: Lib

Owner: Gazeau family   Château des Rontets, 71960 Fuissé
Claire Gazeau and her Italian husband, Fabio Montrasi, have transformed the wines from this old family property since the mid-1990s. There are just 6 ha but all are planted to Chardonnay. Being well-established, the average vine age is high (45 years in the Clos Varambon, 70 in Les Birbettes). The Clos Varambon is a fine example of Pouilly aged exclusively in large wood. Pierrefolle adds more depth and interest and a spicy component which derives in part from a small percentage of new oak. The top *cuvée*, Les Birbettes, has really superb fruit, which easily takes up the new oak (30 per cent), as well as excellent depth and is one of the most stylish examples of Pouilly-Fuissé. Though it is not inexpensive it outperforms many a more expensive village-level Chassagne or Puligny-Montrachet. (PW)
O **Pouilly-Fuissé** Clos Varambon★★ £C   Pierrefolle★★★ £D   Les Birbettes★★★ £D

CH. THIVIN   Côte de Brouilly   www.chateau-thivin.com   A: RHW, GWW, Wse

Owner: Claude & Evelyne Geoffray   Château Thivin, 69460 Odenas
Château Thivin is renowned for its Côte de Brouilly and is one of Beaujolais' historic properties, with medieval origins. The top *cuvée*, Zaccharie Geoffray, is named for one of Claude Geoffray's ancestors, who purchased the property in 1877. The 24 ha include a second domaine, Manoir du Pavé (from his wife's family), which is the source of a good Beaujolais-Villages. While ripe and supple with fine structures, the wines show real individual expression and distinctive fruit, with a mineral, floral and herbal quality that is unique to the local soils. Several other *cuvées* have been separately bottled recently and are made to the same standards, including La Chapelle, Clos Bertrand and La Croix Dessaigne. Prices are reasonable for the quality. (PW)
● **Côte de Brouilly**★★ £B   Zaccharie Geoffray★★★ £B
● **Brouilly**★ £B   ● **Beaujolais-Villages** Manoir du Pavé★ £B

CLOS DE LA ROILETTE/COUDERT   Fleurie   A: DDr, L&W, Sav

Owner: Coudert family   Clos de la Roilette, La Roilette, 69820 Fleurie
Within their 9.5 ha of vineyard, the Couderts possess the best part of La Roilette, the finest *climat* in Fleurie. The site gives Fleurie of more body, depth and complexity than is typical and theirs is a parcel of very old vines. The grapes are harvested very ripe and in the small amount of a special bottling called Cuvée Tardive there is more intensity and richness. The wines are sleek and supple, with a black fruit character and a subtle mineral streak. Both are consistently fine yet reasonably priced Beaujolais that drink well with anything from one to three years' age, occasionally more. (PW)
● **Fleurie**★★ £B   Cuvée Tardive★★★ £B

DOM. CORDIER PÈRE ET FILS   Pouilly-Fuissé   A: HHB, L&S, WSc

Owner: Cordier family   Les Molards, 71960 Fuissé

Since Christophe Cordier joined his father Roger, this estate's inherent potential has been further realised. Their vineyards are in the commune of Fuissé, where some of other big Pouilly-Fuissé names such as J A FERRET and CHÂTEAU DE FUISSÉ are to be found. The 13.5 ha also includes some Saint-Véran. The wines are very powerful, many of them high in alcohol, being made from very ripe, low-yielding fruit, but are still remarkably well-balanced. There is progressively more concentration and depth, as well as power, in the top *cuvées*. An intense minerality complements a preserved citrus and oak-derived spiciness in many of the wines. Prices are now high, even in the context of the higher prices Pouilly-Fuissé now commands, but so is the quality. Most of the wines can be drunk young for their dramatic, exuberant richness, though the most structured and profound, Vers Cras and Vers Pouilly, will be better with four or five years' age. As well as some Bourgogne Blanc (Jean de la Vigne) and two other *cuvées* of Pouilly-Fuissé (Au Métertière and Les Schistes), a little of an exotic blockbuster, Juliette la Grande, is also made. (PW)

O **Pouilly-Fuissé** Vignes Blanches★★★★ £D Vers Cras★★★★ £E Vers Pouilly★★★★ £E
O **Pouilly-Fuissé**★★★ £C Vieilles Vignes★★★ £D La Vigne de Mr. Marguin★★★★ £E
O **Saint-Véran** Clos à la Côte★★★ £C En Faux★★★ £C Les Crais★★★★ £D
O **Pouilly-Loché**★★★ £C   O **Mâcon-Fuissé**★★ £C   O **Mâcon Blanc**★★ £B

CORSIN   Pouilly-Fuissé   A: SsG, E&T

Owner: Corsin family   Les Plantes, 71960 Davayé

Gilles and Jean-Jacques Corsin are the current generation making the wines at this long-established Pouilly-Fuissé estate. The 12 ha are split between Pouilly-Fuissé and Saint-Véran. The wines are fermented and aged both partly in vats and partly in oak, and typically show concentrated ripe fruit and a well-integrated oak character. They can provide excellent, relatively inexpensive drinking with two or three years' age. A Cuvée Précoce bottling of Saint-Véran comes from younger vines, is bottled sooner and can be drunk earlier. (PW)

O **Pouilly-Fuissé**★★ £C   O **Saint-Véran**★★ £B   O **Mâcon-Villages**★ £B

DOM. LOUIS-CLAUDE DESVIGNES   Morgon   A: Sav, BBR

Owner: Louis-Claude Desvignes   135 Rue de la Voûte, 69910 Villié-Morgon

Louis-Claude Desvignes was one of the first in Beaujolais to produce separate *cuvées* from the best parcels in his estate. From 1.5 ha of Côte de Py and 2 ha of Javernières (from different soils within the Côte de Py) are regularly produced two rich vibrant, aromatic and distinctly different Morgons that bear little resemblance to most of what comes out of the Beaujolais region. There is undoubted skill and care in their production; low yields and a cold pre-fermentation maceration are just two contributing factors. Though there are now several other versions of Côte de Py (including Jean FOILLARD'S), few rival this one and none at the price, which remains low. These are wines to drink with at least three or four years' age if their full potential is to be realised. (PW)

● **Morgon** La Voûte Saint-Vincent★★ £B Javernières★★ £B Côte de Py★★ £B

DOM. DES DEUX ROCHES   Saint-Véran   A: Fie, BBR

Owner: Christian Collovray & Jean-Luc Terrier   Domaine des Deux Roches, 71960 Davayé

Increasing amounts of very good whites are being made outside the quality heart of Mâconnais, Pouilly-Fuissé. Saint-Véran lies both to the north and south but this estate has long shown that high quality is possible here too. While a number of Pouilly-Fuissé estates make fine Saint-Véran in addition to their top whites, the 35-ha Deux Roches majors on Saint-Véran. As well as attractive, fruity regular *cuvées* a percentage of new oak is used for fermenting and ageing the top wines. Generally there is good ripeness as well as a mineral aspect to most of the wines. There is also a little Pouilly-Fuissé La Roche. (PW)

O **Saint-Véran**★ £B Vieilles Vignes★★ £C Terres Noires★★ £C Cras★★★ £D
O **Mâcon-Villages**★ £B

GEORGES DUBOEUF Beaujolais www.duboeuf.com A: BWC, JNi, Maj

Owner: Georges Duboeuf 71570 Romanèche-Thorins

For many around the world Duboeuf represents Beaujolais, or at least the decent stuff. A production of 30 million bottles is one of the reasons why it can be found in local wine shops and supermarkets almost everywhere. Duboeuf has been admirably consistent despite the phenomenal growth over more than three decades. Many small domaines, including some in every *cru*, come under the Duboeuf umbrella and are marketed and bottled accordingly. Though some of the *cuvées*, especially the generic *crus*, are simple and rather short and firm on the finish, others show more expression, and more succulence and finesse in their structures. The individual *cuvées* (most from single domaines) are nearly always worth the small premium they command, particularly those from Moulin-à-Vent and Fleurie, when compared to regular examples of the more southerly Beaujolais *crus*, Brouilly or Régnié. Individual *crus* can be drunk with a couple of years' ageing but don't need it. Prices of fine wines around the globe may have escalated but those of most of these Beaujolais, like their quality, have remained steady. Some fresh, attractive whites with good substance are also made, as are many Rhône wines and vins de pays from the Languedoc-Roussillon. Below are some of the very best of Duboeuf's Beaujolais/Mâconnais wines. (PW)

● **Moulin-à-Vent**★★ £B Fût de Chêne★★ £B Domaine des Rosiers★★ £B Prestige★★★ £B
● **Moulin-à-Vent** Domaine de la Tour de Bief★★★ £B
● **Fleurie**★ £B Domaine des Quatre Vents★★ £B La Madone★★ £B Château des Déduits★ £B
● **Fleurie** Château des Bachelards★ £B ● **Saint-Amour** Domaine des Sablons★ £B
● **Morgon**★ £B Domaine Jean Descombes★★ £B ● **Juliénas** Domaine de la Seigneurie★ £B
O **Pouilly-Fuissé** Fût de Chêne★ £B Prestige★★ £B O **Saint-Véran**★ £B

DOM. J A FERRET Pouilly-Fuissé A: Bal, JAr, Lay, Rae

Owner: Colette Ferret Le Plan, 71960 Fuissé

This domaine has been bottling its own wine for 60 years, though it had its beginnings more than two decades before the French Revolution. Colette Ferret's Pouilly-Fuissés, made famous by her mother before she died in 1993, have been compared to not just *premier cru* but also *grand cru* Côte de Beaune whites. They are certainly very full-bodied with remarkable concentration and extract and with added finesse and purity in the best examples. As might be expected, yields are low, the average vine age high and the grapes are manually harvested. The wines are barrel-fermented and aged with extended lees-contact for maximum enrichment. From 15 ha are fashioned four great *crus*: Le Clos, Les Ménétrières, Les Perrières and Tournant de Pouilly. These are given the greatest amount of new oak and the longest period of ageing. Other bottlings are also made including three other *crus*, Les Sceles, Les Vernays and Les Moulins, which are sold only in the US. Rich and honeyed, the wines also display fine floral, mineral aspects as well as a classic grilled nuts character. An Hors Classé designation applies only to a selection of old vines in the best years and these wines are slightly more expensive than the Tête de Cru bottlings. Prices reflect what top Pouilly-Fuissé ought to command and are no longer anything like the most expensive from the appellation. (PW)

O **Pouilly-Fuissé** Ménétrières Hors Classé★★★★ £D Tournant de Pouilly Hors Classé★★★★ £D
O **Pouilly-Fuissé** Le Clos Tête de Cru★★★ £D Perrières Tête de Cru★★★ £D

HENRY FESSY Beaujolais   www.vins-henry-fessy.com   A: Cib, For, Frw

Owner: Henry Fessy   Bel Air, 69220 Saint-Jean d'Ardières

With both a domaine of 12 ha and a *négociant* business, Henry and Serges Fessy make a number of ripe, vigorous, perfumed Beaujolais. The estate vineyards are confined to Brouilly and Beaujolais but some fine examples are made from other *crus*. The Brouillys are particularly good for this *cru*, with both intensity and length of flavour in a more forward, supple Cuvée Georges Fessy and a richer Pur Sang. Other wines listed are those regularly encountered but the standard of Beaujolais seems good throughout. Prices are not excessive for the quality. Some white Beaujolais, Saint-Véran and Pouilly-Fuissé are also made but have not been tasted. (PW)

● **Brouilly** Cuvée Georges Fessy★★ £B   Domaine du Plateau de Bel Air★★ £B   Pur Sang★★ £B
● **Morgon** Cuvée Luquet★★ £B   ● **Fleurie**   Mauriers ★★ £B

JEAN FOILLARD Morgon   A: HHB

Owner: Jean Foillard   Le Clachet, 69910 Villié-Morgan

Jean Foillard is a disciple of Jules Chauvet, a noted enologist who believed in fashioning Beaujolais in an altogether different way from what has become the modern standard of semi-carbonic maceration. Foillard's 8 ha include one of the best sites in the whole Beaujolais region, Morgon's Côte du Py. Important to the style are low yields and very ripe grapes, which are subject to a long cool vinification, practically zero use of sulphur, and minimal or no filtration. It's not what you would normally associate with Beaujolais; an intense, spice- and mineral-rich, structured wine that needs five years or more before it is ready. Light years from simple, fruity quaffing Beaujolais, it does achieve real harmony in the best years. (PW)

● **Morgon** Première★★ £B   Côte du Py★★★ £C

DOM. GUFFENS-HEYNEN   Mâcon-Villages   A: C&R, L&S, Far

Owner: Jean-Marie Guffens-Heynen   Domaine Guffens-Heynen, 71960 Vergisson

Jean-Marie Guffens is one of the wine world's larger than life characters but also one of its most exciting winemakers. Both through the substantial *négociant* VERGET operation and a small number of wines made at this, his own private 3-ha estate, he has made a significant impact on the fine wine scene. The grapes are picked very ripe from low-yielding vines that have been meticulously cared for, before being pressed very slowly in an old-fashioned vertical press. A mix of oak, both new and used, small and large, is used in their fermentation and ageing. Not only do the wines have fantastic richness, depth and substance but they also show finesse and elegance. They are not as consistent as some but neither is there uniformity; when these wines are particularly successful (the 2000s are outstanding) they will provide memorable drinking for up to a decade. The Verget Mâconnais wines are also included here. (PW)

Guffens-Heynen:
○ **Pouilly-Fuissé** Les Croux★★★ £E   Roche★★★ £E   Hauts de Vignes★★★★ £F
○ **Mâcon-Pierreclos**★★★ £C   En Chavigne★★★★ £D

Verget:
○ **Pouilly-Fuissé** Terroir de Vergisson★★★ £D   ○ **Pouilly-Vinzelles** Les Quarts★★ £B
○ **Saint-Véran** Terroirs de Davayé★★ £B   Terres Noires★★★ £C   Vignes de Saint-Claude★★★ £C
○ **Mâcon-Bussières** Vieilles Vignes de Montbrison★★★ £B   Les Prusettes★★ £C
○ **Mâcon-Burgy** Les Prusettes★★ £C   En Chatelaine★★★ £C
○ **Mâcon-Vergisson** La Roche★★★ £B   ○ **Mâcon-Charnay** Le Clos Saint-Pierre★★ £B

DOM. PAUL ET ERIC JANIN Moulin-à-Vent

A: DDr, CPp, Rae

Owner: Janin family   71570 Romanèche-Thorins
Eric Janin makes excellent Moulin-à-Vent to a biodynamic recipe. The domaine of 10 ha of old vines are carefully nurtured by father and son and the result is a marvellous fruit quality and good concentration and depth in the wines. Occasionally the tannins can be a little firm in the finish but the Clos du Tremblay (which is a selection of the very best old vines) in particular benefits from a couple of years' age. Two-thirds of production is Moulin-à-Vent, the rest Beaujolais-Villages from the smaller Domaine des Vignes des Jumeaux. Prices, as so often from those most dedicated to the land, are very reasonable. (PW)

● **Moulin-à-Vent** Clos du Tremblay★★ £B Vignes du Tremblay★★ £B
● **Beaujolais-Villages** Domaine des Vignes du Jumeaux★ £B

DOM. ROGER LASSARAT Pouilly-Fuissé www.roger-lassarat.com

A: THt, Mar

Owner: Roger Lassarat   Le Martelet, 71960, Vergisson
Roger Lassarat was inspired by Château de Fuissé and J A FERRET and set out to emulate them as he established his own estate more than 30 years ago. Here as at so many of the best Pouilly-Fuissé estates the secret to the quality of the fruit is manual picking of carefully maintained, low-yielding old vines. The grapes receive a gentle pressing and partial barrel fermentation with prolonged lees enrichment in barrel before the wines are bottled unfiltered. The wines are ripe and richly textured, with increasing definition and better balance and structure in the most recent vintages. The range of wines has very recently been expanded to single out more individual *climats*. (PW)

O **Pouilly-Fuissé** Clos de France★★ £C Cuvée Prestige★★★ £D
O **Saint-Véran** Fournaise★★ £C Cuvée Prestige★★★ £C O **Mâcon-Vergisson** La Roche★★ £B

MERLIN Mâcon-Villages

A: M&V, WSc

Owner: Olivier Merlin   Domaine du Vieux Saint-Sorlin, 71960 La Roche Vineuse
Olivier Merlin's Domaine du Vieux Saint-Sorlin has built a reputation since the late 1980s as one of the Mâcon's most reliable as well as exciting producers. For long this took the form of excellent white Mâcon-La Roche Vineuse but more recently he has made wines to the same high standards from Pouilly-Fuissé. His own 7.5 ha includes a little Pinot Noir for some red Mâcon but is mostly Chardonnay, from which he makes rich, full-bodied whites with deep ripe fruit and a certain finesse and complexity, particularly in the old vine Les Cras. Both Pouilly-Fuissé show excellent structures and the capacity to age for at least five years. The Vergisson, with a fine mineral streak, is marginally the finer of the two. A sophisticated Moulin-à-Vent is rather better than the Mâcon red. (PW)

O **Mâcon-La Roche Vineuse★** £B Vieilles Vignes★★ £B Les Cras★★★ £C
O **Pouilly-Fuissé** Terroir de Fuissé★★★ £D Vergisson★★★ £D O **Saint-Véran** Grand Bussière★★ £C
● **Moulin-à-Vent★★** £C

DOM. RIJCKAERT Viré-Clessé

A: JAr, Lay, BBR

Owner: Jean Rijckaert   En Correaux, 71570 Leynes
Jean Rijckaert is one of the Mâconnais' most exciting new producers. He used to work with Jean-Marie Guffens (GUFFENS-HEYNEN) but he is now giving the Mâconnais a further boost with his own range of wines. Having helped mould the VERGET style, it is no surprise that the same principles of slow pressings, enhanced lees-enrichment and intelligent oak-ageing, are being continued here. Rijckaert also believes passionately in restoring life to the soils and the importance of promoting deep roots in the vines. He makes more than two dozen individual cuvées, mostly from 35-40

year old vines - both from his own 4 ha of vineyards and for other small growers. He seeks precision and minerality in his wines and achieves it with some superb aromatic, concentrated wines that show excellent definition and purity. Also made are a number of excellent whites from the Jura where he has another 4 ha of vineyard and winery facility. Many are of an unprecedented level of quality for the region, both those based on Chardonnay and those from Savagnin. Particularly good and relatively inexpensive are Arbois Pre-Leveron Vieilles Vignes (Chardonnay), Côtes de Jura Vignes des Voies (Chardonnay), Côtes du Jura Les Sarres (both Chardonnay and Savagnin) and Arbois En Paradis Vieilles Vignes (both versions). Rarely is there any need to hurry to drink these wines, most will be better with three or four years' age. A brown label indicate a grower's wine (and also includes their name) while a green label is used for the domaine wines. Only a selection are listed below. The 2002s promise to be particularly fine. (PW)

O **Pouilly-Fuissé** Vers Chânes★★★ £C
O **Saint-Véran** En Avonne★★ £C   L'Epinet★★ £C
O **Viré-Clessé** Les Vercherres Vieilles Vignes★★ £C   En Thurissey Vieilles Vignes★★★ £C

DOM. ROBERT-DENOGENT   Pouilly-Fuissé   www.robert-denogent.com   A: Bib, Gau

Owner: Jean-Jacques Robert   Domaine Robert-Denogent, 71960 Fuissé
Jean-Jacques Robert has rapidly improved quality at this small 5-ha estate since taking over in 1988. There is a tremendous resource of old vines and yields are further reduced through careful pruning. Though new oak is used, all the wines show lovely fruit intensity and fine structures with pronounced minerally, *terroir*-given definition and no two are quite alike. Even the Mâcon-Solutré shows some style, more floral in character than the various Pouilly-Fuissés. The La Croix has a striking mineral component due to more schistous soils, while the Claude Denogent wine is an old-vine selection and Les Carrons comes from an exceptional site with a higher clay content and very old vines. The top wines benefit from at least three to four years' ageing. As well as those listed below, another *cuvée*, Les Taches, is also made. (PW)

O **Pouilly-Fuissé** La Croix★★ £C   Les Reisses★★ £C   Claude Denogent★★★ £D   Les Carrons★★★★ £E
O **Mâcon-Solutré** Clos Bertillonnes★★ £C

SAUMAIZE-MICHELIN   Pouilly-Fuissé   A: Eno, Rae

Owner: Roger & Christine Saumaize   Le Martelet, 71960 Vergisson
Like the wines of Daniel et Martine BARRAUD and others, these wines show that Vergisson has the potential to equal Pouilly-Fuissé's more established and generally highest regarded commune, Fuissé. The Saumaize estate extends to 9 ha and as well as several different *cuvées* of Pouilly-Fuissé, some fine Saint-Véran and Mâcon-Villages are made. There is the utmost attention to detail and hygiene and the resulting consistency, both from year to year and across the range, is very impressive. The wines see some oak but, although they can be quite firm and steely when very young, they have good definition and added richness with age. The best Pouilly-Fuissé *cuvées* come from old vines, including a very small amount of Ampelopsis, the top wine. The Saint-Vérans are two more of an increasing number of good examples from this previously under-performing appellation. (PW)

O **Pouilly-Fuissé** Vigne Blanche★★ £C   Clos sur la Roche★★★ £C   Ronchevats★★★ £C
O **Saint-Véran** Crêches★★ £B   Vieilles Vignes★★ £B   O **Mâcon-Villages** Sertaux★★ £B

DOM. LA SOUFRANDIÈRE   Pouilly-Vinzelles   A: M&V, WSc

Owner: Jean-Guillaume & Jean-Philippe Bert   Domaine La Soufrandière, 71680 Vinzelles
These two young *vignerons* have made the finest wines ever under the small Pouilly-Vinzelles AC,

which together with the contiguous Pouilly-Loché AC has less than 100 ha of vines. The Berts have less than 5 ha but their rich, ripe, structured wines have finally shown that these separate zones at the south-eastern end of Pouilly-Fuissé have similar exciting potential to that being realised elsewhere in the region. The top *cuvées* are moderately expensive but provide a great alternative to much modest-quality village-level wine from the famous Côte de Beaune communes. This is an estate to watch. In addition to those listed below, another *cuvée* of Pouilly-Vinzelles, Longeays, is made, as is a Viré-Clissé, Verchère. (PW)

O **Pouilly-Vinzelles**★★ £B Quarts★★★ £C Quarts Millerandée★★★ £D

JEAN THÉVENET Macon-Villages www.bongran.com A: L&S, GBa, HHB, JNi

Owner: Jean Thévenet Domaine de la Bongran, Quintaine, 71260 Clessé
Jean Thévenet's wines are like no-one else's – atypically rich, very ripe and honeyed but with great structure and vibrancy. The wines from 15 ha of vineyards are the products of two separate domaines, Domaine de la Bongran and Domaine Emilian Gillet. Yields are low and the grapes are harvested manually. The Emilian Gillet is more floral than the Bongran but similarly strikingly honeyed. Previously labelled Mâcon-Clessé and Mâcon-Viré, the wines are now simply labelled Mâcon-Villages as, with a degree of residual sugar, they were denied promotion to the new Viré-Clessé AC despite their evident quality. A Cuvée Levroutée is made from selected overripe grapes in certain years, while a little Cuvée Botrytis (from botrytised grapes) is made when exceptional conditions permit (such as 2000 and 1995). This is a wine of exceptional richness and honeyed, preserved and tropical fruits but with excellent acidity and the ability to keep for more than a decade. (PW)

O **Mâcon-Villages** Tradition Sélection EJ Thévenet Domaine de la Bongran★★★ £D
O **Mâcon-Villages** Quintaine Domaine Emilian Gillet★★★ £C

DOM. THIBERT PÈRE ET FILS Pouilly-Fuissé A: Lay, BBR, Dec, CRs

Owner: Thibert family Le Bourg, 71960 Fuissé
Christophe and his wife Catherine Thibert run this 16-ha estate, which has around half its vineyards in Pouilly-Fuissé. The wines show more finesse and less upfront richness than some but combine a minerally intensity with good concentration in the best years. Oak is used to enhance structure and is less considerably overt in most of the wines than in many a Pouilly-Fuissé. Though less immediate, the wines have excellent ageing potential, especially the top *cuvées*. Recent releases have been a little uneven but always elegant. In addition, as well as some Mâcon-Prissé and Pouilly-Vinzelles, a little of a prestige *cuvée*, Vignes de la Côte, is made. (PW)

O **Pouilly-Fuissé**★★ £C Vieilles Vignes★★ £C Vignes Blanches★★★ £D
O **Mâcon-Fuissé**★ £B

DOM. VALETTE Pouilly-Fuissé A: M&V, WSc

Owner: Valette family Vercheres, 71570 Chaintré
No list of the Mâconnais' best producers would be complete without Gérard Valette. Gérard and his son Philippe run what is effectively an organic estate of 17 ha. Although more than half of it is in Mâcon-Chaintré, the rest is in Pouilly-Fuissé, producing full-bodied, very ripe-fruited blockbusters. The grapes are harvested very late from often very low-yielding old vines and a percentage of new oak is used for fermenting the two Réserve *cuvées*, resulting in very powerful oaky wines. Despite the rich, almost overwhelming, fruit and lees-enriched character, the wines usually have the necessary balance to provide heady, complex drinking soon after their release and often for another five years' or more. The extended ageing of these *cuvées* before bottling means they become available a year or two later

than other top Pouilly-Fuissé releases – but in the meantime you can enjoy the fresh, fruit-filled Mâcon-Chaintré made for early drinking. A little Pouilly-Vinzelles is also made. (PW)

O **Pouilly-Fuissé** Tradition★★★ £D Clos Reyssie Réserve★★★★ £E
O **Pouilly-Fuissé** Clos de M Noly Vieilles Vignes Réserve★★★★ £E
O **Mâcon-Chaintré** Vieilles Vignes★★ £B

MÂCONNAIS & BEAUJOLAIS/OTHER WINES OF NOTE

Mâconnais

AUVIGUE O **Pouilly-Fuissé** Hors Classé £D Vieilles Vignes £C   O **Mâcon-Solutré** Moulin du Pont £B
CH. DE BEAUREGARD/JOSEPH BURRIER O **Pouilly-Fuissé** £C Les Châtaigniers £D
DOM. DE LA CROIX SENAILLET O **Pouilly-Fuissé** £C   O **Saint-Véran** £C Les Rochats £C
CORINNE ET THIERRY DROUIN O **Pouilly-Fuissé** Vieilles Vignes £C
MICHEL FOREST O **Pouilly-Fuissé** £C La Roche £C Les Crays £D Vieilles Vignes £D
O **Mâcon-Vergisson** £B
DOM. DES GERBEAUX/JEAN-MICHEL DROUIN O **Pouilly-Fuissé** Solutré Vieilles Vignes £C
O **Saint-Véran** £B
PIERETTE ET MARC GUILLEMOT-MICHEL O **Mâcon-Villages** Quintaine £B
DOM. DES HÉRITIERS COMTES LAFON O **Mâcon** Milly Lamartine £B
JEAN MANCIAT O **Mâcon-Charnay** £B
MANCIAT-PONCET O **Pouilly-Fuissé** La Roche Vieilles Vignes £C Vieilles Vignes £C
O **Pouilly-Fuissé** Les Crays Vieilles Vignes £C
GILLES NOBLET O **Pouilly-Fuissé** £C Vieilles Vignes Les Champs £C   O **Mâcon-Fuissé** £B
DOM. DE ROALLY O **Mâcon-Montbellet** £B   O **Mâcon-Villages** £B
JACQUES ET NATALIE SAUMAIZE O **Pouilly-Fuissé** Vieilles Vignes £C
DOM. LA SOUFRANDISE/MELIN O **Pouilly-Fuissé** Vieilles Vignes £C   O **Mâcon-Fuissé** £B
DOM. GÉRALD ET PHILIBERT TALMARD O **Mâcon-Uchizy** £B   O **Mâcon-Chardonnay** £B
DOM. PAUL ET MALLORY TALMARD O **Mâcon-Uchizy** £B
DOM. VESSIGAUD O **Pouilly-Fuissé** Vieilles Vignes £C

Beaujolais

RENÉ BERROD ● **Fleurie** £B
JEAN-MARC BURGAUD ● **Morgon** Côte du Py £B Vieilles Vignes £C
NICOLE CHANRION/DOM. DE LA VOÛTE DES CROZES ● **Côte de Brouilly** £B
GÉRARD CHARVET/DOM. DES ROSIERS ● **Moulin-à-Vent** £B
CH. DE BEAUREGARD/JOSEPH BURRIER ● **Moulin-à-Vent** £C
CH. DE LA CHAIZE ● **Brouilly** £B
DOM. ÉMILE CHEYSSON ● **Chiroubles** £B Prestige £B
MICHEL CHIGNARD ● **Fleurie** Les Moriers £B Spéciale Vieilles Vignes £C
ANDRÉ COLONGE ● **Fleurie** £B
DOM. DIOCHON ● **Moulin-à-Vent** Vieilles Vignes £B
DOM. DUBOST ● **Brouilly** La Bruyère Vieilles Vignes £B
CAVE COOPÉRATIVE DE FLEURIE ● **Fleurie** Cuvée Millésimé £B
DOM. GAY-COPERET ● **Moulin-à-Vent** Réserve Vieilles Vignes £B
PASCAL GRANGER ● **Chénas** £B   ● **Juliénas** Cuvée Speciale £B
JACKY JANODET ● **Moulin-à-Vent** Vieilles Vignes £B Domaine Les Fines Graves £B
MARCEL LAPIERRE ● **Morgon** £B
HUBERT LAPIERRE ● **Chénas** Vieilles Vignes £B   ● **Moulin-à-Vent** Vieilles Vignes £B
DOM. DE LA MADONE ● **Fleurie** Tradition £B Vieilles Vignes £B
JEAN-PIERRE MARGERAND ● **Juliénas** £B
LAURENT MARTRAY ● **Brouilly** Vieilles Vignes £B
DOMAINE BERNARD MÉTRAT ● **Fleurie** Roilette Vieilles Vignes £B
ALBERT MOREL ● **Fleurie** £B

CHÂTEAU DU MOULIN-À-VENT ● **Moulin-à-Vent** £B Cuvée Exceptionelle £B
ALAIN PASSOT/DOM. DE LA GROSSE PIERRE ● **Chiroubles** £B
DOMINIQUE PIRON ● **Morgon** Côte du Py £B
JEAN-CHARLES PIVOT ● **Beaujolais-Villages** £B
POTEL-AVIRON ● **Morgon** Côte du Py Vieilles Vignes £C ● **Fleurie** Vieilles Vignes £C
● **Moulin-à-Vent** Vieilles Vignes £C
DOM. LES ROCHES BLEUES ● **Côte de Brouilly** £B
BERNARD SANTÉ ● **Chénas** £B
DOM. DES TERRES DORÉES/JEAN-PAUL BRUN ● **Moulin-à-Vent** £C
MICHEL TÊTE/DOM. DU CLOS DU FIEF ● **Juliénas** £B Cuvée Prestige £C
● **Saint-Amour** £B
DOM. GEORGES VIORNERY ● **Côte de Brouilly** £B
DOM. DU VISSOUX ● **Fleurie** Les Garants £B Poncié £B ● **Moulin-à-Vent** Rochegrès £B

Author's Choice for Mâconnais & Beaujolais (PW)

15 Great Mâcon Whites
DANIEL ET MARTINE BARRAUD ○ **Pouilly-Fuissé** En Buland Vieilles Vignes
CH. FUISSÉ ○ **Pouilly-Fuissé** Le Clos
CH. DES RONTETS ○ **Pouilly-Fuissé** Les Birbettes
DOM. CORDIER PÈRE ET FILS ○ **Pouilly-Fuissé** Vignes Blanches
DOM. DE LA CROIX SENAILLET ○ **Saint-Véran** Les Rochats
DOM. DES DEUX ROCHES ○ **Saint-Véran** Cras
DOM. J A FERRET ○ **Pouilly-Fuissé** Ménétrières Hors Classé
DOM. GUFFENS-HEYNEN/VERGET ○ **Pouilly-Fuissé** Terroir de Vergisson
MERLIN ○ **Mâcon-La Roche Vineuse** Les Cras
DOM. RIJCKAERT ○ **Viré-Clessé** En Thurissey Vieilles Vignes
DOM. ROBERT-DENOGENT ○ **Pouilly-Fuissé** Claude Denogent
DOM. LA SOUFRANDIÈRE ○ **Pouilly-Vinzelles** Quarts
DOM. LA SOUFRANDISE/MELIN ○ **Pouilly-Fuissé** Vieilles Vignes
JEAN THÉVENET ○ **Mâcon-Villages** Quintaine Domaine Emilian Gillet
DOM. VALETTE ○ **Pouilly-Fuissé** Clos de M Noly Vieilles Vignes Réserve

This is one of France's most unusual and exciting regions. Culturally it is as much German as it is French and twice during the last 130 years or so has been a part of the former. It is one of France's most spectacular regions to visit, with the splendour of the Vosges mountains complemented by the medieval architecture of many towns and villages. Unlike in other regions, the grape varietal plays a key element in wine labelling. The wines themselves can be piercingly aromatic and are quite unique in style. Although there are some substantial merchant operations and large co-ops the area is not a purveyor of bulk wine. However there is still a wide variation in quality and yields generally throughout the region are too high with most wine still coming from flat, over-productive sites. As elsewhere, who produced the wine is the key.

Geography

The region of Alsace is a narrow stretch of vineyards running north-south at the base of and nestled into the eastern foothills of the Vosges mountains. These, along with the Rhine just to the east of the *vignoble*, provide the region with an impressively favourable climate for such a northerly latitude. Sunshine hours are high during the growing season and rainfall low. The vineyard area stretches from just west of Strasbourg in the north to Mulhouse in the south, with the heart of the region centred around the town of Colmar. This is where the greatest concentration of top villages and vineyard sites, particularly *grands crus,* are to be found. These southern stretches are known as the **Haut Rhin**; the northern the **Bas Rhin**. There are fewer great sites in the Bas Rhin but some very fine wine is produced nonetheless. As you travel through it the region is not dissimilar to the Côte d'Or. The finest sites are inevitably on the slopes of the Vosges, with well-drained, meagre soils. By contrast those vineyards planted on the fertile, heavy alluvial soils on the plains towards the Rhine are far less propitious for quality wine production.

Wine Styles

The generic appellation of the region is simply **Alsace** AC. The vast majority of wine is labelled by its grape variety. There is an ongoing debate in the region about the importance of the varieties themselves, as opposed to site and *terroir,* in determining style. There is just one permitted red grape, Pinot Noir, which can be good but is often light and insubstantial, needing a good vintage. The white varietals are the fairly neutral Pinot Blanc and Sylvaner (although there are some impressive old-vine examples) and the more aromatic Riesling, Muscat, Tokay Pinot Gris and Gewurztraminer. There is some Chasselas producing the odd varietal wine, as well as Auxerrois, but both will generally be used with Sylvaner and Pinot Blanc in generic blends. These are covered by the Alsace AC and are labelled either Edelzwicker or Gentil. An unusual rarity in the higher reaches of the Bas Rhin is the Klevner de Heilegenstein. No wines of real note have been produced from it. Confusingly, Auxerrois is often referred to as Klevner.

The 50 *grands crus* here were established in 1983. Wines produced from these are classified **Alsace Grand Cru** AC. The majority of these sites can be found in the heart of the Haut Rhin and were created to pinpoint the best vineyards. Much work still needs to be done with the region's labelling system and although there is talk of it, there is no further official classification. Many wines make reference to their *lieux-dits* in order to emphasise potential quality. A number of these sites produce wines that are comfortably a match for many *grands crus.* The vineyards of the latter must be planted to Gewürztraminer, Muscat, Riesling or Tokay Pinot Gris.

Almost all wines are varietal but there are experiments, particularly those by Jean-Michel Deiss, in establishing field blends.

Some of the region's greatest wines are the late-harvested wines, **Vendange Tardive** (VT) and *Sélection de Grains Nobles* (SGN). Being made from late-harvested grapes, these are generally sweet styles. Noble rot may occur, particularly in the SGNs, but not always. The classification, though, is based on grape ripeness at harvest and some *Vendange Tardive* wines can be surprisingly dry. Indeed the whole question of levels of residual sugar can be confusing. Some producers tend towards a very steely, dry style, while others prefer to let nature take its course, with fermentation stopping naturally. The results in the latter case are wines with often surprising levels of sugar and extract. The best, though, are very well balanced with sometimes remarkable depth. In order to help with this confusion a scale has been established, indicating on the back label the degree of sweetness.

The final style is **Crémant d'Alsace AC**. These are made by the traditional method and are mostly produced from Pinot Blanc and Riesling, although Auxerrois, Pinot Noir and Tokay Pinot Gris are also permitted. The best examples have reasonable depth and structure, often with marked acidity.

Vintages

The region is sunny and warm and, like many of the top areas of France, governed by a marginal climate. While this is important in the development of great wines, there will inevitably be some vintage variation. The lesser whites should be drunk young and certainly by the time they have had four or five years' ageing. Riesling is better in slightly cooler years, Gewürztraminer and Tokay Pinot Gris add dimension in warmer years. The chart below will provide a reliable guide as to what you should expect. The very best *grand cru* and late-harvest styles are remarkably ageworthy. Of the great earlier years to consider are 1983, 1976 and for very top wines 1971 and 1967.

Alsace vintages

	Riesling Grand or Top Cru	Pinot Gris Grand or Top Cru	Gewürztraminer Grand or Top Cru	Late-Harvest Wines Vendange Tardive or SGN
2002	★★★★ A	★★★★/★★★★★ A	★★★★/★★★★★ A	★★★★ A
2001	★★★★ A	★★★★ A	★★★★ A	★★★★ A
2000	★★★★ A	★★★★ A	★★★★ A	★★★★ A
1999	★★★★ A	★★★/★★★★ B	★★★/★★★★ B	★★★★ A
1998	★★★★/★★★★★ A	★★★★ B	★★★★ B	★★★★/★★★★★ A
1997	★★★★ B	★★★★/★★★★★ B	★★★★/★★★★★ B	★★★★/★★★★★ A
1996	★★★★/★★★★★ B	★★★★/★★★★★ B	★★★★ B	★★★★/★★★★★ B
1995	★★★★/★★★★★ B	★★★★/★★★★★ B	★★★★ C	★★★★/★★★★★ B
1994	★★★ C	★★★ C	★★★ C	★★★★ B
1990	★★★★/★★★★★ C	★★★★/★★★★★ C	★★★★/★★★★★ C	★★★★/★★★★★ B
1989	★★★★ C	★★★★/★★★★★ C	★★★★/★★★★★ C	★★★★/★★★★★ B
1988	★★★★/★★★★★ C	★★★★C	★★★★ C	★★★★ B
1985	★★★★ C	★★★★/★★★★★ C	★★★★ C	★★★★ C

DOM. LUCIEN ALBRECHT   Orschwihr   www.lucien-albrecht.fr   A: Eno

Owner: Jean Albrecht   9 Grand-Rue, 68500 Orschwihr

There are just over 30 ha of vineyards at this small to medium-sized property. The regular wines are simple, straightforward and emphasise their varietal character well. The best wines are from Grand Cru Pfingtsberg, particularly the special bottlings labelled Cuvée A de Albrecht. Vendange Tardive and SGN can be impressive as well. Top Pinot Gris and Gewürztraminer are quite opulent and reasonably approachable, Riesling is in a tighter, more structured mould – citrussy and intense with some age but relatively austere when young. Prices are very reasonable. (DM)

O **Gewürztraminer** Cuvée Martine Albrecht★★★ £B Pfingstberg Grand Cru Cuvée A de Albrecht★★★ £C
O **Riesling** Pfingstberg Grand Cru Cuvée A de Albrecht★★★ £C Vendange Tardive★★★ £C
O **Tokay Pinot Gris** Grand Cru Pfingstberg★★★ £C Vendange Tardive★★★★ £D
O **Muscat** Bollenberg★★ £B

DOM. JEAN BECKER   Zellenberg   vinsbecker@aol.com

Owner: Marie-José Becker 4 route d'Ostheim, 68340 Zellenberg

Fine old family domaine established in 1610, which now has 18 ha of vineyards in the villages of Zellenberg, Riquewihr, Beblenheim and Ribeauvillé. 4 ha are *Grand Cru* and a small amount of fruit is bought in from other growers around Zellenberg. Among the *Grand Crus* floral, elegant Riesling, Tokay Pinot Gris, Muscat and Gewürztraminer come from Froehn. Riesling and Gewürztraminer from the marl soils of Schoenenbourg can produce excellent late harvest wines. Gewürztraminer is also grown at the Sporen, Sonnenglanz and Praelatenberg sites. Among the *Lieux-dits* fresh fruity Riesling comes from Hagenschlauf and Tokay Pinot Gris and Gewürztraminer, often produced as Vendange Tardive and occasionally SGN, from Rimelsberg. Good fruit driven Pinot Blanc and regular Tokay Pinot Gris are produced organically. The style of the wines is traditional but they all show good fruit intensity. The top *crus* have a fine mineral complexity to them and you can expect them to age well. (DM)

O **Gewürztraminer** Grand Cru Sonnenglanz★★ £C Vendange Tardive★★★★ £D
O **Gewürztraminer** Grand Cru Schoenenbourg SGN★★★★ £E
O **Riesling** Hagenschlauf★★ £C Grand Cru Froehn★★★ £C
O **Tokay Pinot Gris**★★ £B Grand Cru Froehn★★★ £C
O **Muscat** Grand Cru Froehn★★★ £C
O **Pinot Blanc**★ £B

LÉON BEYER   Eguisheim   www.leonbeyer.fr   A: Hal, BBR

Owner: Léon Beyer   2 Rue de la Première-Arnée, 68420 Eguisheim

This is quite a substantial property producing wines from its own 20 ha of vineyards and buying in grapes for its *négociant* wines also. Vineyard holdings include the Grands Crus Eichberg and Pfersigberg but as at HUGEL no wines are released as such. Output is around 60,000 cases a year. As one would expect, the generic bottlings do not set the world on fire but are generally well crafted and offer a particularly dry, almost austere style. They will develop well in bottle. Better are the Grandes Cuvées Comtes d'Eguisheim labels which are rich and reasonably concentrated. Riesling Ecaillers and Gewürztraminer Réserve also stand out. VT Gewürztraminer is good but just lacks some of the weight one might hope for. Sélection de Grains Nobles from the same variety is very impressive. The Pinot Gris SGN is remarkable: structured, rich and very ageworthy. (DM)

O **Gewürztraminer** Comtes d'Eguisheim★★ £D Vendange Tardive★★★ £E SGN★★★★ £F
O **Riesling** Ecaillers★★ £C Comtes d'Eguisheim★★ £D
O **Tokay Pinot Gris** SGN✪✪✪✪✪ £F

DOM. PAUL BLANCK   Kaysersberg   www.blanck.com   A: Lay

Owner: Blanck family   32 Grand-Rue, 68240 Kientzheim
Medium-sized family producer with an output approaching 20,000 cases a year. Quality is generally
good to very good across the board and the wines tend to be made in an opulent, rich vein. Often
quite marked levels of residual sugar can be found in the drier styles. Generic labels including Riesling
and Pinot Blanc are sound but can be a little simple. Very good is an intense, green-apple Sylvaner
from old vines. There are a range of *vieilles vignes, grand cru*, VT and SGN bottlings. You can expect
almost all *grand cru* bottles to be at least three stars. Very good examples are produced from the Grands
Crus Furstentum, Sommerberg and Schlossberg and there are fine wines produced from other
lieux-dits as well. Fine VT is almost invariably of four-star quality and there is an explosive rich and
opulent Pinot Gris SGN. Make sure you get the right address; there is more than one Blanck in
Kientzheim. (DM)

O **Pinot Auxerrois**★ £B
O **Gewürztraminer** Furstentum Grand Cru Vieilles Vignes★★★★ £E
O **Gewürztraminer** Furstentum Grand Cru Vendange Tardive★★★★★ £E
O **Riesling** Rosenbourg★★ £B Patergarten★★★ £C
O **Riesling** Furstentum Grand Cru★★★★ £D Schlossberg Grand Cru★★★★ £D
O **Tokay Pinot Gris** Patergarten★★ £B Furstentum Grand Cru★★★ £E SGN⬤⬤⬤⬤⬤ £G

DOM. BOTT-GEYL   Beblenheim   bottgeyl@libertysurf.fr   A: CTy

Owner: Bott-Geyl family   1 Rue du Petit-Château, 68980 Beblenheim
Impressive small family domaine that has some 12.5 ha of estate vineyards producing close to 8,000
cases a year. The quality is nearly always very sound right across the range. The style is almost
explosively rich and the wines will often have marked residual sugar. Harvesting as ripe as possible and
letting nature and indigenous yeasts run their natural course produces such results. Good generic Pinot
Auxerrois and Gewürztraminer Beblenheim as well as Muscat Riquewihr offer very good value. There
are also considerable *grand cru* holdings. Gewürztraminer and Pinot Gris comes from Furstentum and
Sonnenglanz and also the excellent *lieu-dit* of Schlosselreben, the *grand cru* bottles always three stars,
often better. Riesling comes from Mandelberg, Schoenenbourg and Grafenreben. The Mandelberg
tends to be fullest – rich and weighty with a marvellously pure mineral core. While the Gewürztraminer
VT is quite tight and restrained in style, the Pinot Gris SGN from Sonnenglanz can be explosive, rich
and sumptuous but with a marvellous fresh, structured backbone. The top wines will inevitably age
extraordinarily well. Most offer very good value. (DM)

O **Pinot d'Alsace** Beblenheim★ £B O **Muscat** Riquewihr★★ £B
O **Riesling** Mandelberg Grand Cru★★★★ £C
O **Gewürztraminer** Furstentum Grand Cru★★★ £C Sonnenglanz Grand Cru Vieilles Vignes★★★★ £D
O **Gewürztraminer** Sonnenglanz Grand Cru Vendange Tardive★★★★★ £D
O **Tokay Pinot Gris** de Beblenheim★★★ £B Furstentum Grand Cru★★★★ £C
O **Tokay Pinot Gris** Sonnenglanz Grand Cru SGN⬤⬤⬤⬤⬤ £F

ALBERT BOXLER   Niedermorschwihr   albert.boxler@9online.fr   A: Gau

Owner: Jean-Marc Boxler   78 Rue des Trois-Epis, 68230 Niedermorschwihr
Jean-Marc Boxler's small domaine, nearly 14 ha, produces just over 4,000 cases across a small but
well-made range. Generics including Riesling and Pinot Blanc are very good, but Gewürztraminer
can occasionally disappoint. Top Gewürztraminer and Pinot Gris comes from the Brand vineyard,
Riesling from Brand and Sommerberg. The Rieslings particularly stand out. The style is for very dry,
almost austere wines with a restrained, youthful, green-apple and markedly mineral character. Pinot

Gris and Gewürztraminer, even at *grand cru* level, do not have the formidable structure and depth of the Rieslings. They tend more towards a simpler, riper if more opulent style. Riesling VT and SGN can be stunning as can a very impressive Pinot Gris – all are four stars, often five or occasionally super-five. The top Rieslings will age magnificently and should not be broached without six or seven years' ageing. (DM)

- ● **Pinot Blanc★★** £B
- ● **Gewürztraminer** Brand Grand Cru★★★ £D
- ○ **Riesling★★** £B Brand Grand Cru★★★ £D Sommerberg Grand Cru★★★★ £D
- ○ **Tokay Pinot Gris★** £B Brand Grand Cru★★★ £C

ERNEST BURN Gueberschwihr www.domaine-burn.fr A: Has, HHB, NYg, Gau

Owner: Joseph et Francis Burn 8 Rue Basse, 68420 Gueberschwihr
This is a very impressive, small, traditional domaine with a holding of just 10 ha. The wholly owned *monopole* Clos Saint Imer is part of the Grand Cru Goldert and this accounts for over half the vineyard holdings. A fine Pinot Blanc is joined by some very well crafted, rich and stylish Muscat, Pinot Gris, Gewürztraminer and Riesling. The latter tends to be at its best in the cooler years. The style of the *grand cru* wines is for rich, very late-harvested fruit with real density and imense depth. They can almost seem overblown but always retain a fine, structured undercurrent. Riesling can be a touch overwhelmed in this style when the vintage produces very ripe, soft wines, as in 1997. Some very fine, sumptuous and honeyed VT is made from Gewürztraminer and Pinot Gris. (DM)

- ○ **Pinot Blanc★★** £B
- ○ **Gewürztraminer** Goldert Grand Cru Cuvée de la Chapelle★★★★ £E
- ○ **Riesling** Goldert Grand Cru Cuvée de la Chapelle★★★ £D
- ○ **Tokay Pinot Gris★★** £B Goldert Grand Cru Cuvée de la Chapelle★★★★ £D

MARCEL DEISS Bergheim www.marceldeiss.com A: Res, Bal, L&S

Owner: Deiss family 15 Route du Vin, 68750 Bergheim
The Deiss family has been producing wines here for over 50 years. Jean-Michel Deiss is now in charge of the property and running the domaine along biodynamic lines. He is unquestionably now one of the three or four best producers in the entire region. An exemplary range of wines is made from very low yields from a range of sites including *grand cru* holdings at the Altenberg, Mambourg and Schoenenbourg sites. A very good generic Pinot Blanc is made, as well as Riesling from Saint-Hippolyte and Pinot Gris and Gewürztraminer from Bergheim. The *grands crus* are very fine. Riesling comes from Altenberg and Schoenenbourg, Gewürztraminer and Pinot Gris from Altenberg. Jean-Michel Deiss also produces three remarkable and very rich *grands crus* from Altenberg, Mambourg and Schoenenbourg that are field blends of the noble varieties. As well as these, there is a very good Gentil from the Burg site. The intention is to increase the complexity of the wines and emphasise their *terroir* rather than their varietal character. The approach throughout is to achieve very ripe fruit and the wines regularly have very marked sugar levels. Occasional super-rich VT and SGN are made. (DM)

- ○ **Pinot Blanc★★★** £C ○ **Altenberg Grand Cru**●●●●● £F
- ○ **Gewürztraminer** Bergheim★★★★ £D Altenberg Grand Cru★★★★ £F
- ○ **Riesling** Saint-Hippolyte★★★ £C Altenberg Grand Cru●●●●● £F
- ○ **Tokay Pinot Gris** Bergheim★★★★ £E Altenberg Grand Cru★★★★★ £F

HUGEL ET FILS   Riquewihr   www.hugel.fr   A: Day, OWL, BBR, PFx, WSc

Owner: Hugel family   3 Rue de la Premiere-Armee-Française, B.P. 32, 68340 Riquewihr
Along with TRIMBACH one of the two best-known names in the region. As well as being a substantial merchant operation Hugel also has extensive vineyard holdings – some 127 ha. The top wines here are good to exceptional and are excellent, structured examples of the region. What disappoints most is the very average, at times downright poor, quality of the generics. The Gentil basics and the Tradition cuvées struggle to stand up to much of their competition. Gewürztraminer Tradition is sound with good varietal character, as is Pinot Gris. The Jubilee wines and the VT and SGN cuvées are of an entirely different class. Riesling Jubilee is taut and intense, minerally with great structure; Pinot Gris is powerful and with subtle, honeyed notes; the Jubilee Gewürztraminer floral and spicy with classic but youthfully restrained lychee character. These are wines that should be cellared for at least four or five years as they will continue to develop very well in bottle. Pinot Noir is less successful. VTs are very intense. The style tends towards the drier end of the spectrum but they have remarkable depth. Both Pinot Gris and Riesling SGN are quite splendid wines with remarkable depth and complexity. The Riesling is perhaps the finest, with astonishing toasty, citrus and mineral character. (DM)

O **Gewürztraminer** Tradition★★ £B   Jubilee★★★ £F   Vendange Tardive★★★★ £F
O **Riesling** Jubilee★★★ £C   Vendange Tardive★★★★ £F   SGN✪✪✪✪✪ £H
O **Tokay Pinot Gris** Tradition★ £B   Jubilee★★★ £F   Vendange Tardive★★★★ £F   SGN✪✪✪✪✪ £H

ANDRÉ KIENTZLER   Ribeauvillé   A: JAr, Res, HHB

Owner: André Kientzler   50 Route de Bergheim, 68150 Ribeauvillé
André Kientzler makes around 6,500 cases across a small but very impressive range of wines. They are marked by their purity of fruit and elegant structure at all levels. The top *grand cru* bottles are very ageworthy and require cellaring. No varieties stand out but the Rieslings, particularly from the Grands Crus Geisberg and Osterberg, are truly profound. On occasion Geisberg produces a Riesling VT and SGN. Wines of remarkable complexity, the latter is astonishingly rich while the former is very structured, almost dry. You can expect these to be four stars, often five or super-five. Very good Muscat and Pinot Gris is made from Kirchberg. Gewürztraminer is not *grand cru* but there are occasional bottles of VT and SGN. Even the lesser Pinot Blanc, Auxerrois and Chasselas offer excellent quality and value. (DM)

O **Chasselas★** £B   O **Auxerrois★★** £B   O **Pinot Blanc★★** £B
O **Gewürztraminer★★** £B   Vendange Tardive★★★★ £E
O **Riesling** Réserve Particulière★★★ £B   Geisberg Grand Cru★★★★ £D
O **Tokay Pinot Gris★★** £B   Kirchberg Grand Cru★★★★ £E

MARC KREYDENWEISS   Andlau   marc.kreydenweiss@wanadoo.fr   A: C&C, Vig

Owner: Marc Kreydenweiss   12 Rue Deharbe, 67140 Andlau
Marc Kreydenweiss's 12-ha domaine is in the north of the region in the Bas Rhin. He produces around 5,000 cases using biodynamic principles in the vineyard. In addition to the Alsace property, Marc and his wife Emmanuelle own the Costières de Nîmes property Domaine des PERRIÈRES (see Languedoc-Roussillon & Provence). The approach at both properties is the same: to achieve elegance and refinement rather than weight and power. The wines here are marked most by their intense fruit purity. Taut and with an almost gripping structure the top wines should be cellared for six or seven years, sometimes more. Marc produces an unusual blend of mainly Riesling and some Pinot Gris labelled Le Clos du Val d'Eléon, which technically is an Edelzwicker but is unlike almost

all you're likely to encounter elsewhere. Plots are farmed in a considerable number of sites, both *lieux-dits* and *grands crus*. Supreme examples include Tokay Pinot Gris from Moenchberg, and Riesling from Kastelberg and Wiebelsberg. Among the great *lieux-dits* are Gewürztraminer from Kritt and Pinot Gris from both Rebberg and Lerchenberg. Fine Muscat Clos Rebgarten is intense, floral and musky and there is also a most unusual, very impressive Klevner from the Kritt site. Very stylish VT and SGN are produced from Gewürztraminer and VT Riesling from Kastelberg. (DM)

O **Le Clos du Val d'Eléon**★★★ £D   O **Klevner** Kritt★★★ £C
O **Gewürztraminer** Kritt★★★ £C
O **Riesling** Wiebelsberg Grand Cru★★★ £E   Kastelberg Grand Cru★★★★ £E
O **Tokay Pinot Gris** Rebberg★★★ £C   Lerchenberg★★★ £C   Moenchberg Grand Cru★★★★ £E

DOM. ALBERT MANN   Wettolsheim   vins@mann-albert.com   A: NYg

Owner: Barthelmé family 13 Rue du Château, 68920 Wettolsheim
Very fine producer with a bewildering array of wines from just under 19 ha of vineyards, which are now, like so many others, being tended organically. The style is for very ripe, full-bodied, traditional wines. Generics can be very good: Pinot Blanc/Auxerrois is one of the best in the region. Gewürztraminer at the generic level also impresses and the 2001 was three stars. Rieslings have considerable weight and depth, more so than most, and you do feel they work best in a cooler vintage. The great Grand Cru Furstentum is a source not only of Riesling but of very rich and concentrated Gewürztraminer too, full of lychee and spice. Pinot Gris is very important and there is an excellent regular *cuvée* from old vines as well as first-class bottles from Altenbourg, Furstentum and Hengst. VT can be stunning and both the Grand Cru Hengst and Furstentum SGNs are remarkable wines, immensely rich and concentrated with substantial toffee, honey and peach. The style throughout is rich, opulent, almost extracted and the wines can be approached quite young, though the top examples age very well indeed. Prices are very fair. (DM)

O **Pinot Blanc/Auxerrois** Vieilles Vignes★★ £B   O **Muscat**★★ £B
O **Gewürztraminer**★★ £B   Steingrubler Grand Cru★★★★ £D
O **Gewürztraminer** Furstentum Grand Cru Vieilles Vignes★★★★ £D
O **Riesling** Schlossberg Grand Cru★★★ £C   Furstentum Grand Cru★★★ £D
O **Riesling** Pfleck Vendange Tardive★★★ £D
O **Tokay Pinot Gris** Vieilles Vignes★★★ £C   Hengst Grand Cru★★★★ £C
O **Tokay Pinot Gris** Altenbourg Vendange Tardive★★★★ £D
O **Tokay Pinot Gris** Hengst Grand Cru SGN✪✪✪✪✪ £E   Furstentum Grand Cru SGN✪✪✪✪✪ £E
● **Pinot Noir** Vieilles Vignes★★ £D

RENÉ MURÉ   Rouffach   www.mure.com   A: BWC, Gau

Owner: Muré family   Clos Saint Landelin, Route du Vin, 68250 Rouffach
René Muré's total production is not vast but sizeable for the area, at close to 25,000 cases per year. There are two distinct sides to the operation here. Domaine wines are labelled Clos Saint-Landelin and produced from 20 ha of estate vineyards at the Grand Cru Vorbourg and a number of neighbouring sites. The Muré family solely own the Clos Saint-Landelin vineyard, a *monopole* within the Vorbourg. The quality and price of the wines are substantially above that of the *négoçiant* wines under the René Muré label. There are a range of generics which generally offer good value along with a decent Crémant d'Alsace. Superior bottlings of varieties go under the Côte de Rouffach label. Among the Domaine wines there is impressively steely Sylvaner from the *clos* which is full of ripe, green fruits and minerals and one of the finest examples in the region. Intense, long-lived Riesling comes from Vorbourg and Clos Saint-Landelin. Rich, spicy and opulent Gewürztraminer from the *lieu-dit* Schultzengass as well as Vorbourg and Pinot Gris from Lutzeltal as well as the *clos*. Some better-than-average Pinot Noir is also produced,

plus some very fine Muscat, as both VT and SGN, along with Riesling, Gewürztraminer and Tokay Pinot Gris. Clos Saint-Landelin is favoured by the regular occurrence of noble rot. The Gewürztraminer and Pinot Gris are more approachable than the Rieslings, which really will benefit from six or seven years in bottle. The generic René Muré labels will be enjoyable on release, the Côte de Rouffach wines will be better for two or three years' ageing. (DM)

Domaine du Clos Saint-Landelin
O **Sylvaner** Cuvée Oscar★★ £B
O **Gewürztraminer** Schulzengass★★★ £C Vorbourg Grand Cru★★★ £D
O **Riesling** Vorbourg Grand Cru★★★ £C Clos Saint Landelin Vorbourg Grand Cru★★★★ £E
O **Tokay Pinot Gris** Lutzeltal★★ £D Clos Saint Landelin Vorbourg Grand Cru★★★ £D
● **Pinot Noir** V★★ £D

René Muré
O **Muscat** Côte de Rouffach★★ £C
O **Gewürztraminer**★ £B Côte de Rouffach★★ £C
O **Riesling** Côte de Rouffach★★ £C
O **Tokay Pinot Gris** Côte de Rouffach★★ £D
O **Crémant d'Alsace**★★ £C
● **Pinot Noir** Côte de Rouffach★★ £C

OSTERTAG Epfig   A: M&V

Owner: André Ostertag 87 Rue Finckwiller, 67680 Epfig
For more than ten years André Ostertag has taken a radical approach to winemaking in the region. The vineyards are now farmed biodynamically but of greater significance has been the creation of wines that are given barrique treatment, including Pinot Blanc, Pinot Gris and Pinot Noir. Some of his experiments have brought him into open conflict with the appellation bureaucrats in the past. The generic labels he classifies as *vins du fruit*, the *lieux-dits* and *grands crus* as *vins du terroir*, and his late-harvest bottlings are *vins du temps*. In general the oak-handled wines work well. He also makes very good Rieslings with no recourse to wood, most notably from the Grand Cru Muenchberg, and some very fine Gewürztraminer. Ostertag favours producing a dry style but the Gewürztraminer will often have a touch of residual sugar for balance. Sylvaner from very old vines is arguably the best example in the region. Top wines are not only very ageworthy but require five or six years' cellaring at a minimum. (DM)

O **Sylvaner** Vieilles Vignes★★ £B O **Pinot Blanc** Barriques★ £B
O **Gewürztraminer** d'Epfig★★★ £C Fronholz Vendange Tardive★★★★ £E
O **Riesling** Fronholz★★★ £D Muenchberg Grand Cru★★★★ £E
O **Riesling** Muenchberg Grand Cru Vendange Tardive★★★★ £F
O **Tokay Pinot Gris** Barriques★★ £C Zellberg★★★ £E Muenchberg Grand Cru★★★★ £E

ROLLY-GASSMANN Rorschwihr rollygassmann@wanadoo.fr   A: RsW, Bib, Rae, WSc

Owner: Rolly-Gassmann family 2 Rue de l'Eglise, 68950 Rorschwihr
An extensive range of very good, traditionally produced wines emerges from this family domaine. There are no *grand cru* vineyards but a number of wines from some excellent *lieux-dits*. As well as the varietal and vineyard-labelled wines, including a good Edelzwicker, there are some particularly fine VT and SGN bottlings. The Muscat, Pinot Gris and Gewürztraminer are marked by pungent and concentrated varietal character. Riesling is intense and lightly mineral in style but with a piercing citrus character regularly showing through. The top wines need some cellaring to show at their best. Release dates can be confusing with a number of bottlings held back in the cellar and released with several years' age. This is is however a rare source for purchasing top wines approaching their peak. (DM)

O **Pinot Blanc Auxerrois** Moenchreben★★ £B
O **Muscat** Moenchreben★★★ £C Moenchreben Vendange Tardive★★★★ £E
O **Gewürztraminer** SGN★★★★ £F
O **Riesling** Kappelweg★★★ £C Kappelweg Vendange Tardive★★★★ £E Pflaenzereben★★★ £C
O **Tokay Pinot Gris**★★ £B Réserve★★★ £C

DOM. SCHOFFIT Colmar   A: HBJ,BBR,Gau

Owner: Schoffit family   66-68 Nonnenholzweg, 6800 Colmar

There are some 16 ha planted at this brilliant domaine based in Colmar, with production now running at around 8,000 cases a year. The regular bottlings are all very good. Pinot Blanc and particularly the humble Chasselas produced from venerable vines really stand out. Indeed, throughout the range all the cuvées represent excellent quality and value. A significant part of the Schoffit's vineyard holding is in lesser sites but quality is still admirable. The focal point of the domaine, though, is the fine volcanic soil of the Clos Saint-Théobald in the Grand Cru Rangen. The resulting wines are structured but have a remarkable array of exotic fruit aromas and always a pure mineral undercurrent. VT and SGN are very fine to exceptional. Given the extraordinary quality, prices are extremely reasonable. (DM)

O **Pinot Blanc** Cuvée Caroline★★ £B O **Muscat** Tradition★★ £B
O **Chasselas** Vieilles Vignes★★ £B
O **Gewürztraminer** Harth Cuvée Alexandre Vieilles Vignes★★★ £C
O **Gewürztraminer** Clos Saint-Théobald Rangen Grand Cru★★★★ £E
O **Gewürztraminer** Clos Saint-Théobald Rangen Grand Cru Vendange Tardive★★★★★ £F
O **Riesling** Harth Cuvée Alexandre★★ £B Clos Saint-Théobald Rangen Grand Cru★★★★ £E
O **Riesling** Clos Saint-Théobald Rangen Grand Cru Vendange Tardive❂❂❂❂❂ £F
O **Tokay Pinot Gris** Cuvée Alexandre Vieilles Vignes★★★ £C
O **Tokay Pinot Gris** Clos Saint-Théobald Rangen Grand Cru★★★★★ £E
O **Tokay Pinot Gris** Clos Saint-Théobald Rangen Grand Cru SGN❂❂❂❂❂ £F

TRIMBACH Ribeauvillé www.maison-trimbach.fr   A: Par, BBR,WSc

Owner: Trimbach family   15 Route de Bergheim, 68150 Ribeauvillé

Large well-established merchant house producing close to 100,000 cases a year. Like HUGEL, the top wines are very impressive, although perhaps of not quite the same dimension. This is with the exception of the remarkable Riesling Clos Sainte-Hune, arguably the greatest dry expression of the variety in the region and one of the greatest anywhere in the world. Indeed, the Rieslings are the most successful of the varietals. They are structured, very dry in style and have a pure and intense mineral depth. They age remarkably well. The Gewürztraminer Seigneurs de Ribeaupierre is in a similarly dry, structured style. Rich, aromatic, lychee notes and an increasingly honeyed character will emerge with five or six years' cellaring. VT and SGN bottlings are certainly impressive. They are structured and rich, just a little way short of the very best. The generics are less exciting than many equivalents you may find from smaller domaines and the prices for these are quite steep. (DM)

O **Muscat** Réserve★ £B
O **Gewürztraminer**★ £C Seigneurs de Ribeaupierre★★★ £E Vendange Tardive★★★★ £F
O **Riesling**★★ £B Réserve★★ £C Clos Sainte-Hune❂❂❂❂❂ £G
O **Riesling** Cuvée Frédéric Émile★★★★ £E
O **Tokay Pinot Gris** Réserve★★ £B Réserve Personnelle★★★ £C SGN★★★★ £G

DOMAINE WEINBACH Kaysersberg www.domaineweinbach.com A: J&B, Tan, NYg

Owner: Mme Faller & family 25 route du Vin, 68240 Kaysersberg

Weinbach is another of the great names of Alsace. Madame Faller and her daughters run an impressive 26-ha estate partly converted to biodynamic cultivation since 1998. The wines are stylistically different from those of Trimbach or Zind-Humbrecht, not the elegance or reserve of the former nor the same degree of definition and nuance of terroir seen in the Zind-Humbrecht wines, yet they are rich, powerful and complex, particularly concentrated and impressive in the top cuvées, and they are rarely disappointing. The richest styles can be magnificent. The two most important holdings are those of the 5-ha walled Clos des Capucins and 10 ha in the Grand Cru Schlossberg, but outstanding wines are also made from *lieu-dit* Altenbourg. The number of bottlings is extensive and somewhat complicated with special cuvées named after family members. Cuvée Theo Gewürztraminer and Riesling (named after the late Theo Faller) come only from the Clos. Cuvée Sainte-Catherine is a rich Riesling from the lower part of Schlossberg, usually harvested in late November, but a more select bottling is additionally labelled Grand Cru Schlossberg while L'Inédit represents the very best selection of this vineyard. Regular Cuvée Laurence Tokay Pinot Gris and Gewürztraminer comes from the foot of Altenbourg, while those additionally labelled Altenbourg come from the vineyard itself. A small amount of Gewürztraminer also comes from the Grand Cru Furstentum. VT and SGN styles add more sweetness to the usual Weinbach concentration and depth whilst retaining good balance. Cuvée d'Or Quintessence SGN is reserved for formidable rich and sweet cuvées made when conditions allow it, such as an intensely sweet and spicy botrytised Gewürztraminer. A scented, stylish Muscat Réserve Personelle is also very good if drunk fairly young. (PW)

O **Riesling** Cuvée Theo★★★ £C Schlossberg Grand Cru Cuvée Sainte-Catherine★★★★★ £E
O **Riesling** Schlossberg Grand Cru Cuvée Sainte-Catherine l'Inédit★★★★★ £F Vendange Tardive★★★★★ £F
O **Gewürztraminer** Cuvée Theo★★★ £D Altenbourg Cuvée Laurence★★★★ £E
O **Gewürztraminer** Furstentum Vendange Tardive✪✪✪✪✪ £F
O **Gewürztraminer** Cuvée d'Or Quintessence SGN✪✪✪✪✪ £G
O **Tokay Pinot Gris** Cuvée Sainte-Catherine Fut II★★★★ £E O **Pinot Blanc** Réserve★★ £C
O **Muscat** Réserve Personelle★★★ £D

ZIND-HUMBRECHT Turckheim o.humbrecht@wanadoo.fr A: ABy, BBR

Owner: Olivier Zind-Humbrecht 4 Route de Colmar, 68230 Turckheim

It is very easy to eulogise about both the wines and the winemaking ethos of Olivier Humbrecht. The family's 40 ha of vineyards cultivated by Oliver's father Léonard (and biodynamic since 1997) offer an enviable resource from which individual *terroir* have been given expression. In fact, from a combination of several different grape varieties and many excellent sites, one of France's, indeed the world's great white wine producers has created a miniature vinous wonderland. More than 30 wines are produced in every vintage – multiply that by the different vintage permutations that a non-interventionist winemaking approach emphasises and you might not ever find time to taste anything else. The wines, made only from fully ripe grapes, are full, concentrated and intense, each expressing something of the essence of their origins. Some of Zind-Humbrecht's *crus* are also produced in late-harvested VT and SGN styles and although even regular versions can vary in the degree of residual sugar there is almost always the necessary balance between sweetness and acidity. If the range and variable levels of sweetness can make it difficult to choose an individual bottle, the new scale of sweetness being introduced in Alsace will help make it a little less bewildering. Highlights include a fascinating array of fine Riesling: Clos Saint-Urbain combines breadth and a fine minerality; Brand has great structure and power that unfurls slowly with age; Clos Windsbuhl shows an intense fruit depth; while Clos Hauserer can be more classically crisp and stimulating. Fine Pinot Gris include a very rich, creamy Vieilles Vignes example, potent Rotenberg, vibrant and deeply fruity Clos

Windsbuhl, and the smoky, minerally Clos Saint-Urbain, all of which are surpassed by the Clos Jebsal for sheer richness and substance. Impressively rich and aromatic Gewürztraminers include fine, minerally Wintzerheim, broad and powerful Herrenweg, rich, almost overwhelming Heimbourg, exotic Goldert and marvellously deep and concentrated Clos Windsbuhl. There is also a very small amount of Grand Cru Rangen Clos Saint-Urbain. Fine Muscat is also made, both deeply grapey Herrenweg and a more expressive, floral Goldert. Muscat excepted, almost all the wines need a decent amount of bottle-age to show at their best. Regular bottlings should have at least two or three years' ageing; most *lieu-dit*-labelled wines or *grands crus* (whether in regular versions or either VT or SGN styles) deserve at least five or six years. The list below includes most but not all of the extensive range. When made VT or SGN this can add a considerable premium to prices, especially the latter style. (PW)

O **Riesling** Rangen Grand Cru Clos Saint-Urbain★★★★ £F Brand Grand Cru✪✪✪✪✪ £F
O **Riesling** Turckheim★ £B Clos Hauserer★★★★ £E Clos Windsbuhl★★★★ £E
O **Tokay Pinot Gris** Rangen Grand Cru Clos Saint-Urbain★★★★★ £F Clos Windsbuhl★★★★★ £F
O **Tokay Pinot Gris** Vieilles Vignes★★★ £C Rotenberg★★★ £E Heimbourg★★★ £E Clos Jebsal★★★★ £E
O **Gewürztraminer** Heimbourg★★★★ £E Goldert Grand Cru★★★★ £E Clos Windsbuhl★★★★ £E
O **Gewürztraminer** Herrenweg★★★ £D Wintzenheim★★★ £D Hengst Grand Cru★★★★★ £F
O **Muscat** Herrenweg★★★ £D Goldert Grand Cru★★★★ £D
O **Pinot d'Alsace** ★★ £C   O **Sylvaner**★ £B

OTHER WINES OF NOTE

JEAN-BAPTISTE ADAM O **Muscat** Réserve £B   O **Riesling** Kaefferkopf Vieilles Vignes £C
O **Gewürztraminer** Vendange Tardive £E
ALLIMANT-LAUGNER O **Muscat** £B   O **Riesling** £B   O **Gewürztraminer** £C
DOM. AUTHER O **Muscat** £B   O **Riesling** £B
JEAN-PIERRE BECHTOLD O **Gewürztraminer** Silberberg £C   O **Riesling** Engelberg Grand Cru £C
DOM. BERHHARD-RIEBEL O **Riesling** Rittersberg £B   O **Tokay Pinot Gris** Rittersberg £C
LÉON BOESCH O **Sylvaner** £B   O **Gewürztraminer** Zinnkoepflé Grand Cru £D
CAVE DE CLEEBOURG O **Gewürztraminer** Sigillé £B   O **Muscat** Sigillé £B
DOM. DIRLER-CADÉ O **Sylvaner** VV £B   O **Muscat** Spiegel Grand Cru £D
O **Riesling** Kessler Grand Cru £C   O **Gewürztraminer** Spiegel Grand Cru SGN £F
DOPFF & IRION O **Tokay Pinot Gris** Maquisards £B   Vorbourg Grand Cru £F
DOPFF AU MOULIN O **Gewürztraminer** Brand Grand Cru £F
PIERRE FRICK O **Pinot Blanc** £B   O **Sylvaner** Précieuse £B   O **Riesling** Steinert Grand Cru £C
A & R GRESSER O **Gewürztraminer** Duttenberg VV £D   O **Riesling** Kastelberg Grand Cru £C
PAUL GINGLINGER O **Riesling** Drei Exa £C Pfersigberg Grand Cru £D
O **Tokay Pinot Gris** Eichberg Grand Cru £D   O **Gewürztraminer** Wahlenbourg £D
O **Gewürztraminer** Pfersigberg Grand Cru Cuvée Saint Léon £D
JOSMEYER O **Pinot Auxerrois H** Vieilles Vignes £C   O **Tokay Pinot Gris** 1854 Fondation £D
O **Gewürztraminer** Les Folastries £D Hengst Grand Cru £E
O **Riesling** Le Kottabe £C Hengst Grand Cru £E
DOM. ROGER JUNG O **Riesling** VV £B Schoenenbourg Grand Cru £C
KUENTZ-BAS O **Tokay Pinot Gris** Eichberg Grand Cru £D Cuvée Caroline Vendange Tardive £E
O **Tokay Pinot Gris** Cuvée Jeremy SGN £F
SEPPI LANDMANN O **Gewürztraminer** Zinnkoepflé Grand Cru £E
O **Gewürztraminer** Zinnkoepflé Grand Cru Vendange Tardive £F
O **Riesling** Zinnkoepflé Grand Cru £E   O **Tokay Pinot Gris** Zinnkoepflé Grand Cru £E
FRANÇOIS LICHTLÉ O **Riesling** Pfersigberg Grand Cru £C SGN £E
O **Gewürztraminer** Réserve Personelle £B   O **Tokay Pinot Gris** Cuvée Leo £C
JEAN-LUC MADER O **Pinot Blanc** Théophile £B   O **Gewürztraminer** Théophile £B
DOM. MATERNE-HAEGELIN O **Gewürztraminer** £B   O **Riesling** Bollenberg £B

MEYER-FONNÉ ○ **Riesling** Katzenthal £B Winneck-Schlossberg Grand Cru £C
○ **Gewürztraminer** Winneck-Schlossberg Grand Cru £C
DOM. MITTNACHT-KLACK ○ **Riesling** Muhlforst £B Schoenenbourg Grand Cru £C
CAVE DE PFAFFENHEIM ○ **Riesling** Goldert Grand Cru £C Zinnkoepflé Grand Cru £C
CAVE DE RIBEAUVILLÉ ○ **Tokay Pinot Gris** £B Gloekelberg Grand Cru £C ○ **Riesling** Prestige £B
DOM. RIEFLÉ ○ **Gewürztraminer** Steinert Grand Cru £E ○ **Riesling** £C Steinert Grand Cru £C
○ **Tokay Pinot Gris** Côte de Rouffach£C Steinert Grand Cru £C
DOMAINE MARTIN SCHAETZEL ○ **Pinot Blanc** Réserve £B ○ **Riesling** Réserve £B
○ **Tokay Pinot Gris** Réserve £B ○ **Gewürztraminer** Kaefferkopf £C
ANDRÉ SCHERER ○ **Riesling** Pfersigberg Grand Cru £C
DOM. CHARLES SCHLERET ○ **Sylvaner** £B ○ **Riesling** Herrenweg £C
○ **Tokay Pinot Gris** Herrenweg £C
DOMAINES SCHLUMBERGER ○ **Tokay Pinot Gris** Cuvée Clarisse £E
○ **Gewürztraminer** Cuvée Christine Vendange Tardive £F
GÉRARD SCHUELLER ○ **Muscat** Reserve £B ○ **Tokay Pinot Gris** Trottacker £C
BRUNO SORG ○ **Gewürztraminer** £B Pfersigberg Grand Cru £C
○ **Tokay Pinot Gris** Florimont Grand Cru £C
PIERRE SPARR ○ **Gewürztraminer** GC Mambourg £C ○ **Pinot Gris** Réserve £B
MARC TEMPÉ ○ **Pinot Blanc** Zellenberg £B ○ **Riesling** Zellenberg £B
CAVE VINICOLE DE TURCKHEIM ○ **Gewürztraminer** Réserve £B Hengst Grand Cru £C
○ **Gewürztraminer** Brand Grand Cru £C Vendange Tardive £D ○ **Tokay Pinot Gris** Vendange Tardive £D
PAUL ZINCK ○ **Riesling** Prestige £B Rangen Grand Cru £C ○ **Tokay Pinot Gris** Prestige £B
○ **Gewürztraminer** Prestige £B Eichberg Grand Cru £C

Author's choice (DM)

A dozen striking dry whites
DOM. PAUL BLANCK ○ **Gewürztraminer** Grand Cru Furstentum Vieilles Vignes
DOM. BOTT-GEYL ○ **Riesling** Mandelburg Grand Cru
ERNEST BURN ○ **Tokay Pinot Gris** Goldert Grand Cru Cuvée de la Chapelle
MARCEL DEISS ○ **Altenberg Grand Cru**
MARC KREYDENWEISS ○ **Le Clos du Val d'Eléon**
DOM. ALBERT MANN ○ **Pinot Blanc/Auxerrois** Vieilles Vignes
RENÉ MURÉ ○ **Riesling** Clos Saint Landelin Vorbourg Grand Cru
OSTERTAG ○ **Sylvaner** Vieilles Vignes
DOM. SCHOFFIT ○ **Gewürztraminer** Harth Cuvée Alexandre Vieilles Vignes
TRIMBACH ○ **Riesling** Clos Sainte-Hune
DOM. WEINBACH ○ **Muscat** Réserve Personelle
ZIND-HUMBRECHT ○ **Tokay Pinot Gris** Clos Windsbuhl

An exciting selection of late harvest whites
DOM. JEAN BECKER ○ **Gewürztraminer** Schoenenbourg Grand Cru SGN
DOM. LÉON BEYER ○ **Tokay Pinot Gris** SGN
DOM. BOTT-GEYL ○ **Tokay Pinot Gris** Sonnenglanz Grand Cru SGN
HUGEL ET FILS ○ **Riesling** SGN
ANDRÉ KIENTZLER ○ **Gewürztraminer** Vendange Tardive
DOM. ALBERT MANN ○ **Tokay Pinot Gris** Hengst Grand Cru SGN
OSTERTAG ○ **Gewürztraminer** Fronholz Vendange Tardive
ROLLY-GASSMANN ○ **Muscat** Moenchreben Vendange Tardive
DOM. SCHOFFIT ○ **Riesling** Clos Saint Théobald Rangen Grand Cru Vendange Tardive
DOM. WEINBACH ○ **Gewürztraminer** Cuvée d'Or Quintessence SGN

The name Champagne carries almost mystical properties for a vast number of people. However, there are a bewildering number of Champagne houses, co-operatives and growers bottling wine under their own labels and a further huge own-label business with wines of immensely variable quality all being bottled under the auspices of just one appellation. The great Champagne houses virtually invented the concept of the brand in winemaking and in most cases they do a very acceptable job. Nonetheless, the area remains a minefield for consumers without a better classification system. There are some 30,000-plus ha under vine with many of the 19,000 growers cultivating no more than a ha or two. Not only in the cellars of the region but also in the vineyards there are inevitably substantial variations in quality.

The Appellation and its Districts

Making sparkling wine is realistically the only consistent vinegrowing activity that can be undertaken here, among the windswept rolling hills of the most northerly of France's wine regions. Alsace may be on a not dissimilar latitude but crucially it is protected by the Vosges Mountains. Ripening the three varieties Pinot Meunier, Pinot Noir and Chardonnay is by no means easy. Pinot Noir and Chardonnay are at their optimum in the production of the great wines of the Côte d'Or some 240 km (150 miles) to the south. The vital requirement here is to provide grapes that are physiologically ripe and of sufficient intensity to produce at least good wine. That means controlling yields and harvesting properly ripened fruit, which remains a problem.

Within the appellation the communes have been classified as Grand Cru, Premier Cru or Deuxième Cru. This does not however give an indication of quality or the potential of a given *terroir* as it does in Burgundy but works more as a means by which to establish the price a grower gets for his harvest. You may have an outstanding performer in a second-classed village and a moderate grower in a *grand cru*.

The appellation falls into five main districts, which account for some two-thirds of the working vineyard area. These five districts may yet become their own sub-appellations in a desired move to establish better regional identity within this geographically extensive AC. The rest of the appellation is spread across a vast area. Indeed the idea that all Champagne comes from fabled chalk soils is not the case. Much of the *vignoble* is clay, sand or marl. The **Montagne de Reims** is just to the south of that city and the aspect of the vineyards improves as you move south. Pinot Noir and Pinot Meunier are the predominant varieties here and are famed for producing rich, full-bodied Champagnes. The village of **Bouzy** is as well known for producing the best, still Coteaux Champenois reds as it is sparkling wines.

The **Vallée de la Marne** to north-west from the Montagne de Reims stretches east along the River Marne. The centre of the district is the town of Épernay and the best vineyard sites are to the east. Red grapes are predominant here and the wines tend to be a touch lighter than those from the Montagne de Reims, with more elegance and refinement. The **Côte des Blancs** is, unsurprisingly, white wine territory. Chardonnay is virtually the exclusive grape here with very few red plantings. The vineyards are largely sited with an easterly aspect. The great Chardonnay villages of Avize, Le Mesnil-sur-Oger and Vertus are found here.

In the far south-west of the main Champagne area, north of Troyes, is the **Côte de Sézanne**, with the small town of the same name at its heart. The vineyards are dominated by Chardonnay, which accounts for some seven out of ten vines. As in the Côte des Blancs there is extensive chalk in the soil but not to the same degree. Way to the south of Troyes and away from the main Champagne appellation boundaries is the **Aube**. The area is one hundred miles from Reims. The soil is different, there is no chalk but more of the Kimmeridgian clay and limestone soils of Sancerre and Chablis. The latter is in fact a good deal closer to the Aube than any of the other Champagne vineyards.

At present the Aube is largely planted to Pinot Noir. There is a case for a considerable increase in Chardonnay. The area could potentially make extremely rich and powerful Blanc de Blancs.

The Styles

The range of different styles available take in sparkling white and rosé along with the still red wines which use the Coteaux Champenois appellation. While the role of the master blender in Champagne remains as significant as ever, the development of wines that come from single *terroirs* or from the same, very specific sources when vintage conditions favour – like the great Salon wines – seems likely to accelerate as time goes on. The sheer quality of many of the emerging small growers is a signal of things to come.

The styles and method outlined below should only be used as a very general guide; there can be significant variation within these. It is quite possible to find deluxe super-premium *cuvées* that are non-vintage, Blanc de Blancs that may be from a single vineyard or a blend of many, or Blanc de Noirs in vintage and non-vintage versions.

Most common and providing the bulk of the output of the great Champagne houses are the regular **non-vintage** blends. The use of reserve wine stocks is an undoubted asset, but a huge variation in quality exists. Available vineyard resources (and consequent fruit quality) and the length of time on lees in bottle are just two of the factors that affect the style of these wines. You should expect **vintage** *cuvées* to be a significant step up. They should be denser and richer with significantly greater structure. Inevitably there will be more variation in style with these as they reflect the nature of the year. Generally they should only be released after good harvests.

Blanc de Blancs is produced solely from Chardonnay while **Blanc de Noirs** is produced from Pinot Noir and/or Pinot Meunier, to the complete exclusion of Chardonnay. Blanc de Blancs are more refined and elegant and often have a tighter structure when young, whereas a Blanc de Noirs is fuller, with richer, more opulent flavours. The pink **Rosés** can be made either by blending in a little red wine (the only AC where this is permitted) or, and generally with better results, by the normal manner of a short maceration on skins. The best rosé generally comes from pure Pinot Noir.

The most expensive Champagnes are the deluxe bottlings. There are a wide range of styles but the best are among the finest white or rosé wines in the world. The latter are generally more expensive and made in minute quantities.

Vintages

Because of the variable and challenging climate there is much vintage variation. Vintage wines are only produced when conditions permit. Among recent years 2002 looks very promising. 2001, though, was a disaster with unprecedented rainfall. From 1995 to 2000 the Champenois were very lucky, having a string of good to very good vintages. 1996 and 1998 were outstanding. 1996 was uniformly good, very warm and sunny with ideal ripening conditions. There was some variation in 1998. 1996 and 1997 are now emerging on the market. Prior to 1995 the only really halfway presentable year was 1993. There were an alarming number of 1992s which were green and hard. 1990 is a classic. There are stunning wines on release now, like the Bollinger RD. 1989 and 1988 were both very good but not quite on a par with 1990. 1989 has less structure and should be drunk now. 1985, 1983 and 1982 are all great earlier years and top wines encountered from these will be worth considering, although '85 and '83 particularly do need drinking now.

PAUL BARA

A: OWL

Owner: Bara family   4 Rue Yvonnet, 51150 Bouzy

Very good small and traditional producer with vineyard holdings in the *grand cru* village of Bouzy. The wines have a high level of Pinot Noir in the blend and this tends to show through with weight and substance. The Grand Cru Vintage is rich and bready, the Vintage Club shows extra depth and there is a very impressive, intense rosé. The Comtesse Marie de France is lighter and more elegant. The wines are all good value. (DM)

○ **Brut Réserve Grand Cru** Non-Vintage★★ £C   ○ **Brut Grand Cru** Vintage★★★ £D
○ **Brut Grand Cru Comtesse Marie de France** Vintage★★★★ £E
○ **Grand Cru Vintage Club** Vintage★★★★ £E
◉ **Brut Grand Cru Grand** Rosé de Bouzy★★★ £D

EDMOND BARNAUT   www.champagne-barnaut.com

A: L&S, GFy

Owner: Philippe Secondé   2 Rue Gambetta, BP 19, 51150 Bouzy

The 14 ha of vineyards are, like those of the Bara family, around the village of Bouzy. Unlike the Bara vineyards, though, there is a high proportion of Chardonnay planted. This gives an added finesse and grip although the wines are of an impressively weighty, substantial style. There are two fine non-vintage wines: the Sélection-Extra and Grand Réserve. The former has a higher proportion of Pinot Noir which is evident, as it is in a rich, bready Blanc de Noirs. The Authentique Rosé gains its colour from the Pinot Noir skins rather than from blending with red base wine. There is also a limited-production special Cuvée Edmond Brut, a 1995 is the latest release, a Cuvée Douceur Sec and a fruity Bouzy Rouge. (DM)

○ **Brut Sélection-Extra** Non-Vintage★★★ £D   ○ **Grand Réserve** Non-Vintage★★★ £D
○ **Blanc de Noirs** Non-Vintage★★★ £D
◉ **Brut Authentique** Non-Vintage★★ £D

BILLECART-SALMON   www.champagne-billecart.fr

A: B-S

Owner: Billecart family   40 Rue Carnot, 51160 Mareuil-sur-Aÿ

A medium-sized and very impressive house, family-owned Billecart-Salmon produces 100,000 cases a year. The house was founded in 1818. The Brut Réserve non-vintage is classy stuff at this level and the top wines are very intense and marvellously refined. There is a sizeable proportion of Chardonnay used and this helps the wines' balance and classic Champagne structure. The elegant non-vintage Blanc de Blancs is sourced from Le Mesnil-sur-Oger and is normally a blend of two vintages. The super Cuvée Nicolas-François Billecart is a very complex and elegant blend of 40 per cent Chardonnay and 60 per cent Pinot Noir. A vintage Blanc de Blancs is also produced along with a vintage Grande Cuvée the current release of which is 1990. There is also a tiny amount of prestige rosé Cuvée Elisabeth Salmon. (DM)

○ **Brut Réserve** Non-Vintage★★★ £E   ○ **Blancs de Blancs Grand Cru** Non-Vintage★★★★ £F
○ **Brut Cuvée Nicolas-François Billecart** Vintage★★★★★ £F
◉ **Brut Rosé**★★★ £F

BOLLINGER   www.champagne-bollinger.fr

A: Men

Owner: Bollinger family   16 Rue Jules-Lobet, BP4, 51160 Aÿ

One of the greatest names in sparkling wine production. Bollinger produces around 150,000 cases a year. It is one of just a handful of producers here who still ferment base wines in wood. A high proportion of

Pinot Noir is used and the non-vintaged Special Cuvée is always full and rich in style. The vintage Grande Année can almost take on a hint of Burgundian gaminess with age, as can the remarkable RD *(récemment dégorgé)*. This wine is kept in bottle on its yeast sediment for up to 10 years and possesses a rich toastiness; it is both concentrated and exceptionally well balanced. 1990 is the current release. A tiny amount of a 100 per cent Pinot Noir *cuvée*, Vieilles Vignes, is made from ungrafted, very low-yielding old vines and there is a decent Coteaux Champenois red, Côte aux Enfants. (DM)

O **Brut Spécial Cuvée** Non-Vintage★★★ £E
O **Brut Grande Année** Vintage★★★★★ £G   O **RD**✪✪✪✪✪ £H
◉ **Brut Grande Année** Rosé Vintage★★★ £G

DEUTZ   www.champagne-deutz.com   A: BWC, Lay

Owner: Louis Roederer   16 Rue Jeanson, BP 9, 51160 Aÿ
Now owned by Louis Roederer, Deutz also has a successful sparkling wine partnership in New Zealand with MONTANA. By comparison with many of the other great houses the annual production here is relatively modest at some 80,000 cases or so. Quality is generally good to very good indeed and the wines are well-priced, perhaps with the exception of the luxury *cuvées* William Deutz and Blanc de Blancs Amour de Deutz. The non-vintage Brut Classic is a good and well-structured, yeasty style; the vintage wines are tighter, more refined. (DM)

O **Brut Classic** Non-Vintage★★ £E
O **Brut** Vintage★★★ £F   O **William Deutz** Vintage★★★★★ £G
O **Blanc de Blancs** Vintage★★★★ £F
◉ **Brut** Rosé Vintage★★★ £F

EGLY-OURIET

Owner: Michel et Francis Egly-Ouriet   9-15. Rue de Trépail, 51150 Ambonnay
Very impressive, small family-run property with some 7 ha of Pinot Noir and 2 ha of Chardonnay. Production is tiny at some 5,500 cases a year. Quality is high, with well-aged vineyards that are over 30 years old and a dedicated, generally organic approach to viticulture. Yields are carefully tempered and a partial *vendange vert* is practised. In the cellar minimal handling extends to an absence of either fining or filtration for the base wines. The result is wonderfully pure, full-bodied wines of great character. A very good example of Coteaux Champenois is also produced but available only in very limited quantities. (DM)

O **Brut Tradition** Non-Vintage★★★ £D   O **Grand Cru** Vintage★★★★★ £E
O **Blanc de Noirs Vieilles Vignes** Non-Vintage★★★★ £E
◉ **Brut** Rosé Non-Vintage★★★ £D

PIERRE GIMONNET ET FILS   www.champagne-gimmonet.com   A: Oas

Owner: Gimonnet family   1 Rue de la République, 51530 Cuis
Family domaine that possesses 26 ha of very well-sited vineyards in the Côte des Blancs populated exclusively with old Chardonnay vines. Part of the vineyard holding is *premier cru* and part *grand cru*. This provides the property with a superb resource of base wine material. The style varies from the fresh, taut and lightly toasty Cuis Premier Cru to the weightier and richer Fleuron and Club Premier Cru labels. The Extra-Brut Oenophile, bottled without *dosage*, is very tight and lean but elegant. (DM)

O **Blanc de Blancs Puis** Premier Cru Non-Vintage★★ £D
O **Brut Fleuron** Premier Cru Vintage★★★ £E   O **Brut Club** Premier Cru Vintage★★★ £E
O **Brut Gastronome** Vintage★★ £D
O **Extra-Brut Oenophile** Vintage★★★ £E

GOSSET www.champagne-gosset.com A: McK

Owner: Cointreau family   69 Rue Jules-Blondeau, 51160 Aÿ
This is among the very oldest of the Champagne houses, its commercial origins going back to 1584. The regular non-vintage Excellence can be good but isn't always. The Grande Réserve and Grand Rosé, both non-vintage, and the vintage offerings here are a step up. The style is one of weight and a rich toastiness in the top wines but unfortunately a lack of elegance can creep in as well. Celebris is clearly a cut above the rest. (DM)

O **Brut Excellence** Non-Vintage★ £D
O **Grande Réserve** Non-Vintage★★★ £F   **Grande Millésime** Vintage★★★ £F
O **Celebris** Vintage★★★★ £G
◉ **Grand Rosé** Non-Vintage★★★ £F

ALFRED GRATIEN www.alfredgratien.com A: Wit, WSc

Owner: Henkell and Sohnlein   30 Rue Maurice Cerveaux, BP 3, 51201 Épernay
Very good, small, traditional house which produces barely 15,000 cases a year. The base wines are vinified in wood and all cellar operations are still carried out by hand. The malolactic fermentation is blocked and this provides the taught, structured style. The wines, even the non-vintage, are ageworthy. The purchase by German *sekt* producer Henkell and Sohnlein is a recent development and it remains to be seen whether the house style will remain faithful and equally whether production will soar. (DM)

O **Brut** Réserve Non-Vintage★★★ £E   O **Paradis** Non-Vintage★★★★ £F
O **Brut** Vintage★★★★★ £F
◉ **Brut Rosé Paradis** Non-Vintage★★★ £F

CHARLES HEIDSIECK www.charlesheidsieck.com A: Max

Owner: Remy Cointreau   4 Boulevard Henri-Vasnier, 51100 Reims
Under the ownersip of Remy-Cointreau, the quality of the wine at this house over the past 15 years has been very impressive. The non-vintaged Brut Réserve Mis-en-Cave is arguably the best of its style in the appellation. The wine draws on a considerable amount of reserve wine and unusually gives the date of bottling so that the consumer has some idea of the age of the wine. Much of the consummate skill in creating this wine was achieved by the late Daniel Thibaut, one of the great modern master blenders of Champagne. There are two first-class vintage reserves: the elegant, superbly-crafted Blanc des Millénaires made from Chardonnay and the Pinot-dominated Charlie, a powerful, concentrated, weighty but very refined wine. (DM)

O **Brut Réserve Mis-en-Cave** Non-Vintage★★★★ £E   O **Charlie** Vintage★★★★★ £G
O **Blanc des Millénaires Vintage★★★★★** £G

HENRIOT contact@champagne-henriot.com A: JEF

Owner: Joseph Henriot   81 Rue Coquebert, 51100 Reims
Medium-sized producer accounting for some 80,000 cases a year of moderately-priced Champagne. The quality reflects the price here but the top vintage wines are reasonably impressive. The wines, including the straightforward Brut Souverain non-vintage, are weighty enough but lack a certain amount of refinement. The Cuvée des Enchanteleurs is a marked step up in both elegance and depth. (DM)

O **Blanc de Blancs** Non-Vintage★ £D   **Brut** Vintage★★★ £E
O **Cuvée des Enchanteleurs★★★** £F   ◉ **Brut** Rosé Vintage★★ £E

JACQUESSON   champagne.jacquesson@wanadoo.fr   A: May

Owner: Chiquet family   68 Rue du Colonel-Fabien, 51530 Dizy
This is a good, small-scale family-run operation producing around 25,000 cases a year of good to
very good Champagnes. Barrel-fermentation is used for the base wine and the resulting Champagnes
are characterful and refined. The style is rich, full-bodied and harmonious. The Brut Signature
vintage bottlings are very serious and structured and there is a very impressive vintage Blanc de
Blancs as well. A complex and very pricey Dégorgement Tardif is now being produced, which is given
extended ageing on lees. (DM)
O **Brut Perfection** Non-Vintage★★ £E   O **Signature** Vintage★★★★ £G
O **Blanc de Blancs Vintage**★★★★ £G
◉ **Brut Perfection Rosé** Non-Vintage★★ £E

KRUG   krug@krug.fr   A: Par

Owner: LMVH   5 Rue Coquebert, 51100 Reims
Still run by Rémy Krug, this is arguably the most prestigious of all the great Champagne houses.
However, production remains quite small at just over 40,000 cases a year. It is to be hoped that the
exceptional quality standards here will remain under LMVH ownership and that volume will not
escalate. These are quite remarkably impressive and structured wines. Tight and very restrained,
perhaps more so than all other Champagnes, they demand cellaring. Even the non-vintage Grande
Cuvée will benefit from at least five years after release. The wine often on the cusp of a super-five
rating. The Clos du Mesnil is that rare breed in this appellation, a wine from a small single vineyard.
The range is completed by the tiny-production and undoubtedly very fine non-vintage Rosé. (DM)
O **Grande Cuvée** Non-Vintage★★★★★ £H   O **Clos du Mesnil** Vintage✪✪✪✪✪ £H
O **Vintage**✪✪✪✪✪ £H

LANSON   www.lanson.fr   A: MCD

*Owner: **Marne et Champagne**   12 Boulevard Lundy, 51100 Reims*
Production here is vast at close to some 600,000 cases a year. In the light of that, quality has been at
least solid. The Black Label Brut is probably the best-known Champagne brand after the MOËT ET
CHANDON Brut Impérial; quality has been variable to say the least but across recent releases there has
been a sound upturn in form – by no means where it could be, but a marked improvement. As well as
the big brand a non-vintage rosé is fairly unexciting but there is a stylish Blanc de Blancs vintage and a
decent enough Ivory Label Demi-Sec. The Brut Gold Label vintage was good rather than spectacular
in 1995 but the quality of the wines currently does seem to indicate real progress. The Noble Cuvée is
a seriously structured and impressive Champagne. (DM)
O **Brut Black Label** Non-Vintage★ £D   O **Gold Label** Vintage★★ £E
O **Blanc de Blancs** Vintage★★★ £F
O **Noble Cuvée** Vintage★★★★ £G

LARMANDIER-BERNIER   larmandier@terre-net.fr   A: VTr

Owner: Larmandier-Bernier family   43 Rue de 28 Août, 51130 Vertus
Small, top-class grower based in the Côte des Blancs, with an understandably large proportion of
Chardonnay plantings. Like most really quality-conscious winemakers around the world Pierre
Larmandier keeps the human input to a minimum. The style is for very structured, minerally, intense
Champagnes that have been given extra weight and depth through cask-ageing (no new wood is

used) prior to bottling and further cellaring prior to release. Very low *dosage* is the approach here, with the Né d'Un Terre de Vertus being bone dry. The wines have the depth and texture to support the style but will reward cellaring, the vintage wines for many years. A very small amount of red Coteaux Champenois is also produced and is among the very best examples of the style. The fact that the wines are excellent value is another plus. (DM)

O **Brut Tradition** Non-Vintage★★★£D   O **Blanc de Blancs** Non-Vintage★★★£D
O **Extra Brut Vieille Vignes de Cramant** Vintage★★★★★£E
O **Né d'Un Terre de Vertus Non Dosé** Non-Vintage★★★★£D

LAURENT-PERRIER   www.laurent-perrier.co.uk   A: L-P

Owner: De Nonancourt family   151150 Tour-sur-Marne
Still very much a family-run operation, although interests also include the other Champagne houses of DE CASTELLANE, DELAMOTTE and the super-prestige SALON. The great wines here are the Grand Siècle labels; they are immensely refined, the two whites having a rich, powerful, bready character underpinned by a pure mineral structure. The rosé is refined and very complex with a remarkable array of berry-fruit aromas. The regular Brut non-vintage is sound with quite a heavy *dosage* but lacks a bit of grip. The non-vintaged rosé, though, is stylish and fresh, with attractive fruit. The Ultra Brut is impressively piercing and will develop well with some bottle-age. (DM)

O **Brut LP** Non-Vintage★£E   O **Vintage**★★£F   O **Ultra Brut** Non-Vintage★★★£F
O **Grand Siècle La Cuvée** Non-Vintage★★★★★£G
O **Grand Siècle** Vintage★★★★★£H
◉ **Brut Rosé** Non-Vintage★★★★£H
◉ **Grand Siècle Alexandra Rosé** Vintage★★★★£H

SERGE MATHIEU   champagne.mathieu@wanadoo.fr

Owner: Mathieu family   6 Rue des Vignes, 10340 Avirey-Lingey
Small but very good property based in the Aube. Pinot Noir is the key component here and the wines certainly display a real weight and concentration. However, what marks them out is their elegance and refinement, something that a great many of their near neighbours struggle to achieve. The vintage Brut is impressively concentrated, rich, bready and toasty but with a fine mineral backbone. The Tête de Cuvée is subtler, more refined, with a higher proportion of Chardonnay and a shorter period on lees. Both are ageworthy. (DM)

O **Brut Tradition** Non-Vintage★★£C   O **Brut Prestige** Non-Vintage★★£D
O **Brut Millésime** Vintage★★★£E   O **Tête de Cuvée** Non-Vintage★★★£E
O **Blanc de Noirs** Non-Vintage★★★£D
◉ **Brut Rosé** Non-Vintage★★£D

MOËT ET CHANDON   www.moet.com   A: MHn

Owner: LMVH   20 Rue avenue de Champagne, 51220 Épernay
Of all the Champagne houses this is the one that most readily comes to most consumers' minds. The tendency among the majority of occasional wine drinkers is to think of Moët as a brand rather than understanding it as a great Champagne house. Production is considerable, around 2,500,000 cases a year. Brut Impérial can be a lot more impressive than it is often given credit for. The White Star is marketed in the US and contains a higher *dosage*. The vintage Brut is well made with reasonable yeasty complexity and will age well over the medium term. Like the house itself, Dom Pérignon is the most established of the region's luxury *cuvées* and production is not small. The wine is very good

and consistent, becoming increasingly complex and harmonious with age. There is a fine vintage rosé and a very small amount of the Dom Perignon Rosé, every bit as impressive as the white. Three expensive additions have also been made from *grand cru* villages: Champs de Romont is based on Pinot Meunier, Vignes de Saran is from Chardonnay and Sarment d'Aÿ is a Pinot Noir. All are non-vintage. There is also now a non-vintage *premier cru* bottling blended from all three Champagne varieties. (DM)

O **Brut Impérial** Non-Vintage★★ £E   O **Brut White Star** Non-Vintage★ £E
O **Brut Impérial** Vintage★★★ £E
O **Dom Pérignon** Vintage★★★★★ £E
◉ **Brut Rosé** Vintage★★ £H

PIERRE MONCUIT   A: HHB

Owner: Nicole & Yves Moncuit   11 Rue Persault-Maheu, 51190 Le Mesnil-sur-Oger
The Moncuits produce two very fine Blanc de Blancs at their 20-ha property at Le Mesnil-sur-Oger. The Grand Cru Vintage bottling is superbly crafted, intense and refined with not a hint of austerity, rather a rich, biscuity approachability. The Vieilles Vignes is a very fine expression of Champagne hand-crafted from Chardonnay – intense, refined and very ageworthy. Sadly very little is made. What makes these wines all the more remarkable is the reasonable prices. (DM)

O **Blanc de Blancs** Grand Cru Vintage★★★ £D   O **Nicole Moncuit Vieilles Vignes** Vintage★★★★ £E

G H MUMM   www.mumm.com   A: ADo

*Owner: **Allied Domecq**   29 Rue du Champs-de-Mar, 51100 Reims*
Allied Domecq purchased this old house in 2001 and it now joins PERRIER-JOUËT in the same stable. It will be interesting to see how the operations perform. The main brand, Cordon Rouge, was for a long time a serious underperformer. However during the late 1990s the quality has been altogether sounder. The wine is not complex but has a good core of appley fruit and is bottled with quite a high *dosage*. The vintage bottling is really only marginally better but the Grand Cordon vintage is a classier proposition. There is also now a vintage-blended Grand Cru, a decent Brut Rosé and of course the prestige, non-vintaged Mumm de Cramant. (DM)

O **Cordon Rouge** Non-Vintage★ £E   O **Cordon Rouge** Vintage★ £E
O **Grand Cordon** Vintage★★★ £F   O **Grand Cru** Vintage★★ £E
O **Mumm de Cramant** Non-Vintage★★★★ £G
◉ **Brut Rosé** Non-Vintage★ £E

BRUNO PAILLARD   www.champagnebrunopaillard.com   A: Bib

Owner: Bruno Paillard   Avenue de Champagne, 51100 Reims
Bruno Paillard runs a modern, well-organised cellar producing towards 45,000 cases a year. The style is relatively austere but these are wines, particularly the vintage bottlings, that should develop well in bottle. The prestige NPU (Nec Plus Ultra) is undoubtedly a serious step up from the rest of the range but is also very pricey. The wines are labelled with a date of disgorging which gives a clear idea about when to drink the non-vintaged wines. (DM)

O **Brut Première Cuvée** Non-Vintage★ £E   O **Brut Millésime** Vintage★★★ £F
O **Chardonnay** Réserve Privée★★ £E
O **Nec Plus Ultra** Vintage★★★★ £H
◉ **Brut Rosé Première Cuvée** Non-Vintage★ £E

JOSEPH PERRIER josephperrier@wanadoo.fr A: CHk, FSA, GWW

Owner: Alain Thienot 69 Avenue de Paris, 51016 Châlons-en-Champagne

Relatively small among the big Champagne houses, Joseph Perrier is noted for traditional, medium- to full-bodied wines, with the Brut Royale non-vintage marked by a considerable amount of Pinot Meunier and Pinot Noir in the blend, providing a full, fruity style. The vintage Royale is more complex. There is no Pinot Meunier and the wine is tighter, more structured. The Joséphine vintage is of a different order. The concentrated Pinot fruit is beautifully balanced by a refined, nutty quality with its Chardonnay component providing finesse and a real depth and mineral purity. This will cellar well. (DM)

O **Brut Royale** Non-Vintage★★ £E O **Brut Royale** Vintage★★★ £F
O **Joséphine** Vintage★★★★ £G
◉ **Brut Royale** Non-Vintage★★ £E

PERRIER-JOUËT www.perrier-jouet.com A: ADo

Owner: Allied Domecq 51201 Epernay

Like G H MUMM this house, nearly 200 years old, has only been under the Allied Domecq banner since 2001. The wines have a relatively high proportion of Chardonnay but at the lower level they struggle to offer a great deal. The basic non-vintage Brut is a straightforward and simple offering with more green apple than complex, yeast-developed flavours. The Brut Rosé is a touch more impressive and there is a non-vintaged Blason white which provides a hint of bready complexity with a little time in bottle. The Blason Rosé is marked by very simple straightforward fruit, no more. The vintage Brut has better depth than the regular and a hint of toastiness but there should be greater dimension. The prestige *cuvée* La Belle Époque has a stylish bottle design and impressively tight, Chardonnay-based fruit. It achieves good to very good complex characters with age. There's a very good Belle Époque rosé as well. (DM)

O **Brut Blason de France** Non-Vintage★ £E O **Grand Brut** Vintage★ £F
O **La Belle Époque** Vintage★★★★ £G
◉ **Grand Brut** Non-Vintage★★ £E

PHILIPPONNAT www.champagnephilipponnat.com A: Eur

Owner: Bruno Paillard 13 Rue du Pont, 51160 Mareuil-sur-Aÿ

This is a relatively small *négociant-manipulant* with an output of just 50,000 cases a year. Until its acquisition by Bruno PAILLARD, the range was decidedly ordinary – with the exception of the great prestige *cuvée* Brut Clos de Goisses, a wine of super-five quality in extravagant vintages like 1990. However things appear to be making a turn for the better. A good, attractive, strawberry-fruited rosé is joined by the Royale Réserve, which has reasonable depth and a light nutty, biscuity character. The vintage is clearly a step up, more complete and complex, while the impressive Grand Blanc is a tight and structured Blanc de Blancs that needs time. The Clos des Goisses should be given additional cellaring, up to five years' ageing after release. (DM)

O **Brut Royale Réserve** Non-Vintage★ £E O **Brut Réserve Spécial** Vintage★★ £F
O **Grand Blanc** Vintage★★★ £F O **Clos des Goisses** Vintage★★★★★ £H
◉ **Brut Réserve** Non-Vintage★ £E

PIPER-HEIDSIECK   www.piper-heidsieck.com   A: Max

*Owner: **Remy Cointreau**   52 Boulevard Henry-Vasnier, 51100 Reims*
Under the same ownership as Charles HEIDSIECK but the Champagne here is a very different proposition. The non-vintage Brut is a simple, fruit-driven style, now produced without malolactic fermentation to retain its fresh, forward character. In recent years it has been better than of old – some releases used to be basically dilute. The Brut Rosé is simple and straightforward, with some pleasant red-berry fruit showing through. The Brut vintage is a good deal better – the wine has structure and depth with some complex toasty, yeasty notes evolving – while the Rare prestige *cuvée* is tight, structured and displays some real class. (DM)
O **Brut** Vintage★★ £F   O **Rare** Vintage★★★★ £G

POL ROGER   www.polroger.co.uk   A: Pol

Owner: Pol Roger family   1 Rue Henri-de-Large, 51206 Epernay
Family-owned, sizeable house with a production of approaching some 125,000 cases a year. The non-vintage White Foil is now consistently good, a style with real depth and a refined biscuity character but, like all the wines here, elegance and intensity is displayed more than weight. The vintage is just that little bit more complex and structured, very good and intense. There is a first class Blanc de Blancs Chardonnay vintage offering which is lighter still in style but impeccably balanced. Sir Winston Churchill is a very impressive prestige *cuvée* which demands to be cellared. (DM)
O **Brut White Foil** Non-Vintage★★★ £E   O **Brut** Vintage★★★★ £F
O **Brut Chardonnay** Vintage★★★ £F   O **Sir Winston Churchill** Vintage★★★★★ £H
◉ **Brut** Vintage★★★ £F

POMMERY   www.pommery.fr   A: MMD

*Owner: **Vranken**   5. Place du Général Gouraud, 51100 Reims*
Production is considerable at this large house with a volume of some 500,000 cases a year. However the LMVH group have sold their interest to Vranken who, while commercially successful throughout the appellation, have not so far established themselves as a beacon of top quality. Under LMVH ownership the quality throughout the range has been at least sound. There is a straightforward non-vintage Brut Royal, biscuity with a slightly raw edge to it, a better non-vintage Apanage and a sound rosé. The Blanc de Blancs Summertime is tight and structured, really quite elegant and the Blanc de Noirs Wintertime fuller and weightier. The vintage Grand Cru is refined and very well-balanced in the best years, not overly weighty but long and intense. The Cuvée Louise is very impressive, not a full style but very long harmonious and ageworthy. There is also a very fine Louise Rosé as well. Time will tell how the style and quality of the house will develop as a part of the Vranken empire. (DM)
O **Brut Royal** Non-Vintage★★ £E   O **Brut Apanage** Non-Vintage★★ £E
O **Blanc de Blancs Summertime** Non-Vintage★★★ £E
O **Blanc de Noirs Wintertime** Non-Vintage★★★ £E
O **Brut Grand Cru** Vintage★★★ £F   O **Louise** Vintage★★★★ £G
◉ **Brut** Non-Vintage★ £E

LOUIS ROEDERER   www.champagne-roederer.com   A: MMD

*Owner: **Champagne Louis Roederer**   21 Boulevard Lundy, 51100 Reims*
This has long been established as one of the great Champagne houses. Still family-owned, the company has invested heavily in other projects. As well as the ROEDERER ESTATE venture in California's Anderson

Valley (see California North Coast), much closer to home they have acquired DEUTZ, along with Château de PEZ in the Médoc and in Portugal the Port house RAMOS PINTO. The style here is weighty and rich with a considerable influence of Pinot Noir. The Blanc de Blancs is the most obviously restrained style and has its malolactic blocked for freshness and to achieve balance and harmony. A considerable holding of reserve wine helps the non-vintage Brut Premier while the Cristal prestige *cuvée* is one of the greatest and most refined sparkling wines in the world. It needs time. (DM)

○ **Brut Premier** Non-Vintage★★★ £E   ○ **Brut** Vintage★★★★ £F
○ **Blanc de Blancs** Vintage★★★ £F
○ **Cristal** Vintage✪✪✪✪✪ £H
◉ **Brut** Vintage★★★ £F

RUINART   www.ruinart.com
A: Rui

Owner: LMVH   4 Rue des Crayères, BP 85, 51053 Reims-Cedex

Among the big houses Ruinart has maintained a relatively low profile in recent years despite being under the same ownership as MOËT ET CHANDON and more recently KRUG. Surprisingly its production is relatively large at close to 200,000 cases a year. The wines, though, are good to excellent, with the prestige *cuvées* (both Blanc de Blancs Dom Ruinart and the Rosé) worthy of a super-five rating on occasion. Chardonnay is an important part of the blending equation here and the wines are both refined and powerful, particularly the vintage *cuvées*, due to some extended ageing of the base wines. The non-vintage Brut is consistently one of the best of its kind. Newly added is a luxury blend of six *grands crus* and five vintages all from Chardonnay, l'Exclusive de Ruinart. Rare and pricey. (DM)

○ **Brut R de Ruinart** Non-Vintage★★★ £E   ○ **Brut R de Ruinart** Vintage★★★★ £F
○ **Blanc de Blancs** Non-Vintage★★★ £F
○ **Dom Ruinart** Vintage★★★★★ £H
◉ **Brut R de Ruinart** Non-Vintage★★ £F   ◉ **Dom Ruinart** Vintage★★★★★ £H

SALON
A: C&B

Owner: Laurent-Perrier   5 Rue de la Brèche-d'Oger, 51190 Le Mesnil-sur-Oger

Now owned by Laurent-Perrier, just one exceptional wine is produced here: a Blanc de Blancs, in fact the first created, sourced entirely from selected vineyard plots in the village of Le Mesnil. Only bottled in the very best vintage years (the average through the last century was just over one year in four), an exceptional 1990 is the current release. Surprisingly rich and intense, but of course as well structured as you would expect, the wine should be cellared for at least a decade after release. (DM)

○ **Salon** Vintage✪✪✪✪✪ £H

FRANÇOIS SECONDÉ

Owner: François Secondé   6 Rue des Galipes, 51500 Sillery

Based in the Marne village of Sillery François Secondé produces very well-priced and finely structured Champagne from just 5 ha. Around three-quarters of the vineyard is planted to Pinot Noir, with the balance Chardonnay but the style is for tight, restrained, wines which need a little time to show at their best. The vineyards are farmed organically and with vines approaching 35 years age this helps in providing excellent raw material. The wines are traditionally made with manual *remuage*. They offer very good value. (DM)

○ **Brut** Non-Vintage★★★ £C   ○ **Brut Clavier** Non-Vintage★★★ £D
◉ **Brut Rosé** Non-Vintage★★ £C

JACQUES SELOSSE
A: O-F

Owner: Corinne & Anselme Selosse   22 Rue Ernest-Vallé, 51190 Avize

Remarkable small producer. Anselme Selosse bottles less than 4,000 cases of very impressive Champagne every year. The approach in the vineyard is biodynamic and yields are severely resticted to provide the purest, greatest intensity of fruit possible. What makes the approach here radical is to use new as well as old oak to barrel-ferment the base wine. Extensively aged prior to release, these are massive and powerful wines for Champagne but none the less impressive for that. On occasion the presence of oak can almost overwhelm, particularly in young or newly released wines, but there is no doubt that they are some of the most exciting and original wines of the appellation. (DM)

O **Blanc de Blancs Tradition** Non-Vintage★★★ £E   O **Originale** Extra-Brut Non-Vintage★★★★ £E
O **Grand Cru Substance** Non-Vintage★★★★ £E
O **Blanc de Noirs Contraste** Non-Vintage★★★★ £E   O **Blanc de Blancs** Vintage★★★★★ £F

TAITTINGER   www.taittinger.com
A: HMA

Owner: Taittinger family   9 Place Saint-Nicaise, 51100 Reims

A large house producing around 400,000 cases a year of generally reliable if rather unexciting non- vintage Brut Réserve. Better are some really very fine Vintage and an exceptional Blanc de Blancs prestige *cuvée* Comtes de Champagne, matched by an equally exquisite and very rare rosé. In the Loire Valley, Taittinger owns the sparkling wine house BOUVET-LADUBAY and in California Domaine CARNEROS. (DM)

O **Brut Réserve** Non-Vintage★ £E   O **Brut Millésime** Vintage★★★ £F
O **Blanc de Blanc Comtes de Champagne** Vintage✪✪✪✪✪ £H
◉ **Brut Prestige** Non-Vintage★ £E

VEUVE CLICQUOT   www.veuve-clicquot.fr
A: Par

Owner: LVMH   12 Rue du Temple, 51100 Reims

The second-tier producer in volume behind MOËT ET CHANDON in the LVMH hierarchy but most certainly not in terms of quality. Throughout the last five or six years the quality here has always been good, even for the regular Carte Jaune (Yellow Label). The vintage wines have weight and structure, full of rich, toasty character. La Grande Dame is exceptional wine, both the more easily available white and the scarce rosé. Both are rich, heady blends of Pinot Noir and Chardonnay. A number of prestige wineries around the world originally purchased by Veuve Clicquot now fall within the LVMH banner. These include CLOUDY BAY in New Zealand, CAPE MENTELLE in Western Australia and NEWTON in the Napa Valley. The house of Canard-Duchêne, which continues to disappoint of late, has long been under the Clicquot wing. (DM)

O **Brut Carte Jaune** Non-Vintage★★★ £E
O **Vintage Réserve**★★★ £F   O **Rich Réserve** Vintage★★★ £F
O **La Grande Dame** Vintage✪✪✪✪✪ £H
◉ **Rosé Réserve** Vintage★★★ £F

OTHER WINES OF NOTE

AGRAPART O **Blanc de Blancs Grand** Cru Non-Vintage £C   O Réserve Vintage £E
AYALA O **Brut** Non-Vintage £D
BEAUMONT DES CRAYÈRES O **Cuvée Nostalgie** Vintage £E
H BLIN O **Brut** Vintage £E

ALEXANDRE BONNET O Madrigal Vintage £E
CHARLES DE CAZENOVE O Brut Azur Premier Cru Non-Vintage £E
GUY CHARBAUT O Brut Vintage £E
GUY CHARLEMAGNE O Blanc de Blancs Grand Cru Vintage £E
JACKY CHARPENTIER O Brut Prestige Non-Vintage £E
DE CASTELLANE O Cuvée Florens Vintage £F
DELAMOTTE O Brut Vintage £E
DELBECK O Brut Vintage £E
DE SOUSA O Blanc de Blancs Réserve £D   O Brut Vintage £F
PAUL DÉTHUNE O Grand Cru Non-Vintage £C
DE VENOGE O Blanc de Noirs Non-Vintage £D
DOQUET-JEANMAIRE O Blanc de Blancs Couer de Terroir Vintage £D
DRAPPIER O Brut Carte d'Or Vintage £F   O Grande Sendrée Vintage £G
JACKY DUMANGIN O Brut Grande Réserve Premier Cru Non-Vintage £D
DUVAL-LEROY O Fleur de Champagne Blanc de Chardonnay Vintage £E
GARDET O Brut Cuvée Charles Gardet Vintage £E
GATINOIS O Grand Cru Vintage £E
RENE GEOFFROY O Brut Réserve Non-Vintage £D
HENRI GIRAUD O Brut Grand Cru Tradition Non-Vintage £D
GEORGES GOULET O Brut Non-Vintage £D
HENRI GOUTORBE O Brut Cuvée Tradition Non-Vintage £D
JACQUART O Blanc de Blancs Mosaïque Vintage £E
A. JACQUART O Blanc de Blancs Vintage £E
JEAN LALLEMENT O Brut Réserve Non-Vintage £D
LECLERC BRIANT O Brut Réserve Non-Vintage £D
LEGRAS O Blanc de Blancs Grand Cru Non-Vintage £D
LILBERT O Blanc de Blancs Grand Cru Non-Vintage £D
MAILLY GRAND CRU O Brut Réserve Non-Vintage £D   O Echansons Vintage £G
MARGAINE O Brut Premier Cru Non-Vintage £C   O Special Cuvée Club Vintage £E
NICOLAS FEUILLATTE O Cuvée Spéciale Vintage £F   O Cuvée Palmes d'Or Vintage £G
PALMER O Amazone de Palmer Non-Vintage £D
ALAIN ROBERT O Blanc de Blancs Le Mesnil Vintage £F
SOUTIRAN-PELLETIER O Blanc de Blancs Grand Cru Non-Vintage £E
TARLANT O Brut Réserve Non-Vintage £D   Brut Vintage £E
JEAN VESSELLE O Brut Réserve Non-Vintage £D
VILMART O Couer de Cuvée Vintage £F

Author's Choice (DM)
A selection of lesser known Champagnes
PAUL BARA O Brut Grand Cru Vintage
EDMOND BARNAUT O Blancs de Noirs Non-Vintage
EGLY-OURIET O Brut Tradition Non-Vintage
PIERRE GIMONNET ET FILS O Blanc de Blancs Puis Premier Cru Non-Vintage
ALFRED GRATIEN O Paradis Non-Vintage
LARMANDIER-BERNIER O Blanc de Blancs Non-Vintage
SERGE MATHIEU O Brut Millésime Vintage
PIERRE MONCUIT O Blanc de Blancs Grand Cru Vintage
FRANÇOIS SECONDÉ O Brut Clavier Non-Vintage
JACQUES SELOSSE O Blanc de Blancs Tradition Non-Vintage

Pick of the luxury cuvée's

BILLECART-SALMON O **Brut Cuvée Nicolas-François Billecart** Vintage
BOLLINGER O **RD** Vintage
CHARLES HEIDSIECK O **Charlie** Vintage
KRUG O **Clos du Mesnil** Vintage
LAURENT-PERRIER O **Grand Siécle** Vintage
MOËT ET CHANDON O **Dom Pérignon** Vintage
POL ROGER O **Sir Winston Churchill** Vintage
LOUIS ROEDERER O **Cristal** Vintage
SALON O **Salon** Vintage
VEUVE CLICQUOT O **La Grande Dame** Vintage

The Loire is perhaps the most diverse and certainly geographically the most extensive of all France's classic wine regions. Inevitably there is a vast difference in style from wines produced and vines grown from Nantes on the Atlantic coast to those in the heart of the Auvergne. Much of the region is steeped in tradition but, while you won't find the wave of new developments that are happening in the Midi for instance, there are new high-quality producers emerging in almost all appellations. A number of them are committed to either organic farming practices or indeed biodynamic viticulture. Applying these principles in this northerly climate is a far taller order than in, say, dry and sunny Provence.

Pays Nantais

The Pays Nantais generally means just one wine to the majority of people: Muscadet. Generic **Muscadet** can be pretty dire stuff, but there are a number of beacons of quality; names like Domaine de l'Ecu and Louis Métaireau. From a quality perspective the most important appellation is **Muscadet de Sèvre-et-Maine** with the best wines bottled *sur lie*. This means the wine spends a period of time on its lees for added richness. There are two other superior ACs, **Muscadet-Coteaux de la Loire** and **Muscadet Côtes de Grandlieu.** Covering the same area is the **Gros Plant VDQS**, producing simple, austere wines and to the south is the **Fiefs Vendéens VDQS** – you might consider these if you're on holiday in the area but they're not very exciting. Further east and stretching towards the south of Anjou and Saumur is the heart of the **Vin de Pays du Jardin de la France,** although this covers the whole of the valley; the odd fine white is appearing here. To the south is the VDQS of **Haut-Poitou**, where there are some relatively unexciting whites in vineyards surrounding the town of Poitiers. Good Muscadet can be crisp, minerally and with a real green-fruited depth, not dissimilar to sound village Chablis.

Anjou and Saumur

The **Anjou** appellation includes red, rosé and white wines. It covers a vast area north and south of the River Loire, from the west of Angers east to beyond Saumur. The quality can range from dire to very impressive, with some stylish barrel-fermented whites from the major white variety of the region, Chenin Blanc. Reds tend to be light, but the best is ripe and juicy with an odd more serious example and can be made from Gamay, Cabernets Sauvignon and Franc and Pineau d'Aunis. The medium to sweet rosé is generally very average, but an odd well-made example turns up under the Cabernet d'Anjou AC. The best red now has its own AC, **Anjou-Villages** and some very good wines are being made from Cabernet Franc and Cabernet Sauvignon. New oak is increasingly favoured.

The great wines here, though, are the steely, intense dry whites of **Savennières** and the sweet botrytised wines of the **Coteaux du Layon**. Those from the **Coteaux de l'Aubance** are less impressive but there are good examples. Within the Coteaux du Layon are the ACs of **Quarts de Chaume** and **Bonnezeaux** along with a number of communes which may append their names. These sweet wines tend to be traditional, quite restrained and very ageworthy or, increasingly, wines of immense extract and honeyed richness. Producers of the latter have become known as the sugar hunters. The best of these wines are marvellously rich and refined but some seem overblown and not entirely balanced and you have to wonder how they will age. A small amount of fine sweet Chenin Blanc is also made at Saumur and labelled as **Coteaux de Saumur.**

The vineyards of Saumur are also a haven for sparkling wine production. As well as sparkling Saumur there is also the catch-all appellation of **Crémant de Loire**. The attraction in making sparkling Chenin, as opposed to still, is the option it offers in poor vintages like those of the late 1990s. Many small producers take this route and there are some sizeable merchant houses and commercial offshoots of the big Champagne houses in Saumur. Quality can be quite good. The wines are generally more green apple than rich and biscuity.

The best wines from Saumur, though, are the impressive barrel-fermented still white Chenin Blancs of the **Saumur** AC and the rich, ripe and supple reds of **Saumur-Champigny** produced from Cabernet Franc and Cabernet Sauvignon. These tend to be softer and lusher in texture than the equally impressive reds from Bourgueil, Chinon and Saint-Nicolas-de-Bourgueil. Chinon is produced exclusively from Cabernet Franc and tends to be tighter and leaner. However, that said, there is still an alarming amount of dull, over-sulphured white and under-ripe, green-flavoured red throughout Anjou. The producer rather than the appellation is all-important.

Touraine

In the same way as Anjou there is a catch-all **Touraine** AC that encompasses most of the region. Sauvignon Blanc is as important for whites here as Chenin and is common under the Touraine banner. In the far west of the region are the red wine appellations of **Bourgueil, Saint-Nicolas-de-Bourgueil** north of the river Loire and **Chinon** just to the south. The best of these wines are very good indeed and new oak is increasingly favoured. Bourgueil tends to be the fullest, Saint-Nicolas often shows greater elegance while Chinon grown on the limestone *coteaux* is equally refined.

Just to the east of the city of Tours are the vineyards of **Vouvray** amd **Mountlouis**. Vouvray is found on the north of the river, Montlouis just to the south. Depending on the vintage conditions and there have been some very moderate years since 1997 – dry, *demi-sec* and *moelleux* styles are all created. The latter can be some of the greatest and longest-lived sweet wines in the world. Green and minerally in their youth, the dry and medium styles become increasingly rich and honeyed with age. The dry styles can be very austere when young and the searing acidity can be almost overwhelming. This can be the same with the *moelleux* wines – it's just better disguised by the residual sugar. Like many of the sweet wines along the valley the dependence on liberal sulphur additions is beginning to wane and you don't need to wait 20 years now for it to dissipate.

There are a number of lesser Touraine appellations. To the west of Tours can be found **Touraine Azay-le-Rideau** and to the immediate east of Vouvray and Montlouis **Touraine-Amboise** and **Touraine-Mesland**. Gamay, Cabernet Franc and Cabernet Sauvignon feature for the reds and Chenin Blanc for the whites. There are a few good examples. To the south of Blois are the regions of **Cheverny** and **Cour-Cheverny**. Similar reds are planted at Cheverny but the whites include Sauvignon Blanc and the unusual Romorantin. Cour-Cheverny is a white-only appellation planted to Romorantin.

To the north of Tours and the Touraine appellation are the regions of the **Coteaux du Loir** and its sub-region of **Jasnières**. The climate here is extremely marginal. The best wines – dry and late-havested Chenin Blancs – come from Jasnières from vines planted on south-facing aspects with a protected mesoclimate. A handful of very good wines are made.

Central Vineyards and the South

The main wines of consequence are the Sauvignon Blancs from **Quincy, Reuilly, Menetou-Salon, Sancerre** and **Poully-Fumé**. Good Pinot Noir is also made at Sancerre and to a lesser extent at Menetou-Salon. While a considerable amount of very average white wine is made from these appellations there are some seriously good wines too. Those whites that are barrel-fermented and kept on lees are capable of considerable age and bottle development.

To the south is the Auvergne. The best wines come from the **Côte Roannaise**, where the odd decent example of Gamay is produced. Indeed the vineyards are nearer to and have more similarity geographically with Beaujolais than the rest of the Loire. Gamay is also produced in the **Côtes du Forez VDQS**.

A-Z producers by appellation/region

Anjou
DOM. OGEREAU
DOM. DE LA SANSONNIÈRE

Anjou-Saumur
DOM. DES BAUMARD

Bonnezeaux
CH. DE FESLES

Bourgueil
YANNICK AMIRAULT
PIERRE-JACQUES DRUET
DOM. DES OUCHES

Chinon
PHILIPPE ALLIET
BERNARD BAUDRY

Coteaux du Layon
PATRICK BAUDOUIN
CH. PIERRE-BISE
PHILIPPE DELESVAUX
DOM. DES FORGES
YVES SOULEZ/CH. DE LA GENAISERIE

Jasnières
JOËL GIGOU/DOM. DE LA CHARRIÈRE

Montlouis
OLIVIER DELÉTANG
VINCENT PINARD
TAILLE AUX LOUPS

Menetou-Salon
HENRY PELLÉ

Pouilly-Fumé
ALAIN CAILBOURDIN
JEAN-CLAUDE CHATELAIN
CH. DE TRACY
DIDIER DAGUENEAU

Quincy
SILICES DE QUINCY

Sancerre
DOM. HENRI BOURGEOIS
PASCAL COTAT
LUCIEN CROCHET
ALPHONSE MELLOT
DOM. HENRY NATTER
VINCENT PINARD
DOM. VACHERON

Saumur-Champigny
CH. DU HUREAU
DOM. DES ROCHES NEUVES
CH. DE VILLENEUVE
CLOS ROUGEARD

Savennières
CH. D'EPIRÉ
CLOS DE LA COULÉE DE SERRANT
DOM. DU CLOSEL

Vouvray
DOM. DES AUBUISIÈRES
DOM. BOURILLON-DORLÉANS
DIDIER CHAMPALOU
DOM. DU CLOS NAUDIN
HUET L'ECHANSONNE

Loire Valley Vintages

With an area as geographically extensive and as diverse in climate as the Loire it is difficult to generalise about its wines or individual years. Cooler conditions in a given year may favour dry whites, while sweet whites and reds need warm vintages. 2002 has turned out to be very good across the region A huge amount of the general output of the region is best drunk young. You will, though, find the odd top Muscadet as well as those wines listed below which will age well. Of the former 2000 and 1997 were good.

The best red and white wines will age very well. They have great structure and the marked acidity that is characteristic of such a marginal climate. The reds are more marked by their acidity than their tannin. The great dry whites of Savennières and top *demi-secs* from Vouvray and Montlouis are capable of being held in your cellar for well over three decades. They will generally need at least six to seven years before they show their more exotic honeyed characters, though increasing use of oak, new and old, and *macération pellicullaire* are providing more accessible styles. Top Sancerre and Pouilly-Fumé, particularly those wines that are barrel-fermented are surprisingly ageworthy and a far cry from the kind of tropical, gooseberry-laden examples of Sauvignon Blanc from the southern hemisphere that will barely make it past their first birthday.

Of the great earlier vintages Savennières was particularly impressive in 1985, 1983, 1982, 1978 and 1976. The great sweet wine vintages to consider were 1985, 1983, 1982, 1976, 1971, 1959, 1949, 1947 and 1921. Top reds were made in 1986, 1985, 1983, 1982, 1978 and 1976.

Loire Valley vintages

	Anjou & Touraine	Anjou & Touraine	Saumur & Touraine	Sancerre & Pouilly-Fume
	Top Dry Whites inc Savennières	Sweet Whites	Top Red Cuvees	Whites
2002	★★★★ A	★★★★ A	★★★/★★★★ A	★★★★/★★★★★ A
2001	★★★ A	★★★/★★★★ A	★★★/★★★★ A	★★★ A
2000	★★★/★★★★ A	★★★ A	★★★ A	★★★★/★★★★★ A
1999	★★★ B	★★★ B	★★★ A	★★★★/★★★★★ B
1998	★★★ B	★★★ B	★★★ B	★★★★/★★★★★ B
1997	★★★/★★★★ B	★★★★/★★★★★ A	★★★★ B	★★★★ C
1996	★★★★/★★★★★ A	★★★★/★★★★★ A	★★★★/★★★★★ B	★★★★ C
1995	★★★★ B	★★★★ A	★★★★/★★★★★ B	★★★★ C
1993	★★★ C	★★/★★★ C	★★★ D	★★★ D
1990	★★★★/★★★★★ B	★★★★/★★★★★ B	★★★★/★★★★★ C	★★★★/★★★★★ D
1989	★★★★/★★★★★ C	★★★★★ A	★★★★/★★★★★ C	–
1988	★★★★ C	★★★★ B	★★★★ C	–

PHILIPPE ALLIET Chinon   A: Lay

Owner: Philippe Alliet   L'Ouche Monde, 37500 Cravant-les-Coteaux
One of the very best producers in Chinon with 9 ha of Cabernet Franc planted on the *coteaux* at
Cravant. In the vineyard Alliet severely restricts his yields and looks to produce a full, powerful style
with an extended fermentation and maceration. The resulting wines possess marvellously pure
blackcurrant and cedar fruit all underpinned by supple, velvety tannins. New oak is avoided as are
fining and filtration. The top wines possess additional depth and weight. The Coteau de Noiré and
Vieilles Vignes are the sturdiest and longest-lived. (DM)
● **Chinon**★★ £B Coteau de Noiré★★★ £B Vieilles Vignes★★★ £C

YANNICK AMIRAULT Bourgueil   A: L&S, SVS

Owner: Yannick Amirault   5 Pavillon du Grand Clos, 37140 Bourgueil
The Amirault family domaine possesses some 17 ha spread throughout both Bourgueil and
Saint-Nicolas-de-Bourgueil. The wines are among the very best produced in either appellation. The
Bourgueils are marginally deeper, more brawny wines, the Saint-Nicolas bottlings a touch more
elegant and tightly structured. La Petite Cave is a splendid, dark and complex wine produced from old
vines. Malagagnes is the denser, more tannic of the two Saint-Nicolas-de-Bourgueils. Young-vine
cuvées of both are also produced. The top wines are very ageworthy and will improve in bottle for 10
years or more. (DM)
● **Bourgueil** Quartiers★★★ £B La Petite Cave★★★ £C
● **Saint Nicolas-de-Bourgueil** Graviers★★ £B Malgagnes★★★ £C

DOM. DES AUBUISIÈRES Vouvray   www.vouvrayfouquet.com   A: C&R

Owner: Bernard Fouquet   Rue de la Vallée-de-Nouy, 37210 Vouvray
Very good Vouvray from bone dry to lusciously sweet is made at this 22-ha domaine. Production is
relatively small at around 9,000 cases a year and an extensive range is produced when conditions are
favourable. Silex is dry, almost austere and very pure, while the stylish Marigny Sec is barrel-
fermented. The Girardières shows a sweet citrus and mineral style and is refined and well-balanced.
Current vintages have'nt favoured the production of any sweet Moelleux. When the right conditions
do occur the magnificent top bottling is the Cuvée Alexandre. All of the wines will age very well.
(DM)
○ **Vouvray** Silex Sec★★ £B Marigny Sec★★★ £C
○ **Vouvray** Girardières Demi-Sec★★★ £B
○ **Vouvray** Brut★★ £C

PATRICK BAUDOUIN Coteaux du Layon   www.patrick-baudouin-layon.com   A: WTs

Owner: Patrick Baudouin   Princé, 49290 Chaudefonds-sur-Layon
Baudouin is one of the Layon's "sugar hunters", and the style here is rich, heady and unctuously sweet.
What impresses though is the balance and elegance achieved at the same time. He also produces two
very decent reds. The Anjou is solely from Cabernet Franc and displays some attractive, berry and
leafy notes. The Anjou-Villages is more serious and structured; a blend of both Cabernets, it is part
oak-aged. Neither is filtered. Of the great sweet wines the regular Bruandières is intense and honeyed
and it just needs a little extra dimension for true class. The Grains Nobles and Maria Juby are
seriously impressive. Both are honeyed with marked botrytis and the Maria Juby has a marvellously
fresh mineral balance. Aprés Minuit, made in tiny quantities, is an astonishing wine. Selected by berry

by berry it is very opulent, concentrated and complex. It should not only age well but is surprisingly approachable when young. (DM)

● **Anjou**★ £B ● **Anjou-Villages**★★ £B
O **Coteaux du Layon** Les Bruandières★★★ £D Grains Nobles★★★★ £F
O **Coteaux du Layon** Maria Juby★★★★★ £F Aprés Minuit❂❂❂❂❂ £G

BERNARD BAUDRY Chinon www.bernard-baudry@chinon.com A: L&S

Owner: Bernard Baudry 13 Coteau de Sonnay, Cravant-les-Coteaux, 37500 Chinon
Bernard Baudry has 25 ha under vine at Chinon with a tiny amount planted to Chenin Blanc, from which he makes an impressive white Chinon Croix Boisée. Good regular red Chinon is marked by approachable leafy, berry fruit and a hint of spiciness. Les Granges is soft, vibrant and forward. It is the three top *cuvées* that stand out, though. Clos Guillot is sturdy and dense, Grézeaux deep and extracted but supple and sufficiently soft too. The top red Croix Boisée is dark, dense and complex and needs three to four years' ageing. (DM)

● **Chinon**★ £B Les Granges★★ £B Clos Guillot★★★ £B Grézeaux★★★ £C Croix Boisée★★★ £C

DOM. DES BAUMARD Anjou-Saumur www.baumard.fr A: Res

Owner: Florent Baumard 8 Rue de l'Abbaye, 49190 Rochefort-sur-Loire
One of the Loire Valley's great and noble properties and among Anjou's best producers of dry and sweet wines. The range is fairly extensive despite a production of barely more than 10,000 cases a year. Anjou red and white, Rosé de Loire, Cabernet d'Anjou rosé and Crémant de Loire are all produced. The latter can be good but on the whole are somewhat unexciting. The real gems here are the Layon sweet wines and the various *cuvées* of Savennières. The latter are impressively steely and formidably structured in great years like 1997. Top years also see the release of a Trie Spéciale. Among the sweet whites there are four Layons including the impressive Cuvée Le Paon and Clos Sainte-Catherine bottlings, as well as the unquestioned star, the magnificent Quarts de Chaumes – a sublime, restrained and extraordinarily subtle sweet wine, a super-five in great years. (DM)

O **Savennières**★★ £B Clos du Papillon★★★★ £C
O **Coteaux du Layon** Carte d'Or★★ £B Clos Sainte-Catherine★★★★ £D
O **Quarts de Chaume**★★★★★ £E

DOM. HENRI BOURGEOIS Sancerre www.bourgeois-sancerre.com A: WSS

Owner: Jean-Marie Bourgeois Chavignol, 18300 Sancerre
This is a reasonably substantial but very impressive Sancerre producer and *négociant*. The domaine covers a total of some 60 ha, 50 ha planted to Sauvignon Blanc, the balance Pinot Noir. The Bonnes Bouches and Grande Réserve are the regular *cuvées* of Sancerre, while the MD de Bourgeois (named after the local Mont Damnés slopes) and Bourgeoise are a level up. There is a good Pouilly Fumé as well. Among the top *cuvées* d'Antan is very concentrated, made from 65-year-old vines, Jadis is intense and minerally from vines planted in Kimmeridgian marl. The top wine, produced in extremely small quantities, is the very intense, flinty and lightly nutty Étienne Henri, vinified in oak for 12 months on fine lees. The red Sancerre Bourgeoise can be good but needs the benefit of a warm, sunny vintage. (DM)

● **Sancerre** Bourgeoise★★ £C
O **Pouilly Fumé**★★ £B Demoiselle de Bourgeoise★★★ £C
O **Sancerre** Grande Réserve★★ £B Bonne Bouches★★ £B La Côte des Monts Damnés★★★ £C
O **Sancerre** Bourgeoise★★★ £C Jadis★★★★ £D d'Antan★★★★ £E

DOM. BOURILLON-DORLÉANS Vouvray www.bourillon.com A: TWS, M&V

Owner: Frédéric Bourillon-Dorléans 4 Rue de Chalateau, 37210 Rochcordon

There are some 18 ha at this Vouvray property where the emphasis is on dry demi-sec Chenin wines. A Moelleux bottling is made on occasion when the vintage conditions allow, as is a sparkling Brut. The dry styles are very tight and minerally in their youth with piercing green-apple aromas. The Coulée d'Argent gets a touch more oak during vinification, some of it new. The Demi-Sec is minerally and honeyed, it will become rich and profound with age. Handling is kept to a minimum and there is a light filtration prior to bottling. (DM)

O **Vouvray** Argilo Sec★★ £B Coulée d'Argent Sec★★★ £C
O **Vouvray** Cuvée Gaston Dorléans Demi-Sec★★★ £C

ALAIN CAILBOURDIN Pouilly-Fumé A: THT

Owner: Alain Cailbourdin Maltaverne, 58150 Tracy-sur-Loire

Alain Cailbourdin has 16 ha under vine at Pouilly Fumé from which he produces around 8,000 cases a year of fine tight, minerally white. The vineyards, some up to 65 years old, are tended as naturally as possible and there are varied soils including limestone and flint. Temperature control is used during fermentation and the wines are very lightly filterred before bottling. The Cuvée de Boisfleury is the lightest and most floral of the three bottlings, Les Cris, fuller and more structured becoming lightly tropical and richer with two or three years' age. Les Cornets, grown in clay-limestone is the sturdiest and most backward when young. All will evolve well over five years or more.

O **Pouilly Fumé** Les Cris★★ £C Cuvée de Boisfleury★★★ £C Les Cornets★★★ £C

DIDIER CHAMPALOU Vouvray champalou@wanadoo.fr A: GWW, Tan

Owner: Didier et Cathérine Champalou 7 Rue du Grand Ormeau, 37210 Vouvray

The Champalous run a model Vouvray property from their 20 ha of vineyards. Total output is around 8,000 to 8,500 cases a year. The regular Vouvray and the Fondraux are vinified in stainless steel and aged in old wooden casks. They are generally *sec* in style but can have a fair level of residual sugar depending on the nature and conditions of the vintage. In cooler years such as 2000 a stylish sparkling Brut is produced and in great years for sweet wines such as 1995 and 1997 a *moelleux* style, labelled Moelleuse, and a very sweet and late-harvested Trie de Vendange are made. Both these are rich, honeyed and very long-lived. (DM)

● **Vouvray**★★ £B Fondraux★★★ £B

JEAN-CLAUDE CHATELAIN Pouilly-Fumé jean-claude.chatelain@wanadoo.fr A: CTy

Owner: Jean-Claude Chatelain Les Berthiers, 58150 Saint-Andelain

Father and son Jean-Claude and Vincent have 20 ha of vines in the Pouilly Fumé AC and act as small-scale *négociants,* buying in fruit to supplement their needs. They are now producing a regular Sancerre as well as the Pouilly and if anything it's the better of the two. Les Charmes is a level up, richer and with a hint of oak (10 per cent is barrel-fermented) while the top *cuvée*, the Prestige, from old vines is tight and structured and very classy. It is vinified in stainless steel but gets six to seven months on lees. Pilou, an unusual and concentrated barrel-fermented style, is occasionally produced from late-harvest dried grapes if vintage conditions permit. (DM)

O **Pouilly Fumé**★★ £B Les Charmes★★★ £C Préstige★★★ £C
O **Sancerre**★★ £B

185

CH. D'EPIRÉ   Savennières   www.chateau-epire.com

Owner: Luc Bizard   49170 Savennières

Luc Bizard turns out just Savennieres, around 4,000 to 5,000 cases a year from his 11 ha of vineyards. Viticulture is traditional and the harvest hand picked with up to three *tries*. The wines are vinified in *inox* and aged on lees in barrel. A small production bottling Hu-Boyau is also now produced which is sourced from the oldest parcel in the vineyard and is barrel-aged for nine months. Cuvée Spéciale is usually just 15 per cent of the harvest and is generally sourced from parcels that are closest to COULÉE DE SERRANT. These are fine, tightly structured, minerally examples and all show impressive depth and intensity. They are also very fairly priced. (DM)

O **Savennières**★★ £B   Cuvéé Spéciale★★★ £C   Moëlleux★★★ £C

CH. DE FESLES   Bonnezeaux   www.vgas.com   A:Bsh, BBR, WTs

Owner: Bernard Germain   Château de Festes, 49380 Thouarcé

Bordeaux *négociant* Bernard Germain purchased Château de Fesles in 1996. At that time the property had been through a period of serious decline. In the 1970s and 1980s the top Bonnezeaux had been labelled La Chapelle and ef you encounter any old vintages prior to 1985 they can be superb. The Bonnezeaux is now just labelled as such and is very good once more despite poor recent vintages. Two other properties also acquired by Germain, the Châteaux de la Guimonière and de la Roulerie, are both turning out impressive Coteaux du Layon and there are some classy reds from Anjou, particularly the dense and chunky Fesles Anjou-Villages. There is also a very stylish, minerally Savennières Clos de Varennes made from 7 ha of vines that Germain has bought from Pierre SOULEZ at Château de Chamboreau. (DM)

Château de Fesles
● **Anjou** Vieilles Vignes★★ £B   ● **Anjou-Villages**★★★ £C
O **Bonnezeaux**★★★★★ £F

Château de la Guimonière
● **Anjou**★ £B
O **Coteaux du Layon Chaume** Julines★★★ £E

Château de la Roulerie
● **Anjou**★ £B
O **Coteaux du Layon Chaume** Aunis★★★★ £E

Clos de Varenne
O **Savennières**★★★ £C

CH. DU HUREAU   Saumur-Champigny   www.domaine-hureau.fr   A:GWW

Owner: Philippe Vatan   Dampierre-sur-Loire, 49400 Saumur

Philippe Vatan produces excellent Saumur Blanc and sumptuous and supple Saumur-Champigny. He possesses 21 ha planted in tufa/limestone soils, which are particularly suitable for producing first-rate Cabernet Franc. As well as the regular red *cuvée* there are two very fine wines produced from old vines. Cuvée des Fevettes gets new wood treatment, whereas the Lisgathe has more exuberant, fleshy dark berry fruit and is aged in old barrels. The white is everything that good dry Chenin Blanc should be. Minerals, citrus and honey are all in evidence. These are approachable but ageworthy wines, keeping well for 10 years and more in the best vintages. (DM)

● **Saumur-Champigny** Grande Cuvée★★ £B   Fevettes★★★ £C   Lisgathe★★★£C
O **Saumur**★★★£B

CH. PIERRE-BISE Coteaux du Layon   A: L&S

Owner: Claude Papin 49750 Beaulieu-sur-Layon
Based in sleepy Beaulieu-sur-Layon, Claude Papin possesses 53 ha of vines spread across the Anjou-Villages, Coteaux du Layon and Savennières appellations. He is one of the best-established quality producers in the region. The wines are well-crafted and offer great value for money. The reds are full of rich, blackberry and mulberry fruit, and are aged in a small proportion of new oak. The Coteaux du Layon *cuvées* are full of peach, honey and nutmeg in the best years and are always well structured, refined and ageworthy. The Quarts de Chaume is richer still, with formidable depth. The intense, ageworthy, Clos de Coulaine Savennières is not only remarkably well-priced but it has marvellous citrus and mineral aromas. It will be better with five or six years' cellaring. (DM)

● **Anjou-Villages** Clos de Coulaine★★ £B Sur Spilite★★★ £B
O **Anjou** Haut de la Garde★★ £B   O **Savennières** Clos de Coulaine★★★ £B
O **Coteaux du Layon-Beaulieu** Rouannières★★★★£D
O **Coteaux du Layon-Rochefort** Rayelles★★★★ £D
O **Quarts de Chaume**★★★★ £E

CH. DE TRACY Pouilly-Fumé tracy@wanadoo.fr   A: JBa, Lay

Owner: Comtesse Alain d'Estutt d'Assay Château de Tracy, 58150 Tracy-sur-Loire
Historic property with a Renaissance château whose origins date back to 1396. There are approximately 28 ha under vine, all of which are Sauvignon Blanc. There's no compunction in not producing Pouilly-sur-Loire here. Just the one wine is made; a steely, flinty style with surprisingly exotic fruit emerging with age. Structured and refined it needs a year or two in your cellar. (DM)

● **Pouilly-Fumé**★★★ £D

CH. DE VILLENEUVE Saumur-Champigny www.chateau-de-villeneuve.com   A: THt

Owner: Jean-Pierre Chevallier Château de Villeneuve, 49400 Souzay-Champigny
Very good property producing red and white from the Saumur-Champigny and Saumur ACs . The vineyards are run organically and partly on biodynamic principles. The focus here is the quality of the fruit, its intensity and concentration achieved through careful viticulture, a tight control on yields and minimal handling in the cellar. The white Cormiers is subtly oaked and barrel-fermented with a period on lees. The reds are concentrated, dark and spicy examples of the very best Loire Cabernet Franc. A special *cuvée*, Grand Clos, is a super-rich special bottling made in the greatest years only. These are all very ageworthy, improving in bottle for five to ten years. (DM)

● **Saumur-Champigny**★★★ £B Vieille Vignes★★★ £C
O **Saumur** Cormiers★★★ £B

CLOS DE LA COULÉE DE SERRANT Savennières www.coulée-de-serrant.com A: Yap

Owner: Nicolas Joly Château de la Roche-aux-Moines, 49170 Savennières
Nicolas Joly has 14.5 ha of Chenin Blanc which is tended biodynamically. Indeed, Joly is one of the most outspoken proponents of this concept of organic farming. In the past he has been criticised for being more concerned with the application of biodynamic principles than in his wines. This would appear to be unjustified because these are some of the finest expressions of dry Chenin to be found anywhere. The supremely structured and refined Coulée de Serrant is loaded with subtle citrus, mineral and flint. Very fine and with a remarkable capacity to age. It is not really ready for 10 years and will keep with ease for more than twice that time. The Clos de la Bergerie is also impressive and more accessible although it still ages very well. When vintage conditions allow, there is a small amount of Moelleux. (DM)

O **Savennières**★★★ £D
O **Savennières Coulée de Serrant**✪✪✪✪ £F
O **Savennières Roches aux Moines** Clos de la Bergerie★★★★ £E

DOM. DU CLOS NAUDIN Vouvray   A: Gau, SVS

Owner: Philippe Foreau   14 Rue de la Croix Buisée, 37210 Vouvray
A marvellous traditional producer of the some of the greatest Vouvrays made in recent decades. Only the wines of HUËT L'ECHANSONNE bear comparison. Currently production is focused on very well-crafted *sec* and *demi-sec*, wines which are tight and superbly structured. They need time to emerge from their shell and will age for decades. Very good sparkling Méthode Traditionelle and a limited amount of a vintage sparkler are also made. When the gods are favourable in this most marginal of climates for great sweet wines, Foreau produces precisely that, magnificent Moelleux Réserve. (DM)

O **Vouvray** Sec★★★ £B Demi-Sec★★★ £B Méthode Traditionelle★★★ £C

CLOS ROUGEARD Saumur-Champigny   A: HHB

Owner: Foucault family   15 Rue de l'Église, 49400 Chacé
There are 10 ha under vine and just one of those is planted with Chenin Blanc the balance being Cabernet Franc. Inevitably the impressive Saumur Blanc Brezé is encountered rarely. It is a subtly barrel-fermented style and strikingly intense. There is a very good regular Saumur-Champigny with ripe, dark fruit and soft and supple tannins. The two superior *cuvées*, Bourg and Poyeux, are equally velvety in texture but with greater depth and power. Le Bourg offers slightly darker and more overt notes of cassis while the Poyeux is the more elegant with classic leafy, Loire spice. (DM)

● **Saumur-Champigny**★★★ £B Bourg★★★★ £C Poyeux★★★★ £C

DOM. DU CLOSEL Savennières www.savennieres-closel.com   A: Yap, BBR

Owner: De Jessey family   Château des Vaults, 1 Place du Mail, 49170 Savennières
The de Jessey family produce decent, solid, fruity Anjou-Villages red and more importantly some impressive, rich, and mineral-laden Savennières. The regular Savennières is good if lacking real depth, the Caillardières is a solid step up. The Clos du Papillon is very impressive indeed; intense and minerally but with a remarkable depth of citrus and rich honeyed aromas emerging with age. These are cellarworthy, particularly the Clos du Papillon. An occasional Vieilles Vignes bottling is produced in the best years as well as a moelleux Cuvée Isa. (DM)

● **Savennières** Les Vaults★★ £B Caillardières★★★ £C Clos du Papillon★★★★ £C

PASCAL COTAT Sancerre   A: Bal, Gau, Rae, SVS

Owner: Pascal/Francis Cotat   98 Chemin de Grous, 18300 Sancerre
The Cotats make some of the very finest Sancerres. Their production is tiny at just 1,200 to 1,300 cases a year with minimal intervention in either vineyard or cellar. Their sites are superb and naturally low yielding and all that is required is to ensure the vines to stay in balance. The wine is fermented naturally and no fining or filtration is undertaken. These are rich, explosive Sauvignon Blancs which need at least a year or two to show at their best. A remarkable Cuvée Spéciale is produced in the greatest years. (DM)

O **Sancerre** Grande Côte★★★★ £C Monts Damnés★★★★★ £D

LUCIEN CROCHET   Sancerre   lcrochet@terres-net.fr   A: BSh, EoR

Owner: Gilles Crochet   Place de l'Église, 18300 Bué
The Crochets have 35 ha of their own vineyards in Sancerre and also act as *négociants*. Inevitably the best wines here are from their own vineyards. As well as the white Sancerre, which is vinified without new oak, the reds are also noteworthy. So often Pinot Noir fails to perform in this climate and red Sancerre is frequently light and insubstantial, but not so here. Late harvesting and ripe fruit is always the key to quality. The Cuvée Prestige white and red are both old-vine bottlings and most impressive. The white Le Chêne Marchand is lighter but very intense and minerally. The Prestige labels will be better given four or five years' ageing. (DM)

O **Sancerre** Le Chêne Marchand★★★ £C   Cuvée Prestige★★★ £D
● **Sancerre** Le Croix du Roy★★ £C   Cuvée Prestige★★★ £D

DIDIER DAGUENEAU   Pouilly-Fumé   silex@wanadoo.fr   A: HHB, Tan, BBR

Owner: Didier Dagueneau   Le Bourg, 58150 Saint-Andelain
Didier Dagueneau is the finest producer in Pouilly Fumé and while he has a few rivals in Sancerre he stands out as the region's standard bearer for magnificent, complex and very ageworthy Sauvignon Blanc. These wines are light years away from the simple gooseberry and tropical flavours many associate with the variety. Immense care is taken in the vineyard, yields are low, harvesting only at peak maturity, passing through the vines several times, and absolutely minimal handling in the cellar. Buisson Renard, Pur-Sang and the magnificent Silex are all barrel-fermented but in no way does the oak become intrusive. What you are left with is an intense and very complex mix of green fruits and minerals. Superbly structured, these are wines that demand cellaring for half a dozen years or more. (DM)

O **Pouilly-Fumé** En Chailloux★★★★ £E   Buisson Renard★★★★★ £E
O **Pouilly-Fumé** Pur-Sang★★★★★ £E   Silex❂❂❂❂❂ £F

PHILIPPE DELESVAUX   Coteaux du Layon   dom.delesvaux.philippe@wanadoo.fr   A: Gau

Owner: Philippe et Catherine Delesvaux   49190 Saint-Aubin-de-Luigné
Philippe Delesvaux is one of a small new breed of dedicated and quality-conscious wine producers in the sleepy Coteaux du Layon. Recent vintages have not been kind to sweet wine makers here but Delesvaux continues to hand-craft intense, stylish examples. The Anjou reds are deeper and with better grip and structure than most. The Anjou bottling is Cabernet Franc, the more substantial Anjou-Villages is Cabernet Sauvignon. Both are vinified in *inox*. There is a very stylish barrel-fermented Anjou Blanc as well as the sweet Layons. What marks these wines out is not just their rich, honeyed botrytised character but their intensity, refinement and balance. In exceptional vintages two remarkable special *cuvées*, Anthologie and Carbonifera, are produced, both comfortably five-star wines. The former is just that touch more unctuous and heady. (DM)

● **Anjou**★★ £B   ● **Anjou-Villages**★★ £B
O **Anjou** Feuille d'Or★★★ £B
O **Coteaux du Layon**★★★ £C
O **Coteaux du Layon-Saint-Aubin** Clos de la Guiberderie★★★★ £D
O **Coteaux du Layon** Grains Nobles★★★★ £E

OLIVIER DELÉTANG Montlouis www.domaine-deletang.com

Owner: Olivier Delétang 19 Rue d'Amboise, 37270 Saint-Martin-Beau
Olivier Delétang produces very good Montlouis from three different sites – his own 20 ha vineyard, Les Batisses and Les Petits Boulay. The vineyard and the climate conditions are the key here rather than individual wines. He produces *sec* and often *demi-sec* regularly from each site. Some very special sweet wines have been made in great years but none since 1997, when great Moelleux, Moelleux Réserve and Garde Réserve of very fine quality indeed were produced. As well as the Montlouis bottlings there are some simple straightforward Touraines, a white from Sauvignon Blanc and a red from Cabernet Franc. There is also a regular sparkling Brut, called Effervescent, which is clean, appley and fresh. (DM)

O **Montlouis** Sec★★ £B Demi-Sec★★★ £B Les Batisses Sec★★★ £B Les Batisses Demi-Sec★★★ £B
O **Montlouis** Les Petits Boulay Sec★★ £B

PIERRE-JACQUES DRUET Bourgueil   A: J&B, Bal, HHB, ABy

Owner: Pierre-Jacques Druet 7 Rue de la Croix-Rouge, 37140 Benais
A brilliant source of top Cabernet Franc. The Bourgueil rosé is delicious and fruity, far better than most of its kind. There are three *cuvées* of Bourgueil as well as the marvellously elegant and pure Chinon Clos de Danzay, which is aged in *demi-muids*. The Bourgueil Cent Boisselées is handled entirely in stainless steel and displays classic blackcurrant fruit and just a subtle hint of leafiness. The Grand Mont is refined and elegant with hints of cassis and cedar. Produced from chalk vineyards the tannin is supple and well-balanced. The top red Vaumoreau comes from nearly 100-year-old vines. It is an unfiltered, dense, very powerful and concentrated red, full of ripe intense cassis and cedar. A wine of immense class and finesse, it is only produced in top years. (DM)

● **Bourgueil** Cent Boisselées★★ £B Grand Mont★★★ £C Vaumoreau★★★★ £D
● **Chinon** Clos de Danzay★★★ £C
◉ **Bourgueil**★ £B

DOM. DES FORGES Coteaux du Layon   A: M&V, Tan, SVS

Owner: Branchereau family Vignoble Branchereau, 49190 Saint-Aubin-de-Luigné
A wide range of Anjou wines are made at this underrated property: good straightforward Sauvignon Blanc and Chardonnay Vin de Pays de la Jardin de France, along with supple fruity Anjou reds and some decent Anjou white. But best of all are the impressive sweet whites – stylish, rich but restrained Coteaux du Layon and Quarts de Chaume. The top wines are the Quarts de Chaume and Coteaux du Layon-Chaume. There is also a good well-crafted Savennières which is tight and flinty. Recent moderate vintages have prevented the domaine from producing great sweet wines. (DM)

O **Coteaux du Layon**★★ £C Coteaux du Layon-Saint-Aubin★★★ £C
O **Coteaux du Layon-Chaume**★★★★ £D Les Onnis★★★★ £E
O **Quarts de Chaume**★★★★ £F
O **Savennières** Clos des Mauriers★★ £B

JOËL GIGOU/DOM. DE LA CHARRIÈRE Jasnières joel-gigou@libertysurf.fr   A: Yap

Owner: Joël Gigou 4 Rue des Caves, 72340 La Chartre-sur-le-Loir
Joël Gigou is an immensely dedicated grower in this most marginal and extreme of Loire Valley climates. The vineyard is close to organic, yields are kept in check and balanced vines means no *vendange vert*. There are two intense and almost austere dry whites. A real mineral backbone runs through the wines

and they have piercing acidity but are very ageworthy. The Clos Saint-Jacques will take on a marvellously rich, citrus and honeyed character with age. Also produced is a very fine late-harvest white which is far removed from a Bonnezeaux or a Quarts de Chaume. The wine is tightly structured, lightly honeyed but very long and intense. It is extraordinarily long lived. (DM)

O **Jasnières** Cuvée Trois Clos★★ £B Cuvée Clos Saint-Jacques Vieilles-Vignes★★★ £C
O **Jasnières** Sélection de Grains Nobles★★★★ £D

HUET L'ECHANSONNE   Vouvray   www.huet-echansonne.com   A: RsW, WSc, SVS

Owner: Huet family   11–13 Rue de la Croix Buisée, 37210 Vouvray
There may be a rising tide of new quality conscious producers emerging in Vouvray but this domaine still remains the standard bearer for the appellation. The property has a total of 40 ha and sources its fruit from three different sites; Clos du Bourg, Haut-Lieu and Le Mont. Eighty per cent of the domaine has now been purchased by the partnership of Istvan SZEPSY and American financier Antony Hwang, who are helping to revolutionise sweet wine production in Hungary's Tokaji region. The wines are made as *sec, demi-sec* and when conditions allow, like those in 1997, some magnificent *moelleux* including the extraordinary Cuvée Constance. A new 5-ha property, Domaine de Vodanis, was recently purchased and this is now run biodynamically as are all the vineyards. The dry wines are intense, minerally and very backward when young. They will, though, evolve into superb, complex, honeyed masterpieces with time, but you have to be patient. The *demi-sec* and *moelleux* are more immediately approachable, drinking with three or four years' ageing but very fine indeed. (DM)

O **Vouvray** Clos du Bourg Sec★★★ £B Clos du Bourg Demi-Sec★★★ £C
O **Vouvray** Clos du Bourg Moelleux★★★★★ £E
O **Vouvray** Haut-Lieu Sec★★★ £B Haut-Lieu Demi-Sec★★★★ £C Haut-Lieu Moelleux★★★★★ £E
O **Vouvray** Le Mont Sec★★★ £B Le Mont Demi-Sec★★★ £C Le Mont Moelleux★★★★★ £E
O **Vouvray** Cuvée Constance❂❂❂❂❂ £F

ALPHONSE MELLOT   Sancerre   mellot@sifiedi.fr   A: Hal, GVF

Owner: Alphonse Mellot   La Moussière, 18300 Sancerre
Mellot is one of the leading producers in Sancerre. There are *négociant* wines including good Menetou-Salon and Pouilly Fumé but the domaine wines which are of a different order, particularly the top *cuvées*. The white Edmond and Génération XIX, made from very old vines and vinified in oak, are wines of real dimension. The Pinot Noirs are increasingly impressive, displaying considerable depth and a round, supple texture, especially the brilliant, subtly oaked Génération XIX. The top wines will undoubtedly develop very well in bottle. (DM)

O **Sancerre** La Moussière★★★ £C Edmond★★★★ £E Génération XIX★★★★ £E
● **Sancerre** Génération XIX★★★★ £F

DOM. HENRY NATTER   Sancerre   www.henrynatter.com   A: L&W

Owner: Henry Natter   Place de l'Eglise, 18250 Montigny
Established in 1974, this is one of the best domaines now for fine quality white Sancerre based in the top village of Montigny. As well as the regular white there is a small volume special bottling Cuvée François de la Grange de Montigny and a fruity rouge and rosé. Vinification of the whites is traditional with fermentation in large oak vats. The regular white is then aged in stainless steel, François de la Grange de Montigny sees 12 months in oak. The wines have been consistently good in recent years and will develop well with short bottle age. (DM)

O **Sancerre**★★★ £C

DOM. OGEREAU Anjou   A: CdP

Owner: Vincent Ogereau   44 Rue de la Belle-Angevine, 49750 Saint-Lambert-du-Lattay
Vincent Ogereau produces very good Anjou-Villages reds, decent minerally dry white Anjou and
rich, well-crafted Coteaux du Layon. The regular Anjou-Villages is a blend of Cabernet Franc and
Cabernet Sauvignon whereas the Côte de la Houssaye is a dense and powerful, brambly Cabernet
Sauvignon. Both will be the better for five years' ageing. The Coteaux du Layon is powerful, sweet
and unctuous and achieves a really intense botrytised peachy character in the very best years. A
special selection, Clos de Bonnes Blanches, is now produced too. (DM)

● **Anjou**★★ £B ● **Anjou-Villages**★★★ £B Côte de la Houssaye★★★ £C
O **Anjou** Prestige Sec★★ £B
O **Coteaux du Layon-Saint-Lambert-du-Lattay**★★★★ £C

DOM. DES OUCHES Bourgueil perso.wanadoo.fr/gambier   A: THT

Owner: Denis Gambier 3 Rue des Ouches, 37140 Ingrandes-de-Touraine
First class Bourgueil producer offering classic, restrained and ageworthy examples of the appellation
at very keen prices indeed. The style is tighter and more backward than many, even from this cool
climate red growing region. All the wines have a youthfully angular character as much from their
high acidity as from their tannin which requires a few years ageing to add flesh. The top two cuvées
in particular should be cellared for at least four to five years. Cabernet Franc is the mainstay variety
but there is a little (10 per cent) Cabernet Sauvignon in the Grande Réserve. Some of the vines are
remarkably old here, up to 100 years and this undoubtedly contributes to quality. With exception of the
Grande Réserve which is aged in new oak (50 per cent) with malolactic in barrel the wines are
traditionally vinified and aged in *foudres*. (DM)

● **Bourgueil**★★ £B Clos Princé★★ £B Vieilles Vignes★★★ £B Grande Réserve★★★★ £C

HENRY PELLÉ Menetou-Salon www.henry-pelle.com   A: PBW, M&V, HHB, GVF

Owner: Pellé family 18220 Morogues
The leading estate in Menetou-Salon and a producer of Sancerre as well. There are some 40 ha under vine
and these split roughly two-thirds to one-third Sauvignon Blanc to Pinot Noir. The vineyards in Menetou-
Salon are planted on Kimmeridgian clay and tended organically, and green harvesting is practised. There
are now straightforward Menetou-Salon and Sancerre white and red from a mix of estate and bought-in
grapes. Of the estate-grown wines, the white Menetou-Salon tends to impress more than the Sancerre,
the vineyards of which are younger. White Clos de Ratier is from a single parcel as is the rich and intense
Clos des Blanchais, which is from the domaine's oldest vines and possesses an impressive depth of ripe
gooseberry fruit and a fine, mineral structure. The reds, while fruity enough, can be insubstantial. (DM)

● **Menetou-Salon** Les Cris★ £B Sancerre La Croix au Garde★ £C
O **Menetou-Salon** Morogues★★ £B Clos de Ratier★★ £B Clos des Blanchais★★★ £C
O **Sancerre** La Croix au Garde★ £C

VINCENT PINARD Sancerre   A: GWW, HHB, Han

Owner: Vincent Pinard 42 Rue Saint-Vincent, 18300 Bué
There are some 15 ha at this model Sancerre domaine where Vincent Pinard produces good to very good
white and red Sancerre. The regular red is good, light but exuberantly fruity with attractive berry fruit.
Charlouise is denser, richer. Of the whites the Cuvée Florès emphasises ripe classic gooseberry fruit. The
two top whites are fuller and more complex, and both are vinified in wood. Harmonie in particular is spicy
and toasty in its youth, needing three or four years to achieve a balance of fruit and oak. (DM)

● **Sancerre**★★ £C Charlouise★★★ £D
○ **Sancerre** Cuvée Florés★★£D Nuance★★★ £C Harmonie★★★ £D

DOM. DES ROCHES NEUVES Saumur-Champigny www.roches-neuves.com

Owner: Thierry Germain   56 Boulevard Saint-Vincent, 49400 Varrains
Thierry Germain's father Bernard has owned CHÂTEAU DE FESLES in Bonnezeaux since 1996 but his son has been established in Anjou for longer. He produces opulent, powerful, ripely extracted reds from Cabernet Franc. The wines are deeply coloured, dense and oaky. Vinification is aimed at maximum extraction, with the fruit getting a pre-fermentation cold soak and the wine staying on its skins in order to achieve rounded, supple tannins. He notably succeeds in reducing some of the austere youthful characteristics that can often show in other young Loire Cabernet. He also makes a very good barrel-fermented white Saumur which is stylish and refined with a nice balance of toasty, citrus fruit and a fresh mineral structure. The Terres Chaudes and the Marginale are the two top reds. The latter is marked by new oak in its youth and needs time. (DM)
● **Saumur-Champigny**★★ £B Terres Chaudes★★★ £C Marginale★★★ £C
○ **Saumur** Insolite★★★ £C

DOM. DE LA SANSONNIÈRE Anjou

Owner: Marc Angeli   49380 Thouarcé
Marc Angeli has 7 ha, which he farms biodynamically, almost all of which is planted under the Anjou appellation where he makes some of the very finest examples of this humble AC. He has produced tiny amounts (from less than a hectare) of exquisite Bonnezeaux that are released as Les Blanderies and Le Coteau du Houet. The largest volume here is saved for his Anjou La Lune which accounts for nearly half his holding at 3.10 ha. The wine is produced from low yields and is vinified in 400 to 600 litre barrels. It is remarkably pure with an intense mineral quality amidst complex, very subtly tropical fruit. It is occasionally bottled with just a hint of residual sugar. Les Fouchardes and Les Vieilles Vignes des Blanderies are produced from much smaller holdings and therefore very hard to find. The range is completed by a Cabernet Sauvignon Les Gelinettes and a Rosé d'Anjou, Coteau du Houet. (DM)
○ **Anjou** La Lune★★★ £E

SILICES DE QUINCY Quincy   A: Gau, THT

Owner: Jacques Sallé   Place de L'Echuzeau, 18120 Quincy
From his tiny holding of 5.5 ha Jacques Sallé produces around 1,000 cases of Quincy which is the benchmark for the appellation. In order to ensure the integrity of the main wine a second label Silicette is also made. The vineyard is tended biodynamically and the vines are very old. The wine possesses an intense mineral, green-fruit character underpinned by tight gripping acidity. The depth and structure here suggest the top wine will develop surprisingly well over at least four or five years. (DM)
○ **Quincy**★★★ £C

YVES SOULEZ/CH. DE LA GENAISERIE Coteaux du Layon   A: GVF

Owner: Yves Soulez   Ch. de la Genaiserie, 49190 Saint-Aubin-de-Luigné
Yves Soulez makes very good, stylish and refined Coteaux du Layon in a more restrained style than most of his peers. His wines are quite different to the new wave of super-ripe and unctuous styles achieved elsewhere by the likes of Patrick BAUDOUIN or Jo PITHON. They are tight and often quite

backward when young but have a real intensity and finesse also. There are three very fine special *cuvées* in addition to the regular bottling. Les Simonelles is elegant and minerally with subtle botrytis and comes from vines grown on volcanic, schistous soils. La Roche is from a vineyard with a high charcoal content and is very restrained. Les Tetuères is the fullest and most obviously honeyed of the three and generally has more marked botrytis character. There are also good Anjou reds from Gamay and Cabernet Franc and a fruity, fresh medium-sweet Cabernet d'Anjou; a revelation in comparison with so many wines sold under this label. (DM)

● **Anjou**★ £B   ○ **Coteaux du Layon-Chaume**★★★ £C
○ **Coteaux du Layon-Chaume** Les Simonelles★★★★ £D   La Roche★★★★ £D   Les Tetuères★★★★ £D

TAILLE AUX LOUPS   Montlouis   A: M&V

Owner: Jacky Blot   8 Rue des Aitres, Husseau, 37270 Montlouis-sur-Loire
One of the best domaines in Montlouis. A varying small range of *sec, demi-sec* and sweet wines are made both in Montlouis and Vouvray. Recent vintages have seen the production of mainly dry and medium styles along with good sparkling wines including Brut Tradition and a very dry Pétillant. The Montlouis Remus *sec* is barrel-fermented in new oak and aged on lees with *bâtonnage*. The impressive *demi-sec* is not oversweet and when nature is kind there are some remarkable *moelleux*. The Montlouis Cuvée des Loups and particularly Montlouis Cuvée Romulus can be explosively rich. (DM)

○ **Montlouis** Brut Tradition★★ £B   Pétillant★★ £B   Sec★★ £B   Demi-Sec★★★ £C
○ **Montlouis** Moelleux★★★ £D   Cuvée des Loups★★★★ £E
○ **Vouvray** Clos de Venise Sec★★★ £C

DOM. VACHERON   Sancerre   A: E&T, SsG, TWS

Owner: Vacheron family   1 Rue du Puis Poulton, 18300 Sancerre
The Vacherons have some 37 ha under vine with no less than 11 ha planted to Pinot Noir. They are one of only a handful of growers here who make impressive examples of red Sancerre. There are regular red and white Sancerres and two very impressive reserve *cuvées*; the white Romains and the dense and surprisingly powerfully structured red Belle Dame. Good rosé is also produced. The white Sancerre has fine grass and mineral notes and the Romains an impressive depth with subtle, nutty, oak-derived notes and real finesse. Both the top wines have the structure to develop well with five years' cellaring. (DM)

● **Sancerre**★★ £C   Belle Dame★★★ £C
○ **Sancerre**★★ £C   Romains★★★ £D

OTHER WINES OF NOTE

PIERRE AGUILAS ○ **Coteaux du Layon** Cuvée Claire £D
DOM. DE BABLUT ○ **Coteaux de l'Aubance** Vin Noble £D
DOM. BALLAND ○ **Sancerre** £B
BALLAND-CHAPUIS ○ **Sancerre** Le Chêne Marchand £B
DOM. J & C BAUDRY ● **Chinon** £B
DOM. DE BELLIVIÈRE ○ **Coteaux du Loir** Vieilles-Vignes Eparses £C   ○ **Jasnières** Les Rosiers £C
BOUVET-LADUBAY ○ **Saumur Mousseux** Crémant Excellence   Brut Saphir Vintage £B
○ **Saumur Mousseux** Brut Trésor £B   ● **Saumur Mousseux** Brut Rubis £C
DOM. BRETON ● **Bourgueil** Clos Senechal £B
CH. DE L'AULÉE ● **Chinon** Cèdre £B
CH. DE COULAINE ● **Chinon** La Diablesse £C

CH. GAILLARD ○ Touraine-Mesland £B
CH. GAUDRELLE ○ Vouvray Réserve Spéciale £B
CH. LA VARIÈRE ● Anjou-Villages-Brissac Grand Chevalerie £B
CH. DE LA RAGOTIÈRE ○ Muscadet-de-Sèvre-et-Maine Sur Lie Auguste Couillaude £B
CH. DE SAINTE-LOUAND ● Chinon Réserve des Trompegueux £B
CH. DE SOUCHERIE ○ Coteaux du Layon-Beaulieu £E
CH. DE SURONDE ○ Quarts de Chaume £E
CH. DE TIGNÉ ● Anjou-Villages Mozart £C Cyrano £C
LAURENT CHATENAY ○ Montlouis Sec £B Demi-Sec £C
DOM. DE CHATENOY ○ Menetou-Salon £B
CHÉREAU-CARRÉ ○ Muscadet-de-Sèvre-et-Maine Chateau Chasseloir £B
FRANÇOIS CHIDAINE ○ Montlouis Demi-Sec Clos Habert £B
CLOS BAUDOIN ○ Vouvray Aigle Sec £B
CLOS DE LA BRIDERIE ○ Touraine-Meslands Vieilles-Vignes £B
CLOS ROCHE BLANCHE ● Touraine Cabernet £B Closerie £B
MAX COGNARD ● Saint-Nicolas-de-Bourgueil Malgagnes £B
DOM. DU COLLIER ○ Saumur £B
DOM. DE CORBILLÈRES ○ Touraine Sauvignon £B
COULY-DUTHEIL ● Chinon Clos de l'Echo £B
JEAN-CLAUDE DAGUENEAU ○ Pouilly-Fumé £C
VINCENT DELAPORTE ○ Sancerre £C
DOM. DELAUNAY ● Bourgueil Prestige £B
DOM DES DORICES ○ Muscadet-de-Sèvre-et-Maine Sur Lie £B
DOM. DE L'ÉCU ○ Muscadet-de-Sèvre-et-Maine Sur Lie £B Expression de Gneiss £B
ANDRE DÉZAT ○ Sancerre £C ● Sancerre £C
FILLIATREAU ● Saumur-Champigny £B ● Saumur-Champigny Vieilles-Vignes £C
DOM. FOURNIER ○ Menetou-Salon £B
DOM. GADAIS ○ Muscadet-de-Sèvre-et-Maine Sur Lie Vieilles Vignes £B
PIERRE GIRAULT ○ Sancerre Chêne du Roy £C
DOM. GITTON ○ Sancerre Les Belles Dames £C
GRATIEN & MEYER ○ Crémant de Loire £B
DOM. GUINDON ○ Muscadet-Coteaux de la Loire Sur Lie Tradition £B
DOM. JEAN-CLAUDE GUYOT ○ Pouilly-Fumé Les Loges £C
DOM. DE LA HAUTE BORNE ○ Vouvray Sec £B Tendre £B
DOM. CHARLES JOGUET ● Chinon Clos de la Cure £B Clos du Chêne Vert £B
● Chinon Clos de la Dioterie £B
DE LADOUCETTE ○ Pouilly-Fumé £C Baron de L £E
DOM. LAME DELISLE BOUCARD ● Bourgueil Prestige £B Vieilles Vignes £B
LANGLOIS-CHÂTEAU ○ Saumur Vieilles-Vignes £B ● Saumur-Champigny Château de Varrains £B
LA TOUR SAINT MARTIN ○ Menetou-Salon Morogues
RENÉ-NOËL LEGRAND ● Saumur-Champigny Terrages £B Rogelins £B
J Y LEBRETON ● Anjou-Villages Croix de Mission £B
DOM. DES LIARDS ○ Montlouis Demi-Sec Vieilles-Vignes £B
PIERRE LUNEAU ○ Muscadet-de-Sèvre-et-Maine Le L d'Or £B
ALAIN MARCADET ● Touraine Sauvignon £B
HENRY MARIONNET ● Touraine Premiere Vendange £B ○ Touraine M de Marionnet £C
MASSON-BLONDELET ○ Pouilly-Fumé Angelots £C Cullus £D
DOM. MERLIN CHERRIER ○ Sancerre £B
LOUIS MÉTAIREAU ○ Muscadet-de-Sèvre-et-Maine Cuvée LM £B
FLORIAN MOLLET ○ Sancerre £C ○ Pouilly-Fumé £C
DOM. DE MONTGILET ○ Coteaux de l'Aubance £B
DOM. AUX MOINES ○ Savennières Roches-aux-Moines £C
DOM. DE LA MONNAIE ○ Savennières £C
ROGER NEVEU ○ Sancerre £B
DOM. JEAN PABIOT ○ Pouilly-Fumé £C

DOM. DU PETIT VAL ○ **Bonnezeaux** La Montagne £D
DOM. DES PETITS QUARTS ○ **Bonnezeaux** £D
DOM. PICHOT ○ **Vouvray** Sec Coteau de la Biche £B Demi-Sec Peu de la Moriette £B
DOM. PINON ○ **Vouvray** Sec Tradtion £B
JO PITHON ○ **Coteaux du Layon-Lambert** Clos des Bonnes Blanches £E ○ **Quarts de Chaume** £G
DOM. PAUL PRIEUR ○ **Sancerre** £B ● **Sancerre** £B
DOM. RAIFAULT ● **Chinon** £B Allets £B
DOM. MICHEL REDDE ○ **Sancerre** Les Tuilières £C ○ **Pouilly-Fumé** La Moynerie £C
DOM. ROY RENÉ ○ **Coteaux du Layon-Lambert** Le Cormier £C
RENÉ RENOU ○ **Bonnezeaux** Les Mellereses £D
PASCAL ET NICOLAS REVERDY ○ **Sancerre** Vieille-Vignes £C
DOM. RICHOU ○ **Coteaux de l'Aubance** Cuvée Les Trois Desmoiselles £C
CLAUDE RIFFAULT ○ **Sancerre** Cuvée Antique £C
JEAN-MAX ROGER ○ **Sancerre** Cuvee CM £C ○ **Menetou-Salon** £B
DOM. DU RONCÉE ● **Chinon** Clos des Marronniers £B
DOM. DES SABLONNETTES ● **Anjou** £B ○ **Anjou** Genêts £B
○ **Coteaux du Layon** Champ du Cygne £E
DOM. SAINT-VINCENT ● **Saumur-Champigny** Adrialys £B
DOM. SAUTEREAU ○ **Sancerre** Vieilles Vignes £C
PIERRE SOULEZ ○ **Savennières** Château de Chamboreau £C
JOËL TALUAU ● **Saint-Nicolas-de-Bourgueil** Vieilles-Vignes £B
DOM. THIBAULT ○ **Pouilly-Fumé** £C
DOM. ANNICK TINEL ○ **Pouilly-Fumé** £C
DOM. ANDRE VATAN ○ **Sancerre** Les Perriers £C
DOM. VIGNEAU-CHEVREAU ○ **Vouvray** Sec £B Demi-Sec £B

Author's choice (DM)

A diverse selection of sweet whites
PATRICK BAUDOUIN ○ **Coteaux du Layon** Aprés Minuit
DOM. DES BAUMARD ○ **Quarts de Chaume**
CH. DE FESLES ○ **Bonnezeaux**
DOM. DU CLOS NAUDIN ○ **Vouvray** Moelleux
PHILIPPE DELESVAUX ○ **Coteaux du Layon** Grains Nobles
OLIVIER DELÉTANG ○ **Montlouis** Les Petits Boulay Garde Réserve
JOËL GIGOU ○ **Jasnières** Sélection de Grains Nobles
HUET L'ECHANSONNE ○ **Vouvray** Haut-Lieu Moelleux
YVES SOULEZ ○ **Coteaux du Layon** Les Tetuères
TAILLE AUX LOUPS ○ **Montlouis** Cuvée Romulus

A choice of individual dry whites
DOM. HENRI BOURGEOIS ○ **Sancerre** Jadis
CH. D'EPIRÉ ○ **Savennières** Cuveé Spéciale
CH. DE VILLENEUVE ○ **Saumur** Cormiers
JEAN-CLAUDE CHATELAINE ○ **Pouilly Fumé** Prestige
CLOS DE LA COULÉE DE SERRANT ○ **Savennières Coulée de Serrant**
PASCAL COTAT ○ **Sancerre** Monts Damnés
DIDIER DAGUENEAU ○ **Pouilly Fumé** Silex
HENRY PELLÉ ○ **Menetou-Salon** Clos des Blanchais
DOM. DE LA SANSONNIÈRE ○ **Anjou** La Lune
SILICES DE QUINCY ○ **Quincy**

The best of the reds

PHILIPPE ALLIET ● **Chinon** Vieilles-Vignes

YANNICK AMIRAULT ● **Saint-Nicolas-de-Bourgueil** Malgagnes

BERNARD BAUDRY ● **Chinon** Croix Boisée

CH. DU HUREAU ● **Saumur-Champigny** Lisgathe

CLOS ROUGEARD ● **Saumur-Champigny** Poyeux

PIERRE-JACQUES DRUET ● **Bourgueil** Vaumoreau

DOM. OGEREAU ● **Anjou-Villages** Côte de la Houssaye

DOM. DES OUCHES ● **Bourgueil** Grande Réserve

DOM. DES ROCHES NEUVES ● **Saumur-Champigny** Marginale

JOËL TALUAU ● **Saint-Nicolas-de-Bourgueil** Vieilles-Vignes

France/Rhône Valley

No longer undiscovered gems of French wine, the top vineyards of the Rhône are producing increasingly widely distributed wines of world class. The established and increasing number of Rhône super-cuvées are now some of the most exciting as well as expensive wines in the world. However, there remains a vast sea of simple, sometimes disappointingly poor wine at the bottom end of the market. Two-thirds of all wine made throughout the Rhône Valley is generic AC Côtes du Rhône, although the region is improving fast and smart and slick generic marketing is being allied to generally higher quality standards. It is worth seeking out the ever-increasing number of young growers, mainly in the south, who are endeavouring to produce wines of quality and style at still very fair prices, rather than selling to the co-ops or large négociants.

The Northern Rhône

The northern and southern parts of the valley are very different geographically. The Northern Rhône stretches south down the narrow valley of the River Rhône, from Vienne in the north to Valence in the south. The vineyards of **Côte-Rôtie** are on steep, precipitous terraces and provide some of the world's most challenging viticultural conditions. The name Côte-Rôtie means 'roasted slope'. This may be the most northerly of the Rhône appellations, but the vineyards have a superb aspect facing south-east and the soils are ideal for viticulture – high in minerals, relatively infertile and very well drained.

There are only some 200 ha under vine, with a number of *cru* sections identified. The best quality wine comes from the centre of the appellation. Côte Brune to the north of Ampuis produces wines of fuller body, the Côte Blonde to the south lighter more elegant wines often with Viognier blended in, which is permitted here. The style of Côte-Rôtie is perhaps less overtly muscular than the wines of Hermitage and Cornas and its climate can be very marginal in achieving full ripeness. In great years, when everything comes together at vintage, these wines at their best are quite sublime.

Immediately south of Côte-Rôtie, the vineyards of **Condrieu** continue on the western bank of the river. They are planted on granite and sandstone rather than on the schistous soils to the north. The slope becomes less precipitous and the conditions are more suitable for that uniquely perfumed, aromatic variety Viognier. Widely planted now further afield, from the Languedoc to California, the variety has only come into vogue in the last decade or so. While the weight and aromatic power of the wines can be almost overwhelming, Viognier is a difficult variety to grow and Condrieu lacks the structure of other great French whites. The majority are best drunk in their first two or three years. An increasing number are now barrel-fermented on lees with *bâtonnage* and a few more are produced as late-harvest and very occasionally botrytis-affected wines. The best of these can be stunning.

The most extensive appellation in the north is **Saint-Joseph**. It encompasses the southern part of Condrieu and runs right down the western bank of the river to the borders of Cornas, just to the north of Valence. The reds are produced from Syrah, while the whites are a blend of Marsanne and Roussanne. The best wines are produced from the gravel-based soils close to the river. An impressive number of very good wines, both red and white, have been made in recent years and prices are rising. The best sites have real potential.

The great hill of **Hermitage** and its wines, dark, brooding and powerful, are perhaps the quintessential expression of classic northern Rhône reds. There are many fewer producers here than at Côte-Rôtie and a mere 131 ha of vineyards. The hill is split up into seven different *crus* or *lieux-dits* with varying soil types. One grower, Jean-Louis Chave, is able to draw on all seven in blending his reds. The Syrah is joined by whites based on Marsanne with some Roussanne. These can be remarkably long lived, often more so than the reds. New oak and destemming in the cellar are playing an increasing role and the whites often see barrel-fermentation. More often than not here though, the oak is used rather than new. Red Hermitage should be cellared, as it is slow-developing. The white, too, needs years to show at its best. It can be approachable for a couple of years and then mysteriously close up, so if you plan to drink it young, do so within a year or two or else you will be very disappointed.

Surrounding the hill of Hermitage are the vineyards of **Crozes-Hermitage**. The same grapes are used but the vineyard area is much larger and encompasses some 1,238 ha of vines. The better wines are made on isolated outcrops of granite and there can be a wide variation in quality. The best are very good and generally well-priced and there are an increasing number of relatively highly priced special *cuvées*.

To the south and on the west bank of the river opposite Valence, are the appellations of **Cornas**, which borders southern Saint-Joseph, and immediately to its south Saint-Péray. Cornas is dense and muscular Syrah. It shares more in common with Hermitage than Côte-Rôtie, which is not surprising given its near proximity. A wide range of styles are produced, from the modern oak-influenced wines of Jean-Luc Colombo to the fiercely traditional style of Auguste and Pierre-Marie Clape. At their finest, these are dark-fruited, intense and splendidly long-lived expressions of Syrah.

Many of the Cornas growers also produce the still and sparkling wines of **Saint-Péray**; the still having greater potential on the whole. They are blended from Marsanne and Roussanne, like their white counterparts to the north. A further sparkling wine comes from a little further south-east under the **Clairette de Die** AC, which produces lighter semi-sweet sparkling Muscats. **Crémant de Die** is now the AC for dry sparklers from Clairette. At best they are crisp and fresh. There also some dry white still wines produced under the **Châtillon-en-Diois** appellation, from cool-planted Chardonnay and Aligoté in the same area.

The Southern Rhône

While the north meanders down a narrow river valley, giving it its unique viticultural environment, the southern Rhône covers a much greater area, and is extensively planted with vines. The total vineyard area planted in the north is just under 2,700 ha, whereas the total for the whole region is some 75,000 ha and nearly 42,000 ha of that Côtes du Rhône. The climate is altogether warmer in the south and Grenache is the mainstay variety. There can be a significant influence on the region from the cold Mistral wind, which blows down out of the Alps. While it has some influence in the north, it can cause devastation in the south, with not only physical damage to vineyards but stressing of the vines, causing them to shut down. The same Mistral can on occasion help in ripening fruit close to *vendange* and keeping cellars free of humidity.

The most important quality region in the south is **Châteauneuf-du-Pape**. This a sizeable appellation with some 3,084 ha of vineyards. Quality has soared in recent very good vintages and an increasing number of growers are now bottling their own wine. The main Châteauneuf variety is Grenache, but there are 13 permitted varieties in the red blend, a number of them white. Syrah and Mourvèdre are also very important in lending structure and grip. The Châteauneuf soils are varied with clay, gravel and stone all playing a role. The larger *galets roulés* which store up heat and reflect it onto the vines at night are not universally found throughout the appellation and many consider the clay the key component in controlling moisture supply.

Among current trends an increasing number of growers are producing limited-production special *cuvées* from old vines. While some of these are very splendid wines, there is some question as to whether the quality of the regular bottlings suffers as a consequence. The best red Châteauneuf is rich, heady and almost exotic and very ageworthy. The best will easily continue to improve for a decade or more. The white can be good, floral and nutty and there are some more serious structured wines as well, with oak playing a limited role. In general the whites should be drunk young.

To the north and west of Châteauneuf-du-Pape and the ancient Roman town of Orange are the **Côtes du Rhône-Villages** and the separate appellations of **Gigondas** and **Vacqueyras**. The best vineyards of Gigondas are planted on the slopes of the Dentelles de Montmirail, the small range that merges into the hills of the Vaucluse. The wines are dense, massive and brooding. They tend to lack the refinement of the very greatest Châteauneufs, but they can offer not only excellent quality but also value for money. Like Gigondas, Grenache is the most important variety in Vacqueyras, which was awarded its own separate AC in 1990. The wines are generally lighter than Gigondas and an increasing amount of Syrah is now being used. There are even some varietal wines being produced. The best have an intoxicating combination of ripe dark berry fruit and a marked *garrigues* character.

There are 16 villages which can append their names after the Côtes du Rhône-Villages name. Among these are **Cairanne**, **Rasteau**, **Sablet** and **Beaumes-de-Venise** to the south and **Valréas**, **Vinsobres** and **Saint-Maurice** further north where, unsurprisingly, the Syrah is planted with greater success. It is the southern villages, though, and particularly Cairanne which are producing the greatest number of stylish wines. At their best these express vibrant and complex dark fruit and subtle herbal notes. Those wines produced from old vines can be both excellent value and remarkably impressive. Outside these 16 villages there are several thousand hectares of vines producing straight Côtes du Rhône-Villages. A number of very good wines under both this appellation and the humble **Côtes du Rhône** label are now being produced. The latter tend to emphasise their forward fruit, but there are also some very serious and ageworthy wines being produced. Some of the better Rhône-Villages domaines may also have vineyards outside the appellation boundaries, or may chose to label younger-vine *cuvées* as Côtes du Rhône.

There are also two regional specialities, which have their own appellations. **Muscat de Beaumes de Venise** is a floral, grapey fortified Muscat. It is not late-harvested and tends to lack the quality found in the Muscat de Rivesaltes wines of the Roussillon. **Rasteau** is a fortified red *vin doux naturel* produced from Grenache that can develop marked *rancio* notes with cask age. This AC should not be confused with Côtes du Rhône-Villages Rasteau, where some of the best modern southern reds are being made.

To the west of Châteauneuf-du-Pape are the appellations of **Lirac** and **Tavel**. The latter is for rosé only, Lirac for both rosé and, of greater importance from a quality point of view, some very good Grenache-based reds planted in the limestone-rich soils. The rosé can often be excessively high in alcohol and dull. Further to the east is the newly developed appellation of the Costières de Nîmes but this is covered elsewhere (see Languedoc-Roussillon & Provence).

Towards the outer extremities of the Rhône are four other appellations. To the north of the Côtes du Rhône-Villages sector, west and east respectively of the river Rhône, are the **Côtes du Vivarais** and the **Coteaux du Tricastin**. To the south in the Vaucluse are the vineyards of the **Côtes du Ventoux**, where encouraging progress is being made by a number of domaines and reds of some substance are being produced. Immediately south again, on the borders of Provence, is the **Côtes de Lubéron**. The odd exciting red is beginning to emerge and there are some stylish whites as well.

There are a number of vin de pays classifications. In the northern Rhône the important one is the **Vin de Pays des Collines Rhodaniennes**, under which some impressive red and white is produced. Two important southern vins de pays offering wines largely based on Grenache (but also Cabernet Sauvignon in the case of the former) are the **Vin de Pays de la Principauté d'Orange** and further south the **Vin de Pays de Vaucluse**.

A-Z of producers by appellation/commune

Northern Rhône

Château Grillet
CH. GRILLET

Condrieu
DOM. LOUIS CHÈZE
YVES CUILLERON
PIERRE DUMAZET
DOM. YVES GANGLOFF
DOM. DU MONTEILLET
DOM. NIERO-PINCHON
DOM. GEORGES VERNAY
FRANÇOIS VILLARD

Cornas
THIERRY ALLEMAND
DOM. BALTHAZAR
AUGUSTE CLAPE
JEAN-LUC COLOMBO
ERIC ET JOËL DURAND
DOM. DE FAUTERIE
ALAIN VOGE

Côte-Rôtie
GILLES BARGE
DOM. BONNEFOND
DOM. DE BONSERINE
CH. D'AMPUIS
DOM. DU CHÊNE
CLUSEL ROCH
JEAN-MICHEL GERIN
E GUIGAL
DOM. JAMET
DOM. JASMIN
DOM. MICHEL OGIER
DOM. ANDRÉ PERRET
RENÉ ROSTAING
LES VINS DE VIENNE

Crozes Hermitage
DOM. COMBIER
ALAIN GRAILLOT
DOM. DU MURINAIS
ETIENNE POCHON
DOM. DES REMIZIÈRES

Hermitage
ALBERT BELLE
DOM. YANN CHAVE
JEAN-LOUIS CHAVE
DOM. DU COLOMBIER
DELAS FRÈRES
BERNARD FAURIE
PAUL JABOULET AINÉ
MARC SORREL
CAVE DE TAIN L'HERMITAGE

Saint-Péray
DOM. COURBIS

Saint-Joseph
DOM. COURBIS
PIERRE COURSODON
PIERRE GAILLARD
JEAN-LOUIS GRIPPAT

Southern Rhône

Beaumes-de-Venise
DOM. DURBAN

Cairanne
DANIEL ET DENIS ALARY
DOM. AMADIEU
DOM. BRUSSET
CAVE DE CAIRANNE
DOM. DE L'ORATOIRE SAINT-MARTIN
DOM. RABASSE-CHARAVIN
MARCEL RICHAUD
DOMINIQUE ROCHER

Châteauneuf-du-Pape
DOM. LUCIEN BARROT
DOM. DE BEAURENARD
BOIS DE BOURSAN
HENRI BONNEAU
BOSQUETS DES PAPES
DOM. DE LA CHARBONNIÈRE
GÉRARD CHARVIN
CH. DE BEAUCASTEL
CH. LA GARDINE
CH. LA NERTHE
CH. RAYAS
CLOS DU CAILLOU
CLOS DU MONT OLIVET
CLOS DES PAPES
FERAUD-BRUNEL
FONT DE MICHELLE
DOM. DE GRAND TINEL
DOM. DE LA JANASSE
DOM. LA ROQUETTE
LES CAILLOUX
DOM. DE MARCOUX
DOM. DE MONTPERTUIS
CH. MONT-REDON
DOM. DE PEGAÜ
ROGER SABON
PIERRE USSEGLIO
DOM. DE LA VIEILLE-JULIENNE
DOM DU VIEUX TÉLÉGRAPHE

Côtes du Rhône
CH. DE FONSALETTE
CROS DE LA MÛRE
DOM. DE GRAMENON

DOM. PERRIN
DOM DE RENJARDE
DOM. SAINTE-ANNE

Côtes du Rhône-Villages
CH. SAINT-ESTÈVE D'UCHAUX
DOM. LES APHILLANTHES
DOM. RÉMÉJEANNE

Côtes du Ventoux
CH. PESQUIÉ
DOM. DE FONDRÈCHE

Gigondas
DOM. DU CAYRON
CH. REDORTIER
CH. SAINT-COSME
DOM. DE FONT-SANE
DOM. LES GOUBERTS
DOM. GRAPILLON D'OR
LES PALLIÈRES
MOULIN DE LA GARDETTE
DOM. RASPAIL-AY
DOM. SANTA DUC

Rasteau
GOURT DE MAUTENS
DOM. LA SOUMADE
DOM. DU TRAPADIS

DOM. COTEAUX DES TRAVERS

Sablet
DOM. DE PIAUGIER

Tavel
DOM. AMIDO
DOM. LAFOND-ROC-EPINE
DOM. DE LA MORDORÉE

Vacqueyras
DOM. DES AMOURIERS
CH. DES TOURS
CLOS DES CAZAUX
DOM. DES ESPIERS
SANG DES CAILLOUX
DOM. LA GARRIGUE

Valréas
CLOS PETITE BELLANE

Vinsobres
DOM. DE DEURRE
DOM. CHAUME-ARNAUD

Other
PATRICK LESEC SELECTIONS
TARDIEU-LAURENT

Rhône Valley Vintages

The run of vintages from 1998 to 2001 was remarkable in both the north and south of the Rhône Valley. The wines were either been very good or excellent. The best wines from these years are becoming very scarce but it is still well worth your while to hunt around for them. Over the same period, the lesser Rhône-Villages wines have performed in a similarly impressive manner to those at Châteauneuf-du-Pape. The top wines will keep very well, 10 even 20 years in the best examples, the lesser wines from recent years comfortably for five years or more.

2002: After the previous four bountiful vintages this was a disappointment. There was very heavy rain in the North requiring extreme care and selectivity by growers to achieve any real quality. In the South it was a similar tale of woe with heavy flooding. Once again an extremely careful selection was necessary. The wines are likely to be for early drinking.

2001: This was very good throughout the valley, if not quite hitting the heights of 1999 for the northern appellations or 2000 for the south. Nevertheless these are impressive and cellarworthy examples, a smaller than normal yield helping to ensure this. White Hermitage is very ageworthy.

2000: A generally very good year, particularly in the south with good crop levels and some very rich, profound and complex wines being made. The best are ripe, very full and approachable. Not quite the same quality in the north, but good and very ageworthy wines were produced. Côte-Rôtie is the most successful among the reds.

1999: A very good year throughout the north, with well-structured, opulent and heady wines being produced in all the major appellations. Conditions were excellent with a balmy and dry summer and adequate rainfall. The wines are surprisingly forward and approachable but should be long-lived. The south was good to very good but lacked the sheer quality of 1998 and 2000. The wines will be a little lighter but the best will age very well.

1998: The northern appellations fared well, producing very good results after a solid 1997. The wines are generally sizeable and and masculine in structure. They should turn out to be very good cellaring prospects but without the opulence or elegance of 1999. In the south the vintage was spectacularly good. The wines are immensely opulent, ripe and exotic but have a fine balance and structure. They will be enjoyable in their relative youth but are excellent cellaring prospects.

1997: A generally average year at best in the south after spring frost damage. The summer was very hot and the wines have neither perfect balance nor ripeness. Almost all should be drunk now. The north fared better, with good quality. Saint-Joseph and Crozes-Hermitage are drinking well now.

1996: A pretty moderate year with the best results in the north, where the top wines have higher than normal acidity after a cold wet summer and windy ripening period. Some good wines were produced in a relatively austere style. The south produced soft, forward reds somewhat lacking in structure. They are drinking now and are not for ageing.

1995: Generally the best year since 1990 for reds with the exception of the magnificent 1991 Côte-Rôties. Yields were low but a warm and propitious summer and favourable harvest produced wines of impressive density and extract both in the north and the south. Whites were somewhat less impressive and will be surprisingly short-lived. They should be drunk soon except for the best white Hermitage.

1994: Neither north nor south produced wines with the density or structure of the 95s. They are marked more by their soft tannins and elegance than their power and are for the mid-term. Many are drinking well now.

1993: For much of the north this was a disastrous vintage. Côte-Rôtie was a little better but not much. Châteauneuf-du-Pape produced some soft agreeable reds which need finishing up.

1992: Sadly the vintage was badly affected by rain in September and most wines were light and soft. Most should have been drunk by now.

1991: This was a good to very good year in the northern Rhône and in Côte-Rôtie in particular. There was quite marked variation and some producers were more successful than others, particularly in Cornas and Hermitage. The south was disappointing and the wines should by now have been drunk.

1990: A superb year for great long-lived Hermitage. These will need more time to achieve their full potential. Côte-Rôtie did not quite match the superb 91s. Cornas and Côte-Rôtie are both drinking well now, as are some of the excellent wines produced at Châteauneuf-du-Pape.

1989: A good to very good vintage, particularly at Hermitage and Cornas and in the south for top reds. White Hermitage was also good and is drinking well now as are the generally fleshy reds. These are not the great structured wines of 1990 but are perfect now if you have them cellared or come across them.

1988: This was a very good year for classic northern Rhône reds; the best Hermitage will probably benefit from a little more time. Also tremendous exotic white Hermitage which is drinking well now. Impressive in the south but only the top wines will still be at their best.

Earlier Years: 1985 was good in both the north and the south. 1983 produced some excellent long-lived Hermitage. Châteauneuf-du-Pape in 1981 is worth considering from very top producers. A few good 1979s from both north and south are still drinking well. 1978 was a truly great year in the north, with some very fine Châteauneuf also. Other very good earlier years for the north were 1971, 1970, 1969, 1966, 1964 and 1961.

Rhône Valley vintages

	Côte-Rôtie	Red Hermitage	White Hermitage	Châteauneuf-du-Pape
2002	★★ A	★★ A	★★/★★★ A	★★ A
2001	★★★★ A	★★★★ A	★★★★/★★★★★ A	★★★★ A
2000	★★★★/★★★★★ A	★★★★ A	★★★★ A	★★★★/★★★★★ A
1999	★★★★/★★★★★ A	★★★★/★★★★★ A	★★★★/★★★★★ A	★★★★ B
1998	★★★★ A	★★★★ A	★★★★ A	★★★★★ B
1997	★★★/★★★★ B	★★★/★★★★ A	★★★/★★★★ A	★★★ C
1996	★★★ B	★★★ B	★★★/★★★★ A	★★/★★★ C
1995	★★★★ B	★★★★ B	★★★/★★★★ C	★★★★ C
1994	★★★/★★★★ C	★★★/★★★★ C	★★★/★★★★ C	★★★ C
1991	★★★★/★★★★★ B	★★★★ B	★★★★ C	★/★★ D
1990	★★★★ C	★★★★★ B	★★★★/★★★★★ B	★★★★/★★★★★ C
1989	★★★★ C	★★★★/★★★★★ C	★★★★ C	★★★★/★★★★★ C
1988	★★★★ C	★★★★ C	★★★★/★★★★★ C	★★★★ C

Northern Rhône

THIERRY ALLEMAND Cornas   A: Tan, SVS, Gau

Owner: Thierry Allemand   22 Impasse des Granges, 07130 Cornas
Small Cornas domaine with just over 3 ha, producing two rich, sturdy and powerful Syrah wines. Total production is tiny at a mere 1,000 cases a year but the quality is very good to exceptional and among the best in the appellation. The Reynard comes from vines that are over 80 years old. Vinification is traditional with a long *cuvaison* at high temperatures to extract both flavour and supple, well-rounded tannins. The resulting wines are impressive, concentrated and very elegant. They are both bottled unfiltered. Reynard is very ageworthy and will continue to improve for up to a decade, sometimes longer in the best years. (DM).

● **Cornas** Chaillot★★★★ £D   Reynard★★★★★ £E

DOM. BALTHAZAR Cornas   A:Has

Owner: René Balthazar   07130 Cornas
Balthazar produces generally very good traditionally vinified and aged Cornas from very old vines. 2002, 2001 and 2000 are all ripe and structured, with the depth and complexity of dark berry fruit that can only be coaxed from a vineyard planted with very old vines. Aged in large old wood the wine is nevertheless surprisingly ripe, forward and approachable with just four or five years' ageing. Like many producers in this village Balthazar's Cornas offers very good value. (DM)

● **Cornas**★★★ £D

GILLES BARGE Côte-Rôtie   A: Bib, Tan, SVS

Owner: Gilles Barge   8 Boulevard des Allées, 69420 Ampuis
Gilles Barge took over from his father Pierre in the mid-1990s and the wine is now of impressive quality. He has not only reduced yields from his holdings of around 7 ha but has refined the approach in the cellar as well. The wine is still vinified with stems but the tannin is riper and suppler. These are wines characterised by elegance and finesse rather than by raw power; excellent unfiltered Côte-Rôtie, if not in the absolute top flight. The Cuvée du Plessy is the lighter, more forward of the two, elegant and approachable. Both wines are impressively ageworthy and will improve in bottle for seven to ten years. Enjoy his peachy Condrieu and spicy, berry-fruited straightforward Saint-Joseph young. (DM)

● **Côte-Rôtie** Cuvée du Plessy★★★ £D   Côte Brune★★★★ £E

ALBERT BELLE Hermitage   A: Cdp

Owner: Albert Belle   Quartier les Marsuriaux, 26600 Larnage
A young domaine which has produced good red and white now for upwards of a decade. Total vineyard holdings are now close to 18 ha, almost all in Crozes-Hermitage. Reds are made traditionally and destemming is avoided. Good, structured, ageworthy wines result in the best years. There can, though, be an occasional green hint in cooler vintages. The key here is to get the stems as well as the fruit fully ripe at harvest. The white is fully or part-fermented in oak and the Hermitage is fat and toasty with real depth and concentration. The top wines will be all the better for five or six years' cellaring. (DM)

● **Hermitage**★★★ £E
● **Crozes-Hermitage** Les Pierelles★★ £B   Cuvée Louis Belle★★★ £C
O **Hermitage**★★★ £D   O **Crozes-Hermitage**★ £B

DOM. BONNEFOND   Côte-Rôtie   A:SVS

Owner: Patrick & Christophe Bonnefond   Mornas, 69420 Ampuis
From their small holding of 6 ha, the Bonnefond brothers produce very good Condrieu and – in their top bottling, Les Rochains – one of the finest of all Côte-Rôties. The style of the reds is modern, with de-stemming and new oak in the top *cuvée,* and a really elegant spicy, mineral character shows through in all the wines. The regular bottling is a little light in comparison to Côte Rozier and Les Rochains but nonetheless ripe and well-structured with the slightest hint of green pepper. Côte Rozier, with 10 per cent Viognier has a characteristic floral undercurrent but with depth and real dimension. Les Rochains is rich, opulent and firmly structured, needing two to three years longer in bottle than the other reds and should not be broached without five or six years' ageing. Condrieu is opulent, peachy and immediately accessible. (DM)

● **Côte-Rôtie**★★★ £D   Côte Rozier★★★★ £E   Les Rochains★★★★★ £F
O **Condrieu**★★★ £D

DOM. DE BONSERINE   Côte-Rôtie   A:Ear

Owner: Richard Dommerc   Verenay, 69420 Ampuis
This is a large property for the appellation, which has been developed with considerable outside investment, including Georges DUBOEUF. It is now the second largest vineyard owner after GUIGAL. The are a total of just under 10 ha with Syrah (95 per cent) and Viognier (5 per cent) spread accross 17 different parcels. Vinification is modern and the fruit is all de-stemmed before ageing in barrel. The regular cuvée, La Sarrasine has 5 per cent Viognier blended in whereas the two top wines Les Moutonnes and La Garde are both 100 per cent Syrah and both are aged in new oak for 24 months. These are impressive, modern and opulent examples of the appellation which should be aged for five, even as much as seven, years. (DM)

● **Côte-Rôtie**★★★ £D   Les Moutonnes★★★★ £E   La Garde★★★★ £E

BERNARD BURGAUD   Côte-Rôtie   A: BBR, Yap, SVS

Owner: Bernard Burgaud   Le Champin, 69420 Ampuis
Just one wine is produced here but it is among the better examples in the appellation. It is made from a number of different sites that are always vinified separately to maximise the wine's complexity. Bernard Burgaud maintains a strict control of yields, and a portion of the harvest is regularly sold off after careful sorting. Finally a *saignée* of up to 20 per cent of the juice prior to fermentation results in a wine that is both concentrated and full of character, and which benefits from four to five years' ageing. It always offers good value. (DM)

● **Côte-Rôtie**★★★★ £D

M CHAPOUTIER   Hermitage   www.chapoutier.com   A: Men, Tan, Odd, BBR

Owner: Chapoutier family   18 Avenue Dr Paul Durand, 26600 Tain-l'Hermitage
One of the most important *négociants* in the northern Rhône, with the largest vineyard holding on the great Hermitage hill. Interests are not restricted to the Rhône but also include Domaine des BÉATES in Provence and M CHAPOUTIER AUSTRALIA at Mount Benson in South Australia, as well as some fine, chunky Collioure, rich Banyuls and Muscat de Rivesaltes from Roussillon. Amidst the vast array of Rhône labels the top wines are superbly crafted examples of their appellations. New benchmarks have been set in both Crozes-Hermitage – with the dense, muscular and very concentrated Les Varonniers – and Saint-Joseph, with both red and white Les Granits. These are not

cheap but have established new standards that others are following. Côte-Rôtie La Mordorée is a magnificent example of the appellation; even though not quite of the order of the three GUIGAL *super-cuvées* it is still very impressive. Hermitage red and white now comes in a number of guises. Pavillon and L'Ermite are perhaps the finest among the reds and the former is the weightiest and most powerful of the trio. Of the whites Cuvée de l'Orée is now joined by Le Méal. There is no doubting the supreme quality at this level. The wines are remarkably plush, even when relatively young and very different to a Jean-Louis CHAVE Hermitage. The regular Hermitage Monier de la Sizeranne and Chante Alouette white pale in comparison, but at least won't break the bank. In the south, Châteauneuf-du-Pape is good to very good and Barbe Rac is 100 per cent Grenache. At a lower level though the wines from lesser appellations can be disappointing. The generic Côtes du Rhône Belleruche labels are light and insubstantial. The top Hermitage wines are labelled with the traditional spelling, Ermitage. (DM)

● **Côte-Rôtie** Les Bécasses★★★ £D   La Mordorée❂❂❂❂❂ £H
● **Hermitage** Monier de la Sizeranne★★★★ £E   Le Meal❂❂❂❂❂ £H   L'Ermite❂❂❂❂❂ £H
● **Hermitage** Le Pavillon❂❂❂❂❂ £H
○ **Hermitage** Chante Alouette★★★★ £E   Cuvée de l'Orée❂❂❂❂❂ £H   Le Meal❂❂❂❂❂ £H
○ **Hermitage Vin de Paille**❂❂❂❂❂ £H   ○ **Condrieu**★★ £D
● **Crozes-Hermitage** La Petite-Ruche★★ £B   Les Meysonniers★★ £C
● **Crozes-Hermitage** Les Varonniers★★★★ £E
○ **Crozes-Hermitage** La Petite-Ruche★ £B   Les Meysonniers★ £B
● **Cornas**★★★ £D   ● **Saint-Joseph** Deschants★★ £C   Les Granits★★★★ £E
○ **Saint-Joseph** Deschants★★ £C   Les Granits★★★ £D
● **Chateauneuf-du-Pâpe** La Bernadine★★★ £D   Croix de Bois★★★★ £E   Barbe Rac★★★★ £G
○ **Chateauneuf-du-Pâpe** La Bernadine★★ £D
● **Côtes-du-Rhône Villages Rasteau**★ £B   ● **Côtes-du-Rhône Villages Valréas**★ £B
● **Collioure**★★ £B   ● **Banyuls**★★★ £C   Terra Vinya★★★★ £D
○ **Muscat de Beaumes-de-Venise**★★ £C   ○ **Muscat de Rivesaltes**★★★ £C

CH. D'AMPUIS   Côte-Rôtie   www.guigal.com   A: JEF

Owner: Marcel Guigal   Château d'Ampuis, 69420 Ampuis
Guigal is rightly famed for the resurrection of the wines of Côte-Rôtie during the 1970s and 80s. His top three red *cuvées*, La Mouline, La Landonne and La Turque, are now sold under the Château d'Ampuis rather than E. GUIGAL label. Super-rich, very extracted and with loads of new oak, they are produced in very limited quantities and not surprisingly sell for stratospheric prices. However, their balance and extraordinary finesse is more important still. All three are truly profound wines with that extra dimension and depth found in only a handful of truly great wines. Perhaps La Turque is the finest. The vinification of each is quite unique. The Côte-Rôtie Château d'Ampuis and Condrieu La Doriane are very good but not of the same order. In 2001 Marcel Guigal purchased the domaine and vineyards of Jean-Louis GRIPPAT, embellishing his estate with top-class sites in both Saint-Joseph and Hermitage. (DM)

● **Côte-Rôtie** Ch. d'Ampuis★★★★★ £E   La Mouline❂❂❂❂❂ £H   La Turque❂❂❂❂❂ £H
● **Côte-Rôtie** La Landonne❂❂❂❂❂ £H
○ **Condrieu** La Doriane★★★★★ £F

CH. GRILLET   Château Grillet   A: Yap, BBR

Owner: Neyret-Gachet family   42410 Vérin
This is in fact a tiny appellation as well as a single estate and one of the smallest in France at around 3 ha. Like Condrieu the wine is produced solely from Viognier and has always been vinified in barrel on its *lees*. Unlike some Viogniers, at its best this wine can be aged. After a period in the doldrums the

quality at Grillet has improved somewhat. However there is some way to go before the wine offers the same quality and dimension of the best examples in Condrieu. (DM)

O **Château Grillet★★★** £F

DOM. YANN CHAVE   Hermitage   A: HHB, GrD, L&W, SVS, Gau

Owner: Yann Chave   La Burge, 26600 Mercurol

Fine, improving small domaine with 16 ha of Syrah and a tiny amount of Marsanne and Roussanne. The property is now run by Yann Chave and he is producing increasingly impressive supple and structured red wines. Vinification is modern and more new wood is being used both for red and white. These are now wines of finesse and depth and the top reds need cellaring. The Crozes-Hermitage Tête de Cuvée and Hermitage will improve in bottle for up to 10 years, the latter more in great years. (DM)

● **Hermitage★★★** £D
● **Crozes-Hermitage★★** £B Tête de Cuvée★★★ £C
O **Crozes-Hermitage★★** £B

JEAN-LOUIS CHAVE   Hermitage   A: Yap, Adm, WSc, Tan

Owner: Gérard et Jean-Louis Chave   37 Avenue de St-Joseph, 07300 Mauves

Utterly splendid ancient domaine, perhaps the finest in the northern Rhône and among the best in France. The Chave family own plots in all seven *lieux-dits* on the Hermitage hill, which contributes to the marvellous complexity and finesse of their wines. Any of the components felt to be below standard will be sold off in order to protect the integrity of the wine. Cuvée Cathelin is a special selection which sees more new wood and is produced only in top years. Both red and white are extraordinarily ageworthy and are not wines to approach in their youth. Also produced is a very good Saint-Joseph and an extraordinary *vin de paille,* the latter only in tiny quantities. (DM)

● **Hermitage✪✪✪✪✪** £F Ermitage Cuvée Cathelin✪✪✪✪✪ £H
O **Hermitage✪✪✪✪✪** £F
● **Saint-Joseph★★★** £C

DOM. DU CHÊNE   Côte-Rôtie   A: Rev

Owner: Marc & Dominique Rouvière   Le Pêcher, 42410 Chavanay

Marc Rouviere makes small but impressive quantities of both red and white Saint-Joseph, as well as a striking and intensely peachy, honeyed Condrieu. Medium rather than full bodied with a fine lightly mineral structure this will drink well over three to four years. 2002 was impressively concentrated despite the vintage. In addition to the regular Saint-Joseph bottlings, a good fruit driven white produced from Marsanne and a medium weight, spicy, strawberry scented red there is a much deeper special cuvee - Anais. Firm and structured in its youth with rich, dark berry fruit and spicy oak it should be aged for three or four years to show at its best. (DM)

O **Condrieu★★★★** £E   O **Saint-Joseph★★** £C
● **Saint-Joseph★★** £C Cuvée Anais★★★ £D

DOM. LOUIS CHÈZE   Condrieu   A: C&C

Owner: Louis Chèze   Les Chênes Verts, 26600 Pont-de-l'Isère

Louis Chèze has gradually built up a small domaine of some 20 ha, with the largest plots planted to Syrah in Saint-Joseph. His holding of Viognier in Condrieu is mainly young vines but the wines are stylish and well-crafted with good, nicely integrated oak. The Coteau de Brèze, in particular, is very fine with rich, peachy opulent fruit. The white Saint-Joseph emphasises Marsanne's broad, nutty character. The top Saint-Joseph reds are supple and sufficiently structured to provide excellent drinking with a few years' cellaring. (DM)

O **Condrieu**★★★ £D Coteau de Brèze★★★★ £E
● **Saint-Joseph** Ro-Rée★★ £B Cuvée des Anges★★★ £C Caroline★★★ £C
O **Saint-Joseph**★★ £B Ro-Rée★★ £C

AUGUSTE CLAPE Cornas   A: Yap

Owner: Auguste et Pierre-Marie Clape RN 146, 07130 Cornas
Pierre-Marie now makes the wine at this domaine, an established leader in the appellation. The winemaking is fiercely traditional and no new wood is used whatsoever. However, the wines are always supple, any stems retained during vinification are always fully ripened and the tannin and fruit is harmonious and always balanced and very refined. Vines that date from the 1890s contribute to the impressive quality. Cuvée Renaissance is a second wine, made to help maintain the quality of the Cornas. Inevitably from younger vines, it lacks the weight and power of the *grand vin*. Both the spicy Côtes du Rhône red and Saint-Péray offer good value. (DM)

● **Cornas**★★★★★ £D Cuvée Renaissance★★ £C
O **Saint-Péray**★★ £B
● **Côtes du Rhône**★★ £B

CLUSEL ROCH Côte-Rôtie   A: L&S

Owner: Gilbert Clusel et Brigitte Roch 15 Route du Lacat, Verenay, 69420 Ampuis
Among the leading handful of small domaines in Côte-Rôtie, this tiny operation with just 4 ha of Syrah and Viognier produces barely more than 1,000 cases a year. Côte-Rôtie is powerful and structured for the long haul, particularly Les Grandes Places, made from 65- to 70-year-old vines and occasionally of super-five quality. Neither are for drinking young. The Condrieu is good, with attractive peachy Viognier fruit, but lacks the intensity and depth of the reds. (DM)

● **Côte-Rôtie**★★★★ £D Les Grandes Places★★★★★ £F
O **Condrieu**★★★ £D

DOM. DU COLOMBIER Hermitage   A: Bib, Gau, J&B, Tan, HHB, BBR, Bal

Owner: Florent Viale 2 Route de Chantemerle, 26600 Tain L'Hermitage
Another small, improving northern Rhône domaine. The Viale family own almost 15 ha of vineyards, some with very old vines on the Hermitage hill. They produce around 5,000 cases of wine including a cool-fermented white Crozes-Hermitage, vinified with a touch of oak, and three stylish, complex reds. The Crozes-Hermitage Cuvée Gaby and in particular the Hermitage are powerful, structured reds that benefit from five or six years' cellaring. The Hermitage keeps extremely well. Prices are very fair indeed. (DM)

● **Crozes-Hermitage**★★★ £B Cuvée Gaby★★★ £C ● **Hermitage**★★★★ £D
O **Crozes-Hermitage**★★ £B

JEAN-LUC COLOMBO Cornas   A: L&W, HHB

Owner: Jean-Luc Colombo Chemin Pied la Vigne, 07130 Cornas

This operation is essentially now split into two. Domaine Jean-Luc Colombo produces wines from vineyards in and around Cornas and Saint-Péray, whereas the Jean-Luc Colombo label is reserved for an extensive range of *négociant* wines. There are also two separate domaines in the Midi; Domaine de Salente in the Languedoc producing red and white Vins de Pays d'Oc from Syrah and Viognier as well as a Coteaux du Languedoc red, L'Ame de Salente, a structured blend of Syrah, Carignan, Grenache and a smattering of Mourvedre. Good red Côtes du Roussillon and Muscat de Rivesaltes are produced at Domaine de Saint-Luc where there a premium red La Mission Saint-Luc has been added. New reds are also now produced from vineyards in Provence's Coteaux d'Aix-en-Provence and there is a good white Vin de Pays des Bouches-du-Rhône, Les Pins Couchés. The wines are labelled Domaine de la Côte Bleue. Of the Rhône merchant wines, which range ordinary to very good, the Chateauneuf-du-Pape Bartavelles stands out, a powerful, dense, Grenache based red. Top Cornas cuvées Les Ruchets and La Louvée are most impressive. Aged in new oak, the wines are always well-balanced and are some of the best in the appellation. (DM)

Domaine Jean-Luc Colombo
● **Cornas** Les Mejeans★★★ £E Terres Brûlées★★★ £E Les Ruchets★★★★ £F La Louvée★★★★★ £F

Jean-Luc Colombo
● **Hermitage** Le Louet★★★ £E O **Hermitage** Le Louet★★★ £E
● **Saint-Joseph** Le Prieuré★★ £C Les Lauves★★ £C
O **Condrieu**★★★ £E O **Vin de Pays Viognier** Les Ramilles Blanche★★ £B
● **Crozes-Hermitage** La Tuilière★★ £B O **Crozes-Hermitage**★ £B
● **Vin de Pays des Collines Rhodaniennes** Collines de Laure★ £B Syrah la Serine Pointue★★ £B
● **Chateauneuf-du-Pape** Les Bartavelles★★★★ £D
● **Côtes du Rhône** Abeilles★★ £B Les Forots★★★ £C O **Côtes du Rhône** Les Figuières★★ £B
● **Vin de Pays Syrah** Les Ramilles★★ £B

Domaine de Sait-Luc
● **Côtes du Roussillon** La Chance de Saint-Luc ★★ £B O **Muscat de Rivesaltes** Les Saintes★★★ £C

DOM. COMBIER Crozes-Hermitage   A: Eno

Owner: Maurice et Laurent Combier RN 7, 26600 Pont de l'Isère

Good stylish and concentrated wines are made at this recently established domaine. The regular red and white wines are well-crafted and see some new wood during maturation. The Clos des Grives is altogether more serious and amongst the best in the appellation. The red, which is macerated for around 30 days on skins, is dense and muscular, with refined fruit and supple, balanced tannins. The wine is aged in new oak and requires a little patience before it is ready. The whites are mainly Roussanne, barrel-fermented and kept on their lees with *bâtonnage*. Both will develop well in the medium term. (DM)

● **Crozes-Hermitage**★★ £B Clos des Grives★★★ £C
O **Crozes-Hermitage**★★ £B Clos des Grives★★★ £C
● **Saint-Joseph**★★ £C

DOM. COURBIS Saint-Joseph   A: Ege, HHB, Res, SVS

Owner: Dominique Courbis Les Ravières, 07130 Chateaubourg

The bulk of this estate's 23 ha is in Saint-Joseph, with just over 4 ha planted to white varieties. The average vine age is fairly young. This is to some extent illustrated in the wines, which as yet do not have quite the density or complexity of the best in the appellation. The Cornas bottlings, though, are of a different order. Les Eygats and La Sabarotte are wines of dense muscular power. The latter comes from old vine plantings and is very ageworthy. It is close to five stars in top years like 2001. Both top Cornas will improve for up to a decade with ease. (DM)

● **Saint-Joseph**★★ £B Domaine Les Royes★★★ £C
○ **Saint-Joseph**★★ £B
● **Cornas** Champelrose★★★ £C Les Eygats★★★★ £D La Sabarotte★★★★ £E

DOM. PIERRE COURSODON Saint-Joseph   A: Win, WSc

Owner: Pierre et Gilbert Coursodon 3 place du Marché, 07300 Mauves
During the early to mid-1990s the Coursodon wines were sound enough but often possessed a raw, harsh undercurrent. De-stemming was not practised and old *foudres* were the order of the day. Jérôme Coursodon has now taken over the winemaking and the results in the late 90s have been impressive, particularly the top red *cuvées*. The wines have concentrated dark fruit but are more refined and better balanced than of old. The very fine bottling of La Sensonne is produced in association with Patrick LESEC. (DM)

● **Saint-Joseph**★★ £B L'Olivaie★★★ £C Le Paradis St-Pierre★★★ £C La Sensonne★★★ £C
○ **Saint-Joseph**★ £B Le Paradis St-Pierre★★ £C

YVES CUILLERON Condrieu www.cuilleron.com   A: Eno, BBR

Owner: Yves Cuilleron Verlieu, 42140 Chavanay
One of the new younger superstars of the northern Rhône, Cuilleron is best known for superb Condrieu made in a number of guises including Essences d'Automne, a very intense and distinctive sweet botrytised example that spends eight months in wood. A new dry wine labelled Vertige was added to the range of Condrieus with the 2001 vintage. He also produces a small range of first-class Saint-Joseph, both red and white, and is working with François VILLARD and Pierre GAILLARD in a new small-scale *négociant* venture, Les VINS DE VIENNE. An additional Côte-Rôtie and a small range of vins de pays are the latest additions. The wines offer generally very good value. (DM)

● **Côte-Rôtie** Coteau de Bassenon★★★★ £E Terres Sombres★★★★★ £F
○ **Vin de Pays Marsanne**★ £B
○ **Condrieu** La Petite Côte★★★★ £D Chaillets Vieilles Vignes★★★★★ £E
○ **Condrieu** Les Ayguets✪✪✪✪✪ £F Fleur d'Automne✪✪✪✪✪ £G
● **Saint-Joseph** Les Pierres Sèches★★ £C Les Serines★★★ £C L'Amarybelle★★★ £C
○ **Saint-Joseph** Coteaux Saint-Pierre★★★ £C Le Lombard★★★★ £C Lyseras★★★ £C

DELAS FRÈRES Hermitage   A: BWC, BBR

Owner: Maison Louis Roederer 2 Allée de l'Olivet, 07300 Saint-Jean-de-Muzols
Once one of the northern Rhône's under-performers, Delas is now a serious player among the top Rhône *négociants*. With the purchase by leading Champagne house Louis ROEDERER and the arrival of Jacques Grange as winemaking chief, the wines have radically improved. The range is comprehensive and even the humbler wines are now sound and well-crafted. Far better fruit quality and well-handled new oak in the better wines are just two of the keys here to the transformation in fortune and quality. Star turns are the top *cuvées*, which are densely textured and explosively rich and concentrated. The outstanding Hermitage Les Bessards and Côte-Rôtie La Landonne are remarkably ageworthy propositions now, demanding at least six to seven years' cellaring. (DM)

● **Côte-Rôtie** Seigneur de Maugiron★★★★ £E La Landonne✪✪✪✪✪ £G
○ **Condrieu** Galopine★★★ £D Clos Boucher★★★★ £F

O **Condrieu** Vendange Tardive Brumaire de Bruyère★★★★ £F
● **Hermitage** Marquise de la Tourette★★★ £E Les Bessards✪✪✪✪✪ £H
O **Hermitage** Marquise de la Tourette✪✪✪✪✪ £E
● **Crozes-Hermitage** Les Launes★★ £B Tour d'Albon★★★ £D Le Clos★★★★ £E
O **Crozes-Hermitage** Les Launes★★ £B
● **Saint-Joseph** François de Tournon★★★ £C Les Challeys★★★ £C Sainte-Épine★★★ £D
O **Saint-Joseph** François de Tournon★★ £B Les Challeys★★★ £C
● **Cornas** Chante Perdrix★★★ £D
● **Châteauneuf-du-Pape**★★ £C ● **Gigondas**★★★ £C
● **Vacqueyras** Domaine des Genêts★ £B ● **Côtes du Ventoux**★ £A ● **Côtes du Rhône** Saint-Esprit★£B
O **Côtes du Rhône** Saint-Esprit★ £A

PIERRE DUMAZET Condrieu   A: Bib

Owner: Pierre Dumazet RN 86, 07340 Limony
Somewhat controversial among Condrieu producers, Dumazet produces wines which are rich, dense and full of classic Viognier dried peaches, spices and minerals. Don't expect modern squeaky-clean fruit-driven wines here. The vin de pays and Cuvée du Zenith offer similar style at a lower level than the Condrieus. Old-fashioned in style, quite heavily oaked, they are at times almost rustic. However they are also characterful, powerful and structured. This is an excellent source of traditional Condrieu. (DM)

O **Condrieu**★★★ £D Côte de Fournet★★★★ £E
O **Vin de Pays Viognier**★★ £B O **Côtes du Rhône** Cuvée du Zenith★★ £B

ERIC ET JOËL DURAND Cornas   A: N&P

Owner: Eric et Joël Durand 07130 Châteaubourg
Just two reds are made here from a small holding of some 7 ha. They are traditionally vinified and are bottled unfiltered. Ageing at present is in older barrels and, while dense and impressively concentrated, they are not quite in the first division. However, the vineyard is still relatively young and the best has probably yet to emerge. Both wines are firmly structured and will age well in the medium term. The Cornas requires four to five years at a minimum. (DM)

● **Cornas**★★★ £C ● **Saint-Joseph** Les Coteaux★★★ £C

BERNARD FAURIE Hermitage   A: THt, J&B, HHC

Owner: Bernard Faurie 27 Avenue Hélène de Tournon, 07300 Tournon
Producer of old-style Hermitage and Saint-Joseph from a tiny holding of just 3 ha of vines. The wines are at their best in great years, when they are both ripe and powerful. In lesser vintages the odd green note can creep in. The Hermitage Le Méal packs a real punch of complex old-vine fruit. They demand cellaring for 10 years or more. (DM)

● **Hermitage**★★★ £D Le Méal★★★★ £E O **Hermitage**★★★ £D
● **Saint-Joseph**★★ £B Cuvée Vieilles-Vignes★★★ £D

DOM. DE FAUTERIE Cornas   A: M&V, Yap

Owner: Sylvain Bernard 07130 Saint-Péray
Recently established but assuredly traditional domaine in its approach to viticulture. Sylvain Bernard trained with Jean-Louis CHAVE before establishing his own small holding of vineyards in Saint-Peray, Saint-Joseph and now of most interest in Cornas. The vines in the latter, leased from Guy de Barjac,

are around 100 years old and are grown in ideal sandy granite soils with an exceptional and very sunny mesoclimate. The result is a wine with considerable depth, complexity and some power. It will be all the better for five years' ageing. The 1999 was particularly impressive. (DM)

● **Cornas**★★★ £D   **O Saint-Péray** Les Hauts de Fauterie★★ £B

PIERRE GAILLARD   Saint-Joseph   A: HHB, JAr, L&S

Owner: Pierre Gaillard   Chez Favier, 42520 Malleval
A diverse range of wines from a scattered 16 ha in Saint-Joseph, Côte-Rôtie and Condrieu. Gaillard also runs to a good Côtes du Rhône Viognier and, when conditions permit, an excellent late-harvest Condrieu and a rare *vin de paille* Jean-Elise. Though small, this is an expanding domaine. The wines are modern and stylish and, given the relative youth of the vines, it is clear the best is yet to come. New oak is present but not overdone in the best reds. The regular Côte-Rôtie is lighter and more elegant, with the inclusion of Viognier, the Rose Poupre dense and firmly structured. It requires five or six years' cellaring. Gaillard is also the inspiration and one of the partners behind LES VINS DE VIENNE. (DM)

● **Côte-Rôtie**★★★ £D   Rose Pourpre★★★★ £E
O **Condrieu**★★★★ £E
● **Saint-Joseph**★★★ £C   Les Pierres★★★ £C   Clos du Cuminaille★★★★ £C
O **Saint-Joseph**★★★ £C   **O Côtes du Rhône** Viognier★★★ £C

DOM.YVES GANGLOFF   Condrieu   A: M&V

Owner: Mathilde & Yves Gangloff   2 Rue de la Garenne, 69420 Condrieu
Yves Gangloff has been established here for nearly twenty years and has built up a small holding like many of his neighbours. He now has 3.5 ha. The rich and opulent Condrieu is sourced from two separate parcels, La Bonnette and Chéry, adding to the wines complexity. For Viognier it is finely structured with sufficient grip to develop well over four or five years. There are two Côte-Rôtie's, Barbarine, which is blended with a little Viognier and produced from younger vines, and the sturdier Sereine Noir which is partly aged in new wood. Both are very impressive with the Sereine Noir requiring five years or so to show at its best. (DM)

● **Côte-Rôtie** Barbarine★★★★ £D   Sereine Noir★★★★★ £E
O **Condrieu**★★★★ £E

JEAN-MICHEL GERIN   Côte-Rôtie   A: C&C

Owner: Jean-Michel Gerin   19 Rue de Montmain, Verenay, 69420 Ampuis
Jean-Michel Gerin's 9 ha are the source of some fine rich and modern Côte-Rôtie with an emphasis on dark, brambly and chocolaty fruit. New oak is not used sparingly either. La Landonne and Les Grandes Places, which is produced from vines that are over 80 years old, are very good indeed. Modern and oaky they may be but the wines are superbly crafted and display a fine balance of complex fruit and firm but supple rounded tannins. These top *cuvées* need five years or so of ageing. (DM)

● **Côte-Rôtie** Champin Junior★★ £C   Champin Le Seigneur★★★ £E
● **Côte-Rôtie** Les Grandes Places★★★★★ £F   La Landonne★★★★★ £F
O **Condrieu** Coteau de la Loye★★ £D
● **Côtes du Rhône**★ £B

ALAIN GRAILLOT   Crozes-Hermitage   A: Yap, L&W, ABy

Owner: Alain Graillot   Les Chênes Verts, 26600 Pont-de-l'Isère
In barely two decades Alain Graillot has become a benchmark producer for Crozes-Hermitage, both
white and red. Yields are kept in check but green harvesting is not practised. The more traditional
winter pruning will set the yield for the year. The white is vinified in wood and *inox* and kept on lees
and the reds given an extended maceration of up to 21 days. The special cuvée La Guiraude is a very
impressive barrel selection. The reds, particularly La Guiraude, will age very well. (DM)

- **Crozes-Hermitage★★★** £B La Guiraude★★★★ £C   O **Crozes-Hermitage★★** £B
- **Hermitage★★★** £D   **Saint-Joseph★★★** £C

JEAN-LOUIS GRIPPAT   Saint-Joseph   A: WSc

Owner: Marcel Guigal   La Sauva, 07300 Tournon
For the past two decades this has been one of the leading domaines in Saint-Joseph, producing good
traditional Hermitage as well. Jean-Louis Grippat has now sold his vineyards to Marcel Guigal at
CHÂTEAU D'AMPUIS. With no previous vineyards of their own in these ACs, Guigal is sure to
maintain quality. The wines are now vinified at Ampuis and the Grippat name will be retained, the
intention being to label them as Lieu-Dit or Ancien Domaine Jean-Louis Grippat. (DM)

- **Hermitage★★★★** £D   O **Hermitage★★★** £D
- **Saint-Joseph★★** £C Cuvée des Hospices★★★★ £C   O **Saint-Joseph★★** £C

E GUIGAL   Côte-Rôtie   www.guigal.com   A: JEF

Owner: Marcel Guigal   Château d'Ampuis, 69420 Ampuis
The E. Guigal label covers an extensive range produced from the length and breadth of the Rhône
Valley. The firm is far and away the largest producer of Côte-Rôtie and also owns Domaine de
VALLOUIT as well as the merchant house of VIDAL FLEURY. The vibrant red Côtes du Rhône, if not
quite of the quality of a decade ago, remains a model of consistency. The top Guigal wines are supplied
under the CHÂTEAU D'AMPUIS label and include the three magnificent *super-cuvées* for which he
himself and the appellation have become particularly famous. As a part of Château d'Ampuis Guigal also
acquired the Domaine of Jean-Louis GRIPPAT in 2001. The Côte-Rôtie Brune et Blonde, which is
sourced mainly from bought-in fruit, is good rather than great. More impressive is the Hermitage, which
is dense and concentrated. It generally offers very fair value for the appellation. The southern Rhône
wines lack the quality and refinement of their northern counterparts. (DM)

- **Côte-Rôtie** Brune et Blonde★★★ £D   O **Condrieu★★★** £D
- **Hermitage★★★★** £D   O **Hermitage★★★** £D
- **Châteauneuf-du-Pape★★★** £D   ● **Gigondas★★** £C
- **Côtes du Rhône★** £B   O **Côtes du Rhône★** £B

PAUL JABOULET AINÉ   Hermitage   www.jaboulet.com   A: Tan, OWL, ,BBR, DAy, WSc

Owner: Jaboulet family   Les Jalets, La Roche-sur-Glun, 26600 Tain-l'Hermitage
Large *négociant* operation with some 100 ha of their own vineyards. An extensive range is produced
but the main focus is the northern Rhône appellations. The Jaboulet name is most famous for one
massive and very ageworthy cuvée of red Hermitage, La Chapelle. With dense and dark fruit, the wine
is more approachable than, say, a Jean-Louis CHAVE but not as modern and opulent as a top
CHAPOUTIER. Recent vintages have not been quite so good, although 2000 looks to be back on fine
form. There is a much lighter second red Hermitage, Le Pied de La Côte, produced from younger

vines. During the 1990s the Raymond Roure property was added to the portfolio and with the dense and chocolaty Thalabert offers good to very good quality in Crozes-Hermitage. Domaine de Saint-Pierre Cornas is powerful and tannic in its youth and the Châteauneuf-du-Pape Les Cèdres has been better of late. Top wines are ageworthy but the lesser appellations should be approached young. (DM)

- ● **Côte-Rôtie** Les Jumelles★★ £E
- O **Condrieu** Les Cassines★★ £D
- ● **Hermitage** La Chapelle✪✪✪✪✪ £G   O **Hermitage** Chevalier de Sterimberg★★★★ £E
- ● **Crozes-Hermitage** Les Jalets★ £B Raymond Roure★★★ £C Thalabert★★★ £C
- O **Crozes-Hermitage**★ £B Raymond Roure★★ £C Mules Blanche★★ £C
- ● **Cornas** Les Grandes Terrasses★★ £C Domaine de St Pierre★★★ £D
- ● **Saint-Joseph** La Grand Pompée★ £B   O **Saint-Joseph** La Grand Pompée★★ £B
- ● **Châteauneuf-du-Pape** Les Cèdres★★★ £D   ● **Vacqueyras**★★ £B
- ● **Gigondas** Pierre Aiguille★★ £C
- O **Muscat de Beaumes-de-Venise**★★★ £C

DOM. JAMET   Côte-Rôtie   A: Bib

Owner: Jean-Paul et Jean-Luc Jamet   Le Vallin, 69420 Ampuis
Brothers Jean-Luc and Jean-Paul Jamet own 6.5ha of Syrah and a tiny amount of Viognier. They make a sumptuous, almost opulent Côte-Rôtie which has marvellous balance and poise. The oak is seamlessly handled and the wine is bottled unfiltered. Not only is this one of the finest examples of the appellation but it also represents excellent value for money. 1999 was of super-five quality. An attractive light and vibrant Syrah is also produced from young vines and classified as Vin de Pays des Collines Rhodaniennes. (DM)

- ● **Côte-Rôtie**★★★★★ £E

DOM. JASMIN   Côte-Rôtie   A: Yap

Owner: Patrick Jasmin   14 Rue des Maraîchers, 69420 Ampuis
Patrick Jasmin took over the running of this fine, traditional domaine after his late father Robert's early death. Patrick continues to make the wines in a traditional and elegant style. De-stemming is now employed and this helps in lesser years and the wine is aged for around two years in mainly old wood. Never blockbusters, there is always great purity of fruit and impressive intensity and depth. Top years like 2001 and 2000 require seven to ten years ageing. (DM)

- ● **Côte-Rôtie**★★★★ £

DOM. DU MONTEILLET   Condrieu   A: Cdp, Goe, GWW, Gau, SVS

Owner: Antoine et Stéphane Montez   Le Montelier, 42140 Chavanay
Stéphane Montez runs this small family domaine in Condrieu. The property consists of some 7ha in Condrieu, Côte-Rôtie and Saint-Joseph. Vinification is modern and plenty of new oak is used in the top *cuvées*. The Condrieu is rich and peachy but has a fine minerally backbone. The top *cuvée* Les Grandes Chaillées is particularly impressive. Both should develop well over three or four years. A late-harvest label, Tries Grains de Folie, is also now produced when conditions permit. The reds are ripe and spicy; both the Cuvée Papy and Côte-Rôtie are wines of considerable dimension and should be cellared for a good four or five years. (DM)

- ● **Côte-Rôtie**★★★★ £E
- O **Condrieu**★★★★ £D Les Grands Chaillees★★★★★ £E Tries Grains de Folie★★★★ £F
- ● **Saint-Joseph**★★ £B Cuvée Papy★★★ £C   O **Saint-Joseph**★★ £C

DOM. DU MURINAIS Crozes-Hermitage   A: OWL

Owner: Catherine & Luc Tardy   Quartier Champ Bernard, 26600 Beaumont-Monteux
This is an impressive producer of well priced Crozes-Hermitage. There are 12.5 ha under vine with
a mere 0.5 ha planted to Marsanne, the balance is Syrah. The Tardys produce a little under 4,000
cases a year. The white is good and lightly nutty with moderate depth and intensity. The 2001 was
particularly good of the style. The reds though are a step up, particularly the densely structured
Vieilles Vignes bottling which comes from vines that are over 30 years old. A special selection Cuvée
Valentin will also now be produced in exceptional years. (DM)

● **Crozes-Hermitage** Cuvée Amandier★★ £B
○ **Crozes-Hermitage** Cuvée Marine★★★ £B Vieilles Vignes★★★ £C

DOM. NIERO-PINCHON Condrieu   A:M&V, SVS

Owner: Robert Niero   20 Rue Cuvillère, 69420 Condrieu
Robert Niero has now been in charge of this fine domaine since the 1980s. The vineyard holding is
typically small. There are some 3 ha in Condrieu and a small parcel within Les Viaillères in Côte-
Rôtie. Insecticides are never used and the vines tended as naturally as possible. Les Ravines is part
vinified in *inox* and part in old wood and is elegant and lightly mineral with less overt peachy,
honeyed character than others. The Coteau de Chéry comes from old vines, some approaching 60
years and the wine is fuller and more opulent with an added dimension and greater weight and
concentration. The Côte-Rôtie is lighter than some of his neighbours examples but very
elegant, not least because of the 10 per cent Viognier in the blend. Both Condrieu should be drunk
young the Côte-Rôtie will benefit from five years cellaring. (DM)

● **Côte-Rôtie★★★★** £E
○ **Condrieu** Les Ravines★★★ £D Coteau de Chéry★★★★ £B

DOM. MICHEL OGIER Côte-Rôtie sogier@club-internet.fr   A: CTy, BBR

Owner: Michel & Stephane Ogier 3 Chemin du Bac, 69420 Ampuis
Very good Vin de Pays as well as some exceptional Côte-Rôtie is made at this small 3.5 ha property.
The vineyards for La Rosine are to be found just to the south of Ampuis towards Condrieu.
Winemaking is modern and the fruit is always de-stemmed prior to fermentation. New oak is used
both for the regular Côte-Rôtie as well as for the limited release special bottling, Belle Helene. The
wines are supple and velvety, with a real dimension to the fruit. The Belle Helene has become
established as one of the super-cuvées of the appellation and as such is very pricey.   (DM)

● **Côte-Rôtie★★★★** £E ● **Vin de Pays des Collines Rhodaniennes** La Rosine★★★ £C

DOM. ANDRÉ PERRET Côte-Rôtie   A:CTy, WTs, M&V

Owner: André Perret Verlieu, 42410 Chavanay
André Perret took over the family domaine in 1982 and now has some 10 ha of vines from which
he produces Condrieu, Saint-Joseph, Côtes du Rhône and varietals. The Condrieus are some of the
finest of the AC. These and the white Saint-Joseph are vinified in a combination of *inox* and oak,
some of it new and kept on lees. The reds are fully destemmed and spend two to three weeks on their
skins. Some late-harvest grapes are also included in the blend, adding greater complexity. Les
Grissières is dense and dark with ripe, black pepper notes. It will age well. Varietal Syrah and
Marsanne are produced as vins de pays and offer attractive early drinking. (DM)

○ **Condrieu★★★** £D Clos Chanson★★★★ £E Coteau du Chéry★★★★ £F
● **Saint-Joseph★★** £B Les Grissières★★★ £C ○ **Saint-Joseph★★** £B

DOM. ÉTIENNE POCHON   Crozes-Hermitage

A:L&W,WSc

Owner: Etienne Pochon   Château de Curson, 26600 Chanos Curson

Étienne Pochon makes straightforward attractively fruity regular Crozes-Hermitage and a special bottling of both red and white which are labelled Chateau de Curson. Both are vinified using more oak and are a significant step up in quality. The property consists of a total of 18 ha with 14 planted to Syrah and with around 3 ha of Roussanne and a single ha of Marsanne. The Curson white is dominated by Roussanne and is enticingly floral as well as lightly toasty and spicy. The red Curson is weighty but supple and will benefit from two or three years cellaring. (DM)

● **Crozes-Hermitage**★★ £B   Cuvée Château de Curson★★★ £C
O **Crozes-Hermitage**★ £B   Cuvée Château de Curson★★★ £C

DOM. DES REMIZIÈRES   Crozes-Hermitage

A: Bib, SVS

Owner: Philippe Desmeure   Route de Romans, 26600 Mercurol

This 27-ha property has greatly improved in recent vintages. At best the wines used to be no more than middle-ranking examples of their appellations. The reds are now deep and intense. The Hermitage Émilie is powerful and structured with considerable grip but there is also real concentration and old-vine complexity here. Patrick LESEC also produces his own *cuvée* of the same wine in association with Philippe Desmeure. The Cuvée Christophe red is ripe and full of dark fruit, needing three or four years' ageing, while the whites display all the nutty, pure character of Marsanne at its best. The wines also represent very good value. (DM)

● **Hermitage** Cuvée Émilie★★★★ £E   O **Hermitage**★★★★ £D
● **Crozes-Hermitage** Cuvée Christophe★★★ £C   O **Crozes-Hermitage** Cuvée Christophe★★★ £B
● **Saint-Joseph**★★ £C

RENÉ ROSTAING   Côte-Rôtie

A: Mis, BBR, J&B, HHB, GBa,SVS

Owner: René Rostaing   69420 Ampuis

Rostaing is now one of the very finest producers of great Côte-Rôtie. He is continually seeking to keep yields in check, to harvest at optimum ripeness and to minimize handling in the cellar. The wines are uniformly bottled without filtration. He has tremendous vineyards to draw upon, having taken over the running of those of Albert Dervieux-Thaize as well as Marius Gentaz-Dervieux. The wines are deep and extracted but always refined and with supple, finely crafted, velvety tannins. The top *cuvées* are very ageworthy. They will improve in bottle for a decade or more. La Landonne is dense, massive in its youth, the Côte Blonde lighter but typically more elegant as one might expect from vines planted in these soils. The Condrieu is marked by glorious ripe, peachy varietal fruit and should be drunk young. (DM)

● **Côte-Rôtie**★★★ £D   Classique★★★ £E   La Viallières★★★★ £E
● **Côte-Rôtie** La Landonne★★★★★ £F   Côte Blonde✪✪✪✪✪ £G
O **Condrieu** La Bonnette★★★★ £E

MARC SORREL   Hermitage   marc.sorrel@wanadoo.fr

A: CTy, Gau

Owner: Marc Sorrel   Avenue Jean-Jaurès, 26600 Tain-l'Hermitage

The top *cuvées* both red and white are some of the finest expressions of the great wines of the Hermitage hill. The regular bottlings, in particular the red, can be a touch disappointing and should often have more depth and substance. 2001, though, looks to be more impressive and Le Greal potentially exceptional. The red Crozes-Hermitage is a reasonable example with moderately intense, dark berry fruit in a lighter style than some but stylish for what it is. What marks out Le Gréal is its powerful, dense and complex fruit and backward structure. If you give it seven or eight years at least you'll be rewarded with a great example of the appellation. In exceptional years, among them 1998, 1991 and 1990, this can be legendary. Les Rocoules is an equally fine, but equally backward example of great Marsanne. Honeyed, nutty and complex with age; this really needs at least ten years. (DM)

● **Hermitage**★★★ £D Le Greal★★★★★ £F
O **Hermitage**★★★ £D Les Rocoules★★★★★ £F
● **Crozes-Hermitage**★★ £B O **Crozes-Hermitage**★ £B

CAVE DE TAIN L'HERMITAGE Hermitage   A: PBW

Owner: Co-operative members 22 Route de Larnage, BP 3, 26601 Tain-l'Hermitage Cedex
The growers belonging to this co-operative have a considerable holding, in total some 1,000 ha, planted throughout the region and production is considerable at around 475,000 cases a year. The range is fairly extensive and there are varietal vins de pays as well as AC bottlings. These are sound but relatively unexciting. It is the top bottlings within each appellation, labelled as Nobles Rives, which particularly stand out. There are also special superior *cuvées* of Hermitage and Crozes-Hermitage red. The former, Gambert de Loche, is from an individual plot of old vines. It is dense, rich and very complex, impressive indeed for a co-op wine. Occasionally a little *vin de paille* is also produced. (DM)

● **Hermitage** Les Nobles Rives★★ £D Gambert de Loche★★★ £E
O **Hermitage** Les Nobles Rives★★★ £D
● **Crozes-Hermitage** Les Nobles Rives★ £B Les Hauts du Fief★★ £C
O **Crozes-Hermitage** Les Nobles Rives★ £B
● **Cornas** Les Nobles Rives★★ £C
● **Saint-Joseph** Les Nobles Rives★ £B

DOM. DU TUNNEL Saint-Péray   A:HHB, Gau, Lib

Owner: Stéphane Robert 20 Rue de la République, 07130 Saint-Péray
Very good Saint-Péray as well as Cornas are made at this small 3.5 ha property which was established as recently as 1996. The regular Saint-Péray is fresh, forward and attractively nutty, the Prestige, denser and altogether more concentrated. The two Cornas are both splendid wines made from ancient vineyard plantings, in the case of the Prestige the vines are 80 years old. This parcel originally being farmed by Marcel JUGE. The wines are dense, sumptuous and full of classic dark fruit, spice and black pepper, the Prestige characterised by complex old viney fruit. The 2001 was particularly impressive. A small amount of well crafted Saint-Joseph is also made (DM)

● **Cornas**★★★ £D Prestige★★★★ £E ● **Saint-Joseph**★★★ £C
O **Saint-Péray**★★ £B Prestige★★★ £C

DOM. GEORGES VERNAY Condrieu   A: Yap, Win, Cco

Owner: Georges Vernay 1 Route National, Condrieu 69420
Vernay is one of the great Condrieu producers. His daughter Christine now runs the domaine and they possess some 9 ha of Viognier and a further 7 ha of Syrah from which they are making increasingly impressive Côte-Rôtie, an appellation they used to struggle with. There has been some consultancy for the reds from Jean-Luc COLOMBO. Good vin de pays Viognier is made from the youngest vines but it is the three Condieus which are the main focus here. Terasses de l'Empire, the regular bottling, is well-crafted but lacks a little depth. The other two wines are part barrel-fermented and of serious depth and weight; Chaillées de L'Enfer is just a little more opulent and heady. Both will develop well in the short term. (DM)

● **Côte-Rôtie**★★★ £D Cuvée Maison Rouge★★★★ £E
O **Condrieu** Les Terrasses de L'Empire★★★ £D Les Chaillées de L'Enfer★★★★ £E
O **Condrieu** Coteau du Vernon★★★★ £E O **Vin de Pays** Viognier★★ £C
● **Saint-Joseph**★ £B

FRANÇOIS VILLARD Condrieu   A: HHB

Owner: François Villard Montjoux, 42410 Saint-Michel-sur-Rhône
3.5 ha of a total of 7 ha vineyards are in Condrieu where three fine dry examples of the appellation
are produced. Vinified in new oak on their lees with careful *bâtonnage,* they they have considerable
depth and structure for Viognier and age uncharacteristically well. A sweet Condrieu, Quintessence,
is also made as are very good Côte-Rôtie and red and white Saint-Joseph. François is involved with
Pierre GAILLARD and Yves CUILLERON in Les VINS DE VIENNE. (DM)
● **Côte-Rôtie** la Brocarde★★★★★ £E
● **Vin de Pays des Collines Rhodaniennes** Syrah★★ £B
O **Vin de Pays des Collines Rhodaniennes** Viognier★★★ £C
O **Condrieu** Grand Vallon★★★ £D Les Terrasses du Palat★★★★ £E Coteaux de Poncin★★★★ £E
O **Condrieu** Quintessence❂❂❂❂❂ £G
● **Saint-Joseph** Reflet★★★ £C Côtes de Mairlant★★★ £C
O **Saint-Joseph** Côtes de Mairlant★★★★ £C

LES VINS DE VIENNE Côte-Rôtie   A: Goe, C&B, NYg

Owner: Yves Cuilleron, Pierre Gaillard & François Villard Le Bas de Seyssuel, 38200 Seyssuel
A recently established small-scale operation that is part domaine and part *négociant.* The three partners
are re-establishing the pre-phylloxera vineyards of the Côteaux du Seyssuel to the west of Vienne. This once
famous area, known to Pliny and Plutarch, produces the red Sotanum, a wine of real potential and a
partially barrel-aged Viognier, Taburnum. The vines are as yet very young at six years. and the wines are
likely to improve considerably as the vines age. The *négociant* offerings range from good to exciting.
New oak is evident in all the wines but is well handled. One criticism might be that the character of
the individual appellations can struggle to show through. The Côte-Rôtie Les Essartailles and Condrieu
La Chambée particularly stand out. The best are undoubtedly very ageworthy. (DM)
● **Vin de Pays des Collines Rhodaniennes** Sotanum★★★★ £C
O **Vin de Pays des Collines Rhodaniennes** Taburnum★★★ £C
● **Côte-Rôtie** Les Essartailles★★★★★ £E
O **Condrieu** La Chambée★★★★ £E
● **Hermitage** Les Chirats de Saint-Christophe★★★ £D
O **Hermitage** La Bachole★★★ £D
● **Crozes-Hermitage** Les Palignons★★ £C ● **Cornas** Les Barcillants★★★ £D
● **Châteauneuf du Pape** Les Oteliées★★★ £C
● **Gigondas** Les Pimpignoles★★ £C ● **Vacqueyras** La Sillote★★ £B
● **Côtes du Rhône** Les Cranilles★★ £B ● **Cairanne** La Perpendaille★★★ £B
O **Saint-Péray** Les Bialères★★★ £B

ALAIN VOGE Cornas   A: GWW, VTr, SVS

Owner: Alain Voge 4 Rue de l'Equerre, 07130 Cornas
As well as his very powerful and muscular Cornas, Alain Voge also produces some of the best Saint-
Péray, both dry and sparkling. The Mélodie William and Harmonie are unoaked and marked by
impressive nutty Marsanne fruit, while the Cuvée Boisée sees some new oak. The top Fleur du
Crussol is amongst the very finest in the appellation. His Cornas vineyards are of increasingly

venerable age and this is showing through in the wines with immensely complex smoky dark fruits and black spices emerging in the Vieilles Vignes and Vieille Fontaines bottlings. A very small amount of new oak is used to barrel-age the wines, which you should expect to cellar for five years or more. (DM)

● **Cornas★★★** £D Vieilles Vignes★★★★ £D Vieille Fontaines★★★★ £E

○ **Saint-Péray** Cuvée Mélodie William★★ £B Cuvée Harmonie★★ £B Cuvée Boisée★★★ £B

○ **Saint-Péray** Cuvée Fleur du Crussol★★★ £B Dry Vintage★ £B

NORTHERN RHÔNE/OTHER WINES OF NOTE

GUY DE BARJAC ● **Cornas** £D

DOM. DE BIGUET ● **Cornas** £D

DOM. BOISSEYT-CHOL ● **Côte-Rôtie** £E

DOM. FRÉDÉRIC BOISSONET ○ **Condrieu** £E Les Rochains £E

JOEL CHAMPET ● **Côte-Rôtie** £E

CH. MONTLYS ● **Côte-Rôtie** £E

CH. DU ROZAY ○ **Condrieu** £D

CAVE DES CLAIRMONTS ● **Crozes-Hermitage** £B ○ **Crozes-Hermitage** £B

MARTIN DAUBRÉE ● **Côte-Rôtie** Côte Brune £D

EDMOND ET DAVID DUCLAUX ● **Côte-Rôtie** £E

OLIVIER DUMAINE ● **Crozes-Hermitage** £B ○ **Crozes-Hermitage** £B

DOM. DUMIEN-SURETTE ● **Cornas** Vieilles Vignes £D

CHRISTIAN FACCHIN ○ **Condrieu** Les Grands-Maison £E

PHILIPPE FAURY ● **Saint-Joseph** £C ● **Côte-Rôtie** £E ○ **Condrieu** La Berne £E

CAVE FAYOLLE ● **Hermitage** £D ○ **Hermitage** £D

DOM. FERRATON ● **Hermitage** Les Miaux £E Le Méal £F ○ **Hermitage** Le Méal £F

GILLES FLACHER ● **Saint-Joseph** Prestige £C ○ **Condrieu** £D Cuvée Lea £E

DOM. GACHON ● **Saint-Joseph** £C

HENRI GALLET ● **Côte-Rôtie** £E

VINCENT GASSE ● **Saint-Joseph** £C ● **Côte-Rôtie** £D Vieilles Vignes £E

DOM. GONON ● **Saint-Joseph** £C ○ **Saint-Joseph** Les Oliviers £C

DOM. BERNARD GRIPA ● **Saint-Joseph** £C Le Berceau £C ○ **Saint-Joseph** Le Berceau £C

○ **Saint-Péray** £B Les Figuières £C

DOM. MARCEL JUGE ● **Cornas** Cuvée C £D

JACQUES LEMENCIER ● **Cornas** £D

BERNARD LEVET ● **Côte-Rôtie** £D La Chavaroche £E

DOM. JEAN LIONNET ● **Cornas** £C Rochepertuis £E

ROBERT MICHEL ● **Cornas** Cuvée de Coteaux £C La Geynale £D

DOM. MOUTON ● **Côte-Rôtie** £E ○ **Condrieu** Côte Bonnette £E Côte Chatillons £E

ALAIN PARET ● **Côtes du Rhône** Valvigneyre £B ○ **Condrieu** Lys de Volan £D

VINCENT PARIS ● **Cornas** Granit 60 £E

DOM. PAVILLON-MERCUROL ● **Crozes-Hermitage** £B

CHRISTOPHE PICHON ● **Saint-Joseph** £C ○ **Condrieu** £D

PHILIPPE PICHON ● **Saint-Joseph** £C ○ **Condrieu** £D

JEAN-PAUL REMILLIER ● **Côte-Rôtie** £E

HERVÉ RICHARD ● **Côte-Rôtie** L'Amarage £D

GILLES ROBIN ● **Crozes-Hermitage** Alberic Bouvet £B ● **Crozes-Hermitage** Les Marelles £B

DOM. ERIC ROCHER ● **Saint-Joseph** Terroir de Champal £C

CAVE CO-OPÉRATIVE DE SAINT DÉSIRAT ● **Saint-Joseph** £B

JEAN-MICHEL STEPHAN ● **Côte-Rôtie** £D Coteau de Tupin £E Vieilles Vignes En Coteau £F

JEAN-LOUIS THIERS ● **Cornas** £D

DOM. DE VALLOUIT ● **Côte-Rôtie** Les Roziers £E ● **Hermitage** Les Greffières £F

DANIEL VERNAY ● **Côte-Rôtie** £D
NOËL VERSET ● **Cornas** £D
VIDAL FLEURY ● **Côte-Rôtie** £D La Chatillon £F O **Condrieu** £E

Author's choice (DM)

10 of the Northern Rhone's most distinguished reds
THIERRY ALLEMAND ● **Cornas** Reynard
M CHAPOUTIER ● **Hermitage** Le Pavillon
CH. D' AMPUIS ● **Côte-Rôtie** La Turque
JEAN-LOUIS CHAVE ● **Hermitage** Ermitage Cuvée Cathelin
AUGUSTE CLAPE ● **Cornas**
CLUSEL ROCH ● **Côte-Rôtie** Les Grandes Places
PAUL JABOULET AINÉ ● **Hermitage** La Chapelle
DOM. JAMET ● **Côte-Rôtie**
RENÉ ROSTAING ● **Côte-Rôtie** Côte Blonde
MARC SORREL ● **Hermitage** Le Gréal

A choice of opulent dry whites
M CHAPOUTIER O **Hermitage** Cuveé de l'Orée
JEAN-LOUIS CHAVE O **Hermitage**
DOM. DU CHENE O **Condrieu**
YVES CUILLERON O **Condrieu** Chaillets Vieilles Vignes
DOM. YVES GANGLOFF O **Condrieu**
DOM. DU MURINAIS O **Crozes Hermitage** Vieilles Vignes
ANDRÉ PERRET O **Condrieu** Coteaux du Chéry
GEORGES VERNAY O **Condrieu** Les Chaillées de L'Enfer
FRANÇOIS VILLARD O **Saint-Joseph** Côtes de Mairlant
ALAIN VOGE O **Saint-Péray** Cuvée Fleur du Crussol

A selection of up and coming reds and whites
ALBERT BELLE ● **Crozes-Hermitage** Cuvée Louis Belle
M CHAPOUTIER ● **Saint-Joseph** Les Granits
YANN CHAVE ● **Crozes-Hermitage** Tête de Cuvée
JEAN-LUC COLOMBO O **Hermitage** Le Louet
DOM. COMBIER O **Crozes-Hermitage** Clos des Grives
YVES CUILLERON O **Saint-Joseph** Le Lombard
DELAS FRÈRES ● **Crozes-Hermitage** Le Clos
PIERRE GAILLARD O **Côtes du Rhône** Viognier
DOM. MICHEL OGIER ● **Vin de Pays des Collines Rhodaniennes** La Rosine
DOM. DU TUNNEL O **Saint-Peray** Prestige

Southern Rhône

DANIEL ET DENIS ALARY Cairanne   A: HHB

Owner: Daniel & Denis Alary   Font d'Estevenas, Route de Rasteau, 84290 Cairanne
A comprehensive and impressive range of Côtes du Rhône and Cairanne village wines are made here from the Alarys' 25 ha. Nearly 90 per cent of the vineyard is planted to red varieties, with some of the plantings now of notable age. The floral, forward white Côtes du Rhône blends Clairette with

221

Bourboulenc. The Font d'Estevenas white is a step up, a rich, nutty and complex blend of mainly Roussanne with some Viognier. The reds are unfiltered, full of dense and aromatic *garrigue* scents and complex, heady, berry fruit. The Font d'Estevenas and Jean de Verde are among the best expressions of old-vine Grenache outside Châteauneuf-du-Pape. The former usually has a proportion of Syrah, whereas La Jean de Verde is 100 per cent Grenache. The overall quality across all the wines is very good indeed. The top two reds will age well. (DM)

● **Côtes du Rhône**★ £B ● **Côtes du Rhône-Villages Cairanne**★★ £B
● **Côtes du Rhône-Villages Cairanne** Réserve du Vigneron★★★ £B
● **Côtes du Rhône-Villages Cairanne** La Jean de Verde★★★ £C
● **Côtes du Rhône-Villages Cairanne** La Font d'Estevenas★★★★ £C
O **Côtes du Rhône** La Chevre d'Or★★ £B
O **Côtes du Rhône-Villages Cairanne** La Font d'Estevenas★★★ £C
◉ **Côtes du Rhône**★ £A

DOM. DES AMADIEU   Cairanne   www.achiary.com   A:P-F

Owner: Marylène & Michel Achiary   Quartier Beauregard, 84290 Cairanne
Small 7 ha domaine established in 1984 which produces some excellent value Cairanne. The property is planted to Grenache, Syrah and Mourvedre and the Grenache vines now average 50 years. Yields are restricted, averaging 35 hl/ha and pigeage employed during vinification. With output a mere 1,500 cases or so the wines will not be the easiest to find. The small range consists of two wines which are labelled Vitalis and Vieilles Vignes. Vitalis generally blends all three of the varieties planted and is the softer, more vibrantly fruit driven example of the two. The Vieilles Vignes is usually crafted from an equal amount of Syrah and Grenache. It is denser, firmer and will age well in the medium term. The 2001 was nudging three stars. (DM)

● **Côtes du Rhône-Villages Cairanne** Vitalis★★ £B
● **Côtes du Rhône-Villages Cairanne** Vieilles Vignes★★ £B

DOM. AMIDO   Tavel

Owner: Christian Amido   Rue des Carrières, 30126 Tavel
This is the most significant domaine in Tavel from a quality point of view producing one of the best examples of the appellation. The wine undergoes a 36 hour pre-fermentation maceration and is fermented cool to preserve its attractive fresh berry fruit, something many in the AC fail to achieve. More important though from a quality perspective is a fine Côtes du Rhône-Villages which is a blend of Grenache (70 per cent) and Syrah (30 per cent) as well as benchmark red Lirac. This is produced from 50 year old Grenache, which accounts for just over half of the blend with the balance Syrah and Mourvèdre. It is aged traditionally, first in cement tanks and then transferred to used oak. The wine shows rich dark berry fruit, classic southern herbal spice and will benefit from a year or two of bottle age. (DM)

● **Lirac**★★★ £B ● **Côtes du Rhône-Villages**★★ £B
◉ **Tavel** Les Amandines★★ £A

DOM. DES AMOURIERS   Vacqueyras   A: EoR, HHB

Owner: Patrick Gras   Les Garrigues, 84260 Sarrians
First class operation run by Patrick Gras, producing very stylish balanced wines. Up until the mid-1990s the estate fruit was sold on but in only a few years this has become one of the finest sources in the AC. A sizeable planting of Syrah produces wines of depth and rich savoury fruit and considerable

structure, with new oak playing a large part in the style. The 1998, 1999 and now 2000 Genestes are benchmarks for the appellation and will age very well. 2001 seems to be showing similar promise. All are moving towards four stars. (DM)

● **Vin de Pays du Vaucluse★** £A   ● **Côtes du Rhône★** £B
● **Vacqueyras★★** £B   Signature★★ £B   Les Hautes Terrasses★★★ £C   Les Genestes★★★ £C

DOM. LUCIEN BARROT   Châteauneuf-du-Pape   A: M&V, Maj, Bal

Owner: Barrot family   Chemin du Clos, 84230 Châteauneuf-du-Pape
This is a small family run operation with 20 ha of vineyards spread across the Châteauneuf-du-Pape appellation. The Barrots have been established as winemakers here since the late 17th century. The vines are old, approaching 50 years, planted in limestones soils with a *galet* stone topsoil. The resulting wine is dense, complex and stylish and with a classic rich, savoury, *garrigue*-scented character. It is blended from Grenache, Syrah, Mourvèdre and Cinsault and vinification is traditional: the grapes are not destemmed and maceration lasts up to four weeks in top years. The wine is then aged in foudres for around 18 months. Firmly structured when young, it will drink well at five years or so. Excellent value. (DM)

● **Châteauneuf du Pape★★★** £C

DOM. DE BEAURENARD   Châteauneuf-du-Pape   www.beaurenard.fr   A: BWC

Owner: Paul Coulon   Avenue Pierre-de-Luxembourg, 84231 Châteauneuf-du-Pape
The Coulon family make an impressive range of stylish reds and whites in modern, well-equipped cellars. The lighter reds and white Châteauneuf-du-Pape are forward and full of fruit, the latter enjoying some lees-enrichment. The Côtes du Rhône Rasteau has 20 per cent Syrah as well Grenache, to add to the wine's structure. The regular Châteauneuf-du-Pape red is supple, rich and forward, whereas the Boisrenard is a dense powerful wine produced from very low yields of 15 to 20 hl/ha. It requires six or seven years' ageing in years such as 1998, 1999 and 2000. The fortified Rasteau is one of the better examples. (DM)

● **Côtes du Rhône★** £A   ● **Côtes du Rhône-Villages Rasteau★** £B
● **Rasteau★** £B
● **Châteauneuf du Pape★★★** £D   Boisrenard★★★★ £F
○ **Châteauneuf du Pape★★★** £C

BOIS DE BOURSAN   Châteauneuf-du-Pape

Owner: Jean et Jean-Paul Versino   Quartier Saint-Pierre, 84230 Châteauneuf-du-Pape
Small, extremely quality-conscious Châteauneuf producer with around 15 ha planted mainly to Grenache, Syrah and Mourvèdre. The white is relatively unexciting but both the reds are dense, powerful wines needing time to soften their youthful tannins and fiery character. Both are bottled without filtration. The Cuvée Felix is particularly ageworthy. (DM)

● **Châteauneuf du Pape★★★★** £C   Cuvée des Felix★★★★★ £E

HENRI BONNEAU   Châteauneuf-du-Pape   A: HHB, BBR, Sec

Owner: Henri Bonneau   35 Rue Joseph-Ducos, 84230 Châteauneuf-du-Pape
A Somewhat controversial producer, M. Bonneau is, as was the late Jacques Reynaud at CHÂTEAU RAYAS, one of Châteauneufs more interesting characters. The two special *cuvées*, which are produced from a high proportion of Grenache, are generally only bottled if the vintage justifies it – otherwise

a regular Chateauneuf-du-Pape is produced – and he sells to *négociants* to maintain quality. Both the Marie Beurrier and Réserve des Célestins wines will improve with a decade or more in bottle. (DM)

● **Châteauneuf du Pape**★★ £C Marie Beurrier★★★★★ £F Réserve des Célestins❂❂❂❂❂ £G

BOSQUETS DES PAPES Châteauneuf-du-Pape A: Cty, HHB, Res, SVS, OWL

Owner: Boiron Family 18 Route d'Orange, BP 50, 84232 Châteauneuf-du-Pape
The Boiron family own 8 ha of vineyards but also lease from other properties. There is a relatively dull white as well as three potentially classic dense and rich reds. Vinification is traditional and the fruit is not destemmed. They can be some of the most impressive traditional Châteauneufs, particularly the old-vine Cuvée Chantemerle. Bottling is carried out according to demand, so there can be considerable variation. A recent tasting of the 1998 Chantemerle revealed excessive oxidation. Buy as close to the vintage as possible. (DM)

● **Châteauneuf -du-Pape**★★★ £C Cuvée Grenache★★★ £E Cuvée Chantemerle★★★★ £F

DOM. BRUSSET Cairanne www.domaine brusset.fr A: Eno, NYg

Owner: Daniel & Laurent Brusset Le Village, 84290 Cairanne
The Brusset family make an excellent range of wines, producing some 30,000 cases annually from a total vineyard holding of 84 ha. The top wines are modern in style with pre-fermentation maceration, ageing on lees and no filtration. They are marked by rich, concentrated fruit and ripe but powerful tannins; they need to be cellared to show of their best but are less backward than some. Les Hauts de Montmirail is a magnificent, complex old-vine *cuvée* mainly from Grenache. In contrast lesser *cuvées* exhibit vibrant juicy fruit and are great youthful gluggers. (DM)

● **Gigondas** Le Grand Montmirail★★★ £C   Les Hauts de Montmirail★★★★ £D
● **Côtes du Rhône-Villages Cairanne** Travers★★ £B Hommage à André Brusset★★★★ £D
○ **Côtes du Rhône-Villages Cairanne**★ £B
● **Côtes du Rhône** Laurent Brusset★ £A ○ **Côtes du Rhône** Viognier★★ £C
● **Cotes du Ventoux** La Boudale★ £A

CAVE DE CAIRANNE Cairanne A: RSo

Owner: Co-operative members 84290 Cairanne
Very good modern co-op producing an extensive range of wines from this important southern Rhône village as well as decent straightforward Côtes du Rhône. The basic *cuvées* represent good value with attractive berry fruit and are best drunk young, while the top wines are a notch up in quality. Les Voconces is made from 40-year-old vines. The red Salyens sees 30 per cent new oak while the Cuvée Antique is quite firmly structured and will benefit from three or four years of ageing. The top reds are bottled unfiltered and represent very fair value for money. (DM)

● **Côtes du Rhône-Villages Cairanne** Temptation★ £B Grand Réserve★ £B
● **Côtes du Rhône-Villages Cairanne** Réserve des Voconces★★ £B
● **Côtes du Rhône-Villages Cairanne** Cuvée Antique★★ £B Cuvée Salyens★★ £B
○ **Côtes du Rhône-Villages Cairanne** Cuvée Salyens★★ £B

DOM. DU CAYRON Gigondas A: JAr

Owner: Michel Faraud 84190 Gigondas
Just one wine is made at this traditional estate, and very good it is in most years. With vines close to

50 years old and very well-drained stony soils producing exceptional quality fruit, this is one of the best estates in the appellation. Surprisingly the 1998 was less than impressive, although recent vintages seem to be back on form. (DM)

● Gigondas★★★ £C

DOM. DE LA CHARBONNIÈRE　Châteauneuf-du-Pape　　　A: GWW,VWs, BBR

Owner: Michel Maret　84230 Châteauneuf-du-Pape
Generally good, if not in the top division. The wines are produced from a total of 21 ha of vines. Michel Maret avoids filtration and in the best years such as 1998 and 1999 the results are very impressive. The Mourre de Perdrix is partially aged in new wood, but it is the impressively concentrated Haut Brusquières (blending a proportion of Syrah with Grenache) and the Vieilles Vignes bottlings that really stand out. The Vacqueyras is a good chunky, earthy example and represents good value for money. (DM)

● Vacqueyras★★ £B
● Châteauneuf-du-Pape★★£C　Mourre des Perdrix★★★ £D
● Châteauneuf-du-Pape　Haut Brusquières★★★★ £E　Vieilles Vignes★★★★ £E
○ Châteauneuf-du-Pape★ £C

GÉRARD CHARVIN　Châteauneuf-du-Pape　　　　　　　A:VTr

Owner: Gérard Charvin　Quartier Maucoil, 84100 Orange
Small, high-quality domaine now run by Laurent Charvin, producing full-blown, rich spicy reds. Both the Côtes du Rhône and the Châteauneuf-du-Pape offer quality and value. The latter is a blend of Grenache with a little Syrah, Mourvèdre and Vaccarese adding both definition and a firm youthful structure. The wine has been particularly impressive in the current run of fine vintages – a real blockbuster style, it will age very well. (DM)

● Côtes du Rhone★★ £B　● Châteauneuf-du-Pape★★★★ £D

CH. DE BEAUCASTEL　Châteauneuf-du-Pape　www.beaucastel.com　A: Mis, Far,Tan, Rae

Owner: Perrin family　84350 Courthezon
Among the very top echelon of producers in the southern Rhône. Notable for the organic approach in their 131 ha estate vineyards, the Perrins also employ a process called *vinification a chaud* for their red Châteauneuf, which extracts good colour and fruit and guards against bacteria and oxidation. Unusually here all 13 permitted varieties are planted. The very finest quality is achieved in both red and white, the former unusually dominated by Mourvèdre and Syrah and there is a good secondary label Coudoulet de Beaucastel. The red is not filtered but is given a light fining to help soften the very firm structure of the wine in its youth. Also produced are a range of *négociant* wines under the Domaines PERRIN label, while the Côtes du Rhône property Château du Grand Prebois is a recent acquisition. Further afield the Perrins have a partnership in the Californian Paso Robles winery TABLAS CREEK. Both the Châteauneuf red and white must be cellared, up to eight to ten years in top vintages. (DM)

● Châteauneuf-du-Pape★★★★★ £E　Homage à Jacques Perrin✪✪✪✪✪ £H
○ Châteauneuf-du-Pape★★★★ £E　Vieilles Vignes✪✪✪✪✪ £G
● Côtes du Rhône Coudoulet du Beaucastel★★★ £C
○ Côtes du Rhône Coudoulet du Beaucastel★★ £C

CH. DE FONSALETTE   Côtes du Rhône   A: Sec, Blx

Owner: Reynaud family   84290 Lagarde-Pareol

Benchmark 11-ha Côtes du Rhône property owned by the Reynaud family of CHÂTEAU RAYAS. Emmanuel Reynaud also undertakes vinification here now as well as at Rayas and his own Vacqueyras property, CHÂTEAU DES TOURS. The regular bottling is a blend of mainly Grenache with a sizeable dollop of Cinsault. The Syrah is a varietal bottling. These are fine, intense and firmly structured examples, they are long lived albeit expensive examples of the AC. (DM)

● **Côtes du Rhône**★★★ £C Syrah★★★★ £D
O **Côtes du Rhône**★★★ £C

CH. LA GARDINE   Châteauneuf-du-Pape   www.gardine.com   A: T&W

Owner: Brunel family   Route de Roquemaure, BP 35, 84231 Châteauneuf-du-Pape

A modern approach to vinification here allied to a dedication to *terroir* results in an impressive range of wines. The reds are dense and deeply coloured when young but supple and impeccably balanced. In their youth they are sturdy and firm and require several years' ageing. Temperature control is used in producing fruity, gloriously nutty whites, with new oak in abundance in the top *cuvées*. The Brunels purchased the Lirac property Domaine SAINT-ROCH in 1998 and have already started to bring about improvements. (DM)

● **Côtes du Rhône-Villages**★ £B
● **Châteauneuf-du-Pape** Tradition★★★ £C Cuvée des Générations Gaston Philippe★★★★ £E
O **Châteauneuf-du-Pape** Tradition★★★ £C Cuvée des Generations Marie-Léoncie★★★★ £D

CH. LA NERTHE   Châteauneuf-du-Pape   A: BBR, C&C

Owner: Richard family   Route de Sourgues, 84230 Châteauneuf-d-Pape

This large (for Châteauneuf) property has been performing at a high level since it was purchased by the Richard family in the mid-1980s. Annual production is now around 25,000 cases. There tends to be less Grenache in the reds here than elsewhere. The Cadettes is a sturdy blend of 100-year-old Grenache and Mourvèdre. Throughout the small range there is a modern, sophisticated approach to vinification, with destemming and extended vatting for reds and increasing use of barriques for both red and white, which has produced excellent results. (DM)

● **Châteauneuf-du-Pape**★★★★ £D Cuvée des Cadettes★★★★ £E
O **Châteauneuf-du-Pape**★★★ £C Clos de Beauvenir★★★★ £D

CH. MONT-REDON   Châteauneuf-du-Pape   www.chateaumontredon.fr   A: PFx

Owner: Abeille-Fabre family   BP 10, 84321 Châteauneuf-du-Pape

By the standards of the appellation this is a large property producing good to very good rather than exceptional wines. Vinification is now modern, using a mix of *inox* and some barriques for the Châteauneuf bottlings. A Lirac property, Château Cantegril, has recently been purchased and these wines are now to be marketed under the Mont-Redon label. Expect quality at Cantegril to improve. The red Châteauneuf ages well over the medium term, acquiring additional depth and finesse. These are very fairly priced wines. (DM)

● **Côtes du Rhône**★★ £B ● **Châteauneuf-du-Pape**★★★ £C ● **Lirac**★★ £B
O **Châteauneuf-du-Pape**★★★ £C
O **Côtes du Rhône**★ £B Viognier★ £B

CH. PESQUIÉ Côtes du Ventoux   A: VWs, OWL

Owner: Chaudière Bastide family 84570 Mormoiron
Medium-sized property with over 70 ha of vineyards producing some 25,000 cases a year across a
range of wines from this lesser appellation. Quality is generally good across the board with attractive
forward, fruit-driven styles being the order of the day. The Terrasses labels are simple and straightforward. There is a very decent fresh and characterful rosé, Perle de Roses. The real stars here,
though, are the Prestige and Quintessence. These are a serious step up and are among the best
examples of the appellation. Prestige is dominated by old-vine Grenache with a dollop of Syrah
lending structure and grip. Quintessence is mainly Syrah. Both are impressively cellarworthy. Ageing
for four or five years is advisable. (DM)

● **Cotes du Ventoux** Terre Précieuse★ £B Prestige★★★ £B Quintessence★★★ £B
◉ **Cotes du Ventoux** Perle de Roses★ £A
O **Vin de Pays** Chardonnay du Pesquié★ £B Viognier du Pesquié★ £B

CH. RAYAS Châteauneuf-du-Pape   A: OWL, BBR

Owner: Reynaud family Route de Courthézon, 84230 Châteauneuf-du-Pape
Legendary estate, producing stunning red and white Châteauneuf for decades under the late Jacques
Reynaud. The second label, Pignan, is also very impressive. The wines are now vinified by Emmanuel
Reynaud, Jacques' nephew, of CHATEAU DES TOURS who also produces the wines at the Rayas sister
property CHATEAU DE FONSALETTE. The wines have unquestionably been very fine in the late 1990s
but lack some of the sublime quality of earlier years. (DM)

● **Châteauneuf-du-Pape**✪✪✪✪✪ £F Pignan★★★★★ £E
O **Châteauneuf-du-Pape**★★★★★ £E

CH. REDORTIER Gigondas   A: BRW

Owner: Étienne & Sabine de Menthon 84190 Suzette
Although a little white is produced it is the reds that show real refinement and class at this excellent
property. As yet the overall vine age is younger than some other estates, at around 25 years, so there
should be more to to look forward to. The blend for the Gigondas is dominated by Grenache but there
is a hefty dollop of Syrah as well. The wine is firmer and more structured than some of its neighbours,
with extended cask-ageing and requiring a few years of patience. The Beaumes-de-Venise Cuvée
Prestige is an undoubted star of that village. (DM)

● **Cotes du Rhone-Villages Beaumes-de-Venise**★★ £B Cuvée Prestige★★ £C
● **Gigondas**★★★ £C

CH. SAINT-COSME Gigondas louis@chateau-st-cosme.com   A: Dec, NYg, Han

Owner: Louis Barruol 84190 Gigondas
Louis Barruol owns vines only in Gigondas but in recent years he has made an excellent small range
of *négociant* wines as well. The Côtes du Rhône offerings represent excellent value, notably the reds,
whereas the Gigondas Cuvée Valbelle and Côte-Rôtie are both impressively concentrated and
ageworthy. The Gigondas bottlings are dense and powerful and quite marked by youthful new oak.
At their best they are both intense and complex. There is also decent if not yet top-flight Condrieu
but the potential here is exciting and current releases are very fairly priced. (DM)

● **Côtes du Rhone**★★ £B Les Deux Albions★★ £B
O **Côtes du Rhone**★ £A
● **Gigondas**★★ £C Cuvée Valbelle★★★ £D

● Côte-Rôtie★★★ £D
○ Condrieu★★ £D

CH. SAINT-ESTÈVE D'UCHAUX   Côtes du Rhône-Villages   A:HBJ

Owner: Marc Français Route de Sérignan, 84100 Uchaux
Some very good reds and whites are made at this sizeable 60 ha property in the far south of the Côtes du Rhône-Villages appellation in the northern Vaucluse. There are three regular reds and the same number of whites. There is a straightforward white Côtes du Rhône which is a blend of mainly Grenache Blanc and Roussanne. There are also two fine Viognier-based whites, one from young vines which is blended with a little Grenache Blanc and a very striking top cuvée Dionysos, which is 100 per cent varietal. There is a good straightforward fruit driven red Côtes du Rhône as well as two more serious Côtes du Rhône-Villages. Grande Réserve is 60 per cent Grenache and 40 per cent Syrah whereas the dense and impressively structured Vieilles Vignes is the reverse blend. The range is completed by a straightforward juicy rosé and a Méthode Traditionelle Blanc de Blancs sparkler. There is also a very limited production, pricey, oak aged Viognier Cuvée Thérèse. Top reds will benefit from two or three years ageing. (DM)
● **Côtes du Rhône** Tradition★ £B
● **Côtes du Rhône-Villages** Grande Réserve★★ £C Vieilles Vignes★★★ £C
○ **Côtes du Rhône**★ £B Viognier Jeune Vignes★★ £B
○ **Côtes du Rhône-Villages** Vionysos★★★ £C

CH. DES TOURS   Vacqueyras   A: Yap, Bib, Rae

Owner: Emmanuel Reynaud Quartier des Sablons, 84260 Sarrians
As well as owning this excellent 40-ha property, Emmanuel Reynaud, the nephew of the late Jacques Reynaud, is now vinifying the wines at Château RAYAS and Château de FONSALETTE. His Vacqueyras has long been a yardstick example for the AC and is produced from mainly Grenache from very low-yielding old vines. Always emphasising classic *garrigue* aromas, these are complex, even refined wines, in marked contrast to some of the more extracted examples of some of his neighbours. (DM)
● **Côtes du Rhône**★★ £B ● **Vacqueyras**★★★ £C
○ **Côtes du Rhône**★ £B

DOM. CHAUME-ARNAUD   Vinsobres   A:M&V

Owner: Valérie & Philippe Chaume-Arnaud 26110 Vinsobres
This is a good source of well-priced southern Rhône red and white. The domaine is small with 13.5 ha situated around the lesser known village of Vinsobres. Reds are dominated by Grenache and Syrah and there is a little Viognier and Marsanne for the white. Quality is key, yields are kept low and no artificial fertilizers are used on the soil. The property also benefits from some very old vines. The small amount of Carignan used in the Vinsobres red is now over 60 years old. Both the Vinsobres reds will develop well in bottle with three or four years age. (DM)
● **Côtes du Rhône**★★ £B
● **Côtes du Rhône-Villages Vinsobres**★★ £B La Cadene★★★ £C
○ **Côtes du Rhône-Villages Vinsobres**★★ £B

CLOS DU CAILLOU   Châteauneuf-du-Pape

A: HHB, BBR, NYg

Owner: Jean-Denis Vacheron   84350 Courthezon

Jean-Denis Vacheron (related to the VACHERONS of Sancerre) has been in charge of the winemaking at this domaine throughout the late 1990s and quality has gone from strength to strength. Careful vineyard management, modern vinification with some malolactic in cask and a tight control of yields are producing excellent results. Les Quartz is tight and firmly structured, the Réserve bottling richer and more opulent with added dimension from a large dollop of Mourvèdre. The top two *cuvées* will age very well. (DM)

● **Côtes du Rhône** Bouquet des Garrigues★ £B
● **Châteauneuf-du-Pape**★★★ £C Les Quartz★★★★ £E Réserve Clos du Caillou★★★★★ £F

CLOS DES CAZAUX   Vacqueyras

A: CBg, Lay, VWs, Tan

Owner: Jean-Michel & Frédéric Archimbaud-Vache   84190 Vacqueyras

The Archimbaud-Vache family make a surprisingly diverse range of wines from their holdings in Vacqueyras and Gigondas. There is a very good nutty white, a blend of Clairette and Roussanne in equal proportions. The Cuvée Saint-Roche is mainly Grenache, whereas the other two Vacqueyras bottlings are dominated by Syrah. Green harvesting (*vendange vert*) is practised and there is minimal intervention in the cellar. Particularly unusual and generally successful is a late-harvest Vacqueyras produced from Grenache infected by noble rot. It has great depth and intensity. (DM)

● **Vacqueyras** Cuvée des Templiers★★★ £B Cuvée St Roche★★★ £B Réserve★★★ £B
● **Vacqueyras** Grénat Noble★★★★ £C
O **Vacqueyras**★★ £B
● **Gigondas** La Tour Sarrazine★★★ £C

CLOS DU MONT OLIVET   Châteauneuf-du-Pape

A: Hal, Res, Rae

Owner: Sabon family   Chemin Bois la Ville, 84230 Châteauneuf-du-Pape

These are very traditional, old fashioned examples of the appellation. The regular bottling is moderately dense with some marked dark fruit and herbal scents and reasonable depth. The Cuvée du Papet is bigger and fuller. The fruit is not destemmed, which works very well in the best years, but occasionally the wines can show a marked rusticity and some hard and green tannin in more challenging years. Bottling occurs in several stages, so the fruit will not be consistent. Buy as soon after the vintage as you can. (DM)

● **Châteauneuf-du-Pape**★★★ £C Cuvée du Papet★★★★ £D
O **Châteauneuf-du-Pape**★★ £C

CLOS DES PAPES   Châteauneuf-du-Pape

A: RsW, Rae, SVS, BBR

Owner: Avril family   13 Avenue Pierre-de-Luxembourg, BP 8, 84231 Châteauneuf-du-Pape

One of the great benchmark names in Châteauneuf-du-Pape, producing just one white and one red. Considerable investment in the cellar during the 1990s has enabled the property to go from strength to strength. The red is a very structured, ageworthy example of the AC. It is always destemmed and the different varieties are fermented together, which the Avrils feel adds complexity. Vincent has now taken over the winemaking from his father Paul. (DM)

● **Châteauneuf-du-Pape**★★★★★ £D O **Châteauneuf-du-Pape**★★★★ £C

CLOS PETITE BELLANE Valréas   A:Odd

Owner: Olivier Peuchot   Chemin de Sainte-Croix, 84600 Valréas
Impressive property producing modern stylish wines with classic Rhône fruit. The vineyard covers
an area of 44 ha and some of the vines, particularly the Grenache, are up to 65 years old. The white
Côtes du Rhône is half Roussanne and half Viognier and like all the whites given a period of *macération
pelliculaire.* The white Les Echalas is finer and purer, produced from 100 per cent Roussanne. The
red Côtes du Rhône is ripe, forward and brambly, the Valréas bottlings fuller and more
concentrated. The top two reds have real depth and concentration. Les Echalas is 100 per cent Syrah
and can show a hint of reduction when young, Vieilles Vignes is very fine and complex, full of
old-viney character and spicy, herbal scents. Both will age well. (DM)

● **Côtes du Rhône**★★ £B ● **Côtes du Rhône Valréas**★★ £B
● **Côtes du Rhône Valréas** Les Echalas★★★ £D Vieilles Vignes★★★ £D
O **Côtes du Rhône**★★ £B O **Côtes du RhôneValréas** Les Echalas★★★ £D

DOM. COTEAUX DES TRAVERS Rasteau

Owner: Robert Charavin   84110 Rasteau
Robert Charavin produces some of the best examples from this Rhône village which itself is a
candidate for its own AC for dry wines as well as the fortifieds the Rasteau AC currently covers. He
has 20 ha under vine which includes a sizeable planting of old vines and produces around 5,000 cases
a year. In the vineyard everything is as natural as possible and no fertilizers are used on the soil. There
is a good, nutty white which blends equal parts of Marsanne, Grenache Blanc, Roussanne and
Viognier. The soft, forward, red Côtes du Rhône is produced from young vines and is mainly
Grenache with some Carignan. More serious are the Rasteau reds. Prestige is made from 60 year
old vines, a blend of Grenache, Syrah and Mourvèdre which gets 12 months in wood. The top
wine is the complex, structured Cuvée Paul, full of old-vine character and very ageworthy.
Produced from 50 to 100 year old vines it blends Syrah with a little Mourvèdre and Grenache. It
needs a year or two of bottle ageing to integrate the 24 months spent in oak. (DM)

● **Côtes du Rhône**★ £B
● **Côtes du Rhône Rasteau**★★ £B Prestige★★★ £C Cuvée Paul★★★ £C
O **Côtes du Rhône Rasteau** Cuvee Marie★★ £D

CROS DE LA MÛRE Côtes du Rhône   A: JAr, CBg

Owner: Eric Michel   Hameau de Derboux, 84430 Mondragon
Small estate making stylish, elegant Côtes du Rhône, Côtes du Rhône-Villages and denser fuller
Gigondas. These wines are not blockbusters but display very good classic *garrigue*-scented red-berry
fruit. The Côtes du Rhône has a high proportion of old-vine Grenache and will drink well in the
short to medium term. The Villages bottling has a higher proportion of Syrah and a touch more
density and structure. The Gigondas is the sturdiest of the wines and will benefit from tucking away
for four or five years. All the wines offer good value. (DM)

● **Cotes du Rhone**★★ £B ● **Côtes du Rhône-Villages**★★★ £B
● **Gigondas**★★★ £B

DOM. DE DEURRE Vinsobres   A: MtC, SVS

Owner: Hubert Valayer   26110 Vinsobres
Hubert Valayer's property is newly established but the results are very promising and the wines show

increasing potential with every vintage. The 2001s and 2000s are all stunning. As well as the southern Rhône wines a Cornas is produced as a result of a leasehold agreement with a cousin. As yet it does not show the same potential as Valayer's other wines. The Saint-Maurice is supple and well-structured, with around 30 per cent Syrah in the blend, and the Vinsobres richer, more savoury, with a touch of Mourvèdre. Both are edging towards three stars. There are two splendid Côtes du Rhônes. Les Oliviers is 100 per cent Syrah, the brilliant Les Rabasses 100per cent Grenache. Newly added Cuvée J.M. Valayer, which is aged in used barriques, resembles a very good Châteuneuf-du-Pape. (DM)

● **Côtes du Rhône**★ £B Les Oliviers★★★ £C Les Rabasses★★★★ £C
● **Côtes du Rhône-Villages Saint-Maurice**★★ £B
● **Côtes du Rhône-Villages Vinsobres**★★ £B Cuvee JM Valayer★★★ £B
● **Cornas**★★ £C

DOM. DURBAN Beaumes-de-Venise   A: Yap, BBR

Owner: Jean-Pierre Leydier 84190 Beaumes-de-Venise
The Beaumes-de-Venise Vieilles Vignes here is a good, spicy, nicely intense red dominated by Grenache. However it is the fortified Muscat de Beaumes-de-Venise that marks out this estate. One of the very best examples made, it is richly intense and gloriously honeyed but has a real finesse and elegance very rarely encountered in these wines. It should, though, in the style of the appellation, be drunk young and fresh. (DM)

● **Côtes du Rhône-Villages Beaumes-de-Venise**★★ £B
O **Muscat de Beaumes-de-Venise**★★★ £C

DOM. DES ESPIERS Vacqueyras   A: Bal

Owner: Philippe Cartoux 84190 Vacqueyras
With cellars based in the village of Vacqueyras, M. Cartoux crafts his excellent wines from parcels totalling some 10 ha around Gigondas and Sablet. A little white and rosé Côtes du Rhône is produced but it is the top reds that particularly impress. The Cuvée des Blâches is wonderfully dense and gamey with some attractive herbal *garrigue* notes. It is produced from 35-year-old vines. Both Gigondas *cuvées* will be the better for four or five years' cellaring; the Sablet too will benefit from short ageing. (DM)

● **Côtes du Rhône** ★ £B ● **Côtes du Rhône-Villages Sablet**★★ £B
● **Gigondas**★★★ £B Cuvée des Blâches★★★★ £C

FERAUD-BRUNEL Châteauneuf-du-Pape

Owner: Feraud/Brunel families 84230 Châteauneuf-du-Pape
Fine quality small *négociant* operation run by Laurence Feraud of Domaine du PEGAÜ and André Brunel of LES CAILLOUX in Châteauneuf-du-Pape. The wines are vinified by the Brunel *oenologue*, Philippe Cambie, and the style is traditional but impressive across the board, with the wines made in a manner similar to that at Pegaü and Les Cailloux. They also produce the joint venture vin de table, Images du Sud, an attractive, spicy, forward red blend. All represent good value. (DM)

● **Vin de Table** Image du Sud★★ £B
● **Côtes du Rhône-Villages Cairanne**★★ £B
● **Côtes du Rhône-Villages Rasteau**★★ £B ● **Vacqueyras**★★ £B
● **Gigondas**★★★ £C ● **Châteauneuf-du-Pape**★★★ £C

DOM. DE FONDRÈCHE   Côtes du Ventoux   A: N&P

Owner: Sébastien Barthélémy   Quartier Fondrèche, 84380 Mazan
With their 30-odd ha Sébastien and Nanou Barthélémy are rivals to CHÂTEAU PESQUIÉ – both are making benchmark wines for the appellation. Careful viticulture with increasingly old vines (now averaging 40 years) and minimal interference throughout vinification and *élévage* is now delivering in an impressive range. The regular red, blended from Grenache, Syrah and Cinsault, is silky and forward. The Fayard, similarly aged in tank, adds Carignan to Grenache and Syrah. The Persia red is mainly Syrah and aged in barriques, some new. Nadal is roughly equal proportions of Syrah and Grenache, a blockbuster style often marked by alcohol but generally well-balanced. A number of single varietal bottlings of reds have also been produced in recent vintages. Roussanne is an important component of the two whites. The regular bottling blends in some Clairette as well, whereas the Persia is almost exclusively Rousanne, aged in barrel on its lees. The wines are well worth seeking out and very good value. (DM)

● **Côtes du Ventoux★** £A   Cuvée Fayard★★ £B   Cuvée Persia★★★ £B
● **Côtes du Ventoux** Cuvée Carles Nadal★★★ £B
○ **Côtes du Ventoux★** £A   Cuvée Persia★★ £B

FONT DE MICHELLE   Châteauneuf-du-Pape   A: JAr, Yng, Tan, WSS

Owner: Gonnet family   14 Impasse de Vignerons, 84370 Bedarrides
There has been a marked step up in quality here since the late 1990s, not least because of considerable investment in the cellar. The F de Font de Michelle, both red and white, are fruity and approachable. The regular Châteauneuf-du-Pape used to lack real depth and substance, with part being vinified by carbonic maceration. The style now, though, is for sturdier, longer lived wines. The whites are for earlier drinking, although the stylish Cuvée Etienne Gonnet, vinified with a high proportion of Rousanne, will develop well over the short term. The Gonnets have produced serious red Châteauneuf-du- Pape in recent vintages. Cuvée Etienne Gonnet red is now very ageworthy and will improve for a decade or more. (DM)

● **Côtes du Rhône** F de Font de Michelle★★ £B
○ **Côtes du Rhône** F de Font de Michelle★★ £B
● **Châteauneuf-du-Pape★★★** £C   Cuvée Etienne Gonnet★★★★ £D
○ **Châteauneuf-du-Pape★★** £C   Cuvée Etienne Gonnet★★★★ £C

DOM. DE FONT SANE   Gigondas   A: Bib, GBa

Owner: Peysson family   Route Sablet, 84190 Gigondas
First-class producer of both Gigondas and Côtes du Ventoux, the latter among the very best in the AC and excellent value for money. The regular Gigondas is a spicy herb-laden blend of Grenache, Syrah, Mourvèdre and Cinsault, while the oak-aged barrel selection Cuvée Futée is dense, powerful and very ageworthy. It is generally made from the oldest vines on the property and requires five years' patience to show at its best. (DM)

● **Cotes du Ventoux★** £A
● **Gigondas★★★** £C   Cuvée Futée★★★★ £C

DOM. LA GARRIGUE   Vacqueyras

Owner: Bernard family   84190 Vacqueyras
Very good traditional domaine with 65 ha of vineyard spread across Vacqueyras and Gigondas with

additional holdings simply classified as Côtes du Rhône. Grenache dominates the red plantings with a smattering of Syrah, Mourvèdre and Cinsault. Clairette and Grenache Blanc make up the blend of the Vacqueyras blanc. It is the red Vacqueyras and Gigondas bottlings though that are the focal point of the property. Vinification is traditional, no de-stemming and no fining or filtration either. There is a 20 day *cuvaison* and the resulting wines are sturdy and powerful. The Cuvée de Hostellerie is particularly fine and in 2001 close to four stars. (DM)

● **Vacqueyras★★★** £B Cuvée Hostellerie★★★ £C
● **Gigondas★★★** £C

GOURT DE MAUTENS Rasteau   A: Rae, SVS

Owner: Jérôme Bressy 84110 Rasteau
Enormously impressive producer with some 14 ha planted almost exclusively to red varieties: Grenache, Carignan, Syrah, Mourvedre and a few others. The rich, dense and ageworthy red is produced from vines that are up to 80 years old. The Bressy style is to create wines with considerable extraction, producing fiery almost ferocious examples which always show not only concentration but are complex, dark and spicy too. In recent vintages it has been quite as good as many a top Châteauneuf. The white, a blend of Bourboulenc and Grenache Blanc, doesn't quite hit the same stellar heights but is still among the more interesting and structured examples of the region. In keeping with the approach, the wines are bottled unfiltered. (DM)

● **Côtes du Rhône-Villages Rasteau★★★★** £D
O **Côtes du Rhône-Villages Rasteau★★★** £C

DOM. GRAMENON Côtes du Rhône   A: BRW, HHB, Rae, SVS

Owner: Laurent family 26770 Monbrison-sur-Lez
Long established as one of the great producers in the lesser area of the Côtes du Rhône. Michèle Laurent has now taken over the running of this domaine from her late husband. The vineyard is planted to Grenache and Syrah with a little Cinsault and Carignan for the reds and a little Clairette and Viognier for the whites. Yields are very low and minimal handling and an absence of filtration in the cellar produces wines of both density, concentration and finesse. The remarkable Ceps Centenaires Cuvée Mémé, produced from very old vines, is as fine as the very best from the southern Rhône. Prices are very reasonable as well. (DM)

● **Côtes du Rhône** Le Gramenon★★ £B Les Laurentides★★★ £B
● **Côtes du Rhône** La Sagesse★★★ £B La Sierra du Sud★★★ £B
● **Côtes du Rhône** Ceps Centenaires Cuvée Mémé★★★★ £C
● **Côtes du Rhône-Villages** Les Hauts de Gramenon★★★★ £C
O **Côtes du Rhône** Vie on y est★ £B

DOM. DE GRAND TINEL Châteauneuf-du-Pape   A: NoG, EoR, OWL, WSc

Owner: Jeune family Route de Bedarrides, 84230 Châteauneuf-du-Pape
Fine, traditional old Châteauneuf property producing earthy, robust reds, albeit without the power of their counterparts a decade ago. Alexis Establet is produced from the family's parcels of particularly old vines and shows greater complexity. Bottling here is staged and it's worth trying to purchase as close to the vintage as possible. (DM)

● **Châteauneuf-du-Pape Traditionelle★★★** £C Cuvée Alexis Establet★★★ £D

DOM. GRAPILLON D'OR Gigondas

A:CTy

Owner: Bernard Chauvet 84190 Gigondas

Good traditional Gigondas and Vacqueyras are produced by Bernard Chauvet. He has around 15 ha in Gigondas including several different parcels and a further 9 ha in Vacqueyras. As is the practice in a number of properties, the varieties, which are dominated by Grenache but also include Syrah and Cinsault, are vinified together. The fruit is not de-stemmed and there is a long *cuvaison* of up to 20 days for the Gigondas. The Vacqueyras is the lighter of the wines and will drink well with two or three years age, the Gigondas is sturdy and masculine, and will add increasing complexity with up to 10 years' age. The wines are bottled without filtration after ageing in old *foudres*. (DM)

● **Gigondas**★★★ £C   ● **Vacqueyras**★★ £B

DOM. DE LA JANASSE Châteauneuf-du-Pape

A: Eno, N&P, NYg, WSc

Owner: Aimé Sabon   27 Chemin de Moulin, 84350 Courthezon

Splendid, medium-sized domaine producing good to excellent wines across the board. A total of some 12,500 cases are produced annually from 50 ha of vines. The Châteauneuf vines are planted on ideal, free-draining stony soils and this, together with a vine age averaging over 60 years, results in lovely supple, dense and powerful wines. Vinification is a good deal more modern than at some properties in the region. Jean-Luc COLOMBO has consulted here and part of the red crop is always destemmed. Ageing is in an assortment of vessels with some new oak being used for the red and white Châteauneuf-du-Pape. The Chaupin and Vieilles-Vignes reds develop very well in bottle and should be given four or five years. (DM)

● **Côtes du Rhône** Tradition★ £B Les Garrigues★★ £B   O **Côtes du Rhône**★ £B
● **Châteauneuf-du-Pape**★★★ £D Cuvée Chaupin★★★★ £E Vieilles-Vignes★★★★ £F
O **Châteauneuf-du-Pape** Tradition★★ £C Prestige★★★ £E
● **Vin de Pays de la Principaute d'Orange**★★ £B
O **Vin de Pays de la Principaute d'Orange** Viognier★★ £C

DOM. LAFOND-ROC-EPINE Tavel www.lafond.roc-epine.com

A:CTy, BBR

Owner: Jean-Pierre & Pascal Lafond   Route des Vignobles, 30126 Tavel

Excellent value wines produced from both Lirac and the Côtes du Rhône as well as one of the better Tavels which shows some vibrant fresh fruit. The Lirac is blended from a mix of Grenache, Syrah and Mourvèdre, the Côtes du Rhône just Grenache and Syrah. Vinification of the reds is modern with fermentation in stainless steel before ageing in a mix of large and small oak. In addition, the Lafonds produce a straightforward pleasant white Lirac from a blend of Grenache Blanc, Viognier and Roussanne and a sumptuously rich special cuvée La Ferme Romaine, which is aged in small oak for a year. The Liracs will evolve well in the medium term. (DM)

● **Lirac**★★ £B La Ferme Romaine★★★ £C
● **Côtes du Rhône**★★ £B
O **Lirac**★ £B

DOM. LA ROQUETTE Châteauneuf-du-Pape www.vignoblesbrunier.fr

A:L&W, BBR

Owner: Brunier family   Avenue Louis Pasteur, 84230 Châteauneuf-du-Pape

While this property is owned by the Bruniers it is quite separate to VIEUX-TÉLÉGRAPHE. Produced from vineyard parcels spread throughout the appellation, these are unfiltered modern wines of some class and finesse. The average vine age is now around 40 years and this undoubtedly helps quality. The white should be broached young, the red with a little age. It is marked particularly by its vibrant, attractive, dark, spicy fruit character, supple velvety tannin and approachable style. (DM)

● Châteauneuf-du-Pape★★★ £D   O Châteauneuf-du-Pape★★★ £D

DOM. LA SOUMADE   Rasteau   A: BBR,HHB, NYg, Hal

Owner: Andre Romero   84110 Rasteau
A great range of wines, especially the impressive reds from Rasteau and Gigondas. These are vinified as true *vins de garde*. Romero goes for maximum extraction but the results are almost always very good indeed. Even the lesser wines have an abundance of vibrant, crunchy fruit. With the best *cuvées* the lengthy vatting, allied to extensive parcels of old vines (some up to 100 years), provides for dense, chewy, powerful reds in need of five years' cellaring. Romero also produces fine *vins doux naturels* under the Rasteau AC. (DM)

● **Vin de Pays de la Principauté d'Orange**★ £B   ● **Vin de Pays** Cabernet Sauvignon★ £B
● **Côtes du Rhône** Les Violettes★ £B
● **Côtes du Rhône-Villages Rasteau** Prestige★★★ £C   Confiance★★★★ £C
● **Côtes du Rhône-Villages Rasteau** Fleur de Confiance★★★★ £E
● **Gigondas**★★★★ £C   ● **Rasteau**★★ £C

DOM. LES APHILLANTHES   Travaillan   A:Sec

Owner: Daniel Boulle   Quartier Saint Jean, 84850 Travaillan
This is one of the new rising stars of the southern Rhône based in the village of Travaillan. Les Galets is mainly Grenache and is the most open and approachable of the wines. The more seriously structured Trois Cepages blends Grenache, Syrah and Mourvèdre. The Cuvée du Cros is produced solely from Syrah while the Vieilles Vignes is made from very old Grenache with around 20 per cent Mourvèdre. Bottled with neither fining nor filtration all the wines show real depth and very impressive concentration and will develop very well in bottle. (DM)

● **Côtes du Rhône-Villages** Les Galets★★★ £C Trois Cépages★★★ £C
● **Côtes du Rhône-Villages** Cuvée du Cros★★★ £C Vieilles Vignes★★★★ £C

LES CAILLOUX   Châteauneuf-du-Pape   A: Hal, SVS

Owner: André Brunel   84230 Châteauneuf-du-Pape
Very fine traditional producer of Côtes du Rhône and Châteauneuf-du-Pape. The Côtes du Rhônes are produced at the Brunel family property Domaine de l'Enclos. The profound Cuvée Centenaire produced from 100-year-old vines is one of the great wines of the appellation, while the regular red is dense and powerful and lacks just a little of the depth of the centenarian. The Brunel family are also involved with the Feraud family of Domaine du PEGAÜ in an excellent small-scale *négociant* venture, FERAUD-BRUNEL. (DM)

Domaine de l'Enclos
● **Côtes du Rhône**★★£B Cuvée Sommelongue★★★ £B

Les Cailloux
● **Châteauneuf-du-Pape**★★★★ £C Cuvée Centenaire✪✪✪✪ £E

PATRICK LESEC SELECTIONS   A: JAr, NYg

Owner: Patrick Lesec   15 bis, Rue Hégésippe Moreau, 75018 Paris
Wine broker Patrick Lesec works in association with fine quality-conscious domaines in Languedoc

and Roussillon as well as the Rhône Valley producing wines which are released under his own label. He is spreading his wings to take in Burgundy, Bordeaux, Alsace and South-West France as well. As a part of his portfolio he produces top *cuvées* from a number of properties, such as Domaine des Remizières with their Cuvée Emilie, just varying these slightly to match his own style of ripe, elegant, approachable wines. Some of the Rhône *cuvées* are very, very good indeed but as yet the wines from the Languedoc are not of the same order. There is, however, real potential here at all levels. (DM)

● **Côtes du Rhône-Villages Beaumes-de-Venise**★ £B   ● **Côtes du Rhône-Villages Rasteau**★★ £B
● **Coteaux du Languedoc** Château Roumanière Tonneaux★★ £C Domaine de Granoupiac★★★ £C
● **Saint-Chinian** Domaine Rognet Tonneaux★★ £C   ● **Faugères** J.C. Estève Tonneaux★★★ £C
● **Gigondas** Les Blaches★★★ £C   ● **Châteauneuf-du-Pape** Les Galets Blonds★★★★ £E
● **Hermitage** Domaine des Remizières Cuvée Émilie★★★★ £D

DOM. LES GOUBERT   Gigondas   A: BRW

Owner: Jean-Pierre Cartier   84190 Gigondas
An extensive range of Côtes du Rhône and-Villages wines are made by this domaine with the quality generally good to sometimes very good. There are 23 ha under vine, of which 20 or so are red with the majority Grenache but a decent planting of Syrah as well. Barrel-fermentation is used to produce the Viognier, which has real depth and some gloriously ripe, peachy fruit. It is best drunk young. Vinification of the reds is modern without a hint of rusticity emerging in the wines and new oak used to age the Gigondas Cuvée Florence. Both Gigondas wines are good cellaring prospects. (DM)

● **Gigondas**★★ £C Cuvee Florence★★★ £C
● **Côtes du Rhône-Villages Sablet**★★ £B   O **Cotes du Rhone-Villages Sablet**★★ £B
● **Côtes du Rhône-Villages Beaumes de Venise**★★ £B
● **Côtes du Rhône**★ £B
O **Côtes du Rhône**★ £B Viognier   Cuvée de V★★★ £C

LES PALLIÈRES   Gigondas   www.vignoblesbrunier.fr   A: THt

Owner: Brunier family/Kermit Lynch   84190 Gigondas
Now owned as a joint venture between the Bruniers of VIEUX-TÉLÉGRAPHE and US wine merchant Kermit Lynch. The potential of the *terroir* is beginning to be fully explored – the vineyards are ideally located in limestone soils on the precipitous slopes of the Dentelles de Montmirail. The 50-year-old vines produce wines which are now less rustic and increasingly impressive. Some de-stemming has been introduced and there is a careful control in the cellar. The wines are bottled after 15 months in *cuve* and *foudres* without filtration. (DM)

● **Gigondas**★★★ £C

DOM. DE MARCOUX   Châteauneuf-du-Pape   A: HHB, CCC, Alo

Owner: Armenier family   Chemin de la Gironde, 84100 Orange
Model property run on biodynamic lines since 1990. The main purpose of this viticultural approach is to optimise the fruit quality of the late-ripening Grenache and Mourvèdre in particular. There can be no question about the results. Vieilles Vignes has for a decade been one of the benchmark wines of the appellation. Very ageworthy and extraordinarily complex. (DM)

● **Châteauneuf-du-Pape**★★★★ £E Vieilles Vignes❂❂❂❂❂ £F
O **Châteauneuf-du-Pape**★★★ £D

DOM. DE MONTPERTUIS Châteauneuf-du-Pape   A: L&W, SVS

Owner: Paul Jeune   84230 Châteauneuf-du-Pape
Paul Jeune produces impressively deep and concentrated red Châteauneuf-du-Pape, which is
occasionally labelled Domaine de Croze. The wine, a blend of Grenache, Mourvèdre, Syrah and
Cinsault is a powerful, structured example with intense, dark berry fruit and spicy, herbal *garrigue*
scents. A white Chateauneuf produced from Clairette, Bourboulenc, Grenache Blanc and Roussanne
is full, weighty and soft. It should be drunk relatively young. There are also forward, fruit-driven
Côtes du Rhône and vin de pays. Paul Jeune now also has an interest in the Côtes du Ventoux
property Château de Valcombe, where some increasingly impressive dense and structured examples
of this lesser appellation are now being made. The Cuvée Genevrières is very good. Montpertuis's
winemaker, Gilles Basq, is also making a dense, richly concentrated, new Côtes du Rhône under his
own label, Domaine La Manarine. (DM)

Domaine de Montpertuis
● **Châteauneuf-du-Pape★★★** £D ● **Vin de Pays du Gard** Counoise★ £B ● **Cotes du Rhone★** £B
O **Châteauneuf-du-Pape★★** £C O **Côtes du Rhône★** £B

Château de Valcombe
● **Côtes du Ventoux** Signature★ £B Cuvée Genevrières★★ £B

Domaine La Manarine
● **Côtes du Rhône★★** £B

DOM. DE LA MORDORÉE Tavel   A: L&S, Bal, Box, Rae, HHB

Owner: Christophe Delorme   Chemin des Oliviers, 30126 Tavel
Christophe Delorme produces an extensive and impressive range of wines from his fully organic
domaine in Lirac. A total of over 55 ha spread across Lirac, Tavel and Châteauneuf-du-Pape produces
an excellent range of wines. The Tavel is a benchmark wine and the Reine des Bois *cuvées* are both very
refined and characterful and will improve in bottle for five to ten years. A superb source of very
well-priced wines. (DM)
● **Côtes du Rhône★★** £B O **Côtes du Rhône★** £B
● **Lirac★★★** £C Reine des Bois★★★★ £C O **Lirac** Reine des Bois★★★ £C
● **Châteauneuf-du-Pape★★★★** £D Reine des Bois★★★★ £E
◉ **Tavel★★** £B

MOULIN DE LA GARDETTE Gigondas   A: A&B

Owner: Jean-Baptiste Meunier   Place de la Mairie, 84190 Gigondas
These are powerful, traditionally slightly rustic styles of Gigondas. Grenache (90 per cent) and
Mourvèdre comprise the blend of the regular *cuvée,* whereas Syrah is blended with Grenache and
Cinsault in the Ventabren, which is also aged in barrique rather than the larger vats used for the
regular bottling. Only a relatively small proportion is new and the wine is not overwhelmed by
the wood, although some vintages need time for the fruit to show through. There is a general
dedication to quality – the wines are neither fined nor filtered and are produced from vines that are
over 50 years old. Fine and very intense, they drink very well over the medium term. (DM)
● **Gigondas★★** £C Cuvée Ventabren★★★ £C

DOM. DE L'ORATOIRE SAINT-MARTIN   Cairanne   A: Car

Owner: Frédéric and François Alary   Route de Saint-Roman, 84290 Cairanne

Frédéric and François are cousins of Daniel and Denis ALARY and produce equally exciting results in this outperforming Rhône village. The main Rhône varieties are planted and there are various blends. All the Cairanne bottlings are very impressive. The white Haut Coustias is a rich, nutty, almost honeyed blend of Marsanne, Roussanne and Viognier. The lesser reds have a high proportion of Grenache but are intense and heady. The Haut Coustias red is lent considerable depth and structure by its large Mourvèdre/Syrah component (60 and 20 per cent respectively). It can hold its own against top-quality Châteauneuf-du-Papes and is rich, concentrated, powerful and very ageworthy. (DM)

- Côtes du Rhône★★ £B   O Côtes du Rhône★ £B
- Côtes du Rhône-Villages Cairanne Prestige★★★ £B Réserve des Seigneurs★★★ £C
- Côtes du Rhône-Villages Cairanne Haut Coustias★★★★ £C
- O Côtes du Rhône-Villages Cairanne Haut Coustias★★★ £C

DOM. DU PEGAÜ   Châteauneuf-du-Pape   www.pegau.com   A: Gau, H&B, GrD,SVS, NYg

Owner: Feraud family   Avenue Impériale, 84230 Châteauneuf-du-Pape

Very fine traditional domaine now run largely by Laurence Feraud. The vin de table Plan Pegaü is good, if a little light, but in the traditional style of the property. The red Châteauneuf-du-Papes are classic, formidably structured wines. The white is honeyed, nutty and concentrated. The Cuvée Réservée is in fact the regular red bottling but is full of impressive super-ripe, dark berry Grenache character and loaded with muscular tannin in its youth. The immensely concentrated Cuvée da Capo has emerged as one of the Rhône Valley's great reds – dense, massively powerful but surprisingly refined as well. The Ferauds are also involved with André Brunel of LES CAILLOUX in a fine new *négociant* venture (FERAUD-BRUNEL). (DM)

- Vin de Table Plan Pegau Non-Filtré★ £B
- Châteauneuf-du-Pape Cuvée Réservée★★★★★ £E Cuvée da Capo✪✪✪✪ £F
- O Châteauneuf-du-Pape Cuvée Réservée★★★ £D

DOM. PERRIN   Côtes du Rhône   www.beaucastel.com   A:Bib, JAr, Mis, BRW, BBR

Owner: Perrin Brothers   84350 Courthezon

This is the *négociant* arm of the Perrin brothers of CHÂTEAU DE BEAUCASTEL. Most famous among the wines is the long-established brand, La Vieille Ferme, an original trendsetter for quality in the Côtes du Ventoux, although other producers have now taken quality there to higher levels. They also now produce reliable to good examples from a number of southern Rhône ACs along with a sound Crozes-Hermitage. The wines offer an attractive, approachable style with forward, juicy fruit but fail to sing in the way that some of the best small growers in these appellations now do. (DM)

- Crozes-Hermitage★ £B
- Côtes du Rhône★ £B   ● Côtes du Rhône-Villages Réserve★ £B
- O Côtes du Rhône-Villages Réserve★ £B
- Vacqueyras★★ £B   ● Gigondas★★ £C   ● Châteauneuf-du-Pape Les Sinards★★ £C

DOM. DE PIAUGIER   Sablet   piaugier@wanadoo.fr   A: GVF

Owner: Jean-Marc Autran   3 Route de Gigondas, 84110 Sablet

Jean-Marc Autran possesses some 30 ha of vineyards in Sablet and Gigondas, almost all of which are planted to red varieties. A very small amount of very good, nutty and lightly herbal white Sablet is made from Grenache Blanc, Roussanne, Viognier and Clairette, which lends a fresh grip to the wine. Among the reds the real star turns are the special *cuvées* from Sablet. All of these are dense, rich, powerful and very impressive for the appellation. Ténébi is an unusual 100 per cent Counoise, Réserve de Maude 100 per cent Syrah. The other Sablets blend Grenache with Mourvèdre. The approach to vinification is traditional and the fruit is not destemmed. The result, though, is never rustic. In the lesser regular Sablet, Côtes du Rhône and even the Gigondas – which are all significantly lighter – a green undercurrent can occur in lighter vintages. The Gigondas was very good in 2001. The top Sablet reds and the Gigondas all improve with three or four years' ageing. (DM)

● **Côtes du Rhône★** £A ● **Côtes du Rhône-Villages Sablet★** £B
● **Côtes du Rhône-Villages Sablet** Montmartel★★★ £C Ténébi★★★ £C Les Briquières★★★★ £C
● **Côtes du Rhône-Villages Sablet** Réserve de Maude★★★ £D Réserve Alphonse Vautour★★★★ £D
● **Gigondas★★** £B

DOM. RABASSE-CHARAVIN   Cairanne   A: THt

Owner: Corinne Couturier   La Font d'Estevenas, 84290 Cairanne
A good small range here with fairly extensive vineyards (over 65 ha) and a surprisingly large annual production of around 15,000 cases. All but 2 ha are planted to red varieties. The average vine age is now over 50 years, which no doubt ably assists in maintaining wine quality. The approach to vinifying the reds is traditional, with no destemming and ageing in vat. The wines are well made, with good dark berry fruit and a typically intense herbal component. Cuvée Estevenas has impressive depth and firm tannin in its youth. It is a good medium-term cellar prospect. (DM)

O **Côtes du Rhône-Villages Cairanne★** £B
● **Côtes du Rhône-Villages Cairanne★★** £B Estevenas★★★ £B
● **Côtes du Rhône-Villages Rasteau★★** £B

DOM. RASPAIL-AY   Gigondas   A: Has

Owner: Dominique Ay   Le Colombier, 84190 Gigondas
Dominique Ay produces just two wines from his 18 ha in Gigondas. There is a little rosé but the real interest here is the burly, powerful but elegant and very ageworthy Gigondas. The fruit is all destemmed and the result is not at all rustic. The wine is aged in large vats rather than in barrique but is none the worse for that. On occasion the wine can lack the intensity and power of the very best. 2000 lacked ripeness whereas 2001 was very impressive indeed. (DM)

● **Gigondas★★★** £C

DOM. RÉMÉJEANNE   Côtes du Rhône-Villages   remejeanne@wanadoo.fr   A: CTy

Owner: Remy Klein   Cadignac, 30200 Sabran
A real benchmark for other Côtes du Rhône properties. This medium-sized domaine makes some 12,500 cases annually, 90 per cent of it red, from 35 ha of vineyards. Les Arbousiers red and white are classic southern Rhône blends – the red is vibrant and spicy, the white subtly nutty. Les Chevrefeuilles adds Carignan and Counoise from old vines to Syrah and Grenache. The top two *cuvées* are Les Églantiers (100 per cent Syrah) and Les Génevriers, a blend of Grenache, Syrah and Mourvèdre. Vinification is high-tech and modern and micro-oygenation is used during *élevage*. The top wines are rich, concentrated and develop well in bottle after three to five years' ageing. (DM)

● **Côtes du Rhône** Les Arbousiers★★ £B Les Chèvrefeuilles★★★ £B Les Églantiers★★★★ £C
O **Côtes du Rhône** Les Arbousiers★ £B
● **Côtes du Rhône-Villages** Les Génevriers★★★ £B

DOM. DE RENJARDE   Côtes du Rhône   www.chateau-la-nerthe.com   A: BBR, C&C

Owner: Richard family   Route d'Uchaux, 84830 Serignan du Comtat
Good, well-priced reds from a sister property to CHÂTEAU LA NERTHE. There are 50 ha under vine so this is quite a substantial operation with an annual output of around 20,000 cases in all. The vineyard is planted to a blend of Grenache, Syrah, Cinsault, Carignan and Mourvèdre. Alain Dugas, the director of Château La Nerthe, also guides operations here. Unlike at its sister property, vinfication of each variety is separate, emphasising the quality of the fruit, with assemblage prior to bottling. Undoubtedly the quality stamp of the Richard family shows through, with a good, medium-weight, attractive fruit-driven Côtes du Rhône of some style and the Réserve de Cassagne, which is a particularly well-priced, concentrated and structured red. (DM)

● **Côtes du Rhône**★★ £B
● **Côtes du Rhône-Villages** Réserve de Cassagne★★★ £B

MARCEL RICHAUD   Cairanne   A: Lib

Owner: Marcel Richaud   Route de Rasteau, 84290 Cairanne
Marcel Richaud is one of a number of excellent producers from this top-performing village. He has a reasonably sizeable vineyard holding of over 40 ha, some of which date back over 100 years, so the potential of his raw material is remarkable and this shows through in his wines. All show impressive, spicy berry fruit with intense notes of thyme and the classic scent of *garrigues* from a range offering very fair prices. The top two *cuvées* are impressively structured; the Estrambords is aged in barriques, while the Côtes du Rhône Les Garrigues is particularly good value. (DM)

● **Côtes du Rhône**★ £B Terres d'Aigues★★ £B Les Garrigues★★★ £B
O **Côtes du Rhône**★ £B
● **Côtes du Rhône-Villages Cairanne**★★★ £B L'Ebrescade★★★★ £C Les Estrambords★★★★ £C
O **Côtes du Rhône-Villages Cairanne**★★ £B

DOMINIQUE ROCHER   Cairanne   www.rochervin.com   A: WTs

Owner: Dominique Rocher   Route de Saint-Roman, 84290 Cairanne
Stylish modern domaine with some superbly sited vineyards totalling around 14 ha or so. The Côtes du Rhône wines are both full of fruit, the red as appealing in its youth as the nutty, herbal white. The Cairanne labels are more serious. Cuvée Monsieur Paul is firmly structured, but it can appear a touch over-extracted on occasions. The vinification is modern – virtually all the crop is destemmed and many of the cellar operations are carried out by gravity. This is an good source and the Cairanne wines will improve for several years. (DM)

● **Côtes du Rhône-Villages Cairanne**★★ £B Cuvée Monsieur Paul★★ £B
● **Côtes du Rhône**★ £B O **Côtes du Rhône**★ £B

ROGER SABON   Châteauneuf-du-Pape   A: Gau, Rae, BBR, Bal

Owner: Roger Sabon   Avenue Impérial, BP 57, 84230 Châteauneuf-du-Pape
While there is good to very good regular Lirac and Châteauneuf-du-Pape here it is the marvellous old-vine Cuvée Prestige and Le Secret de Sabon that show real intensity and sheer class. They are produced from very low-yielding, superbly sited, venerable vines. The latter is one of the great wines of the appellation. The wines are all bottled without filtration. (DM)

● **Châteauneuf-du-Pape** Les Olivets★★ £D Cuvée Réservée★★★ £D
● **Châteauneuf-du-Pape** Cuvée Prestige★★★★ £E Le Secret de Sabon★★★★★ £F
● **Lirac**★★ £B

SANG DES CAILLOUX   Vacqueyras   A: CPp

Owner: Serge Férigoule 84260 Sarrians
The performance at this estate represents one of the region's notable turnarounds in recent years. Quality in the early to mid-1990s was acceptable but only just. The wines were light, lacked dimension and appeared heavily processed. Now, though, they have minimal manipulation and are all the better for it. A barrel-fermented white is made from Grenache Blanc, Bourboulenc, Clairette and Roussanne but in tiny quantities, fewer than 200 cases a year. It is the two excellent-value reds which demand attention, particularly for their availability. They are now rich, dense and loaded with black fruit and spicy, *garrigue* scents. The Classique has been variously named Doucinello, Azalais and Floureto over recent vintages (since 1995). It is blended from Grenache, Syrah, Mourvèdre and Cinsault and is the mainstay of the domaine. The Cuvée Lopy is produced from the oldest vines of Grenache (75 years) and Syrah. It is firmly structured and requires three or four years. Both reds keep very well. (DM)
● **Vacqueyras** Classique★★★ £B Cuvée Lopy Vieilles Vignes★★★ £C

DOM. SANTA DUC   Gigondas   A: Bib, Rae, HHB

Owner: Yves Gras 84190 Gigondas
For the past decade or more Santa Duc has been one of the finest and most reliable names in Gigondas. Even in some of the lesser vintages of the 1990s the Gigondas showed impressively well. The red vin de pays is attractively fruity with crunchy strawberry and cherry to the fore. Just over half of Yves Gras's holding is in Gigondas. The Côtes du Rhône is lighter than some but has intensity and a marked scent of *garrigues*. The wines are given a cold soak prior to fermentation and are bottled unfined and unfiltered after being aged on lees. There is a solid *negoçiant* wine La Garancières but it is the two domaine wines which really stand out. The regular *cuvée* is the softer, more forward of the two, with the more structured and very, very fine Les Hautes Garrigues seeing around one-third new oak. The balance is aged in *foudres*. (DM)
● **Vin de Pays de la Principauté d'Orange★** £B ● **Côtes du Rhône★★** £B
● **Gigondas★★★** £C La Garancières★★ £B Les Hautes Garrigues★★★★ £D

DOM. SAINTE-ANNE   Côtes du Rhône   A: OWL, Tan, SVS, BBR

Owner: Steinmaier family   Les Cellettes, 30200 Saint-Gervais
Quality has been of a high order here throughout the 1990s but the wines still remain very good value. There are some 33 ha under vine and Syrah and Mourvèdre as well as Grenache are important in shaping the style of the reds. These are full-bodied and dense; the top two *cuvées* in particular will benefit from medium-term ageing. The Viognier is important here and is one of the better southern Rhône examples. It should always be enjoyed young and fresh, when it will be both exotic and peachy. (DM)
● **Côtes du Rhône-Villages★★** £B Cuvée St Gervais★★★ £B Cuvée Notre-Dame des Celettes★★★ £B
O **Côtes du Rhône** Viognier★★ £C

TARDIEU-LAURENT   A: HBJ, Vig, Rae, BBR

Owner: Michel Tardieu/Dominique Laurent   Qtr. Les Ferailles, Route de Cucuron, 84160 Lourmarin
An exceptional range of wines from throughout the Rhône Valley are produced by the partnership of Michel Tardieu and Dominique LAURENT of Burgundy. Along with wines from the Rhône there are selected bottlings from the Costières de Nimes, Provence and the Languedoc. Almost everything

is of at least two- to three-star quality. Top wines from Hermitage, Côte-Rôtie and Cornas in the north and Châteauneuf-du-Pape, Gigondas and Vacqueyras in the south invariably rate at least three and often four stars, particularly the Vieilles Vignes labels. (DM)

● **Côtes du Rhône** Guy Louis★★★ £C   ● **Saint-Joseph** Vieilles Vignes★★★ £D
● **Côtes du Rhône-Villages Rasteau** Vieilles-Vignes★★★ £C
● **Costieres de Nimes**★★★ £B   ● **Corbieres** Roquefort★★★ £B

DOM. DU TRAPADIS   Rasteau   A: GrD, H&B, VTr, SVS

Owner: Michèle Charavin & Helen Durand   Route d'Orange, 84110 Rasteau
Helen Durand has been in charge here since 1994 and the estate is now run with minimal interference in vineyard or cellar. Les Adrès is a classic, Grenache-based southern Rhône blend while Harys is produced from Syrah. Traditional vinification (no destemming) produces wines which are both rich and structured. Even the Côtes du Rhône will benefit from short cellaring. In short these are powerful and complex wines. (DM)

● **Côtes du Rhône**★★ £B
● **Côtes du Rhône-Villages Rasteau**★★★ £B Les Adrès★★★ £C Harys★★★ £C

PIERRE USSEGLIO   Châteauneuf-du-Pape   A: Gau, BBR

Owner: Jean-Pierre & Thierry Usseglio   Route d'Orange, 84230 Châteauneuf-du-Pape
Jean-Pierre and Thierry are now running their father's property of some 23 ha, where they produce around 4,500 cases a year. The white is sound but it is the reds which excel. They include very good regular red Châteauneuf as well as the super-dense and rich old-vine Mon Aïeul and an exceptional Cuvée Cinquantenaire which was produced in 1999. Réserve des Deux-Frères, an expensive reserve bottling that replaces the Cinquantenaire as the top label, was made in 2000 and 2001. (DM)

● **Châteauneuf-du-Pape** Tradition★★★ £C Cuvée de Mon Aïeul★★★★ £E
O **Châteauneuf-du-Pape** Tradition★★ £C

DOM. DE LA VIEILLE-JULIENNE   Châteauneuf-du-Pape   A:SVS, OWL

Owner: Jean-Paul Daumen   84100 Orange
The wines here are now of a different order to those of a few years back. The vin de pays is still from relatively young vines but for the Côtes du Rhône and Châteauneuf-du-Pape bottlings the vines are old to very old. The Vieilles Vignes Côtes du Rhône is produced from 60-year-old plantings and is a blend of Grenache, Syrah and Mourvèdre. It is very intense and complex. The regular Châteauneuf-du-Pape is sweet, spicy and intense, full of *garrigue* and super-ripe dark berry fruit – the 2000 rated four stars. The top two *cuvées* are remarkable. The Vieille Vignes is immensely powerful and structured and it needs time. The Vieilles Vignes Réservé is extraordinary – ninety-five per cent Grenache, heady and super-rich. It's the more open and approachable of the two but immensely ageworthy. (DM)

● **Châteauneuf-du-Pape**★★★ £C Vieilles Vignes★★★★★ £F Vieilles Vignes Réservé❂❂❂❂❂ £H
● **Cotes du Rhône**★★ £B Vieilles Vignes★★★ £B
● **Vin de Pays de la Principauté d'Orange**★ £B

DOM. DU VIEUX-TÉLÉGRAPHE   Châteauneuf-du-Pape   A: J&B, BBR THt, Lay, Tan, SVS

Owner: Brunier family   3 Route de Châteauneuf-du-Pape, 84370 Bedarrides
The Bruniers have been benchmark producers here for two decades. They now own the Domaine

LA ROQUETTE also in Châteauneuf, and have an interest in the revitalised LES PALLIÈRES in Gigondas. The 70-ha estate is planted largely to reds, understandably, with a little Clairette, Grenache Blanc, Bourboulenc and Roussanne which are used to produce a spicy, intensely nutty and surprisingly refined white Châteauneuf. The Vieux Mas des Papes is a very impressive second wine. The approach is to maximise the potential of the *grand vin*, rather than bottling small plots as special individual *cuvées*. The Châteauneuf-du-Pape red is now denser and more powerful than of old but with marvellous depth and refinement. There have been significant improvements at many properties throughout the appellation in recent years but few of these wines can achieve the balance and harmony of those of the Bruniers. (DM)

● **Châteauneuf-du-Pape**●●●●● £E Le Vieux Mas des Papes★★★ £C
O **Châteauneuf-du-Pape**★★★★ £E
● **Vin de Pays de Vaucluse** Le Pigeoulet★★ £B

SOUTHERN RHÔNE/OTHER WINES OF NOTE

DOM. D'AÉRIA ● **Côtes du Rhône-Villages Cairanne** Tradition £B
DOM. DE L'AMEILLAUD ● **Côtes du Rhône-Villages Cairanne** £B
DOM. DES ANGES ● **Côtes du Ventoux** £A Clos de l'Archange £B
DOM. PAUL AUTARD ● **Châteauneuf-du-Pape** £C La Côte Ronde £E
LES DOMAINES BERNARD ● **Châteauneuf-du-Pape** Louis Bernard £C
DOM. DES BERNARDINS O **Muscat de Beaumes-de-Venise** £C
DOM. BERTHET-RAYNE ● **Châteauneuf-du-Pape** £C
BOIS DAUPHIN ● **Châteauneuf-du-Pape** £C
DOM. DES BOSQUETS ● **Gigondas** £C
DOM. BOUCHASSY ● **Lirac** £B
DOM. DE LA BOUISSIÈRE ● **Gigondas** £B Cuvée La Font du Tonin £C
DOM. BRESSY MASSON ● **Côtes du Rhône-Villages** Envée Paul-Emile£B
DOM. DES BUISSERONS ● **Côtes du Rhône-Villages Cairanne** £B
DOM. DE CABASSE ● **Côtes du Rhône-Villages Séguret** £B Casa Bassa £B ● **Gigondas** £C
DOM. DE CASSAN ● **Gigondas** £B
DOM. DE CHANABAS ● **Châteauneuf-du-Pape** £C
CHANTE PERDRIX ● **Châteauneuf-du-Pape** £C
DIDIER CHARAVIN ● **Côtes du Rhône Villages Rasteau**£B Prestige£B
CH. D'ACQUERIA ◉ **Tavel** £B ● **Lirac** £B
CH. CABRIÈRES ● **Châteauneuf-du-Pape** £C Tête de Cru £E
CH. LA CANORGUE ● **Côtes du Luberon** £B ● **Côtes du Rhône** £B
● **Côtes du Rhône-Villages Laudun** £B
CH. FONTSÉGUGNE ● **Côtes du Rhône** £B Santo Estello £B
CH. FORTIA ● **Châteauneuf-du-Pape** £C
CH. DE GRAND MOULAS ● **Côtes du Rhône** £B ● **Côtes du Rhône-Villages** £B
CH. MAUCOIL ● **Châteauneuf-du-Pape** £C Cuvée Privilège £C
CH. DE MONTMIRAIL ● **Vacqueyras** l'Ermite £B St Papes £B ● **Gigondas** Beauchamp £B
CH. DE ROUANNE ● **Côtes du Rhône-Villages Vinsobres** £B
CH. DES ROQUES ● **Vacqueyras** £B
CH. SAINT-ROCH ● **Lirac** Cuvée Confidentielle £C
CH. DE SEGRIES ● **Côtes du Rhône** Clos de l'Hermitage £B ● **Lirac** Cuvée Reservée £C
CH. SIGNAC ● **Côtes du Rhone-Villages** £B Combe d'Enfer £B Terra Amata £B
CH. DU TRIGNON ● **Côtes du Rhône-Villages Sablet** £B ● **Gigondas** £C
CH. VAL JOANIS ● **Côtes du Luberon** Réserve Les Griottes £B
CH. DE LA VERRERIE ● **Côtes du Luberon** £B
DOM. DE LA CITADELLE ● **Cotes du Luberon** £B Cuvée de Gouverneur £C
CLOS DU JONCUAS ● **Gigondas** Esprit de Grenache £B
CLOS DE L'ORATOIRE DES PAPES ● **Châteauneuf-du-Pape** £C
CLOS SAINT-MICHEL ● **Châteauneuf-du-Pape** £C Cuvée Réservée £D
DOM. DES CORIANCON ● **Côtes du Rhône-Villages Vinsobres** £B Cuvée Claude Vallot £B

DOM DU CORNE-LOUP ● Lirac £B

DOM. DU COUROULU ● Vacqueyras £B Vieilles Vignes £B

DOM. DE CRISTIA ● Châteauneuf-du-Pape £C

DOM. OLIVIER CUILLERON ● Côtes du Rhône-Villages Visan £B

DOM. DE LA DAYSSE ● Gigondas £B

DIFFONTY ET FILS ● Châteauneuf-du-Pape £C Réserve Sixteen £D

DOMAINE DUCLAUX ● Châteauneuf-du-Pape £C

CAVE D'ESTÉZARGUES ● Côtes du Rhône Dom. d'Andezon £B

DOM. DE FERRAND ● Châteauneuf-du-Pape £C

DOM. DE FONTENILLE ● Côtes du Luberon £B Vieilles Vignes £B Prestige £B

DOM. LOU FREJAU ● Châteauneuf-du-Pape £C

GALET DES PAPES ● Châteauneuf-du-Pape £C Vieilles Vignes £D

DOM. GRAND BOURJASSOT ● Gigondas £B

DOM. DES GRAND DEVERS ● Côtes du Rhône Enclave des Papes £ La Suranne £C
● Côtes du Rhône-Villages Valreas £B ● Côtes du Rhône-Villages Visan £B

DOM. GRAND VENEUR ● Châteauneuf-du-Pape £C Cuvée Les Origines £D

DOM. DE GRANGENEUVE ● Coteaux du Tricastin Vieilles Vignes £B La Truffiere £B

DOM. DU JONCIER ● Lirac £B

DOM. LA BASTIDE SAINT DOMINIQUE ● Châteauneuf-du-Pape £C

DOM. LA CABOTTE ● Côtes du Rhône-Villages £B Élevé en Futs de Chene £B

DOM. LA FOURMONE ● Vacqueyras £B ● Gigondas l'Oustau Fauquet £B

DOM. LA NAVETTE ● Gigondas £C

DOM. LA ROCALIÈRE ● Lirac Cuvée Prestige £B

DOM. LE CLOS DE CAVEAU ● Vacqueyras £B Cuvée Lao Muse £C

DOM. CATHERINE LEGOEUIL ● Côtes du Rhône-Villages Cairanne Cuvée Lea Felsch £B
Cuvée Marie Rouvière £B Les Beauchières £B

DOM. LES CLEFS D'OR ● Châteauneuf-du-Pape £C

DOM. LES GRANDS BOIS ● Côtes du Rhône-Villages Cairanne Cuvée Mireille £B
Cuvée Eloise £B

DOM. LES HAUTES CANCES ● Côtes du Rhône-Villages Cairanne £B Vieilles Vignes £B

LE VIEUX DONJON ● Châteauneuf-du-Pape £D

DOM. LONGUE TOQUE ● Gigondas £C

MAS DE BOISLAUZON ● Châteauneuf-du-Pape £C

MAS DE LIBIAN ● Côtes du Rhone £B ● Côtes du Rhône-Villages £B La Calade £C

DOM. MATHIEU ● Châteauneuf-du-Pape £C Marquis Anselm Mathieu £D

DOM. DE LA MONARDIÈRE ● Vacqueyras £B Les Calades £B Vieilles Vignes £B

DOM. MONTIRIUS ● Vacqueyras £B

DOM. DE MONTVAC ● Vacqueyras £B Cuvée Vincilan £C ● Gigondas £C

DOM. DU MOULIN ● Côtes du Rhône-Villages Vinsobres Charles Joseph £B
O Côtes du Rhône-Villages Vinsobres £B

DOM. DE NALYS ● Châteauneuf-du-Pape £C

DOM. PÉLAQUIÉ ● Lirac £B O Côtes du Rhône-Villages Laudun £B

DOM. PÈRE CABOCHE ● Châteauneuf-du-Pape £C Cuvée Elisabeth Chambellan £C

DOM. DU PÈRE PAPE ● Châteauneuf-du-Pape £C La Crau de Ma Mère £D

ROGER PERRIN ● Côtes du Rhône £B Prestige £B ● Châteauneuf-du-Pape £C Vieilles Vignes £E

DOM. PESQUIER ● Gigondas £C

DOM. DES RELAGNES ● Châteauneuf-du-Pape £C Cuvée Vigneronne £D

DOM. ROUGE GARANCE ● Côtes du Rhone-Villages £B

DOM SAINT-AMANT ● Côtes du Rhône Les Clapas £B
● Côtes du Rhône-Villages Rasteau Grangeneuve £C O Côtes du Rhône La Borry £B
O Côtes du Rhône-Villages Rasteau La Tabardonne £C

DOM. SAINT-GAYAN ● Côtes du Rhône-Villages Rasteau £B ● Gigondas £C Fontmaria £C

DOM. SAINT-ROCH O Lirac Cuvée Boisée £C ● Lirac £B ● Châteauneuf-du-Pape £D

DOM. DE LA SOLITUDE ● Châteauneuf-du-Pape £C

DOM. SAINT-BENOIT ● Châteauneuf-du-Pape La Truffière £C Grand Garde £C

DOM. DE SAINT-LUC ● Coteaux du Tricastin Syrah £B ● Côtes du Rhône-Villages £B

DOM. DES SAINT-SIFFREIN ● **Châteauneuf-du-Pape** £C
DOM. DU TERME ● **Gigondas** £C
DOM. LES TEYSSONIERES ● **Gigondas** Cuvée Alexandre £C
DOM. LES TOURELLES ● **Gigondas** £B
DOM. DE VERQUIERE ● **Côtes du Rhône-Villages Sablet** £B
DOM. DE VILLENEUVE ● **Châteauneuf-du-Pape** £D Vieilles Vignes £E
DOM. RAYMOND USSEGLIO ● **Châteauneuf-du-Pape** Girard £C Impériale £E
DOM VERDA ● **Lirac** Cuvée Prestige £B
DOM. DE LA VERRIÈRE ● **Côtes du Ventoux** £B

Author's choice (DM)

12 benchmark Châteauneuf-du-Papes

DOM. DE BEAURENARD ● **Châteauneuf du Pape** Boisrenard
M CHAPOUTIER ● **Châteauneuf du Pape** Barbe Rac
CH. DE BEAUCASTEL ● **Châteauneuf du Pape** Hommage à Jacques`Perrin
CH. LA NERTHE ● **Châteauneuf du Pape** Cuvée des Cadettes
CH. RAYAS ● **Châteauneuf du Pape**
CLOS DES CAILLOU ● **Châteauneuf du Pape** Réserve
CLOS DES PAPES ● **Châteauneuf du Pape**
DOM DE LA JANASSE ● **Châteauneuf du Pape** Vieilles Vignes
DOM. DE MARCOUX ● **Châteauneuf du Pape** Vieilles Vignes
DOM. DE LA MORDORÉE ● **Châteauneuf du Pape** Reine des Bois
DOM. DE LA VIEILLE-JULIENNE ● **Châteauneuf du Pape** Vieilles Vignes Réservé
DOM. DU VIEUX TÉLÉGRAPHE ● **Châteauneuf du Pape**

A diverse selection of a dozen emerging reds

DANIEL ET DENIS ALARY ● **Côtes du Rhône-Villages Cairanne** La Font d'Estevenas
DOM. BRUSSET ● **Gigondas**   Les Hauts de Montmirail
CLOS DES CAZAUX ● **Vacqueyras** Grénat Noble
CLOS PETITE BELLANE ● **Cotes du Rhone Valréas** Vieilles Vignes
DOM. DE DEURRE ● **Côtes du Rhône** Les Rabasses
GOURT DE MAUTENS ● **Côtes du Rhône-Villages Rasteau**
DOM. LA SOUMADE ● **Côtes du Rhône-Villages Rasteau** Fleur de Confiance
DOM. LES APHILLANTHES ● **Côtes du Rhône-Villages** Vieilles Vignes
DOM. DE L'ORATOIRE SAINT-MARTIN ● **Côtes du Rhône-Villages Cairanne** Haut Coustias
DOM. DE PIAUGIER ● **Côtes du Rhône-Villages Sablet** Réserve Alphonse Vautour
MARCEL RICHAUD ● **Côtes du Rhône-Villages Cairanne** Les Estrambords
DOM. SANTA-DUC ● **Gigondas** Les Hautes Garrigues

A selection of good value reds and whites

CH. SAINT-COSME ● **Côtes du Rhone** Les Deux Albions
DOM. CHAUME-ARNAUD O **Côtes du Rhône-Villages Vinsobres**
CROS DE LA MÛRE ● **Côtes du Rhône-Villages**
DOM. DE FONDRÈCHE ● **Côtes du Ventoux** Cuvée Persia
FONT DE MICHELLE O **Côtes du Rhône** F de Font de Michelle
DOM. LA GARRIGUE ● **Vacqueyras**
DOM. GRAMENON O **Côtes du Rhône** Vie on y est
DOM. GRAPILLON D'OR ● **Gigondas**
DOM. RABASSE-CHARAVIN ● **Côtes du Rhône-Villages Cairanne** Estevenas
DOM. DE RÉMÉJEANNE ● **Côtes du Rhone** Les Génevriers
SANG DES CAILLOUX ● **Vacqueyras** Classique
DOM. SAINTE-ANNE O **Côtes du Rhône** Viognier
DOM. DE LA VERRIÈRE ● **Côtes du Ventoux**

France/Languedoc-Roussillon & Provence

The focus here is on established pioneers, as well as the many new small domaines now placing the Mediterranean coast of France solidly on the country's quality wine map. Many appellations here are of long standing but only recently have widespread improvements been made in the standard of the wines. The transformation in Languedoc-Roussillon is unique in France. The change in Provence is less dramatic, but here too many quality-minded individuals are bringing a new focus to viticulture and expressing the potential of their terroirs. The role of Provence as a purveyor of easy-drinking pink plonk to sun-seeking tourists is gradually changing, although the importance of rosé in the region's wine production is still depressingly high.

Provence and Corsica

While rosé remains the mainstay of Provençal wine production, exciting reds and some very well-made whites have emerged over the last fifteen years or so. In the foothills of the Alpes-Maritimes inland of Nice the tiny appellation of **Bellet,** with a total of a mere 39 ha under vine, offers some unusual albeit pricey, well-structured reds and lightly floral nutty whites and fruity rosés. The proximity of neighbouring Italy shows itself with the Braquet (Brachetto) among the varieties that make up the permitted red blend, along with Folle Noir and the more usual Grenache and Cinsault. The vineyards are planted at altitude of some 300 m, moderating the climate.This provides an unusual opportunity in ripening Chardonnay in such a southerly maritime climate, which in the whites is blended with Rolle.

The vast bulk of central Provence is covered by the appellations of **Côtes de Provence** and **Coteaux Varois.** While both produce vast amounts of glugging rosé, some very impressive reds are being produced from blends of Rhône varieties, some with the addition of Cabernet Sauvignon. The **Coteaux d'Aix en Provence** and the spectacularly sited vineyards of **Les Baux de Provence** produce similar wines. Domaine de Trevallon, now forced to label its wine as Vin de Pays des Bouches du Rhône, set the trend with a stunning blend of Cabernet and Syrah. There are a number of other such blends now; some like Trevallon use more traditional ageing in large vats while others are seduced by new oak. Whatever the approach an exciting array of different styles is emerging.

Palette is another tiny AC of just 40 ha for both red and white and with only two established producers, although others are emerging. Château Crémade has yet to challenge Château Simone, thus far the only producer of wines of real quality. An extensive number of varieties can be planted but increasingly replanting is concentrated on Syrah, Grenache and Mourvèdre.

The two coastal appellations of **Cassis** and **Bandol** between Marseilles and Toulon are sources of red, white and rosé. Generally Cassis tends to be pretty dull fare but there is the odd impressive white. The best whites and rosés from Bandol are good but it is the reds that you should look out for. The appellation is situated in the foothills just inland of the port of Bandol in a natural coastal amphitheatre. The vineyards stretch from La Ciotat in the east to Sanary-sur-Mer in the west and enjoy a unique warm, dry maritime climate. The style of the wine itself varies surprisingly due to differing calcareous, gravel and clay soils and varying levels of Mourvèdre, the main grape variety. Established Bandol leaders Domaine Tempier and Château Pibarnon are now being joined by a new wave of small, high-quality growers. This is an exciting area to follow. Remember, though, that these wines need cellaring, often for up to a decade.

There are three main appellations on the island of Corsica; **Vin de Corse, Patrimonio** and **Ajaccio.** Almost all viticulture is carried out around the coast. The forested, mountainous interior is far too extreme for viticulture. There are also a number of *crus* within the Vin de Corse appellation: **Calvi, Sartène, Figari, Porto-Vecchio** and **Coteaux du Cap Corse.** Both Coteaux du Cap Corse and Patrimonio are entitled to the Muscat du Cap Corse appellation and it is some of these good to very good rich fortified Muscats which offer the greatest excitement here. Some good reds, albeit somewhat rustic, are also produced from the native Nielluccio along with Grenache, Carignan and Cinsault.

Languedoc

Some truly great wine is now being made in the Languedoc. Most but by no means all of this is produced under a number of different appellations. For reasons of practicality and location a number of splendid new-wave wines, particularly red, are being produced as vins de pays. A number are **Vins de Pays d'Oc** but **Vin de Pays du Gard** and **Vin de Pays de l'Hérault** also feature, including two of the greatest properties in the Languedoc, Mas de Daumas Gassac and Domaine de La Grange des Pères. Just to the west of the River Rhône is the emerging region of the **Costières de Nîmes.** Not surprisingly the wine here has more in common with the blends of the southern Rhône than the rest of the Languedoc. Intense, strawberry-scented, Grenache-based reds are being produced by a number of good domaines and increasing use is being made of Mourvèdre. Many of these properties are also making rich, stylish blends of Cabernet Sauvignon and Syrah, generally labelled as Vins de Pays du Gard.

To the west of the Costières de Nîmes is the giant spread of the **Coteaux du Languedoc** AC. Vast and sprawling, it stretches from Nîmes in the east around the coastline to Narbonne and a considerable distance into the hills of the Gard and Hérault *départements*. There are twelve communes which are allowed to add their village names as *crus* and these include **La Clape, Picpoul de Pinet, Cabrières, Montpeyroux, Pic-Saint-Loup** and **Saint-Drézéry.** At best there are some splendid wines, generally blends of Syrah, Grenache and Mourvèdre for the reds and a host of white varieties including Roussanne, Grenache Blanc and Clairette. Sadly, you are also likely to encounter a great many moderate to average bottles as well, so always try to buy from a good source.

Just to the north of Béziers and to the west of the Coteaux du Languedoc are the small appellations of **Faugères** and **Saint-Chinian.** Some very fine small properties are now producing great reds, the most important variety being Syrah (which performs superbly in the schistous soils of Faugères) although Grenache, Mourvèdre and old vine Carignan all play an important role in the local viticulture. There are a number of Muscat-based *vins doux naturels* as well but none are comparable to their peers from Muscat de Rivesaltes in the Roussillon. They include **Muscat de Frontignan, Muscat de Mireval** and **Muscat de Lunel.**

South of Narbonne and stretching down to the hills of the Roussillon are a number of key appellations. **Minervois, Corbières** and **Fitou** had for a long time been regarded as little more than Midi workhorse wines, vinified by unambitious local co-ops or volume *négociants.* This has to a large extent changed for the better. The wines of Minervois have shown the most potential and within that appellation is the new *cru* sub-zone of **La Livinière,** the source of generally the densest and most substantial wines of the AC. Old-vine Carignan plays an important role here although plantings of the Rhône *cépages améliorateurs* continue apace with some vineyards now possessing some increasingly old Syrah, Grenache and Mourvèdre. Carbonic maceration is widely used for Carignan, particularly in Corbières.

To the west of Minervois, the smaller new AC of **Cabardès** has real potential and the Bordeaux varieties Cabernet Sauvignon, Merlot and Cabernet Franc are important here. The biggest disappointment over the past decade has been the performance of Fitou, one of the first ACs established in the region. The co-op at Mont-Tauch has always been a solid source but other promising new producers are emerging.

To the west of Fitou, in the hills around the town of **Limoux,** cool hillside vineyards are planted to Chardonnay and Mauzac. Good sparkling wine is made here, both **Blanquette de Limoux** and **Crémant de Limoux,** but it is the barrel-fermented Chardonnays that have emerged in recent years that impress most.

Roussillon

Until recently the vineyards in the Pyrenées-Orientales *département* were best known in quality wine terms for the production of fine *vins doux naturels*. This situation is changing apace though, and there seems perhaps even more potential here than in the Languedoc. Some stunning reds have appeared over the past decade and the emergence of exciting new small producers continues unabated. One of the region's great strengths is the extensive hillside vineyards planted to both old-vine Carignan and equally importantly Grenache. This is because of the traditional importance of fortified Rivesaltes and Maury, from north of Perpignan, and of Banyuls-sur-Mer, another fortified wine further south on the coast.

Exciting wines are being made throughout the **Côtes du Roussillon** and the **Côtes du Roussillon-Villages** ACs. As well as Grenache, the other Rhône varieties are important too, and a number of top *cuvées* vinified largely from Syrah and aged in high-quality new oak are also emerging, along with the occasional exceptional blend dominated by Mourvèdre. On the coast around the village of Banyuls-sur-Mer the **Collioure** appellation shares the same vineyard area as **Banyuls**. Syrah, Carignan, Mourvèdre and Cinsault are all cultivated here but interestingly it is Mourvèdre planted in close proximity to the sea that has performed particularly well, as it does in Bandol. The **Vin de Pays des Côtes Catalanes** is also increasingly important for red blends and these include Cabernet Sauvignon and Merlot. A new and very exciting region that covers much of the physical area shared by the Maury sweet wine appellation is the newly established **Vin de Pays des Coteaux de Fenouillèdes** in the Agly valley in the north western section of the Côtes du Roussillon. There is a tremendous resource of old vine Grenache and Carignan.

The great traditional wines of the Roussillon are the fortified **Maury**, **Rivesaltes** and **Banyuls**, which in their most exquisite and aged manifestations are characterised by an intense baked, raisiny, *rancio* character. A whole range of styles are produced, with small differences between the appellations. Almost all these wines depend on Grenache as the backbone of the blend; indeed, many are produced solely from the variety. There are youthful, fruit-driven styles that spend only a limited time in cask, wines that are aged for an extended time and wines that are made from a blend of vintages very much in a *solera*-style system. The wines of Maury tend to be more overtly tannic when young and those earlier-released vintages will need more cellaring. Most wines are aged in cool cellars but in Rivesaltes they are also left out for a period in the summer sun in large glass containers, *bonbonnes,* to encourage the development of those complex *rancio* aromas.

As well as the Grenache-based wines there is some very impressive **Muscat de Rivesaltes**, which is markedly different in style. At their best these wines emphasise Muscat's rich grapy character, and are heady and impressively perfumed. Indeed, the best examples are better generally than their equivalents in the Languedoc and the Rhône Valley at Beaumes-de-Venise.

A-Z of Producers by appellation

Bandol
CH. DE PIBARNON
CH. PRADEAUX
CH. VANNIÈRES
DOM. DU GROS NORÉ
DOM. LA BASTIDE BLANCHE
DOM. LAFRAN VEYROLLES
DOM. TEMPIER
DOM. DE TERREBRUNE
DOM DE LA TOUR DU BON

Banyuls
CELLIER DES TEMPLIERS
DOM. LA TOUR VIELLE
DOM. DU MAS BLANC
DOM. DE LA RECTORIE

Bellet
CH. DE BELLET

Collioure
DOM. LA TOUR VIEILLE
DOM. DU MAS BLANC
CELLIER DES TEMPLIERS
DOM. DE LA RECTORIE

Corbières
CH. LA VOULTE-GASPARETS

Costières de Nîmes
CH. MOURGUES DU GRÈS
DOM. DES PERRIÈRES
CH. MAS NEUF
CH D'OR ET DE GUEULES

Coteaux d'Aix-en-Provence
DOM. DES BÉATES

Coteaux du Languedoc
CH. CAPITOUL
CH. DE CAZENEUVE
CH. L'EUZIÈRE
CH. GRÈS SAINT-PAUL
CH. DE JONQUIÈRES
DOM. CLAVEL
DOM. FONT-CAUDE
DOM. DE L'HORTUS
DOM. DE LA MARFÉE
MAS BRUGUIÈRE
MAS CAL DEMOURA
MAS HAUT BUIS
MAS JULLIEN
MAS DE MORTIÈS
MAS MOURIES
DOM. DE PEYRE ROSE
PRIEURÉ DE SAINT-JEAN-DE-BÉBIAN

Coteaux Varois
CH. ROUTAS

Côtes de Provence
DOM DE LA COURTADE
DOM. RABIEGA
DOMAINE RICHEAUME

Côtes du Roussillon
DOM. DE CASENOVE

Côtes du Roussillon-Villages
DOM. DES CHÊNES
DOM. DU CLOS DES FÉES
DOM. FONTANEL
DOM. GARDIES

DOM. GAUBY
DOM. DES SCHISTES
DOM. SEGUELA

Faugères
JEAN-MICHEL ALQUIER
CH. DES ESTANILLES

Les Baux-de-Provence
MAS DE LA DAME
DOM. DE TREVALLON

Limoux
SIEUR D'ARQUES

Minervois
CLOS CENTEILLES
CH. BELGRAVE

Palette
CH. SIMONE

Rivesaltes
DOM. CAZES

Saint-Chinian
DOM. BORIE LA VITARÈLE
DOM. CANET-VALETTE
MAS CHAMPART
MOULIN DE CIFFRE
DOM. RIMBERT

Vin de Pays de Gard
DOM. LEA

Vin de Pays de l'Hérault
DOM. DE LA GRANGE DES PÈRES
DOM. LES CREISSES
MAS DE DAUMAS GASSAC

Vin de Pays d'Oc
MAS D'ESPANET

Other
M CHAPOUTIER
JEAN-LUC COLOMBO
TARDIEU-LAURENT
DOM. TERRE INCONNUE
VAL D'ORBIEU

Languedoc-Roussillon and Provence Vintages

It is extremely difficult in a vast region such as this to make specific vintage assessments. Also much of the development that has been made in recent years makes a longer term assessment of the wines more erratic. However, there have been significant changes in vintage conditions from one year to another throughout the region. These variations are more pronounced as you move further inland. Provence, particularly, has a very benign maritime climate and is reasonably consistent.

In terms of the wines, the best red examples from year to year have the potential to age. Some Languedoc-Roussillon wines have shown a recent tendency to fade prematurely, particularly those from the Coteaux du Languedoc. The *cépages améliorateurs* varieties planted in the Languedoc are generally still young and the wines made from them can be over-extracted. There is no question that as these vines age and the Midi's keen young producers develop their craft the wines will become increasingly refined and cellarworthy.

The more established Provençal red appellations have consistently produced wines that develop well with age. Bandol, particularly, with its high percentage of the structured and noble Mourvèdre, is a very ageworthy red. Among the top older years for premium Provençal reds (mainly Bandol) are 1989, 1988, 1985, 1982, 1978, 1975 and 1970. Top earlier years in the Languedoc include 1989, 1988, 1986 and 1985 but these really only apply to Mas de Daumas Gassac and Prieuré de Saint-Jean-de-Bébian.

The whites throughout the area are generally intended for drinking young, although the best traditional examples from the likes of Château Simone in Palette will keep for a decade. There are increasing numbers of barrel-fermented styles in the Midi and these will develop over three or four years in bottle.

Languedoc-Roussillon and Provence vintages

	Bandol	Côtes de Provence Top Reds	Coteaux du Languedoc	Côtes du Roussillon-Villages including Collioure
2002	★★★ A	★★★ A	★★★ A	★★★/★★★★ A
2001	★★★★ A	★★★★ A	★★★★/★★★★★ A	★★★★/★★★★★ A
2000	★★★★/★★★★★ A	★★★★/★★★★★ A	★★★★/★★★★★ A	★★★★ A
1999	★★★★ A	★★★★ A	★★★/★★★★ B	★★★★ B
1998	★★★★/★★★★★ A	★★★★/★★★★★ B	★★★★/★★★★★ B	★★★★★ B
1997	★★★/★★★★ A	★★★ C	★★/★★★C	★★★C
1996	★★★/★★★★ B	★★★/★★★★ B	★★★ C	★★★ C
1995	★★★/★★★★ B	★★★/★★★★ B	★★★★ C	★★★★ C
1994	★★★ C	★★★ C	★★★ D	★★★/★★★★ C
1993	★★★/★★★★ C	★★/★★★ D	★★★/★★★★C	★★★/★★★★ C
1991	★★★/★★★★ C	★★★ D	★★/★★★ D	★★/★★★ D
1990	★★★★★ B	★★★★★ C	★★★★ C	★★★★ C

JEAN-MICHEL ALQUIER Faugères   A: Rae

Owner: Alquier family   4 Route de Pézenes-les-Mines, 34600 Faugères
Long-established quality producer in this appellation. These are impressive wines, almost rustic in the case of the reds – but in the best sense. There are some 12 ha under vine with the vast majority of this planted to red varieties. Syrah accounts for 40 per cent of the *vignoble* and does very well in the meagre, well-drained, soils. The average vine age of the *cépages ameliorateurs* is increasing and this along with a healthy planting of very old Carignan provides tremendous raw material. The regular red Faugères, a blend of Syrah, Grenache and Carignan, is good if austere when very young, while there is an extra dimension in the two top reds. La Réserve La Maison Jaune is a mix of Syrah and Mourvèdre whereas Les Bastides is aged in some new oak and has a smattering of Grenache adding a touch of red-berry character. These two wines will age well over six or seven years. The basic white vin de pays Roussanne/Marsanne is attractively fruity while the Domaine Jean-Michel Alquier bottling is a gloriously nutty and complex southern-style white. Both of these should be drunk young. (DM)

● **Faugères**★★ £B   La Réserve La Maison Jaune★★★ £C   Les Bastides★★★ £C
O **Vin de Pays de l'Hérault** Roussanne/Marsanne★ £B   Domaine Jean-Michel Alquier★★★ £C

DOM. DES BÉATES Coteaux d'Aix-en-Provence   www.chapoutier.com   A: Men

Owner: M Chapoutier   Route de Caireval, 13410 Lambesc
Biodynamic operation that attracted the interest of Michel CHAPOUTIER of the Rhône Valley in the late 1990s. Four labels are now produced here. The soft, fruity Les Béatines red, white and rosé are easygoing, drink-me-now styles. The Domaine Saint-Estève red and white are more serious, the former now characteristic of the Chapoutier style, providing a typically forward supple, rounded red. These should be drunk young although the red will benefit from keeping a year or two. Domaines des Béates and Terra d'Or are two superior labels which are blends of Cabernet Sauvignon, Syrah and Grenache. The fruit from the oldest vines, which are around 45 years old, is reserved for the top *cru*. The Domaine label is structured, dense and powerful but with supple, well-rounded, ripe tannin. It will develop well in the medium term. Terra d'Or, vinified and aged in new oak, is a serious step up, surprisingly approachable but rich and concentrated with a velvety texture. Complex dark berry fruit, herbal spice and subtle oak are all seamlessly integrated. (DM)

● **Coteaux d'Aix-en-Provence** Béates★★★ £C   Terra d'Or★★★★ £E
● **Coteaux d'Aix-en-Provence** Domaine Saint-Estève★ £B   Les Béatines★ £B

DOM. BORIE LA VITARÈLE Saint-Chinian   A: Odd

Owner: Jean-François Izarn & Cathy Izarn Plane   34490 Saint-Nazaire de Ladarez
The Izarns have some 30 ha under vine now, of which a mere 2 ha are planted with white varieties. Most are in Saint-Chinian but some extend into the Coteaux du Languedoc. Powerful, dense and muscular reds are the order of the day, achieved through controlling yields, which rarely exceed 30 hl/ha. Coteaux du Languedoc Les Terres Blanches is supple, approachable and full of spicy dark fruit, whereas the vin de pays bottlings, including Cabernet Sauvignon and Merlot, are softer and show more overt fruit character. La Combe is the more serious and structured of the two. Of the two Saint-Chinians Les Schistes, mainly Grenache with Syrah and a touch of Carignan, has depth and a firm structure. Give it two or three years. The top wine Les Crès, like all the wines here, is named after the soil in which the vines are grown; in this case it comprises the *galet*-type stones found at Châteauneuf-du-Pape. The wine is a blend of Syrah, Grenache and Mourvèdre and comes from vines yielding less than 20 hl/ha. No new wood is used and it is all the better for it, emphasising its dark,

brooding, spicy fruit character. There is real depth and concentration with the structure to ensure ageing for up to a decade or more. (DM)

● **Saint-Chinian** Les Schistes★★★ £C Les Crès★★★ £C
● **Coteaux du Languedoc** Les Terres Blanches★★ £B
● **Vin de Pays Coteaux de Murviel** Bouïsset★ £B La Combe★★ £B

DOM. CANET-VALETTE Saint-Chinian earl-canet-valette@wanadoo.fr A: C&C, SVS

Owner: Marc Valette Route de Causses-et-Veyran, 34460 Cessenon
There are 18 ha under vine here, all of it planted to red varieties. Along with BORIE LA VITARÈLE this is a benchmark for Saint-Chinian and the top red here, Le Vin Maghani, is arguably the finest in the AC. Minimal handling in the cellar with neither fining nor filtration helps to achieve this. No new oak is used and as a result the character of the impressively intense fruit really shines through in the wines. Une et Mille Nuits is a blend of Grenache, Mourvèdre, Syrah, Carignan and Cinsault. Aged in a mix of *inox* and older oak it is vibrant and approachable, but with sufficient structure to develop well over four or five years. Le Vin Maghani is more serious; dense, rich and very complex. The wine is full of dark fruits, spice and black pepper. Cellaring for five years is a must to enjoy this at its best. (DM)

● **Saint-Chinian** Une et Mille Nuits★★ £B Le Vin Maghani★★★★ £D

DOM. DE CASENOVE Côtes du Roussillon

Owner: Etienne Montes Mas Sabole, 66300 Trouillas
An ancient estate which, unlike many in the Midi, has been in the same family for generations. However, impressive modern fruit-driven wines are now being made at this fine property, where owner Etienne Montes has enjoyed consultancy input from Jean-Luc COLOMBO. There are a total of some 50 ha of vines planted on the property, including 16 ha of whites comprising Grenache Blanc, Maccabeo, Muscat and the rare Torbat. Rich, honeyed Muscat de Rivesaltes and raisiny Rivesaltes are produced as well as a rather dull Côtes du Roussillon white. The red Commandant François Jaubert, produced from mainly Syrah and partly aged in new oak, is powerful, dense and smoky. The Garrigue bottling is spicy and approachable. (DM)

● **Côtes du Roussillon** Garrigue★★ £B Commandant François Jaubert★★★ £E

DOM. CAZES Rivesaltes www.cazes-rivesaltes.com A: Eno

Owner: André & Bernard Cazes 4 Rue Francisco-Ferrer, BP 61, 66602 Rivesaltes
In a region marked by new arrivals and vinegrowers becoming winemakers, this venerable and substantial property with some 160 ha of vineyards produces close to 70,000 cases of both table and fortified wines a year and has done so consistently for decades. An extensive range is produced here, including good red Vin de Pays des Côtes Catalanes. Le Credo is a decent blend of Cabernet Sauvignon and Merlot. There are red and white Côtes du Roussillons, red Côtes du Roussillon-Villages and Muscat de Rivesaltes, with some splendid aged examples, along with very good Rivesaltes. These have an intense nutty complexity and will keep very well. There are some remarkable and expensive limited-release old vintages available under the Aimé Cazes label. (DM)

● **Côtes du Roussillon**★ £B ● **Côtes du Roussillon-Villages** Alter★★ £B Trilogy★★ £C
● **Vin de Pays des Côtes Catalanes** Le Credo★★ £C
● **Rivesaltes** Tuilé★★★ £C Ambré★★★ £C
O **Muscat de Rivesaltes**★★★ £B

CELLIER DES TEMPLIERS Banyuls & Collioure

Owner: 'Co-operative' Route du Mas-Reig, 66650 Banyuls-sur-Mer
This is the largest co-operative in the Banyuls and Collioure regions, producing traditional Collioure and some impressive fortifieds. The ownership consists of over 750 growers who between them farm close to 900 ha in Banyuls and Collioure, producing wines under both appellations along with a vin de pays white. The majority of the fortified production is relatively ordinary and the Collioure bottlings are sound rather than really inspiring, although the domaine wines are altogether more serious. The top Banyuls Grand Cru *cuvées,* though, are a big step up in quality and are labelled Cuvées de Prestige. These are wines with a real nutty complexity and often marked by a dry tangy finish. The Henri Caris is a *demi-sec* style. (DM)

● **Collioure** Château des Abelles★★ £C Abbaye de Valbonne★★ £C
● **Banyuls Grand Cru** Henri Caris★★★ £E Henri Vidal★★★★ £E Vivianne Lerof ★★★ £E

CH. DE BELLET Bellet chateaudebellet@aol.com

Owner: Ghislain de Charnacé Quartier Saint-Roman, 440 Route de Saquier, 06200 Nice
One of a handful of properties in the tiny appellation of Bellet in the Provençal hills inland of Nice. As at neighbouring CHATEAU DE CRÉMAT, a red, white and rosé are produced. Because the vineyards are in a protected *mesoclimate* and planted at altitude, they are cooler than their southerly location would suggest. This enables Chardonnay to ripen successfully as well as the local Rolle that completes the white blend. The red and rosé are produced from Folle Noire, Bracquet, Cinsaut and Grenache. The Bracquet variety can also be found further east in Piedmont in Italy, where it is known as Brachetto. The wines are good; the red perfumed, supple and approachable and the white lightly floral and aromatic with an underlying nutty character. They may be approached young but will benefit from a year or two in the cellar. The rosé should be drunk young. (DM)

● **Bellet**★★ £D O **Bellet**★★ £D ◉ **Bellet**★ £C

CH. CAPITOUL Coteaux du Languedoc La Clape www.chateau-capitoul.com

Owner: Charles Hock Route de Gruissan, 11000 Narbonne
The bulk of the production at this organically farmed 65 ha property is red and white Coteaux du Languedoc La Clape, with some rosé produced as well under the same appellation. The Lavandines white blends Marsanne and Roussanne while the more complex barrel aged Rocailles adds Viognier, to mostly Roussanne. The Les Lavandines red is almost equal proportions of Grenache, Syrah and Carignan whereas the striking Les Rocailles is 40 per cent Grenache, 40 per cent Mourvèdre and 20 per cent Carignan adding some peppery spice. Richly concentrated, the wine is given a very lengthy period on skins for up to 45 days and is aged in *cuve* using micro-oxygenation rather than racking during *élevage*. It offers very good value for money. A small volume red, mainly Mourvèdre and Carignan, Maelma is also produced as are two luscious late harvest Viogniers, Les Oubliées and Les Tardives. The yield for Les Oubliées is barely more than 5 hl/ha. Not surprisingly fewer than 60 cases are produced. (DM)

● **Coteaux du Languedoc Pic Saint-Loup** Les Lavandines★ £B Les Rocailles★★★ £C
O **Coteaux du Languedoc** Les Rocailles★★ £B

CH. DE CAZENEUVE Coteaux du Languedoc Pic Saint-Loup A: CBg,Bal,Lay

Owner: André Leenhardt 34270 Lauret
First class Languedoc property with some 35 ha under vine. Since acquiring Cazeneuve in the late

1980s André Leenhardt has been actively planting the top red Rhône varieties. His reds come in a number of guises. Syrah features strongly in the blend of Les Calcaires and the oak-aged Le Roc des Mates. Le Sang du Calcaire, now the top red, is an individual selection of the best the harvest has to offer. It too is aged in oak. The white is a stylish, nutty barrel-fermented blend of Roussanne, Grenache Blanc and Viognier. Top reds are ageworthy. (DM)

● **Coteaux du Languedoc Pic Saint-Loup** Les Terres Rouges★ £B Les Calcaires★★ £B
● **Coteaux du Languedoc Pic Saint-Loup** le Roc des Mates★★★ £C
○ **Coteaux du Languedoc Pic Saint-Loup**★ £B

CH. DES ESTANILLES Faugères   A: THt

Owner: Michel Louison   Lenthéric, 34480 Caberolles

Michel Louison produces upwards of 15,000 cases of Faugères and a white Coteaux du Languedoc each year, a sizeable production for a high quality Midi property. Syrah now dominates the plantings and, as with the wines of Jean-Michel ALQUIER, the variety is notably successful here. Grenache and Mourvèdre are also important among the reds and the white is a blend of Marsanne, Roussanne and Viognier. The Préstige and Syrah cuvées, the latter seeing around a year in oak, will both stand some age, while the other wines are best approached young. (DM)

● **Faugères** Tradition★ £B Préstige★★ £B Cuvée Syrah★★★ £C
○ **Coteaux du Languedoc**★ £B
◉ **Faugères**★ £B

CH. L'EUZIÈRE Coteaux du Languedoc Pic Saint-Loup   A: Lib

Owner: Michel & Marcel Causse   34270 Fontanes

The Causse siblings are, in fact, the fourth generation of vinegrowers at this impressive Languedoc property but it is only much more recently that they have established themselves as quality wine producers. They have some 22 ha under vine and produce around 5,000 cases a year. A good nutty, lightly floral white, Grains de Lune, is produced from young vines – the average age is still only six years – and is an unusual blend of Roussanne, Vermentino, Rolle and Grenache Blanc. After *macération pelliculaire* it is cool-fermented with limited lees-ageing. Of the three reds, Cuvée Tourmaline is a blend of Syrah and Grenache, whereas the more serious and structured Cuvées l'Almandin and Les Escarboucles are neither fined nor filtered and have a small dollop of Mourvèdre. They are both marvellously expressive with a fine balance of herb, spice and complex berry fruits and each will benefit from three or four years' ageing. (DM)

● **Coteaux du Languedoc** La Tourmaline★★ £B
● **Coteaux du Languedoc Pic Saint-Loup** Cuvée l'Almandin★★★ £B Cuvée Les Escarboucles★★★ £B
○ **Coteaux du Languedoc** Grains de Lune★★ £B

CH. GRÈS SAINT-PAUL Coteaux du Languedoc www.gres-saint-paul.com   A: FCA

Owner: Jean-Philippe Servière   Route de Restinclières, 34400 Lunel

Small to medium sized property with 24 ha of vineyards which are farmed along organic lines. Total production is now around 10,000 cases a year. An extensive range of wines is produced including some straightforward well-priced, fruit-driven Vin de Pays Chardonnay, Sauvignon Blanc and Merlot. It is the red Coteaux du Languedoc wines that are most important though from a quality point of view. Of the four cuvées La Grange Philippe is 90 per cent Syrah and 10 per cent Grenache and is vinified with some *macération carbonique* for the Syrah. It is soft, brambly and forward. Romanis, like all the red Languedocs, is dominated by Syrah with Grenache and Mourvèdre. Aged for 12 months in *cuve*, it is denser, more structured. The excellent value Antonin is between 80 and 90 per cent Syrah, the balance Grenache and Mourvèdre. The wine, produced from a yield of 25 to 30 hl/ha is dark, concentrated and spicy with subtle hints of black pepper and just a touch of oak spice from the 16 months spent in one-third new barrels. The top wine is the impressive but pricey Syrhus, a varietal Syrah produced from a yield of less than 20 hl/ha. It needs two or three years cellaring to integrate the 100 per cent new oak it is aged in. Of the sweet white Muscats the Bohémienne has moderate depth, the Sévillane greater weight and intensity. These are well made but lack the depth of a good Muscat de Rivesaltes. (DM)

● **Coteaux du Languedoc** Syrhus★★★ £E Antonin★★★ £C Romanis★★ £B La Grange Phlippe★★ £B
○ **Muscat de Lunel** Sévillane★★ £B ○ **Muscat Moelleux** Bohémienne★ £B

CH. DE JONQUIÈRES   Coteaux du Languedoc

Owner: Isabelle & François de Cabissole   34725 Jonquières
This 23-ha property located in the foothills of the Plateau de Gassac now has 19 ha planted to vines. The small range includes a good straightforward white, which is barrel-fermented and aged with *battonage* and has the malolactic blocked to preserve freshness. There is a juicy, soft, easygoing Vin de Pays de l'Hérault red Domaine de Jonquières dominated by Cinsault and Carignan, along with a more serious Coteaux du Languedoc and the Syrah-dominated Renaissance. The top two red labels are dark, powerful and supple wines with a sufficiently firm structure and depth to ensure limited bottle-development with age, while at the same time retaining their core vibrant fruit quality. (DM)

● **Vin de Pays de l'Hérault** Domaine de Jonquières★★ £B
● **Coteaux du Languedoc**★★★ £C
○ **Coteaux du Languedoc**★ £B

CH. MAS NEUF   Costières de Nîmes   www.chateaumasneuf.com

Owner: Luc Baudet   30600 Gallician
Luc Baudet has a sizeable property of 60 ha, 53 ha of which are planted to red varieties. Of the whites the regular Costières de Nîmes is straightforward and fruity with some nutty, spicy tones. Richer and fuller are the Compostelle Blanc, a blend of Grenache Blanc and Roussanne which is lent some additional weight from ageing in oak, and the Vin de Pays Chardonnay/Viognier blend which is leaner but more aromatic. The regular red is a sturdy, forward blend of Syrah, Grenache, Mourvèdre and a hint of Carignan adding some herbal spice notes. The Compostelle red is a serious step up: a blend of Syrah, Grenache and Mourvèdre it is neither fined nor filtered and is aged in barriques for eight to 12 months. It will benefit from two or three years further cellaring. (DM)

● **Costières de Nîmes**★★ £B Compostelle★★★ £C
○ **Costières de Nîmes** Compostelle★★ £B ○ **Vin de Pays d'Oc** Chardonnay/Viognier★★ £B

CH. MOURGUES DU GRÈS   Costières de Nîmes   mourguesdugres@wanadoo.fr   A:WTs

Owner: François Collard   Route de Bellegarde, 30300 Beaucaire
Some 20,000 cases of red, white and rosé are now made here each year. As one would expect the majority of planting is to red varieties, mainly Syrah. Galets is the label for the basic red, white and rosé and these are straightforward wines characterised by their approachable, forward fruit. The second tier Terre d'Argence wines are more serious. There is a nutty, floral white dominated by Roussanne and a dense, powerful red. The top wine is Capitelles des Mourgues, which spends a year in barrel. There is also a premium rosé under the same label. The top reds will improve with short ageing. (DM)

● **Costières de Nîmes** Galets Rouge★★ £B Terre d'Argence★★★ £B Capitelles des Mourgues★★★ £C
○ **Costières de Nîmes** Terre d'Argence★★ £B

CH. D'OR ET DE GUEULES   Costières de Nîmes   www.chateau-or-et-gueules.com

Owner: Diane de Puymorin   Chemin des Cassagnes, Route de Générac, 30800 Saint-Gilles
This property was very recently established in 1998 and the wines appear to be improving with every vintage. The vineyards have an excellent south-to south-east exposure and its large pebbles and stones retain heat well, aiding ripening. A couple of rosés are produced including a Cuvée Trassegum which is part barrel-fermented. The Cep de Diane Chardonnay is full, rich and toasty, with an almost toffeed character. It is vinified in barrel on lees. There are two lower level Costières de Nîmes reds. The Tradition has more dimension than the Classique, it blends Grenache, Carignan and Mourvèdre. Some of the Carignan being very old and adding real, dark and spicy complexity. Les Cimels produced from yields of 35 hl/ha blends Syrah with very old Carignan. The wine is dark, spicy and full of old viney character. Top of the line are the Cuvee Trassegum red (formerly Cuvée Prestige) and La Bolida. Trassegum is now aged in less oak than in the debut 1998 vintage and is the better for it. La Bolida is a blend of 90 per cent very old Mourvèdre and 10 per cent Syrah. Rich and supple it could do with just a little more refinement but is a wine of great potential. (DM)

● **Costières de Nîmes** Tradition★★ £B Les Cimels★★ £B Cuvée Trassegum★★★ £C
● **Costières de Nîmes** La Bolida★★★ £D
O **Vin de Pays d'Oc** Le Ceps de Diane★★★ £C

CH. DE PIBARNON   Bandol   pibarnon@wanadoo.fr   A: Bal, ABy

Owner: Eric de Saint-Victor   410, Chemin de la Croix-des-Signaux, 83740 La Cadière d'Azur
One of the two best and most established properties in the appellation, the other being Domaine TEMPIER. The style of wine is quite different, though. The red here is powerful and structured, very backward in its youth, requiring up to a decade to fully develop. A very large proportion of Mourvèdre (90 to 95 per cent) accounts for the dark, brambly and mineral style of its wine, dense but very, very refined as well. The site is ideal for ripening the variety; well drained, limestone-based soils and vineyards that are cooled by elevation as well as being very sunny, ensure fruit loaded with intense flavour and fine, well-ripened tannins. The 2001 looks to be quite exceptional. While the red excels, the white and rosé are a touch less exciting but good nonetheless. (DM)

● **Bandol★★★★** £D O **Bandol★★** £C
◉ **Bandol★** £C

CH. PRADEAUX   Bandol   A: HHB

Owner: Cyrille Portallis   676 Chemin des Pradeaux, 83270 Saint-Cyr-sur-Mer
Just over 4,000 cases of red are made here from 20 ha of prime Bandol vineyard that is permanently being encroached upon by urban planners. A small amount of rosé is also produced. The blend is almost exclusively Mourvèdre with a little Grenache. Traditionally vinified, the fruit is not de-stemmed, and the wine is aged in large wooden *foudres* for over three years which helps in softening its raw youthful tannin. It is a wine that demands a minimum of six to seven years in the cellar. Anything less would be to miss the point of it. (DM)

● **Bandol★★★★** £D

CH. ROUTAS   Coteaux Varois   www.routas.com   A: Col

Owner: Philippe Bieler   Chateauvert, 83149 Bras
Established now for upwards of a decade, Routas is located in the wild inland Provençal hills of the Coteaux Varois and has vineyards that are just that bit cooler than its neighbours'. Philippe Bieler

has invested considerably in both the vineyard and the cellar, with state of the art vinification equipment and consultancy advice from Bob Lindquist of QUPE in California. Production now runs at around 20,000 cases and the wines, particularly the top reds, are good to very good. Fashioned in a full but approachable style, they will nevertheless improve with some cellar time. Infernet is a blend of Grenache, Syrah and Cabernet Sauvignon whereas Agrippa is just Syrah and Cabernet Sauvignon. Pyramus is a typical white blend of southern French grapes. The two best wines truly stand out: Cyrano, a spicy, smoky 100 per cent Syrah, and Coquelicot, a nutty, subtly oaked, herb-scented blend of Viognier and Chardonnay. (DM)

● **Coteaux Varois** Carignane★★ £B Wild Boar Cabernet Sauvignon★★ £B
● **Coteaux Varois** Cuvée Infernet★★★ £C Cuvée Agrippa★★★ £C
● **Vin de Pays du Var** Cuvée Cyrano★★★ £C
O **Coteaux Varois** Cuvée Pyramus★★ £B
O **Vin de Pays du Var** Cuvée Coquelicot★★★ £C

CH. SIMONE Palette   A: Yap, Vig

Owner: Rougier family 13590 Meyreuil
This is the benchmark property in the tiny appellation of Palette just outside Aix-en-Provence. The property has around 17 ha of vineyard and there are a bewildering number of permitted red varieties under the appellation regulations. Small quantities of some of the rarer ones are still planted but the emphasis is increasingly on Grenache, Mourvèdre and Syrah. White varieties are dominated by Clairette and it is the white which is the most exciting of the wines. Full, rich and decidedly old fashioned, it nevertheless possesses some marvellous nutty, spicy and honeyed notes which increase with age. The red is good but can be somewhat rustic and four-square. There's a small amount of decent but pricy rosé. (DM)

● **Palette★★★ £E** O **Palette★★★★ £E**

CH. VANNIÈRES Bandol www.chateauvannieres.com   A: C&O

Owner: Colette & Eric Boisseaux 83740 La Cadière d'Azur
One of the best of the current generation of Bandol producers. Along with the likes of CHATEAU PRADEAUX and Domaine du GROS NORÉ this is another property that's knocking on the door of PIBARNON and TEMPIER. The wine is a powerful but stylish example of the appellation. All its intense, dark-berry Mourvèdre character and intense herbal, garrigue scents will shine through when the tannin has had time to soften and the wine achieves real balance and harmony. Good floral white Bandol is produced along with a good rosé and recently a red Côtes de Provence, a junior version of the *grand vin*.

● **Bandol★★★★ £E**

CH. LA VOULTE-GASPARETS Corbières   A: C&C

Owner: Patrick Reverdy 11200 Boutenac
One of the longer-established quality producers in Corbières, whose wine is distributed and marketed by VAL D'ORBIEU. There are 42 ha under vine and decent regular red and white are produced, along with two special *cuvées*, Réservé and Romain Parc. The Réservé is good, stylish and shows some class and refinement but the Romain Parc is clearly the benchmark wine here. Quality is helped by some very old vines, and the wine displays a rich, savoury concentration with marked vanilla oak and real complexity. A powerful spicy red that will age well in the medium term. (DM)

● **Corbières** Cuvée Réservé★★ £B Cuvée Romain Pauc★★★ £C

DOM. DES CHÊNES Côtes du Roussillon-Villages A: L&S

Owner: Razungles & Fils 7 Rue de Maréchal-Joffre, 66600 Vingrau
The 38 ha under vine here is fairly evenly divided between red and white and 8,000 or so cases are
produced. Sturdy Côtes du Roussillon-Villages red, Alzines is a blend of varieties, Grands Mères is
vinified from Carignan and the rich and spicy Tautavel from Syrah and Mourvèdre. A limited-release
Carissa is produced from the latter. Stylish barrel-fermented white vin de pays is joined by an impressive
white Côtes du Roussillon Magdaleniens. The range is completed by a Muscat and two well priced
Rivesaltes fortifieds. (DM)
- ● **Côtes du Roussillon-Villages** Grands Mères★ £B Alzines★★ £B Tautavel★★★ £C
- ● **Rivesaltes** Ambré★★ £B Tuilé★★★ £C
- O **Vin de Pays** Val d'Agly Sorbiers★★ £B
- O **Muscat de Rivesaltes★★★** £B

DOM. CLAVEL Coteaux du Languedoc A: CBg, N&P, Odd, Tan

Owner: Pierre Clavel 34160 Saint-Bauzilles de Montimes
This property is situated just beyond the suburbs of the city of Montpellier. Some 40 ha are planted
to Syrah, Grenache, Mourvèdre and Carignan among the reds, along with white varieties Roussanne,
Grenache Blanc and Rolle. The latter are blended into a lightly herb-scented, nutty, fruit-driven
white. It is the reds, though, that stand out here. Both Le Mas and Les Garrigues are ripe and
sturdy with well integrated, dark blackberry and herb-spiced fruit and supple tannin, while the
old-vine Copa Santa, regularly on the cusp of four stars, is a splendid ageworthy blend of Syrah,
Grenache and Mourvèdre. (DM)
- ● **Coteaux du Languedoc** Le Mas★ £B Les Garrigues★★ £B Copa Santa★★★ £C

CLOS CENTEILLES Minervois

Owner: Daniel & Patricia Domergue 34210 Siran
Stylish Minervois has been produced at this property for a decade and the Domergues have been
established considerably longer than some of their competitors who go for a much fuller and more
extracted style. There is a minimum of new wood here and the wines are restrained, intentionally so,
but are good and well-crafted, with elegant fruit and well-honed and ripened tannins. A number of
cuvées are produced. Carignanissime is made from 100 per cent old-vine Carignan vinified in part
by *macération carbonique.* It shows just what old-vine Carignan properly ripened can achieve.
Capitelle de Centeilles is a juicy, vibrant 100 per cent Cinsault that, like Carignanissime, is aged for
a couple of years in *cuve* before bottling. Campagne de Centeilles is a straightforward soft, fruit-
driven blend of Cinsault and a little Syrah. The top wine is the Minervois La Livinière which is
structured and refined and needs three to four years. The Guigniers de Centeilles Pinot Noir is less
impressive, possessing relatively simple red-berry fruit and a touch one dimensional. (DM)
- ● **Minervois** Campagne de Centeilles★ £B Carignanissime★★ £B Capitelle de Centeilles★★ £B
- ● **Minervois** La Livinière★★ £C

DOM. DU CLOS DES FÉES Côtes du Roussillon-Villages www.closdesfees.com A: Odd

Owner: Claudine & Hervé Bizeul 69 Rue du Maréchal-Joffre, 66600 Vingrau
Very impressive newly established domaine producing good to stunning red Roussillons from 11 ha
of Carignan, Grenache, Syrah, Mourvèdre and Lladoner Pelut; the latter is not exactly a regular point
of discussion around most dinner tables. Even the entry level Les Sorcières is full of dark, spicy

bramble and herbs. Approachable and supple, it is mainly aged in *cuve* with a small portion put in new oak. The Vieilles Vignes, a blend produced from very old vines, many 50 to 100 years old, is not racked; instead micro-oxygenation is used, as it is with Le Clos des Fées, the domaine's flagship wine. The latter is a blend of Syrah, Mourvèdre, Grenache and Carignan aged in oak for 18 months. A tiny amount of a remarkable 100 per cent Grenache, La Petite Sibérie, is also produced. Very intense and concentrated, it displays more piercing pure berry-fruit intensity than a top Châteauneuf-du-Pape but is softer and more approachable and is very stylish indeed. The vineyard plot of some 1 ha and 17 ares yields a mere 175 cases of this wine a year. (DM)

- **Côtes du Roussillon-Villages** Les Sorcières★★£B Vieilles Vignes★★★£D
- **Côtes du Roussillon-Villages** Clos des Fées★★★★£E La Petite Sibérie★★★★★£F

DOM. DE LA COURTADE Côtes de Provence   A: Vig, GBa

Owner: Henri Vidal   83400 Ile-de-Porquerolles
The Ile de Porquerolles is best known as a secluded destination for holidaying Mediterranean yachtsmen. The island lies off the coast of Provence between Bandol and Saint-Tropez. There are some 30 ha of vines, 13 ha of them the white Rolle. This is used exclusively to vinify the white Côtes de Provence, which is lightly oaked and displays some ripe tropical notes as well as a more typically southern nutty character. It will stand a little age as will the red Alycastre, which is the second wine here, produced to ensure the integrity of the red *grand vin*. The latter is a rich, brambly, spicy blend of Mourvèdre, Grenache and Syrah and is impressive, concentrated and worth seeking out. (DM)

- **Côtes de Provence**★★★£D Alycastre★★£B
- O **Côtes de Provence**★★£D

DOM. FONT CAUDE Coteaux du Languedoc Montpeyroux

Owner: Alain Chabanon   34150 Lagamas
From his small Montpeyroux property Alain Chabanon produces somewhat less than 3,000 cases a year of three very good reds and a tiny amount of a white labelled Trelans that is classified as vin de table. The Vin de Pays d'Oc Merle aux Alouettes is a fleshy, vibrant Merlot aged in *cuve* to emphasise its plum and blackberry fruit, which is nicely supported by fine, well-rounded tannins. The supple and well-structured Les Boissières is produced from Grenache. It is ripe and bold with an impressive depth of fruit. The third red is L'Esprit de Font Caude. Generally produced from a blend of Syrah and Mourvèdre this is a marvellously rich, dense red, full of smoky dark berry fruit and just a subtle hint of oak. In 2001 the wine was dominated by Mourvèdre rather than Syrah, although there was some of the latter in the blend and the wine showed more elegance and less overt concentration and extract. It will be interesting to see how the style develops here. (DM)

- **Coteaux du Languedoc Montpeyroux** Les Boissieres★★★£C L'Esprit de Font Caude★★★£D
- **Vin de Pays d'Oc** Merle aux Alouettes★★★£D

DOM. FONTANEL Côtes du Roussillon-Villages

Owner: Pierre Fontanel   25 avenue Jean-Jaurés, 66720 Tautavel
A good small range of wine is produced in the commune of Tautavel by the Fontanels, who have a total of some 35 ha from which they produce approaching 15,000 cases a year. Rich and heady fortifieds are fine examples and good value for money, as are the two Roussillon reds. Cistes is the lighter of the two, with upfront, nicely ripe brambly, spicy fruit, whereas the Prieuré is denser and more powerful, a real medium-term cellaring prospect. However it shows remarkably well in its youth, with opulent dark-berry fruit and a velvety, rounded, supple texture. (DM)

● **Côtes du Roussillon-Villages** Cistes★★ £B Prieuré★★★ £B
● **Rivesaltes** ★★★ £B O **Muscat de Rivesaltes**★★★ £B

DOM. GARDIES Côtes du Roussillon-Villages   A: GVF, Bal, Odd

Owner: Jean Gardies 1 Rue Millères, 66600 Vingrau
A really first class 30-ha property among an increasing number in this exciting appellation. Some good Muscat de Rivesaltes is produced here but it is the reds which are particularly noteworthy. The property has superbly drained limestone and schistous soils and these provide ideal growing conditions. The Millères, a blend of all four red varieties, is vibrant and approachable. The Vieilles Vignes has a high proportion of Grenache from old vines while La Torre is a massive and dense dark, brooding mix of Mourvèdre and Carignan. The most expensive wine, La Falaise is an extremely ageworthy and powerful expression of Syrah. (DM)

● **Côtes du Roussillon-Villages** Millères★★★ £B Vieilles Vignes★★★ £C
● **Côtes du Roussillon-Villages** La Torre★★★★ £D Falaises★★★★ £E

DOM. GAUBY Côtes du Roussillon-Villages   A: A&B, F&R, Rae

Owner: Gérard Gauby La Faradjal, 66600 Calce
Gérard Gauby and his wife Ghislaine produce a stunning range of reds and whites from the Roussillon. The white La Jasse is a crisp, piercing dry Muscat, the Vieilles Vignes a powerful nutty blend of southern varieties including Grenache Blanc, Maccabeo and Viognier, a wine of depth and great value for money. The top white Coume Gineste is sourced from a single vineyard and is produced from Grenache Blanc. Among the reds Les Calcinaires is a juicy, vibrant red made from Grenache, Syrah and Carignan and laden with sumptuous raspberry fruit, while the marvellous Vieilles Vignes is a structured dense, powerful expression of intensely complex old-vine Grenache and Carignan with a smattering of Syrah, Mourvèdre and Cinsault. The top red, and among the most expensive wines in the South of France, is the magnificent Muntada. This is a superbly crafted Syrah, very rich, concentrated and powerful but increasingly refined and no doubt very long lived. (DM)

● **Côtes du Roussillon** Les Calcinaires★★ £B
● **Côtes du Roussillon-Villages** Vieilles Vignes★★★★ £D Muntada★★★★★ £F
O **Vin de Pays de Côtes Catalanes** La Jasse★★ £B Vieille Vignes★★★ £C Coume Gineste★★★★ £E

DOM. DE LA GRANGE DES PÈRES Vin de Pays de l'Hérault   A: Vig, Gun

Owner: Laurent Vaillé 34150 Aniane
The wine here now rivals the long-established leader among Languedoc-Roussillon producers, MAS DE DAUMAS GASSAC. There is no doubt that Grange des Pères is every bit as impressive as its near neighbour. The production is much smaller, though, and Laurent Vaillé has just 10 ha under vine, the majority planted to Mourvèdre, Syrah and Cabernet Sauvignon farmed to almost organic standards. The wine is surprisingly approachable in its youth but has all the density, velvety tannin and class to age gracefully. Although matured in 100 per cent new oak this is very well-integrated and the wine is, of course, bottled without fining or filtration. There is a tiny amount of a very fine Roussanne-based white with equally deftly handled oak. (DM)

● **Vin de Pays de l'Hérault**★★★★★ £F

DOM. DU GROS NORÉ   Bandol   www.gros-nore.com   A: Vig

Owner: Alain Pascal   675 Chemin de l'Argile, 83740 La Cadière d'Azur
The first vintage at this newly established Bandol producer was as recent as 1997, but it was still one of real class and style. Almost all of the 11.5 ha are planted to red varieties but a small amount of white is also produced, a typically fat wine with broad, warm, nutty fruit, as well as a reasonable rosé. It is the red Bandol, though, that is the important wine here. It is a big, brooding unfiltered blend of Mourvèdre, Grenache and Cinsault and full of dark, savoury, roasted aromas with real intensity. Backward in its youth it needs time. Very characterful and likely to improve in bottle for up to a decade or more. (DM)

● Bandol★★★★£C   O Bandol★★£C

DOM. DE L'HORTUS   Coteaux du Languedoc Pic Saint-Loup   A: CdP, L&S, HHB

Owner: Jean Orliac   34270 Valflaunes
Jean Orliac established this 54-ha property in the late 1970s but only began producing wine himself in 1990. This is now one of the benchmark producers for Pic Saint-Loup, an appellation with a depressingly large number of average wines that should be better. The red Grande Cuvée, blended mainly from Syrah and Mourvèdre, is aged in two-thirds new wood but is surprisingly tight and restrained in its youth. The Grande Cuvée white is ripe, almost tropical and produced from barrel-fermented and aged Viognier and Chardonnay. There is a second label, Bergerie de l'Hortus which offers decent value with an approachable straightforward red and white. (DM)

● Coteaux du Languedoc Pic Saint-Loup Grande Cuvée★★★£C
O Vin de Pays Val de Montferrand Grande Cuvée★★★£C

DOM. LA BASTIDE BLANCHE   Bandol   bastide.blanche@libertysurf.fr

Owner: EARL Bronzo   367 Route des Oratoires, 83330 Sainte-Anne-du-Castellet
Red, white and rosé are produced under the Bandol AC at this 28 ha property, established by the Bronzo family over 30 years ago. The vineyards are cultivated largely organically and great care is taken at harvesting in selecting the best fruit. The three reds here inevitably stand out. The sturdy Longue Garde is around three-quarters Grenache with the balance Mourvèdre. Both the Fontanieu and Estagnol are Mourvèdre bottlings. These last two wines are produced from vines grown on different soils. The reds will all develop very well for a decade or longer and require cellaring for four or five years. (DM)

● Bandol Longue Garde★★★£C Fontanieu★★★★£D Estagnol★★★★£D

DOM. LAFRAN VEYROLLES   Bandol   A: Vig

Owner: Mme Jouve-Férec   2115 Route de l'Aigle, 83740 La Cadière-d'Azur
Very impressive red Bandol is now being made at this 10 ha property, with production small at less than 4,000 cases per year. Mourvèdre dominates the red plantings, while the whites are a mix of Clairette and Ugni Blanc. The vineyards are farmed organically and the argile-calcareous soils provide an excellent base for growing fruit of the highest quality. The white is one of the better examples produced in the appellation as is the softly strawberry-scented rosé. It is the two reds with their sizeable Mourvèdre component that stand out though. Both are dense, powerful and finely structured. Firm youthful tannin will be seamlessly integrated with five or six years ageing. 2001 looks to be quite exceptional with the Tradition, effortlessly of five star quality. (DM)

● **Bandol** Tradition★★★★ £D   Spéciale★★★★ £D
◉ **Bandol** ★ £C

DOM. LA TOUR VIEILLE   Banyuls & Collioure   A: Yap

Owner: Vincent Cantié & Christine Campadieu 66190 Collioure
Well-established producer of both Collioure and Banyuls, the quality of which is consistently good.
There are two red labels as well as a nutty honeyed white, Les Canadells, blended from Grenache
Gris and Blanc as well as some Maccabeo. The red La Pinède, from Grenache, Carignan and
Mourvèdre is a full, dense, spicy black-fruit style, while the Puig Oriol, which is 70 per cent
Grenache and the balance Syrah, is more fragrant with a marvellous garrigue scent to the deep berry
fruit, the Grenache very prominent. Good Banyuls comes in two guises: the Cuvée Francis Cantié is
the more serious with sophisticated nutty *rancio* characters from extended time in cask. (DM)
● **Collioure** La Pinède★★ £B   Puig Oriol★★★ £C
● **Banyuls** Cuvée Francis Cantié★★★ £C
O **Vin de Pays de la Côte Vermeille** Les Canadells★★★ £C

DOM. LEA   Vin de Pays de Gard   www.domaine-lea.com

Owner: Vincent Auquier 30260 Cannes et Clairan
Very new small property of some 18 ha planted to a range of varieties including Cabernet Sauvignon,
Syrah, Grenache, Cinsault and Carignan among the reds, along with Sauvignon Blanc, Chardonnay
and Ugni Blanc. At present just one wine is produced, a blend of Merlot and Syrah. Broad, fleshy
and approachable with black fruits, pepper and spice, this is marked by its fruit more than anything
and the wine is excellent value. Vinification is carefully controlled and temperature during the
20-day maceration is restricted to ensure its style. (DM)
● **Vin de Pays d'Oc**★★ £B

DOM. LES CREISSES   Vin de Pays de l'Hérault   A: Vig

Owner: Philippe Chesnelong 34290 Valros
Recently established domaine just outside the village of Valros, inland to the north-east of Béziers. Just
two reds are produced here. The regular Domaine Les Creisses bottling is a blend of Syrah, Grenache
and Cabernet Sauvignon. Produced from grapes grown in calcareous soils, the wine has excellent
definition and structure with just a slight raw edge to its youthful tannin. It will be better with two
or three years' ageing. Les Brunes is a considerable step up in quality and has a price tag to match.
Approaching four stars, this is a dense, rich, cedary blend of Cabernet Sauvignon and Syrah. 1999 was
the third vintage and as yet there is a feeling that the structure overpowers the wine. Great potential
here, though. (DM)
● **Vin de Pays d'Oc** Les Creisses★★ £B   Les Brunes★★★ £D

DOM. DE LA MARFÉE   Coteaux du Languedoc   A: Vig

Owner: Thierry Hasard 34570 Murviel-lès-Montpellier
Very small new property: the first vintage was in 1997, with just 6-ha of vines. Two wines are
produced and they are sturdy, powerful and very extracted in style. There is no doubt that there is
real depth and power and an absolute commitment to quality but at the moment here I feel the tannin
plays a greater role than it should. Les Champs Murmurés is a southern Rhône-style blend with some
Cabernet Sauvignon thrown in, while Les Vignes qu'on Abat is dominated by old-vine Carignan.

With a little more refinement these could be very classy wines indeed. (DM)

● **Coteaux du Languedoc** Les Champs Murmurés★★★ £D   Les Vignes qu'on Abat★★★ £D

MAS AMIEL Maury   A: L&S

Owner: Olivier Decelle 66460 Maury

A historic 155-ha property that is understandably best known for its remarkable range of Maury *vins doux naturels*. Two stylish and impressive red Côtes du Roussillons are also produced here in addition to a well-priced, vibrant vin de pays, Plaisir, and a white Côtes du Roussillon. The two Roussillon reds are impressively large, structured wines. The range of fortified Maury is extensive from young minimally aged current vintages through to old vintage bottles. The top *cuvées* are Réserve, Privilège and the immensely rich Charles Dupuy. The wines are marked by a classic burnt raisiny, toffeed *rancio* character. The top wines are extraordinarily intense. (DM)

● **Côtes du Roussillon** Hautes Terres★★★ £B ● **Côtes du Roussillon-Villages** Carrerade★★★ £C
● **Vin de Pays des Côtes Catalanes** Plaisir★★ £B
● **Maury** 10 Ans d'Age★★★ £C 15 Ans d'Age★★★★ £E
● **Maury** Vintage★★ £C Vintage Réserve★★★ £D Privilège★★★★ £E Charles Dupuy★★★★★ £E
○ **Côtes du Roussillon** Altaïr★★★ £D

DOM. DU MAS BLANC Banyuls & Collioure   A: VTr, C&R

Owner: Jean-Michel Parcé 9 Avenue du Général-de-Gaulle, 66650 Banyuls-sur-Mer

Splendid 21-ha Banyuls and Collioure property developed by the late Dr André Parcé and now run by his son Jean-Michel. There are four Collioures. La Llose is the regular bottling while there are three very fine single-vineyard wines; the Cosprons Levant is an old-vine blend of Mourvèdre, Syrah and Counoise, Clos du Moulin is produced from Mourvèdre and Counoise and Les Junquets is from Syrah with a hint of Roussanne and Marsanne for fragrance. Production of these three is small but they are very impressive, refined reds. Some of the very best Banyuls is also created here. There are two Rimage bottlings that have spent less time in cask, the sumptuous Cuvée de la Saint-Martin, which has intense, nutty, *rancio* notes and the Hors d'Age de Solera, resembling a great old Oloroso from a *solera* of old wines. These are expensive. (DM)

● **Collioure** La Llose★★ £B Clos du Moulin★★★ £C Cosprons Levant★★★ £C
● **Banyuls** Rimage★★★★ £E La Coume★★★★ £F

MAS BRUGUIÈRE Coteaux du Languedoc Pic Saint-Loup   A: HHB

Owner: Guilhem Bruguière La Plaine, 34270 Valflaunes

Guilhem Bruguière is one of the best producers in the Pic Saint-Loup sub-region. This is a small property of just over 9 ha and Guilhem now produces a total of some 4,000 cases a year. Syrah, Grenache and Mourvèdre are grown, along with Roussanne for the white Les Muriers; a nutty, floral, medium-weight spicy white. The basic Cuvée Calcadiz is well-priced but can be raw with some aggressive green notes creeping through. L'Arbouse is round, suppler and fuller while the flagship La Grenadière is a blockbuster red; spicy and dense, with a solid chunk of vanilla oak. (DM)

● **Coteaux du Languedoc Pic Saint-Loup** Cuvée Calcadiz★ £B L'Arbouse★★ £B La Grenadière★★★ £C
○ **Coteaux du Languedoc Pic Saint -Loup** Les Muriers★★ £B

MAS CAL DEMOURA Coteaux du Languedoc   A: GVF

Owner: Jean-Pierre Jullien Chemin du Mas Jullien, 34725 Jonquières
Like so many growers, Jean-Pierre Jullien used to sell his grapes to the local co-op. Now he produces a very good red and a simple, vibrant, berry-fruited rosé from his 6 ha or so, which are all planted to red varieties. It is the cuvée L'Infidèle, though, that is the serious business here, a blend of Syrah, Mourvèdre, Grenache, Cinsault and Carignan, of which the Syrah, Grenache and Mourvèdre see some new oak during the 12 months of ageing. The wine is full, rich and quite extracted, with supple tannins and real depth. The 1999 was particularly good. It will be interesting to see how it ages. (DM)

● **Coteaux du Languedoc** L'Infidèle★★★ £D
◉ **Coteaux du Languedoc** Qu'es Aquo★★ £B

MAS CHAMPART Saint-Chinian   A:RsW, SVS

Owner: Isabelle & Matthieu Champart 34360 Saint-Chinian
There are now 16 ha planted at this fine Saint-Chinian property where the Champarts produce a fruity rosé and a rich, lightly oaked white from Roussanne, Marsanne, Viognier, Bourboulenc and Grenache, as well as four reds. Up until 1988 they sold their crop to the local co-op and a small proportion of the harvest is still sold on. The four reds are blends of different terroirs across the property. The wines are only lightly fined with egg whites while the top two reds are bottled without filtration. The Vin de Pays d'Oc is an unusual blend of Cabernet Franc (80 per cent) with the balance Syrah. It is lightly leafy with attractive ripe berry fruit. The brambly, forward Côte d'Arbo comprises Syrah, old vine Carignan, young Grenache and a tiny amount of Graziano. The top two wines are more serious and firmly structured. Causse du Bouquet blends Syrah with Mourvèdre, Grenache and, in certain vintages, some Carignan. It is aged for a year in barrel and then six months in vat. The impressively dense and concentrated Clos de la Simonette is mainly Mourvèdre with some Grenache. It is aged in oak, some new, for around 18 months. The top two reds will develop well for a decade at least. (DM)

● **Saint-Chinian** Côte d'Arbo★★ £B Causse de Bousque★★★ £B Clos de La Simonette★★★★ £C
● **Vin de Pays d'Oc**★ £B

MAS DE LA DAME Les Baux www.masdeladame.com   A: L&W, HHB, AVn

Owner: Anne Ponitowski & Caroline Missoffe 13520 Les Baux-de-Provence
Good quality producer from Les Baux-de-Provence with 57 ha of vineyards. The property was immortalised by Vincent Van Gogh when he painted it in 1889. As one would expect the great majority of vines are red varieties but there are 5 ha of whites including some Semillon. You can also look out for very good olive oils from the estate's 25 ha of olive groves. A relatively extensive range of wines is made here with consultancy provided by Jean-Luc COLOMBO. The red Réserve and white Cuvée de la Stèle offer reasonable value and straightforward drinking. The Coin Caché white is very stylish, floral, nutty and perfumed, the Cuvée de la Stèle red rich and chunky with hints of garrigue and smoke. The Coin Caché red is a supple, smoky, powerful, old-vine blend of Grenache and Syrah. (DM)

● **Les Baux-de-Provence** Réserve★★ £B Cuvée de la Stèle★★★ £C Coin Caché★★★ £D
○ **Les Baux-de-Provence** Coin Caché★★★ £D
○ **Coteaux d'Aix-en-Provence** Cuvée de la Stèle★★ £B
◉ **Les Baux-de-Provence** Rosé Mas★ £B

MAS DE DAUMAS GASSAC   Vin de Pays de l'Hérault   www.daumas-gassac.com   A: Adm

Owner: Aimé & Véronique Guibert   Guibert de la Vaissière, 34150 Aniane

Undoubtedly the most famous property in the Midi and the inspiration for the many high-quality winemakers now spread throughout Languedoc and Roussillon. There are some 26 ha of red varieties and 12 ha of white. The vineyard potential here in the upper Gassac Valley was discovered in 1970. The key is soil that is mineral-rich, superbly drained and that stresses the vines just sufficiently to produce grapes of remarkable flavour, the key to all great wine. The red is a dense and immensely powerful but refined blend of mainly Cabernet Sauvignon (80 per cent) blended with a plethora of other varieties. Very backward and even austere when young this is best left for a decade or more. The white is an intense, nutty, complex blend dominated by Viognier, Petit Manseng and Chardonnay. Finely structured with a piercing mineral core the wine needs three or four years and will keep comfortably for a great deal longer. A tiny amount of a limited red *cuvée* Emile Peynaud, in honour of the great Bordeaux enology professor, was produced in 2001. Aimé Guibert also produces a range of simple and straightforward wines under the Terrasses label. (DM)

● **Vin de Pays de l'Hérault**★★★★★ £F   O **Vin de Pays de l'Hérault**★★★★★ £F

MAS D'ESPANET   Vin de Pays d'Oc

Owner: Agnès & Denys Armand   30730 Saint-Mamert-du-Gard

The Armand property is located just inland between Picpoul de Pinet and Nîmes. Production is spread across two reds and a white, all of which take the Vin de Pays d'Oc classification. The white Eolienne is a part tank- and part barrel-fermented blend of Sauvignon Blanc, Grenache Blanc and Viognier. The vines are grown in calcareous soils and from a yield of just 25 hl/ha the wine has a fine grassy, nutty intensity and is best enjoyed young. Les Lens is an exuberant, fruit-driven blend of Cinsault, Grenache and Syrah. It displays a marvellous pure strawberry character and will drink well over three to four years. The top red, Bois du Roi, is a Syrah-based oak-aged red. In 1999 it was blended with just Grenache, whereas in 2000 the *assemblage* included 10 per cent Carignan. It is an impressive wine with complexity, a fine balance of dark berry fruit and herbs, subtly oaked with a supple tannic structure. The Carignan adds a greater depth to the wine. It was very good in 2000. (DM)

● **Vin de Pays d'Oc** Les Lens★★ £B Bois du Roi★★★ £C
● **Vin de Pays d'Oc** Eolienne★★ £B

MAS HAUT BUIS   Coteaux du Languedoc

Owner: Olivier Jeantet   34520 Lavacquerie-et-Saint-Martin

The production at Olivier Jeantet's property is tiny, barely more than 1,200 cases a year for just one wine. It is, though, among the better examples in the appellation. Costa Caoude is a blend of Syrah, Grenache and Cabernet Sauvignon. Seventy per cent of the wine is aged in barrique and 30 per cent in *cuve* for up to 12 months. Deep, dense and powerful but with well-judged oak and supple, well-rounded tannins. Balanced and surprisingly refined, the wine is aged for a further year in *demi-muids* before bottling. (DM)

● **Coteaux du Languedoc** Costa Caoude★★★ £D

MAS JULLIEN   Coteaux du Languedoc   A: Vig, Gun

Owner: Olivier Jullien   34725 Jonquières

Now one of the most established properties in the Coteaux du Languedoc. The wine style and indeed the labels have changed over the years. Two reds and a floral white Vin de Pays de l'Hérault are produced and the approach is one of restraint, in quite marked contrast to some of the extracted wines of Olivier Jullien's neighbours. The top Coteaux du Languedoc is tight, restrained and with a refined, intense mineral quality, whereas the États d'Âme is in a supple and forward fruit-driven style. The reds, particularly the Coteaux du Languedoc, should age very well. (DM)

● **Coteaux du Languedoc**★★★ £C États d' Âme★★★£B
O **Vin de Pay de l'Hérault**★★ £C

MAS DE MORTIÈS Coteaux du Languedoc   A: HHB

Owner: Isabelle & Rémi Duchemin Route de Cazevieille, 34270 Saint-Jean-de-Cuculles
This is a very good property with some 20 ha under vine in the southern sector of the Pic Saint-Loup sub-region. The estate has been continually improved over the last six or seven years with a careful replanting programme to improve quality in the vineyard. Good white as well as vibrant dark and chunky Coteaux du Languedoc are produced as well as a first-class Syrah Que Sera Sera. The wines here are very reasonably priced. (DM)

● **Coteaux du Languedoc Pic Saint-Loup** Que Sera Sera★★★ £B

MAS MOURIES Coteaux du Languedoc

Owner: Solange & Eric Bouet 30260 Vic le Fesq
Fine new property located 25 km north-west of Nîmes with organically tended vineyards planted in well-drained calcareous soils. There are two wines produced, both red. Mas Mouries Coteaux du Languedoc is a blend of Syrah and Grenache. The varieties are vinified separately before blending and ageing in *cuve*. The fruit is forward and accessible, but the tannin is just a touch hard – perhaps 30 days vatting is too much here. The top cuvée Les Myrthes, which is aged in part new wood, is of the same blend of Syrah and Grenache but at a lower yield; some 25 hl/ha rather than 40. The wine displays excellent black fruits with nicely handled vanilla oak; in short plenty of depth and class. (DM)

● **Coteaux du Languedoc**★★ £B Les Myrthes★★★ £C

MOULIN DE CIFFRE Saint-Chinian www.moulindeciffre.com   A:WSc

Owner: Bernadette & Jacques Lesineau 34480 Autignac
Small to medium sized estate producing around 10,000 cases a year from 30 ha across a number of appellations. The vineyards are dominated by red varieties with just 1.5 ha planted to Viognier from which a good spicy barrel-fermented Vin de Pays Viognier is produced. Ageing on lees with *bâtonnage* adds extra richness. Reds are produced under three appellations, Coteaux du Languedoc, Saint-Chinian and Faugères. A richly textured Vin de Pays red Val Taurou is also produced from a blend of Cabernet Sauvignon, Syrah and Grenache. The oak aged Saint-Chinian and Faugères cuvées add a round suppler character, while the Eole is a step up. Firmly structured when young this blend of Syrah, Grenache and Mourvèdre, produced from the best parcels the estate has in the AC, is aged in a mix of new and old barriques. The wines offer good value and the Eole and Val Taurou will develop well with three to five years' ageing. (DM)

● **Faugères**★★ £B Élevé en Fûts de Chêne★★ £B Eole★★★ £C
● **Saint-Chinian**★★ £B Élevé en Fûts de Chêne★★ £B
● **Coteaux du Languedoc**★★ £B ● **Vin de Pays des Coteaux de Murviel** Val Taurou★★★ £C
O **Vin de Pays des Coteaux de Murviel** Viognier★★ £C

DOM. DES PERRIÈRES   Costières de Nîmes

Owner: Emmanuelle & Marc Kreydenweiss   30129 Manduel

Marc Kreydenweiss and his wife Emmanuelle are better known for their stylish Alsace domaine but here in the Costières de Nîmes they produce two good to very good elegant reds in quite marked contrast to many of their neighbours. The approach is one of refinement not muscle. Marc Kreydenweiss feels many of the current new wave of Mediterranean reds are over-extracted and alcoholic. How will they age? The Domaine de Grimaud bottling is Emmanuelle's baby and comes from its own 7-ha vineyard. Blended from 50 per cent Carignan, 25 Cinsault and 25 Grenache, it is full of upfront brambly fruit. Domaine des Perrières is a refined and harmonious blend of Carignan, Syrah and Grenache with vines ranging from 25 to 70 years. It has more depth and a firmer structure and will age well for five or six years. (DM)

● **Costières de Nîmes** Domaine des Perrières★★★ £C Domaine de Grimaud★★ £B

DOM. DE PEYRE ROSE   Coteaux du Languedoc

Owner: Marlène Soria   34230 Saint-Pargoire

This 25-ha property is responsible for two of the most renowned reds in the Languedoc and they certainly have a price tag to match their reputation. The vineyard is planted in ideal sparse, rocky soils and there is a commitment to low-yielding fruit of the highest quality. Of the two reds Clos des Cistes has a hint of Grenache and is the more forward of the two. It is supple and full of piercing fruit. Clos Syrah Léone is the more structured, denser, darker and on occasion showing real animal aromas. The wines are certainly very impressive in their youth, although it has to be said very marked by oak and highly extracted in style. It remains to be seen how they will develop. A stylish, nutty white is also now produced from Rolle, Roussanne and Viognier. (DM)

● **Coteaux du Languedoc** Clos de Cistes★★★ £E Clos Syrah Léone★★★ £E

PRIEURÉ DE SAINT-JEAN-DE-BÉBIAN   www.bebian.com   A: RsW

Owner: Chantal Lecouty & Jean-Claude Lebrun   Route de Nizas, 34120 Pezenas

This has long been one of the esteemed names of the Languedoc but it is only in the last few years, under the stewardship of Chantal Lecouty and Jean-Claude Lebrun, that quality has been back to where it was in the mid- to late 1980s. The early 90s were vintages to avoid here. The current estate bottlings of both red from Syrah, Grenache and Mourvèdre and white from mainly Roussanne are very rich and stylish, especially the white. Perhaps the real disappointment is the Chapelle de Bébian, a second wine that has on occasion shown a fierce angular austerity. (DM)

● **Coteaux du Languedoc★★★** £D Chapelle de Bébian★ £B ○ **Coteaux du Languedoc★★★★** £D

DOM. RABIEGA   Côtes de Provence   www.rabiega.com   A: L&S

*Owner: **Vin & Spirit AB Sweden**   Clos d'Ière Méridional, 83300 Draguinan*

Owned by the Swedish Vin & Spirit operation since 1988, this property, along with its sister operation Château d'Esclans, produces good to very good red and white and a fascinating Vin Toussaint sweet red from Carignan. This wine is outside any appellation regulations and therefore labelled as vin de table. The vineyards are planted on limestone and clay soils near Draguignan. The property is farmed organically and there are some 9 ha under vine, with production small at a mere 1,600 to 1,700 cases a year. Volume is around twice this at the leased d'Esclans, where the red Mourbase and Grebase, produced respectively from Mourvèdre and Grenache, stand out. At Rabiega a fine ripe, tropical scented, barrel-fermented white, Clos d'Ière Blanc, produced from Sauvignon Blanc, Chardonnay and Viognier, is impressive, as is the second tier red Clos d'Ière II, a blend of Grenache, Cabernet Sauvignon and Carignan. Pride of place, though, is undoubtedly the Clos d'Ière I, a powerful, dense oak-aged Syrah. (DM)

● **Côtes de Provence** Clos d'Ière I★★★★ £E Clos d'Ière II★★★ £D
● **Vin Toussaint**★★★ £D
O **Vin de Pays du Var** Clos d'Ière★★★ £E

DOM. DE LA RECTORIE Banyuls & Collioure larectorie@wanadoo.fr A: A&B, Bal

Owner: Parcé Frères 54 Avenue du Puig-Delmas, 66650 Banyuls-sur-Mer

One of the finest producers of Collioure and Banyuls. There are three *cuvées* of red Collioure and a presentable rosé. Of the reds Col de Bast is the lightest and made from 100 per cent Grenache, whereas the denser and more structured La Coume Pascole is a blend of Grenache, Syrah and Carignan. The sturdiest of the three, Le Seris is produced from very old Carignan and Grenache vines. Even the latter two are not in any way overblown; they are more wines of refinement and elegance. These are complemented by a white vin de pays, L'Argile, a powerfully oaked Grenache Gris. Very good Banyuls includes two regular *cuvées* – the best is Cuvée Léon Parcé, which is aged for around a year in cask and an altogether different, less evolved style to that found at MAS BLANC – and an aged wine, L'Oublée, which is understandably pricey. (DM)

● **Collioure** Col de Bast★★ £B La Coume Pascole★★★ £D Le Seris★★★ £C
● **Banyuls** Cuvée Léon Parcé★★★ £C
O **Vin de Pays de la Côte Vermeille** L'Argile★★★ £C

DOM. RICHEAUME Côtes de Provence A: BGL

Owner: Henning Hoesch 13114 Puyloubier

Very good estate that has been producing consistently excellent wine under the Côtes de Provence appellation for years. The property consists of some 25 ha planted largely to Cabernet Sauvignon, Syrah, Grenache and Merlot. There is also a little Viognier, from which a decent white is made. The Tradition includes all four red varieties, complemented by fine varietal Cabernet and Syrah bottlings and a splendid *grand vin,* Cuvée Columelle, massive, dense and very concentrated and one of the best reds in Provence. (DM)

● **Côtes de Provence** Tradition★★★ £C Cuvée Columelle★★★★ £D

DOM. RIMBERT Saint-Chinian www.domainerimbert.com A:FWW, SVS

Owner: Jean-Marie Rimbert 4 Avenue des Mimosas, 34360 Berlou

Jean-Marie Rimbert's domaine was only established in 1997 but he is proving to be one of the really exciting producers of the appellation. He now has 20 ha under vine and is producing between 7,000 and 8,000 cases per year. He has some very well-sited terroirs planted in impoverished schistous soils planted to Carignan, Syrah, Grenache, Cinsault and Mourvèdre. Most of the vines are over 40 years and some Carignan is extremely venerable. Three wines are made. There is a good regular Saint-Chinian, Les Travers de Marceau which is blended from 40 per cent each of Carignan and Cinsault, 15 per cent Syrah and 5 per cent Grenache. It is a finely structured, elegant example, not at all over-extracted and with a pure mineral undercurrent running through it. There are also two very fine pure Carignan wines which are simply labelled as Vin de Table. Le Chant de Marjolaine comes from old vines in some of the best parcels, whereas the extraordinary Carignator is blended from two vintages and is sourced from 50 to 70 year old vines and is fermented in barriques. Heady and exotic it is one of the most characterful wines of the region. (DM)

● **Saint Chinian** Les Travers de Marceau★★ £B
● **Carignator**★★★★ £D

DOM. DES SCHISTES Côtes du Roussillon-Villages sire-schistes@wanadoo.fr A: M&V

Owner: Jacques Sire 1 Avenue Jean-Lurçat, 66310 Estagel
A small, first-class range of both table and fortified wines are produced at this 44-ha property. The reds are characterised by the old-vine quality of the fruit, which adds an extra dimension. Indeed some of the oldest vines are approaching 80 years. Tradition is a forward, fruit-driven style blended from Syrah, Grenache and Carignan and vinified both traditionally and with some carbonic maceration. Les Terrasses is produced from the same varieties but with a higher proportion of Syrah aged in one-year-old oak, the balance in *cuve*. Stylish and intense, there is a real mineral quality running through the wine. La Coumeille, the top red, is 100 per cent Syrah, aged in oak of which only a small portion is new and the wine is very fine with a really spicy, dark, intense fruit quality. There's a lovely nutty and raisiny Maury and a very good floral but powerful and concentrated Muscat de Rivesaltes. (DM)

● **Côtes du Roussillon-Villages** Tradition★★ £B Les Terrasses★★★ £B La Coumeille★★★ £C
● **Maury** Cerisaie★★★ £C
○ **Muscat de Rivesaltes**★★★ £B

DOM. SEGUELA Côtes du Roussillon-Villages

Owner: Trinidad & Jean-Pierre Seguela 12 Avenue de Caramany, 66720 Rasiguères
Production is small at this dedicated Roussillon producer, with a total of less than 3,000 cases made annually. Yields are kept very low, fruit is carefully sorted prior to vinification and in the cellar filtration is avoided. What marks these wines out is the depth and purity of their fruit. At present they don't quite have the structure of the very best but are impressive nevertheless. Les Condalies is a blend mainly of Carignan but with some Syrah and Grenache also. Soft easy tannins and spicy brambly fruit mark the style of the wine. Cuvée Jean-Julien is a dense old-vine blend of Syrah and Carignan partly aged in new oak (but this is seamlessly handled), while the Planète-Seguela is an astonishingly low-yielding (as low as 12 hl/ha) *assemblage* of Carignan, Syrah, Grenache and Cinsault and is refined, long and well-structured. (DM)

● **Côtes du Roussillon-Villages** Les Condalies★★ £B Cuvée Jean-Julien★★★ £B Planète-Seguela★★★ £C

SIEUR D'ARQUES Limoux   A: PVF

Owner: 'Co-operative' Avenue de Mauzac, 11303 Limoux
A very sizeable but well organized co-op that produces close to a million cases a year. Its membership controls around 3,000 ha of vineyards, the vast majority of the whole Limoux appellation. Good, well-made Blanquette de Limoux is produced as well as Crémant de Limoux. There is a good lightly oaked regular Chardonnay but the top wines are four well-crafted individual Toques et Clochers bottlings. These are barrel-fermented and aged partly in new wood, on lees and with *bâtonnage*. With a number of decidedly cool mesoclimates within the AC these are surprisingly elegant and tight, with a fine piercing mineral undercurrent to the fruit. (DM)

Toques et Clochers
○ **Chardonnay** Terroir Océanique★★★ £B Terroir d'Autan★★ £B Terroir Haute Vallée★★ £B
○ **Chardonnay** Terroir Méditerranéen★★ £B

DOM. TEMPIER Bandol

A: Sav

Owner: Peyraud family Le Plan du Castellet, 83330 Le Castellet

This is one of the great Bandol producers and has remained so for the past two decades despite the emergence of newer names such as PIBARNON and more recently GROS NORÉ. More than anything these wines are characterised by their elegance and refinement as opposed to the sheer power and density often achieved elsewhere. There are around 28 ha planted to red varieties but a mere 1 ha to white. Along with the five reds there is also a very decent rosé. The regular *cuvée* produced from the youngest vines on the property, though, is somewhat light in comparison to the other wines. Cuvée Spéciale is denser and richer, with altogether greater concentration. It is, though, the three single vineyard wines, La Tourtine, Migoua and Cabassou that stand out. The latter with the highest proportion of Mourvèdre is the sturdiest of the trio, the Migoua the most stylish and elegant. All will age gracefully for well over a decade. (DM)

● **Bandol** Cuvée Classique★★£C Cuvée Spéciale★★★£D
● **Bandol** La Tourtine★★★★£E Migoua★★★★£E Cabassou★★★★★£E
◉ **Bandol**★★£C

DOM. TERRE INCONNUE Gard

Owner: Robert Creus 62 Rue des Albizzias, 34400 Saint Séries

Robert Creus is based in the eastern borders of the Coteaux du Languedoc but has little interest in concerning himself with the bureaucracy of appellation regulations. As a result his tiny production of garage style wines are simply labelled as Vin de Table. His production is still very small but jumped dramatically in 2003 rising to 1,000 cases from the previous vintage which had been a mere 300 or so. He now has 4 ha of vines and these are handled as naturally as possible but he will have no truck with biodynamism. The wines are vinified with a minimum of sulphur and aged in barriques for 16 to 18 months. Handling is by gravity, fining is avoided and the wines are bottled without filtration. There are three main cuvées as well as a second wine Les Bruyères for lots which are not felt to be up to scratch. Léonie is an astonishingly heady and rich 100 per cent Carignan, in many ways the most exciting and shocking of Creus's wines. Los Abuelos is 100 per cent Grenache, rich and characterful, always super ripe. Alcohol levels for any of the top cuvées can easily be 15 per cent or more but always balance and purity are maintained. Sylvie is dominated by Syrah with 12 per cent Grenache and 5 per cent Carignan blended in. More opulent than the wines of the northern Rhone and loaded with super-ripe fruit, perhaps a slightly firmer structure would add a further dimension. The wines are very good value. (DM)

● **Sylvie**★★★★ £E ● **Los Abuelos**★★★★ £E ● **Léonie**★★★★ £D

DOM. DE TERREBRUNE Bandol

Owner: Georges Delille 724 Chemin de la Tourelle, 83190 Ollioulles

The red Bandol produced by Georges Delille from his 25-ha vineyard is a massive, muscular and brooding example of the appellation. The vineyards have an ideal aspect with finely drained calcareous soils and the average vine age is now moving towards 30 years, adding intensity, depth and character to the fruit. This is a true *vin de garde*; a dense smoky, spicy Mourvèdre requiring seven or eight years at a minimum to achieve true balance and harmony. The small amount of rosé and white produced is of a reasonable quality, the latter capable of some age. (DM)

● **Bandol**★★★★ £D
◉ **Bandol**★★ £C O **Bandol**★★ £C

DOM. DE LA TOUR DU BON   Bandol

Owner: Claude Hocquard   714 Chemin des Olivettes, 83330 Le Brûlat-du-Castellet
A small property with just 12 ha planted to vines. Production is small at some 3,500 cases but the quality of the red Bandols is very good indeed. These are stylish, supple and very well crafted and the Saint-Ferréol is finely structured, refined and very long lived; a wine of not only weight and concentration but wonderful herbal intensity. As with so many properties in the appellation, though, the rosé and white are decent and well enough made but lack the interest of the reds. (DM)

● **Bandol**★★★ £D   Saint-Ferréol★★★★ £E
O **Bandol**★★ £C

DOM. DE TREVALLON   Les Baux-de-Provence   www.trevallon.fr   A: Yap

Owner: Eloi Dürrbach   13103 Saint-Étienne-du-Grès
It remains one of the ludicrous features of the appellation contrôlée regulations that this benchmark Provençal red is now only entitled to vin de pays status. Theoretically there should be some Grenache planted but the vineyard with north-facing calcareous slopes will not ripen the variety adequately. The *mesoclimate* here is remarkably cool, much more so than one would imagine. The resulting red blend of Cabernet and Syrah and the tiny amount of white produced (barely more than a couple of barrels) are very impressive and remarkably refined wines. Cask-aging of the red is in large older wood and it needs at least five years to unfurl. The wine is a classic Provençal example of the blend with floral garrigue scents underpinning the concentrated, dark, cedary fruit. The white is a barrel-fermented blend of Marsanne, Roussanne and Chardonnay, very fine and intense with concentrated, lightly floral, nutty fruit. (DM)

● **Vin de Pays des Bouches-du-Rhône**★★★★ £F
O **Vin de Pays des Bouches-du-Rhône**★★★★ £D

VAL D'ORBIEU   Narbonne   A: VOC

Owner: Les Vignerons du Val d'Orbieu   11100 Narbonne
This vast organisation has among its membership many of the major co-ops of the Midi as well as a number of individual growers. Interests spread as far as Bordeaux, where Val d'Orbieu now owns GRAND-PUY-DUCASSE and RAYNE-VIGNEAU among others. It is responsible as well for the marketing and distribution of a number of small quality domaines. These include the Château de Jau in the Roussillon, Clos Paulliles Collioures and fine Corbières produced at CH. LA VOULTE GASPARETS. The prestige Val d'Orbieu label is the Cuvée Mythique, a red blend from varying sources and varieties. It is inevitably labelled as Vin de Pays d'Oc. Good stylish and moderately fleshy, it has reasonable depth for drinking over the short to medium term. (DM)

Val d'Orbieu
● **Vin de Pays d'Oc** Cuvée Mythique★★ £C
O **Vin de Pays d'Oc Chardonnay** Réserve Saint-Martin Vin de Pays d'Oc★ £B

Ch. de Jau
● **Côtes du Roussillon** Talon★★★ £B

Also see the following Rhône *négociants* with an entry in the section *Rhône Valley:*
M CHAPOUTIER
JEAN-LUC COLOMBO
TARDIEU-LAURENT

OTHER WINES OF NOTE

L'ABBAYE SYLVA PLANA ● **Faugères** La Closeraie £B

ABBAYE DE THOLOMIES ● **Minervois** £B ● **Minervois La Livinière** £C

ABBOTTS WINES ● **Minervois** Cumulo Nimbus £B

DOM. DE L'AIGLE O **Limoux** les Aigles £C

DOM. DE L'AIGUELIÈRE ● **Coteaux du Languedoc** Côte Dorée £C Côte Rousse £C

DOM. DES AIRES HAUTES ● **Minervois La Livinière** £B

DOM. DES ALYSSES ● **Coteaux Varois** £C

DOM. D'ANTUGNAC O **Limoux** £C

ANTOINE ARENA ● **Patrimonio** Carco di Sole £B Carco £C O **Muscat du Cap Corse** £C

DOM. DE L'ARJOLLE ● **Vin de Pays Côtes de Thongue** Cabernet £B Paradoxe £C

DOM. D'AUPILHAC ● **Coteaux du Languedoc-Montpeyroux** £C

DOM. DES AURELLES ● **Coteaux du Languedoc** Solen £C Aurel £C

DOM. LEON BARRAL● **Faugères** Cuvée Tradition £B Cuvée Jadis £C

DOM. BERTRAND BERGÉ ● **Fitou** Ancestrale £B

DOM. BORIE DE MAUREL ● **Minervois** Esprit d'Automne £B Scylla £D

DOMAINES BUNAN ● **Bandol** Moulin des Costes £C Château de La Rouvière £D

DOM. DE CABROL ● **Cabardès** Vent d'Ouest £B

DOM. CAPION ● **Syrah** Vin de Pays de l'Hérault £B O **Chardonnay** Vin de Pays de l'Hérault £B

CAVES DE CASTELMAURE ● **Corbières** Cuvée No 3 £D

DOM. DE CLOVALLON ● **Vin de Pays d'Oc** Pinot Noir £B O **Vin de Pays d'Oc** Viognier £B

DOM. CULOMBU O **Calvi** £B

CH. DE L'AMARINE ● **Costières de Nîmes** Cuvée de Bernis £B

CH. BAS ● **Coteaux d'Aix-en-Provence** Cuvée du Temple £C

CH. BONHOMME ● **Minervois** Les Amandiers £B Les Oliviers £C

CH. DE CALADROY ● **Côtes du Roussillon-Villages** Cuvée La Juliane £B

CH. CALISSANNE ● **Coteaux d'Aix-en-Provence** Clos Victoire £D

CH. CAMPLAZENS ● **Coteaux du Languedoc La Clape** La Reserve £B

CH. CAMPUGET ● **Costières de Nîmes** Cuvée Prestige £B

CH. CASCADAIS ● **Corbières** £B

CH. CAZAL-VIEL ● **Saint-Chinian** Cuvée des Fées £B Larmes des Fées £E

CH. DE COMBEBELLE ● **Saint-Chinian** Tradition £B Réserve £C

CH. COUPE ROSES ● **Minervois** Les Plots £B

CH. D'ESCLANS ● **Côtes de Provence** Grebase £C Mourbase £C

CH. FLAUGERGUES ● **Coteaux du Languedoc** £B

CH. GLÉON MONTANIE ● **Corbières** Gaston Bonnes £C Combe de Berre £B

CH. DE GOURGAZAUD ● **Minervois La Livinière** Réserve £B

CH. GRANDE-CASSAGNE ● **Costières de Nîmes** £B

CH. GRAND MOULIN ● **Corbières** Vieilles Vignes £B

CH. GRÉZAN ● **Faugères** Cuvée Arnaud Lubac £B

CH. LA BARONNE ● **Corbières** Montagne d'Alaric Unfiltered £B

CH. LA BASTIDE ● **Corbières** Optimé £B

CH. LA TUILERIE ● **Costières de Nîmes** Cuvée Eole £B

CH. LA SAUVAGEONNE ● **Coteaux du Languedoc** Cuvée Prestige £C

CH. DE LASCAUX ● **Coteaux du Languedoc Pic Saint-Loup** Les Nobles Pierres £C

CH. DE LASTOURS ● **Corbières** Cuvée Simon Descamps £B Fûts de Chêne £B

CH. LE THOU ● **Coteaux du Languedoc** £B

CH. LES PALAIS ● **Corbières** Les Randolin Vieille Vignes £B

CH. DE LA LIQUIERE ● **Faugères** Cistus £B

CH. MANSENOBLE ● **Corbières** Réserve £B

CH. MARIS ● **Minervois La Livinière** £C Vieilles Vignes £C

CH. DE MONTPEZAT ● **Coteaux du Languedoc** £B Cuvée Prestige £C

CH. DE LA NÉGLY ● **Coteaux du Languedoc** La Falaise £C Porte du Ciel £F

CH DE NOUVELLES ● **Fitou** Vieilles Vignes £B

CH. D'OUPIA ● **Minervois** Les Barons £B

CH. PECH-CELEYRAN ● **Coteaux du Languedoc La Clape** Réserve £C

CH. PECH-LATT ● **Corbières** Cuvée Vieille Vignes £B Cuvée Alix £C

CH. PUECH-HAUT ● **Coteaux du Languedoc** Tête de Cuvée £D

CH. PLANÈRES ● **Côtes du Roussillon** £B

CH. REAL MARTIN ● **Côtes de Provence** £C Optimum £D

CH. ROCHE REDONNE ● **Bandol** Guilhem £D

CH. ROMANIN ● **Les Baux-de-Provence** £B

CH. LA ROQUE ● **Coteaux du Languedoc Pic Saint-Loup** Cuvée Mourvèdre £B

CH. DE ROQUEFORT ● **Côtes de Provence** £C

CH. ROUMANIÈRES ● **Coteaux du Languedoc** £B

CH. SAINT-AURIOL ● **Corbières** Les Terrassettes £B

CH. SAINTE-EULALIE ● **Minervois La Livinière** £B

CH. DES SARRINS ● **Côtes de Provence** £B

CH. DE VALCOMBE ● **Costières de Nîmes** Cuvée Prestige £B

CH. VEYRAN ● **Saint-Chinian** Cuvée Henri £B

CH. VIGNELAURE ● **Coteaux d'Aix-en-Provence** £C

CH. VILLERAMBERT-JULIEN ● **Minervois** £B

CH. VIRGILE ● **Costières de Nîmes** £B

CLOS DE L'ANHEL ● **Corbières** Les Terrassettes £B Dimanches £B

CLOS BAGATELLE ● **Saint-Chinian** La Gloire de Mon Père £B

CLOS MARIE ● **Coteaux du Languedoc** L'Olivette £B Cuvée Simon £D

CLOS DEL REY ● **Vin de Pays d'Oc** £D

CLOS SAINTE-MAGDELEINE ○ **Cassis** £C

COMMANDERIE DE PEYRASSOL ● **Côtes de Provence** Cuvée Marie-Estelle £C

DOM. DE LA COMBE-BLANCHE ● **Minervois** La Chandelière £B
● **Vin de Pays d'Oc** Le Dessous de l'Enfer £B

DOM. DE COURTILLES ● **Corbières** £C Côte 125 £B

JEAN-LOUIS DENOIS ● **Vin de Pays d'Oc** £B Grand Cuvée £C

DOM. ERMITAGE DU PIC SAINT LOUP ● **Coteaux du Languedoc**
Pic Saint-Loup Cuvée Saint-Agnes £C

DOM. FERRER-RIBIÈRE ● **Côtes du Roussillon** £B Mémoire des Temps £C

DOM. FONTEDICTO ● **Coteaux du Languedoc** Coulisses £C Cuvée Promise £D

DOM. FORÇA-REAL ● **Côtes du Roussillon-Villages** £B ● **Rivesaltes** Hors d'Age £B

JEAN-PIERRE GAUSSEN ● **Bandol** Longue Garde £D

DOM. DU GRAND CRÈS ● **Corbières** £B

DOM. DES GRECAUX ● **Coteaux du Languedoc** Hemera £D

DOM. HENRY ● **Coteaux du Languedoc** Les Chailles £D

DOM. DE L'HERMITAGE ● **Bandol** £C

DOM. VIRGILE JOLY ● **Coteaux du Languedoc** £D

LA FERME BLANCHE ○ **Cassis** £C

DOM. LA GALANTIN ● **Bandol** £C

DOM. DE LA GARANCE ● **Vin de Pays de l'Hérault** Les Armières £C

DOM. GAVOTY ● **Côtes de Provence** Cuvée Clarendon £C

DOM. LACROIX-VANEL ● **Coteaux du Languedoc** Clos Fine Amour £B

LA GRANGE DE QUATRE SOUS ● **Vin de Pays d'Oc** Lo Molin £B

LA JASSE CASTEL ● **Coteaux du Languedoc** £C

DOM. LUC LAPEYRE ● **Minervois** L'Amourier £B

DOM. LAPORTE ● **Côtes du Roussillon** Domitia £B

LA PRÉCEPTORIE DE CENTERNACH ● **Vin de Pays des Côtes de Catalanes** Terre Promise £B
● **Côtes du Roussillon-Villages** ● **Bandol** Cuvée des Bartavelles £D

DOM. LA SUFFRENE ● **Bandol** £D

DOM. LA TERRASSE D'ELISE ● **Vin de Pays de l'Herault** £E

DOM. LECCIA ● **Patrimonio** £B Petra Bianca £C

L'ETOILE ● **Banyuls** Extra Vieux £D

DOM. L'HÉRITIER ● **Côtes du Roussillon** Romani £C

MAÎTRES VIGNERONNES DE SAINT-TROPEZ ● **Bandol** La Roque £C

DOM MARCEVOL ● **Côtes du Roussillon** £B Prestige £C

MAS DES BRESSADES ● **Costières de Nîmes** £B ● **Vin de Pays du Gard** Cabernet/Syrah £B

DOM. DU MAS CARLOT ● **Costières de Nîmes** £B

MAS DES CHIMÈRES ● **Vin de Pays du Salagou** Oeillades £B Marie et Joseph £B

MAS CRÉMAT ● **Côtes du Roussillon** £B Fût de Chêne £C

MAS FOULAQUIER ● **Coteaux du Languedoc** Le Rollier £B

MAS DE FOURNEL ● **Coteaux du Languedoc Pic Saint-Loup** Classique £B Cuvée Pierre £B

MAS DE GOURGONNIER ● **Les Baux-de-Provence** Réserve £D

MAS GRANIER ● **Coteaux du Languedoc** Les Gres £B

MAS DE GUIOT ● **Vin de Pays du Gard** Cabernet Syrah £B

MAS DE L'ECRITURE ● **Coteaux du Languedoc** £E

MAS DE MARTIN ● **Coteaux du Languedoc** £B

GUY MOULINIER ● **Saint-Chinian** Les Sigillaires £B Les Terrasses Grillées £D

CAVES DU MONT TAUCH ● **Fitou** Les Crouzels £B Terroir de Tuchan £B

ORENGA DE GAFFORY ● **Patrimonio** £B ○ **Muscat de Cap Corse** £C

DOMAINES OTT ○ **Côtes de Provence** Clos Mireille L'Insolent £E

DOM. PICCININI ● **Minervois La Livinière** Line et Laetitia £B

DOM. PIÉTRI-GÉRAUD ● **Collioure** £B ● **Banyuls** £C ○ **Muscat de Rivesaltes** £B

DOM. OLIVIER PITHON ● **Côtes du Roussillon** £B Vignes de Saturne £C

DOM. POUDÉROUX ● **Côtes du Roussillon** Terre Brune £C

DOM. DE LA PROSE ● **Coteaux du Languedoc** Cuvée Prestige £B Les Embruns £B

DOM. DES RAVANÈS ● **Merlot** Les Gravières de Taurol Vin de Pays Coteaux de Murviel £B

ROC D'ANGLADE ● **Coteaux du Languedoc** £E

DOM. SAINT-ANDRÉ DE FIGUIÈRE ● **Côtes de Provence** Grande Cuvée VV £C

DOM SAINT-ANDRIEU ● **Coteaux du Languedoc** Les Roches Blanches £B

DOM. SAINT-ANTOINE ● **Costières de Nîmes** Cuvée des Oliviers £B

DOM. SAINT-MARTIN LA GARRIGUE ● **Coteaux du Languedoc** £B

DOM. SARDA-MALET ● **Côtes du Roussillon** Réserve £C Terroi ● Mailloles £D

DOM. SERRES MAZARD ● **Corbières** Cuvée Henri Serres £B

SKALLI-FORTANT DE FRANCE ● **Cabernet Sauvignon** Réserve Édition Limité F £C

DOM. SORIN ● **Côtes de Provence** Cuvée Privée £C

DOM. DE TORRACCIA ● **Vin de Corse Porto-Vecchio** £C

DOM. DE LA TOUR-BOISÉE ● **Minervois** Cuvée Marie-Claude £B

DOM. DE TRIENNES ● **Vin de Pays des Var** Les Auréliens £B

DOM. VAQUER ● **Vin de Pays des Côtes de Catalanes** £C

DOM. VIAL-MAGNÈRES ● **Banyuls** Vintage £B

Author's choice (DM)

The new wave from the Languedoc

DOM. CANET-VALETTE ● **Saint-Chinian** Le Vin Maghani

CH. L'EUZIÈRE ● **Coteaux du Languedoc Pic Saint-Loup** Cuvée Les Escarboucles

CH. DES ESTANILLES ● **Faugères** Cuvée Syrah

CH. MOURGUES DU GRÈS ● **Costières de Nîmes** Capitelles des Mourgues

DOM. CLAVEL ● **Coteaux du Languedoc** Copa Santa

DOM. FONT CAUDE ● **Coteaux du Languedoc Montpeyroux** L'Esprit de Font Caude

DOM. DE LA GRANGE DES PÈRES ● **Vin de Pays de l'Hérault**

DOM. DE L'HORTUS ○ **Vin de Pays Val de Montferrand** Grande Cuvée

MAS CHAMPART ● **Saint-Chinian** Clos de La Simonette

MAS DE DAUMAS GASSAC ○ Vin de Pays de l'Hérault

PRIEURÉ DE SAINT-JEAN-DE-BÉBIAN ○ Coteaux du Languedoc

DOM. RIMBERT ● Carignator

DOM. TERRE INCONNUE ● Sylvie

Emerging classics from Provence

DOM. DES BÉATES ● Coteaux d'Aix-en-Provence Terra d'Or

CH. DE PIBARNON ● Bandol

CH. PRADEAUX ● Bandol

CH. ROUTAS ○ Vin de Pays du Var Cuvée Coquelicot

CH. SIMONE ○ Palette

DOM. DE LA COURTADE ● Côtes de Provence

DOM. DU GROS NORÉ ● Bandol

DOM. LAFRAN-VEYROLLES ● Bandol Tradition

DOM. RABIEGA ● Côtes de Provence Clos d'Ière I

DOM. RICHEAUME ● Côtes de Provence Cuvée Columelle

DOM. TEMPIER ● Bandol Cabassou

DOM. DE TREVALLON ● Vin de Pays des Bouches-du-Rhône

Dry and fortifieds from the Roussillon

CELLIER DES TEMPLIERS ● Banyuls Grand Cru Henri Vidal

DOM. DE CASENOVE ● Côtes du Roussillon Commandant François Jaubert

DOM. DES CHÊNES ● Côtes du Roussillon-Villages Tautavel

DOM. DU CLOS DES FÉES ● Côtes du Roussillon-Villages La Petite Sibérie

DOM. FONTANEL ● Côtes du Roussillon-Villages Prieuré

DOM. GARDIES ● Côtes du Roussillon-Villages La Torre

DOM. GAUBY ○ Vin de Pays de Côtes Catalanes Coume Gineste

DOM. LA TOUR VIEILLE ● Collioure Puig Oriol

MAS AMIEL ● Maury Charles Dupuy

DOM. DU MAS BLANC ● Banyuls La Coume

DOM. DE LA RECTORIE ● Collioure La Coume Pascole

DOM. DES SCHISTES ○ Muscat de Rivesaltes

Regional France

This section of the guide covers south-western France along with the alpine vineyards of the Jura and Savoie. The latter are steeped in tradition and relatively unknown but some fine and very diverse styles are produced. A number of the regions in the south-west are close neighbours of Bordeaux and the style inevitably mirrors that of the Bordelais. Further south, both in the Lot Valley at Cahors and south towards the Pyrenees at Madiran and Jurançon, first-class dry and sweet whites and rich, stylish reds are becoming justifiably known to a wider audience.

Jura

Located to the west of Burgundy's Côte d'Or, the vineyard area is situated at altitude on the western slopes of the Jura mountains. There are a number of appellations here. The **Côte du Jura** AC encompasses the whole region and produces red, rosé and white wine. Reds and rosés are produced from the local Poulsard and Trousseau as well as Pinot Noir. Those produced from Pinot are the best bets. Among the whites, Chardonnay is good but of more interest are the nutty, characterful Savagnin-based wines. Some oak is used but it tends to be subtle and restrained. The speciality of the region is *vin jaune*. This is not dissimilar to fino sherry in character as it is aged under a yeast film, yet it remains unfortified. The wine is remarkably ageworthy. *Vin jaune* can also be found under the **Arbois**, **Château Chalon** and **L'Étoile** AC's. At Arbois good red and white (from the same varieties as in the Côte du Jura), *vin de paille* and sparkling wines are also produced. Château-Chalon and L'Étoile are much smaller appellations. The former is solely for the production of *vin jaune*. In L'Étoile dry whites from Chardonnay and Savagnin and some moderate sparkling wine are produced as well as *vin jaune*. The rare *vin de paille* is, like those in the northern Rhône, a late-harvested sweet white with a hint of nutty oxidation. Most sparkling wine is made by the traditional method and is labelled as **Crémant de Jura**. There is the odd decent example.

Savoie

This high alpine vineyard area is located just to the south-west of Geneva. The regional AC is **Vin de Savoie**. There are some good whites from the Altesse grape which are fresh and floral and reds from Pinot Noir and Mondeuse. The latter particularly are worth considering. Good light, fresh, dry whites from Altesse and sparkling wines from Molette (with some Altesse) are produced under the **Seyssel AC**. The Chasselas-based whites at **Crepy AC** are generally unexciting.

South-West France

Immediately to the east of Bordeaux on the river Dordogne is Bergerac . There are a number of ACs north and south of the river, but the large, generic **Bergerac AC** encompasses all the smaller sub-regions. Red, white and rosé are produced from the Bordeaux varieties. Quality is fairly pedestrian with high yields and widespread mechanical harvesting. The number of good reds and whites being produced here is, however, increasing. Lees-enrichment and *bâtonnage* are now being used for whites and new oak is increasingly common for both reds and whites. The **Côtes de Bergerac** and **Pécharmant** are immediately to the north of the town of Bergerac. The former is a source of some good reds and sweet whites (labelled as Côtes de Bergerac Moelleux). Pécharmant should do better than it does with its well-drained sandy, limestone soils. To the south of the river are the sweet-white ACs of **Monbazillac** and **Saussignac**. The former is worth considering as an alternative to Sauternes. The wines can be remarkably rich and complex with heady levels of botrytis. Be aware though that they are becoming more established and prices are rising. Both ACs are a blend of Sémillon and Sauvignon Blanc. Some good red and dry white is made at **Montravel** in vineyards bordering the Côtes de Castillon in Bordeaux. Sweet styles are also produced here and in the small ACs of **Côtes de Montravel** and **Haut-Montravel**. Thus far they lack the richness and depth found in Monbazillac.

South of Bergerac are the appellations of the **Côtes de Duras**, **Côtes du Marmandais** and **Buzet**. Both red and white are produced in the vineyards around Duras, with an occasional late-harvest white. As at Bergerac, Bordeaux varieties are planted. The reds tend towards a vegetal character and the whites are at best fresh and grassy. More new oak is being used, with varying success. Marmandais and Buzet appellations are red only, with more interest in the Côtes du Marmandais, where as well as Bordeaux grapes some indigenous south-western varieties are also permitted.

To the south-east of Bergerac along a 30-mile stretch of the river Lot are the vineyards of **Cahors**. Some of the finest red wines of the south-west are now produced here. Auxerrois (Malbec) dominates plantings, with some Merlot and Tannat. Expect anything from light, plummy, easy-drinking wines (occasionally with a green vegetal note) to serious and very structured ageworthy reds. Prices of the best examples seem to be surging upwards. West of Cahors the AC of **Marcillac** produces spicy reds from Fer-Servadou, while to the south the VDQS of the **Coteaux du Quercy** produces reds of some potential. further south, towards Toulouse, are the VDQS of both the **Côtes du Brulhois** and **Lavilledieu**; and the **Côtes du Frontonnais** AC. The latter has turned out a number of interesting reds based on the Negrette grape. The wines are both perfumed and spicy, the best impressively structured. To the north-east of Toulouse, **Gaillac** AC offers some unusual and diverse styles; Mauzac is the key white variety, although Muscadelle is also important. Good dry and sweet wines are produced along with *perlé* (a lightly sparkling white) and Gaillac Mousseux, produced by the *méthode rural*. The majority of the red is light and generally disappointing.

To the south are the great red and white wines of Gascony. This is also bulk-white **Vin de Pays des Côtes de Gasgogne** country. The **Madiran** and **Pacherenc du Vic-Bilh** ACs share the same geographical area and many growers produce both. Pacherenc can be dry or sweet and is produced from Gros and Petit Manseng, Petit Courbu and Arrufiac, with the odd touch of Sémillon and Sauvignon Blanc (for *moelleux*) blended in. The best are very good. Madiran itself produces powerful, dense and ageworthy reds based on Tannat and often blended with a bit of Cabernets Franc and Sauvignon and Fer-Servadou. It was here that the technique of micro-oxygenation was developed to harness and soften the Tannat's often aggressive and sturdy tannins. Some of the wines are world-class and provide very good value. **Jurançon** is without doubt the finest white-wine appellation of the south-west. Gros and Petit Manseng as well as Petit Courbu are planted. The wines can be sublime, particularly the sweet styles. Yields are low and inevitably prices are rising. The reds of nearby **Béarn** are generally light and insubstantial. To the south-west of Jurançon, nestled into the foothills of the Pyrenees, **Irouléguy** provides some good reds and whites from the same varieties as at Madiran and Jurançon.

Vintages

In general most red and white should be drunk young and only a number of appellations provide wines with the substance for real ageing. However, in the Jura, *vin jaune* is remarkably long-lived; it is typically released with 10 years age. Other Savagnin-based white also develops well for a decade or so. Top Cahors needs several years in bottle and evolves well. Jurançon, both dry and sweet, will improve over half a decade or more and keep much longer. Top Madiran, more approachable than in the past, needs five years at least, particularly the top cuvées. Top years in the Jura have been 2000, 1999, 1996, 1995, 1990, 1989, 1988 and 1985. Throughout the south-west 2002, 2001, 2000, 1999, 1998, 1996 and 1995 were good. 1993, 1990 and 1988 are worth considering for top Jurançon and the trio of 1990, 1989 and 1988 for top Madiran.

DOM. BERTHET-BONDET Château-Chalon

Owner: Jean Berthet-Bondet 39210 Château-Chalon

First class traditional Jura producer, making top quality whites from Chardonnay and the local white Savagnin. Of the two Côtes du Jura dry whites, Alliance is produced from Chardonnay, the more complex and structured Tradition from a blend of Savagnin and Chardonnay. Both wines offer marvellously pure and intense mineral and lightly citrussy fruit characters. In the Tradition an almost salty like tang underpins the wine. The Château-Chalon, a *Vin Jaune*, is not dissimilar to a top level fino and has an earthy, salty character derived from the flor yeast it is aged under in cask. Unlike Fino sherry, these wines have a piercing acidity, lending them the structure for very long ageing. The wines require time to show at their best. (DM)

O **Côtes du Jura** Alliance★★★ £B Tradition★★★★ £C
O **Château-Chalon**★★★★ £E

DOM. BERTHOUMIEU Madiran barre.didier@wanadoo.fr   A: CdP, AVn

Owner: Didier Barré Dutour, 32400 Viella

Impressive 25-ha Madiran property producing around 15,000 cases a year. The main focus of the property and, it has to be said, the best wines are the two Madiran cuvées. Vinification is traditional and the wines have considerable extract and youthful tannin after a maceration of three weeks or so. The Tradition is spicy, dense and structured with an earthy, mineral core. A blend of Tannat, Cabernet Sauvignon, Cabernet Franc and Fer-Servadou, it is arged partly in wood and partly in *cuve*. The old-vine Charles de Batz is a rich, brooding wine with sweet, chocolatey notes. It sees a large portion of new oak. The wines here are extensively racked as opposed to using micro-oxygenation to minimise those burly, aggressive Tannat tannins. The result is uniformly ripe and supple. The Pacherenc Sec is crisp and fresh, the sweet Symphonie d'Automne is weighty, rich and more aromatic. (DM)

● **Madiran** Tradition★★ £B Charles de Batz★★★ £C
O **Pacherenc de Vic-Bilh** Sec★ £B Cuvée Symphonie d'Automne Doux★★ £C

ALAIN BRUMONT Madiran www.montus-madiran.com   A: CdP, HHB, N&P

Owner: Alain Brumont Château Bouscassé, 32400 Maumusson

With a large vineyard holding of some 140 ha and a total production of 65,000 to 70,000 cases, Alain Brumont makes impressively structured, rich and very concentrated Madiran under the Montus and Bouscassé labels. He also produces good dry Pacherenc de Vic Bilh under the Montus label. Mainly Petit Courbu, the wine is barrel-fermented and aged and is rich, nutty and intensely honeyed in character. There is also a Bouscassé white that is not vinified in oak and is understandably more aromatic in nature. A number of very good late-harvest Pacherencs are produced as well. Bouscassé is the secondary property and there is a well-priced regular Madiran and a dense and powerful Vieilles Vignes. The approach to vinification emphasises power and extraction. Maceration lasts for over four weeks and no micro-oxygentation is employed during maturation.The regular Château Montus is full of firm, dark-fruited Tannat character. The Cuvée Prestige is pricey but a serious step up. Very, powerful and structured it demands seven or eight years ageing to achieve a harmonious balance of fruit and tannin. It will show great refinement with time. (DM)

Château Montus
● **Madiran**★★★ £C Cuvée Prestige★★★★ £F
O **Pacherenc de Vic-Bilh**★★★ £C

Château Bouscassé

● **Madiran**★★ £B   Vieilles Vignes★★★ £D
○ **Pacherenc de Vic-Bilh**★★ £B

DOM. CAUHAPÉ   Jurançon   domainecauhape@wanadoo.fr   A: SsG, M&V, N&P

Owner: Henri Ramonteu   Quartier Castet, 64360 Monein

Henri Ramonteu's domaine is sizeable for the region at some 40 ha but he is arguably the finest exponent of the appellation. He makes an extensive range with two dry and four sweet wines from very low-yielding vineyards. The sweet wines are classified according the harvesting of the grapes. The dry styles are produced mainly from Gros Manseng and vinified with some skin contact, with the Sève d'Automne being barrel-fermented, and all the wines are kept on their lees. The sweet wines, with a high Petit Manseng content are increasingly luscious and richly concentrated but with a fine, fresh acid backbone. They are structured and very ageworthy. Rare and only produced when conditions favour it from fruit harvested close to the year's end, Quintessence is among the great wines not only of Jurançon but of France as well. (DM)

○ **Jurançon** Chant des Vignes★★ £B   Sève d'Automne★★★ £C
○ **Jurançon** Ballet d'Octobre★★★ £C   Symphonie de Novembre★★★★ £C   Noblesse du Temps★★★★ £E

CHAPELLE LENCLOS   Madiran   A: THt, CdP

Owner: Patrick Ducournau   32400 Maumusson Laguian

Patrick Ducournau has 18 ha of vineyards of which a mere 2.5 ha are planted to white varieties, from which he produces decent, lightly honeyed and intense Pacherenc de Vic-Bilh, occasionally as a *moelleux*. The main focus is on the Madiran reds. There are two wines here. The Domaine Mouréou is supple and surprisingly approachable for the appellation. The wine is mainly aged in tank and requires a little time to take the hard edge off its tannins. La Chapelle Lenclos is denser and more structured; it will be better with four or five years' ageing. The wine is partly aged in *cuve* and partly in large 400-litre barrels. Winemaker Damiens Sartori is trying to emphasise the wine's fruit and underplay the oak influence that is increasingly evident in some of his neighbours. Much of the style is achieved by the process of micro-oxygenation, which Ducournau is responsible for developing. (DM)

● **Madiran** Domaine Mouréou★★ £B   la Chapelle Lenclos★★★ £C
○ **Pacherenc de Vic-Bilh** Moelleux★★ £B

CH. D'AYDIE   Madiran   A: GBa, AVn

Owner: Laplace family   64330 Aydie

A small but fine range of Madirans and Pacherenc de Vic-Bilhs are produced at this sizeable property. There are 45 ha of vineyards; 35 ha are devoted to producing Madiran. Decent, straightforward red Madiran is released as Fleury-Laplace, which is produced from bought-in fruit and offers a soft, accessible example of the appellation. Odé d'Aydie is the second label and is reasonably dense and powerful. The Château d'Aydie is a serious step up, full of dark fruit, well-judged oak and firm, youthful tannin. Five or six years' ageing is needed. The wine is kept on its lees in barrel and micro-oxygenation employed. Pacherenc is produced in a dry style under the Frédéric Laplace label, which is both aromatic and intense, with piercing, green nettly fruit. Rich and impressively concentrated *moelleux* is also made. (DM)

● **Madiran** Odé d'Aydie★★ £B   Château d'Aydie★★★ £C
○ **Pacherenc de Vic-Bilh** Frédéric Laplace★★ £B

CH. BARRÉJAT   Madiran

Owner: Denis Capmartin   32400 Maumusson
Good to very good Madiran is made by Denis Capmartin at his 22 ha domaine. One of the important keys to quality here is the impressive age of some of the vineyards which are farmed along organic principles. In the remarkable top label Vieux ceps some of the vines utilised are up to an astounding 200 years of age. The regular Madiran Tradition is as forward as Madiran tends to be, it still needs a year or two to soften its hard youthful edge which is promoted by a lengthy 21 day cuvaison and ageing in *cuve*. Richer and lusher in texture is the Séduction, a blend of 60 per cent Tannat and 40 per cent Cabernets Sauvignon and Franc. Aged in small oak barriques, a small proportion new, it is ripe and full of deep, dark, cedary fruit and subtle spicy oak. The Vieux ceps has just 20 per cent of the Cabernets blended with Tannat. It is both rich and understandably very complex. The top two wines will benefit from at leasts five years ageing. (DM)

● **Madiran** Tradition★★ £B   Séduction★★★ £C   Vieux ceps★★★★ £C

CH. BEAULIEU   Côtes du Marmandais

Owner: Robert Schulte   32400 Maumusson
Robert Schulte's property is among a small handful of producers independently striving for fine quality in this lesser known appellation. Most of his neighbours choose to sell to the local co-op. Beaulieu's 26.5 ha of vineyards have great potential and are planted on a mix of gravel and calcareous soils. The vineyard is also being replanted to achieve a density of up to 6,000 vines per hectare which will improve quality further. Three reds are made here and the style is traditional, particularly for the Côtes du Marmandais and top Cuvée de l'Oratoire. You need to give them at least four or five years ageing to soften their firm youthful edge. These latter two wines are about structure rather than fruit. The Galapian de Beaulieu produced from young vines, is softer, more obviously fruit driven. The Cuvée de l'Oratoire comes from vines up to 40 years old and is produced from a yield of just 18 to 20 hl/ha. It is impressively dense, rich and concentrated. (DM).

● **Côtes du Marmandais**★★ £B   l'Oratoire★★★ £C   Galapian de Beaulieu★ £B

CH. DU CÈDRE   Cahors   chateauducedre@wanadoo.fr   A: CdP, GWW

Owner: Pascal et Jean-Marc Verhaeghe   46700 Vire-sur-Lot
The Verhaegue family possesses some 25 ha of vineyards and produces three good to very good reds. The regular Cahors is made from the youngest vines. It is a ripe, brambly, forward style for drinking young. The Prestige cuvée is altogether sturdier and denser. The top wine, Le Cèdre, is now fairly pricey, particularly for the appellation. Produced entirely from old Malbec vines and aged in 100 per cent new oak, it is powerful, structured and very ageworthy – best with five years in the cellar or more. There are also ongoing experiments here with lees-ageing for reds and the use of micro-oxygenation. (DM)

● **Cahors**★ £B   Prestige★★ £C   Le Cèdre★★★★ £E

CH. LAGREZETTE   Cahors   www.chateau-lagrezette.tm.fr   A:CCC

Owner: Alain-Dominique Perrin   46140 Caillac
Another recent top-quality performer in Cahors, Alain-Dominique Perrin is a wealthy entrepreneur whose portfolio includes prestige jewellery operation Cartier. No expense is spared at this 65-ha property and roving consultant Michel Rolland provides guidance over vinification. Classic Rolland

techniques are all evident including pre-fermentation maceration,extended vatting, malolactic in barrel and judicious use of new oak. A number a soft fruity Cahors are made under the *négociant* Domaine de Lagrezette label: Grezette, Expression de Grezette and Chevalier-Lagrezette. Grezette is a straightforward commune wine, Expression and Chevalier get a touch of used oak for ageing. The rich and impressively concentrated Château Lagrezette is a regular Cahors given an extended maceration of up to four weeks. The two prestige cuvées, Dame Honneur and the very pricey Pigeonnier, are a step up, particularly the deep and saturated Pigeonnier, which is nudging five stars. It is 100 per cent Malbec, sourced from the property's oldest vines and produced from a yield of barely more than 15 hl/ha. The Dame Honneur will benefit from five years or so, the Pigeonnier a year or two longer. (DM)

● **Cahors**★★★ £C Dame Honneur★★★★ £E Pigeonnier★★★ £E

CH. TIRECUL-LA-GRAVIÈRE Monbazillac   A:L&S

Owner: Claudie et Bruno Billancini 24240 Monbazillac
Arguably the top property for sweet Monbazillac. The Billancinis have just 9 ha or so planted and produce a tiny amount – some 1,500 cases in total every year. The style is radically different from their neighbours' with intensely honeyed wines full of rich fruit, quince, toast and very marked botrytis. They achieve this by controlling yields and conducting a succession of *tris* as extensive as any top Sauternes property. The regular bottling is very impressive with rich fruit and spicy, vanilla notes from new oak. There is also a tiny volume of the special and very pricey Cuvée Madame. The wines may be enjoyed young but will keep very well. (DM)

● **Monbazillac**★★★★ £E Cuvée Madame★★★★★ £F

CH. TOUR DES GENDRES Bergerac   A:CdP,GWW,HHB

Owner: De Conti family Les Gendres, 24240 Ribagnac
Very impressive Bergerac property with a range of red and white produced as Bergerac as well as a red Côtes de Bergerac, the stylish and concentrated Gloire de Mon Père. There are a total of some 43 ha of vineyards with more than half planted to red varieties. Production is now over 25,000 cases a year, which is in no way detrimental to quality. White planting is typically Bordelais, mainly Sémillon with Sauvignon Blanc and around 10 per cent Muscadelle; reds are dominated by Merlot and full of rich, plummy fruit. In addition to the regular range, Casanova des Conti wines – a simple fruit-driven white blend of Sémillon, Sauvignon and Muscadelle and a red comprising mainly Merlot with some Cabernet Sauvignon – are produced exclusively for the UK market. The top cuvées have real dimension and class. The Anthologia bottlings are as impressive as anything yet produced from the region, the red adding a round, supple character through partial barrel-fermentation. The white is marvellously intense and pure with beautifully balanced oak. It has only been released in 1996 and 2001. Some of the vineyards are now being farmed biodynamically. (DM)

● **Bergerac**★ £B Moulin des Dames★★★ £D Cuvée Anthologia★★★★ £E
● **Côtes de Bergerac** Gloire de Mon Père★★★ £B
O **Bergerac** Cuvée des Conti★★ £B Moulin des Dames★★★ £C Cuvée Anthologia★★★★ £E
◎ **Bergerac**★ £B

CH. VIELLA Madiran

Owner: Alain Bortolussi Les Gendres, 24240 Ribagnac
The Bortolussi family is in the course of renovating the splendid old Château at this property. They make a simple very straightforward Bearn rosé but of more importance is a good barrel-fermented dry

Pacherenc du Vic-Bilh from mainly Arrufiac, as well as a little Gros and Petit Manseng and a very fine late harvest Pacherenc which is fully Petit Manseng. The latter is luscious but very finely structured, with a glorious ripe citrus and mineral character. The regular Madiran is good, aged in *cuve* with 40 per cent Cabernets Franc and Sauvignon blended with Tannat. It needs a year or two to add some flesh. The Cuvée Prestige is rich, dense and powerfully structured. It is 100 per cent Tannat and aged in new wood. A minimum of four to five years is needed to achieve an equilibrium of fruit and oak. The wines are all very fairly priced. (DM)

● **Madiran**★★ £B Cuvée Prestige★★★ £C
O **Pacherenc du Vic-Bilh**★ £B Moelleux★★★ £C

CLOS LAPEYRE Jurançon jean-bernard.larrieu@wanadoo.fr A: HHB

Owner: Jean-Bernard Larrieu La Chapelle de Rousse, 64110 Jurançon
There are 12 ha under vine here and both dry and sweet styles are produced. The regular Jurançon *sec* is fermented in stainless steel and kept on its lees for added depth. The old-vine Vitatge Vielh is barrel-fermented, adding additional weight. Three sweet wines are made. The regular Moelleux is full and spicy with nicely balanced acidity; the barrel Sélection is richer and more intensely citrusy with subtle oak in the background. The top late-harvested wine, Vent Balaguer, is produced solely from Petit Manseng grapes that are marked by *passerillage*. Remarkably rich and concentrated it is only produced in the most exceptional years. (DM)

O **Jurançon** Sec★ £B Vitatge Vielh★★ £B Moelleux★★ £B Sélection Petit Manseng★★★ £C

CLOS TRIGUEDINA Cahors www.clos-triguedina.com A: CdP, HHB

Owner: Jean-Luc Baldés 46700 Puy l'Evêque
The Baldés family has been in the region for nearly two centuries and in the Prince Probus cuvée they produced one of the benchmark wines of the appellation long before some of the more recently established names. There are 57 ha of reds and just 2 ha of whites. From the latter they produce a good barrel-fermented, blended vin de pays white from Chardonnay and Viognier and a small amount of late-harvest Chenin Blanc. Some rosé is also produced but it is the red Cahors which defines quality here. In order to maintain the standard of the top wines, two secondary labels are also released, which are forward and fruit driven. Of these, Domaine Labrande comes from a separate property, while Balmont de Cahors is produced at Clos Triguedina. The estate red is a structured and impressively ageworthy example of the appellation. Aged in used oak, it is full of spicy tobacco and red berry fruit. Prince Probus is fuller, darker and with a marked vanilla undercurrent from new wood. (DM)

● **Cahors**★★ £C Prince Probus★★★ £D

CLOS UROULAT Jurançon A: HHB

Owner: Charles Hours Quartier Trouilh, 64360 Monein
Charles Hours possesses a small holding of some 7 ha with the bulk planted to Petit Manseng and the balancing 25 per cent Gros Manseng with a bit of Courbu. Just two wines are produced here and very good and attractively priced they are too. Both wines are barrel-fermented. The dry Cuvée Marie is full of intense, citrus character and subtle, vanilla oak. The sweet Clos Uroulat is unctuous and rich with a few years in bottle but has marvellously fresh acidity cutting through it. Both will develop well with time. (DM)

● **Jurançon** Cuvée Marie★★ £B Clos Uroulat★★★ £C

PRIMO PALATUM   Vin de Pays d'Oc   xavier.copel@primo-palatum.fr   A: N&P

Owner: Xavier Copel   1 Cirette, 33190 Morizes

Xavier Copel has now established himself as a very successful small scale merchant and *négociant*, specialising in limited production bottlings from the important South-West appellations as well as as in Languedoc and Roussillon. He makes a considerable range which includes additional wines from Bordeaux, Graves, Sauternes and in the Midi, Minervois and the Côtes du Roussillon. The regular, or lesser bottlings are labelled Classica and the top cuvées within an appellation are usually labelled Mythologia. Xavier sources fruit from some of the best growers in each of the appellations he works in. His production is less than 6,000 cases a year, so these are small scale bottlings, some barely more than micro-cuvées. The wines though are very impressive: modern and stylish, with an emphasis on terroir but always impeccably made in the various growers own cellars. (DM)

● **Cahors** Classica★★★ £C Mythologia★★★★ £D
● **Vin de Pays d'Oc** Classica★★ £C Mythologia★★★ £C
O **Limoux** Anthologie★★★ £D **Jurançon** Classica★★★ £D

Also see **JEAN RIJCKAERT** (Burgundy, Mâconnais and Beaujolais)

OTHER WINES OF NOTE

DOM. ABOTIA ● **Irouléguy** £B
DOM. DE L'ANCIENNE CURE ● **Bergerac** L'Extrase £D O **Monbazillac** £B Cuvée de l'Abbaye £E
DOM. ARRETXIA ● **Irouléguy** £B
DOM. BELLEGARDE O **Jurançon** £B Cuvée Thibaut £C
DOM. BRANA ● **Irouléguy** £B
DOM. BRU-BACHÉ O **Jurançon** Casterrasses £B Quintessence £C
DOM. GUY CAPMARTIN ● **Madiran** Tradition £B Cuvée de Couvent £B
DOM. CASTERA O **Jurançon** £B
DOM. DE CAUSSE-MARINES O **Gaillac** Greilles £B Délires d'Automne £D
CH. BAUDARE ● **Côtes du Frontonnais** Tradition £B
CH. BÉLINGARD O **Bergerac** Blanche de Bosredon £B O **Monbazillac** Blanche de Bosredon £D
CH. BELLEVUE-LA-FORÊT ● **Côtes du Frontonnais** £B Préstige £B
CH. BOUISSEL ● **Côtes du Frontonnais** £B Cuvée d'Or £B Cuvée Sélection £B
CH. LAFITTE-TESTON ● **Madiran** £B Vieilles Vignes £B
O **Pacherenc de Vic-Bilh** Ericka £B
CH. LES MIADOUX O **Bergerac** £B
CH. LAMARTINE ● **Cahors** £B Cuvée Particulière £C Expression £D
CH. LA MOULIÈRE ● **Côtes de Duras** £B O **Côtes de Duras** £B
CH. LE ROC ● **Côtes du Frontonnais** £B Cuvée Reservée £B Cuvée Don Quichotte £B
CH. MASBUREL O **Montravel** £B ● **Côtes de Bergerac** £C
CH. PEYROS ● **Madiran** £B
CH. PLAISANCE ● **Côtes du Frontonnais** £B Cuvée Thibaut £B
CH. LES RIGALETS ● **Cahors** Cuvée Prestige £B Cuvée Quintessence £D
CH. DE RIPAILLE O **Vin de Savoie** £B
CH. THEULET ● **Bergerac** £B O **Monbazillac** £C
CH. DE TIREGAND ● **Pécharmant** £C
CLOS DE GAMOT ● **Cahors** £B
CLOS LA COUTALE ● **Cahors** £B
CLOS THOU O **Jurançon** Sec £C
CAVE DE COCUMONT ● **Côtes du Marmandais** Béroy £B
DOM. DU CRAMPILH ● **Madiran** Vieilles vignes £B Cuvée Baron £B
DOM. DURAND-PERRON O **Château-Chalon** £E

DOM. ETXEGARAYA ● **Irouléguy** £B
DOM. DE GINESTE O **Gaillac** Grande Cuvée £B ● **Gaillac** Grande Cuvée £B
DOM. ILARRIA ● **Irouléguy** £B
DOM. LABET O **Côtes du Jura** Chardonnay/Savagnin £B Fleur de Chardonnay £B Les Varrons £C
DOM. LABRANCHE-LAFFONT ● **Madiran** Vieilles Vignes £B
DOM. LARREDYA O **Jurançon** Sec £B Sélections des Terrasses £C
DOM. DE LAULAN O **Côtes de Duras** £B
LES VERDOTS O **Bergerac** Clos des Verdots £B Grand Vin Les Verdots £D
● **Côtes de Bergerac** Clos des Verdots £B Grand Vin Les Verdots £E
DOM. JEAN MACLE O **Cotes du Jura** £B O **Château-Chalon** £E
DOM. LOUIS MAGNIN O **Roussette de Savoie** £B ● **Vin de Savoie** Mondeuse Vieilles Vignes £B
DOM. PINERAIE ● **Cahors** Château Pineraie £B
ROBERT PLAGEOLES O **Gaillac** Mauzac Vert £B Vin d'Autan £F
PRODUCTEURS PLAIMONT ● **Côtes de Saint-Mont** Château de Sabazan £B
DOM. JACQUES PUFFENEY O **Arbois** Chardonnay £B
ANDRÉ ET MICHEL QUÉNARD O **Roussette de Savoie Altesse** £B
● **Vin de Savoie** Mondeuse Vieilles Vignes £B Pinot Noir £B
DOM. ROLET O **Côtes du Jura** Chardonnay/Savagnin £C O **Arbois** Tradition £C Vin Jaune £E
DOM. ELIAN DA ROS O **Côtes du Marmandais** Chante Coucou £C

Author's choice (DM)

Cellarworthy South West reds
DOM. BERTHOUMIEU ● **Madiran** Charles de Batz
ALAIN BRUMONT ● **Madiran** Château Montus Cuvée Prestige
CHAPELLE LENCLOS ● **Madiran** la Chapelle Lenclos
CH. D'AYDIE ● **Madiran** Château d'Aydie
CH. BARREJAT ● **Madiran** Vieux ceps
CH. BEAULIEU ● **Côtes du Marmandais** L'Oratoire
CH. DU CÈDRE ● **Cahors** Le Cèdre
CH. LAGREZETTE ● **Cahors** Pigeonnier
CH. TOUR DES GENDRES ● **Bergerac** Moulin des Dames
CH. VIELLA ● **Madiran** Cuvée Prestige
CLOS TRIGUEDINA ● **Cahors** Prince Probus
PRIMO PALATUM ● **Cahors** Mythologia

Six diverse regional whites
DOM. BERTHET-BONDET O **Château-Chalon**
DOM. CAUHAPÉ O **Jurançon** Noblesse du Temps
CH. TIRECUL-LA-GRAVIÈRE O **Monbazillac** Cuvée Madame
CH. TOUR DES GENDRES O **Bergerac** Cuvée Anthologia
CH. VIELLA O **Pacherenc du Vic-Bilh** Moelleux
CLOS UROULAT O **Jurançon** Clos Uroulat

Piedmont has made progress like almost no other wine region over the past 20 years. There is both outstanding quality and considerable diversity. What is really wonderful about Piedmont is man's connection with the land and the importance of the link between fine wine, the physical environment and the human endeavour therein. It is illustrated as well here as in any wine region in the world.

Red wines

At the heart of Piedmont viticulture are the Langhe hills. The finest grape is Nebbiolo. The two great wines are **Barolo** and **Barbaresco**, both DOCG, though some of the best wines from these zones are now sold under the **Langhe** DOC. One of the region's greatest strengths derives from its peasant landholding heritage. While *commerciante* or large *négociant* houses flogged the grapes of any number of small growers under generic labels in the 1950s and 60s, the subsequent success andleadership of Angelo Gaja and others paved the way for small growers to do likewise – a trend that really gained momentum in the 80s and 90s. Outside money tends to be the exception in Piedmont yetsome producers have been highly receptive to new ideas. Both Barolo (a little over 1,300 ha) and Barbaresco (not much more than 500 ha) are fairly small wine regions and it is common for growers here to have just one or two hectares of this or that *cru*.

Barolo is spread for the most part over five communes: La Morra, Barolo, Castiglione Falletto, Monforte d'Alba and Serralunga. Verduno is the most significant of six other communes that encroach on the DOCG. The southern part of Monforte and Serralunga (in the east) have mostly the older Helvetian soils, said to favour strength and structure. La Morra soils are predominantly on younger Tortonian soils, a chalky marl giving greater perfume and a less rigorous structure. Between the two there tends to be a mix of the two with varying amounts of sand and clay. More clay can help in very hot years but a higher sand component can improve drainage in cool, wet years.

Barbaresco is almost exclusively restricted to just three communes. Almost half of it comes from the commune of Barbaresco, where 60 per cent of the vineyard area is is given over to Barbaresco production, compared to only a little over 20 per cent of the vineyard area in neighbouring Neive and Treiso. Barbaresco generally, is slightly less powerful than Barolo, more perfumed and ready to drink a little sooner, but producer and site are the real determinants of style and character. The wines are required to have a minimum of nine months' wood-ageing and are released a year earlier than Barolo (which must have two years in wood).

In both zones much is made of a modern versus traditional approach to winemaking yet the reality is less distinct, with a range of different approaches to vinification and winemaking. The important differences centre around the length of maceration; the type and use of oak (size, age and origin); temperature and style of fermentation; and the type of fermentation vessel – we have tried to highlight some of these differences within the individual producer profiles. Of course these differences apply as much in Burgundy but in this relatively isolated, conservative area the differences of opinion have taken on an extra intensity. There are many outstanding wines across the spectrum.

Nebbiolo under other guises includes **Carema**, **Gattinara**, **Ghemme** and **Roero** in Piedmont and **Valtellina Superiore** in Lombardy. In the latter the wines may also be identified by one of four sub-zones: Grumello, Inferno, Sassella or Valgella. But nowhere is the combination of soils, elevation and mesoclimate as predisposing as in the Langhe hills. The majority of other good examples currently come from Roero and Valtellina.

Piedmont's second great grape is Barbera, which can take on a number of guises. The leading two appellations are **Barbera d'Alba** and **Barbera d'Asti**. The Superiore version of the latter is now redefined by three subzones: Colli Astiani, Nizza and Tinella. Barbera has a great affinity with new oak and many of the top examples have spent around 12 months in *barriques*. Barbera also combines well with Nebbiolo and there are many good oak-aged, deeply fruity, lush examples (typically **Langhe** DOC) that can be drunk quite young or kept. The more northerly hills of the Asti and Alessandria provinces include similar interesting blends under the **Monferrato** DOC.

Dolcetto doesn't quite make the cut in fine wine terms. It does, however, make both wonderfully fruity everyday wine or something more intense and concentrated and often better with a year or two of bottle-age, depending on its maker. There are three leading manifestations: **Dolcetto d'Alba**, the small **Dolcetto di Diano d'Alba** and **Dolcetto di Dogliani**. Dolcetto is also included in the Monferrato DOC, while **Dolcetto di Ovada** is mostly of the fruity, juicy type.

What else is there? Other natives varieties include Freisa and Grignolino, both sold under most of the regional DOCs, but exciting examples are few. There's also sparkling red fizz, actually DOCG in **Brachetto d'Acqui** (from Brachetto) and **Malvasia di Castelnuovo Don Bosco** from Malvasia Nera. How significant are the French imports? Not very, but Cabernet Sauvignon features in many a Langhe or Monferrato blend (see above), Merlot to a lesser extent. Pinot Nero (Pinot Noir) has yet to really impress, while only a very small amount of Syrah is planted.

Beyond Piedmont, in Lombardy Pinot Nero, Bonarda and Barbera figure in the rarely other than ordinary **Oltrepò Pavese**. Cabernet Franc (or, as likely, Carmenère), Merlot, Cabernet Sauvignon and Pinot Nero are also used for sometimes very good **Terre di Franciacorta** reds.

Leading Barolo crus

La Morra
Arborina, Brunate, Cerequio, Conca di Annunziata, Fossati, Gattera, Giachini, La Serra, Rocche di Annunziata

Barolo
Brunate, Cerequio, Fossati (all three are shared with La Morra) Bricco Viole, Cannubi, Cannubi Boschis, Le Coste, Sarmassa

Castiglione Falletto
Bricco Boschis, Fiasco, Monprivato, Villero, Rocche

Monforte d'Alba
Bussia Soprana, Bricco Cicala, Colonello, Gavarini, Ginestra, Mosconi, Pianpolvere

Serralunga d'Alba
Cerretta, Falletto, Francia, Lazzarito, Marenca-Rivette, Parafada, Prapò, Vigna Rionda

---

Leading Barbaresco crus:

Barbaresco
Asili, Martinenga, Montefico, Montestefano, Ovello, Pajé, Pora, Rabajà, Rio Sordo, Roncagliette, Secondine

Neive
Bricco, Gallina, Marcorino, Messoirano, Santo Stefano, Serraboella and Starderi

Treiso
Pajoré, Valeirano

White and sparkling wines

The perfumed and characterful Arneis (frequently as **Roero Arneis**) and relatively high acid Cortese (the best examples sold as **Gavi del Comune di Gavi** – those at the heart of a wider zone) are the leading native whites. Other natives include Favorita, a distinctive herb-scented wine, and Erbaluce as **Erbaluce di Caluso** or the better sweet version from dried grapes, **Caluso Passito**. Pigato and Vermentino are important in Liguria as **Rivera Ligure di Ponente** varietals, but the latter also in **Colli di Luni** and **Cinqueterre**. In the east of Lombardy some attractive dry white **Lugana** is made from Trebbiano di Lugana (*see* North-East Italy).

Yet the most important white grape in North-West Italy is Moscato Bianco. This, the 'good' Muscat (Muscat Blanc à Petits Grains), is very widely planted in the Asti and Alba hills in Piedmont. Good **Asti** is a well-made, sweet party fizz and much better than some of the nasty acidic and green branded stuff made in Germany, France and elsewhere. But **Moscato d'Asti**, made on a different scale, can be incomparably better. Delightfully perfumed and low in alcohol, it is excellent with fresh fruit. A very small amount of *passito*-style Muscat is made in an Asti enclave called **Loazzolo**. Chambave Moscato is another sweet example from the Valle d'Aosta.

The closest Italy has to top Champagne in quality is **Franciacorta**. Here, near Lake Iseo in Lombardy, Chardonnay, Pinot Bianco and Pinot Nero grapes are combined in serious *metodo classico* sparkling wines. Satèn is a softer, creamier, low-pressure version.

Of imports, Chardonnay is the leading variety, usually appearing as **Langhe** Chardonnay but occasionally under the regionwide **Piemonte** DOC. Really top examples are relatively few but there is potential here. It is also increasingly important in Oltrepò Pavese and Terre di Franciacorta whites. There are small amounts of Sauvignon and even less Riesling, Viognier and other Rhône varietals.

A-Z of Producers by appellation

Asti
CONTRATTO

Barbaresco
PRODUTTORI DEL BARBARESCO
PIERO BUSSO
FRATELLI CIGLIUTI
GAJA
BRUNO GIACOSA
LA SPINETTA
MARCHESI DI GRÉSY
MOCCAGATTA
FIORENZO NADA
PAITIN
PELISSERO
VIGNAIOLI ELVIO PERTINACE
ALBINO ROCCA
BRUNO ROCCA
SOTTIMANO

Barbera d'Asti
ARALDICA VINI PIEMONTESI
BAVA
BERTELLI
BRAIDA
CASTELLO DI CALOSSO
LUIGI COPPO & FIGLI

ICARDI
LA BARBATELLA
FRANCO M MARTINETTI
TENUTA LA TENAGLIA

Barolo
GIANFRANCO ALESSANDRIA
ELIO ALTARE
ASCHERI
AZELIA
LUIGI BAUDANA
ENZO BOGLIETTI
BONGIOVANNI
BROVIA
BUSSIA SOPRANA
CAVALOTTO
CERETTO
MICHELE CHIARLO
DOMENICO CLERICO
ELVIO COGNO
ALDO CONTERNO
GIACOMO CONTERNO
CONTERNO-FANTINO
CORDERO DI MONTEZEMOLO
GIOVANNI CORINO
FONTANAFREDDA
ETTORE GERMANO
ATTILIO GHISOLFI

ELIO GRASSO
SILVIO GRASSO
GIOVANNI MANZONE
MARCARINI
BARTOLO MASCARELLO
GIUSEPPE MASCARELLO & FIGLIO
MAURO MOLINO
ANDREA OBERTO
FRATELLI ODDERO
ARMANDO PARUSSO
PIO CESARE
E PIRA & FIGLI
LUIGI PIRA
FERDINANDO PRINCIPIANO
PRUNOTTO
RENATO RATTI
FRATELLI REVELLO
ROCCHE DEI MANZONI
LUCIANO SANDRONE
PAOLO SCAVINO
ALDO & RICCARDO SEGHESIO
G D VAJRA
MAURO VEGLIO
VIETTI
VIGNA RIONDA - MASSOLINO
GIANNI VOERZIO
ROBERTO VOERZIO

Dolcetto d'Alba
CA' VIOLA

Dolcetto di Diano d'Alba
CLAUDIO ALARIO
BRICCO MAIOLICA

Dolcetto di Dogliani
ANNA MARIA ABBONA
M & E ABBONA
QUINTO CHIONETTI
LUIGI EINAUDI
FRATELLI PECCHENINO
SAN FEREOLO

Erbaluce di Caluso
ORSOLANI

Franciacorta
BELLAVISTA
CA' DEL BOSCO

Gavi
LA GIUSTINIANA
LA SCOLCA

Ghemme
ANTICHI VIGNETI DI CANTALUPO

Loazzolo
FORTETO DELLA LUJA

Moscato d'Asti
CAUDRINA
SARACCO

Roero
CASCINA CHICCO
CASCINA VAL DEL PRETE
MATTEO CORREGGIA
FILIPPO GALLINO
MALVIRÀ
ANGELO NEGRO & FIGLI

Valtellina Superiore
NINO NEGRI
ALDO RAINOLDI
TRIACCA

Piedmont vintages

There's never been a better time to add a selection of the best Piedmont wines to a wine cellar. Not just great Barolo and Barbaresco for the medium- and long-term (8 to 30 years) but much excellent Langhe and Barbera for the short- and medium-term (4 to 12 years). When to drink depends on a producer's own style but also on your own preference, whether for the fruit intensity and boldness of youth or the more mellow complexity that comes with age.

2002: There's not much enthusiasm for this vintage given the poor summer which was atypically wet and cool. If this were not enough some prize vineyards were devastated by hail, severely denting production as well as quality. Nonetheless those most dedicated to quality in the vineyard and a rigorous selection will make good, if not great wine.

2001: A very promising vintage and the last in a long string of fine vintages in Piedmont that began with 1995. A hot summer followed a wet spring and hopes were very high. But from September intermittent rain and hail had a negative effect on quality for some. Likely to be more variable than other top vintages.

2000: There's evident quality in barrel from Barolo and Barbaresco. A very hot August followed a cool July. The consequent rapid ripenening seems to have harmed the Dolcetto more than anything else yet plenty of these are good too.

1999: Opinion is somewhat divided but this vintage seems to combine the fruit richness and ripeness of 97 with more of the structure of 96. Many exciting wines to look out for. Good for Nebbiolo, Barbera and Dolcetto.

1998: A smallish crop from a hot dry summer that concluded with some rain. Colours are more evolved, more typical for the Nebbiolo-based wines; many are full, ripe and balanced. Another very fine vintage for medium- to long-term cellaring.

1997: Two words characterise this vintage: hot and dry. The very ripe, occasionally overripe fruit has resulted in wines with a sweet, lush fruit character and relatively low acidities. Generally the tannins are good and ripe but in some instances are quite marked (a lack of physiological ripeness due to the heat) and this will only become more apparent as the primary fruit evolves. Some won't keep but many will, given the chance.

1996: Cool and classic, with gradual even ripening. Many growers picked very late to produce wines that are fully ripe but powerfully structured. One to cellar for at least 10 to 15 years particularly from the so-called traditional producers. Pretty consistent too, though a few of the newer names were still finding their way. Hail hit some badly and reduced quantities overall.

1995: The first of an unprecedented run of good to great vintages. Though not at the same level as 1996 - 2001, attractive, well-structured if slightly leaner Barolo and Barbaresco. The best are only just beginning to show well.

1994: If generally weak, with a lack of real fruit concentration, there are some attractive, forward Nebbiolo-based wines. Go for a specific recommendation or expect to be disappointed.

1993: The best vintage between 90 and 95. Worth a punt from a grower with a good track record but some are too firm for the fruit levels. Some good if not great Riservas have been released in the past couple of years.

1992: Wet, depressing – the poorest vintage of the 90s. No longer one to take a chance on (if you ever could) – even for the best Barolos – but there were rare successes.

1991: A lack of balance seems to be typical of 91, the first weak vintage in a gloomy spell for

Piedmont. How different it all seems now. Generally poorly balanced wines emerged from a wet vintage.

1990: The last outstanding vintage prior to 1996. Sustained hot weather gave rise to rich, ripe wines. The first wave of exciting new producers (Clerico, Sandrone, R Voerzio *et al*) became well-established stars. A good vintage to discover how great Barolo/Barbaresco begins to evolve.

1989: Another classic year with powerful, structured wines. Most should still be kept but it depends on the signature of the grower or producer.

1988: Some Nebbiolo was compromised by rain but the best are dense sturdy wines that have aged well. Many will still keep.

Earlier years: Few **1987s**★★ ever achieved real harmony but **1986**★★★ provided some very attractive Barolo and Barbaresco – but stick with the top wines now, others are past it. **1985**★★★ and **1982** ★★★★ were excellent vintages but there were nothing like the number of top examples now being made. Beware of many of the *négociant* labels; seek out a classic from a small grower instead. **1979**★★★ provided some refined wines but most of the rare remaining bottles are past their best. Though long-lived, both **1978**★★★ and **1974**★★★ can be rather tough and old-fashioned – taste before buying any quantity and be sure of its provenance. Well-stored examples from **1971** can still be classic while **1970, 67, 64** and **61** might tempt the intrepid.

Piedmont & North-West Italy vintages

	Barolo	Barbaresco	Barbera (premium)
2002	NYR	NYR	NYR
2001	NYR	★★★★ A	★★★★ A
2000	★★★★/★★★★★ A	★★★★/★★★★★ A	★★★★/★★★★★ B
1999	★★★★/★★★★★ A	★★★★/★★★★★ A	★★★/★★★★ B
1998	★★★★ A	★★★★ B	★★★★ B
1997	★★★★/★★★★★ B	★★★★/★★★★★ B	★★★★ /★★★★★ C
1996	★★★★/★★★★★ A	★★★★/★★★★★ B	★★★ C
1995	★★★/★★★★ B	★★★/★★★★ B	★★★/★★★★ C
1994	★★/★★★ C	★★/★★★ C	★★/★★★ D
1993	★★★ B	★★★ B	★★★ C
1992	★/★★ C	★/★★ C	★/★★ D
1991	★★/★★★ C	★★ C	★★★ D
1990	★★★★/★★★★★ B	★★★★/★★★★★ B	★★★★/★★★★★ C
1989	★★★★/★★★★★ B	★★★★/★★★★★ B	★★★★/★★★★★ C
1988	★★★/★★★★ C	★★★/★★★★ C	★★★/★★★★ D

ANNA MARIA ABBONA   Dolcetto di Dogliani   www.amabbona.com   A: Mgi

Owner: Anna Maria Abbona & Franco Schellino   Fraz. Moncucco 21, 12060 Farigliano (CN)
The historic zone of Dogliani has undergone a considerable resurgence in the past decade. It's easy
to be dismissive about a zone dedicated to Dolcetto, but the best are very good indeed. Anna Maria's
Maioli is made from vines planted in 1935; rich, almost velvety with lovely fruit, but powerful too
with a refined structure. An oak-aged Superiore adds smoke and spice and is equally good, though
it benefits from an extra year or two's age. An attractive fleshy Barbera, Cadò, which doesn't qualify
as Barbera d'Alba due to the location, includes 10 per cent Dolcetto. (PW)
- **Dolcetto di Dogliani** Sorì dij But★★ £B   Maioli★★★ £C   Superiore★★★ £C
- **Langhe** Cadò★★ £D   ● **Langhe** Dolcetto★ £B

M & E ABBONA   Dolcetto di Dogliani   A: LoW

Owner: Marziano Abbona   Via Torino 242, 12063 Dogliani (CN)
Marziano Abbona is one of the stars of Dogliani, but also does justice to two small plots of Barolo
and Barbaresco, the latter which sees a percentage of new oak. Old vines in the Dariolo vineyard are
source for the top (unoaked) Dolcetto Papà Celso which shows a breadth uncommon to most
examples of the variety. I Due Ricu combines Barbera, Nebbiolo and Cabernet. Also made is a white,
Cinerino Bianco, from Viognier. (PW)
- **Dolcetto di Dogliani** Papà Celso★★★ £B   Vigna Dariolo★★ £B   Vigneto Muntâ★★ £B
- **Barbaresco** Faset★★★ £E   ● **Barolo** Terlo Ravera★★★ £E
- **Barbera d'Alba** Rinaldi★★ £C   ● **Langhe** I Due Ricu★★ £D

CLAUDIO ALARIO   Dolcetto di Diano d'Alba   A:WTs

Owner: Claudio Alario   Via Santa Croce 23, 12055 Diano d'Alba (CN)
This estate and BRICCO MAIOLICA are champions of the small Dolcetto zone that lies between
Barolo and Barbaresco yet both are as notable for their Nebbiolo as for Dolcetto. Here both the
Nebbiolo d'Alba and Barolo are perfumed, balanced and ageworthy. Of the Dolcetto, Costa Fiore is
the more concentrated but backward version and is best with an extra year or two. (PW)
- **Dolcetto di Diano d'Alba** Costa Fiore★★★ £B   Montegrillo★★ £B
- **Barbera d'Alba** Valletta★★ £C   ● **Nebbiolo d'Alba** Cascinotto★★ £C
- **Barolo** Riva★★★ £E

GIANFRANCO ALESSANDRIA   Barolo   A:Win

Owner: Gianfranco Alessandria   Loc. Manzoni 12, 12065 Monforte d'Alba (CN)
Inspired young grower with a range of ripe, full and stylish reds. The top wines all show a measure
of new oak but it is never obvious or allowed to dominate. An intense Barbera Vittoria from
65-year-old vines, and beautifully balanced Barolo San Giovanni (a special selection rather than
vineyard specific) are particularly worthy but all of the wines deliver good fruit in a modern accessible
style. Gianfranco's version of Insieme (see ALTARE), 40 per cent Nebbiolo with the balance 'Vittoria'
Barbera and Cabernet, is one of the best. (PW)
- **Barolo**★★★ £E   San Giovanni★★★★ £F
- **Barbera d'Alba**★★ £B   Vittoria★★★ £C   ● **Dolcetto d'Alba**★ £B
- **Insieme**★★★★ £F

ELIO ALTARE Barolo   A: DWS, J&B, Fal, F&R

Owner: Elio Altare   Fraz. Annunziata 51, 12064 La Morra (CN)

La Morra's and Barolo's great moderniser as well as mentor to a group of other small growers –
ALESSANDRIA, CORINO, Silvio GRASSO, MOLINO, REVELLO and VEGLIO. Radically low yields,
short maceration times and rows of barriques are now common to all but nobody else quite manages
to get the extra depth and concentration of Altare. It is not a purist's Barolo that emerges yet one of
terrific concentration and balance that still conveys something of its origins. Super-Langhes Arborina
(Nebbiolo), Larigi (Barbera) and La Villa (Nebbiolo/Barbera) take the new oak theme to its logical
(or illogical, depending on your viewpoint) conclusion. Altare was also the proponent behind
Insieme. The band of seven producers share winemaking resources and expertise to produce
delicious, concentrated modern oak-aged blends – variations on a Nebbiolo, Barbera, Cabernet
and/or Merlot theme – a percentage of the proceeds go to local cultural and artisanal causes. The
setback of cork contamination problems (though no fault of his own) that ruined potentially
wonderful 1997 Barolos and 1998 Langhe reds has done little to dent Elio Altare's resolve and the
maintenance of his very high standards. (PW)

● **Barolo**★★★ £E Arborina★★★★ £F Brunate★★★★ £F
● **Langhe** Arborina★★★ £F Larigi★★★★ £F La Villa★★★★ £F
● **Barbera d'Alba**★★ £C ● **Dolcetto d'Alba**★★ £B
● **Insieme**★★★★ £F

ANTICHI VIGNETI DI CANTALUPO Ghemme www.cantalupovigneti.it   A: AIF

Owner: Arlunno family   Via Michelangelo Buonarroti 5, 28074 Montelupo Albese (NO)

Ghemme's one producer that gives real credibility to the zone's DOCG status. Input from top
enologist Donato Lanati helps even if in the main the wines follow a fairly traditional, unadventurous
vinification. Typically rather austere and firm when young, the wines mellow with age and their
already enticing perfumes become ever more complex. While the regular Ghemme includes a little
Vespolina and Uva Rara, special bottlings are pure Nebbiolo. Carellae and Breclemae are vineyard-
specific, while Signore di Bayard is a special selction which is aged in French barriques (a third new).
The latter is often the most flattering when young but also has the greatest dimension, intensity and
sheer style. Colline Novaresi wines, Agamium (Nebbiolo) and Primigenia (Nebbiolo/Uva
Rara/Vespolina), are characterful but not at the same level. Unoaked white Carolus combines Arneis,
Greco and Chardonnay. There is much quality Ghemme from recent good vintages though there is
no Collis Carellae in 1998 or 2001 and no Ghemme at all is likely from the 2002 vintage! (PW)

● **Ghemme**★ £D Collis Carellae★★ £E Collis Breclamae★★★ £E Signore di Bayard★★★ £E

ARALDICA VINI PIEMONTESI Barbera d'Asti www.araldicavini.com   A: Mer

Owner: 'Cooperative'   Viale Laudano 2, 14040 Castel Boglione (AT)

Big co-op, well actually three rather than one, but increasingly respected under the direction of
Claudio Manera. Widely seen Alasia varietals, first developed by Australian Martin Shaw (SHAW &
SMITH) include bright, clean fruity Barbera, Dolcetto, Chardonnay and Cortese. More recently
some of the best vineyards have been identified, the best are bottled under the Poderi Alasia label.
(PW)

● **Barbera d'Asti** Poderi Alasia Rive★★ £B Ceppi Storici★ £B Vigneti Croja★★ £B
● **Nebbiolo d'Alba** Poderi Alasia Castellero★ £B
O **Roero Arneis** Podere Alasia Sorilaria★ £B

ASCHERI   Barolo   www.ascherivini.it   A: Eno

Owner: Ascheri family   Via Piumati 23, 12042 Bra (CN)

Matteo Ascheri has an energy to match his bear-like stature. A list of his accomplishments includes planting Viognier and Syrah at Bra (outside the Barolo zone), creating the Osteria Murivecchi in the family's old cellars, promoting the Langhe at home and abroad – yet all the while maintaining realistic prices and good quality. Matteo believes strongly in natural winemaking, and recent vintages show improvement from the regeneration of the family's vineyards, with wines of bright, pure varietal character. Of two *cru* Barolos, Vigna dei Pola comes from the Pisapolla *cru* in the Verduno vineyards that lie south of Ascheri's base in Bra. The more traditional (moderately long fermentation, ageing in mostly old wood) Sorano comes from Serralunga and has more depth, grip and class. In 1999 fruit from the best vines within Sorano was vinified separately to produce Coste & Bricco. First impressions are of yet more style and expression. (PW)

● **Barolo** Sorano★★★ £E Vigna dei Pola★★★ £E
● **Barbera d'Alba** Vigna Fontanelle★★ £C
● **Dolcetto d'Alba** Vigna Nirane★ £B ● **Nebbiolo d'Alba** Bricco San Giacomo★ £C
● **Montalupa Syrah**★★ £D O **Montalupa Viognier**★★ £D

AZELIA   Barolo   A: J&B

Owner: Luigi Scavino   Via Alba-Barolo 27, 12060 Castiglione Falletto (CN)

Less well-known than Enrico Scavino, Luigi similarly owns a decent chunk of the excellently positioned Fiasco vineyard, which has certain similarities to the nearby Monprivato and Villero *crus*. The regular Barolo, made from younger vines, sees mostly large wood (*botte grande*) but the two *crus* Bricco Fiasco and San Rocco (the latter from Serralunga) both receive 50 per cent new oak. There is evident structure but the wines are balanced with good weight, depth and dimension and definite class. A name to seek out – consistently fine in successive top vintages from 95 onwards. (PW)

● **Barolo**★★★ £E Bricco Fiasco★★★★ £F San Rocco★★★★ £F
● **Barbera d'Alba** Vigneto Punta★★ £D ● **Dolcetto d'Alba** Bricco dell'Oriolo★ £C

PRODUTTORI DEL BARBARESCO   Barbaresco   www.produttori-barbaresco.it A: V&C

Owner: 'Cooperative'   Via Torino 52, 12050 Barbaresco (CN)

This super co-op manages around a fifth (100 ha) of Barbaresco's relatively tiny vineyard area (509 ha). It is dDmocratically run and winemaker Gianni Testa adheres to traditional lines with lengthy maceration and ageing in large *botti*. But what perfume, grace and charm they achieve in the top *crus* in a good vintage! These wines are a purist's delight, capturing much of the essence of Nebbiolo and a splendid expression of the grape in some of the most hallowed patches of soil in Barbaresco. What's more, the single-vineyard Riservas sell for less than many other producers' regular Barbaresco. All will keep for, and sometimes need, a decade or more. For the uninitiated, try the love-ly 1997s, which have great vinosity and lowish acidity. Other recent vintages are also proving very promising but older bottles from more difficult years are likely to be more variable. (PW)

● **Barbaresco Riserva** Asili★★★★ £E Moccagatta★★★★ £E Montefico★★★★ £E
● **Barbaresco Riserva** Montestefano★★★★ £E Rabajà★★★★ £E Ovello★★★ £E
● **Barbaresco Riserva** Pajé★★★ £E Pora★★★ £E   Rio Sordo★★★ £E
● **Barbaresco**★★ £D ● **Langhe Nebbiolo**★ £B

LUIGI BAUDANA Barolo   A: THt

Owner: Luigi Baudana   Fraz. Baudana 43, 12050 Serralunga d'Alba (CN)

With barely 5 ha of vineyards, Luigi Baudana's small output nonetheless encompasses most of the main styles common to Langhe producers. Full ripeness and a particular intensity are common to all. A solid regular Barolo (if slightly weaker in 1998) is surpassed by Cerretta Piani, which has the extract and power associated with Serralunga but also a certain elegance that vintages such as 96 or 99 seem certain to accentuate with a decade's age. A Baudana *cru* from 99, more meaty but balanced, shows promise too. Barbera (with some barrique-influence) and Dolcetto are of a good standard, while Lorenso Rosso is a satisfactory example of the oak-influenced Nebbiolo/Barbera/Merlot blend. Any charm the white Lorenzo, from Sauvignon and Chardonnay, might have, however, is masked by oak. A varietal Chardonnay, on the other hand, delivers good fruit and intensity for the price. (PW)

● **Barolo**★★★ £E Cerretta Piani★★★★ £E
● **Barbera d'Alba** Donatella★★ £C ● **Dolcetto d'Alba** Sorì Baudana★★ £B
● **Langhe** Lorenso★★★ £C O **Langhe Chardonnay**★★ £B

BAVA Barbera d'Asti www.bava.com   A: BWC

Owner: Bava family   Strada Monferrato 2, 14023 Cocconato d'Asti (AT)

Advertising and marketing have given this medium-sized producer a higher profile than many in Piedmont, despite its being closer to Torino than any of the leading wine towns. Barbera is the leading variety and usually impressive if not that cheap in the two top examples, Pianalto and Stradivario. Other wines, including Moscato d'Asti, are less exciting if typically sound, safe bets, although the sweet, fragrant, *frizzante* red Malvasia di Castelnuovo Don Bosco is fun if drunk very young. (PW)

● **Barbera d'Asti** Libera★ £C Arbest★ £C
● **Barbera d'Asti** Superiore Pianalto★★ £D Superiore Stradivario★★ £D
● **Malvasia di Castelnuovo Don Bosco**★ £B O **Monferrato** Alteserre★ £C

BELLAVISTA Franciacorta www.bellavistasrl.it   A: Alv

Owner: Vittorio Moretti   Via Bellavista 5, 25030 Erbusco (BS)

Under the direction of Vittorio Moretti and winemaker Mattia Vezzola, Bellavista make brilliant, refined yet full-flavoured sparkling wines that deservedly sell for the same prices as good non-vintage Champagne. Most include at least a component of barrel-fermentation to add further complexity. The non-vintage Brut Cuvée (predominantly Chardonnay with a little Pinot Noir and Pinot Blanc) is the most affordable, and made in by far the greatest quantities, of the DOCG Franciacorta. Gran Cuvée Brut is a step up, three parts Chardonnay to one of Pinot Noir. The Rosé is a sheer delight (60/40 Pinot Noir and Chardonnay) while the soft, creamy and delicately sparkling non-vintage Satèn is a lovely example of this low-pressure style. Pas Operé has no final addition of sugar, making it the driest of the range. A Riserva named after the owner has extended ageing on its lees (around six years). The still wines are sold under the Terre di Franciacorta DOC. The best of these is the rich, complex Chardonnay and Pinot Bianco blend, Convento della Santissima Annunciata. Varietal Chardonnay Uccellanda is rich and oaky while a Pinot Noir, Casotte, has good texture but is not among the best Italian examples (see North-East Italy). A powerful Cabernet/Merlot blend, Solesine, can show well with five to ten years' age when from a warm vintage. None of the still wines offers particularly good value for money but try the very classy fizz at least. (PW)

O **Franciacorta** Brut Cuvée★★ £D Gran Cuvée Brut★★★ £E
O **Franciacorta** Gran Cuvée Pas Operé★★★ £E Gran Cuvée Satèn★★★ £E
◉ **Franciacorta** Gran Cuvée Brut Rosé★★★

O **Terre di Franciacorta** Convento della Santissima Annunciata★★★ £E
O **Terre di Franciacorta** Uccellanda★★ £E
● **Terre di Franciacorta** Rosso★ £C
● **Casotte**★★ £E ● **Solesine**★★ £E

BERTELLI Barbera d'Asti   A: J&B

Owner: Aldo & Alberto Bertelli Fraz. San Carlo 38, 14055 Costiglione d'Asti (AT)
Aldo and his son Alberto make only a few barrels of this and that, but what there is can be very very good even if it isn't always so. Barbera aside, it's as if France (her grape varieties and a few oaks too) has come to Piedmont. Deep, rich and characterful Chardonnay is very powerful if sometimes slightly at the expense of better defintion and expression. The Barberas are often rich, very ripe and always oaky, but in San Antonio Vieilles Vignes the marvellous old vine fruit depth easily contains the oak with a resultant complexity, seamless structure and a very long finish. Red I Fossaretti is a big, extracted Cabernet that usually works with plenty of age while the white Fossaretti from Sauvignon Blanc is similarly in an outsized Bordeaux mould. St. Marsan is the label for a Rhône pair, the red a very intense Hermitage-like Syrah of marginal balance. The white, a Roussanne/Marsanne blend was produced in a one-off moderately sweet, rich (but balanced) style in 2000 from late-harvested grapes. Mon Mayor is usually a well-oaked but fruit-intense Nebbiolo/Cabernet but is not convincing in 99. Such occasional blips in the wines' technical soundness however, has done nothing to dampen the prices they command. (PW)

● **Barbera d'Asti** Giarone★★★ £E Montetusa★★★ £E San Antonio Vieilles Vignes★★★★ £E
● **Monferrato** I Fossaretti★★★ £E Mon Mayor★★★ £E
O **Piemonte Chardonnay** Giarone★★★★ £E O **Monferrato** I Fossaretti★★ £E
● **St Marsan**★★★ £E O **St Marsan**★★★ £E

ENZO BOGLIETTI Barolo   A: L&W

Owner: Enzo Boglietti Via Roma 37, 12064 La Morra (CN)
A young grower with only a modest patchwork of vines but those sites include Brunate, Case Nere and Fossati (noted for Barbera as much as Nebbiolo). Full of fruit, oak-enriched, and with relatively soft but abundant tannin, these are good examples of the modern style – perhaps why the old-vine Barbera Vigna dei Romani (from Fossati) can impress almost as much as the Barolos. Fossati and Case Nere see a lot of new oak (50 and 80 per cent respectively) and the structure can suffer a little from the treatment, though there is better harmony with age. Brunate, subject to only a small percentage of new oak but a longer maceration, is intense and compact when young but the most expressive and stylish of the three. All need eight to ten years' age. Ripe, potent Dolcetto Tiglineri oozes delicious old-vine fruit but needs a couple of years' age. Langhe Buio, Nebbiolo with some Barbera (80/20), spends 18 months in mostly new barriques but has considerable charm and style, especially with three or four years' age. (PW)

● **Barolo** Brunate★★★★ £F Case Nere★★★ £F Fossati★★★ £F
● **Barbera d'Alba**★★ £B Vigna dei Romani★★★ £E Roscaleto★★★ £E
● **Dolcetto d'Alba**★ £B Tiglineri★★ £C ● **Langhe Nebbiolo**★ £B ● **Langhe** Buio★★★ £D

BONGIOVANNI Barolo

Owner: Davide Mozzoni Via Alba-Barolo 4, 12060 Castiglione Falletto (CN)
Davide Mozzoni is not afraid to experiment and takes diverse approaches to making each of his Barolos. The regular version (from three different plots), subject to cold maceration and a short fermentation, is relatively light but modern with some charm. With Pernanno the total maceration

is longer and the temperature allowed to rise to the mid-30s as the fermentation reaches completion. The extract, weight and richness evident on the palate is reinforced by ageing in (60 per cent) new barriques. Micro-oxygenation is employed for the two fruity Dolcettos; the more compact, structured Diano d'Alba deserves to be drunk with an extra year or two's age. Faletto (Cabernet, Merlot and Barbera) is fruit-rich and oaky. While these moderately priced wines are good rather than exciting, it will be interesting to see how the styles evolve. (PW)

● **Barolo★★** £E Pernanno★★★ £E
● **Langhe** Faletto★★★ £D ● **Barbera d'Alba★★** £C
● **Dolcetto d'Alba★★** £B ● **Dolcetto di Diano d'Alba★★** £B

BRAIDA Barbera d'Asti www.braida.it A: SCh, GFy, Bal, Gau, L&W, BBR, N&P

Owner: Anna Bologna Via Roma 94, 14030 Rocchetta Tanaro (CN)
Plenty has been written about Giacomo Bologna, who was one of Piedmont's great characters as well as innovators. Bricco dell'Uccellone, first made in 1982, is the original oak-aged Barbera of outsized proportions. Bricco della Bigotta can often match it, while Ai Suma, which incorporates late-harvested grapes, can be even richer and more powerful. All should but don't always improve for a decade and my feeling is they are often best after six to eight years. There seems to be a real return to form from the late nineties but stick to the top vintages. Il Bacialé adds Pinot Nero to Barbera. Braida are also one of the Hastae five. Working with CHIARLO, COPPO, PRUNOTTO and VIETTI, this is an Asti/Alba axis to promote Barbera. A single wine, Quorum, is made by Riccardo Cotarella. While it is rich, oaky and flattering, as yet it lacks the depth and style of the very best. The serious stuff aside, Barbera La Monella, Brachetto and Moscato are great examples of their effervescent type but the latter two (as ever with these styles) are best within six months of the vintage. (PW)

● **Barbera d'Asti** Bricco della Bigotta★★★ £E Bricco dell' Uccellone★★★ £E Ai Suma★★★★ £F
● **Barbera d'Asti** Quorum★★★ £G
● **Barbera del Monferrato** La Monella★ £B ● **Monferrato** Rosso Il Bacialé★★ £C
● **Brachetto d'Acqui★★** £B **O Moscato d'Asti** Vigna Senza Nome★ £B

BRICCO MAIOLICA Dolcetto di Diano d'Alba A: L&S

Owner: Angelo Accomo Fraz. Ricca, Via Bolangino 7, 12055 Diano d'Alba (CN)
It's just as much the really good examples of Barbera, Dolcetto and Moscato that make this the top estate in this zone even if the Nebbiolo, like CORREGGIA'S or CASCINA CHICCO'S (both in Roero), is one of the few in the Langhe outside Barolo and Barbaresco to be taken seriously. The oak in the best wines is taken up by decent ripe, intense fruit and consistently so. The Briccolero Barbera in fact doesn't see any wood, while the Vigna Vigia receives 50 per cent new, 50 per cent used and Il Cumot Nebbiolo is put in 'second use' barriques. There is splendid fruit in both Dolcettos; the *cru* has a little more amplitude and some gentle spice from six months in used wood. The oak-influenced white Langhe combines Chardonnay and Sauvignon, wile the red Langhe Lorié is one of the best Piedmont Pinots made. (PW)

● **Nebbiolo d'Alba** Il Cumot★★★ £E
● **Barbera d'Alba** Briccolero★★ £B Vigna Vigia★★ £C
● **Dolcetto di Diano d'Alba★** £B Sorì Bricco Maiolica★★ £B
● **Langhe** Lorié★ £D **O Langhe** Rolando★ £C **O Moscato d'Asti** Valdavì★ £B

BROVIA   Barolo   www.brovia.net   A: VDu, Gau

Owner: Brovia family   Via Alba-Barolo 54, 12060 Castiglione Falletto (CN)
Sisters Elena and Cristina Brovia, aided by their father Giacinto, regularly produce full, muscular but
ageworthy Barolo from local plots and another (Cà Mia) in Serralunga, all without the aid of small
new oak barrels. Instead, large 3,000-litre French oak is used following a relatively long maceration
of around 20 days. The elegance of Rocche (di Castiglione) may be contrasted with the intensity of
Villero or the build of Ca' Mia. Barriques are reserved for Dolcetto, especially the remarkable Solatio.
Late-harvested, this purple, high-ethanol monster is typically deep, smooth and balanced. Scarce it
is, but like those from other champions of intense Dolcetto (CA' VIOLA, MARCARINI,
G MASCARELLO, VAJRA *et al*) it deserves to be tasted. Barberas are good too. Through the efforts of
Elena's husband, Alex Sanchez, who hails from Cataluña, this fine range should become more wide-
ly seen. (PW)
- **Barolo** Ca' Mia★★★★ £F Rocche dei Brovia★★★★ £F Villero★★★★ £F
- **Barbera d'Alba** Brea★★★ £E Sorì del Drago★★ £D
- **Dolcetto d'Alba** Vignavillej★★ £C Solatio★★★ £E

BUSSIA SOPRANA   Barolo

Owner: S Casiraghi & G Rossi   Loc. Bussia 81, 12065 Monforte d'Alba (CN)
Silvano Casiraghi has a minority stake in some of the *crus* made famous by ALDO CONTERNO.
With help from roving consultant Giuseppe Caviola (CA' VIOLA) these are wines to look out for
from the mid-nineties vintages. Lesser-known Mosconi, from the south of the commune, is a match
for the Bussia wines at present. (PW)
- **Barolo** Bussia Soprana★★★ £F Mosconi★★★ £F Vigna Colonello★★★ £F
- **Barbera d'Alba**★ £C Vin del Ross★★ £D ● **Dolcetto d'Alba**★ £C

PIERO BUSSO   Barbaresco

Owner: Piero Busso   Via Albesani 8, 12057 Neive (CN)
Piero Busso controls 7 ha from the heart of the Neive commune and believes in a natural expression
of each variety and the importance of place (or *tipicità*). He has little time for technology but does
use barriques (50 per cent new) for Barbaresco Bricco Mondino. While the oak does show in this
cru, all the wines have classic perfumes and structure typical to their variety and add richness and
complexity with age. At least six to eight years' is needed for the Barbarescos. New from 1999 is a
third *cru,* Gallina. Dolcetto and Barbera sometimes struggle for full ripeness and usually need a year
or two to soften. The Langhe white is a blend of Chardonnay and Sauvignon Blanc, the Chardonnay
component fermented and aged in barrique; while not special it will keep at least three to four years.
(PW)
- **Barbaresco** Bricco Mondino★★ £E Vigna Borgese★★★ £E
- **Barbera d'Alba** Vigna Majano★★ £C ● **Dolcetto d'Alba**Vigna Majano★ £B
- O **Langhe** Bianco di Busso★ £C

CA' DEL BOSCO   Franciacorta   www.cadelbosco.com   A: Eno, N&P

*Owner: **Santa Margherita group**   Via Case Sparse 20, 25030 Erbusco (BS)*
Maurizio Zanella was one of Italy's modern pioneers for quality wine and was already receiving wide
acclaim by the early 1980s. Now one of two outstanding, prestigious Franciacorta sparkling wine
producers, Maurizio continues to direct and inspire. While BELLAVISTA sparkling wines are at least

as good, the still wines here remain a good notch or two higher. Pinèro (Pinot Nero or Pinot Noir), the Bordeaux blend, Maurizio Zanella, and Chardonnay have more competition than a decade ago but remain among the best Italian examples. The most recent innovation is Carmenero, a varietal Carmenère and a first for Italy (though it seems likely that, as in Chile, there could be a good deal of this variety planted, particularly in the North-East). Red and white Terre di Franciacorta are also good. All the grapes are estate-grown from some 140 ha of vineyard. For the sparklers, fermentation of the base wine is finished in barrique following by some ageing before the second fermentation. The regular Brut combines Chardonnay, Pinot Blanc and a little Pinot Noir, while the Rosé is more Pinot Noir-based. As at Bellavista there's a very fine Satèn but the finest sparkler is the rich, complex, mouthfilling Cuvée Annamaria Clementi. Only the regular Brut is non-vintage. Prices have always been high. (PW)

O **Franciacorta** Brut Non-Vintage★★ £D Brut Vintage★★ £E
O **Franciacorta** Dosage Zero★★ £E Cuvée Annamaria Clementi★★★★ £F
O **Franciacorta** Satèn★★★ £F ◎ **Franciacorta** Rosé★★ £E
O **Terre di Franciacorta Chardonnay**★★★ £F
O **Terre di Franciacorta Bianco**★ £C ● **Terre di Franciacorta**Curtefranca Rosso★ £C
● **Carmenero**★★★ £F ● **Maurizio Zanella**★★★★ £F ● **Pinero**★★★ £F

CASCINA CHICCO Roero www.cascinachicco.com

Owner: Enrico & Marco Faccenda Via Valentino 144, 12043 Canale (CN)
A Roero producer that makes better Barbera than anything else (especially a suave, spicy and scented Bric Loira), yet Roero (Valmaggiore) and Nebbiolo d'Alba can show similar flair when the conditions are right. Barrique-ageing is reserved for top *cuvées*. Roero Arneis can be good too. (PW)

● **Barbera d'Alba**★ £B Granera Alta★★ £C Bric Loira★★★
● **Roero** Mulino della Costa★★ £C Valmaggiore★★ £D
O **Roero Arneis** Anterisio★ £B
● **Nebbiolo d'Alba** Mompissano★★ £C

CASCINA VAL DEL PRETE Roero

Owner: Mario Roagna Strada Santuario 2, 12040 Priocca (CN)
Mario Roagna has transformed the grapes from 8 ha of family vineyards into a small fine range of wines in recent years, maximising the potential from a natural amphitheatre of vines first worked, then purchased back in 1977, by his late father, Lino (Bartolomeo). A delightful fruit-driven, unoaked regular Barbera contrasts with Carolina (named for his mother) which comes from a single parcel of vines and is aged for 16 months in new barriques. The oak is evident but there is fabulous style to its smoke and plum richness too. A small amount of Roero has been made since 1998 though its oak/fruit balance is more marginal. Better is the Nebbiolo expression in Vigna di Lino; vintages such as 2000 and 2001 should be super with five years' age or more. Arneis has more weight and structure than usual and will keep a year or two. Quantities are small, even the bigger-volume Arneis and Barbera *normale* don't much exceed 1,000 cases each. (PW)

● **Barbera d'Alba**★★ £B Superiore Carolina★★★ £C ● **Roero**★★ £C
● **Nebbiolo d'Alba** Vigna di Lino★★★ £C O **Roero Arneis** Luèt★★ £B

CA'VIOLA Dolcetto d'Alba www.caviola.com   A: HHB

Owner: Giuseppe Caviola Via Langa 17, 12050 Montelupo Albese (CN)
Beppe Caviola has given many a small grower the technical help to produce wines of the standard to

ensure they are sought out both in Italy and abroad. Though a modernist he earns respect particularly because he doesn't impose a formula but adapts his expertise to the philosophy of the individual producer. His own material centres on Barbera, for the excellent Bric du Luv, and Dolcetto, in various guises (Barturot is from old vines and subtly enhanced by oak). All are ripe, lush and fruit-rich, very easy to drink but with good structure. Rangone is from Pinot Nero. (PW)

- **Dolcetto d'Alba★** £B Barturot★★ £C Vilot★ £C
- **Langhe** Bric du Luv★★★ £E Rangone★ £E

CASTELLO DI CALOSSO Barbera d'Asti   www.castellodicalosso.it   A: Orb

Owner: (an association of producers) Piazza del Castello 7, 14052 Calosso (AT)
What do you do if you have at most a few hectares and produce high quality Barbera d'Asti but need a stronger identity while still making your wine? The ten growers of the Castello di Calosso all have a small parcel of old-vine Barbera (ranging from 40 to 70 years old) but share the same label under which they promote their own bottlings. The standard is high but not uniform and stylistically there are important differences too. While at least another vintage is needed before passing judgement on the individual wines, most seem deserving of at least a three-star rating. While one or two struggle for balance nearly all are concentrated with a measure of oak and have a rich, ripe fruit intensity as well as impressive breadth and length. The growers (or estates) followed by their single-vineyard Barberas are: Due Colline (Rodotiglia), Maurizio Domanda (Crevacuore), Fabio Fidanza (Rodotiglia), Giorgio Fogliati (La Cascinetta), Mauro Grasso (Rodotiglia), Renzo Grasso (Camp Maìna), La Badia (Belletta), L'Armangia (Vignali), Roberto Paschina (Musiano) and Tenuta dei Fiori (Rodotiglia). Some of these, such as Ignazio Giovine of L'ARMANGIA, make other wines of a standard to be worthy of a separate entry in the future. (PW)

CAUDRINA   Moscato d'Asti   www.caudrina.it

Owner: Romano Dogliotti Strada Brosia 20, 12053 Castiglione Tinella (CN)
Moscato d'Asti may not age but Romano Dogliotti has been making some of the finest examples for over 20 years. He applied new technologies to grapes (off steep slopes to the east of Barbaresco) first vinified by his father. Wonderfully fragrant with appie, citrus, grape and musk scents, the intense, tangy La Galeisa is exquisite when drunk with just a few months' bottle-age. Barbera d'Asti is increasingly good too (in both versions), while oaked Chardonnay and a very good fully sparkling Asti are also made. (PW)

- **Barbera d'Asti** La Solista★ £C Superiore Montevenere★★ £D
- O **Moscato d'Asti** La Caudrina★★ £B La Galeisa★★★ £C
- O **Asti** La Selvatica★★ £C
- O **Piemonte Chardonnay** Mej★ £C

CAVALOTTO Barolo   A: Goe

Owner: O & G Cavalotto Loc. Bricco Boschis, 12060 Castiglione Falletto (CN)
In the past Cavalotto's wines have tended to lack excitement. But the most recent releases have made the most of nature's beneficence. A traditionally minded producer, money saved by not buying new oak seems to have been invested instead in more care in the vineyard (which includes the nearly 4 ha solely owned Vigna San Giuseppe) and winery. Barolos recommended from 1997. (PW)

- **Barolo** Bricco Boschis★★ £E Riserva Vignolo★★ £F
- **Barolo** Riserva Bricco Boschis Vigna San Giuseppe★★★ £F
- **Dolcetto d'Alba** Vigna Melera★ £B Vigna Scot★ £B ● **Langhe Freisa★** £C

CERETTO Barolo www.ceretto.com

A: BcV

Owner: Bruno & Marcello Ceretto   Loc. San Cassiano 34, 12051 Alba (CN)

In the 1970s Ceretto evolved from an old-style merchant house into a modern one owning most of its grape sources. Of the many fabulous sites, the most famous perhaps is the Bricco Asili *cru*, (confusingly nearly all the Barbarescos produced carry this name) but it is in Barolo's Bricco Rocche (which adjoins Villero in Castiglione Falletto), Prapò and Brunate that the brothers Ceretto usually have their top wines. Each property is overseen from the impressive headquarters at the La Bernadina estate where Riesling (Arbarei), and also Cabernet, Merlot and Pinot Nero (the three combined in Monsordo Rosso with a little Nebbiolo) are vinified. New oak is used in all the top wines, which when on form are sleek and concentrated but veer towards being hard and lean when not. 1997s are particularly recommended. (PW)

● **Barolo** Brunate★★★ £F   Prapò★★★★ £F   Zonchera★★★ £F   Bricco Rocche★★★★ £H
● **Barbaresco** Asij★★ £G   Bernadot★★ £G   Fasêt★★ £F   Bricco Asili★★★ £H
● **Langhe** Monsordo★★ £E   **O Langhe Arneis** Blangé★ £C
● **Barbera d'Alba** Piana★ £D   ● **Dolcetto d'Alba** Rossana★ £B
● **Nebbiolo d'Alba** Lantasco★ £D   **O Piemonte** Brut La Bernardina★ £D

MICHELE CHIARLO Barolo www.chiarlo.it

A: Hal, Odd

Owner: Michele Chiarlo   Stada Nizza-Canelli 99, 14042 Calamandrana (AT)

With 110 ha, Chiarlo is one of the most substantial vineyard owners in Piedmont. A major part of this is for Barbera d'Asti production but it also includes some top *crus* for Nebbiolo and a chunk of Gavi. While the wines are competently made, the Barbaresco and Barolos, despite their origins, are rather inelegant when tasted alongside their peers. Often encountered are the oak-aged Nebbiolo/Barbera, Barilot, and Cabernet/Nebbiolo/Barbera, Countacc!. (PW)

● **Barolo** Cannubi★★★ £F   Cerequio★★★ £F
● **Barbaresco** Asili★★★ £F
● **Barbera d'Asti** Superiore Cipressi della Court★★ £B   La Court★★★ £D   Tardiva★★ £D
● **Langhe** Barilot★★ £D   ● **Monferrato** Countacc!★★★ £D
O Gavi del Comune del Gavi Fornaci di Tassarolo★ £C   **O Moscato d'Asti** Smentiò★ £C   Nivole★ £C

QUINTO CHIONETTI Dolcetto di Dogliani

Owner: Quinto Chionetti   Fraz. San Luigi, 12063 Dogliani (CN)

The benchmark producer in Dogliani now has plenty of competition (Anna Maria ABBONA, M&E ABBONA, Luigi EINAUDI, PECCHENINO and others). Of some 14 ha, six are designated Briccolero, but these are often given a close run by the rest, sold as San Luigi. Both are delicious, perfumed, full of fruit and best with one to two years' age. (PW)

● **Dolcetto di Dogliani** Briccolero★★★ £C   San Luigi★★★ £C

FRATELLI CIGLIUTI Barbaresco

A: HHB, M&V, PWa, The

Owner: Renato Cigliuti   Via Serraboella 17, 12057 Neive (CN)

The *cru* of Serraboella occupies slopes south-east of, and across from the town of Neive. It is shared between Cigliuti and PAITIN. Of Renato Cigliuti's few hectares, 2.5 with a south-west aspect are planted to Nebbiolo. The resultant Barbaresco shows the craft of a dedicated grower. Concentrated, it shows some oak influence and quite powerful but ripe tannnins which enable it to improve for a decade or more. Briccoserra (a Barbera/Nebbiolo blend sourced mostly from the

nearby Bricco vineyards), Dolcetto and Barbera rarely disappoint. (PW)
- **Barbaresco** Bricco★★★ £E Serraboella★★★★ £E
- **Langhe** Briccoserra★★★ £D
- **Barbera d'Alba** Serraboella★★ £C ● **Dolcetto d'Alba** Serraboella★ £B

DOMENICO CLERICO Barolo   A: J&B, N&P

Owner: Domenico Clerico Loc. Manzoni 67, 12065 Monforte d'Alba (CN)
Domenico Clerico shot to prominence in the 1980s and has been one of Barolo's most consistent superstars ever since. Even from the miserable early nineties, the wines stand out. Maceration times are relatively short and most of the small oak is new but the wines don't lack for stuffing or structure. Clerico has built up 15 ha, more than 40 per cent of it for three fabulous Barolos. The Ginestra *cru* provides both classy Ciabot Mentin Ginestra and more international Pajana; Mosconi, a stone's throw to the south, the rich, fleshy Per Cristina. Also very worthy, in descending order of value for money, are Barbera, Dolcetto and Arte (barrique-aged, 90 per cent Nebbiolo topped up with Barbera, and, since 99 Cabernet too). (PW)
- **Barolo** Ciabot Mentin Ginestra★★★★★ £F Pajana★★★★★ £F Riserva Per Cristina★★★★★ £F
- **Langhe** Arte★★★ £E ● **Langhe Dolcetto** Visadì★★ £B
- **Barbera d'Alba** Trevigne★★★ £C

ELVIO COGNO Barolo   A: PaV

Owner: Nadia Cogno & Valter Fissore Loc. Ravera 2, 12060 Novello (CN)
Wedged against the Monforte and Barolo communes in the south-west of the Barolo zone is a decent chunk of the Novello commune. It's sole significant and historic *cru*, Ravera, is given expression by both Cogno and M&E ABBONA. Nadia Cogno's husband, Walter Fissore, makes robustly flavoured wines with an extra intensity to the fruit than most. All are deep, well-balanced and benefit from a little extra bottle-age. Ravera, with a muted barrique influence, assumes an earthy, truffly, savoury complexity with even a little age. Barolo Vigna Elena, first made in 1997, is unusual in being produced solely from the Rosé clone of Nebbiolo. Montegrilli is a barrique-aged blend, half Nebbiolo and half Barbera. Nas-cetta is from the obscure local grape Nascetta, a portion of the grapes barrique-fermented and aged; it is attractively perfumed and gently creamy. (PW)
- **Barolo** Ravera★★★ £E Vigna Elena★★★★ £E
- **Barbera d'Alba** Bricco dei Merli★★ £C
- **Dolcetto d'Alba** Vigna del Mandorlo★ £B ● **Langhe** Montegrilli★★ £D
- O **Nas-cetta**★★ £B

ALDO CONTERNO Barolo   A: Lib, ACh, Vne

Owner: Aldo Conterno Loc. Bussia 48, 12065 Monforte d'Alba (CN)
In the more than 30 years since going it alone, Aldo Conterno has established a house of formidable reputation but also inspiration. Barolos are considered traditional because they are aged in large Slavonian oak but aspects of their vinification are more modern. The wines are made by sons Franco and Stefano. All, but particularly Cicala, Colonello and Granbussia (a Riserva selection of all plots), show lovely style and dimension on the palate, and the ensuing complexity and nuance most other examples miss. Barriques come into play for Barbera, Chardonnay Bussiador and Langhe blends Il Favot (Nebbiolo) and Quartetto (Nebbiolo, Barbera, Cabernet and Merlot). Printanié (a second Chardonnay) and Dolcetto are unoaked. (PW)
- **Barolo** Bussia Soprana★★★★ £F Cicala✪✪✪✪✪ £G

● **Barolo** Colonello✪✪✪✪✪ £G Riserva Granbussia✪✪✪✪✪ £H
● **Langhe** Il Favot★★★ £E Quartetto★★★ £E
○ **Langhe** Bussiador★★★ £D Printanié★ £C
● **Barbera d'Alba** Conca Tre Pile★★★ £D ● **Dolcetto d'Alba**★ £B

GIACOMO CONTERNO Barolo   A: JAr

Owner: Giovanni Conterno Loc. Ornati 2, 12065 Monforte d'Alba (CN)
Giovanni Conterno is the arch-traditionalist, famed for the legendary Monfortino. Long maceration times (five to six weeks) and extended ageing (six to seven years) in large, old oak barrels are two essential elements, producing a wine of sometimes unequalled intensity, power and longevity. Cascina Francia, a little easier to obtain, is also a great wine. Though there has been some moderation in the winemaking,the wines still show great breadth, intensity and persistence in a robust and tannic style: macho Barolo. Gutsy Dolcetto and Barbera are true to the house style. (PW)
● **Barolo** Cascina Francia★★★★★ £G Riserva Monfortino✪✪✪✪✪ £H
● **Barbera d'Alba**★★ £D ● **Dolcetto d'Alba**★★ £C

CONTERNO-FANTINO Barolo www.conternofantino.it   A: Eno, N&P

Owner: G Fantino & C Conterno Via Ginestra 1, 12065 Monforte d'Alba (CN)
A partnership that serves as a beacon to others determined to producer flawless, modern-style Barolos. The rich and complete Sorì Ginestra is a great wine if not quite among Barolo's élite. Vigna del Gris is almost at the same level and can show a more floral, exquisite perfume but just misses the extra depth and structure of Sorì Ginestra. Parussi is new from 1997. Monprà (Nebbiolo/Barbera Cabernet) is a usually a good example of the barrique-aged Langhe blend, while the Chardonnay is one of the better Piedmont examples. (PW)
● **Barolo** Sorì Ginestra★★★★★ £F Vigna del Gris★★★★ £F Vigna Parussi★★★ £E
● **Langhe** Monprà★★★ £E ○ **Langhe Chardonnay** Bastia★★★ £D
● **Barbera d'Alba** Vignota★★ £C ● **Dolcetto d'Alba** Bricco Bastia★★ £B

CONTRATTO Asti www.contratto.it   A: Vex

Owner: C & A Micca-Bocchino Via G B Giuliani 56, 14053 Canelli (AT)
A producer of Asti in the 19th century Contratto has been rejuvenated following its purchase in 1994 by the Bocchino Grappa house. Winemaker Giancarlo Scaglione (FORTETO DELLA LUJA) has revived the production of a vineyard-specific Asti (De Miranda) made by a variation on the traditional or Champagne method. This elegant, wonderfully perfumed sparkler will actually keep a year or two. A number of other *metodo classico* wines are made from Pinot Nero and Chardonnay. Barolo and Barbera Solus Ad are modern and well-made if still lacking a little individuality. (PW)
● **Barolo** Cerequio Secolo★★★ £F
● **Barbera d'Asti** Panta Rei★ £B Solus Ad★★ £D
○ **Piemonte** Chardonnay Sabauda★ £C
○ **Asti** De Miranda★★★ £C ○ **Brut Riserva Giuseppe Contratto**★★ £D

LUIGI COPPO & FIGLI Barbera d'Asti www.coppo.it   A: Res

Owner: Coppo family Via Alba 68, 14053 Canelli (AT)
Brilliant Barberas have been made here for a number of years. Pomorosso is a deep, rich and complex example and often among the best made, it shows what a match good Barbera fruit is for new oak.

Other Barbera can be good but are not of the same order but Alterego (Cabernet/Barbera) adds more richness in late 90s vintages and Mondaccione is one of the few serious still, dry Freisas (see also VAJRA). Also notable are one of the best oak-fermented and aged Piedmont Chardonnays (Monteriolo) and ripe fizz. (PW)

- **Barbera d'Asti** Pomorosso★★★★ £E Camp du Rouss★★ £C L'Avvocata★ £B
- **Langhe** Mondaccione★★ £C ● **Monferrato** Alterego★★★ £D
- O **Piemonte Chardonnay** Costebianche★ £B Monteriolo★★★ £D
- O **Riserva Brut Coppo**★★ £C

CORDERO DI MONTEZEMOLO Barolo www.corderodimontezemolo.com A:Eur

Owner: G & E Cordero di Montezemolo Fraz. Annunziata 67, 12064 La Morra (CN)
Well-directed estate with modern, pristine cellars, drawing on 29 ha of vineyard (much of it owned) centred on the spur of Monfalletto in Annunziata. The property has been transformed over two decades and the wines since 1995 are impressive. Maceration times are now very short and there is much experimentation with different types of new oak but the approach remains flexible. It remains to be seen how well the current crop of fine vintages will age. Enrico VI shows the class of the Villero *cru* in Castiglione Falletto, while a promising Bricco Gattera from the Lebanese cedar-topped knoll of Monfalletto has been made since 1997. Curdè is an estate blended red. Very good Barbera Funtanì. (PW)

- **Barolo** Monfalletto★★★ £E Bricco Gattera★★★★ £F Enrico VI★★★★ £F
- **Barbera d'Alba**★ £C Superiore Funtanì★★★ £D
- **Dolcetto d'Alba**★ £B
- O **Langhe Arneis**★ £B O **Langhe Chardonnay** Elioro★ £C

GIOVANNI CORINO Barolo A: DWS, J&B, F&R

Owner: Giovanni Corino Fraz. Annunziata 24, 12064 La Morra (CN)
Another producer of the Annunziata subzone in La Morra making modern-styled, fruit-rich Barolo. Since the mid-1980s brothers Renato and Giuliano have highlighted the quality inherent in Giachini, a small 3.5-ha *cru*, immediately east of Rocche dell'Annunziata. Raspberry, coffee and earth are typical aromas, the tannins tight but ripe. Vecchie Vigne is a superior selection made since 1997. Many of the modern vanguard produce excellent Barbera and Corino is no exception. Insieme is pretty good here too (see ALTARE), this one mostly Nebbiolo and Barbera with a little Cabernet and Merlot. (PW)

- **Barolo**★★ £E Arborina★★★ £E Giachini★★★ £E Rocche★★★ £E Vecchie Vigne★★★★ £F
- **Barbera d'Alba**★ £B Pozzo★★★ £D ● **Dolcetto d'Alba**★ £B ● **Insieme**★★★ £F

MATTEO CORREGGIA Roero www.matteocorreggia.com A: J&B

Owner: Ornella Correggia Case Sparse Gabinetto 2, 12043 Canale (CN)
Roero's inspirational grower died tragically in June 2001. His legacy from 14 years of undinting effort is Nebbiolo and Barbera of unprecedented quality from the 'other' (northern) side of the Tanaro river. Both undergo a relatively short maceration before being aged in new oak. Like others of modernist leanings who have really succeeded, there is a density and quality to the fruit that ensure the wines have real character, structure and aroma. The *cru* Roero red, made since 1996 adds further breadth to a quality range. Anthos is a dry version of Brachetto. (PW)

- **Roero**★ £B Ròche d'Ampsèj★★★ £C O **Roero Arneis**★ £B
- **Nebbiolo d'Alba** La Val di Preti★★★ £C
- **Barbera d'Alba** Marun★★★ £C

LUIGI EINAUDI   Dolcetto di Dogliani   A: L&S, Bal

Owner: P & R Einaudi   Borgata Gombe 31, 12063 Dogliani (CN)
Made famous by the first president of the Italian republic, but recently reinvigorated by Paola
Einaudi and her husband Giorgio Ruffo, this 'Dolcetto' estate is now making top-flight Barolo.
Costa Grimaldi from 1997 or 1998 is a very complete and harmonious Barolo with great intensity
and a match for that from the recently acquired Cannubi vines. Both show real class and have
excellent cellaring potential. Dense, intense Dolcetto needs a year or two but the *crus* are consistently
among the best of the zone. The fruit-rich, oak-aged Langhe Luigi Einaudi blends Cabernet,
Nebbiolo, Barbera and Merlot together. (PW)
● **Barolo**★★★ £E   Costa Grimaldi★★★★ £E   Nei Cannubi★★★★ £F
● **Langhe Nebbiolo**★★ £C ● **Langhe** Luigi Einaudi★★★ £E ● **Piemonte Barbera**★★★ £C
● **Dolcetto di Dogliani**★ £B   I Filari★★★ £C   Vigna Tecc★★★ £C

FONTANAFREDDA   Barolo   www.fontanafredda.it   A: Eno, JNi

Owner: Monte dei Paschi di Siena Bank   Via Alba 15, 12050 Serralunga d'Alba (CN)
Directed by Giovanni Minetti, Fontanafredda is one of the heavyweights of the Barolo region.
Tenementi Fontanafredda refers specifically to the premium wines, now being bottled with new
labels in a heavy Bordeaux format. Many vineyards are owned, particularly in Serralunga where the
massive winery complex is found, but much is bought in too. There are highs and lows – very recently
(1997, 1998) Barolos (Serralunga and the four *crus* therein) have been pretty good, but they have
not always been so. A moderately long fermentation and extended maceration are favoured. Barbera
Papagena and Dolcetto di Diano d'Alba are the best-value wines, but Barolo Serralunga is reasonably
priced too. Decent *metodo classico* sparklers are rather better than the ubiquitous Asti. (PW)
● **Barolo** Serralunga d'Alba★★ £D   Vigna La Delizia★★★ £F   Vigna La Rosa★★★ £F   Vigna La Villa★★★ £F
● **Barolo** Vigna Lazzarito★★★ £F ● **Barbaresco** Coste Rubin★ £D
● **Barbera d'Alba** Papagena★★ £C ● **Langhe** Eremo★ £B
● **Dolcetto di Diano d'Alba** Vigna La Lepre★★ £B

FORTETO DELLA LUJA   Loazzolo   A: Vim

Owner: Giancarlo Scaglione   Regione Bricco, Borgata Rosso, 14050 Loazzolo (AT)
Giancarlo Scaglione has put more than a few producers on the map. One wine, a late-harvest
(Vendemmia Tardiva) Muscat (with its distinctive 'wound ribbon' label) was until recently what both
this tiny DOC and its producer were all about. Production is now in the hands of son Gianni. Half the
grapes are dried and half are late-harvested and botrytis-affected. A slow, very extended fermentation
adds an oxidative component and honey, nuts and dried figs complement a rich fruit core. Other
unusual but good quality wines include a late-harvest Brachetto and a partly barrique-aged blend of
Barbera and Pinot Nero, Le Grive. (PW)
○ **Loazzolo** Piasa Rischei★★★ £E
○ **Moscato d'Asti** Piasa San Maurizio★ £C
● **Monferrato** Le Grive★★ £D ● **Piemonte Brachetto** Forteto Pian dei Sogni★★ £E

GAJA   Barbaresco   A: L&W, JAr

Owner: Angelo Gaja   Via Torino 36 A, 12050 Barbaresco (CN)
Piedmont's numero uno, Gaja has been a veritable phenomenon in the pursuit of quality and the
promotion of his native region. Consumption of the the often stupendous single-vineyard wines,

especially the trio from Barbaresco vineyards but also Sperss, is pretty much restricted to the wealthy. The first to be made (from 1967) was Sorì San Lorenzo; the most austere in its youth, it is based on the Secondine *cru*. Both Sorì Tildin (made from 1970, the year winemaker Giudo Rivella arrived), often the richest and deepest, and the more forward Costa Russi (1978) derive from the Roncagliette *cru*. Sperss, the ex-Barolo, is sourced from the Marenca and Rivette *crus* in Serralunga. All these former Barbaresco and Barolo *crus* may now include a very small percentage of Barbera. The most notable other wine for me is the Gaia e Rey Chardonnay, rich and expressive without mimicking the classic Burgundian style. Interestingly it is fermented in stainless steel before being aged for six to eight months in oak barriques of mixed European origin. Darmagi is pure Cabernet while Sito Rey is from Barbera. Sito Moresco combines Nebbiolo, Merlot and Barbera. This trio of reds are also of good quality if missing the hallmarks of greatness. Gaja, it would seem, only needs time before reaching the peak of whichever vinous summit he attempts. Brunello (PIEVE SANTA RESTITUTA) is now (since 1995) showing the Gaja stamp of elegance together with characteristic breadth and structure. CA' MARCANDA will shift the spotlight to Bolgheri. Quantities of the top wines remains small and the prices necessarily high. (PW)

- **Barbaresco**✪✪✪✪✪ £H
- **Langhe Nebbiolo** Costa Russi★★★★★ £H   Sorì San Lorenzo✪✪✪✪✪ £H   Sorì Tildin✪✪✪✪✪ £H
- **Langhe Nebbiolo** Sperss✪✪✪✪✪ £H   Conteisa★★★★★ £H
- **Langhe Rosso** Darmagi★★★ £H   Sito Moresco★★★ £D   Sito Rey★★★ £F
- O **Langhe Chardonnay** Gaia e Rey★★★★ £G   Rossj-Bass★★★ £E

FILIPPO GALLINO Roero   A: Gau

Owner: Gianni Gallino   Valle del Pozzo 63, 12043 Canale d'Alba (CN)
Production here is confined to red and white Roero and Barbera but quality has shot up and like CORREGGIA, CASCINA CHICCO or MALVIRÀ shows what's possible from the best of Roero's soils. The Gallino family now have 12 ha of vineyards and production of around 5,000 cases is likely to increase a little from 2003. Both Barbera and Nebbiolo are strengths, the Superiore versions, in particular, are increasingly full but well-structured with fine tannins. (PW)

- **Barbera d'Alba**★ £B ● **Barbera d'Alba** Superiore★★★ £C
- **Roero**★ £B   Superiore★★★ £C
- O **Roero Arneis**★ £B

ETTORE GERMANO Barolo www.germanoettore.com   A: Ast, P&S

Owner: Sergio Germano   Loc. Cerretta 1, 12050 Serralunga d'Alba (CN)
Compared to La Morra, Serralunga is somewhat bereft of top-flight small growers but Sergio Germano, who has relatively recently assumed control and ownership from his father Ettore, is certainly one. Renovation and expansion have aided the emergence of dense but well-structured Barolos. New small oak is restricted to the *cru* Cerretta, an impressive Barbera, and Langhe Balau, an unusual blend of Dolcetto and Barbera. A white Langhe, Binel, is also unusual in combining Chardonnay and Riesling. Prapò, the sturdier of the two Barolos, needs more bottle age. (PW)

- **Barolo**★★ £E   Cerretta★★★ £E   Prapò★★★ £E
- **Barbera d'Alba** Vigna della Madre★★ £C
- **Langhe** Balau★★ £C   O **Langhe** Binel★ £C
- **Dolcetto d'Alba** Lorenzino★ £B   Pra di Pò★★ £B

ATTILIO GHISOLFI Barolo   A: Ock

Owner: Gian Marco Ghisolfi Fraz. Bussia 27, 12065 Monforte d'Alba (CN)

Gian Marco is one of a number of talented young Piedmont winemakers able to harness the fruit potential that results from his father's viticultural expertise. The Barolo vines are located in the lesser known Visette *cru* (a sub *cru* of Bussia) and the wine shows lovely weight and richness with deep, intense fruit. Though it can be drunk reasonably young, it should improve for a decade. Barriques are used for two Langhe reds: a rich, expansive Alta Bussia is 80 per cent Barbera, 20 Nebbiolo, while a very individual, if firm, Carlin adds Freisa to Nebbiolo. Barbera Vigna Lisi comes from old vines, receives 50 per cent new oak and is sleek and stylish with three or four years' age. All show a similarly deft winemaking touch and fine fruit. Pinay is a Pinot Nero of some promise but the vines are as yet very young. A new Barolo *cru*, Fantini will appear from the 2000 vintage. (PW)

● **Barolo** Bricco Visette★★★★ £E
● **Langhe** Alta Bussia★★★ £E Carlin★★ £D ● **Barbera d'Alba**★ £B Vigna Lisi★★ £B

BRUNO GIACOSA Barbaresco www.brunogiacosa.it   A: JAr

Owner: Bruno Giacosa Via XX Settembre 52, 12057 Neive (CN)

Bruno Giacosa has made many of the great bottles of Barolo and Barbaresco over the last 40 years. Much of his reputation rests on buying the best grapes from an intimate knowledge of the best vineyards. The renown of Barbaresco *crus* Asili, Rabajà, Santo Stefano and Barolo *crus* Vigna Rionda, Falletto and Villero owes much to Giacosa's supremely complex and harmonious renditions of Nebbiolo. With so many growers now making their own wines Giacosa has also acquired vineyards of his own – some 15 ha includes some of the best sites, namely Asili in Barbaresco and Falletto in Serralunga. Riservas made from both sites in 1996 were only released in 2001 (Riserva bottles have a red label rather than the usual white). Winemaker Dante Scaglione still employs a fairly traditional winemaking practice but the maceration times are now only moderately long and he uses large French oak rather than the once much-favoured Slavonian casks. These are not wines for drinking young, though they might show well with six or seven years. Keep all the *cru* Barbaresco and Barolo for a decade from the vintage date – only then will it be possible to see if current releases stack up against some of the legendary older bottlings. The prices they obtain tends to reflect their sought-after status. Barbera, Dolcetto and Roero Arneis are consistently good among several other wines made. (PW)

● **Barbaresco** Rabajà★★★★ £G Asili★★★★★ £G Santo Stefano di Neive★★★★★ £G
● **Barolo** Falletto di Serralunga★★★★ £H Rocche del Falletto di Serralunga✪✪✪✪✪ £H
● **Nebbiolo d'Alba** Valmaggiore★★ £C ● **Barbera d'Alba** Falletto di Serralunga★★★ £C
● **Dolcetto d Alba** Falletto di Serralunga★ £B **O Roero Arneis**★★ £C

ELIO GRASSO Barolo   A: Mgi

Owner: Elio Grasso Loc. Ginestra 40, 12065 Monforte d Alba (CN)

Elio Grasso has 14 ha of prized steep hillside vineyards in the east of the Monforte commune. He has spent more than 20 years working his historic family vineyards and has recently relinquished the winemaking responsibility to his son Gianluca. An exisiting pair of refined, scented Barolos have been complemented by a barrique-aged Barolo from the replanted Runcot, a superior plot within Gavarini. As with other top barrique-aged examples from this area (CLERICO or CONTERNO-FANTINO) there is an inherent richness and structure from the fruit to marry with that from the oak. Maceration times are longer than for his neighbours' wines and Runcot seems likely to achieve greatness as the vines age. Barbera, Dolcetto and a little Chardonnay are very worthy too. (PW)

● **Barolo** Gavarini Vigna Chiniera★★★ £E Runcot★★★ £E Ginestra Casa Matè★★★★ £E

● **Barbera d'Alba** Vigna Martina★★★ £C ● **Dolcetto d'Alba** Vigna dei Grassi★★ £B
○ **Langhe Chardonnay** Educato★ £B

SILVIO GRASSO Barolo

A: Fal, N&P

Owner: Alessio Grasso Cascina Luciani 112, 12064 La Morra (CN)
A modern, small estate run by Federico Grasso that can be relied on for very well-made Barolos. Both the Luciani and Manzoni *crus* lie near the eastern periphery of La Morra at slightly lower altitudes than some of the more celebrated *crus* in the zone. Though of the modern type, both show full, ripe fruit and excellent balance with well-integrated oak on the palate. Of the two, Ciabot Manzoni sometimes has the edge but it depends on the vintage. Both are best with five to ten years' age. Federico's Insieme (see ALTARE) is a blend of almost half Nebbiolo with roughly equal parts of Barbera, Cabernet and Merlot – aged entirely in new oak. (PW)
● **Barolo**★★ £E Bricco Luciani★★★ £E Ciabot Manzoni★★★ £F
● **Barbera d'Alba**★ £B Vigna Fontanile★★ £C ● **Dolcetto d'Alba**★ £B
● **Insieme**★★ £F

ICARDI Barbera d'Asti

A: Ast, Odd

Owner: Pierino Icardi Via Balbi 30, 12053 Castiglione Tinella (CN)
This sizeable 65-ha estate to the east of Barbaresco is run by Claudio and Ornella Icardi and makes an extraordinary plethora of pleasurable wines, most in small quantities. The wines often combine remarkable drinkability and good varietal character with a succulent fruit richness, though occasionally at the cost of character. Yet quality is high and the wines' opulence and vinosity could be suited to palates that find most Piemonte wines too demanding. Barolo Parej shows increasing depth and structure, particularly in the 1999. A new Barbaresco Montubert (from 2000) is a fine fruit-rich expression of Nebbiolo as is Langhe Pafoj. Bricco del Sole combines Barbera, Nebbiolo and Cabernet. Langhe Nej is 100 per cent Pinot Nero, while the white Pafoj is partially barriqued Chardonnay/Sauvignon. Moscato and Brachetto are light and moderately sweet – fresh and splendidly scented if drunk young. Grignolino (Bric du Su) and Cortese (Balera) are also produced. (PW)
● **Barolo** Parej★★★★ £F
● **Barbera d'Alba** Surì di Mù★★ £C ● **Barbera d'Asti** Tabarin★★ £B Nuj Suj★★★ £D
● **Langhe** Nej★★ £D Pafoj★★★ £E ● **Dolcetto d'Alba** Rousori★★ £B
● **Monferrato** Cascina Bricco del Sole★★★ £E
○ **Monferrato** Pafoj★ £D ○ **Piemonte** Chardonnay Surissara★ £D
○ **Moscato d'Asti** La Rosa Selvatica★★ £B ● **Piemonte Brachetto** Surì Vigin★★ £B

LA BARBATELLA Barbera d'Asti

Owner: Sonvico family Strada Annunziata 55, 14049 Nizza Monferrato (AT)
Giuliano Noè, a top consultant enologist, is the winemaker here. What he has done with Angelo Sonvico's few well-situated hectares showcases his skills. One of the most celebrated Barbera d'Asti together with Sonvico, the Barbera/Cabernet blend for long known as La Vigna di Sonvico, have earned this estate an enviable celebrity in the heart of Asti's hills. The wines have proven ageing potential and possess power and concentration but without excess. New is Mystère, another pricey but highly promising red that adds Pinot Nero to Barbera and Cabernet. Whites Noè and new Non è combine Cortese with Sauvignon. (PW)
● **Barbera d'Asti**★★ £C
● **Barbera d'Asti** Superiore Vigna dell'Angelo★★★ £E
● **Monferrato** Sonvico★★★★ £F ○ **Monferrato** Noè★ £C

LA GIUSTINIANA Gavi   A: Lib, Vne

Owner: Lombardini family   Fraz. Rovereto 5, 15066 Gavi (AL)

Few Gavi producers are worth making a fuss about. La Giustiniana are the exception. Enrico Tomalino with help from Donato Lanati is now producing consistently full, concentrated unwooded Gavi. Lugarara is the mainstay; better, though, is slightly minerally, appley Montessora, with more intensity and persistence. A special selection, Just (for a time sold outside the DOCG), in which a relatively small percentage of the wine goes into barrique, is full, creamy and that much better again. New (since 1998) is a red version of Just – barrique-aged, ripe and balanced, and predominantly from Barbera. Whites are best within a couple of years of the vintage. For immediate drinking there's some good fizzy Brachetto d'Acqui and Moscato d'Asti from the Contero estate at Strevi. (PW)

O **Gavi del Comune di Gavi** Lugarara★ £C Montessora★★ £C Just★★★ £D
● **Monferrato** Rosso Just★★ £D

LA SCOLCA Gavi www.scolca.it   A: Alv

Owner: Giorgio Soldati   Fraz. Rovereto 170/R, 15066 Gavi (AL)

La Scolca has long been Gavi's most widely admired estate but others (Gian Piero Broglia, Castellari Bergaglio, LA GIUSTINIANA and Villa Sparina) have, with expert help, surpassed it for quality. Regular and Villa Scolca versions lack personality and concentration and even the Etichetta Nera (Black Label) can be found wanting. What is interesting is the regular and high quality of the sparkling wines. The Gavi Spumante are well-balanced and attractively toasty with a fine bead. Soldati La Scolca, released around eight years after the vintage is refined and complex (PW)

O **Gavi** Etichetta Nera★ £D
O **Gavi Spumante** Brut Soldati★★ £C Pas Dosé★ £C
O **Soldati La Scolca Brut Millesimato★★** £C

LA SPINETTA Barbaresco   A: Eno, WTs, Res, JNi, NYg, UnC, P&S, Han

Owner: Rivetti family   Via Annunziata 17, 14054 Castagnole Lanze (AT)

Giorgio Rivetti has become one of Italy's most talked-about winemakers. Being based just north of the Barbaresco zone, he, with brothers Carlo and Bruno, first made his mark with excellent Moscato, Barbera and a blend called Pin (Nebbiolo, Barbera and Cabernet). But the creation of new Barbaresco wines from the *crus* Gallina and Starderi (in Neive) and Valeirano (in Treiso) has rocketed the Rivetti name to fame. The wines are unequivocally modern. Moscato apart, nearly all the wines see the inside of a barrique, but they are profound with super fruit. Of the Barbarescos, Starderi is the most structured of the three, Valeirano perhaps most concentrated while Gallina is a touch softer and more expressive. Yet I'd as happily drink the smoky, old-vine Barbera d'Asti Superiore or the consistently brilliant Pin. New is a Sauvignon sold under the Langhe DOC, a sweet Moscato from dried grapes, a Barolo and even Tuscan Sangiovese (CASANOVA DELLA SPINETTA) from 2001. (PW)

● **Barbaresco** Vigneto Gallina★★★★★ £G Vigneto Starderi★★★★★ £G Vigneto Valeirano★★★★★ £G
● **Barbera d'Asti** Ca' di Pian★★★ £D Superiore★★★★ £E
● **Barbera d'Alba** Vigneto Gallina★★★★ £E
● **Monferrato** Pin★★★★ £E
O **Langhe** Bianco★★ £E   O **Piemonte** Chardonnay Lidia★ £C
O **Moscato d'Asti** Biancospino★★ £B Bricco Quaglia★★ £B
O **Moscato d'Asti** Passito★★ £E

TENUTA LA TENAGLIA   Barbera d'Asti   www.latenaglia.com

Owner: A & E Ehrmann   Via Sanctuario di Crea 6, 15020 Serralunga di Crea (AL)
La Tenaglia rose to prominence in the 1980s on the basis of very good Barbera, championing the Monferrato hills not far south of the River Po. 18 ha of a 33-ha estate are planted to vines at an altitude of 450 m. The pursuit of quality is reinforced with the use of outside expertise, including the services of eminent Tuscan enologist Attilio Pagli. Barbera is still the top wine, particularly the sumptuous, complex barrique-aged Emozioni from a single vineyard of 70-year-old vines. Giorgio Tenaglia comes from a selection of the best vines and is leaner but stylish, needing a year or two to soften. A third, the Monferrato Barbera is firmly textured (and a little overoaked in 2000). Crea is a simpler, unoaked Barbera d'Asti. Half a hectare is dedicated to Syrah and the resulting Paradiso is peppery and black-fruited. Chardonnay (Oltre) is not unlike a good Pouilly-Fuissé but only a little is made. Regular uoaked Piemonte Chardonnay is adequate but no more, as is Grignolino. (PW)

- **Barbera d'Asti** Giorgio Tenaglia★★ £C Emozioni★★★ £D
- **Barbera del Monferrato** Superiore Tenaglia è★★ £C
- **Paradiso**★★ £D   **O Piemonte Chardonnay** Oltre★★ £E

MALVIRÀ   Roero   www.malvira.com   A: Alv

Owner: R & M Damonte   Via Carse Sparse-Loc. Canova 144, 12043 Canale (CN)
Brothers Roberto and Massimo consistently produce as good Arneis as any. Renesio is an unwooded version, while Trinità sees some oak and Saglietto is oak-fermented and aged. All three can show real personality and style. Reds too, are of a good standard, making the most of the recent string of fine vintages. The Roero Superiore has been bottled as two separate *crus* from the 1999 vintage and both combine intensity with real elegance and should be drunk with five years' age. The remaining Nebbiolo is sold as Langhe Nebbiolo. San Guglielmo is an unwooded, perfumed and reasonably priced example of the Langhe Barbera/Nebbiolo blend. The oak-aged Treuve combines Sauvignon and Chardonnay with Arneis. (PW)

- **Roero Superiore** Mombeltramo★★★ £D Trinità★★★ £D
- **Barbera d'Alba**★ £C   **Langhe Nebbiolo**★ £C   **Langhe Nebbiolo**San Guglielmo★★ £D
- **O Roero Arneis** Renesio★★ £B Trinità★★ £B Saglietto★★ £C
- **O Langhe** Treuve★★ £C

GIOVANNI MANZONE   Barolo

Owner: Giovanni Manzone   Via Castelletto 9, 12065 Monforte d'Alba (CN)
Giovanni Manzone's 7.6 ha centre on the *cru* Gramolere in the Castelletto part of the Monforte commune. A special part of it is bottled as Bricat and a Riserva is also made in the best years. A tiny amount of elegant, floral Barolo from nearby Santo Stefano (Perno) has been recently added. There is partial use of French *tonneaux* (new and used) but maceration times are moderately long and Giovanni is avowedly not in the modern camp. While there seems to be some variation in quality and the cleanliness of some wines, the potential is clearly here. A distinctive wild mint and woodsmoke character seems typical of Gramolere (rather than a lack of ripeness as some have suggested), with extra intensity and dimension in Bricat. A concentrated old-vine Barbera La Serra is the pick of the rest. Tris unusually combines the Piedmont trio of Nebbiolo, Barbera and Dolcetto. A very interesting white, Rosserto, is made from Rossese Bianco and unique in Piedmont. (PW)

- **Barolo** Gramolere★★ £D Bricat★★★ £E Riserva★★★ £E Perno Santo Stefano★★★ £E
- **Barbera d'Alba**★ £B La Serra★★★ £C
- **Dolcetto d'Alba** La Serra★★ £B
- **Langhe** Tris★★ £C   **O Rosserto**★★ £C

MARCARINI   Barolo   www.marcarini.it   A: RsW

Owner: L & M Marchetti   Piazza Martiri 2, 12064 La Morra (CN)
The Barolo here is traditionally styled, with no new oak. Though a little firm and unexpressive when young, the wines can often age impressively from a good vintage. Yet given the inherent quality of the *crus* and examples like those from VOERZIO, there should be more. As much attention is now paid to the Dolcettos especially the rich Boschi di Berri made from vines over a 100 years old grown on their own roots – a factor which may account for the distinctive almondy, slightly earthy streak running through the intense berry-fruit flavours. One to try at least once. Langhe Nebbiolo and Moscato d'Asti are also made. (PW)

● **Barolo** Brunate★★★ £E   La Serra★★★ £E
● **Barbera d'Alba** Ciabot Camerano★★ £C
● **Dolcetto d'Alba** Fontanazza★ £B   Boschi di Berri★★★ £C

MARCHESI DI GRÉSY   Barbaresco   www.marchesidigresy.com

Owner: Marchesi di Grésy   Via Rabajà 43, 12050 Barbaresco (CN)
The Tenute Cisa Asinari actually comprises three estates but the centrepiece is the famous Martinenga *cru*. Though not ultra-consistent, the tight, dense, compact impression the individual plots – Camp Gros (adjoining Rabajà) and Gaiun (an extension of Asili) – give when young can lead to splendid graceful and complex drinking after a decade or more. There is some use of barriques, though more for Virtus (Barbera/Cabernet) and Villa Martis (Nebbiolo/Barbera) than for the Barbarescos. Other wines, sourced from Monte Aribaldo at Treiso, include two Chardonnays and one of Piedmont's best Sauvignons. Both a Moscato d'Asti and a Moscato Passito (L'Altro) are produced from the third estate, La Serra. (PW)

● **Barbaresco** Martinenga★★ £F   Camp Gros★★★★ £F   Gaiun★★★★ £F
● **Langhe** Virtus★★ £E   Villa Martis★★ £E   ● **Dolcetto d'Alba** Monte Aribaldo★ £B
○ **Langhe Chardonnay**★ £C   Grésy★ £E   ○ **Langhe Sauvignon**★★ £C

FRANCO M MARTINETTI   Barbera d'Asti   A:VDu

Owner: Franco Martinetti   Via San Francesco da Paola 18, 10123 Torino
Martinetti employs the father and daughter team of Giuliano and Elena Noè (see LA BARBATELLA) to make top quality wines from leased vineyards. A string of good vintages of Barbera (Montruc) and Barbera/Cabernet (Sul Bric) have been made. These are powerful, concentrated reds with breadth and refinement. They are characterised by the seamless quality of their tannins whilst capable of ageing for a decade or more from top vintages. Whites are impressive too. Minaia, once again being sold as Gavi, is very classy for this generally overrated appellation; Martin, from the obscure local variety Timorasso, offers ripe pear, quince, citrus peel and exotic fruits – both are barrique-aged, ripe, concentrated and sophisticated. Marasco (named for the Marasco cherry), a Barolo blended from the sites in the Barolo commune, has been made since 1997 and is very modern and seductive yet not superficial, albeit without the dimension or expression of the best. The appealing fruity Banditi Barbera is one for everyday. (PW)

● **Barbera d'Asti** Bric dei Banditi★ £B   Superiore Montruc★★★★ £E
● **Monferrato** Sulbric★★★★ £E   ● **Barolo** Marasco★★★ £F
○ **Gavi** Minaia★★★ £D   ○ **Colli Tortonesi** Martin★★★ £E

BARTOLO MASCARELLO Barolo   A :LaC

Owner: Bartolo Mascarello Via Roma 15, 12060 Barolo (CN)

Classic traditionally styled Barolo, made without concession to the modernists. Not for wimps, these are always powerful, broad and firmly tannic yet harmonious and superbly expressive wines. Don't even think about drinking it young (wait at least a decade) – or indeed at all if those from the likes of REVELLO are your ideal Barolo. Barbera and Dolcetto are also sturdy but balanced and *terroir*-derived. Bartolo's 1996 Barolo featured the controversial 'No Barrique No Berlusconi' label that is now a collector's item worldwide. (PW)

● **Barolo**★★★★★ £F
● **Barbera d'Alba** Vigna San Lorenzo★★ £C ● **Dolcetto d'Alba** Monrobiolo e Rué★★ £C

GIUSEPPE MASCARELLO & FIGLIO Barolo www.mascarello1881.com   A: Wtr

Owner: Mauro Mascarello Via Borgonuovo 108, 12060 Monchiero (CN)

Monprivato is one of the great *crus* of Castiglione Falletto and the entire Barolo zone. Superbly situated, its 6 ha face south-west at around 280 m. The wines in the best years combine superb fruit quality with an effortless structure and balance. A Riserva Ca' d' Morissio, first produced in 1993, is made only from the Michet subvariety of Nebbiolo and undergoes longer ageing in large oak. Mauro, now aided by his son Giuseppe (Christian names are passed from grandfather to grandson in Piedmont) also makes very small amounts of Barolo from nearby Bricco and Villero as well as Santo Stefano di Perno. Barbera and Dolcetto show great character and extract and benefit from bottle-age. Barbera Codana (which adjoins Monprivato) is from old vines, as is Scudetto, a selection from Santo Stefano di Perno. Langhe Status is Nebbiolo with a little Barbera and Freisa added in. (PW)

● **Barolo** Monprivato★★★★★ £F Riserva Ca' d' Morissio★★★★★ £F
● **Barolo** Bricco★★★ £E Santo Stefano di Perno★★★ £ Villero★★★★ £F
● **Langhe Nebbiolo**★ £B ● **Langhe** Status★★ £C
● **Barbera d'Alba** Santo Stefano di Perno★★ £C Scudetto★★★ £D Codana★★★ £D
● **Dolcetto d'Alba** Bricco★★ £C Santo Stefano di Perno★★ £C

MOCCAGATTA Barbaresco

Owner: Franco & Sergio Minuto Via Rabajà 24, 12050 Barbaresco (CN)

The Minuto brothers are a reliable source for good modern-style wines. Barbarescos are ripe and intense but with a certain style and elegance too. Cole shows the most structure and dimension, Balin is the most supple but there is little to chose between them. All deserve to be kept for five to ten years. The Basarin Barbera adds a breadth and lushness to the perfumed regular version of this grape. Dolcetto is more of a quaffing wine but the barrique-fermented and aged version of Chardonnay is increasingly good and will keep a year or two. (PW)

● **Barbaresco** Basarin★★★ £E Bric Balin★★★ £E Cole★★★ £E
● **Barbera d'Alba**★ £C Basarin★★ £D ● **Dolcetto d'Alba**★ £B
O **Langhe Chardonnay**★ £B Buschet★★ £D

MAURO MOLINO Barolo   A:N&P

Owner: Mauro Molino Fraz. Annunziata 111, 12064 Barolo (CN)

Though based in the Annunziata part of La Morra, Mauro Molino also has a few rows of vines in Monforte. As with other Altare disciples, short maceration times and barrique-aging are employed but the fruit quality he gets after 10 years of being at it full-time makes for good Barolo. Of two *crus*, it is considered that the higher calcareous content of Gancia gives rise to its firmer tannic structure but both show real weight and complexity in addition to fine aromatic character. Mauro's Insieme is a fairly typical blend, 40 per cent Nebbiolo with the balance equal parts Barbera, Cabernet and Merlot. He is also not alone in planting Chardonnay where the Piedmontese red grapes simply don't work. Accanzio is mostly Barbera and Nebbiolo. (PW)

- **Barolo★★** £E Vigna Conca★★★ £F Gancia★★★ £F
- **Barbera d'Alba★** £B Gattere★★ £D ● **Dolcetto d'Alba★** £B
- **Langhe** Accanzio★★ £D ● **Insieme★★★** £F

O **Langhe Chardonnay** Livrot★★ £C

FIORENZO NADA Barbaresco www.nada.it   A: HSA

Owner: Fiorenzo Nada Loc. Rombone, 12050 Treiso (CN)
Bruno Nada (Fiorenzo's son) runs a small 6-ha operation. The fruit quality and intensity resulting from much diligence in the vineyard is, with some assistance from Giuseppe Caviola (CA' VIOLA), harnessed into fine, elegant yet structured reds that add richness with age. Rombone, a potentially great *cru*, faces south-west; the Nadas' superior selection from these slopes is aged in barriques but evolves into a very refined classy example with five to ten years' age. Seifile, a Barbera/Nebbiolo blend also gets the small oak treatment and is characterised by its complexity and fruit intensity. Dolcetto and Barbera, the latter of which sees some oak, are ripe-fruited but could sometimes use a little more weight. An estate that deserves to be better known. (PW)

- **Barbaresco★★★** £E Rombone★★★★ £F
- **Langhe** Seifile★★★ £F ● **Dolcetto d'Alba★** £C **Barbera d'Alba★** £C

NINO NEGRI Valtellina Superiore www.giv.it   A: Eno

Owner: GIV Via Ghebellini 3, 23030 Chiuro (SO)
Nino Negri is owned by Italy's largest wine group – GIV or Gruppo Italiano Vini – and is directed by the respected enologist Casimiro Maule. There are good examples of all four Valtellina Superiore DOCG sub-zones: Grumello, Inferno, Sassella and Valgella. Though traditionally vinified, most are partly aged in barrique; of light to medium body, at their best they are intense, perfumed and elegant. Sfursat or Sforzato is a high-alcohol version (typically 14.5°) made from semi-dried grapes; in the top wine, Sfursat 5 Stelle, the grapes spend three-and-a-half weeks on their skins prior to ageing exclusively in new barriques. Drunk young it can be a bit overwhelming, with its sweet, intense fruit and evident tannin and acidity, yet it is enticingly perfumed with floral and preserved raspberry and cherry aromas. The oak-aged, perfumed white Ca' Brione is based on Nebbiolo vinified as a white wine and can show unusual structure and weight. (PW)

- **Valtellina** Sfursat★★★ £C Sfursat 5 Stelle★★★★ £E
- **Valtellina Superiore** Grumello Vigna Sassorosso★★ £C Inferno Mazér★★ £C
- **Valtellina Superiore** Sassella Le Tense★★ £C Valgella Fracia Oro★ £C

O **Ca' Brione★★** £C

ANGELO NEGRO & FIGLI Roero www.negroangelo.it   A: GWW

Owner: Giovanni Negro Fraz. Sant'Anna 1, 12040 Monteu Roero (CN)
Giovanni Negro's Roero estate is one of the appellation's leaders. While half of the 50-odd ha are planted to Arneis, it is the Barbera and Nebbiolo that have really forged a reputation for this family. The top wine, Sudisfà, is deep and powerful with ripe, smooth tannins but there is good quality throughout the reds. Good examples of Arneis are also produced, a fresh slightly spicy regular ver-

sion contrasts with fuller more characterful single-vineyard Gianat and Perdaudin examples. A small amount of grapes for the latter are dried for a sweet version. In addition to those below, Birbet (Brachetto), and Favorita are also made. Bric Millon is a promising new red based on Croatina but includes some Barbera and Cabernet Sauvignon. (PW)

● **Roero**★★ £B Prachiosso★★ £C Sudisfà★★★ £D
● **Barbera d'Alba** Nicolon★★ £B Bric Bertu★★★ £C
○ **Roero Arneis**★★ £B Gianat★★ £C Perdaudin★★ £C ○ **Perdaudin Passito** £D

ANDREA OBERTO Barolo   A: Alv

Owner: Andrea Oberto Via G Marconi, 25, 12064 La Morra (CN)
The father and son team of Andrea and Fabio Oberto make excellent examples of Barbera, Dolcetto and Barolo. Rotofermenters have been used since 2000 but maceration times are moderate rather than short. Andrea Oberto initially made his name with Barbera especially for the very rich, ripe barrique-aged Giada (from 60- to 70-year-old vines) though even the regular version is based on relatively old vines and is decidedly good value. New oak is used for all the Barolos as well as the 60/40 Nebbiolo/Barbera blend Seifile. Rocche, from a parcel directly below SCAVINO's, is a lovely example of the *cru*, with the unique Rocche perfumed, floral character around a deep fruit core. Delicious *cru* Dolcetto will keep a year or two. (PW)

● **Barolo**★★★ £E Albarella★★★ £F Rocche★★★★ £F
● **Langhe** Rosso Fabio★★★ £D
● **Barbera d'Alba**★★ £B Giada★★★ £D
● **Dolcetto d'Alba**★ £B Vantrino Albarella★★ £C San Francesco★★ £C

FRATELLI ODDERO Barolo www.odderofratelli.it   A: Alv

Owner: Giacomo & Luigi Oddero Via Santa Maria, 28, 12064 La Morra (CN)
The Oddero's are long-time vineyard owners, now with a very significant 60 ha, a proportion of it in some of Barolo's most notable *crus*. Some examples of these, such as (Mondoca di) Bussia Soprana (from Monforte) or Vigna Rionda (Serralunga) are now starting to realise their true potential – they had a tendency to be rather rustic and rugged in the past. Some input from leading consultant Donato Lanati has helped. Vineyards less suited to Nebbiolo have been planted to Barbera, Dolcetto and even Cabernet (Furesté is 100 per cent Cabernet from La Morra vineyards) and Chardonnay (Collaretto). If the wines remain reasonably priced, this promises to be a good label for characterful, structured, and widely available, Barolo – but stick to the *crus* as regular bottlings are a bit dull. (PW)

● **Barolo** Mondoca di Bussia Soprana★★★ £E Rocche di Castiglione★★★ £E
● **Barolo** Rocche dei Rivera★★★ £E Vigna Rionda★★★ £E
● **Langhe** Furesté★★ £D ○ **Langhe Chardonnay** Collaretto★ £C

ORSOLANI Erbaluce di Caluso   A: Mgi

Owner: G-F Orsolani Via Michele Chiesa 12, 10090 San Giorgio Canavese (TO)
Orsolani have become the main proponents of the Erbaluce grape and the small zone created for it north of Torino. Around half of 15 ha on glacial morraine are owned and in recent vintages the wines have benefited from Donato Lanati's technical assistance. La Rustìa is now the name for a tangy dry version with a lightly herbal spice and dried peach character. Vignot Sant'Antonio is more concentrated with some barrique influence. The top wine though is Sulé (since 1995, previously sold as La Rustìa), a rich sweet honeyed version of Erbaluce made from dried grapes and fermented in barriques before spending three years in barrels. A new Carema (from Nebbiolo), while relatively light, shows some promise. There's

also sparkling wine from Erbaluce, Orsolani Brut Cuvée Storica. (PW)

O **Erbaluce di Caluso** La Rustìa★ £B Vignot Sant' Antonio★★ £D
O **Caluso Passito** Sulé★★★ £E ● **Carema** Le Tabbie★ £D

PAITIN Barbaresco   A: Win, BBR

Owner: Secondo Pasquero-Elia Via Serra Boella 20, 12057 Neive (CN)
The Pasquero-Elia have 10 ha in the *cru* of Serraboella (next to CIGLIUTI). There was acclaim for
their Barbaresco back in the 1980s and after the difficult early nineties, quality has taken another
step forward. Dense and firm when young, though increasingly accessible too, it promises a lovely
style and complexity with eight to ten years' age. Other wines are made to high standards too: in the
Langhe red, Paitin, a little Cabernet and Syrah are now added to Barbera and Nebbiolo in a sleek
barrique-aged blend. Barbera, especially Campolive, and Dolcetto show a touch of class too. A white
Campolive is from Sauvignon and Chardonnay. (PW)

● **Barbaresco** Sorì Paitin★★★ £E
● **Langhe** Paitin★★★ £D
● **Barbera d'Alba** Campolive★★★ £C Serra Boella★★ £C
● **Dolcetto d'Alba** Sorì Paitin★★ £B ● **Nebbiolo d'Alba** Ca'Veja★ £C

ARMANDO PARUSSO Barolo www.parusso.com   A: Eno, N&P

Owner: Marco & Tiziano Parusso Loc. Bussia 55, 12065 Monforte d'Alba (CN)
From 20 ha of vineyards Marco Parusso fashions a high quality range of wines. Vinification and
ageing are modern: 24 months in new French barriques for the Barolos though oak rarely dominates
the top examples (plots within Bussia), Vigna Munie, Vigna Rocche and since 1998, Vigna Fiurin.
There is a weight and depth to go with their evident style, complexity and length on the palate. They
are a step-up from the less expensive but perfumed, sometimes oaky, Mariondino and attractively
fruity Piccole Vigne which comes from young vines. Other wines include excellent Barberas (the
superior Superiore is from old vines) and Langhe Bricco Rovella, a Nebbiolo, Barbera and Cabernet
blend, especially good in 99. There's a good example of Langhe Nebbiolo too while a white Bricco
Rovella is barrique-fermented Sauvignon. (PW)

● **Barolo** Bussia Vigne Rocche★★★★ £F Bussia Vigne Munie★★★★ £F
● **Barolo** Piccole Vigne★★★ £E Mariondino★★★ £E Bussia Vigna Fiurin★★★★ £F
● **Barbera d'Alba** Ornati★★★ £C ● **Barbera d'Alba** Superiore★★★ £E
● **Dolcetto d'Alba** Piani Noce★★ £B ● **Langhe Nebbiolo**★★ £C
● **Langhe** Bricco Rovella★★ £D O **Langhe** Bricco Rovella★★ £C

FRATELLI PECCHENINO Dolcetto di Dogliani   A: Odd

Owner: Orlando & Attilio Pecchenino Borgata Valdiberti 59, 12063 Dogliani (CN)
Tireless efforts go into making better and better Dolcetto at this 25-ha estate. Of the dense yet
succulent Dolcettos, San Luigi is unoaked, the classy Sirì d'Jermu sees some oak and half the Bricco
Botti is aged in new oak. La Castella is Barbera, Nebbiolo and Cabernet, while the white Vigna
Maestro is Chardonnay-based. Prices are proportionate to quality. (PW)

● **Dolcetto di Dogliani** San Luigi★★ £B Siri d'Jermu★★★ £C
● **Dolcetto di Dogliani** Superiore Bricco Botti★★★ £D
● **Langhe** La Castella★★★ £D O **Langhe** Vigna Maestro★ £C

PELISSERO Barbaresco www.pelissero.com   A: Alv, Odd

Owner: Giorgio Pelissero Via Ferrere 19, 12050 Treiso (CN)
Under Giorgio Pelissero, quality at this 20-ha estate has soared dramatically in recent years. At its heart is Vanotu, a vineyard at the intersection of Barbaresco's three main communes and the source of an increasingly complex and stylish Barbaresco. It spends 18 months in mostly new oak but this is increasingly well-integrated into a rich, ripe fruit core. The regular Barbaresco is attractive with good substance and reasonable depth. The 99s show slightly better definition and depth than the 2000s but will require more time. There's plenty of fruit in Dolcetto too, especially Augenta – a vibrant, perfumed and expressive example of the grape. Barbera is ripe and long while Langhe Nebbiolo shows a fine preserved raspberry fruit intensity. Barbera and Nebbiolo are harmoniously combined in 'Long Now' – named for the Long Now Foundation clock (www.longnow.org) – a modern, oaky example of this blend. Freisa (a lightly fizzy style), Grignolino and Favorita are also made. (PW)
● **Barbaresco**★★★ £E Vanotu★★★★ £F
● **Langhe Nebbiolo**★★ £C ● **Langhe** Long Now★★★ £D
● **Dolcetto d'Alba** Munfrina★★ £B Augenta★★ £C ● **Barbera d'Alba** Piani★★ £C

VIGNAIOLI ELVIO PERTINACE Barbaresco

Owner: 'Cooperative' Loc. Pertinace 2, 12050 Treiso (CN)
Named for a Roman emperor (Pertinax) of very brief reign, this co-op established in the 1970s controls some 80 ha of vineyards. Cesare Barbero supervises the making of a very reasonably priced Barbaresco and three relatively inexpensive *crus*. The use of some new oak complements the natural density and structure in the wines, and all show good *tipicità*. This being a Treiso-based operation, Dolcetto also features prominently in wines that are firm but with good fruit. (PW)
● **Barbaresco**★★ £D Vigneto Castellizzano★★★ £E Vigneto Marcarini★★★ £E Vigneto Nervo★★★ £E
● **Dolcetto d'Alba**★ £B Vigneto Castellizzano★ £B Vigneto Nervo★★ £B

PIO CESARE Barolo www.piocesare.it   A: Cib, Maj, F&R

Owner: Pio Boffa Via Cesare Balbo 6, 12051 Alba (CN)
Cesare Pio established this house in the 19th century and its success as a *commerciante* or *négociant* make it a well-known name. 30 ha are now owned, including the prized Il Bricco and Ornato *crus*. This pair of wines, in particular, can show real depth and a certain stylishness together with the propensity to age. Barbera Fides and Chardonnay Piodilei absorb a good measure of oak but consistently show depth and character too. On the down side Dolcetto, regular Barbera, Nebbiolo and Arneis, and sometimes even the house Barolo and Barbaresco, could be more. (PW)
● **Barbaresco**★★ £E Il Bricco★★★ £F
● **Barolo**★★ £F Ornato★★★★ £G
● **Barbera d'Alba** Fides★★ £D
O **Langhe Chardonnay** Piodilei★★ £D O **Piemonte Chardonnay** L'Altro★ £C

E PIRA & FIGLI Barolo   A: Eno, JNi

Owner: Chiara Boschis Via Vittorio Veneto 1, 12060 Barolo (CN)
Chiara Boschis has only recently assumed control of this old Barolo producer. The prize here is 2 ha of Cannubi and recent efforts display definite class. There is impressive complexity and considerable elegance and purity that reflect its origins. The wines build in richness and depth with age and

despite the use of new oak there is an underlying structure that demands cellaring. Recent vintages have been very good and suggest an even higher rating in the future. Barbera shows increasing style and purity from 2001 and is best with three years' age or more. Dolcetto is less exciting. (PW)

● **Barolo** Cannubi★★★★ £F

● **Barbera d'Alba**★★ £C   ● **Dolcetto d'Alba**★ £C

LUIGI PIRA   Barolo   A: Bal, N&P, F&R

Owner: Luigi Pira   Via XX Septembre 9, 12050 Serralunga d'Alba (CN)

Giampaolo Pira is rightly considered the hottest young winemaker in Serralunga and with his brother, Romolo, and father, Luigi, is forging one of Barolo's most exciting new estates (albeit just 6 ha). Since 1995 he has further underlined the potential of Serralunga with excellent wines from the Marenca, Margheria and (since 1997) Vigna Rionda *crus*. Having cut yields and modified the vinification, he is now producing dense, structured Barolos that are extremely concentrated and powerful with great cellaring potential. A mix of barriques, *tonneaux* (both new and used) and large wood is used; Vigneto Margheria sees 60 per cent new oak, while the minute quantities of Vigna Rionda receive 100 per cent new oak. Both deserve 10 years' cellaring. A tiny amount of Langhe Nebbiolo is also made, with a seductive fruit and texture that more examples should show. Unoaked Dolcetto is good too. (PW)

● **Barolo** Margheria★★★★ £F Vigna Rionda★★★★★ £G

● **Barolo**★★★ £E Marenca★★★★ £F

● **Nebbiolo d'Alba** Le Ombre★★★ £F   ● **Dolcetto d'Alba**★★ £C

FERDINANDO PRINCIPIANO   Barolo   A: HSA

Owner: Americo Principiano   Via Alba 19, 12065 Monforte d'Alba (CN)

Thanks to his dad, young Ferdinando has 9 ha of well-tended, mostly old vines in the south-eastern corner of the Barolo zone to work with. The main Barolo is the Boscareto *cru*, adjacent to Cascina Francia of GIACOMO CONTERNO. Despite an overoaked 96 this can be a wine of great character, complexity (including woodsmoke and truffles) and structure too. The same *cru* also provides half the Barbera for La Romualda – the rest coming from the celebrated Barbera vineyard Pian Romualdo (see PRUNOTTO). Rich, ripe and lush with old-vine blackberry fruit, it is best with at least two or three years' age. With some help from Giuseppe Caviola, the wines from the most recent vintages are really starting to shine. (PW)

● **Barolo** Boscareto★★★★ £E Le Coste★★★ £E

● **Barbera d'Alba** La Romualda★★★ £D   ● **Dolcetto d'Alba** Sant'Anna★ £B

PRUNOTTO   Barolo   www.prunotto.it   A: BWC

Owner: Antinori   Reg. San Cassiano 4/G, 12051 Alba (CN)

One of the best known names from the Langhe – and that was before ANTINORI (see Tuscany) took over. Once a traditional *commerciante*, Prunotto now owns an increasing percentage of the vineyard sources and there is some use of 500-litre French oak. Yet stylistically Antinori seem to be building on the legacy of the celebrated Beppe Colla rather than imposing a new order. A consistent and not excessively priced range is headed by the *cru* Barolo Bussia. At least something of the harmony and balance, if not the concentration or size of this Barolo can be seen in nearly all the wines. Noted Barbera d'Alba Pian Romualdo has recently been surpassed by the super Barbera d'Asti Costamiole, albeit with a considerable price differential. (PW)

● **Barbaresco**★★ £E Bric Turot★★★ £F

● **Barolo**★★★ £E Bussia★★★★ £F

● **Nebbiolo d'Alba** Occhetti★★ £B ● **Barbera d'Alba**★ £B Pian Romualdo★★★ £C
● **Barbera d'Asti** Fiulot★★ £B Costamiole★★★★ £E
● **Dolcetto d'Alba**★ £B Mosesco★★ £B O **Moscato d'Asti**★ £B O **Roero Arneis**★ £B

ALDO RAINOLDI Valtellina Superiore www.rainoldi.com   A: VDu

Owner: Giuseppe Rainoldi Via Stelvio 128, 23030 Chiuro (SO)
The wines have been improved and modernised here to the extent that this narrow alpine valley
might yet receive more attention. The length and flavour intensity in the top wines is striking. The
barrique-aged Il Crespino (from 100 per cent Nebbiolo) is but one of several Valtellina Superiore. As
well as an Inferno Barrique (aged in the same) there are versions of Grumello and Sassella; the Sasella
Riserva delivers a lovely savoury complexity with age. As at NINO NEGRI it is the Sfursat that shows
the most power and concentration. The Fruttaio Ca' Rizzieri is similarly aged in barriques and is
dense and powerful with excellent depth and intensity. (PW)
● **Vatellina** Sfursat★★ £D Sfursat Fruttaio Ca' Rizzieri★★★★ £E
● **Valtellina Superiore** Il Crespino★★ £C Inferno Riserva Barrique★★★ £D Sassella Riserva★★★ £C

RENATO RATTI Barolo www.renatoratti.com   A: ViV

Owner: Pietro Ratti & Massimo Martinelli Fraz. Annunziata 7, 12064 La Morra (CN)
Renato Ratti was one of the key modernisers in Barolo in the 80s. The estate (Marcenasco) vineyards
continue to be competently run and are supplemented by vineyards in the Asti hills. Barolos can at
times lack a little weight and richness yet have an understated charm and personality. Production of
Conca resumed in 98, after replanting. Villa Pattono, a blend of Barbera (at least half) with Cabernet
and Merlot is much more showy, with a succulent, almost creamy, ripe red and black fruit character.
Barbera d'Alba and other wines show good intense fruit and sound structure. (PW)
● **Barolo** Marcenasco★★ £E Conca Marcenasco★★ £F Rocche Marcenasco★★★ £F
● **Monferrato** Villa Pattono★★★ £D
● **Barbera d'Alba** Torriglione★★ £C ● **Dolcetto d'Alba** Colombè★ £B

FRATELLI REVELLO Barolo   A: DWS

Owner: Fratelli Revello Fraz. Annunziata 103, 12064 La Morra (CN)
Fruit-bomb Barolo? Revello represents a softer face to Barolo with almost unbelievably short maceration
times (albeit in rotofermenters) and plenty of new oak. There's no denying the wines' accessibility and
upfront fruit appeal when very young but there's a disturbing lack of substance from the noble Nebbiolo
and sometimes some firm tannins too. It is possible that they will age quite well but I doubt much of it
will get the chance given the fruit charm. It does feel slightly as if we've been given the icing minus the
cake, and there are ways of achieving fine tannins and fruit-rich wine without sacrificing depth and
breadth of structure. Despite these reservations the wines might well widen Nebbiolo's appeal. Gattera is
new from 1999. Regular Barbera and Dolcetto are aged in stainless steel but the small quantities of an
explosively fruity Ciabot du Re (from 25-year-old vines) spend 16 months in barrique. (PW)
● **Barolo**★★ £E Vigna Conca★★★ £F Vigna Giachini★★★ £F Rocche★★★ £F
● **Barbera d'Alba**★ £C Ciabot du Re★★★ £D ● **Dolcetto d'Alba**★ £B
● **Insieme**★★★ £F

ALBINO ROCCA Barbaresco   A: CKr

Owner: Albino Rocca Via Rabajà 15, 12050 Barbaresco (CN)
Albino Rocca and his son Angelo now have 12 ha (2 ha leased) and make two contrasting and very good Barbarescos. The richer, more lush but also more structured Brich Ronchi, made in greater quantities, receives the new barrique treatment, while Loreto, aged only in large oak, is a more pure, elegant expression of Nebbiolo. Barbera is also first class here; the white La Rocca, a barrique-aged Cortese, is better than most Gavi. All are reasonably priced. (PW)
- **Barbaresco** Vigneto Brich Ronchi★★★★ £E Vigneto Loreto★★★★ £E
- **Barbera d'Alba** Gèpin★★★ £D ● **Dolcetto d'Alba** Vignalunga★★ £B
○ **Langhe** La Rocca★★ £C ○ **Langhe Chardonnay** Da Bertü★ £B

BRUNO ROCCA Barbaresco   A: Lib, HHB

Owner: Bruno Rocca Via Rabajà 29, 12050 Barbaresco (CN)
Bruno Rocca makes a modern interpretation of one of Barbaresco's leading *crus*, Rabajà (the name derives from his family's estate). It is ripe, concentrated and with a more restrained oak character and better depth since 1998. A second Barbaresco, called Coparossa and made since 1995, includes grapes from the Fausoni and Pajorè *crus*; from 1998 it is approaching Rabajà in quality. The quality and promise of the 1999 vintage can be seen in Langhe red Rabajolo (Cabernet, Barbera and Nebbiolo). Barbera, Dolcetto and a Chardonnay are also very competently made. (PW)
- **Barbaresco** Coparossa★★★ £F Rabajà★★★★ £F
- **Barbera d'Alba**★★ £C ● **Dolcetto d'Alba** Vigna Trifolè★ £B
- **Langhe** Rabajolo★★★ £E ○ **Langhe Chardonnay** Cadet★★ £C

ROCCHE DEI MANZONI Barolo www.rocchedeimanzoni.it   A: Alv

Owner: Valentino & Iolanda Migliorini Loc. Manzoni Soprani 3, 12065 Monforte d'Alba (CN)
Production here, from in excess of 40 ha spread over four separate estates, is quite substantial by the usual standard for a Piedmont grower. The imposing and well-financed cellar turns out modern, bold and oaky wines that are good examples of their type. Of an ever-expanding range of Barolos, Cappella di Santo Stefano (made since 1996) is emerging with the most class and depth. The relatively forward Bricco Manzoni combines Nebbiolo with Barbera while Quatr Nas is composed of Nebbiolo, Cabernet Sauvignon, Merlot and Pinot Nero. While the latter has been a little over-hyped in the past, the 99, with its complex black fruits character and deceptively supple texture, has plenty of underlying substance. Pinònero is pure Pinot Nero. Chardonnay is oaky but distinctly Piemontese, while the sparkling wine is creamy, toasty and yeasty. (PW)
- **Barolo** Vigna Big★★★ £F Vigna d'la Roul★★★ £F Bussia Pianpolvere Soprano★★★ £F
- **Barolo** Cappella di Santo Stefano★★★★ £F
- **Barbera d'Alba** Sorito Mosconi★★ £C
- **Langhe** Bricco Manzoni★★ £E Quatr Nas★★★ £E Pinònero★ £E
○ **Langhe Chardonnay** L'Angelica★★ £E ○ **Valentino Brut** Riserva Elena★ £E

LUCIANO SANDRONE Barolo www.sandroneluciano.com   A: RsW, WTs

Owner: Luciano Sandrone Via Pugnane 4, 12060 Barolo (CN)
Luciano Sandrone remains as progressive and open-minded as ever yet continues to bring out greatness of both place and grape. The vines are tended by Luciano's brother Luca. Barolos are always super with splendid complexity and terrific breadth on the palate but also balanced and harmonious, with great

length and a fine tannic backbone. Maceration times are quite lengthy and 600-litre oak is favoured. More or less equal amounts are made of both the famous *cru* Cannubi Boschis and sometimes equally fine Le Vigne (blended from the Brunate, Bussia, Cerretta and Vignane *crus*). The wines generally are also expressive of the vintage, unlike others that are forced into the same mould each year. Sandrone's 16 ha also provide good fruit-rich expressions of Barbera and Dolcetto while Nebbiolo d'Alba is one of a relatively few decent examples of this appellation. Since 1999, Pe Mol, a Langhe blend of Barbera and Nebbiolo (60/40) has also been made. (PW)

● **Barolo** Cannubi Boschis✪✪✪✪✪ £H Le Vigne★★★★★ £G
● **Barbera d'Alba**★★★ £D ● **Dolcetto d'Alba**★★ £C
● **Langhe** Pe Mol★★ £E ● **Nebbiolo d'Alba** Valmaggiore★★ £C

SAN FEREOLO   Dolcetto di Dogliani

Owner: Nicoletta Bocca & Francesco Stralla   Borgata Valdibà 59, 12063 Dogliani (CN)
As with most Dogliani producers the focus here is Dolcetto. The deep, dense Dolcetto, among the best of the zone or anywhere for that matter, seems to improve with every vintage. The 7 ha also provide a rich, intense Barbera that is aged partly in new oak and sold under the Langhe DOC as Brumaio. Both barriques and the larger *tonneaux* are used. Another Dolcetto di Dogliani, Valdibà was produced in 2001. (PW)

● **Dolcetto di Dogliani** San Fereolo★★★ £C
● **Langhe** Brumaio★★ £C

SARACCO   Moscato d'Asti   www.paolosaracco.com

Owner: Paolo & Roberto Saracco   Via Circonvallazione 6, 12053 Castiglione Tinella (CN)
No reds here, just one of several small producers making exquisite Moscato d'Asti (CAUDRINA, LA MORANDINA and Elio PERRONE are others) that deserves to be better known in English-speaking countries. Saracco also make good Chardonnay, both an unoaked Prasuè and a stylishly oaked Bianch del Luv with attractive peach, spice and melon notes. A perfumed, herbal white, Graffagno combines Riesling with Sauvignon and Chardonnay. (PW)

O **Moscato d'Asti**★★ £B Moscato d'Autunno★★★ £B
O **Langhe Chardonnay** Prasuè★ £B Bianch del Luv★★ £C
O **Langhe** Graffagno★ £C

PAOLO SCAVINO   Barolo   A: J&B, DWS, N&P

Owner: Enrico Scavino   Via Alba-Barolo 59, 12060 Castiglione Falletto (CN)
Enrico Scavino, like CLERICO, SANDRONE and others who shot to prominence in the 1980s, has proved to be very successful and the premium prices are a reflection of the continued high demand for his wines. He makes arguably the definitive example of Barolo Rocche dell'Annunziata, adding power and breadth to the *cru's* classic perfume. Also often superb, Cannubi and Bric del Fiasc show a little more of the structure indicative of their origins. Scavino is more 'modern' than most and occasionally the wines can show an excess of oak, though ageing includes both barriques and larger wood. The Barbera now has many rivals but still rewards cellaring of at least five to six years. Corale is a barrique-aged blend of Nebbiolo, Barbera and Cabernet. Recent vineyard acquisitions on the slopes of Roddi in the very north of the Barolo zone promise to highlight a previously unrealised potential. (PW)

● **Barolo**★★★ £E Carobric★★★ £G Bric del Fiasc★★★★ £G Cannubi★★★★ £G
● **Barolo Riserva** Rocche dell'Annunziata★★★★★ £G

● **Barbera d'Alba** Affinato in Carati★★★ £E ● **Dolcetto d'Alba**★ £B
● **Langhe** Corale★★★ £E

ALDO & RICCARDO SEGHESIO Barolo   A: Fal, N&P

Owner: Aldo & Riccardo Seghesio Fraz. Castelletto 19, 12065 Monforte d'Alba (CN)
Brothers Aldo and Riccardo make seductive, showy and accessible Barolo in the modern style, which
somewhat belies their location in the Castelletto subzone of Monforte where the wines more often
are noted for their structure and rigour. I feel there could be more in terms of stuffing yet apart from
the slightly excessive oak it does have obvious appeal. An oaky but rich, deep Barbera works better
and is similarly remarkably approachable. Bouquet, a blend of Nebbiolo, Cabernet and Merlot, is
much in the same mould while ripe, fruity unoaked Barbera and Dolcetto are also made. (PW)
● **Barolo** Vigneto La Villa★★★ £E
● **Barbera d'Alba**★★★ £C Vigneto della Chiesa★★★ £D
● **Langhe** Bouquet★★ £D ● **Dolcetto d'Alba** Vigneto della Chiesa★★ £B

SOTTIMANO Barbaresco   A: F&R

Owner: Sottimano family Loc. Cottà 21, 12057 Neive (CN)
A 14-ha estate run by Rino Sottimano and his son Andrea that has taken a significant leap in quality
in the recent run of top vintages. Small amounts of ripe barrique-aged Barbaresco are made from the
Cottà, Currà, Fausoni and Pajoré *crus*. Barbera and Dolcetto also reflect the new standards being
attained here. Maté is a dry, fruity Brachetto. (PW)
● **Barbaresco** Cottà★★★ £E Currà★★★ £E Fausoni★★★ £E Pajoré★★★ £E
● **Barbera d'Alba** Pairolero★★★ £C
● **Dolcetto d'Alba** Bric del Salto★★ £B Cottà★★ £B

TRIACCA Valtellina Superiore www.triacca.com

Owner: Triacca brothers Via Nazionale 121, 23030 Villa di Tirano (SO)
Domenico Triacca is one of a few who show what Valtellina is capable of (NINO NEGRI, Mamete
PREVOSTINI, RAINOLDI and Conti SERTOLI SALIS are others worth a try). As much work is going
into improving the vineyards as the cellar, reducing yields and improving the canopy to obtain better
light penetration and subsequently better, riper Nebbiolo fruit. Typically it is the Sfursat/Sforzato
that is one of the best wines, but the barrique-aged Prestigio is of comparable quality. Del Frate, a
herbal, minerally Sauvignon, shows there's potential for this grape here too. (PW)
● **Valtellina** Sforzato★★ £E
● **Valtellina Superiore** Prestigio★★ £E Riserva Triacca★ £C
○ **Del Frate**★★ £C

G D VAJRA Barolo   A: Lib, ACh, Vne

Owner: Aldo Vaira Via delle Viole 25, 12060 Barolo (CN)
Based in the Vergne subzone of the Barolo commune, those of Aldo Vaira's vines grown locally are
at an altitude atypically high for Barolo. The protected, south-facing Bricco delle Viole ripens
Nebbiolo with a distinctive floral, plum and cherry fruit character but equally Barbera of great vigour
and intensity. This altitude suits Dolcetto too and the best grapes from two nearby plots, Coste di
Vergne and Fossati, have long produced a magnificent spicy, earthy Dolcetto with intense black plum
fruit. Wait at least five years for this or keep as long again – it will outlive many Barberas and a few

Barolos too. Aldo's Langhe Bianco is a very pure perfumed Riesling, tinged with lime, while Kyé is a wonderfully expressive and increasingly refined, powerful dry Freisa. Wood is used for ageing most wines, but almost exclusively large Slavonian oak. As a result the wines are not lush or soft but have both a varietal fruit intensity and a *terroir*-derived character. Great care goes into all wines and regular Dolcetto, Barbera and Nebbiolo are also a delight to drink. (PW)

● **Barolo**★★ £E Bricco delle Viole★★★★ £F
● **Barbera d'Alba**★ £C Bricco delle Viole★★★ £D
● **Dolcetto d'Alba**★ £B Coste & Fossati★★★★ £C
● **Langhe Freisa** Kyé★★ £C ● **Langhe Nebbiolo**★ £C
○ **Langhe** Bianco★★ £D

MAURO VEGLIO Barolo   A: Win

Owner: Mauro & Daniele Veglio   Fraz. Annunziata 50, 12064 La Morra (CN)
ELIO ALTARE'S neighbour, the serious, dedicated Mauro Veglio might just be his truest disciple. The 10 ha combines plots from both Mauro's and his wife, Daniele's, families. Barolos have relatively short maceration in rotofermenters prior to ageing in 225-litre barriques (60 per cent new). Castelletto, from Monforte vineyards and the most fleshy and perhaps most characterful, and Arborina, sourced from outside the winery doors, are made in the greatest quantities. Gattera is a relatively forward, attractive, poised example, while a tiny amount of floral, elegant and cherry-flavoured Rocche is also made. In general there are very good 97s but slightly less exciting 98s and promising 99s. Cascina Nuova Barbera is aged only in barriques and is best with at least three to four years' age. Good regular Barbera and Dolcetto can be drunk very young. Insieme is Nebbiolo, Barbera and Cabernet. (PW)

● **Barolo** Arborina★★★ £F Castelletto★★★ £E Gattera★★★ £E Rocche★★★ £E
● **Barbera d'Alba**★ £B Cascina Nuova★★ £D
● **Dolcetto d'Alba**★ £B ● **Insieme**★★★ £F

VIETTI Barolo www.vietti.com   A: Vim

Owner: Currado-Vietti & Cordero family   Piazza V Veneto 5, 12060 Castiglione Falletto (CN)
Established for more than a century this house came to prominence under the direction of Alfredo Currado. 22 ha of vineyards have gradually been acquired and less than a third of its grapes are now bought in. Single-vineyard Barolos are sourced from top *crus*. While traditionally vinified most are now partly barrique-aged and Lazzarito in particular can show more than a hint of oak when young. Yet there is a big difference between these and some of the more forward, easy modern examples from other producers. They add real weight and richness with cellaring. Rocche is the most traditionally styled and often the most classic but it is worth waiting at least seven years before drinking any of them. Often superb, Barbera d'Alba Scarrone Vigna Vecchia usually repays similar ageing. Barbera d'Asti La Crena is a notable single-vineyard example while other wines are soundly made. (PW)

● **Barolo** Castiglione★★ £E Brunate★★★ £F Lazzarito★★★★ £F Rocche★★★★ £F
● **Barbaresco** Masseria★★ £E
● **Barbera d'Alba** Scarrone★★ £D Scarrone Vigna Vecchia★★★ £E
● **Barbera d'Asti** Tre Vigne★ £C La Crena★★★ £E
● **Dolcetto d'Alba** Tre Vigne★ £B Sant'Anna★ £B
○ **Roero Arneis**★ £B ○ **Moscato d'Asti** Cascinetta★★ £B

VIGNA RIONDA – MASSOLINO   Barolo   A: Lib, Vne

Owner: Massolino brothers   Piazza Cappellano 8, 12050 Serralunga d'Alba (CN)
One of Langhe's best traditional producers, based around one of her top *crus* – Vigna Rionda.
Barolos tend to show a more typical Nebbiolo colour than from those who use lots of new oak and
can be deceptive and difficult to assess in their youth. Plump and flattering they are not, but the
breadth and length is apparent even when young and the tight, intense core builds with age to give
fullness and a marvellous complexity after a decade or so. Margheria is intense and tannic, with a
certain elegance. Parafada, a more modern style with a short but high-temperature maceration and
partial barrique-ageing, adds more breadth and weight allied to great length. Vigna Rionda Riserva
subject to a three-week maceration can show still more fullness and complexity. Barriques are also
used for Barbera, Chardonnay and Langhe blend Piria (Barbera/Nebbiolo). All are good examples of
their type. (PW)

- **Barolo★★★** £E Margheria★★★★ £F Parafada★★★★ £F
- **Barolo Riserva** Vigna Rionda★★★★★ £F
- **Barbera d'Alba** Gisep★★ £D ● **Dolcetto d'Alba** Barilot★★ £B
- **Langhe** Nebbiolo★ £C ● **Langhe** Piria★★ £E

O **Langhe** Chardonnay★★ £C

GIANNI VOERZIO   Barolo   A: JAr

Owner: Gianni Voerzio   Strada Loreto 1, 12064 La Morra (CN)
Gianni Voerzio doesn't make the blockbuster, super-concentrated wines of his brother, ROBERTO
VOERZIO, but he does produce a consistent and diverse range of very fine, even elegant wines. All
have great vigour, deep fruit and good balance. Arneis and Dolcetto are excellent examples, both alive
and intense, the Dolcetto with splendid definition and uncommon style for this grape. Barbera and
the Nebbiolo/Barbera blend, Serrapiù, show the most marked oak influence but this melts into the
the rich pure fruit with a little age. Barolo La Serra is dense and intriguing when young, inviting at
least eight to ten years' cellaring. Prices are on the high side but not out of step with quality. (PW)

- **Barolo** La Serra★★★★★ £G ● **Langhe** Serrapiù★★★ £E
- **Barbera d'Alba** Ciabot della Luna★★★ £D ● **Dolcetto d'Alba** Rochettevino★★★ £C
- **Langhe Freisa** Sotto I Bastioni★★ £C ● **Langhe Nebbiolo** Ciabot della Luna★★ £D

O **Roero Arneis** Bricco Cappellina★★ £C O **Moscato d'Asti** Vignasergente★ £C

ROBERTO VOERZIO   Barolo   A: Eno, WTs, JNi

Owner: Roberto Voerzio   Loc. Cerreto 1, 12064 La Morra (CN)
Voerzio's prices have inevitably risen in line with his seeming unending ascent of the Piedmont
hierarchy. In fact he took a little longer to achieve greatness in his wines than other stars. Relentless
in his pusuit of low yields and very concentrated fruit and unwavering in his use of new oak, he now
achieves balance and harmony in all wines that earlier vintages sometimes lacked. New, from 1998,
is a bottling of the *cru* Sarmassa, which lies immediately below Cerequio and therefore in the Barolo
commune. Next to appear (first vintage 2000) is a version of Rocche dell'Annunziata while a tiny
amount of a Riserva, Vecchie Viti dei Capalot e delle Brunate, is bottled only in magnums. Voerzio's
mega Barbera is the most powerful and concentrated made anywhere. Vignaserra is Nebbiolo with
Cabernet Sauvignon (and/or Barbera) and is regularly among the best of its type. (PW)

- **Barolo** Brunate✪✪✪✪✪ £H Cerequio✪✪✪✪✪ £H
- **Barolo** La Serra★★★★★ £H Sarmassa★★★★★ £H
- **Barbera d'Alba Riserva** Vigneto Pozzo dell'Annunziata✪✪✪✪✪ £F
- **Dolcetto d'Alba** Priavino★★ £B
- **Langhe** Vignaserra★★★ £D

OTHER WINES OF NOTE

GIOVANNI ABRIGO ● **Barbera d'Alba** Marminela £B ● **Dolcetto Diano d'Alba** Garabei £B
ORLANDO ABRIGO ● **Barbaresco** Vigna Montersino £D
G ACCORNERO & FIGLI ● **Barbera del Monferrato** Superiore Bricco Bastista £E Cima £E
● **Monferrato** Centenario (Cabernet Sauvignon/Barbera) £E
GIOVANNI ALMONDO ● **Roero** Bric Valdiana £C ● **Barbera d'Alba** Valbianchera £C
BATASIOLO ● **Barolo** Bofani £F Boscareto £F Cerequio £F Corda della Briccolina £F
CARLO BENOTTO ● **Barbera d'Asti** Superiore Balau £B Vigneto Casot £B Rupestris £C
NICOLA BERGAGLIO ● **Gavi del Comune di Gavi** La Minaia £C
BERSANO ● **Barbera d'Asti** Superiore Nizza £C Superiore Generala £D
GUIDO BERTA ● **Barbera d'Asti** Superiore Canto di Luna £C
FRANCO BOASSO GABUTTI ● **Barolo** Gabutti £E
S & E BOROLI ● **Barolo** Bussia £E Villero £E ● **Barbera d'Alba** Bricco dei Fagiani £C
● **Dolcetto d'Alba** Madonna di Como £B O **Moscato d'Asti** Aureum £B
FRANCESCO BOSCHIS ● **Dolcetto di Dogliani** Sorì San Martino £B Vigna dei Prey £B
BOVIO ● **Barolo** Arborina £F Gattera £F Rocchettevino £E ● **Barbera d'Alba** Regia Veja £C
GIACOMO BREZZA ● **Barolo** Bricco Sarmassa £F Cannubi £F
BRICCO MONDALINO ● **Barbera del Monferrato** Gaudium Magnum £D
● **Barbera d'Asti** Il Bergantino £B
GIAN PIERO BROGLIA - LA MEIRANO O **Gavi** Bruno Broglia £C
● **Monferrato** Bruno Broglia (Barbera/Merlot/Cabernet Sauvignon) £C
BRUNA O **Riviera Ligure di Ponente** Pigato U Bacan £C Le Russeghine £B
CABUTTO - TENUTA LA VOLTA ● **Barolo** Vigna La Volta £E
● **Langhe** Vendemmiaio (Nebbiolo/Barbera) £C
CAPPELLANO ● **Barolo** Gabutti £E Gabutti Franco £E
TENUTA CARRETTA ● **Barbaresco** Cascina Bordino £E ● **Barolo** Cannubi £E
CA' ROSSA ● **Roero** Audinaggio £C Mompissano £C ● **Barbera d'Alba** Mulassa £C
CASCINA CASTLÈT ● **Barbera d'Asti** Superiore Litina £C Passum £D
● **Monferrato** Policalpo (Barbera/Cabernet Sauvignon) £C O **Piemonte Moscato Passito** Avié £E
CASCINA CUCCO ● **Barolo** Vigna Cucco £E
CASCINA FONDA O **Moscato d'Asti** £B O **Driveri Moscato Spumante** £C
O **Vendemmia Tardiva** (Moscato) £C
CASCINA GARITINA ● **Barbera d'Asti** Bricco Garitta £B
CASCINA LA GHERSA ● **Barbera d'Asti** Superiore Camparò £B La Vignassa £D
● **Monferrato** La Ghersa (Barbera/Cabernet Sauvignon/Merlot) £E
CASCINA MONREALE ● **Barbera d'Asti** Superiore Valentina £C
CASTELLARI BERGAGLIO O **Gavi** Fornaci £B Rolona £B Rovereto V Vecchia £C O **Pilìn** £D
CAVALLERI O **Franciacorta** Brut Collezione Eslusiva £D Satèn £C
PODERI COLLA ● **Barolo** Bussia Dardi Le Rose £F ● **Barbaresco** Roncaglia £F
PAOLO CONTERNO ● **Barolo** Ginestra £F ● **Barolo** Riserva Ginestra £G
● **Barbera d'Alba** Ginestra £D ● **Dolcetto d'Alba** Ginestra £B
GIUSEPPE CORTESE ● **Barbaresco** Rabajà £E
DAMILANO ● **Barolo** Cannubi £E ● **Barbera d'Alba** £C ● **Dolcetto d'Alba** £B
WALTER DE BATTÉ O **Cinque Terre** £C O **Cinque Terre Sciacchetrà** £D
DELTETTO ● **Roero** Braja £C ● **Barbera d'Alba** Bramé £C O **Roero Arneis** San Michele £C
ALESSANDRO & GIAN NATALE FANTINO ● **Barolo** Vigna dei Dardi £E
FERRANDO ● **Carema** Etichetta Nera £E O **Erbaluce di Caluso** Cariola Etichetta Nera £C
O **Caluso Passito** Vigneto Cariola £F
FONTANABIANCA ● **Barbaresco** Sorì Burdin £E
TENUTA GARETTO ● **Barbera d'Asti Superiore** In Pectore £B Favà £C
GASTALDI ● **Barbaresco** £E ● **Langhe** Castlè (Nebbiolo) £F O **Langhe Chardonnay** £C
O **Langhe** Gastaldi (Chardonnay/Sauvignon) £D
FRATELLI GIACOSA ● **Barbaresco** Rio Sordo £E ● **Barolo** Vigna Mandorlo £E

● **Barbera d'Alba** Maria Gioana £B
GILLARDI ● **Dolcetto di Dogliani** Cursalet £B Vigneto Maestra £B
● **Langhe** Yeta (Dolcetto/Cabernet Sauvignon) £D ● **Harys** (Syrah/Cabernet Sauvignon) £E
FRATELLI GRASSO ● **Barbaresco** Bricco Spessa £D Sorì Valgrande £D
GIACOMO GRIMALDI ● **Barolo** Le Coste £E
HILBERG - PASQUERO ● **Barbera d'Alba** Superiore £C ● **Nebbiolo d'Alba** £C
HOHLER ● **Barbera d'Asti** Pian Bosco £C Pian Bosco Barrique £D
I PAGLIERI - ROAGNA ● **Barbaresco** Crichet Pajé £E
ISABELLA ● **Barbera d'Asti** Superiore Bric Stupui £C
OTTAVIANO LAMBRUSCHI ○ **Colli di Luna Vermentino** Colle Marina £C Sarticola £C
LA MORANDINA ● **Barbera d'Asti** Varmat £C ○ **Moscato d'Asti** £B
GIANLUIGI LANO ● **Barbaresco** £E ● **Barbera d'Alba** Fondo Prà £C
L'ARMANGIA ● **Barbera d'Asti** Vignali Castello di Calosso £D
○ **Piemonte Chardonnay** Robi e Robi £C
LES CRÊTES ● **Valle d'Aosta Fumin** Vigne La Tour £C ● **Valle d'Aosta Syrah** Coteau La Tour £C;
○ **Valle d'Aosta Chardonnay** Frissonière Cuvée Bois £C
MARCHESI ALFIERI ● **Barbera d'Asti** La Tota £B ● **Barbera d'Asti** Superiore Alfiera £C
● **Monferrato** San Germano £D
MARCHESI DI BAROLO ● **Barolo** Cannubi £E Sarmassa £E ● **Langhe** Picit £D
MARIO MARENGO ● **Barolo** Bricco Viole £E Brunate £E
LUIGI MINUTO - CASCINA LUISIN ● **Barbaresco** Rabajà £F Sorì Paolin £F
● **Barbera d'Alba** Maggiur £B Asili £D
MONCHIERO CARBONE ● **Roero** Printi £C Srü £C ● **Barbera d'Alba** Mon Birone £B
○ **Roero Arneis** Re Cit £B
MONTARIBALDI ● **Barbaresco** Sorì Montaribaldi £E ● **Barbera d'Alba** dü Gir £B
● **Dolcetto d'Alba** Niccolini £B
MONTE ROSSA ○ **Franciacorta** Brut Cabochon £E Brut Satèn £D
◉ **Franciacorta** Brut Cabochon Rosé £E
MONTI ● **Barbera d'Alba** £C ● **Langhe** (Cabernet Sauvignon/Merlot/Nebbiolo) Dossi Rossi £D
○ **Langhe** (Chardonnay/Riesling) L'Aura £C
MORGASSI SUPERIORE ● **Sarastro** (Barbera/Cabernet Sauvignon) £C ● **Tamino** (Syrah) £D
FRATELLI MOSSIO ● **Dolcetto d'Alba** Bricco Caramelli £B Piano delli Perdoni £B
TENUTE NEIRANO ● **Barbera d'Asti** Superiore Le Croci £C
PALLADINO ● **Barolo** San Bernardo £E Vigna Broglio £E
ELIO PERRONE ○ **Moscato d'Asti** Clarté £B Sourgal £B ● **Barbera d'Asti** Grivò £C
PIRA ● **Dolcetto di Dogliani** Vigna Bricco dei Botti £B Vigna Landes £B
● **Dolcetto d'Alba** Vigna Fornaci £B ● **Piemonte** Barbera Briccobotti £C
MAMETE PREVOSTINI ● **Valtellina Superiore** Corte di Cama £E Sassella Sommarovina £D
● **Valtellina** Sforzato Albareda £E
PUNSET ● **Barbaresco** Campo Quadro £E
RICCHINO ● **Dolcetto Diano d'Alba** Rizieri £B
RICCI CURBASTRO ○ **Franciacorta** Satèn Brut £C Extra Brut £C
GIUSEPPE RINALDI ● **Barolo** Brunate - Le Coste £F Cannubi - San Lorenzo - Ravera £F
ROCCHE COSTAMAGNA ● **Barolo** Rocche dell'Annunziata Bricco Francesco £F
● **Barbera d'Alba** Annunziata £B Rocche delle Rocche £D ● **Dolcetto d'Alba** Rubis £B
SAN ROMANO ● **Dolcetto di Dogliani** £B Vigna del Pilone £B Superiore Dolianum £C
CANTINE SANT' AGATA ● **Barbera d'Asti** Superiore Cavalé £C
CANTINE SANT' EVASIO ● **Barbera d'Asti** Superiore Nizza £C
SCAGLIOLA ● **Barbera d'Asti** SanSì £C Selezione £C ○ **Moscato d'Asti** Volo di Farfalle £B
GIORGIO SCARZELLO E FIGLI ● **Barolo** Vigna Merenda £F ● **Barbera d'Alba Sup.** £C
F & M SCRIMAGLIO ● **Barbera d'Asti Superiore** Acsé £D Crutin £C Bricco Sant'Ippolito £B
● **Monferrato** Tantra (Barbera/Cabernet Sauvignon) £D
MAURO SEBASTE ● **Barolo** Monvigliero £E Prapò £E
SYLLA SEBASTE ● **Barolo** Bussia £E
SERTOLIS SALIS ● **Valtellina Superiore** Inferno £C Sassella £C Corte della Meridiana £D

● **Valtellina** Sforzato Canua £F

MICHELE TALIANO ● **Barbaresco** Ad Altiora £E ● **Barbera d'Alba** Laboriosa £B

TERRE DA VINO ● **Barolo** Paesi Tuoi £D Poderi Parussi £E

● **Barbera d'Asti** La Luna e i Falò £B

TERRE ROSSE O **Rivera delle Ligure Ponente** Pigato £B Pigato Apogèo £C Vermentino £B

● **Solitario** (Rossese/Grenache/Barbera) £E

GIANCARLO TRAVAGLINI ● **Gattinara** £D Riserva £E Tre Vigne £E

UBERTI O **Franciacorta** Brut Francesco I £C Brut Magnificentia £E Extra Brut Comarì del Salem £E

RINO VARALDO ● **Barbaresco** Bricco Libero £E Sorì Loreto £E ● **Barbera d'Alba** £C

ERALDO VIBERTI ● **Barolo** £E ● **Barbera d'Alba** Vigna Clara £C

VILLA SPARINA O **Gavi** Monte Rotondo £D ● **Dolcetto d'Acqui** d'Giusep £B

● **Monferrato** Rivalta (Barbera) £D

Author's choice (PW)

Two dozen outstanding Barolo

AZELIA ● **Barolo** San Rocco

ENZO BOGLIETTI ● **Barolo** Brunate

BROVIA ● **Barolo** Rocche dei Brovia

ELVIO COGNO ● **Barolo** Vigna Elena

DOMENICO CLERICO ● **Barolo** Ciabot Mentin Ginestra

ALDO CONTERNO ● **Barolo** Colonello

GIACOMO CONTERNO ● **Barolo** Riserva Monfortino

CONTERNO-FANTINO ● **Barolo** Sorì Ginestra

CORDERO DI MONTEZEMOLO ● **Barolo** Bricco Gattera

LUIGI EINAUDI ● **Barolo** Nei Cannubi

ETTORE GERMANO ● **Barolo** Cerretta

ATTILIO GHISOLFI ● **Barolo** Bricco Visette

BRUNO GIACOSA ● **Barolo** Rocche del Falletto di Serralunga

ELIO GRASSO ● **Barolo** Ginestra Casa Matè

BARTOLO MASCARELLO ● **Barolo**

GIUSEPPE MASCARELLO & FIGLIO ● **Barolo** Monprivato

ARMANDO PARUSSO ● **Barolo** Bussia Vigne Rocche

E PIRA & FIGLI ● **Barolo** Cannubi

LUIGI PIRA ● **Barolo** Margheria

LUCIANO SANDRONE ● **Barolo** Le Vigne

PAOLO SCAVINO ● **Barolo** Bric del Fiasc

VIGNA RIONDA - MASSOLINO ● **Barolo** Parafada

GIANNI VOERZIO ● **Barolo** La Serra

ROBERTO VOERZIO ● **Barolo** Brunate

12 exciting Barbaresco

PRODUTTORI DEL BARBARESCO ● **Barbaresco** Riserva Montefico

PIERO BUSSO ● **Barbaresco** Vigna Borghese

CERETTO ● **Barbaresco** Bricco Asili

GAJA ● **Barbaresco**

BRUNO GIACOSA ● **Barbaresco** Santo Stefano di Neive

LA SPINETTA ● **Barbaresco** Vigneto Starderi

MARCHESI DI GRESY ● **Barbaresco** Martinenga Camp Gros

MOCCAGATTA ● **Barbaresco** Bric Balin

PAITIN ● **Barbaresco** Sorì Paitin

PELISSERO ● **Barbaresco** Vanotu

ALBINO ROCCA ● **Barbaresco** Brich Ronchi
BRUNO ROCCA ● **Barbaresco** Rabajà

10 other special North-West reds
ANTICHI VIGNETI DI CANTALUPO ● **Ghemme** Signore di Bayard
MATTEO CORREGGIA ● **Nebbiolo d'Alba** La Val di Preti
ELIO ALTARE ● **Insieme**
BRICCO MAIOLICA ● **Nebbiolo d'Alba** Il Cumot
CA' DEL BOSCO ● **Maurizio Zanella**
LA SPINETTA ● **Monferrato Rosso** Pin
MALVIRÀ ● **Roero Superiore** Mombeltramo
NINO NEGRI ● **Valtellina** Sfursat 5 Stelle
ANGELO NEGRO & FIGLI ● **Roero** Sudisfà
ALDO RAINOLDI ● **Valtellina** Sfursat Fruttaio Ca' Rizzieri

15 super Barbera
GIANFRANCO ALESSANDRIA ● **Barbera d'Alba** Vittoria
BERTELLI ● **Barbera d'Asti** San Antonio Vieilles Vignes
BRAIDA ● **Barbera d'Asti** Ai Suma
CASCINA VAL DEL PRETE ● **Barbera d'Alba** Superiore Carolina
CASTELLO DI CALOSSO/MAURO GRASSO ● **Barbera d'Asti** Rodotiglia
LUIGI COPPO & FIGLI ● **Barbera d'Asti** Pomorosso
HASTAE ● **Barbera d'Asti** Quorum
LA BARBATELLA ● **Barbera d'Asti** Superiore Vigna dell'Angelo
LA SPINETTA ● **Barbera d'Asti** Superiore
TENUTA LA TENAGLIA ● **Barbera d'Asti** Emozioni
FRANCO M MARTINETTI ● **Barbera d'Asti** Superiore Montruc
ANDREA OBERTO ● **Barbera d'Alba** Giada
FERDINANDO PRINCIPIANO ● **Barbera d'Alba** La Romualda
VIETTI ● **Barbera d'Alba Scarrone** Vigna Vecchia
ROBERTO VOERZIO ● **Barbera d'Alba** Riserva Vigneto Pozzo dell'Annunziata

10 diverse Dolcetto
ANNA MARIA ABBONA ● **Dolcetto di Dogliani** Maioli
CLAUDIO ALARIO ● **Dolcetto di Diano d'Alba** Costa Fiore
ENZO BOGLIETTI ● **Dolcetto d'Alba** Tiglineri
BROVIA ● **Dolcetto d'Alba** Solatio
CA' VIOLA ● **Dolcetto d'Alba** Barturot
LUIGI EINAUDI ● **Dolcetto di Dogliani** I Filari
MARCARINI ● **Dolcetto d'Alba** Boschi di Berri
SAN FEREOLO ● **Dolcetto di Dogliani** San Fereolo
G D VAJRA ● **Dolcetto d'Alba** Coste & Fossati
GIANNI VOERZIO ● **Dolcetto d'Alba** Rochettevino

Rinascimento

Appropriately Tuscany's wine renaissance or rinascimento could be said to have its beginnings in Florence, thanks to the firm of Antinori. Its artists include individual producers but of as much importance are the highly trained and experienced enologists that are consulted by the majority of producers to a greater or lesser degree. Over the past three decades Tuscany has also attracted a fair amount of outside investment and talent, including Swiss and English winemakers and entrepreneurs. In the new millennium, with winemaking of a generally high standard, there is increasing emphasis placed on style, including the appropriateness of international varieties and the importance of expressing something of the wine's origins or tipicità (typicality). As well as unprecedented quality from Sangiovese, and very good Cabernet Sauvignon, Merlot and Syrah, more effort is being spent on achieving not just good varietal expression but also maximising the different manifestations possible from permutations of place, soil and climate. While the best wines show richness and concentration it is not at the expense of finesse and elegance.

Red Wines

Central Tuscany & The Classic Appellations

The heart of Tuscany is **Chianti Classico**, its most historic and still its most important wine zone. The blunder of massive replanting in the 1960s with productive but poor-quality clones has started to be atoned for by recent replantings that have benefited from the research project known as Chianti Classico 2000. While the Chianti Classico DOCG now permits increasing amounts of other, foreign, varieties (usually at the expense of natives such as Canaiolo and Colorino), it is still based for the most part on Sangiovese (with pure examples possible since 1996). The leading communes are Greve in Chianti, Barberino Val d'Elsa, Castellina in Chianti, Radda in Chianti, Gaiole in Chianti and Castelnuovo Berardenga. Part of the communes of Tavarnelle Val di Pesa and San Casciano Val di Pesa are also included. While there are some discernable differences between each, as important are elevation, specific mesoclimates and soil types (there is much variation within each commune), better identified in sub-zones such as Monti (Gaiole) and Panzano (Greve). Interestingly, in a 'Chianti Classico 2000' tasting demonstrating the characteristics of different trialled clones there was as much affinity between wines from different clones grown in the same location, as those from the same clones but different sites. But arguably still more important is the style of winemaking. The use of new oak and variations in fermentation length, type, temperature, etc. all play a significant part in emphasising or smothering differences in *terroir*. Regular or *normale* Chianti Classico can be sold with a year's age, whereas Riservas, which are more likely to have been barrique-aged, are only released from the beginning of the third year after the vintage (i.e. the 2001s from January 2004). While a few high-profile estates have re-established Chianti Classico as their leading wine, others promote a so-called Super-Tuscan, first created as a vino da tavola when the laws were more restrictive and now often sold under the Toscana IGT. These include varietal Cabernet Sauvignon and Merlot, blends of the two together and blends of each with Sangiovese. There is also varietal Syrah and even Pinot Nero. This profusion of wine types is repeated in almost every important wine zone in Tuscany.

Chianti Classico is surrounded by several viticultural zones of differing size and importance. Immediately north in the hills closest to Florence, is **Chianti Colli Fiorentini**. North-east of Florence, from hills on either side of the river Sieve (but pressing up against the Apennines) is the small zone of **Chianti Rufina** where a small number of producers make a soaring, elegant expression of Sangiovese. Intruding into Rufina's eastern flank is the high-altitude **Pomino**, notable for its historical inclusion of French varieties and its domination by Frescobaldi. From the other side of Florence are another minor Chianti zone, **Chianti Montalbano** and the small but high-quality zone of **Carmignano**. Though revived only since the 1970s there are historical references both to its quality and to the planting of Cabernet Sauvignon, of which 20 per cent may be added to Sangiovese. South of Carmignano and west of Colli Fiorentini is another small Chianti zone, **Chianti Montespertoli**. West of Chianti Classico are the medieval towers of San Gimignano. Having only limited success with the white Vernaccia (see below) the surrounding vineyards are increasingly planted to red varieties. Some fine blends, mostly Sangiovese, Cabernet Sauvignon or Merlot, or a combination of these are sold as mainly Toscana IGT in preference to a newish **San Gimignano** DOC. Lesser examples of Sangiovese tend to be sold as **Chianti Colli Senesi**. This zone extends from here south around the lower reaches of Chianti Classico and also surrounds the Brunello and Vino Nobile zones – these southern examples are the fullest and most meaty of non-Classico Chianti.

Brunello di Montalcino DOCG is a wine like no other in Tuscany. Here it is hotter and drier than in any other major zone and the bigger, more muscular wines, produced by an ever growing number of producers, have maintained high prices thanks in part to a more singular, focused image that has been effectively promoted both locally and on foreign markets. Yet the quality of these pure Sangiovese (locally called Brunello) wines varies greatly. Excessive wood-ageing requirements were blamed for the wines drying out, especially in lighter years when there is insufficient fruit to support it. However, though the wines are only available from the fifth year after the vintage (the 1998s in 2003) there is now much greater flexibility about the type of wood used to age the wines and some styles are characterised by their use of new oak. The introduction of **Rosso di Montalcino** DOC, effectively a second wine, has helped cash flow. Its more accessible, fruit-driven style also means these wines can be drunk much younger, though some examples have better structure and depth than lighter, more forward Brunello and need at least three to five years' age. The most structured and ageworthy Brunello tends to come from the higher ridges and many individual sub-zones are beginning to emerge. **Sant'Antimo** DOC covers examples of blends of Sangiovese and other (foreign) varieties as well as varietal examples from other grapes grown in the zone, though some are sold as Toscana IGT.

Vino Nobile di Montepulciano DOCG lies to the east of Montalcino around its own small historic town. Unlike Brunello, pure Sangiovese (here called Prugnolo Gentile) was not permitted until very recently and many examples contain a percentage of Canaiolo and sometimes Mammolo. Vino Nobile has had difficulty reclaiming its historic status but is currently good value from one of the leading producers. Lesser vineyards are assigned as **Rosso di Montepulciano** which is not the same as Rosso di Montalcino and most examples are much more modestly structured and for drinking within a couple of years of the vintage. Further east in the Val di Chiana a new **Cortona** DOC has been created with provision for varietal Merlot, Syrah (and Chardonnay – see below), among other varieties, and is already being utilised by Antinori, Avignonesi and Tenementi D'Alessandro. Further north in the Valdarno (and east of Chianti Classico) is another minor Chianti zone, **Chianti Colli Aretini**, currently being rescued from its former obscurity by Petrolo and others, though the best wines are sold as Toscana IGT.

Many of Tuscany's new stars come from within the areas discussed above but increasingly important are the mostly unexploited western and southern areas of viticulture first highlighted by Sassicaia but developed at an accelerating pace over the past couple of decades.

The Tuscan coast and the new Tuscany

The most northern of the Tuscan coastal zones is the **Colline Lucchesi** for wines from slopes on either side of the historic and beautiful town of Lucca. As in the east at Rufina, the vineyards lie close to the Apennines and there is a growing number of progressive producers. Plantings in the more restrictive zone around the town of **Montecarlo**, include several French varieties and many of the best wines from both DOCs, are sold as Toscana IGT. Some way south and east of Pisa the hills are demarcated as **Colline Pisane** for another of the minor Chianti zones but Sangiovese, Cabernet Sauvignon and

Merlot blends of high quality are made. Similarly promising wines are being produced from within the **Montescudaio** DOC, though again both these and the Pisane wines tend to be sold as Toscana IGT. From Castello del Terriccio, located on the periphery of these zones but one of the most high-profile producers in the area, it is but a short distance south to the famous zone of Bolgheri.

Bolgheri (and the commune of Castagneto Carducci) is where the narrow strip of the coastal Maremma might be said to start properly. Cabernet Sauvignon and Merlot dominate but Sangiovese is not completely ignored and the DOC (which includes a single-wine sub-zone for Sassicaia) covers blends from each grape. There is a mix of both smaller producers, such as Michele Satta, Grattamacco and Le Macchiole, and big powerful names including Antinori (Guado al Tasso), Gaja (Ca' Marcanda), Mondavi (Ornellaia) and A & G Folonari (Campo del Mare). There is still more potential to the south of Bolgheri. One such hotspot is **Suvereto**, where Cabernet and Merlot again are favoured and the wines of Tua Rita, Montepeloso and Gualdo del Re have incited others such as Vittorio Moretti of Bellavista (Petra) to join the action. The wider, encompassing DOC of **Val di Cornia** adjoins Bolgheri in the north but also contains a southern outcrop north of Piombino on the coast.

The next step south on an emerging coastal patchwork is Massa Marittima which opens out into the southern Maremma. It has its own extensive DOC, **Monteregio di Massa Marittima**, with some good reds but is likely to assume even greater importance in the next few years. South of Grosseto is **Morellino di Scansano** DOC, the most important appellation in the southern Maremma for Sangiovese-based reds (led by Le Pupille). Cabernet Sauvignon and Merlot are also important here and sold as Toscana Maremma IGT or simply Toscana IGT. The area between these two DOCs is also demarcated, as **Montecucco**, and connects up with Brunello. Other southern appellations include **Parrina**, overlooking the coast at Orbetello and centred around the vineyards of one producer, La Parrina. **Sovana** DOC extends to the Lazio border and makes provision not only for Sangiovese-based reds but also varietal Sangiovese, Cabernet Sauvignon and Merlot. One further zone, to the east of Sovana near the Umbria border, is Sarteano, worthy of mention for the new reds being developed by Tenuta di Trinoro.

White wines

Most of Italy's best as well as original, dry whites can be found under the North-East, Central & Southern Italy section. In Tuscany there is generally less excitement even if there are reasonable quantities of attractive everyday whites. The problem for long has been the dominance of the humdrum Trebbiano grape. Deciding what to replace it with is rarely a priority for producers in this very 'red' region. Many have worked with Chardonnay (and the new **Cortona** DOC embraces it) but while a small number of examples are very good, most lack the elegance or class that might inspire greater dedication and even better results. Equally only a handful of examples have emerged with the structure that would guarantee greater longevity. The most important white wine appellation is **Vernaccia di San Gimignano** which can be reasonably characterful but the majority of examples lack the depth or style that it's DOCG status implies. Several of the coastal appellations offer whites, including Colline Lucchesi and Montecarlo whose grapes include Sémillon and Roussanne. From Montescudaio, Trebbiano is complemented by Sauvignon Blanc and Vermentino and both of the latter show good style in Bolgheri. Val di Cornia sanctions Vermentino with Trebbiano and further south in the Maremma some of the best producers are working with Vermentino though have to resort to IGT status for their whites. **Bianco di Pitigliano,** which overlaps with the most southern red DOC, Sovana, is a dedicated white wine zone for occasionally characterful Procanico/Greco/Malvasia blends.

Tuscany's best and most individual wine from white grapes has to be **Vin Santo** though it varies enormously in quality, style and sweetness. Made from dried grapes, usually hung from rafters, the best examples tend to be predominantly Malvasia rather than Trebbiano. They range from dry to rich, concentrated and sweet and from the gently oxidised and fruit-rich (preserved fruits and citrus peel) to more old-fashioned, more overtly nutty oxidised examples. Like the best extra virgin olive oils, few taste alike. As exciting as it can be, price and quality are often a reflection of the efforts that have gone into their production. The one or two good examples of the sweet wine **Moscadello di Montalcino** (from Moscato Bianco grapes grown in the Brunello zone) are also worth a try.

A-Z of Producers by appellation

Bolgheri
GRATTAMACCO/COLLE MASSARI
LE MACCHIOLE
TENUTA DELL' ORNELLAIA
SASSICAIA/TENUTA SAN GUIDO
ENRICO SANTINI
MICHELE SATTA

Brunello di Montalcino
ALTESINO
ARGIANO
BANFI
BIONDI-SANTI
TENUTA CAPARZO
CASANOVA DI NERI
CERBAIONA
CIACCI PICCOLOMINI D'ARAGONA
COL D'ORCIA
COSTANTI
FULIGNI
IL POGGIONE
MAURIZIO LAMBARDI
LISINI
MASTROJANNI
SIRO PACENTI
PERTIMALI/LIVIO SASSETTI
PIEVE SANTA RESTITUTA
SALVIONI/LA CERBAIOLA
SAN FILIPPO - FANTI
SOLDERA
TALENTI
VALDICAVA

Carmignano
CAPEZZANA

Chianti
CORZANO & PATERNO

Chianti Classico
CAPANNELLE
CASALOSTE
CASTELLARE DI CASTELLINA
CASTELLO DELLA PANERETTA
CASTELLO DI AMA
CASTELLO DI FONTERUTOLI
CASTELLO DEI RAMPOLLA
CASTELLO DI MONSANTO

CASTELLO DI VOLPAIA
CASTELLO VICCHIOMAGGIO
COLOMBAIO DI CENCIO
FATTORIA DI FELSINA
FONTODI
IL PALAZZINO
ISOLE E OLENA
LA BRANCAIA
LA MASSA
LANCIOLA
LE CORTI/PRINCIPE CORSINI
LE FILIGARE
FATTORIA LE FONTI
MONTE BERNARDI
POGGERINO
POGGIO AL SOLE
POGGIOPIANO
QUERCIABELLA
BARONE RICASOLI/CASTELLO DI BROLIO
RIECINE
ROCCA DI MONTEGROSSI
SAN FABIANO CALCINAIA
SAN FELICE
SAN GIUSTO A RENTENNANO
FATTORIA VALTELLINA
VECCHIE TERRE DI MONTEFILI
VILLA CAFAGGIO

Colli Fiorentini
CASTELLO DI POPPIANO

Colline Pisane
TENUTA DI GHIZZANO
SAN GERVASIO

Chianti Rufina
FATTORIA DI BASCIANO
FATTORIA SELVAPIANA

Colline Lucchesi
TENUTA DI VALGIANO

Cortona
LUIGI D'ALESSANDRO

Montecarlo
FATTORIA DEL BUONAMICO

Monteregio di Massa Marittima
MORIS FARMS

Morellino di Scansano
ERIK BANTI
LE PUPILLE

Val di Cornia/Suvereto
GUALDO DEL RE
MONTEPELOSO
TUA RITA

Vino Nobile di Montepulciano
AVIGNONESI
BOSCARELLI
DEI
POLIZIANO

Other
ANTINORI
CASTELLO DEL TERRICCIO
TENUTE DI A & G FOLONARI
FRESCOBALDI
GAGLIOLE
BIBI GRAETZ
LIVERNANO
MONTEVERTINE
PETROLO
POGGIO SCALETTE
RUFFINO
SETTE PONTI
TENUTA DI TRINORO
VILLA PILLO

Tuscany vintages

Tuscany produces plenty of red wine for short and medium-term cellaring but to date not that much that has provided real pleasure for a 15- or 20-year celebration. Many of the best reds, be it Chianti Classico Riserva, the best Vino Nobile, reds from the Tuscan coast or other blends including Cabernet or Merlot, are at or near their best with five to 10 years age, the very best with 10 to 15 years' age. Certainly some of the most sought-after labels will last longer but how much they will continue to improve is more debatable. Brunello from 1990, 93, 95 and 97 should go the distance of two decades though most also have the balance to be ready to drink at half that age. A good Rosso di Montalcino will age better than a weaker, more forward Brunello and give a lot more satisfaction. The style of any producer's wines is as important as location or the primary grape variety so where possible the comments should be considered together.

2002: As for most but not all of Italy this was a difficult vintage in Tuscany. However despite being plagued by rain and cool temperatures it's a mixed picture with some pockets of quality (especially the southern zones) and the best producers will still make good wine though many of the region's top reds neither should nor will be made. In theory this could make for some good value at lower levels as the best fruit cascades down. But as in 92, a little good fruit can too easily be wasted if blended into vats of poor, dilute and unripe wine.

2001: Like 2000 this was another vintage affected by heat stress due to a very hot, dry summer. Late rains were, in some instances, detrimental rather than beneficial to the quality of the fruit. Quantities are down on average and quality is likely to be variable, ranging from the dilute and out of balance to fully ripe, very concentrated reds. A vintage that will highlight those producers who have their vineyards in the best shape.

2000: Not of the order of 99 or 97, with the characteristics typical of lack of full physiological ripeness resulting in part from a very hot August. Many Chianti Classico *normale* show an over-ripe fruit character with less intensity than usual and a slight hollowness and high alcohol levels. There is also a lack of complete ripeness in their tannins. Those from a recommended producer however are less likely to show these defects and will have good richness and ripeness.

1999: A very fine vintage if not quite of the standard of 1997. If the fruit is less immediately seductive there is excellent drinking now at the lower levels and excellent ageing potential from good acidities, ripe tannins and ample fruit densities in more serious examples. A vintage to buy before the wines disappear, like the 97s. The fine Rosso di Montalcino, most of which will have been consumed, suggests a very good vintage for Brunello.

1998: Another highly successful but much more variable vintage. Some weakness and a slightly hard edge to some Vino Nobile but generally pretty good from the best producers; if anything more uneven in Chianti Classico. Already seems likely to be characterised as a vintage of greater elegance than is typical with real style and complexity where there was full ripeness. 98 Brunello is generally good and, though not all will keep, much richer and more consistent than 96.

1997: An outstanding vintage, and the best of the 20th century in terms of the amount of high quality red wine produced. Though most of the best Chianti Classico *normale* have been consumed with gusto there remains much that should be cellared including both regular and Riserva Brunello (very rich, powerful and tannic) but also other premium examples from all over Tuscany. The top wines have excellent ageing potential and a fair number will be at or near their best with 10 years.

1996: A good if generally overrated Tuscan vintage with some surprisingly weak, relatively forward wines in most zones. The best producers, however, did very well, the greatest consistency coming from Bolgheri. The greatest disappointments are in Brunello, where apart from Siro Pacenti and a handful of others, this is a decidedly poor vintage. The majority are fast-evolving wines that lack substance and balance and will need to be drunk soon.

1995: A poor growing season but saved by fine October weather. Elegant, stylish Chianti Classico and fine quality in the premium blends or Super-Tuscans. Many Chianti Classico Riserva or their equivalents are now emerging with considerable charm and style where they previously appeared a bit slight. Brunello, if occasionally too structured, has classic keeping qualities and has yet to approach its peak.

1994: Rain-affected growing season, though picked in mostly dry conditions; the reds are generally lighter than 1993 though there is often more elegance. Never the most concentrated, most wines from Chianti Classico and the surrounding areas are already at or near their best. A reasonable vintage in Brunello, too, with more weight and richness than the 96s but a lack of complete ripeness in fruit and tannins takes the edge off some. Not one to pay over the odds for.

1993: Though poorly received, 1993 has proved to be the source of rich, gutsy if slightly rough-hewn reds. The best have good richness and are capable of further development. Some solid powerful Brunello, too, the best examples still need more time to soften and add further complexity.

1992: The worst vintage of the last decade or so in Tuscany though some of the lesser wines were better than expected as some producers opted not to produce their Super-Tuscan blends. A vintage for drinking up, if at all.

1991: An uneven vintage and although some wines showed good intensity, a lack of balance characterised many. Only the best have aged with style, most should have been drunk up.

1990: A great year – but only in the context of the period. There are many more fine wines from 1997, the next great year, due to more widespread winemaking know-how and viticultural improvements. Nonetheless many of the celebrated properties produced marvellous wines with fabulous ripeness and balance. All the top wines may be drunk now but some bottles ought to be kept in order to see what is possible with further age.

1989: A surprisingly light and forward vintage in Tuscany (best for Brunello), not matching the generally high quality seen in other leading European wine regions in 89. The best provided attractive early drinking but little was worth keeping.

1988: Always a firm, relatively austere vintage and there are still a fair number of top wines that have mellowed with age, allowing an intense ripe fruit to emerge more fully with age. Some fine Super-Tuscans and Brunello, in particular, to drink now and in some cases, keep a little longer.

Earlier years: For earlier vintages the picture is decidedly bleak. Much of what was very good is now past its best. This is true of 1986 which with a decade's age provided some excellent Chianti Classico Riservas and Super-Tuscan blends. 1985 was a generally outstanding vintage with very ripe, flamboyant wines but only a handful of classics are likely to drink well or improve further. 1983 and 1982 were also very good vintages yet, other than the occasional Brunello, few had the stuffing or structure for two decades' ageing. Of still older vintages only 75, 71 or 70 are worth taking a chance on.

Tuscany vintages

	Chianti Classico (Riserva)	Vino Nobile di Montepulciano	Brunello di di Montalcino	Bolgheri/Suvereto
2002	NYR	NYR	NYR	NYR
2001	★★★/★★★★ A	★★★/★★★★ A	NYR	★★★/★★★★ A
2000	★★★/★★★★ A	★★★★ A	NYR	★★★★ A
1999	★★★★/★★★★★ A	★★★★/★★★★★ A	★★★★/★★★★★ B	★★★★/★★★★★ B
1998	★★★ B	★★★/★★★★ B	★★★ A	★★★/★★★★ B
1997	★★★★★ B	★★★★★ B	★★★★★ A	★★★★/★★★★★ B
1996	★★★ B	★★★ C	★★ C	★★★★ B
1995	★★★★ B	★★★/★★★★ C	★★★★ B	★★★/★★★★ C
1994	★★★ C	★★★ C	★★★ C	★★★ C
1993	★★★/★★★★ C	★★★ C	★★★★ B	★★★/★★★★ C
1992	★★ D	★/★★ D	★/★★ C	★★ C
1991	★★★ C	★★★ C	★★★/★★★★ C	★★★ C
1990	★★★★/★★★★★ C	★★★★/★★★★★ C	★★★★/★★★★★ B	★★★★/★★★★★ C
1989	★★/★★★ D	★★/★★★ D	★★★/★★★★ C	★★★ C
1988	★★★★ C	★★★★ C	★★★★ C	★★★★ C

ALTESINO   Brunello di Montalcino   A: PFx, N&P

Owner: Elisabetta Angelini Gnudi   Fraz. Torrenieri, Loc. Altesino, 53028 Montalcino (SI)

Altesino are a well-established and well-respected source of Brunello. A recent change of ownership has brought Altesino under the same ownership as CAPARZO but it continues to be directed by Claudio Basla. As well as Sangiovese, Cabernet Sauvignon and Merlot also form part of the estate's 28 ha but, though the resulting wines are often attractive and well-made, they rarely challenge a barrique-aged Sangiovese, Palazzo d'Altesi, a wine devised when the mandatory ageing for Brunello was too long. Alte di Altesi is a blend of Sangiovese and Cabernet (70/30), Borgo d'Altesi 100 per cent Cabernet, while Quarto d'Altesi is based on Merlot. Of recent Brunellos, after an adequate 94, a superior 95 and 97, and stylish 98 are typical of what is possible here; full, ripe and meaty, approachable soon after release but best with seven to ten years' age. In certain years both a powerful Riserva and Montosoli have been produced. The latter comes from a particularly favoured sub-zone in the northern part of the Brunello zone. Made only in top years it adds both concentration, depth and finesse. Rosso di Altesino, an inexpensive blend of Sangiovese and Cabernet, should not be confused with the (mostly dependable) fruit-driven Rosso di Montalcino. (PW)

- **Brunello di Montalcino**★★★ £E Riserva★★★★ £F Montosoli★★★★ £F
- **Palazzo d'Altesi**★★★ £D ● Alte d'Altesi★★ £D ● Borgo d'Altesi★★ £E ● Quarto d'Altesi★★ £E
- **Rosso di Montalcino**★ £C ○Vin Santo★★ £E

ANTINORI   www.antinori.it   A: BWC

Owner: Piero Antinori   Piazza degli Antinori 3, 50123 Firenze

It's been said many times that no-one has done more for Tuscan wine than Piero Antinori and this is well born out in the radical innovation, experimentation as well as expansion he has brought about. He and his daughters continue to promote quality and to enlarge the empire. The Tuscan estates are covered below but see also PRUNOTTO (Piedmont & NW Italy), CASTELLO DELLA SALA (Central Italy) and TORMARESCA (Southern Italy). In common with many large producers, quality at the lower levels is consistent, if not very exciting. Most famous are the wines of the Santa Cristina estate, Tignanello and Solaia. Tignanello, for many the original Super-Tuscan, was first made in 1971 and has been a blend of Sangiovese and Cabernet Sauvignon since 1975 (typically 80/20 but five per cent of the 20 is sometimes Cabernet Franc). Not every vintage has qualified as great but it's still a very good wine, as the 1999 shows. Solaia is Antinori's flagship and usually a very worthy one at that with added breadth and class; it is primarily Cabernet Sauvignon with support from Sangiovese and Cabernet Franc. Syrah is now produced from Antinori's Cortona vineyards, and the impressive Bramasole 2000 confirms the grape's potential in this part of Tuscany (see Luigi D'ALESSANDRO). Vino Nobile di Montepulciano comes from the large La Braccesca estate and is consistently a good, full and stylish example of the DOCG. New 60-ha Brunello estate Pian delle Vigne was only purchased in 1995. The wine is sophisticated, modern but not classically Brunello if atypically good in 96 and very good in 97 and 98 too. Guado al Tasso is Antinori's vast estate in Bolgheri and produces a consistently excellent red from Cabernet Sauvignon and Merlot. There are also other properties scattered about Tuscany for whites and lesser reds including vineyards in the fashionable Maremma. Antinori's interests also extend abroad, into Hungary and California. (PW)

Antinori:
- **Solaia**✪✪✪✪✪ £H ● **Tignanello**★★★★ £G
- **Chianti Classico** Riserva Badia a Passignano★★ £C Riserva Marchese Antinori★★ £D

La Braccesca:
- **Vino Nobile di Montepulciano**★★ £C ● **Merlot**★★ £E

Pian delle Vigne:
- **Brunello di Montalcino**★★★ £E

Guado al Tasso:
● **Bolgheri Rosso**★★★★ £G   O **Bolgheri** Vermentino★★ £B

ARGIANO   Brunello di Montalcino   www.argiano.net   A: Lib, P&S

Owner: Contessa Noemi Marone Cinzano   Loc. Argiano, 53024 Montalcino (SI)

It is now more than a decade since this historic estate (with 48 ha of vineyards) came under new ownership and direction but the improvements from changes overseen by Giacomon Tachis (instrumental in the success of SASSICAIA) during the 1990s continue to accrue. The Brunello is structured and powerful, with considerably more depth and dimension than most, especially evident in the 1995 and backward, tannic but exciting 1997 vintage. While lighter vintages do not reach the same standard they are nonetheless well made. The barrique-aged Solengo, a blend of Cabernet Sauvignon, Syrah and Merlot (and previously Sangiovese), has been consistently rich and stylish since first created from the 1995 vintage. With the help of Hans Vinding-Diers, 3,000 bottles of a special barrique-aged *cuvée* of Sangiovese, Suolo was produced in the 2000 vintage. It should be noted that this property, the Tenuta di Argiano with its own 16th-century villa, should not be confused with the neighbouring SESTI/CASTELLO DI ARGIANO. (PW)

● **Brunello di Montalcino**★★★★ £F
● **Solengo**★★★★ £F   ● **Rosso di Montalcino**★★ £C

AVIGNONESI   Vino Nobile di Montepulciano   www.avignonesi.it   A: Lib, P&S, N&P

Owner: Falvo brothers   Via Gracciano nel Corso 91, 53040 Montepulciano (SI)

With 109 ha spread over four estates, Avignonesi continue to be the most important producer in Montepulciano. At one point they were as well-known for their production of non-indigenous varieties as for Vino Nobile but in recent years they have been experimenting with local varieties and gradually improving the quality of the Prugnolo (Sangiovese) in their vineyards. The other varieties in the classic Vino Nobile blend have also been retained. The result is a regular Vino Nobile of increasing consistency, purity and real class. Some of the austerity of past vintages has gone but there is still a structure that ensures fine drinking with five years' age or more. Riserva Grandi Annate applies only to the best years and usually adds considerable depth and dimension. Though one of the estates is planted to international varieties they are now given less prominence in the range of wines. Grifi, a famous Sangiovese/Cabernet blend, was discontinued after the 1996 vintage though the '50 & 50' joint production Merlot/Sangiovese with CAPANNELLE continues. International and native varieties are also combined in a more everyday Avignonesi Rosso (Sangiovese/Cabernet Sauvignon/ Merlot). Desiderio, previously varietal Merlot now includes up to 15 per cent Cabernet while Il Marzocco is a bold, powerful, toasty Chardonnay. Production of Vin Santo, one from Malvasia, Trebbiano and Grechetto grapes and Occhio di Pernice from Prugnolo (Sangiovese), is tiny (around 3,000 half-bottles of the first, 1,000 of the latter), but the richness, texture and complexity in these wines is incomparable. They ferment and age over eight and ten years respectively so the latest releases are from vintages more than a decade ago. Light, fresh cherryish Rosso di Montepulciano is also made. (PW)

● **Vino Nobile di Montepulciano**★★★ £C   Riserva Grandi Annate★★★★★ £E
● **Cortona** Merlot Desiderio★★★ £F   ● **Avignonesi Rosso**★ £B
O **Cortona** Chardonnay Il Marzocco★★★ £C
O **Vin Santo**✪✪✪✪ £H   ● **Vin Santo** Occhio di Pernice✪✪✪✪✪£H

BANFI Brunello di Montalcino   www.castellobanfi.com   A: Vim

Owner: Mariani family   Loc. Sant'Angelo Scalo, 53020 Montalcino (SI)
No-one has made an impact on Montalcino and Tuscan viticulture like Banfi. Millions of American
dollars have been poured in to reshape the entire south-western corner of the Brunello zone. There are
800 ha planted to vines and superb facilities for making great wine. However the inherent potential
(or lack of it) of some of these vineyards and the varieties to which they have been planted has caused
the greatest contention. What does work with increasing consistency is Sangiovese for Brunello, which
despite the volumes – more than 40,000 cases of the regular example – is rich, ripe and well-balanced
if missing the extra depth and breadth of the best examples. The excellent Riserva Poggio all'Oro is
more complex, structured and elegant, while another single-vineyard example, Poggio alle Mura, has
also been made since the 1997 vintage. Rosso di Montalcino can show good Brunello-like breadth and
depth in the best years, while Florus is a flavoursome, well-balanced example of Moscadello di
Montalcino. Of the international wines, the premium blends are the most successful. Summus
combines Sangiovese, Cabernet Sauvignon and Syrah, while Excelsus is composed of Cabernet and
Merlot in equal measure. As varietals, Cabernet Sauvignon Tavernelle shows good richness, Syrah
Colvecchio shows the most promise but Merlot Mandrielle is less convincing. A Pinot Nero, Belnero,
is also made. Chardonnay Fontanelle can show real richness and depth but seems most successful
(with better strucure) in the less good years for reds. Lesser whites and reds are well-made but only
occasionally have sufficient quality to their fruit. Centine is an adequate blend of Sangiovese (60 per
cent), Cabernet Sauvignon and Merlot, Col di Sasso just Sangiovese and Cabernet. New is a mid-priced
blend, Cum Laude comprised of Sangiovese, Cabernet Sauvignon, Merlot and Syrah. (PW)

● **Brunello di Montalcino**★★★ £E Poggio alle Mura★★★★ £F Riserva Poggio all'Oro★★★★ £G
● **Rosso di Montalcino**★★ £C ● **Summus**★★★★ £E ● **Excelsus**★★★★ £F
● **Sant'Antimo** Cabernet Sauvignon Tavernelle★★ £D Syrah Colvecchio★★ £D Merlot Mandrielle★ £D
O **Sant'Antimo** Chardonnay Fontanelle★★ £C O **Moscadello di Montalcino** Florus★★ £D

ERIK BANTI Morellino di Scansano   www.erikbanti.com

Owner: Erik Banti   Loc. Fosso dei Molini, 58054 Scansano (GR)
Erik Banti, a pioneer of viticulture in the southern Maremma, makes good Morellino di Scansano
from 55 ha of vineyards. Moderately long maceration, 15 days for the Riserva, and the use of
Slavonian oak are favoured. Carato, previously IGT, is particularly good value and includes 15 per
cent of other varieties (in addition to Sangiovese). The Riserva, pure Sangiovese, comes from the
Ciabatta vineyard and is intense and extracted, with the herb scents and fruit quality typical of the
Maremma. Poggio Maestrino, from a vineyard of the same name, was previously named only for the
successive year of its production (2000 is the fourth, Annoquarto). Well-oaked (in French barriques)
and including 10 per cent Merlot, it misses the character of Ciabatta. Banti also makes the range of
food products, Italia & Gusto. (PW)

● **Morellino di Scansano**★★ £B Carato★★★ £C Riserva Ciabatta★★★ £D
● **Poggio Maestrino**★★★ £E

FATTORIA DI BASCIANO Chianti Rufina   A: Bib

Owner: Renzo Masi   Viale Duca della Vittoria 159, 50068 Rufina (FI)
Paolo Masi (son of Renzo) made major improvements to the estate's viticulture and winemaking from
the early 1990s and the quality is evident in the good vintages of the late 90s. High-quality fruit and
careful handling as well as long macerations and malolactic fermentation in barrique for the top wines
are key components. While the major part of 30 ha is planted to Sangiovese, there is also some Cabernet

Sauvignon, and Merlot and Syrah coming on stream. The regular Chianti Rufina shows ripe, lively fruit with a couple of years' age, without being overly austere, and is a good example of the zone. Chianti Rufina Riserva and two special *cuvées* are better still, with added richness and style; Vigna Il Corto and I Pini are currently blends of Sangiovese and Cabernet (90/10 and 50/50 respectively). Perhaps reflecting the predisposition of these soils (and climate) for Sangiovese, I Pini is the least vibrant and individual of the three top wines. While not yet challenging the supremacy of SELVAPIANA or Nipozzana's best (see FRESCOBALDI), Basciano delivers both fine quality and value. A good source for Vin Santo too. Wines sold under the Renzo Masi label are made from bought-in grapes and if not generally of the same standard can provide good-value drinking, particularly the Sangiovese/Cabernet blend, Erta & China. (PW)

● **Chianti Rufina**★★ £B Riserva★★★ £C
● **Vigna Il Corto**★★★ £C ● **I Pini**★★★ £C
O **Vin Santo**★★ £C

BIONDI-SANTI Brunello di Montalcino www.biondisanti.it A: Alv

Owner: Franco Biondi-Santi Loc. Greppo, 53024 Montalcino (SI)

This is still Montalcino's most famous estate, even if the wines are no longer the most expensive (see SOLDERA). Franco Biondi-Santi continues to make the wines to a traditional non-interventionist approach and without any outside assistance. The wines don't lack for power or depth or indeed complexity but can be quite forbidding when young, with a structure that makes you wonder if there's enough stuffing to match. Certainly in top vintages it would seem that they have but patience is required. Rosso di Montalcino comes in two bottlings, a white label from young-vine fruit, and a red stripe from fruit not used for Brunello. Franco's son Jacopo handles the wines' distribution along with those of Pierluigi Tagliabue, which he has helped to make at the estate of his wife's family, Villa Poggio Salvi. Here, with input from Vittorio Fiore, a more forward, approachable but flavousome Brunello is made but it is also where two very good barrique-aged reds were first created. They are now produced from Jacopo's own estate in the Maremma, Castello di Montepò. Schidione is Sangiovese with some Cabernet Sauvignon and Merlot while Sassoalloro, produced in much greater quantities, is pure Sangiovese. Rich and oak-influenced, the best examples of both also have considerable structure and ageing potential. (PW)

Tenuta Greppo:
● **Brunello di Montalcino**★★★ £H Riserva★★★★ £H
Villa Poggio Salvi:
● **Brunello di Montalcino**★★★ £F
Castello di Montepò:
● **Schidione**★★★ £E ● **Sassoalloro**★★★ £D

BOSCARELLI Vino Nobile di Montepulciano www.poderiboscarelli.com A: Bal, BBR

Owner: Paola De Ferrari Corradi Loc. Cervognano, Via di Montenero 28, 53045 Montepulciano (SI)

Luca and Niccolò work with their mother and long-time consultant Maurizio Castelli to keep this small estate (just 13 ha of vineyards) at the top of the hierarchy of Montepulciano estates. They are rivalled only by POLIZIANO and AVIGNONESI, though there are an increasing number of good estates (among others also see DEI). There is not only extra richness and depth but also better proportions and greater refinement, while the regular bottling has no equal at this level. There is an on-going commitment to quality, with increased planting densities and improvements to vinification. 'Boscarelli', like the Vino Nobile and single-vineyard Vigna del Nocio, is based on Sangiovese but is the only wine to see barriques. There is great consistency in vintages of the mid- to late 1990s and if prices are at a slight premium over some producers, the wines are good value both in a Tuscan and a wider sense. Rosso de Ferrari is the more everyday wine but better than most Rosso di Montepulciano. (PW)

● **Vino Nobile di Montepulciano★★★** £C Vigna del Nocio★★★★ £D
● **Boscarelli★★★★** £E ● **Rosso de Ferrari★** £B

FATTORIA DEL BUONAMICO Montecarlo www.buonamico.it A: Rec

*Owner: **Gruppo Concerto Hotels** Via Provinciale di Montecarlo 43, 55015 Montecarlo (LU)*
Directed by Vasco Grassi and Francesco Berti, Buonamico is one of the leaders of the relatively unsung DOC of Montecarlo, which has been growing both Tuscan and French grape varieties for several hundred years. 24 ha of the 37 ha estate are planted to vines and include Sémillon, Sauvignon Blanc, Pinot Bianco, Cabernet Sauvignon, Syrah and Merlot as well as Sangiovese, Canaiolo and Trebbiano. The Montecarlo red and white are the well-made basic wines, while Il Fortino is produced from 80-year-old Syrah vines and shows marvellous fruit intensity in a medium-bodied style that will keep for up to a decade. Cercatoja Rosso combines Sangiovese, Cabernet Sauvignon, Merlot and Syrah and is aged in small French oak; if missing some richness at first, it opens out with a little age. Vasario Bianco, based on Pinot Bianco is barrique-fermented and aged. It also shows plenty of flavour intensity and has the structure to improve for at least two or three years. Oro di Re, a late-harvested blend of mostly Sauvignon Blanc and Sémillon with a little Pinot Bianco, was first made in 1997 and again in 1999. It is a light- to medium-bodied, individual, complex and very fine sweet wine (with the finest honeycomb and dried exotic fruit flavours). It is made in just a few hundred half-bottles – quite delightful if you should come across it. A little Cercatoja Rosato, based on Sangiovese, is also made. (PW)

● **Il Fortino★★** £D ● **Cercatoja Rosso★★** £D
O **Vasario Bianco★★** £C O **Oro di Re★★★** £E

CAPANNELLE Chianti Classico A: N&P

Owner: James Sherwood Loc. Capannelle, 53013 Gaiole in Chianti (SI)
This estate with 15 ha of vineyards achieved a high profile under Raffaele Rossetti during Tuscany's wine revolution. Under the ownership of American James Sherwood since 1997, the wines continue to be very good but Capannelle, one of the most prominent vini da tavola, is no longer made and now forms part of a Chianti Classico Riserva thus marking a return to the once (and arguably rightly) vilified DOCG. The style has always been for very ripe fruit and lots of oak, at times to excess. However all the wines have terrific flavour complexity and style particularly when given the eight to ten years' age they deserve. The best wine is the rich, complex '50 & 50', a collaboration with AVIGNONESI, who provide the Merlot component to complement Capannelle's Sangiovese. Solare is a bold innovation, containing as it does a significant percentage of Malvasia Nera. Chardonnay is also made. (PW)

● **Chianti Classico** Riserva★★★ £E ● **50 & 50★★★★** £E
● **Solare★★★** £F

TENUTA CAPARZO Brunello di Montalcino www.caparzo.com A: Ast, P&S, UnC, N&P

Owner: Elisabetta Angelini Gnudi Strada Provinciale del Brunello, 53024 Montalcino (SI)
Almost half of this 180-ha estate is planted to vines, making Caparzo one of Brunello's more significant producers. It is directed by Nuccio Turone with ongoing consultancy from Vittorio Fiore. Quality is high, sometimes very high indeed, as in certain vintages of Vigna La Casa. With the exception of the 96s, which, though adequate, are not of the standard at which the wines are rated below, the vintages of the mid-1990s at least maintain their considerable reputation. Occasionally there is a question mark

over the balance and stability but there is also remarkable concentration, depth and power with very ripe, fine tannins in the best years. Formerly vini da tavola, now Sant'Antimo red and white, Ca' del Pazzo (Sangiovese/Cabernet Sauvignon) and Le Grance (mostly Chardonnay but also Sauvignon and Gewürztraminer) were innovative Tuscan wines that still show good fruit and the intelligent use of new oak. Caparzo also owns the Chianti Classico estate of Borgo Scopeto (a large estate but with only 37 ha of vines) in Castelnuovo Berardenga. The most recent releases reflect a new winemaking direction and, as well as Chianti Classico and Riserva, from 1998 there is a new single-vineyard Riserva, Misciano, and Super-Tuscan, Borgonero, from Sangiovese, Syrah and Cabernet Sauvignon. (PW)

Tenuta Caparzo:
- **Brunello di Montalcino**★★★ £E Riserva★★★★★ £F Vigna La Casa❂❂❂❂❂ £F
- **Rosso di Montalcino**★★ £C Vigna La Caduta★★★ £C ● **Rosso Caparzo Sangiovese**★★ £B
- **Sant'Antimo** Ca' del Pazzo★★★ £D O **Sant'Antimo** Le Grance★★ £C
- O **Moscadello di Montalcino** Vendemmia Tardiva★ £E

Borgo Scopeto:
- **Chianti Classico** Riserva Misciano★★ £D

CAPEZZANA   Carmignano   www.capezzana.it   A: Lib, ACh, Res, N&P

Owner: Contini Bonacossi family   Loc. Seano, Via Capezzana 100, 59015 Carmignano (PO)
Thanks to the direction of Count Ugo Contini Bonacossi, Capezzana has long been the foremost estate in the small Carmignano zone west of Florence. As if in response to the increasing quality from other local estates (ENRICO PIERAZZUOLI, AMBRA and others) quality has taken another step forward. Actually it's down to a younger generation taking charge and the hiring of Stefano Chioccioli as consultant. While there's no longer a Riserva, the Carmignano (around 20 per cent Cabernet Sauvignon and 10 per cent Canaiolo in addition to Sangiovese) has a refined structure, lovely depth and a touch of class missing in many other Tuscan reds, particularly some of the 'showy fruit and oak-rich' wines favoured by some wine critics, and has achieved a new level of excellence with the 99 vintage (four stars). Ghiaie della Furba, originally a sort of Tuscan Bordeaux blend now adds a little Syrah to Cabernet Sauvignon and Merlot, and is a wine of persuasive style. Both benefit from five years' ageing or more. Barco Reale, a lighter style based on Sangiovese and pioneered by Capezzana, can have delicious forward fruit but is best with just a couple of years' age. Capezzana's Vin Santo is elegant and refined with a classic, aged, gently oxidised character, though not the richness of some. Vin Ruspo is a relatively rare Rosato from this part of Italy and Chardonnay is also made. Non-wine products include impressive grappa and extra virgin olive oil. (PW)
- **Carmignano** Villa di Capezzana★★★ £D ● **Ghiaie della Furba**★★★ £E
- **Barco Reale di Carmignano**★ £B O **Carmignano Vin Santo**★★★ £E

CASALOSTE   Chianti Classico   www.casaloste.it   A: RsW, Rae, SVS

Owner: Giovanni Battista & Emilia d'Orsi   Via Montagliari 32, 50020 Panzano (FI)
A small 10.5-ha estate in Panzano that has recently turned out a string of fine Chianti with greater depth, weight and interest than many better-known estates. The efforts and commitment of Giovanni Battista and the results of his collaboration with consultant Gabriella Tani (whose efforts have produced fine Chianti at nearby CAROBBIO as well) deserve to be more well-known. Chianti Classico *normale* benefits from a little age and has the potential to improve for five years or so from a vintage like 1999. Two Riservas are even better but must be given at least three to five years' ageing. (PW)
- **Chianti Classico**★★ £C Riserva★★★ £D Riserva Don VincEnzo★★★ £E

CASANOVA DI NERI   Brunello di Montalcino   A: Eur, Far, JAr, Tur

Owner: Giacomo Neri   Podere Casanova, Loc. Torrenieri, 53028 Montalcino (SI)
Another of Brunello's relatively new stars and not a one-vintage wonder, Giacomo Neri works with
the widely consulted Carlo Ferrini to produce increasingly rich, stylish meaty Brunello even in more
difficult vintages like 94 and 96. There is some use of new wood as well as the traditional large *botti*
but this only enhances the structure not the flavours. The 27 ha are not confined to one site, which
makes it possible to produce both Tenuta Nuova and Riserva Cerretalto as well as a regular Brunello.
The superb 97 Tenuta Nuova is the finest wine to date but there is little doubt that these wines can
get even better. The Rosso is full and stylish too, better than much widely exported Brunello, but
should be drunk with three to five years' age. (PW)
● **Brunello di Montalcino**★★★ £E Tenuta Nuova★★★★ £F Riserva Cerretalto★★★★ £F
● **Rosso di Montalcino**★★ £C

CASTELLARE DI CASTELLINA   Chianti Classico   A: Bal

*Owner: **Nettuno srl** Loc. Castellare, 53011 Castellina in Chianti (SI)*
Directed by Paolo Panerai, Castellare first became well known for one of Tuscany's most innovative
Super-Tuscans, I Sodi di San Niccolò, and for the elegant labels that feature a different bird with each
vintage. The 25 ha of vineyards are well sited and both renewed investment and the retention of
Maurizio Castelli as consultant should ensure continued success. However the wines can be a bit
uneven, even if very satisfying with considerable finesse and elegance when they are on song. Regular
Chianti Classico is typically bright and attractive but has been a little lean of late, despite some excellent
vintages. The regular Riserva has only been at the level of a decent *normale*, though a single-vineyard
version, Il Poggiale, is rather better. It is the distinctive, perfumed and complex I Sodi that still
provides the greatest interest; its balance, depth and style make it a worthy flagship wine. Versions of
international varieties are also made but only in very small quantities. These include Sauvignon Blanc
(Spartito di Castellare), Chardonnay (Canonico di Castellare) and Cabernet Sauvignon (Coniale di
Castellare) but only the latter is regularly convincing. The best wines are reasonable value though a
new Merlot, Poggio ai Merli is pricey. (PW)
● **Chianti Classico Riserva**★ £C Riserva Vigna Il Poggiale★★ £C
● **I Sodi di San Niccolò**★★★ £D ● **Coniale di Castellare**★★ £D

CASTELLO DEL TERRICCIO   www.terriccio.it   A: L&S

Owner: G A Rossi de Medelana e Serrafini Ferri   Via Bagnoli 56040 Castellina Marittima (PI)
Castello del Terriccio lies not far to the north of Bolgheri and was one of the first of the many other
fine estates that now dot the Tuscan coastline. Thanks to considerable investment and a determination
to produce wines of the highest order, the estate, with 44 ha of vines, is now well-known in fine wine
circles. Winemaking expertise has come from Carlo Ferrini and Terricio's fame has been spearheaded
by two fine reds. Lupicaia is the high-priced flagship red (Cabernet Sauvignon with around 10 per
cent Merlot) and is intended to compete with Bordeaux's best. It is powerful, intense and oaky with
deep lush blackcurrant and black cherry fruit but plenty of structure too, and though of high quality
gives only a hint of its origins. The considerably cheaper Tassinaia, from equal parts Cabernet
Sauvignon, Merlot and Sangiovese, is similarly flattering, developing delicious chocolate and plum
flavours with a little age. There is similar ambition to produce great whites but, while both show
some lovely ripe fruit, there's not enough structure or depth. Con Vento is 100 per cent Sauvignon
Blanc while Saluccio is a barrel-fermented and aged Chardonnay.

Help with the most recent whites has been sought from Hans Terzer (SAN MICHELE APPIANO co-op) in Alto Adige. (PW)

● **Lupicaia★★★★** £G ● **Tassinaia★★★** £D
○ **Saluccio★★** £D ○ **Con Vento★★** £C

CASTELLO DELLA PANERETTA Chianti Classico   A: Vim

Owner: Maria Carla Musso Strada della Paneretta 35, Barberino Val d'Elsa (FI)
Located in the very west of Chianti Classico, this historic estate produces a range of wines often notable for the age and quality of the fruit. The vines are planted on fine *galestro-alberese* soils, pockets of which are found in other estates in Barberino Val d'Elsa. All the wines have good concentration and ripe, intense fruit, though can lack a little for structure. The 98 Chianti Classico Riservas, which include both a regular Riserva and a single-vineyard wine, Torre a Destra, lack the balance and refinement of the better vintages. However, the quality is generally very high and the plump, rich fruit is in stark contrast to other lean, underripe efforts still too prevalent in the Classico zone. Terrine is unusual in consisting of equal parts Canaiolo and Sangiovese and shows a fine fusion of floral, black fruit and oak-given characters. Quattrocentenario by contrast is 100 per cent Sangiovese from the estate's best old-vine fruit. Vin Santo is also made. (PW)

● **Chianti Classico★★** £C Riserva★★ £C Riserva Torre a Destra★★★ £D
● **Terrine★★★** £D ● **Quattrocentenario★★★★** £E

CASTELLO DI AMA Chianti Classico www.castellodiama.com   A: WTs, JAr

Owner: Lorenza Sebasti (& others) Loc. Ama, Fraz. Lecchi in Chianti, 53010 Gaiole in Chianti (SI)
During the explosion of Super-Tuscans in the 1980s, Castello di Ama instead chose to emphasise Chianti Classico, producing four single-vineyard versions that were the equal of the best vini da tavola. Winemaker Marco Pallanti, who has been involved with Ama for 20 years and is married to director Lorenza Sebasti, still makes two single-vineyard versions but now only in small quantities and only in the best years. Both Bellavista (which includes a percentage of Malvasia Nera) and La Casuccia (Merlot complements the Sangiovese) combine intensity with nuance and elegance but the latter is the richer of the two. As at a number of top estates attention is now focused on a single bottling of Chianti Classico, more in the manner of a Bordeaux château. Ama's Chianti Classico starts out quite firm but with good intensity and depth as well as a certain class others lack. Given the vineyards' elevation (450–480 m), more difficult vintages such as 98 can be a little lean but the wines gain richness with age and a top vintage such as 97 or 99 will improve for at least five years. Tuscany's first great Merlot, L'Apparita, was produced here and it continues to be one of the very best. Relatively high fermentation temperatures and a long maceration precede ageing in 100 per cent new Allier oak. This now sizeable (90-ha) estate also provides an attractive, well-balanced Chardonnay, Al Poggio, capable of a little age, and some Pinot Nero, Il Chiuso. (PW)

● **Chianti Classico★★** £C Vigneto Bellavista★★★★ £E Vigneto La Casuccia★★★★ £E
● **L'Apparita ★★★★** £F ○ **Al Poggio★★** £B

CASTELLO DI FONTERUTOLI Chianti Classico www.fonterutoli.it   A: Eno, JNi

Owner: Mazzei family Loc. Fonterutoli, 53011 Castellina in Chianti (SI)
The Fonterutoli estate, one of Chianti's finest, dates from 1435. In recent times (from the 1995 vintage) it has taken the lead in attempting to restore the reputation of Chianti Classico, sacrificing a well-established Super-Tuscan, Concerto (a Sangiovese/Cabernet blend) and a previously made Riserva Ser Lapo to this end. The focus of production from 62 ha of vines, under the direction of

brothers Filippo and Francesco and the continued winemaking expertise of the respected Carlo Ferrini, is the Castello di Fonterutoli estate wine, a premium selection of the two best plots of Sangiovese (dubbed by some a super-Chianti Classico). It is barrique-aged and a rich, ripe modernstyle example with excellent intensity and depth and on a different level from most Chianti Classico (including Riservas). A second selection is labelled simply Fonterutoli but is of similar quality to much good Chianti Classico. One Super-Tuscan still made is Siepi (from a vineyard of this name) – a wonderfully rich, enticing blend of equal parts of Sangiovese and Merlot. The same direction is employed at the 30-ha Belguardo estate in the southern Maremma where ever better Morellino di Scansano is made. In addition from the 2000 vintage a major new Cabernet Sauvignon-based estate wine show great promise, as does a well-priced, scented and characterful Serrata di Belguardo (Merlot/Sangiovese/Cabernet Sauvignon). The Mazzei also have close links with the neighbouring estate of LA BRANCAIA as well as GHIZZANO in the Pisa hills. (PW)

Castello di Fonterutoli:
● **Chianti Classico** Castello di Fonterutoli★★★★ £E
● **Chianti Classico** Fonterutoli★★ £C
● **Siepi**★★★★ £F   ● **Poggio alla Badiola**★ £B
Tenuta Belguardo:
● **Morellino di Scansano** Poggio Bronzone★★★ £C

CASTELLO DI POPPIANO   Colli Fiorentini   A: GWW

Owner: Conte Ferdinando Guicciardini   Via di Fezzana 43, 50025 Montespertoli (FI)
This Colli Fiorentini estate belonged to the Guicciardini from the mid-12th century and the current count Ferdinando can claim an ancestor who corresponded regularly with Machiavelli, who lived nearby. In wine terms this location is too often associated with something less impressive but the 120 ha of vines here produce some of the best wines of the Colli Fiorentini. The traditional wines include some Canaiolo and Colorino along with the Sangiovese. Il Cortile is a fine example of Chianti from these hills. A denser Riserva must be given at least five years' age, yet misses a little of the style of the *normale*. Of the new style reds two in particular stand out. In Tricorno, Sangiovese combines with Cabernet Sauvignon and Merlot; well-oaked, concentrated and powerful, it is quite individual for this blend. Increasingly impressive Syrah, with a dash of blueberry and white pepper, includes 10 per cent Sangiovese. In Tosco Forte the proportions are reversed. Vin Santo, produced from Malvasia, is of the old-fashioned style; very biscuity, nutty yet with good concentration. Ancient as Poppiano is, it sustains new life in a seven-year-old property with 35 ha of vines in the Maremma. Adding to a regular Morellino di Scansano, the first Riserva was produced from the 2001 vintage. (PW)

Castello di Poppiano:
● **Chianti Colli Fiorentini** Il Cortile★★ £B   ● **Chianti Colli Fiorentini** Riserva★★ £C
● **Tricorno**★★★★ £D   ● **Syrah**★★★ £C   ● **Tosco Forte**★★ £C
O **Vernaccia**★ £B   O **Vin Santo** della Torre Grande★★ £E
Massi di Mandorlaia:
● **Morellino di Scansano**★★ £B

CASTELLO DEI RAMPOLLA   Chianti Classico   A: Bal, Wgg

Owner: Di Napoli Rampolla family   Via Santa Lucia in Faulle, 50020 Panzano (FI)
The Conca d'Oro south of the town of Panzano has long been considered one of Chianti Classico's finest sub-zones. Principe (Prince) Alceo Di Napoli Rampolla favoured Cabernet Sauvignon over Sangiovese and more than half the current 42 ha of vineyard are planted to it. Sammarco was the wine that made the estate famous and only includes 20 per cent Sangiovese with the Cabernet. It continues to be a firm, powerful and aristocratic red with great dimension and fine blackcurrant, herb and

small-berried fruit. The estate is now run along biodynamic lines by son Luca and daughter Maurizia (with continued guidance from Giacomo Tachis), who have brought to fruition a project started by their father, La Vigna d'Alceo. Of particular interest is the high-density (8–10,000 vines per hectare: twice that of many Tuscan vineyards) and low spur-training. The wine is a blend of 85 per cent Cabernet and 15 per cent Petit Verdot. It has been sensational since its first vintage in 1996: Vigna d'Alceo spends less time in wood than Sammarco and has quite a contrasting texture and profile, but there is terrific purity, depth and intensity in a superb 99. Chianti Classico Riserva which included a little Cabernet is being phased out but it would be wrong to overlook the regular Chianti Classico, which shows how well Sangiovese does in these soils. With lots of class and intensity within a sturdy frame, it needs to be kept for at least five years from a good vintage. (PW)

● **Vigna d'Alceo**✪✪✪✪✪ £G   ● **Sammarco**★★★★★ £F
● **Chianti Classico**★★★ £C

CASTELLO DI MONSANTO   Chianti Classico   www.castellodimonsanto.it   A: CKr

Owner: Fabrizio Bianchi   Via Monsanto 8, 50021 Barberino Val d'Elsa (FI)
Fabrizio Bianchi bought this estate in 1961 and in the years that followed the focus on producing a great Chianti Classico led to Monsanto's illustrious reputation. That wine, Il Poggio, is still very good but is not of the lush, new oak style favoured by some (less than half the wine goes into second-use barriques, the rest into large Slavonian oak) and the resulting lighter, more evolved colour precedes a palate of good breadth and excellent flavour depth. Based on a 5.5-ha vineyard it is also a true Chianti Classico in the sense that it is mostly Sangiovese with some Canaiolo and a little Colorino and it will evolve slowly for many years. There is no doubt that this stylistically diverse Chianti Classico is not in vogue and it could be that denser planting and winemaking changes could better express its potential. From the rest of the estate's 70 ha are produced a regular Riserva and three other premium reds. Fabrizio Bianchi lends his name to both a pure Sangiovese and a Chardonnay. Tinscvil is a blend of Sangiovese and Cabernet Sauvignon but can display an earthy, herbal aspect, while Nemo can be a very distinctive cedary, but also Tuscan-scented, Cabernet Sauvignon with intense sweet fruit within a muscular frame. (PW)

● **Chianti Classico** Riserva★ £D Riserva Il Poggio★★★ £E
● **Fabrizio Bianchi**★★ £E   ● **Tinscvil**★ £D   ● **Nemo**★★★ £E
O **Fabrizio Bianchi Chardonnay**★ £C

CASTELLO DI VOLPAIA   Chianti Classico   www.volpaia.com   A: Alv

Owner: Giovanella Stianti   Loc. Volpaia, 53017 Radda in Chianti (SI)
While much is made of sub-zones like Panzano and Monti, there are many other good small areas within the Chianti Classico zone such as the cluster of fine small estates in the hills north-east of Radda. Giovanella Stianti and her husband Carlo Mascheroni, assisted by Maurizio Castelli, have long made elegant stylish wines, including Super-Tuscans Coltassala (Sangiovese and a little Mammolo) and Balifico (Sangiovese with a third from the two Cabernets). Coltassala, in particular, has shown the elegance, refinement and grace that Sangiovese can attain. The downside is that some of the wines struggle for ripeness and adequate richness in poorer vintages and there is not the consistency that some critics have suggested. Changes have taken place, including the recent recruitment of Riccardo Cotarella. From a top recent vintage such as 97 or 99 there is delightful drinking at all levels. Coltassala has been redesignated a Chianti Classico Riserva since the 98 vintage, while the regular Chianti Classico is now labelled simply as Volpaia. Some Vin Santo is also made. (PW)

● **Chianti Classico**★ £B Riserva★★ £C Riserva Coltassala★★★ £E
● **Balifico**★★★ £E

CASTELLO VICCHIOMAGGIO   Chianti Classico   www.vicchiomaggio.it   A: Hal

Owner: John Matta   Via Vicchiomaggio 4, 50022 Greve in Chianti (FI)
John Matta's well-sited estate, topped by an impressive Renaissance castle, has been transformed since it was bought by his family in 1966. It now runs to 30 ha and with help from Giorgio Marone, produces three very good Sangiovese-based reds. Arguably the best of these is the Chianti Classico Riserva La Prima which comes from the estate's oldest vines. The wine consistently shows good richness, depth and a preserved black fruits character. Made in greater quantities is the Riserva Petri, which complements Sangiovese with a small percentage of Cabernet rather than the native Canaiolo and Colorino used in La Prima. While good, it hasn't quite the extra intensity or structure of La Prima. Both are partly raised in barrique, while a fine pure Sangiovese, Ripa delle More, is entirely so. Ripa delle Mandorle is a blend of Sangiovese and Cabernet Sauvignon while Chianti Classico San Jacopo can provide adequate everyday drinking. (PW)

● **Chianti Classico** Riserva Petri★★ £C   Riserva La Prima★★★ £D
● **Ripa delle Mandorle**★ £C   ● **Ripa delle More**★★★ £E

CERBAIONA   Brunello di Montalcino   A: Bal

Owner: Diego Molinari   Loc. Cerbaiona, 53024 Montalcino (SI)
Diego Molinara's small 7-ha estate can be one of Brunello's greats. The concentration, depth and power combined with a thrilling aromatic and flavour complexity make it a superb cellaring investment even at the price. However, of those vintages tasted there is marked variation and the wines can lack for balance and cleanliness. The rating therefore only applies to certifiable great vintages such as 1997 and 1990. Though the estate now seems to be hitting its stride, other older vintages should only be bought in any quantity (not that there's much to be had) once tasted. A second wine labelled simply Cerbaiona adds Cabernet Sauvignon, Merlot, Syrah and Malvasia Nera to Sangiovese, and can also be variable. (PW)

● **Brunello di Montalcino**★★★★★ £F   ● **Cerbaiona**★★★ £E

CIACCI PICCOLOMINI D'ARAGONA   Brunello di Montalcino   A: Bal

Owner: Giuseppe Bianchini   Via Borgo di Mezzo, Loc. Castelnuovo dell'Abate, 53020 Montalcino (SI)
This substantial estate with a fine 17th-century *palazzo* and 35 ha of vineyards is in the favoured south-east corner of the Brunello zone. After making waves with the 1988 and 90 vintages it has continued, first under Roberto Cipresso and now Paolo Vagaggini, to make fine modern-styled Brunello and Rosso. Brunello is ripe and full-textured, with good breadth and depth, relatively approachable when released but generally better with ten years' age. Good examples were made in 94, 95, 97 and 98, though a 96 is not of the usual standard and faster evolving, Riservas from 95 and 97 add more extract and weight over the regular example. The ripe, smoky, meaty Rosso is high in alcohol but typically has good richness and depth and with three to five years' age makes a better bet than many a poor Brunello. The estate also has plantings of French varieties, used in Ateo, a Sangiovese/Merlot/ Cabernet Sauvignon blend, and Fabius, which is based on Syrah and sold under the Sant'Antimo DOC. A new estate, Santo Stefano, in the Montecucco DOC, has been acquired and is run by Giuseppe's son Paolo. (PW)

● **Brunello di Montalcino** Vigna di Pianrosso★★★ £E   Riserva★★★★ £F
● **Rosso di Montalcino** Vigna della Fonte★★ £C   ● **Ateo**★★ £C

COL D'ORCIA Brunello di Montalcino   A: Alv

Owner: Francesco Marone Cinzano   Fraz. Sant'Angelo in Colle, 53020 Montalcino (SI)
Col d'Orcia is one of the best known and most respected names in Montalcino. The large estate includes 130 ha of vines but the wines are made to a high standard. Ex-BANFI winemaker Pablo Harri now directs winemaking and there is consultancy from Maurizio Castelli. The vintages of regular Brunello in the mid-1990s shows plenty of fruit, slightly more evolved in 94 and 96, more tannic but richer in 95 and 97. A tendency to firm, slightly drying tannins can detract and structure can be too dominant in the regular Riserva. The Riserva Poggio al Vento comes from 5.5 ha of south-facing slopes and can develop a marvellous complexity with a decade's ageing. As well as Brunello there is a consistent and gutsy, characterful Rosso di Montalcino, while Rosso degli Spezieri is a bright, fruity blend of Sangiovese, Ciliegiolo and Merlot for early consumption. Olmaia is the major concession to foreign varieties and is a very powerful, rich oaky Cabernet Sauvignon, although it still wants for a little more refinement both in its structure and flavours. Moscadello di Montalcino is very honeyed with intense, very ripe fruit yet is not in the least heavy. Some Chardonnay (Ghiaie) and Pinot Grigio are also made. (PW)
- ● **Brunello di Montalcino**★★★ £E Riserva Poggio al Vento★★★★ £F
- ● **Rosso di Montalcino**★★ £C ● **Rosso degli Spezieri**★ £B ● **Olmaia**★★★ £F
- ○ **Moscadello di Montalcino** Pascena★★★ £D

COLOMBAIO DI CENCIO Chianti Classico   A: L&S

Owner: Werner Wikhelm   Loc. Cornia, 53013 Gaiole in Chianti (SI)
It is not every day that interesting new estates emerge from the more established order of Chianti Classico's hillsides. The focus here is on just two reds, a Chianti Classico (originally a Riserva but no longer given this designation) from Sangiovese (and a little Merlot) and a Cabernet Sauvignon, Sangiovese and Merlot blend, Il Futuro. Winemaking is directed by Jacopo Morganti with input from established enologist Paolo Vagaggini (FULIGNI and others). There's no mistaking the oak in Il Futuro but there's also powerful, ripe, deep, lush berry richness and a sleek texture. The length, intensity and promise is there but time is needed to see how much expression and finesse will be apparent with the five years' age or more. Chianti Classico is good but not of the previous standard in 2001. (PW)
- ● **Chianti Classico** I Massi★★★ £D ● **Il Futuro**★★★★ £E

CORZANO & PATERNO Chianti   A: THt, Han, UnC

Owner: Gelpke family   Fraz. San Pancrazio, Via Paterno 8, 50020 San Casciano Val di Pesa (FI)
For sleek, pure Tuscan reds, Corzano & Paterno is a label to seek out. From 15 ha of vineyard on the outer rim of the Classico zone, Alijoscha Goldschmidt produces a small but fine range of wines. Il Corzano, the premium red, is the finest expression and, though international in its composition and modern vinification, it is far removed from the more bland examples of this genre. A wine of splendid texture and complexity it is a blend of mostly Sangiovese and Cabernet Sauvignon but including a little Merlot (40/45/15 in the 2000). Oak is also present in stylish Chianti and Chianti Riserva but again it is offset against pure fruit and good depth. The quality possible from Malvasia and Trebbiano grapes can be seen in a very fine intense sweet white, Passito di Corzano (or in older vintages as Vin Santo). For dry whites there's barrique-aged Chardonnay, Aglaia and Il Corzanello. (PW)
- ● **Il Corzano**★★★★ £E
- ● **Chianti** Terre di Corzano★★ £B Riserva Tre Borri★★★ £D
- ○ **Aglaia**★★ £E ○ **Passito di Corzano**★★★ £E

COSTANTI Brunello di Montalcino   A: Lib

Owner: Andrea Costanti Loc. Colle al Matrichese, 53024 Montalcino (SI)

Costanti was one of the first recorded producers of Brunello. Andrea Costanti, who has run this estate for close on two decades, now oversees both the small 7-ha, high-altitude vineyard area of Colle al Matrichese, east of Montalcino itself, and a further 4 ha in the Calbello vineyard at Montosoli, purchased in 1997. He works with Vittorio Fiore to produce elegant but long-lasting Brunello that starts out a little forbidding but shows considerable finesse and style with ten years' age or more. There is richer fruit and less austerity than previously but similar ageing capacity from the intense fruit. A Riserva is only produced in really exceptional years. Rosso di Montalcino shows both more breadth and refinement than is usual but needs at least five years' age. From the Calbello property are produced a second very good Rosso di Montalcino and a Merlot/Cabernet Sauvignon blend, Ardingo. The latter shows excellent ripe black fruit and a fine structure and promises to be at its best with six to ten years' age. Vermiglio is a partly barrique-aged Sangiovese with the emphasis on the fruit character. (PW)

● **Brunello di Montalcino**★★★ £E Riserva★★★★ £F
● **Rosso di Montalcino**★★ £D Calbello★★ £E
● **Ardingo**★★★ £E

LUIGI D'ALESSANDRO Cortona   A: L&S

Owner: D'Alessandro family Loc. Camucia, Via Manzano 15, 52042 Cortona (AR)

It must have taken not only money but also plenty of courage to establish a new wine estate in the relative viticultural wilderness of eastern Tuscany. Chardonnay, Viognier and Syrah and even some Gamay were planted at high densities for Tuscany (7,000 vines per hectare), but the range has gradually evolved to focus on Fontarca, a rich, blended white from Chardonnay and Viognier, and Il Bosco, pure Syrah. The Chardonnay component (60–85 per cent) of Fontarca is barrique-fermented and the wine is ripe and aromatic, powerful and high in alcohol and, if not a keeper, provides marvellous exotic, peachy fruit within a couple of years of the vintage. The red offers similarly impressive fruit of the black plum, herb, spice and floral spectrum, a lovely intensity and richness but, importantly, within a more complete structure that suggests as much pleasure with five years' age or more. Il Vescovo was made from Gamay but Il Vescovo II is intended as a second wine for Il Bosco and is similarly 100 per cent Syrah, but mostly from younger vines. It provides an alternative to a good Côtes du Rhône Syrah. The wines now come under the new Cortona DOC. A traditional wine also gets a look in as a little Vin Santo (from the classic Trebbiano and Malvasia) is also made. Production is relatively modest and prices proportionate to quality. (PW)

● **Cortona Syrah** Il Bosco★★★★ £D Il Vescovo II★★ £B
O **Fontarca**★★★ £C

DEI Vino Nobile di Montepulciano   A: L&S

Owner: Dei family Via di Martiena 35, 53045 Montepulciano (SI)

Catherina Dei has 37 ha over which she lavishes much attention and the fruit intensity she procures is of a different order to run-of-the-mill Vino Nobile. Consultancy comes from one of Tuscany's best, Niccolò D'Afflitto, and the regular Vino Nobile, if only on the cusp of three stars, has been supremely consistent since the mid-1990s. There is ripe, stylish, concentrated fruit but also an initial firmness that makes for better drinking with three to five years' age, when it has developed a spicy, savoury complexity. A Riserva adds more weight and structure and shows a little barrique influence but the new oak is mostly reserved for an unusual premium blend from a single vineyard of Sangiovese, Syrah, Cabernet Sauvignon and Petit Verdot, Sancta Catharina. If more variable this has generally been a lush, ripe characterful wine since its inception in 1994. Rosso di Montepulciano is also made and is light (if with a little more richness in the best years), round and fresh if drunk with a couple of years' age. Prices are very reasonable but any reckoning. (PW)

● **Vino Nobile di Montepulciano**★★★ £C   Riserva★★★ £C
● **Sancta Catharina**★★★ £D

FATTORIA DI FELSINA   Chianti Classico   A: Lib, ACh, N&P, Vne

Owner: Poggiali family   Strada Chiantigiana 484, 53019 Castelnuovo Berardenga (SI)
Under Giuseppe Mazzocolin (whose wife's family also own CASTELLO DI FARNETELLA) and consultant Franco Bernabei this now substantial property (82 ha) has become one of Chianti Classico's quality heavyweights. Felsina always shows off the best of this southern commune, where the wines are more earthy, gutsy and fleshy (hinting at Brunello) than the more elevated, more northerly zones. The best wines, Riserva Vigneto Rancia, and the premium oak-aged Sangiovese, Fontalloro, and increasingly the rich Cabernet Sauvignon, Maestro Raro, all show greater complexity and add a touch of refinement but there are no wimps here. A Chardonnay, I Sistri, has never lacked for flavour either. Recent releases have been a little uneven, occasionally wanting for more finesse in their structures. Regular Chianti Classico is best with at least three years' age, others with five or more. Renown has also brought higher prices and the value for money of old is no longer there. (PW)

● **Chianti Classico**★★ £C   Riserva★★ £D   Riserva Vigneto Rancia★★★ £E
● **Fontalloro**★★★★ £F   ● **Maestro Raro**★★★ £F
O **Chardonnay** I Sistri★★ £C

TENUTE DI AMBROGIO E GIOVANNI FOLONARI   www.tenutefolonari.com

Owner: Ambrogio & Giovanni Folonari   Via De Bardi 28, 50125 Firenze (FI)
This is the new project of the Folonari family members who were formerly part of RUFFINO. As well as taking possession of the Cabreo and Nozzole estates, the father and son team of Ambrogio and Giovanni Folonari have moved quickly to embellish their holdings. New Vino Nobile estate Gracciano Svetoni and Brunello producer La Fuga are complemented by an estate being developed in Bolgheri, Campo del Mare. The most outstanding of the ex-Ruffino wines is the Cabernet Sauvignon, Il Pareto, from the Nozzole estate but a Sangiovese/Cabernet Sauvignon blend (70/30), Cabreo Il Borgo, is just as well known and can show similar intensity and depth of fruit in top vintages. Both need five years' age but will keep for much longer. Cabreo La Pietra is a barrique-fermented and aged Chardonnay of long-standing and is typically rich and creamy with ripe fruit and plenty of depth and good length, but can be a little ungainly. The Spalletti estate in Chianti Rufina also forms part of the holdings. (PW)

Tenuta di Nozzole:
● **Chianti Classico** Riserva La Forra★★ £C   ● **Il Pareto**★★★★ £F

Tenute del Cabreo:
● **Cabreo Il Borgo**★★★ £E   O **Cabreo La Pietra**★★★ £D

Tenuta La Fuga:
● **Brunello di Montalcino**★★★ £E

FONTODI   Chianti Classico   www.fontodi.com   A: Lib, ACh, Res, BBR

Owner: Manetti family   Via San Leolino 89, 50020 Panzano (FI)
Fontodi Chianti Classico is a benchmark example that most other producers, except a few making super-Chianti Classico, should be aiming to emulate. At its price position it is rarely (if ever) matched

and shows marvellous vigour, intensity and style. Fontodi, with 67 ha of vineyards, is fortunate to have not only a great location (Panzano's Conca d'Oro) but also the dedication of Giovanni Manetti in the vineyards and long-term winemaking direction from Franco Bernabei. Chianti Classico Riserva Vigna del Sorbo includes 10 per cent Cabernet Sauvignon and shows great refinement and style. Flaccianello della Pieve was one of the first great pure-Sangiovese Tuscan wines and still shows lovely dimension and evident class (if a slightly overripe character in the 99) even though it is no longer one of the out and out top examples. Syrah has also been made for several years and is beginning to really hit its stride (since 1998) with an intense fruit core, though it still lacks the refinement and style to compete with similarly priced examples from around the world. Pinot Nero has also improved but is less suited to the soils (and climate) than the Syrah. A white, Meriggio, is made from barrel-fermented Pinot Bianco and some Sauvignon Blanc. (PW)

● **Chianti Classico**★★★ £C Riserva Vigna del Sorbo★★★★ £E
● **Flaccianello**★★★★ £F ● **Syrah Case Via**★★★ £E ● **Pinot Nero**★ £E

FRESCOBALDI www.frescobaldi.it   A: Hal, Odd

Owner: Marchesi de' Frescobaldi   Via Santo Spirito 11, 50125 Firenze
The Frescobaldi empire is one of Tuscany's most historic and important. The 1,000 ha of vineyards spread over nine estates include some prime sites. Subject to the expertise of Lamberto Frescobaldi and Niccolò d'Afflitto many of the wines are richer and riper than they were in the 1980s and early 90s. The best wine is unquestionably the very fine Montesodi (from 20 ha of vineyards) from the Chianti Rufina estate, Nipozzano. Of long-standing reputation, it is a wine of real class with great length and structure; a wine to drink with a decade's age or more. The much bigger volume Nipozzano Riserva can also show a certain style and, with age, charm. Mormoreto, an intense Cabernet Sauvignon that includes some Cabernet Franc is also produced on this estate. From more elevated vineyards in the enclave of Pomino, the whites in particular show recent improvement; Il Benefizio is a barrique-aged blend of predominantly Chardonnay. The other major outpost of quality is the Castelgiocondo estate in Montalcino. However, even if recently improved, many vintages of Brunello have been very disappointing and the Rosso di Montalcino, Campo ai Sassi, is rarely of a quality worthy of its appellation. It seems that more vintages are needed before the improvements translate to consistent high quality. Lamaione is a varietal Merlot of good fruit and consistency. The most over-hyped Italian wine of recent years, Luce della Vite, also has its source in Montalcino. A joint venture with Robert Mondavi, it is a blend of Sangiovese and Merlot in equal measure but, while there is good fruit richness and plenty of oak, there is not the structure or refinement that the price would suggest. Lucente, more Sangiovese than Merlot, is the second wine, while a range of new varietals is being produced under the Danzante label. A promising new premium wine, Giramonte, made since 1999, comes from the Castiglioni estate in the Colli Fiorentini, where Chianti and Cabernet Sauvignon are also produced. Seductive, stylish aromas precede a palate structure of slightly less sophistication but of wide appeal. Basic Frescobaldi brands, including Rèmole Chianti, are just that, basic. Frescobaldi has also recently ventured into Friuli, North-East Italy, taking a controlling interest in Collio producer, Attems. (PW)

Marchesi de' Frescobaldi:
● **Chianti Rufina** Riserva Nipozzano★★ £C Montesodi★★★★ £E
● **Mormoreto**★★★ £E ● **Pomino**★ £C
O **Pomino**★ £B Il Benefizio★★ £C
Tenuta di Castelgiocondo:
● **Brunello di Montalcino**★★ £E Riserva★★★★ £F
● **Lamaione**★★★ £E
Tenuta di Castiglioni:
● **Giramonte**★★★ £F
Frescobaldi/Mondavi:
● **Luce della Vite**★★★ £G ● **Lucente la Vite**★ £D

FULIGNI   Brunello di Montalcino   A: L&S, N&P

Owner: Eredi Fuligni   Via Soccorso Saloni 33, 53024 Montalcino (SI)

At just 8 ha, this is one of the many small Brunello estates and one of the few that are really worth hunting down. The erudite Roberto Guerrini makes wine to contemplate and savour and while there is the classic Brunello muscle and size there is also more elegance than is typical. Despite a modest 96 there is generally good consistency and good wines too in years when many others are disappointing. Currently the regular 97 and the 95 and 97 Riservas are the best examples of the collaboration between Guerrini and his consultant Paolo Vagaggini. The SJ or San Jacopo is lush with a seductive immediacy but not much more and the Rosso oftens shows a similar vibrancy of fruit. Brunello is reasonably priced vis-à-vis the competition. (PW)

● **Brunello di Montalcino** Vigneti dei Cottimelli★★★ £E Riserva★★★★ £F
● **Rosso di Montalcino** Ginestreto★★ £C ● **SJ**★★ £C

GAGLIOLE   www.gagliole.com

Owner: Thomas & Monika Bär-Bettschart   Loc. Gagiole 42, 53011 Castellina in Chianti (SI)

With Swiss banker, Thomas Bär there is a passionate commitment to making fine wine. Seven of 9 ha of vines on slopes in Castellina, not far from LA BRANCAIA, are currently in production. Luca D'Attoma is the consultant of choice. Fermentation is in conical oak vats with a total maceration of three to four weeks. Sangiovese-based, Gagliole includes around 10 per cent Cabernet Sauvignon. The result is a very complete modern, sophisticated red with a lush, creamy texture and rich blackberry fruit but it is also a wine of some style and individuality. Of the most recent vintages, 2001 improves on a 2000 that avoids the defects of that vintage. More original and even better than Gagliole is Pecchia, so far only made in 1999 and from 30-year-old vines, but a candidate for a five-star rating. (PW)

● **Gagliole Rosso**★★★★ £E

TENUTA DI GHIZZANO   Colline Pisane   www.tenutadighizzano.com   A: L&S, Eno

Owner: Pierfrancesco Venerosi Pesciolini   Via della Chiesa 1, 56030 Ghizzano di Peccioli (PI)

Ghizzano is the leading property in the Colline Pisane, an increasingly good source of rich, ripe reds, further up the coast from the famous Bolgheri zone. The large estate (350 ha) has belonged to the noble family since the 14th century and the relatively small vineyard of 16 ha is currently being expanded to 25 ha. The estate is managed by the owner's daughter, Ginevra, and two wines fashioned by enologist Carlo Ferrini have established their reputation as wine producers. Veneroso is primarily a blend of Sangiovese and Cabernet Sauvignon (but with five per cent Merlot in 1999) while Nambrot, originally a varietal Merlot, now includes an increasing amount of Cabernet. Both are aged in new oak and made in a rich, lush modern style. Nambrot is a little fuller and more succulent but Veneroso has the greater class. Chianti Colline Pisane is fruity and stylish while a tiny quantity of Vin Santo, San Germano, is also made. (PW)

● **Nambrot**★★★★ £E ● **Veneroso**★★★★ £E
● **Chianti Colline Pisane**★ £B

GRATTAMACCO/COLLE MASSARI   Bolgheri   www.collemassari.it   A: Sec

Owner: P Meletti Cavallari/Claudio Tipa   Loc. Grattamacco, 57022 Castagneto Carducci (LI)

Grattamacco was only the second estate to commercialise wine from the now famous zone of

Bolgheri. Piermario Meletti Cavallari worked steadily to refine a great red wine of his own but in 2002 leased his estate to Claudia Tipa of Colle Massari (a 300-ha estate in the southern Maremma with young plantings) for 10 years. The red Grattamacco, a blend now dominated by Cabernet Sauvignon with the balance from Sangiovese and Merlot comes from 10 of the 11 ha of gently sloping vineyards on a 30-ha estate. Over recent years the wine has become increasingly refined and harmonious but without losing its individuality, its fine perfume of spice, floral and herb scents and dark berried fruit. There is good depth and a certain rigour to the structure but great length of flavour. Older vintages (pre-1992) contain Malvasia Nera rather than Merlot. Future vintages, following investment and input from Tipa, should be interesting. The perfumed white is from Vermentino, a small portion of it barrique-fermented, and is ripe and full if not that complex. (PW)

● **Bolgheri** Superiore★★★ £E   O **Bolgheri** Bianco★★ £B

BIBI GRAETZ

A: F&R

Owner: Bibi Graetz   Via di Vincigliata, 50014 Fiesole (FI)
Bibi Graetz has 10 ha at Fiesole just outside Florence. If this seems an unlikely place for making fine wines then try his one and only wine, Testamatta. Just 20, 000 bottles of 2001 were produced, with an eye-catching label that is also his own work. Consultancy comes from the highly regarded Alberto Antonini team. The blend is very Tuscan with 70 per cent Sangiovese and the balance between mostly Colorino and Canaiolo but also a little Malvasia Nera and Moscato Nero. The fruit comes from vines that are 30–60 years old and vinification is in open fermenters. The result is an inky black red of marvellous intensity and originality. Powerful and extracted, it should be cellared rather than used to impress your friends. The wine is rated on the basis of just two vintages (2001 and 2000) but this is very promising – if you can find it. (PW)

● **Testamatta**★★★★ £E

GUALDO DEL RE   Val di Cornia

A: L&S, N&P

Owner: N Rossi & M T Cabella   Loc. Notri 77, 57028 Suvereto (LI)
Under Barbara Tamburini's consultancy both the composition and the quality of several wines here have had a serious makeover. Generally there is successively better depth, concentration and intensity in the three premium reds going from 99 to 2000 to 2001. The wines also have better textures and fruit expression. I Rennero is now pure Merlot but included Pinot Nero in the first two vintages (98 and 99). It is more varietal, with a mineral streak to its deep, ripe black-fruit character in 2001. Federico Primo is 100 per cent Cabernet Sauvignon from 2000, having previously included Merlot, while Gualdo del Re is from Sangiovese. Of the whites, Strale, 100 per cent barrique-femented and aged Pinot Bianco, used to be known as Lumen but is a good spicy, creamy, Tuscan example of the variety. Vermentino is very attractive if drunk very young, while basic Eliseo red and white have good character if only moderate structure and substance. A sweet Aleatico, Amansio, is also made. (PW)

● **Val di Cornia Suvereto** Gualdo del Re★★★ £D Federico Primo★★★ £D I Rennero★★★ £D
O **Strale**★★ £C   O **Valentina Vermentino**★★ £B
O **Val di Cornia Bianco** Eliseo★ £B   ● **Val di Cornia Rosso** Eliseo★ £B

IL PALAZZINO   Chianti Classico

A: J&B

Owner: Alessandro & Andrea Sderci   Loc. Monti, 53010 Gaiole in Chianti (SI)
Relatively few estates are as committed to the pursuit of a classic expression of Chianti Classico as Il Palazzino. Alessandro Sderci distinguishes between four different sites and achieves a quite different

expression and level of quality from each. While technical assistance is sought, he is determined to avoid any style imposition from an outside consultant. The Sdercis' finest plot of vines is Grosso Sanese, planted over 30 years ago. 100 per cent Sangiovese and sold as a vino da tavola from 1981 till 1993, it is now among the top flight of Chianti Classico. A small part of Grosso Sanese may be set aside as Riserva and given slightly longer ageing in barriques. These are 10-year wines but currently the excellent 97 or 98 might be broached. La Pieve comes from four parcels around a church, is barrique-aged (a third new) and has impressive depth, although also some of the austerity of the other wines if drunk too young. More fruit-driven but with less structure is Argenina, while La Cascina Girasole (sold as an IGT) is simpler and reflects its cooler origins. (PW)

● **Chianti Classico** Grosso Sanese★★★★ £C Riserva Grosso Sanese★★★★ £D
● **Chianti Classico** Argenina★★ £C La Pieve★★★ £C
● **La Cascina Girasole★** £B

IL POGGIONE Brunello di Montalcino   A: Eno, N&P

Owner: Clemente Leopoldo & Livia Franceschi Fraz. Sant'Angelo in Colle, 53020 Montalcino (SI)
Il Poggione has made some excellent Brunello for 40-odd years, in fact during all the time that Pierluigi Talenti (see TALENTI) was winemaker here – from 1958 until his death in 1999. The large estate with just over 100 ha of vines is now under the direction of Pierluigi's protégé – Fabrizio Bindocci. The wines have been slightly old-fashioned, full and structured, always with a fair amount of tannin but balanced and capable of long ageing, although already exhibiting a deep, savoury complexity and richness soon after their release; in fact everything that lighter, more superficial examples lack. The balance can be more marginal in a lighter vintage but not in recent vintages such as 95 or 97 or even 98. There is even more power, structure and breadth in the long-lived Riserva. The Rosso, too, rarely lacks for depth or intensity but shows more obvious plummy black fruits and plenty of grip (as is evident in a good 99). Future vintages look likely to maintain the fine tradition if perhaps tending to a more overt fruit richness that can also be seen in San Leopoldo, a Sangiovese/Cabernet Sauvignon/Cabernet Franc blend. The wines are very reasonably priced for the quality. (PW)

● **Brunello di Montalcino★★★★** £D Riserva★★★★ £E
● **Rosso di Montalcino★★** £B ● **San Leopoldo★★★** £C

ISOLE E OLENA Chianti Classico   A: Lib, Vne, ACh, Res

Owner: De Marchi family Loc. Isole 1, 50021 Barberino Val d'Elsa (FI)
Paolo De Marchi is perhaps Tuscany's finest ambassador, effortlessly combining dynamism and humility in a tireless pursuit of quality. A *vignaiolo* first and winemaker second, over more than two and a half decades he has poured a massive amount of energy (and intelligence) into reshaping an estate (now with 48 ha of vineyards) bought by his family in the 1960s. The wines have been very good for a long time but having developed his own clones of Sangiovese and reclaimed the most taxing vineyards, the best fruits of his labours are only now being transformed into ever better wines. From the great Cepparello (from Sangiovese) through powerful, long-lived Cabernet Sauvignon and stylish Syrah to vibrant Chianti Classico the wines are intense, complete and expressive with both depth and elegance. The wines also manage to reflect something of the vintage character (without the defects) as a vertical tasting of any of the wines will reveal. Whites as well as reds are made and, though the Chardonnay has had its ups and downs, it is usually one of Tuscany's best examples, while the Vin Santo is consistently brilliant. (PW)

● **Cepparello★★★★★** £F ● **Chianti Classico★★** £C
● **Cabernet Sauvignon** Collezione De Marchi★★★★ £F ● **Syrah** Collezione De Marchi★★★ £E
O **Chardonnay** Collezione De Marchi★★★ £D O **Vin Santo★★★★** £F

LA BRANCAIA   Chianti Classico   www.brancaia.com   A: Eno, JNi, NYg

Owner: Bruno & Brigette Widmer   Loc. Poppi 42b, 53017 Radda in Chianti (SI)
Up until 1997 the La Brancaia wines were made at FONTERUTOLI and there are still close links between the two properties. Since 1999 the estate has been under the direction of Barbara Widmer, daughter of the Swiss owners, who has recently been joined by her husband, Martin Kronenberg. The 19 ha comprises two estates, 9-ha Brancaia (in Castellina) and 10-ha Poppi (in Radda). The Chianti Classico is pure Sangiovese, while Brancaia Il Blu (with a blue label) includes 40 per cent Merlot and 5 per cent Cabernet. Both wines see some new wood and this is evident in the wines but both also show ripe stylish fruit and good depth, the more structured Brancaia better with five years' age or more while the Chianti Classico can be drunk a little sooner. A third wine, Tre, shows fine fruit and structure at the price. While quality has increased so have the prices. As well as developing an estate in the southern Maremma, Poggio al Sasso, Bruno Widmer is involved in CLOS D'AGON on Spain's Costa Brava, whose wines are made by Peter Sisseck (PINGUS). (PW)
● **Chianti Classico★★★** £D   ● **Brancaia Il Blu★★★★** £E
● **Tre★★** £C

LA MASSA   Chianti Classico   A: JAr

Owner: Giampaolo Motta   Via Case Sparse 9, 50020 Panzano (FI)
Neapolitan Giampaolo Motta and enologist Carlo Ferrini make two very good modern-styled Chianti Classicos from 27 ha of vines. Already experienced before purchasing prime vineyards in the much vaunted Panzano sub-zone in 1992, he now has almost a decade of vintages behind him. Both wines are aged in barriques and the wines are always full of ripe, intense fruit. Both wines, while predominantly Sangiovese (85–90 per cent) include some Cabernet Sauvignon and/or Merlot. If less individual than some, they do deliver consistently high quality. The regular version is best with three to five years' age, while the greater depth and structure of Giorgio Primo deserves five or more. The 2000s, while good, miss the balance and fruit succulence of the 99s. Unfortunately prices are high, even given the quality. (PW)
● **Chianti Classico★★** £D   Giorgio Primo★★★★ £F

MAURIZIO LAMBARDI   Brunello di Montalcino

Owner: Maurizio Lambardi   Podere Canalicchio di Sotto 8, 53024 Montalcino (SI)
Maurizio Lambardi's Canalicchio di Sotto, like a number of Brunello's small growers, doesn't produce that much wine but what there is can be very good. A committed winegrower, his wines have a depth and fullness that show off the quality of the fruit he obtains. Their lushness and richness make a vintage like 95 (four star) both accessible now but capable of another 10 years' ageing. Though not all of the same standard, there is good quality across recent vintages. From the best years, an intense vibrant Rosso needs three to five years to show at its best. (PW)
● **Brunello di Montalcino★★★** £E   ● **Rosso di Montalcino★★** £C

LANCIOLA   Chianti Classico   www.lanciola.net   A: HSA, Wat, The

Owner: Guarnieri family   Via Imprunetana 210, 50023 Impruneta (FI)
The 80-ha estate of Lanciola, nearly half of it planted to vines, lies at the top of the Classico zone. By rights the wines ought not be anything special here but in recent vintages these wines have certainly offered plenty of substance and vibrancy. At the level of Chianti Classico Riserva and the

premium red, Terricci (Sangiovese with 15 per cent Cabernet Sauvignon and 5 per cent Cabernet Franc), this translates as broad, muscular wines that can be slightly overdone in terms of oak and extract. Both shouldn't be drunk with less than five years' age. Within their context, regular Chiantis, both Classico and Fiorentini, are, however, more successful, with a vigour and intensity well-matched by a stylish fruit expression. In short, don't expect great finesse here but you will get plenty of wine for your money. Chardonnay, Pinot Nero and Vin Santo are also made. (PW)

● **Terricci**★★★ £D   ● **Chianti Classico** Le Masse di Greve★★ £B Riserva★★ £C
● **Chianti Colli Fiorentini**★★ £B

LE CORTI/PRINCIPE CORSINI   Chianti Classico   www.principecorsini.com   A: Ast

Owner: Principe Corsini   Via Bolgherese 189/A, 57020 Castagneto Carducci (LI)
As recently as 1992, Duccio Corsini the son of Prince Corsini, set out to produce high-quality wine with view to restoring the historic Villa di Corsini. The estate, in the family since Renaissance times, covers 250 ha with 49 ha of vineyards. Duccio Corsini is assisted by one of Tuscany's best consultant winemakers, Carlo Ferrini. There are three fine Chianti Classicos, a good *normale* (Le Corti), a more structured Riserva (Cortevecchia) and the premium bottling, Don Tommaso. The wines are ripe, intense and modern but typically Chianti Classico, with particularly good structure and depth in Don Tommaso. The family also have a holding in the Maremma, Tenuta Marsiliana, producing a deep, penetrating and characterful IGT primarily from Cabernet Sauvignon, Merlot and Sangiovese. (PW)

Le Corti:
● **Chianti Classico** Le Corti★★ £B Riserva Cortevecchia★★ £C Don Tommaso★★★ £D

Tenuta Marsiliana:
● **Marsiliana**★★★ £E

LE FILIGARE   Chianti Classico   A: M&V, HHB

*Owner: **Del Conte srl**   Via Sicelle 37, Loc. San Donato in Poggio, 50020 Barberino Val d'Elsa (FI)*
This attractive estate is at a relatively high altitude on lean, stony soils and shows increasing promise with its wines. Carlo Burchi has doubled the original vineyard area to 12 ha and now works with his son Filippo and enologist Dr Luciano Bandini. Though the wines can be a little tight and compact if tasted very young, there is usually an underlying fruit richness which makes for sleek, elegant and stylish fruity Chianti with a little age. In the regular version the Sangiovese is complemented by Canaiolo and Colorino, while the Riserva includes Colorino and Merlot and spends longer in oak. Podere Le Rocce is a blend of Cabernet Sauvignon and Sangiovese (65/35) that is quite sturdy but with the potential to add richness with age. *Normale* is best with two or three years, Riserva with three to five, while even more time is needed for the Podere Le Rocce. A small amount of Vin Santo is also made. (PW)

● **Chianti Classico**★ £C Riserva Maria Vittoria★★ £D
● **Podere Le Rocce**★★★ £D

FATTORIA LE FONTI   Chianti Classico

Owner: Imberti family   Loc. San Giorgio, 53036 Poggibonsi (SI)
Tuscany needs more producers like this – small estates that are maximising the potential of a small but coherent range of wines. Le Fonti's success seems to owe much to Lorenzo Bernini, responsible for the 22 ha of vineyards, and consultant Paolo Caciorgna, who makes the wines. Vito Arturo is named for the Imberti brothers' father, who bought the estate in 1956. The single-vineyard, 100 per cent Sangiovese wine struggled a little for balance in the difficult 2000 vintage but there is a quality and

intensity to the fruit that promise a four-star rating in the near future. Only a notch or two lower is the Chianti Classico Riserva, also pure Sangiovese. The *normale* (with 5 per cent Canailolo) starts out a little lean but will fill out if given three years' age. Rather traditionally styled and of moderate sweetness, Vin Santo has a roasted nuts, date and walnut character but also dried citrus and a honeyed intensity. These wines shouldn't be confused with those of Azienda Agricola LE FONTI. (PW)

- **Chianti Classico**★ £B Riserva★★★ £C
- **Vito Arturo**★★★ £D **O Vin Santo del Chianti Classico**★★ £E

LE MACCHIOLE Bolgheri www.lemacchiole.it   A: L&S, F&R

Owner: Cinzia Campolmi   Via Bolgherese 189/A, 57020 Castagneto Carducci (LI)

Le Macchiole is as outstanding a producer of Bolgheri as its neighbours ORNELLAIA or SASSICAIA. Eugenio Campolmi transformed both the 18-ha estate and the way the wines were made before his recent early death. His success owes much to enologist Luca D'Attoma, responsible for several of Tuscany's more exciting recent creations. Made in the greatest quantities, the estate red, Macchiole, is Sangiovese-based but with 5 per cent Cabernet Sauvignon in 99 and 10 per cent each of Merlot and Cabernet Franc in 2000. The latter in particular seems to add character; sleek and compact, it opens out with age. Three other reds are made in small quantities, each less than 1,000 cases in the 2001 vintage. Paléo Rosso was originally a Cabernet Sauvignon-based wine complemented by Sangiovese and Cabernet Franc. However the Cabernet Franc increased from15 per cent in 1999 to 30 in 2000, while the 2001 is entirely from Cabernet Franc. Despite this evolution, a mineral-imbued, intense, small-berry fruit character within a structured frame is characteristic. At least five years' age is recommended as it is for two reds that fully deserve their cult status. The quality of the tremendously rich, classically varietal Merlot, Messorio, and deep, structured minerally Syrah, Scrio, is quite spellbinding. Paléo Bianco, from Chardonnay and Sauvignon, is ripe and stylish. (PW)

- **Bolgheri** Rosso Superiore Paléo★★★★ £E ● **Macchiole Rosso**★★★ £D
- **Messorio**★★★★★ £E ● **Scrio**★★★★★ £D
- **O Paléo Bianco**★★ £D

LE PUPILLE Morellino di Scansano   A: Lib, Res, Vne, P&S, NYg

Owner: Elisabetta Geppetti   Piagge del Maiano 92/A, 58040 Istia d'Ombrone (GR)

The one outstanding producer from the heart of the southern Maremma, Le Pupille was well-established before a recent wave of newcomers from other parts of Tuscany rushed to join in. Quality (already good) soared in the 1990s under a string of top-flight consultants, the latest being ex-technical director of Château LAFITE, Christian Le Sommer. Regular Morellino di Scansano has always shown off the character of Sangiovese in this zone with its wild herb and delightful berry fruit character. A fine Riserva with extra weight and structure was produced until 1998 but efforts are now going into making an even better regular example and further improving the quality of the excellent single-vineyard Poggio Valente, introduced in 1997. There is marvellous style and complexity in this wine that newer producers in Morellino will take some time to emulate. Even better and now a marvellously rich, concentrated wine is Saffredi, a blend of Cabernet Sauvignon and Merlot (70/30). All three reds need a little age: three years for the regular Morellino, five or more for Poggio Valente and Saffredi. Solalto, a delicious sweet wine with gently spicy dried peach and apricot fruit, is a late-harvested blend of Sauvignon and Traminer. (PW)

- **Morellino di Scansano**★★ £C Poggio Valente★★★ £D
- **Saffredi**★★★★ £F **O Solalto**★★★ £E

LISINI Brunello di Montalcino www.lisini.com A: N&P, RsW

Owner: Lisini family Fraz. Sant'Angelo in Colle, 53020 Montalcino (SI)
Franco Bernabei is the consultant of choice for the Lisinis. From 11.5 ha he ensures good consistency and attractive wines even in lesser vintages. Though there is real Brunello complexity and weight the wines are generally more for the medium than long term. The exception is the single-vineyard wine Ugolaia. Potentially very exciting, it can be just a little overdone in terms of structure, though the necessary balance for long keeping is usually there. The regular Brunello was very good in 97 (as are many but certainly not all), and the 95 and 97 Ugolaia show great depth and dimension. The Rosso can impress for its forward, lush and vibrant black fruit character. (PW)
● **Brunello di Montalcino★★★** £F Ugolaia★★★★ £F
● **Rosso di Montalcino★★** £C

LIVERNANO Radda in Chianti www.livernano.it A: L&S

Owner: Marco Montanari Loc. Livernano, 53017 Radda in Chianti (SI)
Livernano is a restored medieval hamlet that, like a number of others, was abandoned in the post-war migration to the cities. Marco Montanari is Swiss, one of several making an impression on the Tuscan wine scene. He has just 5.5 ha of vines that have been replanted at higher densities. The Livernano blend (Cabernet/Merlot/Sangiovese) shows good intensity and structure but much more exciting and aptly named is Puro Sangue, a very pure, powerful expression of Sangiovese which promises much with five to seven years' age. Small amounts of a white, Anima, a barrique-aged blend of Chardonnay, Sauvignon and Traminer, are also made. (PW)
● **Purosangue★★★** £E ● **Livernano★★** £E

MASTROJANNI Brunello di Montalcino A: Col, F&R

Owner: Mastrojanni family Podere Loreto, Fraz. Castelnuovo dell' Abate, 53020 Montalcino (SI)
One of the few really great Brunello producers, Mastrojanni commands almost 19 ha of steep stony slopes in the south-eastern confines of the Brunello di Montalcino DOCG. Both large and small wood is used for ageing but it's not obvious in these deep, dark monsters. Structured, with dense but ripe tannins, the wines always show an expansive quality in the mouth that few of the more modern, oak-influenced styles even approach. Sometimes the balance is not quite there or the wine is a bit deficient, as in 96, or relatively advanced though good (98), but the depth, class and complexity from vintages like 90, 93, 95 or 97 make this an excellent investment for keeping at least 10 years (five more after release). Very small quantities of a rich, complex Riserva are made in the best years and occasionally produced is a special selection, Schiena d'Asino (which may need closer to two decades). San Pio (Sangiovese/Cabernet Sauvignon) is more accessible in the short-term as is a Rosso which can be excellent in good vintages, with Brunello-like fullness but always needing another two or three years after its release (at two years). Botrys is a late-harvested blend of Moscato and Malvasia. (PW)
● **Brunello di Montalcino★★★★** £F Riserva★★★★ £F Schiena d'Asino★★★★ £F
● **Rosso di Montalcino★★** £D ● **San Pio★★★** £D

MONTE BERNARDI Chianti Classico www.montebernardi.com A: RsW, UnC

Owner: Stak Aivaliotis Via Chiantigiana, 50020 Panzano (FI)
Stak Aivaliotis is passionate about wine and has developed Monte Bernardi since the late 1980s with the aim of producing the best wine in the region. Under the winemaking direction of Giorgio

Marone, the intention is to produce pure wines with minimal interference. A rigorous selection and – relatively unusual for Tuscany – a prolonged pre-fermentation maceration are employed as well as the use of a basket press. High-quality French oak, some of it new, is used in the ageing of all the wines and this is evident in their structures and flavours. The wines are increasingly rich and intense but could still use a little more sophistication. Sa'etta is, like the Chianti Classico, 100 per cent Sangiovese, and ripe, oaky, intense and vibrant, the 99 the most promising to date. Tzingana is a blend of Merlot and Cabernet Sauvignon but also includes Cabernet Franc and Petit Verdot. Prices are high but there is promise in the wines that suggests quality may soon gain parity. (PW)

● **Chianti Classico** Paris★★ £D
● **Sa'etta★★★** £E ● **Tzingana★★★** £F

MONTEPELOSO   Val di Cornia   A: Bal, UnC

Owner: Fabio Chiarelotto   Loc. Montepeloso 82, 57020 Suvereto (LI)

This estate is one of Suvereto's stars, making wines of extraordinary concentration from well-sited vineyards. Low yields and barrique-ageing make for wines with deep, rich, powerful fruit and fine, ripe tannins. Though the alcohol levels are high, there is enough substance and balance to support it. Gabbro is 100 per cent Cabernet Sauvignon while Nardo is predominantly Sangiovese but with a little Cabernet Sauvignon (10–20 per cent). Both are made in very small quantities and highly sought after, so are not cheap. More is made of Eneo, predominantly Sangiovese but also including a little Canaiolo and Ciliegiolo. This is increasingly fine and good value (labelled Val di Cornia Rosso prior to 2000). (PW)

● **Gabbro★★★★** £F ● **Nardo★★★★** £F
● **Eneo★★★** £C

MONTEVERTINE   www.montevertine.it   A: N&P, Res

Owner: Martino Manetti   Loc. Montevertine, 53017 Radda in Chianti (SI)

Sergio Manetti became one of the legends of the modern Tuscan wine renaissance after creating the pure-Sangiovese, single-vineyard Super-Tuscan Le Pergole Torte. The striking labels are the work of artist Alberto Manfredi. The small estate now has 10 ha of vineyards at high altitude, though not all of it is fully in production. Le Pergole Torte is subject to a lengthy maceration (25–30 days) before ageing, only initially in barriques. Besides Le Pergole Torte there are two other top reds – Il Sodaccio, which is also from a single vineyard, and Montevertine Riserva, which approximates to a regular traditional Chianti Classico, albeit a very good one. Both include a little Canaiolo. All three can show marvellous quality, at once very stylish and harmonious, complex with excellent dimension on the palate, gaining in richness with age and with great length of flavour. It can be easy to underestimate quality when the wines are very young but usually with five to eight years' age the full potential becomes apparent. Quality is not entirely consistent but tends to follow the best vintages. Pian del Ciampolo is a recently introduced cheaper red with a bright, more forward, floral fruit character. Following his father's death in 2000, it will be inter-esting to see where Martino Manetti takes this fine estate as he continues to be assisted by the venerable Giulio Gambelli. A very small amount of white wine is also produced. (PW)

● **Le Pergole Torte★★★★★** £F ● **Il Sodaccio★★★★** £E
● **Montevertine Riserva★★★** £E ● **Pian del Ciampolo★** £B

MORIS FARMS   Monteregio di Massa Marittima   www.morisfarms.it   A: C&B

Owner: Moris family   Loc. Curanuova, 58024 Massa Marittima (GR)

The Moris family's substantial landholding in the Maremma includes 70 ha of vineyards. 40 of these fall under the Monteregio di Massa Marittima DOC and 30 ha qualify as Morellino di Scansano. Generally sound if robust examples of both are produced, particularly an intense, extracted Riserva of the latter. The real star however is Avvoltore, a powerhouse Sangiovese-based wine of great vigour and depth. Cabernet Sauvignon and Syrah (20 and 5 per cent respectively) play an important part in its consistently rich, floral and crushed-berry fruit complexity. It is balanced with great length and usually best with six to eight years age. (PW)

● **Avvoltore**★★★★ £E
● **Morellino di Scansano**★ £B Riserva★★ £C ● **Monteregio di Massa Marittima**★ £B

TENUTA DELL' ORNELLAIA Bolgheri www.ornellaia.it A: JAr

Owner: Robert Mondavi & Frescobaldi Via Bolgherese 191, 57020 Bolgheri (LI)
Lodovico, Piero ANTINORI's younger brother, was able to set up on his own in the 1980s due to his inheritance from his mother's family. No expense was spared transforming 70 ha of mostly scrubby countryside into a model wine estate. Various talented wine people have also been recruited over the years. The main focus of production is the Cabernet Sauvignon/Merlot/Cabernet Franc blend, Ornellaia, which is now made well in excess of 10,000 cases a year. Le Serre Nuove, positioned as a second wine, has been made since 1997. Large volumes are made of Le Volte, the least expensive wine and a blend of Cabernet Sauvignon, Sangiovese, and Merlot; it has been somewhat irregular in terms of quality, rarely providing value for money. Made in more modest quantities, if not quite as scarce as it once was, is the pure Merlot, Masseto – the estate's most sought after wine. There's little doubt about the quality of this or of Ornellaia, though the ratings below only apply to the best vintages. The more classically structured Ornellaia requires the greater patience, the sheer opulence of the fruit in Masseto has no equal for some of its more impassioned fans. Poggio alle Gazze is the Sauvignon-based white. Though ripe and zesty with good fruit if drunk young it is perhaps no longer of the standard it used to be when it was first made by then winemaker, Tibor Gal. ROBERT MONDAVI took a controlling interest in 2002. (PW)

● **Bolgheri** Rosso Superiore Ornellaia★★★★★ £G ● **Masseto**✪✪✪✪✪ £H
● **Bolgheri** Rosso Le Serre Nuove★★★ £E ● **Le Volte**★ £B
O **Poggio alle Gazze**★★ £C

SIRO PACENTI Brunello di Montalcino A: Lay, BBR, Far

Owner: Giancarlo Pacenti Loc. Pelagrilli 1, 53024 Montalcino (SI)
Giancarlo Pacenti has turned a good estate into an outstanding one in just a few short years. In recent vintages quality has been exemplary, in fact arguably it has become the best regular Brunello since 1995, including an excellent 96 and an outstanding 97 and 98. Some new oak is used but this does not over-whelm the marvellous quality of the fruit and extract. Not only is there superb richness, breadth and power but great length, really fine tannins and impeccable balance. He also makes a rich, concentrated Brunello-like Rosso, with the weight if not the dimension of a really decent example at that. Unfortunately certain wine brokers are only too aware of the quality and its speculative potential but prices are not crazy when a merchant or retailer has bought first-hand. At least these wines can be bought in the confidence of finding out what great Brunello tastes like, whether drunk now or with another 10 to 15 years' age. A little Riserva is sometimes made but has not been tasted from recent vintages. (PW)

● **Brunello di Montalcino**✪✪✪✪✪ £F
● **Rosso di Montalcino**★★★ £D

PERTIMALI/LIVIO SASSETTI Brunello di Montalcino   A: F&R, Far

Owner: Livio Sassetti Loc. Pertimali, 53024 Montalcino (SI)
Pertimali is a small 9-ha estate producing slightly old-fashioned Brunello of great richness and depth within a sturdy frame. Rosso too can be full, ripe and savoury with a little age, showing the true character of Sangiovese in this zone. Vigna dei Fili di Seta, a blend of Sangiovese and Cabernet Sauvignon, is the only wine likely to have seen any small wood and is more modern, with rich, dense fruit to the fore. However, a note of caution, particularly for the Brunello – despite some really fine examples (for which the rating is given) such as the 1995, quality can be uneven with sometimes questionable balance (a slightly bruising, monolithic 98) and stability. Individual vintages should be tasted before buying by the case (the 96 is best avoided). A very small amount of Riserva is also made but can be superb as in 97. (PW)
● **Brunello di Montalcino**★★★★ £F   Riserva★★★★★ £F
● **Rosso di Montalcino**★★ £C ● **Vigna dei Fili di Seta**★★★ £D

PETROLO   A: Lib, Vne, But, P&S

Owner: L. Bazzocchi Sanjust & L. Sanjust Fraz. Mercatale Valdarno, 52020 Montevarchi (AR)
From the wine zone of Chianti Colli Aretini comes one of Tuscany's finest pure Merlots. Made in very small quantities, Galatrona has not only remarkable richness and concentration but a depth, spice and individuality that compares with the very best Pomerol. But while the Merlot joins the spiral of cult wines, Luca Sanjust and his mother, with expert help, have tried to ensure that the entire production (from a total of 31 ha) bears little relation to the humble status of the Colli Aretini zone in which they are based. Torrione is for Sangiovese what Galatrona is for Merlot. Made in much greater quantities it has been very impressive since 1997, if not of the same concentration or proportions as Galatrona. Terre di Galatrona is the regular wine and combines Sangiovese (70 per cent) with Merlot as well as a little Cabernet Sauvignon but is always likely to be at its ripest and fullest in the best vintages. (PW)
● **Galatrona**★★★★ £F
● **Torrione**★★★ £D ● **Terre di Galatrona**★ £B

PIEVE SANTA RESTITUTA Brunello di Montalcino   A: JAr, F&R

Owner: Gaja family Loc. Chiesa Santa Restituta, 53024 Montalcino (SI)
Angelo GAJA's first venture into Tuscany was this small, wonderfully sited Brunello estate. While all eyes are now on what comes out of his major undertaking in Bolgheri, CA' MARCANDA, the wines here are beginning to show the impact of his winemaker, Guido Rivella. Two Brunellos are made – Rennina, a superior selection from the best vines, and Sugarille, from a single-vineyard site. The original 11 ha have been expanded and will eventually total 35 ha, still small by comparison with the zone's biggest producers. The wines already command high prices, whether by design or demand, but show an elegance and structure that since 1995 have set them apart from most other Brunello. There's nothing with the Gaja magic ready for drinking now, as both wines need at least 10 years' age (and can be expected to keep for considerably longer). (PW)
● **Brunello di Montalcino** Rennina★★★★★ £G Sugarille★★★★★ £G

POGGERINO Chianti Classico www.poggerino.com   A: L&S

Owner: Piero & Benedetta Lanza Via Poggerino 6, 53017 Radda in Chianti (SI)
This fine, small 11-ha estate is in some of Chianti Classico's highest hills (between 400 and 500 m

above sea-level) north-east of Radda. After a remarkable Riserva made in 1990, the wines have maintained a high standard under the continued efforts and winemaking skill of Piero Lanza. A small amount of Merlot supplements the plantings of Sangiovese and is used in both a minor supporting role in the Chianti Classico and as an equal partner in the premium cuvée, Primamateria. While new oak and concentrated ripe fruit are much in evidence, there is also an elegance and stylishness to the wines derived at least in part from the elevation, aspect and soil of the vineyards. The Chianti Classico shows the fine spice, cherry and herb notes characteristic of Sangiovese and deserves two or three years' age. A small amount of a fine Riserva from a single vineyard, Bugialla, is made in good years – recently in 1999 and 97 and deserves five years' age. Primamateria, with intense sweet berry fruit depth, great length and superfine tannins is very approachable but best with five years or more. It was only produced in magnums in its first two vintages, 97 and 98. Il Labirinto, for everyday drinking, is made from young vines and intended as a 'second' selection for the Chianti Classico. (PW)

● **Chianti Classico**★★ £B Riserva Bugialla★★★ £D
● **Primamateria**★★★★ £D

POGGIO AL SOLE   Chianti Classico   A: THt, Res, The

Owner: Giovanni Davaz   Fraz. Sambuca, Loc. Badia a Passignano, 50020 Tavarnelle Val di Pesa (FI)
Giovanni Davaz is one of a special group of Tuscan winemakers whose dedication in the vineyard and great care in maximising the potential of the grapes from a favoured site results in wines a breed apart from the increasing amounts of well-made wine in Tuscany. The 14 ha are in the vicinity of ANTINORI'S most famous vineyards. The majority of production is Chianti Classico, both a splendid, sleek, intense and stylish *normale* and a poised, elegant but graceful and beautifully defined Casasilia. There are also two concessions to international varieties: Selvasera is a Merlot/Cabernet Sauvignon blend but with similar refinement to Casasilia, while a Syrah, although lacking the concentration of a top Côte-Rôtie, has fine fruit and intensity and the length of flavour that characterises all the wines. Don't expect blockbusters or immediate gratification in these wines; instead, elegance triumphs over power. At least three years is needed for the regular Chianti Classico and five or more for the other wines. (PW)

● **Chianti Classico**★★★ £C Casasilia★★★★ £E
● **Seraselva**★★★ £E ● **Syrah**★★★ £E

POGGIO SCALETTE   A: Mgi

Owner: Adriana Assjé Di Marcorà-Fiore   Loc. Ruffoli, Via Barbiano 7, 50022 Greve in Chianti (FI)
Only one wine is made here by consultant Vittorio Fiore, who put together this small 12.5-ha estate close to QUERCIABELLA in the 1990s. Resurrecting an old vineyard with some very old vines he was able to expand the estate and keeps only the best grapes for Il Carbonaione. The wine has always been 100 per cent Sangiovese and is a very fine example, with pure fruit, ample breadth and depth and lovely harmony. It has been consistently good since its first vintage in the difficult 1992 vintage and it was very impressive in the somewhat uneven 98 vintage. Vittorio's son Jurij is now responsible for the vineyards and the day-to-day running of the estate. Though the wine now qualifies as Chianti Classico, it retains IGT status as Alta Valle delle Greve, giving it some regional definition in the absence of Chianti Classico sub-zones. (PW)

● **Il Carbonaione**★★★★ £F

POGGIOPIANO Chianti Classico   A: Mer, Con, Fal

Owner: Bartoli family   Via di Pisignano 29, 50025 San Casciano Val di Pesa (FI)
Not to be confused with Fattoria di Poggiopiano, this small property (Azienda Agricola Poggiopiano) is found in San Casciano Val di Pesa in the north-west of the Chianti Classico zone and is run by Stefano Bartoli and his brother Alessandro. Consultancy for the two wines comes from Luca D'Attoma. Most remarkable is the premium red, Rosso di Sera, which combines a high 15 per cent of Colorino (an exciting grape but seldomly used in a significant percentage) with Sangiovese. The wine has a delicious spicy, black-fruited depth and a lush texture but with a floral cherry character that distinguishes it from more boring efforts that include Merlot instead. A second vineyard now supplements the estate vineyards of only 9 ha but production of Rosso di Sera is limited to around 1,000 cases a year. Having made the effort to acquire some, particularly from the most recent vintages, it is worth waiting at least five years before drinking it. In the interim there's 1999 Chianti Classico, with excellent breadth, intensity and depth. A slightly more robust 2000 will need a little more time to harmonise completely. (PW)
● **Chianti Classico★★** £C ● **Rosso di Sera★★★★** £E

POLIZIANO Vino Nobile di Montepulciano www.carlettipoliziano.com A: Eno, JNi, Res,N&P

Owner: Federico Carletti   Via Fontago 1, Loc. Montepulciano Stazione, 53040 Montepulciano (SI)
In the past two decades Poliziano (named for the Renaissance poet, Politian) has been propelled to the top echelon of producers, not just in Montepulciano but in all of Tuscany, by its owner Federico Carletti. Assisted for the past eight years by the brilliant Carlo Ferrini, he has given the wine range greater focus and taken the quality consistently higher. Most encouraging has been the quality of the regular Vino Nobile, with its atypical intensity and weight, which has continued to improve despite being made in increased quantities (in excess of 10,000 cases). However, it is the top two wines that are most exciting. Asinone, from a 9-ha vineyard, adds more breadth, complexity and sheer style over the regular version but with similar preserved-cherry fruit intensity. Le Stanze is an outstanding Tuscan Cabernet Sauvignon (close to five stars) with wonderful depth and intensity but also shows increasing elegance and style. Other wines include a Rosso di Montepulciano that is fuller and fleshier than any other versions and most resembles a good Chianti Classico *normale*. Elegia, was a fine oak-aged Sangiovese made until 1995. The estate's 120 ha of vineyard also includes a new project in the Maremma from which is produced the Morellino di Scansano Lohsa. It includes 10 per cent Ciliegiolo and has a spicy, vibrant pure fruit character and is adding more depth as new vines come on stream. (PW)

Poliziano:
● **Vino Nobile di Montepulciano★★★** £C Asinone★★★★ £E
● **Le Stanze★★★★** £E ● **Rosso di Montepulciano★** £B
Azienda Agricola Lohsa:
● **Morellino di Scansano★★★** £C

QUERCIABELLA Chianti Classico www.querciabella.com   A: JAr, SVS, Fal, F&R

Owner: G. Castiglioni & S. Cossia Castiglioni   Via di Barbiano 17, 50022 Greve in Chianti (FI)
One of Chianti Classico's grand estates, Querciabella is now run by Sebastiano, son of its founder Giuseppe Castiglioni, who is gently guided by winemaker Guido De Santi. The range was until very recently restricted to just four wines: Chianti Classico, a Riserva and red and white Super-Tuscans. All the wines have a certain strength as well as individuality – the structure amply supports a considerable richness of fine intense fruit (from low yields). The Chiantis include a little Cabernet

Sauvignon and Merlot in their composition yet retain a distinctive Tuscan character. The most praise, however, has been reserved for the red Camartina, which adds a little Syrah as well as slightly more significant percentages of Cabernet and Merlot to Sangiovese, and the white, Batàr, produced from Pinot Bianco and Chardonnay. This is a very rich, powerful, toasty, creamy white with an almost exotic fruit character. Sometimes a little overblown, it is not for those seeking elegance or refinement but there is depth and flavour and reasonable ageing potential. That said, there has been less oak and more elegance since 1998. Of the reds, even the *normale* Chianti needs three years' ageing or more, Riserva and Camartina a minimum of five. Querciabella has also established vineyards at Alberese in the Maremma. A promising new, if modern, blend of Merlot and Sangiovese called Palafreno was first made from the 2000 vintage. (PW)

● **Chianti Classico**★★ £C Riserva★★★ £D
● **Camartina**★★★★ £F **O Batàr**★★★ £E

BARONE RICASOLI/CASTELLO DI BROLIO   Chianti Classico   A: Eno, Cam, F&R

Owner: Ricasoli family Loc. Cantine del Castello di Brolio, 53013 Gaiole in Chianti (SI)
This noble property had a rough ride under corporate ownership for a couple of decades until it was re-acquired in 1993 by the Ricasoli family, led by Francesco Ricasoli. Brolio's importance in the modern era (Baron Bettino Ricasoli set out the parameters for Chianti Classico in the 1870s) added more clout to a decision taken four years later to establish a flagship Chianti Classico in a move to try to restore the pre-eminence of that name in the zone. The wine is made from 100 per cent Sangiovese from a selection of the best vineyards and aged in predominantly new French oak. Successive vintages, if quite oaky, are increasingly expansive and stylish and as the vineyards (the vast estate includes 227 ha of vines) continue to improve, so should the wine. That labelled simply Brolio is a 'second' wine. A classic nutty, biscuity Vin Santo is also made under the Castello di Brolio label. The Barone Ricasoli label, which also includes wine from bought-in grapes, includes Casalferro (recently a blend of Sangiovese with a little Merlot), a consistently impressive red which shows typical concentration, intensity and ageing potential in the 1999 vintage. Torricella is a barrique-aged Chardonnay of increasing refinement while other wines of improving quality include the inexpensive Formulae, based on Sangiovese. (PW)

Castello di Brolio:
● **Chianti Classico** Brolio★★ £C Castello di Brolio★★★ £E
O Vin Santo★★★ £D

Barone Ricasoli:
● **Chianti Classico** Riserva Rocca Guicciarda★ £C
● **Casalferro**★★★ £D **O Torricella**★★ £C

RIECINE   Chianti Classico   www.riecine.com   A: Dec, THt, Han

Owner: Gary Baumann & Sean O'Callaghan Loc. Riecine, 53013 Gaiole in Chianti (SI)
Owned for more than two decades by Englishman John Dunkley, this small jewel already had a considerable reputation before its purchase by Americans Gary and Lindsay Baumann. Dunkley had the good fortune to buy a vineyard already planted to a remarkably high-quality clone of Sangiovese and further increases in vineyard area from elsewhere in the commune have brought in more good fruit. The wines have always shown great concentration, intensity and a purity and elegance that have set them apart from most examples. More recently they have shed some of the austerity that some tasters found overwhelming, though they were never intended to be drunk in their youth. The wines will still age very well but now have a richer texture and greater suppleness. Chianti Classico is still best with three to five years' ageing, Riserva and La Gioia (also Sangiovese) with six to ten,

sometimes more. The wines have always commanded prices that reflect their quality. (PW)

● **Chianti Classico**★★★ £D Riserva★★★★ £E
● **La Gioia**★★★★ £F

ROCCA DI MONTEGROSSI Chianti Classico   A: HSA, UnC

Owner: Ricasoli-Firidolfi family & Marco Ricasoli   Loc. Monti in Chianti 53010 Gaiole in Chianti (SI)
Marco Ricasoli's 18 ha have been cleaved off from those of CASTELLO DI CACCHIANO, which is
now under the control of his brother Giovanni. They are related to the Ricasoli family of the area's
most famous estate, Castello di Brolio (see RICASOLI). Ever finer Chianti Classico (Sangiovese with
10 per cent Canaiolo, and the only wine produced in 2000) and Riserva (entirely Sangiovese from
1999) are becoming classic pure Tuscan wines. Geremia, 100 per cent Sangiovese up to and including
98, included 7 per cent Merlot in a transitional 99 but from the 2001 vintage will be a Cabernet
Sauvignon and Merlot blend. This emphasis on establishing the purity and typicity of Chianti
Classico is to be admired and will hopefully set an example that others will follow. There is real
distinction to the bright, vibrant fruit character in these composed, refined wines, as well as a depth
and structure that ensures they age well. Regular Chianti Classico needs two to three years' ageing;
the Riserva five; and most Geremia need closer to 10. Marvellously rich Vin Santo is made in very
small quantities. This is now a first-division estate and one to follow. (PW)

● **Chianti Classico**★★★ £C Riserva San Marcellino★★★★ £D
● **Geremia**★★★★ £E   O **Vin Santo**★★★★ £E

RUFFINO www.ruffino.com   A: Alv

Owner: Marco & Paolo Folonari   Via Aretina 42/44, 50065 Pontassieve (FI)
One of the most famous Tuscan houses, Ruffino was divided in 2000 (see Ambrogio e Giovanni
FOLONARI) and some of its prized vineyards, including those of the Nozzole estate, have been lost.
Yet there are still great swathes of vineyard scattered around the leading wine zones. Vino Nobile di
Montepulciano Lodola Nuova is not overly concentrated but shows some of the character of the
appellation, while Brunello from Il Greppone Mazzi can be an attractive, savoury example in a good
vintage. The real excitement comes from the Chianti Classico zone, which produces a wine of great
class and breadth in top vintages, Riserva Ducale Oro. Slightly old-fashioned in style, it needs at least
five to eight years' age but can last considerably longer. That without the gold (Oro) label is not of
the same standard. Better still is Romitorio di Santedame (Colorino/Sangiovese), a highly original
wine of great character and superb fruit but needing similar age to the Oro. Following the loss of the
Cabreo wines, a new Chardonnay, Il Solatio, has been added. Modus is a relatively new red
combining Sangiovese, Cabernet Sauvignon and Merlot with good balance and increasing style.
Ruffino also makes an attractive white, Libaio (Chardonnay with a little Pinot Grigio) and the
large-scale production Chianti Classico Aziano. (PW)

Tenimenti Ruffino:
● **Chianti Classico** Santedame★★ £C Riserva Ducale★★ £C Riserva Ducale Oro★★★★ £E
● **Romitorio di Santedame**★★★★★ £F   ● **Modus**★★★ £E

Il Greppone Mazzi:
● **Brunello di Montalcino**★★ £E

Lodola Nuova:
● **Vino Nobile di Montepulciano**★★ £E

SALVIONI/LA CERBAIOLA   Brunello di Montalcino   A: Lay, JAr

Owner: Giulio Salvioni   Piazza Cavour 20, 53024 Montalcino (SI)
This classic Brunello is made in small quantities but such is the quality and expression of Sangiovese in the Montalcino zone it deserves to be tasted at least once. Given the dedication of its makers, there is no need to track down the most raved-about vintage either, as the quality of the wines from the mid-1990s (including an atypically fine 96) seems likely to be maintained. Traditionally produced without any new oak, the wine undergoes a long maceration followed by around two years in the traditional large Slavonian oak casks. The wine is rich, deep and powerful with superb texture and definition and great expression both in aroma and flavour. The elevated 2.26-ha site of Cerbaiola yields little more than 5,000 bottles a year but all depends on the vintage as the production of Rosso is used to help maintain the very high standards. Hand-made Brunello of great elegance and complexity. (PW)

● **Brunello di Montalcino**✪✪✪✪✪ £G

SAN FABIANO CALCINAIA   Chianti Classico   www.sanfabianocalcinaia.com   A: Gal

Owner: Guido Serio   Loc. Cellole, 53011 Castellina in Chianti (SI)
Cellole is one of two estates that make up 34 ha of vineyard; the second, San Fabiano, is at lower altitude and 10 km from Castellina. Top consultant Carlo Ferrini has helped elevate the quality of the reds. His hand is most evident in Cerviolo Rosso, a very worthy flagship wine. Seemingly somewhat boring in its make-up, with Sangiovese mixed with large helpings of Cabernet Sauvignon and Merlot (50/25/25 in 2000), it is nevertheless a very distinguished red of excellent concentration and density. Old-vine fruit, earth and mineral notes add class and complexity. Regular Chianti Classico, aged only in one- and two-year oak is typically supple and stylish. The Riserva is potentially a lush, flattering red but is marked by too much oak in both 1999 and 2000. A Chardonnay is also made but the balance isn't quite right yet in this either. (PW)

● **Cerviolo Rosso**★★★★ £E
●   **Chianti Classico**★★ £B   Riserva★★ £D

SAN FELICE   Chianti Classico   www.agricolasanfelice.com   A: Cib

Owner: RAS SpA   Loc. San Felice, 53019 Castelnuovo Berardenga (SI)
The property of insurance company Reunione Adriatica Sicurtà, this grand estate, only partly planted to vines (200 ha), is noted for its experiments with Sangiovese and other grapes (especially native varieties). During a long period of development under Enzo Morganti, both Vigorello, a Sangiovese/ Cabernet Sauvignon blend, and a single-vineyard Chianti Classico Riserva Poggio Rosso (containing 10 per cent of Colorino) were created. Both wines can be long-lived, intense and stylish, but though richer, Vigorello can be dominated by its Cabernet component. A second Chianti Classico Riserva, Il Grigio, made in much greater quantities, is not of comparable quality but can offer a dense, chewy mouthful. The regular Chianti Classico, though a big volume wine (50,000 cases), can show good fruit and perfume, especially in good vintages. Two whites are also made, a Chardonnay, Ancherona and a Vermentino/Sauvignon Blanc blend, Belcaro. Also included in San Felice's production are 14 ha of vineyards of the Campogiovanni estate in Montalcino from which some fine Brunello has been produced, including an excellent 1995, as well as a little Riserva Il Quercione. (PW)

● **Chianti Classico** Riserva Poggio Rosso★★ £C   ● **Vigorello**★★ £E
● **Brunello di Montalcino** Campogiovanni★★★★ £E

SAN FILIPPO - FANTI Brunello di Montalcino   A: LaC

Owner: Filippo Baldassare Fanti   Loc. San Filippo, 53020 Montalcino (SI)
The Tenuta San Filippo includes 14 ha of vineyards in the south-east corner of the Montalcino zone.
It may be just one of several rising stars in Montalcino (FOSSACOLLE, LA FIORITA and LA TOGATA
are others) but the depth, drive and structure in 1997 and 98 Brunellos reveal the influence of Attilio
Pagli. The deep colour and oak influence are characteristic but there's also the promise of marvellous
complexity and texture with 10 years' age or more. Vin Santo is also made and a barrique-aged selection of Sangiovese called Svoltone was produced in 1995. (PW)

● **Brunello di Montalcino★★★★** £E   ● **Rosso di Montalcino★★** £C

SAN GERVASIO Colline Pisane www.sangervasio.com   A: L&W, Maj

Owner: Tommasini family   Loc. San Gervasio, 56036 Palaia (SI)
San Gervasio is just one of several estates in the Pisa hills giving credence to this zone relatively close
to the Tuscan coast. Part of a large estate, 22 ha of vineyards are cultivated organically (biodynamic
from 2003) and planting densities are being radically increased. The great potential here seems
certain to be realised by Luca Tomassini, who currently employs top consultant Luca D'Attoma (who
works at LE MACCHIOLE among others) to produce two intense, tightly structured reds. 'A Sirio' is
Sangiovese-based but including five per cent Cabernet Sauvignon while 'I Renai' is oaky, powerful
Merlot, which has a lot of extract but good ageing potential. Both wines need at least five years to
show at their best. A good inexpensive Chianti, Le Stoppie has been replaced from 2002 with an
estate 'second wine', Sangervasio (from Sangiovese, Merlot and Cabernet not used for the top reds).
Also produced are Vin Santo, Recinaio, a dry white, Marna (Chardonnay, Vermentino and
Sauvignon) and rosé, Aprico. (PW)

● **A Sirio★★★** £E   ● **I Renai★★★** £E
● **Chianti Colline Pisane** Le Stoppie★ £B

SAN GIUSTO A RENTENNANO Chianti Classico   A: Bal, UnC, NYg

Owner: Martini di Cigala family   Loc. Monti, 53013 Gaiole in Chianti (SI)
This is a much venerated estate run by brothers Francesco and Luca Martini di Cigala and all the
wines are made to a very high standard. The focus is very much on Sangiovese and as natural as
possible an expression of it. The wines are particularly notable for strength allied to an intense
preserved-fruit quality which makes for complex, classy wines with the necessary age. In top years
even the Chianti Classico *normale* shows these attributes and easily surpasses some of the more
expensive offerings. The Riserva (with five per cent Canaiolo) is more muscular but shows exquisite
fruit and great length and is only bettered by the premium Sangiovese, Percarlo, made from 5.5 ha of
the estate's 30 ha of vineyards. With a great track record this big, structured wine, made from very ripe
fruit is subject to long ageing in barrique (more than 50 per cent new), and more closely resembles a
top Brunello in style than most wines from the Classico zone. There's also an outstanding, wonderfully
complex example of Vin Santo (based primarily on Malvasia) and from recent vintages a varietal
blockbuster Merlot, La Ricolma (aged in 100 per cent new oak), but quantities of both are minuscule.
Regular Chianti Classico excepted, don't drink any of the wines with less than six years' age; ten or
more is often better. Prices are very fair. (PW)

● **Chianti Classico★★** £B Riserva★★★ £C
● **Percarlo★★★★** £E   ● **La Ricolma★★★★** £F
O **Vin Santo★★★★** £F

ENRICO SANTINI Bolgheri

A: C&B

Owner: Enrico Santini   Loc. Campo alla Casa 74, 57022 Castagneto Carducci (LI)
Enrico Santini has 10 ha in Bolgheri and is its most interesting new star. His first vintage was as recent as 2000 and the vines are young but the leading wine, Montepergoli, is worth contrasting with the zone's heavyweights. Advice from near neighbour Michele SATTA and consultancy from Attilio Pagli have helped in producing a profound red of real vigour and intensity and lovely berry fruit aroma and flavour. The blend is mostly Cabernet Sauvignon, Merlot and Syrah with some Sangiovese. The latter contributes more to an attractive spicy perfumed second wine, Poggio al Moro, that represents much better value than equivalent wines from other Bolgheri producers. Both reds also show a refinement that Satta's can lack. Santini's white has good weight but could be more focused; from Sauvignon and Vermentino, the latter seems to contribute more to its character. (PW)
● **Bolgheri Rosso** Poggio al Moro★★ £C Montepergoli★★★ £E
● **Bolgheri Bianco** Campo alla Casa★ £C

SASSICAIA/TENUTA SAN GUIDO Bolgheri www.sassicaia.com A: Lib, JAr, BBR, Sec

Owner: Marchese Nicolò Incisa della Rocchetta   Loc. Capanne 27, 57020 Bolgheri (LI)
Much has been written about what is arguably Italy's single most famous wine, including a book (by Marco Fini). Its production has been much expanded from the original elevated Castiglioncello vineyard that provided the first commercial and much celebrated vintage, 1968. The vast San Guido estate now has about 60 ha of vineyards spread over four main plots, resulting in excess of 12,000 cases a year. The wine, for long sold as a vino da tavola, since 1994 has had its own special zone in the Bolgheri DOC, which the Marchese has done much to promote. It is now a blend of 85 per cent Cabernet Sauvignon and 15 per cent Cabernet Franc and aged for up to two years in French barriques (a third new). The five-star rating applies only to outstanding vintages and, while efforts in the 1990s generally don't match exceptional vintages like 1985, most years still reveal a beautifully composed wine with a delicious sweet black fruits intensity and elegant complexity that is sustained on a very long finish. Five years' ageing is a minimum, the best will improve for twenty or more. A new wine called Guidalberto, more modestly priced and from different vineyards, was first made in the 2000 vintage. Composed of Merlot, Cabernet Sauvignon and Sangiovese (50/30/20), it is aged for 12 months in barriques and shows cool fruit and some sophistication. (PW)
● **Bolgheri Sassicaia★★★★★** £G
● **Guidalberto★★★** £E

MICHELE SATTA Bolgheri

A: SCh

Owner: Michele Satta   Loc. Vigna al Cavaliere 61, 57022 Castagneto Carducci (LI)
Michele Satta isn't one of Bolgheri's big names but makes some good wines from 30 ha of vineyards. Piastraia is the top wine, a blend of Sangiovese, Cabernet Sauvignon, Merlot and Syrah. It doesn't lack for extract or depth but sometimes wants for more refined tannins. Nonetheless it is usually full, complex and characterful. Cavaliere (previously Vigna al Cavaliere) is unusual in the zone in being pure Sangiovese and, if again characterful, it can be more angular than Piastraia. Whites have always been important: Costa di Guilia, from Vermentino and Sauvignon, is aromatic and attractive if no more; Giovin Re, a varietal Viognier, is very ripe and oak-influenced but lacks the structure and definition of good Condrieu. Basic Bolgheri Rosato and Bianco are also produced. (PW)
● **Bolgheri Rosso** Piastraia★★★ £E ● **Cavaliere★★** £D
● **Giovin Re★★** £C ● **Costa di Giulia★** £B

FATTORIA SELVAPIANA   Chianti Rufina   A: Lib, Vne, ACh

Owner: Francesco Giuntini Antinori   Via Selvapiana 3, 50068 Rufina (FI)
For years this noble estate, in the Giuntini family since 1827, was the only rival to FRESCOBALDI in the small but exciting zone of Chianti Rufina. The combination of energy and austerity in the wines when young can seem daunting to wine drinkers used to soft, oak-rich reds but there is both a purity to the fruit and refinement in the wines that sets them apart from all but the best Chianti Classico. From 25 ha of vineyards, Federico Masseti and consultant Franco Bernabei have been producing very good wines for a number of years, especially a single vineyard Riserva Bucerchiale. It shows great intensity and depth but always deserves to be kept for at least six or seven years and will keep for as long again. A second single-vineyard wine, Fornace includes 10 per cent Cabernet and is more obvious and fleshy but shows similar fruit quality and depth. A regular Riserva was last made in 1997 and was particularly good in the absence of Bucerchiale in that year due to frost. This wine now enriches a very good *normale* that always requires a couple of years' age before drinking. A traditional-styled Vin Santo is both richer and fresher than previously. (PW)

● **Chianti Rufina**★★ £B   Riserva Bucerchiale★★★★ £D   Riserva Fornace★★★ £E
○ **Vin Santo**★★★ £E

SETTE PONTI   www.tenutasetteponti.com   A: C&C, Res

Owner: Moretti family   Loc. Oreno, Fraz. San Giustino Valdarno, 52020 Terranuova Bracciolini (AR)
This is a very slick and professional operation which has produced fabulous wines from the eastern side of the Valdarno in a very short space of time. Some 64 ha of vineyards are a mix of new and well-established plantings. The estimable Carlo Ferrini is the consultant winemaker. Oreno (3,000 cases) is from Sangiovese, Cabernet Sauvignon and Merlot (50/25/25 in 2000). Crognolo, produced in slightly greater quantity (almost 4,000 cases), is 90 per cent Sangiovese with the balance partly from Merlot. Both are rich yet gently textured wines with a beautifully detailed fruit intensity. Oreno, as might be expected, is the more international of the two but is very harmonious; Crognolo expresses more of its origins in a sweet-fruited expression of Sangiovese. It will be interesting to see if quality can be at least maintained as volume grows. Slightly baffling is the disparity in price when these wines are so close in quality. Watch out too for a blended red, Poggio al Lupo, from a second property, Le Fornaci. (PW)

● **Oreno**★★★★ £F   ● **Crognolo**★★★★ £D

SOLDERA   Brunello di Montalcino   www.soldera.it   A: Bal, Fal, Sec, F&R

Owner: Gianfranco Soldera   Case Basse, Loc. Villa Santa Restituta, 53024 Montalcino (SI)
Gianfranco Soldera's small 8-ha estate is Brunello's most controversial. In the best years like 1995, Riservas are now produced from the two different vineyards of Intistieti and Case Basse but are not released until six to seven years after the vintage. Sourced from some of Montalcino's best slopes (next to Gaja's PIEVE SANTA RESTITUTA) the grapes are grown organically with great effort going into not only maximising the fruit quality but also enriching the ecosystem. The winemaking is natural, with no temperature control, and a long and rigorous maceration precedes a stay of (often) more than five years in large oak *botti*. The resulting wines of, at times, extraordinary breadth and complexity can make most modern-styled efforts seem rather simplistic and one-dimensional. In lesser vintages a single Brunello is likely to be produced (designated Riserva if considered worthy) but not necessarily of the same standard as great vintages like 95 or 90 (five stars). Problems of stability due to high levels of volatility have occasionally been an issue in the past, but the greatest dilemma for most would-be-drinkers is which car to sell in order to buy a case or two. (Prices are always £H). (PW)

TALENTI Brunello di Montalcino   A: Bib

Owner: Riccardo Talenti Loc. Pian di Conte, Fraz. Sant'Angelo in Colle, 53020 Montalcino (SI)
Riccardo Talenti's father was one of those instrumental in creating a worldwide reputation for
Brunello. The small 13-ha estate created by Pierluigi Talenti, after receiving great acclaim for the
Brunello of IL POGGIONE, has been a reliable source of fine Brunello for nearly two decades.
Enologist Carlo Ferrini now works with Riccardo and it will take some time to see how the style
evolves. In the meantime, recent vintages show classic character, breadth and style with nicely covered
tannins and will maintain the reputation for ageing very well. 1996 was a little weaker but by no
means poor, 98 good for the vintage, while both regular and Riserva versions in 95 and97 can be drunk
reasonably soon or kept for another 10 years. Talenti Rosso is a fruit-centred blend of Sangiovese,
Syrah, Canaiolo and Colorino. (PW)
● **Brunello di Montalcino★★★★** £E Riserva★★★★ £F
● **Rosso di Montalcino★★** £C ● **Talenti★★** £C

TENUTA DI TRINORO www.trinoro.com   A: Sec, C&B, F&R

Owner: Andrea Franchetti Via Ribattola 9, 53047 Sarteano (SI)
From high up in the hills, a little way south of Montepulciano, come some of Tuscany's currently
most talked about wines. Andrea Franchetti is the creator of this estate established from virgin wine
territory in 1992. Passing over Sangiovese, Bordeaux varieties, particularly Cabernet Franc, Merlot
and Petit Verdot were chosen to be planted at high densities. At around 600 m the 16 ha of
vineyards would be too high further north in Tuscany, but the cool nights counter the summer heat
experienced near the Umbrian and Lazio borders. Trinoro is the main wine and based primarily on
Cabernet Franc (70 per cent) with about 20 per cent Merlot and the balance Cabernet Sauvignon
and Petit Verdot. Clearly the terroir is something special, given not only the richness but also the
originality of the wine. While the vines are still young, yields are very low and there is marvellously
pure concentrated black fruit and a hint of wild herbs in a refined structure. That said, prices have
run ahead of quality somewhat. A new 'second' wine, Le Cupole di Trinoro has been introduced and
a tiny amount of Cincinnato, from the local variety, Cesanese d'Affile, has also been made. Palazzi,
a blend of roughly equal parts Merlot and Cabernet Franc, was made until 1999. (PW)
● **Tenuta di Trinoro★★★★** £G

TUA RITA Val di Cornia   A: L&S, JAr, Fal, F&R

Owner: Rita Tua Loc. Notri 81, 57028 Suvereto (LI)
Tua Rita is now firmly established as the brightest new star in one of Tuscany's brightest new zones.
The Merlot, Redigaffi, is among Tuscany's half-dozen top Merlots but continues to be made in tiny
quantities that make it of somewhat academic interest to most wine drinkers. Rather more of the
Cabernet/Merlot blend (roughly two parts Cabernet to one of Merlot), Giusto di Notri, is produced,
but in an equally powerful, dense, expansive style and with similarly excellent texture and balance.
While some patience is needed, both wines promise to keep for at least a decade. Quantities can be
expected to increase as newly planted vineyards come into production in the next few years. The
wine currently made in the greatest quantity (albeit just 1,000 cases) and often overlooked in all the
hype is the red Perlato del Bosco. Produced from Sangiovese, it is also considerably more affordable and
has seductive, forward fruit but good depth and style too. Whites, too, are worthy; a blend of
Chardonnay, Gewürztraminer and Riesling previously known as Sileno but since 1999 as Lodano, is
aromatic and attractive. White Perlato del Bosco is now Trebbiano with some Vermentino. (PW)
● **Redigaffi★★★★★** £G ● **Giusto di Notri★★★★** £F
● **Perlato del Bosco★★★** £C O **Perlato del Bosco★** £B O **Lodano★★** £C

VALDICAVA   Brunello di Montalcino   A: VDu, Tur

Owner: Vincenzo Abbruzzese   Fraz. Valdicava, 53024 Montalcino (SI)
Another of Brunello's small growers, this estate has come to the fore under the direction of Vincenzo
Abbruzzese (though it has belonged to his family for half a century) and the winemaking skills of
Attilio Pagli. The style is for Brunello of real weight, power and richness without recourse to new oak
and there is excellent complexity and dimension. The wines don't usually lack for depth yet that
something extra, an added intensity that would place them among the very best, is missing. There is
usually the structure to improve for at least a decade, longer in the Riserva Madonna del Piano (from
1995 or 90). Regular Brunello was very good in 95 and 97, but, though savoury and flavoursome,
also much more advanced in 96 and to a lesser extent in 98. Improvements are ongoing and if the
outstanding 97 Riserva is anything to go by the best is still to come. (PW)
● **Brunello di Montalcino**★★★ £F Riserva Madonna del Piano★★★★ £G
● **Rosso di Montalcino**★★ £C

TENUTA DI VALGIANO   Colline Lucchesi   www.valgiano.it   A: Sec

Owner: Petrini & C.,   Via di Valgiano 7, Loc. Valgiano, 55010 Capannori (LU)
The Lucchese hills are the northernmost of several pockets of viticulture gaining prominence on the
western coastal rim of Tuscany. Valgiano is arguably the leading estate but it is only one of several of
emerging importance in the area. The 14 ha of vineyards are on poor gravelly soils at around 250 m
altitude, between the coast and the Apennines. Much importance is placed on ensuring the wines express
their origins and a sense of place and organic practices are employed to this end. The estate red is 60 per
cent Sangiovese with 20 per cent of both Merlot and Syrah and is rich and succulent with good depth
and balance. Palistorti is a similar blend but from younger vines; effectively a second wine, it is lighter
and more perfumed but has good depth and intensity too. The most stylish red however is the racy Scasso
dei Cesari, a pure Sangiovese from 40-year-old vines from two contrasting soil types. A cooling Apennine
influence favours the retention of acidity and the production of a characterful white, Giallo dei Muri, a
blend of Trebbiano, Vermentino and Malvasia but also including a little barrique-fermented
Chardonnay. (PW)
● **Tenuta di Valgiano**★★★ £E ● **Scasso dei Cesari**★★★ £E
● **Palistorti**★★ £C ○ **Giallo dei Muri**★ £B

FATTORIA VALTELLINA   Chianti Classico

Owner: Christoph Schneider   Loc. Rietine, 53013 Gaiole in Chianti (SI)
Valtellina is a small estate whose wines have always commanded a premium. The wines are made by
Andreas Stössel with some input from the much-consulted Vittorio Fiore. They are not of the easy-going,
quaffing type but rather firm, dense, powerful wines with lots of extract and can require some patience.
There is a tendency to overripeness in the top wines in the best years but this doesn't compromise their
ageing potential. If the wines could occasionally use a little more harmony and finesse they don't want
for flavour, complexity or power. Convivio is three parts Sangiovese to one part Cabernet Sauvignon
while the newer Il Duca swells the ranks of varietal Tuscan Merlots. (PW)
● **Chianti Classico**★★ £C Riserva★★★ £E
● **Convivio**★★★ £E ● **Il Duca**★★★ £G

VECCHIE TERRE DI MONTEFILI   Chianti Classico   A: RsW, Rae, N&P

Owner: Roccaldo Acuti   Via San Cresci 47, 50022 Greve in Chianti (FI)
The reputation of this estate, the property of the Acuti family since 1979, rests primarily with two very fine Super-Tuscans. The quality and symmetry of the wines was recognised in the 1980s and has been maintained due to the skill of Vittorio Fiore. Bruno di Rocca is a Cabernet Sauvignon/Sangiovese blend and usually a stylish but concentrated blend of berryish fruit and elegant oak after some ageing. More distinctive, with a lovely complexity and acquiring an increasingly rich and smooth texture with age, is a pure Sangiovese, Anfiteatro. Regular Chianti Classico also shows a stylish complexity but evolves more quickly than some *normale*. A white, Villa Regis, is a barrique-aged blend of Chardonnay that includes some Sauvignon Blanc and Traminer; while attractive and well-made, it is not for long-keeping. (PW)

● **Bruno di Rocca★★★★** £F   ● **Anfiteatro★★★★** £F
● **Chianti Classico★** £C   O **Vigna Regis★** £D

VILLA CAFAGGIO   Chianti Classico   A: BBR, N&P, Vne

Owner: **Basilica Cafaggio (Casa Girelli)** *Via San Martino in Cecione 5, 50020 Panzano (FI)*
A very professionally directed estate, Villa Cafaggio is a dependable name for high-quality Chianti Classico and Tuscan blends. Stefano Farkas produces ripe, vibrant, almost chewy wines with lovely perfume and sweet fruit on the palate. There are 30 ha of vineyards in Panzano's Conca d'Oro as well as a further 10 ha that are leased; they are planted mostly to Sangiovese but also to some Cabernet Sauvignon and Merlot. Efforts to maximise fruit quality include the selection of, and replanting with, superior clones as well as the adoption of green-harvesting. In the winery, the use of concentrated must adds richness in lighter years, while micro-oxygenation has also been employed since the 1999 vintage. New oak is important to the style of the wines, enhancing both structure and flavour – 100 per cent is used in the top two wines. San Martino, from a single vineyard, is now pure Sangiovese, though older vintages include a little Cabernet, while Cortaccio is 100 per cent Cabernet Sauvignon but used to include a little Sangiovese. Both add a little more concentration and style over a very good Chianti Classico Riserva. A single-vineyard Riserva Solatio Basilica (from 4 ha) is even better but has not been made in the most recent vintages due to replanting. All the wines benefit from a little extra age, Chianti Classico *normale* is best with three years, Riserva with four or five and Cortaccio and San Martino with at least five years. Prices are reasonable for the quality. (PW)

● **Chianti Classico★★** £B   Riserva★★★ £C   Riserva Solatio Basilica★★★ £D
● **Cortaccio★★★** £E   ● **San Martino★★★** £E

VILLA PILLO   www.villapillo.com   A: L&S

Owner: **John & Kathe Dyson** *Via Volterrana 24, 50050 Gambassi Terme (FI)*
Villa Pillo is another of those estates who show that good wine is not restricted to the well established or even the newer areas of the coastal or southern Maremma. Being off the beaten track, north of San Gimignano, and with reds from non-native varieties may not endear them to everyone but the wines are both interesting and of good quality. Marco Chellini now makes the wines but 90s vintages were made by Paolo di Marchi of ISOLE E OLENA. Syrah has been the star wine with some lovely pepper, berry and mineral character as well as a fleshy succulence. Merlot too, shows good fruit intensity while Vivaldaia from Cabernet Franc has an overly herbaceous, green component yet can also show good depth and texture. Vin Santo, only released with five years' age has good dried fruit, brazils and walnut complexity but promises more fruit richness than previously in the 1997 version. Borgoforte is a simple fruity red of variable composition. (PW)

● **Syrah★★★** £E   ● **Merlot** Sant'Adele★★★ £E
● **Vivaldaia★** £E   O **Vin Santo del Chianti★★★** £E

OTHER WINES OF NOTE

FATTORIA AMBRA ● **Carmignano** Vigna Santa Cristina in Pilli £B Riserva Le Vigne Alte Montalbiolo £C
● **Carmignano** Riserva Elzana £C
BADIA A COLTIBUONO ● **Chianti Classico** Riserva £D   ● **Sangioveto** (Sangiovese) £F
BADIA DI MORRONA ● **Vigna Alta** (Sangiovese) £D
● **N'Antia** (Sangiovese/Cabernet Sauvignon/Merlot) £D
FATTORIA DEI BARBI ● **Brunello di Montalcino** Riserva Vigna del Fiore £E
BARICCI ● **Brunello di Montalcino** £E
BINDELLA ● **Vino Nobile di Montepulciano** £C   ● **Vallocaia** (Sangiovese/Cabernet Sauvignon) £D
BORGO SALCETINO ● **Chianti Classico** Riserva Lucarello £D   ● **Rossole** (Sangiovese/Merlot) £D
CA' MARCANDA ● **Promis** (Merlot/Syrah/Sangiovese) £C
● **Magari** (Merlot/Cabernet Sauvignon/Cabernet Franc) £E
PODERE CAPACCIA ● **Chianti Classico** £C Riserva £D   ● **Querciagrande** (Sangiovese) £E
G FUSO CARMIGNANI ● **For Duke** (Syrah/Sangiovese) £D   O **Vin Santo** £E
CAROBBIO ● **Chianti Classico** £C Riserva £D   ● **Leone** (Sangiovese) £D
● **Pietraforte** (Cabernet Sauvignon) £D
CARPINETO ● **Chianti Classico** Riserva £D   ● **Farnito** (Cabernet Sauvignon) £E
CASA EMMA ● **Chianti Classico** £C Riserva £E   ● **Soloio** (Merlot) £F
CASAFRASSI ● **Chianti Classico** £C
CASALE-FALCHINI O **Vernaccia di San Gimignano** Ab Vinea Doni £B
● **Campora** (Cabernet Sauvignon) £C
CASTEL RUGGERO ● **Chianti Classico** £C
CASTELLO D'ALBOLA (Zonin) ● **Chianti Classico** Riserva £D
● **Acciaiolo** (Sangiovese/Cabernet Sauvignon) £E
CASTELLO DEL TREBBIO ● **Chianti Rufina** Riserva Lastricato £C
● **Pazzesco** (Merlot/Syrah/Sangiovese) £C
CASTELLO DI BOSSI ● **Chianti Classico** £B Riserva Berardo £D   ● **Girolamo** (Merlot) £E
● **Corbaia** (Sangiovese/Cabernet Sauvignon) £F
CASTELLO DI CACCHIANO ● **Chianti Classico** Millennio £D
CASTELLO DI FARNETELLA ● **Chianti Colli Senesi** £B   ● **Lucilla** (Sangiovese/Merlot) £B
● **Poggio Granoni** (Sangiovese/Cabernet Sauvignon/Syrah) £F
CASTELLO DI MELETO ● **Fiore** (Sangiovese) £D
CASTELLO DI QUERCETO ● **Cignale** (Cabernet Sauvignon/Merlot) £E
● **Il Querciolaia** (Sangiovese/Cabernet Sauvignon) £E   ● **La Corte** (Sangiovese) £E
CECCHI ● **Spargolo** (Sangiovese) £E   ● **Morellino di Scansano** Riserva Val delle Rose £C
CENNATOIO ● **Chianti Classico Riserva** £D Riserva O'Leandro £D   ● **Etrusco** (Sangiovese) £E
CENTOLANI ● **Brunello di Montalcino** Tenuta Friggiali £E Pietranera £E
CESANI ● **Luenzo** (Sangiovese/Colorino) £C O **Vernaccia di San Gimignano** Sanice £B
GIOVANNI CHIAPPINI ● **Guado de' Gemoli** (Cabernet Sauvignon/Merlot) £E
CIMA O **Vermentino** £C O **Candia dei Colli Apuani** Vigneto Candia Alto £C
● **Anchigi** (Sangiovese) £C   ● **Romalbo** (Sangiovese/Massaretta) £D   ● **Montervo** (Merlot) £D
DONATELLA CINELLI COLOMBINI ● **Brunello di Montalcino** £E
● **Brunello di Montalcino** Progetto Prime Donne £E
COLIBERTO ● **Monteregio di Massa Marittima** Riserva Thesan (Sangiovese/Cabernet Sauvignon) £C
COLLE SANTA MUSTIOLA ● **Poggio Ai Chiari** (Sangiovese/Colorino) £D
COLLELUNGO ● **Chianti Classico** £C Riserva £D Roveto £E
COLLEMATTONI ● **Brunello di Montalcino** £D
COLLESORBO ● **Brunello di Montalcino** £E
CONTUCCI ● **Vino Nobile di Montepulciano** £C
CUSONA/GUICCIARDINI STROZZI ● **Millanni** (Sangiovese/Cabernet Sauvignon/Merlot) £D
● **Sòdole** (Sangiovese) £C
DEL CERRO (Saiagricola) ● **Vino Nobile di Montepulciano** £C Antica Chiusina £E
● **Manero** (Sangiovese) £E   ● **Poggio Golo** (Merlot) £E

FASSATI (Fazi Battaglia) ● **Vino Nobile di Montepulciano** Pasiteo £C Riserva Salarco £D
FASSATI (Fazi Battaglia) ● **Vino Nobile di Montepulciano** Pasiteo £C Riserva Salarco £D
FATTORIA DI FIANO/UGO BING ● **Chianti Colli Fiorentini** £B
● **Fianesco** (Sangiovese & others) £D
GUALDO AL MELO ● **Bolgheri** £C
I BALZINI/FILIPUTTI & D'ISANTO ● **I Balzini** (Sangiovese/Cabernet Sauvignon) £E
I GIUSTI & ZANZA ● **Dulcamara** (Cabernet/Merlot) £E ● **Belcore** (Sangiovese/Merlot) £C
IL BORRO ● **Il Borro** (Merlot/Cabernet Sauvignon/Syrah/Petit Verdot) £F
IL BRUSCELLO ● **Val di Cornia** Loco dei Frati £D
IL CARNASCIALE ● **Caberlot** £F
IL MACCHIONE ● **Vino Nobile di Montepulciano** Riserva Caggiole £C
INCONTRI (Martelli & Busdraghi) ● **Val di Cornia** Lago Bruno £D
LA CIARLIANA ● **Vino Nobile di Montepulciano** £C Riserva £D
LA COMANDINA ● **Vintore** (Sangiovese/Colorino) £D
LA FIORITA ● **Brunello di Montalcino** £F
LA GERLA ● **Brunello di Montalcino** £E Riserva £F
LA NOVELLA ● **Chianti Classico** £B Riserva £D
LA PARRINA ● **Parrina Rosso** Muraccio £B Riserva £C
LA PODERINA (Saiagricola) ● **Brunello di Montalcino** £E Riserva £F
LA QUERCE ● **Chianti Colli Fiorentini** La Torretta £C ● **La Querce** (Sangiovese/Colorino) £D
LA RAMPA DI FUGNANO ● **Bombereto** (Sangiovese) £C ● **Gisèle** (Merlot) £E
LA REGOLA ● **Montescudaio** La Regola (Sangiovese/Merlot/Cabernet Sauvignon) £C
LA SELVA ● **Prima Causa** (Cabernet Sauvignon/Merlot) £D
LA TOGATA/TENUTA CARLINA ● **Brunello di Montalcino** £F
LAVACCHIO ● **Chianti Rufina** £B Riserva £C
● **Cortigiano** (Cabernet Sauvignon/Merlot/Sangiovese) £D
PODERE LE BONCIE/LE TRAME ● **Chianti Classico** Le Trame £C
LE CALCINAIE O **Vernaccia di San Gimignano** Vigna ai Sassi £C
● **Teodoro** (Sangiovese/Merlot/Cabernet Sauvignon) £C
LE CALVANE ● **Chianti Colli Fiorentini** Riserva Il Trecione £C
● **Borro del Boscone** (Cabernet Sauvignon) £D
LE CASALTE ● **Vino Nobile di Montepulicano** £C Riserva £C
LE CINCIOLE ● **Chianti Classico** £B Riserva Petresco £D
LE FONTI ● **Chianti Classico** Riserva £C ● **Fontissimo** (Sangiovese/Cabernet) £D
LE SORGENTI ● **Chianti Colli Fiorentini** £B ● **Scirus** (Merlot/Cabernet) £D
CANTINE LEONARDO DA VINCI ● **Chianti Riserva** £C ● **San Zio** (Sangiovese) £C
● **Sant' Ippolito** (Merlot/Syrah) £D O **Ser Piero** (Chardonnay) £B
COSTANZA MALFATTI ● **Morellino di Scansano** £D
MANTELLASSI ● **Morellino di Scansano** Riserva £C Riserva Le Sentinelle £C
● **Querciolaia** (Alicante) £C
MARCHESI PANCRAZI/TENUTA DI BAGNOLO ● **Pinot Nero Villa di Bagnolo** £D
MASSIA VECCHIA ● **Terziere** (Alicante) £D ● **La Fonte di Pietrarsa** (Cabernet Sauvignon/Merlot) £E
MELINI ● **Chianti Classico** Riserva Vigneti La Selvanella £D
MERLINI ● **Guadi Piani** (Sangiovese/Cabernet Sauvignon) £C
CANTINA DI MONTALCINO ● **Brunello di Montalcino** £E
MONTECALVI ● **Montecalvi** (Sangiovese & other) £E
SILVIO NARDI ● **Brunello di Montalcino** Vigneto Manachiara £F
NITTARDI ● **Chianti Classico** Riserva £D
NOTTOLA ● **Vino Nobile di Montepulciano** Vigna del Fattore £C
OLIVETO ● **Brunello di Montalcino** £F ● **Rosso di Montalcino** Il Roccolo £B
PALAZZO VECCHIO ● **Vino Nobile di Montepulciano** £B
PANIZZI O **Vernaccia di San Gimignano** Riserva £C
● **San Gimignano** Folgóre (Sangiovese/Merlot/Cabernet Sauvignon) £D
PANZANELLO ● **Chianti Classico** £B Riserva £C
PARADISO ● **Paterno II** (Sangiovese) £D ● **Saxa Calida** (Cabernet Sauvignon/Merlot) £E

PETRA ● **Val di Cornia** £C

FATTORIA DI PETROIO ● **Chianti Classico** £B Riserva £D

PIAGGIA/MAURO VANNUCCI ● **Carmignano** Riserva £D

PIANCORNELLO ● **Brunello di Montalcino** £E

PIAZZANO ● **Chianti** Riserva Rio Camerata £C

ENRICO PIERAZZUOLI ● **Carmignano** Riserva Le Farnete £E ● **Chianti Montalbano** Riserva £C
● **Chianti Classico** Matroneo £C

AGOSTINA PIERI ● **Brunello di Montalcino** £E

POGGIO ANTICO ● **Brunello di Montalcino** £E Altero £E Riserva £F

POGGIO ARGENTIERA ● **Morellino di Scansano** Bellamarsilia £C Capatosta £D

POGGIO GAGLIARDO ○ **Montescudaio** Vignalontana (Chardonnay) £B
● **Montescudaio** Rovo (Sangiovese) £C Gobbo ai Pianacci (Merlot/Cabernet Sauvignon/Sangiovese) £C

POGGIOLUNGO ● **Morellino di Scansano** Riserva £C

POGGIO DI SOTTO ● **Brunello di Montalcino** £G

POGGIO SAN POLO ● **Brunello di Montalcino** £E
● **Mezzo Pane** (Sangiovese/Cabernet Sauvignon) £E

PRATESI ● **Carmignano** £D

QUERCIA AL POGGIO ● **Chianti Classico** £C Riserva £D

RISECCOLI ● **Chianti Classico** Riserva £D ● **Saeculum** (Sangiovese/Cabernet Sauvignon/Merlot) £F

ROCCA DELLE MACÌE ● **Roccato** (Sangiovese/Cabernet Sauvignon) £E
● **Ser Gioveto** (Sangiovese) £E

ROCCA DI CASTAGNOLI ● **Chianti Classico** £B Riserva Capraia £C
● **Buriano** (Cabernet Sauvignon) £F ● **Stielle** (Sangiovese/Cabernet Sauvignon) £E

ROCCACCIA ● **Fontenova** (Sangiovese/Ciliegiolo) £C ● **Poggio Cavalluccio** (Ciliegiolo) £D

RUSSO ● **Val di Cornia** Ceppitaio £B Riserva Barbicone (Sangiovese) £D
● **Sassobucato** (Merlot/Cabernet Sauvignon) £D

PODERE SALICUTTI ● **Brunello di Montalcino** £F ● **Rosso di Montalcino** £C
● **Dopoteatro** (Cabernet Sauvignon/Sangiovese/Canaiolo) £D

SAN FILIPPO – ROSI ● **Brunello di Montalcino** £F

SASSOTONDO ● **Sovana** Superiore Franze (Sangiovese) £C ● **San Lorenzo** (Ciliegiolo) £D

SCOPETONE ● **Brunello di Montalcino** £E ● **Rosso di Montalcino** £C

SERRAIOLA ○ **Monteregio di Massa Marittima** Violina (Vermentino) £C
● **Monteregio di Massa Marittima** Lentisco (Sangiovese) £C
● **Campo Montecristo** (Sangiovese/Merlot/Syrah) £D

SESTI/CASTELLO DI ARGIANO ● **Brunello di Montalcino** £E ● **Rosso di Montalcino** £C

SORBAIANO ○ **Montescudaio** Lucestraia (Sauvignon/Vermentino/Trebbiano) £C
● **Pian di Conte** (Sangiovese) £C ● **Montescudaio** Rosso delle Miniere £D

SUVERAIA ● **Monteregio di Massa Marittima** Bacucco di Suveraia £D

TERRABIANCA ● **Chianti Classico** Riserva Croce £C ● **Piano del Cipresso** (Sangiovese) £C
● **Ceppate** (Cabernet Sauvignon/Merlot) £E ● **Campaccio Riserva** (Sangiovese/Cabernet Sauvignon) £E

TERRE DEL SILLABO ● **Niffo** (Cabernets/Sangiovese/Merlot) £E

TERUZZI E PUTHOD ○ **Terre di Tufi** (Vernaccia/Malvasia/Vermentino) £C
○ **Carmen** (Sangiovese – vinified as a white) £C

GIULIANO TIBERI ● **Le Vespe** (Sangiovese based) £C

TORRACCIA DI PRESURA ● **Chianti Classico** Il Tarocco £B Riserva Il Tarocco £C

TREROSE (Tenementi Angelini) ● **Vino Nobile di Montepulciano** La Villa £D Simposio £E

FATTORIA UCCELLIERA ● **Castellaccio** (Sangiovese/Cabernet Sauvignon) £D

VAL DI SUGA (Tenementi Angelini) ● **Brunello di Montalcino** £E

VALDIPIATTA ● **Vino Nobile di Montepulciano** Riserva £E
● **Tre Fonti** (Cabernet Sauvignon/Sangiovese/Canaiolo) £D

FATTORIA VARRAMISTA ● **Varramista** (Syrah/Merlot/Sangiovese) £D

VIGNAMAGGIO ● **Chianti Classico** Riserva Monna Lisa £C
● **Obsession** (Cabernet Sauvignon/Merlot) £E ○ **Vin Santo** £E

VILLA ARCENO ● **Chianti Classico** Riserva £C
● **Arguzzio** (Merlot/Cabernet Sauvignon/Sangiovese) £E

VILLA MONTE RICO ● Val di Cornia £C
VILLA SANT' ANNA ● Rosso di Montepulciano £B ● I Valloni (Sangiovese/Cabernet Sauvignon) £D
WANDANNA ● Montecarlo Rosso Terre dei Cascinieri £C
● Virente (Syrah/Merlot/Cabernet Sauvignon) £D

Author's Choice (PW)

20 classic Tuscans reds
ANTINORI ● Solaia
AVIGNONESI ● Vino Nobile di Montepulciano Riserva Grandi Annate
BOSCARELLI ● Vino Nobile di Montepulciano Vigna del Nocio
CAPANNELLE ● 50 & 50
CASTELLO DI RAMPOLLA ● Vigna d'Alceo
CORZANO & PATERNO ● Il Corzano
GAGLIOLE ● Gagliole Rosso
ISOLE E OLENA ● Cepparello
LE PUPILLE ● Saffredi
MONTEVERTINE ● Le Pergole Torte
PETROLO ● Galatrona
POGGIOPIANO ● Rosso di Sera
POLIZIANO ● Vino Nobile di Montepulciano Asinone
RIECINE ● La Gioia
RUFFINO ● Romitorio di Santedame
QUERCIABELLA ● Camartina
SAN GIUSTO A RENTENNANO ● Percarlo
SETTE PONTI ● Crognolo
TENUTA DI TRINORO ● Tenuta di Trinoro
VECCHIE TERRE DI MONTEFILI ● Anfiteatro

12 outstanding Chianti
CASTELLO DI AMA ● Chianti Classico Vigneto Bellavista
CASTELLO DI FONTERUTOLI ● Chianti Classico Castello di Fonterutoli
CASTELLO DI VOLPAIA ● Chianti Classico Riserva Coltassala
CASTELLO VICCHIOMAGGIO ● Chianti Classico Riserva La Prima
FATTORIA DI FELSINA ● Chianti Classico Riserva Vigneto Rancia
FONTODI ● Chianti Classico
FRESCOBALDI ● Chianti Rufina Montesodi
IL PALAZZINO ● Chianti Classico Grosso Sanese
LA MASSA ● Chianti Classico Giorgio Primo
POGGIO AL SOLE ● Chianti Classico Casasilia
FATTORIA SELVAPIANA ● Chianti Rufina Riserva Bucerchiale
ROCCA DI MONTEGROSSI ● Chianti Classico Riserva San Marcellino

12 diverse top quality Brunello
BANFI ● Brunello di Montalcino Riserva Poggio all'Oro
TENUTA CAPARZO ● Brunello di Montalcino Vigna La Casa
CASANOVA DI NERI ● Brunello di Montalcino Tenuta Nuova
COL D'ORCIA ● Brunello di Montalcino Riserva Poggio al Vento
COSTANTI ● Brunello di Montalcino Riserva
FULIGNI ● Brunello di Montalcino Vigneti dei Cottimelli
MASTROJANNI ● Brunello di Montalcino Schiena d'Asino
SIRO PACENTI ● Brunello di Montalcino

PERTIMALI/LIVIO SASSETTI ● Brunello di Montalcino Riserva
PIEVE SANTA RESTITUTA ● Brunello di Montalcino Sugarille
SALVIONI/LA CERBAIOLA ● Brunello di Montalcino
SAN FILIPPO - FANTI ● Brunello di Montalcino

12 coastal marvels

ANTINORI/GUADO AL TASSO ● Bolgheri Rosso
CASTELLO DEL TERRICCIO ● Lupicaia
TENUTA DI GHIZZANO ● Veneroso
GRATTAMACCO/COLLE MASSARI ● Bolgheri Rosso Superiore
LE MACCHIOLE ● Scrio
MONTEPELOSO ● Nardo
TENUTA DELL'ORNELLAIA ● Bolgheri Rosso Superiore Ornellaia
SAN GERVASIO ● A Sirio
ENRICO SANTINI ● Bolgheri Rosso Montepergoli
SASSICAIA/TENUTA SAN GUIDO ● Bolgheri Sassicaia
TUA RITA ● Redigaffi
TENUTA DI VALGIANO ● Tenuta di Valgiano

If Italy contained only the viticultural resources of Piedmont and Tuscany, that would be wealth enough, but there is much, much more even if a large part of it is too often ignored by an increasingly homogenised wider world. In North-East Italy fine, elegant whites are produced in the Alto Adige, fuller and more concentrated examples in Friuli-Venezia-Giulia, from a mix of both local and international varieties. Some of Italy's finest sweet wines also come from the North-East while all three provinces now also provide high-quality reds. While some come from the like of Cabernet Sauvignon or Merlot, more and more outstanding original reds result from a realization of the true potential of the native grapes; not just Corvina in the Veneto for Valpolicella and powerful Amarone but also Lagrein and Teroldego in Trentino-Alto Adige and even the previously obscure Pignolo and Schiopettino in Friuli.

The regions of North-East Italy

Trentino-Alto Adige

The German-speaking South Tyrol (Südtirol) is becoming an increasingly reliable source of elegant, perfumed dry white wines. Most of the wines are varietal and while there are several different grape varieties, many are familar to wine drinkers and the wines are labelled as **Alto Adige** DOC. The best examples of Chardonnay, Sauvignon, Gewürztraminer, Pinot Bianco and Pinot Grigio are both concentrated and elegant and are complemented by some ripe reds from Cabernet Sauvignon and Merlot as well as one or two genuinely good examples of Pinot Nero. The native Lagrein has emerged over the past decade as a superior grape variety and most of the top producers now offer a premium oak-aged version, often in addition to simpler, supple, spicy, brambly-fruited examples. Lago di Caldaro (or Kalterersee) which now comes under the Alto Adige DOC can be a light but attractive perfumed red from the Schiava grape. *Scelto* (or Auslese) indicates a higher degree of ripeness.The quality of the co-operative wines tended to be consistent if unexciting in the past but many have taken a big leap forward in the last decade, adding to the supply of quality wines forged by Lageder and Hofstätter.

As in the Alto Adige, the regional **Trentino** DOC covers a wide range of varietals and though the standard is generally lower than in the Alto Adige several small producers signal the quality possible. The greatest originality comes in the shape of an excellent red in **Teroldego Rotaliano** (from the Teroldego grape). Regrettably there are not that many examples yet but the superb wines of Foradori show what is possible with higher-density planting and low yields. The potential of another native variety, Marzemino, remains unrealised but some attractively floral, plummy examples do exist. Though Trentino is a major producer of sparkling wine, few **Trento** examples have the quality to compete with the best examples from around the world.

Veneto

The Adige river swings out of Trentino-Alto Adige and turns more easterly as it runs through Verona. On the lowest reaches of the Lessini Mountains to the north are the hills of Valpolicella, merging with Soave to the east. A number of producers have turned their backs on these classic appellations (using instead a regional IGT) as they believe they have failed to shed an image of cheap, simple plonk. In terms of quality wine the international reputation of this noble Italian province has come to depend chiefly on **Amarone della Valpolicella**. From a still relatively small number of producers, top examples of this powerful red, made from partially-dried grapes, are among Italy's finest reds. When not fully fermented out dry this results in the sweeter **Recioto della Valpolicella** while *Amandorlato* is sometimes used to describe an in-between style. The biggest problem for producers of Amarone is retaining some of the typicity of the style while losing the rusticity that has plagued its image. The excessively raisiny character and high levels of volatile acidity have become less apparent as more care has gone into eliminating grapes affected by rot and generally better hygiene. Many are now aged in new oak but whether more modern or traditional in style, Amarone's strength and character don't give it the greatest versatility. Fortunately, despite the trend to increased quantities of Amarone, a few producers have radically improved the quality of **Valpolicella**. Modern producers have thrown out the lesser of the traditional grapes, concentrating on Corvina, but are also introducing small percentages of other grapes – such as Syrah in the case of Allegrini. Most of the best examples have benefited from some sort of enrichment. The technique known as *ripasso* (the name is exclusive to Masi) involves passing the finished wine over fermented Amarone skins, improving both the texture and character of the wine. Many a producer's premium version of Valpolicella (sometimes from a single vineyard and usually as Valpolicella Classico Superiore) benefits from it but not all – others directly incorporate a percentage of dried grapes at some point during the fermentation, producing a sort of hybrid Valpolicella/Amarone. The best Amarone need at least five to six years' age and will keep for 10 to 15. Recioto is often better drunk younger but top examples will keep as long. Top examples of Valpolicella generally drink well with three to five years' age but exceptionally will keep for more than a decade. The best recent vintages are 2000, 97, 95, 93, 90, 88 and 85 but from a top producer wines from most other years are also very good.

Soave at its best is much more than an anonymous dry white – instead it can be a concentrated and stylish medium-bodied white, capable of some age in the best examples, which are produced either solely from Garganega or with a small amount of Chardonnay. Wine from dried grapes, as **Recioto di Soave,** can be an excellent sweet white. **Bianco di Custoza** and **Bardolino** to the west, on the eastern and southern fringes of Lake Garda, are sometimes cited as substitutes for Soave and Valpolicella but usually only compare with basic examples of each. From the western shores of Lake Garda one or two producers make quite concentrated, stylish **Lugana** as well as other blends (that incorporate Chardonnay and Sauvignon in the case of Ca' dei Frati). North of historic Vicenza is **Breganze** which owes its reputation to one producer, Maculan. As well as splendid sweet whites from the native white Vespaiolo, good quality has been realised from Cabernet Sauvignon and Merlot. Vignalta in the **Colli Euganei**, found south of Padova (Padua), have also been successful with both Merlot and Cabernet but make good dry whites too. **Prosecco** is the region's fizz and from a good producer can be fresh and attractive if drunk young.

Friuli-Venezia Giulia

Friuli's production (like that of Trentino-Alto Adige) is dwarfed by that of the Veneto but in terms of the number of top-quality producers is its equal. French varieties have been planted for many years in the hilly **Collio** and **Colli Orientali del Friuli** DOCs, but despite the quality of the wines produced from them they fail to give the region a distinctive stamp. Yet beyond Chardonnay, Sauvignon (Blanc), Pinot Grigio and Pinot Bianco there are ever-better examples of Tocai Friulano, Ribolla Gialla and Malvasia Istriana of distinctive character – and high quality from a top producer. The flatter **Friuli Isonzo** has emerged over the past decade as the third major quality zone, led by a young generation of growers making some of the most concentrated and structured whites anywhere in the region. While a good number of the wines are made in the prevalent unoaked fashion, an increasing number of the best wines have added structure from some use of oak. Fine light, sweet whites from the native grapes Picolit and Verduzzo are made by several producers. Red wines are increasingly important and with better training, higher density planting and lower yields the grassy character once common to so many of the reds from Cabernet Sauvignon, Cabernet Franc and Merlot has been replaced by a lush, ripe berry fruit richness in best examples. Also showing much promise in the most recent vintages are some intense and concentrated examples of native varieties, Pignolo, Refosco and Schioppettino. Soundly made but rarely exciting whites and reds are produced in the large, mostly flat zone of **Friuli Grave** or even the smaller southern zones of **Friuli Aquileia** or **Friuli Latisana**.

A-Z of Producers by region

Alto Adige
COLTERENZIO
FRANZ HAAS
HOFSTÄTTER
ALOIS LAGEDER
JOSEF NIEDERMAYR
PRODUTTORI SAN MICHELE APPIANO
CANTINA TERLANO

Friuli-Venezia Giulia
BORGO DEL TIGLIO
BORGO SAN DANIELE
GIROLAMO DORIGO
LIVIO FELLUGA
WALTER FILIPUTTI
IL CARPINO
VINNAIOLI JERMANN
RONCHI DI MANZANO
RONCO DEL GELSO
RUSSIZ SUPERIORE
SCHIOPETTO
MATIJAZ TERCIC
VIE DI ROMANS
VILLA RUSSIZ
LE VIGNE DI ZAMÒ

Lombardia
CA' DEI FRATI

Trentino
CESCONI
FORADORI
POJER & SANDRI
SAN LEONARDO

Veneto
ALLEGRINI
ANSELMI
TOMMASO BUSSOLA
CORTE SANT' ALDA
ROMANO DAL FORNO
INAMA
LA SALETTE
MACULAN
MASI
PIEROPAN
QUINTARELLI
ROCCOLO GRASSI
TEDESCHI
VIGNALTA
ZENATO

ALLEGRINI Veneto www.allegrini.it A: Lib, ACh, Vne, UnC, Con, P&S, BBR

Owner: Walter, Franco & Marilisa Allegrini   Corte Giara, 37022 Fumane di Valpolicella (VR)
The 70-ha Allegrini estate is Valpolicella's leading producer of modern-style reds. The wines have excellent fruit, balance, depth and intensity and develop marvellously smooth velvety textures with age. While a good regular Valpolicella is based on the three traditional grapes, two single-vineyard reds, previously Valpolicella *crus* but now sold as Veronese IGT, continue to evolve. Both are based on Corvina (70 percent) and Rondinella, but La Grola also includes 10 per cent Syrah and five per cent Sangiovese since 1998. Palazzo della Torre, a *ripasso*-style version (but enriched by dried grapes rather than Amarone lees) also includes a Sangiovese component. Oak is also a feature of the best wines, including the Amarone, which shows marvellous richness and concentration in the most recent releases. La Poja is a pure Corvina red made from late-harvested grapes grown on the top of the La Grola hill, a wine of striking intensity and depth, now with a long-established record of production. The sweet Recioto, Giovanni Allegrini, is dedicated to the memory of the Allegrini father who founded the company. Amarone, La Grola and Palazzo della Torre are all made in significant quantities and should be easy to obtain. (PW)
- **Amarone della Valpolicella Classico★★★★★** £F ● **La Poja★★★★★** £F
- **La Grola★★★** £D ● **Palazzo della Torre★★★** £D
- **Recioto della Valpolicella Classico** Giovanni Allegrini★★★ £F

ANSELMI Veneto A: Eno, NYg, N&P, FWC

Owner: Roberto Anselmi   Via San Carlo 46, 37032 Monteforte d'Alpone (VR)
Roberto Anselmi used to make Soave. 'Used to' because all the wines are now Veneto IGT as one of the Veneto's, indeed Italy's pioneers for quality continues the pursuit of excellence beyond the restraints of the appellation. Only the regular bottling of San Vicenzo is made in substantial quantities but quality is consistently high. Two former *crus* offer a marked contrast in style with two or three years' age: Capitel Foscarino offers a lovely pure citrus and yellow plum fruit, while Capitel Croce divides opinion somewhat with its slightly exaggerated oak-influenced style with some spice, even coconut character. Foscarino and San Vicenzo include a little Chardonnay. The star, though, is the wonderfully elegant pure-fruited and classy sweet wine, I Capitelli. A red from Cabernet Sauvignon, Realda, shows concentrated blackcurrant fruit and a leafy influence. (PW)
- O **Capitel Foscarino★★★** £C   O **Capitel Croce★★** £C
- O **San Vicenzo★** £B   O **I Capitelli★★★★** £D
- ● **Cabernet Sauvignon Realda★★** £C

BORGO DEL TIGLIO Friuli-Venezia Giulia A: Ast, P&S, UnC, But

Owner: Nicola Manferrari   Via San Giorgio 71, 34070 Brazzano di Cormóns (GO)
Nicola Manferrari has 9 ha spread across three distinct vineyard sites. The cooler sites are planted to Riesling, Sauvignon and Chardonnay while those more warmed by the Adriatic include the red grape varieties. Whites in particular are made to a high standard with good ripeness, intensity as well as the capacity to age. In addition to regular varietal examples of good varietal character, superior versions are also made. Tocai, for instance, in Ronco della Chiesa shows more oak-influence and much better structure, while Chardonnay Selezione adds more depth, complexity and richness, over the standard bottling. In Studio di Bianco, Tocai, Sauvignon and Riesling are deftly combined in a stylish, ripe white with both depth and intensity. Reds are more variable, sometimes not quite achieving full ripeness in both fruit and tannins yet when they do there is good supple plummy, berry fruited depth. Rosso della Centa is a pure Merlot while Collio Rosso Riserva adds 25 to 30 per cent

Cabernet Sauvignon to Merlot. (PW)

O **Collio** Chardonnay★★ £D Chardonnay Selezione★★★ £E
O **Collio** Tocai★★ £C Tocai Ronco della Chiesa★★★ £E
O **Collio** Malvasia Selezione★★ £C   O **Collio Bianco** Studio di Bianco★★★ £E
● **Collio** Rosso della Centa★★ £E   ● **Collio Rosso** Riserva★★ £E

BORGO SAN DANIELE Friuli-Venezia Giulia   A: Ast

Owner: Mauro Mauri   Via San Daniele 16, 34071 Cormòns (GO)
Mauro Mauri and his sister Alessandra make a small but uniformly high-quality range of wines from
19 ha of vineyards. They undertake staggered picking to produce whites that impress both for their
individuality and structure. Most singular is a smoky, scented Tocai fermented and aged in *botti
grandi* that combines citrus with exotic flavours. Both the Pinot Grigio and Arbis (Chardonnay,
Sauvignon, Pinot Bianco and Tocai) have a measure of barrique influence and show a little more
breadth if less flair. A little red is also made, Arbis Rosso from the two Cabernets and Pignolo. A new
red will combine Pignolo and other native varieties with Merlot. (PW)

O **Fruili Isonzo** Tocai★★★ £C Pinot Grigio★★ £C
O **Fruili Isonzo Bianco** Arbis★★ £D

TOMMASO BUSSOLA Veneto   A: Bal, But, The, P&S, UnC, Fal, NYg, Res

Owner: Tommaso Bussola   Loc. San Peretto, Via Molino Turri 30, 37024 Negrar (VR)
A brilliant, young, dedicated grower, Tommaso Bussola only started on his own in the early 1990s
yet is now one of the stars of Valpolicella. As well as a regular bottling (BG – named for his uncle,
Giuseppe Bussola with whom he started out) of each wine, there are premium wines labelled 'TB'
made from the finest fruit. Amarone Vigneto Alto vies with the moderately sweet Recioto TB as the
best of the lot. The wines are wonderfully perfumed with ever more depth and concentration in the
most recent releases. Production is small and prices already high; older vintages, while good, are not
at the same level as that seen since 1997. (PW)

● **Amarone della Valpolicella Classico**★★★ £E TB★★★★★ £F TB Vigneto Alto★★★★★ £F
● **Recioto della Valpolicella Classico** TB★★★★ £F   ● **Valpolicella Classico** Superiore TB★★★ £C

CA' DEI FRATI Lombardia   www.cadeifrati.it   A: Lib, Con, Vne, Res

Owner: Dal Cero family   Fraz. Lugana, Via Frati 22, 25010 Sirmione (BS)
Ca' dei Frati have set high standards for Lugana in the same way Anselmi and Pieropan have done
for Soave. Wines range from a consistently stylish and characterful Lugana I Frati through Brolettino
which is distinguished by its elegance and texture, to Pratto, an IGT white blend of Lugana,
Chardonnay and Sauvignon, which is lush and exotic with great length of flavour. The sweet Tre Filer
is made from the same varieties as Pratto but the grapes are dried for three months prior to being
fermented and aged in barriques. Aside from the excellent whites, a little red Ronchedone (from the
two Cabernets and Merlot), rosé (Chiaretto) and sparkling wine are also made. (PW)

O **Lugana** I Frati★★ £B Brolettino★★★ £C
O **Pratto**★★★ £D   O **Tre Filer**★★ £D

CESCONI Trentino   A: Lib, Gau, Vne, SVS

Owner: Paolo Cesconi   Loc. Pressano, Via Marconi 39, 38015 Lavis (TN)
The Cesconi family have been grape-growers for generations but it is the current generation, four

young brothers, Alessandro, Franco, Lorenzo and Roberto, that have transformed this small 11.5-ha estate. Producing wines of an atypical ripeness and richness, they have risen quickly to be one of Trentino-Alto Adige's best. All the wines show good depth and intensity with good varietal definition, if not yet the extra finesse or flair to compete with the very best from Friuli. Oak is employed with restraint in an aromatic Sauvignon, weighty Chardonnay and full, creamy Pinot Grigio. An unoaked Traminer is at least the equal of any of these. Olivar, a blend of Pinot Bianco, Pinot Grigio and Chardonnay can be the most complete and complex while a Merlot with cool fruit but good depth, has been made since the 1998 vintage. (PW)

○ **Olivar**★★★ £D ○ **Trentino** Chardonnay★★★ £C ○ **Trentino** Traminer Aromatico★★★ £C
○ **Trentino** Pinot Grigio★★ £C ○ **Trentino** Sauvignon★★ £C ○ **Trentino** Nosiola★ £C
● **Trentino** Merlot★★ £C

COLTERENZIO Alto Adige www.colterenzio.com A: Eno

Owner: 'Co-operative' Loc. Cornaiano / Girlan, Strada del Vino 8, 39050 Appiano / Eppan (BZ)
The Cantina Produttori Colterenzio is amongst the finest of the Alto Adige's many good co-ops, though has rivals in the like of SAN MICHELE APPIANO and TERLANO. Under the direction of Luis Raifer the image and profile of Colterenzio has been transformed and investment realised. Improved fruit quality from the 370 ha of vineyards has resulted in good quality at a regular 'classic' varietal level though the wines can be a little simple and sometimes lacking concentration. A step up are the 'vineyard series' Praedium-labelled wines which bridge the gap between the 'classic' wines and the premium Cornell label. Cornell wines, though more pricy, are consistently impressive and show the influence of expert enologist Donato Lanati. Chardonnay Cornell in particular stands out for its excellent concentration, depth and balance over a string of recent vintages. Also good are the top reds, both the blended Cornelius (Cabernet/Merlot) and a powerful but less harmonious Cabernet Sauvignon Lafoa. Lagrein Cornell, suggestive of old vines, has the greatest character though, showing off the smoky, earthy, roasted qualities this grape can produce. In fact even the 'classic' range example of Lagrein is most attractive. Varietal Merlot (Riserva) and Pinot Nero (Riserva St Daniel) are also made. (PW)

○ **Alto Adige** Chardonnay Cornell★★★ £D Pinot Grigio Cornell★★ £C Gewürztraminer Cornell★★ £C
○ **Alto Adige** Sauvignon Prail★★ £C Sauvignon Lafoa★★ £D Pinot Bianco Weisshaus★★ £C
● **Alto Adige** Cabernet/Merlot Cornelius★★★ £E Cabernet Sauvignon Lafoa★★★ £E
● **Alto Adige** Lagrein Grieser★★ £B Lagrein Cornell★★★ £D

CORTE SANT'ALDA Veneto A: Wtr, DWS, BBR, Fal

Owner: Marinella Camerani Loc. Fioi, Via Capovilla 28, 37030 Mezzane di Sotto (VR)
For those who insist there is only a handful of really good producers of Valpolicella and Amarone, Corte Sant'Alda is likely to be one of several good producers they have missed. Much of the 15 ha of vineyard has been newly replanted employing single Guyot training (rather than the traditional pergola system) for better quality fruit. In addition oak vats are now being used for fermentation in a multi-faceted approach to further improving quality. Since the late nineties these sleek, elegant wines have been of indisputably good quality, with excellent expression but no lack of intensity or concentration either. For composed, balanced examples of Valpolicella (especially Mithas and Ripasso versions), Amarone and Recioto look no further. A dry white, Retratto, is made from Sauvignon complemented by Chardonnay and Garganega. (PW)

● **Amarone della Valpolicella**★★★★ £E ● **Recioto della Valpolicella**★★★★ £E
● **Valpolicella** Superiore Mithas★★★ £C ● **Valpolicella** Superiore Ripasso★★★ £C
● **Valpolicella** Ca' Fiui★★ £B

ROMANO DAL FORNO Veneto

A: JAr, Far, BBR, Fal

Owner: Romano Dal Forno   Fraz. Cellore, Via Lodoletta 4, 37030 Illasi (VR)

Valpolicella's most sought-after producer doesn't even hail from the Classico hills north-west of Verona but from slopes further to the east. It is not yet clear how his own site compares to the best slopes in the Classico zone but a radical retraining of the vines (trained low at very high densities) in order to obtain fully ripe, concentrated fruit and the use of new oak set his wines apart from the rest. The Valpolicella shows an extract and concentration missing in most Amarone and bears no resemblance to much of what shares the name. The quality is stunning and not simply showy and fruit-rich but deep and structured, with remarkable character and complexity. Extraordinary Amarone and Recioto set the standard for others to follow. Quantities are very small, reflected in their 'cult status' prices. (PW)

● **Amarone della Valpolicella** Vigneto di Monte Lodoletta✪✪✪✪✪ £H
● **Recioto della Valpolicella** Vigneto di Monte Lodoletta✪✪✪✪✪ £H
● **Valpolicella Superiore** Vigneto di Monte Lodoletta★★★★ £F

GIROLAMO DORIGO Friuli-Venezia Giulia

A: LaC

Owner: Girolamo Dorigo   Via del Pozzo 5, 33042 Buttrio (UD)

All of Dorigo's excellent wines are labelled for either one of two hillside sources, both acquired in 1966: Montscalape and Ronc di Juri. Girolamo's son, Alessio is now assuming greater responsibility for a range encompassing international as well as several local varieties. Chardonnay has a definite oak accent but delicious fruit, balance and refinement and there's a good Bordeaux style Sauvignon. Yet it is for reds as much as whites that these wines should be tried. Successful examples of Refosco and Tazzelenghe have great fruit expression and relatively harmonious structures for these difficult grapes and if you can't afford Moschioni's Schioppettino, Dorigo's appealing example shows a lovely peppery varietal expression. A little powerful, extracted Pignolo is also made. The top red, however is the Bordeaux blend labelled simply Montscalapade, a very composed example, with cedary crushed berry fruit, that oozes style. Brilliant in 1999 it could be drunk now or kept another five years. Dorigo's Picolit is one of the best examples of this elegant sweet white, though the honeyed Verduzzo isn't far behind. Sparkling wine from Chardonnay and Pinot Nero is also made. (PW)

○ **Colli Orientali del Friuli** Chardonnay Vigneto Ronc di Juri★★★ £D
○ **Colli Orientali del Friuli** Sauvignon Ronc di Juri★★ £D
○ **Colli Orientali del Friuli** Picolit Vigneto Montsclapade★★★ £E Verduzzo Vigneto Ronc di Juri★★ £E
● **Colli Orientali del Friuli Rosso** Montsclapade★★★ £E
● **Colli Orientali del Friuli** Schioppettino Vigneto Montscalapade★★ £C
● **Colli Orientali del Friuli** Refosco Vigneto Montsclapade★★ £C Tazzelenghe Vigneto Ronc di Juri★★ £D

LIVIO FELLUGA Friuli-Venezia Giulia   www.liviofelluga.it

A: Lib, Vne

Owner: Livio Felluga   Fraz. Brazzano, Via Risorgimento 1, 34071 Cormòns (GO)

This is one of the grand estates of Friuli, having been established by Livio Felluga in the 1950s. It is now being taken to new heights by his offspring, who have 135 ha to manage but with the expertise of consultant Stefano Chioccioli to assist them. The most widely acclaimed white, Terre Alte, is a blend of Tocai, Pinot Bianco and Sauvignon Blanc, a white of exquisite balance and elegance rather than concentration. Previously unoaked, a portion of the wine now receives some time in barriques but the finely nuanced complex fruit characters continue long on the finish. At a lower level is a well-concentrated, aromatic and characterful blend of Chardonnay and Ribolla Gialla, Shàrjs. Unoaked varietals are also of a high standard. The Picolit is a fine if pricy, medium-sweet white with honeyed, vanilla, wild flowers and dried fruit character – both long and refined not in the least bit coarse or heavy. Reds include an attractive Merlot/Cabernet Sauvignon, Vertigo and a deep, polished lushly berry-fruited Merlot, Sossò. More characterful but less refined in flavour is an excellent example of Refosco. First made in 1999 is a new oak-aged Pinot Bianco, Il Livio. (PW)

O **Colli Orientali del Friuli Rosazzo Bianco** Terre Alte★★★ £E O **Sharjs**★★ £C
O **Colli Orientali del Friuli** Pinot Grigio★★ £C Sauvignon★★ £C Tocai★★ £C Picolit Riserva★★★ £G
● **Colli Orientali del Friuli** Merlot Riserva Sossò★★★ £F Refosco dal Peduncolo Rosso★★★ £F
● **Vertigo**★★ £C

WALTER FILIPUTTI Friuli-Venezia Giulia   A: Bal

Owner: Walter Filiputti Loc. Rosazzo, Piazza dell'Abbazia 15, 33044 Manzano (UD)
One of Friuli most experienced winemakers, Walter Filiputti (who has also written extensively on the region's wines) is able to draw on the highly regarded vineyards of the historic Abbazia di Rosazzo, having gained full control over them with the 1997 vintage. As well as some good, fresh aromatic varietals, white blends of note include Ronco degli Agostiniani, a stylish barrique-aged blend of Chardonnay with lesser amounts of Pinot Bianco and Tocai Friulano. By contrast Ronco del Monastero is unoaked and restricted to the native varieties, Malvasia, Tocai and Ribolla Gialla. A barrique-aged red blend, Ronco dei Domeniciani, is based mainly on Cabernet Sauvignon but includes a little Tazzelenghe, Franconia and Refosco. It is a little firm and cool but shows some potential. Ronco dei Benedettini is a varietal Merlot. The reds generally flesh out and soften with a little bottle-age and also include a cool, peppery, berryish Merlot/Refosco blend, Broili di Filip. The top wines, though, are the native varietals, the sweet white Picolit – one of the best of a number of fine examples now made in Friuli – and the powerful, brambly, earthy, barrique-aged Pignolo Riserva (a grape variety Filiputti is credited with saving from extinction). A little of a single-vineyard version of the latter was made in 1999, Prima Vigna. (PW)

O **Colli Orientali del Friuli Bianco** Ronco degli Agostiniani★★ £C Ronco del Monastero★ £C
O **Colli Orientali del Friuli** Ribolla Gialla★ £C Sauvignon Suvignis★★ £C Pinot Grigio★★ £B
O **Colli Orientali del Friuli** Picolit Monastrium Rosarium★★★ £D
● **Colli Orientali del Friuli Rosso** Ronco dei Domeniciani★★ £D Ronco dei Benedettini★★ £D
● **Colli Orientali del Friuli** Pignolo Riserva★★★ £E ● **Broili di Filip**★★ £B

FORADORI Trentino   A: JAr

Owner: Elisabetta Foradori Via Damiano Chiesa 1, 38017 Mezzolombardo (TN)
Foradori is one of the top estates in all of Italy yet come from a zone that is little known outside the country. Elisabetta Foradori is something of a celebrity in Italy for her renditions of Teroldego Rotaliano. Previously two single-vineyard versions (Vigneto Sgarzon, Vigneto Morei) were made, surpassed only by Granato, the top selection, but since 1997 only the regular version and Granato have been retained. Where the regular version now shows real poise and persistence allied to a deep, smoky, bramble and mineral character (especially good in 2001), in Granato, a wine of great style and class, are added tobacco, spice and cedar, beautifully harmonised oak, and dense but fine, ripe tannins that ensure long ageing. An increasingly fine white is also made. Myrto contains 40 per cent each of Chardonnay and Sauvignon Blanc complemented by 20 per cent of Pinot Bianco; it is well-defined with attractive floral and fruit characters. Under the Vigneti delle Dolomiti IGT come very small quantities of very good Ailanpa, from Syrah, and Karanar, a blend of Cabernet Sauvignon, Syrah, Petit Verdot and Merlot. Prices are very reasonable for the quality. (PW)

● **Teroldego Rotaliano**★★ £B Granato★★★★ £D
● **Ailanpa**★★★ £D ● **Karanar**★★★ £D O **Myrto**★★ £C

FRANZ HAAS Alto Adige   A: Lib, Vne

Owner: Franz Haas   Via Villa 6, 39040 Montagna (BZ)

This 40-ha estate has become one of the most consistent in the Alto Adige, producing good reds as well as whites nearly every year. It is the quality of the fruit and the harmony in the wines that give them an extra edge over other good examples. The excellent Manna, a beautifully composed blend of Riesling, Chardonnay, Traminer Aromatico (or Gewürztraminer) and Sauvignon, shows a marvellous aromatic fruit quality with a Chardonnay-like weight in the mouth yet is intense and vibrant. There's good depth and flavour in the varietals too. Istante is a structured but distinctive red from Cabernet Franc, Cabernet Sauvignon and Merlot, ripe and stylish in recent vintages, with enticing ripe Cabernet Franc aromatics. The moderately sweet Moscato Rosa is a fine, perfumed, delicious and generally well-balanced example of its type. Wines labelled Cru (or Schweizer) indicate a superior bottling. Lagrein Scuro (or Dunkel) and Pinot Nero can also be good. (PW)

O **Alto Adig**e Pinot Bianco★ £B Traminer Aromatico★★ £C   O **Manna**★★★ £D
◉ **Alto Adige** Moscato Rosa★★★ £E
● **Alto Adige** Merlot Cru★★ £D   ● **Istante**★★★ £D

HOFSTÄTTER Alto Adige www.hofstatter.com   A: Mgi

Owner: Foradori (Hofstätter) family   Piazza Municipio 5, 39040 Termeno (BZ)

Hofstätter produce both Italy's best Pinot Noir and one of the best Gewürztraminers. Though not a world-beater, the top Pinot Noir, from Vigna Sant'Urbano on high slopes at Mazon, shows a depth and texture uncommon to Italian examples and is increasingly successful even in more difficult vintages. Martin Foradori, who has assumed the direction of the estate from his father, has the fortune to have one or two particularly favoured sites among the estate's 45 ha of vineyards and the training is gradually being switched from pergola to *guyot*-trained vines. The stunningly sited 3.5-ha Crozzol vineyards, acquired in 1995, are organically cultivated. The Kolbenhof Gewürztraminer from the village of Söll shows a depth and richness not found in many Alto Adige examples (the poorest of which are based on ordinary Traminer). Bianco Vigna San Michele, a blend of Pinot Bianco, Chardonnay and Riesling partly aged in barriques, shows similar weight and style and a subtle oak influence. Yngram is a blend of Cabernet Sauvignon (75 per cent) and Petit Verdot. (PW)

● **Alto Adige** Pinot Nero Riserva★ £C Pinot Nero Barthenau Vigna Sant'Urbano★★★ £E
● **Alto Adige** Lagrein Steinraffler★★ £C
O **Alto Adige** Gewürztraminer★★ £C Gewürztraminer Kolbenhof Söll★★★ £D
O **Alto Adige** Pinot Bianco★★ £C   O **Alto Adige Bianco** Barthenau Vigna San Michele★★ £C

IL CARPINO Friuli-Venezia Giulia www.ilcarpino.com

Owner: Silvano Cibini & Franco Sosol   Loc. Sovenza 14/A, 34070 San Floriano del Collio (GO)

Over the past couple of years this has become one of the most exciting estates in Friuli. Excellent white and red wines, predominantly varietal, show a combination of superb fruit and fine balance. A fine gentle, stylish Chardonnay is complemented by a partially oaked Sauvignon which has excellent definition, rich, ripe fruit and a lingering finish. Bianco Carpino is an equal blend of both with good harmony. A fine citrusy, herbal Ribolla Gialla is also produced as is some Malvasia. In red the wines are based on Merlot. A plush brambly Rosso Carpino includes 20 per cent Cabernet Sauvignon and shows lots of promise. Even better is Rubrum (potentially four stars), a sumptuous, black plum-fruited Merlot that tastes not unlike a young Pomerol. Both reds show good ageing potential. While all the Il Carpino wines see some French oak, Vigna Runc, a promising second label, is for unoaked varietals. These include Chardonnay, Pinot Grigio and an aromatic, floral, gooseberryish, concentrated Sauvignon Blanc. (PW)

Il Carpino
O **Collio** Sauvignon★★★ £C Chardonnay★★★ £C Pinot Grigio★★ £C Ribolla Gialla★★ £C
O **Bianco Carpino**★★ £C ● **Rosso Carpino**★★ £C ● **Rubrum**★★★ £D

Vigna Runc
O **Collio** Sauvignon★★ £B

INAMA Veneto www.inamaaziendaagricola.it A: Wtr, JAr

Owner: Inama family Via IV Novembre 1, 37047 San Bonifacio (VR)
Stefano Inama assumed control of the winemaking here in the early nineties and the wines have
attracted plenty of attention ever since. Two single vineyard Soaves are barrique-fermented and aged
while an unoaked regular (Vin Soave) Superiore version can be very good with citrusy, grapefruit notes,
fine balance and subtle leesy and minerally hints. The championing of Chardonnay and Sauvignon in
the Soave district has attracted a fair amount of controversy. Both are produced in oaked and unoaked
versions. Stefano Inama also makes Bradisismo, a blend of 70 per cent Cabernet Sauvignon and 30 per
cent Carmenère from the Colli Berici. It displays intense wild plum, bramble fruit but also a touch of
austerity and leafy herbaceousness though this will be less pronounced with age. Vulcaia Après is a late-
harvested version of Sauvignon while BINOMIO Montepulciano d'Abruzzo is produced in conjunction
with La Valentina (see Central Italy). (PW)

O **Soave Classico Superiore** Vin Soave★★ £B Vigneti di Foscarino★★★ £C Vigneto du Lot★★★ £D
O **Vulcaia Sauvignon**★★ £C O **Vulcaia Fumé**★★ £D
O **Chardonnay**★★ £C Campo dei Tovi★★ £D
● **Bradisismo**★★★ £E

VINNAIOLI JERMANN Friuli-Venezia Giulia www.jermannvinnaioli.it A: Eno, Vne, N&P

Owner: Silvio Jermann Loc. Villanova, Via Monte Fortino 21, 34070 Farra d'Isonzo
Silvio Jermann is the long-time champion of Friuli, having been making excellent whites for an age.
These are not just wines of good concentration and ripe fruit but ones with good definition and
character and with an added elegance and refinement in the top examples that other powerful
examples lack. The prices have always been a little ahead of others but when Jermann is on form,
which is most of the time, they deserve to be. Vinnae, the least expensive of the blended whites,
combines Ribolla Gialla, Malvasia and Riesling and is balanced and characterful. Capo Martino,
which adds a lot more richness, is a blend of Pinot Bianco and Tocai with a little Malvasia and Picolit.
Better though and often the top wine is Vintage Tunina (Sauvignon, Chardonnay, Ribolla Gialla,
Malvasia and Picolit), which shows intense stylish fruit, wonderful elegance and refinement, and
superb length of flavour. Though it might be drunk young it is best with five years' age. Dreams
('Were Dreams, now it is just wine!' – to give it its full name – and originally sold as 'Where the
Dreams have no end', in homage to U2's Bono) is a Chardonnay with rich oak spice and ripe fruit
that can show real precision and lovely harmony on the palate and is a rare Italian example that can
stand comparison with a fine Burgundian white. As well as those varietals below other whites include
Müller-Thurgau and Sauvignon. For red, a little intense Pinot Nero (Red Angel on the Moonlight)
and flavoursome, if extracted Pignolo (Pignacolusse) are produced. (PW)

O **Vintage Tunina**★★★★ £E O **Dreams**★★★★ £E
O **Capo Martino**★★★ £E O **Pinot Bianco**★★ £C O **Pinot Grigio**★★★ £C
O **Vinnae**★★ £C O **Traminer Aromatico**★★ £C O **Riesling Afix**★ £C

ALOIS LAGEDER Alto Adige www.lageder.com A: Bib

Owner: Lageder family Tenuta Löwengang, 39040 Magre' (BZ)
Lageder is the Alto Adige's leading private estate, driven on to exacting standards by the dynamic 'current' Alois Lageder (fifth generation). Though owning a relatively small percentage of their own vineyards, through close links with growers they are converting from pergola-trained vines to *spalliera* training on an increasingly organic basis. While the wines can be a little simple and dilute at the 'classic' varietal level, there are some fine examples of single-vineyard wines (especially the Sauvignon Lehenhof, Pinot Bianco Haberlehof and Pinot Grigio Benefizium Porer) and the estate premium varietals and blends. The elegant, perfumed whites show real style with three years' bottle age or more. Cor Römingberg is the top red from a high-density, *guyot*-trained vineyard, a rich, ripe and concentrated Cabernet Sauvignon (with three per cent Petit Verdot) with a fine minerally depth and class with few rivals in North-East Italy. Though from older vines and of some style and intensity, the Cabernet Sauvignon blend, Löwengang (including 15 per cent each of Cabernet Franc and Merlot) rather pales beside it. Much better is the white equivalent, a marvellously rich, deep, tightly structured and ageworthy Chardonnay. Also emerging with some promise are the Pinot Noir, Krafuss, and a rich Chardonnay and Sauvignon blend, Tannhammer. Casòn Hirschprunn is a separate single estate of 32 ha purchased in 1991. The blended whites and reds, especially the 'Reserves' Contest (Pinot Grigio, Chardonnay, Sauvignon and a little Viognier and other Rhône varietals) and Casòn (Merlot, both Cabernets, Lagrein and others) show lovely fruit and real style and composure. The regular white Etelle and red Corolle are similar blends but see less oak. All four are sold under the Mitterberg IGT. (PW)

Lageder
○ **Alto Adige** Sauvignon Terlaner★ £B Sauvignon Lehenhof★★★ £C
○ **Alto Adige** Chardonnay Buchholz★ £B Chardonnay Löwengang★★★ £D
○ **Alto Adige** Gewürztraminer★ £B Gewürztraminer Am Sand★★ £C
○ **Alto Adige** Pinot Bianco Haberlehof★★ £B Pinot Grigio Benefizium Porer★★ £C
● **Alto Adige** Cabernet Löwengang★★ £E Cabernet Sauvignon Cor Römigberg★★★ £E

Casòn Hirschprunn
● **Corolle**★ £C ● **Casòn**★★ £D
○ **Etelle**★★ £C ○ **Contest**★★★ £D

LE SALETTE Veneto A: Ast

Owner: F Scamperle & M Grisi Via Pio Brugnoli 11/C, 37022 Fumane di Valpolicella (VR)
Franco Scamperle makes consistent, stylish and very drinkable Valpolicella and Amarone. Apart from regular Valpolicella Classico all the wines are vineyard specific. Of two single vineyard Valpolicella, Ca' Carnocchio is produced solely from dried grapes and combines the supple texture of a good Valpolicella with more of the flavour depth associated with Amarone. There are also two versions of both Amarone and Recioto. The intense but only moderately concentrated La Marega Amarone is aged only partly in barrique while the Pergole Vece version (made only in the best years) is aged entirely in barriques. Both Amarone and Recioto wines have significantly more depth and complexity in the Pergole Vece versions. A sweet white, Cesare Passito, is made from dried Garganega, Malvasia and Moscato grapes. (PW)

● **Amarone della Valpolicella Classico** La Marega★★★ £E Pergole Vece★★★★ £F
● **Valpolicella Classico Superiore** I Progni★★ £C Ca' Carnocchio★★★ £C
● **Recioto della Valpolicella Classico** Le Traversagne★★ £E Pergole Vece★★★ £F

MACULAN   Veneto   A: BWC, Odd, Vts

Owner: Fausto & Franca Maculan   Via Castelletto 3, 36042 Breganze (VI)
A brother-and-sister partnership runs the well-known 35-ha Maculan estate, the only producer of real
note in the Breganze zone some way north of Vincenza. Famed for their production of some of Italy's
finest sweet wines, they also make very good reds, initially as Cabernet Sauvignon Ferrata but more
recently as simply Fratta, the premium blend of Cabernet Sauvignon and Merlot. Other reds include
Brentino, a fruit-driven Merlot/Cabernet blend and varietal Merlot, Marchesante. Dry whites are less
impressive with a rather oaky Ferrata and reliable if unexciting Breganze di Breganze. Pino & Toi is
an unoaked blend of Pinot Bianco, Pinot Grigio and Tocai. Sweet whites include the grapy, aromatic
Dindarella from a strain of Moscato, Fior d'Arancio, while Torcolato is made from dried Vespaiola,
Garganega and Tocai grapes. Only the botrytis-affected grapes are selected for Acininobili which is
aged (but not fermented) in new French oak barriques. There is an extra intensity to its sweet
dried-fruit richness, well checked by acidity, but it is made in much smaller quantities than the
sometimes equally impressive Torcolato. (PW)

● **Fratta**★★★ £F   ● **Breganze** Merlot Marchesante★★ £D
● **Breganze** Cabernet Sauvignon Palazzotto★★ £C   ● **Brentino**★ £B
○ **Breganze** Chardonnay Ferrata★★ £D   Chardonnay Riale★ £C
○ **Breganze Bianco** Breganze di Breganze★ £B
○ **Acininobili**★★★★ £G   ○ **Breganze** Torcolato★★★ £E   ○ **Dindarello**★★★ £D

MASI   Veneto   www.masi.it   A: BWC, Odd, Vts

Owner: Boscaini family   Fraz. Gargagnago, Via Monteleone, 37020 Sant'Ambrogio della Valpolicella
This large family firm is synonymous with Valpolicella and Amarone and has been a leader in
experimentation and innovation in the Valpolicella zone. Firsts include the bottling of single-vineyard
Amarone and Recioto (Campolongo di Torbe, Mazzano and Mezzanella), the re-introduction of the
ripasso method in Campofiorin (and for which they have the registered trademark) and the revised
dried-grape variation for enrichment (a refermentation) in Brolo di Campofiorin from a special parcel
of the same vineyard. Then there are the new wines from 'rescued' grape varieties, the best of which
is Osar, based on Oseleta (80 per cent – though complemented by the main Valpolicella grape,
Corvina). Toar from Corvina and Rondinella also includes some Oseleta. Both wines show some
new-oak influence. However, as impressive as early releases of many of the wines have been, down
the years there has been a tendency for quality to gradually slip away and at times the wines have also
been characterised by a somewhat high-toned character, leading sometimes to excessive levels of
volatile acidity as the wines have aged. At a lower level there is better value to be had elsewhere and
even many of the well-established premium wines can lack depth and richness when tasted against
some of the zone's leading wines. Production is large; as well as wines from 160 ha of vineyards, the
range also includes the wines of the Serègo Alighieri estate. The latest impressive release is a new red
from dried grapes, Grandarella Appassimento, with powerful, intense fruit and excellent flavour
length; it is a blend of Refosco (75 per cent) complemented by Carmenère and Corvina. Two wines
have also been produced from Argentina's Tupungato Valley in Mendoza. Corbec Appassimento
from semi-dried Corvina and Malbec grapes (70/30) and Passo Doble, essentially reverse proportions
using a dried-grape component for enrichment. (PW)

Masi
● **Amarone della Valpolicella** Campolongo di Torbe★★ £E   Costasera★★ £E   Mazzano★★★ £F
● **Recioto della Valpolicella Classico** Amandorlato Mezzanella★★ £E
● **Brolo di Campofiorin**★★ £C   ● **Toar**★★ £B   ● **Osar**★★★ £E

Serègo Alighieri
● **Amarone della Valpolicella** Vaio Armaron★★ £E   ● **Recioto della Valpolicella** Casal dei Ronchi★★ £E

JOSEF NIEDERMAYR   Alto Adige   www.niedermayr.it   A: LaC

Owner: Josef Niedermayr   Via Casa di Gesù, Cornaiano 39050 Appiano (BZ)

This long established producer manages to produce good quality across a large range, especially in the top reds but also good flavour intensity in simple but soundly made basic varietals. The leading whites are the premium examples of Gewürztraminer and Sauvignon with excellent structures and distinctive penetrating aromas. Less successful are Terlano Hof Zu Pramol and Perelle which though flavoursome and characterful show a touch of coarseness too and seem a bit overdone though may appeal to some palates. Both are made from Pinot Bianco and Chardonnay as is a very well-made sparkling Talento Comitissa Brut Riserva made by Niedermayr's enologist Lorenz Martini. Here the flavours are kept more in check, while the structure and length underscore its quality. Aureus is a blend of Chardonnay, Sauvignon and some Gewürztraminer and has deservedly received wide acclaim. All of Niedermayr's versions of Lagrein are good examples. To complement a very good Lagrein Riserva is Euforius which also adds Merlot and Cabernet Sauvignon; this works a lot better than it might be expected and is typically complex and composed. As well as a simple but flavoursome regular Pinot Nero, also made is a more structured Pinot Nero Riserva. (PW)

Josef Niedermayr
O **Alto Adige** Gewürztraminer Doss★★★ £C   O **Alto Adige** Sylvaner★ £B
O **Alto Adige** Sauvignon Naun★★ £C   Sauvignon Allure★★★ £C
O **Alto Adige Terlano** Hof Zu Pramol★ £C   O **Perelle**★★ £C
● **Alto Adige** Lagrein Aus Gries★ £B   Lagrein Aus Gries Blacedelle★★ £C
● **Alto Adige** Lagrein Aus Gries Riserva★★★ £D   ● **Euforius**★★★ £D
Lorenz Martini
O **Alto Adige Talento** Comitissa Brut Riserva Vintage★★ £C

PIEROPAN   Veneto   www.pieropan.it   A: Lib, Vne, BBR, ACh, Res

Owner: Leonildo Pieropan   Via Camuzzoni 3, 37038 Soave (VR)

The Pieropan Soaves are made in the vineyard, in the sense that the greatest efforts have gone into producing ever better-quality grapes from this 30-ha estate. Both a reliably good Soave Classico and single vineyard Calvarino are unoaked and based on Garganega but complemented by a superior type of Trebbiano, Trebbiano di Soave. In recent years La Rocca, made solely from Garganega from a 5.5 ha slope, has been fermented and aged in double-sized barriques and has added more richness to its pure-fruited expression. Both this and Calvarino may be drunk young but typically keep for at least five years. The dry whites are completed by a fine Recioto di Soave Le Colombare, for which the ripest Garganega grapes are dried for several months producing a rich, ripe and delicately nutty sweet wine after two years in large wood. Passito della Rocca, in contrast, is based on Sauvignon and Riesling grapes (with smaller percentages of Trebbiano di Soave and Garganega) and aged in barriques producing a more intense exotic fruit and honeyed richness. A little of another sweet wine, Santa Lucia is made when conditions favour the formation of late-harvested botrytis-affected Garganega grapes. (PW)

O **Soave Classico** Superiore★★ £B   Vigneto Calvarino★★★ £C   Vigneto La Rocca★★★ £D
O **Recioto di Soave** Le Colombare★★★ £E   O **Passito della Rocca**★★★ £F

POJER & SANDRI   Trentino   A: Ast

Owner: M Pojer & F Sandri   Loc. Molini 4-6, 38010 Faedo (TN)

Mario Pojer and Fiorentino Sandri make as refined wines as anyone in North-East Italy and have been quietly maintaining high standards for close on three decades. For something unusual, the attractive unoaked varietals include a floral and herb scented Nosiola but even Müller Thurgau is good in the context of the variety. Whites culminate in Faye, Chardonnay with 10 per cent Pinot Bianco. Elegant and classy, with a lovely fruit expression, building gently in texture and complexity with age. The red version of Faye is not a blockbuster but a very stylish, beautifully textured wine from Cabernet Sauvignon, Cabernet Franc, Merlot and Lagrein. A new project in the Cembra valley involves the production of just a single white blend and a single red blend from what will be 4.5 ha of vineyards. The barrique-aged white is very promising with fine perfume, weight and intensity from a mix of Pinot Bianco, Sauvignon, Riesling, Incrocio Manzoni and Kerner. Pojer & Sandri's long established, often exquisite sweet wine, Essenzia typically includes Chardonnay, Sauvignon, Riesling, Gewürztraminer and Kerner. A sparkling Brut Cuvée is also made, from Chardonnay and Pinot Nero. Most of the wines are sold under the Vigneti delle Dolomiti IGT. (PW)

Pojer & Sandri
O **Chardonnay**★★ £B   O **Faye**★★★★ £D
O **Trentino** Traminer Aromatico★★ £C
O **Sauvignon**★★ £C   O **Nosiola**★★ £B   O **Müller Thurgau** Palai★ £B
O **Essenzia**★★★ £E   ● **Rosso Faye**★★★ £D

Maso Besler
O **Besler Bianck**★★★ £D

QUINTARELLI   Veneto   A: Bib, Wtr, Fal

Owner: Giuseppe Quintarelli   Via Cerè 1, 37024 Negrar (VR)
Already a legend, Giuseppe Quintarelli is Valpolicella's greatest advocate of artisanal winemaking. The wines, still bottled and labelled by hand, are based on the three classic grapes of Valpolicella but with a few interlopers. They have great power, extract and intensity, needing long barrel-ageing to evolve into something complex yet demanding. Good (sometimes great) as the wines have been in the past, the ratings reflect their current quality – which has been surpassed by those showing greating winemaking sophistication. Nonetheless, the wines will always attract those in search of sheer intensity and extract even if the balance and texture are sometimes found wanting. Alzero is made from partially dried Cabernet Franc grapes while a very small amount of a white from dried grapes is also made. Prices reflect the wines' cult status. (PW)

● **Amarone della Valpolicella Classico** Monte Ca' Paletta★★★★ £H
● **Recioto della Valpolicella Classico** Monte Ca' Paletta★★★ £H
● **Valpolicella Classico** Superiore Monte Ca' Paletta★★★ £E   ● **Alzero**★★★ £H

ROCCOLO GRASSI   Veneto

Owner: Bruno & Marco Sartori   Via San Giovanni di Dio 21, 37030 Mezzane di Sotto (VR)
Marco Sartori is a rapidly rising star of Valpolicella even if his 8 ha of Valpolicella vineyard, Roccolo Grassi (not all of it yet in production) lie well to the east of the Classico zone (and North-East of Verona - DAL FORNO is in the adjacent valley to the east). There is a real focus on quality in the vineyard, in pursuing low yields per vine and in obtaining fully ripe fruit. A rigorous selection is apparent in the wines which are clean, modern and very fruit-driven yet with classic flavours. The tannins are ripe and there is good balancing acidity. In Amarone there is real richness and depth and it is almost overwhelming in its intensity if drunk young. The sheer impact of the fruit to some extent obscures any elegance the wines might otherwise show but the real test will be to see how recent releases mature. Marco also has 4 ha of Vigneto La Broia for the production of Soave and Recioto di Soave. The latter is almost decadent in its ripe, over-ripe exotic fruit character. There is guava, quince, over-ripe apple and pear, preserved citrus and muscovado sugar but it avoids being raisiny. The wines previously appeared under the name Bruno Sartori, which could easily have been confused with the large commercial operation of Sartori. (PW)

● **Amarone della Valpolicella**★★★ £E   ● **Recioto della Valpolicella**★★★ £E

● **Valpolicella** Superiore Roccolo Grassi★★★ £C
○ **Soave** Superiore La Broia★ £B ○ **Recioto di Soave** La Broia★★★ £E

RONCHI DI MANZANO Friuli-Venezia Giulia

Owner: Roberta Borghese Via Orsaria 42, 33044 Manzano (UD)
This moderately large, 60-ha estate in the Colli Orientali del Friuli zone produces a wide range of whites and reds, for the most part reasonably priced and well-defined examples of their type. Varietal whites are most impressive; vigorous, expressive and fruit-centred, having been aged intelligently (whether in stainless steel, large wood or barrique or some combination of these) according to the grape's character. The Ronc di Rosazzo white blends Sauvignon, Chardonnay, Tocai and Picolit in a ripe, stylish, vibrant harmonious whole that can be drunk young or kept for three or four years. Among the reds, while regular varietal examples of Cabernet Sauvignon, Cabernet Franc and Merlot could use more richness and ripeness, a very promising young vine Ronc di Subule from new vineyards planted at much higher densities (8,000 vines/ha) shows opulent, pure fruit well-integrated with new oak. Le Zuccule, a blend of Cabernet Sauvignon and Merlot, and the Ronc di Rosazzo red, which adds Refosco to the blend, show good fruit intensity and lush textures but are not overwhelmed by oak. A varietal Refosco is more robust and earthy but also more characterful than the blends. Two Ronc di Rosazzo sweet whites are good examples of Verduzzo and Picolit respectively, the former slightly more perfumed and refined, the latter more raisiny. (PW)

○ **Colli Orientali del Friuli Rosazzo Bianco** Ronc di Rosazzo★★★ £C
○ **Colli Orientali del Friuli** Tocai Superiore★★ £B Pinot Grigio★★ £B Chardonnay★★ £B Sauvignon★★£B
○ **Colli Orientali del Friuli Rosazzo** Picolit Ronc di Rosazzo★★★ £E Verduzzo Ronc di Rosazzo★★★ £E
● **Colli Orientali del Friuli** Refosco dal Peduncolo Rosso★★ £B Merlot Ronc di Subule★★★ £D
● **Colli Orientali del Friuli Rosazzo Rosso** Ronc di Rosazzo★★ £C ● **Le Zuccule★★** £D

RONCO DEL GELSO Friuli-Venezia Giulia   A: Ock, The

Owner: Giorgio Badin Via Isonzo 117, 34071 Cormòns (GO)
Giorgio Badin is a dedicated vigneron who has done much to improve quality down the years on his family's estate. He makes mostly unoaked whites with good purity and intensity from 20ha of vines. Most of the varietals can be a little reticent when first bottled showing at their best with at least two years' age. Latimis, a blend of Tocai, Pinot Bianco and Riesling, and also fermented and aged in stainless steel, along with the Pinot Bianco can be drunk soonest. Giorgio Badin believes Pinot Grigio can lack for aromatic complexity and as a consequence his Sot Lis Rivis benefits from small oak treatment and shows real weight and a stylish complexity. The one red, a Merlot also benefits from oak ageing and though can start out a little cool and angular is usually soft and plummy with a little age. A new winery should give quality a further boost. (PW)

○ **Friuli Isonzo Bianco** Latimis★ £B ○ **Friuli Isonzo** Pinot Bianco★★ £B
○ **Friuli Isonzo** Sauvignon★★ £C Tocai Friulano★★ £C Riesling★★ £C
○ **Friuli Isonzo** Pinot Grigio Sot Lis Rivis★★ £C ● **Friuli Isonzo** Merlot★ £C

RUSSIZ SUPERIORE Friuli-Venezia Giulia www.marcofelluga.it   A: BWC

Owner: Marco Felluga & family Via Russiz 7, 34070 Capriva del Friuli (GO)
Russiz Superiore is the leading estate of the Marco Felluga family. Like his older brother (Livio FELLUGA), Marco Felluga has Friulian viticulture in his blood and has similarly made an important contribution to establishing the region as Italy's leading area for white wines. His son Roberto and daughter Alessandra continue to expand the family's influence and holdings (another daughter,

Patrizia, is behind the promising blended estate white of ZUANI).The wine that has done the most for the reputation of Russiz Superiore is the red Riserva degli Orzoni, a Cabernet Sauvignon-based red complemented by Cabernet Franc and Merlot. Rich and structured, it has good depth and ripeness but impresses most in top vintages like 1997. As well as some consistently fine varietals, a blended white, Russiz Disôre, is made from from Pinot Bianco, Tocai, Sauvignon and Ribolla Gialla. The leading wines from the 130-ha Marco Felluga estate are Carantan, a stylish plummy red from Cabernet Franc, Cabernet Sauvignon and Merlot, and Molamotta, a blend of Pinot Bianco, Tocai and Ribolla Gialla. Good varietals include Chardonnay, Sauvignon, Tocai, Refosco and unusually (for Friuli), Moscato Rosa. Since 1994, the historic Castello di Buttrio, with 20 ha of vineyards, has been developed to become the source of a single red (Marburg, from Pignolo and Refosco) and white (Overstein, from Tocai and Ribolla Gialla).The family has also acquired an estate on the western fringe of Chianti Classico – San Niccolò a Pisignano is the source of a new red, Sorripa, from Sangiovese, Cabernet Sauvignon and Merlot. (PW)

Russiz Superiore
O **Collio** Pinot Grigio★★ £C Sauvignon★★ £C
O **Collio Bianco** Russiz Disôre★★★ £D ● **Collio Rosso** Riserva degli Orzoni★★★ £E
● **Collio** Cabernet Franc★★ £D Merlot★★ £D

Marco Felluga
● **Carantan★★★** £E ● **Refosco★★** £C O **Collio Bianco** Molamotta★★ £C
O **Collio** Tocai★★ £C Sauvignon★★ £C Chardonnay★★ £C

SAN LEONARDO Trentino www.sanleonardo.it A: JAr, Res

Owner: Marchese Carlo Guerrieri Gonzaga Loc. Borghetto, 38060 Avio (TN)
There are only 18 ha of vineyards but this large 300-ha estate dates back to the Middle Ages, being originally the site of a monastery. It is held in high regard for a single red wine that has been developed by the current owner with help from the enologist Giacomo Tachis. Improvements to both the vineyard and vinification have been ongoing and in a good year (such as 1997) can result in a complex, refined yet rich, full expression of a cooler climate blend of Cabernet Sauvignon, Cabernet Franc and Merlot (60/30/10). With deep blackcurrant, spice, plum and subtle herbal character it adds further complexity and fullness with another three or four years after its release (six to eight years' age). In some years it is not made at all and it has occasionally been disappointing, but good 1990s vintages have been of a generally very high standard. A varietal Merlot is effectively a second wine and though lighter, typically shows good style with attractive berry fruit and soft, supple tannins. (PW)
● **San Leonardo★★★★** £E ● **Merlot di San Leonardo★★** £C

PRODUTTORI SAN MICHELE APPIANO Alto Adige www.stmichael.it A: Eur

Owner: 'Cooperative' Via Circonvallazione 17/19, 39057 Appiano (BZ)
The wines of St Michael Eppan, the more usually seen form of the name, are made under the direction of one of Italy's great white winemakers, Hans Terzer. Drawing on 300 ha of vineyards, all the whites show good fruit and the mid-range varietals are defined by the vineyard area from which they are sourced. At the premium level the wines from the prized Sanct Valentin vineyards show greater aromatic complexity as well as an extra precision and refinement that put them ahead of most other Alto Adige examples. Gewürztraminer and Sauvignon are particularly stylish but quality of all the varietals is exemplary. An exquisite sweet white, Passito Comtess', from dried Gewürztraminer, Riesling, Sauvignon and Pinot Bianco grapes, is wonderfully perfumed but finely balanced and concentrated too. Reds can be very good as well, ripe with good expression and supple textures after at least two or three years' ageing. Released in 2003 was a very promising new Lagrein under the Sanct Valentin range. (PW)

O **Alto Adige** Chardonnay Merol★★ £D Chardonnay Sanct Valentin★★★ £D
O **Alto Adige** Sauvignon Lahn★★ £C Sauvignon Sanct Valentin★★★ £D
O **Alto Adige** Pinot Bianco Schulthauser★★ £C Pinot Grigio Sanct Valentin★★ £D
O **Alto Adige** Riesling Montiggl★★ £C Gewürztraminer Sanct Valentin★★★ £D
O **Alto Adige Bianco** Passito Comtess' Sanct Valentin★★★★ £E
● **Alto Adige** Pinot Nero Riserva★★ £C Pinot Nero Sanct Valentin★★ £E
● **Alto Adige** Cabernet Sanct Valentin★★ £E

SCHIOPETTO Friuli-Venezia Giulia www.schiopetto.it A: L&S, N&P

Owner: Mario Schiopetto Via Palazzo Arcivescovile 1, 34070 Capriva del Friuli (GO)
Mario Schiopetto was one of the great figures of Friulian viticulture. Up until his recent death he continued to work with his family and winemaker Stefano Menotti, to make some of Friuli's best unoaked white varietals, something he has done since the 1970s. His Pinot Bianco, Pinot Grigio, Malvasia, Sauvignon and Tocai Friulano in particular show the intense clear-fruited expressions that have earned such respect. Though based in Collio, the small estate of Podere dei Blumeri was added in 1996, to make a total of 30 ha of vineyards. Here Sauvignon, Chardonnay and Pinot Grigio have been made with a similar intensity, excellent concentration and individual expression. Wary of the flavours of new oak, Mario Schiopetto has only recently made any use of oak. Large Slavonian casks are now use for a series of wood-fermented and aged varietals. Amrità (Pinot Bianco), Pardes (Tocai) and Tarsia (Sauvignon) are richer, creamier and fuller; less pure perhaps but more complex and likely to last for up to a decade. Also made is an impressive, harmonious, unoaked blended white, Blanc des Rosis, from Pinot Bianco, Tocai, Sauvignon and Malvasia while the best red is the blended Rivarossa from Merlot, Cabernet Sauvignon and Cabernet Franc. (PW)

O **Collio** Pinot Bianco★★★ £C Pinot Bianco Amrità★★★ £E Sauvignon★★ £C Sauvignon Tarsia★★★ £E
O **Collio** Tocai Friulano★★ £C Tocai Friulano Pardes★★★ £E Pinot Grigio★★ £C Malvasia★★ £C
O **Colli Orientali del Friuli** Sauvignon Podere dei Blumeri★★★ £C Pinot Grigio Podere dei Blumeri★★ £C
O **Colli Orientali del Friuli** Chardonnay Podere dei Blumeri★★ £C
O **Blanc des Rosis**★★★ £E ● **Rivarossa**★★ £C

TEDESCHI Veneto www.tedeschiwines.com A: Hal, N&P

Owner: Tedeschi family Fraz. Pedemonte, Via Verdi 4, 37020 San Pietro in Cariano (VR)
The fifth generation of Tedeschis to be involved in making wine in the heart of the Valpolicella zone is now in charge here. They control 67 ha of vineyards, 22 ha of which are owned. Of a substantial range, the best wines are the premium Amarone and Recioto which show classic vigour, flavour intensity and power. More occasionally made is a Fabriseria Amarone Classico, effectively a Riserva. The modern-styled barrique-aged Rosso La Fabriseria adds a small amount of Cabernet Sauvignon to Corvina, Corvinone, Rondinella and Dindarella. Also made are a sweet white from Garganega and Soarin grapes, Vin de la Fabriseria, a ripasso red, Capitel San Rocco, of variable quality and basic generics of Valpolicella, Bardolino, Soave etc. (PW)

● **Amarone della Valpolicella Classico**★★ £D Capitel Monte Olmi★★★★ £E La Fabriseria★★★★ £E
● **Recioto della Valpolicella Classico** Capitel Monte Fontana★★★ £E
● **Valpolicella Classico** Superiore Capitel dei Nicolò★★ £C ● **Rosso La Fabriseria**★★★ £D

MATIJAZ TERCIC Friuli-Venezia Giulia A: Mgi, L&W

Owner: Matijaz Tercic Loc. Bucuie 9, 34070 San Floriano del Collio (GO)
This is an increasingly good and reasonably priced source of Fruili wines with a perceptible increase in quality year on year. To impressive intensity and concentration have been added more expression

and better balance. The best wine is the Collio Bianco Planta, Chardonnay with 10 per cent Pinot Bianco. This combines a gently creamy texture with good complexity and has the structure to improve for at least four or five years. Vino degli Orti is produced from Tocai, Malvasia and Riesling and manages to be delightfully aromatic but concentrated too. This as with all the white varietals is vinified and aged in stainless steel - all are ripe, intense and stylish. Merlot is usually cool with a touch of herbaceous green pepper character to its smoky plummy fruit yet characterful and well-made. A varietal Ribolla Gialla is also made. (PW)

O **Collio Bianco** Planta★★★ £C   O **Vino degli Orti**★★ £C
O **Collio** Pinot Grigio★★ £C Sauvignon★★ £C Chardonnay★★ £C   ● **Collio** Merlot★★ £C

CANTINA TERLANO Alto Adige   www.cantina-terlano.com   A: Ast, But, P&S

Owner: 'Cooperative' Via Silberleiten 7, 39018 Terlano (BZ)
The Terlan or Terlano cooperative is another of the Alto Adige's dynamic co-ops. The wines made by Hartmann Donà are in a bold and flavoursome mould in contrast to the refinement and subtlety sought by others in the region. Above a regular (Classico) series of varietals is an extensive range of vineyard designated varietals and four premium releases with prices to match. While oak can be a little too intrusive in the these top cuvées, it does further enhance their structure, and one-off releases of Terlano and Sauvignon with more than a decade's age give an indication of their some-times exceptional ageing potential. Both the Terlano Classico and the premium Nova Domus achieve good harmony between Pinot Bianco, Sauvignon and Chardonnay. The best of the reds are two versions of Lagrein but there's also Merlot (Riserva Siebeneich), Pinot Nero (Riserva Montigl), Cabernet (Riserva Siemegg) and other native varieties. (PW)

O **Alto Adige** Pinot Bianco Vorberg★★ £C Sauvignon Quarz★★★ £D Gewürztraminer Lunare★★ £D
O **Alto Adige Terlano** Classico★★ £B Nova Domus★★★ £D
● **Alto Adige** Lagrein Riserva Gries★ £C Lagrein Riserva Porphyr★★ £D

VIGNALTA Veneto   A: Ast

Owner: L Gomiero, F Zanovello & G Cardin Fraz. Luvigliano, Via dei Vescovi 5, 35038 Torreglia
Many wine lovers would have trouble locating Valpolicella in the Veneto so what chance has Colli Euganei? The hills south-west of Padova don't in fact have much of a reputation yet for more than a decade Vignalta has produced fine reds and interesting whites. The top red is Gemola, 70 per cent Merlot complemented by Cabernet Franc. A cool but ripe, elegant Bordeaux like red that ages gracefully. A Rosso Riserva from a similar blend hasn't the same depth or concentration but is typically supple and expressive. Small quantities of an unusual blend of Petite Sirah, Primitivo and Barbera was first made in 1998. The varieties suggest a deep coloured robust, earthy but characterful red which in fact it is. Just a little more concentration and it could be very good indeed. Of the whites the Chardonnay comes from a 30 year old vineyard and is barrique-fermented and aged. The best white is the refined sweet Moscato, Fior d'Arancio Alpinae. (PW)

● **Colli Euganei Rosso** Rosso Riserva★★ £C Gemola★★★ £D
● **Agno Tinto**★★ £D
O **Colli Euganei** Pinot Bianco★★ £C Pinot Bianco Agno Casto★★ £C Chardonnay★★ £C
O **Colli Euganei** Fior d'Arancio Alpinae★★★ £E   O **Moscato Sirio**★ £B

VIE DI ROMANS Friuli-Venezia Giulia   A: Lib, Vne

Owner: Gianfranco Gallo Loc. Vie di Romans 1, 34070 Mariano del Friuli (GO)
For those dismissive of the quality of Chardonnay and Sauvignon produced in Friuli, those of

Gianfranco Gallo need to be tasted. From 30 ha of vines the grapes are turned into wines with a richness, intensity – but even more importantly a breadth and a structure – that few other examples approach. Of two Chardonnay, Ciampagnis Vieris, with a tangy pure fruit intensity is the unoaked version; the richer, more complex and structured Vie di Romans spends 12 months in French oak. Piere is the unoaked Sauvignon, concentrated and intense with good grip. if less flattering than the delicately creamy, ripe and harmonious Vieris. Two other whites are made, a very flavoursome characterful blend of Malvasia, Tocai, Riesling and Chardonnay (each vinified separately), Flor di Uis, and a barrique-aged and fermented Pinot Grigio, Dessimis, that is rich and creamy with a lot of depth but arguably the least refined of the whites. There is real depth and intensity to a red, Voos dai Ciamps, (from Merlot) too. (PW)

O **Friuli Isonzo** Chardonnay Ciampagnis Vieris★★★ £D Chardonnay Vie di Romans★★★★ £E
O **Friuli Isonzo** Sauvignon Piere★★★ £E Sauvignon Vieris★★★ £E Pinot Grigio Dessimis★★★ £E
O **Friuli Isonzo Bianco** Flor di Uis★★★ £E ● **Friuli Isonzo Rosso** Voos dai Ciamps★★★ £E

VILLA RUSSIZ Friuli-Venezia Giulia www.villarussiz.it A: HHB

Owner: Instituto Adele Cerruti Via Russiz 6, 34070 Capriva del Friuli (GO)
The dynamic Gianni Menotti directs this very professionally run estate and winery for the charitable institute Adele Cerruti. Whilst there is excellent intensity and varietal expression in the regular bottlings, it is only in the special versions that an extra depth and structure is truly evident. All the varietal-labelled whites are vinified in stainless steel and don't see any oak. Regular Sauvignon is particularly good - long and tangy, intense and aromatic while Sauvignon de la Tour adds more breadth and structure from 10 months on its lees. Oak is employed for a very small production of Gräfin de la Tour, a Chardonnay which spends 12 months in barriques. Similarly small quantities are made of the red Graf de la Tour from 100 per cent Merlot. With two years in barrique it typically shows a richness and ripeness that can be missing in the regular Merlot and Cabernet which are aged in a mix of small and large oak, the Cabernet being a blend of both Cabernet Sauvignon and Cabernet Franc. Other varietals usually made to a high standard are Riesling, Malvasia and Ribolla Gialla. (PW)

O **Collio** Tocai Friulano★★ £B Pinot Bianco★★ £B Pinot Grigio★★ £B
O **Collio** Sauvignon★★ £B Sauvignon de la Tour★★★ £D
O **Collio** Chardonnay Gräfin de la Tour★★★ £D ● **Collio** Merlot Graf de la Tour★★ £E

LE VIGNE DI ZAMÒ Friuli-Venezia Giulia www.levignedizamo.com A: HSA

Owner: Zamò family Loc. Rosazzo, Via Abate Corrado 4, 33044 Manzano (GO)
The Zamò family commenced wine production in the late seventies but their roots in the Friuli hills stretch back to 1924. Their now sizeable operation has undergone many changes over the past decade with a transformation in vineyard resources which now total 55 ha, either owned or leased from the zones around Rocca Bernarda, Buttrio and Rosazzo. A modern winery with a battery of stainless steel tanks underpins the cleanliness and freshness of regular varietals while oak is employed for the premium Pinot Bianco. Tullio Zamò (the family patriarch), and Ronco delle Acacie, from Tocai, Chardonnay and Pinot Bianco. Both can show impressive texture and complexity if missing the balance and elegance for more. Tocai is nearly always good whether in the regular version or the old vine, Cinquant'Anni. 40 per cent of the vineyard is planted to red grapes and the quality of the special bottlings no doubt owes much to consultancy from top enologist Franco Bernabei, better known for his Tuscan endeavours. The characterful Ronco dei Roseti is mostly from Merlot and the two Cabernets. The best red is usually the richly textured and concentrated Merlot Cinquant' Anni with a structure to improve for five to ten years. Tiny amounts of Pignolo and Schioppettino are also made. (PW)

○ **Colli Orientali del Friuli** Tocai Friulano★★ £C Tocai Friulano Vigne Cinquant' Anni★★★ £C
○ **Colli Orientali del Friuli** Sauvignon★★ £C Pinot Bianco Tullio Zamò★★ £C
○ **Colli Orientali del Friuli Bianco** Ronco delle Acacie★★★ £C
● **Colli Orientali del Friuli** Merlot Vigne Cinquant' Anni★★★ £E
● **Colli Orientali del Friuli Rosso** Ronco dei Roseti★★★ £D

ZENATO Veneto www.zenato.it   A: Eur

Owner: Sergio Zenato Via San Benedetto 8, 337019 Peschiera del Garda (VR)
Sergio Zenato established this well-known house in 1960 which though Lugana-based also includes a
significant production from Valpolicella. Whilst the regular cuvées only rarely offer much excitement,
the special bottlings can be very good indeed. As well as vibrant, chewy Ripassa Valpolicella there are
the 'signature' Riserva wines - powerful Amarone and a concentrated Lugana. New is a barrique-aged
and fermented Riserva Chardonnay. Good Lugana (Vigneto Massoni) is also made from the Santa
Cristina estate where production also includes Cabernet Sauvignon, Chardonnay, and sweet white,
Rigoletto made from dried Lugana grapes. La Sansonina is an estate owned by by Carla Prospero, the
wife of Sergio Zenato. The existing Merlot vines were supplementd by further plantings and her first
vintage 1997 (sold in magnums) was 100 per cent Merlot. The 98 adds in Cabernet Sauvignon. This
stylish red is fully ripe and shows a chocolatey, cedary complexity with five years' age or more. (PW)

Zenato
○ **Lugana** Vigneto Massoni★★ £C Riserva Sergio Zenato★★ £C
● **Valpolicella Classico** Superiore★ £B ● **Valpolicella** Superiore Ripassa★★ £C
● **Amarone della Valpolicella Classico**★ £E Riserva Sergio Zenato★★★ £F

La Sansonina
● **Sansonina**★★★ £D

OTHER WINES OF NOTE

IGINO ACCORDINI ● **Amarone della Valpolicella Classico** Le Bessole £E
STEFANO ACCORDINI ● **Amarone della Valpolicella** Acinatico £E
● **Recioto della Valpolicella** Acinatico £E
BASTANICH ○ **Colli Orientali del Friuli** Pinot Plus (Pinot Grigio/Pinot Bianco) £C Tocai Plus £C
○ **Vespa Bianco** (Chardonnay/Sauvignon/Picolit) £C
● **Calabrone** (Refosco/Pignolo/Cabernet Franc/Merlot) £C
BERTANI ● **Amarone della Valpolicella** Classico £F
CARLO BOGONI ○ **Soave Classico** Superiore La Ponsara £B
BRIGALDARA ● **Amarone della Valpolicella** Classico £D
VITICOLTORI CALDARO ○ **Alto Adige** Gewürztraminer Campaner £C
CANTINA DEL CASTELLO ○ **Soave Classico Superiore** £B Pressoni £C
○ **Soave Classico Superiore** Acini Soavi (late-harvested, dry) £D
MICHELE CASTELLANI & FIGLI ● **Amarone della Valpolicella** I Castei Campo Casalin £E
● **Recioto della Valpolicella** I Castei Campo Casalin £D
CORTEFORTE ● **Amarone della Valpolicella** £E ● **Recioto della Valpolicella** Amandorlato £E
DAMIJAN ○ **Collio Bianco** Kaplja (Chardonnay/Malvasia Istriana/Tocai Friulano) £C
○ **Collio** Ribolla Gialla £C ● **Collio Rosso** Prelit (Cabernet Sauvignon/Merlot) £C
PETER DIPOLI ○ **Alto Adige** Sauvignon Voglar £D
MAURO DRIUS ○ **Collio** Pinot Bianco £C Sauvignon £C Tocai Friulano £C
○ **Collio Bianco** Vignis di Siris (Sauvignon/Tocai/Pinot Bianco) £C
ERSTE & NEUE – PRIMA & NUOVA ○ **Alto Adige** Gewürztraminer Puntay £C
FERRARI ○ **Trento** Brut Giulio Ferrari Riserva del Fondatore £C
GINI ○ **Soave Classico** Superiore £B La Froscà £B Contrada Salvarenza Vecchie Vigne £C
○ **Recioto di Soave** Col Foscarin £E Renobilis £E

JOSKO GRAVNER ○ **Collio** Ribolla £F
○ **Collio Bianco** Breg (Sauvignon/Chardonnay/Pinot Grigio/Ribolla) £F
GUERRIERI RIZZARDI ● **Amarone della Valpolicella** £E
EDI KANTE ○ **Carso** Malvasia £C Chardonnay £C Sauvignon £C
LA CAPPUCINA ○ **Soave** Superiore Fontégo £B Superiore San Brizio £C
LA CASTELLADA ○ **Collio** Chardonnay £C Ribolla Gialla £C
○ **Collio Bianco** Bianco della Castellada (Sauvignon/Tocai/Pinot Grigio/Ribolla Gialla) £D
LE RAGOSE ● **Valpolicella Classico** Superiore Le Sassine £B ● **Amarone della Valpolicella** £E
LE VIGNE DI SAN PIETRO ● **Cabernet Sauvignon Refolà** £E
○ **Bianco di Custoza** San Pietro £C ○ **Due Cuori** (sweet – Moscato Giallo) £F
LIS NERIS ○ **Friuli Isonzo** Chardonnay Sant' Jurosa £D Pinot Grigio Gris £C Sauvignon Picol £C
○ **Lis** (Pinot Grigio/Chardonnay/Sauvignon) £C
○ **Confini** (Pinot Grigio/Riesling/Malvasia/Traminer) £D ○ **Tal Lùc** (sweet – Verduzzo) £F
LIVON ○ **Collio** Chardonnay Braide Mate £C Pinot Grigio Braide Grande £C
○ **Braide Alte** (Chardonnay/Sauvignon/Moscato Giallo/Picolit) £C
LOREDAN GASPARINI ● **Capo di Stato** (Cabernets/Merlot/Malbec) £E
LORENZON/I FEUDI DI ROMANS ○ **Friuli Isonzo** Sauvignon Blanc £B Pinot Grigio £B
● **Friuli Isonzo** Merlot £B
MARION ● **Valpolicella Superiore** £D ● **Teroldego** £D
MIANI ○ **Colli Orientali del Friuli** Tocai Friulano £C Sauvignon £C
● **Colli Orientali del Friuli** Merlot £D
ORNELLA MOLON TRAVERSO ○ **Sauvignon** £C ○ **Traminer** £C ● **Piave** Merlot £C
● **Vite Rossa** (Merlot/Cabernets) £C ● **Riserva Rosso di Villa** (Merlot/Cabernet Sauvignon) £D
DAVIDE MOSCHIONI ● **Colli Orientali del Friuli** Pignolo £F Schioppettino £F
MURI-GRIES ○ **Alto Adige** Lagrein Riserva Abtei £D
PIERPAOLO PECORARI ○ **Friuli Isonzo** Chardonnay Soris £C Sauvignon Kolaus £C
● **Friuli Isonzo** Merlot Baolar £D
PRÀ ○ **Soave Classico** Superiore £B Vigneto Monte Grande £B Colle Sant'Antonio £C
PUIATTI ○ **Collio** Sauvignon Ruttars £C ● **Friuli Isonzo** Cabernet Franc Le Zuccole £B
DARIO RACCARO ○ **Collio** Tocai Friulano £C
RONCO DEL GNEMIZ ○ **Colli Orientali del Friuli** Chardonnay £D
RONCO DELLE BETULLE ○ **Colli Orientali del Friuli** Sauvignon £B Tocai Friulano £B
● **Colli Orientali del Friuli** Cabernet Franc £C Franconia £C
RUSSOLO ○ **Pinot Grigio** Ronco Calaj £B ○ **Tocai Friulano** Ronco Calaj £B
○ **Malvasia Istriana** £B ○ **Doi Raps** (Pinot Grigio/Sauvignon/Moscato Giallo) £C
● **Pinot Nero** Grifo Nero £C ● **Borgo di Peuma** (Merlot/Cabernet Franc/Refosco) £C
TENUTA SANT' ANTONIO ● **Amarone della Valpolicella** Campo dei Gigli £E
● **Valpolicella Superiore** La Bandina £C
SERAFINI & VIDOTTO ● **Rosso dell' Abazia** (Cabernet Sauvignon/Cabernet Franc/Merlot) £E
● **Pinot Nero** £E ● **Phigaia After The Red** (Cabernet Franc/Merlot) £C
SPECOGNA ○ **Colli** Orientali del Friuli Tocai £C ○ **Pinot Grigio** £C
SPERI ● **Amarone della Valpolicella** Vigneto Monte Sant'Urbano £E
● **Recioto della Valpolicella** I Communai £E
SUAVIA ○ **Soave Classico** Superiore Monte Carbonare £C Superiore Le Rive £D
○ **Recioto di Soave Classico** Acinatum £F
TAMELLINI ○ **Soave** Superiore £B ○ **Soave Classico** Anguane £B Le Bine £C
CANTINA PRODUTTORI TERMENO ● **Alto Adige** Lagrein Urban £D
○ **Alto Adige** Gewürztraminer Maratsch £C Gewürztraminer Nussbaumer £D
○ **Alto Adige** Pinot Grigio Unterebner £C Sauvignon £C
TIEFENBRUNNER ○ **Feldmarschall Von Fenner** (Müller Thurgau) £D
● **Linticlarus Cuvée** (Lagrein/Cabernet Sauvignon/Merlot) £D
TRABUCCHI ● **Valpolicella Superiore** Terre del Cereolo £C ● **Amarone della Valpolicella** £E
● **Recioto della Valpolicella** £E
VALLAROM ○ **Trentino** Chardonnay Riserva Vigna di Brioni £C
CANTINA VALPANTENA/FALASCO ● **Valpolicella** Valpantena Ripasso £B

● Amarone della Valpolicella £D
C. S. VALPOLICELLA ● Amarone della Valpolicella Domini Veneti £D Vigneti di Jago £E
● Recioto della Valpolicella Domini Veneti £D Vigneti di Moron £E
VILLA MONTELEONE ● Amarone della Valpolicella Classico £E
ELENA WALCH O Alto Adige Gewürztraminer Kastelaz £D Pinot Bianco Kastelaz £C
O Alto Adige Pinot Grigio Castel Ringberg £C Riesling Castel Ringberg £C
VISTORTA ● Merlot £C
ZUANI O Collio Bianco (Tocai/Pinot Grigio/Sauvignon Blanc/Chardonnay) £D Zuani Vigne £C

Author's Choice (PW)

10 premium reds
ALLEGRINI ● La Poja
GIROLAMO DORIGO ● Colli Orientali del Friuli Rosso Montscalapade
LIVIO FELLUGA ● Colli Orientali del Fruili Merlot Riserva Sossò
FORADORI ● Teroldego Rotaliano Granato
HOFSTÄTTER ● Alto Adige Pinot Nero Barthenau Vigna Sant'Urbano
ALOIS LAGEDER ● Alto Adige Cabernet Sauvignon Cor Römigberg
JOSEF NIEDERMAYR ● Alto Adige Lagrein Aus Gries Riserva
RUSSIZ SUPERIORE ● Collio Rosso Riserva degli Orzoni
SAN LEONARDO ● San Leonardo
VIGNALTA ● Gemola

10 superior Valpolicella (or equivalent)
ALLEGRINI ● La Grola
TOMMASO BUSSOLA ● Valpolicella Classico Superiore TB
CORTE SANT'ALDA ● Valpolicella Superiore Mithas
ROMANO DAL FORNO ● Valpolicella Superiore Vigneto di Monte Lodoletta
LE SALETTE ● Valpolicella Classico Superiore Ca' Carnocchio
MARION ● Valpolicella Superiore
QUINTARELLI ● Valpolicella Classico Superiore Monte Ca' Paletta
ROCCOLO GRASSI ● Valpolicella Superiore Roccolo Grassi
TRABUCCHI ● Valpolicella Superiore Terre di Cereolo
ZENATO ● Valpolicella Superiore Ripassa

10 reds for meditation
ALLEGRINI ● Amarone della Valpolicella Classico
TOMMASO BUSSOLA ● Recioto della Valpolicella Classico TB
MICHELE CASTELLANI ● Amarone della Valpolicella Classico Campo Casalin I Castei
CORTE SANT'ALDA ● Recioto della Valpolicella
LE SALETTE ● Amarone della Valpolicella Classico Pergole Vece
QUINTARELLI ● Amarone della Valpolicella Classico Monte Ca' Paletta
SPERI ● Amarone della Valpolicella Classico Vigneto Monte Sant' Urbano
TENUTA SANT' ANTONIO ● Amarone della Valpolicella Campo dei Gigli
TEDESCHI ● Amarone della Valpolicella Classico Capitel Monte Olmi
ZENATO ● Amarone della Valpolicella Classico Riserva Sergio Zenato

20 first class whites
BORGO DEL TIGLIO O Collio Bianco Studio di Bianco
CA' DEI FRATI O Pratto
CESCONI O Trentino Chardonnay
COLTERENZIO O Alto Adige Chardonnay Cornell

LIVIO FELLUGA O Colli Orientali del Fruili Rosazzo Bianco Terre Alte
FRANZ HAAS O Manna
HOFSTÄTTER O Alto Adige Gewürztraminer Kolbenhof Söll
IL CARPINO O Collio Chardonnay
VINNAIOLI JERMANN O Vintage Tunina
PIEROPAN O Soave Classico Superiore La Rocca
POJER & SANDRI O Faye
RONCHI DI MANZANO O Colli Orientali del Friuli Rosazzo Bianco Ronc di Rosazzo
RUSSIZ SUPERIORE O Collio Bianco Russiz Disôre
PRODUTTORI SAN MICHELE APPIANO O Alto Adige Gewürztraminer Sanct Valentin
SCHIOPETTO O Collio Pinot Bianco Amrità
MATIJAZ TERCIC O Collio Bianco Planta
CANTINA TERLANO O Alto Adige Sauvignon Quarz
VIE DI ROMANS O Friuli Isonzo Chardonnay Vie di Romans
VILLA RUSSIZ O Collio Sauvignon de la Tour
LE VIGNE DI ZAMÒ O Colli Orientali del Friuli Tocai Friulano Vigne Cinquant'Anni

6 fine sweet whites
ANSELMI O I Capitelli
GIROLAMO DORIGO O Colli Orientali del Friuli Picolit Vigneto Montscalapade
MACULAN O Breganze Torcolato
PIEROPAN O Passito della Rocca
POJER & SANDRI O Essenzia
PRODUTTORI SAN MICHELE APPIANO O Alto Adige Bianco Passito Comtess' Sanct Valentin

Central Italy

Just as culturally there is so much to be discovered just beyond the bounds of Tuscany so it is when it comes to viticulturally derived masterpieces. This is not a section of also-rans but includes exciting top-quality producers – some working in a Tuscan vein but with much more to offer besides. Away from those famous appellations can be found an increasing number of fine reds from not only from the likes of Sangiovese, Sagrantino and Montepulciano, native in these diverse regions, but also Cabernet Sauvignon and Merlot, as well as stylish whites from Verdicchio.

The regions of Central Italy

Emilia-Romagna

Emilia has, besides **Lambrusco** (with four DOC zones of its own), two significant DOCs for hillsides to the south of the cities of Piacenza and Bologna. Both the **Colli Piacentini** (contiguous with Lombardy's Oltrepò Pavese) and **Colli Bolognesi** can produce decent Cabernet Sauvignon and Barbera as well as Chardonnay, Sauvignon and Malvasia. **Gutturnio** is a speciality of the former, a blend of Barbera and Bonarda of good character and quality from a handful of producers. Much more exciting in viticulture terms is Romagna, where the best Sangioveses outside Tuscany are now produced. Though much **Sangiovese di Romagna** is pretty basic, the best examples have depth, intensity and excellent texture and concentration where there is denser planting and lower yields. Top producers also make good wines from Chardonnay, Cabernet Sauvignon and other imports. Both a slightly nutty, dry and a sweet version of **Albana di Romagna** are made; the latter, as *passito*, made from dried grapes, is usually far superior.

Marche

the region is best-known for **Verdicchio dei Castelli di Jesi** and both the wines from this zone and the more inland **Verdicchio di Matelica** show increasing concentration, structure and style from a top producer. Late-harvested, *passito* (from dried grapes) and sparkling versions highlight the grape's versatility, although most of the best are dry and subtly oaked. With odd exceptions, **Falerio di Colli Ascolani** tends to be much more ordinary, its blend usually dominated by the boring Trebbiano. The Marche's best red is **Rosso Conero**, an often spicy, sturdy red based on the Montepulciano grape. Produced from a wider zone, there are fewer good examples of **Rosso Piceno**, which incorporates a greater percentage of Sangiovese. Foreign varieties or unusual blends tend to be sold under the region-wide Marche IGT.

Umbria

Sangiovese is the leading red variety in Umbria and the regular red from region's most important zone, Montefalco is based on it. **Montefalco Rosso** also includes a small percentage of Sagrantino and in the very best examples offers a characterful alternative to similarly priced Chianti or other Tuscan equivalents. Other Sangiovese-based appellations include **Colli Amerini** and **Colli del Trasimeno,** though both are becoming better known for rich, ripe, modern reds based on Cabernet Sauvignon and/or Merlot. The best wine from Montefalco is **Sagrantino di Montefalco**, from a grape that gives remarkable colour, extract, acid and alcohol. It needs careful vinification but at best produces an intense, concentrated, powerful yet original Italian red and the small plantings are on the increase. Sweet versions from dried grapes are labelled *passito*. **Colli Martani,** a much more extensive zone lying mostly to the west of Montefalco, can produce attractive whites from Grechetto. South of Perugia is the small zone of **Torgiano** (DOCG for a Riserva version) for reds based on Sangiovese but also including Canaiolo and Ciliegiolo. The Lungarotti reds responsible for its status are not currently making the most of their their potential.

Lazio

The most important appellation in Lazio is now the regional IGT. Whether from the border with Umbria and Tuscany, the coast (Cerveteri) or the Colli Albani (Alban hills) many new wines are appearing. The majority are reds made from Cabernet Sauvignon and/or Merlot, though Sangiovese occasionally forms the main component. The established DOCs of **Est! Est!! Est!!!**, **Orvieto** (shared with Umbria) and **Frascati** are for the most part all based on the Trebbiano grape and offer little in terms of serious quality, but there are some reasonable examples of each and some good, late-harvested sweet styles. Frascati based on Malvasia tends to be much better.

Abruzzo & Molise

Abruzzo has two region-wide DOCs and most wines are either **Montepulciano d'Abruzzo**, if red, or **Trebbiano d'Abruzzo**, if white. There are an increasing number of good examples of the red; characterful, peppery, if not that refined (Valentini's excepted), but a source of good value. Decent examples of other varietals and blends can appear under the **Controguerra** DOC. In Molise, **Biferno** was until recently its one important DOC. Like the reds of Abruzzo it is based on Montepulciano but additionally includes some Aglianico. The white is similar to Trebbiano d'Abruzzo. Newly created is a region-wide **Molise** DOC including essentially varietal examples of Aglianico, Montepulciano, Falanghina, Greco and Moscato, given life by its one important producer, Di Majo Norante.

A-Z of Producers by region

Abruzzo
PODERE CASTORANI
ANTONIO & ELIO MONTI
VALENTINI

Lazio
FALESCO

Marche
BOCCADIGABBIA
CORONCINO
GAROFOLI
LA MONACESCA
LE TERRAZZE
FATTORIA MANCINI
OASI DEGLI ANGELI
SARTARELLI
UMANI RONCHI

Molise
DI MAJO NORANTE

Romagna
STEFANO BERTI
CASTELLUCCIO
DREI DONÀ - LA PALAZZA
SAN PATRIGNANO
ZERBINA

Umbria
ARNALDO CAPRAI
CASTELLO DELLA SALA
LA FIORITA LAMBORGHINI
PIEVE DEL VESCOVO
SPORTOLETTI

STEFANO BERTI Romagna

Owner: Stefano Berti Loc. Ravaldino in Monte, Via La Scagna 18, 47100 Forlì
Stefano Berti has only been making his own wine since 2000 but in the 2001 Calisto in particular, has made a Sangiovese di Romagna of such character and intensity as to add further proof of the quality possible from this zone. Winemaking help is provided by Leonardo Conti of the Attilo Pagli - Alberto Antonini consultancy team. Fruit comes from both older vines and newer plantings but easily absorbs the 12 months in new oak the wine is given. The wine has drive, intensity and a stylish mineral, herb and black fruits complexity. If there is not yet the extra breadth of the very best examples, future vintages should add it. Quantities are small if increasing. Not made in 2002, a second red, Ravaldo which is only partially barrique-aged benefitted from the inclusion of the grapes instead. This too, has plenty of style and appeal. (PW)
● **Sangiovese di Romagna Superiore** Ravaldo★★ £C Calisto★★★ £D

BOCCADIGABBIA Marche www.boccadigabbia.com   A: L&S

Owner: Elvidio Alessandri Contrada Castelletta 56, 62012 Civitanova Marche (MC)
There is not one but two estates here, the 12-ha Boccadigabbia estate and the more recently acquired 18-ha Villamagna estate. Under the extremely competent winemaking of Fabrizio Ciufoli, both produce some of the best Rosso Piceno going. Boccadigabbia's single-vineyard Saltapicchio (previously sold as Rosso Piceno) now, like most of the other wines, appears under the Marche IGT. It shows some herbs, smoke and cherry fruit together with good acidity and well-balanced tannin. The Rosso Piceno from Villamagna is a little more fleshy. A white, Monsanulus from Villamagna, is based on Verdicchio. French varieties have been planted at Boccadigabbia since the early 19th century (introduced when the region was under Napoleonic rule), so foreign varieties are no recent sell-out. Their quality is of a high standard, too – all the wines show ripe fruit and some oak influence but with good balance. Pinot Grigio, with ripe citrus, pear and spicy notes, is a rare good example outside North-East Italy but the best wine is a stylish, powerful but elegant, pure blackcurrant-fruited Cabernet Sauvignon that has few rivals outside Tuscany. New is a varietal Merlot called Pix. (PW)

Boccadigabbia
● **Akronte★★★** £D ● **Pinot Nero Il Girone★** £D
● **Rosso Piceno★** £B ● **Sangiovese Saltapicchio★★** £C
O **Chardonnay Montalperti★★** £C O **Pinot Grigio La Castelletta★★** £B
Villamagna
● **Rosso Piceno★★** £C O **Monsanulus★** £C

ARNALDO CAPRAI Umbria www.arnaldocaprai.it   A: JAr

Owner: Arnaldo Caprai Val di Maggio, Loc. Torre, 06036 Montefalco (PG)
This modern powerhouse operation has brought the small Montefalco zone and its Sagrantino grape wide recognition both within Italy and on foreign markets. Since the late 1980s the winery, vineyards (90 ha in production) and the wines have been transformed under Marco Caprai (Arnaldo's son) and his winemaking consultant Attilio Pagli. The leading Sagrantino wines are extremely concentrated, powerful and structured wines, not wines for early drinking but are complex and demanding, needing at least seven to ten years' age. The Sagrantino 25 Anni is an Italian classic, utterly compelling with terrific aromatic complexity, and superb texture and dimension in the mouth. An unusual sweet (*passito*) version is very intense, with much of the wild berry character of Sagrantino but a certain finesse too. Montefalco Rosso Riserva, in contrast, is based on Sangiovese (70 per cent) with the balance from Sagrantino and Merlot. Subject to a long maceration, this shows

in the wine's breadth and rich texture. Lesser wines are also very good, including a stylish, intense regular Montefalco Rosso and a fresh citrusy white from Grechetto. Montefalco Bianco combines Chardonnay, Trebbiano and Sauvignon with Grechetto. There are ongoing experiments with other varieties including international ones such as Syrah and Malbec. A Pinot Nero, Nero Outsider, was produced from the 1998 vintage and sold exclusively over the internet. New and most accessible of all the reds is Poggio Belvedere, an unoaked blend of Sangiovese and Ciliegiolo (80/20). (PW)

● **Sagrantino di Montefalco** Colle Piano★★★★ £E 25 Anni✪✪✪✪✪ £F Passito★★★£F
● **Montefalco Rosso**★★ £C Riserva★★★ £D
○ **Grechetto dei Colli Martini** Grecante★★ £B   ○ **Montefalco Bianco**★ £B

CASTELLO DELLA SALA   Umbria   www.antinori.it   A: BWC

Owner: Antinori   Loc. Sala, 05016 Ficulle (TR)

The Castello della Sala is a major outpost of the ANTINORI family, with 160 ha in the vicinity of the 14th-century castle after which the estate is named. It was acquired by Niccolò Antinori (father of Piero) in 1940. The principal wine, Cervaro della Sala, has an established track record as one of Italy's best Chardonnays, with a refinement missing from most of the bigger, concentrated examples. As much as 20 per cent of the wine is Grechetto but its relative propensity to age also sets it apart from others. A second selection is sold as Chardonnay under the Umbria IGT as are a Sauvignon Blanc and a Pinot Nero. Muffato della Sala is an oak-aged, botrytised sweet wine of moderate richness and good sweetness made from varying percentages of Sauvignon, Grechetto, Gewürztraminer and Riesling. Orvieto is made in three versions: Superiore, Campogrande and an *amabile* (medium-dry) version, Casasole. (PW)

○ **Cervaro della Sala**★★★ £E
○ **Chardonnay**★★ £C   ○ **Sauvignon**★ £C   ● **Pinot Nero**★★ £E
○ **Muffato della Sala**★★ £E   ○ **Orvieto** Classico Superiore★ £B

CASTELLUCCIO   Romagna   www.ronchidicastelluccio.it   A: Bal

Owner: Vittorio, Ermanno & Gian Michele Fiore   Via Tramonto 15, 47015 Modigliana (FC)

This was the first estate in Romagna to undertake changes to prove Sangiovese from Romagna could compete with top examples from Tuscany. Renowned Tuscan consultant Vittorio Fiore (POGGIO SCALETTE), already involved with making the wines to a standard not previously associated with Romagna, bought into the 16-ha estate in 1999. The wines, made by Vittorio's son, Claudio used to be sold as vino da tavola in order to distance them from the lowly perception of the Sangiovese di Romagna DOC but most are now sold under the Forlì IGT. As well as revamping the winemaking efforts, single *crus* – Ronco delle Ciliegi and Ronco delle Ginestre – were planted as long ago as 1975 to high-quality clones at a higher density and continue to be improved by the viticulturalist, Remigio Bordini. A third *cru*, Ronco della Simia, was also made until very recently but there are now just the two original *crus*. Ciliegi shows more class and elegance than an increasingly rich-fruited and good-value Sangiovese di Romagna, Le More. Ginestre, the top wine, comes from a 2-ha site and adds more weight, power and complexity. Sauvignon Blanc is the other variety of choice, Lunaria is a very distinctive mineral and very ripe citrus example that is partially barrel-fermented, resulting in a gentle leesy influence. Though not classically varietal, it can be more convincing than the richer, more 'barriqued' Ronco del Re. All the reds need at least two or three years to get going, the *crus* are best with five or more. Whites can be drunk young but don't fall apart if kept for a year or two. (PW)

● **Sangiovese di Romagna** Le More★★ £B
● **Ronco dei Ciliegi**★★★ £C   ● **Ronco delle Ginestre**★★★ £D
○ **Lunaria**★★£B   ○ **Ronco del Re**★★ £D

PODERE CASTORANI Abruzzo   A:Eno

Owner: B Cavuto, L Cavuto, L Petricelli & E Trulli   Contrada Oratorio 1, 65020 Alanno
First-rate Montepulciano d'Abruzzo is a relatively rare beast but this new partnership promises something special. The name has a ring of motor racing about it and the owners include Formula One
racing driver Jarno Trulli's father and his manager. Also on board is expert viticulturalist Bruno
Cavuto who oversees the estate's 30 ha of well-established vines. The wines are made by the fourth
partner, Luca Petricelli whose experience includes winemaking in Bordeaux and Spain. A very good
2000, beautifully made with concentrated black cherry and spice, has been followed by an even more
convincing 2001. Rich and deep with lots of Montepulciano flesh and individuality, it shows just
what is possible with a good site and the right know-how in Abruzzo. One to follow. (PW)
● **Montepulciano d'Abruzzo**★★★ £E

CORONCINO Marche   A: Mgi, L&W

Owner: Lucio Canestrari & Fiorella De Nardo   Contrada Coroncino 7, 60039 Staffolo (AN)
A better Verdicchio than Coroncino's Gaiospino is hard to find. The husband and wife team started
out in 1982 and have just 7 ha of vineyards. Gaiospino is sourced from the best vineyard, Spescia – a
steep 2.7-ha site – and part is fermented and aged in double-sized barriques. Though high in alcohol,
the wine has a gentle pear and quince fruit intensity, definition and style that belie its body. A Fumé
version was also made in 1998. A second Verdicchio, Il Coroncino, comes from vineyards around the
winery and if less refined has good fruit richness. Two other well-made Verdicchios are also produced:
Bacco and Staffilo. (PW)
O **Verdicchio dei Castelli di Jesi Classico** Superiore Il Coroncino★★ £B Gaiospino★★★ £C
O **Verdicchio dei Castelli di Jesi Classico** Bacco★ £B Staffilo★ £B

DI MAJO NORANTE Molise   A: L&S

Owner: Di Majo Norante family   Contrada Ramitelli 4, 86042 Campomarino (CB)
Alessio Di Majo's 60 ha estate is essentially organic and has been Molise's one really notable producer
for more than a decade. Yet only more recently, since the input of consultant Riccardo Cotarella, has
there been real consistency and a further increase in quality across the range. Reds are now led by a
premium example of greater breadth and intensity than previously seen. Don Luigi comes from 90
per cent Montepulciano with the balance from Tintilia and is a rich, oaky cuvée - just occasionally
a little overdone. The long-established blend Ramitello Rosso is produced from Sangiovese and
Aglianico and is ripe, balanced and characterful. Contado shows plenty of Aglianico fruit and style
if not yet the depth and structure synonymous with the best examples of this grape while another
varietal, from Sangiovese, needs a little more refinement. Whites are ripe, clean with plenty of fruit:
a Greco has dried peach, apricot and spice if modest structure while the partially oaked, lightly
creamy Biblos from Falanghina and Greco (70/30) remedies this deficiency if slightly to the cost of
its character. Don Luigi excepted, the wines continue to be well-priced for the fruit and character
they deliver. (PW)
● **Molise** Don Luigi★★★ £D Aglianico Contado★★ £B   ● **Biferno Rosso** Ramitello★★ £B
● **Sangiovese**★ £B   O **Greco**★★ £B   O **Biblos**★★ £B

DREI DONÀ - LA PALAZZA Romagna

Owner: Claudio Drei Donà   Loc. Massa di Vecchiazzano, Via del Tesoro 23, 47100 Forlì
Claudio Drei Donà together with his son, Enrico, and Tuscan consultant Franco Bernabei make a

small but very competent range of wines from 27 ha of vineyards. Pruno, the best if not the most expensive wine, is made from the oldest part of a single vineyard. Notturno, Sangiovese from younger vines, is effectively the second wine and reveals plenty of very attractive plum and cherry fruit. Magnificat is varietal Cabernet Sauvignon with plenty of substance and style and a chocolaty-coffee complexity from a vineyard planted in the late 1980s. Graf Noir is a rich, characterful blend of Sangiovese, Cabernet Sauvignon, Cabernet Franc and Negretto Longanesi, while Il Tornese is Chardonnay aged in double-sized barriques and large wood and, although it is intense and ripe, the leesy aspect is slightly overdone. (PW)

● **Sangiovese di Romagna** Superiore Riserva Pruno★★★ £D   ● **Notturno Sangiovese**★★ £B
● **Magnificat**★★★ £E   ● **Graf Noir**★★★ £F   O Il **Tornese**★ £C

FALESCO   Lazio   A: BWC, Res, N&P

Owner: Renzo & Riccardo Cotarella   S S Cassia Km 94, 155, 01027 Montefiascone (VT)
This substantial 250-ha estate on the Lazio/Umbria border belongs to two of Italy's most famous winemaker brothers. Renzo Cotarella, ANTINORI's winemaker, and the widely consulted enologist Riccardo Cotarella. The local appellation is the normally nondescript Est! Est!! Est!!! but Poggio dei Gelsi is a bright, perfumed and fruity white of some style. It is also made in a late-harvest version while a good, characterful if oaky, dry white is made from one of the local grapes, Roscetto. There is also an attractive Grechetto. But it is the reds have caused the most interest (especially in the US). Montiano is a high-quality, showy Merlot which has that combination of lush new oak and very rich succulent fruit that instantly seduces many wine lovers. The 1999 was more profound and structured but can be drunk fairly young or with five years' age or more. At a more affordable level is a 'second' richly fruity Merlot and Vitiano, a blend of Cabernet Sauvignon, Merlot and Sangiovese made in large quantities. Marciliano is a new (from 1999) Cabernet Sauvignon as yet produced only in very small quantities. (PW)

● **Montiano**★★★★ £E
● **Merlot**★★ £C   ● **Vitiano**★ £B
O **Est! Est!! Est!!!** Poggio dei Gelsi★★ £B   Poggio dei Gelsi Vendemmia Tardiva★★ £D

GAROFOLI   Marche   www.garofolivini.it   A: Hal

Owner: Garofoli family   Via Arno 9, 60025 Loreto (AN)
Fourth-generation Carlo and Gianfranco Garofoli now head this family firm which was founded in 1871 and has been making wines for over a century. They focus on producing top-quality Verdicchio from low yields. Serra Fiorese is a Riserva aged in oak and can show considerably richness and depth with three or four years' age, but the best Verdicchio is the unoaked Podium, with lovely breadth, weight and a refinement only seen in a handful of examples. A *passito* version from dried grapes, Le Brume, is also made as is sparkling wine from Verdicchio. Of some well-made reds the Grosso Agontano, 100 per cent Montepulciano and aged in barriques for 12 months, particularly impresses for its breadth and complexity and should be drunk with five years' age or more. All the wines, but particularly the whites, are very well-priced for the quality. (PW)

O **Verdicchio dei Castelli di Jesi Classico** Superiore Macrina★★ £B   Podium★★★ £B
O **Verdicchio dei Castelli di Jesi Classico** Riserva Serra Fiorese★★★ £C
● **Rosso Conero** Vigna Piancarda★ £B   Riserva Grosso Agontano★★★ £D
● **Rosso Piceno** Colle Ambro★ £B

LA FIORITA LAMBORGHINI Umbria www.lamborghini.cc   A: SCh

Owner: Patrizia Lamborghini Loc. Soderi 1, 06064 Panicale (PG)

A pair of very good reds are made at this beautiful estate at the southern end of Lago Trasimeno purchased by Ferruccio Lamborghini (Patrizia's father) in 1971. Riccardo Cotarella (see FALESCO) has made the wines in recent vintages – the 1999s and 2000s are a further improvement on his highly acclaimed but overhyped 1997s. Campoleone, an equal blend of Sangiovese and Merlot, is the more international of the two reds but shows terrific intensity, powerful new oak and crushed small-berry fruit within a vibrant structure. It is a wine of great potential if not originality. The second wine, Trescone, is sleek and an intense blend of Sangiovese, Ciliegiolo and Merlot (50/30/20) with distinctive plum and cherry fruit. Both reds are subject to a long maceration. Trescone is aged in large wood as against the one year's ageing in new barriques that the Campoleone receives. Trescone needs at least three years' ageing in bottle, Campoleone twice that. Both are sold under the Umbria IGT. (PW)

● **Campoleone★★★★** £F ● **Trescone★★** £C

LA MONACESCA Marche   A: Wtr

Owner: Casimiro Cifola Contrada Monacesca, 62012 Matelica (MC)

La Monacesca is located in Matelica, the smaller, lesser known of Marche's two Verdicchio zones. Ripe and concentrated Verdicchio with good depth and character are produced from 27 ha of high vineyards (400 m). The superior bottling, gently nutty and buttery with spice, citrus and a minerally quality, shows greater refinement and definition than a well-made regular version. The top white, Mirum, is produced from late-harvested grapes, including a little Chardonnay and Sauvignon Blanc. All three can be drunk young but, though unoaked, keep well. An increasingly good red from Sangiovese and Merlot, Camerte, is also made, as is a varietal Chardonnay, Ecclesia. (PW)

O **Verdicchio di Matelica★★** £B La Monacesca★★ £B O **Mirum★★★** £C
● **Camerte★★★** £D

LE TERRAZZE Marche   A: Fie

Owner: Antonio Terni Via Musone 4, 60026 Numana (AN)

To rhythms of Bob Dylan, the laid-back Antonio Terni is steadily building production towards 10,000 cases of wine a year. Under the winemaking expertise of Attilio Pagli, Rosso Conero (from 100 per cent Montepulciano) shows better ripeness and richness than is usually encountered in this relatively modest appellation. The Sassi Neri, in particular, with an extended maceration (three weeks) and a year in barriques (a third new) shows both real depth and succulence as well as elegance with three years' age or more. Chaos is a lush, black-fruited blend of Montepulciano (50 per cent), Syrah and Merlot aged in new oak. Visions of J, which rapidly sold out from the 1997 vintage, is made when conditions are most favourable. A little Chardonnay, Le Cave, is also made. (PW)

● **Rosso Conero★** £B Sassi Neri★★★ £D
● **Chaos★★★** £E

FATTORIA MANCINI Marche www.fattoriamancini.com   A: BWC, P&S, Vts

Owner: Mancini family Strada dei Colli 35, 61100 Pesaro (MC)

Luigi Mancini has got all sorts of weird things going on here, but the intent and results deserve to be taken seriously. From slopes high above the rim of the Adriatic, Pinot Nero, which came with Napoleon's troops nearly 200 years ago, is the grape of choice. From it is made a white wine of exotic, almost decadent fruit character, vaguely similar to an over-the-top Alsace Pinot Gris. In a second white, the unoaked Roncaglia, Pinot Nero is again vinified as a white wine where it complements Albanella, a little-known variety said to have Albariño as a parent – though of modest structure, it is full of ripe nectarine and exotic fruits. The best Pinot however is kept for three reds. Impero Rosso has rather old-fashioned Burgundian flavours without the finesse of which Pinot is capable but there's no disputing the character and complexity of these ripe, meaty but well-balanced examples. A 2001 Riserva shows more oak as well as a lot of extract and intensity and should be put aside for at least five more years. Blu, previously half Pinot Nero and half Ancellotto, now includes a little Montepulciano. This powerful black-fruited wine also needs time but shows great promise. Sangiovese is also made. (PW)

● **Blu★★★** £D ● **Colli Pesaresi Focara Pinot Nero Impero★★★** £D
O **Colli Pesaresi** Roncaglia★★ £B O **Pinot Nero Impero Bianco★★** £B

ANTONIO & ELIO MONTI Abruzzo

Owner: Antonio & Elio Monti Contrada Pignotto 62, 64010 Controguerra (TE)
This small operation draws from 15 ha of vineyards to make around 7000 cases of wine each year. With something of a reputation for powerful, structured if somewhat rustic reds, recently there has been input from Riccardo Cotarella and the wines show more oak influence but also more vigour and fruit purity without sacrificing their marvellous complexity and flavour expression. The single vineyard Pignotto of which only 11,000 bottles are made is potentially an outstanding wine. Following a very long maceration, it is aged in French barriques. Wonderfully complex with earth, coffee, wild herbs, oak spice, plum and other black fruits, it also powerful and extracted. There is good integration between fruit and structure but it does demand ten years' ageing from all but the most masochistic of drinkers of such big reds. A little white is also made. Beyond a decent Trebbiano d'Abruzzo, Dorato del Sole, there's Raggio di Luna, a characterful white in which Chardonnay is added to Trebbiano and some local varieties. Cerasuolo (Montepulciano vinified as a white) has more the colour of a light red rather than a rosé and has pretty fruit. (PW)

● **Montepulciano d'Abruzzo★★★** £C Pignotto★★★★ £E
O **Controguerra** Raggio di Luna★ £B

OASI DEGLI ANGELI Marche www.kurni.it   A: Wtr, PaV, BBR, F&R

Owner: Eleonora Rossi Contrada Sant' Egidio 50, 63012 Cupra Marittima (AP)
Marco Casolanetti and Eleonora Rossi produce just one very sought after wine. Kurni was first made in 1997 (a white from Trebbiano, Esedra was also made in the first two vintages) and can be a powerful, very complex expression of the Montepulciano grape. Winemaker Giovanni Basso takes a rigorous approach to quality both in the vineyard and cellar which along with the tiny production has fuelled the wine's cult status. Due to some variability in the most recent vintages, a rating will be given only after further more consistent scores are obtained. Production, currently less than 5000 bottles, is slowly increasing, though despite relatively high prices (£F), seems unlikely to ever satisfy the demand for it. (PW)

PIEVE DEL VESCOVO Umbria

*Owner: **Pieve del Vescovo srl** Via G Leopardi 82, 06073 Corciano (PG)*
Two very good wines are now made on this estate named for the 14th century Castello di Pieve di Vescovo. Much of the vineyard area (22 ha of 120 ha estate) has recently been replanted, particularly that used to make the premium red, Lucciaio. A blend of roughly equal parts Merlot and Cabernet

Sauvignon with 15 per cent Sangiovese (in 2000), it is aged for 12 months in barrique, a third new. It shows both substance and style with good terroir expression but needs time to harmonise its structure. Piovano by contrast is based on Sangiovese complemented by Canaiolo and Ciliegiolo and shows excellent, stylish fruit character but promises to be very appealing with three to four years' age.(PW)

● **Colli del Trasimeno** Piovano★★ £B   ● **Lucciaio**★★★ £D

SAN PATRIGNANO   Romagna   www.sanpatrignano.org   A: LaC

Owner: Cooperativa San Patrignano   Loc. Ospedaletto, Via San Patrignano 53, 47852 Coriano (RN)
This remarkable community, founded by Vincenzo Muccioli and now run by his son, Andrea, is a centre of drug and social rehabilitation near Rimini. Part of the international Rainbow network, it is financed through private donations and activities such as wine production, where it is fortunate to have the services of Riccardo Cotarella (see FALESCO). The wines are very good indeed, from mostly older vineyards, but new vineyards are coming on stream and a total of 100 ha is planned, half of it planted to Sangiovese. The top wine, Sangiovese di Romagna Riserva Avi, is bottled with a different label every year. The four-star 1999 comes from new vineyards that are more densely planted to higher-quality clones. It is very concentrated, dense and structured but with a sleek and elegant texture and shows great promise. Also impressive is a second Riserva, Zarricante, which is aged in a mixture of old and new oak. A regular version, Aulente, spends eight months in large wood and exhibits lovely pure cherry fruit and good depth. All three wines need time, three years for Aulente, at least five for the Riservas. A classy Bordeaux blend Montepirolo is also made and combines Cabernet Sauvignon (50 per cent), Merlot (30), Cabernet Franc (15) and Petit Verdot (5). Structured but concentrated with great length, it has great promise but needs five years or more. (PW)

● **Sangiovese di Romagna** Aulente★★ £C   Riserva Zarricante★★★ £D   Riserva Avi★★★ £E
● **Montepirolo**★★★ £E

SARTARELLI   Marche   www.sartarelli.it   A: Ast, P&S, UnC

Owner: D. Sartarelli & C. Pozzi   Via Coste del Mulino 24, 60030 Poggio San Marcello (AN)
This 51 ha estate is one of the best sources in the Marche for ripe, flavoursome Verdicchio. The regular example is typically bright, fresh and fruit-driven with ripe apple, floral and yellow plum flavours. Tralivio is partially barrique-aged resulting in a richer texture but more of a leesy influence and less refinement and fruit purity but is better with at least three years' age. The Contrada Balciana which has a year in barrique, can start out a little awkwardly too but has good intensity and lots of depth and character though still seems to miss a little refinement that would ensure a higher rating. (PW)

O **Verdicchio dei Castelli di Jesi Classico**★★ £B   Tralivio★★ £C   Contrada Balciana★★ £D

SPORTOLETTI   Umbria   www.sportoletti.com   A: L&S

Owner: Ernesto & Remo Sportoletti   Via Lombardia 1, Capitanloreto, 06038 Spello (PG)
One of the best of a new wave of producers in Umbria and Lazio, many of whom have been helped by Riccardo Cotarella in producing high-quality reds. Brothers Ernesto and Remo have 20 ha of vines at around 400 m on the hills of Spello and Assisi in central-eastern Umbria (north of Montefalco) within a new Assisi DOC. The leading red is an oak-aged blend of Merlot with Cabernet Sauvignon and Cabernet Franc (typically 70/20/10) from 4 ha of vineyards and shows all the richness, depth and concentrated fruit of the best Cotarella reds. A second red, Assisi Rosso (Merlot/Sangiovese) is ripe and plummy with a typical lush, supple 'Cotarella' mouthfeel and is intense and stylish, particularly

for what can be a rather boring blend. Villa Fidelia Bianco is an increasingly good white, an oak-aged blend of Chardonnay and Grechetto while the texture of a varietal skin-contacted Grechetto has been subtly enhanced by oak. New is a Pinot Nero, Vallegloria. (PW)

● **Villa Fidelia Rosso**★★★★ £E   ● **Assisi** Rosso★★ £B
O **Villa Fidelia Bianco**★★ £C   O **Assisi** Grechetto Vigna della Maestà★ £B

UMANI RONCHI   Marche   www.umanironchi.it   A: Eno, Vne, Vts

Owner: Bianchi Bernetti family   S.S 16 Km 310+400, 60027 Osimo (AN)
Despite being a big volume producer in its more basic brands, in its best wines Umani Ronchi offers a good quality introduction to the wines from the central Adriatic coast. These include good Verdicchio, both stainless steel fermented examples, Villa Bianchi and single vineyard Casal di Serra, and a partially oak-aged and fermented version in the Riserva Plenio. Verdicchio is also combined with Chardonnay in the oak-aged Le Busche. Reds from the Montepulciano grape show good character too, especially in Rosso Conero San Lorenzo and Cúmaro. In Pelago the flagship wine, a richer, oakier red, Montepulciano has been successfully combined with Cabernet Sauvignon and Merlot (typically 50/40/10). Yet despite a pretty good record for consistency and flavour there's not quite the value for money of old. The wines can also sometimes lack for balance and definition. As well made as they can be, it seems there should be more life and intensity to most of the range. Among other wines made are a varietal Sangiovese, Medoro, and a sweet white from botrytised Sauvignon grapes, Maximo. (PW)

O **Verdicchio dei Castelli di Jesi** Casla di Serra★ £B Riserva Plenio★★ £C   O **Le Busche**★ £C
● **Rosso Conero** San Lorenzo★ £B Cúmaro★★ £C   ● **Pelago**★★★ £E
● **Montepulciano d'Abruzzo** Jorio★ £B

VALENTINI   Abruzzo   A: Wtr

Owner: Edoardo & Francesco Paolo Valentini   Via del Baio 2, 65014 Loreto Aprutino (PE)
The Valentinis, father and son, offer one of the great alternatives to the modern school of winemaking. The greatest care goes into producing high-quality fruit from *tendone* trained vines planted at low densities. From a total of 64 ha of vines, only a small quantity is released under Valentini's distinctive label. Much of the wine is sold off in bulk and if it is not up to standard then no wine is produced at all. There is no temperature control, only large old wood, and no fining or filtration, After the wine is bottled it is kept until it is considered ready to drink. At it's best, the red (100 per cent Montepulciano) is a wine of great power and dimension that slowly releases it's complex aromas and flavours that include dried flowers, cedar, coffee, spice, pepper and berry fruit. It is best with around a decade's age and recent good vintages include 1995, 92, 90, 88 and 85. The white from Trebbiano shows a subtle range of floral, herbal and fruit-derived scents but is more notable for its texture than its depth or richness. Some pink Cerasuolo is also made. (PW)

● **Montepulciano d'Abruzzo**★★★★ £F   O **Trebbiano d'Abruzzo**★★★ £F

ZERBINA   Romagna   www.zerbina.com   A: Mgi

Owner: Germiniani family   Loc. Marzeno, Via Vicchio 11, 48010 Faenza (RA)
If wine lovers have heard of one estate in Romagna it is probably Zerbina, and with good reason. The 40-ha estate is brilliantly run by Cristina Geminiani who has been able to call on the advice of consultant winemaker, Vittorio Fiore, over the years. The standard of the wines has become ever higher in recent vintages. The top wine, Pietramora, from a single vineyard of old vines, shows an extra level of richness and dimension since 1997. Torre di Ceparano comes from more densely planted

alberello (bush-trained) vines and is beginning to gain weight as the vines age. The greatest part of the Sangiovese production comes in the shape of the unoaked Ceregio, a supple, fruity, earlier-drinking example. Cabernet Sauvignon is added to Sangiovese in Marzieno, rounder than Pietramora but with not quite the same style. Scacco Matto is an excellent rich, concentrated botrytised sweet wine, remarkable given how ordinary the Albana grape usually is when made as a dry wine. Arrocco is a lighter version made from second choice fruit or in lesser vintages. An attractive, partly oak-fermented and aged dry white, Tergeno, is made from (mostly) Chardonnay with a little Sauvignon Blanc. (PW)

● **Sangiovese di Romagna Superiore** Ceregio★ £B Torre di Ceparano★★ £C Riserva Pietramora★★★★ £E
● **Marzieno★★★** £E ○ **Tergeno★★** £C
○ **Albana di Romagna** Passito Arrocco★ £D Scacco Matto★★★ £F

OTHER WINES OF NOTE

ADANTI ● **Montefalco Sagrantino** £C Passito £D
AGRIVERDE ● **Montepulciano d'Abruzzo** Riseis £B Plateo £C
ANTONELLI ● **Montefalco Rosso** £B ● **Montefalco Sagrantino** £D
BARBERANI ○ **Orvieto Classico** Superiore Calcaia Muffa Nobile £E
● **Lago di Corbara** Foresco (Sangiovese/Cabernets) £D
BELISARIO ○ **Verdicchio di Matelica** Vigneti Belisario £B Vigneti del Cerro £B
○ **Verdicchio di Matelica** Riserva Cambrugiano £C
BINOMIO (INAMA & LA VALENTINA) ● **Montepulciano d'Abruzzo** Binomio £E
BISCI ○ **Verdicchio di Matelica** Vigneto Fogliano £B
MARIO & GIORGIO BRUNORI ○ **Verdicchio dei Castelli di Jesi Classico** Superiore San Niccolò £B
BUCCI ○ **Verdicchio dei Castelli di Jesi Classico** Riserva Villa Bucci £C
TENUTA CARACCIOLO ● **Montepulciano d'Abruzzo** Duchi di Castelluccio £B
CASTEL DE PAOLIS ○ **Frascati** Superiore Vigna Adriana (Malvasia/Viognier) £C
● **Quattro Mori** (Syrah/Merlot/Cabernet Sauvignon/Petit Verdot) £D
CATALDI MADONNA ● **Montepulciano d'Abruzzo** Tonì £C
CANTINA COLLI AMERINI ● **Torraccio** (Sangiovese) £B
COLPETRONE (Saiagricola) ● **Montefalco Rosso** £B ● **Montefalco Sagrantino** £D
LEONE CONTI ○ **Albana di Romagna** Passito Non Ti Scordar di Me £D
CONTRADA CASTELLETTA ● **Contrada Castelletta** (Montepulciano/Syrah) £C
PIERO COSTANTINI/VILLA SIMONE ○ **Frascati** Superiore Villa dei Preti £B Vigneto Filonardi £C
TENUTA DE ANGELIS ● **Anghelos** (Montepulciano/Sangiovese/Cabernet Sauvignon) £D
DECUGNANO DEI BARBI ○ **Orvieto Classico** Superiore IL £B
● **IL** (Sangiovese/Montepulciano/Canaiolo) £C
DEZI ● **Solo** (Sangiovese) £D ● **Regina del Bosco** (Montepulciano) £C
PAOLA DI MAURO ● **Colle Picchioni Vigna del Vassallo** (Merlot/Cabernets) £C
FAZI BATTAGLIA ● **Rosso Conero** Riserva Passo del Lupo £C
○ **Verdicchio dei Castelli di Jesi Classico** Superiore Le Moie £B Riserva San Sisto £C
FONTANA CANDIDA ○ **Frascati** Superiore Terre dei Grifi £B Superiore Vigneto Santa Teresa £B
● **Kron** (Merlot/Sangiovese) £C
ILLUMINATI ● **Montepulciano d'Abruzzo** Zanna £C ● **Controguerra Rosso** Riserva Lumen £E
CANTINE INTESI ● **I Calanchi - Numi** (Cabernet Sauvignon) £C
LA BERTA ● **Sangiovese di Romagna** Superiore Solano £B Riserva Olmatello £C
● **Almante** (Alicante) £C
LA CARRAIA ○ **Orvieto Classico** Poggio Calvelli £B
● **Sangiovese** £B ● **Fobiano** (Merlot/Cabernet Sauvignon) £D
LA PALAZZOLA ● **Merlot** £D ● **Rubino** (Cabernet Sauvignon/Merlot) £D
LA TOSA ● **Colli Piacentini** Cabernet Sauvignon Luna Selvatica £C
● **Colli Piacentini Gutturnio** Vignamorello £C
LA VALENTINA ● **Montepulciano d'Abruzzo** Spelt £C Bellovedere £F

LA VIOLA ● Sangiovese di Romagna £C

LANARI ● Rosso Conero Fibbio £C

LE CANIETTE ● Rosso Piceno Morellone £C ● Rosso Piceno Nero di Vite £D

LEOPARDI DITTAJUTI ● Rosso Conero Vigneti del Coppo £B Pigmento £C

LUNGAROTTI ● Giubilante (Cabernets/Sangiovese/Canaiolo/Montepulciano) £D

● San Giorgio (Cabernet Sauvignon/Sangiovese/Canaiolo) £E

● Torgiano Riserva Rubesco Vigna Monticchio £E O Chardonnay Palazzi £C

GIOVANNA MADONIA ● Sangiovese di Romagna Superiore Riserva Ombroso £C

MASCIARELLI ● Montepulciano d'Abruzzo Villa Gemma £C

O Trebbiano d'Abruzzo Marina Cvetic £C

MONTE SCHIAVO ● Rosso Conero Adeodato £D

● Esio (Cabernet Sauvignon/Montepulciano/Merlot) £C

MORODER ● Rosso Conero Dorico £C

PALAZZONE O Orvieto Classico Terre Vineate £B Campo del Guardiano £C

● Armaleo (Cabernet Sauvignon) £D

PARADISO ● Mito (Cabernet Sauvignon/Merlot/Syrah) £E ● Barbarossa £D

POGGIO BERTAIO ● Sangiovese Cimbolo £C

CASA VINICOLA ROXAN ● Montepulciano d'Abruzzo Galelle £B

SALADINI PILASTRI ● Rosso Piceno Vigna Montetinello £B Vigna Monteprandone £C

● Pregio del Conte (Aglianico/Montepulciano) £B

SALVIANO O Lago di Corbara Turlò £B

SANTA BARBARA O Verdicchio dei Castelli di Jesi Classico Le Vaglie £B Stefano Antonucci £C

● Stefano Antonucci (Merlot/Cabernet Sauvignon/Montepulciano/Syrah) £C

● Pathos (Merlot/Cabernet Sauvignon/Syrah) £C

SPOLETODUCALE ● Montefalco Sagrantino Casale Triocco £D

LUCANGELI AYMERICH DI LACONI/TAVIGNANO ● Rosso Piceno £B

O Verdicchio dei Castelli di Jesi Misco £C

TERRA GENS ● Romio £C

TERRE CORTESI MONCARO O Verdicchio dei Castelli di Jesi Classico Verde di Cà Ruptae £B

O Verdicchio dei Castelli di Jesi Riserva Vigna Novali £C Passito Tordiruta £D

● Rosso Conero Riserva Vigneto del Parco £C

VIGNETO DELLE TERRE ROSSE ● Colli Bolognesi Cabernet Sauvignon Enrico Vallania £D

O Colli Bolognesi Chardonnay Giovanni Vallania £C

TRAPPOLINI ● Sangiovese Paterno £D

TRE MONTI ● Sangiovese di Romagna Superiore Thea £C Riserva £C

ERCOLE VELENOSI O Falerio dei Colli Ascolani Vigna Solaria £B

● Ludi (Montepulciano/Cabernet Sauvignon/Merlot) £D ● Rosso Piceno Superiore Roggio del Filare £C

ZACCAGNINI & C. O Verdicchio dei Castelli di Jesi Classico Salmàgina £B Pier delle Vigne £C

CICCIO ZACCAGNINI ● Montepulciano d'Abruzzo Castello di Salle £B

● Montepulciano d'Abruzzo Cuvée dell'Abate £C San Clemente £C

Author's Choice (PW)

10 excellent Sangiovese di Romagna

STEFANO BERTI ● Sangiovese di Romagna Superiore Calisto

CASTELLUCCIO ● Ronco dei Ciliegi

CASTELLUCCIO ● Ronco delle Ginestre

DREI DONÀ - LA PALAZZA ● Sangiovese di Romagna Superiore Riserva Pruno

LA BERTA ● Sangiovese di Romagna Superiore Riserva Olmatello

LA VIOLA ● Sangiovese di Romagna

GIOVANNA MADONIA ● Sangiovese di Romagna Superiore Riserva Ombroso

SAN PATRIGNANO ● Sangiovese di Romagna Riserva Avi

SAN PATRIGNANO ● Sangiovese di Romagna Riserva Zarricante

ZERBINA ● Sangiovese di Romagna Riserva Pietramora

10 Montepulciano based reds

PODERE CASTORANI ● Montepulciano d'Abruzzo
CATALDI MADONNA ● Montepulciano d'Abruzzo Tonì
DI MAJO NORANTE ● Molise Don Luigi
GAROFOLI ● Rosso Conero Riserva Grosso Agontano
LANARI ● Rosso Conero Fibbio
LE TERRAZZE ● Rosso Conero Sassi Neri
MASCIARELLI ● Montepulciano d'Abruzzo Villa Gemma
ANTONIO & ELIO MONTI ● Montepulciano d'Abruzzo Pignotto
OASI DEGLI ANGELI ● Kurni
VALENTINI ● Montepulciano d'Abruzzo

10 individual stars

BOCCADIGABBIA ● Akronte Cabernet Sauvignon
CAPRAI ● Sagrantino di Montefalco 25 Anni
CASTELLO DELLA SALA ○ Cervaro della Sala
FALESCO ● Montiano
LA FIORITA LAMBORGHINI ● Campoleone
LE TERRAZZE ● Chaos
FATTORIA MANCINI ● Blu
PIEVE DEL VESCOVO ● Lucciaio
SPORTOLETTI ● Villa Fidelia Rosso
ZERBINA ● Marzieno

10 alternatives to Chardonnay

CASTEL DE PAOLIS ○ Vigna Adriana
CORONCINO ○ Verdicchio dei Castelli di Jesi Classico Superiore Gaiospino
FALESCO ○ Est! Est!! Est!!! Poggio dei Gelsi
GAROFOLI ○ Verdicchio dei Castelli di Jesi Classico Superiore Podium
LA MONACESCA ○ Verdicchio di Matelica La Monacesca
FATTORIA MANCINI ○ Pinot Nero Impero Bianco
PALAZZONE ○ Orvieto Classico Campo del Guardiano
SARTARELLI ○ Verdicchio dei Castelli di Jesi Classico Superiore Contrada Balciana
UMANI RONCHI ○ Verdicchio dei Castelli di Jesi Classico Riserva Plenio
VALENTINI ○ Trebbiano d'Abruzzo

For years fans of Italian wine have glimpsed the quality and originality of the south but have been frustrated by a lack of consistently fine examples. Since the mid- to late nineties, the once-isolated pockets of quality have been growing and spreading and with this edition it has been possible to add several more of the now many excellent producers of the Mezzogiorno. As in much of Italy the general standard of winemaking is at an unprecedented level. Add this to some high-quality vineyard sources, both new and old, and a rich hoard of native grape varieties and you begin to glimpse what is possible. Campania vies with Puglia and Sicily as the south's most important quality wine producing area but there are now both good-value and world-class wines, often with prices to match, to be had in all regions.

The regions of Southern Italy & Islands

Campania
Taurasi is Campania's leading appellation based on its most important grape, Aglianico. Its DOCG status may have once wanted for endorsement but now there are many good examples and a few outstanding wines which show the depth, structure and class of the grape that result when winemaking expertise is employed and the fruit quality has been maximised. Increasing amounts of good (DOC) **Greco di Tufo** and **Fiano di Avellino** are also produced in the Avellino hills but many of the best wines from this exciting area appear under the Irpinia IGT, the ancient name for the zone. In the neighbouring province of Benevento another white, Falanghina, is starting to show real promise under the DOCs of **Sannio**, **Sant'Agata dei Goti**, **Solopaca** and **Taburno**. More good Aglianico also appears under each, especially the **Aglianico del Taburno**. From vineyards closer to Lazio, Aglianico is complemented by Piedirosso in **Falerno del Massico**. The **Lacryma Christi del Vesuvio** red is also based on Piedirosso. Whites from **Ischia** (such as those from D'Ambra) and the wines of the **Costa d'Amalfi** show potential too. What seems certain is that an increasing number of names will take on greater meaning as the rise in quality continues to become more widespread.

Basilicata & Calabria
In Basilicata, as in Campania, the great red grape is Aglianico and at last there are now several good sources of high quality examples of **Aglianico del Vulture** from the elevated slopes of Monte Vulture. Recent vintages from Le Querce or Cantine del Notaio, amongst others, may now be compared with those from Paternoster or D'Angelo, who are invariably the only sources of older wines of quality. In Calabria there has also been a paucity of good wine but the most important DOC is **Cirò**. The characterful red is based almost exlusively on Gaglioppo, the more ordinary white on Greco Bianco, but there are only three significant producers including Librandi. Two other DOCs, **Savuto** and **Scavigna**, used by Odoardi, include a substantial proportion of Gaglioppo in the blend. Scavigna can also include significant percentages of Aglianico, Cabernet Sauvignon and Merlot.

Puglia
Salice Salentino is the best-known of the many DOCs on the Salento peninsula based on the Negroamaro grape, but topped up with some Malvasia Nera. The others, Alezio, Copertino, Leverano and Squinzano, are not as good but even the best gutsy, baked, raisiny Salice Salentinos, while lush and sweet-fruited, are not to everyone's taste. The best Negroamaro comes from *alberello* (bush-trained) vines and the reds of **Brindisi** are also based on it. **Primitivo di Manduria** is the most important DOC on the peninsula for Primitivo (a grape said to be identical to California's Zinfandel if of discernably different character according to some winemakers). Primitivo also appears under broader IGTs such as Tarantino and several of the Salento peninsula's best wines are sold as Salento IGT. On the high plateau of central Puglia, Primitivo is also DOC in **Gioia del Colle**. To the north lies **Castel del Monte** and here Uva di Troia, Montepulciano and Aglianico feature. Antinori's Tormaresca operation is also using Cabernet Sauvignon.

Sicily

The sea of vines in the west of Sicily is why the island vies with Puglia as Italy's most productive region. Most of it is pretty simple, dilute stuff but both here in the DOC zones of **Marsala** and **Alcamo,** and in pockets all over the island, some excellent new producers are emerging. Cabernet Sauvignon, Merlot, Syrah and Chardonnay are the foreign stars while Nero d'Avola and Nerello Mascalese are increasingly important native red grapes. The latter two are combined in a small zone near Messina called **Faro** but the majority of the new wave of fine Sicilian reds are sold as Sicilia IGT. Other DOCs include **Cerasuolo di Vittoria,** where Frappato is usually combined with Nero d'Avola in a characterful, concentrated and perfumed red; **Contessa Entellina** DOC covers a wide range of reds and whites of the producer Donnafugata; while the vineyards on the lower slopes of Mount Etna are **Etna** DOC. While some producers focus on the international varieties, others are more committed to promoting the native varieties and what is most exciting about Sicily is this very mix of quality-minded producers – to be certain it needs them all. Success and acclaim with international varieties at worst serves as a kind of Trojan horse facilitating a more sustained assault of native varieties in foreign markets. From off-shore come **Malvasia delle Lipari** from this volcanic island group to the north and **Moscato di Pantelleria** from an especially windswept volcanic island that lies closer to Tunisia than Sicily. The richer, sweeter **Passito di Pantelleria** versions from dried grapes are the most exciting.

Sardinia

Several of Sardinia's DOCs are region-wide and typically account for everyday reds and whites of reasonable value if from a good source. These include **Cannonau di Sardegna, Monica di Sardegna** and **Vermentino di Sardegna.** The best wines containing Cannonau (a clone of Grenache), from Argiolas and Sella & Mosca, do not come under the regional DOC but are wines of much greater depth, complexity and longevity. **Vermentino di Gallura,** from a more restricted northern zone, is the island's only DOCG but examples of both Vermentinos can be wonderfully fresh and aromatic. The rest of Sella & Mosca's production falls under **Alghero** DOC, named for the town on the north-west coast. **Carignano del Sulcis** is also a more defined zone (in the south-west corner) where the best of Sardinia's many co-ops is based and makes some remarkably good Carignano-based reds that bear little resemblance to most Carignan from the Languedoc-Roussillon. Cagnulari is another Sardinian red variety of some potential if Giovanni Cherchi's results can be emulated. **Vernaccia di Oristano** is a small zone producing oxidised, sherry-like wines – those from Attilio Contini are of high quality.

A-Z of Producers by region

Basilicata
CANTINE DEL NOTAIO
D'ANGELO
TENUTE LE QUERCE
PATERNOSTER

Calabria
LIBRANDI

Campania
ANTONIO CAGGIANO
FEUDI DI SAN GREGORIO
GALARDI
MASTROBERARDINO
MONTEVETRANO
TELARO/LAVORO & SALUTE

Puglia
ACCADEMIA DEI RACEMI
LA CORTE
COSIMO TAURINO
TORMARESCA
VALLONE
CONTI ZECCA

Sardinia
ARGIOLAS
GIOVANNI CHERCHI
DETTORI
SANTADI
SELLA & MOSCA

Sicily
ABBAZIA SANTA ANASTASIA
BENANTI
CEUSO
COTTANERA
CUSUMANO
MARCO DE BARTOLI
DONNAFUGATA

PALARI
MORGANTE
SALVATORE MURANA
PLANETA
TASCA D'ALMERITA

ABBAZIA SANTA ANASTASIA Sicilia www.abbaziasantanastasia.it A: L&S

Owner: Francesco Lena Contrada Santa Anastasia, 90013 Castelbuono (PA)
Superbly sited estate high above the sea on the north coast of Sicily and one of the island's brightest
new stars. It wines first grabbed attention after help from the Tuscan enologist Giacomo Tachis and
are now made under guidance from Riccardo Cotarella (see FALESCO). Most impressive is the top
wine, Litra, previously produced from Cabernet Sauvignon and Nero d'Avola but 100 per cent
Cabernet in the 1999 version. It is intense and ripe, with blackcurrant, black plum, mineral and a
hint of herbs within a full, structured but balanced frame. Montenero adds Merlot and Syrah (20 per
cent of each) to Nero d'Avola, while the still-improving Passomaggio is Nero d'Avola with just the
Merlot component. The most basic red is straight Nero d'Avola and recently much improved. Given
the vineyards' altitude of 400–500 m above sea level, whites also have potential here. Baccante is a
late-harvested Chardonnay fermented in new oak and fairly rich from some residual sugar, while
Gemelli, first made in 2000, is Chardonnnay with a little Sauvignon Blanc. Zurrica is an unoaked
blend of Inzolia with a percentage of Chardonnay and Pinot Bianco. Drink Litra with five years' age
or more, others wines can be drunk young. (PW)
● **Litra**★★★ £E ● **Montenero**★★ £C ● **Passomaggio**★★ £B

ACCADEMIA DEI RACEMI Puglia www.accademiadeiracemi.it A: Mer

Owner: (an association of producers) Via Santo Stasi Primo, ZI, 74024 Manduria (TA)
The idea of an umbrella organisation for a network of growers in Puglia's Salento peninsula was
conceived and then realised by Gregory (Gregorio) Perrucci of Pervini. Launched as recently as 1999
it has done much to promote the good-value reds, particularly from old Primitivo vines. of this area.
Pervini itself is the operation fired by the new younger generation of the Perrucci family. Fabrizio
Perrucci is the winemaker and has worked closely with highy regarded consultant Roberto Cipresso
since 1996 on the wines of the family's own 45-ha estate, Felline, as well as making the wines for the
rest of the association. Typically all the wines have good fruit, balance and real character. Pervini's
Bizantino Rosso is a blend of Negroamaro and Primitivo, as is Felline's Alberello while the promising
new L'Evangelista is Primitivo with a little Montepulciano (90/10). Felline's Vigna del Feudo,
previously a blend of Primitivo, Montepulciano and a little Cabernet and Merlot, is now Primitivo,
Malvasia Nera and Ottavianello in equal proportions. Primo Amore is a sweet version of Primitivo.
La Quadratura del Cerchio has been developed by Roberto Cipresso – a blend of Primitivo and
Sangiovese (70/30), it is now in its third incarnation (*terze viaggio*). Wines from five producers are
listed below but new wines include those from Tenuta Pozzopalo (Primitivo di Manduria Giravolta)
and Torre Guaceto (Sum from Susumaniello, and Dedalo from Ottavianello). (PW)

Pervini
● **Primitivo di Manduria** Archidamo★★ £B Primo Amore★★ £C
● **Bizantino Rosso**★★ £B ● **Squinzano** L'Evangelista★★ £B
Felline
● **Primitivo di Manduria**★★ £B ● **Vigna del Feudo**★★ £B
● **Alberello**★ £B ● **La Quadratura del Cerchio**★★ £C
Masseria Pepe
● **Primitivo di Manduria** Dunico★★ £C ● **Primitivo del Tarantino Portile**★★ £B
Sinfarosa
● **Primitivo di Manduria** Zinfandel★★ £B ● **Primitivo**★ £B
Casale Bevagna
● **Salice Salentino** Te Deum Laudamus★★ £B

ARGIOLAS   Sardegna   www.cantine-argiolas.it   A: Eur, L&W

Owner: Antonio Argiolas   Via Roma 56-58, 09040 Serdiana (CA)

Argiolas is one of Sardinia's three leading producers (the others are SANTADI and SELLA & MOSCA). It is run by Franco and Giuseppe Argiolas, sons of Antonio Argiolas, but with assistance from leading enologist Giacomo Tachis. Since 1985 the 230-ha estate has been completely replanted with the emphasis on local Sardinian varieties. There are good examples of some of the island's more widely seen DOCs including Costamolino (Vermentino di Sardegna); Costera (Cannonau di Sardegna); Perdera (Monica di Sardegna); and Selegas (Nuragus di Cagliari), a crisp dry white. The best wines, however, are sold under the IGT Isola dei Nuraghi. Argiolas is a stylish blend of Vermentino, Sauvignon Blanc and Chardonnay while Angialis, a fine light sweet wine, is made from (mostly) Nasco and Malvasia. The top red is the deep but structured Turriga, based on Cannonau but with five per cent of each of Carignano, Malvasia Nera and the Sardinian variety Bovale. Similarly structured is Korem, from Cannonau, Carignano, Bovale, Syrah and Merlot. Most wines should be drunk young but Korem and Turriga (subject to a delayed release) usually need more bottle-age after release; the Turriga is best with 10 years' age. (PW)

● **Turriga**★★★ £E   ● **Korem**★★ £D
● **Monica di Sardegna** Perdera★ £B   ● **Cannonau di Sardegna** Costera★ £C
○ **Angialis**★★ £D   ○ **Argiolas**★ £B   ○ **Vermentino di Sardegna** Costamolino★ £B

BENANTI   Sicilia   www.vinicolabenanti.it

Owner: Giuseppe Benanti   Via Garibaldi 475, 95029 Viagrande (CT)

The Benanti family have had vines on the lower slopes of Mount Etna since the late nineteeth century. Since 1988 Giuseppe Benanti has identified some of the best densely planted old-vine vineyards from the northern, southern and eastern slopes of Etna and experimented with, primarily, the local varieties in order to produce wines of great character and individuality. Some new single varietal reds, with at times too firm and ungiving structure, are not so convincing. Nero d'Avola is the most composed but both Nerello Mascalese and Nerello Cappuccio show a delightful complexity, if difficult to enjoy. If these and other wines need more supple textures and tannins Benanti deserve space here on the basis of the excellent Lamorèmio red alone. From equal parts Nerello Mascalese, Nero d'Avola and Cabernet Sauvignon, it has a fascinating black fruits, mineral and herbs complexity and is also much more profound and better balanced than the varietals. Rosso di Verzella, Rovittello and Serra della Contessa all combine Nerello Mascalese and Nerello Cappuccio but come from quite diverse locations and altitudes, the last having perhaps the most agreeable structure. Whites are generally soundly made and individual, including a varietal Carricante, the scented and intense Pietramarina, a Carricante/Chardonnay blend in the flavoursome if unsubtle Edèlmio, as well as the only known example of the obscure Minnella grape made from vines growing amongst the Nerello Mascalese. Better though is the sweet Passito di Pantelleria that combines intensity and refinement in its spiced honeyed apricot fruit, one of the best going. (PW)

● **Lamorèmio**★★★★ £E   ● **Etna Rosso** Serra della Contessa★★ £D   Rovittello★★ £C
● **Nero d'Avola**★★ £D   ● **Nerello Cappuccio**★★ £D
○ **Etna Bianco** Superiore Pietramarina★★ £C   ○ **Edèlmio**★★ £C   ○ **Minnella**★ £C
○ **Passito di Pantelleria** Coste di Mueggen★★★ £E

ANTONIO CAGGIANO   Campania   www.cantinecaggiano.it   A: J&B

Owner: Antonio Caggiano   Contrada Sala, 83030 Taurasi (AV)

Antonio Caggiano is one of the stars of Taurasi yet only turned his attention to making fine wines in 1990. Now he makes a range of reds and whites, all to a consistently high standard. Foremost is the single-vineyard Taurasi Vigna Macchia dei Goti, from Aglianico which is then aged in one- and two-year-old wood. It shows some classic tar, earth, smoke and black plum fruit characters, with no lack of depth or character and fine tannins in a good vintage like 1998, and promises plum, chocolate and pepper with age. Also from a single vineyard comes Salae Domini with 10–12 months in barrique and sold under the IGT Aglianico dell' Irpinia. Though oak is apparent it integrates well with a fine, ripe fruit character. Taurì, an inexpensive version of Aglianico displaying some of the grape's classic character, is also sold under the IGT. Béchar is a fruit-intense Fiano di Avellino that is not too structured – as wines from this appellation sometimes can be. There is no pure Greco but rather FiaGre, a blend of 70 per cent Fiano and 30 per cent Greco that is barrique-aged. Fresh when young, it will also keep a couple of years. Also made is a lovely, elegant sweet white, Mel, from dried Fiano and Greco grapes, with lightly spicy pear and quince among its delicious flavours. (PW)

● **Taurasi** Vigna Macchia dei Goti★★★ £E
● **Salae Dominii**★★★ £D ● **Taurì**★★ £C
O **Fiano di Avellino** Béchar★★ £C O **FiaGre**★ £B O **Mel**★★★ £E

CANTINE DEL NOTAIO Basilcata www.cantinedelnotaio.com A: BBR

Owner: G Giuratrabochetti Via Roma 159, 85028 Rionero in Vulture (PZ)

This a very new operation but one already making exciting Aglianico del Vulture. The owner is one of several producers working with Aglianico to profit from the expertise of Luigi Moio, a professor of oenology in Naples. The premium example La Firma is subject to a lengthy maceration and has 12 months in new French oak which adds complexity to a splendid expression of Aglianico fruit. The wine hasn't yet quite the same sophistication in structure as some of its rivals but is very promsing in both 2000 and 2001. Both deserve at least five or six years' age. A second example, Il Repetorio, has less depth but is more immeditate and fruit-accented with attractive pepper, spice and berry notes though still benefits from a little bottle age. A sweet wine, L'Autentica, comes from Moscato and Malvasia grapes and is very apricotty and fruit intense if relatively straightforward. (PW)

● **Aglianico del Vulture** Il Repetorio★★ £C La Firma★★★★ £D
O **L'Autentica**★★ £E

CEUSO Sicilia www.ceuso.it

Owner: Antonino, Giuseppe & Vincenzo Melia Via Enea 18, 91011 Alcamo (TP)

Though based in the Alcamo zone in western Sicily, best known for its dilute whites, Ceuso make just two very good reds. They combine the best of the traditional and modern and the native Nero d'Avola grape with Cabernet Sauvignon and Merlot. Custera (50/30/20) is a wonderfully characterful, concentrated and powerful red with deep smoky, earthy aromas.Though given 12 months in barrique, it is freshened up in vats before 18 months' bottle-age prior to release. 25.5 ha of the estate is planted to vines. The average age of those used for Custera (from 8.5 ha) is only 12 years so the wines can be expected to show further richness in coming vintages. Production is small – just 3,000 cases at present. Added in 2000, a second wine, Fastaia, from 70 per cent Nero d'Avola and 15 per cent each of Merlot and Cabernet Franc shows a deep smoky and powerful southern character as well as polished tannins. Both wines may be drunk young but will keep, Custera perhaps 10 years. (PW)

● **Custera**★★★ £D ● **Fastaia**★★ £C

GIOVANNI CHERCHI Sardegna   A: LaC

Owner: Giovanni Cherchi Loc. Sa pala e sa chessa, 07049 Usini (SS)
This small Sardinian operation is worth tracking down for the quality of its Vermentinos alone but the soft, appealing, scented reds have a similar intensity and the same ability to evoke something of the essence of the island. The sage, pear, citrus and spice character Cherchi achieves in his Vermentino makes for delightful whites for relatively early drinking. The barrique-aged Boghes, also from Vermentino shows a deft use of oak and lovely complexity with a couple of years' age. Most intriguing of the reds, a varietal Cagnulari is not a wine of great depth or structure but its delightful fruit character is now inspiring other growers to plant it. Luzzana is a blend of equal parts Cannonau and Cagnulari; scented and oak-influenced with preserved berry-fruit character, it is deserving of at least three to four years' age. The non-DOC wines are sold under the Isola dei Nuraghi IGT. (PW)
● **Cannonau di Sardegna★★** £C ● **Cagnulari★★** £C ● **Luzzana★★★** £C
O **Vermentino di Sardegna** Pigalva★★ £B Tuvaoes★★★ £C O **Boghes★★★** £C

COTTANERA Sicilia   A: Ast, Res, L&W

Owner: Guglielmo & Vincenzo Cambria Contrada Iannazzo, 95030 Castiglione di Sicilia (CT)
An exciting new operation on the northern side of Mount Etna at 700 m. Since 1995 the Cambria brothers have begun to transform the 43 ha of vines bought by their father some 40 years ago. Consultancy comes from Leonardo Valenti and the first vintage was as recent as 1999. The wines at the top level – including Grammonte, a varietal Merlot; Sole di Sesta, varietal Syrah; and L'Ardenza, varietal Mondeuse (surely Sicily's if not Italy's only example) – show remarkable fruit intensity, concentration and definition. All are aged in new French oak for 18 months. They are powerful and vibrant with great potential, but it is still early days and it remains to be seen how well the wines age and how much finesse they will add. They should be given at least five years from the vintage. A less expensive Fatagione, a blend of Nerello Mascalese and Nero d'Avola (80/20), shows very intense fruit and good potential too. Barbazzale is produced in both red and white versions: the red is a similar blend to Fatagione but is less convincing, while the promising unoaked white is produced from old vineyards of Inzolia, perhaps Sicily's most interesting native variety. (PW)
● **Grammonte★★★** £E ● **L'Ardenza★★★** £E ● **Sole di Sesta★★★** £E
● **Fatagione★★** £D

CUSUMANO Sicilia www.cusumano.it   A: Eur, WTs, Odd

Owner: Alberto Cusumano & Diego Cusumano S.S. 113, Contrada San Carlo, 90047 Partinico (PA)
Alberto and Diego Cusumano control 140 ha of vineyards and with the help of consultant Mario Ronco are proving to be another of Sicily's new revelations. Three reds are based on Nero d'Avola, though the French varieties are also proving their worth here. Sàgana is a varietal Nero d'Avola fermented and aged in 20hl barrels and shows the ripe, intense fruit. In contrast, Noà, which adds Cabernet Sauvignon and Merlot to Nero d'Avola, is aged in French barriques but is even better, with more depth and complexiy in a seamless harmonious blend. Produced without any wood but good value are a brambly, spicy blackberry Benuara, which adds Syrah to Nero d'Avola, and a fresh, stylish white from Inzolia and Chardonnay, called Angimbé. A barrique-fermented Chardonnay, Jalé, and varietal Inzolia, Cubìa, show fine fruit and each spends 6 months on its lees though this works less well in the latter. Inexpensive varietal examples of Nero d'Avola, Merlot and Syrah produced under the Nadarìa label are more everyday but could use a little more ripeness and richness. Inzolia under the same label is more appealing. (PW)
● **Benuara★** £C ● **Sàgana★★** £D ● **Noà★★★** £D

○ **Angimbé**★★ £C   ○ **Cubìa**★★ £C   ○ **Jalé**★★ £C
○ **Alcamo** Nadarìa★ £B   ○ **Nadarìa Inzolia**★ £B

D'ANGELO   Basilicata   A: Alv

Owner: Donato & Lucio D'Angelo   Via Provinciale 8, 85028 Rionero in Vulture
The secret to appreciating the D'Angelo reds is patience for although the Aglianico del Vulture reds show impressive fruit and complexity when young they add greater richness, harmony and a deep, savoury complexity with long ageing. An increasing percentage of the wines is now produced from estate fruit, including the single-vineyard Riserva, Caselle, from a 5-ha site. Canneto is a selection of Aglianico from old vines and is aged in barriques but has a similarly profound structure and good ageing potential. Another estate vineyard, Serra delle Querce (6.2 ha), is the source of an increasingly persuasive barrique-aged blend of Aglianico and Merlot. Intense and minerally with smoke, pepper and berry fruit character, despite the oak influence this too deserves at least five years' age. New Donato d'Angelo is expansive and very long in the 2000 vintage but will need time to fill in. Vigna dei Pini is a fresh attractive white if drunk young. (PW)
● **Aglianico del Vulture**★★ £B   Riserva Vigna Caselle★★★ £C
● **Canneto**★★★★ £C   ● **Serra delle Querce**★★★★ £D

MARCO DE BARTOLI   Sicilia   A: Cib

Owner: Marco de Bartoli   Contrada Fornara 292, 91025 Marsala (TP)
A crusader for the original unfortified Marsala, for five years between 1995 and 2000 Marco De Bartoli was prevented by the authorities from making any wine. He now continues with his sons Renato (a trained winemaker) and Sebastiano and currently produces Vigna La Miccia, the youngest and freshest style fortified with a little *mistella*, and a Marsala Superiore (also fortified) from wines aged for around 10 years in a sort of *solera* system. Small amounts of extraordinary old wines are used for blending with younger wines, some of which are used for Vecchio Samperi Ventennale, an unsweetened and unfortified blend of older and younger vintages but with an average age of 20 years. This is the best expression of what very ripe Grillo grapes can achieve with considerable age and is full of rich, toffeed, dry fruits, candied peel, dates, nuts and other nuances of flavour. Other wines include some from the island of Pantelleria (the production of which was the source of the controversy), the very good Passito di Pantelleria Bukkuram, and a fine dry version of Zibibbo (Muscat of Alexandria) called Pietranera. New are a dry white from Grillo, Grappoli del Grillo and a Merlot, Rosso di Marco. (PW)
○ **Vigna La Miccia**★★ £C   ○ **Marsala Superiore**★★★ £D   ○ **Vecchio Samperi** Ventennale★★★★ £D
○ **Passito di Pantelleria** Bukkuram★★★ £D   ○ **Pietranera**★★ £B

DETTORI   Sardegna   www.tenutedettori.it   A: LaC

Owner: Dettori family   Loc. Badde Nigolosu, 07036 Sénnori (SS)
To appreciate these fabulous wines be prepared to take some time and leave your preconceptions behind. Alessandro Dettori is uncompromising in the making of his wine. His 13 ha of very low yielding *alberello* or bush-trained vines lie close to the sea (but at 250m altitude) in Sénnori in north-west Sardinia. There is no oak whatsoever, no filtration, no fining, no additions or adjustments and Alessandro accepts it might not always work but is undeterred. All the wines are high in alcohol yet well-balanced. Vermentino shows uncommon weight and texture for this wine and pure, cool fruit. Three Cannonau from three different plots show diverse character. 'Tuderi', from 40 year old vines is full, powerful yet mellow with deep fruit. Of the vintage tasted, the intense licoricey 'Tenores' (from

40-60 year old vines) is the most extracted and discernably tannic, with highish acidity too, needing at least five years' age. 'Dettori' (from 60-120 year old vines) has a fabulous red fruit and lightly mineral, floral complexity. There is lovely breadth and purity - a wine to savour and savour (in a decent glass) before trying to procure another bottle. The Moscadeddu, from a local variant of Moscato, has a gorgeous nose, purest honeycomb, delicate apricot and allspice. Medium-dry, it is not as concentrated as might be expected but more vintages need to be tasted - as do all the wines in order to be able to rate them. The wines are not cheap (whites £D, Tuderi, Tenores £E, Dettori £F) but they are very special indeed. (PW)

DONNAFUGATA Sicilia www.donnafugata.it   A: Vim

Owner: Rallo family Via Sebastiano Lipari 18, 91025 Marsala (TP)

The Rallo family left only their name in Marsala production having devoted themselves to making only table wines in the last decade. They even have effectively their own DOC for their top reds and whites at altitude in western Sicily. The best reds had a tendency to overextraction but the recent hiring of Carlo Ferrini, one of Tuscany's very best consultants, should continue the trend to richer, softer examples with finer tannins. This augurs particularly well for the already complex and classy Mille e Una Notte, based on Nero d'Avola, while Tancredi (Nero d'Avola with some Cabernet Sauvignon) seemed to be already showing more refinement with the 2000 vintage and should get even better. Angheli adds Merlot to Nero d'Avola and seems fullest and ripest when the Merlot is most successful. Whites include the scented Vigna di Gabri from 100 per cent Ansonica (Inzolia) has real style and length while the Chardonnay Chiarandà del Merlo shows a southern richness but also has more structure and better balance than some. The usually fresh and aromatic Anthìlia is produced from Ansonica and Cataratto. From the family's vineyards in Pantelleria, Ben Ryé is very much in the dried fruit, apricot spectrum of these sweet wines but has excellent intensity and balance. (PW)

O **Contessa Entellina** Vigna di Gabri★★ £C Chiarandà del Merlo★★ £E O **Anthìlia**★ £B
O **Moscato di Pantelleria** Kabir★★ £D O **Passito di Pantelleria** Ben Ryé★★★ £E
● **Contessa Entellina** Tancredi★★★ £D Mille e Una Notte★★★ £F ● **Angheli**★★ £C

FEUDI DI SAN GREGORIO Campania www.feudi.it   A: Alv

Owner: Capaldo & Ercolino families Loc. Cerza Grossa, 83050 Sorbo Serpico (AV)

In a short space of time this winery based in the Avellino hills of Campania has risen to be the region's leading producer and one of the most exciting in Italy. Viticultural help has come from the esteemed Attilio Scienza, while the wines are made by Mario Ercolino. Plenty of oak is used and the reds are modern but with fabulous fruit, concentration and depth. Two single-vineyard versions of Taurasi are particularly fine, while Serpico is arguably southern Italy's finest red, a wine of majestic depth and length of flavour. The range of whites, which formerly included late-harvested versions of Fiano di Avellino (Pietracalda) and Greco di Tufo (Cutizzi), is being simplified. Falanghina, Greco and, in particular, Fiano grapes are used here to make some remarkable whites and are a much better bet than many overpriced, poorly structured versions of Viognier that now abound from all parts of the globe. Campanaro is late-harvested Fiano that has been fermented to dryness and partially barrique-aged; a rich, exotic-flavoured but balanced wine. A sweet version from partly botrytised grapes, Privilegio, reveals intense ripe fruit and moderate sweetness. Idem is also sweet but includes Moscato, Greco, Falanghina and Coda di Volpe as well as Fiano. It is all the more remarkable that all this quality is based on the native local varieties. New is a prodigious varietal Merlot, Pàtrimo, with marvellous fruit and depth if not quite the breadth of Serpico. The top wines are no longer cheap but there's both quality and value in the more moderately priced Rubrato, an Aglianico that is sold, along with many of the more unusual wines, under the Irpinia IGT. More is to come as operations in Basilicata, Puglia and Molise reach fruition including an excellent Primitivo di Manduria, Ognisole. (PW)

● **Taurasi★★★** £C Piano di Montevergine★★★★ £E Selve di Luoti★★★★ £E
● **Serpico★★★★★** £F ● **Pàtrimo★★★★** £F ● **Rubrato★★** £B
O **Fiano di Avellino★★★** £C O **Greco di Tufo★★** £C O **Sannio Falanghina★★** £C
O **Campanaro★★★** £D O **Idem★★★** £E O **Privilegio★★★** £E

GALARDI Campania

Owner: F Catello, D Catello & M L Murena S P Sessa Mignano, 81030 Sessa Aurunca (CE)
In the north of Campania, between the volcano of Roccamonfina and the sea, Galardi produces tiny quantities of just one wine, Terra di Lavoro, from Aglianico (80 per cent) and Piedirosso. Only now do the plots of vines wedged between groves of chestnut trees at 400 m total 9 ha. Eventually there will be 40,000 bottles of this new classic but just 9,000 were made in 2001. With help from Riccardo Cotarella, Terra di Lavoro (Roccamonfina IGT) is now a superb, fabulously complex red with great depth and stunning length, with a wealth of black fruits, mineral and earth, spice and herbs. It has improved in nearly every vintage since it was first made in 1994 and shows, along with some of the other stunning wines of this region, what tremendous potential there is here. Cult status means high prices, try from 1999 if you can first find it and then afford it. (PW)

● **Terra di Lavoro★★★★★** £F

LA CORTE Puglia www.renideo.com   A: Ast, Res

*Owner: **Renideo** Via Trepuzzi, 73051 Novoli (LE)*
Chris Ringland of the cult Barossa winery Three Rivers has been recruited to work with La Corte's winemaker Giuseppe Caragnulo. Their aim is to produce great wines from Primitivo and Negroamaro. Primitivo is labelled as Zinfandel to the irritation of some Californian winemakers but the quality at least does their name no harm. Grapes are both bought-in and sourced from leased vineyards. The superior bottlings are labelled simply La Corte and come from old vine fruit that has 12 months in oak. Both show very ripe fruit, considerable intensity and extract and while needing more age are a significant step-up from the more affordable Zinfandel Anfora and Negroamaro Solyss. A selection of the best Negroamaro and Primitivo is now blended together in Ré, first made in 2001 and the most promising wine yet with greater complexity and style. The Renideo group also comprises LA RENDOLA in Tuscany but these wines still want for both consistency and excitement. (PW)

● **Zinfandel Anfora★★** £B ● **Zinfandel La Corte★★★** £C
● **Negroamaro Solyss★★** £B ● **Negroamaro La Corte★★** £B

TENUTE LE QUERCE Basilicata www.tenutalequerce.com   A: Ast

Owner: Pietrafesa family Contrada Le Querce, 85100 Barile (PZ)
Le Querce are a major new star and part of the wider wine revolution in Basilicata. 60 ha of a 100 ha estate is planted to vines averaging 35 years age at an elevation of 450m. The regular example, Il Viola is produced in ample quantities (10,000 cases) yet has good fruit intensity and some style. Rosso di Costanza adds more density and shows impressive length as well as an oak influence from 12 months in barrique and needs five years' age. The crowning glory is, however, Vigna della Corona of which just 7000 bottles are produced from a single plot of vines. This is a marvellously expansive wine but with a structure that demands at least six to eight years' age following a very long maceration and 18 months in French oak. Much of the complexity, expression and nobility of Aglianico is

ensnared here. The Pietrafesa family also produce the wines of Cantina Sasso, source of reasonably priced, soundly made Aglianico del Vulture. (PW)

Tenute Le Querce

● **Aglianico del Vulture** Il Viola★★ £B Rosso di Costanza★★★ £D Vigna Corona★★★★ £F

LIBRANDI Calabria www.librandi.it   A: Eno

Owner: Librandi family   Contrada San Gennaro, S S 106, 88811 Cirò Marina (KR)
Librandi is the leading producer of Calabria from a base near Cirò Marina on the Ionian coast. A long-established enterprise, the family gradually moved from being growers into production of bulk wines before bottling their own wines. The biggest boost to quality followed the involvement of enologist Severino Garofano, responsible for much of the early quality from Puglia. Vineyards have been gradually expanded to the present 230 ha and expertise since 1998 has come from top Piedmontese enologist, Donato Lanati. After initially planting international varieties which resulted in their top red, Gravello (Gaglioppo/Cabernet Sauvignon), much thought (with advice from Attilio Scienza) has gone into the planting of a 160-ha site at Rosaneti, where many Calabrian varieties are being revived. The first great success of this strategy is Magno Megonio, a barrique-aged varietal Magliocco – a wine of distinctive, preserved black fruit character, quite tannic but with good ageing potential. Best value is the Cirò Riserva Duca San Felice, a characterful red with gamey, earthy, black plum and herb characters and intense chocolaty flavours; slightly rustic but good. The non-DOC wines are sold under the Val di Neto IGT. Critone is a fresh, well-made blend of Chardonnay and Sauvignon Blanc, while Le Passule is a light yet intense honeyed and refined sweet wine from Mantonico. Simple Cirò Bianco, Rosso and Rosato are also made. It's clear that there is more still to come. (PW)

● **Gravello**★★★ £D ● **Magno Megonio**★★★ £E
● **Cirò Rosso** Riserva Duca San Felice★★ £B
O **Le Passule**★★★ £D

MASTROBERARDINO Campania www.mastroberardino.com   A: Cib

Owner: Mastroberardino family   Via Manfredi 75-81, 83042 Atripalda (AV)
For decades Mastroberardino was Campania's one producer of note and the first to promote the wines of Taurasi, Fiano di Avellino and Greco di Tufo. Having rebuilt following a devastating earthquake in 1980, the family now control 350 ha of vineyards and produce around 200,000 cases of wine a year. The estate is now run by the tenth generation Carlo and Piero Mastroberardino but winemaking is still overseen by their father, Antonio. A split between brothers Antonio and Walter Mastroberardino in 1994 led to Walter and his family establishing the promising TERREDORA DI PAOLO. The leading wine is the Taurasi Radici, which is aged in a mixture of large and small oak. A rather austere yet balanced wine, it only shows at its best with around a decade's age. This is now complemented by a new wine, Naturalis Historia (after Pliny's great work) which adds 15 per cent Piedirosso to Aglianico. It spends two years in small oak and is richer and more modern in style. A varietal Aglianico, Avellanio, also shows good fruit. Several bottlings of Fiano di Avellino are produced – More Maiorum is unusual in being oak-fermented and aged before a long bottle refinement (two-and-a-half years) prior to release. Whites generally lack the fruit intensity and balance of the best examples. Mastroberardino were given responsibility for replanting historic vineyard sites among the ruins of ancient Pompei from which a new, oak-fermented white from Coda di Volpe, and oak-aged red from Piedirosso (with 10 per cent Aglianico) are now being produced under the Avalon label (and the Pompeiano IGT). Relatively large volumes of Lacryma Christi del Vesuvio are also produced, the white from Coda di Volpe, the red from Piedirosso. (PW)

● **Taurasi** Radici★★★ £E   ● **Naturalis Historia**★★★ £F
● **Avellanio Aglianico**★ £C
O **Fiano di Avellino** Radici★ £C   More Maiorum★ £D
O **Greco di Tufo** Vignadangelo★ £C

MONTEVETRANO   Campania   A: Wtr

Owner: Silvia Imparato   Via Montevetrano, 84099 San Cipriano Picentino (SA)
Production of Montevetrano is only slightly higher (at 20,000 bottles ayear) than GALARDI's Terra di Lavoro, another of the super-Campanian wines made by Riccardo Cotarella. Silvia Imparato's few hectares are at San Cipriano Picentino in hills behind the bustling coastal city of Salerno. Here Cabernet Sauvignon (60 per cent of the blend) and Merlot (30 per cent) hold sway, while Aglianico makes up the balance. The wine sold under the Colli di Salerno IGT has great structure and depth and is not simply another internationally styled red but shows considerable complexity and elegance. If this wine and others like it have little connection with commercial realities, they do provide the inspiration for others, while the rise and rise of FEUDI DI SAN GREGORIO for example, shows that both quality and quantity is also possible. (PW)

● **Montevetrano**★★★★ £F

MORGANTE   Sicilia   www.morgante-vini.it   A: Lib

Owner: Morgante family   Contrada Racalmare, 92020 Grotte (AG)
Former growers and suppliers of wine for blending, the Morgante family have been producing their own wine since 1998 under the winemaking expertise of Riccardo Cotarella. There are some 30 ha of vines. Nero d'Avola is made in two versions: a regular version (10,000 cases a year) has four months of oak-ageing, while Don Antonio (1,700 cases) is a superior selection which spends 12 months in new French oak. The oak is quite prominent in the latter but there is depth and intensity too in a sleek and stylish structure. The regular example, with good character and intensity, can be drunk quite young, Don Antonio is better with three to five years' age but will keep for longer. (PW)

● **Nero d'Avola**★★ £B   ● **Don Antonio**★★★ £D

SALVATORE MURANA   Sicilia   A: Eno

Owner: Salvatore Murana   Contrada Kamma 276, 91017 Pantelleria (TP)
Salvatore Murana is the top producer of Passito di Pantelleria, a delicious sweet wine from Zibibbo grapes made on the windswept volcanic island of Pantelleria between Sicily and Tunisia. The wines, especially at the top level, show greater refinement than others now being exported in increasing numbers. Murana's wines are named for the sub-zones from which they are produced. Martingana is the most concentrated and raisiny, a very powerful but stylish example. Khamma is also an excellent example with classic dried apricot and date aromas and flavours. Moscato di Pantelleria is a lighter style with lower alcohol and from grapes subjected to a shorter drying period. Murana's Mueggen has good intensity and a spicy, dried-fruit character. (PW)

O **Passito di Pantelleria** Khamma★★★ £E   Martingana★★★★ £F
O **Moscato di Pantelleria** Mueggen★★ £D

PALARI   Sicilia

Owner: Salvatore Geraci   Loc. Santo Stefano Briga, 98137 Messina
In the premium wine from the Palari estate we are witnessing the revival of a wine name famous in

the 14th century: Faro. From steep slopes high above the Straits of Messina, Salvatore Geraci undertook to breath life back into a DOC that had almost ceased to exist. Working with his brother, Giampiero, he also enlisted the winemaking expertise of Donato Lanati. Only local grapes have been used - Nerello Mascalese and Nerello Cappuccio as well as smaller amounts of other obscure varieties - though vinification and maturation are modern with ageing in French barriques. The wine impresses most with its nuanced complexity, which includes red fruits, coffee, herb and dried flowers, and its dimension and length but also for its refined, discreet structure. Don't come seeking colour, extract or incredible fruit richness, this is from a different part of the quality spectrum. Rosso del Soprano is a stylish second wine that can be drunk young or kept. (PW)

● **Rosso del Soprano**★★ £C   ● **Faro**★★★★ £E

PATERNOSTER Basilicata   www.paternostervini1925.com   A:Eno

Owner: Giuseppe Paternoster & family   Via Nazionale 23, 85022 Barile (PZ)
In the rush for a new wave of quality wines now coming out of Basilicata this venerable producer should not be overlooked. This is still very much a family winemaking enterprise, the wines being first commercialized back in 1925. Vinification and ageing is relatively traditional and in the top example, Don Anselmo, produces a deep, powerful wine, classically tight and closed in youth but rich and mesmerising with age. Almost as good but in a different, more modern style is Rotondo which is subject to a shorter maceration and spends 14 months in barriques. The wine is richer, more immediate but stylish and sophisticated too. The bigger volume Synthesi (aged mostly in large Slavonian casks) is ripe and supple, not a big wine but with good structure and needs just a couple of years' age. Also made is a partially barrique-fermented white from Fiano, Bianco di Corte, and a sweet white from Moscato grapes, Clivus. (PW)

● **Aglianico del Vulture** Synthesi★★ £C   Rotondo★★★★ £E   Don Anselmo★★★★ £E

PLANETA Sicilia   www.planeta.it   A: Eno, JNi, Vne

Owner: Alessio, Francesca & Santi Planeta   Contrada Dispensa, 92013 Menfi (AG)
There are now two Planeta wineries powering the seemingly unstoppable engine that is producing marvellously consistent quality and doing wonders for Sicily's image in foreign markets. Both the Ulmo winery, near Sambuca, and the newer (2001) Dispensa winery near Menfi, are in the west of the island but grapes are sourced from several major vineyard areas. The estate has expanded rapidly to more than 300 ha and the dynamic young Planetas have a wise and gifted winemaker in Carlo Corino. Despite an initial reputation for international varieties some of the finest wines already come from native varieties and more are being developed. The top wines are relatively expensive; the Santa Cecilia, from Nero d'Avola, and a pure Syrah are the most impressive with excellent fruit and length. Cabernet Sauvignon is very good too though a rich, intense Merlot misses a little finesse. Chardonnay, while complex and powerful, could use more refinement (though this is seen in cooler vintages such as 2002). La Segreta Rosso and Bianco are much cheaper yet made to a high standard and represent the best value for money. The red is a blend of Nero d'Avola, Merlot and Syrah (60/20/20) and is consistently good. The white is based on Grecanico but includes 20 per cent Chardonnay and 10 each of Viognier and Sauvignon Blanc and the combination of citrus and more exotic fruit really sings out. Another white, Alastro, combines Grecanico and Chardonnay but a barrique-fermented component of the latter overwhelms the fruit somewhat. Cometa is an impressive powerful, concentrated, partly barrel-fermented and oak-aged white from Fiano grapes – not subtle but rich in exotic and dried stone-fruits aromas and flavours. New from 2001 Cerasuolo di Vittoria is a classic blend of Nero d'Avola and Frappato (60/40) with distinctive perfume, spice and very ripe red fruits. (PW)

● **Santa Cecilia**★★★ £D   ● **La Segreta**★★ £B   ● **Cerasuolo di Vittoria**★★ £B

● **Burdese Cabernet Sauvignon**★★★ £D ● **Syrah**★★★ £D ● **Merlot**★★ £D
O **Chardonnay**★★★ £D O **Cometa**★★★ £C O **La Segreta**★★ £B O **Alastro**★ £B

SANTADI Sardegna www.cantinadisantadi.it   A: Eno, Vne

Owner: 'Co-operative' Via Su Pranu 12, 09010 Santadi (CA)
The success and renown of the Santadi co-op is based around the Carignano grape (France's humble
Carignan). The key seems to be that here it fully ripens unlike many of the efforts in the Languedoc-
Roussillon. Santadi have received many plaudits and a deservedly loyal following for the way they have
combined quantity and quality. The top wine is Terre Brune which also includes a tiny amount of
Bovaleddu and is aged for 16–18 months in new French barriques. It is rich, powerful and structured,
southern in its warmth and flavours and usually needs another three to five years' ageing after it is
released (so is best with eight years' age or more). Baie Rosse is a collaboration with the co-op on the
island of Calasetta and is more herb-scented with ripe black fruits but also needs time to show its full
potential. Rocca Rubia is made in much greater quantities (more than 12,000 cases) has less weight
and structure but plenty of style and can be drunk a little sooner. Both are aged in used barriques.
Araja is an unoaked Carignano that includes 15 per cent Sangiovese. A basic yet stylish Carignano
Grotta Rossa can be a good quaffing wine. Several good whites are also made, the Cala Silente has
some lees contact for added complexity. Very fresh and appealing if drunk young is a citrusy, herbal
Pedraia from Nuragus grapes while Villa di Chiesa is a barrel-fermented blend of Vermentino and
Chardonnay. The best white, however, is a sweet wine based on Nasco (as is the ARGIOLAS sweet
wine). Latinia has lovely ripe fruit, real intensity, style and balance. (PW)
● **Carignano del Sulcis** Grotta Rossa★ £B Riserva Rocca Rubia★★★ £C Superiore Terre Brune★★★★ £E
● **Baie Rosse**★★★ £C ● **Araja**★ £B
O **Vermentino di Sardegna** Villa Solais★ £B Cala Silente★★ £B
O **Villa di Chiesa**★ £C O **Latinia**★★★ £E

SELLA & MOSCA Sardegna www.sellaemosca.com   A: Alv

Owner: Sella & Mosca Loc. I Piani, 07041 Alghero (SS)
Sella & Mosca make a diverse range of wines from around 500 ha of vineyards in the north-west of
Sardinia. Operations are directed by Mario Consorte, who combines the traditional and modern to
produce an unusual range of wines. Most intriguing is Anghelu Ruju, a fortified wine produced from
Cannonau grapes that have been dried in the sun for 15 days and spends eight years in large oak
casks before it is released. Though it has developed complex tertiary flavours there are powerful spice
and dried-fruit characters too. Other reds include the firmly structured Tanca Farrà from Cannonau
and Cabernet Sauvignon and Marchese di Villamarina, a varietal Cabernet. Terrerare is a red from
Carignano del Sulcis but in common with most of Sella & Mosca's reds, it could use a little more
refinement. Good examples of Vermentino are made while Le Arenarie is from Sauvignon Blanc.
Terre Bianche is from Torbato, only grown in the Alghero zone on Sardinia. Many of the wines were
previously sold as vino da tavola. (PW)
● **Alghero** Riserva Anghelu Ruju★★ £D
● **Alghero** Tanca Farrà★★ £C Marchese di Villamarina★★ £E
O **Vermentino di Gallura** Monteoro★ £B O **Vermentino di Sardegna** La Cala★ £B

TASCA D'ALMERITA Sicilia www.tascadalmerita.it   A: BWC

Owner: Tasca d'Almerita family Contrada Regaleali, 90020 Sclafani Bagni (PA)
This large estate was acquired as long ago as 1830 and though much reduced by land reform in the

1950s still boasts 500 ha, over 300 of it given over to vineyards. Giuseppe Tasca, son of the current Count, Lucio Tasca d'Almerita, works tirelessly in the high-altitude vineyards to maintain a high-quality fruit source, but there is a whole team (including the recently recruited Gaetano Zangara) dedicated to continuing the standards that set them apart when wine from Sicily meant nothing more than plonk. Nero d'Avola is the most important red grape but there is ongoing research into other varieties. Rosso del Conte (Nero d'Avola with a little Perricone) and Cabernet Sauvignon are the two leading reds, made to a consistently high standard. The Rosso del Conte is full of bramble, plum and spice fruit, fleshy, ripe and adding chocolate and coffee flavours with age – composed yet characterful. The Cabernet is both powerful and remarkably refined. Nero d'Avola has been combined with Cabernet in Cygnus; and Merlot to make Camastra. Whites are led by a rich, powerful Chardonnay which has good depth and well-integrated oak. Nozze d'Oro is a flavoursome white from Inzolia and unidentified varieties (called Tasca) while Leone d'Almerita combines Chardonnay and Inzolia. The top wines now have their own DOC, Contea di Sclafani but were previously sold as Sicilia IGT as the rest of the wines are. The basic range, made in big quantities, are very acceptable characterful quaffing wines. (PW)

● **Contea di Sclafani** Rosso del Conte★★★★ £D   Cabernet Sauvignon★★★★ £E
O **Contea di Sclafani** Chardonnay★★★ £E   Nozze d'Oro★★ £C
● **Camastra★** £D   O **Leone d'Almerita★** £B

COSIMO TAURINO Puglia   A: Hal

Owner: Taurino family   SS 605, 73010 Guagnano (LE)

Francesco Taurino works with the estate's long-serving consultant, Severino Garofano, who helped to produce some of Puglia's few memorable wines before its recent awakening. Rich, robust yet harmonious reds are made based on the principles of picking very ripe fruit at low yields and the intelligent use of new oak. It is now a 140-ha estate but the top wine Patriglione comes from just 15 ha of vines, with a high average vine age. Its quality is surely the best argument in favour of the Negroamaro grape (though the wine also includes 10 per cent Malvasia Nera). It is a wonderfully rich, complex and beautifully structured expression of southern Italy. The modestly priced Notarpanaro, a similar blend, is also produced from old vines and is dense and flavoursome. Both wines qualify for the DOC Brindisi but are sold as Salento IGT. There is typically good intensity of flavour in a popular Salice Salentino Riserva produced in a fair quantity (60,000 cases). A little Chardonnay, I Sierri, is also produced as is a rare decent Rosato (Rosé), Scaloti. (PW)

● **Patriglione★★★★** £E   ● **Notarpanaro★★** £B   ● **Salice Salentino** Riserva★ £B

TELARO/LAVORO & SALUTE Campania   www.vinitelaro.it

Owner: Telaro family   Via Cinque Pietre, 81045 Galluccio (CE)

The three Telaro brothers produce a distinctive range of reasonably priced wines from Campania's leading grape varieties. The 35 ha of vines on their 85 ha estate on the lower slopes of the Roccamonfina volcano in northern Campania are treated organically with Aglianico forming the basis of the reds and Falanghina, Fiano and Greco, the whites. The top two reds are two Riservas, Aramundi from 100 per cent Aglianico and Calivierno which includes some 10-15 per cent Piedirosso. Both show deep earth, mineral, herb and ripe fruit complexity, good density and ripe tannins as well as a proven ability to age well. Of similar style and character but more immediate and fruit-driven is Montecaruso which also includes a little Piedirosso. In the whites the examples of Fiano and Greco are well-made with good fruit, a Falanghina shows extra style when made in a late-harvested, Vendemmia Tardiva version. Unusual is a sweet Aglianico-based red made from dried grapes, Passito delle Cinque Pietre. Concentrated, intense it shows reasonable balance if some astringency, avoids being too raisiny and releases a fusion of red fruit flavours and spice. (PW)

● **Galluccio Riserva** Ara Mundi★★★ £D Calivierno★★★£D
● **Galluccio** Montecaruso★★ £B ● **Passito delle Cinque Pietre**★★ £D
○ **Galluccio** Ripabianca Falanghina★ £B ○ **Falanghina Vendemmia Tardiva**★★ £B
○ **Greco Le Cinque Pietre**★★ £B ○ **Fiano Le Cinque Pietre**★★ £B

TORMARESCA Puglia www.tormaresca.it   A: BWC, Vts

Owner: Vigneti del Sud (Antinori) Via Matenità ed Infanzia 21, 72027 San Pietro Vernotico (BR)
I wouldn't expect anything less than an unqualified success from an ANTINORI venture into Puglia
and so it's proving. From 350 ha of vineyard split between two estates, the top two reds, both the
100 per cent Negroamaro Masseria Maime, and Bocca di Lupo (90 per cent Aglianico
complemented by Cabernet Sauvignon in the 2000) show great fruit definition, excellent texture and
balance. Modern, yes, but characterful too. The deep spice and berry fruit of the Maime is one to
contrast with the pure Negroamaro from Avignonesi's MASSERIA LI VELI, Pezzo Morgana. On a
simpler level, there's good intensity (if also a slightly underripe aspect in the 2001) in the regular and
relatively inexpensive Tormaresca Rosso, variously a blend of Negroamaro with Cabernet Sauvignon
or Merlot in its early vintages. Beyond a sound, attractive regular Chardonnay is an impressively rich
if only moderately complex, Pietrabianca. To be sure, there's more to come. (PW)

● **Masseria Maime**★★★ £D ● **Castel del Monte** Bocca di Lupo★★★ £C
● **Tormaresca Rosso**★ £B
○ **Castel del Monte** Pietrabianca★★★ £C ○ **Tormaresca Chardonnay**★ £B

VALLONE Puglia   A: Mer, L&W

Owner: Vallone family Via XXV Luglio 5, 73100 Lecce
This large estate includes 150 ha of vines among its other crops. Another of Puglia's top estates to
employ Severino Garofano, the wines are made to a consistently high standard. The outstanding
wine, Graticciaia, is a red made from (mostly) Negroamaro grapes that have been dried for around
three weeks on mats (*graticci*) in the warm autumn sun. The resulting partially barrique-aged wine
has powerful aromas of rich spice, very ripe berry, dried fruit and tobacco. There is rich, concentrated
sweet fruit, depth and power but good balance and it may be drunk soon after release or kept. Other
wines include Brindisi Rosso Vigna Flaminio (also made as a Rosato), which shows very ripe fruit in
a very supple structure while intensely flavoured Salice Salentino is one of the best made. Some
Sauvignon Blanc is grown for both a dry white, Corte Valesio and a *passito* (dried grapes) version,
Passo delle Viscarde. (PW)

● **Graticciaia**★★★ £E ● **Brindisi** Vigna Flaminio★★ £B
● **Salice Salentino** Vereto★ £B

CONTI ZECCA Puglia www.contizecca.it   A: HHB

Owner: Alcibiade Zecca Via Cesarea, 73045 Leverano (LE)
From across the Salento peninsula in Puglia, Conti Zecca do some fairly serious volume across their basic
range, Donna Marzia but this also affords enologist Dr Fernando Antonio Romano the opportunity to
make more modest volumes of progressively better wines from the DOCs Salice Salentino and
Leverano at slightly higher prices. From a fine wine point of view it also makes possible a
premium red called simply Nero of very impressive fruit richness and complexity. Only 25,000
bottles are made. Based on Negroamaro it also includes 30 per cent Cabernet Sauvignon. Slightly
less rich but more oaky yet very stylish is Terra which substitutes Aglianico for the Cabernet

component. Both deserve five years' age. Also of commendable quality (and similarly striking labels) are a soft yet concentrated and characterful Primitivo and Cantalupi Riserva, a Salice Salentino of quite serious quality for the appellation (80 per cent Negroamaro and 20 per cent Malvasia Nera). The latter seems particularly good value. (PW)

● **Nero**★★★ £D   ● **Leverano Riserva** Terra★★★ £C
● **Primitivo**★★ £B   ● **Salice Salentino Riserva** Cantalupi★★ £B
● **Leverano** Vigna del Saraceno★ £B   O **Leverano** Vigna del Saraceno★ £B

OTHER WINES OF NOTE

APOLLONIO ● **Copertino Rosso Riserva** Divoto £B   ● **Primitivo Terragnolo** £B
● **Valle Cupa** (Negroamaro /Primitivo) £B
BASILISCO ● **Aglianico del Vulture** £D
BOTROMAGNO O **Gravina** (Greco/Malvasia Bianca) £B
● **Pier delle Vigne** (Aglianico/Montepulciano) £B   ● **Primitivo** £B
CALATRASI ● **D'Istinto Magnifico** (Sangiovese/Cabernet Sauvignon/Syrah/Merlot) £C
CANDIDO ● **Cappello di Prete** (Negroamaro/Malvasia Nera) £B
● **Duca di Aragona** (Negroamaro/Montepulciano) £C
● **Immensum** (Negroamaro/Cabernet Sauvignon) £C
CANTELE ● **Amativo** (Negroamaro/Primitivo) £B
● **Varius** (Negroamaro/Cabernet Sauvignon/Montepulciano) £B
TENUTE DI CAPICHERA O **Vermentino di Gallura** Vigna 'Ngena £D
O **Capichera** (Vermentino) £D   O **Capichera Vendemmia Tardiva** (Vermentino) £E
CARPARELLI ● **Primitivo** I Pastini £B
CANTINE COLOSI O **Malvasia delle Lipari** Naturale di Salina £C Passito di Salina £D
O **Moscato di Pantelleria** £C   O **Passito di Pantelleria** £D
COLLI DI LAPIO/CLELIA ROMANO O **Fiano di Avellino** £D
ATTILIO CONTINI O **Vernaccia di Oristano** Riserva £C Antico Gregori £E
COS ● **Cerasuolo di Vittoria** £B   ● **Scyri** (Nero d'Avola) £C   O **Ramí** (Inzolia/Grecanico) £B
DE CONCILIIS ● **Donnaluna Aglianico** £B   ● **Naima** (Aglianico) £D
DUCA DI SALAPARUTA ● **Duca Enriico** (Nero d'Avola) £D
O **Bianco di Valguarnera** (Inzolia) £B
FEOTTO DELLO JATO ● **Rosso di Turi** (Merlot) £C   ● **Syrae** (Syrah) £C
O **Zabbya** (Cataratto - mod. sweet) £D
BENITO FERRARA O **Greco di Tufo** £C Vigna Cicogna £D
FEUDO PRINCIPI DI BUTERA (Zonin) ● **Nero d'Avola Deliella** £E
● **Merlot Calat** £E   ● **Cabernet Sauvignon San Rocco** £E
FIRRIATO ● **Harmonium** (Nero d'Avola) £D   ● **Camelot** (Cabernet Sauvignon/Merlot) £C
CANTINE FLORIO O **Marsala** Vergine Oro Terre Arse £C Vergine Oro Baglio Florio £C
O **Marsala Superiore** Riserva Vecchioflorio £C
O **Vino Liquoroso di Pantelleria** Morsi di Luce £C
CANTINA SOCIALE GALLURA O **Vermentino di Gallura** Canayli £B
HAUNER O **Malvasia delle Lipari** Passito £E
LEONE DE CASTRIS ● **Salice Salentino** Riserva £B Riserva Donna Lisa £C
● **Primitivo di Manduria** Santera £B   ● **Illemos** (Primitivo/Montepulciano/Merlot/Negroamaro) £B
LUIGI MAFFINI O **Kràtos** (Fiano) £B   ● **Klèos** (Piedirosso/Sangiovese/Aglianico) £B
● **Cenito** (Piedirosso/Aglianico) £D
MASSERIA LI VELI ● **Salice Salentino** Pezzo Morgana (Negroamaro) £C
SALVATORE MOLETTIERI ● **Taurasi** Vigna Cinque Querce £C
ODOARDI ● **Savuto** £B   ● **Scavigna** Garrone £C
RIVERA ● **Castel del Monte** Riserva Il Falcone £C Aglianico Riserva Cappellaccio £C
ROSA DEL GOLFO ⊙ **Rosato Rosa del Golfo** £B
● **Quarantale Riserva Mino Calò** (Negroamaro/Primitivo) £D

TENUTE RUBINO ● **Marmorelle Rosso** (Negroamaro/Malvasia Nera) £B
● **Jaddico** (Negroamaro/Montepulciano/Malvasia Nera) £C ● **Visellio** (Primitivo) £C
O **Marmorelle Bianco** (Chardonnay/Malvasia Bianca) £B
FATTORIA SAN FRANCESCO ● **Cirò Rosso** Rondo dei Quattro Venti £C
SETTESOLI ● **Mandrarossa Bonera** (Nero d'Avola/Cabernet Sauvignon) £B
SPADAFORA ● **Don Pietro** (Nero d'Avola/Cabernet Sauvignon/Merlot) £C
● **Virzì Rosso** (Nero d'Avola/Syrah) £C ● **Schietto** (Cabernet Sauvignon) £D
CANTINA DEL TABURNO ● **Aglianico del Taburno** Fidelis £B ● **Delius** (Aglianico) £D
O **Serra Docile** Coda di Volpe £C O **Falanghina** £B O **Greco** £B
TERRE DEGLI SVEVI ● **Aglianico del Vulture** Re Manfredi £B
TERREDORA DI PAOLO ● **Taurasi** Fatica Contadina £D
O **Fiano di Avellino** Terre di Dora £C Campo Re £C
TORRE QUARTO ● **Tarabuso** (Primitivo) £C ● **Bottaccia** (Uva di Troia) £C
● **Quarto Ducale** (Primitivo/Uva di Troia) £C
TORREVENTO ● **Castel del Monte** Vigna Pedale £B
VALLE DELL' ACATE ● **Cerasuolo di Vittoria** £C ● **Il Moro** (Nero d'Avola) £C
CANTINA SOCIALE VERMENTINO O **Vermentino di Gallura** Funtanaliras £B
VILLA MATILDE O **Falerno del Massico** Vigna Caracci £B
● **Falerno del Massico** £B ● **Vigna Camarato** (Aglianico) £D
CONSORZIO VITICOLTORI ASSOCIATI DEL VULTURE ● **Aglianico del Vulture** Carpe Diem £B
● Vetusto £C

Author's choice (PW)

15 southern red stars
ABBAZIA SANTA ANASTASIA ● **Litra**
ARGIOLAS ● **Turriga**
BENANTI ● **Lamorèmio**
CEUSO ● **Custera**
DETTORI ● **Cannonau Dettori**
DONNAFUGATA ● **Contessa Entellina Mille e Una Notte**
LIBRANDI ● **Gravello**
MONTEVETRANO ● **Montevetrano**
MORGANTE ● **Don Antonio**
PALARI ● **Faro**
SANTADI ● **Carignano del Sulcis** Superiore Terre Brune
TASCA D'ALMERITA ● **Contea di Sclafani** Rosso del Conte
COSIMO TAURINO ● **Patriglione**
VALLONE ● **Graticciaia**
CONTI ZECCA ● **Nero**

10 superior expressions of Aglianico
BASILISCO ● **Aglianico del Vulture**
ANTONIO CAGGIANO ● **Taurasi** Vigna Macchia dei Goti
CANTINE DEL NOTAIO ● **Aglianico del Vulture** La Firma
D'ANGELO ● **Canneto**
FEUDI DI SAN GREGORIO ● **Taurasi** Selve di Luoti
GALARDI ● **Terra di Lavoro**
TENUTA LE QUERCE ● **Aglianico del Vulture** Vigna Corona
SALVATORE MOLETTIERI ● **Taurasi** Vigna Cinque Querce
PATERNOSTER ● **Aglianico del Vulture** Rotondo
TELARO/LAVORO & SALUTE ● **Galluccio** Riserva Ara Mundi

10 captivating whites

BENANTI ○ **Etna Bianco** Superiore Pietramarina
ANTONIO CAGGIANO ○ **Fiano di Avellino** Béchar
GIOVANNI CHERCHI ○ **Vermentino di Sardegna** Tuvaoes
COS ○ **Ramì**
CUSUMANO ○ **Cubìa**
FEUDI DI SAN GREGORIO ○ **Sannio** Falanghina
PLANETA ○ **Cometa**
SANTADI ○ **Vermentino di Sardegna** Cala Silente
TASCA D'ALMERITA ○ **Contea di Sclafani** Nozze d'Oro
TORMARESCA ○ **Castel del Monte** Pietrabianca

10 brilliant inexpensive reds

ACCADEMIA DEI RACEMI/FELLINE ● **Vigna del Feudo**
ACCADEMIA DEI RACEMI/SINFAROSA ● **Primitivo di Mandura** Zinfandel
APOLLONIO ● **Vale Cupa**
TENUTA LE QUERCE ● **Aglianico del Vulture** Il Viola
MORGANTE ● **Nero d'Avola**
PLANETA ● **La Segreta Rosso**
COSIMO TAURINO ● **Notarpanaro**
TELARO/LAVORO & SALUTE ● **Galluccio** Montecaruso
VALLONE ● **Salice Salentino** Vereto
CONTI ZECCA ● **Salice Salentino** Riserva Cantalupi

6 delicious sweet whites

ARGIOLAS ○ **Angialis**
BENANTI ○ **Passito di Pantelleria** Coste di Mueggen
ANTONIO CAGGIANO ○ **Mel**
DONNAFUGATA ○ **Passito di Pantelleria** Ben Ryé
FEUDI DI SAN GREGORIO ○ **Privilegio**
SALVATORE MURANA ○ **Passito di Pantelleria** Martingana

Spain

While for years the quality of Spanish wine in the more established regions and DOs had been acceptable it could also have fairly been said that the real potential in the country remained untapped. However, the past half-decade or so has seen dramatic change both in fine-wine production and in lesser regions. There are new-wave Riojas and an abundance of great reds from Castilla y Leon, but other, smaller regions like Priorat have also been providing some remarkable and striking wines in recent years. Further south, in the great centre of the country, relaxation of the regulations governing irrigation and a desire to harness the potential of some fine, old bush-vine plantings of regional varieties has brought small but commendable change. It remains depressing, however that with all this there is still a vast amount of very poor wine being produced in almost all the established regions.

The North-East

País Vasco is the Spanish Basque country and home to two tiny DOs with barely 125 ha between them. Both are close to the coast between Bilbao and San Sebastien. **Getariako Txakolina** is the more western of the two and slightly larger than **Bizkaiko Txakolina**. The best are dry, quite steely whites based on Hondarribi Zuri. The north-western sector of the **Rioja** DO stretches into País Vasco and includes some of the best of the region's sites in the Rioja Alavesa. The Rioja wine zone spreads out of the administrative region of Rioja, its borders stretching into Navarra to its north-east and Castilla y León to the west. The wine area is split into three sub-regions: Alavesa, Alta and Baja. Tempranillo performs well in the limestone soils of the Alavesa, which is moderated by cooling breezes, as is the Alta. The latter, though, has heavier clay soils more suitable for Garnacha, which dominates the plantings in the hotter Baja sub-region. Graciano is also planted and makes an important impact on many blends as well as providing the odd varietal. Most wines are a blend of the regions and, while generally the fruit of the Alavesa is the finest, there are outposts of quality in all three. Whites are dominated by Viura with some Garnacha Blanca and Malvasia but few are of anything like the quality of the reds. Of equal importance is the approach of the bodegas. The area has some very substantial producers but quality remains variable. The original ageing classifications of Crianza, Reserva and Gran Reserva are still in place but varietal labels are becoming far more commonplace and many fine new-wave premium wines are being produced, which are generally vinified with French rather than American oak. Some, it has to be said, are very pricey.

Navarra shares the native Tempranillo, Garnacha and Viura with Rioja but also has considerable plantings of the international varieties; Cabernet Sauvignon, Merlot and Chardonnay are all found in abundance here. Some impressive wines are produced but one often feels price is a key in the producer's approach and there should be more excitement than there is. To the east and stretching far towards the south of Navarra are the arid plains of Aragón. Bulk wine is generally the order of the day but there are two DOs worth considering: **Campo de Borja** and **Somontano**. There is nothing spectacular but some good reds and the occasional Chardonnay stand out.

Running south from the Pyrenees and along the Mediterranean coast on the Costa Brava is Cataluña, home to a diverse number of wine regions. Right up close to the French border a few fine, traditional reds are made in the **Empordà-Costa Brava** DO. Some good red and white is produced from the **Costers del Segre** DO and a vast array of indigenous and international grapes are planted. To the immediate east are the vineyards of **Conca de Barberá**, cooled by altitude and source of good Chardonnay and Pinot Noir, but most of the fruit is sold on. Just inland from the coast and south-west of Barcelona are the vineyards of **Penedès**, established in a global sense by the efforts of Miguel Torres. Some fine red and white is produced, again from a mix of local and international varieties but much of the output is relatively pedestrian. Interestingly the odd low-volume, garage-style red is appearing too. Penedès is also the centre of the vast **Cava** DO. These sparkling wines are made by the traditional method from a combination of local Macabeo, Parellada and Xarel-lo as well as Chardonnay and Pinot Noir. Some well-crafted vintage bottlings are produced but generally the quality is sound at best. Many operations are very substantial and automation in the cellars is common. Cava at the lower levels can often display a marked rubbery character.

Immediately to the west of Penedès are the vineyards of **Tarragona**, which has a superior new sub-region, **Monsant DO**, and the small, very high-quality region of **Priorat**. Tarragona is planted to a range of varieties and fortified wines are still produced here. It is the reds, though, that excel and none more so than the suberb old-vine plantings of Garnacha. The best can rival top-quality Châteauneuf-du-Pape. The reds in Priorat are the wines with the greatest potential. They include a fascinatingly variable blend comprising Garnacha, Cariñena, Cabernet Sauvignon, Syrah, Merlot and Pinot Noir. The vineyards are ideally planted in finely drained, stony soils and the climate is warm but not excessively so.

The North-West

The wines of north-western Spain are produced in Castilla y León and Galicia. Immediately to the west of Rioja is **Ribera del Duero** which, along with exceptional examples in Rioja and Priorat, produces the finest reds in the country. The historic Vega Sicilia bodega is based here and top reds are produced in and around the region as vino de mesa as well as DO. While the greatest Ribera del Duero wines are both magnificent and pricey, a vast number remain depressingly mediocre. The wines are based on Tinto Fino (Tempranillo) but may also include Cabernet Sauvignon, Merlot and Malbec in the blend.

To the north-west is the small DO of **Cigales**, where light, simple reds are made, and to the west the white-wine DO of **Rueda**. Interesting barrel-fermented wines from both Sauvignon Blanc and the local Verdejo are produced. The latter can be responsible for some very striking and potentially ageworthy whites. Immediately west of Rueda and also centred on the Duero river towards Zamora and Portugal is the warm red-wine area of **Toro**. The vineyard area here has always promised much but it is only recently that wines of real depth have begun to emerge, some world-class. A local strain of Tempranillo, Tinto de Toro, is the mainstay of blends but Garnacha is also permitted. In the far west of the Castilla y León region is the small DO of **Bierzo** which produces easy-drinking reds and a little white.

Next to Bierzo but in fact in Galicia is **Valdeorras**. Reds are produced, like those in Bierzo, from Mencía but of particular note are the whites produced from the unusual, indigenous Godello. The best are floral, ripe and respond well to handling in oak. Some attractive, fruity whites are also produced in **Ribeiro** but the greatest interest lies in the coastal vineyards of **Rías Baixas**. These strikingly aromatic whites are generally best enjoyed young but the odd example is successfully barrel-fermented and will keep in the short- to medium-term, not dissimilar in this respect to Condrieu.

Central Spain

The vast central plains and particularly **La Mancha** are not generally associated with wines of any substance. Things are beginning to change, though, and new and interesting wines are emerging. Identifying cooler mesoclimates, harnessing the sheer quality of some of the old bush vines and outcrops of well-drained soils are some of the keys. The introduction of irrigation over the last decade has also given this arid area greater scope. It would appear so far that the best potential for reds is to the east of the area nearer the coast in **Valencia**, in the DOs of **Utiel-Requena** and **Jumilla**. The indigenous Bobal and Monastrell are both proving very successful. Some good fortified wine is produced from Monastrell at **Alicante,** as are some fine, sweet Moscatels. Cabernet Sauvignon, Merlot and Syrah are also grown with the aid of irrigation to the north of La Mancha. **Valdepeñas** used to be considered a beacon amongst the other wine regions of the area but nothing of real consequence has emerged recently.

The South

The south is fortified-wine country, most specifically the sherries of **Jerez y Manzanilla.** Andalucía is also home to the fortified wines of **Montilla-Moriles** and **Málaga.** Most of the former are decidedly ordinary but there are some exceptional wines from old *soleras.* The wines of Málaga are very rare, a blend of sweet wine and grape juice, some of which is fortified. The sherry industry is centred around the towns of Jerez and Sanlúcar de Barrameda to the north of Cádiz. The wines are all brought up in a *solera* system which is maintained by fresh young wines. Fino sherry in Jerez is very similar to Manzanilla at Sanlúcar. Both are best drunk on release for their fresh, salty character imbued by a period under flor yeast. Manzanilla Pasada is a rich, nutty, aged wine, having been exposed to flor influence, as is Amontillado. Oloroso will have no flor character at all, having been immediately fortified above 18 degrees alcohol. Palo Cortado is halfway in style between Fino and Amontillado. Rich and concentrated fortified Moscatel is also produced in the area as well as Pedro Ximènez. The latter is often close to technically not being wine: it can be fortified at just a few degrees alcohol and is astonishingly, sometimes overpoweringly sweet.

A-Z of Producers by region

Castilla la Mancha
MARQUÉS DE GRIÑÓN

Castilla y León
ABADÍA RETUERTA
MAURO
LEDA VINAS VIEJAS

Costers del Segre
CASTELL DEL REMEI

Jerez y Manzanilla
BARBADILLO
PEDRO DOMECQ
GONZÃLEZ BYASS
HIDALGO
EMILIO LUSTAU
VALDESPINO

Jumilla
CASA CASTILLO

Penedès
TORRES

Priorat
CELLER VALL LLACH
CELLERS J.M. FUENTES
CIMS DE PORRERA

CLOS I TERASSES
CLOS MOGADOR
COSTERS DEL SIURANA
MAS MARTINET
ALVARO PALACIOS

Rías Baixas
AGRO DE BAZAN
TERRAS GAUDA

Ribera del Duero
AALTO
ISMAEL ARROYO
DOMINIO DE PINGUS
HERMANOS CUADRADO
ALEJANDRO FERNÃNDEZ
PÉREZ PASCUAS
VEGA SICILIA

Rioja
FINCA ALLENDE
ARTADI
CONTINO
IJALBA
MARQUÉS DE MURRIETA
MARQUÉS DE RISCAL
MUGA
PALACIOS REMONDO
REMELLURI
LA RIOJA ALTA
RODA

Rueda
BODEGAS DE CRIANZA CASTILLA LA VIEJA

Toro
MAURODOS

Tarragona
CELLER DE CAPÇANES

Valencia
MUSTIGUILLO

Vintages

Although there is a reasonably uniform climate in most of Spain's more southerly regions, the chart below should provide a good guide as to what to expect with the premium red-wine areas. The maturity guide applies to top wines. Dry whites generally should be drunk on or shortly after release.

Spanish vintages

	Rioja	Ribera del Duero	Priorat
2002	★★★/★★★★ A	★★★/★★★★ A	★★★/★★★★ A
2001	★★★★/★★★★★ A	★★★★/★★★★★ A	★★★★ A
2000	★★★ A	★★★ A	★★★/★★★★ A
1999	★★★/★★★★ B	★★★/★★★★ A	★★★/★★★★ A
1998	★★★ B	★★★/★★★★ A	★★★★/★★★★★ A
1997	★★★ B	★★★ B	★★★ B
1996	★★★ B	★★★★ B	★★★★ B
1995	★★★★ B	★★★★ B	★★★★ B
1994	★★★★/★★★★★ B	★★★★ B	★★★★/★★★★★ B
1993	★★★ C	★★/★★★ B	★★★/★★★★ B
1992	★★★ C	★★/★★★ C	★★★ C
1990	★★★/★★★★ C	★★★★ C	★★★★ C

AALTO   Ribera del Duero   www.aalto.es

Owner: Aalto Bodegas y Vinedos SA   Roa de Duero, 09300 Burgos
Very impressive new estate producing richly concentrated, dense, modern style Ribera del Duero. The operation is relatively small with production between 8,000 and 9,000 cases a year produced from 82 ha of vineyards. Aalto own 32 ha and lease a further 50 ha and both are effectively farmed organically. All the vines are over 40 years old and yields can easily be kept to a minimum. Among the small group of partners Mariano Garcia looks after winemaking and had for 30 years been the enologist at VEGA SICILIA. His regime ensures careful sorting and ageing in 70 per cent new French oak. The wine is powerful, supple and very complex, full of dark fruits and oriental spices. The PS bottling adds an extra dimension and will only be released in the best vintages. (DM)
● **Ribera del Duero** Aalto★★★★ £E Aalto PS★★★★★ £F

ABADÍA RETUERTA   Castilla y León   www.abadia-retuerta.com   A: JAr

Owner: Novartis Group   Sardon de Duero, 47540 Valladolid
Ambitious but very impressive project based just outside the boundaries of Ribera del Duero. There are now over 200 ha of vineyards and although the range is extensive, quality is uniformly impressive. Considerable investment has been put into the operation, which includes a state-of-the-art, gravity-fed winery. The Bordeaux red varieties are planted as well as Tempranillo and Syrah. Viña Arnaldo, Primicia and Rivola offer attractive early drinking, while the Abadía Retuerta Especial red is fuller, more structured and with more oak. El Campanario Reserva is produced from Tempranillo, El Palomar from Tempranillo and Cabernet Sauvignon. Limited amounts of three special top cuvées represent the pinnacle here: Pago Valdebellón from Cabernet Sauvignon, Pago Negrallada from Tempranillo and PV produced from Petit Verdot. The top reds are very ageworthy. (DM)
● **Primicia** Vino de Mesa★ £B ● **Viña Arnaldo** Vino de Mesa★★ £B ● **Rivola** Vino de Mesa★★ £C
● **Selección Especial** Vino de Mesa★★★ £D ● **Cuvée El Campanario** Vino de Mesa★★★ £E
● **El Palomar** Vino de Mesa★★★★ £F

AGRO DE BAZÁN   Rías Baixas

Owner: Agro de Bazan S.A.   Tromoedo 46, Villanueva de Arosa, 36628 Pontevedra
Small, first-class producer in this potentially high-quality appellation in Galicia, with a mere 13 ha under vine. Many Albariño-based whites are produced for early consumption and can lack grip and structure, as is the case with the approachable, but attractively aromatic Granbazán Verde. However, the Granbazán Ambar is richer and more concentrated, resembling a good Condrieu. It has a pure mineral structure and the depth to develop well over two or three years – not long-lived but richly harmonious with a little bottle-development. (DM)
O **Rías Baixas** Granbazán Verde★★ £B Granbazán Ambar★★★ £C

FINCA ALLENDE   Rioja   fallende@fer.es   A: M&V

Owner: Miguel Angel de Gregorio   Pl. Ibarra 1, Briones, 26330 La Rioja
One of the very best producers in Rioja. The first wine was actually only produced here in 1995. Most of the fruit comes from their own vineyards in the Rioja Alta although some other growers are used also. Impressive Rioja Blanco, blended from Viura and Malvasia is fermented and aged for a year in French oak. The Rioja Tinto gets just over a year in a combination of French and American wood. There are two other very concentrated and complex reds. Calvario is Tempranillo with a bit of Garnacha and Graciano and comes from a single vineyard planted in 1945. The top wine, the

pricey Aurus from 60-year-old vines, is equally impressive – unfiltered and vinified with some whole bunches as well as being given a lengthy conventional maceration of around four weeks, thus adding weight and a supple texture. Both very complex and harmonious, it will age gracefully. (DM)

● **Rioja**★★ £B Calvario★★★★ £F Aurus★★★★ £G
○ **Rioja** Blanco★★ £B

ISMAEL ARROYO Ribera del Duero www.valsotillo.com A: N&P, NYg

Owner: Arroyo family Los Lagares 71, Sotillo de la Ribera, 09441 Burgos
Fine, quality producer of dense, powerful and tannic Ribera del Duero. The wines can be among the best in the DO. Top wines go under the Val Sotillo label and include Crianza, Reserva and Gran Reserva from the small 16-ha estate vineyard holding. Even the Crianza is very structured while the Gran Reserva has formidable extract with concentrated, dark fruit, subtle, spicy oak and real refinement. Wines that demand to be cellared. (DM)

● **Ribera de Duero** Val Sotillo★★ £B Val Sotillo Crianza★★★ £C Val Sotillo Reserva★★★ £E
● **Ribera de Duero** Val Sotillo Gran Reserva★★★★ £F

ARTADI Rioja A: BBR, GWW, NYg, Bal

Owner: Cosecheros Alaveses S.A. Ctra. Logroño, Laguardia, 01300 Alava
This is the brand name of the Cosecheros Alaveses bodega and an impressive range of new-wave Rioja is produced here from 75 ha of vineyards. The range includes well-crafted regular white and red; the former is barrel-fermented while the latter sees no oak. A level up are the Viñas de Gain Crianza and the more expensive Pagos Viejos Reserva. Both are rich, ripe and concentrated reds in marked contrast to the many other disappointing examples emanating from the region in recent years. There are also two other very impressive Reservas: Viña El Pisón comes from a single vineyard whereas the Grandes Añadas is a very limited, special bottling. It is only released in the greatest years and is very pricey. A fine modern source. (DM)

● **Rioja** Viñas de Gain★ £B Viñas de Gain Crianza★★ £C Pagos Viejos Reserva★★★ £E
● **Rioja** Viña El Pisón Reserva★★★★ £F
○ **Rioja** Viñas de Gain★ £B

BARBADILLO Jerez y Manzanilla www.barbadillo.com A: JEF

Owner: Antonio Barbadillo S.A. Luis de Eguilaz 11, Sanlúcar de Barrameda, 11540 Cádiz
This producer is based in Sanlúcar de Barrameda and the key focus is the production of good and often exceptional Manzanilla. There are two lighter styles, Solear and En Rama, which resemble Jerez Fino. The En Rama is very intense with a real salty, yeasty depth and a piercing, background citrus character. In addition there is an excellent, nutty, aged style of Amontillado de Sanlúcar – bone-dry, almost austere but marvellously intense – a Manzanilla Pasada and the rich, powerful and heady Cuco Oloroso. A number of remarkable old wines from venerable *soleras* are available and labelled as Relics, including Amontillado, Oloroso, Palo Cortado and Pedro Ximénez. They are understandably very pricey but are surely at the pinnacle of great sherries. (DM)

○ **Solear** Manzanilla★★ £B ○ **En Rama** Manzanilla★★ £B ○ **Principe** Amontillado★★★ £C
○ **Cuco** Oloroso Seco★★★ £C ○ **Amontillado de Sanlúcar**★★★ £C ○ **Manzanilla Pasada**★★★ £C
○ **Obispo Gascón** Palo Cortado★★ £C ○ **La Cilla** Pedro Ximénez★★ £C

BODEGAS DE CRIANZA CASTILLA LA VIEJA   www.palaciodebornas.com   A: Res

Owner: Sanz family   Ctra. Madrid-A Coruña, Rueda, 47490 Valladolid
This is one of the best modern producers of Rueda. As well as white-wine interests in Rueda it also produces impressive Toro at the Bodegas Toresanas, including the Toro Amant Barrica – a supple, modern, fruit-driven style with some depth and substance. Among a fine line-up of Rueda whites under the Palacio de Bornos label there are a grassy, fresh Sauvignon Blanc that should be drunk young and three wines based on Verdejo. The Superior, which has a touch of Viura, is similarly fresh, grassy and herbaceous in style. Other wines are handled in oak. The Fermentado en Barrica is rich, toasty and buttery, while the Vendimia Seleccionada is more structured, with the pure green Verdejo fruit always making itself felt. (DM)

O **Rueda** Bornos Sauvignon Blanc★★ £B Superior Palacio de Bornos★★ £B
O **Rueda** Palacio de Bornos Fermentado en Barrica★★ £B Palacio de Bornos Vendimia Selecionnada★★★ £C

Bodegas Toresanas
● **Toro** Amant Barrica★★ £B

CELLER DE CAPÇANES   Tarragona   capsanes@retemail.es   A: Vni

Owner: Co-operatve   Llabería, Capçanes, 43776 Tarragona
Arguably Spain's finest co-operative, established way back in 1933, it must also be regarded as among the very best in Europe. It is really only in 1995 that high quality was achieved as a result of the production of a remakable Kosher wine, Flor de Primavera. This initiative was promoted by the Jewish community of Barcelona who wished to produce a high quality wine under strict *Lo mebushal* conditions, everything carried out by a rabbi and no pasteurization of the wine. It is now a splendid blend of Cabernet Sauvignon, Garnacha, Tempranillo and Cariñena. With the resulting new investment that this development brought the range of reds here is now extensive and generally very impressive. The 120- strong membership provides some splendid old-vine Garnacha, Tempranillo and Cariñena as well as Merlot, Syrah and Cabernet Sauvignon, drawing on close to 250 ha of vine-yards between them. The top-labelled reds are now classified under the recently established Monsant DO. Among the best wines are two ripe, berry-fruited styles – Mas Collet and Lasendal – which have a big dollop of Garnacha. Lasendal has some Syrah adding firm, tannic depth. Costers del Gravet is fuller and more structured – a blend of Cabernet Sauvignon, Garnacha, Cariñena and Tempranillo – but the tannin can be a touch raw in its youth. The Vall de Calàs, a blend of Merlot, Garnacha and Tempranillo is suppler and rounder with dark plum fruit. The top two wines, Mas Turtò and Cabrida, are both massively extracted, dense and powerful reds. The former is dominated by old-vine Garnacha, with Cabernet Sauvignon and Syrah lending structure and perfume. Cabrida, 100 per cent very old-vine Garnacha (some close to 100 years), is macerated on skins for four to five weeks and has a modern touch with malolactic in barrel, most of the oak being French. It is immensely concentrated, just lacking that element of extra refinement for true greatness but very impressive and ageworthy nonetheless. All of the wines offer excellent value for money. (DM)

● **Monsant** Mas Collet★★ £B Lasendal★ £B Costers del Gravet★★★ £B Vall de Calàs★★ £B
● **Monsant** Mas Turtò★★★ £C Flor de Primavera★★★ £D Cabrida★★★★ £E

CASA CASTILLO   Jumilla   A: M&V

Owner: Sánchez-Cerezo Roch family   Ctra. Jumilla-Hellín, Jumilla, Murcia
Among a number of rising stars from Spain's lesser-known southern regions. Despite the hot, arid climate of the area the vineyards here are planted at an altitude of over 700 m and this elevation and the limestone soils provide old bush-vine Monastrell (Mourvèdre) of exceptional quality. Vendimia,

a blend of Tempranillo as well as Monastrell, is full of vibrant juicy fruit; the varietal Monastrell is richer, fuller but equally approachable young. The top two wines are impressively concentrated and structured. Las Gravas has 40 per cent Cabernet Sauvignon and 10 per cent Syrah in the blend to lend grip to the dark, brambly old-vine fruit. It is aged in French oak. Pie Franco is 100 per cent Monastrell from ungrafted vines that are over 60 years old. Rich, dense and spicy, the wine is aged in mainly American oak. So far these all offer very good value. (DM)

● **Jumilla** Vendimia★ £B Monastrell★★ £B Las Gravas★★★★ £C Pie Franco★★★★ £D

CASTELL DEL REMEI Costers de Segre www.castelldelremei.com A: Mor, His

Owner: Cusiné family 25333 Lleida
Along with RAIMAT, this is the other major quality producer in this DO and arguably the best. Good to very good reds are made here along with Blanc Panell a tank fermented blend of Macabeo, Sauvignon Blanc and Chardonnay and Oda Blanc which is vinified and aged on lees for six months in American oak. It is the reds though that really stand out. Gotim Bru is a ripe, forward blend of Tempranillo, Merlot and Cabernet Sauvignon, which a spicy hint of cinnamon from 10 months ageing in American wood, as are all the reds here. Oda, is denser, more structured, a blend of Merlot, Cabernet Sauvignon and Tempranillo. The top label 1780 is a firmly structured blend of Cabernet Sauvignon, Tempranillo and Merlot. The top two reds will benefit from two or three years cellaring after release. (DM)

● **Costers del Segre** Gotim Bru★★ £B Oda★★ £C 1780★★★ £D

CIMS DE PORRERA Priorat cims@arrakis.es A: JAr

Owner: Cims de Porerra SL Ctra. Torroja, s.n. Porrera, 43739 Valladolid
One of an increasing number of top quality performers from this small but great appellation. There are 55 ha of vines here producing a firmly structured, rich and concentrated Priorat Classic dominated by Cariñena and blended with Garnacha and just a touch of Cabernet Sauvignon. Dark, spicy and beguiling in its fiery complexity. Two small scale single vineyard bottlings are also produced, Finca Pigat and Finca La Tena are both 100 per cent Cariñena. There is a good, much more forward second wine, Solanes. Produced from younger vines it will provide an exciting example of what the DO has to offer at a relatively affordable price. (DM)

● **Priorat** Classic★★★★ £F Solanes★★★ £D

CLOS I TERASSES Priorat closeramus@terra.es A: JAr, F&R

Owner: Daphne Glorian Valls 24, Gratallops, 43737 Tarragona
Very small but very impressive 10-ha Priorat property, established in 1989 and one of a number of emerging operations that have transformed this small DO from rustic backwater to important, quality wine region. Two wines are made here: the top wine, Clos Eramus, is a super-rich blend of Garnacha, Cabernet Sauvignon and Cariñena; the well-priced second wine, Laurel, is produced from Cabernet Sauvignon. Clos Erasmus is given extended ageing in new oak and is a massively dense, powerful and exotic style of red. It is both very concentrated and complex, but very firm when young and requires six to seven years' ageing. (DM)

● **Priorat** Clos Erasmus★★★★★ £F

CLOS MOGADOR Priorat closmogador@sendanet.es   A: Bal, GBa

Owner: René Barbier Ferrer Camí Manyetes, Gratallops, 43737 Tarragona

Talented owner and winemaker René Barbier Ferrer advises at a number of other wineries, including Daphne Glorian's CLOS I TERASSES, as well as producing wine here at his own 20-ha property. Clos Mogador is yet another super-rich, extracted, deep and dense example of this exciting appellation. The blend is Garnacha, Cabernet Sauvignon, Syrah and, unusually, Pinot Noir just adding a piercingly fragrant note. A big, structured wine, it will develop very well with age. (DM)

● **Priorat** Clos Mogador★★★★★ £F

CONTINO Rioja www.contini-sa.com   A: L&W, Frt

*Owner: **Viñedos del Contino S.A.** Finca San Gregorio, Laserna, 01321 Alava*

This traditional Rioja property is part-owned by CVNE and the wines are made by them. There is a total of some 60 ha of vineyards, 4 ha of which are Graciano. There were some cellar problems in the late 1980s but these have now been eradicated. There are now straightforward Crianza and Reservas which have reasonable depth and are supple and velvety in texture. As well as these, there is a varietal Graciano which is firmer and less approachable along with the single-vineyard Viña del Olivo. Both of these will develop well in the medium-term. (DM)

● **Rioja** Crianza★ £B Reserva★★ £D Graciano★★ £E Viña del Olivo★★★ £E

COSTERS DEL SIURANA Priorat   A: LyS, NYg, Vne

Owner: Carlos Pastrana Manyetes, s/n Gratallops, 43737 Tarragona

Sizeable operation by Priorat standards with 40 ha of estate vineyards. Carlos Pastrana was one of the earlier pioneers of the appellation establishing his estate in the 1980s. Of the wines the dense and powerful Clos de l'Obac is a dark, fiery and impressively structured blend of Garnacha and Cabernet Sauvignon in equal parts, with a little Merlot, Syrah and Cariñena. Dolç de l'Obac is an unusual sweet red blended from Syrah, Garnacha and Cabernet Sauvignon. The Miserere bottling, while good is lighter with reasonable depth and a soft rounded structure but with a leaner edge than others. Blended from Cabernet Sauvignon, Garnacha, Tempranillo, Merlot as well as Cariñena you feel there should be more. (DM)

● **Priorat** Miserere★★★ £E Clos de l'Obac★★★★ £F Dolç de l'Obac★★★★ £G

DOMINIO DE PINGUS Ribera del Duero   A: C&B, BBR

Owner: Peter Sisseck Hospital, Quintanilla de Onésimo, 47350 Valladolid

Now a cult wine among the top Ribera del Duero reds and rivalled for price only by VEGA SICILIA and the top limited *cuvées* from Priorat. Pingus was in fact only established as recently as 1995. Very modern in style and approach, the wine is massively extracted but has remarkably intense, pure, dark and spicy fruit. Malolactic fermentation in barrel provides a supple, velvety texture resulting in a wine which is not only approachable but very ageworthy. The second label, Fleur de Pingus, is also impressive. Sisseck is also the consultant overseeing the production of the wines of CLOS D'AGON . (DM)

● **Ribera del Duero** Pingus✪✪✪✪✪ £H

HERMANOS CUADRADO   Ribera del Duero   A: N&P

Owner: Cuadrado family Finca Villacreces, Ctra. de Soria, Quintanilla de Onésimo, 47350 Valladolid
This new Ribera del Duero property is producing some of the best wine in the DO. The vineyard is planted to Tinto Fino (Tempranillo), Merlot and Cabernet Sauvignon but thus far the wine has been produced solely from Tinto Fino. Just 2,000 cases are made and the Finca Villacreces is a powerful, firm, ageworthy example of the appellation. A new, tiny-production super-cuvée, Nebro, is also being made. It is very pricey. (DM)
● **Ribera del Duero** Finca Villacreces★★★ £D

PEDRO DOMECQ   Jerez y Manzanilla   A: PLB, ADo

*Owner: **Allied Domecq** San Ildefonso 3, Jerez de la Frontera, 11404 Cádiz*
Among the largest companies in Jerez de la Frontera with 1,100 ha of vineyards and a huge commercial range of sherry. The Fino La Ina is very well-known and is a good example of the style: light and fresh with an attractive salty, almost nutty tang. Better though are the rich, dry and austere Amontillado 51-1A, the Palo Cortado Capuchino, the Oloroso Sibarita and the Venerable Pedro Ximénez. All of these are now classified as VORS. Some pretty average Rioja is made under the Marqués de Arienzo label and the company has interests as far afield as Mexico. (DM)
O **La Ina** Fino★ £B   O **Amontillado 51-1A**★★★ £D   O **Sibarita** Oloroso★★★ £D

CELLERS J.M. FUENTES   Priorat   granclos@airtel.net   A:Bal

*Owner: **Cellers Fuentes Hernandez** Monsant 2, Bellmont del Priorat, Tarragona*
Small Priorat producer established in 1995 making an impressively structured and concentrated Gran Clos cuvée as well as a decent second wine, El Puig, and a straightforward nutty white Vinya Llisarda. There are 11 ha under vine planted in schistous soils and much of the production is sold internationally. Gran Clos is blended from mainly Garnacha with Carinena and a touch of Cabernet Sauvignon. A wine of formidable extract but with beguiling dark spicy berry fruit, it will develop well with five to seven years' ageing. (DM)
● **Priorat** Gran Clos Joset Maria Fuentes★★★★ £E

ALEJANDRO FERNÁNDEZ   Ribera del Duero   www.pesqueraafernandez.com   A:JAr, May

Owner: Alejandro Fernández Real 2, Pesquera de Duero, 47315 Valladolid
VEGA SICILIA may be the most famous property in this potentially great DO but Alejandro Fernández isn't far behind. His two wineries, Pesquera and Condado de Haza, produce some of the best examples here at all quality levels. The Pesquera Crianza is stylish and concentrated whereas the Reserva and Gran Reserva are real benchmarks – very dark, powerful and marked by subtle, cedary oak and, in the case of the Gran Reserva, a formidable structure. The Cuvée Janus is made only in great years and is not only massive in extract but remarkably fine. Sadly it is made in tiny quantities. The Condado de Haza wines don't quite match their stablemates but are impressive nonetheless. The Crianza is surprisingly forward in style, the Alenza more extracted and inevitably rich and heady. The Reservas and Gran Reservas demand to be cellared. Two interesting new projects are DEJHESA LA GRANJA and EL VINICULO. At the former in the region of Zamora, Fernández is producing a 100 per cent Tempranillo that is aged for 24 months in American oak. At El Viniculo in La Mancha he produces two further Tempranillo varietals, one a Crianza aged for six months, the other a Reserva which sees 12 months in cask. In both cases American oak is used to complement the rich, and ripe warm-grown fruit. (DM)

Pesquera
● **Ribera del Duero** Crianza★★★ £C Reserva★★★★ £E Gran Reserva✪✪✪✪✪ £G

Condado de Haza
● **Ribera del Duero** Crianza★★ £C Alenza★★★ £G

GONZÁLEZ BYASS Jerez y Manzanilla www.gonzalezbyass.com

Owner: González Byass S.A. Manuel MªGonzález 12, Jerez de la Frontera, 11403 Cádiz
One of the most famous names in sherry production with a large volume of regular Fino and Amontillado that is sound but somewhat unexciting. However, the Tio Pepe brand, while produced in very large quantity, is nonetheless an impressive Fino – salty and intense with piercing citrus notes. Of a different order are a number of super-rich Amontillados and Olorosos. These include the refined Oloroso Añada, as well as the full, rich Alfonso, Apóstoles, and most notably Matusalem. Two other very impressive, full-bodied styles are made. The Amontillado Del Duque is dry, very intense and almost overwhelms one with its full, rich and toffeed *rancio* character. The Noé Pedro Ximénez is unctuously sweet, very rich and heady but refined too. The Rioja firm BODEGA BRETÓN is also run by González Byass. The wines, with the exception of the Alba de Bretón, are fairly uninspiring, though. (DM)

○ **Tio Pepe** Fino★★ £B
○ **Alfonso** Oloroso★★ £C **Añada** Oloroso★★★ £E ○ **Apóstoles** Oloroso★★★★ £E
○ **Matusalem** Oloroso★★★★★ £F ○ **Del Duque** Amontillado✪✪✪✪✪ £F
○ **Noé Pedro** Pedro Ximénez★★★★ £E

HIDALGO Jerez y Manzanilla www.lagitana.es

Owner: Hidalgo family Banda de la Playa 42, Sanlúcar de Barrameda, 11540 Cádiz
Large Sanlúcar-based operation with some impressive sherry brands. Best-known is La Gitana Manzanilla, which provides consistently good value with fresh, tangy, lightly salty fruit. It particularly needs to be drunk young. There are two volume ranges and the better wines go under the Napoleon label. The Amontillado is slightly toffeed and nutty but dry, and there is a fresh Fino Superior and an evolved and nutty Oloroso Abocado. Generic sherry styles are produced simply under the Hidalgo label. Jerez Cortado is a soft, round style but from a very old *solera*. There are also two single-vineyard wines: Amontillado and Manzanilla Pastrana. The Manzanilla is an aged Pasada, with an evolved, nutty character as well as an underlying hint of citrus. The Amontillado is a wine that originally started life as a Manzanilla. The former is now VOS. The range is completed by the impressive collection of rare Viejo wines. The Amontillado and Oloroso are now classified as VORS. The latter is almost bone dry but full of evolved *rancio* notes. Impressively complex. (DM)

○ **La Gitana** Manzanilla★ £B ○ **Napoleon** Amontillado★★ £B **Napoleon** Fino Superior★★ £B
○ **Amontillado Pastrana**★★★★ £E ○ **Manzanilla Pastrana**★★★ £B ○ **Jerez Cortado**★★★ £C
○ **Amontillado Viejo**★★★★ £E ○ **Palo Cortado Viejo**★★★ £D ○ **Oloroso Viejo**★★★★ £E

IJALBA Rioja www.ijalba.com   A: HHB, VRt

Owner: Dionisio Ruiz Ijalba Ctra. Pamplona, Logroño, 26006 La Rioja
Three reds and a decent fruity white, Genoli, are produced at this 70-ha property. The Múrice Tinto Crianza is a good modern, fruit-driven style. The Graciano Tinto is precisely that, an unusual varietal Graciano which is full of dark brambly fruit. It is structured and will age well and is quite unlike most Rioja in style. A level up, the Reserva is 90 per cent Tempranillo, the small-production Reserva Especial is an equal blend of Tempranillo and Graciano. Both are full, deep and extracted

styles with surprising weight and depth. Better with four or five years' ageing. (DM)

● **Rioja** Múrice Tinto Crianza★ £B   Graciano★★ £B   Reserva★★★ £D

LEDA VIÑAS VIEJAS   Castilla y Leon

*Owner: **Leda Viñas Viejas SL**   47320 Tudela de Duero, Valladolid*
This is an exciting new project along the lines of Mauro and Abadia Retuerta, producing first class red wine not just from within the boundaries of the Ribera del Duero DO. Winemaker César Munoz, who is also responsible for the up and coming Ribera wines at Bodegas MONTEBACO is one of the partners here. Currently some of the fruit is sourced from Ribera and some from the Cigales DO. Produced from 100 per cent Tinto Fino, the average age of the vines is 50 years. The resulting wine is deep, dark and formidably extracted but with a fine balance and supple structure. It will age very well for a decade or so. (DM)

● **Viña Leda★★★★** £E

EMILIO LUSTAU   Jerez y Manzanilla   www.emilio-lustau.com   A: M&V

*Owner: **Emilio Lustau S.A.**   Pl. del Cubo,4 Jerez de la Frontera, 11403 Cádiz*
Sizeable sherry operation supplying a considerable international own-label market. It also has a splendid range of high-quality sherries sold under its own label. A good Solera Reserva range includes salty, good-value Puerto Fino, Palo Cortado Peninsula and Amontillado Escuadrilla. The Almacenista label offers very impressive, nutty Manzanilla Amontillado, a beautifully evolved, very lightly salty Manzanilla Pasada and the richly concentrated Amontillado del Puerto. The Emperatriz Eugenia Oloroso is more developed and shows greater *rancio* character. The Old East India Solera is full of nutty, burnt toffee aromas. Very unusual and very rich, almost overly so, is the Moscatel Superior Emilin. A considerable range of very fine old wines are also offered from the company's oldest *soleras* under the Very Old, Very Old Rare and Single Cask labels. (DM)

O **Puerto Fino** Solera Reserva★★ £B   O **Palo Cortado Peninsula** Solera Reserva★★ £B
O **Almacenista** Manzanilla Pasada★★★ £D   O **Almacenista** Manzanilla Amontillado★★★ £D
O **Empertriz Eugenia** Oloroso★★★ £D   O **Old East India Solera** Oloroso★★★★ £D
O **Moscatel Superior** Emilin★★★ £D

MARQUÉS DE GRIÑÓN   Castilla la Mancha   www.marquesdegrinon.com   A: Arc, BWC

*Owner: **Marqués de Griñón S.A.**   Avenida del Ebro, 26540 Alfaro, La Rioja*
Based in Rioja and part-owned by the giant Arco Bodegas Unidas group (whose brands include Berberana and Marqués de Monistrol). The main focus of interest are the Dominio de Valdepusa wines produced on the Marqués's private 30-ha estate to the south of Madrid. These are very well-crafted and stylish reds in one of Spain's large, arid and far from fancied wine regions. The key here is the use of irrigation and a commitment to viticulture with sophisticated modern trellising. Four good to very good reds are produced: Cabernet Sauvignon, Petit Verdot, Syrah and a blend of all three, Eméritus. The Syrah is rich and smoky and the Petit Verdot scented yet firm – it needs more time than the others, five or six years. The Cabernet, surprisingly, has quite a green note which can show through in the Eméritus as well. The Marqués de Griñón label is also used for the straightforward Durius brands; red and white are produced and the white from Rueda fruit can be good. Marqués de Griñón Rioja is also well-established: the Alea Crianza is simple but a bit one-dimensional, the Reserva is good, with depth and some concentration. (DM)

Dominio de Valdepusa
● **Cabernet Sauvignon** Montes de Toledo★★ £C   ● **Petit Verdot** Montes de Toledo★★★ £C

● **Syrah** Montes de Toledo★★★ £C ● **Émeritus** Montes de Toledo★★★★ £E

Marqués de Griñón Rioja
● **Rioja** Reserva Colección Personal★★ £D

MARQUÉS DE MURRIETA Rioja rrpp@marquesdemurrieta.com A: MMD

Owner: Creixell family Ctra. Zaragoza, Km.5 Logroño, 26006 La Rioja
This most conservative of the Rioja bodegas produces traditional reds and whites which are exposed
to considerable periods of oak-ageing. There are some 300 ha of vineyards and production is sizeable
at 250,000 cases or so a year. Gran Reservas are now all released under the Castillo d'Ygay label and
Reservas are now simply Murrieta. The white Reserva El Dorado is citrusy with very marked vanilla
essence – oaky but good. The Castillo d'Ygay white is more evolved but very intense. The red Reserva
and Gran Reserva can be more variable with occasionally very high volatile acidity. At their best they
are splendidly rich, particularly the Castillo d'Ygay Especial which can be of a different order. In a
concession to new-wave Rioja styles a premium red, Dalmau, is now produced. It is firm, structured
and above all elegant and it should develop well with five or six years' cellaring. A less oaked, straightforward white Misela is also produced in Rioja, and in Rías Baixas a peachy, lightly exotic white Pazo
de Barrantes, which should be drunk young. (DM)
● **Rioja** Reserva★★ £C Gran Reserva Especial Castillo d'Ygay★★★ £E Dalmau Reserva★★★★ £F
O **Rioja** Reserva El Dorado★★ £B

MARQUÉS DE RISCAL Rioja www.marquesderiscal.com A: L-P, His

Owner: Herederos del Marqués de Riscal   Torrea 1, Elciego, 01340 Alava
Much development and expense has been put into this noble old bodega in recent years. Paul
Pontallier of CHATEAU MARGAUX has provided additional guidance in the winery. Some of the
releases in the early 1990s were variable to say the least, but things seem to be taking a welcome turn
for the better. The Riojas under the Marqués de Riscal label can still disappoint but the Barón de
Chirel Reserva is very impressive: rich but structured and youthfully firm in style. It will make excellent
drinking with five or six years' bottle-development. Riscal's Rueda has been consistently good in
recent years. The fresh Superior and Sauvignon should both be enjoyed young, the Limousin is lightly
oaky and leesy and will benefit from keeping for two or three years. (DM)
● **Rioja** Gran Reseva★ £D Reserva Baron de Chirel★★★ £F
O **Rueda** Sauvignon Blanc★ £B Superior★ £B Limousin★★ £B

MAS MARTINET Priorat martinet@arrakis.es A:N&P, Rae

Owner: Pérez Overjero family   Ctra, Falset-Gratallops, Falset, 43730 Tarragona
Small family run operation producing some excellent results in this high quality DO. The Perez
Ovejero family possesses some 7 ha of vineyards producing a marvellously complex,
structured example of the appellation. In Clos Martinet they handcraft a wine with more elegance
and less raw power than some of the wines of their neighbours but raely less intensity or finesse. It
is a blend of Garnacha, Syrah, Cabernet Sauvignon and Cariñena. One of the winemakers here Jose
Luis Perez was also involved with CIMS DE PORRERA. The second wine Martinet Bru, like the Clos
Martinet itself, is very well priced and relatively soft and accessible, if lacking the depth and quality
of some of the other secondary labels now emerging. (DM)
● **Priorat** Martinet Bru★★ £C Clos Martinet★★★★ £F

MAURO   Castilla y León   www.bodegasmauro.com   A: JAr

Owner: Bodegas Mauro S.A.   Cervantes 12, Tudela de Duero, 47320 Valladolid
Like that other top-quality Castilla y León producer ABADIA RETUERTA, this property is also producing fine quality reds under the vino de mesa classification. A total of slightly more than 15,000 cases are made from 35 ha. The vineyards are planted mainly to Tempranillo but also to Syrah and Garnacha and soils are well-drained and stony. Three reds are produced: a supple, opulent, forward style simply labelled Mauro; a Vendimia Seleccionada, which is richer and firmer; and a single-vineyard cuvée, Terreus, which is limited and produced only when the vintage conditions are particularly fine. It comes from very old vines and requires medium-term cellaring. There is also a new Toro property, Bodega MAURODÓS, established by Mariano Garcia, one of the partners as well as the winemaker here. The red Viña San Román shows great potential. (DM)
● **Mauro** Vino de Mesa★★★ £D Vendimia Seleccionada Vino de Mesa★★★★ £F Terreus★★★★★ £F

MAURODOS   Toro

Owner: Garcia family   Carretera N-122, Villaester, Valladolid
As well as the excellent wines he has been involved in developing at MAURO, enologist Mariano Garcia established this benchmark Toro property in the mid 1990s. Just one wine is made, Vina San Roman, which is varietal Tinta de Toro, with production still small at just over 4,000 cases a year. It is a marvellously dense, opulent and richly textured red, full of dark berry fruit and supple tannin. The considerable structure, youthfully firm grip from both the tannins and oak will necessitate a little patience. Given five or six years ageing the wine should provide ample reward. (DM)
● **Toro** Viña San Román★★★★ £F

MUGA   Rioja   www.bodegasmuga.com   A: Res

Owner: Muga family   Barrio de la Estación, Haro, 26200 La Rioja
This is a small (by Rioja standards), family-owned bodega. The approach is fiercely traditional for most of the range and at best the wines can be very good. There can also be infuriating variations in quality with oxidation and high volatile acidity being regularly encountered. Fermentation is in wooden vats and ageing in oak. Nevertheless the Reserva and Gran Reserva can display classically mellow, rounded Tempranillo character with vanilla and coconut notes infused from extended time in cask. Tempranillo is blended with Garnacha, Mazuelo and Graciano in the Reserva and Prado Enea; with Mazuelo and Graciano in the impressive and expensive new, modern-style Torre Muga, which is loaded with vibrant, blackberry fruit and velvety tannin. Good white Fermentado en Barrica shows some depth and some decent, fruity rosé completes the range. (DM)
● **Rioja** Reserva★★ £C Gran Reserva Prado Enea★★ £D Torre Muga★★★ £F
O **Rioja** Bianco★ £B

MUSTIGUILLO   Valencia   mustiguillo@inicia.es   A: Lib, NYg

Owner: Sarríon family   Chera 20, Requena, 46340 Valencia
Recently established but very impressive new producer with some 80 ha of vineyards in unheralded Valencia. Much of the vineyard is planted to very old, unirrigated Bobal, which provides potentially exceptional raw material. Currently production is less than 2,000 cases but this will rise. Tempranillo, which is by no means young at 30 years, and Cabernet Sauvignon are also planted. Two wines are produced. Finca Terrerazu is the suppler and more forward of the two; it is a blend of Bobal,

Tempranillo and Cabernet and is aged for 16 months in a mix of mainly French and American oak. The pricier Quincha Corral is more structured and firm, a blend of both Bobal and Tempranillo. Winemaking is distinctly modern, with fermentation completed in barrel followed by the malolactic. These are rich, concentrated wines full of dark fruit and cedar. They are likely to improve in bottle for five years or more. (DM)

● **Finca Terrerazu** Valencia ★★★ £D   ● **Quincha Corral**★★★★ £F

PALACIOS REMONDO   Rioja   www.ddnet.esvinhos/herenciaremondo   A: M&V

Owner: Palacios Remondo family   Avenida Zargosa 8, Alfaro, 26540 La Rioja

As well as producing his own range in Priorat, Alvaro PALACIOS has also had a significant recent contribution to the family property in the Rioja Baja. The 150 ha of vineyards are planted in large, pebbly soils and provide a formidable resource for intensely flavoured fruit. There is a relatively simple, lightly oaked white Plácet, but it is the reds here which impress. La Vendimia is partly vinified by carbonic maceration, which provides a wine of immediate appeal. Dark and spicy La Montesa Crianza spends a year in oak. Propriedad is fermented in large wooden casks and then transferred to barrique for malolactic. It is supple and richly extracted. Dos Viñedos is a blend of varieties – Tempranillo with some Garnacha and Graciano sourced from two higher-altitude vineyards. Rich and concentrated, it is aged in both French and, for a shorter time, American oak. It will benefit from three or four years' cellaring. (DM)

● **Rioja** Herencia Remondo La Vendimia★ £B   Herencia Remondo La Montesa Crianza★★ £B
● **Rioja** Propriedad H Remondo★★★ £C   Dos Viñedos★★★ £F
○ **Rioja** Plácet★ £B

ALVARO PALACIOS   Priorat   alvaropalacios@ctv.es   A: C&B, BBR

Owner: Alvaro Palacios   Finca El Colomé, Gratallops, 43737 Tarragona

Alvaro Palacios established this excellent property in the late 1980s and he produces some very good to quite exceptional examples of the Priorat DO from his small 10 ha of vineyards. Experience gained in the Napa Valley has enabled him to produce modern, very finely crafted examples from this small but great region. Les Terasses is produced from fruit sourced throughout the area. The result is always harmonious and impressive, the wine displaying supple tannin and an exotic, dark fruit quality. The magnificently concentrated L'Ermita, produced from very old vines, is dominated by Garnacha with a hint of Garnacha Blanco, Cabernet Sauvignon and Cariñena. Finca Dofi has less Garnacha, although that is still the main variety, with a firm structure provided by the inclusion of Cabernet Sauvignon, Syrah, Merlot and Cariñena. It is very complex, with an almost floral, cedary character as well as the rich, dark fruit of the Garnacha. Finca Dofi and L'Ermita are both refined and very ageworthy, improving effortlessly for a decade or more. (DM)

● **Priorat** Les Terasses★★★ £C   Finca Dofi★★★★★ £F   L'Ermita✪✪✪✪✪ £H

PÉREZ PASCUAS   Ribera del Duero   A: RsW, BBR

Owner: Perez Pascuas family   Ctra. Roa, Pedrosa de Duero, 09314 Burgos

One of a regrettably still small number of top-quality producers in this great north-western appellation. Established in 1980 with some 100 ha of vineyards planted mainly to Tempranillo but also some Cabernet Sauvignon and Merlot. The wines are powerful and quite extracted and are now aged in a mix of French and American oak. Under the Viña Pedrosa label there are fine, structured Crianza and Reserva, as well as a denser, richer Gran Reserva with considerable tannin – a wine that demands patience. Pérez Pascuas, from a single vineyard is very refined and complex as well as powerful and firmly tannic when young. A silky, velvety texture will emerge with age, though. Gran Reservas particularly should be cellared for at least seven or eight years. A very small amount of a Pérez Pascuas Gran Seleccion limited *cuvée* is also made. (DM)

● **Ribera del Duero** Viña Pedrosa★★ £C Viña Pedrosa Crianza★★★ £D Viña Pedrosa Reserva★★★ £E
● **Ribera del Duero** Viña Pedrosa Gran Reserva★★★★ £G
● **Ribera del Duero** Pérez Pascuas Gran Reserva★★★★ £G

REMELLURI Rioja remelluri@sea.es A:Adm

Owner: Rodríguez family Ctra. Rivas de Tereso, s/n Labastida, 01330 Alava
This has now been established as one of the best of the new-wave Rioja producers for more than a decade. Telmo RODRIGUEZ, responsible for building the reputation of the bodega, has a number of other projects as well, producing wines in many of Spain's major appellations. There are 90 ha planted in the Rioja Alavesa and the vineyards are tended organically. French rather than American oak is used during the wine's *élevage* and the style provides greater fruit than is normally the case in the region. The Reserva and Gran Reserva, particularly, are structured and will stand some ageing – the latter will be all the better for five or six years in your cellar. The Crianza is supple and approachable. (DM)

● **Rioja** Crianza★★ £C Reserva★★★ £D Gran Reserva★★★ £E

LA RIOJA ALTA Rioja www.riojaalta.com A:LyS, NYg, BBR

*Owner: **La Rioja Alta Group S.A.** Avda de Vizcaya, s/n 26200, Haro-La Rioja*
This is one of the most fiercely traditional of the old Rioja Bodegas. It is a moderately sizeable operation with a production of around 40,000 cases a year. It was originally founded in 1890 and some founding families still have a share in the company. It is renowned for some of the very best traditional Reservas and Gran Reservas. Interests include the Bodega Torre de Oña, also in Rioja, where a modern, fruit-driven Baron de Oña is made and the Rías Baixas property Lagar de Fornelos, where a straightforward, peachy, fruit-driven white is produced. At the La Rioja Alta winery the wines are given considerable cask-ageing. The Viña Alberdi Reserva is the most modern with a mere two years in oak, a high proportion of it new. The Gran Reservas 904 and 890 spend respectively five and eight years in cask. There is no doubt that the sheer quality of the fruit and the wines' intensity is exemplary but releases tasted throughout the last five years have been patchy. A new state-of- the-art winery has also been completed in the Ribera del Duero and the first wines from the 76-ha vineyard there are yet to be released. Two vintages have now been vinified. Prior to this the fruit from the first seven harvests was sold. (DM)

La Rioja Alta
● **Rioja** Viña Alberdi Reserva★★ £D Viña Arana Reserva★★ £D Viña Ardanza Reserva★★ £D
● **Rioja** 904 Gran Reserva★★★ £E 890 Gran Reserva★★★ £F

Bodega Torre de Oña
● Rioja Barón de Oña Reserva★★ £D

RODA Rioja A: JAr

Owner: Rottlan-Daurella family Av.Vizcaya, 5 Haro, 26200 La Rioja
Impressive 50-ha Rioja property producing two Reservas and a new-wave Rioja *super-cuvée*, the very pricey Cirsion. The property was established in 1986 but much of the vineyard is over 30 years old. Current plantings comprise mainly Tempanillo with a smattering of Graciano and Garnacha. Roda I is the flagship of the two Reservas, powerful and concentrated but with the characteristic

underlying spicy, berry-fruit character of Tempranillo. Roda II is lighter but still much more than a second wine. Cirsion is rich, structured and cedary – a wine of great finesse and breeding. (DM)

● **Rioja** Roda I Reserva★★★ £E Roda II Reserva★★★ £E Cirsion★★★★ £G

TERRAS GAUDA Rías Baixas www.terrasgauda.com

Owner: Bodegas Terras Gauda S.A. Ctra. Tui-AGuarda, Rosal, 36760 Pontevedra
Founded in 1990, this is one the best properties in Rías Baixas. The vineyards in the Rosal Valley are to be found close to the River Miño, which provides a benevolent mesoclimate. All of the wines are based on the aromatic Albariño, with a small amount of Loureiro and Caiño Blanco. The Abadía de San Campio is marked by its piercing, almost peachy, aromatic fruit, while the Terras Gauda label offers more depth and concentration. Both are cool-fermented to emphasise their fruit. The Terras Gauda Black Label is vinified in oak, a portion new with *bâtonnage*. The wine has a weighty oak character but loses some of its exuberant fruit in the process. (DM)

O **Rias Baixas** Abadía de San Campio★★ £B Terras Gauda★★★£C Terras Gauda Black Label★ £C

TORRES Penedès www.torres.es

Owner: Torres family Comercio 20, Vilafranca del Penedès, 08720 Barcelona
Very important producer, now making wines from grapes sourced throughout Cataluña. The Penedès firm of Jean León has now been added to the operation. The Cabernet Sauvignon from Jean León has been decidedly patchy over the last decade but the Chardonnay can provide some attractive if toasty, rich, almost honeyed drinking. Overseas interests have been established in Chile with the MIGUEL TORRES brand but for many years now these have continued to disappoint. By contrast Miguel Torres' sister MARIMAR TORRES produces well-made and well-priced, cool-climate Chardonnay and Pinot Noir in California's Sonoma Green Valley. The Torres range is extensive and the regular wines are often less exhilarating than they might be. You have to look for the mid-range and top-flight labels to find real excitement. Among the reds, Atrium is a plummy, ripe Merlot, and Gran Coronas a blend of mainly Cabernet Sauvignon and Tempranillo. New to the range is Nerola, mainly Syrah with some Monastrell. The top reds include the Mas Borrás Pinot Noir which has still to show the quality achieved elsewhere with this tricky variety. The Mas la Plana Cabernet Sauvignon is structured and cedary, and the Grans Muralles is of real interest – a very local blend of Monastrell, Garnacha Tinta, Cariñena, Garró and Samsó, full of exotic dark fruit. Reserva Real is a very impressive blend of Cabernet Sauvignon, Merlot and Cabernet Franc. Of the whites, the commercial Viña Esmeralda is a blend of Moscatel and Gewürztraminer and has a dollop of residual sugar. More serious is Fransola, a lightly-oaked blend of mainly Sauvignon Blanc with some local Parellada. Milmanda is the pricey top Chardonnay from Conca de Barberá and Waltraud is a fine lime- and mineral-scented Riesling. Top reds are undoubtedly ageworthy; Reserva Real requires considerable patience. (DM)

Torres
● **Gran Coronas** Penedès★ £B ● **Atrium Merlot** Penedès★ £B
● **Mas la Plana** Penedès★★★ £E ● **Reserva Real** Penedès★★★★ £H
● **Grans Muralles** Conca de Barberá★★★ £E
O **Gran Viña Sol** Penedès★ £B O **Waltraud** Penedès★★★ £C O **Fransola** Penedès★★★ £D
O **Milmanda** Conca de Barberá★★★ £E

Jean León
O **Chardonnay** Penedès★★ £C

VALDESPINO Jerez y Manzanilla   A: HWC

Owner: A.R. Valdespino S.A. Pozo del Olivar 16, Jerez de la Frontera, 11480 Cádiz

Marvellous, old-fashioned sherry producer with an impressive holding of old *soleras* to provide some of the best examples to be found in Jerez. The salty and intense Fino Inocente has a marked *flor* yeast character but should be drunk as soon after purchase as possible to enjoy its fresh, pungent, citrus character. There is a very rich and toffee-like Pedro Ximénez Solera Superior which can only really be sipped. The Palo Cortado Cardenal is one of the very best examples of this unusual style. There are a number of rich and dry Amontillados. Tio Diego has an almost austere, tangy finish; Don Tomás has greater depth and concentration. By far the most interesting of the three is the remarkable, intense, nutty and fragrant Coliseo, one of the greatest sherries. This along with the Palo Cortado Cardenal and the rich and concentrated Oloroso su Majestad are now VORS. (DM)

O **Inocente** Fino★★ £B   O **Cardenal** Palo Cortado★★★ £C   O **Solera Superior** Pedro Ximénez★★★ £C
O **Tio Diego** Amontillado★★ £B   O **Don Tomás** Amontillado★★★ £C   O **Coliseo** Amontillado✪✪✪✪✪£E
O **Su Majestad** Oloroso★★★★ £D

CELLER VALL LLACH Priorat www.fm2.com/vallllach

Owner: Luis Llach 43739 Porrera, Tarragona

Singer Luis Llach founded this first class Priorat property in the early 1990s. He also has an interest in CIMS DE PORRERA. The first vintage bottled at Vall Llach was 1998. Much of the key to quality here has been the acquisition of some very old vineyards, varying from 60 to 90 years of age grown on slatey soil slopes. Viticulture is generally organic and chemicals are avoided. New plantings of Garnacha, Cabernet Sauvignon, Merlot and Syrah have been undertaken and these generally make up the bulk of the second wine Embruix. They also contribute texture and complexity to the main wine. Vall Llach itself is dominated by old vine Carinena, with Garnacha and Cabernet Sauvignon blended in. It is a dark, spicy, brooding beast, full of fiery *sauvage* character. It will require four or five years cellaring to soften its raw youthful edge. (DM)

● **Priorat**★★★★★ £F Embruix★★★ £C

VEGA SICILIA Ribera del Duero www.vega-sicilia.com   A: M&V, BBR

Owner: Alvarez family Ctra. N-122, Valbuena de Duero, 47359 Valladolid

Spain's most famous red wine producer. The quality of its wines in Ribera del Duero in recent years has been challenged by the likes of ALEJANDRO FERNANDEZ and DOMINIO DE PINGUS but Vega Sicilia remains quite distinct in style and approach. The top wine, Unico, which is a blend of Tinto Fino with Cabernet Sauvignon, Malbec and Merlot, is still given extended cask-maturation, although this has been reduced to help preserve the wine's fruit character. A non-vintaged Reserva Especial is also produced – very expensive and evolved in style. The second wine, Valbuena, produced from Tinto Fino and Merlot, has more obvious fruit character. In a move to provide a more contemporary approach but to retain the style of Vega Sicilia, a new winery, Alión, was established in 1991. These are impressive, structured and dense modern examples of the DO produced solely from Tinto Fino and full of dark, spicy fruit, supple tannin and cedary oak. Alión will benefit from at least five years' cellaring. Both Unico and Valbuena are accessible on release but will develop very well in bottle. The Alvarez family have also invested in Hungary in the Tokaji operation OREMUS. (DM)

Bodegas Vega Sicilia
● **Ribera del Duero** Valbuena★★★★ £F Unico✪✪✪✪✪ £H Reserva Especial★★★★★ £H
Bodegas y Viñedos Alión
● **Ribera del Duero** Alión★★★★★ £E

OTHER WINES OF NOTE

ALBET I NOYA O **Chardonnay** Collecció £B ● **Penedès** Reserva Marti £C

ALEMANY I CORRIO ● **Sot Lefriec** Catalunya £F

ALVEAR O **Montilla-Moriles** Alvear CB £C

ANTAÑO O **Rueda** Viña Mocén £B

HEREDEROS DE ARGÜESO O **San León** Manzanilla £B

BELONDRADE Y LURTON O **Rueda** £B Oak Aged £B

BODEGAS BILBAINAS ● **Rioja** la Vicalanda Reseva £B

BORSAO ● **Campo de Borja** Crianza £B Reserva £B

BODEGAS BRETÓN ● **Rioja** Alba de Bretón £F

CAMPILLO ● **Rioja** Reserva £C Gran Reserva £D

CAMPO VIEJO ● **Rioja** Gran Reserva Marqués de Villamanga £D

CAN FEIXES O **Chardonnay** Penedès £B

CAN RÀFOLS DELS CAUS ● **Penedès** Gran Caus £D Caus Lubis £D

CASA DE LA ERMITA ● **Jumilla** £B

CELLER DE CANTONELLA ● **Costers del Segre** Cérvoles £B

CELLER DEL PONT ● **Priorat** Lo Givot £E

CHIVITE O **Navarra** Colección Reserva Blanco £E

CLOS D'AGON ● **Clos d'Agon** Tinto Vino de Mesa £F O **Clos d'Agon** Blanco Vino de Mesa £E

CLOS FIGUERAS ● **Priorat** £F Font de la Figuiere £C

CODORNÍU O **Cava** Jaume Brut Non-Vintage £C

CVNE ● **Rioja Viña** Real Reserva £D Imperial Reserva £D

DELGADO ZULETA O **La Goya** Manzanilla £B

ENATE ● **Somontano** Reserva £E Reserva Especial £F

EUROPVIN FALSET ● **Monsant** Laurona £C 6 Vinyes de Laurona £E

FREIXENET O **Cava** Reserva Vintage £C

GRAND RECOSIND ● **Ampurdan Costa Brava** Crianza £B Gran Reserva £C

GRANJA FILLABOA O **Rias Baixas** Albariño £C

GUELBENZU ● **Navarra** Evo £C Lautus £E

GUTIÉRREZ DE LA VEGA ● **Viña Ulises** £C O **Casta Diva** £D

HACIENDA MONASTERIO ● **Ribera del Duero** £D

JUAN DE LA BARREDA ● **Torre de Barreda** Vino de la Tierra £B

LA TAPADA ● **Valdeorras** Guitián Fermentado en Barrica £C

LÓPEZ DE HEREDIA/VIÑA TONDONIA O **Rioja Crianza** Viña Gravonia £B

LUSCO DO MIÑO O **Rías Baixas** £C

MAGAÑA ● **Navarra** Dignus Crianza £B

MARQUÉS DE CÁCERES ● **Rioja** Gaudium £C

MARQUES DE VARGAS ● **Rioja** Reserva £D

MARTÍNEZ BUJANDA ● **Rioja** Conde de Valdemar Reserva £B Reserva £C Gran Reserva £D

MAS D'EN COMPTE ● **Priorat** Negre £E O **Priorat** Garnacha Blanca £E

MAS D'EN GIL ● **Priorat** Coma Vella £C Clos Fontà £E O **Priorat** Coma Blanca £D

MAS IGNEUS ● **Priorat** Fa 112 £E

MATARROMERA ● **Ribera del Duero** Crianza £C Reserva £E

MIGUEL MERINO ● **Rioja** Reserva £E

BODEGAS MONTEBACO ● **Ribera del Duero** Montebaco £E

MONTICELLO ● **Rioja** Viña Cumbrero £B Reserva £C

OSBORNE O **Solera India** Oloroso £E O **Alonso el Sabia** Oloroso £G

OTAZU ● **Navarra** Crianza £B Reserva £C O **Chardonnay** Navarra £B

PAGO DE CARRAOVEJAS ● **Ribera del Duero** Crianza £C Reserva £E

BODEGAS PALACIO ● **Rioja** Cosme Palacio y Hermanos £D

PAZO DE SEÑORANS O **Rías Baixas** £C

PIRINEOS ● **Somomontano** Moristel £B Merlot-Cabernet £B

RAÏMAT ● **Costers del Segre** Mas Castell £D Vallcorba £D

REMIREZ DE GANUZA ● **Rioja** Reserva £E
TEÓFILO REYES ● **Ribera del Duero** Crianza £C
BODEGAS RIOJANAS ● **Rioja Gran** Albina £C
TELMO RODRIGUEZ ● **Ribera del Duero** Valderiz £C ● **Rioja** Altas de Lanzaga £C
● **Toro** Dehesa Gago £E
SANCHEZ ROMATE O **Amontillado NPU** £C
ROTLLÁN I TORRA ● **Priorat** Amadis £D Tirant £F
SCALA DEI ● **Priorat** Negre Garnacha £C
SEÑORÍO DE SAN VICENTE ● **Rioja** San Vicente £E Sierra Cantabria Coleccion Privada £E
TARSUS ● **Ribera del Duero** Quinta de Tarsus £B Tarsus £D
TORO ALBALÁ O **Montilla-Moriles** Pedro Ximénez Don PX £C
VALPICULATA ● **Toro** £D
JANE VENTURA ● **Penedes** Margalló £C Finca Els Camps £D Mas Vilella £D
VIÑA BAJOZ ● **Toro** Crianza £B Reserva £C
VIÑAS DEL VERO ● **Somontano** Gran Vos £C
VIÑA SOLORCA ● **Ribera del Duero** Crianza £C
VINICOLA DEL PRIORAT ● **Priorat** Onix £C
WILLIAMS & HUMBERT O **Dos Cortados** Palo Cortado £C **Dry Sack Solera Especial** £D

Author's choice (DM)

The Spanish new wave
AALTO ● **Ribera del Duero** Aalto PS
ABADÍA RETUERTA ● **Pago Valdellón** Vino de Mesa
AGRO DE BAZÁN O **Rías Baixas** Granbazán Ambar
CELLER DE CAPÇANES ● **Monsant** Flor de Primavera
CASA CASTILLO ● **Jumilla** Pie Franco
CLOS I TERASSES ● **Priorat** Clos Erasmus
CLOS MOGADOR ● **Priorat** Clos Mogador
LEDA VINAS VIEJAS ● **Vina Leda**
DOMINIO DE VALDEPUSA ● **Émeritus** Montes de Toledo
MAURO ● **Mauro** Terreus
MAURODOS ● **Toro** Viña San Román
CELLER VALL LLACH ● **Priorat**

Established and emerging classics
FINCA ALLENDE ● **Rioja** Aurus
ISMAEL ARROYO ● **Ribera de Duero** Val Sotillo Gran Reserva
ARTADI ● **Rioja** Viña El Pisón Reserva
DOMINIO DE PINGUS ● **Ribera del Duero** Pingus
ALEJANDRO FERNÁNDEZ - PESQUERA ● **Ribera del Duero** Gran Reserva
MARQUÉS DE MURRIETA ● **Rioja** Gran Reserva Especial Castillo d'Ygay
MARQUÉS DE RISCAL ● **Rioja** Reserva Baron de Chirel
ALVARO PALACIOS ● **Priorat** L'Ermita
PÉREZ PASCUAS ● **Ribera del Duero** Pérez Pascuas Gran Reserva
LA RIOJA ALTA ● **Rioja** 890 Gran Reserva
RODA ● **Rioja** Cirsion
VEGA SICILIA ● **Ribera del Duero** Unico

A handful of great Sherries

BARBADILLO O Manzanilla Pasada
PEDRO DOMECQ O Amontillado 51-1A
GONZÁLEZ BYASS O Del Duque Amontillado
HIDALGO O Amontillado Pastrana
EMILIO LUSTAU O Old East India Solera Oloroso
VALDESPINO O Coliseo Amontillado

There is a fantastic revolution taking place in the quality of Portuguese wines. At the cutting edge are some brilliant winemakers making both everyday wines of great value and character and also exciting new wines of unprecedented quality for this ancient wine-producing country. The Douro, followed by Alentejo, provides the greatest riches but there are exciting wines from nearly all the major regions. There is still much poor wine at lower levels and even moderately ambitious efforts can show winemaking faults or a lack of balance – but the best wines from leading producers can be tried with confidence. Portugal's burgeoning middle classes account for the lion's share of the best wines and have pushed up prices but small quantities are exported and many new wines are being introduced every year.

Port & the Douro

The five leading varieties in this spectacular region were identified in the 1970s as Touriga Nacional, Tinta Roriz, Touriga Franca (previously called Touriga Francesa), Tinta Barroca and Tinto Cão. Some consider a sixth, Tinta Amarela, to be equally important. Though all were often planted as field blends that might include any number of other varieties, there has been an increasing trend towards planting by single variety. Where it is feasible on the steep schistous slopes, quality-conscious producers now favour vertical plantings (as used in the Mosel) with a resultant increase in density. But these vineyards co-exist with old-fashioned (occasionally single-row) terracing (*socalcos*) and the bulldozed terracing (*patamares*) that was introduced in the 1970s and allowed for greater mechanization.

In the west of the region the Serra do Marão range of mountains has a significant effect on the climate. There is a successive drop-off in average rainfall in stages from relatively rain-soaked Porto to Régua (Baixo Corgo – the westernmost of three sections), to Pinhão (Cima Corgo), to the dry, flatter lands of the Douro Superior (close to Spain) where there is some use of irrigation. Producers have shown it is possible to get grapes fully ripe in the Baixo Corgo around Régua though they are likely to be hardest hit in rain-affected vintages. Cima Corgo is the classic port country with the greatest concentration of 'A' classified vineyards (vines are classified A to F) and most of the famous *quintas*. A *quinta* defines a farm or estate which may be composed of vineyards of more than one grade. The *quintas* overlooking the Douro are important but so are those found on several small tributaries, especially those from the valleys of the Rio Pinhão and the Rio Torto. Here the greatest differences in character, structure and style are discernible from individual *terroirs*. Although many of the classic Vintage Ports are sourced from here fine port is also made in the Douro Superior.

Port has traditionally been stored at the port lodges in Vila Nova da Gaia (opposite Porto), but since 1986 it has been permitted to make, store and ship port at its source in the Douro. Quinta do Noval and Quinta de la Rosa were two of the first to take advantage of this but it is necessary to have cool cellars if the wines are not to take on a distinctive baked character known as Douro bake. Although autovinification is common for most ports, the best Vintage Ports are made by fermenting in *lagares*. Traditionally this involves treading by foot (though this is now being closely imitated by robotic devices) which allows the rapid but gentle extraction of colour, tannin and extract in the 48 hours or so before the fermentation is arrested by the addition of port brandy. Temperature control of *lagares* and the chilling of brandy are also used to harmonise this addition and avoid a spirity component in the resulting port.

Most table reds were previously made from inferior grapes or sites, but in the past decade leading producers have established potentially high-quality sites (or harnessed the potential of existing sites) specifically for Douro reds, resulting in a remarkable revolution in both the quality and quantity of premium examples. The best wines impress not only with splendid fruit, depth and structure but also the stylish minerality that the Douro's soils can bring. As with port, some of it is coarse, baked or unattractively earthy but the best are rich, complex and characterful.

Other regions

Good **Vinho Verde**, made in the Rios do Minho region, is rare. Despite changes to viticulture, the damp climate makes it difficult to get Alvarinho (the best grape), Loureiro, Trajadura or other grapes fully ripe for the white version that is widely exported. **Beiras**, a large region to the south of the Douro, includes both the DOCs Bairrada and Dão. Labels showing simply Beiras Vinho Regional can be wines that fall outside the regulations for these DOCs as well as wines from the wider region. Excellent vintages can be few and far between in **Bairrada**. The biggest problem is rain and the diseases which can result from it. The clay soils are largely planted to the Baga grape which is high in both tannin and acidity and it can be difficult to achieve full ripeness in its tannins. Nonetheless wines of great depth and character, if idiosyncratic style and flavour, are possible and much progress has been in recent years. The **Dão** has granitic sandy soils and is less exposed to the coast than Bairrada. Though once associated with tough, tannic reds that only occasionally showed well with considerable age, the last six or seven years have seen a dramatic improvement in quality and there has been increased planting of Touriga Nacional and Tinta Roriz on well-sited hillsides. Both grapes have been produced varietally as have Jaen, Alfrocheiro Preto and even some Tinta Cão, though these grapes generally perform better as part of a blend. The best estates now offer rich, ripe, modern but characterful reds. Fine quality whites have also been made from Malvasia Fina and Encruzado, the latter particularly promising in gently oaked varietal examples.

Estremadura covers undulating hillsides north of Lisbon but despite its proximity to the coast it avoids much of the cloud cover and rain of more northerly maritime-influenced areas such as Bairrada and Vinho Verde. It has long produced more wine than any other region, much of it from large co-ops. But here, too, things have improved and a handful of individual estates are emerging with some creditable wines. **Alenquer** is the most important sub-regional DOC. In the Ribatejo, despite many high-yielding vineyards, there is some good value to be had where a top winemaker has been contracted to make the wines. Both regions have a smattering of foreign varieties, including Cabernet Sauvignon and Syrah, but premium, sometimes varietal, examples of Portugal's best grapes are far more important.

One grape, Castelão (Periquita), brought to the region by José Maria da Fonseca in 1830, dominates production in **Terras do Sado** and nowhere else does it work varietally quite so well. The best smoky, minerally, earthy, spicy examples are sold as **Palmela** (a more defined area of mostly sandy soils on the Setúbal peninsula) or Terras do Sado. Based on Muscat of Alexandria variants, **Setúbal** and **Moscatel de Setúbal** (predominantly Moscatel) are famous fortified wines of good quality, particularly from José Maria da Fonseca. The still relatively small, scattered vineyards of **Alentejo** lie close to the Spanish border and are drier and less maritime-influenced. Most of the top Alentejo reds are blends based on Trincadeira and Aragonês (Tinta Roriz), with Castelão, Alicante Bouschet or even Cabernet Sauvignon as minor components. Syrah has been made varietally and shows promise in a rich, powerful if slightly earthy, robust way. Ripe, sound, attractive whites are on the increase from the Alentejo (grapes include Roupeiro and Arinto) but only a handful show sufficient depth or structure to improve beyond a couple of years' age.

Madeira

Madeira is made by a small number of shippers who for the most part buy grapes from the island's many small growers. Tinta Negra Mole dominates their vineyards but the best Madeira comes from the slowly increasing amounts of the traditional varieties. The wine needs to be made from at least 85 per cent of either Malvasia (Malmsey), Bual (Boal), Verdelho or Sercial to be labelled as such. As well as being fortified, fundamental to Madeira's style is a high level of acidity and a degree of caramelisation due to the heating process that the wines must undergo. *Estufagem*, the heating in hot stores (*estufas*) is central to the production of most Madeira, especially the stuff used for cooking. The best wines, however, are made by the *canteiro* system, whereby the wine is only subject to natural heating in cask over a period of three years or more. As a result the wines are less coarse and have less of a burnt-sugar flavour.

Each of the traditional varieties is associated with a certain degree of sweetness. The greater the sweetness, the higher the percentage of spirit in the wine as the fermentation is arrested at an earlier stage to retain a higher sugar level. The richest and sweetest, Malmsey – often pungent, full and toffeed – is usually the most easily appreciated but most examples miss the elegance and definition associated with the smoky, spicy, dried-fruits Bual (Boal), which is less sweet but still a dessert-style wine. The best Verdelho (of moderate sweetness) is often tangy yet lightly honeyed with dried citrus fruits and a certain delicacy of flavour and aroma. The dry Sercial, often with daunting acidity, can show a fine citrusy (orangey), nutty and dried-fruit complexity with age.

The best commercial styles are the 10-year-old and 15-year-old wines. The age indicated will be an average as the wines are blended to maintain a consistent style. Even from the best shippers, 3-year-old Madeira will almost invariably be made from Tinta Negra Mole and is likely to involve the addition of caramel and the use of concentrated must. Vintage Madeira will have spent at least 20 years in cask but many of the very best have spent 50 years or even 100 years in wood. Once bottled it continues to age but at a very slow rate. As they are only made in tiny quantities it is imperative to consult a specialist before parting with the considerable sums needed to secure a bottle. Rare examples of two other traditional grapes, Moscatel and Terrantez, are also occasionally encountered.

Port styles

There are two basic styles of port: those matured in bottle and those aged in wood. Of the first, **Vintage Port** applies to any port that meets the requirements of the IVP (Instituto do Vinho do Porto or Port Wine Institute) and is usually bottled before the summer of the second year after the harvest. It applies as much to single-quinta ports and 'off-vintage' ports (or 'second label' – a shipper's port from a non-declared year, increasingly made as a true single-quinta example) as to the declared ports. These wines, which may be bought through a wine merchant or agent prior to being shipped, will always require decanting. Late Bottled Vintage Port (or **LBV**) spends four to six years in large vats and the majority are fined and filtered to avoid any sediment forming in the bottle and are ready to be consumed when released. 'Traditional' examples, however, more closely resemble Vintage Ports in character and depth and, though they must be aged for a further three years in bottle, are not necessarily ready to drink when released. Some, having only the minimum bottle-age, will improve for a further five or six years. **Crusted Port**, like Traditional LBVs and Vintage Port, will throw a sediment but is a blend of two or three vintages rather than one and the year given is that of its bottling.

Of the wood-matured styles the most credible are those tawnies with an indication of age. Though extensively blended to maintain a house style, these gently oxidised styles can show considerable complexity and refinement. The quality of **10-year-old Tawny Port** is, however, extremely variable and in many instances the quality doesn't match the price. At worst they are simple, coarse and tired but better, fresher, balanced examples can show a date, nut, fig and toasty complexity that is seen more often in examples of the more pricey **20-year-old Tawny Port**. 30-and 40-year-old examples are variable (sometimes excessively volatile) and expensive but at their best have an intense, nutty rancio character and complexity not dissimilar to an aged sherry. **Colheita Port** is effectively a tawny port of a single vintage and is labelled with both the year of the *colheita* (harvest) and bottling year. They have a minimum of seven years in cask and can have all the qualities of the best tawnies with an indication of age but don't always have the fruit to further improve with extended bottle age. The most commercially important port is the relatively inexpensive **Vintage Character** or **Premium**

Ruby. The best offer good fruit intensity in an easy-drinking style and their brand names are more familiar to many consumers than the style of port. Regular **Ruby Port** is very young, fruity port (at best) while some basic Tawny Port is simply a poor Ruby cut with some **White Port**. The latter, from white grapes but turning amber with age, is usually best avoided as many taste sweet and doctored. A few are dry and nutty with some refinement.

A-Z Producers by region

Alentejo
CORTES DE CIMA
ESPORÃO
JOAO PORTUGAL RAMOS

Bairrada
LUIS PATO
SIDONIO DE SOUSA

Beiras
CAVES ALIANCA

Dão
QUINTA DE CABRIZ / DÃO SUL
QUINTA DOS ROQUES

Douro/Port
DOMINGOS ALVES DE SOUSA
CHURCHILL
COCKBURN
CROFT
DELAFORCE
DOW
FERREIRA
FOJO
FONSECA
GRAHAM
NIEPOORT
PINTAS
QUINTA DE LA ROSA
QUINTA DE RORIZ
QUINTA DO COTTO

QUINTA DO CRASTO
QUINTA DO INFANTADO
QUINTA DO NOVAL
QUINTA DO PORTAL
QUINTA DO VALE DONA MARIA
QUINTA DO VALE MEAO
QUINTA DO VALLADO
QUINTA DO VESUVIO
RAMOS PINTO
REAL COMPANHIA VELHA
SANDEMAN
SMITH WOODHOUSE
TAYLOR'S
WARRE

Estremadura
QUINTA DA CORTEZIA

Madeira
BARBEITO
HENRIQUES & HENRIQUES
MADEIRA WINE COMPANY

Terras do Sado
JOSE MARIA DA FONSECA
J P VINHOS

Other
SOGRAPE
SYMINGTON

Port vintages

It used to be so simple. Vintage port was made when the port shippers 'declared' a particular vintage was of sufficient quality to justify the bottling of a house port from that year. In other years, the same wine would be bottled under the name of a leading estate or quinta. But in a swing towards estate-based ports, some true single quintas make a port more in the mould of a Bordeaux château, that is to say in almost every year. Nonetheless general declarations are still important and still tend to highlight the very best years, though examples from a top source – whether a true single quinta or that of an 'off-vintage' quinta name – can surpass weaker efforts from a declared year. As the declarations are made 15 months to two years after the harvest there is always a second vintage coming under consideration, leading sometimes to a so-called 'split declaration' as some shippers decide to wait and declare the younger wine instead. For a true guide to longevity both the vintage assessment and that of the individual producer's style and reputation must be taken together. **Those years underlined denote a wide declaration.**

2001: The winter preceding this growing season was incredibly wet resulting in the widely televised, tragic bridge collapse over the river on March 4. Despite the reasonably dry growing season and good harvest conditions, the moisture absorbed in the early part of the year has dampened quality to some extent, though volumes are up.

2000: Rain in the early part of the growing season and a poor flowering were compensated for by a hot, dry ripening period. Yields were very low but the best wines have an incredible intensity of fruit and fine ripe tannins. There is not perhaps quite the size or power of certain other excellent vintages but the wines promise to be long-lived with great expression and classic character in the top names.

1999: Though characterised by irregular, low rainfall much of it fell at harvest as the rain set in from mid-September. Top quality was hard to achieve and while most small estates made Vintage Port, the shippers opted for their single-quinta ports. Good quality but it will be overshadowed by 2000.

1998: Due to an irregular growing season with intermittent heavy rain at harvest, and despite very low yields, this year is one of good rather than great quality. The best single-quinta ports are reasonably concentrated and intense but more modestly structured and lack real stuffing. Nonetheless some will be attractive in the medium term where there is good winemaking.

1997: The season had something of a hole in the middle, with a cool, wet mid-summer period. The return of the sun and real heat more than saved the vintage. The wines have quite firm but ripe structures and the best are well-concentrated too. Less than 94 or 2000 yet still a very promising vintage with many excellent wines. The very best may come from Fonseca, Niepoort and Noval (Nacional) as well as Dow, Graham, Taylor and Vesúvio.

1995: A very hot August ensured a vintage of good concentration to follow 1994. The wines are often very ripe and there are more raisiny characters and a lack of flavour finesse in some. At least half a dozen shippers declared, though most of the top names opted for single-quinta port instead.

1994: The most outstanding port vintage in recent times. Universally declared, the wines initially showed a remarkably seductive fruit but a deep, tannic backbone that suggests classic wines with 20, 30 or more years' age. Now is not the time to drink them, especially when many older vintages, that are drinking so well, often cost less.

1992: A very high-quality vintage declared by a few who preferred this to 1991. The cynical dismissed Taylor-Fonseca motives in the Tricentenary year of Taylor's founding yet, as at Vesúvio and Niepoort, port of real class and concentration was made.

1991: Given the mixed form of the 80s, 1991 is emerging as something of a turning point in vintage fortunes. It was also the start of a much brighter era for port's commercial prospects. The wines are full and firm, not a seductive or elegant vintage but with plenty of power in the best examples. Despite more than a decade's age the best examples such as Dow, Graham and Warre deserve considerably longer.

1987: Few declarations but whether Vintage or single-quinta, one for drinking now.

1985: A much-touted vintage on the basis of extremely favourable vintage conditions but while exceptional for a few, generally it is very patchy. The heat at vintage time precipitated winemaking problems which, though remedied in subsequent vintages, led to washed-out, sometimes volatile wines. Generally a success for the well-equipped Symington group (Graham is superb); only a few others, including Fonseca capitalised on nature's benevolence.

1983: Muscle and structure typified many of the wines from this vintage but the best have added flesh and richness with age. Another Symington year and while Taylor and Niepoort are also very good, bottles from Cockburn and Ramos Pinto can be more variable.

1982: The more hasty chose to declare this instead of the superior 1983 and got it badly wrong. A few, including Sandeman and Niepoort, did rather better but these and the best singe-quinta are attractive drinking now and not for keeping.

1980: A year unjustly overlooked and for a time considered second-rate but those from the Symington stable in particular have done much to restore its reputation. To those in the know, Dow, Graham and Warre have long provided a remarkably good and well-priced source of port.

1977: A classic year but with many examples now near their best, it doesn't seem to have quite the staying power of 1966 or 63. Variation has been noted in Taylor and more recently in Dow. Fonseca has been consistently brilliant and both Graham and Smith Woodhouse seem to have got better and better while Warre too has proven its worth down the years.

1975: Few exceptions to what has turned out to be a relatively light and fast-maturing vintage.

1970: Up until and including 1970 much Vintage port was bottled in the UK rather than at source and this fine vintage does sometimes show the variations in quality this can bring. Nonetheless a very good vintage with most wines showing excellent balance and fine tannins, often displaying the particular style of a shipper's port to good effect. The likes of Dow, Graham, Fonseca, Noval's Nacional, Niepoort and Taylor will continue to improve.

1966: An excellent vintage of very powerful ports, the best of which are likely to last even longer than the classic 1963. However there are slightly fewer really great wines and of those most do not possess the extra finesse or harmony of its predecessor. Nonetheless very fine examples from Cálem, Delaforce, Dow, Fonseca, Graham, Noval's Nacional and Taylor. Drink now or keep.

1963: The finest proven vintage of the second half of the 20th century, and remarkably consistent too. Cockburn, Croft, Delaforce, Dow, Fonseca, Graham, Noval's Nacional, Taylor and Warre provide the evidence. Of recent declarations only 1994 poses any sort of threat to its supremacy. As well as continued ageworthiness, it is the balance and marvellous refinement in the wines that set them apart from other top years. Drink now or keep.

Earlier Years: Great port years extend back the length of the entire 20th century but those still truly alive and great become increasingly scarce with the years (as well as hard to find and prohibitively expensive). 1960 is a fully mature vintage but good bottles exist from a number of shippers; Cockburn's seems the most likely to keep a lot longer. 1955 has always had more vigour and richness and while many are tiring, well-sourced bottles of Dow, Graham, Fonseca and the regular Noval will live on. Older vintages (48, 45, 35, 34, 31, 27 and others) should only be be bought where the wines have been impeccably stored and from a reliable bottler (see 1970).

Portuguese red wine vintages

While not covered in the vintage commentary above, the best Portuguese table wines have considerable ageing potential. In general, the best reds, whatever their origins, will keep for five to ten years but the majority of such wines have been made in the last few years and do not come from earlier vintages. Therefore while the vintage chart needs to be considered in conjunction with comments in the specific producer entry, in most instances buy from a recent good vintage whether for drinking young or to cellar for a substantial period.

Port vintages

Portuguese red vintages

			Douro	Dão	Alentejo
2000	★★★★/★★★★★ A	2001	★★★★ A	★★★★ A	★★★★ A
1997	★★★/★★★★ A	2000	★★★★/★★★★★ A	★★★★ A	★★★★ A
1995	★★★ B	1999	★★★/★★★★ A	★★★ A	★★★/★★★★ B
1994	★★★★★ A	1998	★★/★★★ B	★★ C	★★/★★★ B
1992	★★★★ B	1997	★★★★ B	★★★★/★★★★★ B	★★★★ C
1991	★★★/★★★★ B	1996	★★/★★★ B	★★★★ B	★★/★★★ C
1987	★★/★★★ C	1995	★★★/★★★★ B	★★★★/★★★★ C	★★★★ C
1985	★★/★★★★ A	1994	★★★★/★★★★★ C	★★★/★★★★ C	★★★ C
1983	★★★★ C	1992	★★★★ C	★★★/★★★★ C	★★/★★★ D
1980	★★★ C	1991	★★★★ C	★★★/★★★★ C	★★★/★★★★ C
1977	★★★★/★★★★★ C	1990	★★★ C	★★/★★★ D	★★★★ C
1970	★★★★ C				
1966	★★★★/★★★★★ C				
1963	★★★★★ C				

DOMINGOS ALVES DE SOUSA   Douro

Owner: Domingos Alves de Sousa   Quinta da Gaivosa, Apartado 15, 5031 SantaMartadePenaguião
Quinta da Gaivosa is one of two leading estates of Domingos Alves de Sousa located in the Lower Douro, north of Régua. The Gaivosa wine is one of the most stylish and refined reds of the Douro; there is not the weight or richness of other examples but it is long and distinguished and drinks well with three years' age or more. The smaller Quinta do Vale da Raposa is the source of several reds, including a round, fruity, regular Douro, two good varietal expressions and a deep, powerful Grande Escolha, which has excellent ageing potential. Like Gaivosa it is based on Touriga Nacional, Tinta Cão and Tinta Roriz. Three other estates, Estação, Caldas and Aveleira provide inexpensive but generally well-made reds. New and very promising is an Alves de Sousa Reserva Pessoal from the Gaivosa vineyards; a 1999 shows more powerful, earthy character than Gaivosa if less refinement and composure. White wine is also made if of more variable quality. (PW)

Quinta da Gaivosa
● **Douro★★★** £C
Quinta do Vale da Raposa
● **Douro★** £B   Tinta Roriz★★ £B   Touriga Nacional★★ £B   Grande Escolha★★★ £C

BARBEITO   Madeira   A: RyR, BBR

*Owner: De Freitas family & **Kinoshita Shoji** Estrada Monumental 145, 9000-098 Funchal, Madeira*
Barbeito have a interesting range of commercial Madeiras as well as small stock of very old vintage examples. Operations are directed by Riccardo de Freitas, who has been involved in the winemaking since 1991. All the grapes are bought in and all the wines are *canteiro* wines, subject only to natural heating. The wines are generally drier and with higher acidities than some due to a policy of not de-acidifying. Nor are the wines caramelised as is more usually the case. Single Harvest, made only from Tinta Negra Mole, and with dried fruits, nut, fig and date flavours, shows what is possible from this variety. The Boal (Bual) Veramar which averages five years' age has excellent fruit and intensity for this level. For more classic fire-power, the range of 10-year-old wines should be tried. Again the Boal is fine, while a Special Reserve 20-year-old adds still more power, intensity and length. The breadth and potency of both of these contrast with the elegance and purity in a very small-production single cask example, 1993 Malvasia Colheita Cask 3a. These and other treasures besides deserve a wider audience. (PW)

O **Single Harvest★★★** £D   O **Madeira** Boal Veramar★★★ £C
O **Madeira** 10-year-old Boal★★★ £E
O **Madeira** 20-year-old Special Reserve Malvasia★★★★ £F

CAVES ALIANÇA   Beiras   www.caves-alianca.com   A: Mer

*Owner: **Dão**S.A   Apartado 6, 3781-908 Sangalhos*
Once associated with the mediocrity of much Portuguese table wine, Caves Aliança has undergone a major transformation in the past decade and now provides much-improved quality at all levels. The company owns large estates in the Douro Superior, Beiras Interior, Dão and Alentejo. The basics are simple but increasingly well-made, but much more interesting are the reasonably-priced Bairrada Garrafeira, Douro Foral Grande Escolha, Palmela Particular and Dão Particular which from a good vintage, show good regional character and a savoury intensity with three to five years' age. New premium wines see winemaker Francisco Antunes working with Michel Rolland to produce flagship reds from three estates: Quinta das Baceladas (Bairrada), Quinta dos Quatro Ventos (Douro) and Quinta da Terrugem in Alentejo. The latter, a blend of Aragonês (Tinta Roriz) and Trincadeira (70:30),

is very fine, with smoke, earth and black plum, good breadth and an excellent expression of the Alentejo. T da Terrugem (first made in 1999) is very classy, combining power and finesse and promises to be a new classic Portuguese red. Quatro Ventos, primarily Touriga Franca and Tinta Barocca shows real potential while the Baceladas Merlot/Cabernet Sauvignon/Baga blend is individual and distinctly Bairrada in expression. A new Dão red, Quinta da Garrida is also promising. Caves Aliança has also helped make and distribute the early vintages of QUINTA DA CORTEZIA. (PW)

● **Douro** Foral Grande Escolha★★ £B ● **Bairrada** Garrafeira★★ £B
● **Dão** Particular★★ £B ● **Palmela** Particular★★ £B

Quinta da Terrugem
● **Alentejo** Quinta da Terrugem★★★ £C

CHURCHILL Port www.churchills-port.com   A: HHB, L&S, Tan

Owner: Churchill Graham Lda Rua da Fonte Nova 5, 4400 Vila Nova de Gaia
In just over 20 years the port house established by Johnny Graham and his brothers has come a long way. In the early years port was made in rented, cramped quarters and solely from bought-in grapes but now the company has expanded, acquiring an important quinta of its own in 1999, Quinta da Gricha. The ports have always been made to a high standard, for a time sourcing grapes from the Fojo and Manuela quintas, and generally show rich, ripe fruit and good balance, avoiding overripeness or an excessive spirity character. The Vintage Port, in particular, has got better with successive declarations. Best recent years are 2000, 97, 94 and 91. Other ports are competitively priced and often better-value than the equivalents from the biggest names. Served slightly chilled, the amber-coloured dry white port is a rare good example. The single-quinta Quinta da Gricha port now complements the fine Agua Alta made in 1998, 96, 95 and 92. (PW)

● **Vintage Port**★★★★ £F ● **Late Bottled Vintage Port** Traditional★★ £C
● **10-year-old Tawny Port**★★ £C ● **Finest Vintage Character Port**★ £B
● **Crusted Port**★★ £C O **White Port** Dry Aperitif★ £B

COCKBURN Port   A: BBR, J&B

Owner: Cockburn Smithes Ca (Allied Domecq) Rua das Coradas 13, 4400 Vila Nova de Gaia
Established in 1815, Cockburn is one of the best-known port names. Much of its recent popularity is down to the success of the simple, sweet Special Reserve, a premium Ruby. Quinta do Tua and, since 1989, Quinta dos Canais are two excellent quintas that form part of a substantial vineyard resource. The Vintage Port, for many years of only moderate quality or worse, has returned to form – good in 1991 and 97, excellent in 94 and 2000. Mature vintages such as 1963, 60 and 55 or even older bottles can be superb (the rating only applies to the best vintages). The single-quinta Quinta dos Canais shows a lovely fruit purity and intensity and if it is a more medium-term port than the Vintage it shows the quality of fruit that it brings to the blend. LBV is modest but tawnies show good intensity and length of flavour. (PW)

● **Vintage Port**★★★★ £F Quinta dos Canais★★★ £E
● **10-year-old Tawny Port**★ £C ● **20-year-old Tawny Port**★★ £E

CORTES DE CIMA Alentejo www.cortesdecima.pt   A: Adm, Odd, JNi

Owner: Hans Kristian Jørgensen & family Cortes de Cima, 7960-999 Vidigueira
The 35-ha Cortes de Cima is in the southernmost of the Alentejo's sub-zones, Vidigueira. For ripe, modern-styled reds, they are one of Alentejo's leaders. Though the wines are made by Dane Hans Kristian Jørgensen, outside help has been sought from the likes of viticultural expert Richard Smart.

Since 1997 there have been consistently excellent, fruit-driven wines with plenty of Portuguese character, seen in both the ripe, fleshy Cortes de Cima and a more forward but fruity Chaminé red. A dark, dense Reserva marries new oak to a complex fruit character and is often the top wine. The 2001 was produced from Aragonês and Syrah. A powerful varietal Syrah, Incógnito, is concentrated and adequately balanced despite being high in alcohol. It has lots of character but is at the very ripe end of the spectrum and lacks the finesse of a top Rhône example. From the 2002 vintage an enticingly aromatic Touriga Nacional was made as was a second varietal Syrah. Varietal Aragonês (labelled Aragonez) is usually impressive too but then there are no poor wines here. (PW)

● **Cortes de Cima**★★ £C **Reserva**★★★ £D
● **Incógnito**★★★ £D ● **Aragonez**★★★ £D
● **Chaminé**★ £B

CROFT Port www.croftport.com A: BBR, N&P

Owner: Fladgate partnership Apartado 5, 4401 Vila Nova de Gaia
What later became known as Croft had its beginnings in 1678 and its leading quinta, Quinta da Roêda, has provided the backbone of all its best Vintage Ports in the 20th century. Prior to the 1990s it is necessary to go back to 1977, 70, 66, 63, 60 or 55 for a really great Croft port but recent improvements, due in part to the winemaking of Nick Delaforce, have improved the standard here. Yet despite making better ports recently (1991, 94 and 2000 for Vintage Port and 95 and 97 for Roêda) there still seems to be some variability in the wines and Croft's real salvation seems likely to come from its recent purchase by the estimable Taylor-Fonseca group. Croft's Vintage has often been characterised by a certain muscularity stemming from its Roêda base. Of the other ports, a 20-year-old Tawny is the most exciting, the LBV with some upfront fruit is of the filtered type. Triple Crown and Fine Tawny are the big-volume basic ports. (PW)

● **Vintage Port**★★★ £F Quinta da Roêda★★ £E
● **20-year-old Tawny Port**★★ £E

DELAFORCE Port A: Blx, N&P

Owner: Fladgate partnership Largo Joaquim Magalhaes, 4401-501 Vila Nova de Gaia
Though relinquishing family ownership in 1968 in what was a very difficult time for the port trade, the Delaforce family continues to shape wines that are fruit-rich, stylish and refined at their best. Nick Delaforce is the sixth generation and also makes the ports at Croft because of their shared ownership over recent decades, assumed by the Taylor-Fonseca group in 2001. That 'best' vanished after 1977 but 92, 94 and 2000 show some lovely fruit, although they are not in the blockbuster mould. Older vintages still very much alive are 1966, 63, 60 and 55. The sculptured terraces of Quinta da Corte (adjoining Ramos Pinto's Bom-Retiro), under contract over many years, are a key component of fruit quality and have been the source of a delicious if relatively forward, medium-weight, single-quinta port when a vintage isn't declared. Recent vintages are 1997, 95 and 91. Late Bottled Vintage, if more superficial, can also reveal good fruit, while the tawnies show more finesse than most yet have good intensity too. (PW)

● **Vintage Port**★★★ £E Quinta da Corte★★ £E
● **20-year-old Tawny Port** Curious and Ancient★★★ £E
● **10-year-old Tawny Port** His Eminence's Choice★★ £C ● **Late Bottled Vintage Port**★ £C

DOW Port www.dows-port.com A: JEF

Owner: Symington group Travesso Barão de Forrester, Apartado 10, 4401-997 Vila Nova de Gaia
Though a part of the Symington empire, as Silva & Cosens, the Dow port brand has a very distinct

profile. There is a weight and dimension to the top years that, combined with an elegance and poise, puts them among the best made, recently seen in 1994, 97 and 2000. Though a quite structured port, its fine tannins are covered in layers of ripe fruit. In lesser years the wine can appear more muscular and occasionally a hint of spirit can also show through but other vintages to try include 1985, 83, 80, 77, 70, 66, 63, 55 and 45. Even older vintages can still have some life, as does a fully-mature 1960 – although the 77 is now showing some variability. Quinta do Bomfim, from slopes close to Pinhão in the heart of the Douro, was, until recently, the most important quinta in the region and some fine ports have been made under this name in non-declared years including 1998, 95, 92, 90, 87, 86 and 84. Dow also includes the exciting Quinta Senhora da Ribeira, which lies across the Douro from Quinta da Vesúvio in the Douro Superior. Once owned by Silva & Cosens and still part of its grape resources in recent years, its acquisition by the Symingtons in 1998 has resulted in excellent single-quinta ports from 98 and 99. Winemaking facilities have been boosted by the high-tech Quinta do Sol, where many of the other ports are made. Crusted Port shows something of the Dow style at a moderate price and Late Bottled Vintage, though of the filtered type, can have good fruit richness and some depth. Tawnies tend to be quite vigorous but with good complexity at the 20-and 30-year level, while Trademark is an acceptable Vintage Character port. (PW)

● **Vintage Port**✪✪✪✪✪ £F Quinta do Bomfim★★★★ £E Quinta Senhora da Ribeira★★★★ £E
● **30-year-old Tawny Port**★★★ £F ● **20-year-old Tawny Port**★★ £D
● **10-year-old Tawny Port**★ £C ● **Crusted Port**★★★ £C ● **Late Bottled Vintage Port**★★ £C

ESPORÃO Alentejo www.esporao.com   A: JEF

*Owner: **Finagra** Apartado 31, 7200-999 Reguengos de Monsaraz*
Herdade do Esporão represents a massive investment and real faith in the potential of the Alentejo region but the Roquette family (behind QUINTA DO CRASTO) has been very successful in developing what is now 550 ha of vineyards spread across five different sites. Despite the size, winemaker David Baverstock (a leading influence in the development of modern, quality Portuguese wines) has set a high standard in both red and white wines. The Esporão Reserva is currently a blend of Trincadeira, Aragonês and Cabernet Sauvignon aged in American oak for 12 months. It can be a little reticent when young but shows good richness and depth with at least four years' age. Varietal examples of these three red varieties are also made as are a Bastardo, Touriga Nacional and a new Syrah. Vinha da Defesa is based on Aragonês but includes Syrah. The white equivalent, with good tangy, citrusy fruit, is produced from Antão Vaz, Arinto and Roupeiro and the same varieties are oak-aged to give a ripe, spicy, creamy and peachy Esporão Reserva that can improve for at least two or three years. Unoaked varietal examples of Arinto and Roupeiro are well-balanced with good fruit intensity, the latter revealing a more exotic character. New Private Selection estate red and white promise three star quality. The best vintages of Monte Velho red can provide remarkably good value. Least expensive are the Alandra red and white. (PW)

● **Alentejo** Esporão Reserva★★ £B
● **Cabernet Sauvignon**★ £C ● **Aragonês**★★ £C ● **Trincadeira**★★ £C
● **Touriga Nacional**★★ £C ● **Vinha da Defesa**★ £B ● **Monte Velho**★ £A
○ **Alentejo** Esporão Reserva★★ £B
○ **Roupeiro**★ £B ○ **Arinto**★ £B ○ **Vinha da Defesa**★ £B

FERREIRA Port   A: BWC

*Owner: **Sogrape** Rua da Carvalhosa 19, 4400 Vila Nova de Gaia*
Ferreira was built up by one of the legends of the Douro, Dona Antónia Adelaide Ferreira (from whom comes the diminutive name Ferreirinha that lends itself to the company' table-wine production). Ferreira makes the most gutsy, earthy example among the leading Vintage Ports, often very ripe and raisiny but with plenty of raw intensity and it can age impressively. It is declared more

frequently than most, including good non-declared years (recently 1999 and 95) as well as 2000, 97, 94 and 91. Late Bottled Vintage with character and depth is not shy, while the tawnies maintain fruit intensity; spice and dried fruits in the Quinta do Porto, adding a refined, nutty complexity in the Duque de Bragança. Four important quintas are included in the Ferreira holdings: Quinta do Porto, Quinta do Seixo, Quinta do Caedo and Quinta da Leda. The last is the centre of table-wine production that includes Barca Velha, first produced in 1952 and for long Portugal's most famous red. It is based on Tinta Roriz, but with increasing amounts of Touriga Nacional as well as some Touriga Franca, Tinta Barroca and Tinta Amarela, and aged for around 18 months in new French (previously Portuguese) oak. The component parts are only blended and subsequently released when deemed ready (with five to ten years' age), which can mean that the few years considered good enough don't necessarily appear sequentially. The fruit source may be changing (see QUINTA DO VALE MEÃO) but the current promise of the Leda reds suggests that future vintages will be at least as good as the best to date. 1991 is the vintage currently available but the good (rather than great) years are released as Casa Ferreirinha Reserva (previously Reserva Especial) although some vintages of this have had finesse at the expense of richness. Of the new reds, Quinta da Leda and Callabriga are based on Touriga Nacional but complemented by varying percentages of Tinta Roriz and Touriga Franca. Together with a varietal Touriga Nacional these wines show more power and greater depth and structure than many of the new wave of Douro reds but need seven to ten years to develop fully. (PW)

Ferreira
● **Vintage Port**★★★ £E ● **Late Bottled Vintage Port**★★ £C
● **Tawny Port** 10-year-old Quinta do Porto★★ £D
● **20-year-old Tawny Port** Duque de Bragança★★★ £E

Casa Ferreirinha
● **Douro** Casa Ferreirinha Reserva★★ £E Barca Velha★★★★ £F
● **Douro** Quinta da Leda★★★ £C Quinta da Leda Touriga Nacional★★★ £C
● **Douro** Callabriga★★ £C Vinha Grande★★ £B

FOJO Douro   A: ARe, Vne

Owner: Maria Doroteia Serôdio Borges Fermentoes, 5060 Sabrosa
A small property in the heart of the Douro already with an excellent reputation established around an estate red produced in the 1996 vintage. Jorge and his sister Margarida Serôdio Borges actually manage two quintas, Fojo and Manuela. Fojo was intended to be made in only the best vintages and there has been no rush to follow the initial release, the grapes instead going into a supple, characterful second wine, Vinha do Fojo. Grapes (previously sold to CHURCHILL) from very old vines of Touriga Franca and Tinta Roriz are foot-trodden in *lagares* before being finished in open fermenters. While Fojo (£F) cannot be rated on the basis of a single vintage it is nonetheless a wine of four-star quality, with great power, depth and complexity, particularly striking in the quality and intensity of its fruit. While it can be drunk now it should continue to keep for another five years at least. The more accessible Vinha do Fojo can be drunk with just two or three years' age but will also keep. (PW)
● **Vinha do Fojo**★★ £C

FONSECA Port www.fonseca.pt   A: Men

Owner: Fonseca Guimaraens Rua Barão de Forrester 404, 4400 Vila Nova de Gaia
Fonseca is one of the truly great Vintage Ports and a name most serious port drinkers have good experience of. Though under the same ownership as Taylor it has a very distinct identity of its own. Fruit comes from the Cruzeiro, Santo António (both in the Pinhão valley) and Panascal quintas and

the wines have recently been fashioned by David Guimaraens, following the successful tenure by his father (Bruce Guimaraens) before him. Fonseca has a rich and expansive style with often explosive fruit intensity and marvellous depth of flavour yet doesn't lack for structure. Great vintages include 2000, 97, 94, 92, 85, 77, 70, 66, 63 and 55. Fonseca Guimaraens is the name of the 'off-vintage' port, made in good years when there isn't a Vintage declaration; consistently very fine it can generally be bought with confidence at a somewhat more affordable price. A single-quinta, Quinta do Panascal (which may be visited), is also sometimes made in these years. The standard is generally high in the other ports, too, with good vigour and intensity in the tawnies and usually good fruit in a filtered-type LBV. Bin 27 is one of the best of the big-brand Vintage Character ports while a dry White Port, Siroco, is also made. (PW)

● **Vintage Port✪✪✪✪✪** £G Fonseca Guimaraens★★★ £E Quinta do Panascal★★★ £E
● **10-year-old Tawny Port★★** £C ● **20-year-old Tawny Port★★★** £E
● **Late Bottled Vintage Port★** £C ● **Bin No. 27★** £B

JOSÉ MARIA DA FONSECA Terras do Sado www.jmf.pt A: Che

Owner: Soares Franco family Apartado 8, Vila Nogueira de Azeitão, 2925 Azeitão
This long-established family producer has 850 ha of vines at its disposal between the two regions of Terras do Sado and Alentejo, including the large Algeruz vineyard purchased in 1989 and subsequently used to develop better clones of the leading southern Portuguese varieties but also trialling Syrah, Tannat, Viognier and Sauvignon Blanc. The wines are made by seventh-generation Domingos Soares Franco. Some of the big-volume brands can show attractive fruit if lacking the structure and concentration for more. Whites including Septimus, Quinta de Camarate and Primum are generally sound but like the reds want for more intensity and excitement. Periquita (Castelão) and red Primum (from Touriga Nacional and Touriga Franca) could use a little more richness. Periquita Clássico, released with some age, shows more of the classic spicy, berry, savoury and chocolaty Castelão character. Better still are the not so widely seen Garrafeira wines, RA and CO (more oaky and from Castelão), and more recently FSF (from Tinta Cão, Tannat and Trincadeira), which show excellent complexity, depth and intensity; all are best with six to ten years' age. New are promising Colecção Privada Domingos Soares Franco red varietals Touriga Nacional, Touriga Franca and a white Alvarinho. From the Douro comes the Domini wines, a joint venture with Cristiano van Zeller (QUINTA DO VALE DOÑA MARIA). Domini Plus shows classic Douro character and intensity in a modern style; better in 2001 than 00. The other great strength is Setúbal (fortified sweet Moscatel and other varieties), ranging from a youngish vintage-dated Alambre that is grapey and fresh with citrus peel, ripest peach and apricot character, to a deep-coloured, honeyed Moscatel Roxo with an orange peel aroma through to a rich, gently oxidised Superior (recent vintages are 1962, 64, 65 and 66) with a sweet intensity of dates and nuts. Most extraordinary, however, is a limited-release bottling called Trilogia (a blend of 1900, 34 and 65). Very intense yet not excessively sweet, it has marvellous finesse to its honeyed, citrus peel and nutty aromas and flavours. (PW)

José Maria da Fonseca
● **Periquita** Clássico★★ £C
● **Garrafeira** CO★ £C RA★★ £C FSF★★★ £C
O **Setúbal** Superior★★ £E Moscatel Roxo 20-year-old★★ £E
O **Moscatel de Setúbal** Alambre★ £B

Domingos Soares Franco & Cristiano Van Zeller
● **Douro** Domini★ £B Domini Plus★★★ £E

GRAHAM Port www.grahams-port.com

A: JEF

Owner: Symington group Travesso Barão de Forrester, Apartado 19, 4401-997 Vila Nova de Gaia
In terms of quality if not quantity, Grahams reputation is anchored by its brilliant Vintage Port. If not quite as sought after as Taylor or Fonseca in the last decade, it nonetheless has proven itself to be one of the top ports in almost every widely declared vintage, perhaps the most consistently fine of all. The wines are big, rich and sweet-fruited with a lush opulence that conceals ripe, compact tannins. The same intensity of fruit holds up magnificently over 20, 30, 40 years or more. Excellent vintages include 2000, 97, 94, 91, 85, 83, 80, 77, 70, 66, 63, 55 and 45. In non-declared years the wine has long been produced as the often excellent Malvedos Vintage Port, named for Quinta dos Malvedos (at Tua, up-river from Pinhão) where 70 ha of vineyards were replanted in the 1980s. Therefore only more recently has a significant percentage of the grapes come from Malvedos; other important components of the Vintage Ports are Quinta das Lages and Quinta da Vila Velha in the Rio Torto, south of Pinhão. Graham's aged tawnies are adequate with quite an evolved character in the 20-year-old version. Small amounts of 30- and 40-year-old versions are also made. The LBV (of the filtered type) is fruity, round and agreeable if lacking real depth. An intense, grapey Six Grapes is one of the better examples of the Premium Ruby or Vintage Character style. A Crusted Port is now also made. (PW)

● **Vintage Port**✪✪✪✪✪ £F Malvedos★★★★ £E
● **10-year-old Tawny Port**★ £D ● **20-year-old Tawny Port**★★ £E
● **Late Bottled Vintage Port**★ £C ● **Six Grapes**★ £B

HENRIQUES & HENRIQUES Madeira

A: HWC

Owner: Henriques & Henriques SA PO Box 4296, 9053 Funchal, Madeira
A leading Madeira producer equipped with a modern winery and making excellent, consistent commercial Madeiras, especially the 10-year-old and 15-year-old versions of the noble varieties, Sercial, Verdelho, Malmsey and Bual. The historic family firm was started in 1850 but the family have been landowners on Madeira for centuries. Most impressive is their ability to produce high quality in all styles (some shippers are impressive with one or two only) across vibrant citrusy Sercial, elegant honeyed Verdelho, rich nutty Bual and still richer, sweeter but less refined Malmsey. The 15-year-old versions generally add that bit more intensity and richness which better balances the assertive acidities. Very small amounts of outstanding Vintage Madeira (at very high prices) are available from specialist stockists, some vintage-dated from the late 19th century and other even more venerable examples without a specific vintage date. (PW)

O **Madeira** 15-year-old Sercial★★★ £E 15-year-old Verdelho★★★ £E
O **Madeira** 15-year-old Bual★★★ £E 15-year-old Malmsey★★★ £E
O **Madeira** 10-year-old Sercial★★ £D 10-year-old Verdelho★★★ £D 5-year-old Verdelho★ £C
O **Madeira** 10-year-old Bual★★★ £D 5-year-old Bual★★ £C 10-year-old Malmsey★★ £D

J P VINHOS Terras do Sado www.jpvinhos.com

A: Ehr

Owner: J P Vinhos SA Apartado 54, Vila Norgueira de Azeitão, 2925-901 Azeitão
J P Vinhos is the other significant and sizeable producer in the Terras do Sado, with some 500–600 ha of vineyards, some of it in the neighbouring regions of Alentejo and Estremadura. Though there are no outstanding wines, the best have good flavour and intensity. Tinto da Ânfora is a good, occasionally variable, gutsy example of Alentejo fruit and personality – mostly Aragonês (Tinta Roriz) with a little Trincadeira, Castelão and Alfrocheiro Preto, oak-aged in wood of mixed origins. Much better but at a price is a Grande Escolha version made in the best years. Full and concentrated with deep spice, cedar and savoury notes, it is aged in 100 per cent new Allier oak for eight months. Quinta do Bacalhôa is a

single-estate wine, mostly Cabernet Sauvignon but with 10 per cent Merlot, that tastes not unlike a slightly rustic, earthy Graves – a ripe, meaty, characterful example with ample earthy blackcurrant fruit and depth. Má Partilha, a varietal Merlot, can be slightly raisiny if savoury while Meia Pipa is an equal blend of Cabernet and Castelão. Whites, too, are not without character. Cova da Ursa is a barrel-fermented Chardonnay that is flavoursome but better balanced and more restrained than in early efforts. Other well-known brands include a light, dry Catarina based on Fernão Pires with a barrel-fermented Chardonnay component, and adequate fruity Monte das Ânforas red and white. J P Tinto and Branco are the basic red and white. Sparkling wine, both Loridos Bruto, (from Castelão and Fernão Pires), and Loridos Chardonnay are produced from grapes grown in Estremadura. A new Syrah, Só, has character and some intensity but could use further refinement both in flavour and structure. (PW)

● Tinto da Ânfora★ £B Grande Escolha★★★ £D
● Quinta do Bacalhôa★★ £C   ● Má Partilha★ £C
O Cova da Ursa★ £B   O **Moscatel de Setúbal**★★ £C

MADEIRA WINE COMPANY Madeira www.madeirawinecompany.com   A: JEF

Owner: Symington group   Old Blandy Wine Lodge, Avenida Arriaga 32, Funchal, Madeira
This is the leading producer of Madeira and includes the well-known brand names of Blandy's, Cossart Gordon and Leacocks. Some marvellous Vintage Madeiras are made but only in small quantities, usually only a few thousand bottles at best. The bigger volume, so-called commercial Madeiras with an indication of age can show plenty of style too, if not the same concentration or complexity. Wines labelled with one of the noble varieties (most are almost 100 per cent rather than the required minimum of 85 per cent) are now only made using the *canteiro* system and used American oak casks are used for ageing. Blandy's wines are generally richer and sweeter than those of Cossart Gordon but the wines are similarly made. Cossart Gordon's 10-year-old Verdelho and Bual are particularly fine for this level, the delicacy and harmony of the Verdelho contrasting with the orangey, peel and spice, tangy fruit intensity of the richer Bual. Blandy's 15-year-old Malmsey is both concentrated and elegant and is a significant step-up from the 10-year-old version. For the many fine Vintage Madeiras consult a specialist, but both Cossart Gordon and Blandy's include rare vintages of Terrantez. (PW)

Blandy's
O **Madeira** 15-year-old Malmsey★★★ £E 10-year-old Malmsey★★ £D 5-year-old Malmsey★★ £C
O **Madeira** Dry Duke of Sussex★ £C

Cossart Gordon
O **Madeira** 15-year-old Bual★★★ £E 10-year-old Bual★★★ £D 5-year-old Bual★★ £C
O **Madeira** 10-year-old Verdelho★★★ £D

Leacocks
O **Madeira** 10-year-old Bual★★ £D

NIEPOORT Port   A: RyR, Bib, Rae, Res

Owner: Niepoort family   Rua Infante D. Henrique 39, 4050 Porto
Dirk Niepoort, fifth generation of this Dutch-owned shipper, is obsessed with wine to the benefit of wine lovers everywhere. Working with winemaker Jorge Serôdio Borges he produces an extraordinary array of fine port in almost every style imaginable. The Vintage Port is marked by its raw power and vigour in youth but with almost unequalled intensity and length of flavour. Niepoort has two quintas of its own (Quinta de Nápoles and Quinta do Carril) as well as control of an expanding Quinta do Passadouro and from the latter produces a single-quinta port in good years. Since 1999, Secundum has been produced as a second selection to the Vintage Port; as might be expected this is

in a lighter style yet, like the Vintage Port, seems likely to add richness with age. Much of Niepoort's early reputation was for tawnies and *colheitas* of great refinement. An extremely fine 10-year-old Tawny Port shows great subtlety and complexity in a class of port that is too often overpriced for the quality. The very fine *colheitas* are produced from a string of vintages that run from 1990 back to the early part of the 20th century. Dirk Niepoort also makes the best White Port going, with atypical elegance and freshness. Then there are the red wines which, produced from old, low-yielding vines, have excellent structure and weight. Redoma has been produced for a decade and its price has crept up with the quality (four stars in 1999); there is marvellous fruit and complexity but with ever increasing class and elegance too. The Redoma white (also produced as a Reserva in 2000) is quite remarkable for Portugal: from grapes grown at altitude, it is a barrel-fermented and aged white of real depth and structure, capable of ageing for at least three to four years. A Rosé is also produced. A pricey new flagship red, Batuta (of potentially five-star quality), was first produced in 1999; deep, intense and powerful but already splendidly complex, it promises to be one of the great Douro reds. Another new premium wine, Charme, was first made in 2000. Red is also made from Quinta de Nápoles and has been produced from Passadouro (from Tinta Roriz and Touriga Franca grapes foot-trodden in *lagares*). Jorge Serôdio Borges and his wife, Sandra Tavares (see QUINTA DO VALE DOÑA MARIA) have also been making their own red, PINTAS, since 2001. (PW)

- **Vintage Port**✪✪✪✪✪ £F Quinta do Passadouro★★★★ £F Secundum★★★ £E
- **Colheita Port**★★★★ £E ● **10-year-old Tawny Port**★★★ £E ● Senior Fine Old **Tawny Port**★★ £C
- **Late Bottled Vintage Port**★★★ £C ○ **White Port**★★ £C
- **Douro** Passadouro★★★ £D Redoma★★★★ £E Batuta★★★★ £F
○ **Douro** Redoma★★★ £C

LUIS PATO Bairrada   A: LyS, Vne

Owner: Luis Pato Óis do Bairro, 3780 Amoreira da Gândara

Luis Pato has been Bairrada' great moderniser, introducing green harvesting, complete destemming, temperature control and barrique-ageing to fashion the region's and some of Portugal's top wines. The flavours of Baga are not to everyone's taste but these are excellent, ageworthy examples of what is possible. A combination of new and one-year-old Allier barriques are used for the top single-vineyard wines. The best of these, from 70-year-old vines in a 0.7-ha vineyard, is Vinha Barrosa, with terrific intensity and dimension and a remarkable earthy, truffly, old-vine richness. Vinha Pan and Vinha Barrio are almost as good, the Pan perhaps more tannic and intense than the more mineral Barrio. Moinho from younger vines is arguably the least of these wines yet doesn't lack for intensity, breadth or style. A very small amount of wine is produced from ungrafted vines and fermented in new oak and bottled as Baga Pé Franco. Though very structured it has extraordinary aromas and flavour including earth, truffles, smoke, coffee, black plum; it probably needs to be kept for a minimum of a decade before drinking. As might be expected the wine is bottled without fining or filtration. A regular Baga has more forward, spicy, black-plum fruit and is lightly structured. A premium white has also been made since 1998. Again vineyard-specific, Vinha Formal is made from 100-per-cent Bical that is fermented and aged in oak. The oak is not allowed to dominate and the wine reveals subtle yet intense, ripe fruit with excellent breadth and structure to improve for at least three or four years. In recent vintages the wines have been labelled as Vinho Regional Beiras. (PW)

- **Quinta do Ribeirinho Baga Pé Franco**★★★★ £F ● **Baga**★ £B
- **Vinha Barrosa**★★★★ £D ● **Vinha Pan**★★★ £D ● **Vinha Moinho**★★★ £D
- **Vinha Barrio**★★★ £D ○ **Vinha Formal**★★★ £C

PINTAS Douro/Port   A:C&B

Owner: J S Borges & S Tavares   Avenida Júlio de Freitas 6, Vale de Mendiz, 5085-101 Pinhão
From a 1.8-ha south-facing vineyard previously used for Port production comes another profound Douro
red. The small property belongs to Jorge Serôdio Borges (NIEPOORT's winemaker) and his wife,
Sandra Tavares (QUINTA DO VALE DOÑA MARIA). Grapes from a field blend of mixed planting
(more than 30 different grape varieties of 80-year-old vines) are fermented and foot-trodden in
lagares. The malolactic fermentation is completed in barriques in which the wine is aged for 15
months. 2001 is the only vintage tasted but its fabulous fruit and depth suggest at least a four-star rating.
Only 5,000 bottles were made. A 2002 version should be offered, as the grapes were harvested before the
rains. (PW)

QUINTA DA CORTEZIA Estremadura   A: Mer

Owner: José Miguel Clímaco Reis Catarino   2580-101 Aldeia Gavinha (Alenquer)
Miguel Catarino is a trained viticulturalist and winemaker who works as a consultant in the Alentejo
but also has 70 ha of his own vineyards in Estremadura. Here his obsession with light and soils has
resulted in remarkable fruit quality from family vineyards that have been replanted in stages since
1991. Only a small percentage is currently produced under the Cortezia label, led initially by three
varietals (made since 1997). The wines are dense and compact when young but with a pure varietal
intensity and fine, ripe tannins. The wines do seem to lack a little expression or flair but deserve to
be drunk with at least five years' age. More impressive than the varietal examples is a new Reserva
(50 per cent Tinta Roriz, 30 per cent Merlot and 20 per cent Touriga Nacional in the 1999).
Potentially a ★★★★ wine, it is more aggressively oaky and firmly structured but with added depth,
needing time for real harmony. Some white grapes are grown including Chardonnay, Fernão Pires
and Arinto. Early vintages of the wines have been made in cooperation with CAVES ALIANÇA. (PW)
● **Merlot★★★** £C   ● **Touriga Nacional★★★** £C   ● **Tinta Roriz★★★** £C

QUINTA DE CABRIZ / DÃO SUL Dão   A: FWW

*Owner: **Dão Sul** Apartado 28, 3430-909 Carregal do Sal*
Like QUINTA DOS ROQUES, Quinta de Cabriz has benefited enormously from the winemaking
expertise of Professor Virgílio Loureiro, if more recently. Its 38-ha vineyard, recently boosted by a
further 10 ha, yields a decent fruity, regular Dão; good varietal examples are also made and, though
firmly structured when young, will soften with three to five years' age. First made in 1999, Escolha
Virgílio Loureiro is a premium, blended red with great depth, style and complexity. A white
equivalent is a blend of Encruzado, Malvasia Fina and Borrado das Moscas that is fermented and
aged in oak for six months and is full, ripe and concentrated. As Encostas do Douro, Dão Sul also
has two estates in the Douro: Quinta do Brasileiro (Quinta Sá de Baixo) and Quinta das Tecedeiras.
Quinta Sá de Baixo Grande Escolha, first made in 2000, shows lots of Douro character and richness.
A third venture in Bairrada, under winemaker Carlo Rodrigues, also shows promise, as can be
tasted in a richly fruity Quinta do Encontro Touriga Nacional. Homenagem is a new joint venture
between Cabriz and Luis PATO, a blend of 50 per cent Touriga Nacional and 50 per cent Baga
(combined after ageing). A wine of formidable structure but marvellous fruit, depth and character,
time is needed to see how well it ages. There's good potential too in a port-like wine, Vinho Fino
(from Touriga Nacional), which shows lovely sweet, black-plum fruit if not the dimension or depth
of a top Vintage Port. (PW)

Quinta de Cabriz
● **Dão** Escholha Virgílio Loureiro★★★ £E
● **Dão** Alfrocheiro Preto★ £B Tinta Roriz★★ £C Touriga Nacional★★★ £C
O **Dão** Encruzado★ £B Escholha Virgílio Loureiro★★ £D

Quinta do Encontro
●**Touriga Nacional★★** £C

Quinta do Basileiro
● **Douro** Quinta Sá de Baixo Grande Escholha★★★ £E

QUINTA DE LA ROSA Douro/Port www.quintadelarosa.com A: M&V

Owner: Bergqvist family Quinta de la Rosa, 5085-215 Pinhão

The Bergqvist family took back control of its vineyards in the 1980s, producing their own port for the first time in 1988. Quinta de la Rosa has in fact demonstrated how successful a more estate-centred approach can be (given sufficiently cool storage) and makes a Vintage Port in every vintage (1993 excepted) in the manner of a Bordeaux château. Tim Bergqvist, with help from David Baverstock, has steadily improved quality as the extensive winery buildings have been renovated and vineyards upgraded and in some instances replanted. The medium-weight Vintage Port shows the balance but excellent fruit intensity that characterises these ports and the 2000 (four stars) promises to be the best yet. In 1999 an excellent single-vineyard (that is progressing towards organic status) example was made from old vines in Vale do Inferno. Other good vintages include 1997, 96 (as Vinha Velha), 95, 94 and 92. Finest Reserve is essentially a Vintage Character port but far better than the norm, with real elegance and intensity, while Late Bottled Vintage shows more depth than is typical. Quinta de la Rosa table wines are just as important as the ports and both a partially oaked, regular example (from Tinta Roriz, Touriga Franca and Tinta Barocca) and more oaky Reserva (needing at least three to five years' age) are excellent, well-priced Douro reds. A very fine varietal Tinta Roriz was made in 1998. Also made are a perfumed white and a second red, Val da Clara, partly from bought-in grapes. (PW)

● **Vintage Port★★★★** £E
● **10-year-old Tawny Port** Tonel No. 12★★ £C ● **Late Bottled Vintage Port★★** £C
● **Finest Reserve★★** £B ● **Ruby Port** Lote 601★ £B
● **Douro★★** £B Reserva★★★ £C

QUINTA DE RORIZ Douro/Port www.quintaderoriz.com A: JEF

Owner: João van Zeller Quinta de Roriz, Ervedosa do Douro, 5130-113 S. João da Pesqueira

Quinta de Roriz was famous as an individual-quinta port in the 19th century but has only recently been re-established as an independent operation by the van Zeller family – the Vintage Port was made by others for most of the 20th century. There are currently 42 ha within a sheltered amphitheatre some distance up-river from Pinhão but still within the Cima Corgo. Its revival is being achieved with help from the SYMINGTON family – the wines are made at their Quinta do Sol facility. The Vintage Port was particularly exciting in the 2000 vintage, one of the very best going. What marks it out is its sheer class, with a dimension, definition and complexity seen only among the top names. Two Douro table wines have made a good initial impression too. The Reserva has a lot of oak (new French barriques are used) and tannin but suggests better harmony with five years' age or more. (PW)

● **Vintage Port★★★★★** £E
● **Douro** Prazo de Roriz★★ £B Quinta de Roriz Reserva★★★ £C

QUINTA DO CÔTTO Douro/Port   A: LyS

Owner: Montez Champalimaud Lda Cidadelhe, 5040 Mesão Frio

Owner and winemaker Miguel Champalimaud has made Douro reds from the early 1980s, long before the recent explosion in their production. The Côtto wines are concentrated and muscular but with much greater refinement in recent years than the slightly tough, brawny, if characterful efforts from the 1980s and early 1990s. The Grande Escolha does in fact mean what are considered by their maker to be the great years, when a selection of Touriga Nacional, Tinta Roriz and Touriga Franca grapes undergo an extended maceration prior to ageing in new Portuguese oak. Still rather forbidding in its youth, there is good dimension as well as increasing complexity with age; it shouldn't be drunk with less than six to eight years' age. The regular Côtto needs time too, often five years. As well as a flavoursome white Douro, decent Vinho Verde (from a mix of varietals subject to some oak influence) has good fruit and ripeness. Good Vintage Port is also made occasionally. (PW)

Quinta do Côtto
● **Douro★★** £B Grande Escolha★★★ £E
● **Vintage Port★★★** £E
O **Douro★** £B

Paço de Teixeró
O **Vinho Verde★** £B

QUINTA DO CRASTO Douro/Port   A: Adm, Eno, Odd

Owner: Roquette family Gouvinhas Ferrão, 5060 Sabrosa

Crasto, firstly under the expertise of David Baverstock (ESPORÃO) and more recently under another Aussie, Dominic Morris, and Tomas Roquette, makes splendid table wines and fruit-rich ports. The regular Douro red was an exceptional buy in the first vintages but if it has lost a little weight and intensity still offers good Douro character within a modern structure. A somewhat oaky Reserva adds extra intensity but a varietal Tinta Roriz (foot-trodden prior to continuing its fermentation in open fermenters) shows marvellous fruit, oak, smoke and spice and just manages to match its 100 per cent new oak treatment. Two small-volume premium reds were first produced from the 1998 vintage, Vinha da Ponte and Doña Maria Teresa. Both show a structure, depth and dimension that put them among the Douro's very best. Vintage Port (made in 1994, 95, 97, 99 and 2000) is a consistently excellent, medium-weight and medium-term example with a stylish, ripe, fruit intensity. A traditional (i.e. it will throw a sediment) Late Bottled Vintage Port is more forward but with a most attractive, moderately sweet fruit character. Wines from a new property in the Douro Superior are also going to be made at Crasto. (PW)

● **Douro★** £B Reserva★★ £B Tinta Roriz★★★ £D Vinha da Ponte★★★★ £E
● **Vintage Port★★★** £E ● **Late Bottled Vintage Port★★** £C

QUINTA DO INFANTADO Port   A: Lib

Owner: Roseira family 5085-217 Covas de Douro

The Roseira family have been making their own wines since 1978 from 43 ha of vineyards up a small northern tributary of the Douro downstream from Pinhão. João Roseira works with the talented Luis Soares Duarte and all the wines, even a Ruby, are made in *lagares* and are richly extracted. The incremental addition of spirit results in less being added and an avoidance of the spirity character seen in some Vintage Ports. Infantado's Vintage Port is powerful, intense and extracted, with more finesse in vintages since 1997. Also made is a traditional (i.e. throwing a sediment) Late Bottled Vintage Port of great extract and intensity. Needless to say a 10-year-old Tawny is vigorous and refined, unlike some of the rather tired, relatively simple examples that exist. João Roseira is also producing the table wines of Bago de Touriga, again in collaboration with Luis Soares Duarte. (PW)

● **Vintage Port★★★★** £E **Late Bottled Vintage Port★★★** £D
● **10-year-old Tawny Port★★★** £E

QUINTA DO NOVAL Douro/Port www.quintadonoval.com   A: Par

Owner: AXA-Millésimes Avenida Diogo Leite 256, 4400-111 Vila Nova de Gaia
Today Noval is directed by Christian Seely of AXA-Millésimes (owner of CH. PICHON-LONGUEVILLE and other prestigious properties) but it got its start in modern times from António José da Silva, who first planted the famous two hectares of ungrafted vines that produce Nacional, the most sought-after of all ports. A port of great breadth, power and dimension, with a distinctive earthy, spicy dark plum character, it adds flesh and richness with age to become an often riveting port after 20, 30 or more years. As well as 2000, 97, 94, 70, 66, 63 and 62 are great vintages and, if price is a guide, 1931. Production from the low-yielding vines that average 35–40 years' age is tiny (200–300 cases) and bottles hard to secure. The regular Quinta do Noval Vintage (which benefits from Nacional fruit when that wine is not made) has been a very exciting port in recent vintages (2000, 97, 95, 94, 91) after a lean spell prior to the 90s. It, too, is structured but profound and very ageworthy. Silval, though named after one of Noval's own vineyards, is essentially a second selection but still a high-quality, medium-full style. Noval for a time made the ports from the excellent QUINTA DO RORIZ but the property's owners are now making the wines in collaboration with the Symingtons. Noval's Late Bottled Vintage is in the traditional sediment-throwing style and a fine, concentrated example particularly in top vintages. There is also a fine range of tawnies, both aged and vintage-dated *colheitas* with bottling dates ranging from 1987 back half a century. Other commercial styles are adequate if not more. Raven is a new, distinctly packaged premium Ruby port. (PW)

● **Vintage Port★★★★★** £F Nacional✪✪✪✪✪ £H Silval★★★★ £E
● **40-year-old Tawny Port★★★** £G ● **20-year-old Tawny Port★★★** £F
● **10-year-old Tawny Port★★** £D ● **Colheita Port★★★** £E
● **Late-Bottled Vintage Port★★** £C ● **LB★** £B

QUINTA DO PORTAL Douro/Port www.quintadoportal.com   A: CHk, GWW, Vne

Owner: Mansilha family E. N. 323 Celeirós do Douro, 5060 Sabrosa
Quinta do Portal is not one quinta but four. Portal itself was also known as Quinta do Casal de Celeirós while the estates also include the Quinta do Confradeiro at Celeirós in the Rio Pinhão valley. Money and expertise have not been spared and the most recent vintages show that it is now all starting to come together. The style is for oaky wines but recently this has been matched by a ripe, intense fruit expression. Previous wood-taint problems have been addressed with help from one of the leading experts in this field, Pascal Chatonnet. Though they are reasonably pricey, varietal expressions of Tinta Roriz and Touriga Nacional are very attractive, while the 2000 Grande Reserva (the first since 1996) though oaky shows a convincing fruit depth and richness that suggest a three- to four-star quality rating. Vintage Port, from Quinta dos Muros grapes, also shows good promise from the 2000 vintage. This is the vintage to buy from, when all the wines show greater richness, better balance and appear to be free of any taint problems. (PW)

● **Douro** Tinta Roriz★★ £D Touriga Nacional★★★ £D
● **Douro★** £B Reserva★★ £B

QUINTA DO VALE DOÑA MARIA   Douro/Port   A: L&S, C&B

Owner: Joana Lemos & Cristiano van Zeller   Sarzedinho, 5130 S. João da Pesqueira
Cristiano van Zeller's family once owned QUINTA DO NOVAL but now he is involved in some
capacity in the production, direction or distribution of several Douro estates as well as one or two
from further afield. The 10-ha vineyard of Vale Doña Maria (in his wife's family for generations) on
the Rio Torto is an old-fashioned, mixed planting, many of the vines 50–60 years old. The wines,
foot-trodden in *lagares*, include both a rich, fleshy, characterful and seductive red (the rating applies
to the most recent vintages) and increasingly good Vintage Port. They are made by Sandra Tavares
da Silva with some input from Francisco Olazabal of QUINTA DO VALE MEÃO. Cristiano van Zeller
also has a joint venture with Domingos Soares Franco (see José Maria da FONSECA), producing both
a Vintage Port and a new table wine called Domini from properties in the Douro Superior (Alto
Douro). Also located in this harsh, dry area is the large estate of Quinta da Portela da Vilariça
(property of the Morais Vaz family), where the small vineyard among ancient village ruins is being
expanded with input in the winemaking and direction from van Zeller. A fine Vilariça estate red
from Touriga Franca, Touriga Nacional and Tinta Cão is complemented by a varietal Touriga
Nacional; both show splendid perfume, depth and intensity albeit at the very ripe end of the
spectrum. Sandra Tavares, as well as making the wines of another Douro property since 1999 (Casal
de Loivos), also makes a fine estate red for her own family in Estremadura, QUINTA DE
CHOCAPALHA. (PW)

Quinta do Vale Doña Maria
● **Douro★★★★** £C   ● **Vintage Port★★★** £E
Quinta da Portela da Vilariça
● **Douro★★** £B Touriga Nacional★★★ £C

QUINTA DO VALE MEÃO   Douro/Port   A: RyR, C&R

Owner: Francisco Javier de Olazabal   Vila Nova de Foz Côa
Francisco Javier de Olazabal was president of FERREIRA until 1998 and his 62 ha of vineyards (part
of a 270-ha estate established by Olazabal's ancestor, Dona António Adelaide Ferreira) used to
provide the basis of Barca Velha. The best grapes from this estate in a bend in the Douro only 30 km
or so from the Spanish border are now made into an outstanding estate red by his son Francisco, a
trained winemaker. Comprising Touriga Nacional (60 per cent), Touriga Franca (20), Tinta Roriz
(10) and five per cent each of Tinto Cão and Tinta Barroca, the wine is initially foot-trodden and
spends two years in new Allier oak. There is a depth and breadth, as well as elegance and class, to
this potentially five-star wine that sets it apart from all but the best top Douro reds – the same
qualities (not surprisingly) that distinguish the best vintages of Barca Velha. A second wine,
Meandro, aged in used oak, is lighter in weight but reveals good intense, juicy, plummy fruit and can
be drunk quite young. A Vintage Port from 2000 with very ripe, sweet, slightly raisiny fruit shows
lots of promise. (PW)
● **Douro** Quinta do Vale Meão★★★★ £E Meandro★★ £B

QUINTA DO VALLADO   Douro/Port   A: L&S

Owner: Jorge Viterbo Ferreira & Herdeiros   Vilarinho dos Freires, 5050 Peso da Régua
Vallado is a revitalised estate in the Lower Douro (Baixo Corgo) on the Rio Corgo run by Francisco
Ferreira and his uncle, Guilherme Alvares Ribeiro. A new winery was completed in the late 1990s to
handle the fruit from new and restructured vineyards totalling 64 ha. An unwooded, regular estate red
(from a field blend of varieties) shows the earthy, smoky, dark, plum fruit of the Douro in a

well-balanced, concentrated (and affordable) form. The wines are made by QUINTA DO VALE MEÃO's Francisco Olazabal and commercialised by Cristiano van Zeller of QUINTA DO VALE DOÑA MARIA. A Reserva, aged in new French oak, has been made since 1999 and shows more sophistication as well as extra depth and concentration in the 2000 vintage. (PW)

● **Douro★★** £B Reserva★★★ £C

QUINTA DO VESUVIO   Port   www.quinta-do-vesuvio.com   A: JEF

Owner: Symington group   Travessa Barão de Forrester, Apartado 26, 4401-997 Vila Nova de Gaia
This estate of 400-odd ha spread over seven hills was one of the grand properties of the 19th century. In 1989 it was bought by the Symington family and turned into one of the new breed of true (château-like) quintas. The wine from the expanding vineyard (currently 100 ha of vines) is made and matured on the estate. Its massive *lagares* and winery buildings are being renovated but there has been a wine of high quality made in almost every vintage since 1989 (not 93) and these have been outstanding in the top years, including 2000 (which could be the most intense, compressed, tight, densely-fruited example yet), 95, 94 and 92. Other years, including 1997, 96, 91 and 90, can be very good too, there being much less vintage variation in the dry Douro Superior than further down-stream. At its best the extraordinary ripeness in the tannins, as well as the fruit from low-yielding vines, can make the wine tempting in its relative youth but obviously more time is needed to see just how well they'll show at full maturity (20 or 30 years' age). High percentages of Tinta Roriz and Tinta Barroca (along with Touriga Nacional and Touriga Franca) contribute to its unique character. (PW)

● **Vintage Port✪✪✪✪✪** £F

QUINTA DOS ROQUES   Dão   A: RyR, Han, C&R

Owner: Manuel Lopes de Oliveira   Abrunhosa do Mato, 3530 Mangualde
In the space of just a few years, Quinta dos Roques has emerged as arguably the Dão's leading estate, producing modern, accessible wines from on-going experimentation with different varieties, blends and refinements to vinification. Vineyards now total 40 ha and the winemaking still benefits from the expertise of Professor Virgílio Loureiro, now widely recognised as one of Portugal's finest winemakers. The regular characterful, medium-weight dos Roques red is based on Touriga Nacional but also includes Alfrocheiro Preto and Tinta Roriz. All three grapes have also been vinified varietally (since the 1996 vintage but not in 1998), with excellent fruit expression and good concentration and structure. The Touriga Nacional has additional breadth and a deep plum and violet character with a hint of pine and white pepper, and is the best of these. Better still is a Reserva made from an old vineyard of mixed plantings that includes Tinta Roriz and Touriga Nacional. Wine from the nearby estate of Quinta das Maias is also made here, the reds reflecting the importance of the local Jaen in the 12 ha of vineyards at 700 m. Both the regular Maias red and varietal Jaen can show a slightly smoky, spicy, wild berry fruit; the varietal example adds more flesh, intensity and structure. A new 'black label' premium Maias red, Rótulo Preto made in 2000 from very old vines is very exciting. A herb-scented Malvasia is a rare good Dão white but a subtly oaked Encruzado with refined peach and exotic notes is even better. Some sparkling Rosé is also made. (PW)

Quinta dos Roques
● **Dão** Tinto★★ £B Reserva★★★ £D
● **Dão** Tinto Cão★★ £C Alfrocheiro Preto★★ £C Touriga Nacional★★★ £D
○ **Dão Encruzado★★ £C**

Quinta das Maias
● **Dão** Tinto★ £B Jaen★★ £C
○ **Dão** Malvasia Fina★ £B

JOÃO PORTUGAL RAMOS   Alentejo   www.jportugalramos.com   A: Oak, ARe

Owner: João Portugal Ramos   Monte da Caldeira, 7100-149 Estremoz

For more than 20 years, João Ramos has been the leading consultant enologist in the south of Portugal, working for some of Alentejo's best co-operatives. His own project has gained increasing momentum in the past decade, producing wines under his own label on his estate near Estremoz but also working for others as a consultancy. The top wine is the Marqués de Borba Reserva (2000, 99 and 97 are all very good), a powerful but composed blend of Aragonês (Tinta Roriz), Trincadeira and some Alicante Bouschet and Cabernet Sauvignon, with excellent dimension and weight, needing five to ten years to show at its best. Vila Santa, with the same varieties (if more based on Trincadeira), shows style and harmony, even elegance and continues to be excellent value for money. Varietal examples of Trincadeira and Aragonês show good fruit definition and supple structures. A varietal Syrah of considerable black-fruit intensity if more marginal balance has been made since 2000. More unusual, if not unique, is a supple, perfumed varietal Tinta Caiada. A simple Marqués de Borba white and varietal Antão Vaz are good, clean whites for early consumption. Of the other wines, very promising is the very ripe and powerful Quinta de Viçosa Syrah/Trincadeira, also from the Alentejo. The wines from Falua co-op in Ribatejo include Conde de Vimioso Reserva, a characterful, extracted red from Touriga Nacional, Tinta Roriz and Cabernet Sauvignon. Of interest too are the wines of Quinta de Foz de Arouce in the Beiras, owned by João's father-in-law. A new single-vineyard wine, Vinha de Santa Marta, from 100 per cent Baga was produced in 2001. It shows a classic rugged, black-fruited Baga character but will require patience. Production of a white is being resumed in 2004. From the Beira Interior, the blended red (Touriga Nacional, Tinta Roriz and Tinta Barocca) of Almeida Garrett is a big step up from two value-for-money varietals. Pegos Claros, a good example of Palmela, has shown greater consistency and stability since being made by João Ramos. (PW)

João Portugal Ramos:
- **Alentejo** Marqués de Borba★ £B   Marqués de Borba Reserva★★★★ £E
- **Vila Santa★★★** £B   ● **Trincadeira★★** £B   ● **Aragonês★★** £B
- **Syrah★★** £B   ● **Tinta Caiada★★** £B   O **Antão Vaz★** £B

Quinta da Viçosa
- **Syrah/Trincadeira★★★** £C

Quinta de Vimioso
- **Conde de Vimioso** Reserva★★ £C

Quinta de Foz de Arouce
- **Quinta de Foz de Arouce★★** £B

Almeida Garrett
- **Almeida Garrett★★** £C   ● **Touriga Nacional★** £B   ● **Tinta Roriz★** £B

Quinta da Ponte Pedrinho
- **Dão** Reserva★★ £C

Pegos Claros
- **Palmela** Reserva★★ £B

RAMOS PINTO   Douro/Port   A: MMD, BBR

*Owner: **Adriano Ramos Pinto SA**   Avenida Ramos Pinto 380, 4401-997 Vila Nova de Gaia*

It was the father of Ramos Pinto's director and winemaker, João Nicolau de Almeida, who created Barca Velha, the Douro's first great red wine and Ramos Pinto has been one of the leading proponents in the recent revival of table wines (last made in any quantity before port evolved into a fortified style). Duas Quintas wines are named for the high vineyards (600 m) of Bon Ares and the lower Ervamoira (both deep in the Douro Superior). Quality of the regular red has been variable but from certain vintages (1999, 97, 95 and 94) a Reserva (from at least 50 per cent Touriga Nacional) has shown good style, fruit intensity and more refinement than is typical – yet it still doesn't represent value for money. A very good Reserva Especial was made in 1999. A little white table wine is also made. Most consistent and refined of the ports is a 20-year-old Tawny from Quinta do Bom-Retiro, the company's leading estate on the Rio Torto. It has depth and intensity (sometimes missing in this category) as well as complexity and refinement. Vintage Port has been better in recent vintages (1997 and 94 at least) but although it has a certain individuality, it wants for more depth and richness. Late Bottled Vintage can be remarkably full and powerful while a modest Vintage Character port is named for a fourth quinta, Urtiga. (PW)

- **Vintage Port★★★** £E ● **Late Bottled Vintage Port★★** £C
- **20-year-old Tawny Port** Quinta do Bom-Retiro★★★ £E
- **10-year-old Tawny Port** Quinta da Ervamoira★ £D
- **Douro** Duas Quintas Reserva★★ £D

REAL COMPANHIA VELHA Douro/Port www.realcompanhiavelha.pt A: FEM, PLB

Owner: Real Companhia Velha Rua Azevedo Magalhães 314, 4430 Vila Nova de Gaia
The Douro's largest landowner and biggest maker of port enjoys wide distribution around the globe. Its Royal Oporto brand is familiar to most consumers even if they haven't drunk it. Its inclusion here, however, is for its revitalized production of Douro table wines, one or two of which are worthy of more than passing mention. The Evel red offers plenty of fruit while the Porca de Murça Riserva adds more structure and complexity. But for those interested in premium Douro reds it is a Grande Escholha version of Evel (from Touriga Nacional, Touriga Franca and Tinta Cão) and the revived Grantom label (which adds Cabernet Sauvignon to the two Tourigas) that should be tasted. Both these reds have quite a forbidding structure but the Evel Grande Escholha in particular shows a capitivating complexity and intensity that suggest a four-star rating if quality is maintained. Unusual for the Douro is a Chardonnay from low-yielding vines on the Quinta do Cidrô that delivers good flavour and texture. (PW)

- **Douro** Quinta dos Aciprestes★ £B Porca de Murça Reserva★★ £B
- **Douro** Evel★ £B Evel Grande Escholha★★★ £D Grantom★★★ £E
- O **Quinta do Cidrô Chardonnay★** £B

SANDEMAN Port www.sandeman.com

Owner: Sogrape Largo Miguel Bombarda 3, 4400 Vila Nova de Gaia
Like Graham's, Sandeman is of Scottish origins and its familiarity to occasional port drinkers has been reinforced by the famous brand logo of the Sandeman 'Don'. In the fifty years since the company went public it has had a torrid time quality-wise under changing ownership. A revival has been started in the past decade following the purchase, and subsequent replanting, of Quinta do Vau since 1988. Its newest owners perhaps offer the best chance of a sustained revival given the example of Ferreira's form under the same ownership. Since 1994, there has been good richness if not the greatest depth in both the Vintage Port and Vau (made when the Vintage Port isn't declared). Of older vintages, some very good ports were made in the 50s and 60s, although most of these are tiring now and are not as good as the top examples. Tawnies are a strength, however, with particular elegance and finesse in the 20-year-old Tawny. Recently in very good form has been the Vintage Character port, Signature (known as Founders Reserve outside the UK). (PW)

- **Vintage Port Vau ★★★** £E
- **Signature★★** £B
- **Imperial Aged Tawny Port★★** £C ● **20-year-old Tawny Port★★★** £E

SIDÓNIO DE SOUSA   Bairrada

Owner: Sousa family   Largo da Vila, 3780-120 Sangalhos
This small estate of 12 ha has some very old vines (up to 100 years) and the wines are made very traditionally. Winemaker Rui Moura Alves, who also makes the wines at Casa de Saima, Quinta de Baixo and Quinta das Bágeiras, uses natural yeasts, favours the retention of stems, uses concrete *lagares* and wooden plungers, and ages the wine where appropriate in large, old Portuguese wood. This approach, even more than at the other properties, really works – perhaps because of the quality of the fruit. A Reserva shows good intensity, and a silky mouthfeel and a stylish, savoury complexity. The remarkable, powerful Garrafeira, with deep savoury fruit, great depth and intensity and enveloping, but refined tannins, is only made in exceptional vintages (there are just a few thousand bottles of 1995 and 97 currently available). New is a sparkling red made from 100 per cent Baga. (PW)
● **Bairrada** Reserva★★ £C Garrafeira★★★ £D

SMITH WOODHOUSE   Port   www.smithwoodhouse.com   A: JEF

Owner: **Symington group**   *Travessa Barão de Forrester, Apartado 19, 4401-997 Vila Nova de Gaia*
It is to be hoped that the going prices for the ports from this excellent, consistent house continue at the recent level. The Vintage Port, based on the Madalena quinta in the Rio Torto valley, has a certain spicy individuality and is typically succulent, intense and well-balanced. Top recent vintages include 2000, 97, 94, 92, 91, 85, 83, 80 and 77. A good Madalena port has been made in certain non-declared years (such as 1988 and 82) but with more distinction as a true single-quinta port in 1995 and 99. A traditional (i.e. it leaves a sediment) Late Bottled Vintage maintains the house style and integrity. Other wines include Lodge Reserve, which is a decent Vintage Character port, and a 10-year-old Tawny. (PW)
● **Vintage Port**★★★★★ £E Madalena★★★ £D
● **Late Bottled Vintage Port**★★★ £C ● **Lodge Reserve**★ £B

SOGRAPE   www.sogrape.pt   A: SsG

Owner: **Sogrape Vinhos de Portugal SA**   *Rua 5 de Outubro 558, Aldeia Nova, 4430-761 Avintes*
Portugal's largest producer includes the port companies of Ferreira, Offley and Sandeman but the focus of table-wine production is in Dão, where the flagship estate of Quinta dos Carvalhais has been developed. Varietal wines from here have been quite impressive but the vines are still relatively young and, though both Touriga Nacional and Tinta Roriz have been reasonably full with good breadth, they have lacked a little richness. A powerful Carvalhais Reserva from 1996 shows a lot of complexity and depth but has a price to match. A varietal Encruzado, fermented and aged in French oak for six months, adds a little richness with a couple of years' age. Sogrape's 'regional' Reservas can be very good value when on form, as they currently are; softly textured with good flavour intensity and a regional stamp. Also impressive is the Herdade do Peso Aragonês from Alentejo, made in 1997 and 2000. Brands such as Terra Franca, Vila Régia and Duque de Viseu, while inexpensive and very successful, at best show a simple, agreeable fruit character. Adequate Vinho Verde is made at Quinta de Azevedo. (PW)
● **Douro** Reserva★★ £B ● **Dão** Reserva★★ £B ● **Alentejo** Reserva★★ £B
● **Herdade do Peso Aragonês**★★★ £D O **Bairrada** Reserva★★ £B
Quinta dos Carvalhais
● **Dão** Tinta Roriz★★★ £D Touriga Nacional★★★ £D Reserva★★★ £E
O **Dão** Encruzado★★ £D

SYMINGTON www.symington.com

A: JEF

Owner: Symington family Travessa Barão de Forrester 86, 4401-997 Vila Nova de Gaia
The Symington family runs the Douro's leading port shippers, owning DOW, GRAHAM, QUINTA DO VESÚVIO, SMITH WOODHOUSE and WARRE, and, through the MADEIRA WINE COMPANY, is also the leading producer of Madeira. Gould Campbell is one of two lesser labels made in widely declared years. While it has lacked real weight and richness in recent vintages it was very good (three stars) in 1980, 83 and 85. The other minor port brand, Quarles Harris, has been the better of the two in recent declarations (1997 and 2000) and is an attractive, short- to medium-term port for drinking with 10 years' age. The Symingtons are also helping to further realise the potential from QUINTA DE RORIZ. Though late in joining the revival in table-wine production, a basic (inexpensive if disappointing) table red, Altano, has been made since 1999. Chryseia is a new premium table wine made in collaboration with Bruno Prats (the former owner of CH. COS D'ESTOURNEL); 2001 is a big improvement on 2000, the first vintage. Time will be needed to see how it stacks up against the increasingly formidable competition. (PW)

Gould Campbell
● **Vintage Port★★** £E ● **Late Bottled Vintage Port★** £C

Quarles Harris
● **Vintage Port★★★** £E

Prats & Symington
● **Douro** Chryseia★★★★ £E

TAYLOR'S Port www.taylor.pt

A: Men

Owner: Taylor Fladgate & Yeatman SA Rua do Choupelo 250, 4401-501 Vila Nova de Gaia
An exemplary port producer, and with FONSECA, part of an expanding group that now includes CROFT and DELAFORCE. Vintage Port is based on the famous Quinta de Vargellas in the Douro Superior and the larger Terra Feita quinta in the Rio Pinhão valley, but new vineyards have recently been purchased in both of these sectors of the Douro. Fruit from the Pinhão provides the greater structure while the Douro Superior gives a more floral perfume and great intensity of fruit. Taylor's structure, marvellous depth and class set it apart from most other ports and occasionally is unrivalled for its completeness. The classic Taylor's style can best be seen in 2000, 97, 94, 92, 85, 83, 80, 77 (though there is variation in this vintage), 70, 66 and 63. The 1960 and 55 can still be lively and impressive, while the 75 is an excellent example in this lighter vintage and 1948, 45 and 27 are classic older vintages. In good non-declared years, Quinta de Vargellas is made (with a high percentage of very old vines it has recently been made in a Vinha Velha version) and can be a stunning port in its own right, while Terra Feita has also been produced as a single-quinta port. Other ports are generally less exciting, 10-year-old Tawny is disappointing against the best examples, though the 20-year-old is better and 30- and 40-year-old versions are also made in small qauntities. Late Bottled Vintage (a style created by Taylor's) is a spicy, fruity and characterful filtered example while First Estate (Vintage Character) is similarly good of its type. A White Port called Chip Dry is also made. (PW)

● **Vintage Port✪✪✪✪✪** £F Quinta de Vargellas★★★★ £E Quinta de Terra Feita★★★ £D
● **10-year-old Tawny Port★** £C ● **20-year-old Tawny Port★★** £E
● **Late Bottled Vintage Port★★** £B ● **First Estate★** £B

WARRE Port www.warre.com

A: JEF

Owner: Symington group Travessa Barão de Forrester, Apartado 26, 4401-997 Vila Nova de Gaia
Last but not least in the Symington portfolio of great port houses, Warre makes a consistently fine

Vintage Port. It is perfumed, with a rich, spice, fig and black fruit intensity and a lushness that together form part of a distinctive character that alone makes it worth cellaring. In certain top vintages it will age for 40 years or more. The best include 2000, 97, 94, 91, 85, 83, 80, 77, 70, 66, 63, 60 and 55, though the last three of these are tiring. Quinta da Cavadinha in the Rio Pinhão valley, not far from either QUINTA DO NOVAL or TAYLOR's Terra Feita, forms the main component of the Vintage Port and can be excellent when released in non-declared years. The traditional Late Bottled Vintage is rightly considered one of the best made and the current release usually has around 10 years' age yet can still be kept. With the exception of a fine, complex, 20-year-old, tawnies, including the mould-breaking Otima (with a clear-glass bottle), are not overly exciting but the Vintage Character, Warrior, if of a different structure, actually tastes something like the Vintage Port and is one of the best in its category. (PW)

● **Vintage Port★★★★★** £F Quinta da Cavadinha★★★ £E
● **Late Bottled Vintage Port★★★** £C
● **20-year-old Tawny Port★★★** £E ● **10-year-old Tawny Port** Otima★ £C Sir William★ £C
● **Warrior Special Reserve★** £B

OTHER WINES OF NOTE

BOAS QUINTAS ● **Dão** Quinta da Fonte do Ouro (Touriga Nacional/Tinta Roriz/Jaen) £B
● **Dão** Quinta da Fonte do Ouro Touriga Nacional £D
H M BORGES O **Madeira** 10-year-old Sercial Reserve £D 10-year-old Boal Reserve £D
O   **Madeira** 10-year-old Malmsey Reserve £D
BRIGHT BROTHERS ● **Douro** TFN (Touriga Franca/Touriga Nacional) £B
● **Palmela** Reserva (Castelão) £B
BURMESTER ● **Vintage Port** £E Quinta de Nossa Senhora do Carmo £E
● **Late-Bottled-Vintage Port** £C
CÁLEM ● **Vintage Port** £E ● **Colheita Port** £D ● **20-year-old Tawny Port** £E
● **40-year-old Tawny Port** £G
CASA AGRICOLA RUI MADEIRA ● **Douro** Reserva (Touriga Nacional) £C
C.A.R.M.I.M. (Reguengos de Monsaraz co-op) ● **Alentejo** Reguengos Garrafeiras dos Sócios £C
CASA DE SAIMA ● **Bairrada** Reserva £C Garrafeira £C
CASA SANTOS LIMA (Estremadura) ● **Touriga Nacional** £B ● **Tinta Roriz** £B ● **Trincadeira** £B
● **Quinta dos Bons Ventos** (Castelão/Camarate/Tinta Roriz) £B ● **Quinta das Setencostas** £B
● **Touriz** (Touriga Nacional/Tinta Roriz) £C
CASAL BRANCO ● **Ribatejo** Falcoaria (Castelão/Trincadeira) £B
O **Ribatejo** Falcoaria (Fernão Pires) £B
DFJ VINHOS ● **Grand' Arte** Alicante Bouschet £B Trincadeira £B Touriga Franca £B
● **Manta Preta** (Touriga Nacional/Tinta Roriz) £B
FUNDAÇÃO EUGÉNIO DE ALMEIDA (Alentejo) ● **Pera Manca** (Aragonês/Trincadeira) £F
● **Cartuxa** (Aragonês/Trincadeira/Castelão) £C Reserva £D
O **Pera Manca** (Arinto/Antão Vaz Perrum) £D
HERDADE DOS COELHEIROS ● **Tapada de Coelheiros** (Trincadeira/Aragonês/Cabernet S.) £C
MARTINEZ ● **Vintage Port** £E Quinta da Eira Velha £E ● **10-year-old Tawny Port** £C
HERDADE DO MOUCHÃO (Alentejo) ● **Herdade do Mouchão** £D
HERDADE GRANDE (Alentejo) ● **Herdade Grande** £C
PERREIRA D'OLIVEIRA O **Madeira** 10-year-old Verdelho £E 10-year-old Boal £E
POÇAS ● **Vintage Port** £E ● **Late Bottled Vintage Port** £C
● **Douro** Reserva (Touriga Naciona/Touriga Franca/Tinta Roriz/Tinta Barroca) £D
QUINTA DA LAGOALVA (Ribatejo) ● **Reserva** (Cabernet Sauvignon/Castelão) £B
● **Alfrocheiro** £B ● **Syrah** £B
QUINTA DAS BÁGEIRAS ● **Bairrada** Reserva £C
QUINTA DE ABRIGADA ● **Alenquer** (Castelão/Alicante Bouschet) £B

● **Alenquer** Vinha Nobre (Castelão/Camarate/Tinta Miúda) £B
QUINTA DE BAIXO ● **Bairrada** Reserva £C Garrafeira £C
QUINTA DE CHOCAPALHA (Estremadura) ● **Cabernet Sauvignon** £B
● **Chocapalha** (Touriga Nacional/Tinta Roriz/Alicante) £C
QUINTA DE PAÇOS O **Vinho Verde** Casa do Capitão £B   O **Casa de Paços Arinto** £B
QUINTA DE PANCAS ● **Cabernet Sauvignon** Special Selection £D
● **Touriga Nacional** Special Selection £D
QUINTA DA PELLADA ● **Dão** Touriga Nacional £C
QUINTA DO CARMO (Alentejo) ● **Quinta do Carmo** (Aragonês/Trincadeira/Alicante B/Cabernet) £C
QUINTA DO MOURO (Alentejo) ● **Quinta do Mouro** £C
QUINTA DO MOINHO (Algarve) ● **Vida Nova** (Shiraz/Aragonês/Trincadeira/Mourvèdre) £B
CAVES SÃO JOÃO ● **Dão** Reserva Seleccionada Porta dos Cavalheiros £B
VINHA D'ERVIDEIRA (Alentejo) ● **Vinha d'Ervideira** +LC (Trincadeira/Aragonês/Castelão) £B
● **Conde d'Ervideira Reserva** (Aragonês/Trincadeira/Alicante Bouschet) £C

Author's choice (PW)

15 classic Vintage ports
COCKBURN ● Vintage Port
CHURCHILL ● Vintage Port
DOW'S ● Vintage Port
FONSECA ● Vintage Port
GRAHAM'S ● Vintage Port
NIEPOORT ● Vintage Port
POÇAS ● Vintage Port
QUINTA DO INFANTADO ● Vintage Port
QUINTA DE RORIZ ● Vintage Port
QUINTA DO NOVAL ● Vintage Port
QUINTA DO NOVAL ● Vintage Port Nacional
QUINTA DO VESUVIO ● Vintage Port
SMITH WOODHOUSE ● Vintage Port
TAYLOR'S ● Vintage Port
WARRE'S ● Vintage Port

15 alternative 'single Quinta' type ports
COCKBURN ● Vintage Port Quinta dos Canais
CROFT ● Vintage Port Quinta da Roêda
DELAFORCE ● Vintage Port Quinta da Corte
DOW ● Vintage Port Quinta do Bomfim
DOW ● Vintage Port Senhora da Ribeira
FONSECA ● Vintage Port Guimaraens
GRAHAM ● Vintage Port Malvedos
NIEPOORT ● Vintage Port Quinta do Passadouro
QUINTA DE LA ROSA ● Vintage Port
QUINTA DO NOVAL ● Vintage Port Silval
QUINTA DO VALE DOÑA MARIA ● Vintage Port
SANDEMAN ● Vintage Port Vau
SMITH WOODHOUSE ● Vintage Port Madalena
TAYLOR'S ● Vintage Port Quinta de Vargellas
WARRE ● Vintage Port Quinta da Cavadinha

15 new order Portuguese reds

ALVES DE SOUSA ● **Douro** Quinta da Gaivosa
CAVES ALIANÇA ● **Alentejo** Quinta da Terrugem
CORTES DE CIMA ● **Reserva**
FERREIRA ● **Douro** Quinta da Leda
FOJO ● **Douro** Fojo
NIEPOORT ● **Douro** Redoma
NIEPOORT ● **Douro** Batuta
LUIS PATO ● **Vinha** Barrosa
PINTAS ● **Douro**
QUINTA DE CABRIZ ● **Dão** Escholha Virgilio Loureiro
QUINTA DO CRASTO ● **Douro** Vinha da Ponte
QUINTA DO VALE DOÑA MARIA ● **Douro**
QUINTA DO VALE MEÃO ● **Douro**
QUINTA DOS ROQUES ● **Dão** Reserva
JOÃO PORTUGAL RAMOS ● **Alentejo** Marqués de Borba Reserva

15 Good Value Portuguese reds

ALVES DE SOUSA ● **Douro** Quinta do Vale da Raposa Tinta Roriz
CASA SANTOS LIMA ● **Touriz**
CASAL BRANCO ● **Ribatejo** Falcoaria
CAVES ALIANÇA ● **Palmela** Particular
CORTES DE CIMA ● **Chaminé**
DFJ VINHOS ● **Manta Preta**
ESPORÃO ● **Alentejo** Reserva
QUINTA DA PORTELA DA VILARIÇA ● **Douro**
QUINTA DE LA ROSA ● **Douro**
QUINTA DE RORIZ ● **Douro** Prazo de Roriz
QUINTA DO CÔTTO ● **Douro**
QUINTA DO VALLADO ● **Douro**
JOÃO PORTUGAL RAMOS ● **Vila Santa**
SOGRAPE ● **Douro** Reserva
VINHA D'ERVIDEIRA ● **Vinha d'Ervideira**

Germany

Why don't Germany's often exquisite white wines receive wider recognition and support? The difficulty for the consumer in understanding her wine styles and wine names has often been put forward by way of explanation in the past. But there is a much simpler reason. Riesling is one of the world's finest grapes and there are some superlative dry and sweet wines at the premium level. However, there is also a depressing amount of wine that is underripe or dilute, often with harsh, aggressive acidity and typically with a high level of sulphur or dirty sulphides character (most acute when the wines are drunk young, as they usually are). Experience of such wines at worst turns drinkers off completely or at least creates an uncertainty about the quality that will be encountered in future bottles. Poor quality is not restricted to the cheapest wines either. Wines need to be made from moderate- or low-yielding vines and the importance of balance, ripeness and cleanliness cannot be overstated. More clarity in terms of what degree of sweetness to expect would also help the wine drinker. Only the best wines are covered below and we have encountered very little at the lower levels that is worth recommending. There are, however, many outstanding producers making stunning white wines. Those with an established reputation have recently been joined by increasing numbers of fine, usually small, newer operations. Apart from the sweet wines, which are expensive to produce and made in tiny quantities, many of the wines are very reasonably priced for the quality. We are determined to support the best German producers and intend to add considerably to those profiled below in the future, but equally we will only recommend those who turn out wines of high quality whenever conditions permit.

Making sense of German wine styles

There are two basic quality levels, QbA (*Qualitätswein bestimmter Anbaugebiete*) and QmP (*Qualitätswein mit Prädikat*). It is the Prädikat wines that we are concerned with. There are six Prädikat (or classifications) of ripeness included under QmP and for each a minimum must weight (sugar level in the grape) must be obtained. **Kabinett** is the lowest level and should mean a light, dry white but too much Kabinett wine isn't up to scratch – not just from the more marginal Mosel but also the many underperforming estates in the Rheingau and elsewhere. **Spätlese** (meaning late-harvest) wines are riper but critical to quality in all the styles is the balance between residual sugar and acidity. Most Spätlese that are dry will be labelled Trocken or alternatively Halb-Trocken for an off-dry style. From the same producer a straight Spätlese might then be expected to be at least partially sweet. Auslese wines are made from riper grapes again and usually sweeter in style though some producers have made quite dry wines from **Auslese** levels of ripeness. Wines from many sites made this way will finish up lacking balance yet some examples maintain balance and have an individual style and complexity. While Auslese wines only sometimes show some botrytis influence the still riper and sweeter categories of **Beerenauslese** and the rare **Trockenbeerenauslese** are made only from handpicked, shrivelled grapes, almost invariably enriched by noble rot. Eiswein is dependent on freezing conditions (rather than botrytis) for concentrating grapes that are high in both sugar and acidity.

In addition to the different levels of ripeness, most Prädikat wines also come from a single site. In fact almost any German wine of real quality comes from an individual vineyard or site (an *Einzellagen* name) usually suffixed with a village name, though this is now being downplayed in the Pfalz. These names have been emphasized in bold throughout the German section. Certain sites lend themselves to favour the production of one style but not necessarily another. Some top growers also distinguish between different parcels within a top site. The Gold Capsule (*Goldkapsel*) represents what a grower considers higher quality within a specific category of ripeness and it usually indicates a greater degree of botrytis character. It is most common with Auslese wines of which there might be three or four different bottlings only distinguished one from another by the inclusion of small stars on the label. Only where these are being made on a fairly regular basis have they been included within producer entries. They are indicated (to avoid confusion with the wine's rating) as either '1 Stern', '2 Sterne', etc., or simply 'Gold Capsule' (*Goldkapsel*) or even 'Long Gold Capsule' (*Lange Goldkapsel*).

Many of Germany's top estate belong to a consortium usually referred to as the VDP (*Verband Deutsches Prädikatsweingüter*) and their labels carry its emblem of an eagle. Many of the best and rarest sweet wines are set aside for sale at the VDP auction (as *versteigerungswein*). Some wine merchants who specialise in German wines will additionally stock some of these wines following a successful bid. The VDP has also been important in promoting the establishment of a vineyard classification system. Since 1999 an increasing number of producers have labelled some or all of their wines from the best vineyards under the top level of the classification. All must be a minimum of Spätlese must weight. Those from the Rheingau are designated *Erstes Gewächs* (here it is also legally approved) with three Roman arches at the bottom of the label. In the Mosel it is *Erste Lage* while in the Pfalz and other regions the designation is *Grosses Gewächs*. From the 2002 vintage, many of these have started appearing in a special bottle with an embossed symbol: a figure '1' next to a bunch of grapes. In 2000, two new categories were introduced for dry wines. Both basic Classic level and premium Selection wines are varietal but the latter also come from a single vineyard.

When looking for good-quality wines from Germany, it is very important to be aware that village names have also been used in conjunction with a *Grosslage* name (looking much like the name of a specific site but actually referring to a broader sweep of inferior vineyards). Infamous wines such as Piesporter Michelsberg or Niersteiner Gutes Domtal wines have thus been allowed to demean the reputation of a fine village and mislead the consumer.

Germany's wine regions

Mosel-Saar-Ruwer

Riesling is king in the Mosel and the top wines are almost exclusively from this grape. The vines are planted individually on often perilously steep slopes above the exaggerated twists and turns of the river below. The River Mosel flows along the Luxembourg border before turning towards Trier and it is almost immediately joined by the important tributary, the Saar. Viticulture is very marginal and only in the best years, and only then in the best sites, are sublime steely, minerally wines made, sometimes with piercing acidity but developing a marvellous, vibrant, honeyed intensity with age. Farthest from the Mosel are the vineyards of **Serrig**, most notably **Schloss Saarstein**; downstream **Saarburg** is distinguished by the **Rausch** vineyard. These, like most of the top vineyards, lie obliquely to the river. Further downstream are **Ockfener Bockstein**, the **Kupp** vineyard from behind **Ayl**, and **Scharzhofberg** from one of Germany's great names, Egon Müller. The village of **Oberemmel** and its fine vineyards, including **Hütte**, lie in a recess away from the Saar and are often overlooked. **Braune Kupp** by contrast is on the river itself, north of **Wiltingen**, as is **Altenberg**, another great site, opposite the village of **Kanzem**. The Ruwer is a trickle by contrast with the Mosel but boasts some exceptional sites that produce exquisite, elegant wines in exceptional vintages. In the village of **Kasel** are the fine **Kehrnagel** and **Nies'chen** sites but the greatest vineyards are those of **Eitelsbach**, with **Karthäuserhofberg** and the **Abtsberg** vineyard of Maximim Grünhaus/von Schubert.

On the Mosel proper obtaining full ripeness and potential greatness is a problem and only in its middle section, the Mittel Mosel, are the great gems of Mosel viticulture consistently superb. Travelling downstream from Trier, opposite the village of **Leiwen**, the very steep **Laurentiuslay** is the first fine site from which several good interpretations are made. **Trittenheim's** best vineyards are **Leiterchen** and **Apotheke**, which can show a cool, delicate minerality, but the really outstanding sites in this section of the river are the south-facing vineyards either side of **Piesport**, **Goldtröpfchen** and **Domherr**, which can show a marvellous intensity of blackcurrant, peach and citrus fruit. **Kesten** marks another fine stretch of vineyard beginning with **Paulinshofberg** and culminating in the **Juffer** and, especially, the **Juffer-Sonnenuhr** sites opposite the village of **Brauneberg**. These wines show a marvellous mineral intensity from a number of top growers. Between here and Bernkastel are some good vineyards around **Lieser** (Niederberg Helden) and **Mülheim** (Helenenkloster) but the most impressive are on the dramatic steep slopes that run northwards along the Mosel from behind **Bernkastel**. These begin with the small celebrated **Doctor** vineyard, **Graben** and **Lay**, but stretch on to **Domprobst**, the great site of **Graach**, flanked on either side by the fine **Himmelreich** and **Josephshof** vineyards. The same great slope then continues with the **Sonnenuhr** vineyard opposite **Wehlen**, which extends as far as **Zeltingen**. Many of the Mosel's finest producers are located in this section and wines from the likes of Willi Schaefer, Dr Loosen, Markus Molitor, Joh Jos Prum, Max Ferd Richter and Selbach-Oster offer high quality but differing interpretations. The Bernkastel wines can tend either to be very expensive without always showing their full potential or, as this is a much misused name, have little to do with the great vineyards behind the village. Two *Grosslage* names to be aware of are Badstube (often fine as it is restricted to the best sites) and the much wider Kurfürstlay. Just downstream of Zeltingen is arguably the last brilliantly exposed segment of the Mittel Mosel. The last two great village names are **Ürzig**, with its famous **Würzgarten** ('spice garden') vineyard, and **Erden**, which lies opposite the almost sheer **Prälat** and similarly south-facing **Treppchen** vineyard.

The last stretch of the Mosel before it reaches the Rhine at Koblenz is known as the Terrassenmosel for its narrow terraces. Though not held in the same esteem as those vineyards in the Mittel Mosel there is undoubted potential here beginning to be realised by a number of small growers. In particular, quite powerful, minerally examples have been realised from the **Röttgen** and **Uhlen** vineyards of **Winningen**.

Mittelrhein

The scattered vineyards on the picturesque north-running stretch of the Rhine constitute the small region of Mittelrhein. They can be seen both north and south of Koblenz but the best wines come from a handful of producers around **Bacharach** which has several good sites with slatey soils. As in the Mosel, Riesling is king and good examples have a distinctive floral, mineral intensity

Nahe

The Nahe has more land planted to vineyards than the Rheingau but much less Riesling, yet its best examples can combine the best qualities of both the Mosel and Rheingau. The greatest stretch of vineyards lies south of the spa town of **Bad Kreuznach**. The town itself has potentially outstanding sites in **Kahlenberg**, **Krötenpfuhl** and **Brückes** but, though improving, quality has not been maximised. Most famous are the vineyards of **Niederhausen**, especially **Hermannshöhle**. Dönnhoff is a brilliant producer which has also underscored the quality of **Brücke** (associated with **Oberhausen**, across the river) and **Kupfergrube**, which along with **Felsenberg** is one of the great vineyards of **Schlossböckelheim**. The village of **Norheim** has good south-facing sites in **Dellchen**, **Kafels** and **Kirschneck** while **Traisen** has **Bastei** and **Rotenfels** but this section of the Nahe needs others besides Dönnhoff to make more of its inherent potential. Much further upstream, refined Rieslings are produced at **Monzingen** by Emrich-Schönleber from the **Halenberg** and **Frühlingsplätzchen** vineyards. Downstream from Bad Kreuznach, and nearer to the Rhine, is **Dorsheim**, where the top sites of **Burgberg**, **Goldloch** and **Pittermännchen** show good richness from Schlossgut Diel. The **Pittersberg**, **Dautenpflänzer** and **Rheinberg** sites of **Munster**-Sarmsheim can also be a source of good-quality Riesling.

Rheingau

One glance at a map of German wine regions makes it obvious why this particular region has been held in high regard for so long. Tight contours above the Rhine, as it swings west south-west for 30 km, indicate an ideal swathe of vineyards, some of which have long belonged to some of Germany's most aristocratic estates. Despite the potential, quality remains mixed and is as likely to come from an emerging smaller grower with less well-known sites as a more famous name. As the river starts to swing north again, Spätburgunder is planted in the **Höllenberg** vineyard above **Assmannshausen** but Riesling otherwise dominates these vineyards as in no other German region. In the main section, where some of the leading villages are to be found, the vines stretch well back from the river. The best wines can show a riper, richer fruit intensity that contrasts with the generally lighter, more elegant examples from the Mosel. The citrus, apple, white peach and blackcurrant flavours more prevalent in the Mosel are replaced more often by peach, nectarine and apricot, even at Kabinett and Spätlese levels of ripeness.

Rudesheim's best vineyards lie opposite Bingen almost directly above the river, **Berg Schlossberg** and **Berg Rottland** on the steepest slopes are the finest but several others can also produce high quality. Moving east, Geisenheim, famous for its wine school, includes the vineyards of Kläuserweg and Rothenberg, while perched high above it is the historic estate of **Schloss Johannisberg** with its own separate *einzellage* identity. Behind the neighbouring village of Winkel, **Schloss Vollrads** too is an *einzellage* in its own right and efforts are being made to restore its flagging reputation. **Winkel** also has two fine vineyards in **Jesuitengarten** and **Hasensprung**. Further east, **Oestrich** deserves to be better known as both the **Doosberg** and **Lenchen** sites can provide top-quality Riesling in the right hands. The village of Hallgarten lies high above Oestrich but it is only with Hattenheim and Erbach, from vineyards close to the river, that better sites are found. **Hattenheim** includes **Wisselbrunnen**, **Nussbrunnen** and, in Mannberg, has the extension of **Erbacher Marcobrunn**, from which some of the Rheingau's most powerful, flavoursome Rieslings can be made. Erbach also includes fine sites in Siegelsberg, Schlossberg and Hohenrain.

Kiedrich lies a long way back from the river but has steep slopes in **Grafenberg** and a high-profile producer in Robert Weil. The vineyard of **Wasseros** also has the potential for top quality. To the east of Kiedrich is **Rauenthal**, a village from which stylish, spicy, minerally Riesling can be made from several outstanding sites. Currently the potential of **Baiken** and **Gehrn** is not being realised but fine examples of **Nonnenberg** and **Rothenberg** do exist. Neighbouring Martinsthal (Langenberg) and other villages closer to Wiesbaden also contain fine if lesser-known vineyards such as **Wallufer Walkenberg**. At its eastern end, the Rheingau vineyards are not on the Rhine at all but on the river Main as it flows west into the Rhine. **Hochheim** includes several top sites from a relatively narrow wedge of vineyard, including **Domdechaney**, **Kirchenstück** and **Hölle**.

Rheinhessen

Germany's most extensively planted and productive region is where a significant amount of its poorest wine comes from. The leading grapes are Müller-Thurgau and Silvaner, much of it destined for oceans of bland semi-sweet blends. It is yet again Riesling grown at the Rhine's edge that produces the best wines. **Bingen**, in the region's north-west corner, at the juncture of the Nahe and the Rhine rivers, has one important vineyard, the **Schlarlachberg**, but it is a famous stretch of vineyards from around Oppenheim and up to Nackenheim that produces the great Rieslings. The steep east-and south-east-facing escarpment of the Roter Hang hill that runs from behind Nierstein towards Nackenheim includes most of the top sites, particularly those on the sweep of the Rhine itself. Fine *Einzellagen* suffixed **Niersteiner** include the **Orbel**, **Heiligenbaum**, **Ölberg**, **Hipping**, **Brudersberg** and **Pettenthal** vineyards, while **Rothenberg** (whose top producer is Gunderloch) comes under **Nackenheim**. Behind **Oppenheim** (like Nierstein, sullied by a Grosslage name), lie **Herrenberg** and **Sackträger**, two more potentially outstanding sites. At Flörsheim-Dalsheim, in the southern hinterland, Weingut Keller has highlighted the potential of this area and established the reputation of the **Dalsheimer Hubacker** vineyard, while a short distance to the north the Wittmann family are forging a reputation for the best vineyards of Westhofen.

Pfalz

Riesling is the most planted variety in the Pfalz but occupies only 21 per cent of the vineyard, so there are many other grapes that assume an important role here as well. There is very fine Rieslaner and excellent Scheurebe and the wines are noted for a lush richness checked by a vibrant acidity. Good examples of the 'Pinots' – Grauburgunder, Weissburgunder and Spätburgunder – are made too. The Pfalz is effectively a continuation of Alsace and here the Haardt mountains offer protection in the same way as the Vosges, often ensuring a sunny, dry autumn. The region's best producers are no longer confined to the Mittelhaardt, a rich vein of sites long made famous by Bassermann-Jordan, Bürklin-Wolf and von Buhl.

On hillside slopes on the western edge of the villages (running northwards) of Ruppertsberg, Deidesheim and Forst are some of the finest sites. The best from **Ruppertsberg** include **Gaisböhl**, **Hoheburg** and **Reiterpfad**, while those from **Deidesheim** include **Hohenmorgen**, **Leinhöhle**, **Kieselberg**, **Kalkofen** and **Grainhübel**. **Forst** has two outstanding sites in **Jesuitengarten** and **Kirchenstück** but also **Freundstück**, **Pechstein** and **Ungeheuer**. The last fine sites in this stretch are clustered together just south of **Wachenheim** and includes **Gerümpel**, **Goldbächel** and **Rechbächel**. From here the vineyards continue virtually unbroken and north of the spa town Bad Dürkheim, from close to **Ungstein** (**Herrenberg**) and **Kallstadt** (**Saumagen**) there is still more potential for outstanding wines. Many producers now make a Riesling Spätlese Trocken from a top site and label it as Grosses Gewächs (in the manner of an Alsace Grand Cru). A growing number of fine producers make fine Rieslings from outside this particularly well-protected belt. The most high-profile of these, Müller-Catoir, is as successful with Rieslaner, Scheurebe and Muskateller, as Riesling.

Baden

This fast-growing, resurgent region (now Germany's third most important in terms of quantity), lies directly across the Rhine, here forming the border with France, from Alsace. Production is dominated by large co-operatives but exciting small, private producers are more responsible for its growing reputation for quality. Though a quarter of the planting is Müller-Thurgau, the leading variety is red. Spätburgunder (Pinot Noir) accounts for almost a third of the vineyard area. Grauburgunder (or Ruländer as it is also called here) and Weissburgunder in both oaked and unoaked styles are also important, as is Traminer. From this elongated stretch of vineyards, those from the areas of Kaiserstuhl and Ortenau produce some of the finest wines. In Kaiserstuhl's volcanic soils all three 'Pinots' do particularly well from around the towns of **Achkarren**, **Burkheim**, **Ihringen** and **Oberrotweil**. Further north, Riesling (as Klingelberger) assumes some significance in **Durbach** (especially from the **Plauelrain** vineyard) and in the Ortenau, where the quality obtained by Laible suggests its true potential is only just beginning to be realised.

Franken

In Franken, as in the Rheinhessen, the variety that dominates production is Müller-Thurgau, though not from a quality perspective. Silvaner is the most important quality grape and Franken is where this grape shows the greatest interest and complexity. Riesling hardly figures at all, in part because the more continental growing season isn't always long enough to achieve full ripeness. Yet from certain locations, usually close to the broad, snaking Main river, it shows a style and complexity that owes something to the soils (often limestone-rich) as well as the grape. **Escherndorf** has one outstanding site, **Lump**, where brilliant wines from Horst Sauer, including Riesling and Silvaner, deserve the widest recognition. **Iphofen** to the south is blessed with excellent vineyards in **Julius-Echter-Berg** and **Kronsberg**. Other locations with good sites include Würzburg (the famous **Würzburger Stein**) and those of **Randersacker**. Top grower Paul Fürst (Weingut Rudolf Fürst) showcases the quality of **Bürgstadter Centgrafenberg** Riesling and Spätburgunder. If the squat *Bocksbeutel* bottle comes as a suprise, and is more difficult to pour from, don't be dissuaded from trying the quality inside.

Other regions

In the very small region of Ahr, named for a northerly tributary of the Rhine, Spätburgunder dominates production while the wines of Hessische Bergstrasse (not widely seen outside Germany) are likely to be produced from Riesling. There are substantial vineyards areas in Württemberg where reds are more important than whites but there are few wines of even reasonable quality and nothing first-rate. The small Saale-Unstrut and Sachsen regions have experienced something of a revival since Germany's reunification. Riesling from the best steep slopes is showing some potential despite being at the extreme northern latitudes of continental European viticulture.

A-Z producers by region

Baden
WGT. BERCHER
ANDREAS LAIBLE

Franken
JULIUSSPITAL
HORST SAUER

Mittelrhein
WGT. TONI JOST

Mosel-Saar-Ruwer
GRANS-FASSIAN
WGT. FRITZ HAAG
WGT. REINHOLD HAART
HEYMANN-LÖWENSTEIN
KARLSMÜHLE
WGT. KARTHÄUSERHOF
VON KESSELSTATT
DR LOOSEN
MAXIMIN GRÜNHAUS/VON SCHUBERT
MARKUS MOLITOR
MÖNCHHOF/ROBERT EYMAEL
EGON MÜLLER/SCHARZHOF
DR PAULY-BERGWEILER
JOH. JOS. PRÜM
MAX FERD. RICHTER
ST. URBANS-HOF
WILLI SCHAEFER
SCHLOSS LIESER
SELBACH-OSTER

Nahe
DÖNNHOFF
EMRICH-SCHÖNLEBER
WGT. GÖTTELMANN
SCHLOSSGUT DIEL

Pfalz
BASSERMANN-JORDAN
JOSEF BIFFAR
REICHSRAT VON BUHL
BÜRKLIN-WOLF
CHRISTMANN
GEORG MOSBACHER
MÜLLER-CATOIR
ÖKONOMIERAT REBHOLZ

Rheingau
GEORG BREUER
DOMDECHANT WERNER'SCHES
PRINZ VON HESSEN
PETER JAKOB KÜHN
FRANZ KÜNSTLER
WGT. JOSEF LEITZ
SCHLOSS SCHÖNBORN
ROBERT WEIL

Rheinhessen
GUNDERLOCH
FREIHERR HEYL ZU HERRNSHEIM
WGT. KELLER
WGT. WITTMANN

Vintages

What is produced each year from German vineyards is dependent on the climatic conditions – especially the months of October and November. Top years provide greater ripeness and plentiful Spätlese and Auslese and, if the conditions are right, botrytis enrichment for Beerenauslese and Trockenbeerenauslese styles. In a poor year only Kabinett and a little Spätlese might be made. When to drink wines and potential longevity are very producer-dependent but the generalised guide in the table below is based on Spätlese and Auslese levels of ripeness. An example from the Mosel is likely to need a little more time than one from the warmer Rhine but the producer will be of much greater significance. While well-made Kabinett can be drunk within a year or two of the vintage, most Spätlese or Auslese needs three or four years' age to start to show well. Whether they will keep for another couple of years or a further five or 10 or 15 (or more) depends on the specific wine and vintage quality. Eiswein from a great vintage like 1998 can age very impressively but even when well-balanced from the outset it usually retains its penetrating acidity. Recent vintages are very exciting, the outstanding 2001 followed by some exceptional wines in 2002 though very little of the very sweet styles were produced in the latter.

German vintages

	Mosel Riesling	Rhine Riesling	Pfalz Riesling
2002	★★★★/★★★★★★ A	★★★★/★★★★★★ A	★★★★/★★★★★★ A
2001	★★★★★ A	★★★★★ A	★★★★★ A
2000	★★★/★★★★ B	★★★ B	★★/★★★ B
1999	★★★/★★★★ B	★★★/★★★★ B	★★★★ B
1998	★★★★ B	★★★★ B	★★★★/★★★★★ B
1997	★★★★ B	★★★/★★★★ C	★★★/★★★★ C
1996	★★★/★★★★ B	★★★★ B	★★★★/★★★★★ B
1995	★★★★/★★★★★ B	★★★/★★★★ B	★★/★★★ C
1994	★★★★ C	★★★★ C	★★★/★★★★ C
1993	★★★★ C	★★★★ C	★★★★ C
1992	★★★/★★★★ C	★★★/★★★★ C	★★★/★★★★ C
1991	★★★/★★★★ C	★★/★★★ D	★★/★★★ D
1990	★★★★★ C	★★★★★ C	★★★★★ C

BASSERMANN-JORDAN Pfalz www.bassermann-jordan.com   A: Gal

Owner: Margrit & Gabriele von Bassermann-Jordan   Kirchgasse 10, D-67142 Deidesheim
This famous Pfalz estate (Weingut Geheimer Rat Dr. von Bassermann-Jordan is its full name) has
been revitalised since the mid-1990s. With 42 ha, the estate is large but includes vineyards in some
of the best sites of Forst and Deidesheim. Under the winemaking direction of Ulrich Mell come
intense, ripe Rieslings (at the Spätlese levels and higher) with good balanced acidities. The *Grosses
Gewächs* versions are particularly impressive in 2001 and 2002. The wines below are only a selection
of what is made, but almost anything of at least Spätlese level made since 1997 is worth trying. (PW)

- O **Forster Jesuitengarten** Riesling Spätlese Trocken★★ £C
- O **Forster Pechstein** Riesling Kabinett Trocken★ £B
- O **Forster Kirchenstück** Riesling Auslese★★★ £D
- O **Deidesheimer Hohenmorgen** Riesling Spätlese Trocken Grosses Gewächs★★★ £E
- O **Deidesheimer Hohenmorgen** Riesling Auslese★★★ £E Riesling Eiswein★★★ £F
- O **Deidesheimer Kalkofen** Riesling Spätlese Trocken Grosses Gewächs★★★ £E

WGT. BERCHER Baden www.germanwine.de/weingut/bercher/   A: WBn

Owner: Eckhardt & Rainer Bercher   Mittelstadt 13, D-79235 Vogtsburg
Bercher has 22 ha of vines in southern Baden and plantings are dominated by the three Pinots. More
than 70 per cent of production comes from Spätburgunder, Weissburgunder or Grauburgunder.
Burkheimer Feuerberg wines qualify as *Grosses Gewächs* and those labelled 'SE' are particularly good,
with real richness and depth; Weissburgunder is stylish, intense and long, while the Spätburgunder
shows splendid flavour complexity. Some very good, well-balanced Eiswein is also made when
conditions allow; it is intense and tangy, full of ripe nectarine and dried peach fruit. The dry whites
should be drunk within three to four years of the vintage. (PW)

- O **Burkheimer Feuerberg** Weissburgunder Spätlese Trocken SE★★★ £C
- O **Burkheimer Feuerberg** Grauburgunder Spätlese Trocken SE★★ £C
- O **Chardonnay** Spätlese Trocken SE★★ £C
- ● **Burkheimer Feuerberg** Spätburgunder Spätlese Trocken SE★★★ £E

JOSEF BIFFAR Pfalz www.biffar.com

Owner: Gerhard Biffar   Niederkirchener Strasse 13, D-67146 Deidesheim
Gerhard Biffar has 12 ha of vineyards in the heart of the Pfalz, three-quarters of it planted to
Riesling. Some excellent wines were produced from the late 1980s onwards as the cellars were
gradually modernised. If quality tapered off a little at the end of the 90s the most recent wines once
again show a crystalline purity and intensity. Both Wachenheimer Gerümpel and Deidesheimer
Grainhübel Rieslings give full justification to the sites' *Grosses Gewächs* status. There is excellent
defintion too in the racy sweeter styles. Lesser wines have not been tasted here recently but why not
invest in the poise and intensity of the best wines from 2001 or 2002. (PW)

- O **Wachenheimer Gerümpel** Riesling Grosses Gewächs★★★ £C
- O **Deidesheimer Grainhübel** Riesling Grosses Gewächs★★★ £C
- O **Deidesheimer Kieselberg** Riesling Auslese★★★ £E
- O **Deidesheimer Kalkofen** Riesling Eiswein★★★★ £G

GEORG BREUER Rheingau www.georg-breuer.com   A: NYg, N&P

Owner: Bernhard & Heinrich Breuer   Grabenstrasse 8, D-65385 Rüdesheim
This estate of some 26.6 ha of vineyards includes 2.6 ha in the highly-rated Rüdesheimer Berg

Schlossberg, 1 ha in Berg Rottland and the entire 5 ha of Rauenthaler Nonnenberg. All three sites are classified as *Erstes Gewächs* giving ample scope for making fine Rheingau Rieslings. The wines improved considerably in the 1990s and in recent vintages have been particularly good. Sweeter styles generally show good botrytis richness, with good intensity and length of flavour in the Gold Capsule Auslese wines; the Rauenthal Nonnenberg is most stylish and distinctive. Just a little more focus and refinement would put the wines among the very best from the Rheingau. The wines can be a little reduced if drunk very young. Some Grauburgunder and Spätburgunder are also made. Prices are high for the quality. (PW)

O **Rüdesheim Berg Rottland** Riesling Trocken★★ £D   Riesling Auslese Gold Capsule★★★★ £F
O **Rüdesheim Bischofsberg** Riesling Auslese Gold Capsule★★★ £F
O **Rüdesheim Berg Schlossberg** Riesling Trocken★★ £D   Riesling Auslese Gold Capsule★★★ £G
O **Rauenthal Nonnenberg** Riesling Trocken★★ £D   Riesling Auslese Gold Capsule★★★★ £F
O **Riesling** Trocken Montosa★ £B

REICHSRAT VON BUHL   Pfalz   www.reichsrat-von-buhl.de   A: FEM, JNi

Owner: Reichsrat von Buhl GmbH   Weinstrasse 16, D-67146 Deidesheim

It has taken some time but Japanese investment has put this once famous estate back on the map of the Pfalz's best. With 50 ha of vineyards spread across some enviable sites it would be a shame if the wines were not special. Established in 1849, one hundred and fifty years of family production passed before its lease to a consortium of Japanese wine merchants. The Yen having been spent the wines have been back on form since 1994. It is difficult to separate the top Rieslings for quality, coming as they do from some out-and-out top Pfalz vineyards yet no two are alike. The very classy, mineral inbued Forster Pechstein is hard to better in a top vintage like 2002 but the initially more austere Ruppertsberger Reiterpfad has underlying concentration, a white peach fruit intensity and a touch of spice. Others are scarcely less good. As is the trend in the Pfalz there is now much emphasis on the production of Grosses Gewächs but some fine sweet wines are made too, including Riesling from Forster Ungeheuer and Scheurebe from Ruppertsberger Reiterpfad. (PW)

O **Forster Pechstein** Riesling Grosses Gewächs★★★★ £C
O **Forster Kirchenstück** Riesling Grosses Gewächs★★★ £C
O **Deidesheimer Paradiesgarten** Riesling Grosses Gewächs★★★ £C
O **Ruppertsberger Reiterpfad** Riesling Grosses Gewächs★★★ £C
O **Forster Jesuitengarten** Riesling Spätlese★★★ £C

BÜRKLIN-WOLF   Pfalz   www.buerklin-wolf.de   A: Lay, Tan, AWs, CPp

Owner: B Bürklin-von Guradze & C von Guradze   Weinstrasse 65, D-67157 Wachenheim

Since the mid-90s Christian von Guradze has restored the reputation of this large and historic estate. 85.5 ha of vineyards include several of the Pfalz's top sites and the focus has been to produce a top full-bodied, dry Riesling in each. Using the new classification system these have been designated *Grosses Gewächs*. These wines, all Spätlese Trocken, much more closely resemble top Alsace wines than anything from other areas in Germany. Forster Jesuitengarten is rich and minerally with real weight and an Alsace-like oiliness; the Kirschenstück is a brilliant wine with terrific minerality, great intensity, concentration and excellent ageing potential; Deidesheimer Hohenmorgen shows an unusual, spicy character and deep, pure fruit while Ruppertsberger Gaisböhl is broader but long and classy. Less expensive, the 'B'-rated Wachenheimer Rechbächel and Ruppertsberger Hoheburg are a little lighter but have good length and intensity. Cheaper again is a Bürklin Estate Riesling, which offers good fruit character. Other good wines include a very sweet Scheurebe Beerenauslese that is just rescued by its acidity and a very intense sweet Muskateller Trockenbeerenauslese with rich, vibrant, apricotty fruit that also teeters on the brink. Some Chardonnay and Spätburgunder are also made. (PW)

O **Forster Kirchenstück** Riesling Grosses Gewächs★★★★★ £E
O **Forster Ungeheuer** Riesling Grosses Gewächs★★★★ £E
O **Forster Jesuitengarten** Riesling Grosses Gewächs★★★ £D
O **Forster Pechstein** Riesling Grosses Gewächs★★★ £D
O **Deidesheimer Hohenmorgen** Riesling Grosses Gewächs★★★ £D
O **Ruppertsberger Gaisböhl** Riesling Grosses Gewächs★★★ £D
O **Ruppertsberger Hoheburg** Riesling Grosses Gewächs★★★ £C
O **Wachenheimer Rechbächel** Riesling Grosses Gewächs★★★ £C Riesling Trockenbeerenauslese★★★★ £H
O **Bürklin Estate** Riesling★★ £B O **Scheurebe** Beerenauslese★★ £F
O **Muskateller** Trockenbeerenauslese★★★★ £H

CHRISTMANN Pfalz   A: F&R

Owner: Karl-Friedrich & Steffen Christmann Peter-Koch-Strasse 43, D-67435 Gimmeldingen
Steffen Christmann's 14 ha of vineyards include four leading Pfalz vineyard sites (Deidesheimer Hohenmorgen, Gimmeldinger Mandelgarten, Königsbacher Idig and Ruppertsberger Reiterpfad), each designated *Grosses Gewächs*. The wines show intense, ripe fruit and a full, lush, almost creamy character yet with good intensity and acidity. Though made in a Trocken style there is also a little sweetness, similar to many of the Alsace *grands crus* in recent vintages. Christmann's own sweet wines are very sweet, intense and succulent but generally well-balanced, with the richness underpinned by a vibrant structure. Small amounts of Trockenbeerenauslese and Eiswein are also made as is a Spätburgunder (Pinot Noir) from Königsbacher Idig. (PW)

O **Königsbacher Idig** Riesling Trocken Grosses Gewächs★★★ £C Riesling Auslese★★★ £E
O **Gimmeldinger Mandelgarten** Riesling Trocken Grosses Gewächs★★★ £C
O **Ruppertsberger Reiterpfad** Riesling Trocken Grosses Gewächs★★★ £C
O **Deidesheimer Hohenmorgen** Riesling Trocken Grosses Gewächs★★★ £C

DOMDECHANT WERNER'SCHES Rheingau www.domdechantwerner.com

Owner: Dr Franz Werner Michel Rathausstrasse 30, D-65234 Hochheim
This estate of 12.5 ha dates back to 1780 when it was acquired by the dean (Domdechant) of the Cathedral of Mainz. The current Dr Franz Werner Michel provides a solid range of wines particularly from the Domdechaney and Kirchenstück sites. There is plenty of intensity together with spice, citrus and riper fruit flavours and good balance, though in most there is not yet the style, richness or persistence for really fine quality. Additionally in 2001, a superior Riesling Spätlese Trocken Long Gold Cap was made from Domdechaney. Eiswein is made from both Kirchenstück and Domdechaney when conditions permit. (PW)

O **Hochheimer Kirchenstück** Riesling Spätlese★★★ £C Riesling Erstes Gewächs★★★ £D
O **Hochheimer Domdechaney** Riesling Spätlese Trocken★★ £C Riesling Erstes Gewächs★★★ £D
O **Hochheimer Domdechaney** Riesling Spätlese★★★ £C Riesling Auslese★★★ £D

DÖNNHOFF Nahe www.doennhoff.com   A: WSS, HRp, Tan, L&W, L&S, JNi

Owner: Helmut Dönnhoff Bahnhofstrasse 11, D-55585 Oberhausen
Helmut Dönnhoff is quite rightly regarded as one of Germany's most celebrated winemakers. He makes prodigious Rieslings from 14.5 ha of vineyards, mostly from the sites of Schlossböckelheim, Niederhausen and Oberhäusen (the Oberhäuser Brücke is a monopole). While QbA can be distinctive, if more modest in cooler years, excellent examples of Riesling Kabinett are made, including Oberhäuser Leistenberg, which is often wonderfully full and ripe for this level. Spätlese and Auslese wines show splendid concentration, a fine, minerally intensity and considerable elegance. The range of vividly

expressed flavours from cool blackcurrant, apple and citrus to ripe peach, is matched by a lingering intensity of fruit. The reasonably-priced Schlossböckelheimer Kupfergrube Spätlese is intense and long and adds a dash of spice to a delicious, ripe, peach and blackcurrant character. Particularly concentrated, if initially less expressive, are Spätlese and Auslese from Oberhäuser Brücke that can appear with a Gold Capsule designation. The Eiswein from the same vineyard is quite exquisite, very sweet and intense and pure but beautifully balanced with honeyed, spicy, dried stone-fruit flavours that go on and on. Those named for a day of the week add a slight premium. Some Weissburgunder and Grauburgunder are also made. Lovely 2001s here. (PW)

O **Oberhäuser Leistenberg** Riesling Kabinett★★★ £C   O **Vorheimer Dellchen** Riesling Kabinett★★ £B
O **Schlossböckelheimer Kupfergrube** Riesling Spätlese★★★ £C
O **Niederhäusen Hermannshöhle** Riesling Spätlese★★★ £C   Riesling Auslese★★★★ £E
O **Oberhäuser Brücke** Riesling Spätlese★★★ £D   Riesling Auslese★★★★ £F   Riesling Eiswein✪✪✪✪✪ £H

EMRICH-SCHÖNLEBER   Nahe   www.emrich-schoenleber.com   A: CTy, HRp

Owner: H & W Schönleber   Naheweinstrasse 10A, D-55569 Monzingen
This still-small estate of 14.5 ha has been been improved and enlarged by Werner Schönleber. Through careful selection and attentive winemaking he makes tight, intense Rieslings with lovely balance and great length of flavour from the previously unsung village of Monzingen. The wines are not big or particularly concentrated but are sleek and intense. Even a Riesling Kabinett from the Monzinger Frühlingsplätzchen shows a lovely elegant, gently spicy, minerally intensity. The estate also includes 4 ha of the steep Halenberg vineyard, which produces minerally, refined flavours in its wines. A regular Spätlese from this site is medium-dry but both Halbtrocken and Trocken versions are also produced, while an Auslese is produced in a Gold Capsule version. Halenberg Eiswein is beautifully delineated and is one of those where citrus, especially grapefruit and lime, flavours often prevail over riper peach or apricot flavours. A little Eiswein is also produced from the Frühlingsplätzchen vineyard. A Grauburgunder is ripe and fruit-emphasised. (PW)

O **Monzinger Frühlingsplätzchen** Riesling Kabinett★★ £B   Riesling Spätlese★★★ £C
O **Monzinger Halenberg** Riesling Spätlese★★★ £C   Riesling Auslese★★★ £D   Riesling Eiswein★★★★ £G
O **Monzinger** Grauburgunder Spätlese Trocken★ £C

WGT. GÖTTELMANN   Nahe

Owner: Ruth Göttelmann Blessing & Götz Blessing   Rheinstrasse 77, D-55424 Münster-Sarmsheim
Götz Blessing and his wife Ruth Göttelmann-Blessing are both trained enologists and have worked very hard to improve both the quality of their grapes and the resulting wines. There are now 12.5 ha of vineyards (10 of it owned) of classic steep slate covered slopes, 70 per cent of which are planted to Riesling. A long, cool, natural fermentation is favoured resulting in wines of often piercing minerally citrus and blackcurrant fruit. The acidity can be a little too sharp in some of the drier styles but a reduction in yields seems to contribute to good flavour length. The Dautenpflänzer Riesling Spätlese shows a Mosel-like elegance. All the Rieslings need age and promise to be very lively even with five to ten years' age at Spätlese level or higher. A pure lemony, minerally Weissburgunder Spätlese Trocken opens out with a time too. (PW)

O **Münsterer** Riesling Kabinett Trocken★ £B   O **Münsterer Dautenpflänzer** Riesling Spätlese★★ £B
O **Münsterer Kapellenberg** Riesling Spätlese Trocken★★★ £B
O **Münsterer Rheinberg** Riesling Spätlese★★ £B   Riesling Beerenauslese★★★ £F
O **Münsterer** Weissburgunder Spätlese Trocken★ £B

GRANS-FASSIAN Mittel Mosel www.grans-fassian.de

Owner: Gerhard Grans Römerstrasse 28, D-54340 Leiwen

Gerhard Grans is credited with generating greater acclaim for Leiwen and its leading site, Laurentiuslay, following a series of impressive wines in the late 1980s. The estate dates back to 1624 and is located in the tight horseshoe bend of the Mosel between Leiwen and Trittenheim. Just over 9 ha of vineyard also includes the top vineyards of Trittenheimer Apotheke and Piesporter Goldtröpfchen. The wines have ample ripe fruit and excellent structure too, the exotic richness in the sweeter styles well checked by balancing acidity. Grans' efforts received further endorsement in 2001 with membership of the VDP. Some slightly weaker 2000s excepted, recent vintages have been very good. (PW)

O **Leiwener Laurentiuslay** Riesling Spätlese★★'S' £C Riesling Eiswein★★★★ £H
O **Piesporter Goldtröpfchen** Riesling Spätlese★★ £D Riesling Auslese★★★ £D
O **Trittenheimer Apotheke** Riesling Spätlese★★ £D Riesling Auslese★★★ £D
O **Trittenheimer Apotheke** Riesling Beerenauslese★★★★ £D

GUNDERLOCH Rheinhessen www.gunderloch.de   A: WSS, JNi

Owner: Agnes Hasselbach-Usinger Carl-Gunderloch-Platz 1, D-55299 Nackenheim

Fritz and Agnes Hasselbach's 10 ha of vineyards are steeply sloping and well protected. The famed Rothenberg site with its distinctive red, slatey soils is as steep as some of those on the Mosel and produces some of the richest, most intense Rieslings in Germany. There is an explosive richness of fruit at Spätlese level with ever-increasing intensity, power and structure at higher levels of ripeness. Yet the wines are elegant too, and superbly balanced, which enables them to be drunk fairly young, though they can suffer a little from reduction and benefit from aeration. The better wines should be kept for five years or considerably longer. A little wine is also made from the Nierstein Oelberg and Nierstein Pettenthal sites, while Jean-Baptiste is an off-dry Kabinett estate wine. (PW)

O **Nackenheimer Rothenberg** Riesling Trocken★★ £C   O **Jean Baptiste** Riesling Kabinett★ £B
O **Nackenheimer Rothenberg** Riesling Auslese★★★★ £D Riesling Spätlese★★★ £C
O **Nackenheimer Rothenberg** Riesling Auslese Gold Capsule✪✪✪✪✪ £F
O **Nackenheimer Rothenberg** Riesling Beerenauslese✪✪✪✪✪ £H

WGT. FRITZ HAAG Mittel Mosel www.weingut-fritz-haag.de   A: J&B, JAr, HRp, L&W

Owner: Wilhelm Haag Dusemonder Hof, Dusemonder Strasse 44, D-54472 Brauneberg

This estate of 7.5 ha produces some of the finest, most elegant Rieslings in the Mosel from one of its greatest sites, Brauneberger Juffer-Sonnenuhr. Wilhelm Haag is not only one of the region's leading winemakers but also a leader in promoting quality throughout the region. The wines start out very taut and concentrated with a remarkably fine, minerally intensity and gradually open out with age. There is increasing weight and richness in Spätlese level and higher, culminating in a small amount of Beerenauslese. Individually (cask) numbered bottlings of Spätlese wines and higher are also made and prices vary according to the considered quality of each. As extremely fine and elegant as the wines can be, quality can be masked by unpleasant sulphur or sulphides character when young. (PW)

O **Brauneberger Juffer-Sonnenuhr** Riesling Kabinett★ £B Riesling Spätlese★★ £C
O **Brauneberger Juffer-Sonnenuhr** Riesling Auslese★★★ £D Riesling Auslese Gold Capsule★★★★ £E

WGT. REINHOLD HAART   Mittel Mosel   www.haart.de   A: RsW

Owner: Theo Haart   Ausoniusufer 18, D-54498 Piesport
The small 6 ha of estate is centred on Piesporter Goldtröpfchen, one of the great sites of the Mittel Mosel. Piesport, a name shamelessly debased by commercial exploitation in the latter half of the 20th century, actually played an important part in the propagation of Riesling in preference to lesser varieties in the 18th century. Theo Haart's wines are made naturally without any overarching style imposition, maximsing quality in the context of the vintage and by reducing yields. The intensely blackcurrant fruit is characteristic, so too is a profusion of peach, apricot, citrus in many Spätlese and Auslese wines as well as exotic fruits in the sweetest styles. It is this flavour and intensity that marks out the wines' quality, supported by a subtle minerality and perfectly balanced acidity. Other sites such as Dronhofberger give cooler green apple and citrus flavours but share this intensity. Wintrich Ohligsberg (which like Goldtröpfchen qualifies as *Erste Lage*) offers spice and ripe peach at the Auslese level. If tasted young the wines show a little sulphur but this doesn't compromise the quality that is revealed with age. Some Gold capsule bottlings are made as are a little Beerenauslese or Trockenbeerenauslese though the last can be difficult to obtain as they are usually set aside as *Versteigerungswein* (wines for auction). (PW)

O **Dhron Hofberger** Riesling Spätlese★★ £C
O **Piesporter Domherr** Riesling Spätlese★★★ £C Auslese★★★★ £D
O **Piesporter Goldtröpfchen** Riesling Kabinett★★ £B Spätlese★★★ £C Auslese★★★★ £D
O **Wintrich Ohligsberg** Riesling Auslese★★★ £C

PRINZ VON HESSEN   Rheingau   www.prinz-von-hessen.com   A: OWL

Owner: Prinz & Landgraf von Hessen   Grund 1, D-65366 Johannisberg
One of several improving domaines in the Rheingau. Following much investment in renewing the cellars, and direction from Markus Sieben, much more is being made of the potential of 45 ha of vineyards. Sweet styles are now very good indeed and progress can also be seen in several of the drier styles, with better richness and texture in the *Erstes Gewächs*. The wines are increasingly showing the texture and structure as well as the ripe fruit that should be found in all good examples from the Rheingau but sadly aren't. The gentle spice and concentrated very ripe fruit in the sweeter styles of Johannisberger Klaus is particularly captivating. A little red Frühburgunder (a strain of Pinot Noir) is also made. (PW)

O **Johannisberger Klaus** Riesling Auslese★★★ £D Riesling Beerenauslese★★★★ £D
O **Johannisberger Klaus** Riesling Kabinett★ £B Riesling Erstes Gewächs★★★ £B
O **Winkeler Hasensprung** Riesling Erstes Gewächs★★ £C
O **Winkeler Jesuitengarten** Riesling Erstes Gewächs★★ £C

FREIHERR HEYL ZU HERRNSHEIM   Rheinhessen   www.heyl-zu-herrnsheim.de A: WBn

Owner: Ahr family foundation   Mathildenhof, Langgasse 3, D-55283 Nierstein
Nierstein has few estates of real quality but the Rieslings produced here in recent vintages under the direction of Markus Ahr and winemaking of Michael Burgdorf give a real lead to others in the area. The 24 ha of vineyards encompass all the top sites between Nierstein and Nackenheim, including sole ownership of the small Brudersberg site. All the wines are much improved but the riper styles of the vineyard-designated examples, with greater depth and intensity, show the most emphatic progress. They are sweet, intense and concentrated, with ripe fruit in the finish. By contrast, a minerally, dry, but rather austere Niersteiner Pettenthal Grosses Gewächs has been disappointing. Other good wines (from other than the top sites) are now sold as Rotschiefer and these include

Silvaner and Weissburgunder as well as Riesling. A little Beerenauslese and Trockenbeerenauslese from the Pettenthal and Brudersberg sites are also made. (PW)

O **Niersteiner Pettenthal** Riesling Trocken Grosses Gewächs★ £D Riesling Auslese★★★ £E
O **Niersteiner Oelberg** Riesling Auslese Gold Capsule★★★★ £F
O **Niesteiner Brudersberg** Riesling Auslese★★★ £F
O **Riesling** Kabinett★ £C

HEYMANN-LÖWENSTEIN Terrassenmosel www.heymann-loewenstein.com A: M&V

Owner: R. Löwenstein & C. Heymann-Löwenstein Bahnhofstrasse 10, D-56333 Winningen

Reinhard Löwenstein's 12 ha of vineyard cling to extremely steep terraces in the Terrassenmosel, only a short distance from Koblenz and the juncture of the Mosel with the Rhine. He makes some magnificent dry wines from stone walled slopes perfectly angled to the low sun. The atypically warm mesoclimate combined with a long ripening season and low yields produce excellent fruit. The slate soils though are distinct from those in the Mittel Mosel and the resulting wines are a very different expression of the Mosel too. They tend to be either fermented to dryness or made in more fully sweet styles (Auslese and above) though the winemaking approach is very 'hands-off'. Sweet wines show exquisite fruit and definition. The Erste Lage wines from parcels of vines within Winninger Uhlen were very successful in 2001 and 2002. Intense, mineral and elegant in the Laubach, more depth and weight in Roth Lay and cooler promise in Blaufüsser Lay. The length of flavour and complexity in all three is most impressive. Of other names used that don't refer to a vineyard site, Schieferterrassen indicates a vineyard blend while a vom Blauem Schiefer Riesling comes from a different 'blue' type of slate within Uhlen. (PW)

O **Winninger Uhlen** Riesling 'Blaufüsser Lay' Erste Lage★★★ £C Riesling 'Laubach' Erste Lage★★★ £D
O **Winninger Uhlen** Riesling 'Roth Lay' Erste Lage★★★ £D Riesling 'Roth Lay' Auslese★★★★ £F
O **Winninger Rottgen** Riesling★★★ £D Riesling Auslese★★★ £F
O **Hatzenporter Kirchberg** Riesling★★ £C
O **Schieferterrassen** Riesling★ £C Eiswein★★★★★ £H
O **Vom Blauem Schiefer** Riesling★★ £C

WGT. TONI JOST Mittelrhein A: HRp, F&R

Owner: Peter Jost Oberstrasse 14, D-55422 Bacharach am Rhein

Peter Jost, who is the Mittelrhein's one grower of real renown, has 8.5 ha of vineyards and the majority of the wines come from Bacharacher Hahn, the region's the leading site. The wines are perfumed, citrusy and zingy, adding riper peach and apricot flavours in the sweet styles. A basic Riesling Trocken is fleetingly floral and can be a little lean, yet at best is attractive, with green apple and white peach flavours; the Kabinett is riper, with better intensity and a little sweetness. Spätlese and Auslese show intense, mineral and floral characters, with increased sweetness though not always the extra depth and concentration expected at these levels of ripeness. A Beerenauslese, however, is typically very ripe, with an accentuated botrytis character and good balance between intense, sweet fruit and a vibrant acidity that ensures long ageing. A little wine is also made from the Rheingau. (PW)

O **Bacharacher Hahn** Riesling Kabinett★★ £B Riesling Spätlese★★ £C
O **Bacharacher Hahn** Riesling Auslese★★★ £D Riesling Beerenauslese★★★★ £H
O **Riesling** Trocken★ £B

JULIUSSPITAL Franken www.juliusspital.de

Owner: Juliusspital Foundation Klinikstrasse 1, D-97070 Würzburg

Founded in 1576, the hospice of Juliusspital has a long history of wine production as well as care for the needy. With 168 ha of vines, production is not insubstantial. Of the most interest are the top Spätlese wines from some of Franken's best sites. These are elegant and refined, with good definition that lets the fruit sing out with a little bottle age. The Silvaner and Riesling are bottled in the distinctive dark green *Bocksbeutel* bottles. Volkacher Karthäuser Weisser Burgunder is bottled in a Burgundy-type bottle and the light touch employed in the winemaking shows just how well this grape (Pinot Blanc) can perform here. As well as those rated below, good wines are made from other top sites such as Randersackerer Pfülben and Escherndorfer Lump. (PW)

O **Würzburger Stein** Riesling Spätlese Trocken★★★ £D   Rieslaner Auslese★★★ £D
O **Würzburger Stein** Silvaner Spätlese Trocken★★ £C
O **Würzburger Innere Leiste** Silvaner Spätlese Trocken★★ £C
O **Iphöfer Julius-Echter-Berg** Riesling Spätlese Trocken★★ £D   Silvaner Spätlese Trocken★★ £C
O **Volkacher Karthäuser** Weisser Burgunder Spätlese Trocken★★ £D

KARLSMÜHLE   Ruwer   www.karlsmuehle.com   A: HRp, F&R

Owner: Peter Geiben   Im Mühlengrund 1, D-54318 Mertesdorf
Peter Geiben's 12 ha of vineyards are spread over some excellent Ruwer sites, namely those in Lorenshöf (Felsay and Mäuerchen) and Kasel (Nies'chen and Kehrnagel). The wine quality from the late 1990s puts him among the best growers in the Mosel-Saar-Ruwer. The wines have excellent ripeness and intensity from the light yet fruit-intense Kabinett to sweet, concentrated Auslese and incredibly sweet and tangy Eiswein, which has smoky, honeyed, mineral aromas and dried fruit flavours and needs plenty of age. All the wines are extremely well-priced for the quality but sometimes can need a bit of aeration (to throw off some sulphury elements) if drunk fairly young. (PW)

O **Lorenzhöfer Mäuerchen** Riesling Kabinett★★ £B
O **Lorenzhöfer** Riesling Spätlese★★ £B   Riesling Auslese Gold Capsule★★★ £D
O **Kaseler Nies'chen** Riesling Spätlese★★★ £B   Riesling Auslese★★★ £C
O **Kaseler Kehrnagel** Eiswein★★★★ £F

WGT. KARTHÄUSERHOF   Ruwer   www.karthaeuserhof.com   A: CTy, F&R

Owner: Christoph Tyrell   Weingut Karthäuserhof, D-54292 Trier-Eitelsbach
Christoph Tyrell's historic estate based in the Ruwer is one the great names of the Mosel-Saar-Ruwer. The 19 ha of vineyards are based on the famous Eitelsbacher Karthäuserhofberg site, which produces vivid, intense and elegant expressions of Riesling. Ludwig Breiling has made the wines in recent vintages and a very high quality standard has been set. Flavours range from apple, white peach, blackcurrant, citrus and mineral in Kabinett and Spatlese to peach and exotic fruits in Auslese and Eiswein. The latter show marvellous richness as well as the same vibrant acidity and long finish seen in all the wines (even the light but stylish, minerally Riesling Kabinett). In any given vintage several individually (cask) numbered bottlings of Auslese are also made. (PW)

O **Eitelsbacher Karthäuserhofberg** Riesling Kabinett★★ £B
O **Eitelsbacher Karthäuserhofberg** Riesling Spätlese Trocken★★★ £C   Riesling Spätlese★★★ £C
O **Eitelsbacher Karthäuserhofberg** Riesling Riesling Auslese★★★★ £D   Eiswein✪✪✪✪ £H

WGT. KELLER   Rheinhessen   www.weingut-keller.de   A: HRp, F&R

Owner: Klaus Keller   Bahnhofstrasse 1, D-67592 Flörsheim-Dalsheim
Away from the Rheinterrassen (the steep slopes between Oppenheim and Nackenheim), the Rheinhessen doesn't have that much to offer, yet Klaus Keller and his son Klaus-Peter are showing that outstanding wines are possible in the hilly countryside around Flörsheim-Dalsheim. With 12.5

ha, almost half of it Riesling but a quarter to Weissburgunder and Grauburgunder, some fine dry examples are made. Better, though, are the marvellously exuberant, sweeter styles with scintillating fruit richness, excellent balance and length of flavour. There is not perhaps the sheer class or elegance that more northern sites can bring but the rich, exotic fruit intensity is hard to resist. As well as very small amounts of outstanding Trockenbeerenauslese, some Spätburgunder is made. All the better wines deserve some age but will keep for a decade. (PW)

○ **Dalsheimer Hubacker** Riesling Kabinett Trocken★ £B
○ **Dalsheimer Hubacker** Riesling Spätlese★★ £C Riesling Spätlese Trocken★★ £C
○ **Dalsheimer Hubacker** Riesling Auslese★★★ £F Riesling Auslese 3 Sterne★★★★ £G

VON KESSELSTATT Mosel-Saar-Ruwer www.kesselstatt.com A: AHW, Cam, OWL, JNi

Owner: Günther Reh family Schlossgut Marienlay, D-54317 Morscheid
The Günter Reh family possess 38 ha of vineyards in the Mosel, all of it planted to Riesling and much of it in leading sites. Yields are moderate and the aim is for natural, unmanipulated wines. Fermentation is in stainless steel with extended ageing on the fine lees. Typically the wines are properly ripe, clean and fruit-emphasized with good acid balance. They also reflect something of their origins if not necessarily competing with the very best examples from a given site. Those rated below include wines from most but not all the famous sites that are regularly made. There are several more good wines besides. (PW)

○ **Josephöfer** Riesling Kabinett★ £B Riesling Spätlese★★ £C
○ **Graacher Domprobst** Riesling Spätlese★★ £C
○ **Kaseler Nies'chen** Riesling Kabinett★ £B Riesling Spätlese★★ £C Riesling Eiswein★★★★ £G
○ **Piesporter Goldtröpfchen** Riesling Spätlese★★★ £C Riesling Auslese★★★ £D
○ **Scharzhofberger** Riesling Spätlese Long Gold Capsule★★★ £D Riesling Eiswein★★★★ £G

PETER JAKOB KÜHN Rheingau www.weingutpjkuehn.de A: CTy, Tan

Owner: Peter & Angela Jakob Kühn Mühlstrasse 70, D-65375 Oestrich im Rheingau
Quality has been on the up and up here in the past decade and Peter Jakob Kühn now makes quite superb Rheingau Rieslings from his long-established family estate. There are 13 ha of vineyards, all in a village that will now surely receive greater respect for its wines. Kühn's Oestrich wines combine the richness of the Rheingau with the elegance of the Mosel. An Oestricher Lenchen Riesling Kabinett is one of the very best in Germany at this level, with beautifully defined fruit and bright but not harsh acidity. The Spätlese has exquisite sweet fruit and lovely balance, while the Auslese is concentrated, wonderfully poised and complex. A sweet, long and intense Beerenauslese is outstanding, with a waxy, honeyed quality and superb preserved-fruit richness, and contrasts with a vibrant, very sweet, but less rich or complex Eiswein. All the wines deserve some age, the sweeter styles should have at least five years. The debate surrounding closures is also having an impact in Germany. While the Stelvin cap is now increasingly widely used Peter Jakob Kühn has bottled some of his wines under a 'crown seal' in order to eliminate taint of any kind. (PW)

○ **Oestricher Lenchen** Riesling Beerenauslese★★★★★ £H Riesling Eiswein★★★★ £H
○ **Oestricher Lenchen** Riesling Auslese★★★★ £F Riesling Spätlese★★★ £C
○ **Oestricher Doosberg** Riesling Erstes Gewächs★★★ £D
○ **Oestricher Lenchen** Riesling Kabinett★★★ £B

FRANZ KÜNSTLER   Rheingau   www.weingut-kuenstler.de   A: RsW, HRp, DWS, NYg

Owner: Gunter Künstler   Freiherr-vom-Stein-Ring 3/Kirchstrasse 38, D-65239 Hochheim

Since the mid-1990s Gunter Künstler has been able to draw upon extensive vineyards spread over the Hochheim slopes, having added those of the Aschrott estate to an existing estate first established by his father in 1965. The 26 ha include the top sites of Hochheimer Hölle, Kirchenstück and Domdechaney. The more traditionally made wines, such as a fine Kirchenstück Spätlese, show wonderful peach and nectarine richness, well checked by good acidity. Gunter Künstler has also made a feature of the dry Auslese style, making completely dry wines from an Auslese level of ripeness. A characterful, weighty example from the Stielweg vineyard shows a coarser, botrytised influence and is not as convincing as a splendidly complex, ripe and distinctive Hölle version with a waxy, honeyed character. While not to everyone's taste, the quality of the latter cannot be ignored. Non-dry examples of Auslese, such as that from Domdechaney, show lovely fruit richness and depth for those who won't be persuaded. A sweet, intense Beerenauslese from Hölle is surpassed by a very concentrated, deep, raisiny and characterful Trockenbeerenauslese. Other wines include a stylish, elegant if oaky, cherry-fruited Pinot Noir (Spätburgunder) Auslese, its price presumably pushed up by local demand, and an attractive sparkling wine, Non Plus Cuvée M (Pinot Noir/Chardonnay), in which the strawberry, cherry notes of Pinot dominate. (PW)

O **Hochheimer Hölle** Riesling Spätlese Trocken★★ £D   Riesling Auslese Trocken★★★ £E
O **Hochheimer Hölle** Riesling Beerenauslese★★★★ £H   Riesling Trockenbeerenauslese★★★★ £H
O **Hochheimer Kirchenstück** Riesling Spätlese★★★ £D   Riesling Auslese Trocken★★ £E
O **Hochheimer Domdechaney** Riesling Auslese★★★ £E
O **Hochheimer Reichstal** Riesling Kabinett★★ £B   ● **Pinot Noir** Auslese★★ £F
O **Hochheimer Stielweg** Riesling Auslese Trocken★★ £E

ANDREAS LAIBLE   Baden   www.weingut-laible.de

Owner: Andreas & Ingrid Laible   Am Bühl 6, D-77770 Durbach

This relatively little-known (outside of Germany at any rate) producer makes wines of a quality unprecedented in the Ortenau area of Baden. From just 6 ha of vineyards there is consistently high quality, not just in Riesling (Klingelberger as it is called here) but also in Gewürztraminer and Scheurebe. All the wines come from the Durbacher Plauelrain site and the top examples have lovely concentrated, fruit, with depth, body and good acidity. The top wine is the Riesling Auslese Trocken, a rich, honeyed yet dry, concentrated and complex example with great length of flavour. A richer Achat version of Riesling Spätlese Trocken contrasts with a racier regular version that offers a cooler spectrum of fruit flavours. Gewürztraminer is lush, ripe and intense and there is a cocktail of fruit in a rich but well-balanced Scheurebe. Chardonnay, Grauburgunder and Spätburgunder are also made to a high standard. (PW)

O **Durbacher Plauelrain** Riesling Auslese Trocken★★★★ £D
O **Durbacher Plauelrain** Riesling Spätlese Trocken★★ £C   Riesling Spätlese Trocken Achat★★★ £C
O **Durbacher Plauelrain** Gewürztraminer Auslese★★★ £C   Scheurebe Auslese★★★ £C

WGT JOSEF LEITZ   Rheingau   www.leitz-wein.de   A: WSS, L&W, JNi

Owner: Johannes Leitz   Theodor Heuss-Strasse 5, D-65385 Rudesheim

Making wine from less than 6 ha in some of Rudesheim's best vineyards, Johannes Leitz is one of the Rheingau's rising stars. Vineyards such as Berg Schlossberg particularly lend themselves to the elegant, refined style of Rheingau Riesling that Leitz is producing. There is generally excellent quality (and remarkable value at the lower levels) from a poised but intense, citrusy, minerally QbA to richer yet elegant, ripe peach and apricot Spätlese, Auslese and Beerenauslese. Eiswein, such as that from

Klosterberg, is tight, intense and long. (PW)

O **Rudesheimer Berg Roseneck** Riesling Kabinett★★ £B Riesling Spätlese★★★ £
O **Rudesheimer Berg Schlossberg** Riesling Spätlese★★★ £D
O **Rudesheimer Drachenstein** Riesling QbA★ £B Riesling Beerenauslese★★★★ £H
O **Rudesheimer Magdalenenkreuz** Riesling Kabinett★★ £B
O **Rudesheimer Klosterberg** Riesling Eiswein★★★★ £H

DR LOOSEN   Mittel Mosel   www.drloosen.de   A: WSS, HRp, Tan, NYg, L&S, JNi

Owner: Ernst Loosen   St Johannishof, D-54470 Bernkastel-Kues
Probably the best-known quality producer from the Mosel today, Ernst Loosen has achieve a remarkable transformation in both the quality and image of a 12-ha estate with some choice Mittel Mosel plots. The wines have lovely depth and intensity but also real elegance and a distinctive expression of their origins. Whether the splendid succulent fruit richness of Wehlener Sonnenuhr, the spice-lined finesse of Ürziger Würzgarten or the more exotic class of Erdener Prälat, there is excellent ripeness, definition and concentration that owes much to old vines and low yields. Wines are also made from the Erdener Treppchen and Graacher Himmelreich sites. The approach is organic and non-interventionist, though the wines (if drunk young) do sometimes show a little too heavy a use of sulphur (if seemingly less highly dosed when bought in Germany). The same is true, even more so, of the wines of the otherwise radically improved J L Wolf estate, taken over by Loosen in 1996. All the wines should be kept for at least three to four years, except perhaps the widely seen Dr L, which can have good intensity and attractive fruit. A little Beerenauslese and Trockenbeerenauslese is also made. (PW)

O **Ürziger Würzgarten** Riesling Spätlese★★★ £C Riesling Auslese★★★ £D
O **Wehlener Sonnenuhr** Riesling Kabinett★★ £B Riesling Spätlese★★★ £C
O **Wehlener Sonnenuhr** Riesling Auslese★★★ £D Riesling Auslese Gold Capsule★★★★ £F
O **Erdener Prälat** Riesling Auslese★★★ £F Riesling Auslese Gold Capsule★★★★ £F
O **Bernkasteler Lay** Riesling Kabinett★★ £B Riesling Eiswein★★★★ £H

MAXIMIN GRÜNHAUS/VON SCHUBERT   Ruwer   ww.vonschubert.com   A: HRp, F&R

Owner: Dr Carl-Ferdinand von Schubert   Maximin Grünhaus, D-54318 Mertesdorf
The most famous estate of the Ruwer valley is based on the Maximin Grünhaus vineyards which, like those of Karthäuserhof on the other side of the river, face south-east on slopes running obliquely to the small Ruwer river. In possession of the Benedictine monastery of St. Maximin until the early 19th century, the estate has for the past two decades been in the capable hands of Dr Carl-Ferdinand von Schubert and his winemaker Alfons Heinrich. The heart of the solely owned site of 34 ha is the Abtsberg vineyard, which produces sublime Rieslings of outstanding expression and definition. Class and finesse are paramount to the style of the wines; overwhelming power and concentration are not sought. Apart from the ripest styles, delicious flavours including lime, mineral, floral, apple and white peach prevail but there is also the structure and intensity to age for years. Most splendid are the numbered Ausleses of varying richness (and price, £E to £F) but always of at least four-star quality. Some Beerenauslese is also sometimes made. Eiswein shows great finesse and lots of concentration and rich, ripe fruit in the best years but with cooler flavours and less concentration in less successful years. All the wines need at least three to four years' ageing for the fruit to emerge and any lingering fermentation odours to disappear. (PW)

O **Maximim Grünhauser Abtsberg** Riesling Kabinett★★ £C Riesling Spätlese★★★ £C
O **Maximim Grünhauser Abtsberg** Riesling Auslese★★★ £D Riesling Eiswein★★★★ £H
O **Maximim Grünhauser Herrenberg** Riesling Spätlese★★ £C

MARKUS MOLITOR   Mittel Mosel   www.wein-markus-molitor.de   A: F&R

Owner: Markus Molitor   Haus Klosterberg, D-54470 Bernkastel-Wehlen

Markus Molitor has 35 ha of vineyards from which several versions of ripe and sweet styles of Riesling are made. The best of these are from the excellent vineyard site of Zeltinger Sonnenuhr in the heart of the Mittel Mosel. The wines are extraordinarily rich for the Mosel, concentrated, intense and ripe but they succeed in retaining sufficient acidity and balance to allow them to be either drunk young or kept (at least in the medium term). While a Riesling Kabinett can be disappointing, there is a honeyed, ripe, peach richness in versions of Riesling Spätlese and the best Auslese and a Beerenauslese show a deep marmalady botrytis character and a luscious richness. Eiswein has vibrant preserved citrus and grapefruit flavours but lacks the complexity of the very best. Sadly prices are very high and the Trockenbeerenauslese are reserved to be sold as *Versteigerungswein* (at auction). (PW)

O **Zeltinger Sonnenuhr** Riesling Spätlese★★★ £C
O **Zeltinger Sonnenuhr** Riesling Auslese★★★ £E Riesling Auslese 3 Sterne★★★★ £H
O **Zeltinger Sonnenuhr** Riesling Beerenauslese★★★★ £H
O **Bernkasteler Badstube** Riesling Eiswein★★★ £H

MÖNCHHOF/ROBERT EYMAEL   Mittel Mosel   www.moenchhof.de   A: RsW, Rae

Owner: Robert Eymael   Mönchhof, D-54539 Ürzig

Robert Eymael has been running the ancient Mönchhof estate since 1994. His 10 ha of vineyards, planted only to Riesling are concentrated on three of the finest sites of the Mittel Mosel: Ürziger Würzgarten, Erdener Treppchen and the great Erdener Prälat. The wines show classic delicacy, intensity and refined fruit flavours, especially at Spätlese and Auslese levels of ripeness. The spice garden of Urzig is famed for the spice character to be found in the wines that are produced from it. The Mönchhof examples show a characteristic spiciness, as well as hints of mineral, ripe peach and nectarine fruit. While there's currently not the concentration or length of flavour seen in the very best examples from these sites, prices aren't excessive for the quality. (PW)

O **Ürziger Würzgarten** Riesling Spätlese★★ £C Riesling Auslese★★★ £D
O **Erdener Prälat** Riesling Auslese★★★ £D
O **Erdener Treppchen** Riesling Kabinett★★ £B Riesling Spätlese Trocken★★ £C Riesling Auslese★★★ £D

GEORG MOSBACHER   Pfalz   www.georg-mosbacher.de   A: HRp

Owner: Mosbacher family   Weinstrasse 27, D-67147 Forst

The lion's share of the Mosbacher family's 15 ha is planted to Riesling. Richard Mosbacher works with his daughter Sabine and her husband Jürgen Düringer to give excellent expression to plots of vines in some of the leading Pfalz vineyards. In the *Grosses Gewächs* in particular there is a fresh, ripe intense fruit and good flavour depth yet real differentiation between each. There is a striking mineral intensity and depth in the powerful Forster Ungeheuer (mid-slope sandstone soils) which contrasts with the open, expressive Deidesheimer Kieselberg (on stoney sandy soils) which includes some exotic fruit flavours. Vines from the small Forster Freundstück site also provide *Grosses Gewächs* Riesling as well as favouring Eiswein production. In addition to the *Grosses Gewächs* sites wines, good Rieslings are made from several of the lesser known sites around Deidesheim and Forst. There is also some Weissburgunder and Gewürtraminer. More wines will be rated in future editions. (PW)

O **Forster Ungeheuer** Riesling Spätlese Trocken Grosses Gewächs★★★ £D
O **Forster Freundstück** Riesling Spätlese Trocken Grosses Gewächs★★★ £D
O **Deidesheimer Kieselberg** Riesling Spätlese Trocken Grosses Gewächs★★★ £D

MÜLLER-CATOIR Pfalz
A: HRp, F&R, N&P

Owner: Jakob Heinrich Catoir   Mandelring 25, D-67433 Haardt
A wine estate made great through the efforts of winemaker Hans-Günther Schwarz. The wines from 20 ha of vineyards are not from the Pfalz's most famous sites but very intense, fine whites are produced across a range of lesser-known vineyards. The wines provide a real contrast to the exquisite balance and finesse seen in the top Mosel wines as, though well-balanced and fine, they are characterised more by their power and thrilling intensity, which have earned them an almost fanatical following. Those from Rieslaner are the most individual and characterful of all, with remarkable sweetness and power in Auslese level and higher. Riesling, though intense, doesn't always have quite the expected depth or concentration seen in other top Pfalz examples. Sweet, exotic Scheurebe and good dry examples of Grauburgunder, Weissburgunder and Muskateller are also made. (PW)

O **Gimmeldinger Mandelgarten** Riesling Auslese★★★ £F
O **Gimmeldinger Schlössel** Rieslaner Spätlese Trocken★★ £C
O **Mussbacher Eselshaut** Rieslaner Spätlese★★ £D   Rieslaner Auslese★★★ £E
O **Mussbacher Eselshaut** Rieslaner Trockenbeerenauslese✪✪✪✪✪ £H
O **Haardter Bürgergarten** Riesling Spätlese Trocken★ £C   Rieslaner Beerenauslese★★★★ £G
O **Haardter Bürgergarten** Muskateller Trocken★★ £C
O **Haardter Herrenletten** Riesling Spätlese Trocken★ £C
O **Haardter Mandelring** Scheurebe Spätlese★★ £C   Scheurebe Auslese★★★ £F

EGON MÜLLER/SCHARZHOF Saar www.scharzhof.de
A: J&B, DAy, HRp, OWL

Owner: Egon Müller   Scharzhof, D-54459 Wiltingen
Egon Müller IV now runs an estate with a reputation like no other in Germany. The fame of the Scharzhofberg site and the prices the top (sweet) wines command align it with the most prestigious domaines in the world. The closest village to the south-east-facing slopes is Wiltingen but this does not appear as part of the wines' names. As well as the wines from 8 ha of estate vineyards the wines from the 4-ha Le Gallais estate are produced here. The latter come from Braune Kupp north of Wiltingen, which, unlike those of Scharzhofberg (in a side valley), lies above the river Saar itself. The top sweet wines start out firm, intense and taut but have tremendous underlying concentration with the potential to last for decades. Small amounts of Trockenbeerenauslese and Eiswein (both of five-star quality) are made when conditions permit. As well as regular versions of Spätlese and Auslese, several superior, numbered versions are also released. All need at least ten years' age. Almost all the wines are sold at auction (so prices can vary considerably). Only a regular Riesling, a Kabinett and a Spätlese are reasonably affordable, though at this level better value can usually be had elsewhere. (PW)

O **Scharzhofberger** Riesling Auslese★★★★ £G   Riesling Beerenauslese✪✪✪✪✪ £H
O **Scharzhofberger** Riesling Kabinett★★ £C   Riesling Spätlese★★★ £E
Le Gallais
O **Wiltinger Braune Kupp** Riesling Spätlese★★ £D   Riesling Auslese Gold Capsule★★★★ £H

DR PAULY-BERGWEILER Mittel Mosel www.pauly-bergweiler.com
A: OWL

Owner: Dr Peter Pauly   Gestade 15, D-54470 Bernkastel-Kues
This producer comprises two estates. In addition to the Pauly-Bergweiler estate are the vineyards of Peter Nicolay that have come from his wife's family. Lighter, simpler styles of Riesling are better made than most, while there is lovely definition and refinement in the Prädikat wines. The family is fortunate to have nearly 2 ha of vineyards in the Bernkastel Badstube am Doctorberg, whose wines retain a minerally elegance whilst building in richness with age. Riesling of Spätlese level, sometimes

higher, is also made from Graacher Himmelreich and Wehlener Sonnenuhr sites. Wines from the Peter Nicolay estate include Riesling Spätlese and Auslese from Ürziger Goldwingert and Erdener Prälat. (PW)

Dr Pauly-Bergweiler
O **Riesling** Dr Pauly Classic★ £B   O **Riesling** Dr Pauly Noble House★ £B
O **Erdener Treppchen** Riesling Selection★★ £B
O **Bernkasteler Badstube am Doctorberg** Riesling Spätlese★★★ £C   Riesling Auslese★★★ £D

JOH JOS PRÜM   Mittel Mosel   A: J&B, JAr, OWL, HRp

Owner: Dr Manfred & Wolfgang Prüm   Uferallee 19, D-54470 Bernkastel-Wehlen
The famed 14-ha estate of Dr Manfred Prüm is centred on the great Wehlener Sonnenuhr site but also includes Zeltinger Sonnenuhr, Graacher Himmelreich and Bernkasteler Lay. The wines are justly renowned for their longevity and the refinement that ageing brings. In fact, a wonderful, racy intensity and minerally elegance used only to become apparent with several years' age. The most recent vintages, however, can be drunk quite young, while after a decade or more a Spätlese can show a delicate toastiness and subtle, honeyed perfume preceding a beautifully delineated, fruit-filled palate. The Auslese-level wines retain a finesse and delicacy seen in Kabinett and Spätlese wines but add more depth and intensity to riper fruit flavours, including peach and apricot, rather than white peach and apple. Five-star Beerenauslese and Trockenbeerenauslese wines are sold at auction and can be difficult to obtain. Late bottling means the wines are usually a year behind most other producers, becoming available only in the second year after the vintage. (PW)
O **Wehlener Sonnenuhr** Riesling Kabinett★★ £C   Riesling Spätlese★★★ £C
O **Wehlener Sonnenuhr** Riesling Auslese★★★★ £E   Riesling Auslese Gold Capsule✪✪✪✪✪ £H
O **Graacher Himmelreich** Riesling Kabinett★ £C   Riesling Spätlese★★★ £C

ÖKONOMIERAT REBHOLZ   Pfalz   www.oekonomierat-rebholz.de

Owner: Hansjörg Rebholz   Weinstrasse 54, D-76833 Siebeldingen
Despite being based in the less-celebrated southern part of Pfalz, Hansjörg Rebholz manages to make some of the region's best wines. Don't expect the power or weight of the likes of BÜRKLIN-WOLF, rather a very fine, intense, *terroir*-derived expression of Riesling. The cool, pure mineral intensity of the Kastanienbusch from red slate soils contrasts with the minerally warmth derived from the gravel and sandstone of the Im Sonnenschein site. Good as these are, only a little over a third of the estate's 14 ha of vineyard are planted to Riesling. Fifty per cent is comprised of the Pinots (Blanc, Gris and Noir) and Chardonnay. The Siebeldingen Im Sonnenschein Weissburgunder is a superb example of this grape. It comes from a more fossilised part of the vineyard than the Riesling and is very composed and complex, on an altogether different quality level to the boring overoaked examples more commonly encountered. The wines rated below are but a few of those made; more ratings will be added in the future. (PW)
O **Birkweiler Kastanienbusch** Riesling Spätlese Trocken Grosses Gewächs★★★★ £E
O **Siebeldingen im Sonnenschein** Riesling Spätlese Trocken Grosses Gewächs★★★ £D
O **Siebeldingen im Sonnenschein** Weisser Burgunder Spätlese Trocken Grosses Gewächs★★★ £D

MAX FERD. RICHTER   Mittel Mosel   www.maxferdrichter.com   A: CTy, Tan, Res, BBR

Owner: Richter family   Hauptstrasse 37/85, D-54486, Mülheim-Mosel
Dr. Dirk Richter is the current director of this family estate, established over 300 years ago. The family's 15 ha of vineyards are in some of the Mittel Mosel's best sites and there is consistently good quality. There is not perhaps the subtlety or refinement of others yet there is a characteristic ripeness and intensity; fine

acidity and the class of the best vineyards comes through. No two wines are quite the same, a Juffer-Sonnenuhr Spätlese for instance, shows an intense apricotty fruit while the equivalent from Graacher Himmelreich shows a more citrusy elegance. The small vineyard (less than a hectare) of Mülheimer Helenenkloster is solely owned and famed for its ability to consistently produce an outstanding Eiswein – a sweet and tangy potion of citrus peel, dried peach, spice and more exotic flavours that lingers long in the mouth. The Veldenzer Elisenberg vineyard is also under the sole ownership of the family and the source of fine Rieslings. Prices are quite reasonable. (PW)

O **Graacher Domprobst** Riesling Spätlese Halbtrocken★★ £B Riesling Auslese★★★ £C
O **Graacher Himmelreich** Riesling Kabinett★★ £B Riesling Spätlese★★★ £B
O **Oehlener Sonnenuhr** Riesling Kabinett★★ £B Riesling Spätlese★★★ £C
O **Brauneberger Juffer-Sonnenuhr** Riesling Spätlese★★★ £C Riesling Auslese★★★ £C
O **Mülheimer Helenenkloster** Riesling Eiswein★★★★★ £H

ST. URBANS-HOF   Mittel Mosel   www.urbans-hof.de

Owner: Nik Weiss   Urbanusstrasse 16, D-54340, Leiwen

For fine Mosel wines that are fully ripe and with an extra intensity yet without losing their elegance or individuality these wines are hard to beat. The young Nik Weiss is making the most of his family's considerable viticultural resource of 38 ha planted mostly to Riesling to promote high quality production from this part of the Mosel. His winemaker Rudolf Hoffmann is clearly able to harness the potential of fruit that is riper and more concentrated than most. Piesporter Goldtröpfchen wines, from a particularly steep part of the vineyard just above the river's edge show a rich, intense blackcurrant, citrus and peach fruit expression yet elegance too. The Ockener Bockstein wines are splendidly individual with a smokey and mineral, very ripe citrus character at Auslese level. The wines from Leiwener Laurentiuslay are of similar quality. Highish sulphur levels can detract at Kabinett level but these wines too will age and will then taste immeasurably cleaner. A small amount wine is usually designated Gold Capsule and Eiswein is also produced from Leiwener Klostergarten. (PW)

O **Piesporter Goldtröpfchen** Riesling Kabinett★★ £B Riesling Spätlese★★★ £C Riesling Auslese★★★★ £E
O **Leiwener Laurentiuslay** Riesling Spätlese★★ £C
O **Ockfener Bockstein** Riesling Kabinett★ £B Riesling Spätlese★★★ £C Riesling Auslese★★★★ £E
O **Wiltinger Schlangengraben** Riesling Auslese Gold Capsule★★★★ £E

HORST SAUER   Franken   www.weingut-horst-sauer.de   A: NYg, J&B

Owner: Horst Sauer   Bocksbeutelstrasse 14, D-97332 Escherndorf

In the space of a few vintages, Horst Sauer has emerged as the best producer in Franken and one of the new stars of Germany. There is both complexity and individuality in all the better wines with elegance and well-detailed fruit even in Riesling Kabinett. From a total of almost 10 ha of vineyards in one of Franken's most prized vineyard sites, Escherndorfer Lump, there is Silvaner of similar quality to Riesling and both have excellent balance and composure in dry and sweeter styles. Quite superb Riesling Beerenauslese and Riesling and Silvaner Trockenbeerenauslese all combine richness and expression; intense spice, mineral and dried fruit flavours linger long on the finish. A Scheurebe Spätlese is an excellent example of this variety too and even Müller-Thurgau has good intensity and shows a light minerally elegance. Partially barriqued Sennsucht Silvaner is a successful diversion in a more international style. Some Pinot Noir Rosé is also made. (PW)

O **Escherndorfer Lump** Riesling Kabinett Trocken★★ £B Riesling Spätlese Trocken★★★ £C
O **Escherndorfer Lump** Riesling Beerenauslese★★★★★ £F Riesling Eiswein★★★★★ £G
O **Escherndorfer Lump** Riesling Trockenbeerenauslese✪✪✪✪✪ £G
O **Escherndorfer Lump** Silvaner Trockenbeerenauslese✪✪✪✪✪ £G
O **Escherndorfer Lump** Silvaner Spatlese Trocken★★★ £C Silvaner Auslese★★★★ £E

O **Eschendorfer Lump** Scheurebe Spatlese★★★ £C   O **Müller-Thurgau★** £B
O **Sehnsucht** Silvaner Spatlese Trocken★★ £C

WILLI SCHAEFER   Mittel Mosel   A: HRp, Tan, F&R

Owner: Willi Schaefer   Hauptstrasse 130, D-54470 Graach
There are arguably no finer examples of Rieslings from the village of Graach than those from Willi Schaefer's extremely modest 2.7 ha planted to 100 per cent Riesling. These pure, intense wines are not in the least overpowering but are wonderfully expressive and long with more richness at Auslese level. Those from Domprobst are superior to those from Himmelreich, being consistently finer, riper and fuller. That said, even the Himmelreich Kabinett can show fine apple, grapefruit and lemon that contrast with the peachier, mineral intensity in Domprobst Kabinett and Spätlese. A perfect balance of acidity and concentrated, riper fruit is typical in the Domprobst Auslese. Some individually numbered Auslese from both Domprobst and Himmelreich are also made, as is a little Beerenauslese. (PW)
O **Graacher Domprobst** Riesling Kabinett★★ £B   Riesling Spätlese★★★ £C   Riesling Auslese★★★★ £D
O **Graacher Himmelreich** Riesling Kabinett★ £B   Riesling Spätlese★★ £C

SCHLOSSGUT DIEL   Nahe   www.schlossgut-diel.com   A: HRp, F&R

Owner: Armin Diel   Schlossgut Diel, D-55452 Burg Layen
Armin Diel, a leading expert on German wines and a German television celebrity, finds time to make some good wines of his own. His 16 ha is centred on Dorsheim's top sites, from which he makes Riesling that is rich and intense but usually well-balanced. Even the Dorsheimer Goldloch Riesling Kabinett shows ripe nectarine and apricot fruit and is balanced and long. As well as Riesling from the Dorsheimer Pittermännchen site, Diel makes barrique-fermented Grauburgunder and Weissburgunder and Cuvée Victor (a blend of the two). While they show good richness they can be a little overblown at the expense of finesse and can develop quite quickly. (PW)
O **Dorsheimer Goldloch** Riesling Kabinett★★ £B   Riesling Spätlese★★ £C
O **Dorsheimer Pittermännchen** Riesling Spätlese★★ £C   Riesling Auslese★★★ £E
O **Grauburgunder★** £C   O **Weissburgunder★** £C   O **Cuvée Victor★★** £E
O **Dorsheimer Burgberg** Riesling Eiswein★★★ £H

SCHLOSS SCHÖNBORN   Rheingau   www.schoenborn.de   A: C&B

Owner: Graf von Schönborn   Am Markt 1, D-54470 Lieser
Schloss Schönborn has a collection of the very best vineyards in the Rheingau. The vineyard resource of 50 ha in a great many of the Rheingau's top sites including Erbacher Marcobrunn must be the envy of many a small grower. Despite some quality ups and down there are indications of a more sustained revival over recent vintages. As well as improvement in the sweeter styles there is increasing depth and texture in *Erstes Gewächs* bottlings. Most wines show a little sulphur when young but this is less marked with age and the best vintages will age very well indeed. (PW)
O **Erbacher Marcobrunn** Riesling Kabinett★ £C   Riesling Spätlese★★ £C   Riesling Erstes Gewächs★★ £C
O **Hattenheimer Pfaffenberg** Riesling Spätlese★★ £C   Riesling Erstes Gewächs★★ £C
O **Rüdesheimer Berg Schlossberg** Riesling Auslese★★★ £E
O **Rüdesheimer Berg Rottland** Riesling Auslese★★★ £E

SCHLOSS LIESER   Mittel Mosel   www.weingut-schloss-lieser.de   A: J&B, HRp, Tan, F&R

Owner: Thomas Haag   Am Markt 1, D-54470 Lieser

A once-famous, recently revitalised estate making taut, intense and ripe Rieslings that add richness and complexity in the higher Prädikat styles and with age. Thomas Haag, who is the son of Wilhelm Haag of the Fritz HAAG estate, has been responsible for the much-improved quality from 7 ha centred on the Lieser Niederberg Helden site. At the Auslese level (there is typically more than one bottling) in particular, there is the exquisite combination of finesse and richness that the best Mittel Mosel sites produce. The only negative point about some recent releases has been the tendency to an excessive sulphur or sulphides taint, however most should lose this with additional bottle age. A little 3 Sterne Auslese and some Beerenauslese are also made. The wines are reasonably priced. (PW)

O **Lieser Niederberg Helden** Riesling Auslese 1 Stern★★★ £C   Riesling Auslese 2 Sterne★★★ £D
O **Lieser Niederberg Helden** Riesling Spätlese★★ £B
O **Riesling** Kabinett★★ £B

SELBACH-OSTER   Mittel Mosel   www.selbach-oster.de   A: M&V, JAr, HRp, L&W, JNi

Owner: Hans & Johannes Selbach   Uferallee 23, D-54492 Zeltingen

This 13.8-ha estate has been in the family since 1661 and is now run by Johannes Selbach and his wife. Some fine Mosel wines are made, with depth, elegance and fine, cool, apple, citrus and white peach flavours. Particularly stylish is a classy Zeltinger Sonnenuhr Riesling Auslese, though this and other wines can sometimes suffer from a excessive level of sulphur. Though this is usually only detected in the wines when young, sometimes with age a more fixed sulphides character detracts from what are otherwise lovely wines. A little Beerenauslese and Trockenbeerenauslese are also made from Zeltinger Sonnenuhr. Wines labelled J&H Selbach are produced from bought-in grapes as part of a *négociant* business. (PW)

O **Wehlener Sonnenuhr** Riesling Kabinett★★ £B
O **Zeltinger Sonnenuhr** Riesling Spätlese★★★ £C   Riesling Auslese★★★ £D
O **Graacher Domprobst** Riesling Spätlese★★ £C   Riesling Auslese★★ £D

ROBERT WEIL   Rheingau   www.weingut-robert-weil.com   A: HBJ, DWS, N&P

Owner: Suntory   Mühlberg 5, D-65399 Kiedrich

Wilhelm Weil continues the revitalisation of this large Rheingau estate with 65 ha of vineyards planted almost exclusively to Riesling. Since the 1990s the wines have shown remarkable intensity and richness, especially in the sweeter styles. At the top level the wines really excel but also sell for very high prices, at least partly fuelled by an almost cult following. At the heart of the domaine is one of the finest vineyards in the Rheingau, Kiedricher Gräfenberg, a site of historical significance and reputation. Everything possible is done to ensure that grapes are as rich, ripe and concentrated as possible and this is particularly apparent at the Auslese level and higher. The rich, sweet, apricot and dried-peach fruit, braced by tangy acidity, becomes more honeyed and magnificent with age. It is a shame to drink these wines too young. Wines from other vineyards are sold as Weil Estate Riesling and though these wines can be reasonably lush and concentrated they do not show the elegance or lingering fruit intensity of the Kiedricher Gräfenberg wines. An *Erstes Gewächs* bottling from the Grafenberg site has yet to show its full potential. A little Spätburgunder and tiny amounts of Trockenbeerenauslese are also made. (PW)

O **Kiedricher Gräfenberg** Riesling Spätlese★★★ £D   Riesling Erstes Gewächs★★★ £D
O **Kiedricher Gräfenberg** Riesling Auslese★★★★ £F   Riesling Auslese Gold Capsule★★★★★ £H
O **Kiedricher Gräfenberg** Riesling Beerenauslese Gold Capsule★★★★★ £H   Riesling Eiswein❂❂❂❂❂ £H

WGT. WITTMANN   Rheinhessen   www.wittmannweingut.com   A: WBn

Owner: Philipp Wittmann   Mainzer Strasse 19, D-67593 Westhofen

Quality from the 25 ha Wittmann estate has risen steadily over recent years and is like Weingut KELLER breathing new life into the Rheinhessen. It is very much a family enterprise with tireless effort going into improving the health of the vineyard that is certified as organic. Around half the plantings are Riesling, the best examples of which, both dry and sweet, are now really first class and stand comparison with top examples from other regions. 'S' selection wines have an extra intensity and rich fruit on the finish as well as the vibrant acidity that is common to all the wines. The Auslese 'S' from Westhofer Morstein pulsates with honey, botrytis and ripe fruit. Patience is required for the powerful but austere *Grosses Gewächs* bottling from the three top vineyards, Aulerde, Kirschspiel and Morstein. The Aulerde starts out the tightest but has excellent potential, Kirschspiel shows excellent fruit and length of flavour, the stylish Morstein, a subtle spice, mineral and fruit complexity. Given the progress already made and the dedication of the Wittmann family there is every suggestion that the wines will get even better. In addition to good Silvaner and Weisser Burgunder (Pinot Blanc) some Chardonnay is also produced. More esoteric wines include sweet versions of Huxelrebe and Albalonga (a Rieslaner-Silvaner crossing). (PW)

O **Westhofener Kirschspiel** Riesling Grosses Gewächs★★★ £D
O **Westhofener Morstein** Riesling Grosses Gewächs★★★ £D   O **Westhofener** Riesling Trocken 'S'★★ £D
O **Westhofener Morstein** Riesling Spätlese £D   Riesling Auslese 'S'★★★★ £E
O **Westhofener Aulerde** Riesling Grosses Gewächs★★★ £D   Riesling Trockenbeerenauslese★★★★ £H
O **Silvaner** Trocken 'S'★★ £C   O **Weisser Burgunder** Trocken 'S'★★ £C

OTHER WINES OF NOTE

ACHAM-MAGIN O **Forster Kirchenstück** Riesling Trocken Grosses Gewächs £D
O **Ruppertsberger Reiterpfad** Riesling Trocken Grosses Gewächs £D
ALDINGER O **Fellbacher Lämmler** Riesling Spätlese Trocken Grosses Gewächs £D
BASTIAN O **Bacharacher Posten** Riesling Grosses Gewächs £D   Riesling Auslese £D
J B BECKER O **Wallufer Walkenberg** Riesling Spätlese Trocken £C   Riesling Auslese Trocken £C
BERGDOLT O **Kirrweiler Mandelberg** Weissburgunder Spatlese Trocken £B   Grosses Gewächs £C
CASTELL'SCHES DOMÄNENAMT O **Casteller Schlossberg** Riesling Spätlese Grosses Gewächs £D
O **Casteller Schlossberg** Silvaner Grosses Gewächs £D   Rieslaner Auslese £F
JOH JOS CHRISTOFFEL O **Ürziger Würzgarten** Riesling Spätlese £B
O **Ürziger Würzgarten** Riesling Auslese I Stern £C   Riesling Auslese 2 Sterne £D
CRUSIUS O **Schlossböckelheimer Felsenberg** Riesling Spätlese £C
O **Traiser Rotenfels** Riesling Spatlese £C
DIEFENHARD O **Martinsthaler Langenberg** Riesling Erstes Gewächs £C
RUDOLF FÜRST O **Bürgstadter Centgrafenberg** Riesling Spätlese £C   Riesling Eiswein £H
O **Bürgstadter Centgrafenberg** Weissburgunder Trocken £D   ● **Spätburgunder** 'R' £F
KURT HAIN O **Piesporter Goldtröpfchen** Riesling Spätlese £B   Riesling Auslese £C
FREIHERR VON HEDDESDORFF O **Winninger Röttgen** Riesling Spätlese £B   Riesling Auslese £D
DR. HEGER O **Ihringer Winklerberg** Weissburgunder Spätlese 3 sterne £D
O **Ihringer Winklerberg** Muskateller Spätlese 3 Sterne £D
● **Ihringer Winklerberg** Spätburgunder 3 Sterne £E
VON HÖVEL O **Oberemmeler Hütte** Riesling Spätlese £B   Riesling Auslese £C
WEINGUT JOHANNISHOF O **Johannisberger Klaus** Riesling Spätlese £B
O **Rüdesheimer Berg Rottland** Riesling Auslese £E
KARL-HEINZ JOHNER O **Weisser Burgunder** 'SJ' £E   O **Grauer Burgunder** 'SJ' £E
● **Spätburgunder** 'SJ' £E
HERIBERT KERPEN O **Wehlener Sonnenuhr** Riesling Spätlese £B
AUGUST KESSELER O **Rüdesheimer Berg Schlossberg** Riesling Spätlese Trocken £D
O **Rüdesheimer Berg Roseneck** Riesling Spätlese Gold Capsule £D

KNIPSER O **Dirmsteiner 'Himmelsrech' Mandelpfad** Riesling Spätlese Trocken Grosses Gewächs £D

O **Laumersheimer 'Steinbuckel' Mandelberg** Riesling Spätlese Trocken Grosses Gewächs £D

KOEHLER-RUPRECHT O **Kallstadter Saumagen** Riesling Auslese Trocken £D

O **Kallstadter Saumagen** Riesling Auslese 'R' £D Riesling Eiswein £G

KRUGER-RUMPF O **Münsterer Kapellenberg** Riesling Kabinett £B

O **Münsterer Dautenpflänzer** Riesling Spätlese £B Riesling Spätlese Trocken £B

O **Münsterer Pittersberg** Riesling Auslese £E

LANGWERTH VON SIMMERN O **Erbacher Marcobrunn** Riesling Kabinett £B

O **Hattenheimer Wisselbrunnen** Riesling Spätlese £C Riesling Beerenauslese £E

LINGENFELDER O **Freinsheimer Goldberg** Riesling Spätlese Trocken £B

O **Grosskarlbacher Osterberg** Riesling Spätlese Halbtrocken £B

O **Grosskarlbacher Burweg** Scheurebe Kabinett Trocken £B

WEINGUT CARL LOEWEN O **Leiwener Klostergarten** Riesling Kabinett £B Riesling Eiswein £F

FÜRST LÖWENSTEIN O **Hallgarten Schönhell** Riesling Erstes Gewächs £D

O **Homburg Kallmuth** Riesling Spätlese Trocken Grosses Gewächs £D

O **Homburg Kallmuth** Silvaner Spätlese Trocken Grosses Gewächs £D

ALFRED MERKELBACH O **Ürziger Würzgarten** Riesling Spätlese £B

MEULENHOF O **Erdener Treppchen** Riesling Spätlese £B Riesling Auslese £B

O **Erdener Prälat** Riesling Auslese £C

MEYER-NÄKEL ● **Spätburgunder Trocken** 'S' £E

WEINGUT PAULINSHOF O **Brauneberger Juffer-Sonnenuhr** Riesling Spätlese Trocken £C

O **Brauneberger Juffer** Riesling Spätlese £C O **Brauneberger Kammer** Riesling Spätlese Halbtrocken £C

O **Kestener Paulinshofberger** Riesling Auslese £D

WEINGUT PFEFFINGEN O **Ungsteiner Herrenberg** Riesling Spätlese Trocken £B

S A PRÜM O **Wehlener Sonnenuhr** Riesling Spätlese £C Riesling Auslese Gold Capsule £H

O **Graacher Himmelreich** Riesling Eiswein £H

QUERBACH O **Oestrich Lenchen** Riesling Trocken No.1 £B Riesling Trocken No.2 £B

O **Oestrich Doosberg** Riesling Erstes Gewächs £C

JOHANN PETER REINERT O **Kanzemer Altenberg** Riesling Spätlese £B Riesling Auslese £C

BALTHASAR RESS O **Hattenheimer Nussbrunnen** Riesling Erstes Gewächs £D Riesling Auslese £D

O **Rüdesheimer Berg Schlossberg** Riesling Erstes Gewächs £D

O **Rüdesheimer Berg Rottland** Riesling Erstes Gewächs £D

O **Schloss Reichartshausen** Riesling Spätlese £C O **Hattenheimer Schützenhaus** Riesling Kabinett £B

WEINGUT SALWEY O **Chardonnay** Kabinett £C

O **Oberrotweiler Kirchberg** Weissburgunder Spätlese Trocken Grosses Gewächs £D

O **Oberrotweiler Kirchberg** Spätburgunder Spätlese Trocken Grosses Gewächs £E

O **Oberrotweiler Eichberg** Ruländer Trockenbeerenauslese £G Ruländer Eiswein £H

SCHÄFER-FRÖHLICH O **Monzingen Frühlingsplätzchen** Riesling Grosses Gewächs £C

O **Bockenauer Felseneck** Riesling Auslese £E

SCHLOSS JOHANNISBERG O **Riesling** Spätlese £C Auslese £F Beerenauslese £H Eiswein £H

SCHLOSS REINHARTSHAUSEN O **Erbacher Marcobrunn** Riesling Erstes Gewächs £D

SCHLOSS SAARSTEIN O **Serriger Schloss Saarsteiner** Riesling Kabinett £B Riesling Spätlese £C

SCHLOSS VOLLRADS O **Riesling** Spätlese £D Auslese Gold Capsule £F

SCHMITT'S KINDER O **Randersacker Pfülben** Riesling Spätlese Grosses Gewächs £C

WEINGUT AM STEIN O **Würzburger Innere Leiste** Riesling Grosses Gewächs £D

O **Stettener Stein** Riesling Eiswein £H

TESCH O **Laubenheimer Karthäuser** Riesling Spätlese £B Riesling Auslese £C

O **Langenlonsheimer Löhrer Berg** Riesling Spätlese £B

DR H THANISCH (ERBEN THANISCH) O **Bernkasteler Lay** Riesling Spätlese £C

O **Bernkasteler Badstube** Riesling Auslese £F O **Bernkasteler Doctor** Riesling Auslese £F

DR HEINZ WAGNER O **Ockfener Bockstein** Riesling Spätlese £B Riesling Auslese £C

O **Saarburger Rausch** Riesling Spätlese £C

DR WEHRHEIM O **Birkweiler Kastanienbusch** Riesling Spätlese Trocken Grosses Gewächs £D

O **Birkweiler Mandelberg** Weisser Burgunder Trocken Grosses Gewächs £D

GEHEIMRAT J WEGELER O **Bernkasteler Doctor** Riesling Spätlese £E Riesling Auslese £E

O **Wehlener Sonnenuhr** Riesling Auslese £E   O **Winkeler Jesuitengarten** Riesling Grosses Gewächs £C
O **Rüdesheimer Berg Schlossberg** Riesling Grosses Gewächs £C
HANS WIRSCHING O **Iphöfer Julius-Echter-Berg** Riesling Spätlese Trocken Grosses Gewächs £D
O **Iphöfer Julius-Echter-Berg** Silvaner Spätlese Trocken Grosses Gewächs £D
O **Iphöfer Kronsberg** Weisser Burgunder Spätlese Trocken Grosses Gewächs £D
O **Iphöfer Julius-Echter-Berg** Rieslaner Beerenauslese £G
J L WOLF O **Forster Pechstein** Riesling Spätlese Trocken £C
O **Deidesheimer Leinhöhle** Riesling Spätlese Trocken £C
WÖHRWAG O **Untertürkheim Herzogenberg** Riesling Spätlese Trocken Grosses Gewächs £D
ZILLIKEN O **Saarburger Rausch** Riesling Spätlese £C

Author's choice (PW)

10 classic dry or off-dry Mosel Riesling

GRANS-FASSIAN O **Leiwener Laurentiuslay** Riesling Spätlese 'S'
WGT. FRITZ HAAG O **Brauneberger Juffer-Sonnenuhr** Riesling Spätlese
WGT. REINHOLD HAART O **Piesporter Goldtröpfchen** Riesling Spätlese
HEYMANN-LÖWENSTEIN O **Winninger Uhlen** Riesling 'Roth Lay' Erste Lage
KARLSMÜHLE O **Kaseler Nies'chen** Riesling Spätlese
WGT. KARTHÄUSERHOF O **Eitelsbacher Karthäuserhofberg** Riesling Spätlese Trocken
DR LOOSEN O **Wehlener Sonnenuhr** Riesling Spätlese
ST. URBANS-HOF O **Ockfener Bockstein** Riesling Spätlese
WILLI SCHAEFER O **Graacher Domprobst** Riesling Spätlese
SCHLOSS LIESER O **Lieser Niederberg Helden** Riesling Spätlese

15 more superior dry or off-dry Riesling

BASSERMANN-JORDAN O **Deidesheimer Hohenmorgen** Riesling Spätlese Trocken Grosses Gewächs
REICHSRAT VON BUHL O **Forster Pechstein** Riesling Grosses Gewächs
BÜRKLIN-WOLF O **Forster Kirchenstück** Riesling Grosses Gewächs
CHRISTMANN O **Gimmeldingen Mandelgarten** Riesling Trocken Grosses Gewächs
DÖNNHOFF O **Niederhäusen Hermannshöhle** Riesling Spätlese
EMRICH-SCHÖNLEBER O **Monzinger Frühlingsplätzchen** Riesling Spätlese
PETER JAKOB KÜHN O **Oestricher Lenchen** Riesling Kabinett
PRINZ VON HESSEN O **Johannisberger Klaus** Riesling Erstes Gewächs
WGT. KELLER O **Dalsheimer Hubacker** Riesling Spätlese Trocken
FRANZ KÜNSTLER O **Hochheimer Hölle** Riesling Auslese Trocken
ANDREAS LAIBLE O **Durbacher Plauelrain** Riesling Auslese Trocken
WEINGUT JOSEPH LEITZ O **Rudesheimer Berg Schlossberg** Riesling Spätlese
ÖKONOMIERAT REBHOLZ O **Birkweiler Kastanienbusch** Riesling Spätlese Trocken Grosses Gewächs
SCHLOSSGUT DIEL **Dorsheimer Pittermännchen** Riesling Spätlese
WGT. WITTMANN O **Westhofener Kirschspiel** Riesling Grosses Gewächs

10 stupendous German sweet wines

GEORG BREUER O **Rauenthal Nonnenberg** Riesling Auslese Gold Capsule
DÖNNHOFF O **Oberhäuser Brücke** Riesling Eiswein
GUNDERLOCH O **Nackenheimer Rothenberg** Riesling Beerenauslese
DR LOOSEN O **Bernkasteler Lay** Riesling Eiswein
MARKUS MOLITOR O **Zeltinger Sonnenuhr** Riesling Beerenauslese
MÜLLER-CATOIR O **Mussbacher Eselshaut** Rieslaner Trockenbeerenauslese
JOH JOS PRÜM O **Wehlener Sonnenuhr** Riesling Auslese Gold Capsule
MAX FERD. RICHTER O **Mülheimer Helenenkloster** Riesling Eiswein
HORST SAUER O **Escherndorfer Lump** Riesling Trockenbeerenauslese
ROBERT WEIL O **Kiedricher Gräfenberg** Riesling Auslese Gold Capsule

10 fine German whites not from Riesling

WGT. BERCHER O **Burkheimer Feuerberg** Weissburgunder Spätlese Trocken SE

EMRICH-SCHÖNLEBER O **Monzinger Grauburgunder** Spätlese Trocken

DR HEGER O **Ihringer Winklerberg Muskateller** Spätlese 3 sterne

ANDREAS LAIBLE O **Durbacher Plauelrain** Gewürztraminer Auslese

MÜLLER-CATOIR O **Haardter Mandelring** Scheurebe Auslese

HORST SAUER O **Escherndorfer Lump** Silvaner Auslese

JULUISSPITAL O **Würzburger Stein** Silvaner Spätlese Trocken

ÖKONOMIERAT REBHOLZ O **Siebeldingen im Sonnenschein** Weisser Burgunder Spätlese Trocken Grosses Gewächs

WEINGUT SALWEY O **Oberrotweiler Kirchberg** Weissburgunder Spätlese Trocken Grosses Gewächs

HANS WIRSCHING O **Iphofer Julius-Echter-Berg** Rieslaner Beerenauslese

Austria & Switzerland

From a growing band of small producers, Austria provides the world with outstanding dry whites, superb sweet wines and ever more interesting, good quality reds. Yet international recognition and appreciation of the great strides made has been slow in coming. From the steep hillside vineyards above the Danube (Donau) come the great Rieslings and Grüner Veltliners of the Wachau, and to a lesser degree those of the neighbouring Kremstal and Kamptal regions. Around the Neusiedlersee, a broad shallow lake in the east that extends into Hungary, are spread the vineyards providing the grapes for the outstanding sweet wines as well as much of the raw materials for the current revolution in red wine production. Switzerland too has its quality regions and more producers deserving of an international reputation seem certain to emerge.

Austria

Wachau-Kremstal-Kamptal

Led by the Wachau these are the three most important areas of Niederösterreich (Lower Austria). Wachau's Rieslings are generally much closer in style to Alsace than Germany; full and powerful, with a marvellous concentration and purity of fruit within a vibrant structure. The very best have great class and age impressively. The more traditional grape of Grüner Veltliner also excels, with great depth and power to its peppery fruit character. There are three levels within the Wachau's system of ripeness: Steinfeder, Federspiel and Smaragd. The relatively low-alcohol style of Steinfeder is for early drinking but the best Federspiel are more structured and concentrated and will keep for at least three or four years. The best quality however always comes from the Smaragd examples, named after a little green lizard. German classifications of ripeness are used for sweeter styles (Auslese, Beerenauslese, etc.), made in small quantities by some growers when conditions permit. Wines from the leading vineyards are sometimes labelled with only the vineyard, or *Ried*, name (*Ried* Klaus for example) and not the associated village.

Behind Spitz are the top sites of **Hochrain** and **Singerriedel**, given brilliant expression by Hirtzberger, while Weissenkirchen includes the **Steinriegl**, **Achleiten** and **Klaus** sites close to the village. Further downstream are the particularly favoured steep terraces running from Dürnstein around past Oberloiben and Unterloiben; top vineyards include **Kellerberg**, **Loibner Berg** (or Loibner Loibenberg), **Schütt** and **Steinertal** but fine examples are also made from several other sites. Wachau merges seamlessly into Kremstal, though there are not the same number of outstanding vineyards or producers here. In fact much of what is produced is decidedly ordinary. Kamptal in the valley of the Kamp is away from the Danube but the potential of vineyards around the wine town of Langenlois is increasingly being realised. The leading producer is Bründlmayer and the top vineyard **Zöbinger Heiligenstein**, from which several producers make good wines. Traisental, east of the Wachau and centred on another Danube tributary, the Traisen, was only officially recognised as a distinct wine region in 1995 but has at least one good producer in Neumayer.

Burgenland

Formerly part of Hungary, the edge of Burgenland forms all of Austria's border with its eastern neighbour. The best wines are the sweet whites made around the shores of the Neusiedlersee. On its western shore in Neusiedlersee-Hügelland, around the town of **Rust**, the traditional **Ausbruch** style is made, now generally a full, sweet white with higher alcohol than wines made in the Germanic style (but with a must weight between those of Beerenauslese and Trockenbeerenauslese). The leading wine town for sweet whites on the eastern shore of the Neusiedlersee is Illmitz and the low-lying vineyards produce Austria's most stunning examples, led by those of Kracher. In both regions Welschriesling, Muskat Ottonel, Pinot Blanc, Pinot Gris and Chardonnay are the most important white grapes; Chardonnay, unusually, in both sweet and dry styles.

Reds are also increasingly important in Burgenland, both from Neusiedlersee (especially around Gols and Mönchhof) and Neusiedlersee-Hügelland but also from southern Burgenland. Grapes include Zweigelt, St-Laurent, Pinot Noir, Blaufränkisch and also Cabernet Sauvignon and Merlot, all of which can be made either varietally or as a blend of some combination of these, often aged in new oak. Previously rather robust, earthy and brambly, Blaufränkisch-based reds are showing increasing refinement.

Other regions

In Steiermark (Styria), especially Südsteiermark close to the Slovenian border, some aromatic, lively Sauvignon Blanc and Chardonnay (here called Morillon) are made. Lighter, unoaked examples sold as *Steirische Klassik* are often best as more serious efforts can be high in alcohol and overoaked. Vienna has a lot of land planted to vines for everyday dry whites. South of the capital is the Thermenregion, once famous for the sweet whites of Gumpoldskirchen from Zierfandler and Rotgipfler grapes but now making mostly dry whites and reds. North of Vienna is Weinviertel, where again there's little of real excitement, though producers such as Pfaffl and Graf Hardegg show there is potential for good dry whites.

Switzerland

Despite high altitudes, Switzerland has several sheltered, sometimes terraced vineyard regions that owe their existence to the moderating influence of lakes or rivers. In the **Valais**, centred on the River Rhône in its upper reaches, south-facing vineyards provide some interesting reds from unusual native grapes such as Cornalin and Humagne but also Pinot Noir and Syrah. The **Vaud** region arches around Lac Léman (Lake Geneva) and the white Chasselas grape dominates production. Beyond the lake's eastern end is Chablais (with the villages of Aigle and Yvorne) and the north-western shore is known as La Côte, but it is between the two, in Lavaux, where some really intense, minerally examples have been produced. Villages include Chardonne, Cully, Epesses and Saint-Saphorin and extremely good Chasselas from Louis Bovard shows why **Dézaley** and **Calamin**, designated Grands Crus, enjoy such a good reputation. North of Zürich, close to the German border, some Pinot Noir and Chardonnay is made in isolated pockets. Some good examples of Merlot are made in **Ticino** (a wedge of Switzerland in the Italian lakes) but quality is very uneven, due in part to often difficult vintage conditions; the better examples can age prematurely. The best rich, ripe examples come from Christian Zündel and a handful of others. When they include a little Cabernet Sauvigon they are sold as **Rosso del Malcantone**.

A-Z Producers by region

Austria

Wachau
FREIE WEINGÄRTNER WACHAU
FRANZ HIRTZBERGER
EMMERICH KNOLL
NIKOLAIHOF
F-X PICHLER
WEINGUT PRAGER

Kremstal
NIGL

Kamptal
BRÜNDLMAYER
HIRSCH
JURTSCHITSCH SONNHOF
LOIMER
SCHLOSS GOBELSBURG

Traisental
NEUMAYER

Neusiedlersee-Hügelland
FEILER-ARTINGER
KOLLWENTZ-RÖMERHOF

Neusiedlersee
KRACHER
VELICH

Switzerland

Lauvaux
DOMAINE LOUIS BOVARD

Vintages

In Austria vintages are of considerable importance, particularly in the Wachau for its leading Rieslings and Grüner Veltliners. More difficult vintages can not only result in a lack of richness and ripeness but can fail to provide the balance essential for ageing. The ratings given to Wachau Riesling in the chart should be considered for the best Smaragd examples but might also be applied to equivalent examples from Kremstal or Kamptal regions where vintage conditions are usually similar. Good examples are better with three or four years' age but will keep for a decade, sometimes longer from a top vintage. The rarer sweet styles, Auslese and Beerenauslese, made in the Wachau will also prove ageworthy. The dramatic flooding in 2002 ruined grapes from vines on the flat ground but quality appears very promising from terraced vineyards.

The sweet wines of Neusiedlersee and Neusiedlersee-Hügelland, while producer-dependent, will nearly always benefit from at least five years' age and will keep for a decade or more.

Austrian vintages

	Wachau/Kremstal/Kamptal Riesling	Wachau/Kremstal/Kamptal Grüner Veltliner	Neusiedlersee/N-Hügelland Sweet whites
2002	★★★★ A	★★★★ A	★★★★ A
2001	★★★★ A	★★★★/★★★★★ A	★★★/★★★★ A
2000	★★★★ A	★★★★ B	★★★★/★★★★★ A
1999	★★★★/★★★★★ B	★★★★/★★★★★ B	★★★★ B
1998	★★★/★★★★ B	★★★/★★★★ C	★★★★ B
1997	★★★★/★★★★★ B	★★★★/★★★★★ C	★★★★ B*
1996	★★ C	★★ D	★★★ C
1995	★★★★ B	★★★★ C	★★★★★ B
1994	★★★ C	★★★ D	★★/★★★ C
1993	★★★/★★★★ C	★★★/★★★★ C	★★★★ C
1992	★★★ C	★★★ D	★★/★★★ D
1991	★★/★★★ D	★★★ C	★★★★ C
1990	★★★★/★★★★★ C	★★★★/★★★★★ C	

* little produced

DOMAINE LOUIS BOVARD Lavaux   www.domainebovard.com   A: Tan

Owner: Louis Bovard SA   La Maison Rose, Place d'Armes 2, 1096 Cully, Switzerland

The wines of Louis Bovard serve as an inspiration to other Swiss growers. Based in Cully on pretty terraced slopes above Lac Léman, brothers Antoine and Louis-Philippe Bovard produce Chasselas-based wines without equal. The wines are remarkably stylish and finely balanced with mineral, citrus, apple and a delicately nutty character. In the Dézaley Grand Cru Médinette there is added depth, structure and intensity and the wines can easily age for five years or more. From Saint-Saphorin, both a varietal Chasselas, L'Archevesque, and a blend of Chasselas and Chenin Blanc are made. The two grapes work surprisingly well together in the latter, another elegant white with an intense long finish. This too is better with a little age and should keep for five years or more. As well as some Sauvignon, some red is made from Merlot, Pinot Noir and Syrah, and sold as Dézaley Grand Cru. (PW)

O **Dézaley** Grand Cru Médinette★★★ £C   O **Calamin** Cuvée Speciale★★ £C
O **Saint-Saphorin** L'Archevesque★★ £C   Chasselas/Chenin★★ £C
O **Epesses** Terre à Boire★★ £B

BRÜNDLMAYER Kamptal   www.bruendlmayer.com   A: RsW, BWC, NYg, Rae

Owner: Willi Bründlmayer   Zwettlerstrasse 23 A-3550 Langenlois, Austria

Willi Bründlmayer's organically run estate is the best dry white wine producer in Austria outside the Wachau and it rivals the best of those. About 60 ha of lyre-trained vineyards occupy sites around the town of Langenlois. The most outstanding of these is Zöbinger Heiligenstein, producing superb Rieslings with depth, power and vibrant ripe fruit; still fuller and more complex is an Alte Reben (old vines) example. A fine mineral-edged Steinmassel Riesling is also produced but Grüner Veltliner is at least as important, with full, flavoursome examples with green peppercorn and yellow plum fruit, particularly lush and ripe in the Ried Lamm bottling. Top examples of each deserve to be drunk with four to five years' age, while regular Langenloiser examples, which show good fruit if not the same style or concentration, can be drunk young. Though Grüner Veltliner (Ried Loiser Berg and Ried Kaferberg are two more fine examples) and Riesling account for more than half of what is produced, a well-balanced, ripe, medium-weight Chardonnay that avoids being too oaky or leesy is also good. Traditional-method sparkling wine and some Pinot Noir (Cécile) are also made, as are occasional sweet Trockenbeerenauslese from both Grüner Veltliner and Riesling. (PW)

O **Zöbinger Heiligenstein** Riesling★★★ £C   Riesling Alte Reben★★★★ £D
O **Langenloiser Steinmassel** Riesling★★★ £C   O **Langenloiser** Riesling★★ £B   Grüner Veltliner★★ £B
O **Langenloiser Berg Vogelsang** Grüner Veltliner★★ £B   O **Kammerner Lamm** Grüner Veltliner★★★ £D
O **Grüner Veltliner** Alte Reben★★★★ £C   O **Chardonnay**★★ £C

FEILER-ARTINGER Neusiedlersee-Hügelland   www.feiler-artinger.at   A: FWW, SVS

Owner: Hans Feiler   Hauptstrasse 3, A-7071 Rust, Austria

Kurt Feiler works with his father to make fine elegant sweet whites but also dry whites and reds on his family's estate. Ruster Ausbruch, the traditional sweet wine of Rust, is based on Pinot Blanc (Weissburgunder) and Welschriesling while a Pinot Cuvée version (as the name suggests) adds Pinot Gris (Rülander) to Pinot Blanc. True to the style, the wines are more fully fermented than the Germanic styles and have an alcohol level (13.5 per cent) similar to Sauternes. The wines are rich, honeyed and refined with lots of ripe botrytised fruit intensity but can show marked differences in style depending on the vintage; the rich, very sweet 98 Ruster Ausbruch contrasts with a lighter, racier, more elegant 96. The partially barrel-fermented Pinot Cuvée shows a lovely balance between sweetness and acidity. Very good Beerenauslese (from Weissburgunder, Chardonnay and Welschriesling) and a Traminer Beerenauslese were made in 2002. The Feilers also produce better-balanced examples than is typical of the intense gutsy reds with which Burgenland is increasingly associated. The characterful Solitaire, with smoky, peppery, sweet brambly fruit is a blend of Blaufränkisch, Zweigelt, Merlot and Cabernet Sauvignon. The tannins are ripe and fine and it develops increasing complexity with five years' age or more. A very convincing example of Austrian Cabernet Sauvignon/Merlot blend is also made (numbered with successive vintages, the 2001 vintage is 1007) though it doesn't stand comparison in an international context at this price level. Other reds include Zweigelt and Pinot Noir. Several dry varietal whites are made too, including a pretty, grapy, off-dry Muscat Ottonel which is better than most – some examples of this grape can be a bit washed out. The barrel-fermented Cuvée Gustav (from Pinot Gris, Chardonnay and Neuburger) emphasises the oak but has creamy pear, quince and melon fruit. (PW)

O **Ruster Ausbruch★★★** £E Pinot Cuvée★★★★ £F
O **Muscat Ottonel** Halbtrocken★★ £B   O **Cuvée Gustav★★** £C
● **Solitaire★★** £E   ● **Cabernet Sauvignon/Merlot★★** £E   ● **Blaufränkisch Umriss★★** £B

FRANZ HIRTZBERGER   Wachau   A: FWW, NYg, P&S, SVS, N&P

Owner: Franz Hirtzberger   Kremserstrasse 8, A-3620 Spitz an der Donau, Austria
The differences between the Wachau's élite (also see KNOLL, F-X PICHLER and PRAGER) are more stylistic than qualitative and it is common to find that one producer pleases more one year or on one particular occasion and another at a different time. From 12 ha of rocky soils there is a pure pristine fruit intensity to Hirtzberger's examples of Grüner Veltliner and Riesling. The wines are structured examples, taut and concentrated, but beautifully balanced. Of the top Rieslings in the (ripest) Smaragd style, Hochrain is a classic Wachau example with great length of flavour, while the splendid minerally Singerriedel has a fine structure underpinning the fruit richness. There is an underlying strength and intensity to Honivogl Grüner Veltliner that like the Rieslings deserves five years' ageing before drinking. Rotes Tor Federspiel is an excellent, more affordable example of Grüner Veltliner for those who have been put off by some of unbalanced, high-alcohol versions that exist. In addition some Axpoint Grüner Veltliner and some Weissburgunder and Grauburgunder are also produced. (PW)

O **Hochrain** Riesling Smaragd★★★★ £E   O **Singerriedel** Riesling Smaragd★★★★ £E
O **Steinterrassen** Riesling Federspiel★★★ £C
O **Honivogl** Grüner Veltliner Smaragd★★★★ £E
O **Rotes Tor** Grüner Veltliner Federspiel★★★ £C Grüner Veltliner Smaragd★★★ £D

FREIE WEINGÄRTNER WACHAU   Wachau   www.fww.at   A: FWW

Owner: 'Cooperative'   Freie Weingärtner Wachau, A-3601 Dürnstein, Austria
This Wachau co-op with around 600 growers produces some of the most readily available and affordable examples of Grüner Veltliner and Riesling from the Wachau. While the wines are not at the same level as the very best private estates, standards are nonetheless quite impressive. They generally show good definition and intensity though occasionally lack a little zip or suffer from too much sulphur when tasted young. From 2001 the Domäne Wachau label was introduced for wines from individual vineyard sites. As well as the leading wines listed below individual bottlings from other sites such as Singerriedel and 1000-Eimer-Berg are also produced. Dry wines are generally best with between two and five years' age, though will keep longer in top vintages. A sweet Beerenauslese shows good botrytis character if missing the extra style and balance of a top example. (PW)

O **BA** Beerenauslese★★ £D

Domäne Wachau
- O **Terrassen** Grüner Veltliner Federspiel★★ £B Riesling Smaragd★★ £C
- O **Dürnsteiner Kellerberg** Grüner Veltliner Smaragd★★ £C Riesling Smaragd★★ £C
- O **Loibener Loibenberg** Riesling Smaragd★★★ £C
- O **Weissenkirchener Achleiten** Grüner Veltliner Smaragd★★★ £C Riesling Smaragd★★★ £C

HIRSCH Kamptal www.weingut-hirsch.at

Owner: Hirsch family Hauptptstrasse 76, A-3493 Kammern-Langenlois, Austria
Hirsch, with 20 ha of vineyards in production, are one of Austria's rising stars. Great care is taken to achieve full physiological ripeness while natural yeasts and whole-bunch pressing are employed in order to enhance a natural expression of terroir. This can best be seen in two contrasting premium Rieslings. The Gaisberg from mica-schist soils shows a mineral, citrus and subtle spice character while the sandstone of Heiligenstein imparts very ripe fruit, spice as well as a certain minerality. Johannes Hirsch believes in delaying bottling as long as possible and from the 2002 vintage Grüner Veltliner Lamm and Rieslings Gaisberg and Heiligenstein are labelled either April or September. The Grüner Veltliner Lamm is also made in an Alte Reben (old vines) version. The wines are bottled with screwcaps. (PW)
- O **Zöbinger Heiligenstein** Riesling★★★ £D   O **Zöbinger Gaisberg** Riesling★★★ £D
- O **Zöbinger** Riesling★★★ £C   O **Kammerner Lamm** Grüner Veltliner★★★ £D

JURTSCHITSCH SONNHOF Kamptal www.jurtschitsch.com   A:VDu

Owner: Jurtschitsch family Rudolfstrasse 39, A-3550 Langenlois, Austria
This traditional family estate, run along ecological principles and with parcels in some of Kamptal's top sites, is making excellent progress, now producing wines of a quality close to the top tier of Wachau/Kamptal dry whites. Edwin Jurtschitsch, one of three brothers, is responsible for the vineyards and pays particular attention to reducing yields, a dedication reflected in the both the intensity and length of flavour achieved with Grüner Veltliner and the particularly fine fruit and gentle minerality in the best Rieslings. Most wines drink well with just two or three years' age. While the selection of wines varies somewhat from year to year it usually includes those listed below. Small quantities of sweet wines are made when conditions favour it. (PW)
- O **Zöbinger Heiligenstein** Riesling★★★ £D Riesling Auslese★★★ £D   O **Riesling** Alte Reben★★★ £D
- O **Ried Steinhaus** Grüner Veltliner★★ £C   O **Ried Schenkenbickl** Grüner Veltliner★★★ £C
- O **Grüner Veltliner** Alte Reben★★ £C   O **Grüner Veltliner** Reserve★★★ £C

KOLLWENTZ-RÖMERHOF Neusiedlersee-Hügelland www.kollwentz.at

Owner: Anton Kollwentz family Hauptstrasse 120, A-7051 Grosshöflein, Austria
One of Burgenland's leading estates, and well-known in Austria and its German-speaking neighbours, it deserves wider recognition for reds, dry whites and sweet wines. Grapes have been adapted to a range of different soil types in 20 ha of vineyard. Selective picking and much work in the vineyard results in moderate yields of high quality grapes. Perhaps most impressive are the deep, complex and original reds. The Steinzeiler from Blaufränkisch, Cabernet Sauvignon and Zweigelt (60/20/20) has marvellous complexity, with earth, truffle, plum, tobacco and coffee hints, if not the dimension of a world class red. Cabernet Sauvignon is very good in a cooler style with round plump berry fruit and well-integrated oak after a little bottle age, though it can sometimes struggle for fully ripe tannins. Relatively high levels of volatility can sometimes impede their otherwise undoubted ageing potential. Varietal Blaufränkisch and Zweigelt are also produced as is Eichkogel, an equal

blend of the two varieties. Powerful oak-aged single vineyard Chardonnays including Tatschler and Gloria are made from different parts of the Leithagebirge which has calcareous soils. All of these wines, along with a vibrant unoaked Sauvignon Blanc Steinmühle will be rated with further tastings. Very ripe, intense honeyed sweet wines are also made, not of the explosive concentration of Kracher but very sweet, richly botrytised and balanced nonetheless. Prices are high (though are estimates), no doubt fuelled by demand for them in this part of Europe. (PW)

● **Steinzeiler**★★★ £E   ● **Cabernet Sauvignon**★★ £E
O **Welschriesling** Trockenbeerenauslese★★★ £G

EMMERICH KNOLL   Wachau   A: RsW, NYg, Sec, Rae, N&P

Owner: Knoll family A-3601 Loiben, Austria
This historic family vineyard of some 12 ha, planted mostly to Gruner Veltliner and Riesling, is another that shows just how good the top Wachau whites are. Emmerich Knoll's wines can be more difficult to taste when young but can become almost overwhelming in their intensity and concentration with a little age or time in the glass. Any youthful aggression also tends to dissipate as both a strong varietal character and terroir influence emerge. The Smaragd version of Loibenberg Loibner Riesling has great vigour and superb length of flavour. Both this and the slighter, more elegant, refined Dürnsteiner Schütt can age for a decade or more in top vintages. Riesling is also made from Ried Pfaffenberg from outside the Wachau area. Examples of Grüner Veltliner show classic peppery varietal fruit but with only moderately high, and more importantly, balanced, levels of alcohol. Loibner Kreutles Grüner Veltliner hasn't usually the extra concentration or style of the Loibenberg Loibner or Loibner Schütt examples but nonetheless shows a lovely fruit character. A little of a special selection of the ripest (but non-botrytised fruit) is reserved for 'Vinothekfüllung' Grüner Veltliner and Riesling, while some Beerenauslese is also made when conditions permit. (PW)

O **Loibenberg Loibner** Riesling Federspiel★★ £C Riesling Smaragd★★★★ £E
O **Loibenberg Loibner** Grüner Veltliner Smaragd★★★ £D
O **Dürnsteiner Ried Schütt** Riesling Smaragd★★★★ £E
O **Loibner Schütt** Grüner Veltliner Smaragd★★★ £D
O **Loibner Ried Kreutles** Grüner Veltliner Federspiel★★ £B Grüner Veltliner Smaragd★★ £C

KRACHER   Neusiedlersee   A: NYg, P&S, Fal, Bal, N&P

Owner: Alois Kracher Weinlaubenhof, Apetlonerstrasse 37, A-7142 Illmitz, Austria
The sweet wines of Alois Kracher are some of the finest going, not just Austria's best but among the top examples made anywhere. They are consistently fine due to both the winemaking and the favourable conditions for botrytis enrichment that the Neusiedlersee region experiences. Those labelled Zwischen den Seen are unoaked examples – usually from naturally spicy, aromatic indigenous varieties but also including Chardonnay – while the Nouvelle Vague wines are oaked. The pick of several very sweet, very intense Trockenbeerauslese are Zwischen den Seen Welschriesling (combining sweetness and elegance), Zwischen den Seen Chardonnay (the current No. 13 shows incredible sweetness and intensity yet is beautifully balanced), Nouvelle Vague Chardonnay, Nouvelle Vague Chardonnay/Welschriesling and Grande Cuvée (a blend usually composed of Chardonnay, Welschriesling, Scheurebe and Muscat Ottonel). A reasonably affordable introduction is the Cuvée Beerenauslese (mostly Chardonnay and Welschriesling), a good, rich, not excessively sweet example with concentrated botytrised fruit and the finely balanced acidity so characteristic of these wines. Red wines, labelled Blend I and Blend II – from Zweigelt and other local varieties – are also made. Though the sweet wines are numbered, composition can change, so they have been listed below by grape variety (or varieties) only. (PW)

O **Grande Cuvée** Trockenbeerenauslese✪✪✪✪✪ £G
O **Scheurebe Zwischen den Seen** Trockenbeerenauslese★★★ £E
O **Chardonnay/Welschriesling Nouvelle Vague** Trockenbeerenauslese✪✪✪✪✪ £G
O **Chardonnay Zwischen den Seen** Trockenbeerenauslese✪✪✪✪✪ £G
O **Chardonnay Nouvelle Vague** Trockenbeerenauslese✪✪✪✪✪ £G
O **Cuvée Beerenauslese**★★★ £D

LOIMER Kamptal www.loimer.at   A: Lib, ACh, Res

Owner: Fred Loimer Haindorfer Vögerlweg 23, A-3550 Langenlois, Austria
Like most in Kamptal, Fred Loimer has more than half of his estate planted to Grüner Veltliner but
a quarter of his 21 ha is also planted to Riesling. He excels at producing both. The wines are precise
but pure and expressive with real depth and length. On current form Loimer looks set to join the
established Wachau/Kamptal superstars of BRÜNDLMAYER, HIRTZBERGER, KNOLL, F-X PICHLER
and PRAGER. As well as the excellent wines from parcels of vines in Spiegel and Steinmassl, there is
Grüner Veltliner from Käferberg and Riesling from Seeberg. The Langenloiser versions are excellent
value for money (PW)

O **Grüner Veltliner** Lois★ £B
O **Langenlois** Grüner Veltliner★★ £B   O **Langenloiser Spiegel** Grüner Veltliner★★★ £D
O **Langenlois** Riesling★★★ £B   O **Langenloiser Steinmassl** Riesling★★★★ £D

NEUMAYER Traisental

Owner: Ludwig Neumayer Inzerdorf 22, A-3130 Inzerdorf ob der Traisen, Austria
Due east of the Wachau region, on the Traisen, a tributary of the Danube, Ludwig Neumayer has 8
ha of scattered parcels of vineyard. Despite the relative obscurity he makes better wines than some
of those with parcels in the Wachau's highly rated sites. Similarly his best wines are derived from
Grüner Veltliner and Riesling though Weissburgunder, Chardonnay and Sauvignon are also important.
While it is apparent that the wines sometimes struggle for full ripeness and the flavours are cool and
citrusy, there is nonetheless good intensity and length to the wines. The Wein vom Stein wines in
particular, from a selection of the best parcels, if youthfully slightly austere show fine fruit expression,
purity and length of flavour. Both Grüner Veltliner and Riesling are best with at least two or three
years' age. (PW)

O **Rafasetzen** Grüner Veltliner★ £B   O **Berg** Riesling★★ £C
O **Der Wein vom Stein** Grüner Veltliner★★ £C Riesling★★★ £C
O **Chardonnay**★ £B

NIGL Kremstal www.weingutnigl.at

Owner: Martin Nigl Priel 7, A-3541 Senftenberg, Austria
The wines have been good here for some time but seem to have moved up a further notch in quality
in recent vintages. A wide range of Grüner Veltliner and Riesling from top sites in Kremstal are made
and the best are now very good indeed. Contrasting Riesling range from the racy, minerally, elegant
Piri to the taut, intense and concentrated Hochäcker or the deep, pure and stylish Privat (a selection
from Piri and old vines). The Privat version of Grüner Veltliner is full-bodied and powerful with very
ripe fruit yet is balanced while an Alte Reben version is atypically rich and profound for this variety.
All have good ageing potential, Rieslings in particular show at their best with at least three to five
years' age or more. As well as those below, other wines include Grüner Veltliner from Ried Zwelt,
and Riesling from Kremser Kremsleiten. (PW)

O **Kremser Freiheit** Grüner Veltliner★★ £C   O **Senftenberger Hochäcker** Riesling★★★ £E
O **Senftenberger Piri** Grüner Veltliner★★★ £D   Riesling★★★ £D
O **Grüner Veltliner** Privat★★★ £D   O **Riesling** Privat★★★★ £E
O **Grüner Veltliner** Alte Reben★★★★ £D

NIKOLAIHOF   Wachau   www.nikolaihof.at

A: RsW, Rae

Owner: Saahs family   A-3512 Mautern, Austria
Nikolaus and Christine Saahs make fine organically produced Riesling and Grüner Veltliner from 20 ha of vineyards that have been a source of wine for more than a thousand years. The vines have a high average age and recent vintages have added a little extra intensity to wines that have good definition and style. Riesling is particularly long-lived, whether the restrained, minerally vom Stein from the Wachau or steely, elegant Steiner Hund from just outside the area, in Kremstal. Even the fine Federspiel version of vom Stein will improve for five years or more. The Saahs' characterful Grüner Veltliner shows a smoky, earthy influence in a quite full, fat Smaragd version and good ripeness in a Federspiel version. Both can be drunk young and the Smaragd version with up to five years' age. Of other varieties grown, Weissburgunder shows good depth and structure. (PW)
O **vom Stein** Riesling Federspiel★★ £C   Riesling Smaragd★★★ £D
O **Steiner Hund** Riesling Spätlese★★★ £E
O **Im Weingebirge** Grüner Veltliner Federspiel★★ £C   Grüner Veltliner Smaragd★★★ £D
O **Baumgarten** Weissburgunder★★ £C

F-X PICHLER   Wachau

A: NYg, Rae, F&R, N&P, Sec

Owner: Franz Xaver Pichler   Oberloiben 27, A-6301 Dürnstein, Austria
Franz Xaver Pichler is acclaimed by many to be the Wachau's finest producer and it's hard to dispute given the extremely high quality in his top Smaragd Riesling and Grüner Veltliner of great extraction and concentration. Certainly no effort is spared in maximising the quality potential from 7.5 ha of vineyards. The Loibner Berg is consistently the most classy and concentrated of the Rieslings but that from the steep Dürnsteiner Kellerberg vineyard has great refinement, purity and length of flavour, while the von den Terrassen shows terrific richness and intensity in outstanding vintages. If more youthfully austere, Steinertal has a beauty and definition that becomes increasingly apparent after five years or more. The Grüner Veltliners are marvellous too; a deep, dense and structured Loibner Berg is perhaps the finest of several made but a full, vibrant Kellerberg and intense, long von den Terrassen are also top wines. More forward Federspiel examples are produced from the Loibner Klostersatz and Frauenweingarten sites. Of great potential if somewhat less typical are the special supercharged selections of Riesling (Unendlich – endless or never-ending) and Grüner Veltliner ('M'), both highly concentrated old-vine versions that are high in alcohol. (PW)
O **Loibner Berg** Riesling Smaragd✪✪✪✪✪ £E   Grüner Veltliner Smaragd★★★★ £E
O **Dürnsteiner Kellerberg** Riesling Smaragd★★★★ £E   Grüner Veltliner Smaragd★★★★ £E
O **von den Terrassen** Riesling Smaragd★★★★ £E   Grüner Veltliner Smaragd★★★ £E
O **Steinertal** Riesling Smaragd★★★★ £E

PRAGER   Wachau   www.weingutprager.at

A: M&V, NYg, Fal, P&S

Owner: Ilse Prager & Toni Bodenstein   A-3610 Weissenkirchen, Austria
Franz Prager did much to establish the pre-eminence of top dry whites from the Wachau. His daughter Ilse and her winemaker husband Toni Bodenstein have sought to produce dry wines of ever greater harmony and longevity as well as making some fine sweet wines when conditions permit. From the village of Weissenkirchen come several fine Smaragd Rieslings, including a superb minerally, peachy

Steinriegl that is firm when young but with great depth and length, adding richness and complexity with age. Both Riesling and Grüner Veltliner from the Achleiten site are also very fine and can show a little spice as well as an intense fruit depth. Fine Auslese and occasional Trockenbeerenauslese examples are also made from this site. Of the other fine Rieslings, a very refined Wachtum Bodenstein Riesling contrasts with a bolder, more forward Kaiserberg example and a distinctive, minerally, cool-fruited Klaus. All wines benefit from even more age than is typical for the best Wachau whites; Rieslings need five years but will keep for a decade or more from the likes of 97, 99 or 2001. An intense, fruit-rich Chardonnay Smaragd is also made and has good structure and depth. (PW)

O **Weissenkirchen Steinriegl** Riesling Federspiel★★ £C   Riesling Smaragd★★★★ £E
O **Weissenkirchen Achleiten** Riesling Smaragd★★★★ £E   Grüner Veltliner Smaragd★★★ £D
O **Weissenkirchen Klaus** Riesling Smaragd★★★ £E
O **Dürnsteiner Kaiserberg** Riesling Smaragd★★★ £E
O **Weissenkirchen Wachtum Bodenstein** Riesling Smaragd★★★ £E
O **Weissenkirchen Weitenberg** Grüner Veltliner Smaragd★★★ £D

SCHLOSS GOBELSBURG   Kamptal   www.gobelsburg.at   A: FWW, NYg, P&S, SVS

Owner: 'Stift Zwettl'   Schlossstrasse 16, A-3550 Gobelsburg, Austria
This ancient estate still belongs to a Cistercian monastery and the castle itself was built in the early 18th century. Under the winemaking direction of Michael Moosbrugger, with consultancy from Willi BRÜNDLMAYER since 1996, the wines have made much progress over recent vintages. 35 ha of vineyards give both Grüner Veltliner and Riesling that are fully ripe and intense but of increasing definition and concentration too. The style and refinement in a rich yet poised Alte Reben Riesling with a sublime fruit character is arguably the pinnacle of the quality now being obtained. Sparkling wine, reds (Zweigelt, Merlot, Pinot Noir), and *Messwein* (altar wine) are also made. (PW)

O **Zöbinger Heiligenstein** Riesling★★★ £C   Riesling Alte Reben★★★★ £D
O **Kammerner Lamm** Grüner Veltliner★★ £C   O **Kammerner Grub** Grüner Veltliner★★★ £C
O **Kammerner Renner** Grüner Veltliner★★ £C

VELICH   Neusiedlersee   A: Fie, SVS

Owner: Velich family   Seeufergasse 12, A-7143 Apetlon, Austria
From Apetlon in the Neusiedlersee, a short distance from the Hungarian border, the Velich brothers make Austria's finest Chardonnay. Tiglat is a single-vineyard example that combines depth and richness with real poise and elegance. It is neither too ripe nor too oaky or leesy as some Austrian examples are. A second Chardonnay, Darscho, hasn't the same depth or style but is balanced and has good fruit intensity. Cuvée OT (Ohne Titel – without title) is a relatively inexpensive blend of Chardonnay with 20 per cent Welschriesling and a little Muscat Ottonel – a perfumed, peachy white for early drinking. Neusiedlersee is of course more famous for its sweet wine production and Velich make some fine examples. Seewinkel Beerenauslese is based on Chardonnay (with Neuburger and Bouvier) and shows good botrytis richness if not the greatest finesse but a Welschriesling Trockenbeerenauslese is both sweet, intense and very refined in vintages like 1998 and 1995. Richer and more powerful if less scintillating is a Trockenbeerenauslese from the Tiglat vineyard. (PW)

O **Apetlon Chardonnay Darscho**★★ £C   **Chardonnay Tiglat**★★★ £D
O **Cuvée OT**★ £B   O **Seewinkel** Beerenauslese★★★ £D
O **Welshriesling** Trockenbeerenauslese★★★★ £F   O **Tiglat** Trockenbeerenauslese★★★ £F

OTHER WINES OF NOTE

Austria

PAUL ACHS (Neusiedlersee) ● **Pinot Noir** £E

LEO ALZINGER (Wachau) ○ **Loibener Steinertal** Riesling Smaragd £D   Grüner Veltliner Smaragd £D

ALOIS GROSS (Südsteiermark) ○ **Ratscher Nussberg** (Chardonnay / Grauburgunder) £C
○ **Gelber Muskateller** £B   ○ **Grauburgunder** £B

GRAF HARDEGG (Weinviertel) ○ **Pinot MAX** (Pinot Blanc / Chardonnay) £B   ○ **Viognier V** £C

HEINRICH (Neusiedlersee) ● **Gabarinza** (Zweigelt/Blaufränkisch/St. Laurent/Cabernet S./Syrah) £E

HIEDLER (Kamptal) ○ **Langenloiser Steinhaus** Riesling £C
○ **Langenloiser Spiegel** Grüner Veltliner £B   ○ **Thal Novemberlese** Grüner Veltliner £C

JOSEF JAMEK (Wachau) ○ **Ried Achleiten** Grüner Veltliner Smaragd £D
○ **Ried Klaus** Riesling Smaragd £E

JURIS (Neusiedlersee) ● **Pinot Noir Reserve** £E   ● **St. Laurent Reserve** £E

LACKNER-TINNACHER (Südsteiermark) ○ **Steinbach Morillon** (Chardonnay) £C

HELMUT LANG (Neusiedlersee) ○ **Sauvignon** Trockenbeerenauslese £E
○ **Eiswein Cuvée** (Scheurebe) £E

ANITA & HANS NITTNAUS (Neusiedlersee) ● **Heideboden** (Zweigelt/Cabernet Sauvignon) £B
● **Pannobile** (Blaufränkisch/Zweigelt/St. Laurent/Merlot) £C
● **Comondor** (Merlot/Cabernet Sauvignon/Syrah) £E

WILLI OPITZ ○ **Opitz One** Trockenbeerenauslese £G   ○ **Opitz One Vin Paille** £G

PFAFFL (Weinviertel) ○ **Hundsleiten Sandtal** Grüner Veltliner £B

RUDI PICHLER (Wachau) ○ **Hochrain** Grüner Veltliner Smaragd £D
○ **Terrassen** Riesling Smaragd £C

PITTNAUER (Burgenland) ○ **Altenberg Chardonnay** £C
● **Pinot Noir** £C   ● **St. Laurent Alte Reben** £C

JOSEF PÖCKL (Neusiedlersee) ● **Zweigelt Classique** £B

ERICH & WALTER POLZ (Südsteiermark) ○ **Morillon Hochgrassnitzberg** £C
○ **Weissburgunder Grassnitzberg** £B

PRETTEREBNER (Neusiedlersee) ● **Blaufränkisch** £B   ● **St. Laurent** £C

PRIELER (Neusiedlersee-Hügelland) ● **Blaufränkisch Ried Goldberg** £D

UNDHOF SALOMON (Kremstal) ○ **Gelber Traminer Reserve** £C   ○ **Pfaffenberg** Riesling £C
○ **Kremser Kögl** Riesling £C   Reserve £D   ○ **Undhof Wieden** Grüner Veltliner £C

MANFRED TEMENT (Steiermark) ○ **Sauvignon Steirische Klassik** £B
○ **Morillon Steirische Klassik** £B

ERNST TRIEBAUMER ● **Rust** Blaufränkisch Ried Marienthal £E   ○ **Chardonnay Pandkräftn** £C

TINHOF ○ **Fuchsenreigl** (Neuburger/Weissburgunder) £C
● **Feuersteig** (Blaufränkisch/St. Laurent) £C
○ **Trockenbeerenauslese** (Weissburgunder/Neuburger/Welschriesling/Muskat Ottonel) £F

UMATHUM (Neusiedlersee) ● **Frauenkirchener Haideboden** (Zweigelt/Blaufränkisch/Cabernet) £C
● **Frauenkirchener Ried Hallebühl** (Zweigelt/Blaufränkisch) £F

DR. UNGER (Kremstal / Wachau) ○ **Ried Silberbügel** Riesling Reserve £C
○ **Ried Oberfeld** Grüner Veltliner Alte Reben £C   ○ **Ried Innausen** Pinot Gris Reserve £C

Switzerland

GANTENBEIN (Graubünden) ● **Pinot Noir** £E

GIALDI (Ticino) ● **Sassi Grossi** (Merlot) £E

IMESCH VINS (Valais) ○ **Valais** Pinot Noir Loquette £C

DOM. DU MONT D'OR (Valais) ○ **Johannisberg du Valais** £C

CAVES ORSAT (Valais) ● **Cornalin du Valais** Primus Classicus £D

ROUVINEZ (Valais) ● **Le Tourmentin** (Pinot Noir/Cornalin/Humagne/Syrah) £C

CHRISTIAN ZÜNDEL (Ticino) ● **Rosso del Malcantone** Orrizonte £E

Author's choice (PW)

12 superior Austrian Riesling
BRÜNDLMAYER O Zöbinger Heiligenstein Riesling Alte Reben
FRANZ HIRTZBERGER O Singerriedel Riesling Smaragd
FREIE WEINGÄRTNER WACHAU/DOMÄNE WACHAU O Loibener Loibenberg Riesling Smaragd
JURTSCHITSCH SONNHOF O Zöbinger Heiligenstein Riesling Alte Reben
EMMERICH KNOLL O Dürnsteiner Ried Schütt Riesling Smaragd
LOIMER O Langenloiser Steinmassl Riesling
NEUMAYER O Der Wein vom Stein Riesling
NIGL O Riesling Privat
NIKOLAIHOF O vom Stein Riesling Smaragd
F-X PICHLER O Dürnsteiner Kellerberg Riesling Smaragd
PRAGER O Weissenkirchen Achleiten Riesling Smaragd
SCHLOSS GOBELSBURG O Zöbinger Heiligenstein Riesling Alte Reben

10 superb Grüner Veltliner
BRÜNDLMAYER O Kammerner Lamm Grüner Veltliner
FRANZ HIRTZBERGER O Honivogl Grüner Veltliner Smaragd
FREIE WEINGÄRTNER WACHAU/DOMÄNE WACHAU O Weissenkirchen Achleiten Grüner Veltliner Smaragd
EMMERICH KNOLL O Loibenberg Loibner Grüner Veltliner Smaragd
LOIMER O Langenloiser Spiegel Grüner Veltliner
NIGL O Grüner Veltliner Alte Reben
NIKOLAIHOF O Im Weingebirge Grüner Veltliner Smaragd
F-X PICHLER O Loibner Berg Grüner Veltliner Smaragd
PRAGER O Weissenkirchen Achleiten Grüner Veltliner Smaragd
SCHLOSS GOBELSBURG O Kammerner Grub Grüner Veltliner Smaragd

10 eclectic Austrian finds
dry white
VELICH O Chardonnay Tiglat
sweet whites
FEILER-ARTINGER O Ruster Ausbruch Pinot Cuvée
KRACHER O Grande Cuvée Trockenbeerenauslese
KRACHER O Chardonnay Zwischen den Seen Trockenbeerenauslese
VELICH O Welschriesling Trockenbeerenauslese
reds
FEILER-ARTINGER ● Solitaire
HEINRICH ● Gabarinza
JURIS ● St. Laurent Reserve
KOLLWENTZ-RÖMERHOF ● Steinzeiler
PRETTEREBNER ● Blaufränkisch

Other Europe & Middle East

This may seem a somewhat diverse geographical section, but in wine terms the countries covered here are either small and developing, or large, but as yet happy, it would appear, to service the bulk and own-label market places rather than seek to establish any quality reputation of their own. In England the future of fine wine production may very well be in sparkling wine-making. In countries like Greece, Israel and Lebanon their is clear potential thanks to their Mediterrannean climates. Isolated viticultural outposts in Eastern Europe too suggest there is undoubted scope for the future. The sweet wines now being produced at Tokaji in Hungary are an example of just what investment, technology and a commitment to excellence can achieve.

In **England** growers continue to face the annual challenge of bringing in an adequate quality grape harvest. For several decades the industry has struggled with modest varieties and crossings of mostly German origin. The problem is that there is a scarcity of reasonable grapes that will ripen adequately in such a cool and damp northerly climate. One variety that has proved to work particularly well here, producing the occasional wine of depth and character, is the **Seyval Blanc**, although, due to the bizarre machinations of the European quality regulations, it is entitled only to table wine (rather than quality wine) status, the reason being that the variety is a hybrid. The real key, though, has been planting and sourcing fruit from existing vineyards on the southern English downland chalk soils in order to produce some first-class sparkling wines. It is worth considering that less than half the Champagne *vignoble* is planted in the same fabled chalk. Chardonnay and Pinot Noir too are being successfully grown and contributing to some very impressive recent results. It may be that the hot summer of 2003 produces wines of a different dimension here.

In Eastern Europe the **Czech** and **Slovak Republics** both produce some decent dry whites. In the Czech Republic whites from the likes of Grüner Veltliner and Gewürztraminer are produced in **Bohemia** and **Moravia** and in the Slovak Republic some well-made commercial reds originate from the **Nitra** region, as well as good stylish whites from **Pezinok** just north of Bratislava. Further east, nothing of real note has yet emerged from the **Ukraine** or **Moldova** despite there being some modern winemaking input in the latter. In **Romania** the best potential would appear to rest with the sweet botrytised wines of **Cotnari** and **Murfatlar** but some outside investment would be an immense advantage.

In **Hungary**, apart from Tokaji, few wines of real quality have been produced. Again, investment has been centred on the bottom of the market. There is potential, particularly with the reds from the southern **Villány-Siklós** region. **Tokaji**, though, is a different matter. Investment aplenty has flooded into the region and some of the results are stunning. The wines are now altogether fresher, more intense and with some truly splendid botrytis character in the best examples. Among the great recent years to look out for are 2000, 1999, 1996, 1995, 1993 and 1988. It's a shame that the same technology has failed to reach that part of the appellation in the Slovak Republic.

In South-Eastern Europe **Slovenia** produces some crisp dry whites and a few reasonable sweet wines close to the Austrian border, but has struggled to shake off its 'Laski Rizling' image. **Croatia** produces a few gutsy reds, while **Bulgaria** ought to produce much more in the way of quality than it does. **Greece** has real potential and an increasing number of stylish modern whites and rich plummy reds are now being made as well as a few established classics like the sweet **Muscats** from the island of **Samos**. As wine producers begin to exploit more high-potential viticultural sites this may become a very exciting country for wine. The industry in **Israel** is still largely focused on the production of kosher wines, many from the **Golan Heights**, but an increasing number of stylish reds and whites are being produced there as well. In **Lebanon**, after decades of war and strife, new producers are joining the long-established Chateau Musar in producing dense, powerful wines of heady character.

DISZNÓKÖ Tokaji A: PFx

Owner: AXA Millésimes PF 10, 3910 Tokaj
Disznókö was created in 1992 and, as with a number of Tokaji producers, considerable investment has been put into this operation with major new cellars. 100 ha are farmed of which 60 ha are very old vines and a full range of Tokaji styles produced. The top sweet wines have marvellous botrytis complexity. The wines are very opulent and exotic but have comfortably enough acidity for balance. (DM)
O Tokaji Aszú 5 Puttonyos★★★★ £E Aszú 6 Puttonyos★★★★ £F

DENBIES Surrey www.denbiesvineyard.co.uk

Owner: Denbies Wine Estate London Rd, Dorking, Surrey RH5 6AA
Very substantial operation with more than 100 ha planted on limestone soils near Dorking. In selecting the site the potential ripening of the grapes was carefully evaluated. At their best these wines are indeed among the finest the country offers, but the range is extensive and production sizeable, approaching 40,000 cases a year, and some wines are fairly ordinary. As elsewhere, sparkling wines have good potential and there have been some impressive sweet whites over the past few vintages. (DM)
O Classic Brut Vintage★ £B

EVHARIS ESTATE Greece www.evharis.gr A: Han, NYg

Owner: Eva-Maria Boehme & Harris Antoniou 24 Lagoumitzi str. 176 71, Athens
Small 30 ha Greek estate located between Athens and Corinth with vineyards planted in the foothills of the Gerania mountains. Indigenous white Assyrtiko, Roditis and Athiri along with red Aghiorghitiko are joined by international varieties Chardonnay, Sauvignon Blanc, Syrah, Merlot and Grenache. From these they produce a good, floral and intense tank fermented Estate White which blends Assyrtiko with Chardonnay and Sauvignon and an Estate red blend of Syrah, Merlot and Grenache. The white is marked by its native herbal Assyrtiko character. The red displays fine, rich berry fruit, with an under-current of herbs and thyme and impressive intensity. It is aged in French oak for 12 months lending it depth and structure. Estate bottlings of Syrah, Merlot and Chardonnay are also produced and there is a budget label Ilaros for white and red. The Estate red should be aged for a couple of years in bottle. (DM)
O Estate Red Gerania★★ £C
O Estate White Gerania★★ £B

LUMIÈRE Morocco

Owner: Gérard Depardieu c/o Terroirs d'Exception, 33330 Saint-Christophe des Bardes, France
Gérard Depardieu's 6 ha estate at Meknes, based within the appellation of Guerrouane produces this remarkable old vine blend of Grenache, Carignan and Syrah. The actor also owns the fine Domaine de SAINT AUGUSTIN in Algeria and has established new benchmarks for what can be achieved in these unheralded regions. The varieties here are planted in near equal amounts and the average age of the vine-yard is now over 70 years. Despite the warm climate, the vineyard benefits from its 600 metre altitude and yields are restricted to less than 20 hl/ha. Both leaf plucking and green harvesting are carried out to help ensure old vine fruit of the highest quality. In the winery there is minimal interference. *Pigeage* is employed and cellar operations are handled by gravity. The wine is aged in new French oak. It is perhaps the finest expression of richly concentrated old vine red produced in north Africa. Ripe, heady dark, spicy fruit with layers of blackberry, herb and black pepper are finely balanced with a supple, youthfully firm

structure. Attractive young the wine will benefit from four or five years ageing. (DM)

O **Guerrouane** Cuvée Lumière★★★★ £E

NYETIMBER West Sussex

Owner: Stuart and Sandra Moss   Gay Street, West Chiltington, Pulborough, West Sussex RH20 2HH
The ancient Nyetimber Manor, which dates back to before Domesday Book was compiled, is now
the base for one of the very best wine producers in England. Vineyards are planted on ideally exposed
south-facing slopes and were established in the mid-1980s. Some fine sparkling wines are being
being produced here from the Champagne varieties. Both the Classic Cuvée and the Blanc de Blancs
are impressive alternatives to Champagne. (DM)

O **Classic Cuvée** Vintage★★★ £D   **Première Cuvée** Blanc de Blancs Vintage★★★ £D

OREMUS Tokaji   A:M&V

Owner: Alvarez family   Damjanich.u.7, H-3950 Sarospatek
Oremus was created in 1993 as a joint venture between Tojaji Kereskedöhóz (the former state-run
commercial house) and Bodegas VEGA SICILIA (see Spain). A full range of styles is produced, from
basic dry Furmint to exceptional and heady Essencia. This latter wine (and it is on the borderline of
not being classified as such – in 1995 it had only 3% of alcohol) is astonishing, with residual sugar
in excess of 400 g/l but fierce acidity to provide balance. All the sweet wines are impressive. (DM)

O **Tokaji** Aszú 5 Puttonyos★★★ £E   Essencia✪✪✪✪✪ £H

DOM. DE SAINT AUGUSTIN Algeria

Owner: Gérard Depardieu   c/o Terroirs d'Exception, 33330 Saint-Christophe des Bardes, France
Gérard Depardieu produces two impressive reds here and these with his LUMIÈRE wine from
Guerrouane in Morocco are north African benchmarks. The vineyards at Saint Augustin, as in
Morocco are planted at altitude, between 400 and 500 metres and this helps to moderate the high
summer temperatures. The yields are kept low, particularly for the Cuvée Monica, at 16 hl/ha for
2002, and green harvesting is practiced during the growing season. The age of the vineyards at an
average of 40 years also helps. The harvest is conducted by hand and brought into the winery (a converted chapel) in refrigerated trucks to preserve the fruit's freshness. The regular bottling La
Confession blends Grenache, Carignan and Syrah whereas the Cuvée Monica more unusually
comprises Grenache, Carignan and Alicante. Dense, very rich and loaded with dark berry fruit,
almost raisiny but the concentration on the palate is impressive. These are exciting and characterful
wines. (DM)

O **Coteaux de Tlemcen** Cuvée Monica★★★ £E

ISTVAN SZEPSY Tokaji   A:RsW

Owner: Istvan Szepsy
Istvan Szepsy was originally a director of the co-operative in Mád. In recent years though he has been
establishing his own small vineyard holding with some of the best sites in the region. He has reverted
his vineyards to traditional bush vine pruning and keeps his yields under tight control. The quality is
reflected in the wines which are unusually fresh and atypical for the region. Indeed there has been a
general move throughout the region to produce wines with less oxidative character and these perhaps
more than any others really reflect this new approach. The Aszú 6 Puttonyos is remarkably intense.

Szepsy is also involved with American financier Anthony Hwang in a new venture, Kiralyudvar. Similarly impressive fresh Tokaji styles are being produced. They have also recently taken a controlling interest in the top Vouvray estate HUET L'ECHANSONNE. (DM)

O **Tokaji** Noble Late Harvest★★★ £D Aszú 6 Puttonyos✪✪✪✪✪ £G

ROYAL TOKAJI WINE COMPANY Tokaji   A RTo, BBR

Owner: Royal Tokay Wine Co Rakoczi Ut 35, H-3909 Mád
This was the first of the foreign investments in the Tokay region in 1989. A consortium including Danish winemaker Peter Vinding-Diers and wine writer Hugh Johnson formed the company in partnership with 63 growers, providing a formidable resource of top vineyard sites. The attention in the vineyard is undoubtedly paying off and yields have been almost halved to an average of around 40 hl/ha. The wines are rich and intense, without a hint of oxidation, and have a more overtly orange peel and nutty character than other examples. (DM)

O **Tokaji** Blue Label 5 Puttonyos★★ £E Aszú Nyulaszo 6 Puttonyos★★★★ £G Essencia✪✪✪✪✪ £H

THREE CHOIRS Gloucestershire www.three-choirs-vineyards.co.uk

Owner: Three Choirs Vineyards Ltd Newent, Gloucestershire GL18 1LS
Top-quality English property with 28 ha of vineyards. Dry and sweet whites are made as well as sparkling non-vintage and vintage bottlings. Considerable effort goes into grape crossing and hybrid research here because of the vagaries of the English climate and the results are generally fairly successful. (DM)

O **Bacchus** Reserve★★ £B

OTHER WINES OF NOTE

England
BREAKY BOTTOM O Seyval Blanc East Sussex £B
CHAPEL DOWN O Epoch Vintage Brut Kent £C
RIDGEVIEW O Bloomsbury Vintage East Sussex £C
VALLEY VINEYARDS O Ascot Brut Non-Vintage Berkshire £B

Greece
ANTONOPOULOS ● Cabernet Nea Dris Patras £C
GAIA ESTATE ● Estate Red Koutsi Nemea £B
SAMOS CO-OPERATIVE O Samos Nectar Samos £C
HARLAFTIS ● Argilos Attika £B

Hungary
CHÂTEAU MEGYER O Tokaji Aszú 5 Puttonyos £E
CHÂTEAU PAJZOS O Tokaji Aszú 5 Puttonyos £E
CROWN ESTATES O Tokaji Aszú 5 Puttonyos £D

Lebanon
CHÂTEAU KEFRAYA ● Château Kefraya Red £C
MASSAYA ● Selection Red £C
CHÂTEAU MUSAR ● Château Musar Red £C

California North Coast

Dynamic pace among small, high-quality wine producers is evident throughout California, and this is as much the case here as elsewhere in the state. As well as the more established cooler areas like the Russian River, new vineyards are now being developed on the Sonoma Coast with great success. Wine prices have been and remain buoyant – a wealthy local market combined with scarcity among the top wines ensures this. There are great Cabernets here but this is generally Chardonnay and Pinot Noir territory, with some exceptional Zinfandel in warmer sites. Some magnificent wines, yes, but without the stratospheric prices of the Napa Valley collectors' Cabernets.

Geography

The North Coast of California is a vast area. It takes in Mendocino and Lake Counties, over 100 miles to the north of San Francisco, as well as Sonoma County, which runs southwards west of the Mayacamas Mountains and then takes in the western end of Carneros, at the head of San Pablo Bay. The whole viticultural area is encompassed under the **North Coast** AVA. What enables such diverse vinegrowing is cool coastal breezes and sea fogs that drift in through coastal gaps. The most significant of these – the Petaluma gap – provides an effective cooling fan for the vast Sonoma vineyard, north and south of the town of Santa Rosa. It is only thanks to these cooling breezes and sea fogs, which dominate the summer months along the state's coastline all the way south towards Santa Barbara, that fine wine production is possible in California at all.

Mendocino and Lake Counties

Mendocino is a large, sprawling vinegrowing area, mostly cool and particularly suitable for Pinot Noir and Chardonnay. The **Anderson Valley**, which opens up to the ocean, in particular produces a number of restrained, stylish examples and is also an excellent source of sparkling wine. To the north-east of the sector are the warmer AVAs of **Redwood Valley** and **Potter Valley**. Some increasingly impressive Syrah, Zinfandel and Cabernet are grown here. Lake County and the **Clear Lake** AVA, **Guenoc** and **Benmore Valley** sub-AVAs are located to the east, across the Mayacamas Mountains. Clear Lake and Guenoc are best-suited to growing reds – Cabernet Sauvignon and Zinfandel – as well as a ripe style of Chardonnay and Sauvignon Blanc. Benmore Valley by contrast is significantly cooled by elevation and provides tighter, more restrained Chardonnay.

Northern Sonoma

This is really the heartland of North Coast vinegrowing and it includes the warm red-grape areas of **Dry Creek Valley** and **Alexander Valley** to the north-east. These are located to the west and east respectively of the meandering northern sections of the Russian River which runs through the towns of Asti, Geyserville and Healdsburg. Tremendous Zinfandel and Syrah can be found in both AVAs. Excellent restrained Chardonnay, structured Cabernet and meritage styles are all sourced from the higher mountain slopes of the Alexander Valley. To the immediate east of here is the **Knights Valley**, source of some first-class Chardonnay and Cabernet Sauvignon. **Chalk Hill** AVA is just to the south and is dominated by the winery of the same name. South of Healdsburg the considerable expanse of the **Russian River Valley** AVA opens out. To the far west on the Sonoma Coast some very impressive Chardonnay and Pinot Noir is now being produced and takes the **Sonoma Coast** AVA. The Russian River area is now very well established as a source of exemplary Pinot Noir and Chardonnay and, in the warmer eastern sites, very good Syrah and Zinfandel. To the south-west is the distinctly cool

Sonoma Green Valley AVA, a source of top-quality sparkling wines and restrained styles of Chardonnay and Pinot Noir.

Sonoma Valley

The **Sonoma Valley** AVA itself is located to the south of Santa Rosa and is home to some of the largest producers on the North Coast. The valley is bordered by the Mayacamas range to the east and the Sonoma Mountains to the west. The appellation runs from north to south-east through the towns of Oakmount, Kenwood, Glen Ellen and Sonoma itself. The western range has its own AVA, **Sonoma Mountain**, and provides impressive examples of restrained Chardonnay, Pinot Noir and Cabernet Sauvignon. In general the better reds are planted in the warmer northern sections of the AVA while the southern sector that borders Carneros produces stylish whites but also good Pinot Noir. Some of the best and sturdiest Cabernet blends and Zinfandels are sourced from the higher slopes leading into the Mayacamas Mountains.

A-Z Producers by Region

Alexander Valley
CLOS DU BOIS
GEYSER PEAK
SAUSAL
STONESTREET

Anderson Valley
EDMEADES
PACIFIC ECHO
ROEDERER ESTATE

Chalk Hill
CHALK HILL WINERY

Dry Creek Valley
DRY CREEK VINEYARDS
FRICK
FRITZ WINERY
GALLO OF SONOMA
A RAFANELLI
SEGHESIO

Knights Valley
PETER MICHAEL

Lake County
STEELE

Mendocino County
BEHRENS AND HITCHCOCK

Redwood Valley
FETZER VINEYARDS

Russian River Valley
DEHLINGER
GARY FARRELL
FOPPIANO
KISTLER
LA CREMA
LYNMAR WINERY
MARTINELLI
ROBERT MUELLER
PAPAPIETRO PERRY
J ROCHIOLI
SIDURI
SONOMA-CUTRER
WILLIAMS SELYEM

Sonoma Coast
MARCASSIN

Sonoma County
PAUL HOBBS
KENDALL JACKSON
SONOMA COUNTY
WH SMITH

Sonoma Mountain
BENZIGER
SONOMA MOUNTAIN

Sonoma Green Valley
HARTFORD FAMILY WINERY

IRON HORSE VINEYARDS
MARIMAR TORRES

Sonoma Valley
ARROWOOD
CHATEAU ST JEAN
HANZELL
LANDMARK

MOON MOUNTAIN VINEYARD
RAVENSWOOD
ST FRANCIS VINEYARDS
VERITÉ

Vintages

As is the case elsewhere in California, there can be significant variation between mesoclimates within regions with inevitably Cabernet, Zinfandel and other late ripening varieties working best in the warmer sites and early-ripening Chardonnay and Pinot Noir performing best in the cooler parts of the Russian River, Sonoma Coast and Sonoma Green Valley. However the charts below will give you a good general idea of what to expect from recent vintages. With regard to earlier years, the occasional 1987, 1985, 1984 and 1980 Cabernet and perhaps really top-flight Zinfandel might be worth a punt. 1978 and 1970 were also classic Cabernet years.

California North Coast Vintages

	Pinot Noir	Chardonnay	Zinfandel	Cabernet Sauvignon
2002	★★★★ A	★★★★ A	★★★★ A	★★★★ A
2001	★★★★ A	★★★★ B	★★★★ A	★★★★/★★★★★ A
2000	★★★/★★★★B	★★★ B	★★/★★★ B	★★★ A
1999	★★★★ B	★★★/★★★★ B	★★★★ B	★★★/★★★★ A
1998	★★★/★★★★ B	★★★/★★★★ C	★★/★★★ C	★★★ B
1997	★★★★ C	★★★★ C	★★★/★★★★ C	★★★★ B
1996	★★★/★★★★C	★★★ C	★★★/★★★★ C	★★★/★★★★ B
1995	★★★/★★★★C	★★★★ C	★★★/★★★★ C	★★★★ B
1994	★★★★ D	★★★/★★★★ D	★★★★ C	★★★★ B
1993	★★★/★★★★ D	★★★★ D	★★★/★★★★ C	★★★/★★★★ B
1992	★★★/★★★★ D	★★★★ D	★★★/★★★★ C	★★★★ B
1991	★★★/★★★★ D	–	★★★★ C	★★★★ C
1990	–	–	★★★★ D	★★★★ C

ARROWOOD Sonoma Valley www.arrowoodvineyards.com   A: RMi

Owner: Robert Mondavi 14347 Sonoma Highway, Glen Ellen, CA 95442

Dick Arrowood sold his interest in this medium-sized operation in 2000 but will remain as winemaker and direct the style and focus of the winery. There is no doubt that his immense experience, gained not only at Arrowood but also previously as winemaker at CHATEAU ST JEAN, will continue to maintain and drive quality here. The wines themselves are all sourced from Sonoma Valley fruit. There are two ranges: the premium Arrowood wines and those under the Grand Archer label. The latter can offer very good value and are vinified with just a hint of oak, the objective being to emphasise varietal character. There is a fairly extensive range of premium Arrowood bottlings: classy citrussy Chardonnay from Sonoma County as well as Chardonnay, Cabernet and Merlot under the Réserve Spéciale label. Alary Ranch Chardonnay was added with the 2000 vintage and should have real potential. Malbec and Rhône styles are of equal importance, the best of which are from Saralee's vineyard and most recently Syrah from the Kuljian vineyard in Dry Creek. Newly added are red and white Rhône blends Côte de Lune, the latter again sourced from Saralee. The Arrowood range is completed by Gewürztraminer, fine Pinot Blanc and two luscious late harvest Rieslings. (DM)

- ● **Cabernet Sauvignon** Réserve Spéciale★★★★£G Sonoma County★★★£F
- ● **Syrah** Sonoma Valley★★★£F
- ○ **Chardonnay** Sonoma County★★★£E ○ **Viognier** Saralee's Vineyard★★★£D

BEHRENS AND HITCHCOCK Mendocino County   A:THt

Owner: Les Behrens & Bob Hitchcock PO Box 1127, Calistoga, CA 94515

Very impressive small producer specialising in tiny lots, often barely more than 100 cases of a cuvée, of startling and massive, super-rich reds from a number of varieties sourced throughout the North Coast. The range includes top Syrah from the Alder Springs vineyard and Petite Sirah from York Creek, along with some concentrated, powerful blends. Ode to Picasso is a fat, forward combination of Syrah, Cabernet Sauvignon, Merlot and Cabernet Franc. The whole range is marked by a style that emphasises full, sumptuous fruit with immense depth and extract. Although there is a greater structure and grip in the Cabernet-based cuvées, these are wines that offer supple tannins, rich fruit and not inconsiderable alcohol. (DM)

- ● **Cabernet Sauvignon** Kenefick Ranch★★★★★£G ● **Merlot** Fortuna Vineyard★★★★£E

BENZIGER Sonoma Mountain www.benziger.com   A: N&P

Owner: Mike Benziger 1883 London Ranch Road, Glen Ellen, CA 95442

Large, family-run operation producing an extensive range of wines. The best are very good and by comparison with many other California examples, good value. The family also owns the Imagery Estate winery, which sells a good-quality range from lesser varieties at the cellar door only. Sonoma County wines are straightforward and good value whereas the Reserves are blended from the winery's best lots. Numerous limited-production, vineyard-designated wines are made, with some of the vineyards farmed biodynamically. (DM)

- ● **Cabernet Sauvignon** Reserve Sonoma County★★£E ● **Merlot** Reserve Sonoma County★★£E
- ○ **Chardonnay** Reserve Carneros★★★£D ○ **Fume Blanc** Sonoma County★£C

CHALK HILL WINERY Chalk Hill www.chalkhill.com   A: J&B

Owner: Fred Furth 10300 Chalk Hill Road, Healdsburg, Sonoma County, CA 95448

This producer unusually possesses its own AVA and has been for many years committed to maximising the quality of the fruit from estate vineyards. The whites are made in a full, ripe style with judicious use of new oak for both Sauvignon and Chardonnay. Vineyard Selection bottlings of both Pinot Gris and Chardonnay have now been added to the range. The reds are leaner than some, with the odd green hint entering the equation, but at best express attractive, berry fruit character. Library Releases are also offered, along with a very small amount of the expensive Vineyard Selection Adele's Merlot. An equally small production of rich and luscious botrytised Semillon Vineyard Selection is produced when vintage conditions permit. (DM)

● **Cabernet Sauvignon** Estate★★★ £E ● **Merlot** Estate★★ £E
○ **Chardonnay** Estate★★★ £E ○ **Sauvignon Blanc** Estate★★ £D
○ **Pinot Gris** Estate★★ £D

CHATEAU ST JEAN Sonoma Valley www.chateaustjean.com

Owner: Beringer Wine Estates 8555 Sonoma Highway, Kenwood, CA 95452
The original and striking 'Chateau' here was built in 1920, pre-Prohibition. The current winery was founded in 1973 and the estate comprises some 100 ha (250 acres), of which 32 ha (80 acres) are planted to vines. These, along with three additional vineyards, Robert Young, Belle Terre and La Petite Etoile, provide the foundation for the good and pricey Reserve and vineyard-designated wines. Sonoma County wines are well-priced and regularly offer good-value drinking. A number of speciality and limited-release wines are sold exclusively at the tasting room. (DM)

● **Pinot Noir** Sonoma County★★ £C ● **Merlot** Sonoma County★★ £C
○ **Chardonnay** Sonoma County★★ £B Belle Terre Vineyard★★★ £C
○ **Fume Blanc** Sonoma County★★ £B La Petite Etoile★★★ £C
○ **Gewürztraminer** Sonoma County★★ £B

CLOS DU BOIS Alexander Valley www.closdubois.com   A: ADo

Owner: Allied Domecq 19410 Geyserville Avenue, Geyserville, CA 95441
Large-volume winery producing close to half a million cases annually. The straightforward Sonoma County Classic range is the mainstay of the winery but can be impressive on occasion. Appellation Reserve wines are a step up, but it is the vineyard-designated and Winemakers Reserve cuvées which are the benchmark here. Winemakers Reserve Cabernet and Marlstone particularly are dense, concentrated and well structured, the latter a blend of Cabernet Sauvignon, Merlot, Cabernet Franc, Malbec and Petit Verdot from the vineyard of the same name . For value and style the two top Chardonnays are subtly oaked, with good citrussy, leesy depth and a certain finesse. (DM)

● **Merlot** Reserve★ £C ● **Tempranillo** Reserve★ £C
● **Cabernet Sauvignon** Briarcrest Vineyard★★ £E Winemakers Reserve★★★ £F
● **Marlstone** Alexander Valley★★★ £E
○ **Chardonnay** Reserve★ £B Flintwood★★ £D Calcaire★★ £D

DEHLINGER Russian River Valley

Owner: Tom Dehlinger 6300 Guerneville Road., Sebastopol, CA 95472
Dehlinger remains among the very top echelon in the Russian River, continually crafting outstanding unfiltered Pinot Noir, Syrah and Chardonnay. Cabernet Sauvignon does not quite hit the same heady heights, although it is rich, structured and impressive in top years such as 1999 and 1997. The quantities of single-vineyard Pinot Noir from the Octagon and Goldridge sites are tiny but well worth seeking out, as is the Goldridge Syrah. The reds are not only powerful and structured but very refined as well, and will drink well in the medium-term. (DM)

● **Cabernet Sauvignon** Estate★★★ £E ● **Syrah** Estate★★★★ £E
● **Pinot Noir** Estate★★★★ £E Octagon Vineyard★★★★ £E
O **Chardonnay** Estate★★★★ £D

DRY CREEK VINEYARDS Dry Creek www.drycreekvineyard.com A: Alv

Owner: David Stare 3770 Lambert Bridge Road, Healdsburg, CA 95448
Medium-sized winery notable for good, well-priced Fumé Blanc in a very much more herbaceous style than many and a number of rich and impressive Zinfandels. The latter have been produced consistently over a number of vintages and, while full and vibrant, they are rarely overblown. With old-vine Zinfandel fruit increasingly in demand throughout the state, Dry Creek has established its own 'Heritage' clone, propagated from old-vine cuttings on phylloxera-resistant rootstock. From the 1997 vintage, a small quantity – some 500 cases – of a new super-premium Cabernet Endeavour has also been released. (DM)

● **Syrah** Dry Creek★ £C ● **Merlot** Reserve★★ £D ● **Cabernet Sauvignon** Reserve★★ £D
● **Zinfandel** Heritage Clone★★ £C Old Vines★★★ £C Reserve★★★ £D
O **Fume Blanc** DCV3★ £B O **Chardonnay** Reserve★ £C

EDMEADES Anderson Valley www.kjsales.com/brands/edmeades A: KJn, WTs

Owner: Kendall-Jackson 5500 Highway 128, Philo, CA 95403
Mendocino-based winery, producing an extensive range of full, brambly Zinfandels and well structured Petite Sirah and Syrah. The wines are typically big and brawny, offering weight and power rather than finesse. They are vinified using wild yeast fermentation and, as in all the best Jackson family wines, handling is kept to a minimum. Top cuvées can be very impressive. Cool Anderson Valley vineyards provide the source for Pinot Noir and Chardonnay. These are good although they can on occasion lack a little balance and refinement. (DM)

● **Pinot Noir** Anderson Valley★★ £C ● **Syrah** Eaglepoint Vineyard★★ £D
● **Petite Sirah** Eaglepoint Vineyard★★★ £D ● **Zinfandel** Mendocino★ £C Ciapusci★★★ £C
● **Zinfandel** Eaglepoint Vineyard★★★ £D Mendocino Ridge★★★ £D
O **Chardonnay** Anderson Valley★★ £C
O **Gewürztraminer** Anderson Valley★★ £B

GARY FARRELL Russian River Valley www.garyfarrell.com A: Vin

Owner: Gary Farrell 10701 Westside Road, Healdsburg, CA 95448
Formerly the winemaker at ROCHIOLI and DAVIS BYNUM, Gary Farrell has more recently become notable for stylish, elegant Chardonnay and Pinot Noir under his own label. The Rochioli vineyard remains an important source of fruit for him, along with Starr Ridge and Olivet Lane vineyards. A more recent addition is Central Coast Pinot Noir from the famed Bien Nacido vineyard. Chardonnay is made in a rich, tropical style but with well-judged oak, while Pinot is ripe, full and packed with dark plum and berry fruit. Zinfandel is good but can at times lack the quality of the other two varietals. Good too are Encounter, a meritage red blend of Cabernet Savignon, Merlot and Cabernet Franc, and Hillside Select Merlot. (DM)

● **Pinot Noir**★★★ £E Starr Ridge Vineyard★★★ £E Rochioli Vineyard★★★★ £F
● **Zinfandel** Dry Creek★★ £C Bradford Mountain★★★ £E
O **Chardonnay**★★★ £E Westside Farms★★★ £E Rochioli Vineyard★★★ £E

FETZER VINEYARDS Redwood Valley www.fetzer.com A: MCI

Owner: Brown Forman 13601 Eastside Road, Hopland, CA 95449

Large-scale Mendocino County producer with an extensive range and one that champions organic wine production. The Barrel Select and Reserve bottlings are the best bets and generally represent pretty decent value for money. The style is for rich and ripe wines with evident, sometimes unsubtle oak handling. Big and full, they can also be marked by excess alcohol. One feels a touch more refinement would provide a better balance. Fetzer also owns the Bonterra winery which itself produces a fairly large range, particularly among the Rhône varietals. (DM)

Fetzer
- **Zinfandel** Valley Oaks★ £B Barrel Select★★ £B ● **Merlot** Barrel Select★ £B
- **Cabernet Sauvignon** Barrel Select★ £B Napa Valley Reserve★ £C
- **Pinot Noir** Bien Nacido Limited Release Reserve★★ £C
- ○ **Chardonnay** Sundial★ £B Barrel Select★ £B ○ **Gewürztraminer** Echo Ridge★ £B
- ○ **Sauvignon Blanc** Echo Ridge★ £B

Bonterra
- **Syrah** Bonterra★★ £C
- ○ **Chardonnay** Bonterra★★£C ○ **Roussanne** Bonterra★★ £C ○ **Viognier** Bonterra★★ £C

FOPPIANO Russian River Valley www.foppiano.com A: WTs

Owner: Foppiano family 12707 Old Redwood Highway, Healdsburg, CA95448

The Foppiano family own some 80 ha (around 200 acres) of prime Russian River vineyards. There are good solid, earthy reds here: the Sangiovese is one of the better Californian examples but the real stars are the two Petite Sirah cuvées. Both are dense, powerful but supple examples of this sometimes raw and tannic variety. The Russian River bottling, with concentrated dark berry fruit and spicy black pepper undercurrents, represents particularly good value. (DM)

- **Sangiovese** Alexander Valley★★ £C ● **Zinfandel** Dry Creek Valley★ £B Reserve★★ £C
- **Merlot** Sonoma County★ £C Reserve★★ £D ● **Cabernet Sauvignon** Russian River★★ £C
- **Petite Sirah** Russian River★★★ £C Reserve★★★ £E

FRICK Dry Creek Valley www.frickwinery.com

Owner: Bill & Judy Frick 23072 Walling Road, Geyserville, CA 95441

Small Rhône specialist with some Merlot as well. Frick produces just 2,500 cases a year from 2 ha (5 acres) of vines on a small property established in 1976 in a cooler sector of the Dry Creek Valley. Key to the style here is a naturally stressed vineyard, planted on steep, well-drained slopes. The result is vines which struggle just sufficiently in order to achieve fruit with real intensity during ripening. The wines are not huge blockbusters but nevertheless show rich and concentrated fruit with balance and finesse. All offer good value. (DM)

- **Syrah** Dry Creek★★ £C ● **Cinsault** Dry Creek★★ £C ● **Merlot** Dry Creek★★ £C
- ○ **Viognier** Gannon Vineyard★★ £C

FRITZ WINERY Dry Creek Valley www.fritzwinery.com A: WTs

Owner: Fritz family 24691 Dutcher Creek Road, Cloverdale, CA 95425

Fritz was established as long ago as 1979 and production is still small at some 12,000 cases a year. Vineyards are owned in both the Dry Creek Valley and the cooler Russian River, providing an excellent source for Chardonnay, particularly the famed Dutton Ranch. Helen Turley of MARCASSIN spent a couple of years consulting here and the quality shines through. Minimalist practices such as native yeast fermentation are employed. The Zins are vibrant and full of rich fruit, the Chardonnay broad, nutty and toasty and Sauvignon fresh and grassy for drinking young. The range is completed by a well-priced Carignane and a restrained cedary Cabernet Sauvignon from the high altitude Rockpile Vineyard. (DM)

● **Zinfandel** Old Vine★★ £C   Rogers Reserve★★★ £E
○ **Sauvignon Blanc** Sonoma County★★ £B
○ **Chardonnay** Dutton Ranch★★★ £C   Dutton Ranch Shop Block★★★ £E

GALLO OF SONOMA   Dry Creek Valley   www.gallosonoma.com   A: EJG

Owner: Gallo family   3387 Dry Creek Road, Healdsburg, CA 95448
The world's largest wine company, E & J Gallo, is known the world over for its Gallo and Turning Leaf volume labels – the former hugely successful but largely unexciting. There is also a Coastal range from the giant facility at Modesto in California's Central Valley, but it is the wines now produced from the vast Sonoma Valley vineyard holdings which provide the real interest. Seven vineyards are owned, spread throughout Sonoma from Barelli Creek in the north to Two Rock in the south. A sound range produced under the Sonoma label is blended from separate lots and offers reasonable value. Better, though, are the selected single-vineyard wines, particularly the rich and powerful, spicy, berry-fruited Zinfandel and the Estate Vineyard Chardonnay and Cabernet Sauvignon. While the latter is not quite up there with the major super-premium Napa examples, it is an impressive wine and in the context of top quality California Cabernet and meritage blends is moderately priced. (DM)

● **Cabernet Sauvignon** Estate★★★★ £F   Barelli Creek★★ £D   Stefani Vineyard★★ £D
● **Zinfandel** Barelli Creek★★★ £D   Frei Ranch★★★ £D
○ **Chardonnay** Estate★★★ £E   Laguna Vineyard★★ £D   Stefani Vineyard★★ £D   Stefani Vineyard★★ £E

GEYSER PEAK   Alexander Valley   www.geyserpeakwinery.com   A: Max

Owner: Henry Trione   22281 Chianti Road, Geyserville CA 95441
This is a substantial operation with production now running at 600,000 cases annually. Unusually the winemaking team is Australian, led by Daryl Groom who was recruited from PENFOLDS in 1989. The Sonoma County wines are generally sound and tend to emphasise a straightforward fruit character. The extensive range of Block Collection wines are sourced from single vineyards and includes Chardonnay, Merlot and Zinfandel as well as Cabernet Sauvignon and Viognier bottlings. The Reserve wines differ in that they are produced from blending a number of the winery's best lots. At the top of the range is the limited-release Bin Series including Shiraz and Sangiovese. Throughout the range expect big, ripe fruit characters with the top-label reds providing wines with weight and structure. (DM)

● **Shiraz** Sonoma County★ £B   Reserve★★ £D
● **Alexandre** Meritage Reserve★★ £E   Zinfandel Sonoma County★★ £B
● **Cabernet Sauvignon** Block Collection Vallerga Vineyard★★ £D   Reserve★★ £D
○ **Sauvignon Blanc** Sonoma County★ £B   ○ **Chardonnay** Sonoma County★ £B
○ **Viognier** Block Collection Sonoma Moment Vineyard★★ £C

HANZELL   Sonoma Valley   www.hanzell.com   A: Vin

Owner: De Brye Estate Trust   18596 Lomita Avenue, Sonoma, CA 95476
Small producer located high up in the Mayacamas Mountains. Hanzell was established way back in 1953 and has long been a pioneer of first-class Chardonnay and Pinot Noir from its hillside estate vineyard. The operation is built on the quality of this mountain *terroir*. The Chardonnay is a tight, structured example in its youth with well-judged oak and subtle citrus notes, altogether different

from many fuller, fatter examples produced by its neighbours. The Pinot is rich and vibrant, with concentrated dark berry flavours and just a hint of game. Both wines will age well and will benefit from four or five years' ageing. (DM)

● **Pinot Noir** Estate★★★ £F
○ **Chardonnay** Estate★★★★ £F

HARTFORD FAMILY WINERY Sonoma Green Valley www.hartfordcourt.com A: May

Owner: Hartford family 8075 Martinelli Road, Forestville, CA 95436
Founded in 1993 by Don Hartford and his wife Jennifer Jackson-Hartford, of the KENDALL-JACKSON clan, this operation is dedicated to producing Pinot Noir, Zinfandel and Chardonnay. Winemaker Mike Sullivan purposely crafts very Burgundian styles of Chardonnay and Pinot – tighter, more structured wines than many of their neighbours'. Both are good medium-term cellar propositions. Zinfandel is produced in a ripe, full style but retains real finesse. The Hartford label encompasses Chardonnay and Pinot Noir from the Sonoma Coast as well as a range of Russian River Zinfandels from the Hartford, Dina's, Fanucchi-Wood Road and Highwire vineyards. In addition to this an extensive range of single-vineyard cuvées are made under the Hartford Court label. Pinot Noir comes from a range of sources: there is a Marin County bottling, as well as wines from Velvet Sisters Vineyard in Anderson Valley, the Sevens Bench Vineyard in Carneros and Jennifer's Vineyard on the Sonoma Coast. Russian River Pinot is produced from the Arrendell and Dutton-Sanchietti vineyards. Some impressive Chardonnay is produced from the Stone Côte, Laura's and Seascape vineyards on the Sonoma Coast as well as the Three Jacks Vineyards bottling from the Russian River. All stand out. (DM)

Hartford
● **Pinot Noir** Sonoma Coast★★★ £C ● **Zinfandel** Russian River Valley★★★★ £D
○ **Chardonnay** Sonoma Coast★★★ £C

Hartford Court
○ **Chardonnay** Three Jacks Vineyard★★★★ £E
● **Pinot Noir** Marin County★★★ £E Velvet Sisters Vineyard★★★ £E Dutton Sanchietti★★★ £E

PAUL HOBBS Sonoma County www.paulhobbs.com A: Bib

Owner: Paul Hobbs 3355 Gravenstein Highway North, Sebastopol, CA 95472
Winemaker Paul Hobbs spends the northern-hemisphere spring months vinifying wines in South America, where he has helped in shaping the style at VALDIVIESO and CATENA. Equally important, he also produces benchmark wines in California from Cabernet Sauvignon, Merlot, Pinot Noir and Chardonnay. His main focus is on single-vineyard wines, particularly an extensive number from Chardonnay, produced in very small quantities. Handling is minimal and the wines are vinified with natural yeast. Oak is carefully integrated and the primary objective is to provide wines of balance and finesse. Top selections for Chardonnay and Pinot Noir, labelled Cuvée Agustina, are unquestionably very impressive and in short supply. (DM)

● **Cabernet Sauvignon** Napa Valley★★★ £F ● **Pinot Noir** Hyde Vineyard★★★★ £F
○ **Chardonnay** Russian River★★★ £E

IRON HORSE VINEYARDS Sonoma Green Valley www.ironhorsevineyards.com

Owner: Sterling family/Forrest Tancer 9786 Ross Station Road, Sebastopol, CA 95472
Like MARIMAR TORRES, Iron Horse is located in the cool Sonoma Green Valley AVA. As a result it produces some of the very best sparkling wines in California. As well as the regular sparkling cuvées, there is a stylish Blanc de Noirs called Wedding Cuvée. The Russian Cuvée has a slightly higher dosage

and the Tête de Cuvée Brut LD is late disgorged after up to eight years on yeast. An extensive range of still wines is also produced, most notably Cabernet (both a Blend One and Two), Merlot, Sangiovese and Viognier under the T Bar T label, sourced from the vineyard of the same name in the Alexander Valley. Stylish and elegant Chardonnay and Pinot Noir are vinified from cool estate vineyards. (DM)

● **Pinot Noir** Estate★★★ £D
○ **Chardonnay** Estate★★★ £D
○ **Classic Vintage Brut** Sonoma Green Valley★★★ £D   ○ **Blanc de Blancs** Sonoma Green Valley★★★ £E
◎ **Brut Rose Sonoma** Green Valley★★ £D

KENDALL-JACKSON Sonoma County   www.kj.com   A: KJn

Owner: Jackson family   5007 Fulton Road, Fulton, CA 95439
Vast, private wine company, founded by Jess Jackson, producing an extensive range under its own label and also owning or part-owning a considerable number of wine operations in the premium-wine sector throughout California. Leading brands include Camelot (good value from the Central Coast), EDMEADES, LA CREMA and Pepi, and the company also has interests in Italy (VILLA ARCENO), Chile (CALINA), Argentina (Tapiz) and Australia. Jess Jackson and his wife Barbara Banke have connections with the HARTFORD FAMILY WINERY and MATANZAS CREEK, as well as owning CAMBRIA, STONESTREET and VÉRITÉ, and a number of independently run estates have been set up to produce top quality reds. The LOKOYA wines emanate from single-vineyard, benchland and mountain-vineyard sites, while the ATALON labels are drawn from varied sources. The super-premium CARDINALE is blended from Napa and Sonoma fruit sources. Under the Kendall-Jackson logo, more affordable wines include the Collage reds and Vintners Reserve red and whites. The Grand Reserve label is a step up, producing cool-climate wines from coastal vineyards, while the Vineyard Series wines are sourced from select sites that show good potential at a moderate price. The top wines under the K-J label are the Great Estates and the Stature series. At the top end, the wines are good to very good but, with the reds in particular, you feel more finesse and less overt muscle would take them a step further. (DM)

Kendall-Jackson
● **Cabernet Sauvignon** Buckeye Vineyard★★ £E   Great Estates Alexander Valley★★★ £F   Stature★★★★ £G
● **Pinot Noir** Great Estates Monterey★★ £E
● **Zinfandel/Shiraz** Collage California★ £B   ● **Zinfandel** Great Estates Dry Creek Valley★ £E
○ **Chardonnay** Grand Reserve★★ £C   Great Estates Sonoma Coast★★★ £E
○ **Chardonnay** Great Estates Arroyo Seco★★★ £E   Stature★★★★ £F

KISTLER Russian River Valley   A: WTs

Owner: Steve Kistler   4707 Vine Hill Road, Sebastopol, CA 95472
This has long been a name associated with some of the greatest California Chardonnay. More recently Steve Kistler has been producing some marvellous, rich and vibrant Pinot Noirs as well. Both varieties are made in very small lots from a number of different sites throughout Sonoma as well as the Russian River Valley. The Kistler Vineyard, Durrell Vineyard, Dutton Ranch, Hudson Vineyard, McCrea Vineyard, Vine Hill, Hirsch and Camp Meeting Ridge have all been sources of wines that are invariably of at least four-star quality. Cuvée Cathleen is the top Chardonnay, while the ultimate expressions of Pinot Noir here are Cuvée Elizabeth from the Occidental Vineyard and Cuvée Catherine. The Chardonnays are characterised by full, rich, honeyed notes along with an elegant, mineral core; the Pinots can be explosive with youthful, weighty tannins, suggesting real cellaring potential. (DM)

● **Pinot Noir** Sonoma County★★★ £E   Kistler Vineyard✪✪✪✪✪ £F
○ **Chardonnay** Sonoma County★★★ £E   Dutton Ranch★★★★★ £F
○ **Chardonnay** Hudson Vineyard✪✪✪✪✪ £F   Kistler Vineyard✪✪✪✪✪ £F

LA CREMA Russian River Valley www.lacrema.com A: KJn

Owner: Kendall-Jackson 3690 Laughlin Road, Windsor, CA 95492
A smaller winery in the Kendall-Jackson empire, La Crema, owned and run by sisters Laura Jackson-Giron and Jennifer Jackson, produces good, well-crafted and reasonably priced Pinot Noir and Chardonnay, along with Viognier, Zinfandel and now Syrah as well. These are good value, if not wines to set the world alight. The Chardonnay is typically ripe and exotic with tropical notes and evident oak, the reds are marked by forward, ripe berry fruit. Russian River and Carneros bottlings are a step up. (DM)
● **Pinot Noir** Sonoma Coast★★ £C Russian River★★ £D Carneros★★★ £D
● **Zinfandel** Sonoma County★★ £C
O **Chardonnay** Sonoma Coast★★ £C Russian River★★★ £C   O **Viognier** Sonoma Valley★★ £C

LANDMARK Sonoma Valley www.landmarkwine.com A: Lay

Owner: Colhoun family 101 Adobe Canyon Road, Kenwood, CA 95452
Very fine and stylish Chardonnays and Pinot Noirs are made on this property by winemaker Eric Stern. During the mid-1990s roving wine consultant Helen Turley of MARCASSIN provided additional input and direction. There is a commitment here to producing wines from the ripest fruit from low-yielding, meticulously-tended vineyards and with minimal intervention. Chardonnay is the main focus, the Overlook label providing great value. The wines are in the rich, lightly tropical vein with nutty oak but impressive grip and structure as well. The Grand Detour Pinot Noir is sourced from the high-altitude Van der Kamp vineyards of Sonoma Mountain and the wine is structured and concentrated with a gamey undercurrent. In addition a small amount of equally impressive, ripe and forward Pinot Noir is produced from the Kastania Vineyard. (DM)
● **Pinot Noir** Grand Detour★★★★ £E
O **Chardonnay** Overlook Vineyard★★★ £D Damaris Reserve★★★★ £E Lorenzo Vineyard★★★★ £E

LAUREL GLEN Sonoma Mountain www.laurelglen.com A: Eno

Owner: Patrick Campbell Box 1419, Glen Ellen, CA 95442
Small winegrowing operation with some 16 ha (40 acres) of prime vineyards planted to Cabernet Sauvignon, Merlot and Cabernet Franc. Cabernet Sauvignon is very much the dominant variety. The property has thin, rocky and superbly drained soils which provide an excellent base for producing around 3,000 cases a year of explosive Cabernet Sauvignon and a second wine Counterpoint. Patrick Campbell also produces three excellent youthful gluggers. 'Reds' is sourced from a variety of California locations and is based on old-vine Zinfandel, while Terra Rosa is a Cabernet Sauvignon from Chile's Central Valley, as is Villa Santiago, which has a little Malbec in the blend. More serious are Za Zin, produced from ancient vines planted in California's Central Valley, and Quintana, a dark vibrant Cabernet Sauvignon from a number of North Coast vineyard sources. (DM)
● **Cabernet Sauvignon** Sonoma Mountain★★★★ £E ● **Counterpoint** Sonoma Mountain★★ £D
● **Za Zin** Lodi★★ £B

LYNMAR WINERY Russian River Valley www.lynmarwinery.com A: Vin

Owner: Lyn and Mara Fritz 3909 Frei Road, Sebastopol, CA 95472
Very good newly established Russian River winery with vineyards at their own Quail Hill Ranch. The first vintage released was in 1996. Production is solely concentrated on hand-crafted Chardonnay and Pinot Noir. The regular estate bottlings are labelled Quail Vineyard and offer very good value for money. Reserves of both varieties are produced as well as limited bottling Quail Cuvées, which are more

restrained in style. The top wines are the Five Sisters bottlings which are a significant step up in both quality and price. The Chardonnay, particularly, is marked by super-ripe opulent fruit and layer upon layer of flavour. The Pinot Noirs are full of of rich dark berry fruit and spicy oak, varying from around 30 per cent for the regular estate wine to 80 per cent for the Five Sisters. A very limited production Pinot Noir, Requiem is also produced. (DM)

● **Pinot Noir** Quail★★★ £D Reserve★★★★ £E Five Sisters★★★★★ £F
O **Chardonnay** Estate★★★★ £D Quail Cuvée★★★★ £E Five Sisters★★★★★ £F

MARCASSIN Sonoma Coast

Owner: Helen Turley & John Wetlaufer PO Box 332, Calistoga, CA 94515
Helen Turley has achieved a cult reputation among California winemakers, consulting to some of the top producers throughout the North Coast. In 1990 she and her husband John Wetlaufer established the Marcassin winery and have developed their own vineyard, planted to Pinot Noir and Chardonnay. Other Chardonnay cuvées are also produced from the Lorenzo Vineyard, Three Sisters and Upper Barn, with Pinot Noir from Blue Slide Ridge and the Three Sisters vineyards. The wines are produced in tiny amounts, only a couple of hundred cases per bottling, and will be nigh on impossible to find. Their reputation is formidable and you can expect the wines invariably to be of at least four-star quality, often five. They are very expensive. (DM)

MARIMAR TORRES Sonoma Green Valley www.marimarestate.com A: JEF

Owner: Marimar Torres 11400 Graton Road, Sebastopol, CA 95472
Based in the cool Sonoma Green Valley sub-appellation, Miguel TORRES' sister Marimar established this operation in 1986, planting the small 33-ha (81-acre) Don Miguel vineyard equally between Chardonnay and Pinot Noir. A new property in the Freestone Valley on the Sonoma Coast is also being planted to Pinot Noir. There is a European approach to viticulture with high vine density helping to ensure low-yielding, piercing fruit. The vineyards are tended entirely organically. The wines are restrained and well balanced. (DM)

● **Pinot Noir** Don Miguel Vineyard★★★ £E
O **Chardonnay** Don Miguel Vineyard★★★ £E

MARTINELLI Russian River Valley www.martinelliwinery.com A: Vin

Owner: Steve Martinelli 3360 River Road, Windsor, CA 95492
Steve Martinelli and winemaker Helen Turley produce brilliant Zinfandel, some of the very best in the state; the Jackass Hill is a benchmark for all. You can also find very classy Chardonnay and Pinot Noir here sourced from a number of sites. These are wines of real complexity and style. Pinot is pro-duced in very small quantities, barely 300 cases per bottling, but you can invariably expect wines of at least three stars, often four. The Chardonnay is honeyed and toasty but with an intense, mineral complexity. There are a number of bottlings of this too, with Gold Ridge and Woolsey Road again numbering barely 300 to 400 cases each. (DM)

● **Zinfandel** Giuseppe & Luisa★★★★ £E Jackass Hill✪✪✪✪✪ £E
● **Pinot Noir** Blue Slide Ridge★★★★ £F
O **Chardonnay** Charles Ranch★★★★ £E Martinelli Road★★★★ £E
O **Gewürztraminer** Martinelli Vineyard★★★ £C O **Sauvignon Blanc** Martinelli Vineyard★★★ £B

MATANZAS CREEK Sonoma County www.matanzascreek.com A: May

Owner: Jess Jackson & Barbara Banke 6097 Bennett Valley Road, Santa Rosa, CA 95404
Medium-sized operation producing mainly Chardonnay, Sauvignon Blanc, Merlot and an increasing amount of impressive Syrah, with total volume around 40,000 cases annually. The winery produced some stunning wines during the late 1980s and early 90s, but more recent offerings have been disappointing. Indeed, prior to the involvement of Jess Jackson the wines were better known for their lofty prices than their quality, but with the Jackson influence this winery looks like it will be back in the top division. Small amounts of a powerful Reserve Merlot, very pricey Journey meritage blend and a promising Mendocino Viognier are also now being made. (DM)

● **Merlot** Sonoma Valley★★★ £E
O **Sauvignon Blanc** Sonoma Valley★★ £C O **Chardonnay** Sonoma Valley★★ £E

PETER MICHAEL Knights Valley www.petermichaelwinery.com A: Vin

Owner: Peter Michael 12400 Ida Clayton Road, Knights Valley, Calistoga, CA 94515
Sir Peter Michael's Knights Valley winery has, for well over a decade, been producing very fine cool-climate wines, with mountain vineyard sources a key element. The Chardonnay cuvées are all very impressive with a combination of rich, ripe, honeyed fruit and deftly handled oak. The combination of different clones, native yeast fermentation and careful selection in the vineyard and cellar all contribute. Sauvignon Blanc is stylish and not dissimilar to top white Graves – it is barrel-fermented with lees-ageing and *bâtonnage* but is tight and structured with a mineral restraint. The Moulin Rouge Pinot is a more recent addition from the famed Pisoni vineyard in the Santa Lucia Highlands. The top red, Les Pavots, is from the vineyard of the same name and is a dark, brooding blend of Cabernet Sauvignon, Merlot and Cabernet Franc. It is among the finest Bordeaux blends in California and requires a minimum of six to seven years' age to show at its best. (DM)

● **Pinot Noir** Le Moulin Rouge★★★ £F Les Pavots Knights Valley★★★★ £G
O **Sauvignon Blanc** Les Après-Midi★★★★ £F
O **Chardonnay** La Carrière★★★★ £F Belle Côte★★★★ £F Mon Plaisir★★★★ £G
O **Chardonnay** Cuvee Indigene★★★★★ £G

MOON MOUNTAIN VINEYARD Sonoma Valley A: Bib

Owner: Chalone Wine Group 1700 Moon Mountain Drive, Sonoma, CA 95476
In late 2002 the CARMENET winery, where the Moon Mountain Cabernet had been produced, was sold to BERINGER BLASS estates. Included in the sale were the ripe and exuberant Zinfandel Evangelo Vineyard and stylish Sauvignon/Semillon Reserve. Time will tell how the wines fare under new ownership. Chalone retained ownership of the original estate vineyard and winery, as well as Dynamite Vineyards label. The Cabernet Reserve is a classically ripe, full, almost chocolatey style. Powerful certainly, but there could be more finesse. (DM)

● **Cabernet Sauvignon** Moon Mountain Reserve★★★ £F Dynamite North Coast★★ £D

ROBERT MUELLER Russian River Valley A: Vin

Owner: Robert & Lori Mueller 120 Foss Creek Circle, Healdsburg, CA 95448
The Muellers' small family winery, in the centre of Healdsburg, produces good, rich and stylish Pinot Noir and Chardonnay. Chardonnay is in a ripe, classically forward California style and should be approached in its youth. The Pinots show impressive deep berry fruit, with some gamey elements and supple, well-balanced tannins. As well as Emily's Cuvée, tiny quantities of two additional Pinots are

produced: Pearlessence Vineyard and the pricey Summa Vineyard. (DM)

● **Pinot Noir** Emily's Cuvee★★★ £E
○ **Chardonnay** LB★★★ £E

PACIFIC ECHO   Anderson Valley   www.cliquot.com   A: G&C

Owner: LVMH   8501 Hwy 128, Philo, CA 95466
Renamed from Scharffenberger Cellars, this sparkling wine producer is now benefiting from the influence of its parent company and in particular guidance from VEUVE CLICQUOT. These are good, straightforward bubblies, fashioned in a ripe, full-bodied style. Nevertheless, they do possess sufficient acidity to give them balance and grip. (DM)

○ **Brut** Non Vintage★★ £C Vintage Blanc de Blancs★★ £D Vintage Private Reserve★★★ £E
◉ **Brut** Vintage Rose★★ £D

PAPAPIETRO PERRY   Russian River Valley   www.papapietro-perry.com   A: WTs

Owner: Ben Papapietro & Bruce Perry   4441 Westside Road, Healdsburg, CA 95448
Very newly established, small but high quality warehouse winery producing two very good Pinot Noirs and a tiny amount of Chardonnay. Production of the Pinots is a mere 650 cases each. The wines are dark and richly concentrated being aged in 70 per cent new oak which is seamlessly integrated. Both are bottled unfined and unfiltered. The Peters Vineyard, from the Sonoma Coast offers just a little more depth and intensity. (DM)

● **Pinot Noir** Russian River★★★★ £E Peters Vineyard★★★★ £E

A RAFANELLI   Dry Creek Valley

Owner: Dave Rafanelli   4685 West Dry Creek Road, Healdsburg, CA 95448
Dave Rafanelli has some excellent hillside vineyard sites in Dry Creek Valley from which he ensures top quality fruit for his own estate wines. He not only produces superlative old-vine, highly complex and characterful Zinfandel, but some impressive Cabernet Sauvignon as well. The estate vineyards are dry-farmed (i.e.without recourse to irrigation) and yields are always kept to a minimum. (DM)

● **Zinfandel** Dry Creek★★★★ £C
● **Cabernet Sauvignon** Dry Creek★★★ £D

RAVENSWOOD   Sonoma Valley   www.ravenswood-wine.com   A: JAr

Owner: Canandaigua   18701 Gehricke Road, Sonoma, CA 95476
No longer small, with production now at some 400,000 cases a year, this Sonoma winery has a major focus on good to very good Zinfandel. The winery was founded in 1976 by winemaker Joel Peterson and partner Reed Foster, who have now sold a controlling interest to Constellation Brands, a part of Canandaigua. Vintners Blend is a good budget label, including Zinfandel, Merlot and Chardonnay. In the second tier are the County Series wines, sourced from vineyards throughout the state, including several Zinfandels. The top wines are in the vineyard-designated series. Along with the many Zinfandels offered there are two meritage reds, Ranch Salina and Pickberry, plus Icon, a blend of Syrah, Grenache and Mourvèdre. Chardonnay comes from the Sangiacomo Vineyard. Top reds are fine cellar prospects. It will be interesting to see whether quality is maintained under the new ownership. (DM)

● **Cabernet Sauvignon** Sonoma County★★ £D ● **Merlot** Sonoma County★★ £C
● **Rancho Salina** Moon Mountain★★★ £E

● **Zinfandel** Monte Bello ★★★★ £E Old Hill Ranch★★★★ £E
● **Zinfandel** Amador County★★ £C Napa Valley★★ £C Sonoma County Old Vines★★★ £C
O **Chardonnay** Sangiacomo Vineyard★★ £D

J ROCHIOLI   Russian River Valley   A: RsW

Owner: Tom Rochioli   6192 Westside Road, Healdsburg, CA 95448
The Rochioli family have been grape growers for far longer than they have been wine producers. They do however produce some of the best Pinot Noir and Chardonnay from the Russian River, along with impressive Sauvignon Blanc and big, full, very rich Zinfandel, of which there is a striking Sodini Vineyard bottling. As well as the estate Pinot Noir and Chardonnay, there are a number of single-vineyard bottlings of each produced in very small quantities, almost invariably rating three stars or more. (DM)
● **Pinot Noir** Estate★★★★ £E ● **Zinfandel** Estate★★★ £D
O **Chardonnay** Estate★★★★ £D O **Sauvignon Blanc** Estate★★★ £C

ROEDERER ESTATE Anderson Valley www.roederer-estate.com   A: MMD

*Owner: **Louis Roederer SA**   4501 Highway 128, Philo, CA 95466*
Champagne house LOUIS ROEDERER has set up its California outpost in the cool Anderson Valley. Unlike a number of their competitors they concentrate on producing just three wines. The regular Brut NV, made from all three Champagne grapes, and Rosé, from Pinot Noir, provide reasonable value and a riper, fuller style than their French counterparts. The Brut L'Ermitage is altogether more serious, a very well structured blend of Pinot Noir and Chardonnay that is both long and complex. (DM)
O **Brut** L'Ermitage★★★★ £E O **Brut** NV★★ £C
◉ **Brut** Rosé BV★★ £D

SAUSAL   Alexander Valley www.sausalwinery.com   A: L&S

Owner: Sausal family   7370 Highway 128, Healdsburg, CA 95448
The Sausal family produce around 10,000 cases a year from their 50 ha (125 acres) of estate vineyards. As the top Zinfandel label suggests, some of the vines here are over 100 years of age and it shows in the quality of the reds. Both the Private Reserve and Century Vines are barrel-aged in top-class French oak to add complexity and depth. The resulting wines are supple but finely structured. (DM)
● **Cabernet Sauvignon** Estate★★★ £D
● **Zinfandel** Family★★ £C Private Reserve★★★ £D Century Vines★★★★ £D

SEGHESIO   Dry Creek Valley www.seghesio.com   A: Lib

Owner: Seghesio family   14730 Grove Street, Healdsburg , CA 95448
The Seghesio family have been based in the Sonoma Valley since 1895, although they only decided to bottle their own fruit as recently as 1983. Today there are 162 ha (400 acres) of prime vineyard sites which are producing some of the best Zinfandel and Italian-style wines in California. The Zins all have marvellous depth and purity – full of ripe fruit but complex and very intense. There's good to very good Sangiovese, with the newly added Venom from Rattlesnake Hill produced from yields of just 2.5 tons to the acre. The wine stands out among California examples of the variety. Ommagio (meaning 'homage'), like many top cuvées produced by winegrowers around the world, celebrates earlier generations. It is a stylish blend of Barbera, Sangiovese, Merlot and Cabernet Sauvignon. (DM)
● **Pinot Noir** Keyhole Ranch★★★ £D ● **Barbera** California★★ £D

- **Sangiovese** Alexander Valley★★ £C Old Vine "Chianti Station"★★★ £D 'Venom'★★★★ £D
- **Omaggio** Alexander Valley★★★★ £E
- **Zinfandel** Sonoma Valley★★★ £C Home Ranch★★★★ £D Cortina★★★★ £D Old Vine★★★★ £D
- O **Pinot Grigio** Russian River★★ £B O **Arneis** Russian River★★ £B

SIDURI Russian River Valley www.siduri.com   A: Vin

Owner: Diana & Adam Lee 980 Airway Court, Suite C, Santa Rosa, CA 95403

An extensive range of fine and stylish Pinot Noirs, as well as impressive Syrah from Novy vineyard, have been made by this small warehouse operation on the outskirts of Santa Rosa since its first vintage in 1994. The Lees practise an absolutely minimalist approach to winegrowing and to date no wine they have bottled has been either fined or filtered. The objective is to produce wines that are expressive of the region or individual *terroir* from which they have been sourced. A range of single-vineyard bottlings number the Hirsch and high-profile Pisoni vineyards among them. Pinot is now sourced all the way from the Willamette Valley in Oregon down to the new Santa Rita AVA in Santa Barbara County – the only problem being that there's not very much about. (DM)

- **Pinot Noir** Sonoma County★★★ £E Santa Lucia★★★ £E Van der Kamp Vineyard★★★★ £F

WH SMITH Sonoma County   A: Vin

Owner: Bill Smith 13719 Dog Bar Road, Grass Valley, CA 95492

Bill Smith established his reputation for making great California reds when he ran the LA JOTA winery on Howell Mountain, creating massive and powerful Cabernet Sauvignon and Petite Sirah – some of legendary proportions. The Smiths have sold their interest in La Jota in order to pursue their most recent venture, vinifying stylish Pinot Noir on the Sonoma Coast. As well as the intense and complex Hellenthal Vineyard, a Sonoma Coast bottling is also offered. The style is one of elegance rather than power, with an attractive undercurrent of piercing, red-berry fruit and well-judged oak. (DM)

- **Pinot Noir** Hellenthal Vineyard★★★ £E

SONOMA-CUTRER Russian River Valley www.sonomacutrer.com   A: Hal

Owner: Brown Forman 4401 Slusser Road, Windsor, CA 95492

Originally established as a top-notch producer of Chardonnay by Brice Cutrer Jones, the Sonoma-Cutrer star has waned a little, but the wines are nevertheless consistent, particularly the two leading cuvées. The winery refers to these as its Grand Cru program. The tiny production top wine is the Founders Reserve, selected from the five best barrels of the vintage and bottled without filtration. (DM)

- O **Chardonnay** Russian River Ranches★★ £C The Cutrer★★★ £D Les Pierres★★★ £D

ST FRANCIS VINEYARDS Sonoma Valley www.stfrancis.com   A: HMA

Owner: Joe Canton, Lloyd Martin, Kopf family 100 Pythian Road, Santa Rosa, CA 95409

Impressive, medium-sized Sonoma winery. An extensive range is produced and at the top end the quality is striking. Zinfandels, both Old Vines and Pagani Ranch, are huge, brooding, super-ripe examples of the variety. Perhaps just a little more elegance and refinement would take these Zins to a higher level. Nuns Canyon bottlings of both Merlot and Cabernet are impressive and very stylish. The Cabernet Kings Ridge Reserve, the top label, is powerful, refined and very well crafted. It will age gracefully and needs a minimum of six years. (DM)

- **Zinfandel** Old Vines★★★ £D Pagani Ranch★★★ £E

● **Merlot** Sonoma County★ £C   Behler Vineyard★★★ £E   Nuns Canyon Vineyard★★★ £E
● **Cabernet Sauvignon** Sonoma County★★ £C   Nuns Canyon Vineyard★★★ £E
● **Cabernet Sauvignon** Kings Ridge Vineyard Reserve★★★★ £G
O **Chardonnay** Sonoma County★ £C   Behler Vineyard★★ £D

STEELE Lake County   www.steelewines.com   A: Vin

Owner: Jed Steele   4350 Thomas Drive at Highway 29, Kelseyville, CA 95451

Jed Steele has enormous experience of the wine business in California, having previously been the founding winemaker at KENDALL-JACKSON. Under his own label he now produces an extensive range, with the top-of-the-line examples coming from an almost bewildering array of single-vineyard sources. These are not only impressive and stylish but represent very good value for money. Chardonnay is on the one hand rich and opulent, on the other balanced by a fine mineral undercurrent, and there are two unusual late harvest examples from the Dupratt and Sangiacomo vineyards. The reds are supple, well-structured and accessible at a young age. They will however develop well in bottle. Shooting Star is the winery's second label, providing good fruit-driven wines at very fair prices. Often these will be one-, sometimes two-star wines. (DM)

● **Pinot Noir** Carneros★★★ £D   Sangiacomo Vineyard★★★ £D   Bien Nacido★★★ £E
● **Cabernet Franc** Lake County★★ £C   Merlot Lake County★★★ £D
● **Zinfandel** California★★★ £C   Catfish Vineyard★★★ £D
● **Syrah** Lake County★★ £C   Parmalee-Hill★★★ £D
O **Chardonnay** Cuvée California★★★ £C   Lolonis Vineyard★★★ £D   Dupratt Vineyard★★★ £D
O **Chardonnay** Bien Nacido★★★★ £D   Durrell Vineyard★★★★ £D
O **Pinot Blanc** Santa Barbara County★★ £C

STONESTREET Alexander Valley   www.stonestreetwines.com   A: KJn, WTs

Owner: Kendall-Jackson   7111 Highway 128, Healdsburg, CA 95448

One of a number of high-quality, medium-sized wineries in the Jackson family empire. Merlot, Chardonnay and the meritage red Legacy , a blend dominated by Cabernet Sauvignon, are all impressive. Chardonnay is in a rich, tropical style, with the top bottlings showing refinement and the structure for mid-term cellaring. The reds are big, powerful and brooding, marked by high alcohol. They are rich almost chocolatey, with just the occasional green note drifting in, in lesser vintages. A fruit-driven Sauvignon Blanc from the Upper Barn Vineyard has also been added to the range. (DM)

● **Merlot** Alexander Valley★★★ £C   ● **Legacy** Alexander Valley★★★★ £F
● **Cabernet Sauvignon** Alexander Valley★★ £D   Christopher's Vineyard★★★ £G
O **Chardonnay** Sonoma County★★★ £C   Block Sixty-Six★★★ £D   Upper Barn★★★★ £E

VÉRITÉ Sonoma Valley   www.veritewines.com   A: May

Owner: Kendall-Jackson   4611 Thomas Road Healdsburg CA 95448

Recently established Jackson family premium operation specialising in Bordeaux red styles. The wines are all hand-crafted from various sites throughout Sonoma County. The vineyard sources are classic mountain terroirs and winemaker Pierre Seillan is able to source what the winery refers to as micro-crus, producing wines from the very best blocks of a number of estates. Fruit comes from the Alexander, Bennett and Knights Valleys as well as Carneros and Atlas Peak. La Joie emulates the Left Bank of Bordeaux it is a blend of roughly two-thirds Cabernet Sauvignon with the balance Merlot. Youthfully backward and firmly structured, it is nevertheless very concentrated with fine, intense very ripe dark berry fruit. La Muse, 90 per cent Merlot and 10 Cabernet Sauvignon is more forward and opulent. Full of dark plum and spicy oak, the wine is richly textured, supple but finely structured.

Undoubtedly the option of being able to source superb fruit from a number of sites adds complexity. Very impressive, the wines need just an extra dimension to take them into the absolute top division. The third wine in the portfolio Le Desir, a Saint-Émilion style blend of Cabernet Franc and Merlot was released for the first time in the second half of 2003. (DM)

● **La Joie** Sonoma County★★★★★ £G **La Muse** Sonoma County★★★★★ £G

WILLIAMS SELYEM   Russian River Valley   A: Vin

Owner: John & Kathe Dyson   1861 Lewis Street, Ballard CA 93463
The Dysons purchased this classic Sonoma property from founders Burt Williams and Ed Selyem in 1998. Winemaker Bob Cabral has stayed on and continues to make the same artisanal style of Chardonnay and Pinot Noir as Williams and Selyem. The Pinots are rich and concentrated, marked by their powerful, earthy tannins, while the Chardonnay can be lusciously rich but with none of the overt tropical notes found in neighbouring wines. A plethora of single-vineyard labels are produced every vintage and rarely are these less than four stars. These are Sonoma wines for the longer haul. There are two very interesting, rich and intense sweet wines from Gewürztraminer and Muscat. Both are opulent in style but well-structured with a fine mineral-acid balance. (DM)

● **Pinot Noir** Sonoma County★★★★ £E Russian River★★★★★ £F Hirsch Vineyard★★★★★ £F
● **Zinfandel** Russian River★★★★ £E Bacigalupi Vineyard★★★★ £E
O **Chardonnay** North Coast★★★★ £F Allen Vineyard★★★★ £F
O **Gewürztraminer** Late Harvest San Benito County★★★★★ £G
O **Muscat Canelli** Late Harvest Russian River Valley★★★★ £G

OTHER WINES OF NOTE

ALDERBROOK ● **Zinfandel** Russian River Reserve £E O **Sauvignon Blanc** Dry Creek £B
ANCIEN ● **Pinot Noir** Carneros £E O **Chardonnay** Carneros £E
BANNISTER ● **Pinot Noir** Floodgate Mountain £D ● **Zinfandel** Dry Creek £C
BELVEDERE ● **Pinot Noir** Russian River £D O **Chardonnay** Russian River £C
BOEGER ● **Cabernet Sauvignon** Eldorado £C ● **Barbera** Eldorado £C
● **Tempranillo** Reserve £C ● **Zinfandel** Old Vine £C
BOGLE VINEYARDS ● **Zinfandel** Walker Vineyard £B ● **Petite Sirah** California £B
O **Chardonnay** California £B O **Chenin Blanc** California £B
AUGUST BRIGGS ● **Pinot Noir** Russian River £D O **Chardonnay** Russian River £D
CANEPA CELLARS O **Chardonnay** Gauer Ranch Adobe III £E
SEAN CAPIAUX ● **Pinot Noir** Widdoes Vineyard £E Pisoni Vineyard £F
CARLISLE ● **Syrah** Sonoma County £E ● **Zinfandel** Dry Creek £D Two Acres Russian River £E
CARMENET ● **Zinfandel** Evangelo Vineyard £D O **Sauvignon Semillon** Reserve £C
CÈAGO ● **Merlot** Mendocino £E
CHATEAU SOUVERAIN ● **Cabernet Sauvignon** Winemakers Reserve £E
CHRISTOPHER CREEK ● **Petite Sirah** Russian River £D ● **Syrah** Russian River £C
DAVID COFFARO ● **Zinfandel** Dry Creek Valley £C Estate Old Vines £C
BR COHN ● **Cabernet Sauvignon** Olive Hill Special Selection £F O **Chardonnay** Joseph Herman £D
COTURRI ● **Zinfandel** Sonoma Valley P Coturri Family Vineyards £C
DAVIS BYNUM ● **Pinot Noir** Le Pinot Rochioli Vineyard £F
DE LOACH ● **Zinfandel** Russian River OFS £D O **Chardonnay** Russian River OFS £D
DUMOL ● **Pinot Noir** Russian River £F O **Chardonnay** Russian River £E
DUXOUP WINE WORKS ● **Syrah** Dry Creek Valley £C ● **Charbono** Napa Valley £B
MERRY EDWARDS ● **Pinot Noir** Russian River £D Olivet Lane £E Klopp Ranch £E
FAILLA JORDAN ● **Syrah** Que Syrah Vineyard £E
FERRARI CARANO ● **Cabernet Sauvignon** Tre Monte £E O **Chardonnay** Tre Monte £E
FISHER ● **Cabernet Sauvignon** Coach Insignia £F Wedding Vineyard £G

O **Chardonnay** Coach Insignia £D

FLOWERS ● **Pinot Noir** Camp Meeting Ridge £F O **Chardonnay** Porter-Bass £E

ADRIAN FOG ● **Pinot Noir** Floodgate £F C23 Russian River £F Hawkeye Vineyard £F

GREENWOOD RIDGE VINEYARDS ● **Zinfandel** Scherrer Vineyards £C

GUENOC ● **Cabernet Sauvignon** Beckstoffer IV Reserve £E ● **Petite Sirah** Estate £E
O **Chardonnay** Genevieve Magoon Reserve £E

GUNDLACH-BUNDSCHU ● **Zinfandel** Rhinefarm Vineyards £D
● **Cabernet Sauvignon** Rhinefarm Vineyards £D

HANDLEY ● **Pinot Noir** Reserve £E O Brut Anderson Valley Vintage £D

HANNA ● **Cabernet Sauvignon** £E Bismarck Ranch £F ● **Zinfandel** Bismarck Ranch £E

HAYWOOD ● **Zinfandel** Los Chamizal Vineyard £C

HIDDEN CELLARS ● **Petite Sirah** Heritage Eaglepoint Ranch £D ● **Sorcery** £D

HOP KILN ● **Zinfandel** Primitivo Vineyard £C ● **Marty Griffin's Big Red** California £B

J WINE COMPANY O **Chardonnay** Russian River £E O **Pinot Gris** Russian River £C O **Vintage Brut** £D

JORDAN O **Chardonnay** Estate £D ● **Cabernet Sauvignon** Estate £E

KENWOOD VINEYARDS ● **Zinfandel** Jack London £C
● **Cabernet Sauvignon** Jack London £E Artist Series £F

KUNDE ESTATE ● **Cabernet Sauvignon** Reserve £D O **Sauvignon Blanc** Magnolia Lane £C

LAMBERT BRIDGE ● **Zinfandel** Dry Creek £C Crane Creek Cuvee £E

LANCASTER ESTATE ● **Lancaster** Alexander Valley £F

LAZY CREEK O **Gewürztraminer** Anderson Valley £C

LIMERICK LANE ● **Zinfandel** Collins Vineyard £D

LITTORAI ● **Pinot Noir** Hirsch Vineyard £E

MARIETTA CELLARS ● **Syrah** California £C

MAYO FAMILY O **Chardonnay** Barrel Select £D

McCRAY RIDGE ● **Merlot** Two Moon Vineyard £F

McDOWELL ● **Syrah** Reserve £C O **Viognier** Reserve £C

MICHEL-SCHLUMBERGER ● **Cabernet Sauvignon** Reserve Dry Creek Valley £D

MURPHY-GOODE ● **Cabernet Sauvignon** Brenda Block £E O **Chardonnay** Sonoma County £C

NALLE WINERY ● **Zinfandel** Dry Creek Valley £C

NAVARRO VINEYARDS ● **Pinot Noir** Méthode a l'Ancienne £C O **Gewürztraminer** Anderson Valley £B

OPTIMA ● **Cabernet Sauvignon** Alexander Valley £E ● **Pinot Noir** Russian River Valley £E

PEZZI KING ● **Zinfandel** Maple Vineyard £D

RANDOM RIDGE ● **Cabernets** Mount Veeder £D ● **Zinfandel** Old Wave £D

QUIVIRA ● **Zinfandel** Dry Creek £D O **Sauvignon Blanc** Fig Tree Vineyard £B

RUTZ CELLARS ● **Pinot Noir** Weir Vineyards £E O **Chardonnay** Dutton Ranch £D

SCHERRER VINEYARD ● **Cabernet Sauvignon** Alexander Valley £F ● **Pinot Noir** Russian River £E
● **Zinfandel** Old and Mature Vines £E

SEBASTIANI ● **Cabernet Sauvignon** Cherry Block £F ● **Mourvèdre** Domenici Vineyard £D

SEBASTOPOL ● **Pinot Noir** Dutton Ranch £D ● **Syrah** Dutton Ranch £E
O **Chardonnay** Dutton Ranch£D

SIMI ● **Cabernet Sauvignon** Reserve £G O **Sendal** Reserve £C

SKEWIS ● **Pinot Noir** Floodgate Vineyard £F Montgomery Vineyard £F

SOLITUDE ● **Pinot Noir** Sangiacomo Vineyard £D O **Chardonnay** Sangiacomo Vineyard £D

STUHLMULLER ● **Cabernet Sauvignon** Alexander Valley £E O **Chardonnay** Alexander Valley £C

JOSEPH SWAN ● **Pinot Noir** Steiner Vineyard £D ● **Zinfandel** Frati Ranch £D Stellwagen Vineyard £D

TARIUS ● **Pinot Noir** Russian River £E ● **Zinfandel** Aldine Vineyard £D

TRENTADUE ● **Petite Sirah** Alexander Valley £C Old Patch Red £C ● **Zinfandel** Alexander Valley £C

TRIA ● **Zinfandel** Dry Creek £C

WELLINGTON VINEYARDS ● **Zinfandel** Russian River Valley £C ● **Syrah** Sonoma County £C

Author's choice (DM)

A selection of Sonoma blockbuster reds
BEHRENS AND HITCHCOCK ● **Cabernet Sauvignon** Kenefick Ranch
DEHLINGER ● **Syrah** Estate
FOPPIANO ● **Petite Sirah** Russian River Reserve
GALLO OF SONOMA ● **Cabernet Sauvignon** Estate
HARTFORD ● **Zinfandel** Russian River Valley
KENDALL JACKSON ● **Cabernet Sauvignon** Stature
MARTINELLI ● **Zinfandel** Jackass Hill
PETER MICHAEL ● **Les Pavots** Knights Valley
SEGHESIO ● **Omaggio** Alexander Valley
VÉRITÉ ● **La Joie** Sonoma County

Benchmark Pinot Noirs
GARY FARRELL ● **Pinot Noir** Rochioli Vineyard
HANZELL ● **Pinot Noir** Estate
HARTFORD COURT ● **Pinot Noir** Dutton Sanchietti Vineyard
PAUL HOBBS ● **Pinot Noir** Cuvée Agustina
KISTLER ● **Pinot Noir** Kistler Vineyard Vineyard
LYNMAR WINERY ● **Pinot Noir** Five Sisters Vineyard
PAPAPIETRO PERRY ● **Pinot Noir** Peters Vineyard
J ROCHIOLI ● **Pinot Noir** Estate
SIDURI ● **Pinot Noir** Van der Kamp Vineyard
WILLIAMS SELYEM ● **Pinot Noir** Hirsch Vineyard

A selection of cool climate Sonoma whites
ARROWOOD O **Viognier** Saralee's Vineyard
KISTLER O **Chardonnay** Hudson Vineyard
LA CREMA O **Chardonnay** Russian River Valley
LANDMARK O **Chardonnay** Damaris Reserve
LYNMAR WINERY O **Chardonnay** Five Sisters Vineyard
MARCASSIN O **Chardonnay** Marcassin Vineyard
MARTINELLI O **Chardonnay** Charles Ranch
PETER MICHAEL O **Chardonnay** Cuvee Indigene
ROEDERER ESTATE O **Brut** L'Ermitage
STEELE O **Chardonnay** Durrell Vineyard

California/Napa & Carneros

The Napa Valley has now been producing high-quality wine for over three decades and indeed many properties go back to pre-Prohibition times. As in the other major viticultural regions of California, dynamic change is continuous and new operations, particularly boutique and very small scale premium red producers, are emerging all the time. Of one thing there is no doubt: winemakers here and particularly those working with classic Bordeaux varieties, are able to charge super-premium prices. These days the top Bordeaux reds can seem relative bargains in comparison to some of their Napa counterparts. There is no question that an increasing number of truly world-class wines continue to emerge from Napa but also that there are as many that are priced too highly and quite simply struggle to justify their lofty tags. If you are looking for some very serious bottles they're certainly here, but some care and research is needed before purchasing.

Geography

The Napa Valley AVA runs along an extensive river valley stretching from north of Calistoga along the Napa River to south of the town of Napa itself and just edging towards San Pablo Bay at the northern end of San Francisco Bay. South-west of Napa, the Carneros AVA is located south of the Mayacamas Mountains and effectively divides the Sonoma and Napa Counties viticultural regions. In Napa, like Sonoma and Mendocino, the climate is moderated by cool marine breezes and coastal fog.

Northern Napa

Calistoga's benchland vineyards are the warmest in the Napa Valley, because little of the moderating sea breeze drifts this far. The topography becomes semi-mountainous to the west with the **Spring Mountain District** AVA and to the east the **Howell Mountain** AVA, which is an extension of the Coastal Ranges. There are a number of exceptional Cabernet Sauvignons, Merlots and meritage blends, produced from vineyards within these mountain AVAs. Equally impressive wines are also emerging from sites similarly cooled by altitude but on the lower slopes, both to the west, and east of the valley. These sites are characterised by both excellent aspects and soil drainage, both of which are hallmarks in the production of great wine. The key to these wines is their structure; their mountain origin gives them a unique stamp. They can be the least approachable when young but among the longest-lived and most refined of Napa's great reds. This is essentially Cabernet country but there are some good Chardonnays, one or two stylish Syrahs and Viogniers and some very good Zinfandel.

Central Napa

The central section of the Napa Valley is the heart of its best benchland vineyards for Cabernet Sauvignon and Bordeaux-style red blends. This takes in an area that runs from **St Helena** in the north to cooler **Yountville** in the south and encompasses the AVAs of **Rutherford** and **Oakville**. It is difficult to generalise as wine quality is by no means determined by the traditional Rutherford Bench yardstick: the bench is a narrow strip of vineyard stretching north of the town of Rutherford with gravel and sandy-clay soils producing potentially great wines, but in recent years a whole host of other small vineyard sites have proven to have excellent growing conditions, many of these taking the Napa Valley AVA. However, in general the wines to the north at St Helena are the ripest and most opulent, while those from Yountville have the tightest structure. These generalisations are offset by exceptional producers outperforming their neighbours and by many sites which are influenced by the sloping hills of Howell Mountain to the east and Spring Mountain and the Mayacamas to the west. As well as the Bordeaux styles, good Zinfandel and Syrah are grown throughout this stretch of vineyards.

Southern Napa

To the east of Yountville are the AVAs of **Stags Leap District** and **Atlas Peak**. To the west **Mount Veeder** provides sturdy reds with Zinfandel and Syrah increasingly successful; some fine, tightly structured Chardonnay and peachy Viognier are also produced. Stags Leap is somewhat of a conundrum. There are some very fine wines produced in these gravel soils but also a number of underperformers. Atlas Peak has so far disappointed. The winery of the same name has experimented with only moderate success with Sangiovese, Cabernet Sauvignon and Chardonnay. To the west of Napa, towards the Wild Horse Valley, the Bordeaux varieties and Chardonnay have all been successful.

Carneros

Part-Sonoma County and part-Napa County, Carneros AVA is just inland to the north of San Pablo Bay and directly affected by those cool, marine breezes. This is key for the production of sparkling base wine and it is no surprise that a number of sparkling-wine operations are based here including California offshoots of some of the big European names. Pinot Noir and Chardonnay are successful and, more surprisingly, in warmer mesoclimates some spicy, black pepper-styled Syrah, notably from the Hudson Vineyard.

A-Z Producers by region

Carneros
ACACIA
CLINE CELLARS
DOMAINE CARNEROS
GLORIA FERRER
HAVENS
SAINTSBURY

Diamond Mountain
DIAMOND CREEK

Howell Mountain
DUNN VINEYARDS
LA JOTA

Mount Veeder
CHATEAU POTELLE
HESS COLLECTION

Napa County
CARDINALE

Napa Valley
ABREU
ARAUJO
ARIETTA
ATALON
ROBERT BIALE
BLOCKHEADIA RINGNOSII
BRYANT FAMILY
CAFARO
CHAPPELLET
CHATEAU MONTELENA

CORISON
ROBERT CRAIG
CUVAISON
DARIOUSH
GREEN AND RED VINEYARD
HARRISON VINEYARDS
JADE MOUNTAIN
KONGSGAARD
LEWIS CELLARS
LUNA
PAHLMEYER
PATZ AND HALL
JOSEPH PHELPS
SCHRAMSBERG
SILVER OAK CELLARS
STORYBOOK MOUNTAIN VINEYARD
VIADER

Oakville
COLGIN CELLARS
DALLA VALLE
FAR NIENTE
FRANCISCAN
HARLAN ESTATE
LOKOYA
MINER FAMILY VINEYARDS
ROBERT MONDAVI
OPUS ONE
PARADIGM
PLUMPJACK
RAMEY
SCREAMING EAGLE

Rutherford
BACIO DIVINO

BEAULIEU VINEYARD
CAKEBREAD CELLARS
CAYMUS
PETER FRANUS
FROG'S LEAP
GRGICH HILLS
LAIL VINEYARDS
LIVINGSTON MOFFETT
MUMM NAPA
NIEBAUM-COPPOLA ESTATE
QUINTESSA
STAGLIN FAMILY
SWANSON

Spring Mountain
CAIN CELLARS
NEWTON
STONY HILL
PHILIP TOGNI

Stags Leap
PINE RIDGE
SHAFER
STAGS LEAP WINE CELLARS

St Helena
BERINGER
DUCKHORN
FLORA SPRINGS
GRACE FAMILY
HEITZ CELLARS
SPOTTSWOODE
TURLEY CELLARS

Yountville
S ANDERSON
DOMAINE CHANDON
DOMINUS

Vintages

As elsewhere in California, it is difficult to provide a locally specific guide but there is a reasonable consistency through the region and the charts below give a fair indication of what you should expect, both in terms of quality and ageability. If you have cellared or considering purchasing some older top Cabernet then earlier vintages that are looking particularly good are 1987, 1986 and more speculatively 1978, 1974 and 1970.

California Napa & Carneros Vintages

	Cabernet and Meritage Blends	Zinfandel	Pinot Noir	Chardonnay
2002	★★★★ A	★★★★ A	★★★★ A	★★★★ A
2001	★★★★/★★★★★ A	★★★★ A	★★★★ A	★★★★ B
2000	★★/★★★ A	★★/★★★ B	★★★/★★★★ B	★★★/★★★★ B
1999	★★★/★★★★ A	★★★★ B	★★★★ B	★★★/★★★★ C
1998	★★★ B	★★/★★★ C	★★★/★★★★ C	★★★ C
1997	★★★★ A	★★★/★★★★ B	★★★★ C	★★★★ C
1996	★★★/★★★★ B	★★★/★★★★ C	★★★/★★★★ C	★★★ C
1995	★★★★ B	★★★/★★★★ C	★★★/★★★★ C	★★★★ D
1994	★★★★/★★★★★ B	★★★★ C	★★★★ C	★★★/★★★★ D
1993	★★★★ B	★★★/★★★★ C	★★★ D	★★★★ D
1992	★★★★ B	★★★/★★★★ C	★★★/★★★★ D	★★★★ D
1991	★★★★ C	★★★★ C	★★★/★★★★ D	–

ABREU Napa Valley A: THt

Owner: David Abreu 2366 Madrona Avenue, St Helena, CA 94574
David Abreu is best-known among his fellow winegrowers as a superlative viticulturalist. Numbered among his distinguished clientele are GRACE FAMILY, VIADER and PAHLMEYER. As well as his many vineyard-management commitments, he fashions a massive, super-ripe Cabernet with a hint of Merlot and Cabernet Franc from this first-class vineyard. The wine is one of the most 'collectable' in California and as such is very pricey and almost impossible to find. (DM)
● **Cabernet Sauvignon** Madrona Ranch✪✪✪✪✪ £H

ACACIA Carneros www.acaciawinery.com A: Bib

*Owner: **Chalone Group** 2750 Las Amigas Road, Napa, CA 94552*
Acacia has always produced wines that are soundly made and represent reasonable value for money if sometimes lacking a touch of real character. The wines are particularly marked by their ripe fruit and for opulent, tropical styles at competitive prices they are all good bets. Both the Chardonnays and Viognier have good weight and a rich texture. Pinot in its various guises offers bright berry fruit with greater depth and power in the Beckstoffer vineyard and smaller-production, premium De Soto vineyard examples. The range is completed by a good regular sparkling Brut. (DM)
● **Pinot Noir** Carneros★★ £D Beckstoffer Vineyard★★★ £D
○ **Viognier** Napa Valley★★ £D ○ **Chardonnay** Marsh★ £B Carneros★★ £C
○ **Brut Vintage**★★ £E

S ANDERSON Yountville www.4bubbly.com

Owner: Anderson family 1473 Yountville Crossroad, Yountville, CA 94599
Good, small producer of sparkling wines as well as a limited amount of Chardonnay and Cabernet Sauvignon. In addition to the small-volume Richard Chambers Cabernet a limited amount of rich, complex Merlot Reserve can be obtained direct from the winery. The Brut is rich and bready, its yeasty character to the fore, whereas the Blanc de Noirs is tighter and more reserved. (DM)
● **Cabernet Sauvignon** SLD★★★ £D Richard Chambers Vineyard★★★★ £F
○ **Chardonnay** Estate★★ £D ○ **Brut** Napa Valley★★★ £E ○ **Blanc de Noirs** Napa Valley★★★ £E

ARAUJO Napa Valley www.araujoestatewines.com A: THt

Owner: Bart Araujo 2155 Pickett Road, Calistoga, CA 94515
These formidable wines are all produced from the Eisele vineyard, originally owned by JOSEPH PHELPS, in the north-eastern part of the Napa Valley. As well as the Cabernet Sauvignon there is a first class Syrah, sadly produced in tiny quantities. Since its purchase by the Araujos in 1990, a considerable effort has been put into the vineyard with its superbly drained stony soils and mountain-moderated climate. Winemaker Françoise Peschon is aided by roving international wine consultant Michel Rolland. The approach is as one would expect, with rich, immensely concentrated fruit and supple and rounded tannin. The Cabernet is blended with a little Cabernet Franc, Petit Verdot and Merlot. The Sauvignon Blanc unusually has a hint of Viognier. With a total of just 16.6 ha (41 acres) under vine there is an inevitable scarcity here. While these reds are immensely ageworthy you might consider broaching them with five or six years' age. (DM)
● **Cabernet Sauvignon** Eisele Vineyard✪✪✪✪✪ £H
○ **Sauvignon Blanc** Eisele Vineyard★★★ £C

ARIETTA   Napa Valley   www.arietta.com   A: Vin

Owner: John Kongsgaard/Fritz Hatton   PO Box 349, Oakville, CA 94562
John Kongsgaard who both consults widely for other wineries as well as producing some superb Rhône styles under his own label has established a partnership here with Fritz Hatton to produce very small scale, high quality reds modelled mainly on the wines of Bordeaux. The Merlot is 100 per cent varietal, dark, cedary, exceptionally balanced and very long and complex. The Hudson H Block is more Saint-Emilion than Pomerol in style, it blends 60 per cent Cabernet Franc with the balance Merlot. It is the firmest of the trio. The Variation One is dominated by Syrah and blended unusually with Merlot. Opulent, exotic and loaded with smoky, dark fruit it is the most approachable of the wines. Given some of the stratospheric prices elsewhere, the wines look like pretty good value. All will benefit from at least four to five years cellaring and will keep very well. (DM)
● **Merlot** Napa Valley★★★★★£G   ● **H Block One Red** Napa Valley★★★★★£G
● **Variation One Red** Napa Valley★★★★★£G

ATALON   Napa Valley   www.atalon.com   A: May

*Owner: **Kendall-Jackson**   7600 St. Helena Highway, Oakville, CA 94562*
Recently established super-premium winery owned by Jess Jackson, producing wines which are intended to complement his LOKOYA and CARDINALE brands. A wide range of Napa vineyard sources are being called on. Some vineyard-specific wines are only available at the winery, such as the seriously pricey Cabernet Sauvignon Beckstoffer Vineyard bottling. These are very impressive, dense and powerful wines although, as with so many premium California reds, the top labels are very expensive. The Cabernets stand out from the Merlots. (DM)
● **Merlot** Napa Valley★★★£F Napa Mountain Estates★★★★£F
● **Cabernet Sauvignon** Napa Valley★★★★£F Napa Mountain Estates★★★★★£G

BACIO DIVINO   Rutherford   www.baciodivino.com   A: WTs

Owner: Claus Janzen P.O. Box 131, Rutherford, CA 94573
With a total output of just 1,000 cases a year, Claus Janzen's operation is small even by California cult-winery standards. Bacio Divino is a very stylish and impressive blend of Cabernet Sauvignon, Sangiovese and Petite Sirah. Second label Bacio Angelico, by contrast, is a blend of Sangiovese, Zinfandel, Cabernet Sauvignon and Alicante Bouschet produced in a lush, forward style, to be enjoyed sooner rather than later. (DM)
● **Bacio Divino** Napa Valley★★★★★£G

BEAULIEU VINEYARD   Rutherford   www.beaulieuvineyards.com   A: PFx

*Owner: **Diageo Chateau and Estates Wine Co**   1960 St Helena Highway, Rutherford, CA 94573*
Historic Napa winery founded in 1900 and, like STERLING, now a part of the Diageo group. The Beaulieu reputation was established by the legendary André Tchelistcheff. While quality was distinctly variable during the 1980s, the late 90s saw a marked improvement. An enormous range of wine is offered under Coastal, Appellation, Reserve and Speciality labels and some good quality can be found at the lower price levels. Beauzeaux is a juicy blend of Zinfandel, Valdiguié, Charbono, Petite Sirah and Grenache. Ensemble is an attractive, spicy, Southern Rhône-style blend, while the top-end Cabernets are particularly impressive. The premium Tapestry is a typical Bordeaux style blend. (DM)
● **Syrah** California★★£C California Signet Collection★★★£D

● **Beauzeaux** North Coast★★ £C   ● **Ensemble** Napa Valley★★ £C
● **Zinfandel** Napa Valley★ £C   Napa Valley Signet Collection★★★ £D
● **Pinot Noir** Carneros★ £C   Carneros Reserve★ £E   ● **Merlot** Napa Valley ★★ £D
● **Cabernet Sauvignon**★★ £C   Georges de Latour★★★★ £G   Clone 4★★★★ £H   Clone 6★★★★ £H
● **Tapestry** Reserve Napa Valley★★ £E
O **Chardonnay** Carneros Reserve★★ £D

BERINGER   St Helena   www.beringer.com   A: BWC

Owner: Beringer Blass   2000 Main Street, St Helena, CA 94574
Now a part of the global BERINGER BLASS group, this winery was established 125 years ago and has always produced wines of good to very good quality at all price levels. Much of this success must be attributed to the skills of winemaking chief Ed Sbragia. The top cuvées remain some of the very best in California. Estate vineyards continue to be developed and for a number of the premium labels the home St Helena vineyard, planted on well-drained soils in the Spring Mountain foothills, remains a key to quality. Their two entry-level ranges provide sound, everyday drinking wines, if, it has to be said, a touch unexciting. Stone Cellars emphasises the classic varieties whereas the California series focuses on the more unusual including white Zinfandel, Merlot and the gluggable Beringer Nouveau. The Founders Estate range is a level up and generally some oak, new and old, is used to lend structure and an added dimension to the wines. The Appellation series are produced with more of an emphasis on *terroir*, where varieties tend to succeed best. Some new French oak is used for ageing and some good bottles can be found. A further step up, the Alluvium wines are red and white meritage blends, the red dominated by Merlot and, like the white, approachable in its youth. At the pinnacle are the Private Reserve and Limited Release labels. An increasing amount of very good Cabernet Franc from Howell Mountain is also being produced along with North Coast Sangiovese and a fine botrytised dessert Semillon/Sauvignon blend, Nightingale. (DM)

● **Alluvium Red** Knights Valley★★★ £E
● **Cabernet Sauvignon** Knights Valley★★ £D   Private Reserve★★★★★ £G
● **Merlot** Napa Valley★★ £D   Reserve Bancroft Ranch Howell Mountain★★★ £E
● **Pinot Noir** North Coast★ £C   Reserve Stanly Ranch Carneros★★ £D
● **Zinfandel** Clear Lake★ £B
O **Alluvium** Knights Valley★★★ £D
O **Chardonnay** Napa Valley★★ £C   Private Reserve★★★★ £E   Sbragia Limited Release★★★★ £E
O **Sauvignon Blanc** Napa Valley★★ £B
O **Viognier** Napa Valley★★ £D

ROBERT BIALE   Napa Valley   A: OWL

Owner: Robert Biale   2040 Brown Street, Napa, CA 94559
The Biale family have owned vineyards in the Napa Valley for decades but more recently they have established themselves as a very impressive, small producer of mainly old-vine Zinfandel from a range of sources including their home vineyard, along with Petite Sirah and a little Syrah. With so much California Zin now massively extracted and overblown, these examples show remarkable refinement and balance. This is artisan California winegrowing at its best. (DM)

● **Zinfandel** Estate★★★★ £E   Spenker Vineyard★★★ £D   Monte Rosso Vineyard★★★★ £E
● **Petite Sirah** Estate★★★ £E

BLOCKHEADIA RINGNOSII   Napa Valley   A:WTs

Owner: Michael Ouellette   Lorenza Lake Winery, 1764 Scott Street, St Helena, CA 94574
Michael Ouellette founded Blockheadia in 1992. He produces well-priced characterful Zinfandel, Petite Sirah (recently added) and Sauvignon Blanc. Around 11,000 cases are now produced from a number of sources and the fruit is always hand-picked. The wines are very much in the fruit driven mould with minimal oak influence. The Zins are marked by spicy, dark fruits and they are medium weight rather than blockbusters. The Sauvignon Blancs are vinified without oak and offer a mix of lightly tropical fruit with a soft mineral undercurrent, they are also well-balanced and tend to avoid some of the excessively alcoholic levels achieved elsewhere. The wines are all approachable on release. (DM)

● **Zinfandel**★★ California £C Mendocino County★★ £C Napa Valley★★★ £D
O **Sauvignon Blanc** California★★ £C Napa Valley★★ £C

BRYANT FAMILY   Napa Valley

Owner: Bryant family   1567 Sage Canyon Road, St Helena, CA94574
With production of around a 1,000 cases the Bryant Cabernet has become one of a handful of blue- chip California examples of the variety alongside such illustrious names as ARAUJO, COLGIN, GRACE FAMILY, HARLAN and SCREAMING EAGLE. While the wine has immense depth and power, consultant Helen Turley has created a style that is also supple and rounded, approachable at five or six years. Expect the wine to age gracefully and to pay a very high price for it.(DM)

● **Cabernet Sauvignon**✪✪✪✪✪ £H

CAFARO   Napa Valley   www.cafaro.com   A: Lib

Owner: Joe Cafaro   1550 Allyn Avenue, St Helena, CA 94574
Joe Cafaro is a successful consultant winemaker having made wine for the likes of ACACIA and DALLA VALLE. He also owns a small winery where he produces stylish, supple and complex Cabernet, Merlot and most recently a small amount of Syrah from the Cafaro Family vineyard. Ripe, intense berry fruit is well balanced with spicy oak. Compared with many of his competitors these wines are great value. (DM)

● **Merlot** Napa Valley★★★ £E   ● **Cabernet Sauvignon** Napa Valley★★★★ £E

CAIN CELLARS   Spring Mountain   www.cainfive.com   A: J&B

Owner: Jim and Nancy Meadlock   3800 Langtry Road, St. Helena   CA   94574
This is a spectacularly sited Spring Mountain estate with some 34 ha (84 acres) planted to Cabernet Sauvignon, Merlot, Malbec, Cabernet Franc and Petit Verdot, which make up the flagship Cain Five – a medium-full, ripe and lightly cedary blend. The Concept, another meritage blend dominated by Cabernet Sauvignon but with a hint of Syrah for perfume, is sourced from benchland as well as hillside vineyards. This is softer, more approachable than its mountain-grown big brother. Cain Cuvée is a non-vintage blend again assembled with Bordeaux varieties but in a soft, forward style. The range is completed by Musque – a fresh, lightly herbal Sauvignon Blanc. (DM)

● **Cain Five** Napa Valley★★★ £F   ● **Cain Concept** Napa Valley★★ £E   ● **Cain Cuvee** Napa Valley★ £C
O **Cain Musque** Ventana Vineyard★★ £C

CAKEBREAD CELLARS Rutherford www.cakebread.com A:C&B

Owner: Cakebread family 8300 St Helena Highway, Rutherford, CA 94573
Now a fairly substantial operation which the Cakebread family have been running for well over two decades. Production is approaching 100,000 cases, including an extensive premium range. Chardonnay and Sauvignon are both rich and oaky in style, with the Reserve and Rutherford bottlings adding an extra element of depth and texture. Regular Merlot and Cabernet are well crafted and both are big, powerful and quite alcoholic reds. The top cuvées, though, are the three super-premium Cabernets. As well as the Benchland Select, Vine Hill Ranch and Three Sisters are made in very small quantities.(DM)

● **Merlot** Napa Valley★★ £E **Cabernet Sauvignon** Napa Valley★★★ £E Benchland Select★★★★ £G
O **Chardonnay** Napa Valley★★ £D Reserve★★★ £E
O **Sauvignon Blanc** Napa Valley★★ £C Rutherford★★★ £D

CARDINALE Napa County www.cardinale.com A:WTs

Owner: Kendall-Jackson 7600 St Helena Highway, Oakville, CA 94562
This very pricey red is the jewel in the crown of the KENDALL-JACKSON empire. It is actually vinified in the same facility as the single-vineyard wines of the LOKOYA label. It is a blend of Cabernet Sauvignon and Merlot sourced from prime mountain vineyards on Mount Veeder and Howell Mountain as well as the Alexander Valley, which explains the generic California appellation. Without doubt a massively powerful and concentrated red with copious quantities of super-ripe cassis and hints of cedar underpinned by high-toast oak, in the best vintages the wine convincingly earns five stars. Yet you do feel that just a hint more refinement would add that final dimension. (DM)

● **Cardinale Proprietary Red** California★★★★★ £H

CAYMUS Rutherford www.caymus.com A:Vin

Owner: Chuck Wagner PO Box 268, Rutherford, CA 94573
Two good to very good Cabernet Sauvignons are vinified here. Chuck Wagner also produces very stylish Chardonnay at his Central Coast winery MER SOLEIL as well as a late harvest Viognier. Conundrum is a classy white, blended from an unusual mix of Sauvignon Blanc, Semillon, Chardonnay, Viognier and Muscat Canelli. It is ripe and aromatic with a hint of new oak. The Special Selection, one of California's great reds, needs cellaring and will improve in bottle for five to ten years. The grapes are harvested lot by lot and vinified with extended maceration on skins and ageing in new French oak. The 1999 was particularly impressive, 2000 is also seriously worth noting for your cellar. (DM)

● **Cabernet Sauvignon** Napa Valley★★★ £F Special Selection Napa Valley★★★★★ £H
O **Conundrum** California★★★ £C

CHAPPELLET Napa Valley www.chappellet.com

Owner: Chappellet family 1581 Sage Canyon Road, St. Helena, CA 94574
This winery, located on Pritchard Hill close to BRYANT, has had a variable record in recent years. Most interesting is the impressive Chenin Blanc. Vinified from old vines with just a hint of oak this is a striking and unusual example of the variety for California. On occasion a late-harvest version is produced, which can be remarkably rich and intense. Signature Cabernet and Chardonnay have both shown recent form as should be expected from first-class vineyards with meagre, well-drained stony soils. Sangiovese and Zinfandel are also produced as well as an extraordinarily expensive Pritchard

Hill Estate Vineyards Cabernet Sauvignon. (DM)

● **Merlot** Napa Valley★★ £D
● **Cabernet Sauvignon** Signature★★★ £E
O **Chardonnay** Napa Valley★★ £C Signature★★★ £E
O **Chenin Blanc**★★ £B Old Vine Cuvée★★★ £B

CHATEAU MONTELENA   Napa Valley   www.montelena.com   A: Vin

Owner: Jim Barrett   1429 Tubbs Lane, Calistoga, CA 94515
One of a few genuinely historic Napa wineries dating back to the 1880s. Nowadays the winery is best-known for one of the greatest Cabernet-based reds from the US. Even in lesser years the Montelena Estate red has a reputation for real quality. It is a backward and powerfully structured wine that stands in marked contrast to the many ripe and supple, opulent styles that have emerged more recently. A minimum of ten years is required to enjoy it at its best. St Vincent is a ripe, spicy blend of Zinfandel and Sangiovese, the latter succeeding better than neighbouring examples of the variety because of a commitment to reduced yields. The Chardonnay is a wonderfully restrained, tight and mineral-laden example, stylish and impeccably balanced. (DM)

● **St Vincent** Montelena Estate★★★ £D
● **Cabernet Sauvignon** Calistoga Cuvée★★★ £E Montelena Estate★★★★★ £H
O **Chardonnay** Napa Valley★★★ £D

CHATEAU POTELLE   Mount Veeder   www.chateaupotelle.com   A: CKr

Owner: Marketta & Jean-Noël Fourmeaux   3875 Mt Veeder Road, Napa, CA 94558
The Fourmeaux family origins are in the French wine trade but Marketta and Jean-Noël have made a very good job of producing classically original, stylish California wine styles. The VGS labels are particularly impressive, none more so than the Zinfandel and Cabernet Sauvignon vinified from estate-grown mountain fruit. These are big, structured wines which need time, five years or so, to soften their youthfully aggressive, at times angular, tannins.(DM)

● **Zinfandel** Old Vines Amador County★★ £C VGS★★★ £F **Cabernet Sauvignon** VGS★★★ £F
O **Chardonnay** VGS★★★ £E O **Sauvignon Blanc** Napa Valley★★ £B

CLINE CELLARS   Carneros   www.clinecellars.com   A: WTs

Owner: Fred Cline   24737 Highway 121, Sonoma, CA 95476
Along with Randall Grahm of BONNY DOON, Fred Cline was one of the original Rhône Rangers. From his 142-ha (350-acre) Carneros property he produces a plethora of Zins and some first-class Rhône styles. The family have some of the most extensive plantings of Rhône varieties in the state and account for no less than 85 per cent of all Mourvèdre plantings, although fruit is also sourced elsewhere. Some solid whites are also produced but they lack the same excitement as the reds, with their vibrant, spicy, berry fruit character. At the top end they posses not only rich, concentrated fruit but marvellously honed, supple tannins – wines of weight and finesse. The fact that they represent great value is another major plus. (DM)

● **Syrah** Carneros★★★ £C ● **Carignane** Ancient Vines Contra Costa County★★ £C
● **Cotes d'Oakley** Vin Rouge California★ £B
● **Mourvèdre** Ancient Vines Contra Costa County★★★ £D Small Berry Vineyard★★★★ £D
● **Zinfandel** California★★ £B Ancient Vines California★★★ £C Big Break Vineyard★★ £D
● **Zinfandel** Bridgehead Vineyard★★★ £D Jacuzzi Family Vineyard★★★ £D Fulton Road★★★ £E
● **Zinfandel** Live Oak Vineyard★★★ £D
O **Cotes d'Oakley** Vin Blanc California★ £B O **Marsanne** Carneros★ £C O **Viognier** Carneros★★ £C
O **Roussanne** Carneros★★ £C

COLGIN CELLARS Oakville www.colgincellars.com

Owner: Ann Colgin   PO Box 254, St Helena, CA 94574

Colgin now offers three super-premium bottlings. All are based on Cabernet Sauvignon, although the Cariad red is 55 per cent Cabernet Sauvignon, 35 per cent Merlot and 5 per cent Cabernet Franc (all sourced from the Madrona Vineyard) as well as 5 per cent Petit Verdot. Unblended Cabernet Sauvignon in two guises is produced from the Herb Lamb and Tychson Hill vineyards. Total production is barely 1,000 cases annually. The wines are neither fined nor filtered and spend around two years in new French oak. All undoubtedly offer magnificent weight, depth and texture. Helen Turley of MARCASSIN was the guiding force behind the winemaking here up to 1998 when the mantle was taken on by Max Aubert – formerly of another benchmark producer, PETER MICHAEL – who is also making top-quality Chardonnay under his own Aubert label. Expect the wines to be of at least four- to five-star quality and to be very, very expensive if you can get any through the mailing list. (DM)

CORISON Napa Valley www.corison.com   A:DDr

Owner: Cathy Corison   987 St Helena Hwy, St Helena, CA 94574

Cathy Corison produces a small amount of Napa Cabernet Sauvignon sourced from a variety of sites throughout the region. Unlike many wines produced by her Napa neighbours the Corison Cabernet is not overblown and shows considerable depth and finesse. A very limited amount of the special cuvée Kronos Vineyard is also produced, which requires more patience. (DM)

● **Cabernet Sauvignon**★★★★£E

ROBERT CRAIG Napa Valley www.robertcraigwine.com   A:THt

Owner: Robert Craig   830 School Street, Suite 14, Napa, CA 94558

Small, high-quality Napa operation established in 1992 and sourcing fruit from a number of locations. Affinity is a typical Bordeaux-style blend of Cabernet Sauvignon, Merlot and Cabernet Franc. Ripe, supple and surprisingly elegant it can be approached relatively young. The two Cabernets are equally stylish but require more time to tame their mountain tannins. As might be expected from warm-climate Paso Robles, the Syrah is in a rich, vibrant, dark-fruit style and contains a smattering of Merlot. Zinfandel from Amador County was added with the 2000 vintage and looks promising. The Chardonnays are a little less impressive than the reds but have reasonable depth with ripe, citrus fruit and a marked tropical character. Drink over the short to medium term. (DM)

● **Cabernet Sauvignon** Mount Veeder★★★★£E Howell Mountain★★★★£E
● **Affinity** Napa Valley★★★★£E ● **Syrah** Paso Robles★★★£D
O **Chardonnay** Carneros★★£C Russian River★£C

CUVAISON Napa Valley www.cuvaison.com   A:THt

Owner: Schmidheiny family   4550 Silverado Trail, Calistoga, CA 94515

Medium-sized operation producing some 63,000 cases a year of which 65 per cent is Chardonnay. Fruit is sourced from its own vineyards, including a 162-ha (400-acre) property in Carneros, as well as from elsewhere; the recently acquired Brandlin Ranch on Mount Veeder provides an increased resource of estate fruit for vintages to come. The wines are well-crafted, well-priced and always reliable but never really set the world alight. The Estate Selection Chardonnay is the most impressive offering. Syrah from the Carneros estate and Napa Valley fruit and Zinfandel from Napa sources have been added to the the range with the 2000 vintage. Expect both to have reasonable potential. (DM)

● **Cabernet Sauvignon** Napa Valley★★ £D   ● **Merlot** Napa Valley/Carneros★★ £D
● **Pinot Noir** Napa Valley Carneros ★★ £D
O **Chardonnay** Napa Valley/Carneros★★ £C Estate Selection Carneros★★★ £E

DALLA VALLE   Oakville   www.dallevallevineyards.com   A: THt

Owner: Naoko Dalla Vale   7766 Silverado Trail, Napa, CA 95448
One of Napa's small-volume, super-premium wineries with a first-class hillside vineyard to the east of
Oakville. Three wines are produced under the guidance of Mia Klein of SELENE. The main focus of
production is Cabernet Sauvignon plus a small amount of the even more impressive Maya, a meritage
blend of Cabernets Sauvignon and Franc, along with Pietre Rosse, a stylish, dark cherry-laden Sangiovese.
The Cabernet Sauvignon and Maya are dense, massive and hugely extracted wines requiring a minimum
of six to seven years' ageing; the Pietre Rosse can be approached much sooner. (DM)
● **Cabernet Sauvignon** Estate★★★★★ £H

DARIOUSH   Napa Valley   www.darioush.com   A: Lib

Owner: Darioush Khaledi   4240 Silverado Trail, Napa, CA 94558
Darioush Khaledi established this winery very recently (1997) but the results are already impressive.
He owns 13 ha (33 acres) of vineyards around the site of the new winery building, which is in the
course of construction, along with 10 ha (25 acres) in the Mount Veeder and Atlas Peak AVAs. The
top wines are released under the Signature label while there is a secondary Estate label for Chardonnay
and Cabernet Sauvignon. The Signature reds are rich, vibrant and impressively dense and powerful.
Cabernet Sauvignon is blended with Merlot, Cabernet Franc and Petit Verdot. The wines have
minimal handling in the cellar and the Cabernet and Shiraz are bottled without filtration. Expect
them to age well over the medium term. (DM)
● **Cabernet Sauvignon** Signature★★★ £F ● **Merlot** Signature★★★ £E ● **Shiraz** Signature★★★ £F
O **Chardonnay** Signature★★ £E O **Viognier** Signature★★ £D

DIAMOND CREEK   Diamond Mountain   www.diamondcreekvineyards.com   A: L&W

Owner: Al Brounstein   1500 Diamond Mountain Road, Calistoga, CA 94515
Supreme Cabernet Sauvignon has been made here for a great deal longer than most of the new
generation of 'super-cuvées'. These are not just wines of massive extract and weight, sourced from
prime mountain sites and each individually stating its own *terroir*, they are wines of grace, power and
above all, immense refinement. Volcanic Hill is the fullest and longest lived; Red Rock Terrace, like
Volcanic Hill, comes from a warm site and is the most accessible of the trio whereas Gravelly Meadow
– from the coolest of the three sites – is tight and restrained. You would be well-advised to cellar for
at least ten years to enjoy one of these bottles at its best. (DM)
● **Cabernet Sauvignon** Gravelly Meadow✪✪✪✪✪ £H Volcanic Hill✪✪✪✪✪ £H
● **Cabernet Sauvignon** Red Rock Terrace✪✪✪✪✪ £H

DOMAINE CARNEROS   Carneros   www.domaine.com   A: HMA

Owner: Champagne Taittinger 1240 Duhig Rd., Napa, CA 94559
California outpost of the Champagne house TAITTINGER. As well as the sparklers they have recently
been producing some stylish and reasonably impressive Pinot Noirs in a ripe and full, berry fruit style.
Avante-Garde, an entry-level example, has now been added. The Le Rêve Blanc de Blancs is the
pinnacle of the sparkling range. A wine of some considerable style, it is almost exclusively

Chardonnay with a tiny proportion of Pinot Blanc. Real complexity is gained from the five years spent on lees. (DM)

● **Pinot Noir**★★ £E Famous Gate★★★ £E
○ **Brut Non-Vintage**★ £C Vintage Cuvée★★ £D Blanc de Blancs Le Rêve★★★ £E

DOMAINE CHANDON Yountville www.chandon.com

Owner: LVMH 1 California Drive, Yountville, CA 94599
Probably the best-known among the California sparkling wine producers and established way back in 1973, Chandon is also producing a limited amount of Carneros-sourced still wine from the traditional Champagne varieties bottled as varietals. Of the sparkling wines, l'Étoile is refined and reasonably intense; the Vintage is bigger, fuller and with marked toasty, bready notes; while the small amount of the rare Mount Veeder cuvée, a Blanc de Blancs which spends four years on lees, is tight, well structured and stylish. (DM)

○ **Brut** Classic★ £B Reserve★★ £C
○ **Blanc de Noirs** ★★ £B ○ **l'Étoile**★★ £E ○ **Vintage**★★ £F
◉ **l'Étoile**★★ £E

DOMINUS ESTATE Yountville www.dominusestate.com   A: C&B

Owner: Christian Moueix 2570 Napanook Road, Yountville, CA 94599
Christian Moueix is a member of the Bordeaux dynasty responsible for CHATEAU PETRUS. Some of the exotic elements of that great wine show through in Dominus despite it being a blend dominated by Cabernet Sauvignon. The key is in the winemaking and while the ripe fruit character of the Napanook Vineyard shows through it still possesses a classically powerful, tannic structure. It requires up to a decade or more of ageing to show at its best, providing a wine of balance, subtlety and refinement. The Napanook is an impressive second label first produced in 1996. It is considerably more forward than the grand vin and can be approached easily with three or fours years' development. (DM)

● **Dominus**✪✪✪✪✪ £H **Napanook**★★★ £E

DUCKHORN St Helena www.duckhorn.com   A: L&W

Owner: Dan & Margaret Duckhorn 1000 Lodi Lane, St Helena, CA 94574
This has grown into a mid-sized operation since it was founded in 1978. Around 1,000 tons of fruit are crushed and production is now around 60,000 cases. The main focus of the operation is Merlot. A good regular Napa Valley bottling is joined by top-end examples from estate fruit as well as two other premium labels from Howell Mountain and the Three Palms vineyard. The style was of an iron fist but is tamer these days, with suppler tannin. The Paraduxx is an unusual blend of Zinfandel with a touch of Merlot and Cabernet, while the Decoy maintains the integrity of the top wines. The Duckhorns have also purchased vineyards and a winery in the cool Anderson Valley to produce stylish Pinot Noir under the Goldeneye label. (DM)

● **Cabernet Sauvignon** Napa Valley★★★ £F ● **Merlot** Decoy Migration★★ £D Napa Valley★★★ £E
● **Paraduxx** Napa Valley★★★ £E
○ **Sauvignon Blanc** Napa Valley★★ £C

DUNN VINEYARDS Howell Mountain   A: L&W

Owner: Randy Dunn 805 White Cottage Road, Angwin, CA 94508
Randy Dunn was one of the pioneers of great mountain-grown Cabernet. The estate bottling, Howell

Mountain, is a massive wine almost always offering formidable concentration and depth, with real finesse as well. The Napa Valley Cabernet is in a marginally softer style but is nevertheless a considerable and seriously structured wine. Both require cellaring, the Estate Howell Mountain a minimum of a decade. What is also noteworthy is the value offered by both wines in these days of extraordinarily high Napa red prices. (DM)

● **Cabernet Sauvignon** Napa Valley★★★★ £F   Estate Howell Mountain✪✪✪✪✪ £F

FAR NIENTE   Oakville   www.farniente.com   A: Hal, T&W

Owner: Gil Nickel   1350 Acacia Drive, Oakville, CA 94562

There are just two main wines at this well-established (first vintage 1979) estate in the heart of Napa. The original winery here dates back to 1885 and was created from gold-rush money. The Cabernet is a typically powerful Napa expression requiring several years' cellaring to be enjoyed at its best. The Chardonnay has been fine-tuned over recent vintages and offers an unusually elegant and refined style with a well-honed, tight oak influence and the balance to offer real promise with age. (DM)

● **Cabernet Sauvignon**★★★★ £G
O **Chardonnay**★★★ £E

FLORA SPRINGS   St Helena   www.florasprings.com   A: Vin, Win

Owner: Komes family   1978 West Zinfandel Lane, St Helena, CA 94574

Sizeable family-owned and run operation with a broad selection of wines. The Komes' now own nearly 200 ha (500 acres) of Napa vineyards, providing a considerable resource for their range. The two estate flagships are the Cabernet Sauvignon Hillside Reserve and the proprietary red Trilogy, a blend of Cabernet Sauvignon, Merlot, Cabernet Franc and Malbec. Both are ageworthy and display a fine balance of ripe fruit and harmonious tannin. Both these and the Wild Boar Vineyard Cabernet require five years' ageing. The Merlot bottlings are more accessible. Italian styles feature prominently in the range, both red and white. Poggio del Papa, the top Italian red, is a Tuscan-influenced blend of Sangiovese, Merlot and Cabernet Sauvignon and there is well-priced Pinot Grigio as well.(DM)

● **Cabernet Sauvignon** Napa Valley★★★ £D   Wild Boar Vineyard★★★ £E   Hillside Reserve★★★★ £G
● **Merlot** Estate★★★ £D   Windfall Vineyard★★★ £E   ● **Sangiovese** Napa Valley★★ £B
● **Trilogy** Napa Valley★★★★ £F
O **Chardonnay** Barrel Fermented Reserve★★★ £D   O **Soliloquy** Oakville★★★ £D

FRANCISCAN   Oakville   www.franciscan.com   A:PWa

Owner: Canandaigua   1178 Galleron Road, Highway 29 at Galleron Road, St Helena, CA 94574

Agustin Huneeus sold Franciscan to Canandaigua in 1999 along with the two sister wineries ESTANCIA and MOUNT VEEDER WINERY, although he retained his prestige QUINTESSA operation. The wines here are good rather than inspired but in most cases offer reasonable value for money. They are very much in a rich California vein, being very ripe, upfront and fruit-driven. They will show well young. Cuvée Sauvage is in a very rich, high-toast oak style and the Magnificat red will develop well with five years' ageing or so. A small amount of a premium ageworthy Merlot Reserve is also produced and is blended with 20 per cent Cabernet Sauvignon. (DM)

● **Cabernet Sauvignon** Napa Valley★★ £D   ● **Merlot** Napa Valley★★ £C   ● **Magnificat**★★★ £F
O **Chardonnay** Napa Valley★★ £C   Cuvée Sauvage★★★ £E

PETER FRANUS   Rutherford   www.franuswine.com

A: THt

Owner: Peter Franus   P.O. Box 10575, Napa, CA 94581

Impressive small producer with a range sourced from a number of committed grape growers. Total production is now some 7,500 cases. The style is very much one of minimal intervention and the wines are impressive without being overdone. Cabernet comes from a number of Napa sources and a single-vineyard bottling from the Rancho Chimiles vineyard was added with the 1999 vintage. Zinfandel is always stylish and vibrant: Napa-sourced Rancho Chimiles and the Planchon Vineyard label from 100-year-old Contra Costa vines are both impressive but the the best of the three is the stylish and complex Mount Veeder wine from Brandlin Vineyard. Sauvignon comes in two guises: Farella-Park is barrel-fermented; the Stewart Vineyard bottling from Carneros sees no wood. (DM)

- ● **Cabernet Sauvignon** Napa Valley★★★ £E
- ● **Zinfandel** Planchon Vineyard★★★ £C   Rancho Chimiles★★ £C   Brandlin Vineyard★★★ £D
- O **Sauvignon Blanc** Farella-Park Vineyard★★ £C   Stewart Vineyard★ £C

FROG'S LEAP   Rutherford   www.frogsleap.com

A: L&W, M&V

Owner: John Williams   8815 Conn Creek Road, Rutherford, CA 94573

John Williams established Frogs Leap with Larry Turley, who went on to make superstar Zins at TURLEY CELLARS. The emphasis of the marketing of wine here is fun, reflected in the labelling. Pull a cork and you'll see what I mean. However the wine is serious and can be very impressive. The style is for forward, ripe, fleshy reds with sufficient structure to age nicely in the medium term and for rich, fruity whites. The Rutherford red, a blend of Cabernet Sauvignon and Cabernet Franc sourced from a number of dry-farmed vineyards, is serious and powerful. A small amount of Syrah is now produced from Carneros and there is a fun, everyday white Leapfrögmilch made from Riesling and Chardonnay plus a few hundred cases of juicy rosé labelled Pink made from old-vine Valdiguié. (DM)

- ● **Cabernet Sauvignon** Napa Valley★★★ £E   ● **Rutherford** Napa Valley★★★ £F
- ● **Merlot** Napa Valley★★★ £D   ● **Zinfandel** Napa Valley★★★ £C
- O **Chardonnay** Napa Valley★★ £C   O **Sauvignon Blanc** Napa Valley★★★ £C

GLORIA FERRER   Carneros   www.gloriaferrer.com

A: FrT

Owner: Freixenet   23555 Highway 121, Sonoma, CA 95476

The style here is for rich, ripe sparkling wines sourced mainly from estate vineyards in Carneros. While the wines are typically Californian, the impressive winery and cellar, referred to by the Ferrer family as 'Champagne Caves', is designed in an unusual hacienda style. The Chardonnay is a style that should be enjoyed young. The Pinot Noir and Merlot, which also come from Carneros, will stand just a little age. The sparkling wines, which all benefit from sufficiently lengthy lees-ageing, are ready on release. The Royal Cuvée spends an extended six years on its yeast. The flagship Carneros Cuvée has a high proportion of reserve wine and seven years on its lees. (DM)

- O **Chardonnay** Carneros★★ £C
- O **Sonoma Brut** Sonoma County★ £C   O **Blanc de Noirs** Carneros★★ £C
- O **Royal Cuvée** Carneros★★ £C   O **Carneros Cuvée** Carneros★★★ £E
- ◉ **Brut Rosé** Carneros★★ £C

GRACE FAMILY VINEYARDS   St Helena

Owner: Dick Grace   1210 Rockland Drive, St Helena, CA 94574

This is a tiny operation producing barely 200 cases of one of the most exalted premium Cabernets in

California. Part of the production is auctioned for charity so the remainder is extremely rare. Big, richly textured and immensely powerful, it is a wine respected for its balance and finesse as much as its sheer concentration. If you can find any, expect to pay a very high price. (DM)

GREEN AND RED VINEYARD   Napa Valley   www.greenandred.com   A: Win

Owner: Jay Hemingway   3208 Chiles Valley Road, St Helena, CA 94574
Small estate in the Chiles Valley on the eastern side of the Napa Valley whose main focus is Zinfandel. Consultancy input from Helen Turley of MARCASSIN has provided the stimulus for well-crafted ripe and supple examples of the variety. The Chiles Mill is an estate-vineyard bottling and is a level up on the Chiles Valley Zin sourced from a number of neighbouring sites. The California label is the lightest of the three and comes from vineyards in Lake County, Lodi, Paso Robles and Napa County. Chardonnay is barrel-fermented using native yeasts and spends nine months in oak. The range also now includes Sobrante, a blend of Zinfandel and Syrah, as well as Sauvignon Blanc. Sobrante is aged in a combination of French and American oak. The Sauvignon Blanc sees a touch of oak during fermentation and malolactic is blocked to preserve freshness. The wines are all reasonably priced. (DM)
● **Zinfandel** California★★£C Chiles Valley Vineyards★★★£C Chiles Mill Vineyard★★★£C
○ **Chardonnay** Napa Valley★£C

GRGICH HILLS   Rutherford   www.grgich.com   A: Fol

Owner: Mike Grgich   1829 St Helena Highway, Rutherford, CA 94573
Mike Grgich made his reputation at CHATEAU MONTELENA before going on to establish a formidable track record under his own label. His Chardonnay is big, full and typically opulent in a classic ripe and forward tropical Napa style. It is aged for 10 months in French oak and should be enjoyed in its first two or three years. The ripe and lightly grassy Fumé Blanc has its malolactic blocked for freshness and should be drunk young. Two powerful and firmly tannic Cabernets, including a pricey limited-release Yountville Selection, are joined by a Zinfandel that is rich and heavily extracted with vibrant dark-berry fruit, full of depth but a touch short on refinement. A late-harvest white is also produced from Chardonnay and Johannisberg Riesling. (DM)
● **Cabernet Sauvignon** Napa Valley★★£F ● **Merlot** Napa Valley★★£E
● **Zinfandel** Napa and Sonoma Counties★★£D
○ **Chardonnay** Napa Valley★★£E ○ **Fumé Blanc** Napa Valley★£C

HARLAN ESTATE   Oakville   www.harlanestate.com   A: THt

Owner: Bill Harlan   PO Box 352, Oakville, CA 94562
Small, very high-quality producer dedicated solely to super-premium Bordeaux-style reds. The property is located in the western foothills of Oakville and there are around 100 ha (240 acres) under vine. The Harlan Estate meritage is a blend of Cabernet Sauvignon, Merlot, Cabernet Franc and Petit Verdot. Winemaker Bob Levy gets additional consultancy from Michel Rolland and between them they produce a wine not only of immense dimension but of great elegance and finesse. The Maiden is a very impressive second label. (DM)
● **Estate Red** Napa Valley✪✪✪✪✪ £H

HARRISON VINEYARDS   Napa Valley   www.harrisonvineyards.com   A: Vin

Owner: Lyndsey Harrison   1527 Sage Canyon Road, St Helena, CA 94574
Small, family-run producer with an output of just 3,000 cases a year located on Pritchard Hill in the

eastern Napa. Lyndsey Harrison herself is the winemaker, gaining valuable consultancy input from John Kongsgaard of KONGSGAARD and ARIETTA. The full gamut of modern winemaking techniques are utilised, native yeasts are used for fermentation and fining and filtration eschewed. An impressive range now includes Syrah, Merlot Reserve and a meritage blend of Merlot, Cabernets Sauvignon and Franc and, unusually, some Syrah. Chardonnay is barrel-fermented with lees-stirring and also bottled unfined and without filtration. The reserve reds are aged in top-quality French oak. They are finely structured and will develop well in bottle with five to seven years' cellaring. (DM)

● **Cabernet Sauvignon** Estate★★★ £F Reserve★★★ £G ● **Zebra Zinfandel**★ £C
O **Chardonnay** Napa Valley★★★ £E Reserve★★★ £F

HAVENS Carneros www.havenswine.com   A: DDr

Owner: Havens & Scot families 2055 Hoffman Lane, Napa, CA 94558

A good, small range of wines with Merlot a key element in the portfolio. Certainly rich and impressive when at their plummy best, the wines can be marked by oak. As well as the two Merlot cuvées, Bourriquot is a Bordeaux-style blend, but Right Bank rather than Left, being a stylish blend of Cabernet Franc and Merlot. Syrah is sourced from the Hudson vineyard in Carneros, the estate Napa vineyard and the Trubody ranch in northern Napa; the oak here is reined in and the style is ripe and forward. Its also worth looking out for a limited production Syrah sourced from the Hudson T vineyard in Carneros. (DM)

● **Bourriquot** Napa Valley★★★ £E ● **Merlot** Napa Valley★★ £C Reserve Carneros★★★ £E
● **Syrah** Napa Valley★★★ £D

HEITZ CELLARS St Helena www.heitzcellar.com   A: J&B

Owner: Heitz family 500 Taplin Road, St Helena, CA 94574

One of the original benchmark producers of premium Napa reds, particularly the great Martha's Vineyard Cabernets. Quality has been up and down during the 1980s and 1990s but the wines are now sounder and they seem generally to be improving. The Bella Oaks and Trailside bottlings are a touch lighter than Martha's Vineyard but impressive nevertheless. Chardonnay is in a tighter style than some of its neighbours and is only lightly oaked. There are a total of 142 ha (350 acres) of estate vineyards spread throughout Napa and, as well as Cabernet and Chardonnay, some Grignolino and Zinfandel are produced. (DM)

● **Cabernet Sauvignon** Napa Valley★★★ £E Bella Oaks Vineyard★★★ £F Trailside Vineyard★★★ £F
● **Cabernet Sauvignon** Martha's Vineyard★★★★ £H
O **Chardonnay** Napa Valley★★ £C Cellar Selection★★★ £D

HESS COLLECTION Mount Veeder www.hesscollection.com   A: JAr

Owner: Donald Hess 4411 Redwood Road, Napa, CA 94558

Unusual operation in that Donald Hess also provides visitors with access to his extensive art collection. The wines here are impressive, particularly the Cabernet Sauvignon and Chardonnay, produced under the Hess Collection label and vinified from estate Mount Veeder fruit. There are now three ranges. In addition to the Hess Collection wines there is the Hess Estate Cabernet Sauvignon blended from a range of Napa sources in a style that is round and approachable. Cabernet Sauvignon, Merlot, Syrah and Chardonnay under the Hess Select label are produced from a 142-ha (350-acre) estate-owned vineyard in the Pinnacles area of Monterey. Donald Hess also owns or has an interest in GLEN CARLOU in South Africa, Bodega NORTON in Argentina and, closer to home, the BLOCKHEADIA winery. (DM)

● **Cabernet Sauvignon** Napa Valley Collection★★★ £E Collection Reserve★★★★ £F
● **Cabernet Sauvignon** California Select★ £B Napa Valley Hess Estate★★ £C
○ **Chardonnay** Napa Valley Collection★★★ £C California Select★ £B

JADE MOUNTAIN Napa Valley www.chalonewinegroup.com A: M&V

Owner: Chalone Wine Group 621 Airpark Road, Napa, CA 94558
Now part of the Chalone group this exceptional winery has been producing very impressive Rhône styles along with fine Merlot for more than a decade in the highly capable hands of Doug Danielak. These are not the blockbuster, super-extracted ripe fruit offerings which abound elsewhere throughout the state. La Provençale blends Mourvèdre, Syrah and Grenache; Les Jumeaux Cabernet, Syrah and Mourvèdre. Cote du Soleil is a lighter style with a little Merlot added to Mourvèdre and Syrah. The varietal Syrah itself is powerful but restrained. The two single-vineyard wines in particular need time. Merlot is not only rich and concentrated, but finely structured with impeccable balance. The sheer quality here is often misunderstood: these are wines that need time to fully unfurl and show at their best. (DM)
● **La Provençale California** ★★★ £C ● **Merlot** Caldwell Vineyard★★★★ £E Paras Vineyard★★★★ £E
● **Mourvèdre** Contra Costa County★★★★ £C
● **Syrah** Napa Valley★★★★ £D Paras Vineyard★★★★★ £F Hudson Vineyard★★★★★ £F
○ **Viognier** Paras Vineyard★★★★ £D

KONGSGAARD Napa Valley A: Vin

Owner: John Kongsgaard PO Box 349, Oakville, CA 94562
John Kongsgaard produces wines of formidable weight and concentration. Minimal intervention in the cellar allied to wild yeast fermentation and neither fining nor filtration all contribute. The Chardonnay is a very impressive example of the variety, combining the best subtle elements of great Burgundy with a richly textured, almost explosive dose of honeyed Napa fruit. The finish is very long and complex. While the Chardonnay is not exactly made in abundance (less than 1,000 cases), there is only a tiny amount of two Rhône styles – a Roussanne and Viognier blend, rich in texture with a fine, intense nutty complexity, and a very powerful and impressive Syrah produced from Carneros fruit. It will comfortably stand alongside the finest examples of the variety from the Northern Rhône and is of undoubted five-star quality and may in time be compared with the greats such as La Mouline. (DM)
● **Syrah** Napa Valley★★★★★ £H
○ **Chardonnay** Napa Valley★★★★★ £G ○ **Roussanne/Viognier** Napa Valley★★★★★ £G

LAIL VINEYARDS Rutherford www.lailvineyards.com A: Vin

Owner: Robin Daniel Lail PO Box 249, Rutherford, CA 94573
Although this is a newly established small scale winery, owner Robin Daniel Lail's family history goes back to the beginnings of viticulture in Napa itself. One of her ancestors, Gustav Niebaum established the original Inglenook winery in 1879. Just the one wine is made here, a Bordeaux blend of two-thirds Cabernet Sauvignon and one-third Merlot. Sourced from a mere 2.3 ha (5.6 acres) annual production is between 1,200 and 1,500 cases. Winemaker Philippe Melka continues to produce an increasingly stylish, elegant and very finely structured meritage red. (DM)
● **J Daniel Cuvée** Napa Valley★★★★ £F

LA JOTA Howell Mountain www.lajotavineyardco.com

Owner: Markham Vineyards 1102 Las Posadas Road, Angwin, CA 94508

Throughout the 1980s and 90s La Jota has been a source of some of the most powerful and impressive examples produced in the Howell Mountain AVA. The winery has become famed for massive dense and tannic reds that need considerable cellaring but develop very well in bottle. Ownership has passed from Bill Smith (now vinifying Sonoma Valley Pinot Noir under the WH SMITH label) to MARKHAM vineyards. Winemaker Kimberlee Nicholls will continue to maximise the potential of the 11 ha (28 acres) of prime mountain vineyards. As well as the Cabernet Sauvignons, a few hundred cases of Cabernet Franc are also produced. (DM)

● **Cabernet Sauvignon** Howell Mountain★★★ £E Anniversary★★★★ £F

LEWIS CELLARS Napa Valley www.lewiscellars.com   A: Win

Owner: Randy Lewis 524 El Cerrito Avenue, Hillsborough, CA 94010

If like me you're a motor racing fan you'll be delighted by the quality of the powerful dense reds hand-crafted by former Indy 500 star Randy Lewis and his wife Debbie. This small, bespoke range (production is still kept at around 8,500 cases) is marked by power and structure. They are quintessentially Californian wines but serious and very impressive. You need to wait for the tannins to subside but it will be worth it. Good Chardonnay, including an excellent Reserve, is also produced and Syrah and Pinot Noir have been added to the range of reds. 1997 saw the most recent vintage of Cuvee L, the winery's top meritage red produced from Cabernet Sauvignon, Merlot and Cabernet Franc. (DM)

● **Cabernet Sauvignon** Napa Valley★★★★ £F Reserve★★★★ £F
● **Merlot** Napa Valley★★★ £E

LIVINGSTON MOFFETT Rutherford www.livingstonwines.com   A: Win

Owner: Livingston family 1895 Cabernet Lane, St Helena, CA 94574

Originally known as Livingston, the name has been changed because of confusion with the label owned by E & J GALLO who produce volume rather than the hand-crafted premium wines made here. Winemaking is directed by John Kongsgaard who produces exceptional wines under his own KONGSGAARD label. Two very good Cabernets are produced: the Moffett is from the family estate vineyard; the Stanley's Selection is sourced from a number of sites but all providing first-class fruit from vineyards planted on stony, hillside sites. Both are refined and harmonious. Gemstone is the flagship from the vineyard of the same name in Yountville and is a typical Bordeaux blend of Cabernet Sauvignon, Cabernet Franc, Merlot and, unusually for California, a hint of Petit Verdot, all of which are vinified separately. The range is completed by a small amount of Genny's Vineyard Chardonnay, vinified with wild yeasts, and Syrah from the Mitchell Vineyard, with a little Viognier blended in. Top Cabernets are ageworthy and require four or five years' patience – a little more for Moffett and Gemstone. (DM)

● **Cabernet Sauvignon** Moffett Vineyard★★★★ £E Stanley's Selection★★★★ £E
● **Gemstone**★★★★ £F

LOKOYA Oakville www.lokoya.com   A: WTs

Owner: Kendall-Jackson 7600 St Helena Highway, Oakville, CA 94562

This is Jess Jackson's super-premium label, producing distinctive Cabernet Sauvignons that showcase the best single-vineyard characteristics of prime mountain- and benchland-grown fruit. The wines are vinified in the same facility as the flagship CARDINALE, which by contrast is a blend of Napa and Sonoma sources. These are all very big, dense and powerfully structured wines, needing time to shed their early youthful austerity. The Diamond Mountain is the most opulent and has had varying small portions of Merlot and Cabernet Franc blended in depending on the year. The Rutherford is more perfumed, while the Howell Mountain and Mount Veeder are the firmest of the quartet. (DM)

● **Cabernet Sauvignon** Diamond Mountain★★★★£G Howell Mountain★★★★£G
● **Cabernet Sauvignon** Mount Veeder★★★★£G Rutherford★★★★£G

LUNA Napa Valley www.lunavineyards.com   A: WTs

Owner: Michael Moone & George Vare 2921 Silverado Trail, Napa, CA 94558

This is a partnership with John KONGSGAARD focusing on Italian varietals and Merlot. Both the regular Pinot Grigio and Sangiovese are good value for money, while the pricier Canto is a proprietary Super-Tuscan-style blend of Sangiovese and Merlot with a touch of Cabernet Sauvignon for grip. Indigenous yeasts are used, the Pinot Grigio unusually gets just a hint of new barrel-fermentation with lees-enrichment while the reds are all aged in fine-grained French oak and bottled without fining or filtration. (DM)

● **Merlot** Napa Valley★★★£E ● **Canto** Napa Valley★★★£F
● **Sangiovese** Napa Valley★★★£C Riserva★★★£F
O **Pinot Grigio** Napa Valley★★★£C

MINER FAMILY VINEYARDS Oakville www.minerwines.com   A: Vin

Owner: Dave Miner 7850 Silverado Trail, Oakville, CA 94562

Recently established winery, founded in 1998. The principle source of fruit for the range is the Oakville Ranch, where Dave Miner was President. Other Napa vineyards are also used as well as Gary's Vineyard in the Santa Lucia Highlands for striking Pinot Noir, and the Simson Vineyard in Madera County which is the source for a floral medium-bodied Viognier. Zinfandel is straightforward and fruit driven and blended with a little Petite Sirah for structure. The Chardonnays, particularly the top two labels, are very impressive. The wines are barrel fermented, with full maloctic and handled in mainly new oak. The Wild Yeast bottling is exotically tropical, rich and very concentrated. In general the wines are very approachable young, the Cabernet needs a little time. (DM)

● **Zinfandel** Napa Valley★★ £D ● **Pinot Noir** Gary's Vineyard★★★★ £F
● **Cabernet Sauvignon** Oakville★★★ £F
O **Chardonnay** Napa Valley★★ £D Oakville Ranch★★★ £E Wild Yeast★★★★ £F
O **Viognier** Simpson Vineyard★★ £D

ROBERT MONDAVI Oakville www.robertmondavi.com   A: RMi, BBR

Owner: Mondavi family 8575 Orcutt Road, Arroyo Grande, CA 93420

Arguably the most famous wine name in California. Robert Mondavi must take much of the credit for the positive public face of the re-emergence of quality California wine in the 1970s. The company has very widespread wine interests, both in California and with overseas investments and partnerships. In addition to the large-scale premium operation at Oakville the Mondavi family also owns the Woodbridge winery facility in the Central Valley, which produces pretty ordinary everyday reds and whites. At Oakville a new range of Italian varietals has been developed under the La Famiglia di Robert Mondavi label. Among the Robert Mondavi Coastal Private Selection range of varietals, the spicy, berry-laden Zinfandel stands out. The BYRON winery on the Central Coast has been a Mondavi label for some years and the prestigious ARROWOOD operation in Sonoma has also recently been acquired. OPUS ONE was the first of the Mondavi winery partnerships, established in 1979 with MOUTON-ROTHSCHILD. More recently, successful overseas forays have been made with ERRÁZURIZ in Chile to produce the premium-label Seña; with the FRESCOBALDI family in the production of the Super-Tuscan Luce; and in 2002 a controlling interest was taken in Tenuta dell' ORNELLAIA. The core of the Oakville operation, though, is the firm's premium wines and Cabernet has always been exceptional. Recently added is IO from Santa Barbara, a decent Rhône-style blend of Syrah, Grenache and Mourvèdre. These are either classified as Napa or other district bottlings as well as Reserves. A range of limited-release wines is also made and these labels are available only at the winery, some of which are undoubtedly very classy. (DM)

● **Cabernet Sauvignon** Napa Valley★★★ £E   Oakville★★★★ £E   Reserve Napa Valley❂❂❂❂❂ £H
● **Merlot** Napa Valley★★ £D   Carneros★ £E   Stag's Leap District★★★ £E
● **Pinot Noir** Napa Valley★ £C   Carneros★★ £E   Reserve★★★ £F
● **Zinfandel** Coastal Private Selection★★ £B   Napa Valley★★★ £C
● **IO** Santa Barbara County★★ £C
O **Chardonnay** Napa Valley★★ £C   Carneros★★★ £D   Reserve★★★ £E
O **Fumé Blanc** Napa Valley★★ £C   Reserve★★★ £E

MUMM NAPA   Rutherford   www.mummcuveenapa.com   A: ADo

Owner: Champagne GH Mumm   8445 Silverado Trail, Rutherford, CA 94573
Another California sparkling-wine operation with a leading Champagne house as owner. The regular Champagne from the parent can often disappoint but the California Brut Cuvée Prestige offers a very attractive, well-priced alternative. It is fresh and forward with just a touch of bready yeast character. The DVX Vintage cuvée is of a different order, combining forward fruit with a rich, leesy character and a firm, balanced structure for short ageing on release. (DM)

O **Brut Cuvée Prestige** Napa Valley★★ £C   O **Blanc de Blancs** Napa Valley★★ £C
O **Cuvée DVX Vintage** Napa Valley★★★ £F
◉ **Blanc de Noirs** Napa Valley★★ £C

NEWTON   Spring Mountain   www.clicquot.com   A: JAr

Owner: LVMH   2555 Madrona Avenue, St Helena, CA 94574
This well-established Napa operation is now part of the expanding portfolio of Moët Hennessey premium wineries around the world along with such names as CLOUDY BAY and BOUCHARD PÈRE ET FILS. The wines here have always been impressive and reasonably priced if not quite reaching the pinnacles achieved elsewhere. At the lower level there is decent Red Label Chardonnay and Special Cuvée Merlot. The best wines though are the impressive Unfiltered range produced with natural fermentation and handled by gravity in the winery. The low-volume Epic bottling is a firm, power-fully structured Merlot sourced from the best mountainside slopes on the property. (DM)

● **Cabernet Sauvignon** Unfiltered Napa Valley★★★★ £E   ● **Pinot Noir** Unfiltered Napa Valley★★ £D
● **Merlot** Unfiltered★★★ £E   ● **Epic** Napa Valley★★★★ £F
O **Chardonnay** Unfiltered★★★ £E

NIEBAUM-COPPOLA ESTATE   Rutherford   www.niebaum-coppola.com   A: Rws

Owner: Francis Ford Coppola   1991 St Helena Highway, Rutherford, CA 94573
This began as a small operation when film director Francis Ford Coppola first became involved in wine-growing, but there is now a sizeable output. As well as the premium wines under the Estate and Directors Reserve labels two lower-priced ranges are also offered. The Diamond Series wines are varietals sourced throughout the North Coast and there are three wines under the Francis Coppola Presents label:

a Rosso, Bianco and Talia Rosé. These are straightfoward, reliable, fruit-driven wines but it is the top labels under both the Directors Reserve and Estate Wines labels that really impress. As well as the wines listed below there is a small production under the Estate label of Dolcetto and Reserve Syrah. Zinfandel Edizione Pennino is rich and powerful with dense, brambly fruit. At the pinnacle there are two Flagship wines. Blancaneaux is an unusual but impressive blend of Chardonnay, Viognier, Marsanne and Roussanne. Rubicon is a very structured, firm and powerful meritage red aged for 26 months in French oak and requires at least six to seven years' patience. (DM)

● **Cabernet Franc** Estate★★★£E   ● **Cask Cabernet** Estate★★★£F
● **Cabernet Sauvignon** Estate★★★£F   ● **Rubicon** Rutherford★★★★★£G
● **Merlot** Directors Reserve★★£D   ◉ **Zinfandel** Edizione Pennino★★★★£E
O **Blancaneaux** Rutherford★★★£E   O **Chardonnay** Directors Series★★£C

OPUS ONE   Oakville   www.opusonewinery.com   A: Par

Owner: Robert Mondavi/Baron Philip de Rothschild SA   7900 St Helena Hwy, Oakville, CA 94562
This MONDAVI/Rothschild (MOUTON-ROTHSCHILD) joint venture was first conceived in 1978, the first vintage being in 1979. At the time, super-premium Napa styles of Cabernet had not yet materialised and Opus One was uniquely highly priced among its peers. The Mondavi Reserve Cabernet Sauvignon from the great To-Kalon vineyard has, however, consistently been of a higher standard, although the Q Block part of that same vineyard contributes to Opus One. The wine, a blend of all five Bordeaux varieties, has never quite fulfilled its potential but the scale of the production means there aren't the scarcity problems found with some other top Californian reds. The wine is always given a very lengthy cuvaison of up to 40 days and is aged in 100 per cent new French oak. (DM)

● **Opus One** Napa Valley★★★★£H

PAHLMEYER   Napa Valley   www.pahlmeyer.com   A: RWs

Owner: Jayson Pahlmeyer 101 South Combs, Suite 10, Napa, CA 94558
This is a top-quality, low-volume winery producing three super-premium wines, although occasional declassified lots under the Jayson label can also be very good. A commited approach to viticulture throughout Pahlmeyer's vineyard sources, with reduced yields and careful canopy management, along with inventive winemaking by Erin Green results in wines of depth, concentration and great finesse. In the winery the reds are partly whole-bunch fermented, helping to provide both a supple texture and firm structure. While they should undoubtedly be cellared for at least half a decade the tannin is just a touch more balanced and harmonious than in some others. A Sonoma Coast Chardonnay has been added from the 2001 vintage. Both Chardonnays are wild yeast fermented in 100 per cent new oak and bottled with neither fining nor filtration. (DM)

● **Merlot** Napa Valley★★★★★£F   ● **Proprietary Red** Napa Valley★★★★★£F
O **Chardonnay** Napa Valley★★★★£F

PARADIGM   Oakville   www.paradigmwinery.com   A: DDr

Owner: Ren & Marilyn Harris   683 Dwyer Road, Oakville, CA 94562
The Harris's sizeable vineyard property in the heart of Oakville underpins the quality achieved at this excellent small estate. Production is very small at around 5,000 cases and quality is admirable. The Cabernet Sauvignon, blended with Cabernet Franc and Merlot for harmony, is the principle wine produced here but they also handcraft very good Merlot, a tiny amount of Zinfandel and, most recently, Cabernet Franc. (DM)

● **Cabernet Sauvignon** Estate★★★★£E

PATZ AND HALL   Napa Valley   www.patzhall.com   A:T&W

Owner: James Hall and Donald Patz   PO Box 5479, Napa, CA 94581

The two partners here first worked for FLORA SPRINGS and during this association they determined to establish a small winemaking operation in order to produce top-quality Pinot Noir and Chardonnay. The regular bottlings of Pinot Noir (from Sonoma County as well as the Russian River) and Napa Valley Chardonnay are impressive but even more so are the small-volume runs produced from a number of single vineyards. Top Pinot Noir is now sourced from the Hyde and Pisoni vineyards, Chardonnay and Pinot from Alder Springs in Mendocino and, most recently, Durrell Ranch. Chardonnay also comes from Dutton Ranch and Woolsey Road. As with so many top-quality producers now, indigenous yeasts are favoured and the wines are always bottled unfiltered and see a high proportion of new oak. These are big, forward, explosive examples of both varieties. (DM)

● **Pinot Noir** Sonoma County★★★£E Russian River★★★£E
O **Chardonnay** Napa Valley★★★£D Dutton Ranch★★★★£E Woolsey Road Vineyard★★★★£E

JOSEPH PHELPS   Napa Valley   www.jpvwines.com   A:WTs

Owner: Joe Phelps   200 Taplin Road, St Helena, CA 94574

Now a fairly large operation, originally founded in 1972, Phelps has built a reputation based on top-quality, Bordeaux-style red varietals and blends. There is a full range that encompasses those other usual suspects Chardonnay and Sauvignon Blanc, a small volume of an excellent late-harvest Scheurebe white and an extensive range of Rhône-style reds and whites. These are labelled Vin du Mistral (after the fierce Mistral wind that can cause havoc in the Rhône Valley) and along with the regular AVA Cabernet, Chardonnay and Sauvignon Blanc, are good but lack just a little excitement. The top label Cabernet Sauvignon from the Backus Vineyard and the magnificent Insignia are of a different order. The former is produced from 100 per cent Oakville Cabernet Sauvignon and is a massive, structured wine with very ripe, black fruit and supple tannin. The Insignia is a meritage blend of all five Bordeaux red varieties. Equally powerful and dense, this is more sumptuous and exotic than the Backus Cabernet but equally ageworthy. (DM)

● **Merlot** Napa Valley★★★£E ● **Insignia** Napa Valley★★★★★£G
● **Cabernet Sauvignon** Napa Valley★★£E Backus Vineyard★★★★★£G
● **Le Mistral** California★★£D ● **Syrah** Napa Valley★★★£E
O **Chardonnay** Ovation★★★£E Los Carneros★★£D
O **Sauvignon Blanc** Napa Valley★£C O **Viognier** Napa Valley★★£D

PINE RIDGE   Stags Leap   www.pineridgewinery.com   A: Hal

Owner: Nancy Andrus   5901 Silverado Trail, Napa, CA 94558

Founded in 1978 this is now a relatively large property producing just mid- to premium-range wines. There are some 122 ha (300 acres) planted in 16 different vineyard locations throughout the Napa Valley. Indeed, estate-grown grapes account for some 95 per cent of the winery's production. The focus is mainly on the Bordeaux varieties, with the wines often lighter and less substantial than some of their neighbours. A rare blend of Chenin Blanc and Viognier is cool-fermented to emphasise its fruit. Onyx is also unusual for California, a blend of Malbec and Tannat (most commonly associated with the dark wines of Madiran). The winery's flagship wine, the meritage Andrus Reserve, is sourced from close-planted estate vineyards in the Mayacamas. Aged in 100 per cent high-toast new oak with malolactic fermentation in barrel, this is a spicy, big, but at times austere wine. (DM)

● **Cabernet Sauvignon** Rutherford★★£E Stags Leap District★★★£F
● **Andrus** Reserve★★★★£G ● **Merlot** Crimson Creek★★£D
● **Cabernet Franc** Trois Cuvées★★★£D

O **Chardonnay** Stags Leap District★★ £C Dijon Clones★★★ £E
O **Chenin Blanc-Viognier** Estate★ £B

PLUMPJACK Oakville www.plumpjack.com   A: Vin

Owner: Getty Family   620 Oakville Cross Road, Oakville, CA 94562
The Plumpjack winery is just a part of this leisure-based operation that specialises in food and wine along with the luxury Squaw Valley Inn at Olympic Valley. Good to very good Cabernet Sauvignon, Merlot and Chardonnay is produced at the winery, nestled into the hills in the eastern side of the valley surrounded by some 19.5 ha (48 acres) of estate vineyards planted in 1992. The vines are still young and so cannot be excessively restricted in terms of their yield. The best must surely be to come if the same winemaking philosophy is maintained. The Chardonnay is ripe, forward and toasty, the Cabernet powerful and structured. The very expensive Reserve offers an extra dimension at a not inconsiderable premium. A Syrah from the Russian River Valley has also been added with the 2001 vintage. (DM)
● **Merlot** Napa Valley★★ £E ● **Cabernet Sauvignon** Estate★★★ £F
O **Chardonnay** Reserve★★★ £E

QUINTESSA Rutherford www.quintessa.com   A: Fie

Owner: Agustin Huneeus   1601 Silverado Trail, Rutherford, CA 94573
This winery was originally part of FRANCISCAN, itself a part of the giant Canandaigua Group. Quintessa is now solely owned by Agustin Huneeus whose other property is the Chilean winery VERAMONTE. Just one single-estate wine is produced here, a rich and powerful, very ripe Napa meritage blended from Cabernet Sauvignon, Merlot and Cabernet Franc that is loaded with oak. Certainly very good but not yet among the top flight of Napa reds. (DM)
● **Quintessa** Napa Valley★★★ £G

RAMEY Oakville   A: M&V

Owner: David Ramey   Oakville, CA 94562
David Ramey has had a vast winemaking influence on the style of a number of leading winegrowers, among them CHALK HILL and RUDD ESTATE, where he is still the general manager. He produces under his own Ramey label remarkably fine Chardonnay, impressive for its finesse, intensity and sheer quality as much as for its weight and texture. While the same gamut of winery techniques may be employed here as elsewhere – natural yeast fermentation, lees-enrichment, new oak for barrel-fermentation and ageing *et al* – the key to these wines is their sheer balance and refinement. Of the two single-vineyard bottlings the Hudson has greater weight, the Hyde a tighter, more mineral structure. (DM)
O **Chardonnay** Carneros★★★★ £E Russian River★★★★ £E
O **Chardonnay** Hudson Vineyard★★★★★ £F Hyde Vineyard★★★★★ £F

SAINTSBURY Carneros www.saintsbury.com   A: Adm, J&B

Owner: Richard Ward & David Graves   1500 Los Carneros Avenue, Napa, CA 94559
Long established as one of the top producers of the Burgundian varietals in Carneros. Volume has risen from 3,000 cases in 1981 to a current level of 55,000 cases of which two-thirds are Pinot Noir. While the Carneros AVA and Reserve labels of both Chardonnay and Pinot Noir are serious and refined examples of the Carneros style, the Garnet Pinot Noir offers a straightforward, fruit-laden

example of the grape in the way that the best of Bourgogne Rouge should in Burgundy but so rarely does. A very small amount of Pinot Noir from the estate-owned, single-vineyard Brown Ranch is now bottled individually. Despite the fact that yields reach a surprisingly high three-and-a-half to four tons to the acre, the wines retain a real piercing fruit quality. The only other variety produced is a tiny amount of Pinot Gris. (DM)

● **Pinot Noir** Garnet★★ £C Carneros★★★ £D Reserve★★★★ £F Brown Ranch★★★★ £F
○ **Chardonnay** Carneros★★★ £C Reserve★★★ £E

SCHRAMSBERG   Napa Valley   www.schramsberg.com   A: Vin

Owner: Jamie Davies   1400 Schramsberg Road, Calistoga, CA 94515
This was the first California winery to produce quality sparkling wines from the classic varieties of Champagne, the Pinots Noir and Meunier and Chardonnay. Across the range of cuvées all three grapes are used. A straightforward, non-vintage blend, Mirabelle, is vinified from Pinot Noir and Chardonnay and is a fruit-driven style intended for easy drinking. More serious are the Vintage cuvées Blanc de Blancs, Blanc de Noirs, Brut Rosé and the off-dry Crémant Demi-Sec produced from Flora, a hybrid of Gewürztraminer and Semillon. Reserve is a structured and concentrated Blanc de Noirs, while the J Schram cuvée is part barrel-fermented and blended from the very best lots in a single vintage. (DM)

○ **Blanc de Blancs**★★★ £D   ○ **Blanc de Noirs**★★ £D   ○ **Crémant Demi-Sec**★★ £D
○ **Reserve**★★★★ £F **J Schram**★★★★ £F

SCREAMING EAGLE   Oakville   www.screamingeagle.com

Owner: Jean Phillips   PO Box 134, Oakville, CA 94562
Perhaps first among all the recent Cabernet and meritage superstars of the Napa, certainly if rated by price achieved at auction. Jean Phillips cultivates around 20 ha (50 acres) of Cabernet Sauvignon, Merlot and Cabernet Franc around Oakville but retains just enough of her crop to produce some 500 cases of a super-concentrated, immense and profound Cabernet Sauvignon. The wine is currently sold exclusively via a mailing list and is nigh-on impossible to find except at the major auction houses where the prices obtained will defy belief. (DM)

SHAFER   Stags Leap   www.shafervineyards.com   A: THt

Owner: John Shafer   6154 Silverado Trail, Napa, CA 94558
The Shafer family purchased this remarkable 85-ha (210-acre) hillside property in Stags Leap District in 1972, initially establishing themselves as grape growers rather than winemakers. However, the transition to wine producers has seen their status elevated to the very top echelon of vintners in the state. To support the winery's development, new estate vineyards have been established in Oak Knoll and Carneros. The winery is no longer small – it has grown from an output of 1,000 cases in 1978 to 32,000 today. There is no doubting the sheer quality of the wines, though. Red Shoulder Ranch Chardonnay comes from Carneros and is barrel-fermented in both French and American oak. Malolactic is blocked and the wine is ripe and toasty. Napa Cabernet is part-aged in American oak whereas the Merlot sees only French for 18 months. Of two smaller-volume cuvées, Firebreak is a stylish blend of Sangiovese and Cabernet Sauvignon and Relentless is a rich and powerful Syrah, aged in oak for 26 months. Most profound is the remarkable Hillside Select from the finest Stags Leap fruit – a 100 per cent Cabernet Sauvignon of power, finesse and sheer velvety harmony; truly one of California's very great reds. (DM)

● **Cabernet Sauvignon** Napa Valley★★★★ £E Hillside Select❂❂❂❂❂ £H   ● **Merlot** Napa Valley★★★ £E
○ **Chardonnay** Red Shoulder Ranch★★★★ £E

SILVER OAK CELLARS Napa Valley www.silveroak.com A:T&W

Owner: Ray Duncan 915 Oakville Cross Road, Oakville, CA 94562
Two powerful and supple Cabernets are produced at Silver Oak Cellars. The estate was established as a partnership between Ray Duncan and the late Justin Meyer, the original winemaker. Daniel Baron took over those reins and continues to produce wines of substance and quality despite production now running at around 70,000 cases a year. The style is classic northern California: wines that are rich, ripe and full but offer an accessible, rounded texture and surprisingly soft tannins; the Napa Valley label has additional finesse and depth. A new venture sees the production of a premium Merlot from the Soda Canyon Ranch in south-eastern Napa, planted in finely drained volcanic soils. This is marketed under the Twomey label and promises much. (DM)
● **Cabernet Sauvignon** Alexander Valley★★★ £F Napa Valley★★★★ £G

SPOTTSWOODE St Helena www.spottswoode.com A: DDr

Owner: Mary Novak 1902 Madrona Ave, St Helena, CA 94574
This historic estate was originally established in 1882 and comprises a lavish Victorian farmhouse and a modern winery constructed in 1999. The estate has 15 ha (37 acres) planted to Cabernet Sauvignon, Cabernet Franc and Sauvignon Blanc, the latter just a single hectare (2.5 acres). The Cabernet is sourced fully from estate fruit, with a small component of Cabernet Franc in the blend. It is a deep, finely structured wine, with refined tannins and great ageing potential; in top vintages undoubtedly of five-star quality. The Sauvignon, sourced from estate fruit as well as vineyards in Calistoga and Carneros, is in a quintessentially California style: part barrel-fermented with lees-enrichment it is ripe, stylish and long. (DM)
● **Cabernet Sauvignon** Napa Valley★★★★★ £G
○ **Sauvignon Blanc** Napa Valley★★★ £E

STAG'S LEAP WINE CELLARS Stags Leap www.cask23.com A: WTs

Owner: Warren Winiarski 5766 Silverdao Trail, Napa, CA 94558
Warren Winiarski's Stag's Leap Wine Cellars will forever be famous in wine circles as a result of the 1976 Paris tasting, when the Cask 23 outgunned the best from Bordeaux to the astonishment of the French judges on that day. The wine world has come a long way in the last 25 years and while Cask 23 remains an impressive example of hillside Napa Cabernet there is matching quality among its immediate neighbours. The lower-level Fay and SLV bottlings are good rather than great but are not excessively priced. The whites include some good Sauvignon Blanc, particularly the Rancho Chimiles, which is barrel-fermented on lees but is not put through malolactic. The barrel-fermented Beckstoffer Ranch, a particularly stylish and balanced Chardonnay, is now joined by a partly barrel-fermented example from the Arcadia estate-owned vineyard, producing a tighter, fruit-driven wine. The top Cabernets will age very well. (DM)
● **Cabernet Sauvignon** Napa Valley★ £E Fay Estate★★★ £F SLV★★★★ £G Cask 23★★★★ £H
● **Merlot** Napa Valley★★ £E
○ **Chardonnay** Napa Valley★ £D Arcadia★★★ £E Beckstoffer Ranch★★★ £E
○ **Sauvignon Blanc** Napa Valley★ £C

STAGLIN FAMILY Rutherford www.staglinfamily.com A: L&S

Owner: Garen and Shari Staglin 1570 Bella Oaks Lane, Rutherford, CA 94573
The Staglins founded their small winery in 1985 with 20 ha (50 acres) of vineyard which had

originally been a source for André Tschelistcheff when blending his legendary vintages of the BEAULIEU VINEYARDS Private Reserve Georges de la Tour Cabernet. Production now runs at just under 10,000 cases a year, the majority Cabernet Sauvignon, with just a few hundred cases of a Sangiovese Stagliano as well as Chardonnay. The estate Chardonnay and Cabernet are both very impressive. A second label Salus is now released to ensure the integrity of the estate wines. Although the Salus wines are lighter and more obviously fruit-driven, all the wines are marked by weight, rich texture and extract. The Rutherford bottlings achieve this with ease and the Cabernet Sauvignon in particular is very refined. Both reds and whites will age well, the Rutherford Cabernet requiring five years or so. (DM)

● **Cabernet Sauvignon** Salus★★★ £F   Rutherford★★★★★ £G
○ **Chardonnay** Salus★★★ £E   Rutherford★★★★ £F

STONY HILL   Spring Mountain   www.stonyhillvineyard.com   A: Vin

Owner: Peter McCrea   3331 St Helena Highway, St Helena, CA 94574
Mountain-grown Chardonnay has been planted at this property since the 1950s; indeed 2002 marked the 50th anniversary for Stony Hill and the McCrea family has presided over operations here since the winery was established. In California terms this is a veritable dynasty. The style for all the whites remains the same: medium-weight wines of intensity and finesse with a pure, mineral streak running through them. The vineyards are planted on meagre volcanic soils providing the necessary stress in the vines for fruit with piercing intensity. A small amount of Gewürztraminer and Tocai Friulano is also now produced, both promising. (DM)

○ **Chardonnay** Napa Valley★★★ £D   ○ **Riesling** Napa Valley★★ £B

STORYBOOK MOUNTAIN VINEYARD   Napa Valley   www.storybookwines.com

Owner: Jerry Seps   3835 Highway 128, Calistoga, CA 94515
This is a Zinfandel-only winery and a very good one, located on the red-clay, loam slopes of the Mayacamas range. The estate vineyards surrounding the property were originally planted in the 1880s and these hillside plots continue to show the potential of the variety. Insecticides and herbicides are avoided and the wine is vinified and aged in century-old caves which provide an ideal environment with even year-round temperatures and just the right level of humidity. A combination of French, American and Hungarian oak is used to age the wines which are full-bodied and structured, tight and firm in their youth but with the kind of cellaring potential the variety often lacks. A top estate reserve is regularly produced with an occasional limited-production, special vintage selection Eastern Exposures which has a small amount (less than five per cent) of Viognier to add fragrance. (DM)

● **Zinfandel** Atlas Peak★★★ £C   Mayacamas Range★★★ £C

SWANSON   Rutherford   www.swansonvineyards.com   A: L&W

Owner: W Clarke Swanson Jnr   1271 Manley Lane, Rutherford, CA 94573
Impressive and stylish wines are produced at this family-run Napa winery, established in 1985. Production is now at 25,000 cases and quality has remained good to very good. As well as the three principle releases, Sangiovese, Syrah, Cabernet Sauvignon and a Late Harvest Semillon have also been produced in recent vintages. Merlot has been made since the winery was founded; it is crafted in a medium-full, supple style with an emphasis on ripe, forward, plummy fruit and well-judged oak. The premium Alexis blends mainly Cabernet Sauvignon with Syrah and also a little Cabernet Franc and Merlot from the estate Schmitt Ranch. The style is modern with an extending vatting of around four weeks and malolactic in barrel. The wine is ripe and supple with quite marked background oak spice. Give it four to five years. (DM)

● **Merlot** Napa Valley★★★ £D **Alexis** Napa Valley★★★★ £F
○ **Pinot Grigio** Napa Valley★ £C

PHILIP TOGNI   Spring Mountain   A:Vin, JAr,Rew

Owner: Philip Togni   3780 Spring Mountain Road, St Helena, CA 94574
Philip Togni is a vastly experienced winemaker, having worked at a number of major wineries during
a career spanning four decades. From his own estate vineyards on Spring Mountain he produces one
of the more impressive Cabernets to be found in the Napa. It is a dense, powerful wine, with
considerable tannin reinforcing its mountain origins, its texture rounded by malolactic fermentation
in barrel. Powerful and long-lived it requires eight to ten years in the cellar. The 2000 was right on
the cusp of five stars. Togni also produces a tiny amount of a fine sweet dessert wine from Black
Muscat under the Ca Togni label. (DM)
● **Cabernet Sauvignon** Spring Mountain★★★★★ £G

TURLEY CELLARS   St Helena   www.turleywinecellars.com   A:THt

Owner: Larry Turley   3358 St Helena Highway, St Helena, CA 94574
Larry Turley produces perhaps the modern benchmark for Zinfandel – massive, dark, brooding examples
of the variety. The wines are increasingly made from a wide range of sources and generally bottled as
single-vineyard cuvées. What is remarkable about these wines is that despite having alcohol levels more
akin to fortified wines – 16 per cent is not uncommon – there is still a remarkable harmony and finesse
as well as extraordinarily concentrated, ripe, berry fruit. Very good Petite Sirah is also produced from
estate as well as the Napa Valley Hayne and Rattlesnake Acres vineyards. These are very powerful and
long-lived wines whereas the Zins can be approachable with just two or three years. All of the wines are
produced in small lots, often fewer than 200 cases, with the majority sold by mailing list. Some of the
wines can offer remarkable value. (DM)
● **Zinfandel** Juvenile★★★ £C   Duarte★★★★ £D   Old Vines★★★★ £E

VIADER   Napa Valley   www.viader.com   A: DDr

Owner: Delia Viader   1120 Deer Park Road, Deer Park, CA 94576
Very stylish and refined red wines are crafted at this small estate nestled in the foothills of Howell
Mountain. Production is less than 5,000 cases a year. The vineyard is planted on well-drained
volcanic soils producing fruit of real depth and intensity. The Viader red is a blend of Cabernet
Sauvignon and Cabernet Franc and is the mainstay of the winery. It is powerful, intense and supple
with malolactic taking place in barrel and, although there is close to 100 per cent new oak, it is
seamlessly integrated, refined and harmonious. Unusually the Cabernet Franc component is aged in
Russian oak. A very small amount of a Petit Verdot V and some estate Syrah are also produced and
are wines of great potential. A new development is the establishment of a small vineyard in the
Bolgheri region of Tuscany where a wine based on Merlot with a small amount of Cabernet Franc,
Cabernet Sauvignon and Sangiovese is to be produced. The first vintage is planned for 2005 or 2006.
(DM)
● **Viader** Estate★★★★★ £F

OTHER WINES OF NOTE

ATLAS PEAK ● **Sangiovese** Reserve Atlas Peak £D O **Chardonnay** Atlas Peak £C
ALTAMURA ● **Cabernet Sauvignon** Napa Valley £F ● **Sangiovese** California £E
ANDERSONS CONN VALLEY ● **Pinot Noir** Valhalla Vineyard £F ● **Eloge** Napa Valley £G
ARTESA ● **Pinot Noir** Carneros Reserve £E O **Chardonnay** Carneros Reserve £D
BARBOUR ● **Cabernet Sauvignon** Napa Valley £G
BARNETT VINEYARDS ● **Cabernet Sauvignon** Spring Mountain £F O **Chardonnay** Napa Valley £D
BELL WINE CELLARS ● **Cabernet Sauvignon** Napa Valley FD Bartelle Vineyard £F
● **Syrah** Sierra Foothills Canterbury Vineyard £D
BENESSERE ● **Zinfandel** Napa Valley £D
BLANKIET ESTATE ● **Cabernet Sauvignon** Paradise Hills £G
BUEHLER VINEYARDS ● **Cabernet Sauvignon** Napa Valley Estate £E O **Chardonnay** Russian River£C
BURGESS CELLARS ● **Cabernet Sauvignon** Vintage Selection Napa Valley £E
CALDWELL ● **Cabernet Sauvignon** Napa Valley £F ● **Caldwell Red** Napa Valley £G
CARNEROS CREEK ● **Pinot Noir** Carneros Signature Reserve £F O **Chardonnay** Palombo Vineyard£D
CARTLIDGE AND BROWNE ● **Zinfandel** California £B O **Chardonnay** California £B
CHIMNEY ROCK ● **Cabernet Sauvignon** Stags Leap District £E ● **Elevage** Stags Leap District £F
O **Chardonnay** Carneros £C
CLOS DU VAL ● **Zinfandel** Pallisade Vineyard £E ● **Cabernet Sauvignon** Pallisade Vineyard £F
● **Cabernet Sauvignon**Vineyard Georges III £F O **Chardonnay** Carneros £C
CLOS PEGASE ● **Cabernet Sauvignon** Napa Valley £E O **Chardonnay** Hommage Artists Series £E
CONN CREEK ● **Cabernet Sauvignon** Limited Release £D ● **Anthology** £F
CORNERSTONE CELLARS ● **Cabernet Sauvignon** Cornerstone Vineyard £F
COSENTINO ● **The Zin** California £D ● **The Poet** Napa Valley £F
DEL DOTTO ● **Cabernet Sauvignon** Estate Napa Valley £F ● **Giovanni's Tuscan Reserve** Napa Valley£F
EHLER'S GROVE ● **Cabernet Sauvignon** Napa Valley £D
EL MOLINO ● **Pinot Noir** Napa Valley £E O **Chardonnay** Rutherford £F
ELYSE ● **Nero Misto** California £C ● **Cabernet Sauvignon** Morisoli Vineyard £F
ETUDE ● **Cabernet Sauvignon** Napa Valley £F ● **Pinot Noir** Carneros £E
FIFE ● **Max Cuvée** £C ● **Zinfandel** Old Vines £C
FOLIE À DEUX ● **Zinfandel** La Grande Folie Amador County £E
FORMAN ● **Cabernet Sauvignon** Napa Valley £E O **Chardonnay** Napa Valley £D
FREEMARK ABBEY ● **Cabernet Sauvignon** Napa Valley £E Bosché Estate £F
GIRARD ● **Petite Sirah** Napa Valley £C O **Sauvignon Blanc** Napa Valley £C
GROTH ● **Cabernet Sauvignon** Napa Valley £E Reserve £H O **Chardonnay** Napa Valley £C
HARTWELL VINEYARDS ● **Cabernet Sauvignon** Stags Leap District £G O **Chardonnay** Napa Valley£E
HENDRY ● **Zinfandel** Napa Valley £D O **Chardonnay** Napa Valley £D
JARVIS ● **Cabernet Sauvignon** Napa Valley £G O **Chardonnay** Napa Valley £E
JONES FAMILY ● **Cabernet Sauvignon** Napa Valley £F
HOWELL MOUNTAIN VINEYARD ● **Zinfandel** Old Vine £D Beatty Ranch £E
JUDD'S HILL ● **Cabernet Sauvignon** Napa Valley £D ● **Merlot** Summers Ranch £E
ROBERT KEENAN ● **Cabernet Sauvignon** Spring Mouintain £E ● **Merlot** Napa Valley £E
KIRKLAND RANCH ● **Cabernet Sauvignon** Napa Valley £E O **Chardonnay** Napa Valley £D
KOVES-NEWLAN ● **Zinfandel** Napa Valley £C
LAMBOURNE FAMILY ● **Zinfandel** Team Connection £D
LA SIRENA ● **Cabernet Sauvignon** Napa Valley £H ● **Sangiovese** Napa Valley £E
LEWELLING ● **Cabernet Sauvignon** Napa Valley £E
LIPARITA ● **Merlot** Napa Valley £E O **Sauvignon Blanc** Oakville £C
LONG VINEYARDS ● **Cabernet Sauvignon** Estate £F O **Chardonnay** Estate £E
MACROSTIE ● **Syrah** Blue Oaks Vineyard £C O **Chardonnay** Carneros £C
MARKHAM VINEYARDS ● **Cabernet Sauvignon** Reserve £F ● **Petite Sirah** Napa Valley £D
● **Zinfandel** Napa Valley £D ● **Merlot** Napa Valley £D
LOUIS M MARTINI ● **Cabernet Sauvignon** Monte Rosso Vineyard £E

MASON CELLARS ● **Merlot** Napa Valley £D   O **Sauvignon Blanc** Napa Valley £C
MAYACAMUS O **Chardonnay** Napa Valley £E
MELKA ● **Metisse Red** Napa Valley £F   ● **Cabernet Sauvignon** Napa Valley £D
MERRYVALE ● **Merlot** Reserve Napa Valley £G   ● **Cabernet Sauvignon** Reserve Napa Valley £G
● **Profile** Napa Valley £G   O **Chardonnay** Silouette £F
MONTICELLO ● **Cabernet Sauvignon** Jefferson Cuvée £D   O **Chardonnay** Corley Reserve £D
MOUNT VEEDER WINERY ● **Cabernet Sauvignon** Napa Valley £E   ● **Reserve** Napa Valley £F
NEWLAN ● **Cabernet Sauvignon** Napa Valley £F   ● **Pinot Noir** Napa Valley £E
O **Chardonnay** Napa Valley £D
NEYERS ● **Syrah** Hudson Vineyards £F   O **Chardonnay** Napa Valley £D
NOVA ● **Merlot** Marilyn Napa Valley £C
OAKFORD ● **Cabernet Sauvignon** Estate £H
PALOMA ● **Merlot** Spring Mountain Estate £E   ● **Syrah** Spring Mountain Estate £E
PAOLETTI ● **Cabernet Sauvignon** Napa Valley Estate £E   ● **Non Plus Ultra** Napa Valley Estate £G
ROBERT PECOTA ● **Syrah** Monterey £C   O **Muscat Canelli** Moscato d'Andrea £B
PEJU ● **Cabernet Franc** Reserve £F   ● **Cabernet Sauvignon** Reserve £G
O **Chardonnay** Estate £D
PEPI O **Sauvignon Blanc** Two Heart £B   O **Arneis** Central Coast £B
PRIDE MOUNTAIN ● **Cabernet Sauvignon** Napa Valley £F   O **Chardonnay** Napa Valley £E
KENT RASMUSSEN O **Chardonnay** Napa Valley £D
RAYMOND ● **Cabernet Sauvignon** Reserve £E   Generations £G   O **Chardonnay** Reserve £C
REVERIE ● **Cabernet Sauvignon** Diamond Mountain £F   ● **Special Reserve** Napa Valley £G
ROCKING HORSE ● **Zinfandel** Napa Valley £C   ● **Cabernet Sauvignon** Garvey Family Vineyards £E
RUDD ESTATE O **Chardonnay** Russian River £E   O **Sauvignon Blanc** Napa Valley £D
ROMBAUER ● **Zinfandel** Napa Valley £C   O **Chardonnay** Napa Valley £C
SADDLEBACK CELLARS ● **Cabernet Sauvignon** Napa Valley £E   ● **Zinfandel** Old Vines £D
ST CLEMENT ● **Merlot** Napa Valley £D   O **Chardonnay** Abbots Vineyard £C
ST SUPÉRY ● **Merritage Red** Napa Valley £F   ● **Cabernet Sauvignon** Napa Valley £E
O **Sauvignon Blanc** Napa Valley £C   O **Chardonnay** Dollarhide Ranch £D
SEAVEY ● **Cabernet Sauvignon** Napa Valley £F   O **Chardonnay** Napa Valley £E
SELENE ● **Merlot** Napa Valley £E   O **Sauvignon Blanc** Hyde Vineyard £C
SEQUOIA GROVE ● **Cabernet Sauvignon** Napa Valley £E   Reserve Rutherford £F
O **Chardonnay** Carneros £D
SHOWKET ● **Cabernet Sauvignon** Oakville £E
SIGNORELLO ● **Cabernet Sauvignon** Estate Napa Valley £E   ● **Syrah** Estate Napa Valley £F
O **Chardonnay** Carneros £D
SILVERADO VINEYARDS ● **Cabernet Sauvignon** Stags Leap District £F   ● **Merlot** Napa Valley £E
ROBERT SINSKEY ● **Merlot** Reserve £E   ● **Pinot Noir** Carneros £D   O **Chardonnay** Carneros £D
SNOWDEN ● **Cabernet Sauvignon** Napa Valley £F
SPRING MOUNTAIN VINEYARD ● **Syrah** Estate £F
STERLING VINEYARDS ● **Cabernet Sauvignon** Diamond Mountain £E
● **Merlot** Three Palms Vineyard £F
D.R. STEPHENS ● **Cabernet Sauvignon** Napa Valley £G   O **Chardonnay** Napa Valley £F
SUMMERS RANCH ● **Merlot** Knights Valley £C
THE TERRACES ● **Cabernet Sauvignon** Napa Valley £F   ● **Zinfandel** Napa Valley £D
TITUS ● **Cabernet Franc** Napa Valley £D   ● **Petite Sirah** Mendocino County £E
TRUCHARD ● **Merlot** Carneros £D   ● **Syrah** Carneros £E   O **Chardonnay** Carneros £D
TURNBULL ● **Cabernet Sauvignon** Estate £F   O **Chardonnay** Napa Valley £E
VINE CLIFF ● **Cabernet Sauvignon** Napa Valley £F   ● **Merlot** Napa Valley £E
O **Chardonnay** Napa Valley £E
VINEYARD 29 ● **Cabernet Sauvignon** Napa Valley £H
VON STRASSER ● **Cabernet Sauvignon** Diamond Mountain £F
WHITEHALL LANE ● **Cabernet Sauvignon** Napa Valley £E   Reserve £F
O **Sauvignon Blanc** Napa Valley £B
WHITE ROCK ● **White Rock Red** Napa Valley £F   O **Chardonnay** Napa Valley £D
ZD WINES ● **Cabernet Sauvignon** Reserve £G   O **Chardonnay** Reserve £E

Author's Choice (DM)

A dozen supreme Napa reds

ABREU ● **Cabernet Sauvignon** Madrona Ranch

ARAUJO ● **Cabernet Sauvignon** Eisele Vineyard

ARIETTA ● **H Block One Red** Napa Valley

BRYANT FAMILY ● **Cabernet Sauvignon** Napa Valley

CHATEAU MONTELENA ● **Cabernet Sauvignon** Montelena Estate

DALLA VALLE ● **Cabernet Sauvignon** Estate Oakville

DIAMOND CREEK ● **Cabernet Sauvignon** Red Rock Terrace

DOMINUS ESTATE ● **Dominus** Yountville

DUNN VINEYARDS ● **Cabernet Sauvignon** Estate Howell Mountain

HARLAN ESTATE ● **Estate Red** Napa Valley

ROBERT MONDAVI ● **Cabernet Sauvignon** Reserve Napa Valley

SHAFER ● **Cabernet Sauvignon** Hillside Select

A selection of diverse Napa whites

FLORA SPRINGS ○ **Chardonnay** Barrel Fermented Reserve

FROG'S LEAP ○ **Sauvignon Blanc** Napa Valley

HESS COLLECTION ○ **Chardonnay** Napa Valley Collection

JADE MOUNTAIN ○ **Viognier** Para's Vineyard

KONGSGAARD ○ **Roussanne/Viognier** Napa Valley

LUNA ○ **Pinot Grigio** Napa Valley

MINER FAMILY ○ **Chardonnay** Wild Yeast

NIEBAUM-COPPOLA ○ **Blancaneaux** Rutherford

PAHLMEYER ○ **Chardonnay** Napa Valley

STAGLIN FAMILY ○ **Chardonnay** Rutherford

The best of Carneros

ACACIA ● **Pinot Noir** Beckstoffer Vineyard

CLINE CELLARS ● **Mourvedre** Small Berry Vineyard

CUVAISON ○ **Chardonnay** Estate Selection

DOMAINE CARNEROS ● **Pinot Noir** Famous Gate

GLORIA FERRER ○ **Carneros Cuvée** Carneros

HAVENS ● **Syrah** Napa Valley

JADE MOUNTAIN ● **Syrah** Hudson Vineyard

KONGSGAARD ● **Syrah** Napa Valley

SAINTSBURY ● **Pinot Noir** Reserve

RAMEY ○ **Chardonnay** Hudson Vineyard

California Central Coast

The coastline from around Santa Barbara to just south of San Francisco has over the last decade and a half emerged as an excellent alternative to the larger regions on the North Coast and along the Napa Valley for a number of quality wine styles. Production is more scattered but includes some very good cool-climate whites and reds and impressive Rhône styles and Zinfandels and, as elsewhere, new and innovative producers are emerging. Prices are high and rising although only Pinot Noir and, to a lesser extent, Syrah are getting anywhere near the stratospheric levels of the super-premium Cabernet blends on the North Coast. In order to cover the remainder of California's wine growing areas – in addition to the Central Coast – Central Valley and the Temecula region to the south of Los Angeles are also included here, as well as the far superior wines of Amador County, Livermore Valley and the Sierra Foothills.

Santa Barbara County

Santa Barbara County is to the north of Los Angeles and follows the coastline embracing the regional AVAs of **Santa Maria** to the north of the county, **Santa Ynez** and the recently established **Santa Rita Hills**. Santa Rita, located between the towns of Lompoc and Buellton, includes the great Sanford and Benedict Vineyard within its boundaries. This is an excellent source of top Pinot Noir and Chardonnay and is notably affected by cooling sea breezes – more so than the neighbouring Santa Ynez Valley, which is further inland. The coolest western sectors provide ripe, tropical Chardonnay, while further east some increasingly impressive Syrah, Grenache and white Rhône varieties are grown, as well as Cabernet Sauvignon and Merlot. To the north of the county the Santa Maria Valley provides some of the best Pinot Noir in the state and some excellent Chardonnay. Pinot Blanc and Syrah are also successful here.

San Luis Obispo County

The northern tip of the Santa Maria AVA lies within San Luis Obispo County which stretches northwards along the coast and a considerable way inland to north of Paso Robles. Four AVA's are contained within its boundaries. **Arroyo Grande** and **Edna Valley** are both relatively cool. The former a fine source of Chardonnay and Pinot Noir, whereas the Edna Valley has also provided some excellent Rhône styles and Sauvignon Blanc and Semillon. Further to the north **Paso Robles** is warmer and the wines are fuller and riper in style. This is generally red-wine territory with very good Cabernet Sauvignon, Merlot, Zinfandel and Syrah. There are also white Rhône varieties planted closer to the ocean along with good Chardonnay. **York Mountain** to the west of Paso Robles is also cooled by altitude.

Monterey County

Extensive area giving its name to an AVA that stretches down from the coast at the town of Monterey along the Salinas River valley almost to Paso Robles. On the coast just to the south of Monterey are the **Carmel Valley** and, further inland, the **Santa Lucia Highlands** AVAs. The former has a surprisingly protected balmy climate and Cabernet Sauvignon and Merlot are successful; the latter is a source of some of the most impressive recent bottlings of Pinot Noir, some of it very pricey indeed. A number of top producers have sourced from the highly regarded Pisoni Vineyard. To the east of Soledad and the Salinas river is the tiny monopole appellation of **Chalone**. First-class Chardonnay, Pinot Blanc and Pinot Noir are grown here. Going south down the Salinas Valley from Soledad are the AVAs of **Arroyo Seco** and **San Lucas**.

Santa Cruz and Santa Clara Counties

Santa Cruz is the principle AVA taken for the best wines, stretching across these two counties. The area includes a whole range of mesoclimates and runs from the southern San Francisco Bay south to Santa Cruz and inland south-east almost to San Benito County, which has just one winery of note (Calera) and the tiny **Mount Harlan** AVA. Chardonnay and Pinot Noir are successful in Santa Cruz as well as warmer-grown Cabernet Sauvignon. Two of California's great reds originate here: the Ridge Monte Bello and Katherine Kennedy Cabernet Sauvignon.

Sierra Foothills, Central Valley and the South

Huge geographical area that encompasses Amador County and stretches into the Sierra Mountains. The AVAs here are **El Dorado**, **Fiddletown** and the **Shenandoah Valley**. The area is mainly a source of top old bush vine Zinfandel but a number of Italian varieties particularly Barbera also enjoy some success. To the south is the giant irrigated Central Valley heart of California's vast bulk wine industry. To the far south towards San Diego is the region of Temecula but no real wines of note have emerged.

A-Z Producers by Region

Amador County
RENWOOD

Arroyo Grande
LAETITIA
TALLEY VINEYARDS
TESTAROSSA

Carmel Valley
BERNARDUS

Chalone
CHALONE

Edna Valley
ALBAN
EDNA VALLEY

Madera County
QUADY

Monterey County
MER SOLEIL WINERY
MORGAN WINERY
ROBERT TALBOTT

Paso Robles
JUSTIN
PEACHY CANYON WINERY
TABLAS CREEK

San Benito County
CALERA

Santa Cruz Mountains
BONNY DOON
CA DEL SOLO
CLOS LACHANCE
KATHRYN KENNEDY
MOUNT EDEN VINEYARDS
RIDGE VINEYARDS

Santa Maria Valley
AU BON CLIMAT
CAMBRIA
COLD HEAVEN
IL PODERE DELL' OLIVOS
QUPÉ
LANE TANNER

Santa Rita Hills
BABCOCK VINEYARDS
BREWER CLIFTON

Santa Ynez Valley
ANDREW MURRAY
GAINEY
SANFORD WINERY

Shenandoah Valley
DOM. DE LA TERRE ROUGE

Other
EDMUNDS ST JOHN
ROSENBLUM CELLARS
OJAI
SEAN THACKREY

Vintages

In general the chart below should give an overall view of what to expect. The AVAs in the main are large by European standards and there can be significant variation from one mesoclimate to another within a single AVA. With the exception of the top Santa Cruz Cabernets most styles will be fading by 12 years or so.

California Central Coast Vintages

	Pinot Noir South Central Coast	Syrah South Central Coast	Cabernet Sauvignon Santa Cruz Area	Zinfandel Amador County
2002	★★★★ A	★★★★ A	★★★★ A	★★★★ A
2001	★★★/★★★★ A	★★★★ A	★★★★ A	★★★★ A
2000	★★★★ B	★★★/★★★★ B	★★★★ A	★★★★ A
1999	★★★★ B	★★★/★★★★ B	★★★/★★★★ A	★★★/★★★★ B
1998	★★★/★★★★ C	★★★/★★★★ B	★★★★ B	★★★/★★★★ B
1997	★★★★ C	★★★★ B	★★★★ B	★★★★ B
1996	★★★★ C	★★★/★★★★ C	★★★★ B	★★★/★★★★ C
1995	★★★★ C	★★★/★★★★ C	★★★/★★★★ B	★★★/★★★★ C
1994	★★★/★★★★ C	★★★/★★★★ C	★★★★ B	★★★/★★★★ C
1993	★★★/★★★★ D	★★★/★★★★ C	★★★★/★★★★★ B	★★★★ C
1992	★★★/★★★★ D	★★★★ C	★★★★ C	★★★/★★★★ D
1991	★★★★ D	★★★★ D	★★★★/★★★★★ C	★★★/★★★★ D
1990	–	★★★★ D	★★★★ C	–

ALBAN   Edna Valley   A: WTs

Owner: John Alban   8575 Orcutt Road, Arroyo Grande, CA 93420

Over a period of 10 years or so John Alban has established himself as one of the finest Rhône specialists on the Central Coast. He has around 20 ha (50 acres) planted to vines in the Edna Valley from which he has been turning out increasingly fine examples for upwards of a decade. His estate vineyards are located in a cool sector of the Edna Valley, and this is reflected in the style, intensity and refinement of his wines. As well as the estate Viognier he makes a good basic example from various Central Coast sources. The estate Roussanne is one of the state's better examples, while Grenache is sourced from warmer Paso Robles. It is the remarkable Syrah bottlings, though – all of them intense and very well crafted – which stand out. Reva is the most approachable, Lorraine and the pricey Seymour sturdier and more structured. Limited-release Pandora is a cellar blend of Alban's best lots of Syrah and Grenache. (DM)

● **Syrah** Reva★★★★ £E   Lorraine★★★★ £F   Seymour Vineyard★★★★ £F   ● **Grenache** Paso Robles★★★ £D
O **Viognier** Central Coast★★ £C   Estate★★★ £D   O **Roussanne** Estate★★★ £E

ANDREW MURRAY   Santa Ynez Valley   www.andrewmurrayvineyards.com   A: Bib

Owner: Andrew Murray   6701 Foxen Canyon Road, Los Olivos, CA 93441

Andrew Murray Vineyards is a new and very good Rhône specialist. Estate and Les Coteaux Syrah are both impressive and new from 2001 is a further bottling, South Slope, which is big, ripe and forward. A level up but still from the same variety are the marvellously dense, ageworthy and powerful Roasted Slope and the top Syrah, Hillside Reserve. Both will support a decade in the cellar. Esperance is a stylish blend of Grenache, Syrah and Mourvèdre, full of ripe berry fruit, spices and herbs. All the components are vinified separately before final blending and ageing. The white Enchanté comprises slightly more Roussanne than Marsanne. Viognier has also featured in the wine in the past. The wine is held on lees but not stirred prior to bottling. Viognier is cool-fermented to emphasise its peachy, exotic character and like Enchanté it should be drunk young. These are stylish and complex wines which all show a deft handling of fruit and oak. (DM)

● **Esperance** Santa Ynez★★★ £E
● **Syrah** Estate★★★ £D   Les Coteaux★★★★ £E   Roasted Slope★★★★ £E   Hillside Reserve★★★★ £F
O **Enchante** Santa Ynez★★★ £D   O **Roussanne** Estate★★★ £D
O **Viognier** Tous Les Jours★★ £C   Estate★★★ £D

AU BON CLIMAT   Santa Maria Valley   www.info@aubonclimat.com   A: M&V

Owner: Jim Clendenen   2905 Grand Avenue, Los Olivos, CA 93441

One of the very finest exponents of Pinot Noir and Chardonnay in California. Very different to many of their peers, these are wines marked by their restrained, almost Burgundian style. This applies particularly to the Chardonnays, which are tight and surprisingly backward in their youth, the top cuvées needing three or four years to unfold but with a potential and depth rarely found outside the finest examples on the Côte de Beaune. Jim Clendenen will often pick a small portion of the fruit early to increase the natural acidity in the wine. Pinot Noir ranges from the youthful, fruit-filled Wild Boy (blended, unusually, with Mondeuse), to the supreme Cuvée Isabelle and Knox Alexander, the vines for the latter being just seven years old. A whole range of single-vineyard cuvées of both Chardonnay and Pinot are produced. The white Le Bouge d'à Côte and red La Bauge are generally sourced from the vast and sprawling Bien Nacido Vineyard which has been a vital source for Au Bon Climat over the last decade and a half. Both varieties have also been regularly sourced from the great Sanford and Benedict Vineyard. Jim Clendenen also works with his wife Morgan, producing good fruit-driven Viogniers at COLD HEAVEN, and vinifies both Chardonnay and Pinot Noir in

partnership at ICI/LA BAS in Oregon. (DM)
- **Wild Boy** California★★ £C
- **Pinot Noir** Santa Barbara★★★ £D   La Bauge au-dessus★★★★ £E   Laetitia & Rincon★★★★ £E
- **Pinot Noir** Rosemary & Rincon★★★★ £E   Sanford & Benedict★★★★★ £F
- **Pinot Noir** Knox Alexander★★★★★ £F   Cuvée Isabelle❂❂❂❂❂ £F
- O **Hildegard** Santa Maria★★★ £E
- O **Chardonnay** Wild Boy★★ £C   Santa Barbara★★★ £D   Le Bouge d' à côté★★★★ £E
- O **Chardonnay** Talley Vineyard★★★★ £E
- O **Chardonnay** Mt Carmel★★★★ £E   Alban Vineyard★★★★ £E   Talley and Alban★★★★ £E
- O **Chardonnay** Sanford and Benedict★★★★★ £F   Les Nuits Blanches❂❂❂❂❂ £F

BABCOCK VINEYARDS   Santa Rita Hills   www.babcockwinery.com   A: Vin

Owner: Bryan Babcock 5175 East, Highway 246, Lompoc, CA 93436
Small to medium-sized operation producing an extensive range of some 20,000 cases a year. Located in the centre of the newly established Santa Rita AVA, the 32 ha (80 acres) of vineyards close to the ocean are cooled by regular morning mists and afternoon sea breezes. The results are generally impressive, particularly Pinot Noir; limited bottlings come from Mount Carmel and the Carsacchi Vineyard in Santa Barbara County. Equally impressive is the stylish and structured Syrah, Black Label. Fathom is a meritage blend and there is a more serious and pricey Cuvée Lestat. Sangiovese comes from two vineyards: Stolpman and 11 Oaks Ranch. It is partly aged in new oak. Among the whites Pinot Grigio is clean and nutty, Gewürztraminer and Sauvignon Blanc barrel-fermented, the former with a hint of residual sugar. Chardonnay is also barrel-fermented (with a part in tank for the Santa Barbara bottling) and put through malolactic to add weight and texture. A simple, fruit-driven range labelled Troc provides affordable easy drinking. In comparison to many of their peers these wines represent particularly good value for money. (DM)
- **Pinot Noir** Santa Barbara★★ £C   Grand Cuvée★★★★ £E
- **Syrah** Black Label Santa Barbara★★★ £E   ● **Sangiovese** Eleven Oaks★★★ £E
- **Fathom**★★ £D
- O **Gewurztraminer** Cuvee Sublime★ £C   O **Pinot Grigio** Santa Barbara★★ £B
- O **Sauvignon Blanc** Eleven Oaks★★ £C
- O **Chardonnay** Santa Barbara★★ £C   Grand Cuvée★★★ £E

BERNARDUS   Carmel Valley   www.bernardus.com   A:Goe

Owner: Ben Pon 5 West Carmel Valley Rd, Carmel Valley, CA 93924
The 20 ha (50 acres) of estate vineyards here are all planted to the Bordeaux varieties. Winemaker Mark Chesebro is committed to making traditional ageworthy reds. The Marinus, crafted from Cabernet Sauvignon, Merlot, Cabernet Franc and Petit Verdot, spends 12 months in new oak but malolactic is not conducted in barrel. The wine is structured and ageworthy. Pinot Noir has also been sourced from a number of locations including the Bien Nacido Vineyard and currently comes from both Monterey and Santa Barbara. Sauvignon Blanc and Chardonnay sourced from a number of Monterey vineyards are subtly oaked with barrel-fermentation and lees-stirring. Both offer good value. (DM)
- **Merlot** Carmel Valley★★ £E   ● **Marinus** Carmel Valley★★★ £E
- O **Sauvignon Blanc** Monterey County★★★ £C   O **Chardonnay** Monterey County★★★ £D

BONNY DOON Santa Cruz Mountains www.bonnydoonvineyard.com A: M&V

Owner: Randall Grahm 2 Pine Flat Road, Santa Cruz, CA 95060

Randall Grahm's Bonny Doon operation may have an eccentric and off-the-wall approach to marketing and labelling but the wines are impressive and generally very fairly priced. The Rhône varieties are the backbone of the range, indeed Grahm is the original 'Rhone Ranger'; Le Cigare Volant (Grenache and Syrah) and Old Telegram (Mourvèdre) are both modelled on the great wines of Châteauneuf-du-Pape. Riesling plays an increasingly significant role. The 'Critique' and 'Pacific Rim' are respectively dry and steely and a touch off-dry, whereas the 'Heart has its Rieslings' is more Auslese in style. Good Madiran and Syrah Domaine des Blagueurs from the Languedoc are a recent and unusual move under the Euro Doon banner, adding a further dimension to the range. Puglia is also recently the source of a further European label, Uva di Troia. CA' DEL SOLO is Grahm's label for his Italian range. (DM)

● **Le Cigare Volant** California★★★★ £E ● **Old Telegram** California★★★★ £E ● **Syrah** California★★★★ £E
● **Clos de Gilroy** California★★ £B ● **Cardinal Zin**★★ £C ● **Carignane**★★ £C
● **Domaine des Blagueurs Syrah-Sirrah** Vin de Pays d'Oc★★ £B
● **Madiran-Heart of Darkness**★★ £C
○ **Viognier** California★★★ £D ● **Roussanne** California★★★ £D
○ **Critique of Pure Riesling**★★ £B ○ **Pacific Rim Riesling**★★ £B
○ **The Heart has its Rieslings**★★★ £C ○ **Muscat** Vin de Glaciere★★★★ £E

BREWER CLIFTON Santa Rita Hills A: THt

Owner: Greg Brewer & Steve Clifton 1704 Industrial Way, Lompoc, CA 93436

Very small, recently established operation producing tiny amounts of very rich and extracted, full-blown Chardonnay and Pinot Noir. Production is tiny at something less than 1,000 cases in total. The Pinot is fermented with whole clusters, sees some new oak and is neither fined nor filtered. The oak is also reined in on the Chardonnays but they do get full malolactic, producing wines which are both richly textured and very full-bodied. All will stand a little age but can be enjoyed young. (DM)

● **Pinot Noir** Rozak Ranch★★★ £E Melville★★★★ £F
○ **Chardonnay** Sweeney Canyon★★★★ £E Mount Carmel★★★★ £F

CA' DEL SOLO Santa Cruz Mountains www.bonnydoonvineyard.com A: M&V

Owner: Randall Grahm 2 Pine Flat Road, Santa Cruz, CA 95060

Whereas the BONNY DOON label is based around the Rhône, Ca' del Solo is fully focused on Italy. Italian varieties have not performed with any real distinction in California and much of the reason for this is poor planting material. The Ca' del Solo range is better than most with some good, well-crafted varietal wines, both red and white, displaying attractive and abundant fruit. Big House Red is made from a variable mix of Mediterranean varieties with a touch of Cabernet Franc; Big House White is a blend of Italian and Rhône varieties along with Sauvignon Blanc – similar in approach to the more intense and refined Il Pescatore. Both Big House wines are forward and fruit-driven for enjoying young. The varietal reds are sturdier and more structured. All are worth a punt as much for the entertaining labelling as for the wines. (DM)

● **Big House Red**★ £B ● **Barbera**★★ £B ● **Sangiovese**★★ £C ● **Charbono**★★ £C
○ **Big House White**★ £B ○ **Malvasia** Bianca★★ £B
○ **Pinot Grigio**★★ £C ○ **Il Pescatore**★★ £C

CALERA San Benito County A: Bib

Owner: Josh Jensen   11300 Cienega Rd, Hollister, CA 95023
Best-known for its quartet of single-vineyard Pinot Noirs that have at times reached near cult status. Josh Jensen's objective is to hand-craft wines that have more to do with classic Burgundy than with some of the more typically fruit-driven, squeaky-clean examples from other California contemporaries. On occasion the results are less than perfect but generally these are benchmarks for the state. The regular Central Coast wines are good if unspectacular and the Viognier is very good when not overly alcoholic. The winery is extremely unusual, being completely gravity-fed. (DM)

● **Pinot Noir** Central Coast★★ £C Reed★★★ £F Selleck★★★★ £F Jensen★★★★ £F Mills★★★★ £F
O **Chardonnay** Central Coast★★ £C Mount Harlan★★★ £E O **Viognier** Mount Harlan★★★ £E

CAMBRIA Santa Maria Valley www.cambriawine.com A:WTs

*Owner: **Kendall Jackson**   5475 Chardonnay Lane, Santa Maria, CA 93454*
Part of the giant KENDALL JACKSON Group, Cambria is their Central Coast flagship. By no means small, the total area under vine is now some 565 ha (1,400 acres). Good top-flight Pinot Noir, which is ripe and full of red-berry fruit, and in particular a number of Chardonnay bottlings which are barrel-fermented with lees-ageing adding weight and complexity. Rhône varieties from the Tepusquet Vineyard also show promise. Syrah is nicely structured with good brambly fruit intensity, more St-Joseph than Hermitage. (DM)

● **Pinot Noir** Julia's Vineyard★★ £D Bench Break★★★ £E Rae's★★★ £F
● **Syrah** Tepusquet★★ £D ● **Sangiovese** Tepusquet★ £C
O **Chardonnay** Katherine's Vineyard★★★ £D Bench Break★★★ £E Rae's★★★ £E
O **Viognier** Tepusquet★★ £C Late Harvest★★ £C

CHALONE Chalone www.chalonewinegroup.com A: Bib

*Owner: **Chalone Group**   Stonewall Canyon Road & Highway 146, Soledad, CA 93960*
This is the original estate founded by the late Richard Graff who went on to establish the Chalone Wine Group whose interests include CANOE RIDGE in Washington, ACACIA, MOON MOUNTAIN and JADE MOUNTAIN among others in California, and a partnership with Domaines Baron Philippe de Rothschild SA in Château DUHART-MILON in Bordeaux. The Chalone white wines are intense, subtle and slow-developing; the Chardonnay Reserve is particularly fine, the Chenin Blanc a benchmark for the variety in California. However, the Pinot Noir has often disappointed in recent vintages. (DM)

● **Pinot Noir** Estate★★ £E
O **Chardonnay** Estate★★★ £E Reserve★★★★ £F
O **Pinot Blanc** Estate★★★ £D Reserve★★★★ £E
O **Chenin Blanc** Estate★★★ £D

CLOS LACHANCE Santa Cruz Mountains www.closlachance.com A: Fie

Owner: Bill & Brenda Murphy   21511 Saratoga Heights Drive, Saratoga, CA 95070
Founded in 1992 this small operation is producing increasingly impressive Chardonnay in three bottlings. These are earthy, quite traditional styles with marked lees influence. The weighty and concentrated Vanumanutagi bottling is barrel-fermented and aged in mainly new French and American oak. Pinot Noir comes from the Santa Cruz Mountains and there is a very limited and well made special cuvée which is aged in mainly new oak. The estate Cabernet is good and well-priced but it is the berry-laden El Dorado

Zinfandel that has the edge among the reds. (DM)

● **Zinfandel** El Dorado County★★★ £C **Cabernet Sauvignon** Santa Cruz★★ £D
● **Pinot Noir** Santa Cruz★★ £C **Merlot** Central Coast★ £C
O **Chardonnay** Santa Cruz★★★ £C Vanumanutagi★★★ £E Napa Valley★★ £C

COLD HEAVEN   Santa Maria Valley   A: M&V

Owner: Morgan Clendenen   2905 Grand Avenue, Los Olivos, CA 93441
Small, single-varietal operation focused on Viognier, the brainchild of Morgan, wife of Jim Clendenen of AU BON CLIMAT. The Sanford and Benedict has been the best example thus far and the wine is classic cool-climate, fruit-driven Viognier with marked floral perfume and a fine, mineral undercurrent lending depth and finesse. All should be drunk young. (DM)

O **Viognier** Santa Ynez Valley★★ £D Alban Vineyard★★★ £E Sanford and Benedict★★★ £E

EDMUNDS ST JOHN   www.edmundsstjohn.com   A: WTs

Owner: Steve Edmunds   1331 Walnut Street, Berkeley, CA 94709
Small warehouse winery, a benchmark among California Rhône Rangers. Very impressive Syrah, which can stand comparison with the very best of the northern Rhône, is made from a number of sources and the Wylie-Fenaughty was added with the 2000 vintage. Rocks and Gravel, originally labelled as Côtes Sauvages, is a classic southern Rhône blend of Grenache, Mourvèdre, Syrah and, most unusually for California, a hint of Counoise. Steve expects to continue working with these varieties, producing a more structured example, the Los Robles Viejos red, from the Rozet vineyard with its excellent calcareous soils. With the Rhône white of the same name, a nutty and impressive blend of Viognier, Marsanne and Roussanne, he has now established an on-going relationship with the vineyard owners. Pallini Rosso, a spicy blend of mainly Zinfandel with some Grenache, has also been produced from old bush vines. (DM)

● **Syrah** California★★★ £D Parmalee Hill Vineyard★★★★ £E Durell Vineyard★★★★ £E
● **Rocks and Gravel** California★★★ £C ● **Pallini Rosso** Mendocino★★★ £C
O **Los Robles Viejos** Rozet Vineyard★★★ £D O **Pinot Grigio** El Dorado County★★★ £C

EDNA VALLEY   Edna Valley   www.ednavalley.com   A: Bib

Owner: Niven family/Chalone Wine Group   2585 Biddle Ranch Road, San Luis Obispo, CA 93401
Chardonnay dominates the production here of some 120,000 cases and it stands out. Quality remains impressive despite the volume and the wines are well-priced. The approach is minimalist in the vineyard and the wine shows nicely judged lees and oak with subtle tropical and melon fruit notes. The Viognier has attractive peachy character, if lighter than some others, and the Pinot is more marked by forward berry fruit than complex secondary flavours. (DM)

● **Pinot Noir** Paragon★★ £C ● **Syrah** Central Coast★★ £C
O **Chardonnay** Paragon★★★ £C O **Viognier** Fralich Vineyard★★★ £C

GAINEY   Santa Ynez Valley   www.gaineyvineyard.com

Owner: Gainey Family   3950 East Highway 246, Santa Ynez, CA 93460
Small to medium sized operation producing around 18,000 cases a year. The Gainey Home Ranch is planted to the red Bordeaux varieties in addition to Sauvignon Blanc. Chardonnay, Pinot Noir and Syrah have been planted at a new vineyard in the cooler Santa Rita Hills. The Limited Selection Merlot, Pinot Noir, Chardonnay and Sauvignon Blanc bottlings have been impressive in recent

vintages. Sauvignon Blanc gets some oak-ageing and the Limited Selection Chardonnay is fermented and aged in barrel on lees. The wines represent reasonable value and the Limited Selection Merlot is bottled without filtration. (DM)

● **Merlot** Santa Ynez Valley★★ £C
O **Chardonnay** Santa Barbara★★ £C   O **Riesling** Santa Ynez Valley★★ £B
O **Sauvignon Blanc** Santa Ynez Valley★★ £B

IL PODERE DELL' OLIVOS   Santa Maria Valley   info@aubonclimat.com   A: M&V

Owner: Jim Clendenen   PO Box 440, Los Olivos, CA 93441
Best-known for his remarkable AU BON CLIMAT Chardonnays and Pinot Noirs, and his wife Morgan's COLD HEAVEN Viogniers, Jim Clendenen has also maintained a prolonged interest in Italian varieties. The wines have varied with the best examples very good. Decent planting material remains a problem in California and while some vintages show real promise others are less impressive. The top red Ragazzo Legnoso is a richly textured blend of Nebbiolo and Barbera. This is now joined by a new premium label Primogenito. Clendenen's commitment to established, quality viticultural techniques such as mass selection may very well prove him right in the long term. (DM)

● **Barbera** Santa Maria★★ £B   ● **Carignan** Santa Maria★ £B   ● **Nebbiolo** Santa Maria★★ £C
● **Ragazzo Legnoso** California★★★ £D
O **Tocai** Santa Maria★★ £B   O **Pinot Grigio** Santa Maria★★ £B

JUSTIN   Paso Robles   www.justinwine.com   A: Lib

Owner: Justin Baldwin   11680 Chimney Rock Road, Paso Robles, CA 93446
Very good operation producing some of the best Bordeaux-style reds on the Central Coast. These wines may share similar grapes to their French counterparts but are altogether fuller and riper without any hint of the rusticity or jamminess often found in warm-climate Cabernet. Isosceles is a blend of Cabernet Sauvignon, Cabernet Franc and Merlot, marginally more refined than Justification, which is just over half Cabernet Sauvignon, the balance Merlot. The Halter vineyard is a full-on example of Syrah: big, powerful if less refined than a top-flight OJAI or ALBAN. A Paso Robles bottling has also now been added as has Zinfandel. Chardonnay and Sauvignon Blanc are aged in top quality French oak and there is a limited-release reserve Chardonnay bottling which is worth considering. A number of interesting special labels can be sourced directly from the winery. Prices are very fair. (DM)

● **Cabernet Sauvignon** Paso Robles★★★ £D   ● **Syrah** Halter Vineyard★★★★ £E
● **Justification** Paso Robles★★★★ £E   ● **Isosceles** Paso Robles★★★★ £E
O **Chardonnay** Paso Robles★★★ £C   O **Sauvignon Blanc** Paso Robles★★ £B

KATHRYN KENNEDY   Santa Cruz Mountains   www.kathrynkennedywinery.com

Owner: Kathryn Kennedy   13180 Pierce Road, Saratoga, CA 95070
The production here is very small with just over 3 ha (8 acres) under vine. The estate Cabernet is highly sought-after by local collectors and the most likely way of getting hold of any at all is to join their mailing list. A Merlot-based proprietary red, Lateral, is made from bought-in fruit and there is a small amount of Syrah from the Maridon Vineyard. Vinification is in small lots and the approach throughout is one of care and minimal handling. (DM)

● **Cabernet Sauvignon** Estate★★★★ £G

LAETITIA   Arroyo Grande   www.laetitiawine.com   A: JAr

Owner: Selim Zilkha   453 Tower Grove Drive, Arroyo Grande, CA 93420
Selim Zilkha purchased Laetitia from CHAMPAGNE DEUTZ in the late 1990s and sound, well-priced
sparklers are still being produced. The real focus of the winery now though is to produce top-quality
estate Chardonnay and Pinot Noir. The wines are good and well-made but as yet lack the depth and
concentration of the best examples along the Central Coast. They are all fairly priced. (DM)
● **Pinot Noir** San Luis Obispo★★ £D Arroyo Grande Reserve★★ £E
○ **Pinot Blanc** Estate★ £C   ○ **Chardonnay** Central Coast★ £C Estate Reserve★★ £D
○ **Laetitia** XD★★ £C   ◉ **Brut Rose** Arroyo Grande★★★ £D

MER SOLEIL WINERY   Monterey County   Mersoleilwinery@aol.com   A: Vin

Owner: Chuck Wagner   PO Box 35, Rutherford, CA 94573
Several different varieties are cultivated at this small vineyard and winery near Santa Lucia. The focus
is mainly on the full-on Chardonnay which is stylish, powerful and possesses an excellent balance of
ripe fruit and well-judged oak. Chuck Wagner also runs CAYMUS in the Napa Valley and produces
an attractive, nutty Marsanne/Viognier blend in partnership with the Hope family who are Paso
Robles grape growers, under the Treana label. The small range is completed by Santa Barbara Pinot
Noir Belle Glos as well as a sweet white Late Harvest Viognier which is rich and unctuous with
moderate depth and intensity. (DM)
○ **Chardonnay** Central Coast★★★ £D   ○ **Treana** Central Coast★★ £C
○ **Viognier** Late Harvest Monterey★★★ £D
● **Pinot Noir** Belle Glos Santa Barbara★★ £D

MORGAN WINERY   Monterey County   www.morganwinery.com   A: Bib

Owner: Donna & Daniel Morgan Lee   590 Brunken Avenue, Suite C, Salinas, CA 93901
Small to medium-sized warehouse winery. Chardonnay, Pinot Noir and Syrah are mainly sourced
from the Santa Lucia Highlands with a touch of Arroyo Grande Chardonnay also used. These are
first-class sources for the Burgundy varieties. Pinot Noirs come from Rosella's, Double L and Garys
vineyards in the Santa Lucia Highlands and are a step up from the regular bottling. Chardonnays
from three different vineyards – Double L, Metallica and Rosella's – have replaced the Reserve
bottling. The Syrah is classy in a cooler, spicier style and the Sauvignon Blanc is good value, full and
ripe with a hint of Sonoma County, Alexander Valley fruit. It is part barrel-fermented. (DM)
● **Pinot Noir** Santa Lucia Highlands★★ £C   ● **Syrah** Monterey★★★ £C Tierra Mar★★★ £E
○ **Chardonnay** Monterey★★★ £C   ○ **Sauvignon Blanc** Monterey★★★ £B

MOUNT EDEN VINEYARDS   Santa Cruz Mountains   www.mounteden.com   A: Vin

Owner: Jeffrey Patterson   22020 Mt. Eden Road, Saratoga, CA 95070
The whole Mount Eden range is characteristic of the best of the Santa Cruz Mountains. The wines
are deep, powerful and reserved. All will benefit from cellaring. The Pinot is a big, rich style whereas
the Cabernet Sauvignons are tight and backward in their youth with considerable structure and grip.
They need time to shed their youthful, mountain tannins. Chardonnay is in a restrained style with
subtle, citrus fruit and fine-grained nutty oak but with real depth and complexity. (DM)
● **Cabernet Sauvignon** Estate★★★ £D Old Vine Reserve★★★★ £F   ● **Pinot Noir** Estate★★★ £E
○ **Chardonnay** Estate★★★★ £E MacGregor Vineyard★★★ £D

OJAI Ventura County ojaivineyard.com A: THt

Owner: Adam Tolmach P.O. Box 952 Oak View CA 93022

Originally involved with Jim Clendenen at AU BON CLIMAT, Adam Tolmach founded his own operation in the mid-1980s. Top Syrah has always been a major focal point here and these are always classy, superbly crafted wines – subtle and restrained with real depth, and very different to many overblown, overripe examples produced elsewhere. Chardonnay, Pinot Noir and Sauvignon are also very impressive in a bewildering number of vineyard guises. Newly established Vin du Soleil red and white Rhône blends are a change of direction for Tolmach as he seeks to maximise the potential of the southern Rhône styles and move away from what he feels is an overly varietal-dominated marketplace. (DM)

- ● **Pinot Noir** Bien Nacido★★★ £E
- ● **Syrah** Santa Barbara★★★ £D Roll Ranch★★★★ £E Bien Nacido★★★★ £E Stolpman Vineyard★★★★ £E
- O **Chardonnay** Talley Vineyard★★★ £D Bien Nacido★★★ £D Sanford and Benedict★★★★ £E
- O **Sauvignon Blanc** Santa Barbara★★★ £C O **Viognier** Roll Ranch★★★ £D
- O **Vin Gris** California★★★ £B

PEACHY CANYON WINERY Paso Robles www.peachycanyon.com A: Fie

Owner: Beckett family 4045 Peachy Canyon Road, Paso Robles, CA 93446

One of the best Zinfandel specialists on the Central Coast. These are wines that are ripe and spicy with great berry fruit, particularly the dry-farmed Benito Dusi Ranch produced from 75-year-old vines. Doug Beckett also produces a number of other impressive reds. Westside and Paso Robles are very largely Zin but have a touch of Carignan, while the premium Para Siempre is dominated by Merlot, with a little Cabernets Sauvignon and Franc. The Incredible Red is a great-value glugger produced in 2000 from 100 per cent Zinfandel. The range now also includes Central Coast Syrah, Mustang Springs and Old School House Zinfandels. (DM)

- ● **Cabernet Sauvignon** Paso Robles★★ £D **Para Siempre** Paso Robles★★ £E
- ● **Paso Robles Cuvée**★ £B ● **Westside** Paso Robles★★ £C
- ● **Zinfandel** Estate★★ £D Benito Dusi Ranch★★★ £D

QUADY Madera County A: Hal

Owner: Andrew Quady 13181 Road 24, Madera, CA 93639

Fortified- and sweet-wine specialist based in the arid Central Valley. Red Starboard is a port style produced from Amador County Zinfandel while the whites are produced from Muscat: Essencia from Orange Muscat and Elysium from Black Muscat. These are good, well-crafted examples if lacking the richness and finesse of the best European and Australian equivalents. (DM)

- ● **Starboard** Amador County★ £C
- O **Essencia** Madera★★ £C O **Elysium** Madera★★ £C

QUPÉ Santa Maria Valley A: M&V, SVS

Owner: Bob Lindquist 2531 Grand Avenue, Los Olivos, CA 93441

An early and still one of the finest exponents among California's Rhône Rangers. Bob Lindquist shares winemaking facilities and a similar vision with Jim Clendenen at AU BON CLIMAT. All the wines here are of a uniformly high standard; both reds and whites are subtle and elegant and very well crafted. The white Bien Nacido Cuvée blends Chardonnay and Viognier and the red Los Olivos Cuvée is classical southern Rhône style comprising Syrah, Mourvèdre and Grenache. The wine has good weight and texture with an underlying black pepper character. Perhaps the greatest contrast is between the two great Bien Nacido Syrahs, often of five-star quality, and the regular Central Coast bottling which can be light and very peppery. (DM)

● **Syrah** Central Coast★★ £C Bien Nacido★★★★ £D Bien Nacido Reserve★★★★★ £D
● **Los Olivos Cuvee** Santa Barabara★★★ £D
○ **Chardonnay** Bien Nacido★★★ £C Bien Nacido Reserve★★★★ £D
○ **Marsanne** Ibarra Young Vineyard★★★ £C ○ **Viognier** Ibarra Young Vineyard★★★★ £D
○ **Bien Nacido Cuvee** Santa Maria★★★ £C
○ **Roussanne** Alban Vineyard★★★ £D

RENWOOD Amador County www.renwood.com   A: CHk

Owner: Renwood Group   12225 Steiner Road, Plymouth, CA 95669
The Italian and the Rhône style wines here are all impressive but it is the great Zinfandels from old bush vines that really stand out. The magnificent D'Agostini bottling, pushing four stars regularly, is what super-ripe, concentrated old-vine Zinfandel is all about. The excellent Sierra series is sourced from selected vineyards throughout the Sierra Foothills and Santino is a good-value budget label offering mainly simple Rhône styles and one of the best white Zinfandels. (DM)

● **Barbera** Sierra Series★★ £B Estate★★★ £C ● **Nebbiolo** Estate★★ £D
● **Sangiovese** Amador County★★ £C ● **Syrah** Sierra Series★★ £B Estate★★★ £D
● **Zinfandel** Sierra Series★★ £B Old Vine★★★ £C Fiddletown★★ £D Jack Rabbit Flat★★★ £D
● **Zinfandel** Grandpere★★★ £D Grandmere★★★ £D D'Agostini★★★ £E Amador Ice Wine★★★ £E
○ **Viognier** Sierra Series★★ £B Estate★★ £C

RIDGE VINEYARDS Santa Cruz Mountains www.ridgewine.com   A:M&V

Owner: Paul Draper   17100 Monte Bello Road, Cupertino CA 95014
This is one of California's great wineries. Chardonnay is in a classically Burgundian style, intense but restrained. Some utterly superb and very complex Zinfandels are hand-crafted from a range of sources. These include the Pagani Ranch, which contains some Alicante Bouschet and Petite Sirah, and York Creek, with increasing amounts of Petite Sirah. There is also one of the best examples of varietal Petite Sirah (so often hard and unyielding) and a stylish Mataro. The great Geyserville red is usually around two-thirds Zin with both Carignane and Petite Sirah in the blend. Syrah and Grenache are also produced and there are some well-priced varietals under the Coastal Range label. The great Ridge wine though is the meritage Monte Bello, unquestionably one of the state's finest and longest-living Cabernet-based reds. Whether some of the newer Napa Valley super-premium examples will stand the test of time like these remains to be seen. (DM)

● **Cabernet Sauvignon** Santa Cruz Mountains★★★★ £E ● **Monte Bello**✪✪✪✪✪ £G
● **Mataro** California★★★ £E ● **Petite Sirah** York Creek★★★★ £E
● **Zinfandel** Lytton Springs★★★★ £E Pagani★★★★ £E York Creek★★★★£E ● **Geyserville**★★★★★£E
○ **Chardonnay** Santa Cruz Mountains★★★★ £E

ROSENBLUM CELLARS Santa Lucia Highlands www.rosenblumcellars.com   A: Vin

Owner: Kent Rosenblum   2900 Main Street, Alameda, CA 94501
The Rosenblum warehouse winery is located in the San Francisco Bay area in central Alameda. Former veterinary surgeon Kent Rosenblum oversees the crushing of some 400 tons of fruit at harvest time. The main focus here is on Zinfandel and very good it is too. Even in a difficult year like 1998 the wines stood out for their intensity, purity and depth. The top examples show really splendid complexity. There are a considerable number of examples of the variety sourced throughout the state, with bottlings

from diverse regions from Contra Costa to Mount Veeder, Paso Robles to Dry Creek. A number of other wines are also produced with the main focus on the Rhône Valley – good Syrah, Marsanne and Viognier and a fruit-filled blend, Chateau La Paws Côte du Bone Roan, of mainly Carignane with some Syrah, Mourvèdre and Grenache. Holbrook Mitchell Trio is a meritage blend of Bordeaux varieties. There are also some impressive late-harvest bottlings including an excellent Black Muscat from the Gallagher Ranch in Madera County. Winemaker Jeff Cohn also produces a small amount of very good Syrah and Petite Sirah under his own JC CELLARS label. (DM)

● **Zinfandel** Samsel Vineyard Maggie's Reserve★★★★ £E   St Peters Church Vineyard★★★★ £E
● **Zinfandel** Carla's Vineyards★★ £C   Alegria Vineyard★★★ £C   Eagle Point Vineyard★★★ £C
● **Zinfandel** Richard Sauret Vineyard★★★ £C
● **Syrah** England Shaw Vineyard★★★ £D   Hillside Vineyard★★★ £D   Fess Parker Vineyard★★★★ £E
● **Holbrook Mitchell Trio** Napa Valley★★★ £E   ● **Chateau La Paws Côte du Bone Roan** California★ £B
● **Black Muscat** Gallagher Ranch★★★ £E
○ **Marsanne** Dry Creek★★★ £C   ○ **Viognier** Santa Barbara★★ £C

SANFORD WINERY   Santa Ynez Valley   A: WTs

Owner: Richard Sanford   7250 Santa Rosa Road, Buellton, CA 93427
Quality here is good although not perhaps of the same order as it was a decade ago. Richard Sanford is the owner of the great Sanford and Benedict Vineyard, from which a number of winemakers have crafted some of the finest examples of Pinot Noir and Chardonnay to have emerged from California. Pinot Noir, particularly La Rinconada and Sanford and Benedict are laden with intense berry fruit and well judged oak. Chardonnay and Sauvignon Blanc are in a ripe tropical style. (DM)

● **Pinot Noir** Santa Barbara★★ £C   La Riconada★★★★ £F   Sanford and Benedict★★★★ £F
○ **Chardonnay** Santa Barbara★★ £C   Estate Barrel Select★★★ £E   Sanford and Benedict★★★ £E
○ **Sauvignon Blanc** Central Coast★ £C

TABLAS CREEK   Paso Robles   www.tablascreek.com   A: Mis

Owner: Robert Haas, Francois and Jean-Pierre Perrin   9339 Adelaida Road, Paso Robles, CA 93446
This is the first major overseas investment for the Perrin brothers of CHÂTEAU DE BEAUCASTEL. Along with Robert Haas, they have established an important nursery for Rhône Valley planting material and are now producing increasingly impressive red and white blends as the vineyards mature. There have been changes in the range. Reserve Cuvée, originally known as Tablas Creek Rouge, and Clos Blanc as Tablas Creek Blanc were respectively blends of Mourvèdre, Grenache, Syrah and Counoise, and Roussanne, Viognier, Marsanne and Grenache Blanc, but have confusingly now been dropped, although top red and white cuvées Esprit de Beaucastel are blends of the same varieties. Expect similarly impressive wines. There is a 100 per cent Roussanne which is part barrel-fermented and tiny amounts of Antithesis, a full-blown style of Chardonnay, as well as Panoplie, a wine based on Mourvèdre and made when vintage conditions favour. 2000 is the most recent release. The range is completed by red and white Côtes de Tablas which are in the mould of top-quality Côtes du Rhônes. (DM)

● **Reserve Cuvée** Paso Robles★★★★ £E
○ **Clos Blanc** Paso Robles★★★ £E

ROBERT TALBOTT Monterey County   www.talbottvineyards.com   A: Vin

Owner: Robert Talbott   53 West Carmel Valley Road, Carmel Valley, CA 93924
Small operation with vineyard resources in the Salinas Foothills and Santa Lucia Mountains. The

three top Chardonnays, Kali-Hart, Sleepy Hollow and Cuvée Cynthia, are marvellously stylish cool-climate examples, delivering very fine fruit from low yields with very well-judged, fine-grained oak and a rich leesy complexity. A special selection from the Diamond T Estate, bottled unfined and unfiltered, has also now been released, labelled Audrey Cuvée. These are among the very best on the Central Coast. Logan is the regular label for Chardonnay and a recently added Pinot Noir. Expect quality to match the whites. A Kali-Hart Vineyard bottling has now been released. (DM)

O **Chardonnay** Logan★★ £D Kali-Hart Vineyard★★★ £E Diamond T Estate★★★★ £E
O **Chardonnay** Sleepy Hollow Vineyard★★★★ £E Cuvée Cynthia★★★★ £E

TALLEY VINEYARDS Arroyo Grande www.talleyvineyards.com A: Bib

Owner: Don and Rosemary Talley 3031 Lopez Drive, Arroyo Grande, CA 93420
First-class estate Chardonnay and Pinot Noir here. The Rosemary and Rincon vineyards have tremendous potential and as yet are still young. Both are capable at times of providing wines of five-star quality. Pinot Noir is produced from very low yields and wild yeasts and new French oak are used in the winery. Chardonnay is reared in the finest French oak and aged on lees to provide additional weight and a rich texture. The Talleys also produce the variety from their Edna Valley Olivers Vineyard site, which is planted exclusively to the variety. The Sauvignon Blanc has not reached the same stellar heights. It is blended with Semillon and part barrel-fermented. Bishops Peak is their label for a range of nicely-crafted, straightforward budget wines and a Late-Harvest Riesling is also produced. The Talleys are also important suppliers to other producers such as AU BON CLIMAT. (DM)

● **Pinot Noir** Estate★★★ £D Rincon Vineyard★★★★ £E Rosemary's Vineyard★★★★ £E
O **Chardonnay** Estate★★★ £D Rincon Vineyard★★★★ £E Rosemary's Vineyard★★★★ £E
O **Sauvignon Blanc** Estate★★ £B

LANE TANNER Santa Maria Valley lanetanner@sbwines.com

Owner: Lane Tanner PO Box 286, Santa Maria, CA 93456
Lane Tanner operates a small warehouse winery in Santa Maria where she has been making first-rate Pinot Noir for a decade. As well as the Santa Maria and Bien Nacido cuvées there are two other small-volume examples from Melville and Julia's vineyards. She has now added a cool, peppery Syrah from the French Camp Vineyard that shows equally impressive potential. Very good and very fairly priced wines here. (DM)

● **Pinot Noir** Santa Maria★★★ £D Bien Nacido★★★ £D

DOM. DE LA TERRE ROUGE Shenandoah Valley www.terrerougewines.com A: Vin

Owner: Bill Easton PO Box 41, Fiddletown, Amador County, CA 95629
Bill Easton was one of the very first Rhône Rangers, along with the likes of Randall Grahm at BONNY DOON. Today he produces Rhône styles under the Terre Rouge label and under his Easton label some good, fruit driven, spicy Barbera and more serious Zinfandel. Based in Amador County, his Shenandoah vineyards are cooled due to their elevation. Syrah is the dominant red variety but in addition there is a simple fruity rosé and floral, minerally Viognier made from 20 year old vines. The basic Syrah cuvée is the Tête a Tête, which is soft and forward, as is the Cote de l'Ouest. More serious are both the Sierra Foothills and Sentinel Oak Vineyard, Pyramid Block Syrahs. At its best in vintages like 2000 and 1999, the Sentinel bottling is structured and firm with good intensity, more in the style of Côte Rôtie than Hermitage. Ascent is a fine barrel selection which sees more new oak: rich, almost opulent with impressive depth and concentration. Top reds will benefit from four or five

years ageing. (DM)

Domaine de la Terre Rouge
- ● **Syrah** Tête a Tête★★£C   Côte l'Ouest★★£C
- ● **Syrah** Sierra Foothills★★★£D   Sentinel Oak Vineyard Pyramid Block★★★£E
- ● **Syrah** Ascent★★★★£F
- ○ **Viognier** Shenandoah Valley★★★£E

Easton
- ● **Barbera** Shenandoah Valley★★£C
- ● **Zinfandel** Shenandoah Valley★★★£C

TESTAROSSA   Arroyo Grande   www.testarossa.com   A: Lib

Owner: Robert & Diana Jensen   300-A College Avenue, Los Gatos, CA 95030
The focus here is top-quality Pinot Noir and Chardonnay. Originally the wines were sourced from Monterey vineyards but the Jensens now scour the whole Central Coast to produce the best possible examples. The range covers an almost bewildering number of single-vineyard cuvées, which are invariably good to very good indeed, if not possessing the striking intensity of both varieties achieved in the top examples at AU BON CLIMAT. The Pinots are rich and gamey with no shortage of oak; the Chardonnays are riper and fuller than some of the more minerally restrained styles elsewhere. They do though possess a marvellously rich weight and texture. They can be enjoyed with just a year or two in bottle. (DM)
- ● **Pinot Noir** Santa Maria Valley★★★£D   Palazzio★★★★£E   Gary's Vineyard★★★★£E
- ● **Pinot Noir** Sleepy Hollow Vineyard★★★★£E   Pisoni Vineyard★★★★£F
- ○ **Chardonnay** Central Coast★★★£D   Castello★★★£E   Rosella's Vineyard★★★£E
- ○ **Chardonnay** Chalone-Michaud★★★★£E   Bien Nacido★★★★£E
- ○ **Chardonnay** Sleepy Hollow Vineyard★★★★£E   Pisoni Vineyard★★★★£E

SEAN THACKREY   Marin County   www.wine-maker.net   A: WTs

Owner: Sean Thackrey   240 Overlook Drive, Bolina, CA 94924
Sean Thackrey originally produced a small range of top-flight Rhône style wines from Syrah, Mourvèdre and Petite Sirah but now solely concentrates on just two wines. Orion is produced from Syrah sourced from the Rossi Vineyard in St Helena and is a massive, burly wine with tremendous potential requiring at least five years' cellaring to shed its tannin. The Pleiades by contrast is a ripe, altogether more forward, non-vintage blend from a variable mix of Syrah, Grenache, Mourvèdre and Petite Sirah and may be enjoyed on release. (DM)
- ● **Pleiades** California★★★£C   **Orion** Rossi Vineyard★★★★★£F

OTHER WINES OF NOTE

ADELAIDA CELLARS ● **Cabernet Sauvignon** Paso Robles £C ● **Zinfandel** Paso Robles £C
AHLGREN ● **Cabernet Sauvignon** Bates Ranch £F   ● **Zinfandel** Livermore Valley £C
ARCADIAN ● **Pinot Noir** Bien Nacido £E   Pisoni Vineyard £F   ● **Syrah** Gary's Vineyard £F
○ **Chardonnay** Bien Nacido £D   Sleepy Hollow £D
BLACKJACK RANCH ● **Merlot** Billy Goat Hill £E   ○ **Chardonnay** Reserve £D
DAVID BRUCE ● **Pinot Noir** Santa Cruz Estate £F   ● **Petite Sirah** Shell Creek Vineyard £C
BYINGTON ○ **Chardonnay** Dirk Vineyard £D
BYRON ● **Pinot Noir** Byron Vineyard £F   ○ **Chardonnay** Byron Vineyard £D
CASTORO CELLARS ● **Syrah** Paso Robles £C   ● **Zinfandel** Vineyard Tribute £C
○ **Viognier** Reserve £C
CONCANNON ○ **Chardonnay** Central Coast £B   ○ **Viognier** Central Coast £C

CRONIN O **Chardonnay** Santa Cruz Mountains £C Stuhlmuller Vineyard £C

DARK STAR ● **Syrah** Meeker Vineyard £C Ricordati Paso Robles £C

DOMAINE SANTA BARBARA O **Chardonnay** Los Olivos £D

DOVER CANYON ● **Syrah** Paso Robles £D   ● **Zinfandel** Cujo £C

EBERLE WINERY ● **Zinfandel** Sauret £C   ● **Cabernet Sauvignon** Estate £D

ESTANCIA ● **Pinot Noir** Reserve £D   O **Chardonnay** Reserve £C

FESS PARKER ● **Mélange du Rhône** Red £B   ● **Syrah** ATR £D

FIDDLEHEAD CELLARS ● **Pinot Noir** Santa Maria Valley £E Willamette Valley £E

FIRESTONE O **Chardonnay** Santa Ynez Valley £B

THOMAS FOGARTY ● **Pinot Noir** Santa Cruz Mountains £D   O **Chardonnay** Santa Cruz Mountains£D

FOLEY ESTATE O **Chardonnay** Bien Nacido Vineyard £D

FOXEN ● **Pinot Noir** Bien Nacido £D   O **Chardonnay** Tinaquaic £D

GALANTE VINEYARDS ● **Cabernet Sauvignon** Blackjack Pasture £E   ● **Merlot** Carmel £D

DANIEL GEHRS ● **Syrah** Paso Robles £C   O **Pinot Blanc** Monterey £C

HELLER ESTATE ● **Cabernet Sauvignon** Carmel Valley Reserve £E   O **Chardonnay** Carmel Valley £C

JAFFURS CELLARS ● **Syrah** Bien Nacido £E Thompson Vineyard £E

JC CELLARS ● **Syrah** California £D   ● **Zinfandel** Rhodes Vineyard £D

KARLY ● **Syrah** Amador County £C

LOCKWOOD O **Chardonnay** Very Special Reserve £D

LONGORIA ● **Pinot Noir** Bien Nacido £D   O **Chardonnay** Clos Pepé £D

MERIDIAN VINEYARDS ● **Cabernet Sauvignon** Reserve £C   O **Chardonnay** Limited Release £C

MURRIETA'S WELL ● **Zinfandel** Livermore Valley £C   ● **Vendimia Red** £E   O **Vendimia White** £C

MORAGA ● **Cabernet Sauvignon** Bel Air £H

NICHOLS WINERY ● **Pinot Noir** Paragon Vineyard £D   O **Chardonnay** Paragon Vineyard £D

NORMAN ● **Zinfandel** The Monster £C

PARAISO SPRINGS O **Chardonnay** Santa Lucia Highlands £C

STEPHEN ROSS ● **Pinot Noir** Edna Ranch £D Bien Nacido £D   O **Chardonnay** Bien Nacido £D

SANTA BARBARA WINERY ● **Syrah** Santa Ynez £C   O **Chardonnay** Reserve £C

SANTA CRUZ MOUNTAINS VINEYARD ● **Pinot Noir** Matteson Vineyard £D

SAUCELITO CANYON ● **Zinfandel** Arroyo Grande £B

SIERRA VISTA ● **Zinfandel** Reeves Vineyard £C

SINE QUA NON ● **Pinot Noir** A Capella £F   O **The Boot** California £E

VIGIL ● **Zinfandel** Mohr Fry Ranch £C Tres Condados £B

VINO NOCETO ● **Sangiovese** Shenandoah Valley £C

WHITCRAFT ● **Pinot Noir** Bien Nacido £D   O **Chardonnay** Bien Nacido £D

WILD HORSE WINERY ● **Merlot** Paso Robles £C   O **Chardonnay** Central Coast £B

ZACA MESA ● **Z Cuvée** Santa Barbara £B   ● **Syrah** Zaca Vineyards £C Black Bear Block £E

Author's Choice (DM)

A diverse selection of Central Coast reds

ALBAN ● **Syrah** Seymour Vineyard
AU BON CLIMAT ● **Pinot Noir** Cuvée Isabelle
BABCOCK VINEYARDS ● **Syrah** Black Label Santa Barbara
BONNY DOON ● **Old Telegram** California
CALERA ● **Pinot Noir** Jensen Vineyard
EDMUNDS ST JOHN ● **Rocks and Gravel** California
JUSTIN ● **Isosceles** Paso Robles
KATHRYN KENNEDY ● **Cabernet Sauvignon** Estate
OJAI ● **Syrah** Roll Ranch
RIDGE VINEYARDS ● **Monte Bello** Santa Cruz Mountains
SANFORD WINERY ● **Pinot Noir** Sanford and Benedict Vineyard
SEAN THACKREY ● **Orion** Rossi Vineyard

A selection of exciting whites

ANDREW MURRAY O **Enchante** Santa Ynez
BREWER CLIFTON O **Chardonnay** Mount Carmel
CA DEL SOLO O **Il Pescatore**
CHALONE O **Pinot Blanc** Reserve
COLD HEAVEN O **Viognier** Alban Vineyard
MOUNT EDEN VINEYARDS O **Chardonnay** Estate
QUPÉ O **Viognier** Ibarra Young Vineyard
ROSENBLUM CELLARS O **Marsanne** Dry Creek
TALBOTT O **Chardonnay** Diamond T Estate
TESTAROSSA O **Chardonnay** Sleepy Hollow Vineyard

Oregon & Washington State

The total area of vineyards in the north-west of the United States is small, certainly when compared to the sprawling expanses of California, but is nevertheless spread across a vast geographical area. Pinot Noir, along with Pinot Gris, Pinot Blanc and Chardonnay have now been well-established in Oregon for close to a couple of decades. A whole host of small to medium-sized wineries have emerged and new ones continue to do so. Almost all of these are to be found in the Willamette Valley. Washington State is the second largest state in terms of quality-wine production behind California, but has only recently become really well-known. New and exciting sources of top reds, from both the Bordeaux and more recently Rhône varieties, are increasing and it seems certain that the best here is yet to come.

Oregon

As well as the **Willamette Valley** there are two other AVAs to the south, **Umpqua Valley** and **Rogue Valley**. The Umpqua Valley region sits in the river valley of the same name, with coastal ranges to the west and the Cascades range of volcanic peaks to the east. The Rogue Valley is marked by relatively high-altitude vineyards and cool-climate whites, including Gewürztraminer and Pinot Gris, are planted with some success in the westerly sectors of the AVA.

The main viticultural activity, though, is in the Willamette Valley, a vast stretch of vineyards with varied soils and an extensive array of mesoclimates running from Eugene in the south to Portland in the north. At its widest the AVA is in excess of 80 km (50 miles) and it runs north-south for 320 km (200 miles). The majority of vineyards are found in the northern half of the region between Monmouth and Portland; the greatest concentration in Yamhill County, in the centre of that area. This is mainly Pinot Noir country and the hunt for unique sites continues apace as wineries seek to establish different *terroirs* within the AVA. A range of white varieties are also successful, among which Pinot Gris and Pinot Blanc have the best potential. Inevitably Chardonnay is extensively planted but really striking examples are few and far between.

Washington

The vineyard area here is vast and is dominated by the giant **Columbia Valley** AVA, within which there are two sub-AVAs, the **Yakima Valley** in the west and the **Walla Walla Valley** in the east. A sizeable part of both Columbia Valley and Walla Walla in fact stretches into northern Oregon. A newly-established AVA close to the coast is **Puget Sound**, yet it appears too cool and damp to provide wines of any substance. The Columbia Valley by contrast is dry and necessarily irrigated. Located to the east of the Cascade Mountains, it is suitable for quality wine because of its northerly latitude and consequently longer, sunnier days. Excellent Bordeaux-style reds are produced along with good Chardonnay. The Yakima Valley is also successful with these grapes and with Syrah. Perhaps the greatest potential is actually the Rhône varieties rather than those of Bordeaux. Excellent wines of both styles have now been made in Walla Walla as well.

A-Z of Producers by region

Oregon

Willamette Valley
AMITY VINEYARDS
ARCHERY SUMMIT
ARGYLE
BEAUX FRÈRES
CHEHALEM
CRISTOM
DOMAINE DROUHIN
PATRICIA GREEN
KING ESTATE
PANTHER CREEK
PENNER ASH
PONZI
REX HILL
DOMAINE SERENE
KEN WRIGHT

Washington

Columbia Valley
CANOE RIDGE VINEYARD
CHATEAU STE MICHELLE
COLUMBIA CREST

Walla Walla Valley
L'ECOLE NO 41
LEONETTI CELLAR
DOMAINE STE MICHELLE
PEPPER BRIDGE WINERY
QUILCEDA CREEK VINTNERS
WOODWARD CANYON

Other
ANDREW WILL
COLUMBIA WINERY
DELILLE CELLARS

Vintages

With such a sprawling viticultural expanse, providing any meaningful detail on vintages is difficult. The following provide an idea of what to look for. 2001 was reasonable in Oregon; 2002, 2000, 1999 and 1998 were good to very good. Prior to this 1996 and 1994 are reasonable bets but only top Pinot Noir will be holding up. In Washington, particularly for reds, 2002 is very good, and only 1996 looks average over the last eight or nine years. Top reds will hold well for a decade, often longer.

AMITY VINEYARDS Willamette Valley www.amityvineyards.com A: PDn

Owner: Myron Redford 18150 Amity Vineyards Road, Amity, OR 97101
Medium-sized Willamette Valley operation founded in the mid-1970s. Pinot Noir is reasonably fragrant with soft, red-berry fruit but can be lacking in depth and substance. The class act and undoubted value for money here is the stylish, lightly pungent Gewürztraminer, one of the better examples in the state. (DM)

● **Pinot Noir** Willamette Valley★£D Winemakers Reserve★★£E
O **Riesling** Oregon★£B O **Gewurztraminer** Oregon★★£B O **Pinot Blanc** Willamette Valley★£D

ANDREW WILL Washington State A: M&V, NYg

Owner: Chris Camarda 12526 SW Bank Road, Vashon, WA 98070
Very good quality throughout this range. Winemaker Chris Camarda produces elegant, very finely made reds. The Cabernet is ripe, concentrated and displays an excellent mix of black fruit and harmonious, cedary oak. The Sorella is a fine, spicy meritage blend, but the main interest lies in the four single-vineyard Merlots. The Ciel du Cheval and the Klipsun stand out but all are impressive. The former two are just that touch richer and fuller but all show elegance, style and refinement. Although relatively expensive, these wines nevertheless represent good value. (DM)

● **Cabernet Sauvignon** Seven Hills★★★★£E
● **Merlot** Klipsun Vineyard★★★★£E Ciel du Cheval★★★★£E Seven Hills★★★★£E Pepper Bridge★★★★£E
● **Sorella**★★★★£F

ARCHERY SUMMIT Willamette Valley www.archerysummit.com A: Dis

Owner: Pine Ridge Winery 18599 NE Archery Summit Road, Dayton, OR 97114
Small, bespoke operation producing some 10,000 cases and owned by the Andrus family, who also own the large premium PINE RIDGE operation in Napa's Stags Leap District. Very classy Pinot Noir is produced here generally and it feels as if higher standards are being achieved across the range than at the parent winery; perhaps this is down to lower volumes. The focus is on specially selected lots of Pinot Noir, providing not only style and class but individuality. To that end over 40 ha (100 acres) of high-density vineyards have now been established. In addition to Arcus and Premier Cuvée, three other examples are produced from Renegade Ridge, Red Hills and the home Archery Summit estates. The latter is the top premium bottling and very expensive. The Vireton Blanc des Collines Rouges is a blend of the better Oregon white varieties – mainly Pinot Gris, with some Chardonnay and Pinot Blanc – and is an elegant, partly barrel-fermented style. (DM)

● **Pinot Noir** Premier Cuvée★★★£E Arcus Estate★★★★£F
O **Vireton** Blanc des Collines Rouges★★★£D

ARGYLE Willamette Valley www.argylewinery.com A: Men

Owner: Petaluma Group PO Box 280/691, Highway 99W, Dundee, OR 97115
Now a part of the Australian PETALUMA group, good Pinot Noir as well as top-quality sparkling wine is produced at this sizeable operation. For both Chardonnay and Pinot Noir, the bigger-volume Willamette Valley and Reserve bottlings offer good value; limited releases – albeit again not excessively priced – under the Nuthouse and Spirithouse labels both offer a notch up in quality. Also produced are a Cabernet Franc and a Nuthouse-label Merlot. (DM)

● **Pinot Noir** Willamette Valley★★£C Reserve★★★£D
O **Chardonnay** Willamette Valley★£C Reserve★★£D

O **Riesling** Dry Reserve★ £B
O **Brut** Willamette Valley★★ £C Knudsen Vineyard★★★ £D
O **Blanc de Blancs**★★★ £E O **Extended Tirage**★★★ £E

BEAUX FRÈRES Willamette Valley www.beauxfreres.com A: Vin

Owner: Mike Etzel, Robert Parker, Robert Ray 15155 NE North Valley Road, Newberg, OR 97132
Undoubtedly a producer of some of the best Pinot Noir in the Willamette Valley, this operation is
as well-known for the involvement of wine critic Robert M Parker as anything else. There are 10 ha
(24 acres) under vine and the vineyard is still relatively young, having been planted in 1988. As with
most of the current run of new vineyards, vine density is high at over 2,200 vines per acre and the
latest Dijon clones are planted. Vinification occurs naturally with indigenous yeasts from the vineyard and malolactic is also allowed to occur naturally. The results are impressive. The wines are powerful and structured with greater grip and concentration than most of their contemporaries. Belles
Soeurs is not a second label but an addition to the estate wine, sourced from the excellent Shea vineyard. (DM)
● **Pinot Noir** Beaux Frères Vineyard★★★★ £F Belles Souers Vineyard★★★★ £F

CANOE RIDGE VINEYARD Columbia Valley www.canoeridgevineyard.com A: Bib

Owner: Chalone Wine Group PO Box 684, Walla Walla, WA 99362
Owned by the California-based Chalone Wine Group, which numbers among its wineries CHALONE
and ACACIA in California, Canoe Ridge is a reliable rather than cutting-edge producer of good, well-
made, ripe and toasty Chardonnay along with Merlot and Cabernet Sauvignon that are soft, forward
reds enjoyable in their relative youth. Merlot sees American oak; Cabernet is aged in French barrels.
A stylish, more expensive Merlot Reserve is also available in more limited quantity. A straightforward
blend of Cabernet and Merlot is labelled Red Table Wine and a small quantity of Gewürztraminer is
produced from the Oak Ridge Vineyard. (DM)
● **Cabernet Sauvignon** Columbia Valley★★ £D ● **Merlot** Columbia Valley★★ £D
O **Chardonnay** Columbia Valley ★★£ D

CHATEAU STE MICHELLE Columbia Valley www.ste-michelle.com A: PRc

Owner: Stimson Lane PO Box 1976, Woodinville, WA 98072
The largest producer in Washington State and the jewel in the Stimson Lane crown. The wines from
Chateau Ste Michelle seem somehow more complete and exciting than those from sister winery
COLUMBIA CREST, even at the lower levels. A considerable array of wines are produced here, including
a number in overseas partnerships. The Columbia Valley is the focal point of the winery's operations
and there is a new vinification facility at the Canoe Ridge Estate Vineyard, the River Ridge Winery.
Other key vineyard sources are Cold Creek, Horse Heaven and Indian Wells. The regular Columbia
Valley bottlings can offer very good value, particularly among the whites, with the single-vineyard series
offering style, quality and diversity. There are some very good Artists Series and Reserve labels, now
including Syrah sourced from a number of vineyards. Of particular interest are the joint partnerships:
Col Solare is a premium blend of Cabernet Sauvignon, Merlot, Syrah and Malbec produced in
association with Tuscan firm ANTINORI; Eroica is a marvellously intense, opulent but crisp, mineral-
scented Riesling made in partnership with Ernst LOOSEN from the Mosel-Saar-Ruwer. (DM)
● **Cabernet Sauvignon** Columbia Valley★★ £C Cold Creek★★★ £E
● **Merlot** Columbia Valley★ £C Canoe Ridge★★ £E
● **Col Solare** Columbia Valley★★★★ £G

O **Chardonnay** Columbia Valley★★ £C   Canoe Ridge★★★ £D
O **Riesling** Columbia Valley★★ £B   Eroica★★★ £D
O **Sauvignon Blanc** Columbia Valley★ £B   O **Semillon** Columbia Valley★ £B

CHEHALEM   Willamette Valley   www.chehalemwines.com

Owner: Harry Peterson-Nedry   31190 NE Veritas Lane, Newberg OR 97132
This property was originally founded as Ridgecrest Vineyards by Harry Peterson-Nedry in 1980. Winemaking at Chehalem did not commence until 1990. There are now three estate vineyards, Ridgecrest, Stoller and Corral Creek, the total area under vine being some 67 ha (165 acres). Pinot Noir makes up the bulk of the grapes at around 60 per cent, the rest being Chardonnay, Riesling, Pinot Gris and a little Gamay Noir. As well as the three vineyard bottlings of Pinot Noir a special cuvée is produced, the Rion Reserve, which is firmer and impressively structured. It should evolve well over four or five years. The wines are generally very ripe and can have surprising alcohol levels close to 15 degrees and new oak is kept to a minimum. The Chardonnay is barrel-fermented and gets full malolactic and lees ageing and stirring. There is a limited production Ian's Reserve which is a step up in quality. The current range is completed by a little Dry Riesling and Pinot Gris, both in dry and late harvest styles made. (DM)
● **Pinot Noir** Ridgecrest Vineyards★★★ £E   Stoller Vineyards★★★ £E   Rion Reserve★★★★ £E
O **Chardonnay** Willamette Valley★★ £D

COLUMBIA CREST   Columbia Valley   www.columbia-crest.com   A: PRc

*Owner: **Stimson Lane**   Highway 221, Columbia Crest Drive, Paterson WA 99345*
Originally conceived as a junior label for CHATEAU STE MICHELLE this is now a stand-alone operation. The wines are all reasonably crafted, particularly at the top end, although there is a certain uniformity of style and you yearn for a little more character and individuality. The operation draws on extensive estate vineyards for much of its needs across the range. An extensive line-up of varietals appear under the Columbia Valley label. The Grand Estates wines are a step up and the range is completed by some impressive Reserve reds as well as Chardonnay. The Walter Clore Private Reserve is the pinnacle here, a powerful meritage blend of Cabernet Sauvignon and Merlot in almost equal parts. New American oak is a key feature of the style. A small amount of Late-harvest Semillon is produced as well as a rare icewine from the same variety. (DM)
● **Cabernet Sauvignon** Grand Estates★★ £C   Reserve★★★ £D
● **Merlot** Grand Estates★★ £C   ● **Merlot** Reserve★★★ £D
● **Syrah** Reserve★★★ £D   ● **Walter Clore Private Reserve** Columbia Valley★★★ £E
O **Chardonnay** Grand Estates★ £B

COLUMBIA WINERY   Washington State   www.columbiawinery.com   A: For

*Owner: **Associated Vintners**   14030 NE 145th Street, PO Box 1248, Woodinville, WA 98072*
One of the pioneering wineries of Washington State under the winemaking guidance of David Lake MW, established in 1962. A considerable range is now offered. The bulk of the winery's top wines are sourced from four prime vineyards – Red Willow, Otis, Wyckoff and Sagemoor – in both the Yakima and Columbia Valleys. The Signature series represents the best examples, bottled as single-vineyard cuvées. The Mainline label offers decent quality at a lower level. Columbia was one of the first Washington wineries to produce Syrah with impressive results and is now also vinifying Sangiovese, which may prove equally suited to the climate here. (DM)
● **Cabernet Sauvignon** Otis Vineyard★★★ £D   Red Willow Vineyard★★★ £D
● **Merlot** Red Willow Vineyard★★ £D   ● **Syrah** Yakima Valley★ £C   Red Willow Vineyard★★★ £D

O **Chardonnay** Woodburne Cuvée★★£C Otis Vineyard★★★£D
O **Viognier** Red Willow Vineyard★★£C   O **Pinot Gris** Yakima Valley★£B
O **Riesling** Cellarmasters Reserve★★£B

CRISTOM Willamette Valley www.cristomwines.com   A: WTs

Owner: Gerrie family Spring Valley Road, NW Salem, OR 97304
Established in 1992, this small operation is now producing a range of excellent Pinot Noirs and some
very good whites. As well as the lightly oaked, quite restrained Chardonnay and floral Viognier there
is a stylish, mineral-scented Pinot Gris. The main focus is Pinot Noir, produced in a number of
cuvées and from a number of estate-owned single vineyards; the Louise, Jessie and Marjorie bottlings
are impressive. The Reserve is unusual in being sourced from eight different vineyards and comprising
five different clones. A barrel selection, it is a full, opulent style which gets extended cask ageing. (DM)
● **Pinot Noir** Mt Jefferson Cuvée★★★£D Reserve★★★★£E Louise Vineyard★★★★£E
O **Chardonnay** Celilo Vineyard★★★£C   ● **Viognier** Willamette Valley★★£D

DELILLE CELLARS Washington State www.delillecellars.com   A: WTs

Owner: Charles & Greg Lill, Chris Upchurch, Jay Soloff PO Box 2233, Woodinville, WA 98072
The focus here is principally on producing top-quality Bordeaux blends from a range of Yakima Valley
fruit sources. To this end they succeed very well, although the wines are not perhaps quite at the
pinnacle. Both the Chaleur Estate and the D2 are made in an open-knit, ripe, supple style, particularly
the soft, more obviously forward D2. The Estate – Cabernet Sauvignon, Merlot and Cabernet Franc –
certainly has depth and a fine tannic structure, but very much in an upfront, bold fashion with vibrant,
dark chocolatey fruit. Harrison Hill differs from Chaleur in that it is a single-vineyard meritage in a
tighter, more backward style. The impressive white Chaleur Estate is a blend of ripe Sauvignon Blanc
and Semillon and there is also a little Syrah produced under the Doyenne label with a tiny hint of
Viognier for fragrance. (DM)
● **Chaleur Estate**★★★£F ● **Harrison Hill** Yakima Valley★★★£F ● **D2**★★★£D
O **Chaleur Estate**★★★£D

DOMAINE STE MICHELLE Washington State www.domaine-ste-michelle.com A: PRc

Owner: Stimson Lane PO Box 1976Woodinville, WA 98072
This is the Washington sparkling-wine label of Stimson Lane. The focus here is on straightforward,
attractive fizz produced at keen prices. The range comprises a Blanc de Blancs and Blanc de Noirs,
both labelled as such, and there is an Extra Dry as well. The style is for marked fruit character rather
than yeasty, bready complexity and a drink-now style. The Blanc de Blancs is a little more elegant.
(DM)
O **Cuvée Brut** NV★£C O **Blanc de Blanc** NV★★£D

DOMAINE DROUHIN Willamette Valley www.domainedrouhin.com   A: M&V

Owner: Maison Joseph Drouhin PO Box 700, Dundee, OR 97115
Established in the late 1980s by Joseph DROUHIN and run by Véronique Drouhin, who controls
the winemaking. The approach to viticulture from the outset was distinctly Burgundian: at the time
she was one of the few focusing on high-density vineyard planting. The estate has some 35 ha (85
acres) under vine in the Red Hills area, which has a climate remarkably similar to that found on the
Côte d'Or. The resulting wines are in a tight, restrained style but very stylish with real depth and con-

centration. There is a powerful, dark-berry character to the Pinot and the Cuvée Laurène has the refined, tannic structure to promise much with age. The Chardonnay is elegant and understated but with a piercing, mineral and citrus undercurrent. Stylish with well-judged oak. (DM)

● **Pinot Noir** Willamette Valley★★★★ £E   Cuvée Laurene★★★★ £F
O **Chardonnay** Willamette Valley★★★★ £E

PATRICIA GREEN CELLARS   Willamette Valley   www.patriciagreencellars.com

Owner: Patricia Green   15225 NE North Valley Road, Newberg, OR 97132
Impressive new property established by former Torii Mor winemakers Patty Green and Jim Anderson. The focal point of the operation is the estate 21 ha (52 acre) Autumn Wind vineyard in Yamhill County, which the pair purchased in 2000. They have the capacity to produce up to 6,000 cases a year and have produced wines from a range of other vineyards as well as their own. These include Balcombe, Eason, Temperance Hill and Four Winds vineyards. Shea Vineyard has now been added and the estate bottling only accounts for a few hundred cases. The 2002 vintage saw the addition of a further number of tiny lot production labels, including grapes sourced from the Hirsch vineyard in the Russian River. Vinification is carried out with native yeasts and lees are often added back during barrel ageing. These are rich and concentrated, almost animal, gamey styles of Pinot with the Estate and Shea Vineyards showing impressive concentration. Well-priced Chardonnay, Sauvignon Blanc and an Oregon Pinot Noir are also produced. (DM)

● **Pinot Noir** Estate★★★★ £D   Shea Vineyard★★★ £E

KING ESTATE   Willamette Valley   www.kingestate.com   A: SWB

Owner: King family   80854 Territorial Road, Eugene, OR 97405
This is a sizeable operation – the estate is some 332 ha (820 acres) – and the largest producer of Pinot Noir in Oregon. Quality ranges from good to very good. There is a second label, Lorane, under which the winery produces soft, fruit-driven, easy-drinking Pinot Noir and Chardonnay – not complex but well made. The King Estate wines are a serious step up in quality and there a couple of classy limited-volume bottlings under the Tower series: Domaine Pinot Noir and a Pfeiffer Vineyard bottling. Low-volume speciality wines are also produced under the Collection series and include an icewine-style Pinot Gris Vin Glace, Late Harvest Riesling and Zinfandel sourced from the north of the state in the Columbia Valley and Cabernet Sauvignon from a range of warmer locations. (DM)

● **Pinot Noir** Oregon★★ £C   Reserve★★★ £E
O **Chardonnay** Oregon★ £B   Reserve★★ £C   O **Pinot Gris** Oregon★ £B   Reserve★★ £C

L'ECOLE NO 41   Walla Walla Valley   www.lecole.com   A: PDn

Owner: Martin Clubb   PO Box 111, Lowden, WA 99360
Established nearly twenty years ago, L'École No 41 has consistently produced good-quality wine, both red and white. The reds are well-crafted and stylish with refined supple tannins; not block-busters, rather more good, medium-term cellar prospects. The Apogee red is sourced from the Pepper Tree vineyard and is a concentrated, cedary meritage blend of Cabernet Sauvignon and Merlot. Syrah from the Seven Hills Vineyard in Walla Walla is dark and brooding with a spicy black pepper character underpinning the fruit. The principle varieties here are Merlot and Semillon and the winery is one of the very best sources of the latter. Subtle use of oak, and a marvellously waxy, honeyed character show through in the wines. A straightforward red blend Schoolhouse Red is also produced from Merlot, both Cabernets, Carmenère and Syrah. (DM)

● **Cabernet Sauvignon** Columbia Valley★★ £D   Walla Walla Valley★★★ £E

● **Merlot** Columbia Valley★★★ £D Walla Walla Valley★★★ £D Seven Hills★★★ £E
● **Syrah** Seven Hills★★★ £E ● **Apogee** Pepper Tree Bridge★★★ £E
○ **Chardonnay** Columbia Valley★★ £C
○ **Semillon** Columbia Valley★★ £B Seven Hills★★★ £C Fries Vineyard★★★ £C

LEONETTI CELLAR Walla Walla Valley www.leonetticellar.com

Owner: Gary Figgins 1875 Foothills Lane, Walla Walla, WA 99362
One of the very best producers of Bordeaux-style reds in Washington State with just over 77 ha (190 acres) of estate vineyards, making around 6,000 cases annually. Meritage styles are of massive proportions – powerful wines that are sturdy but refined and very long-lived – an approach that has been perpetuated here for 25 years. High quality is maintained in the vineyards, which are on fine, well-drained hillside slopes. Sustainable viticulture is practised and yields are kept down, rarely exceeding three tons to the acre. Although frowned on in some quarters, green harvesting is also practiced. As well as the impressive Cabernet and Merlot, stylish Sangiovese is also produced in a softer, lighter style, displaying very good intense, dark, cherry fruit. The magnificent Reserve meritage red is made in very small quantities, just 665 cases for the 2000 vintage. (DM)

● **Reserve** Walla Walla Valley✪✪✪✪✪ £G ● **Cabernet Sauvignon** Walla Walla Valley★★★★★ £F
● **Merlot** Columbia Valley★★★★ £F ● **Sangiovese** Walla Walla Valley★★★ £F

PANTHER CREEK Willamette Valley www.panthercreekcellars.com

Owner: Kaplan family 455 N Irvine, McMinnville, OR 97128
Excellent producer of first-class Pinot Noir as well as Chardonnay, Pinot Gris and a bit of Melon de Bourgogne. Winemaker Michael Stevenson makes no more than 7,500 cases each year. The winery purchases fruit from 10 different vineyard sources throughout the Willamette Valley and, with long-term arrangements with growers, maintains a tight grip on viticulture. Careful sorting (*triage*) takes place prior to vinification and the practice of minimal intervention is carried through to bottling with virtually no fining or filtration. There is a plethora of single-vineyard bottlings of Pinot Noir, of which Freedom Hill and Shea Vineyard are produced in greater volume. (DM)

● **Pinot Noir** Winemakers Cuvée★★★ £D Reserve★★★★ £E

PENNER-ASH Willamette Valley www.pennerash.com

Owner: Ron & Lynn Penner-Ash PO Box 1207, Newberg, OR 97132
Ron and Lynn Penner-Ash produce some rich and concentrated Willamette Valley Pinot Noir as well as small quantities of hand-crafted Syrah and Viognier. The Syrah comes from several different Oregon growers, while the Viognier has been added with the 2002 vintage and is sourced from the Del Rio Vineyard in the south of the state. The Pinot Noir, a blend from a number of sites gets nine months in French oak, 40 per cent of the barrels being new. The wine is rich and concentrated, firmly structured with dark berry fruit and a savoury edge to the palate. It will keep well for six or seven years and drink well with a few months of release. (DM)

● **Pinot Noir** Willamette Valley★★★★ £E

PEPPER BRIDGE WINERY Walla Walla Valley www.pepperbridge.com

Owner: Norm McKibben 1704 JB George Road, Walla Walla, WA 99362
Recently established, the winemaking facility was only completed in 2000, this estate produces Cabernet Sauvignon and Merlot solely from the Walla Walla Valley AVA and their own Pepper Bridge and Seven

Hills vineyards. These are also an important source for a number of other leading Washington wineries. The winery has been designed to be completely gravity fed from crushing to barrel ageing. Vinification is straightforward with pigeage and seven to eight days on skins. Malolactic is carried out in barrel. As well as French oak, a small amount of American oak is used for ageing. Both wines have reasonable depth and concentration but have a little way to go to match the best of their neighbours. There is also a second label Amavi under which a decent, lightly peppery Cabernet Sauvignon and more impressive Syrah are produced. American as well as French and Hungarian oak are used to age the Cabernet, while just French and American is used for the Syrah, which is dark and spicy with impressive fruit. (DM)

● **Cabernet Sauvignon** Walla Walla Valley★★★ £E   ● **Merlot** Walla Walla Valley★★★ £E
● **Cabernet Sauvignon** Amavi Walla Walla Valley★ £C   ● **Syrah** Amavi Walla Walla Valley★★ £C

PONZI   Willamette Valley   www.ponziwines.com

Owner: Ponzi family   14665 SW Winery Lane, Beaverton, OR 97007
Long-established Willamette Valley producer with a high reputation for its Pinot Noir. Luisa Ponzi has now taken on the winemaking mantle. Pinot Noir is certainly good if on occasion lacking the depth and substance now found in the best examples elsewhere in the valley. There is a superior Reserve bottling, as well as the tiny-production Abetina Vineyard Reserve. Of particular interest here is one of the better Pinot Gris and a good fruit-driven Arneis. These offer particularly good value. (DM)

● **Pinot Noir** Willamette Valley★★ £D   Reserve★★★ £F
O **Chardonnay** Reserve★★ £D   O **Pinot Gris** Willamette Valley★★ £B   **Arneis** Willamette Valley★ £C

QUILCEDA CREEK VINTNERS   Washington State   www.quilcedacreek.com   A: Wgg

Owner: Alex Golitzin   5226 Old Machias Road, Snohomish, WA 98290
For many, this is Washington State's greatest source of Cabernet Sauvignon and Merlot. Certainly along with LEONETTI they vie for that accolade. Originally founded in 1978 the main focus and volume here is the Cabernet Sauvignon, sourced from several different prime vineyards, Ciel du Cheval and Klipsun among them. If not fully Cabernet Sauvignon, it is almost so, occasionally with a tiny proportion of Merlot blended in to add some flesh. In addition to the Cabernet a very small amount of varietal Merlot and a Columbia Red are also produced. (DM)

● **Cabernet Sauvignon** Columbia Valley★★★★★ £F

REX HILL   Willamette Valley   www.rexhill.com   A: Mor

Owner: Paul Hart & Jan Jacobsen   30835 N Highway. 99W, Newberg, OR 97132
With access to 91 ha (225 acres) of top-quality vineyards this winery has consistently produced first-class Pinot Noir from a number of sites. There have been a number of stylish, low-volume, single-vineyard offerings as well as a good regular Willamette Valley bottling and a consistent Reserve. The Reserve and single-vineyard cuvées – including Jacob-Hart, Penner-Ash, Carabella and Seven Springs – possess that extra dimension. While reasonably pricey, they are not excessively so. Of equal interest is a very good Pinot Gris Reserve. (DM)

● **Pinot Noir** Kings Ridge★ £B   Willamette Valley★★ £D   Reserve★★★★ £E
O **Pinot Gris** Reserve★★★ £C

DOMAINE SERENE Willamette Valley www.domaineserene.com A: Vin

Owner: Ken & Grace Evenstad 6555 NE Hilltop Lane, Dayton, OR 97114

Top class producer of both Pinot Noir and Chardonnay. Considerable investment has gone into the estate and the results are impressive. Yields are kept to a minimum, around two tons to the acre and the harvest is always carried out by hand. Minimal intervention in the cellars means the Pinot Noir is only racked at bottling and is neither fined nor filtered. The Dijon clone is solely grown for Chardonnay which is barrel-fermented and aged on its lees for up to 15 months. Tiny lots of various single vineyard bottlings are available through the winery and there is also a flagship Pinot Noir, Grace Vineyard. The Pinot Noirs are marked by their firm structure and dark, rich and concentrated berry fruit. Time is needed to integrate the new oak in both the Evenstad Reserve and Mark Bradford. The two Chardonnays are lightly tropical, with a fine spicy, toasty oak character but with the firm structure that signifies their cool grown origins. The Clos du Soleil is the tighter, more mineral of the two. (DM)

● **Pinot Noir** Yamhill Cuvée★★★ £E Evenstad Reserve★★★★ £E Mark Bradford Vineyard★★★★ £F
O **Chardonnay** Clos du Soleil★★★★ £E Cote Sud★★★★ £E

WOODWARD CANYON Walla Walla Valley woodwardcanyon.com A: Vin

Owner: Rick Small 11920 W Hwy 12, Lowden, WA 99360

In Washington State terms this fine small producer is a relative veteran. Rick Small established the winery in 1981 and production has grown from 1,200 cases in 1981 to 15,000 cases today. An extensive range of wines is produced. In addition to the medium weight, finely structured Artists Series Cabernet Sauvignon there are additional bottlings including the soft, approachable Nelms Road and the premium Old Vines Cabernet. The Charbonneau red blends Merlot and Cabernet Sauvignon, whereas the impressive, dense and firmly structured Estate Red is a blend of the best lots of Cabernet Sauvignon, Merlot and Cabernet Franc. The is a good regular Columbia Valley Chardonnay but the Celilo Vineyard wine is a significant step up. It is almost Burgundian in style but with a rich, toasty character. Small amounts of Barbera, Syrah and Pinot Noir are produced as well as Riesling and an Orange Muscat. The white range is completed by a meritage style, Charbonneau Blanc blended from two-thirds Semillon and one-third Sauvignon Blanc. (DM)

● **Charbonneau Red** Walla Walla Valley★★★ £F ● **Estate Red** Walla Walla Valley★★★★ £E
● **Cabernet Sauvignon** Estate Series★★★ £F ● **Merlot** Walla Walla Valley★★★ £E
O **Chardonnay** Columbia Valley★★★ £E Celilo Vineyard★★★★ £E

KEN WRIGHT Willamette Valley www.kenwrightcellars.com A: Vin

Owner: Ken Wright 239 North Kutch Street, Carlton, OR 97111

Ken Wright has established himself as the Willamette champion of single-vineyard Pinot Noir, seeking to show in his wines the best individual site characteristics in a single bottling, what the French refer to as *terroir*. Now working with a considerable number of vineyard owners, he produces wines from a wide range of Willamette Valley sites. Those from the Dundee Hills in the north of the valley, including Abbey Ridge Vineyard and Nysa Vineyards, tend to produce rich, forward wines with marked red-berry fruit and moderate acidity; those from the Eola Hills are more structured and the Canary Hill bottling will be easiest to find. The Guadalupe Vineyard is among the most successful bottlings here over a number of vintages. Sourced like the Shea and McCrone Vineyard Pinots from the Yamhill foothills this is opulent, lush and forward and will drink well at a young age. A single Chardonnay, Dijon Clones, was produced from Oregon-sourced grapes, but this has been superseded by two separate vineyard bottlings from the Columbia River Celilo Vineyard site – Carabella and McCrone. A small amount of floral, subtly-oaked Pinot Blanc is also produced. Because production is so limited, all these cuvées are incredibly hard to find. However you can expect the wines to be almost invariably of three-star quality, often four-star, and although not cheap, they are priced very fairly. (DM)

● **Pinot Noir** Guadalupe Vineyard★★★★ £E   Shea Vineyard★★★★ £E

OTHER WINES OF NOTE

ADELSHEIM ● **Pinot Noir** Elizabeth's Reserve £E
APEX ● **Merlot** Columbia Valley £E O **Chardonnay** Columbia Valley £C Outlook £D
BARNARD GRIFFIN ● **Merlot** Reserve £D O **Fumé Blanc** Columbia Valley £B
BETHEL HEIGHTS ● **Pinot Noir** Estate £D O **Chardonnay** Estate £D
BRICK HOUSE ● **Pinot Noir** Cuvée du Tonnellier £E
BROADLEY VINEYARDS ● **Pinot Noir** Claudia's Choice £E
CADENCE ● **Spring Valley Red** Walla Walla Valley £E ● **Tapteil Red** Washington £E
● **Ciel du Cheval Red** Washington £E
CAMERON ● **Pinot Noir** Clos Electrique £E
JK CARRIERE ● **Pinot Noir** Willamette Valley £E
CAYUSE ● **Syrah** Cailloux Vineyard £E
COOPER MOUNTAIN VINEYARDS ● **Pinot Noir** Estate Reserve £E
DUNHAM CELLARS ● **Cabernet Sauvignon** Columbia Valley £E
ELK COVE ● **Pinot Noir** Reserve £F Roosevelt Vineyard £E O **Riesling** Willamette Valley £C
EYRIE VINEYARD ● **Pinot Gris** Willamette Valley £B
HEDGES CELLARS ● **Red Mountain Reserve** £E
HENRY ESTATE ● **Pinot Noir** Umpqua Cuvée £E O **Pinot Gris** Umpqua Valley £B
McCREA CELLARS ● **Syrah** Yakima Valley £C O **Viognier** Yakima Valley £C
MCKINLAY ● **Pinot Noir** Special Selection £E
MATTHEWS CELLARS ● **Yakima Valley Red** £E O **Yakima Valley White** £C
REININGER ● **Cabernet Sauvignon** Walla Walla Valley £D
SEVEN HILLS ● **Cabernet Sauvignon** Seven Hills £D Klipsun £D ● **Merlot** Seven Hills £D
SILVAN RIDGE ● **Pinot Noir** Willamette Valley £C O **Early Muscat** £B
SINEANN ● **Zinfandel** Old Vine £E
SOKOL BLOSSER ● **Pinot Noir** Willamette Valley £D Old Vineyard Block £F
ST INNOCENT ● **Pinot Noir** Freedom Hill £E Seven Springs Vineyard £E Shea Vineyard £E
O **Chardonnay** Seven Springs Vineyard £D
TAMARACK CELLARS ● **Cabernet Sauvignon** Columbia Valley £D ● **Merlot** Columbia Valley £D
TORII MOR ● **Pinot Noir** Olson Vineyard West Block £F Olson Vineyard East Slope £F
TUALATIN ● **Pinot Noir** Willamette Valley £D O **Pinot Blanc** Oregon £B
WALLA WALLA VINTNERS ● **Cabernet Sauvignon** Columbia Valley £D
WILLAKENZIE ESTATE ● **Pinot Noir** Willamette Valley £D O **Chardonnay** Estelle £D
WILLAMETTE VALLEY VINEYARD ● **Pinot Noir** Hoodview £E
YAMHILL VALLEY VINEYARDS ● **Pinot Noir** Willamette Valley £E

Author's Choice (DM)

The best of the Willamette Valley
ARCHERY SUMMIT ● **Pinot Noir** Arcus Estate
BEAUX FRÈRES ● **Pinot Noir** Beaux Frères Vineyard
CHEHALEM ● **Pinot Noir** Rion Reserve
CRISTOM ● **Pinot Noir** Louise Vineyard
DOMAINE DROUHIN O **Chardonnay**

PATRICIA GREEN CELLARS ● **Pinot Noir** Estate
PENNER ASH ● **Pinot Noir** Willamette Valley
PONZI ○ **Pinot Gris** Willamette Valley
DOMAINE SERENE ○ **Chardonnay** Clos du Soleil
KEN WRIGHT CELLARS ● **Pinot Noir** Shea Vineyard

A selection of new classics from Washington State

ANDREW WILL ● **Merlot** Klipsun Vineyard
CHATEAU STE MICHELLE ○ **Col Solare** Columbia Valley
COLUMBIA WINERY ● **Syrah** Red Willow Vineyard
DELILLE CELLARS ● **Chaleur Estate**
DUNHAM CELLARS ● **Cabernet Sauvignon** Columbia Valley
L'ECOLE NO 41 ○ **Semillon** Seven Hills
LEONETTI CELLAR ● **Reserve** Walla Walla Valley
PEPPER BRIDGE WINERY ● **Merlot** Walla Walla Valley
QUILCEDA CREEK VINEYARDS ● **Cabernet Sauvignon** Columbia Valley
WOODWARD CANYON ○ **Chardonnay** Celilo Vineyard

Besides California, Oregon and Washington State, quality wine production is limited to just a handful of states. However grapes other than vinifera varieties are grown throughout the country. In New York State, for example, hybrid varieties are popular in the production of kosher wines and grape juice. Wines from these tend to have what is quaintly referred to as a 'foxy' character. A very damp pet dog smells not dissimilar. The best developments have been on New York's Long Island, in Maryland, in Virginia and to the far south in Arizona. The odd reasonable bottle has also emerged from Texas and the state may have real potential. Canadian quality wine has traditionally been Niagara icewine, but the developing region of the Okanagan Valley in British Columbia is also providing an increasing number of stylish dry whites and reds.

USA

New York State remains the best bet for quality wines outside the big sources on the western coast. In the north-west of the state the **Finger Lakes,** just to the south of Lake Ontario, has a protected, very localised climate moderated by the lakes themselves. Both Chardonnay and Riesling are successful here along with a few sparkling wines. Among the best wineries, Fox Run, Dr Konstantin Frank, Lamoreaux Landing and Hermann J Wiemer stand out.

Directly north of New Jersey is the small **Hudson River** AVA where some decent Chardonnay is produced. Perhaps of most significance from a quality point of view are the wineries of **Long Island** and particularly **The North Fork of Long Island**. The climate is strongly maritime and both regions have proved to be impressive sources in recent years of Cabernet Sauvignon, Merlot and Cabernet Franc, along with the occasional striking Chardonnay. Bedell, Corey Creek, Gallucio, Jamesport, Palmer, Paumanok and Pellegrini are all worth a look.

To the south of New York, a few good wines are being produced in **Maryland** which, with its warm maritime climate, has real potential despite the odd wet harvest. Better mesoclimates are being established and one winery in particular, Basignano, stands out for the impressive quality of its Cabernet Sauvignon and meritage wines. There have been attempts to grow vines in **Virginia** since Thomas Jefferson's days, but only recently have these proved to be successful. A string of new wineries have now been established around Charlottesville on the eastern side of the Appalachian Mountains. Piedmont Vineyards is making some impressive **Chardonnay** and others have proved successful with a range of varieties, including those of Rhône and Bordeaux origin. Horton, Prince Michel and Barboursville are also worth looking at.

There is just one winery that stands out in **Arizona**: Callaghan Vineyards, based in the **Sonoita** AVA. The region is cooled by its elevation and the winery has some impressive, well-drained, gravel-dominated vineyards. An extensive range of varieties are planted and the Buena Suerte Cuvée is a notable Bordeaux-style red. From a volume rather than a quality point of view, **Idaho** is significant and home to the giant Ste Chapelle Winery. Quality so far has been sound but uninspirational with simple, straightforward red and white varietals.

Canada

The country has one sizeable wine region at **Niagara** in Ontario and more recently one in the far west in British Columbia. Wine production is now controlled by the VQA (Vintners Quality Alliance) and under these regulations the **Ontario** and generic **British Columbia** appellations were established. As well as in **Niagara Peninsula** good whites and icewine are also produced in Ontario from **Pelee Island** and **Lake Eyrie North Shore**. The vast majority of the vineyard area of the country and wine production is still focused on Ontario. It is the icewines that make the country's wine industry special and give it a unique stamp. In British Columbia and in particular in the **Okanagan Valley**, although those same magnificent icewines are crafted, there are an increasing number of dry table wines of note as well. Pinot Gris, Chardonnay, Merlot and Syrah have all shown potential in this dry, sparse inland region to the immediate north of the international border with Washington State.

Mexico

To date no wine in significant quantities of any substantial quality has been forthcoming here. This is largely down to a scarcity of local consumers to support a small wine industry. However, the potential of the area is there and in particular in the Baja Peninsula. The only wines to have had any worthwhile distribution so far are those of the LA Cetto company.

WINES OF NOTE

Rest of the USA

BASIGNANI ● **Lorenzino Reserve Red** Maryland £C
BEDELL ● **Cupola** Long Island £D   ● **Merlot Reserve** Long Island £D
CALLAGHAN VINEYARDS ● **Buena Suerte Cuvée** Arizona £D   ● **Matthews Cuvée** Arizona £C
COREY CREEK O **Chardonnay** Reserve Long Island £C
FALL CREEK ● **Meritus** Texas Hill Country £C
FOX RUN O **Chardonnay** Reserve Finger Lakes £B
DR. KONSTANTIN FRANK O **Johannisberg Riesling** Finger Lakes £B
GALLUCCIO ● **Merlot** Andys Field Long Island £D
JAMESPORT ● **Merlot** Long Island £C
LAMOREAUX LANDING O **Chardonnay** Reserve Finger Lakes £C
MILLBROOK O **Chardonnay** Proprietor's Special Reserve Hudson River £C
PALMER O **Chardonnay** Reserve Long Island £C
PAUMANOK O **Chardonnay** Barrel Fermented Long Island £C   O **Sauvignon Blanc** Late Harvest £E
PELLEGRINI ● **Cabernet Sauvignon** Long Island £C   ● **Merlot** Long Island £C
PIEDMONT O **Chardonnay** Special Reserve Virginia £C   Native Yeast Virginia £D
HERMANN J WIEMAR O **Johannisberg Riesling** Finger Lakes £B

Canada

BLUE MOUNTAIN   **Pinot Gris Okanagan** Valley £C
BURROWING OWL **Chardonnay** Okanagan Valley £C
CAVE SPRING CELLARS O **Chardonnay** Niagara Peninsula £B
CEDARCREEK O **Riesling** Icewine Okanagan Valley £F
CHATEAU DES CHARMES O **Chardonnay** Niagara Peninsula £C
GEHRINGER BROTHERS O **Riesling** Icewine Okanagan Valley £F   O **Pinot Gris** Private Reserve £B
GRAY MONK O **Chardonnay** Okanagan Valley £B
HAWTHORNE MOUNTAIN O **Gewurztraminer** British Columbia £B
HENRY OF PELHAM O **Riesling** Icewine Niagara Peninsula £F
HILLEBRAND O **Vidal** Icewine Trius Niagara Peninsula £E
INNISKILLIN O **Ice Wine** Niagara Peninsula £F   O **Vidal** Icewine Niagara Peninsula £F
INNISKILLIN OKANAGAN ● **Merlot** Okanagan Valley £D
JACKSON-TRIGGS O **Riesling** Ice Wine Grand Reserve Okanagan Valley £F
KONZELMANN O **Riesling** Ice Wine Niagara Peninsula £F
MISSION HILL O **Chardonnay** Grand Reserve Okanagan Valley £C   ● **Shiraz** Okanagan Valley £D
PELLER ESTATES O **Vidal** Ice Wine Niagara Peninsula £F
PILLITTERI ESTATES O **Riesling** Ice Wine Niagara Peninsula £F
QUAILS' GATE O **Chardonnay** Family Reserve Okanagan Valley £C   O **Riesling** Okanagan Valley £B

REIF ESTATE O **Riesling** Icewine Niagara Peninsula £F
STONEY RIDGE O **Chardonnay** Reserve Niagara Peninsula £C
SUMAC RIDGE O **Sauvignon Blanc** Okanagan Valley £B
VINELAND O **Vidal** Icewine Niagara Peninsula £F

South America

Over the last half decade the wines of both Chile and Argentina have become firmly established on the international wine map. This reputation has been built on value and, particularly in the case of Chilean reds, vibrantly fruity styles. More recently some impressive super-premium wines have emerged, suggesting real potential. There is some way to go before either country can compete in absolute quality terms with either Australia or California but new wines and producers are continuing to surface. The only other county that may also have some potential for fine wine is Uruguay. Tannat is widely planted here but as yet there are only a handful of reasonable examples.

Chile

The country is split into five viticultural zones. Running from north to south, they are: **Atacama**, **Coquimbo**, **Aconcagua**, **Valle Central** and the **Región del Sur**. These zones contain a number of sub- regions and these may also be further subdivided. Atacama and Coquimbo are well to the north of the country. These are hot and dry requiring mass flood irrigation and generally produce basic table grapes as well as Pisco, the local brandy. There are new vineyard plantings at Coquimbo nearer the coast, where the climate is moderated by sea breezes. Some good rich and full-bodied reds are now being produced from both the Bordeaux varieties and Syrah. You have to travel further south, though, to find vineyards capable of providing good quality wines in any volume. The region of Aconcagua includes the important sub-region of **Casablanca**, where the vineyards are cool and nearer the coast. This is now a well-established source for some of the best white wines in the country. Chardonnay, Gewürztraminer and Sauvignon Blanc are all successful here. The **Valle del Aconcagua** itself is warmer and and becomes increasingly hot further inland. Eastern Aconcagua is largely red-wine territory. Some of the best sites are on well-drained slopes, rare here, and the super premium Seña blend is sourced from the area.

The Valle Central is a substantial zone which includes Santiago to the north, the suburbs of Chile's capital city encroaching into the vineyards of **Maipo**, the northernmost of the zone's sub-regions. The Valley runs 400 kilometres north to south, taking in **Rapel**, **Maule** and **Curicó**. The two key elements which influence grape growing here are the coastal fogs, which drift a long way inland and moderate the climate, and the Andes mountains. The latter provide an importance water source for irrigation. One of the problems encountered over the past decade has been over-vigorous and productive vineyards. Increased use of sophisticated drip irrigation systems is helping to overcome such vineyard problems. More wines are offering ripe and vibrant fruit now as opposed to some of the overtly green flavours that were so widespread just a few years ago. The best reds from Maipo have traditionally been Cabernet-based but increased plantings of Rhône varieties is a continuing trend.

Rapel is very promising for fine wine production with Cabernet Sauvignon, Merlot and particularly Carmenère successful in the warmer south of the region at **Colchagua,** while earlier-ripening varieties including Chardonnay, Sauvignon Blanc and Pinot Noir are more successful in cooler **Cachapoal**. There are both promising reds and whites to be found at Curicó. Growing conditions are aided by large mid-season temperature fluctuations which help in preserving the acidity in the grapes. **Maule** to the south is largely dominated by white varieties but there is some good Merlot too.

To the south is the Región del Sur including the two sub-regions Itata and immediately to the south Bío Bío. Unsurprisingly, this being the most southerly of the grape growing regions, the climate is cool and rainfall is also high. Sophisticated trellising and the planting of early-ripening Pinot Noir and Chardonnay as well as Alsace varieties has shown some potential. The best results so far have come from Bío Bío.

Argentina

Argentina is as yet less established internationally than Chile and many wineries seem to have some way to go to match the fruit quality achieved at lower levels by her neighbour across the Andes. The country is, however, the fifth-largest wine producer in the world, with a vast bulk-wine industry centred around the main region of Mendoza, which accounts for around nine out of every ten bottles produced. Argentina does appear to have real promise for good and indeed premium wine production and a number of impressive reds and whites are now being made. Outside expertise from the likes of Michel Rolland is increasing as is investment in new vineyards and wineries.

In the north of the country are the hot and dry vineyards of **Salta**. The lower-lying vineyards are too warm for quality wine production and irrigation is vital. Within the region though, there are a number of better sites with vineyards planted at high altitude, in particular those in the Calchaquies Valley. Some good results are being achieved with both Malbec and Cabernet Sauvignon as well as the aromatic Torrontes, a native of Spain.

Mendoza itself is the main focus for quality wine production. The two sub-regions that are of particular note are **Luján de Cuyo** and **Tupungato**. The vineyard area is planted at altitude and some of the wines, particularly from Luján de Cuyo, are world class. Malbec is very successful here but there are also widespread plantings of Cabernet Sauvignon, Syrah and Sangiovese. Bonarda is important both varietally and as a component in many wine blends and is the most widely planted red variety. Chardonnay inevitably is important and produces really striking wines in cooler sites.

To the south in Patagonia is the **Río Negro**. The climate is cool and early-ripening Sauvignon Blanc, Sémillon and Chardonnay have all been grown with some success here. However, stylish, elegant examples of the red Bordeaux varieties and Syrah are also appearing and there are ongoing efforts to realise the potential complexity of Pinot Noir.

The Rest of South America

The only other country that would appear to have any real potential for quality wine production in South America is Uruguay. Hybrid varieties are still important in terms of the area planted but high quality vinifera varieties are becoming increasingly significant. Cabernet Sauvignon, Merlot, Chardonnay and Sauvignon Blanc are all cultivated successfully. Most important from a quality wine perpective is the Tannat. It is now more widely planted here than in France and some reasonable examples have been produced. Elsewhere the climate is too hot and humid, although vinifera varieties are also grown in the southern tip of Brazil.

A-Z Producers by region

Argentina

Mendoza
ACHAVAL-FERRER
ALTA VISTA
ANUBÍS
CATENA ZAPATA
CLOS DE LOS SIETE
DOMINIO DEL PLATA
NIETO SENETINER

Salta
MICHEL TORINO
YACOCHUYA

Chile

Aconcagua
ERRÁZURIZ
SEÑA

Casablanca
VIÑA CASABLANCA

Curicó
MONTES
VALDIVIESO

Maipo
ALMAVIVA
CARMEN
CONCHA Y TORO
EL PRINCIPAL
ODFJELL VINEYARDS
SANTA RITA

Rapel
CASA LAPOSTOLLE
CASA SILVA
CONO SUR
GRACIA

Vintages

Any vintage assessment within the wine zones and regions here has to be very general because of both size and the effect of local mesoclimtes. In general almost all whites with the exception of the top barrel-fermented Chardonnays should be drunk on release. Top reds, though, can develop well in bottle. 2003 looks very good for Malbec in Argentina, particularly after an equally impressive year in 2002. 2003 looks promising for both red and white in Chile. For earlier vintages of note for top reds in Chile look out for 2002, 2001, 2000, 1999, 1996 and 1995; in Argentina 2000, 1999, 1997, 1996 and 1995 were all good.

ACHAVAL-FERRER Mendoza www.achaval-ferrer.com A: C&B

Owner: Bodega Achaval-Ferrer Azcuenaga 453, Luján de Cuyo, 5507 Mendoza
Small, newly established but top quality Mendoza winery. It is an Argentine/Italian partnership of four friends Santiago Achaval Becu, Manuel Ferrer Minetti, Italian winemaker and roving consultant Roberto Cipresso from LA FIORITA in Brunello in Tuscany and former world rally champion Tiziano Siviero. There are three estate owned vineyards which are planted at altitude, between 730 and 1,100 m and there are some leasing arrangements with a number of other vineyard owners. Vinification includes both pumping over and punching the cap during maceration and malolactic takes place in barrel. The 100per cent Malbec comes from the estate owned Finca Altamira vineyard planted to venerable vines over 80 years old. The Quimera red is a blend of Malbec, Cabernet Sauvignon and Merlot and is the mainstay of the winery with production now around 3,600 cases a year. These are dense and powerful wines which will keep well for a decade or more but can be broached with three or four years' age. (DM)
● **Quimera**★★★★ £E   ● **Malbec** Finca Altamira★★★★ £F

ALMAVIVA Maipo www.conchaytoro.com A: CyT

*Owner: **Viña Almaviva SA** Av Nueva Tajamar 481, Torre Norte Piso 15, Las Condes, Santiago*
Recently established joint venture between CONCHA Y TORO and Baroness Philippine de Rothschild (MOUTON-ROTHSCHILD). The ambitious project is aimed at producing one of, possibly the finest red wine yet from Chile. Considerable investment has already gone into both vineyards and winery. Almaviva is undoubtedly impressive but as yet falls some way short of its lofty price tag and on a global scale faces formidable opposition. It is to be hoped that the style will surpass that other Mouton-Rothschild investment OPUS ONE. Under the MAPA label the Rothschilds are producing some good results at a lower level along with a further impressive red, Escudo Rojo. (DM)
● **Almaviva Red** Maipo Valley★★★★ £G

ALTA VISTA Mendoza www.altavistawines.com A: J&B, L&W

Owner: Patrick d'Aulan Alzagar 3972, Chacras de Corja, 5505 Luján de Cuyo, Mendoza
This new venture in Argentina's high-quality Luján de Cuyo region was established by the late Jean-Michel Arcaute and Patrick d'Aulan with the objective of producing cool-grown Malbec and Cabernet Sauvignon of real style and quality. Additional input is now provided by Michel Rolland of BON PASTEUR. There are around 61 ha of vineyards and a range of wines is produced. Two basic blends, Cosecha Blanco and Tinto, offer attractive, fruity easy drinking. There is a varietal Torrontés and an oaky Chardonnay. Regular Malbec is chunky and full of forward, easy-going, brambly fruit; more serious is the Malbec Grande Reserve. The Alto is a very powerfully structured blend of Malbec and Cabernet Sauvignon and has an excellent balance of dark, spicy fruit, supple firm tannins and well-judged oak. The wine is neither fined nor filtered. (DM)
● **Alto** Vistalba★★★★ £F   ● **Grande Reserve** Vistalba★★ £B   ● **Malbec** Luján de Cuyo★ £B
O **Chardonnay** Luján de Cuyo★ £B

ANUBÍS Mendoza sbalbo@impsat1.com.ar A: Lib

Owner: Susana Balbo/Alberto Antonini Rioja 371, Dpto 5, 5500 Ciudad, Mendoza
The first vintage for this relatively new operation was only 1999 but the results so far have been promising and the wines offer excellent value for money. It is a partnership between Susana Balbo, who also produces wine under her own label with her husband Pedro Marchevsky at DOMINIO DEL

PLATA, and Alberto Antonini, formerly of ANTINORI. Fruit is sourced from Luján de Cuyo and Tupungato and a range of vibrant varietals are now being produced. Syrah/Bonarda and Malbec stand out. These are modern, stylish, richly extracted reds that are approachable and supple and may be enjoyed young. Antonini is also involved with estate owner Rodolfo Massera producing a further Malbec, La Remonta from cool La Consulta to the south of Mendoza. (DM)

● **Syrah/Bonarda** Mendoza★★ £B   ● **Tempranillo** Mendoza★ £B   ● **Malbec** Mendoza★★ £B

CATENA ZAPATA   Mendoza   www.nicolascatena.com   A:Bib

Owner: Dr Nicolás Catena   J Cobos s/n, Agrelo, Luján de Cuyo, Mendoza

The Catena operation is considerable with a number of ranges produced at all price levels. Good straightforward varietal styles are produced under the Argento label, while the Alamos range is a step up. Both the Chardonnay and Malbec are worth considering. Good to very good white and red are produced under the Catena label with real depth and style and are very modern approachable wines. The premium bottlings appear under the Catena Alta label and include Chardonnay, Cabernet Sauvignon and Malbec. The top wine is the super-premium Cabernet Sauvignon Zapata. All are sourced from vineyards at Luján de Cuyo. Daughter Laura produces an impressive range independently under the Luca brand which includes powefully structured Malbec, Syrah and Cabernet Sauvignon and toasty Chardonnay from Mendoza, while son Ernesto produces three stylish, modern reds: Corazon, a blend of Bonarda and Malbec; Jubilo which is based on Cabernet Sauvignon; and Amoria, based on Malbec. These are all comfortably worth two stars and have been three stars in the latest releases. The style throughout the premium ranges is modern and approachable and only limited cellaring will be required. Caro a blend of Malbec and Cabernet Sauvignon is a new joint venture with Baron de Rothschild of LAFITE-ROTHSCHILD. (DM)

Catena

● **Nicolás Catena Zapata** Luján de Cuyo★★★★ £F
● **Cabernet Sauvignon**   Catena Luján de Cuyo★★ £C   Alta Luján de Cuyo★★★ £E
● **Malbec** Alamos Mendoza★ £B   Catena Luján de Cuyo★★ £C   Alta Luján de Cuyo★★★★ £E
O **Chardonnay** Alamos Mendoza★ £B   Catena Luján de Cuyo★★ £C   Alta Luján de Cuyo★★★ £E

Luca

● **Syrah** Mendoza★★★ £E   ● **Malbec**★★★ £E
O **Chardonnay** Mendoza★★★ £E

Tikal

● **Corazon** Mendoza★★★ £D   ● **Jubilo** Mendoza★★★ £D

CARMEN   Maipo   www.carmen.com   A: SsG

Owner: Claro family   Apoquindo, 3669, Piso 6, Santiago

Carmen is owned by the large SANTA RITA operation. Production here itself is not inconsiderable at over 350,000 cases a year and an extensive range is produced, both red and white. The regular whites and particularly the reds are well-crafted and full of vibrant, ripe and crunchy fruit. The best wines, though, are produced under the Reserve and Winemakers Reserve labels along with impressive organic Nativa Chardonnay and the deep, concentrated and minty Nativa Cabernet Sauvignon. The Reserve label also now includes Sauvignon Blanc, Carmenère/Cabernet and Petite Sirah. The flagship red is the impressive Gold Reserve, which is produced from a small 45-year-old parcel of vines in Maipo. Top reds, particularly the Gold Reserve, will improve with cellaring. (DM)

● **Cabernet Sauvignon** Nativa Maipo★★★ £C   Reserve Maipo★★ £C   Gold Reserve Maipo★★★ £E
● **Pinot Noir** Reserve Maipo★★ £B   ● **Merlot** Reserve Rapel★★ £B
● **Cabernet Syrah** Reserve Maipo★★ £C   ● **Winemakers** Reserve Red Maipo★★ £C
O **Chardonnay** Nativa Maipo★ £C   Winemakers Reserve Maipo/Casablanca★★ £C

CASA LAPOSTOLLE Rapel www.casalapostolle.com   A: MMD

Owner: Marnier Lapostolle/Rabat families Benjamin 2935, Of. 801, Las Condes, Santiago
This is now established as one of the best red wine producers in Chile. Winemaking direction has
been provided for a number of years by Michel Rolland of BON PASTEUR. The Chardonnay in both
regular and Cuvée Alexandre versions is moderately rich and oaky, the Sauvignon Blanc quite
piercingly tropical and grassy. Tanao is a recent label addition: the red is a blend of Cabernet
Sauvignon, Merlot and Carmenère and is full of dark, spicy berry fruit, while the white is a fresh,
fruit-driven blend of Chardonnay, Semillon and a hint of Sauvignon Blanc. It is the reds, though,
that lift the winery onto a separate quality plateau. Cabernet Sauvignon Cuvée Alexandre is well
structured but lacks the sheer opulence of the rich, supple, almost exotic Merlot Cuvée Alexandre.
Dark smokey Syrah has also now been added. Currently a serious contender for the best red from
Chile is the dense, powerful, opulent and richly textured Clos Apalta. The wine is structured and
ageworthy but has all those hallmarks of Rolland's great wines from St-Émilion. (DM)
● **Clos Apalta** Rapel★★★★ £E ● **Tanao** Rapel★★ £C
● **Cabernet Sauvignon** Rapel★★ £B Cuvée Alexandre Rapel★★ £C
● **Merlot** Rapel★★ £B Cuvée Alexandre Rapel★★★ £C
O **Chardonnay** Casablanca★ £B Cuvée Alexandre Casablanca★★ £C
O **Tanao** Casablanca/Rapel★★ £C O **Sauvignon Blanc** Rapel★ £B

CASA SILVA Rapel www.casasilva.cl   A: JNV

Owner: Silva family Hijuela Norte, Angostura, Casilla 97, San Fernando
Among Chile's best newly-established winery operations, Casa Silva was set up in 1997 and winemaking is supervised by the experienced Mario Geisse Garcia. The winery owns three different
estates and has a total of some 830 ha of vineyards, so is not a small operation by any means. All of
the vineyards are located in the potentially excellent Colchagua Valley. The top wines are the Reserva
labels with impressive red and white being produced. In particular, the dark, brambly and intensely
spicy Carmenère Reserva and Quinta Generación Gran Reserva Tinto, a blend of both Cabernet and
Carmenère, are both ageworthy and will improve for three or four years. 1999 saw the introduction
of the new flagship Altura, a blend of Cabernet Sauvignon and Carmenère. (DM)
● **Cabernet Sauvignon/Sangiovese** Selected Vines Colchagua★ £B
● **Cabernet Sauvignon** Reserva Colchagua★★ £D ● **Carmenère** Reserva Colchagua★★★ £C
● **Merlot** Reserva Colchagua★ £B ● **Syrah** Colchagua★★ £B
● **Quinta Generación** Colchagua★★★ £C
O **Chardonnay** Reserva Colchagua★ £B O **Quinta Generación** Colchagua★★ £C

CLOS DE LOS SIETE Mendoza   A: Eno

*Owner: **Clos de los Siete SA** Vista Flore s/n, Tunuyan, Mendoza*
This is a major new French investment in Argentina which includes international wine consultant
Michel Rolland, who has already established his own successful YACOCHUYA label. 250 ha have
been planted in total at their Vistaflores estate, 80 km south of Mendoza. The wines are produced at
the Bodega Monteviejo, owned by Catherine Péré-Vergé, the owner of Château MONTVIEL in
Pomerol. Of several wines are now produced, the Clos de Los Siete red, which is a blend of Merlot,
Cabernet Sauvignon, Syrah and Malbec, is full of upfront dark, brambly fruit. It is aged one-third
in vats and two thirds in new oak. The Val de Flores label is a low production selection from selected
plots of some of the best sited Malbec. Rich and spicy it sees 100 per cent new oak. Lindaflor, also
Malbec is a vineyard selection sourced from 52 ha. Yields are very low indeed at 20 hl/ha and winemaking is modern - a cold-soak pre-fermentation, gravity-fed in the winery, 100 per cent new French

oak and neither fining nor filtration. Production of Lindaflor is currently capped at around 1,000 cases a year. There is real potential here and it will be interesting to see how things develop as the vineyard ages. (DM)

● **Clos de los Siete** Mendoza★★★ £C   ● **Val de Flores** Mendoza★★★ £D
● **Lindaflor** Mendoza★★★★ £E

CONCHA Y TORO   Maipo   www.conchaytoro.com   A: CyT

Owner: **Viña Concha y Toro**   *Av Nueva Tajamar 481, Torre Norte Piso 15, Las Condes, Santiago*
This is a massive operation with a huge range of commercial wines throughout the vinous spectrum at all price points. It is also involved with MOUTON-ROTHSCHILD of Bordeaux in the super-premium ALMAVIVA project. Production is now well over 10 million cases a year and the company possess more than 3230 ha of vineyards. Ignacio Recabarren has left VIÑA CASABLANCA to provide consultancy input here and the results are beginning to filter through. Both Trio and Casillero del Diablo offer some good values in both red and white while the Terrunyo label has been created to emphasise real regional character. Of the top labels Amelia Chardonnay is ripely tropical and toasty but with good depth. The Don Melchor Cabernet Sauvignon is sourced from the Puente Alto vineyard in the Maipo. It is a powerful, dusty red with dark berry fruit and a lightly leafy, minty component. You feel though there should be more complexity at the price. (DM)

● **Cabernet Sauvignon** Terrunyo★ £D Don Melchor★★★ £E   ● **Carmenère** Terrunyo★ £C
○ **Chardonnay** Trio★ £B Terrunyo ★★ £B Amelia★★ £C
○ **Gewurztraminer** Trio★ £B
○ **Sauvignon Blanc** Trio★ £B Terrunyo★ £B

CONO SUR   Rapel   www.conosur.com   A: WWs

Owner: **Concha Y Toro**   *Nueva Tajamar 481, Of. 1602, Torre Sur Las Condes, Santiago*
This operation was established in 1993. There are extensive estate-owned vineyards and the company sources fruit from Casablanca, Maipo, Rapel and the Bío Bío Valley. Under the Isla Negra label some attractively fruity reds and whites are produced. Reserve Cabernet Sauvignon, Merlot and Pinot Noir are all decent and well-priced, while the Innovative Visión range is a step up. Top wines are the 20 Barrels Pinot Noir, Merlot and Cabernet Sauvignon. Pinot Noir is also produced in a Limited Edition bottling. The Cabernet and Merlot are characterised by their dark berry fruit-driven style: extracted and forward as is the case with so many premium Chilean reds. The Pinot Noir shows a decent balance of strawberry, lightly savoury fruit with marked high toast oak. (DM)

● **Cabernet Sauvignon** Reserve Colchagua★ £B 20 Barrels Colchagua★★ £C
● **Merlot** 20 Barrels Colchagua★★ £C
● **Pinot Noir** 20 Barrels Colchagua★ £C Limited Edition Colchagua★★ £C

DOMINIO DEL PLATA   Mendoza   www.dominiodelplata.com   A: Lib

Owner: Pedro Marchevsky/Susana Balbo   Cochabamba 7801, Agrelo, Mendoza
This is the home winery of Pedro Marchevsky and Susana Balbo who are the manager and wine-maker at ANUBÍS. The Crios label offers some attractive, fruit driven wines including a fine floral Torrontes and two reds - a Cabernet Sauvignon and a Syrah/Bonarda blend. The top Dominio del Plata wines though are a serious step up in both quality and price. Of the two labels the Susana Balbo wines offer greater depth and power. The Susana Balbo wines are also produced in much smaller volume, around 400 to 500 cases each, whereas 2,000 cases of the Ben Marco wines are produced each year. VMS is a blend of Malbec from cool La Consulta, south of Mendoza as well as Cabernet

Sauvignon, Bonarda, Tannat and a little Merlot. Each variety is vinified separately and the wine aged for 12 months in 50 per cent new wood. The top label Brioso means strength and the wine is both deep and concentrated and with great poise and refinement. It blends Cabernet Sauvignon, Cabernet Franc, Malbec and Petit Verdot and will develop well for up to a decade. (DM)

Crios
○ **Crios Torrontes** Cafayate★ £B

Ben Marco
● **Malbec** Mendoza★★ £D ● **VMS** Mendoza★★★ £E

Susana Balbo
● **Malbec** Mendoza★★★ £E ● **Cabernet Sauvignon** Mendoza★★★ £E
● **Brioso** Mendoza★★★★ £F

EL PRINCIPAL Maipo Valley vinaep@ctcinterneyt.cl A:WEx

Owner: Patrick Valette Casilla 80, Pirque, Santiago
This 53 ha Maipo estate has been developed by Bordelais Patrick Valette, with the vineyard planted to Cabernet Sauvignon, Carmenère and Merlot (85/8/7 per cent). The wine is a modern Bordeaux style and like many of those properties a second wine is produced to ensure the integrity of the *Grand Vin*. Yields are kept low at 30 hl/ha and El Principal is aged in 100 per cent new oak with malolactic in barrel. Memorias is good, medium weight in style if a little leafy in 2000. El Principal was unusually 100 per cent Cabernet Sauvignon in 2000, providing a good but somewhat austere style. When normally blended with Carmenère, the wine offers greater richness and a rounder, suppler texture. (DM)

● **Memorias** Maipo★★ £B ● **El Principal** Maipo★★★★ £E

ERRÁZURIZ Aconcagua www.errazuriz.com A:HMA

Owner: Eduardo Chadwick Nueva Tajamar 481, Of. 503, Torre Sur Las Condes, Santiago
Errázuriz is based in the Panquehue sub-region of Aconcagua and has some 405 ha of vineyards. Fruit is generally sourced from the home vineyards but also from cool Casablanca for whites. The range is comprehensive and there are some well-made, stylish wines at all levels. The regular varietals show well-defined fruit character. Superior selections come under the Max Reserva label and there are two striking Wild Ferment wines: a Chardonnay full of citrus and lightly smoked oak, and a forward, vibrant Pinot Noir marked by sappy cherry and wild strawberry aromas. Sangiovese and Carmenère Single Vineyard labels are both impressively concentrated while the top two reds are the Don Maximiano Founders Reserve and the super premium-partnership with ROBERT MONDAVI, SEÑA, which has real potential. The partnership with Mondavi has also now been extended to include a range of premium varietals at the new LA ARBOLEDA ESTATE. 1999 was also the first vintage of Vinedo Chadwick, a super-premium blend of Cabernet Sauvignon and Carmenère from a 15 ha vineyard in the Maipo Valley. The wine promises much. Also jointly owns CALITERRA. (DM)

● **Merlot/Cabernet Sauvignon** Rapel★ £B ● **Sangiovese** Single Vineyard★★ £C
● **Cabernet Sauvignon** Max Reserva★ £C ● **Carmenère** Single Vineyard★★ £D
● **Merlot** Curico★ £B Max Reserva★★ £C ● **Syrah** Aconcagua★★ £B
● **Pinot Noir** Wild Ferment★★ £C ● **Don Maximiano** Founders Reserve★★★ £E
● **Vinedo Chadwick** Maipo★★★★ £E
○ **Chardonnay** Max Reserva★ £B Wild Ferment★★ £C

GRACIA Rapel www.graciawinery.cl   A: Pat

*Owner: **Viña Gracia de Chile S.A.** Vitacura 4380, Piso 18, Vitacura 667 0169, Santiago*
This is one of the more recently established Chilean operations. Formed in 1992, vineyard planting is ongoing and the objective is to establish up to 1,000 ha of estate-owned vineyards in the Aconcagua, Maipo, Rapel and Bío Bío valleys. There are some well-crafted Reserva wines and the style is full-on and opulent: Chardonnay, is ripe, tropical and toasty; Merlot, plummy and smoky; and Carmenère rich, brambly and supple. The top red is the premium Cabernet Sauvignon RR Reserva Caminante – muscular, dense and powerful. (DM)

- **Carmenère** Reserva Especial Callajero Maipo★ £B
- **Cabernet Sauvignon** Reserva Lo Mejor Porquenó★★ £C   ● RR Reserva Caminante★★★ £D
- **Merlot** Reserva Lo Mejor Porquenó★★ £B
- **Pinot Noir** Reserva Lo Mejor Sereno★ £B
- O **Chardonnay** Reserva Superior Temporal★ £B

MONTES Curicó www.monteswines.com   A: HWC

Owner: Montes family Av. Del Valle 945, Of 2611, Ciudad Empresorial, Huechuraba
This is a large but very variable producer. Some wines have been impressive recently, some decidedly less so. Some 300,000 cases of estate-grown and externally-sourced wines are produced. There is a good brambly and moderately dense Reserve Malbec but the best wines are produced under the Montes Alpha label. Chardonnay is in a rich tropical style but has a little finesse, Cabernet Sauvignon is sound if a little light on occasion. However, it is the Montes Alpha Syrah, premium Montes Folly and premium Montes Alpha M that really stand out. The dark, smoky Syrah is one of Chile's best examples. This has now been joined by the special Montes Folly bottling from the firm's Apalta Mountain Estate in Colchagua, a hand-picked 100 per cent Syrah, aged in new French oak, of which less than 1,000 cases are produced. The flagship Montes Alpha M, a Bordeaux blend from the single La Finca estate in Colchagua, is reasonably rich, earthy, extracted and concentrated. You feel it should show more, though, at this price. (DM)

- ●● **Montes Alpha M** Colchagua★★ £E
- ● **Montes Folly** Santa Cruz★★★★ £D **Montes Alpha Syrah** Santa Cruz★★★ £D
- ● **Alpha Merlot** Colchagua★ £C   ● **Malbec** Reserve Curicó★ £B
- O **Alpha Chardonnay** Curicó★ £B

NIETO SENETINER Mendoza www.nietosenetiner.com   A: Cap

*Owner: **Pérez Companc Group/CDPQ** Vieytes no 2275 Carrodilla – CP 5507 Luján de Cuyo*
This is a large operation, producing an extensive range of both varietal and blended reds and whites under the Finca Las Marius and Santa Isabel labels. These are relatively ordinary with Malbec and Bonarda offering some attractively dark berry-fruit character. Significantly better are the Reservas. These include a smoky, supple and plummy Bonarda, an extracted, oaky, dark Malbec, good stylish Syrah and a good but quite austere Cabernet Sauvignon. New is a lightly oaked Malbec Nieto Reserva as well as a premium Bordeaux blend Con Nicanor produced from 30-year-old vines in Luján de Cuyo. Best of all is a splendid premium Malbec Cadus, made from 80-year-old vines, a rich, long and very characterful wine offering much better value than many of its peers. (DM)

- ● **Malbec** Cadus Tupungato★★★★ £D Reserva Luján de Cayo★★ £B
- ● **Bonarda** Reserva Luján de Cayo★★ £B   ● **Cabernet Sauvignon** Reserva Luján de Cayo★ £B
- ● **Syrah** Reserva★★ £B

ODFJELL VINEYARDS Maipo www.odfjellvineyards.com   A: WTs

Owner: Odfjell Family Camino Viejo Valparaiso, No 7000 PO Box 23, Padre Hurtado
Daniel and Laurence Odfjell have established vineyards in Maipo very recently. By Chilean standards this is a small, almost boutique style of operation with a production of fewer than 40,000 cases a year across their range. Winemaking consultancy input is provided by Paul Hobbs as well as French enologist Arnaud Hereu. There is a simple fruit driven Cabernet, Rojo, and a budget label Armador with a ripe, plummy Merlot standing out. The Orzada wines are a level up and some very characterful Cabernet Franc, Carmenère and unusually a Carignan stand out. The Cabernet Sauvignon is less impressive, with a slightly green note evident in the 2001. Top of the range is a 100 per cent Cabernet Sauvignon Aliara, full, rich and with dark berry fruit and a ripe, chocolatey character. There is oak in abundance in the wines' youth, which needs a couple of years to integrate. This is a good new source in contrast to many of the increasingly homogenised styles that are emerging from Chile. (DM)

● **Cabernet Franc** Orzada Maule★★ £B   ● **Merlot** Armador Maule★ £B
● **Carmenère** Orzada Maule★★★ £B Armaudor Maule★ £B
● **Cabernet Sauvignon** Orzada Maule★★ £B   ● **Carignan** Orzada Maule★★ £B
● **Aliara** Maipo★★★ £D

SANTA RITA Maipo www.santarita.com   A: BWC

*Owner: **Viña Santa Rita** Apoquindo 3669, Of. 601, Santiago*
Long-established, traditional old Chilean winery which had a wake-up call in the late 1990s and is beginning to produce an increasingly fine range of mid-market and premium wines. The 120 range offers some reasonable straightforward easy drinking; the reds are a better bet generally than the whites. Reserva whites are sound but no more, the reds again are better as are the Medalla Real wines. Chardonnay though is well crafted in a tropical, toasty style. Both the Cabernet Sauvignon and Merlot Reservas display attractive, moderately concentrated, dark, spicy fruit. The Floresta reds have recently been added to the range. The two wines that really stand out are the red Triple C and Casa Real Cabernet Sauvignon. Triple C is a blend of Cabernet Franc, Cabernet Sauvignon and Carmenère. Casa Real Cabernet is quite traditional in style with well-judged oak, both concentrated and reasonably refined. (DM)

● **Cabernet Sauvignon Floresta Apalta** Rapel★★ £B Medalla Real Maipo Valley★★ £B
● **Cabernet Sauvignon** Casa Real Maipo★★ £D
● **Syrah/Cabernet/Carmenère Floresta** Maipo★★ £B   ● **Merlot/Cabernet Floresta** Maipo★★ £B
● **Triple C** Maipo★★ £C
O **Chardonnay** Medalla Real Maipo★ £B

SEÑA Aconcagua www.senawines.com   A: HMA

Owner: Eduardo Chadwick/Mondavi family
This wine partnership between Eduardo Chadwick at ERRÁZURIZ and California's ROBERT MONDAVI vies with Clos Apalta from CASA LAPASTOLLE, ALMAVIVA and now EL PRINCIPAL for the accolade of best super-premium red from Chile. It is currently a blend of Cabernet Sauvignon, Merlot and Carmenère. The wine is sourced from, among others, the finest plots of the vineyard that also supplies the Errázuriz Don Maximiano red. Seña itself is impressively dense, structured and concentrated. It is planned that the wine will eventually be sourced entirely from its own single estate. This is a 350-ha property in the western Aconcagua with some ideal north-est facing slopes and high-density vineyard planting. As yet, while it is both rich and powerful, you feel there should be just a little more depth

and complexity. (DM)

● **Seña** Aconcagua Valley★★★★ £F

MICHEL TORINO   Salta   www.micheltorino.com.ar   A:Hal

*Owner: **Bodega La Rosa/Peñflor**   Ruta 40 y Ruta 68, Cafayate, Salta, Mendoza*
Located in the hot Cafayate region in the north of Argentina the vineyards here succeed because of their high altitude. There are 360 ha under vine and the quality end of the spectrum is covered by the Colección and Don David labels. There is a good spicy, brambly Colección Malbec and a better, more concentrated Don David. Cabernet Sauvignon under the Don David label has some piercing blackcurrant character with a lightly herbal note creeping in. Don David Torrontés is sound but not at the same level as the reds. A new flagship red, Altimus combines Malbec, Cabernet Sauvignon and Syrah. (DM)

● **Cabernet Sauvignon** Don David Cafayate★★ £B
● **Malbec** Colección Cafayate★ £B   Don David Cafayate★★ £B

VALDIVIESO   Curicó   www.vinavaldivieso.cl   A: Bib

*Owner: **Viña Valdivieso S.A.**   Juan Mitjans 200, Macul, Santiago*
Successful marketing-driven operation which produces an extensive range of wines at all levels. Regular red and white varietals are produced under the Valdivieso and Casa de Piedra labels. At best these offer straightforward easy glugging. Barrel Selections are a step up and the Syrah and Carmenère are good examples – ripe and with decent weight and flesh. Some impressive red is produced under the Reserve label, though whites disappoint. Good Single Vineyard Cabernet Franc and Merlot particularly stand out. The top wines are The Don which is part aged American and French oak; the non-vintaged Caballo Loco, a blend that changes by the year; and the V wines, Pinot Noir and Malbec. The latter is particularly structured and ageworthy. (DM)

● **Cabernet Franc** Single Vineyard Reserve Curicó★★ £B   ● **Merlot** Single Vineyard Reserve Curicó★ £B
● **Malbec** Single Vineyard Reserve Curicó★★ £B   V Curicó★★★ £D
● **Pinot Noir** V Curicó★★★ £D   ● **Caballo Loco** Curicó★★ £D

VIÑA CASABLANCA   Casablanca   rbeckdor@santacarolina.cl   A: Mor

*Owner: **Viña Santa Carolina**   Rodrigo de Araya 1431, Macul, Santiago*
Established by SANTA CAROLINA over 10 years ago this has been a consistently impressive producer of good, sometimes very good, cool-grown whites. Reds are produced as well but these can be disappointing by comparison; the wines show quite marked evidence of their cool-climate origins and can be peppery at best, green at worst. The best are the Santa Isabel Cabernet Sauvignon and the Neblus, a pricey blend of Cabernet Sauvignon, Merlot and Carmenère. Gewürztraminer is good, with some varietally pungent character; Sauvignon Blanc is equally stylish, with grassy, tropical notes showing through its piercing fruit. Chardonnay is one of the best in the country, particularly the Barrel Fermented label, which is very intense with marked citrus and subtle lees and oak character. It will develop well with limited ageing. (DM)

● **Cabernet Sauvignon** Santa Isabel Estate Casablanca★★ £B   ● **Carmenère** El Bosque★ £B
● **Merlot** Santa Isabel Casablanca★ £B   ● **Neblus** Casablanca★★ £D
O **Chardonnay** Santa Isabel Casablanca★★ £B   Santa Isabel Barrel Fermented Casablanca★★★ £C
O **Gewurztraminer** Santa Isabel Casablanca★ £B   O **Sauvignon Blanc** Santa Isabel Casablanca★★ £B

YACOCHUYA Salta lh@estudioehq.com.ar   A: His

Owner: Michel Rolland   Piso 11, 1425 Buenos Aires
Michel Rolland,s small Yacochuya winery is based in warm Salta, but crucially the Calchaquies Valley vineyards here are planted at high altitude, some 2,000 metres above sea level. Of equal importance is the age of the vines, which are now over 80 years old. The wine, pure Malbec, is very dense with marvellous depth and a rich sumptuous texture on the palate. Malolactic takes place in barrel and the wine is aged on lees with micro-oxygenation. It is bottled with minimal fining and without filtration and will develop very well over a decade or so. It is undoubtedly one of the very finest reds to have emerged from South America in recent years. Rolland the owner of Le BON PASTEUR in Pomerol, is also now involved in the recently established CLOS DE LOS SIETE operation, south of Mendoza. (DM)

● **Yacochuya** Cafayate★★★★★ £F

OTHER WINES OF NOTE

Argentina
ALTOS DE MEDRANO ● **Vigna Hormigas Malbec** Mendoza £C
ALTOS LOS HORMIGAS ● **Malbec** Mendoza £C
LEONCIO ARIZU ● **Malbec Luigi Bosca** Mendoza £B ●**Petit Verdot Viña Alicia** Mendoza £D
VALENTIN BIANCHI ● **Cabernet Sauvignon** Mendoza £C
ETCHART ● **Arnaldo B Reserva** Cafayate £C
FABRE MONTMAYOU ● **Grand Vin** Luján de Cuyo £D
FINCA EL RETIRO ● **Syrah** Mendoza £B ● **Malbec** Mendoza £B
FINCA FLICHMAN ● **Dedicado** Maipú £C
LA AGRICOLA ● **Malbec** Familia Zuccardi Q £C
BODEGA LURTON ● **Gran Lurton** Mendoza £B
MAPEMA ● **Primera Zona** Mendoza £E
BODEGA NORTON ● **Privada** Luján de Cuyo £C ● **Malbec** Reserve £C
FELIPE RUTINI ● **Apartado** Tupungato £D
BODEGAS SALENTEIN● **Malbec** Mendoza £C ● **Shiraz** Mendoza £C
BODEGA TERRAZAS DE LOS ANDES ● **Gran Malbec** Luján de Cuyo £D
TRAPICHE ● **Iscay** Maipú £E
RAUL DAVALOS ● **Colomé** Mendoza £D ● **33 de Davalos** Mendoza £D
● **RD de Davalos** Mendoza £D
VINITERRA ● **Cabernet Sauvignon** Luján de Cuyo £B ● **Malbec** Luján de Cuyo £B
DOMAINE VISTALBA ● **Infinitus Malbec/Syrah** Río Negro £C
WEINERT ● **Malbec** Luján de Cuyo £C ● **Cavas de Weinert** Luján de Cuyo £C

Chile
AGUIRRE ● **Tempus** Reserva Especial £B
ANTIYAL ● **Antiyal** Maipo £B
APALTAGUA ● **Carmenère** Colchagua £B ● **Envero** Colchagua £B ● **Grial** Colchagua £B
ARESTI ● **Cabernet Sauvignon** Family Collection £C
BISQUERTT ● **Carmenère** Gran Reserva Casa La Joya £B
VIÑEDOS JULIO BOUCHON ● **Carmenère** Reserva Especial Maule £B ● **Assemblage**Maule £C
CALITERRA ● **Merlot** Reserva Colchagua £B
CANEPA ● **Cabernet Sauvignon** Magnificum Curicó £C ● **Carmenère** Private Reserve Valle Centrale £B
COUSIÑO MACUL ● **Finis Terrae** Maipo £C
DOMAINE PAUL BRUNO ● **Cabernet Sauvignon** Maipo £B
ECHEVERRIA ● **Cabernet Sauvignon** Molina Reserva £C

LUIS FELIPE EDWARDS ● **Cabernet** Reserva Colchagua £B   ● **Merlot** Reserva Colchagua £B
LA ARBOLEDA O **Chardonnay** Casablanca £B   ● **Carmenère** Colchagua £B
● **Syrah** Colchagua £B
MICHEL LAROCHE/JORGE CODERCHE ● **Piedra Feliz** Casablanca £B
● **Colina Negra** Casablanca £B   O **Rio Azul** Casablanca £B
LOS VASCOS ● **Le Dix de Los Vascos** Colchagua £D
LA ROSA ● **Merlot** Gran Reserve La Palmeria Rapel £B
MAPA ● **Merlot** Rapel £B   ● **Cabernet Sauvignon** Maipo £B
MONTGRAS ● **Ninquen** Colchagua £C
SANTA CAROLINA O **Chardonnay** Reservado Maipo £B
TARAPACÁ ● **Syrah** Privada Reserva Maipo £B   ● **Milenium** Maipo £C
TERRANOBLE ● **Carmenère Gran Reserva** Maule £C
TORREÓN DE PAREDES ● **Don Amado** Cachapoal £D
MIGUEL TORRES ● **Manso de Velasco** Curicó £D
VERAMONTE ● **Primus** Casablanca £C
VILLARD ESTATE ● **Equis** Maipo £C
VIÑA LEYDA ● **Carmenère** Leyda £B   ● **Vintage Selection** Leyda £B
● **Lot 21 Pinot Noir** Leyda £C
VIÑA PÉREZ CRUZ ● **Cot** Reserva Limited Edition £C   ● **Syrah** Reserva Limited Edition £C
VIÑA QUEBRADA DE MACUL ● **Domus Aurea** Maipo £D
VIÑA SAN PEDRO ● **Cabernet Sauvignon** Reserva Castillo di Molina £B
VIU MANENT ● **Malbec** Reserva Colchagua £B

Author's Choice (DM)

A Chilean selection

ALMAVIVA ● **Almaviva Red** Maipo Valley
CASA LAPOSTOLLE ● **Clos Apalta** Rapel
CASA SILVA ● **Quinta Generación** Colchagua
EL PRINCIPAL ● **El Principal** Maipo
ERRÁZURIZ ● **Vinedo Chadwick** Maipo
GRACIA ● **RR Reserva** Caminante
MONTES ● **Montes Folly** Santa Cruz
ODFJELL VINEYARDS ● **Aliara** Maipo
SEÑA ● **Seña** Aconcagua Valley
VIÑA CASABLANCA ● **Chardonnay** Santa Isabel Barrel Fermented Casablanca

An Argentine selection

ACHAVAL-FERRER ● **Malbec** Finca Altamira
ALTA VISTA ● **Alto** Vistalba
SUSANA BALBO ● **Brioso** Mendoza
BEN MARCO ● **VMS** Mendoza
CATENA ZAPATA ● **Nicolás Catena Zapata** Luján de Cuyo
LUCA O **Chardonnay** Mendoza
CLOS DE LOS SIETE ● **Lindaflor** Mendoza
NIETO SENETINER ● **Malbec** Cadus Tupungato
DOMAINE VISTALBA ● **Infinitus Malbec/Syrah** Río Negro
YACOCHUYA ● **Yacochuya Red** Cafayate

Australia's coherent assault on world wine markets owes much to its easy-to-understand appeal – from mostly varietal labelling of wine names to the direct and overt fruitiness that still characterises many of the wines. But does it have the same clout in fine wine terms? The answer is no, at least not to the same extent. There are wines with great depth and structure and others of real style, elegance and nuance but nothing like as many as some of its promoters would have us believe. Nonetheless there are many outstanding wines, red, white and fortified. Arguably there needs to be more differentiation between the good and the great and there is not always a sensible correlation between price and quality, but this will come as competition is more keenly felt and palates mature. Meanwhile there is a growing sophistication and there has never been more premium wine available or greater diversity. Almost half of all Australian wine comes from South Australia. The bulk of the cheaper wine comes from the Riverland area, on the Murray River close to Victoria, while large quantities of premium wines are made from regions that range from baking hot to distinctly cool. From the latest wave of small producers the wines are increasingly vineyard-specific but great wines are also blended from a range of mesoclimates.

Barossa

New life has been breathed into many historic areas of Australian viticulture over the past 30 years but the greatest revival in the past decade or so has occurred in the Barossa, the GI zone that incorporates both the Barossa Valley and the Eden Valley.

Barossa Valley

Since the 1840s both English and Silesian immigrants have played an important part in establishing what has become the heart of the Australian wine industry. But in the modern revival of Australian table wines Barossa lost ground to newer areas and its rich viticultural resource of often unirrigated, old-vine Shiraz, Grenache and Mourvèdre began to rapidly disappear under Vine Pull schemes of the 1980s. Fortunately Peter Lehmann, Grant Burge, Charlie Melton and others rode to the rescue by producing wines of a quality that the world couldn't ignore and has since not been able to get enough of. Besides rich, lushly textured old-vine Shiraz and Rhône-style blends, Cabernet Sauvignon has an important place for its distinctive dense, black-fruited blockbusters; such Barossa classics often owe their sweet casing to ageing in American oak. Barossa also has a great history of fortified wines and very high-quality examples, often blended from old wines, continue to be made by Seppelt and others. Though full-flavoured, whites are less suited to the conditions. Chardonnay, whose appeal in the 80s soon waned, does less well than Semillon in the heat.

Eden Valley

The most successful of the whites in the Barossa zone is Riesling, but from over the eastern ranges of the Barossa Valley in the significantly cooler, more elevated vineyards of the Eden Valley. Riesling excels in the higher, more southern reaches (the Mount Lofty Ranges run through from the Adelaide Hills to the south) where some high-quality Chardonnay, Pinot Noir and Merlot are also produced. Viognier shows real potential too, though current quality has been a little overhyped. Great reds, particularly Shiraz but also Cabernet Sauvignon, are also produced from lower altitudes, most notably those from Henschke.

Mount Lofty Ranges

Though geographically disparate, the Clare Valley and Adelaide Hills both form part of the Mount Lofty Ranges, where altitude plays a significant role in the style of the wines.

Clare Valley

Lying to the north-west of Barossa, the Clare Valley might be expected to be even hotter, but altitude changes the equation and is critical to the success of individual varieties. Several sub-regions have already emerged, including **Polish Hill River**, **Sevenhill**, **Watervale** and around the township of Clare itself. Most Rieslings from the Clare Valley offer less immediate fruit sweetness than those from the Eden Valley but have better structure and greater style. The best examples can be relatively austere in youth but develop an intense limey, mineral toastiness with 10 years' age or more. The elevated Clare vineyards also provide a distinctive Shiraz character of smoke, earth and mineral as well as some good Cabernet Sauvignon and Chardonnay.

Adelaide Hills

The Adelaide Hills, in the ranges along and beyond the eastern edge of the state capital, form part of the southern extension of the Mount Lofty Ranges. Elevation is again critical and the reputation of this relatively small vineyard area grows apace, now way beyond its size, since being pioneered by Brian Croser (Petaluma) in the 1970s. Chardonnay, especially from the sub-regions of **Lenswood** and **Piccadilly Valley**, rivals, even surpasses the best in the country but there has also been compelling quality from Pinot Noir and Sauvignon Blanc. The patchwork of vineyards, resulting in part from the perils of spring frost, contrasts with the swathe of low-altitude vineyards that carpet the floor of the McLaren Vale a short distance to the south.

Fleurieu

The Fleurieu Peninsula is dominated by production from the historic and important McLaren Vale but in the past decade wines of quality have begun to emerge from lesser-known neighbouring regions.

McLaren Vale

In the McLaren Vale, tucked between the hills and the coast, the heat is relieved by sea breezes and Shiraz, Grenache, Mourvèdre and Cabernet Sauvignon assume ascendancy. However, care must be taken if the wines are to show balance and depth as well as a lush texture. A wave of new producers, led arguably by Clarendon Hills, as well as the general revival in the fortunes of Rhône varieties in South Australia have brought greater diversity to quality production in the region. Given the region's mix of soil types it is also encouraging to see increasing identification of the various sub-zones and individual vineyards. Soon the likes of Blewitt Springs, Clarendon and Kangarilla should be as well known for their location as for the wineries named after them. Whites are generally unexciting and, while some producers persist with Sauvignon Blanc and Chardonnay, the long-term success of whites in the area seems more likely to depend on Rhône and other warmer-climate varieties.

Other Fleurieu regions

Flood-irrigated **Langhorne Creek** on the other side of the Fleurieu Peninsula has long provided soft, ripe Shiraz and Cabernet fruit that contributes to many a well-established blended South Australian red. An absence of high profile producers has contributed to a lack of identity but Bremerton, Lake Breeze and others will bring greater recognition. Other pockets of vineyard that have recently been given their own official sanction are **Currency Creek** and **Southern Fleurieu** which lie either side of Langhorne Creek. **Kangaroo Island**, a large, 4,350 km^2 (1680 square miles) sparsely populated island, 110 km (69 miles) south-west of Adelaide, has but a few vines yet shows good potential for Bordeaux style reds.

Limestone Coast

South Australia's other vineyard areas lie a long way to the south in a zone known as the Limestone Coast. This vast expanse is essentially flat yet its magic emerges from low limestone ridges topped with the famous terra rossa soil. The most established of these is, of course, Coonawarra.

Coonawarra

Despite its renown, quality from this elongated, relatively exposed and coolish region with its terra rossa soils and high water table, is highly variable. Much of the mechanically harvested, high-yielding Cabernet Sauvignon fruit (that is not generally fully ripe) goes into high-volume blends. But as well as the viticultural riches from Wynns, a growing number of smaller estates are showing the sort of quality that is possible, and from Shiraz as well as Cabernet. There has been much fuss over Coonawarra boundaries but wiser producers are investing their energies on developing other similar, and very promising regions.

The rest of the Limestone Coast

To the north of Coonawarra is **Wrattonbully** where Cabernet Sauvignon, Merlot and Shiraz plantings are taking hold. The identity of **Padthaway** is dwarfed by that of Coonawarra but given its greater disposition for Chardonnay as well as potential for Sauvignon Blanc and Shiraz more ought to be, and it seems is beginning to be, made of its character. The emergence of the likes of Henry's Drive and increasing regional identification by the industry giants, who dominate plantings, will help. **Mount Benson** (and adjoining **Robe**) lies to the west, right on the coast, and Shiraz from not-long-established vines, is particularly promising. Interest has been heightened by investment made by Chapoutier of the Rhône Valley.

A-Z of Producers by region

Adelaide
PRIMO ESTATE

Adelaide Hills
ASHTON HILLS
BARRATT WINES
CHAIN OF PONDS
HILLSTOWE
KNAPPSTEIN LENSWOOD
NEPENTHE
PETALUMA
RAVENSWOOD LANE
SHAW & SMITH
GEOFF WEAVER

Barossa Valley
BAROSSA VALLEY ESTATE
BETHANY
WOLF BLASS
GRANT BURGE
BURGE FAMILY
CHARLES CIMICKY
DUTSCHKE

ELDERTON
GREENOCK CREEK
TREVOR JONES
PETER LEHMANN
CHARLES MELTON
ORLANDO
PENFOLDS
ROCKFORD
ST HALLETT
SALTRAM
SEPPELT
TORBRECK
TURKEY FLAT
VERITAS
YALUMBA

Clare Valley
TIM ADAMS
ANNIE'S LANE
JIM BARRY
CRABTREE
GROSSET
KILIKANOON
KNAPPSTEIN
LEASINGHAM

MITCHELL
MOUNT HORROCKS
PIKES
WENDOUREE

Coonawarra
BALNAVES
BOWEN ESTATE
BRAND'S OF COONAWARRA
HOLLICK
JAMIESONS RUN/MILDARA
KATNOOK ESTATE
LECONFIELD
MAJELLA
PARKER COONAWARRA
PENLEY ESTATE
RYMILL
WYNNS
ZEMA ESTATE

Eden Valley
HENSCHKE
MOUNTADAM

Langthorne Creek
LAKE BREEZE

McLaren Vale
CASCABEL
CHAPEL HILL
CLARENDON HILLS

CORIOLE
D'ARENBERG
EDWARDS & CHAFFEY
FOX CREEK
HAMILTON
HARDY'S
HASELGROVE
MAGLIERI
MAXWELL
GEOFF MERRILL
REYNELLA/REYNELL
ROSEMOUNT (MCLAREN VALE)
TATACHILLA
WIRRA WIRRA
WOODSTOCK

Mount Benson
RALPH FOWLER
M CHAPOUTIER AUSTRALIA

Padthaway
HENRYS DRIVE
LINDEMANS

Other
BRL HARDY
SOUTHCORP

Some comments on vintages and when to drink

The generalised Vintage charts overleaf cover some of the most ageworthy styles and will prove most useful when taken together with comments on style and ageing within individual producer entries. Many wines can be drunk young but an increasing number will not be at their best for at least five years, whether a powerful full-bodied red or a more structured example of Clare Valley Riesling. Top- quality Chardonnay and Pinot Noir is likely to show at its best only with three to six years' ageing. In terms of longer-term cellaring potential, great Australian Rieslings have been shown to age for a decade or more, while some famous Australian reds have been proven to age for 30 or even 40 years. While it is necessary to be prepared to buy only the best if you want to add breadth to an existing French or European-based cellar, this doesn't always mean purchasing only the most expensive. It should also be noted that those indicated (in producer entries) as needing a minimum amount of ageing should be given it; underestimate their structure at your peril. Both the vintage ratings and when to drink assessments generally only apply to the top rated examples (three star wines or higher).

South Australian vintages

	Barossa/Clare Shiraz	Coonawarra Cabernet	Clare/Eden Valley Riesling	Adelaide Hills Chardonnay
2003	★★★/★★★★ A	★★★★ A	★★★★ A	★★★★/★★★★★ A
2002	★★★★/★★★★★★ A	★★★★ A	★★★★★ A	★★★★/★★★★★ A
2001	★★★★ A	★★★/★★★★ A	★★★/★★★★B	★★★★B
2000	★★/★★★ A	★★★/★★★★ A	★★★/★★★★ B	★★★B
1999	★★★/★★★★ A	★★★★/★★★★★ A	★★★/★★★★ B	★★★/★★★★ C
1998	★★★★★ A	★★★★★ A	★★★★C	★★★/★★★★★ C
1997	★★★★ B	★★★/★★★★ B	★★★★★ C	★★★★ C
1996	★★★★/★★★★★ B	★★★★ B	★★★★/★★★★★ C	★★★★/★★★★★ C
1995	★★★/★★★★ B	★★ C	★★★★ C	★★★★/★★★★★ C
1994	★★★★/★★★★★ B	★★★★ B	★★★★C	★★★/★★★★ D
1993	★★★/★★★★ C	★★★/★★★★ C	★★★/★★★★ D	
1992	★★★ C	★★★/★★★★ C	★★★/★★★★ D	
1991	★★★★/★★★★★ C	★★★★/★★★★★ C	★★★★ C	
1990	★★★★/★★★★★ C	★★★★★ C	★★★★★ C	

TIM ADAMS   Clare Valley   www.timadamswines.com.au   A: AWA, ACh

Owner: Tim & Pam Adams Warenda Road, Clare SA 5453

This is a brilliant Clare Valley producer with marvellously consistent reds and whites of great depth and character. Grapes are sourced both from estate vineyards and local growers and though now up to 15,000 cases annually, production remains small by Australian standards. Sorby (sold only in the UK) is made in conjunction with Tim's brother, Simon, and combines Barossa and Clare fruit. Aberfeldy, the top red, has a certain elegance as well as masses of fruit and American oak, in which it spends the best part of two years. The Fergus takes its name from a grower who first supplied the Grenache around which a little Shiraz, Cabernet Sauvignon and Cabernet Franc are now woven; at once complex and appealing, it has a deserved following. Riesling and Semillon both have excellent varietal definition and good structure. The prices are exemplary for the quality. (PW)

● **Shiraz**★★★ £C Sorby★★★ £C Aberfeldy★★★★ £D
● **The Fergus**★★ £B ● **Cabernet**★★★ £C
○ **Semillon**★★★ £C ○ **Riesling**★★★ £B ○ Botrytis **Riesling**★★★ £C

ANNIE'S LANE   Clare Valley   www.annieslane.com.au   A: BBl, Odd

Owner: Beringer Blass Quelltaler Road, Watervale SA 5452

This Clare Valley range of wines is one of the best of the many in the BERINGER BLASS Australian stable. Named after Annie Wayman, a local personality in the late 19th/early 20th century, the wines were previously made at the historic Quelltaler winery but are now made at the impressive Wolf BLASS facilities in the Barossa. The wines glow with fruit and are full and ripe with good balance and varietal expression. As might be expected for Clare Valley, Riesling and Shiraz particularly shine, as does a Shiraz/Grenache/Mourvèdre blend that contains around 50 per cent Shiraz. The premium Copper Trail Shiraz is made in open fermenters from unirrigated vines with part of the wine receiving an extended maceration prior to two years' ageing in mostly French oak barrels. The Riesling, the best value of the lot, harnesses lovely Clare Valley fruit which is checked by good acidity but like all the whites should be drunk young. A Copper Trail version is more structured with better ageing potential. Reds are better with three years' ageing or more but will keep considerably longer. (PW)

○ **Riesling**★★ £B Copper Trail★★★ £C ○ **Chardonnay**★ £B ○ **Semillon**★ £B
● **Shiraz**★★ £B Copper Trail★★★ £D ● **Shiraz/Grenache/Mourvèdre**★★★ £C
● **Cabernet/Merlot**★★ £B

ASHTON HILLS   Adelaide Hills   A: AWA, Cac, Rae

Owner: Stephen George Tregarthen Road, Ashton SA 5137

Stephen George is a winemaker of considerable talent, especially given the diverse range of wines he produces to a such high standard. To be equally at home producing fine sparkling wines as cool Adelaide Hills Riesling, Pinot Noir and Chardonnay or rich powerfuls reds from the Clare Valley, as he is in forging the GALAH wines, is remarkable. The small estate-based 3.5-ha Ashton Hills is known first and foremost for two refined yet ripely fruity sparkling wines. The pale pink Salmon Brut is three-quarters Chardonnay yet its strawberry and delicate biscuity flavours owe as much to the balance of Pinot Noir. An intense Riesling has a structure that puts it with the best from Eden Valley, Clare or Adelaide Hills; Pinot Noir (occasionally made as a Reserve) shows great fruit intensity, and increasingly a texture and breadth uncommon to most Australian examples. Chardonnay, too, shows off the potential of the Adelaide Hills. A less successful Obliqua Cabernet/Merlot reflects in part how cool this region can be. Released commercially since 1998, Burra Burra Lone Star Shiraz is made from a vineyard owned and developed by Stephen's father. (PW)

O Blanc de Blancs★★ £C ◉ Salmon Brut★★★ £C
O Chardonnay★★★ £C O Riesling★★★★ £C
● Pinot Noir★★★ £D

BALNAVES Coonawarra www.balnaves.com.au A: Lib, Vne, But, The

Owner: Balnaves family Main Road, Coonawarra SA 5263
The combination of a new winemaking facility and new winemaker, Peter Bissell (ex WYNNS COONAWARRA), has given this 47-ha estate near the southern end of Coonawarra extra impetus over the past seven or eight years. Even so, the Coonawarra Blend (typically Merlot/Cabernet Franc/Cabernet Sauvignon) and Cabernet Sauvignon/Merlot, while both ripe, round and pleasurable drinking, are a little undistinguished. The Cabernet Sauvignon, by contrast, adds more breadth and style as well as intensity – a really good expression of Coonawarra fruit. A ripe, concentrated Shiraz is also produced in good vintages. The flagship is The Tally Reserve, a big, powerful, oaky Cabernet Sauvignon made in 1998 and 2000 that needs at least five to eight years' ageing. This being Coonawarra there isn't much white but a Chardonnay with delicious fruit and well-worked oak is amongst the better examples from the Limestone Coast. Sparkling Cabernet is worth a try if Australian sparkling reds appeal. Doug Balnaves and son Peter also manage vineyards (e.g. PARKER COONAWARRA ESTATE) and make wines for others (PUNTERS CORNER) in the district. (PW)
● Coonwarra Blend★★ £C ● Cabernet Sauvignon/Merlot★★ £C
● Cabernet Sauvignon★★★ £D ● Shiraz★★★ £C
O Chardonnay★★ £C ● Sparkling Cabernet★★ £D

BAROSSA VALLEY ESTATE Barossa Valley www.bve.com.au A: BRL, WSc, N&P, Nid

Owner: BRL Hardy & local growers Heaslip Road, Angle Vale SA 5117
Established as a co-op (rare in Australia) by around 80 local growers in 1985, BVE is now in partnership with BRL HARDY. The growers have some of the best parcels of very old Shiraz vines in the Barossa. Ebenezer Shiraz is full of berry fruit and American oak and a good classic expression of the style. Chardonnay and Cabernet have been made in a similarly full-flavoured style but it will be interesting to see what change if any occurs under new winemaker Stuart Bourne. The pricey flagship E & E Black Pepper Shiraz is an explosively rich, powerful but balanced expression of old-vine Barossa fruit, full of preserved black fruits, prunes, licorice and tar and with great length too. Moculta is effectively a second label and includes good Grenache, Shiraz and Chardonnay, while the Spires label is used for competitive, budget-priced red and white. (PW)
● Shiraz Ebenezer★★★ £D E & E Black Pepper★★★★ £F
● Cabernet Sauvignon/Merlot Ebenezer★★ £C
O Chardonnay Ebenezer★ £C

BARRATT WINES Adelaide Hills A: Gun

Owner: Lindsay & Carolyn Barratt Collins Road, Summertown SA 5141
One of the Adelaide Hills' small gems, thanks in part to the services of Jeffrey GROSSET. From just 8 ha in two different vineyards (Uley and Bonython) Barratt encapsulates the aptitude of the Adelaide Hills for Pinot Noir and Chardonnay. Even in the rather uninspiring 2000 vintage both wines show a stylish complexity, adequate ripeness – if a more sappy influence to the Pinot – and good breadth on the palate. In 2001 Pinot Noir production was divided between a single vineyard Bonython version and a much superior Reserve which will be rated with further vintages. Sauvignon also does well in the Adelaide Hills (see the likes of LENSWOOD, NEPENTHE), and Barratt has

introduced its version in the 2002 vintage along with a new Merlot. (PW)
- ● **Pinot Noir**★★★ £D
- ○ **Chardonnay**★★★ £D

JIM BARRY Clare Valley   A: Neg, Tan, ACh

Owner: Barry family Craigs Hill Road, Clare SA 5453

From a large number of some of Clare's best sites Mark Barry continues to build on what his father made famous over four decades, but whether the wines will now show more individuality or refinement remains to be seen. Reds are the mainstay: deep, concentrated if relatively unrefined Shiraz, Cabernet Sauvignon and Cabernet Sauvignon/Malbec under the McRae Wood label. However it is for The Armagh that Jim Barry is best known. Considered one of the region's super-reds, it is an uncompromisingly big, thick, extracted and oaky Shiraz with a long track record dating back to 1985. It is made from very old, unirrigated vines and nearly always achieves the balance that some mega-Shirazes lack but must be kept for a minimum of a decade. Riesling is sourced from the Florita vineyard (in Watervale), first made famous by Leo Buring. Production is a substantial 40,000 cases though much of that is more ordinary red and white. (PW)

- ● **Shiraz** The Armagh★★★★ £F McCrae Wood★★ £C
- ● **Cabernet Sauvignon**★ £C McCrae Wood★★★ £C
- ● **Cabernet/Malbec** McCrae Wood★★ £C ○ **Riesling**★★ £B

BETHANY Barossa Valley www.bethany.com.au   A: D&D, POs, Maj

Owner: Schrapel family Bethany Road, Bethany SA 5352

Though they only established their own winery in 1981, Geoff and Rob Schrapel are fifth-generation descendants of one of Barossa's many original Silesian settlers and vine growers. Three estate vineyard blocks have recently been complemented by plantings in the more elevated Eden Valley and some Chardonnay and Cabernet vines on Kangaroo Island. The wines are always ripe rather than overripe, with plenty of upfront fruit and decent intensity, but more structure and depth could be added; even the flavour-intense, oaky, premium GR (numbered for each successive release) wants for more. GR5 was Cabernet Sauvignon; previous releases, Shiraz. Chardonnay and Semillon are barrel-fermented and aged while Riesling is made both in a dry and a late-harvest style. The Manse is an inexpensive blend of all three varieties. Old Quarry Tawny is a wood-matured Grenache/Shiraz fortified wine, while a sparkling wine is made from Eden Valley Pinot Noir and Chardonnay. Almost all the wines are keenly priced. (PW)

- ● **Shiraz**★★ £B ● **Grenache**★ £B ● **Cabernet/Merlot**★ £B
- ○ **Riesling**★ £B ○ **Chardonnay**★ £B ○ **Semillon**★★ £B

WOLF BLASS Barossa Valley www.beringerblass.com.au   A: BBI, Odd

Owner: Beringer Blass PO Box 396, Nurioopta SA 5355

The Wolf Blass label remains an integral part of the giant BERINGER BLASS wine portfolio but the production of one of the great branded successes of Australian wine now seems to draw little inspiration from the personality and energy of the man himself. Shiraz, Cabernet or blends of the two under the various red, green and yellow labels and Eaglehawk façades have been pretty uninspiring and if no worse than some of their competitors are not of the standard they were a decade or more ago. With the least expensive if recently improved whites too, much better value can be found both elsewhere in Australia and from the likes of Chile. These should not be confused with the wines near the top of the hierarchy where quality is much higher and just occasionally the wines' origins are also more discernable. Presidents

Selection wines offer a lot of upfront fruit and oak and adequate depth and structure. New Platinum label Shiraz and Cabernet (potentially three to four stars), based on single vineyards and aged in French oak, finally deliver on depth, structure and balance, but platinum is also required to buy them. The stylish, richly textured Black Label Cabernet Sauvignon/Shiraz (subjected to a delayed release) is consistently fine, though again at a price. A new Blass regional range hints at better quality and some regional identity at an affordable level. (PW)

● **Cabernet Sauvignon/Shiraz** Black Label★★★ £F
● **Shiraz** President's Selection★★ £C   ● **Cabernet Sauvignon** Presidents Selection★★ £C
○ **Riesling** Gold Label★★ £B   ○ **Chardonnay** Presidents Selection★ £B

BOWEN ESTATE Coonawarra   A: AWA, Tan, NYg, P&S, WVt

Owner: Doug & Joy Bowen   Riddoch Highway, Coonawarra SA 5263
Doug Bowen's smallish 33-ha estate continues to maintain a relatively low profile among the Coonawarra giants, though the wines are widely exported. The reds are of consistently high quality: deep, fleshy and textured with very ripe flavours and a certain idiosyncratic style. The grapes are picked very late and a good dose of oak ensures the wines have a sweet succulence particularly in the warmer years. Perhaps surprisingly for Coonawarra, Shiraz is even better than the Cabernet Sauvignon. The Blend is composed of Cabernet Sauvignon, Merlot and Cabernet Franc. A ripe and creamy Chardonnay is also made while Ampelon is a new single-vineyard Shiraz. (PW)

● **Shiraz**★★★★ £C   ● **Cabernet Sauvignon**★★★ £C   ● The Blend★★★ £C
○ **Chardonnay**★ £B

BRAND'S OF COONAWARRA Coonawarra www.mcwilliams.com.au

Owner: McWilliams Wines   Riddoch Highway, Coonawarra SA 5263
The winery was established by the Brand family but has now become a brand of McWILLIAMS. As well as taking full control of Brands, an additional 100 ha of vineyards are in the process of being developed by McWilliams in Coonawarra (giving a total of 300 ha) and production is set to expand as the new vineyards come on stream. The performance of the Brands reds has been reasonably consistent, with soft fruit and gentle structures, though some have lacked a little ripeness and concentration in weaker vintages. Riesling is the strongest white with intense limey, tropical fruit and a mineral streak, and will sometimes improve with additional bottle age. The top wine, Stentifords Reserve Old Vine Shiraz, known until 1995 as Original Vineyard Shiraz (as it is based on a vineyard established in 1896), has been particularly impressive in recent vintages such as 96 and 98. Patrons Reserve is intended to complement it and is based on Cabernet Sauvignon with lesser amounts of Shiraz, Merlot and Cabernet Franc. Older vintages of all the wines are labelled Brands Laira, as it used to be known. (PW)

● **Shiraz**★★ £B Stentiford's Reserve Old Vine★★★ £D
● **Cabernet Sauvignon**★★ £B   ● **Cabernet/Merlot**★ £B
○ **Riesling**★ £B

GRANT BURGE Barossa Valley www.grantburgewines.com.au   A: SsG, Vne, ACh, Res

Owner: Grant Burge   Jacobs Creek, Tanunda SA 5352
Grant Burge has an impressive resource of 200 ha from which to make top Barossa wines. Nearly all the varietals are now prefixed with a vineyard name, though they may sound more like fantasy names. All are made in the recently reacquired old Krondorf winery. Shiraz is naturally the strongest hand, starting with a sweet-fruited Miamba, progressing to a fuller, richer Filsell, and, from

the same vineyard, a pricey but powerful classic American-oaked, old-vine Barossa Shiraz, Meschach. The Cabernet equivalent to Meschach is Shadrach. Some early efforts of both wines lacked balance but this is not true of recent releases. Holy Trinity, composed of Grenache, Shiraz and Mourvèdre (40/40/20), mercifully is not priced as sky-high as Meschach and Shadrach and is developing into an increasingly refined and characterful red; new French oak and an extended maceration on the skins are now employed to good effect. Chardonnay (Summers) is based primarily on Eden Valley fruit, as is the Riesling (Thorn). Other flavoursome whites include a Sauvignon (Kraft) and late-picked Muscat (Lily Farm). Barossa Vines is a decent second label for varietal Shiraz, Semillon and Chardonnay. Sparkling and fortified wines are also made. (PW)

● **Shiraz** Miamba★ £B   Filsell★★ £C   Meschach★★★ £F
● **Cabernet Sauvignon** Cameron Vale★★ £C   Shadrach★★★ £F
● **Merlot** Hillcot★ £C   ● Holy Trinity★★★ £D
O **Chardonnay** Summers★ £B   O **Semillon** Zerk★ £B   O **Riesling** Thorn★   £B

BURGE FAMILY   Barossa Valley   A: NYg, Fal, UnC

Owner: Rick Burge   Barossa Valley Way, Lyndoch SA 5351
Rick Burge makes classic oak-lined, rich, lush, sweet-fruited Barossa reds. The wines have lots of depth, extract and intensity as well as the varietal expression typical of each grape variety as they perform in the Barossa. The wines have highish alcohol (around 14.5 for most of the reds) but are well-balanced, only occasionally showing an excess of oak. Two wines in particular stand out. Olive Hill, roughly equal proportions of Shiraz, Grenache and Mourvèdre (41/31/28 in 2001), is more complete and characterful than The Renoux which combines Shiraz with Cabernet Sauvignon and Merlot (45/38/17 in 2001). Better still is Draycott Shiraz which has lovely depth and style with a lingering sweet fruit-intense finish. Rick Burge's Garnacha, mostly old vine Grenache but also including a little Shiraz and Mourvèdre, has a sweet crushed berry fruit depth but can struggle to balance the high alcohol. Semillon has plenty of rich Barossa citrus and herb character though is not for long keeping. (PW)

● **Shiraz** Draycott★★★★ £E   ● **Shiraz/Merlot/Cabernet Sauvignon** The Renoux★★   £C
● **Shiraz/Grenache/Mourvèdre** Olive Hill★★★   £D   ● **Grenache** Garnacha★★ £D
O **Semillon** Olive Hill★★ £C

CASCABEL   McLaren Vale   A: Bib

Owner: Duncan Ferguson & Susana Fernandez,   Rogers Road, Willunga SA 5172
This is still a very young operation, having only made wines since the late 1990s, yet this experienced couple seeming to have both the know-how and a clear idea of the sort of wines they wish to fashion. All the wines are characterised by bright pure fruit and definite restraint in terms of alcohol and oak. Round, soft and agreeable, they are not without substance and are always fruit-rich on the finish. Only relatively small quantities are made of each wine, particularly the lime-streaked Riesling. Grenache 'et al' includes Shiraz and Mourvèdre. These are wines to drink relatively young rather than for long keeping. (PW)

O **Riesling** Eden Valley★★ £B
● **Shiraz** Fleurieu Peninsula★★★   £C   ● **Grenache et al**★★ £C

CHAIN OF PONDS   Adelaide Hills   www.chainofpondswines.com.au   A: Bib

Owner: Caj & Genny Amadio   Main Adelaide Road, Gumeracha SA 5233
Established only in 1993 this is a relatively small producer but sizeable grower. The family vineyard,

Kersbrook, was recently joined by the adjacent Gumeracha plot giving a total of 140 ha, the majority of which are still sold off to PENFOLDS. There is an expanding range of now exotically named wines as Zar Brooks, the man behind D'ARENBERG'S roll-call of fantasy names, has repeated the trick upon his recent arrival here. Quality has always been high, particularly for Chardonnay and the Amadeus Cabernet; the latter is remarkably profound and tightly furled when young, revealing a deep fruit core with at least five years' ageing. From Kangaroo Island, the Florance Vineyard Cabernets is a blend of the two Cabernets and a little Merlot, while another vineyard has provided Barque Mars Shiraz since 1999. This can be compared with Adelaide Hills Shirazes, Ledge and Graves Gate, the latter sourced from McLaren Vale in 1999 due to frost in Adelaide Hills. The extensive range also includes an unwooded Chardonnay, Nether Hill, and Sauvignon Blanc, Black Thursday. The Novello label includes red, white and rosé, each with an Italian component. Bianco is Semillon/Pinot Grigio, Rosso (the rosé) Sangiovese/Grenache, while Nero is a Barbera/Grenache/Sangiovese blend. (PW)

● **Cabernet Sauvignon** Amadeus★★★ £C
● **Shiraz** Grave's Gate★★ £C Ledge★★ £C
● **Sangiovese** Jupiter's Blood★ £C ● **Pinot Noir** Jerusalem★ £C
O **Chardonnay** Corkscrew Road★★ £C Morning Star★★★ £D
O **Riesling** Purple Patch★ £B O **Semillon** Square Cut★★ £B

CHAPEL HILL McLaren Vale www.chapelhillwine.com.au A: AWA, ACh, IVi

*Owner: Thomas Schmidheiny (**Holcim**) Chapel Hill Road, McLaren Vale SA 5171*
Under consultant winemaker Pam Dunsford, Chapel Hill, now Swiss owned, has built a solid reputation for consistent Cabernet and Shiraz. Quantity (60,000 cases) may be rising but prices are not excessive for wines based on high-quality fruit from 44 ha of McLaren Vale vineyards. The Shiraz is full, concentrated, and oaky after almost two years in French and American oak (50 per cent of it new). In the same mould and subject to a similar oaking regime is The Vicar, a blend of Cabernet and Shiraz in roughly equal proportions. Some of the Cabernet for both this and a varietal Cabernet Sauvignon comes from Coonawarra, while the Reserve Chardonnay includes a Padthaway component too. An unwooded Chardonnay is simple and less appealing than a tasty Verdelho. (PW)

● **Shiraz**★★ £C ● **The Vicar**★★ £D ● **Cabernet Sauvignon**★★ £B
O **Chardonnay** Reserve★★ £B O **Verdelho**★ £B

M CHAPOUTIER AUSTRALIA Mount Benson www.chapoutier.com A: N&P

Owner: Chapoutier Limestone Coast Road, Mount Benson via Robe SA5276
The prestigious Rhône Valley producer CHAPOUTIER has made a sizeable commitment to investing in Australia including developing 50 ha at Mount Benson. Much of it is being planted to Shiraz as might be expected but there is also a significant percentage of Cabernet Sauvignon and some Marsanne, Viognier and Sauvignon Blanc. Viticultural practices model those in the Rhône and progress has been made towards a fully biodynamic regime. Already the reds show a fine fruit intensity and structure and are improving with each successive vintage, adding more refinement and depth. It is to be expected that Chapoutier will succeed in maximising the potential of its new sites and provide a fascinating contrast to Rhône wines in the future. (PW)

● **Shiraz** Mount Benson★★★ £C ● **Cabernet Sauvignon** Mount Benson★★ £C

CHARLES CIMICKY Barossa Valley A: Lwt, WVt

Owner: Charles Cimicky Gomersal Road, Lyndoch SA 5351
Cimicky is a class act in the Barossa, producing deep, harmonious reds with well-integrated oak from

low-yielding, dry-farmed vines. Shiraz, Merlot and (under the Daylight Chamber label) Grenache and Grenache/Shiraz all show splendid fruit allied to sleek proportions and a certain refinement. French oak is favoured over the usually more common American oak. Red Blend is Cabernet Sauvignon-based but with a significant percentage of Merlot and Cabernet Franc. Whites, including Sauvignon Blanc and Chardonnay, are less likely to be encountered outside Australia. Prices are still reasonable. (PW)

● **Shiraz** Signature★★★ £C   ● **Red Blend**★★★ £C   ● **Grenache** Daylight Chamber★★★ £C
● **Grenache/Shiraz** Daylight Chamber★★★ £C
● **Merlot**★★★ £C   O **Sauvignon Blanc**★★ £B

CLARENDON HILLS McLaren Vale   A: J&B, F&R, N&P, Las

Owner: Roman Bratasiuk   Brookmans Road, Blewitt Springs SA 5171
If you've drunk Australis then either you or your friends are not short of money. Bratasiuk's unfiltered and unfined, ripe, extracted reds, aged in French oak, are subjected to a long *cuvaison* and exhibit a depth and dimension that most Australian reds don't even approach. Some early vintages had questionable balance and marginal levels of volatility but all is being mastered and refined as the range expands and gains better definition through the use of vineyard or sub-regional names. Bratasiuk, though he's not the first to do so, is providing an alternative to the brand-name-only marketeers who reveal precious little about their sources (likewise yields), even at a premium level. Reds are marvellously complex, concentrated and long. Whites are intense and muscular too, but show good ageing potential. Pinot Noir has been attempted but is still a work in progress. All the names refer to a specific vineyard or vineyards. (PW)

● **Shiraz** Australis❂❂❂❂❂ £H Piggot Range★★★★★ £G
● **Shiraz** Brookman★★★★ £F Hickinbotham★★★★ £F Liandra★★★ £F Moritz★★★ £F
● **Grenache** Blewitt Springs★★★★ £E Clarendon★★★★ £E Kangarilla★★★ £E Romas★★★★★ £F
● **Merlot** Brookman★★★ £E Hickinbotham★★★ £E
● **Cabernet Sauvignon** Brookman★★★ £E Hickinbotham★★★★ £E Sandown★★★ £E
O **Chardonnay** Hickinbotham★★ £E Kangarilla★★★ £E   O **Semillon** Hickinbotham★★★ £E

CORIOLE McLaren Vale   A: Sec, Tan, ACh, Res

Owner: Lloyd family   Chaffeys Road, McLaren Vale SA 5171
Coriole has been known for its intense Shiraz almost since its inception in 1967, having inherited some already old vines and planted new ones which now have a few years behind them too. The wine is consistently richly textured with deep, ripe fruit and has been particularly good in recent vintages. Lloyd Reserve Shiraz, made only in very small quantities, is the premium version, with a long-established track record and more structure and oak than the regular version. The powerful, minty Mary Kathleen is an equivalent premium red from Cabernet Sauvignon, Merlot and a little Cabernet Franc, but has a tendency to be excessively structured. Both require much patience. Coriole are also known for their Sangiovese. Lloyd Sangiovese/Cabernet (three-quarters Sangiovese with Cabernet Sauvignon and Merlot) is in the mould of certain Super-Tuscans but also wants for better balance, while a regular version is attractively fruity if lacking the qualities of good Italian examples. Redstone is an appealing blend based on Shiraz but usually including Grenache, Merlot and Cabernet Sauvignon. The rich, concentrated Semillon with both citrus and tropical flavours is easily the best of the whites but a decent fruity Australian Chenin Blanc is also made. (PW)

● **Shiraz**★★★ £C Lloyd Reserve★★★★ £E   ● **Sangiovese/Cabernet** Lloyd★★ £C
● **Mary Kathleen**★★★ £D   O **Semillon** Lalla Rookh★★ £B

CRABTREE Clare Valley

Owner: Robert & Elizabeth Crabtree   North Terrace, Watervale SA 5452

Crabtree of Watervale is a small Clare operation with its own vineyards. The experienced Robert Crabtree produces wines that show good structure and balance without being overdone and give at least a subtle indication of their Watervale origins, though there is a diversity of soils. A tight, minerally but scented Riesling has good potential while Semillon is full, broad and stylish. Grenache displays an enticing fruit character whether as a red or in an off-dry Rosé version and Shiraz has good intensity and complexity. All the wines can be drunk young and the Grenache Rosé certainly needs to be. However, whites will keep and improve and although reds could be drunk from just three to five years' they seem certain to age for twice as long. (PW)

O **Riesling**★★★ £C   O **Semillon**★★ £C
● **Shiraz** Picnic Hill★★★   £C   ● **Cabernet Sauvignon** Windmill★★ £C   ● **Grenache**★★ £C

D'ARENBERG McLaren Vale   www.darenberg.com.au   A: Bib, Odd, WSc, NYg

Owner: Osborn family   Osborn Road, McLaren Vale SA 5171

Jazzed up in recent years, this is a much trumpeted and sizeable producer with a seemingly ever-expanding range totalling 150,000 cases per year. Nearly all the wines are good but only a handful really exciting; some are a little overhyped. The myriad exotic names don't make this an easy range to negotiate but they surely help with sales. The best reds have exuberant fruit and highish alcohol levels (and plenty of oak to help them on their way), making for enjoyable youthful drinking, but with enough structure to stand a bit of age. The flagship red is the Dead Arm Shiraz with super fruit, excellent concentration and tannins, oak and alcohol all in balance; it needs five years' age or more. Footbolt is very easy to appreciate but faces stiff competition as South Australia has an abundance of fine Shiraz at this level, some with better texture and more depth. The powerful Ironstone Pressing can struggle for balance, intense sweet-fruited Custodian Grenache often shows some extraordinary flavours if at the cost of elegance and harmony while varietal Mourvèdre seems more effortless with better depth and structure. Whites, from grapes only planted in 1995, are fruit-driven if sometimes a little coarse and lack the structure for long keeping. Riesling, Semillon and Gewürztraminer have been made in a rich late-harvested style with some success. The Stump Jump red and white are forward, fruity gluggers. New are Lucky Lizard Chardonnay and Feral Fox Pinot Noir. A sparkling Chambourcin, called Peppermint Paddock and a fortified Shiraz are also made. (PW)

O **Sauvignon** Broken Fishplate★ £B   O **Riesling** Dry Dam★   £B   Noble★★★   £D
O **Chardonnay** Olive Grove★ £B   Other Side★★ £C   O **Roussanne** Money Spider★★ £B
O **Viognier** Last Ditch★★ £B   O **Marsanne/Viognier** Hermit Crab★ £B
● **Mourvèdre** Twenty-Eight Road★★★ £C   ● **Grenache** Custodian★★   £B
● **Grenache/Shiraz/Mourvèdre** Ironstone Pressings★★ £D
● **Shiraz/Grenache** D'Arry's Original★★ £B
● **Shiraz** Footbolt★★ £B   Dead Arm★★★★ £D   ● **Shiraz/Viognier** Laughing Magpie★★ £C
● **Cabernet Sauvignon** High Trellis★   £B   Coppermine Road★★★ £D

DUTSCHKE Barossa Valley   A: THt, Bal, C&R

Owner: Dutschke & Semmler   Lyndoch Valley Road, Lyndoch SA 5351

Shiraz is the thrust of this operation for wines made by Wayne Dutschke from vines belonging to his uncle, Ken Semmler. St Jakobi, with an almost coconutty American-oak influence (60 per cent), displays a deep fruit succulence and plenty of extract. Although oaky it has depth and character and deserves to be judged with five years' bottle age or more. By contrast, Oscar Semmler, the top cuvée, is aged in 100 per cent French oak. It is marvellously profound with terrific potential if cellared for at least five to eight years. While not cheap, quality is commensurate with price. Willowbend (a second label) Chardonnay and Shiraz/Merlot/Cabernet are enthusiastically consumed locally. (PW)

● **Shiraz** St Jakobi★★★ £D   Oscar Semmler★★★★ £E

EDWARDS & CHAFFEY   McLaren Vale   www.edwardsandchaffey.com.au   A:ScE

Owner: Southcorp   Chaffeys Road, Mclaren Vale SA 5171

One of the many SOUTHCORP brands, this winery, previously known as Seaview, is now named after its original partners. While fizz is very much the order of the day, from inexpensive non-vintage Seaview Brut and Rosé to higher-quality Edwards & Chaffey sparkling wine, between 1992 and 1998 some very good Edwards & Chaffey Section 353 table wines were also made. Chardonnay, Shiraz and Cabernet Sauvignon all showed classic vibrant ripe McLaren Vale fruit (which once set the humbler Seaview varietals apart from competitors) and well-integrated French oak. Production is now limited to sparkling wine only but there is both good quality and value in an attractive, biscuity Seaview Pinot Chardonnay Brut and the Edwards & Chaffey Section 353 Pinot Chardonnay (predominantly Pinot Noir drawn from cool grape-growing regions) which delivers a rich, leesy complexity and ripe powerful fruit. (PW)

O **Pinot Chardonnay** Edwards & Chaffey Section 353★★★ £C   Seaview★★ £B
O **Blanc de Blancs** Seaview★ £B

ELDERTON   Barossa Valley   www.eldertonwines.com.au   A: Fie, BBR, F&R, Nid

Owner: Lorraine Ashmead   3–5 Tanunda Road, Nurioopta SA 5355

An unashamedly oaky, full-throttle style has earned this winery a devoted following. The wines are not to everyone's taste but the best examples have a rich fruit core as they are based on old-vine Barossa Valley fruit. The estate is small in Australian terms with less than 30 ha of vineyards. American oak is favoured, the oak once found in nearly all South Australian wineries, which adds intense vanilla, spice, even coconut flavours to the wines. The most successful and sought-after wine is the Command Shiraz which epitomises the high-alcohol, oaky, richly extracted and lusciously fruity style. Late 1990s vintages show better harmony than earlier examples. Positioned at the same level is a single-vineyard Cabernet Sauvignon, Ashmead; here the rich fruit has been meshed with the more amenable French oak. Merlot too is aged in French oak. As well as estate Shiraz and Cabernet Sauvignon a cheaper Friends version of each is also made from bought in fruit. CSM is not a Rhône blend but what is now an unusual blend of Cabernet Sauvignon, Shiraz and Merlot. Riesling and Chardonnay are also made and offer plenty of upfront flavour if not much else and are best drunk with just a couple of years' age. An intensely flavoured dessert wine, Botrytis Semillon (or Golden Semillon), is made from Riverina fruit, while Tantalus Shiraz/Cabernet is a flavoursome budget red from wider origins. (PW)

● **Shiraz**★ £C   Command★★★   £E   ● CSM★★ £D
● **Cabernet Sauvignon**★ £C   Ashmead Single Vineyard★★   £E   ● **Merlot**★ £C

RALPH FOWLER   Mount Benson   A: HHB, P&S, Han

Owner: Ralph & Deborah Fowler   Lot 101, Limestone Coast Road, Mount Benson SA 5275

This is a newish operation based in the up-and-coming coastal area of Mount Benson. The 40 ha of estate vineyards include Cabernet Sauvignon, Shiraz and Viognier. Ralph Fowler (of diverse Australian winemaking experience) currently makes both Shiraz and Cabernet Sauvignon from a blend of Mount Benson and Coonawarra fruit. Both reds show good fleshy texture, depth and definition; the Cabernet had a cooler but not excessive minty, herbal component in 1998 and 1999. Fowler has also been recruited to a major new venture undertaken by Kreglinger Australia, the major shareholder in PIPERS BROOK. CHAPOUTIER notwithstanding, this promises to be one of the leading protagonists in Mt Benson over the coming decade. Sauvignon Blanc and Viognier are new. (PW)

● **Shiraz** Limestone Coast★★★ £D
● **Cabernet Sauvignon** Limestone Coast★★★ £D

FOX CREEK   McLaren Vale   www.foxcreekwines.com.au   A: NYg, UnC, F&R, N&P

Owner: J&H Watts, J&L Roberts, P Watts   Malpas Road, Willunga SA 5172
This young but already much acclaimed McLaren Vale operation is based on vineyards established by the Watt family in 1985. Since 1995 Fox Creek has made rich, ripe and succulent reds with a measure of (mostly) American oak, sometimes lacking finesse and real style. The first wines were made by Sparky Marquis of HENRYS DRIVE but are now made by Dan Hills and Tony Walker. Reserve Shiraz is the leading red and more than any other displays the potency and character of McLaren Vale. Though the varieties are different there is also classic expression in a more forward but ripe and stylish JSM Shiraz/Cabernet Franc (and a little Cabernet Sauvignon). Reserve Cabernet is rich and earthy with a firm finish. Other reds are less exciting. Merlot and a new Cabernet/Merlot, Duet, show adequate balance and ripeness but lack style and definition. Vixen is a well-balanced if not first-division example of a sparkling Shiraz-based red (but includes both Cabernets). The pick of the whites is a Verdelho with an intense, flavoursome varietal character. Sauvignon Blanc and Semillon/Sauvignon Blanc have delicious ripe tropical fruit and citrus flavours but need to be drunk very young. (PW)

● **Shiraz** Reserve★★★★ £E   Short Row★★ £D
● **Shiraz/Cabernet Franc** JSM★★★ £C   ● **Sparkling Shiraz/Cabernet Franc** Vixen★★ £C
● **Cabernet Sauvignon** Reserve★★ £D   ● **Merlot** Reserve★ £D
○ **Chardonnay**★ £B   ○ **Verdelho**★★ £B   ○ **Semillon/Sauvignon Blanc**★ £B

GREENOCK CREEK   Barossa Valley   A: THt, Bal, NYg

Owner: Michael & Annabelle Waugh   Radford Road, Seppeltsfield SA 5360
The aim here is for very low yields from unirrigated plots. The grapes are harvested very late, and the wines reveal unusual, almost exotic, ripe flavours and a preserved fruits character. The alcohol levels are high but the wines are balanced. For Shiraz, the Apricot Block is perhaps the most promising vineyard but is quite young; shortcomings in initial releases will be overcome with a little more age. By contrast Creek Block is planted with very old vines, some 80 years old, but the wines are slightly coarse, even jammy, though they don't lack for character. The best wine is the Seven Acre Shiraz. Labelled Special Late Harvest, it has a particularly pronounced preserved fruits profile and reveals real power and intensity on the palate. Grenache (Cornerstone) and Cabernet Sauvignon also show what is possible from the best unirrigated vines. The wines are expensive but probably need to be given the very low yields and their cult status. (PW)

● **Shiraz** Seven Acre★★★★ £F   Creek Block★★★ £F   Apricot Block★★★ £E

GROSSET   Clare Valley   www.grosset.com.au   A: MSd, Bal, BBR, Mar, Tur, WVt, WSc

Owner: Jeffrey Grosset   King Street, Auburn SA 5451
Jeffrey Grosset is an Australian superstar and deserves to be as well-known as the country's many sporting greats (in some circles he is). Outstanding Riesling, Chardonnay and Gaia Bordeaux blend, all show pristine fruit, wonderful symmetry and excellent concentration and have proven ageability.

There are two Rieslings: the fine, intense and limey Polish Hill is made in greater quantity though there is still not much of it; Watervale is fuller and broader. Like the Rieslings and Chardonnay, a delicious Semillon/Sauvignon blend is one of the best Australian examples of its type. The compelling Gaia impresses for its style, complexity and depth; it is no wimp but makes a stark contrast to some of the overoaked, alcoholic monsters made by others. Grosset makes Pinot Noir for the BARRATTs but also produces a little of his own from the same locality in the Adelaide Hills. Given the purity and sheer style of the wines it is perhaps not surprising that Grosset has striven to find the best possible closure for his wines. His choice is Stelvin cap for all but a portion of his production of Gaia. All the wines are made in relatively small quantities and are reasonably priced. (PW)

● **Gaia**★★★★ £E ● **Pinot Noir**★★★ £E
O **Riesling** Polish Hill★★★★ £C Watervale★★★★ £C
O **Chardonnay** Piccadilly★★★★ £D O **Semillon/Sauvignon Blanc**★★★ £C

HAMILTON McLaren Vale www.hamiltonwines.com A: Eno, WVt

*Owner: **Hamilton Wine Group** Main Road, Willunga SA 5172*
Richard Hamilton's McLaren Vale operation shouldn't be confused with Hugh Hamilton or the recently revived Hamilton's Ewell in the Barossa, though the extensive family connections run back to one of South Australia's first winemakers. His winemaking team produce some intense, characterful McLaren Vale wines, even if in some years they have lacked balance. Centurion 100-Year-Old Vines Shiraz, Gumpr's Block Shiraz and Burton's Vineyard Old Bush Vine Grenache/Shiraz show good depth and weight, very ripe fruit and often a measure of mint, eucalyptus and gamey notes. Marion's Vineyard Grenache/Shiraz is, like PENFOLD'S Magill, unusual in being a vineyard in the suburbs of Adelaide and shares Magill's flavour intensity. Other wines include Hut Block Cabernets, which has a percentage of Merlot and Cabernet Franc but a tendency to slightly underripe tannins; and Merlot as Lot 148 but better as a French-oaked Reserve Egremont, made in part from Coonawarra fruit. Of the whites, the Signature Chardonnay accentuates ripe melony flavours and oak but not at the expense of balance while Riesling, Slate Quarry, is also made, somewhat surprisingly from local McLaren Vale fruit. The Hamilton Wine Group also own LECONFIELD. (PW)

● **Shiraz** Centurion 100 Year Old Vines★★★ £D Gumpr's Block★★ £C
● **Grenache/Shiraz** Burton's Vineyard★★★ £C Marion Vineyard★★ £C
O **Chardonnay** Signature★★ £B

HARDY WINE COMPANY www.hardywines.com.au
This is the new name for the BRL Hardy group of mostly Australian wineries and brands now forming a part of Constellation Wines following the merger with the North American multinational, Constellation Brands. Leading wineries/brands include HARDYS, LEASINGHAM, Renmano, REYNELL, Stonehaven and half of BAROSSA VALLEY ESTATE in South Australia; HOUGHTON and Moondah Brook in Western Australia; YARRA BURN in Victoria and Bay of Fires in Tasmania; and Kamberra in the Canberra District (southern New South Wales). Banrock Station, also in South Australia, produces large volumes of decent everyday wines as well as well as developing and maintaining a wetlands site on the Murray River. They also produce the Starvedog Lane wines in conjuction with RAVENSWOOD LANE. Outside Australia, Domaine de la Baume in Languedoc-Roussillon and NOBILO in New Zealand also form part of the group. As well as high-quality wines at mid-level and premium prices, the Hardy group has over recent years had the best record of the big Australians at maintaining quality in its least expensive and ubiquitous brands. (PW)

HARDYS   McLaren Vale   www.hardys.com.au   A: BRL, Vne, P&S, N&P

*Owner: **Hardy Wine Company**   Reynell Road, Reynella SA 5161*

Hardys is one of the great names of Australian wine even if the premium Hardys wines are marginally less well-known than those of some of their rivals. The Eileen Hardy label is reserved for an outstanding Shiraz and a rich, powerful if occasionally slightly over-oaked Chardonnay. The Shiraz, now made from predominantly McLaren Vale fruit, has been consistently outstanding over the past decade. Brawny, extracted Thomas Hardy Cabernet, made since 1989, is now sourced entirely from Coonawarra. It has terrific depth and can evolve into an equally impressive, if less consistent red. Without the cult status of these flagship wines, the Tintara Limited Release Shiraz and Grenache are full, concentrated and more affordable, if difficult to obtain outside Australia. The Shiraz is open-fermented and basket-pressed like the Eileen Hardy and offers rich succulent fruit. Tintara Cellars Shiraz, Cabernet and Chardonnay are more modest. Hardys sparkling wines, however, show an extra degree of finesse and intensity over most Australian sparklers, as seen in the top two examples, the vintage-dated Sir James Vintage and premium Arras, both Tasmania and Yarra Valley-sourced Pinot Noir/Chardonnay blends. Of the cheaper, everyday brands Nottage Hill varietals are slightly more expensive than the Stamps of Australia dual-variety blends, but offer more than the price differential suggests. The special release of 2001 Oomoo McLaren Vale Shiraz, to celebrate Hardys' 150th anniversary in 2003, revives a 19th century label. (PW)

● **Shiraz** Eileen Hardy★★★★★ £F   ● **Cabernet Sauvignon** Thomas Hardy★★★★ £F
● **Shiraz** Tintara Limited Release★★★   £C   ● **Grenache** Tintara Limited Release★★★ £C
O **Chardonnay** Eileen Hardy★★★ £C

HASELGROVE   McLaren Vale   www.haselgrove.com.au   A: BGL

*Owner: **BankWest**   Sand Road, McLaren Vale SA 5171*

Thus far, recurring changes of ownership haven't prevented this historic McLaren Vale operation from maintaining its reputation for full and powerful reds. Winemaking is now overseen by the much experienced Adrian Lockhart who has the opportunity to use good quality McLaren Vale fruit (despite the loss of some prime vineyards along the way) to reproduce the quality of the concentrated, chewy, fleshy reds established by Nick Haselgrove (of the original family owners). During the late nineties as the operation rapidly expanded, Haselgrove produced ever better reds, especially 'H' series Cabernet and Shiraz – both with good ageing potential. 'H' series whites were less good but included a bold Chardonnay and a reasonably varietal if short-lived Viognier. A rich, berryish sparkling red with a long finish and reasonably restrained tannin is also better than many of its type. These wines and other existing ranges are being continued including the Bentwing wines which are sourced from Wrattonbully, and the Picture Series which has provided reasonably priced but well-flavoured varietals. More vintages are needed before passing judgement on current quality; the ratings below apply to reds made prior to 2000. New and positioned as a flagship red is Limelight Syrah (/Shiraz). (PW)

● **Cabernet Sauvignon** 'H'★★★ £D   ● **Shiraz** 'H'★★★ £D
● **Sparkling Garnet SG 7**★★ £C

HENRY'S DRIVE   Padthaway   www.henrysdrive.com   A: THt, Bal, NYg, But, Tur, UnC

*Owner: **Longbottom family**   PO Box 9, Padthaway SA 5271*

Sparky and Sarah Marquis (ex FOX CREEK) make the wines at this large Padthaway estate established in 1998. It is planted in the main to Cabernet Sauvignon and Shiraz but also Chardonnay and Merlot. Given their achievements at Fox Creek it is not surprising that early efforts are promising; Shiraz and Cabernet are both distinctive and intense with good balance and texture. From the 2000 vintage the Shiraz has a gravelly, toasty, spicy, berry fruit in contrast to the cooler more minty, eucalyptus and blackcurrant-leaf character of the Cabernet. The Shiraz is aged in new American oak while the Cabernet receives mostly French oak. Reserve Shiraz was added in 1999 and a Reserve Cabernet has been made since 2000; both are more full-on with more extract and structure. Definitely a producer to watch as this range continues to develop. A Sparkling Shiraz is also made. (PW)

● **Cabernet Sauvignon**★★★ £D   Reserve★★★ £D
● **Shiraz**★★★ £D   Reserve★★★★ £E

HENSCHKE   Eden Valley   www.henschke.com.au   A: L&W, JNi, NYg, WSc

Owner: Stephen & Prue Henschke   Henschke Road, Kyneton SA 5353
In the mid-to-late 1980s many of these fabulous reds could be bought for a song but eventually the rest of the world got to taste them and this, added to the explosion in wine prices in the 90s, now usually means making do with something cheaper. Since 1979, Stephen Henschke has been fine-tuning these already well-established single-vineyard-based reds while his wife Prue has maintained and gradually renewed the existing vineyard resources. There are now 115 ha of estate vineyards, the largest segment (50 ha) in the Eden Valley. Carefully seasoned American oak is favoured and red-wine fermentations are now finished in new oak. Fabulous fruit in a full, supple, lushly textured wine is the classic Henschke style, with additional depth and dimension in the top wines. The most celebrated, and necessarily expensive vineyard, the 8-ha Hill of Grace, includes a parcel of vines (Grandfathers Block) that date in part from the 1860s. From close by, Mount Edelstone (the first to be bottled separately in 1952) is arguably more consistent, with more pepper and spice character, if missing the extra majesty of Hill of Grace. Cyril Henschke Cabernet, previously entirely Cabernet Sauvignon, now includes a little Merlot and Cabernet Franc and shows superb pure blackberry and cassis fruit. The ageing potential of all three top reds is well proven. Abbott's Prayer is based on Merlot but supplemented by both Cabernets and sees only French oak. Like the recently introduced Grenache-dominated blend, Johann's Garden, it is almost immediately drinkable. From a start in the early 1990s whites have steadily improved, particularly the intense, taut and concentrated (and ageworthy) Lenswood Croft Chardonnay and Eden Valley Louis Semillon. There's good varietal intensity in Crane's Chardonnay, Julius Riesling and Joseph' s Hill Gewürztraminer, all from Eden Valley fruit. A second Riesling, Green's Hill is sourced from the Adelaide Hills as is Littlehampton Pinot Gris. Tilly's Vineyard is a very gluggable blend of Semillon, Chardonnay and Sauvignon. (PW)

● **Shiraz** Hill of Grace✪✪✪✪✪ £H   Mount Edelstone★★★★★ £E
● **Cabernet** Cyril Henschke★★★★ £F   ● **Abbott's Prayer**★★★ £E
● **Shiraz/Cabernet/Merlot** Keyneton Estate★★★ £D
● **Grenache/Mourvèdre/Shiraz** Johann's Garden★★★ £C
O **Chardonnay** Croft★★★ £D   Crane's★★ £C
O **Semillon** Louis★★★ £C   O **Riesling** Julius★★ £C   Green's Hill★★ £C
O **Gewürztraminer** Joseph's Hill★ £C   Tilly's Vineyard★ £B

HILLSTOWE   Adelaide Hills   www.hillstowe.com.au   A: D&D, Men, Eno, Lwt

Owner: Lion Nathan   104 Main Road, Hahndorf SA 5245
In 2001, with just two clicks of a pen put to paper, this estate belonging to the Laurie family, which has deep roots in the area, fell into the clutches of a big Australasian brewer. Recent vintages have been made very competently so it is to be hoped that quality and integrity will be at least maintained – certainly, with the likes of PETALUMA, MITCHELTON and STONIER now under the same ownership, they are in good company. Wines labelled Buxton indicate a McLaren Vale origin while Udy's Mill is 17 ha of Lenswood (Adelaide Hills) vineyard. Lenswood Pinot is mostly at the ripe end of the spectrum but is intense and stylish while the Chardonnay has characteristic Adelaide Hills fruit

with a cool citrusy vigour. A tiny amount of Pinch Row Merlot also comes from Lenswood as does a new Pinot Gris. Mary's Hundred Shiraz – a tribute to the legendary Mary Laurie, a Scottish immigrant and probably Australia's first woman winemaker – is not named for the age of the vines but does include some 100-year-old McLaren Vale fruit. It's not overly refined, but is rich and deeply characterful. The Sauvignon needs to be drunk as young as possible. (PW)

● **Shiraz** Mary's Hundred★★★★ £C Buxton★★ £B
● **Pinot Noir** Udy's Mill★★★ £C **O Pinot Gris** Scrub Block★ £B
O **Chardonnay** Udy's Mill★★ £C Buxton★ £B

HOLLICK Coonawarra www.hollick.com   A: Sec, JNi, ACh

Owner: Hollick family Corner Ravenswood Lane & Riddoch Highway, Coonawarra SA 5263
The Hollicks have over 100 ha of vineyards including 50 ha in Coonawarra and another 20 ha in the emerging Wrattonbully region, but these are small amounts by Coonawarra standards. There is a diverse range of well-made wines with good intensity and extra depth in the top (Icon) reds that add refinement and complexity with age. All three have a black label; Ravenswood comes from the best parcels of Cabernet Sauvignon while Wilgha Shiraz and newish Neilson's Block Merlot are site-specific. Ravenswood shows good varietal definition and intelligent use of oak and becomes sleek and stylish with five years' age or more. The range also includes Chardonnay (both Unoaked and an oaked Reserve), toasty, limey, mineral Riesling, Sauvignon Blanc/Semillon and reds Pinot Noir, Shiraz/Cabernet (predominantly Shiraz) and Cabernet/Merlot. This last (80 per cent Cabernet) shows increased richness in the most recent vintages. A little light but attractive sweet wine, The Nectar, is also produced when conditions allow it: the most recent releases, mostly Riesling but also including some Sauvignon Blanc and Semillon, are 2001 and 1999. Some Sparkling Merlot is also made. (PW)

● **Cabernet Sauvignon** Ravenswood★★★ £D ● **Shiraz** Wilgha★★★ £C
● **Merlot** Neilson's Block★★★ £C ● **Cabernet Sauvignon/Merlot**★★ £B
O **Chardonnay** Reserve★★ £B O **Riesling**★★ £B

JAMIESONS RUN/MILDARA Coonawarra www.jamiesonsrun.com.au   A: BBI

Owner: Beringer Blass Riddoch Highway, Coonawarra SA 5263
All the Jamiesons Run/Mildara wines are grown and produced at the Jamiesons Run winery in Coonawarra. Such has been the commercial success of what began as an inexpensive red blend that production is now centred on the Jamieson Run label rather than that of Mildara. The basic red started life with a certain style and complexity (in part from combining Cabernet, Shiraz and Merlot) that similar competitively priced examples lacked, but has, sadly, lost its inspiration. The bright-fruited Chardonnay is rather simple and light but harsh too. An absence of richness and full ripeness seems to have plagued the reds down the years and, although the intention has been to produce wines of refinement and complexity, they have been let down by an inherent lack of real fruit quality. Robertson's Well started out decently enough but, despite the stylish cedary complexity that is some-times achieved, it can be found wanting for richness and depth. Individual vineyard bottlings are significantly better. French oak is now favoured and McShane's Block Shiraz and Alexander's Block Cabernet show real promise from a top vintage like 98. A third, O'Dea's Cabernet, was first made in 2000. Jamieson's Run Reserve has been positioned as the flagship wine. In 1999 it was not dominated by any one varietal but includes both Cabernets, Shiraz, Merlot and Malbec. (PW)

● **Jamieson's Run Reserve**★★★ £D ● **Shiraz** McShane's Block★★★ £D
● **Cabernet** Alexander's Block★★★ £D ● **Cabernet Sauvignon** Robertson's Well★★ £C

TREVOR JONES   Barossa   A: THt, UnC, NYg

Owner: Trevor Jones   Barossa Valley Highway, Lyndoch SA 5351

The grapes for these wines are bought in from diverse sources within South Australia. Experienced Trevor Jones makes very small quantities of varietal wines including a particularly good example of unoaked Chardonnay. This style, though popular, often only makes obvious the lack of really top quality fruit (something that can be partially disguised with sophisticated oak handling); but this example, by contrast, has a tight, pure fruit core and is capable of a little age. Reds tend to be in a big, extracted style but careful blending from different sites aids balance. Wild Witch Shiraz is sourced from a single vineyard of old-vine Barossa Shiraz. (PW)

● **Shiraz** Dry Grown★★★ £C   Wild Witch★★★ £E   ● **Cabernet/Merlot**★★ £C
O **Chardonnay** Virgin ★★★ £C   O **Riesling** Reserve★★ £B

KATNOOK ESTATE   Coonawarra   www.katnookestate.com.au A: Frt, Bib, Tan, WWs, NYg

*Owner: **Freixenet**   Riddoch Highway, Coonawarra SA 5263*

The majority shareholder in this Coonawarra stalwart is the Cava giant FREIXENET but it continues to be directed by Wayne Stehbens, who has made the wine in a 19th-century stone woolshed (used in the region's early vintages) for the past 20-odd years. Much of the grape production has been sold to others but Katnook's reds have been characterised by their intense, concentrated, ripe (often very ripe), sweet fruit and tight structures when young. Whites can show good intensity too but typically lack subtlety and flair. A premium (and pricey) Cabernet (Odyssey) has been complemented by a premium Shiraz (Prodigy) since 1997 and although both show more power and depth than the Katnook Estate versions, they are also markedly oaky – they may be redeemable with moderately long ageing. All the Katnook reds need at least five years' age; Riesling and Chardonnay are usually better with three years. Some very attractive, softly textured fruit-driven wines for early consumption have been made under a second label, Riddoch. (PW)

Katnook Estate:
● **Cabernet Sauvignon**★★ £C   Odyssey★★★   £E   ● **Merlot**★★ £C
● **Shiraz**★★ £C   Prodigy★★★ £E   O **Chardonnay**★★ £C
Riddoch:
● **Shiraz**★ £B   O **Chardonnay**★ £B

KILIKANOON   Clare Valley   www.kilikanoon.com.au   A: THt, NYg, UnC, P&S

Owner: Kevin Mitchell, Nathan Waks & partners   Penna Lane, Penwortham SA 5453

If you want to know what wines from the Clare taste like you could do a lot worse than to taste Kevin Mitchell's excellent range. Though lacking his own winemaking facility until 2004, all the grapes come from estate vineyards. Shiraz in particular is a star, showing off the regional characteristics superbly in both Oracle and Covenant versions. The Oracle has a more berryish accent in contrast to a more classic mineral- and earth-imbued fruit intensity in the Covenant. An expressive Cabernet Sauvignon shows both its orgins and the style and balance typical of the wines here. Riesling has deep fruit intensity if not always the structure of Clare's finest. Second Fiddle is a well-balanced, fruity Grenache-derived rosé. The latest releases are particularly impressive and very good value. (PW)

● **Shiraz** Oracle★★★★ £C   Covenant★★★★ £C   ● **Grenache** Prodigal★★★ £C
● **Cabernet Sauvignon** Blocks Road★★★ £C   O **Riesling** Morts Block★★ £B

KNAPPSTEIN   Clare Valley   www.knappsteinwines.com.au   A: Men, Odd

*Owner: **Lion Nathan**   2 Pioneer Avenue, Clare SA 5453*

Tim Knappstein relinquished his medium-sized winery (to the PETALUMA group) to devote himself full-time to KNAPPSTEIN LENSWOOD VINEYARDS, leaving winemaker Andrew Hardy to draw on the 100 ha of well-established vineyards. The reliable varietals remain moderately priced and widely available but there is now a greater emphasis on Shiraz and a switch to French oak. The premium reds are sold under the Enterprise label, named for the historic former brewery in which the winery is housed. Enterprise Cabernet Sauvignon (which include a very small percentage of Malbec) is made from the best parcels within the 30-year-old Knappstein vineyard and Enterprise Shiraz is made from a selection of small plots in Clare Valley. Both show classic Clare fruit with good depth and concentration. Semillon/Sauvignon is at the rich, ripe end of the spectrum of improving whites, Riesling is adding more intensity and Gewürztraminer is displaying a truer varietal character than in the past. A sparkling Shiraz, rather unnervingly called Chainsaw, has also been introduced! (PW)

- ● **Cabernet Sauvignon** Enterprise★★ £C
- ● **Shiraz**★ £B Enterprise★★ £C ● **Cabernet/Merlot**★ £B
- O **Chardonnay**★ £B O **Semillon/Sauvignon Blanc**★★ £B
- O **Gewürztraminer** Dry Style★ £B O **Riesling** Hand Picked★ £B

KNAPPSTEIN LENSWOOD   Adelaide Hills   www.knappsteinlenswood.com.au   A: McK

*Owner: **Tim & Annie Knappstein**   Croft Road, Lenswood SA5240*

Having gradually abandoned the Clare Valley for the heart of the Adelaide Hills, Tim Knappstein seems to have found a higher love. From 54 ha of two almost equal parts come consistently fine Sauvignon Blanc that is one of Australia's best and taut, attractively herbal, subtly oaked Semillon. The range also includes powerful, oaky, citrus and melon Chardonnay – not as nuanced as some Adelaide Hills examples but nicely concentrated – and a complex, richly textured Pinot Noir that has been particularly impressive since the 1997 vintage. Palatine is a Cabernet/Merlot blend (plus a little Malbec) introduced in the same year, and will be increasingly based on a nearby vineyard of the same name. Given the cool origin of the grapes, a portion of the Cabernet was partially dried prior to fermentation in the 98 vintage. The wine is ripe, shows good balance and should age well for up to a decade. A little Gewürztraminer from a single Adelaide Hills vineyard was first made in 1999 and again since 2001. (PW)

- ● **Pinot Noir**★★★ £D ● **Palatine**★★★ £D
- O **Chardonnay**★★★ £C O **Semillon**★★★ £B O **Sauvignon Blanc**★★★ £B

LAKE BREEZE   Langhorne Creek   www.lakebreeze.com.au   A: THt, UnC, Nid, NYg, Rae

*Owner: **Follett family**   Step Road, Langhorne Creek SA 5255*

One of the emerging quality producers from Langhorne Creek (on the opposite, eastern side of the Fleurieu Peninsula to McLaren Vale). Greg Follett makes the wines from a portion of his family's large holdings, the Folletts having been grape growers since the 1930s. The reds are very competently made; they were even of sound quality in the atypically cool, wet 99 vintage. Bernoota is half Shiraz, half Cabernet Sauvignon with good complexity and a well-defined palate, Cabernet Sauvignon is of similar quality. Under a Winemaker's Selection label, both varietal Cabernet Sauvignon and Shiraz are made in the best years. If more oaky, they are more concentrated too. (PW)

- ● **Cabernet Sauvignon**★★★ £C ● **Cabernet/Shiraz** Bernoota★★★ £C
- ● **Shiraz** Winemaker's Selection★★★ £D

LEASINGHAM   Clare Valley   www.leasingham-wines.com.au   A: BRL

*Owner: **Hardy Wine Company**   7 Dominic Street, Clare SA 5453*
This long-established winery is the HARDY WINE COMPANY's centre for Clare Valley excellence, currently overseen by Kerri Thompson. There are four substantial vineyards (all at least 50 ha) whose fruit is supplemented by bought-in grapes. It is pure speculation, but it might be interesting to see whether any part of any of vineyards is considered to be special enough to be isolated in the future. For the moment the range is simple and consistent. The Classic Clare wines are the most exciting, high in alcohol but packed full of rich, ripe fruit and abundant new oak; the Shiraz comes from the Schobers vineyard and the Cabernet from Provis vineyard. The oak theme continues in very good and reasonably priced Bin 61 Shiraz and Bin 56 Cabernet/Malbec. I suspect few of these reds are drunk with much age but all deserve four or five years. Mind you, a rich, untamed infusion of fruit and oak might appeal on some occasions. Prices of these dense, bold Classic Clare reds have risen considerably. Riesling is good with excellent limey, mineral intensity to the Bin 7. Classic Clare Riesling is made in a tighter, more ageworthy style. (PW)
- **Shiraz** Classic Clare★★★ £E   Bin 61★★ £B
- **Cabernet Sauvignon** Classic Clare★★★ £E   ● **Cabernet/Malbec** Bin 56
- O **Riesling** Bin 7★★ £B   ● **Sparkling Shiraz** Classic Clare★★ £C

LECONFIELD   Coonawarra   www.leconfield.com.au   A: Eno, J&B, Nid, WVt

*Owner: **Hamilton Wine Group**   Riddoch Highway, Coonawarra SA 5263*
Leconfield was established by Sydney Hamilton in the early 1970s but sold to his nephew Richard HAMILTON in 1981. The leading wine over more than two decades has been the Cabernet, which made a lasting impact with the 1980 vintage. Yet while some vintages have been very impressive with a deep, rich, assertive berry fruit character, other years have been somewhat leafy and unpredictably light. Cabernet includes a little Merlot, Cabernet Franc and Petit Verdot but most other wines are 100 per cent varietal. Of these, a more plummy, berryish, at times slightly herbal Merlot has been more consistent than a Shiraz which has occasionally been slightly lean after a much celebrated 95. Recent vintages of a Chardonnay have shown more elegance, if not the intensity of the more one-dimensional early vintages. A very small amount of flavoursome Riesling is also made from surviving 1970s vines. Recent vintages have been made by the Hamilton group winemaker, Pip Treadwell. (PW)
- **Cabernet**★★★ £C   ● **Merlot**★★ £C   ● **Shiraz**★★★ £C
- O **Chardonnay**★★ £B   O **Riesling** Old Vines★★ £B

PETER LEHMANN   Barossa Valley   www.peterlehmannwines.com.au   A: PLh, Odd, WSc

*Owner: **Peter Lehmann Wines Ltd**   Para Road, Tanunda SA 5352*
Peter Lehmann is a Barossa institution and a consistently sound bet for accessible but fruit-rich and well-structured Barossa reds. Now a publicly listed company, its fall to a multinational seems inevitable; one can only hope it'll be into good hands. Production is large with much of the fruit bought in under contract. Winemaking has always favoured an American-oaked, low-tannin style, though less so in the premium wines and less so recently. The numerous small parcels and a relatively limited number of wines puts the emphasis on blends. Stonewell Shiraz, released with five years' age, is based on low-yielding old vines in the Stonewell vineyards but also includes fruit from the Moppa and Ebenezer districts. The wine is aged in American oak and is always very full. It is somewhat showy but has lovely depth and richness with real dimension and well-proportioned tannins. Made since 1996, Eight Songs doesn't yet seem to be of the same calibre as the artistic efforts to which its presentation is linked. It is aged in French oak but misses the breadth and richness of the Stonewell.

Mentor is the premium Cabernet-based blend aged in French and American oak; it includes Merlot, Malbec and Shiraz and is dense, structured and best with at least six to ten years's age. Seven Surveys is an improving but relatively light version of a Grenache, Shiraz and Mourvèdre blend. Barossa Valley Shiraz remains well-priced for an impressive mouthful of fruit, as are the other Barossa-derived reds. A powerful ageworthy Reserve Riesling from Eden Valley, best of the whites, is released with four years' bottle-age. An early-release Eden Valley Riesling (Blue Eden) is also made. Semillon, previously coarse and oaky, is now citrusy and unoaked. Clancy's is a label of wider South Australian derivation; the red is a blend of Shiraz, Cabernet Sauvignon and Cabernet Franc. Weighbridge is a budget label for Shiraz and Chardonnay. (PW)

● **Shiraz**★★ £B Stonewell★★★★ £E Eight Songs★★★ £E ● **Mentor**★★★ £D
● **Grenache**★★ £B ● **Grenache/Shiraz**★ £B ● **Cabernet Sauvignon**★ £B
● **Seven Surveys**★ £B ● **Clancy's**★ £B
O **Riesling** Reserve★★★ £B O **Semillon**★★ £B

LINDEMANS Coonawarra & Padthaway www.southcorp.com.au A: ScE

Owner: Southcorp Coonawarra SA 5263 & Naracoorte Road, Padthaway SA 5271
In Coonawarra, Lindemans (also see Victoria) makes a trio of top reds which can be traced back to the mid-1980s, in the case of Pyrus (a Bordeaux blend), and even longer for St George Cabernet and Limestone Ridge Shiraz/Cabernet. But despite some impressive past vintages these wines don't now stack up against the best from Coonawarra (which includes the premium WYNNS wines from the same stable). An initial fullness and fleshy texture and a pleasing complexity are let down by a lack of fruit intensity on the finish and a stalky, sappy quality that is often apparent. This seems to suggest a mix of good quality fruit and that of more mediocre origins. All three wines are significantly cheaper than the Wynns flagship wines but there are many better Coonawarra wines in their price range. By contrast generally good value is to be had in the Padthaway wines, particularly the Reserve Chardonnay with its pronounced barrel-fermentation character and rich fruit. (PW)

● **Pyrus** Coonawarra★★★ £D ● **Cabernet Sauvignon** St George★★ £D
● **Shiraz/Cabernet** Limestone Ridge★★ £D
● **Shiraz** Padthaway★ £B Padthaway Reserve★★ £C
O **Chardonnay** Limestone Coast★ £B Padthaway Reserve★★ £C

MAGLIERI McLaren Vale www.maglieri.com.au A: BBI

Owner: Beringer Blass Douglas Gully Road, McLaren Flat SA 5171
Captured in 1999 by Mildara Blass in 1999 (now BERINGER BLASS), this relatively small McLaren Vale winery had already made a name for itself for premium reds under the direction of Steve Maglieri as well as a wider local fame for its 'Lambrusco'. The reds, currently made by Trevor Tucker, generally show intense ripe fruit and well-integrated oak. Shiraz displays classic McLaren Vale character with slightly smoky, eucalyptus, very ripe dark berry/cherry/plum fruit and a hint of earth, building up dark-chocolate flavours with age. The Steve Maglieri version is more structured, extracted and oaky and needs the best part of a decade's ageing. Merlot is soundly made but, like many South Australian examples, is hardly a classic expression of the grape. The Cabernet is more convincing. Semillon and Chardonnay are both well-crafted and better than is typical for McLaren Vale. Quality across the range dipped a little in the 99 vintage (which was poor in McLaren Vale) but premium reds should continue to be a good bet if the fruit sources are retained. (PW)

● **Shiraz**★★★ £C Steve Maglieri★★★ £E
● **Cabernet Sauvignon**★★ £B ● **Merlot**★ £B
O **Chardonnay**★ £B O **Semillon**★ £B

MAJELLA   Coonawarra   www.majellawines.com.au   A: Fsp, FFW

Owner: Lynn families   Lynn Road, Coonawarra SA 5263

A label of growing recognition and importance as more and more of the Cabernet and Shiraz grapes from prime Coonawarra land that were previously sold under contract (an important supplier to WYNNS since 1980) are now being used for Majella wines. From the late 1960s vines began to compete with sheep for space and by the early 1990s the first wines were produced. With a new winery and now a full-time winemaker, Bruce Gregory (ex BRAND'S), Majella has increased production to 12,000 cases. The Cabernet/Shiraz blend once common to many premium South Australian wines but now mostly seen in budget wines has, since 1996, been the basis of a very impressive flagship, Malleea. Very dense, rich and concentrated fruit takes up the French oak treatment and fine tannins promise a long life. Varietal Shiraz and Cabernet are in a similar mould with potent berry fruit and evident oak but are a little more accessible when young. Riesling shows a better, tighter structure than is usual in Coonawarra Riesling. Sparkling Shiraz is also made but you may need to visit the winery to get your hands on it. (PW)

● **Malleea★★★** £F ● **Cabernet Sauvignon★★★** £D ● **Shiraz★★★** £D
O **Riesling★** £B

MAXWELL   McLaren Vale   www.maxwellwines.com.au   A: FWC

Owner: Maxwell family   Olivers Road, McLaren Vale SA 5171

Still a relatively modest-sized operation, Maxwell is now equipped with a modern winery in order to maximise the potential of its 16-ha vineyard. Though quality has been slightly variable it has always been at least good, sometimes very good and both Ellen Street Shiraz and Lime Cave Cabernet Sauvignon display fine textures, stylish rich ripe fruit and good structure. A little Reserve Shiraz has also been made in a more extracted, blockbuster style. Whites are full of flavour, with good balance and structure too, but a rich, citrusy, herbal Semillon is better and more consistent than the Chardonnay. Grenache and Verdelho are also made. (PW)

● **Shiraz** Four Roads★ £B Ellen Street★★★ £C
● **Cabernet Sauvignon** Lime Cave★★★ £C ● **Cabernet/Merlot★** £B
O **Chardonnay★** £B O **Semillon** Old Vines★★ £B

CHARLES MELTON   Barossa Valley   www.charlesmeltonwines.com.au A: Lib, Vne, ACh, BBR

Owner: Graeme (Charlie) Melton   Krondorf Road, Tanunda SA 5352

Charlie Melton is one of the saviours of Australian Shiraz along with Rocky O'Callaghan (ROCKFORD), Bob McLean (ST HALLETT) and others. In the late 1980s and early 90s he produced wines of such character and richness from dry-farmed (unirrigated) Barossa old-vine fruit that it rescued the grape from the also-ran category assigned to it in the Cabernet-fixated wine scene that prevailed in Australia at the time. Though Melton is based in the heart of the Barossa, grapes (whether owned, leased or bought-in) are sourced from throughout the area. Both French and American oak are used but the past decade has seen a trend towards the former. Shiraz is arguably the best Melton wine made but a varietal Grenache (from old bush vines) is always very ripe and sweet-fruited. One of Australia's best rosés is also based on Grenache while Nine Popes is a blend of Shiraz, Grenache and Mourvèdre. Cabernet shows the rich, ripe fruit and oak character typical to all the reds. Made by the traditional method and from Cabernet as well as Shiraz, the Sparkling Red is a very good example of its type; it shows a rich plum, berry and chocolate character with a little age. More exotic again is Sotto di Ferro made from Pedro Ximenez and Muscadelle grapes (90/10) dried 'under the iron' – beneath a corrugated iron roof. It is well-balanced and complex, including roasted nuts, honey, nougat and dried apricots, with real depth and intensity. Laura Shiraz comes from grapes bought in from vineyards in the Southern Flinders Ranges (north of Clare Valley) near the township of Laura. The last excepted, all the reds benefit from having at least five years' age. Very promising is a new Kirsche Vineyard Shiraz, also from Flinders fruit. (PW)

● **Nine Popes★★★★** £E ● **Grenache★★★** £C
● **Shiraz★★★★** £E Laura★★ £D ● **Cabernet Sauvignon★★★** £E
◉ **Rose of Virginia★★** £C ● **Sparkling Red★★★** £E ● **Sotto di Ferro★★★** £F

GEOFF MERRILL McLaren Vale www.geoffmerrillwines.com A: Eno, Eve, HWC

Owner: Stratmer Vineyards (G Merrill & A Purbrick) 291 Pimpala Road, Woodcroft SA 5162
Geoff Merrill hardly needs any introduction to many wine consumers as he is one of the most instantly recognisable great characters of the Australian wine scene. The wines, made at the renovated Mount Hurtle winery since 1988, can seem a bit anonymous and simple, apparently at odds with the exuberant personality of their maker. At their best they do achieve a certain elegance and subtlety but more often there isn't the necessary fruit quality there to deliver the regional and varietal expression that is sought. Even the red Reserves, though showing greater intensity and complexity, can taste overly leafy and slightly tired and woody from long oak-ageing. Nevertheless, they are refreshing after some of the more hollow, superficial, high-alcohol efforts that are common in the region. The new Henley Shiraz is being sold at a stratospheric price but does have remarkable depth and complexity within a relatively unobtrusive frame. This, like the Reserves (including Chardonnay), is only released with extended bottle-age. Regular varietals, at their best (when fully ripe), are generally soft, supple and attractive, even if they don't have the greatest weight or intensity. Wines under the Mount Hurtle label can have upfront if simple fruit character. (PW)

● **Shiraz** Reserve★★ £D ● **Cabernet Sauvignon** Reserve★★ £D
○ **Chardonnay★** £B Reserve★★ £C

MITCHELL Clare Valley A: MVs, Tan, ACh

Owner: Andrew & Jane Mitchell Hughes Park Road, Sevenhill via Clare SA 5453
The Mitchell winery was established in 1975 and is now a small to medium-sized Clare producer with a strong track record for consistent, well-structured reds and whites. The whites are made without any oak as is a high-alcohol Grenache from old unirrigated bush vines, while the Shiraz and Cabernet (which includes a little Cabernet Franc and Merlot) show a relatively subdued oak influence. Though the wines sometimes lack a little extra flair or personality they nonetheless show typical Clare characteristics and Cabernet, Shiraz and Riesling are capable of long ageing. After some weaker efforts in the late 90s the Riesling is once again intense and concentrated – an all-too-rare inexpensive wine worth cellaring. (PW)

● **Cabernet Sauvignon** Sevenhill Vineyard★★ £B
● **Shiraz** Peppertree Vineyard★★ £B ● **Grenache** Growers★ £B
○ **Riesling** Watervale★★ £B ○ **Semillon** Growers★ £B

MOUNT HORROCKS Clare Valley www.mounthorrocks.com A: Lib, ACh, WSc

Owner: Stephanie Toole Curling Street, Auburn SA 5451
This is a regular but increasingly classy range of wines which all have good structure and ripeness. In recent years Stephanie Toole has been able to centre her production of just 5,000 cases per year around one Watervale source. Great care is taken in producing the best possible fruit from unirrigated vines and also in their vinification (carried out at Jeffrey GROSSET's winery). Riesling is

getting better and better, taut with vibrant fruit (lime and grapefruit with floral notes) and great length. Both Semillon and Chardonnay are from single plots and show good breadth and weight as well as the firm acidity that gives all the whites a certain austerity when young. Though it is barrel-fermented, the citrus and mineral notes in the Semillon are not in the least overwhelmed. Cabernet/Merlot is what others would call simply Cabernet Sauvignon, as it only contains five per cent Merlot, but lately it has been ripely berryish with fine tannins. Shiraz has excellent definition with a hint of the Clare mineral, earth character. A sweet version of Riesling, Cordon Cut, is made by allowing the grapes to dehydrate on the vine by severing the cane from the trunk (the French term is *passerillage*; there is no botrytis but a *passerillé* or dried-grape character is achieved). The wine shows an intense, pure, limey, honeyed character checked by good acidity. All the wines deserve an extra couple of years' bottle-age. (PW)

O **Riesling** Watervale★★★ £C Cordon Cut★★★ £D
O **Semillon** Watervale★★★ £C O **Chardonnay**★★ £C
● **Cabernet/Merlot**★★ £D ● **Shiraz**★★★ £D

MOUNTADAM Eden Valley www.mountadam.com A: MHn, JNi, N&P, FWC

Owner: LVMH High Eden Road, Eden Valley SA 5235
A high-profile and often overhyped winery, Mountadam has had some successes but has never been totally convincing as one of South Australia's leading small producers. Established by the late David Wynn on the elevated High Eden Ridge, it continues to be run by his son Adam despite being purchased by CAPE MENTELLE (part of LVMH) in 2000. Many of the wines have lacked real depth and complexity but have wowed some wine drinkers with their oak and, at times, beguiling fruit veneer. The Chardonnay has some style and structure and has been the most consistent wine but doesn't match the top Adelaide Hills examples. Eden Valley Riesling can show exquisite fruit flavours though not always the structure to match. The Red is a blend of Cabernet Sauvignon and Merlot and often exhibits rather leafy, underripe characters. The David Wynn label provides less expensive Shiraz and Chardonnay but also the winery's best red in Patriarch Shiraz, a rich, powerful and seductive wine. Eden Ridge is for organically grown varietals. (PW)

● **Shiraz** David Wynn Patriarch★★★ £C
● **Pinot Noir**★ £C ● **The Red**★ £D
O **Chardonnay**★★ £C O **Riesling** Eden Valley★★ £B

NEPENTHE Adelaide Hills www.nepenthe.com.au A: Str, Odd, WSc

Owner: Tweddell family Vickers Road, Lenswood SA 5240
A very switched-on Adelaide Hills producer excelling with almost everything it touches. The widely travelled owners only established this small to medium-sized operation in the mid-1990s yet made an immediate impact both locally and abroad. Winemaker Peter Leske works with Ed Tweddell's son James to maximise the potential of the ripe yet cool Lenswood fruit. Predominantly French oak is used, usually a mix of new and used. All the wines have excellent fruit but good texture and balance too. Pinot Noir is particularly impressive with great breadth and intensity on the palate. Whites are intense and varietal; both Chardonnays are nicely composed with good fruit richness. But as well as pristine varietals, a stylish Cabernet/Merlot blend (with Cabernet Franc from 99), The Fugue, has been joined by a curious Merlot, Cabernet, Shiraz and Pinot blend, The Rogue. A rare but good Zinfandel has so far only been made in very small quantities. In 2001 a new range of wines was produced under the Charleston label, named for a second, larger vineyard site. (PW)

● **Pinot Noir**★★★ £C ● **Zinfandel**★★ £D ● **The Fugue**★★ £C
O **Chardonnay**★★★ £B Unwooded★★ £B

O **Riesling**★★ £B   O **Semillon**★★ £B
O **Sauvignon Blanc**★★ £B   O **Pinot Gris**★ £B

ORLANDO   Barossa Valley   www.jacobscreek.com.au   A: PRc

*Owner: **Orlando Wyndham group (Pernod-Ricard)*** *Barossa Valley Way, Rowland Flat SA 5352*
The success of a single brand, namely Jacob's Creek, seems to have swallowed the image of the parent company here. But beyond the mostly meagre, unnatural-tasting offerings of this world-conquering label some serious wines can still be found. Riesling has long been a strength here and the once out-standing wines of Steingarten continue to be made to a high standard, if no longer based solely on the original steep-sloped vineyard of schist. Top older vintages have improved for as much as two decades, occasionally longer and current vintages will keep too. Other wines of note include those made at the Russet Ridge winery in Wrattonbully. The two Coonawarra-based Cabernets, St Hugo and Jacaranda Ridge, generally display fine fruit and structure and show increasing richness and sophistication since the mid-1990s. Lawson's Padthaway Shiraz is in the big oaky mould but it doesn't lack for fruit or structure either; the St Hilary Chardonnay from the same region can be remarkably good value. Jacob's Creek Reserves are a big improvement on the basics but that's not saying much. Also under the same ownership are Richmond Grove, Montrose and the big-volume sparkling wine brand, Carrington. (PW)
● **Shiraz** Lawson's Padthaway★★★ £D   Jacob's Creek Reserve★ £B
● **Cabernet Sauvignon** St Hugo★ £C   Jacaranda Ridge★ £D
O **Chardonnay** St Hilary Padthaway★★ £B
O **Riesling** Steingarten★★ £C   Jacob's Creek Reserve★ £B

PARKER COONAWARRA   Coonwarra   www.parkercoonawarraestate.com.au   A:C&B

Owner: John Parker & James Fairfax   Riddoch Highway, Coonawarra SA 5263
This singular Coonawarra estate established by John Parker in 1985 produced some great wines during the 1990s, but only very recently added its own winemaking facility. Overall direction now comes from Andrew Pirie (recruited from PIPERS BROOK - see Victoria & Tasmania). The focus of production is a single premium wine, a Bordeaux-like approach that is also reflected in the provocative name, Terra Rossa First Growth. It was first made in 1988 but not in 1992, 1995, and 1997. In those years (unlike Médoc classed growths), only the second wine, Terra Rossa Cabernet Sauvignon, was released as it was felt the requisite quality hadn't been reached. First Growth is based on Cabernet Sauvignon but also includes Merlot and Cabernet Franc and is aged in 100 per cent new French oak. It is fully ripe and concentrated, if at times a little oaky, with an intense pure fruit core that takes the best part of a decade to unfurl. The second wine, which sees some American as well as French oak, has recently been only a shade behind. A Merlot is also made but is only available in very small quantities direct from the winery. (PW)
● **Terra Rossa First Growth**★★★★ £F
● **Cabernet Sauvignon** Terra Rossa★★★ £D

PENFOLDS   Barossa Valley   www.penfolds.com.au   A: ScE, Odd

*Owner: **Southcorp*** *Tanunda Road, Nurioopta SA 5355*
The leading Australian brand since the renaissance of Australian wine in the early 1950s, Penfolds continues to be number one in the mammoth SOUTHCORP. Grange, Australia's most consistently great wine over five decades, is the pinnacle of production. Like all established investment wines, Grange has a crazy price tag but prices of all the top wines here reflect demand as much as production costs or intrinsic quality. Some top Penfolds reds are produced from a wide range of vineyard sources,

which can certainly optimise complexity and aid consistency, although on the downside it might be argued there is less individuality. Importantly, there does seem to be a welcome trend to giving more information about the main components. Further details (i.e regional percentages and specific vineyards used) would offer the drinker (OK, anorak, some might say) more academic pleasure when comparing the top reds or tasting vertically (different years of the same wine). Grange is primarily Barossa and McLaren Vale Shiraz aged in American oak but typically contains around five per cent Cabernet (10 per cent in 1992–94); while not the most refined expression of Shiraz, it is very powerful and complete, and fabulously complex with age. The RWT is 100 per cent Barossa Shiraz aged in French oak; it has good drive and intensity but is oaky too. Intense Magill Estate is vineyard-specific but can be almost overripe and slightly coarse. St Henri, which includes around five per cent Cabernet, is aged in large used oak barrels. The top Cabernet is Bin 707, which includes Coonawarra, Padthaway and Barossa fruit and, like Grange, is aged in American oak; there's terrific flesh and blackberry fruit depth in an uncompromising structure. Bin 407 is based primarily on Coonawarra and Padthaway fruit and aged in both French and American oak. Of the other Bin-labelled reds, the Barossa-sourced Bin 138 Old Vine Shiraz/Grenache/Mourvèdre and long-established Bin 389 stands out. White wines have only taken on real significance here in the last decade. Yattarna, the top Chardonnay, is a classic Australian expression of the grape but while rich and concentrated with lovely fruit and excellent structure it lacks real flair or individuality. A series of Bin-numbered Chardonnays have also been very impressive. For more affordable reds and whites, there are the Koonunga Hill and the slightly cheaper Rawson's Retreat brands which cover some of the same varietals and dual-variety blends. It must take considerable skill to maintain these two ranges, but only occasionally does either brand provide anything particularly interesting or good value. (PW)

● **Grange✪✪✪✪✪** £H
● **Shiraz** RWT★★★★ £F Magill Estate★★★ £E
● **Shiraz** St Henri★★★ £E Bin 28★★ £B Bin 128★ £B
● **Cabernet Sauvignon** Bin 407★★★ £C Bin 707★★★★ £F
● **Shiraz/Grenache/Mourvèdre** Bin 138 Old Vine★★ £C
● **Cabernet Shiraz** Bin 389★★ £C
● **Shiraz/Mourvèdre** Bin 2★ £B ● **Old Vine Red**★★ £C
O **Chardonnay** Adelaide Hills★★ £C Bin 98A★★★ £E Yattarna★★★★ £G

PENLEY ESTATE Coonwarra www.penley.com.au A: L&W, WTs, NYg, N&P

Owner: Kym Tolley McLeans Road, Coonawarra SA 5263

Kym Tolley's ancestry and past link him to Penfolds but since 1991 he has produced a small but consistently high-quality range of wines under his own label. There are more than 90 ha of estate plantings including nearly 40 ha of Coonawarra Cabernet. The style is for rich, ripe, smooth wines with lush fruit and unobtrusive tannins but with good ageing potential. American oak is favoured for Shiraz, French for Merlot, with a mix of the two for Cabernet. Cabernet Sauvignon Reserve (the same wine was known simply as Cabernet Sauvignon before 1998) has been consistently impressive while Ausvetia is a pricey flagship Shiraz, mostly from McLaren Vale fruit, but including 10 per cent Cabernet Sauvignon. Phoenix and Hyland are lighter, more forward versions of Cabernet and Shiraz respectively. Chardonnay lacks a little elegance but is not short of richness or flavour. (PW)

● **Cabernet Sauvignon** Reserve★★★ £D Phoenix★★ £C ● **Merlot**★★ £C
● **Shiraz** Ausvetia★★★ £E Hyland★★ £B ● **Shiraz/Cabernet**★★ £C
O **Chardonnay**★★ £B

PETALUMA Adelaide Hills www.petaluma.com.au A: Men, Tan, Odd, Vne

*Owner: **Lion Nathan** Spring Gully Road, Piccadilly SA 5151*

As long as Brian Croser remains involved here, it seems certain Petaluma will always provide ageworthy wines of subtlety and intensity. The formation of the Petaluma group (also KNAPPSTEIN, MITCHELTON, SMITHBROOK and STONIER) seemed to benefit all participants, at least quality-wise. As part of an expanding wine portfolio within a large Australasian drinks company, only time will tell. Right now there's excellent, tightly structured, minerally Riesling which needs a minimum of two to three years' age but is capable of much more. Best of all is the brilliant, individual Tiers Chardonnay from the first vineyard planted in the Piccadilly Valley. With great depth, power and a mineral, citrus intensity its structure and relative austerity when young demand patience. Regular Piccadilly Valley Chardonnay, from other vineyards as well as Tiers, needs a little age too and adds richness over a number of years. Complex berry-fruited Coonawarra (60 per cent Cabernet, 40 per cent Merlot in 1999 but more Cabernet in hot years) could use a little more weight in cooler years but always reveals greater concentration with age. Croser is an elegant traditional-method sparkling wine, generally around half Chardonnay and half Pinot Noir, that has been consistently fine for more than a decade. A Late Disgorged version has also been produced. All wines have a structure not seen in many of the more immediate premium Australian sparkling wines and must be drunk with some bottle-age. The Petaluma range has always been small and total production is relatively modest. Relatively recent additions are Adelaide Hills Shiraz and Viognier. Sharefarmers red (Cabernet/Merlot-based) and white (Sauvignon/Semillon) is a second label. Bridgewater Mill is now a separate entity. (PW)

● **Coonawarra**★★★ £D ● **Merlot**★★★
O **Chardonnay** Piccadilly Valley★★★ £C Tiers★★★★ £F
O **Riesling**★★★ £B O **Croser**★★★ £C

PIKES Clare Valley www.pikeswines.com.au A: L&S, WVt

Owner: Neil & Andrew Pike Polish Hill River Road, Sevenhill via Clare SA 5453

Pikes is without doubt one of the most reliable names from Clare Valley. A medium-sized producer with 38 ha of estate vineyards at Polish Hill River, these are full, flavoursome wines with weight and intensity across the range. Both Shiraz and Cabernet (which includes five per cent Cabernet Franc) show good Clare character with a mineral, earth influence in the rich berry fruit aromas and are ripe, plush and well-balanced with restrained oak character. Shiraz/Grenache/Mourvèdre (more than half Shiraz) is a fragrant, nicely textured example of this now-common Australian threesome. Whites include a Chardonnay which shows rich ripe fruit but includes a mineral, citrus peel component and is capable of a little age. Riesling typically shows a floral, toasty and minerally intensity if not the purity and structure of the best Clare examples. Sauvignon Blanc lacks a real varietal stamp. The wines are decent value though occasional very good Reserves including Riesling, Cabernet, Shiraz and a Merlot are twice the price. Sauvignon Blanc/Semillon is also made, along with Sangiovese (Premio) and, from 2001, a little Viognier. Luccio (Italian for pike) red and white are inexpensive blends, the red adds Sangiovese to Cabernet Sauvignon and Merlot. Pike & Joyce is a partnership with the Joyce family in Lenswood (Adelaide Hills) yielding Pinot Noir, Chardonnay, Sauvignon Blanc as well as a little Pinot Gris. (PW)

O **Riesling**★★ £B O **Chardonnay**★★★ £B
● **Shiraz**★★★ £B ● **Shiraz/Grenache/Mourvèdre**★★ £B
● **Cabernet Sauvignon**★★★ £B

PRIMO ESTATE Adelaide   www.primoestate.com.au   A: AWA, NYg, ACh, N&P

Owner: Joe Grilli   Old Port Wakefield Road, Virginia SA 5120

From an unpromising location, the hot Adelaide Plains, comes a quite exceptional range of wines, the result of innovation and talent that any wine-producing country would be proud of and cautious winemakers can only dream of. Joe Grilli was clearly no ordinary Roseworthy graduate and he had both the confidence and ability to go where others are still frightened to follow. He took on the running of his father's vineyard in 1979 and hasn't stopped experimenting since. Estate plantings are now supplemented from vineyards just south of Adelaide and in McLaren Vale proper as well as by bought-in grapes. His Cabernet/Merlot (90 per cent Cabernet) uses partially dried grapes mostly from McLaren Vale. Dubbed Moda Amarone by Grilli, this is a richly textured, exuberant wine full of ripest cassis, blackberry and black plum fruit with plenty of oak, at its best with five to 10 years' age. La Magia is a late-harvested Riesling with a long history of experimentation; currently it is composed primarily of botrytised Eden Valley fruit (2001 also includes 25 per cent Traminer). A vibrant fleshy Sparkling Red is produced every two years based on Adelaide Plains Shiraz. New since the 2001 vintage is Pinot Grigio d'Elena. All premium wines are labelled Joseph. Packaging is pretty smart and the prices on the high side yet fair for the quality. Il Briccone, a Shiraz/Sangiovese blend (but also a little Cabernet, Nebbiolo and Barbera), and a zesty tropical and citrus-fruited Colombard white, La Biondina, both under the Primo label are more modestly priced. A tiny amount of fortified Frontignan (Muscat), currently called Fronti IV, is also made, as are vintage-dated olive oils and vinegars. (PW)

● **Cabernet Sauvignon/Merlot** Joseph★★★ £D
● **Shiraz/Sangiovese** Il Briccone★ £B
● **Sparkling Red**★★★ £E
O **Riesling** La Magia Joseph★★★ £C   O **Colombard** La Biondina★ £B

RAVENSWOOD LANE Adelaide Hills   www.ravenswoodlane.com.au   A: Cap

Owner: John Edwards   Ravenswood Lane, Hahndorf SA 5245

John Edwards' estate wines come from 28 ha near Hahndorf in the central part of the Adelaide Hills. Much effort has gone into the packaging and image, and fortunately into the wines too. An exciting lush, peppery, fleshy Shiraz has real potential and does reflect something of the South Australia/Rhône hybrid style claimed for these wines. There is potential too in an intense, lemony Chardonnay that reveals the depth and dimension of a serious Côte de Beaune example. In collaboration with Hardys winemakers, John Edwards makes the Starvedog Lane wines at Hardys' Tintara winery from a combination of vineyard resources. Unlike the Starvedog Lane version, the Ravenswood Lane Sauvignon is barrel-fermented and adds more breadth, but at the cost of some of the vibrant nettly intensity of the unoaked wine. Perhaps the best Starvedog Lane wine is the Cabernet: cool, complex, but ripe too, with blackberry, blackcurrant, mint and chocolate flavours and an attractive cedary complexity, not unlike a top Hawkes Bay Cabernet from an exceptional vintage such as 1998. As well as Merlot and an unwooded, 'No Oak' Chardonnay, a traditional-method sparkling Chardonnay/Pinot Noir/Pinot Meunier is also made. There are no bargains here but nicely textured interesting wines at prices commensurate to quality. (PW)

Ravenswood Lane:
● **Shiraz** Reunion★★★ £E   ● **Cabernet Sauvignon** 19th Meeting★★★ £E
O **Sauvignon Blanc** Gathering★★ £C   O **Chardonnay** Beginning★★★ £D

Stavedog Lane:
● **Cabernet Sauvignon**★★★ £C   ● **Shiraz**★★ £C
O **Chardonnay**★★ £C   O **Sauvignon Blanc**★★ £B

REYNELLA/REYNELL   McLaren Vale   www.brlhardy.com.au   A: BRL

Owner: Hardy Wine Company   Reynell Road, Reynella SA 5161

Reynella or Chateau Reynella is a historic property with its origins dating from 1838 when the nation was still in its infancy (and its story is told in any decent book on Australian wine). Bought by the Thomas Hardy company in 1982, it now serves as the corporate headquarters for the much expanded HARDY WINE COMPANY group. Seemingly forever there has been a wealth of old-vine McLaren Vale material and in the 1990s deep, intense, muscular wines were fashioned. Open fermenters and old basket presses are utilised – Basket Pressed is the name that now adorns the reds. These are now wines of great depth, complexity and structure yet with ripe, smooth tannins. Chardonnay is bold and brash with lots of oak – but a good example if you like this style. The wines are sold in Australia as Reynell. (PW)

● **Cabernet Sauvignon** Basket Pressed★★★ £C
● **Cabernet Sauvignon/Merlot** Basket Pressed★★★ £C
● **Shiraz** Basket Pressed★★★ £C   O **Chardonnay**★★ £B

ROCKFORD   Barossa Valley   www.rockfordwines.com.au   A: AHW, FFW

Owner: Robert O'Callaghan   Krondorf Road, Tanunda SA 5352

Rockford wines still taste like true classics. Having been in the vanguard of the Barossa revival, Rocky O'Callaghan seems to have stayed true to the cause better than most. Commercial expansion to fund a fleet of Ferraris has never been the end goal. As a result the wines can be hard to find but they've not been compromised either. Basket Press Shiraz shows the depth and richness that the best old-vine Barossa fruit delivers with ease. An Eden Valley Riesling is picked late with plenty of skin contact giving a very full-flavoured example, but the wine lacks the finesse and other qualities this grape can deliver. Moppa Springs is a Grenache-based blend with Shiraz and Mourvèdre. The Sparkling Shiraz is one of the most famous examples of all but the difficulty in getting hold of it and its cult status-fuelled price mean there's pain before pleasure. (PW)

● **Shiraz** Basket Press★★★★ £D   ● **Cabernet Sauvignon**★★ £C   ● **Moppa Springs**★★ £C
O **Semillon** Local Growers★★ £C   O **Riesling** Eden Valley★★★ £B
● **Sparkling Shiraz** Black Shiraz★★★★ £F

ROSEMOUNT (MCLAREN VALE)   McLaren Vale   www.rosemountestates.com   A: ScE

Owner: Southcorp   Ingoldby Road, McLaren Flat SA 5171

Rosemount makes several of its best red wines at the McLaren Vale winery. Most famous of these is the McLaren Vale Shiraz sold as Balmoral Syrah, a wine with a real harmony of oak, fruit richness and weight as well as an extra dimension most other Australian examples miss. The Show Reserve Cabernet is sourced from Coonawarra and both French and American oak are utilised in its ageing. Show Reserve Shiraz, by contrast, comes from McLaren Vale and Langhorne Creek and like the Balmoral is aged only in American oak. Traditional is a Bordeaux blend of Cabernet Sauvignon, with 20 per cent Merlot and a smaller amount of Petit Verdot, but the oak used is American not French. GSM stands for Grenache/Shiraz/Mourvèdre (typical percentages 50/40/10), and is one of the most high-profile of these now popular blends. Again, in the classic Australian mould, the oak is American. All the wines show lush fruit and oak, good depth and fine tannins, and if there is less refinement in the GSM there is also more character. Any of these reds will keep for up to 10 years but are most rewarding with just five or six years' age. Also see ROSEMOUNT (under New South Wales & Queensland). (PW)

● **Syrah** Balmoral★★★★★ £F   ● **Shiraz** Show Reserve★★★ £C

● **Cabernet Sauvignon** Show Reserve★★★ £C
● **Traditional**★★★ £C   ● **GSM**★★★ £C

RYMILL   Coonawarra   www.rymill.com.au   A: PLB, Rae, Nid

Owner: Peter Riddoch Rymill & Judy Rymill   The Riddoch Run Vineyards, Coonawarra SA 5263
The Rymills are an accomplished Australian family – Peter Riddoch Rymill is descended directly
from John Riddoch, father of Coonawarra – but only began producing their own wine in the late
1980s. Though they are based at the northern end of the region, around a third of their 170 ha of
vineyards are located in the south near Penola. Recent vintages of the wines made by John Innes have
been particularly good, the reds showing better ripeness, tighter structure and a restrained oak
character. The wines are given a little bottle-age before release and can often be broached shortly
after, a rare thing these days. Even so the top wine, a Cabernet Sauvignon, should keep for a decade
from recent vintages. MC2 is a blend of a third Merlot and a third each of the two Cabernets and
now seems to achieve good ripeness in most vintages. Among whites Sauvignon Blanc is now an
attractive quaffer if drunk very young though usually bettered by a nicely plump Chardonnay that
will keep a year or two. A sweet, richly flavoured if not well-structured, botrytised Gewürztraminer
(or June Traminer) is made from just 2 ha of vines. A traditional method Chardonnay/Pinot
Noir/Pinot Meunier blend and a Sparkling red from Cabernet Franc and Shiraz are also made. All
wines are keenly priced. (PW)
● **Cabernet Sauvignon**★★★ £C
● **Shiraz**★★ £B **MC2** ★★ £B
O **Chardonnay**★ £B   O **Sauvignon Blanc**★ £B   O **Gewürztraminer** Botrytis★ £C

ST HALLETT   Barossa Valley   www.sthallett.com.au   A: D&D, Men, POs, AWA, WSc

Owner: Lion Nathan   St Hallett's Road, Tanunda SA 5352
A decade ago, powered by Bob McLean, St Hallett was one of the bright new stars of Barossa. Now a
successful medium-sized operation, it is perhaps the best-known but compared to Charles MELTON,
ROCKFORD and others it has now lost some of its lustre. Sound, with good fruit and supple
structures, the wines lack flair and individuality. Old Block Shiraz appears to have permanently lost its
previous concentration. It would seem that fruit from the many small plots of very old vines is not of
an equal standard. An intense, rich, weighty, if slightly coarse and irregular Eden Valley Riesling can
be impressive. Other whites include Semillon/Sauvignon Blanc and from the 2001 vintage, a
barrique-fermented Blackwell Semillon that is aged on its lees. Biggest volumes come from the blended
red and white, called Gamekeeper's Reserve and Poacher's Blend respectively. On a more positive note
the wines are widely available and reasonably priced. New from 2002 vintage is GST, unusual in
adding Touriga (Nacional) to Grenache and Shiraz. (PW)
● **Shiraz** Faith★ £B Blackwell★★ £C Old Block★★★ £D
O **Riesling** Eden Valley★★ £B

SALTRAM   Barossa Valley   www.beringerblass.com.au   A: BBl, NYg

Owner: Beringer Blass   Nurioopta Road, Angaston SA 5353
Saltram was once one of the most respected names in Australian wine but commercial growth and a
lack of focus on the leading reds meant it wasn't the first name on the lips of the many new foreign
converts to (high quality) Australian wine in the last decade or so. Since 1992 Nigel Dolan has been
the man taking responsibility for restoring some pride to these historic wines. Occasional great bottles
from the late 50s, 60s and 70s can still be unearthed from Australian cellars (many made by Nigel's

father Brian). BERINGER BLASS took control in 1996, the same year Barossa once again became the sole grape source. The wines, particularly the top two reds, now show great richness and depth; Metala Original Plantings comes from 100-year-old vines. From a top vintage like 1998 they should keep for at least a decade. Mamre Brook now offers good value, at least if the prices hold. Pepperjack is a second label seen in Australia and New Zealand. (PW)

● **Shiraz** No. I Reserve★★★ £D Metala Original Plantings (Black Label)★★★ £D
● **Shiraz** Mamre Brook★★ £B ● **Shiraz/Cabernet** Metala (White Label)★ £B
● **Cabernet Sauvignon** Mamre Brook★★ £B O **Chardonnay** Mamre Brook★ £B

SEPPELT Barossa Valley www.seppelt.com.au A: ScE

Owner: Southcorp PMB 1 Seppeltsfield, via Nurioopta SA 5355
Seppelt's historic Seppeltsfield winery is the centre of production for some marvellous Australian fortified wines but they can be difficult to obtain outside Australia. All are very individual but common to each is a marvellous complexity derived from *rancio* flavours and tertiary bottle-aged characters. The intensity and power of the wines (almost all non-vintage) is not for the faint-hearted. While some approximate to a Spanish or Portuguese equivalent, flavours and structures are quite different. Outstanding examples include 'sherries' Amontillado DP 116, Show Fino DP 117 and Show Oloroso DP 38; and Show 'port' Tawny DP 90. Para Liqueur Port is produced in two versions, non-vintage and a 100-year-old version (1897 is the most recent release). From Rutherglen come outstanding Muscat (Show Reserve DP 63) and Tokay (Show Reserve DP 57). Also see SEPPELT GREAT WESTERN (Victoria & Tasmania). (PW)

SHAW & SMITH Adelaide Hills www.shawandsmith.com A: Lib, Tan, Vne, ACh, FFW

Owner: Matthew & Michael Hill Smith, Martin Shaw Lot 4, Jones Road, Balhannah SA 5242
The warehouse winemaking operation begun by Martin Shaw and Michael Hill Smith in 1989 has evolved into an estate-based (Balhannah and Woodside), small to medium-sized operation with a stunning new winery. Early success was fuelled by a Sauvignon that proved it was possible to make a distinctive and attractive early-drinking example in the Adelaide Hills. The most impressive wine was a deep, complex and ageworthy Reserve Chardonnay, replaced from the 2000 vintage by a single-vineyard example. The M3 vineyard at Woodside is named not for an often frustratingly slow motorway escape from London but for Martin, Matthew and Michael. The wine is crafted around a core of pristine Adelaide Hills fruit and shows much promise. Unoaked Chardonnay typically shows nicely concentrated fruit but there are better examples. Merlot has been released under the Shaw & Smith label since 1999 (previously it had been made only under a second label, Incognito) with ripe, small berry fruit and good structure but missing real varietal distinction. Chardonnay and an Eden Valley Riesling under the Incognito label are attractive if undistinguished. Very recently, Riesling and a Shiraz (Elixir) have also appeared under the Shaw & Smith label. (PW)

Shaw & Smith:
O **Chardonnay** M3 Vineyard★★★ £D Unoaked★★ £B
O **Sauvignon Blanc**★★ £B ● **Merlot**★★ £D

Incognito:
O **Riesling**★ £B O **Chardonnay**★★ £B ● **Merlot**★ £B

SOUTHCORP www.southcorp.com.au

Mammoth Australian company that includes some of Australia's biggest wine names. A merger with ROSEMOUNT (see New South Wales & Queensland) in 2001 has further broadened and enhanced the company's position. Leading brands and wineries in South Australia include, PENFOLDS, ROSEMOUNT (MCLAREN VALE), WYNNS, SEPPELT (SEPPELTSFIELD), LINDEMANS, EDWARDS & CHAFFEY, Leo Buring and Tollana. Victoria provides SEPPELT GREAT WESTERN, LINDEMANS and COLDSTREAM HILLS; Western Australia, DEVIL'S LAIR. Outside Australia, Southcorp owns the James Herrick brand in Languedoc-Roussillon and Seven Peaks in California Central Coast. (PW)

TATACHILLA McLaren Vale www.tatachillawinery.com.au   A: D&D, Maj, Lwt

Owner: **Lion Nathan** *151 Main Road, McLaren Vale SA 5171*

Part of the Lion Nathan-owned Banksia wine group, the relaunched Tatachilla produces a very extensive range of wines totalling over a quarter of a million cases per year. The top two reds don't lack for structure, extract, fruit or oak, though the Foundation Shiraz is more complete and convincing than the somewhat showy Clarendon Merlot. Most of the wines show good fruit and balance but the emphasis is on upfront fruit and pleasing textures and often the wines fall away a little on the palate and at times lack for real concentration. Keystone is a characterful blend of Grenache and a little Shiraz, with rich fruit and balanced oak. Both Chardonnay and Cabernet Sauvignon are sourced from Padthaway and show distinctive fruit. The Cabernet makes an interesting contrast with the richer, deeper more black-fruited McLaren Vale example. A premium 1901 Cabernet Sauvignon is a blend of both sources. The inexpensive Breakneck Creek label includes varietal Cabernet, Merlot, Shiraz and Chardonnay. Those listed below include some but not all the wines made. (PW)

● **Merlot** McLaren Vale★ £B Clarendon★★ £D
● **Shiraz** McLaren Vale★★ £C Foundation★★★ £D
● **Grenache/Shiraz** Keystone★★ £B
● **Cabernet Sauvignon** McLaren Vale★★★ £C Padthaway★★ £B
O **Chardonnay** McLaren Vale★ £B Padthaway★ £B

TORBRECK Barossa Valley www.torbreck.com   A: HBJ, Bal, NYg, Rae, Res, BBR

Owner: David Powell Lot 51, Roennfeldt Road, Marananga SA 5360

Established in the mid-1990s, Torbreck became one of the most raved-about Barossa wineries by the turn of the century and is one of the few which produces genuinely outstanding wines that match some of the hype. David Powell manages to buy small parcels of fruit from very old unirrigated, low-yielding vines and turns into them wine with great aroma, deep fruit, structure and balance. All the reds have highish but balanced alcohol levels and a breadth and extract many other Barossa/Clare/ McLaren Vale blockbusters lack. Runrig, the top wine and first made in 1995, is Shiraz with a little Viognier (three per cent); the fruit here is sensational. As well as great depth and class, this wine has the sort of dimension and structure only encountered in the very best Côte-Rôties and needs eight to 10 years' ageing. Descendant (a vineyard established from Runrig cuttings) includes seven or eight per cent Viognier which contributes to its more open, perfumed character, but it has good extract and intensity too. The Factor, made since 1998 from 100 per cent Shiraz from old unirrigated vines, is tighter, more compact and less expressive yet promises to have the greater ageing potential. The Struie, new from 2001 is a super, stylish blend of equal parts Barossa and Eden Valley fruit while Juveniles and The Steading are southern-Rhône-style blends of Grenache, Shiraz and Mourvèdre (60/20/20 in recent vintages). Both of the latter pair are perfumed with lovely fruit and are supple and long; The Steading, aged in used and large oak, shows the better structure, but not the vibrancy or purity of Juveniles. A new white, VMR (Viognier/Marsanne/Roussanne, 60/20/20 in 2002) keeps to the Rhône theme. Woodcutters red (Shiraz) and white (Semillon) are the more affordable basics and offer good fruit. (PW)

- **Runrig✪✪✪✪✪** £H ● **The Factor★★★★★** £G ● **Descendant★★★★** £G
- **The Struie★★★** £D ● **The Steading★★★** £D ● **Juveniles★★★** £D
- **Woodcutter's Red★★** £C ○ **Woodcutter's White★** £C

TURKEY FLAT Barossa Valley www.turkeyflat.com.au A: Bal, NYg, Tan, P&S, The, Nid, But

Owner: Peter & Christie Schulz Bethany Road, Tanunda SA 5352
Turkey Flat is another producer with a priceless resource of old-vine Barossa fruit. The Schulzes have had the good fortune to have it in the family since 1865 (some planted in the 1840s!) though have only been making their own wines since 1990. A decade later they added their own winery but in the interim established their credentials particularly with Shiraz but also Grenache, Semillon and Cabernet. Shiraz is succulent and full of old-viney fruit without being overwhelmed by oak, Grenache is even more approachable but lacks a little richness and depth by comparison. Butcher's Block is named for a vineyard planted to Mourvèdre, Shiraz and Grenache and although an attractive, perfumed wine it misses the interest and intensity of better examples. Cabernet is powerful but accessible and fleshy with good intensity to its earthy, berry-fruit character. Semillon is unoaked but has good ripe fruit, coming as it does from old vines. An unusual Semillon/Marsanne blend is a new departure. Few rosés are worth seeking out but Turkey Flat's fragrant cherry berry-fruited off-dry example (from Grenache, Cabernet, Shiraz and Dolcetto) is delicious, fresh and balanced if drunk very young. (PW)

- **Shiraz★★★** £D ● **Cabernet Sauvignon★★** £C
- **Grenache Noir★★** £B ● **Mataro/Shiraz/Grenache** Butchers Block★★ £C

VERITAS Barossa Valley www.veritaswinery.com A: L&W, NYg

Owner: Rolf Binder & Christa Deans Seppeltsfield Road, Dorrien SA 5355
Veritas is one of the much lauded new stars of the Barossa. Rolf Binder draws on 40 ha of vines for a still very modest production of deep, powerful, extracted reds primarily from Rhône varieties. The most acclaimed wines to date are the Heysen Vineyard and Hanisch Shirazes, the former combining an intense, preserved black fruits, earth and licorice character with a powerful structure and requiring at least eight to 10 years' age to show its full potential. A Shiraz/Mourvèdre Pressings is of similar size and weight with rich black plum and berry fruit, while a more backward Mourvèdre/ Grenache (around two-thirds Mourvèdre) shows more of a Bandol-like character than is usual from a Barossa Mourvèdre-based wine. A Cabernet/Merlot (predominantly Cabernet Sauvignon) has intense brambly, cassis fruit and ripe tannins to match. One that doesn't need cellaring is a more forward, supple, raspberryish Shiraz/Grenache under the Christa-Rolf label. An attractive Semillon is also made under the same label. The wines remain well-priced despite the hype. (PW)

- **Shiraz** Heysen Vineyard★★★★ £C ● **Shiraz/Mourvèdre** Pressings★★★ £C
- **Mourvèdre/Grenache★★★** £C ● **Cabernet/Merlot★★★** £B
- **Shiraz/Grenache** Christa-Rolf★★ £B ○ **Semillon** Christa-Rolf★★ £B

GEOFF WEAVER Adelaide Hills www.geoffweaver.com.au A: Bal, Res, Nid

Owner: Geoff Weaver 2 Gilpin Lane, Mitcham SA 5062
From 11 ha of Lenswood vineyards established in the mid-1980s and at over 500m elevation, Geoff Weaver (ex HARDYS) makes a modest amount of increasingly good wine. Whites are best although,

while flavoursome and well-made, they can lack the extra breadth and subtlety of the finest from the Adelaide Hills. An intensely flavoured and ageworthy Chardonnay vies with an intense toasty, limey and even more cellar-worthy Riesling as the best of these. A stylish Sauvignon with ripe gooseberry fruit and a hint of smoke and blackcurrant leaf is also good if drunk with no more than a year's age. Cabernet/Merlot (typically more than 80 per cent Cabernet) needs a warm year like 98 to really succeed; otherwise cooler leafy, sappy characters become too dominant and the texture too lean. Pinot Noir shows promising cherry fruit but is as yet a little coarse with a hard underripe component. (PW)

○ Chardonnay★★★ £C   ○ Riesling★★★ £B   ○ Sauvignon Blanc★★ £C
● Cabernet/Merlot★ £C

WENDOUREE   Clare Valley   A: NYg

Owner: Tony & Lita Brady   Wendouree Road, Clare SA 5453
This Clare Valley producer maintains a cult following by sticking rigidly to a formula of maximising the extraordinary fruit produced from 12 ha of vines. The winery dates from 1895 and little seems to have changed in the 100 years or so since. The reds are massive and uncompromising, extracted and tannic yet with dense, earthy impenetrable fruit when young. Balance and ripeness are nearly always there ensuring these wines will, after 20 years or more, be complex and compelling. Shiraz/Mataro (Mourvèdre) and Shiraz/Malbec are predominantly Shiraz-based and, together with the varietal Shiraz, are perhaps more consistent than the Cabernet-based reds. None of the wines are made in much more than 500-case lots, so total production remains tiny. The prices are reasonable for the quality, given the considerable demand for them. Above all they are a cellaring investment for wine drinkers with patience. (PW)

● Shiraz★★★★ £F   ● Shiraz/Mataro★★★★ £F   ● Shiraz/Malbec★★★★ £F
● Cabernet/Malbec★★★ £F   ● Cabernet Sauvignon★★★★ £F

WIRRA WIRRA   McLaren Vale   www.wirra.com.au   A: Neg, Res, WSc

Owner: R G & R T Trott Pty   McMurtrie Road, McLaren Vale SA 5171
This medium-sized operation (70,000 cases) has a reputation way beyond its size. In recent years it has recruited expert help from the likes of Tony Jordan (GREEN POINT/DOMAINE CHANDON and, more recently, Tim James (from HARDYS). The wines are technically very sound with all the components to be really fine, yet they miss a certain flair and a natural expression. That said, quality is uniformly high and the top reds will repay keeping for five to eight years. Flagship Cabernet Sauvignon, The Angelus, and Shiraz, RSW, have been complemented by the creation of a further super-premium range of reds made in very small quantities. The Vineyard Series includes a particularly impressive Cabernet (Penley) and Shiraz (Chook Block) of more specific origins as well as a straight Grenache (Allawah). At a more affordable level, Church Block is a long-standing blend of Cabernet, Shiraz and Merlot (approximately 50/30/20) but it no longer has the vibrant fruit or style of earlier vintages. Original Blend, alluding to the first wine made by the Trott cousins, contains around two-thirds Grenache and has an accentuated berry fruit character. Whites are very well balanced and quite refined, if lacking real richness or character, and include a floral, ripely fruity Riesling and both wooded and unwooded (Sextons Acre) Chardonnay. Some fortifieds are made including VP Vintage Fortified Shiraz and Fine Old Tawny. A sparkling wine, The Cousins, is a flavoursome if not particularly refined blend of Pinot Noir and Chardonnay. The inexpensive Scrubby Rise blends, both red and white, are light, clean and fresh if drunk young. (PW)

● Cabernet Sauvignon The Angelus★★★ £D   Coonawarra Penley★★★★ £E
● Shiraz McLaren Vale★★ £C   RSW★★★   £D   McLaren Vale Chook Block★★★★ £E

● **Grenache** Barossa Valley Allawah★★★ £E   ● **Grenache/Shiraz** Original Blend★★ £B
● **Cabernet/Shiraz/Merlot** Church Block★ £B
O **Chardonnay**★★ £B   O **Riesling** Hand Picked★ £B

WOODSTOCK   McLaren Vale   www.woodstockwine.com.au   A: Ver

Owner: Scott & Anne Collett   Douglas Gully Road, McLaren Flat SA 5171
Woodstock is another of McLaren Vale's well-established wineries able to draw on its own vineyards
for a solid, reasonably priced range of wines. As well as 22 ha in McLaren Flat, 33 ha of vineyards
are located in Langhorne Creek (Angas vineyard) and a further 27 ha in Limestone Coast (Wirrega
vineyard). The leading variety unsurprisingly is Shiraz, particularly The Stocks, made since 1991 and
the flagship wine. The fruit from very old vines stands up very well to the new American oak in
which it is aged. Regular Shiraz and a Cabernet Sauvignon are both rich, ripe and concentrated if
lacking a little flair. More straightforward are a berryish Grenache and Five Feet, an improving blend
of Cabernet, Petit Verdot, Merlot and Shiraz. Whites include Semillon/Sauvignon Blanc, Riesling,
Verdelho, and Chardonnay. All show attractive, ripe, generous flavours but only the latter two can
stand a bit of age. Botrytis Sweet White is a blend of Chenin Blanc, Riesling and Semillon and is
ripe and intense if not that refined. A small amout of fortified wine is also made. (PW)
● **Shiraz**★★ £C   The Stocks★★★ £D
● **Cabernet Sauvignon**★★ £C   ● **Five Feet**★ £B
O **Chardonnay**★ £B   O **Semillon**★ £B   O **Verdelho**★ £B   O **Botrytis Sweet White**★ £C

WYNNS   Coonawarra   www.wynns.com.au   A: ScE, Maj, Odd, Nid, BBR, WSc

*Owner: **Southcorp**   Memorial Drive, Coonawarra SA 5263*
The most famous producer name in Coonawarra is a veritable colossus with 900 ha, around a third
of the terra rossa soils. Wynns' great red is the John Riddoch Cabernet, based on unirrigated vines
in the heart of the region. Made since 1982 but not in every vintage (theres no 95 or 99), it is a
magnificent rich, powerful rendition of Cabernet that makes no apology to any other great Cabernet
region but needs to be drunk with ten years' age or more. Michael Shiraz, made since 1990, is the
Shiraz equivalent of John Riddoch. Equally rich and powerful, it is always steeped in oak which adds
to its appeal for some. The fruit is very good indeed and does take up some of the oak with age but
not all, leaving a coarse, oaky feel to the finish (in the 94 for instance). The 98 is more promising
though still not one for the oak-shy. Both Michael and John Riddoch wines now use only a fraction
of the very best fruit available. The famous (Black Label) estate-based Cabernet is now a big-volume
wine but is still relatively inexpensive with the same intense blackcurrant/blackberry fruit, oak and
tannin balance it has always had. Shiraz is often at least as good and from a top vintage can add the
little extra richness that makes it an excellent buy. Cabernet/Shiraz/Merlot includes only a little
Merlot and the Cabernet and Shiraz components invariably merge for a ripe, supple, fruity red.
Chardonnay delivers fine fruit and real complexity, a far cry from some of the overoaked efforts of
years past. Riesling is often one of Australia's best bargain whites, consistently delivering a floral,
limey, fruit-driven intensity. Despite its size, Wynns stands out because of its remarkable viticultur-
al resources. (PW)
● **Cabernet Sauvignon** Black Label★★★ £C   John Riddoch★★★★★ £F
● **Shiraz**★★ £B   Michael★★★★ £F
● **Cabernet/Shiraz/Merlot**★ £B
O **Chardonnay**★★ £B   O **Riesling**★ £B

YALUMBA   Barossa Valley   www.yalumba.com   A: Neg, BBR, Res, WSc

Owner: Hill Smith family   Eden Valley Road, Angaston SA 5353
Yalumba is the only big Australian wine company to still be family owned. Winemaking has been led by Brian Walsh since the late 1980s, when the company's growth was fuelled by the huge success of the inexpensive sparkling wine, Angas Brut. With more than 650 ha of vines from diverse sources, the range is necessarily large and continually evolving, though some wines have a long history. Whites in particular have improved under Louisa Rose. Generally, none of the wines is excessively expensive and Yalumba can sometimes offer better value at a mid-priced level (£B-£C) than other Australian wineries whether large or small. Premium wines begin with The Reserve, a very limited production Cabernet Sauvignon/Shiraz blend made in 1990, 1992 and 1996. Others produced on a more regular basis include Octavius, an expensive, richly oaky, old-vine Barossa Shiraz, and The Signature (two-thirds Coonawarra Cabernet, one-third Barossa Shiraz), a suave, flattering blend streaked with vanilla (from two years in American oak) but not always as composed or convincing as it might be. Entirely Coonawarra-sourced Cabernet, The Menzies, is characterised by open, generous fruit in good vintages while newer and also Coonawarra-derived is Mawson's, which adds Shiraz and a little Merlot to Cabernet. There is also Adelaide Hills Pinot Noir and Chardonnay, the latter showing some of the stylish complexity and subtlety typical of the best examples. Much has been made of Yalumba's efforts with Viognier (it pioneered plantings of the variety in South Australia) yet even at the premium level (Virgilius) there is some way to go before competing with the best Condrieu producers. Late-harvested/botrytis styles now include Riesling, Semillon and Viognier under a Noble Pick label. Dolcetto, Nebbiolo and other varieties have also been released locally under the Vinnovation Collection label. Y is a new series of relatively inexpensive varietals including an unwooded Chardonnay, Riesling, Viognier, Merlot and Shiraz. Even cheaper is the budget brand, Oxford Landing, produced from Riverlands fruit, but the wines tend to be dilute, simple and rather innocuous. Other wineries owned by the family include the Eden Valley estates of Pewsey Vale and Heggies as well as Jansz from the Pipers River area of northern Tasmania. Pewsey Vale's Riesling has been revived with greater intensity and definition in the most recent vintages, a Contours version released with bottle age is impressive too. The Heggies wines are made by Peter Gambetta and include Riesling (occasionally also made in a botrytised version) with a pure citrus and mineral character, improving Viognier and elegant, complex Chardonnay. The only red is a variable yet sometimes stylish Merlot. Jansz sparkling wines easily surpass the Yalumba sparklers, with cooler, better defined fruit as well as better length and complexity. (PW)

Yalumba:
- **Shiraz** Barossa★ £B   Clare Valley Reserve★ £D   The Octavius★★★ £F
- **Shiraz/Viognier** Handpicked★★ £D
- **Cabernet Sauvignon** Clare Valley Reserve★ £D   Coonawarra The Menzies★★★ £D
- **Cabernet/Shiraz** Barossa★ £B   The Signature★★★ £D   ● **Cabernet/Shiraz/Merlot** Mawson's★★ £B
- **Grenache** Barossa Bush Vine★ £B   Handpicked Tri-centenary Vines★★ £D
- O **Chardonnay** Barossa★ £B   Adelaide Hills★★★ £C
- O **Viognier** Y★ £B   Eden Valley★★ £B   Virgilius★★★ £D   O **Semillon** Noble Pick★ £D
- **Sparkling Cabernet/Shiraz** 'D' Black★ £C   O **Jansz** Non-Vintage★★ £B   Vintage★★★ £C

Heggies:
O **Chardonnay**★★ £B   O **Riesling**★★ £B   O **Viognier**★★ £C   ● **Merlot**★★ £C

Pewsey Vale:
O **Riesling**★★ £B   The Contours★★★ £C

ZEMA ESTATE Coonawarra www.zema.com.au   A: MSd, WVt, Lwt

Owner: Zema family Riddoch Highway, Coonawarra SA 5263

Nearly 50 ha of estate vineyards have been built up in Coonawarra by this family during the 1980s and early 90s, the core being in the very heart of the region. The wines express much of the best of Coonawarra with dense, powerful fruit lent a little more structure from oak ageing. However the oak is restrained, making for less obvious, slightly firmer wines that really benefit from at least three to five years bottle age. The oak is more in evidence, but not overdone, in the lusher Family Reserve Cabernet Sauvignon. Though mechanically-harvested like most vineyards in Coonwarra, the vines are still hand pruned, arguably making a positive impact on quality. If slightly less good in cooler years like 97, the really shine from good to great years such as 2000 through to 98. Cluny, a somewhat lighter, softer-style Bordeaux blend (adding Merlot, Cabernet Franc and Malbec to Cabernet Sauvignon) is the most accessible. A Family Reserve Shiraz was also made in the 2000 vintage. (PW)

● **Cabernet Sauvignon★★★** £C Family Selection★★★ £D
● **Shiraz★★★** £C   ● **Cluny★★** £C

OTHER WINES OF NOTE

AUSTRALIAN DOMAINE WINES (McLaren Vale) ● **The Hattrick** (Shiraz/Grenache/Cabernet) £E
BARLETTA BROS (McLaren Vale) ● **Grenache/Shiraz** £C ● **Shiraz** Clare Valley £C
● **Sheeraz** (Limestone Coast Shiraz) £B
BASEDOW (Barossa Valley) ● **Shiraz** Johannes £E
BRIAN BARRY O **Riesling Jud's** Hill Clare Valley £B ● **Cabernet Sauvignon Jud's** Hill Clare Valley £C
BIRCHWOOD ESTATE ● **Shiraz** Decades McLaren Vale £C
● **Cabernet Sauvignon** Twin Rivers Langhorne Creek £C
BLEASDALE (Langhorne Creek) ● **Frank Potts** £C ● **Shiraz** Generations £D Bremerview £B
BREMERTON (Langhorne Creek) ● **Shiraz** Old Adam £C ● **Cabernet Sauvignon** Walter's £C
LEO BURING O **Riesling** Leonay Eden Valley £D Leonay Watervale £D
CLASSIC MCLAREN (McLaren Vale) ● **La Testa** (Shiraz/Grenache/Cabernet) £D ● **Shiraz** La Testa £F
COLONIAL WINE COMPANY (Barossa Valley) ● **Exile** (Shiraz/Mourvèdre) £G ● **Emigre**
(Shiraz/Grenache/Mourvèdre/Cabernet Sauvignon £E
CRANEFORD ● **Cabernet Sauvignon** Coonawarra £C ● **Shiraz** Barossa Valley £C
O **Riesling** Eden Valley £B
GALAH ● **Cabernet/Malbec/Shiraz** Clare Valley £C ● **Shiraz** Clare Valley £C
● **Cabernet Sauvignon** Clare Valley £C
GLAETZER (Barossa Valley) ● **Shiraz** £C Bishop £C O **Semillon** Bush Vine £B
GLENARA (Adelaide Hills) O **Riesling** £B
TIM GRAMP (Clare Valley) O **Riesling** Watervale £B ● **Cabernet Sauvignon** Watervale £B
HAAN (Barossa Valley) ● **Merlot** Prestige £C O **Viognier** £C
HAMILTON'S EWELL (Barossa Valley) ● **Shiraz** Railway £C ● **Grenache/Shiraz** Stonegarden £B
● **Cabernet Sauvignon** £C
HERITAGE WINES/STEPHEN HOFF ● **Shiraz** Barossa £B ● **Cabernet/Malbec** £B
INGOLDBY (McLaren Vale) ● **Shiraz** Reserve £C
IRVINE (Eden Valley) ● **Merlot Grand** James Irvine £F
JEANNERET (Clare Valley) ● **Shiraz** £B ● **Cabernet Sauvignon** £C
JENKE ● **Shiraz** Barossa £C
STEPHEN JOHN (Clare Valley) O **Riesling** Watervale £B
KANGARILLA ROAD ● **Shiraz** McLaren Vale £B ● **Cabernet Sauvignon** McLaren Vale £B
LENGS & COOTER ● **Shiraz** Old Vines Clare Valley £C
McLEAN'S FARM (Barossa Valley) ● **Barossa Reserve** (Shiraz/Cabernet Sauvignon) £C
● **Shiraz** Barossa Valley £C
MAGPIE ESTATE (Barossa Valley) ● **Shiraz** The Sack £B The Election £E

NOON (McLaren Vale) ● **Shiraz/Grenache** Eclipse £E
PARACOMBE (Adelaide Hills) ● **Cabernet Franc** £C ● **Shiraz** £C
PAULETT (Clare Valley) O **Riesling** Polish Hill River £B
PERTARINGA/GEOFF HARDY (Adelaide Hills) ● **Shiraz** Kuitpo £D ● **Cabernet** Kuitpo £D
PIRRAMIMMA (McLaren Vale) ● **Petit Verdot** Reserve £C ● **Shiraz** Stocks Hill £B
PUNTERS CORNER (Coonawarra) ● **Cabernet Sauvignon** £C ● **Shiraz** £C
PYCNANTHA HILL (Clare Valley) ● **Shiraz** £C
RBJ VINTNERS ● **Theologicum** (Mourvèdre/Grenache) £C
RICHMOND GROVE O **Riesling** Watervale £B ● **Shiraz** Barossa £C
SEVENHILL CELLARS O **Riesling** Clare Valley £B ● **Shiraz** Clare Valley £C
SKILLOGALEE O **Riesling** Clare Valley £C ● **The Cabernets** £C ● **Shiraz** Clare Valley £C
STEP ROAD ● **Shiraz** McLaren Vale £B ● **Sangiovese** Langhorne Creek £B
STONEHAVEN ● **Shiraz** Limestone Coast £C O **Chardonnay** Limestone Coast £B
STRINGY BRAE ● **Riesling** Clare Valley £C ● **Shiraz** Clare Valley £C
TAYLORS/WAKEFIELD CELLARS (Clare Valley) O **Riesling** Clare £B St Andrews £C
● **Shiraz** £B St Andrews £D
TEMPLE BRUER (Langhorne Creek) ● **Grenache/Shiraz/Viognier** £B
● **Cabernet/Petit Verdot** Reserve £C
TWO HANDS ● **Shiraz** Lily's Garden McLaren Vale £E Angel's Share McLaren Vale £C
VIKING (Barossa Valley) ● **Grand Shiraz** £E
WANINGA (Clare Valley) ● **Shiraz** £C
THE WILLOWS VINEYARD (Barossa Valley) ● **Cabernet Sauvignon** Barossa £B ● **Shiraz** Barossa £C
O **Semillon** Barossa £B
WILSON VINEYARD (Clare Valley) O **Riesling** Gallery Series £B

Author's choice (PW)

12 powerful Barossa/Eden Valley Shiraz
BAROSSA VALLEY ESTATE ● **Shiraz** E&E Black Pepper
GRANT BURGE ● **Shiraz** Meschach
BURGE FAMILY ● **Shiraz** Draycott
CHARLES CIMICKY ● **Shiraz** Signature
DUTSCHKE ● **Shiraz** Oscar Semmler
GREENOCK CREEK ● **Shiraz** Seven Acre
HENSCHKE ● **Shiraz** Mount Edelstone
PETER LEHMANN ● **Shiraz** Stonewell
CHARLES MELTON ● **Shiraz**
ROCKFORD ● **Shiraz** Basket Press
TORBRECK ● **Shiraz** The Factor
VERITAS ● **Shiraz** Heysen Vineyard

12 other top Shiraz
TIM ADAMS ● **Shiraz Clare Valley Aberfeldy**
JIM BARRY ● **Shiraz Clare Valley The Armagh**
BOWEN ESTATE ● **Shiraz Coonawarra**
CORIOLE ● **Shiraz McLaren Vale Lloyd Reserve**
D'ARENBERG ● **Shiraz McLaren Vale Dead Arm**
FOX CREEK ● **Shiraz McLaren Vale Reserve**
HARDYS ● **Shiraz Eileen Hardy**
HENRY'S DRIVE ● **Shiraz Padthaway Reserve**
KILIKANOON ● **Shiraz Clare Valley Covenant**

REYNELLA ● **Shiraz** McLaren Vale Basket Pressed
ROSEMOUNT ● **Syrah** McLaren Vale Balmoral
WENDOUREE ● **Shiraz** Clare Valley

12 leading Cabernet-based reds
D'ARENBERG ● **Cabernet Sauvignon** Coppermine Road
GROSSET ● **Gaia**
HENSCHKE ● **Cabernet Sauvignon** Cyril Henschke
HOLLICK ● **Cabernet Sauvignon** Ravenswood
LECONFIELD ● **Cabernet** Coonawarra
MAXWELL ● **Cabernet Sauvignon** Lime Cave
PARKER COONAWARRA ● **Terra Rossa** First Growth
PENFOLDS ● **Cabernet Sauvignon** Bin 707
PENLEY ESTATE ● **Cabernet Sauvignon** Reserve
PRIMO ESTATE ● **Cabernet Sauvignon/Merlot** Joseph
WYNNS ● **Cabernet Sauvignon** John Riddoch
ZEMA ESTATE ● **Cabernet Sauvignon** Coonawarra

10 ageworthy whites
TIM ADAMS O **Semillon** Clare Valley
BARRATT O **Chardonnay** Adelaide Hills
GROSSET O **Chardonnay** Piccadilly
GROSSET O **Riesling** Polish Hill
HARDYS O **Chardonnay** Eileen Hardy
KNAPPSTEIN LENSWOOD O **Chardonnay** Lenswood
MOUNT HORROCKS O **Riesling** Watervale
PETALUMA O **Chardonnay** Tiers
PEWSEY VALE O **Riesling** The Contours
SHAW & SMITH O **Chardonnay** M3 Vineyard

10 best buys
ANNIE'S LANE O **Riesling** Clare Valley
CASCABEL O **Riesling** Eden Valley
D'ARENBERG O **Roussanne** Money Spider
TIM GRAMP O **Riesling** Watervale
KILIKANOON O **Riesling** Clare Valley Morts Block
PETER LEHMANN ● **Shiraz** Barossa Valley
TAYLORS/WAKEFIELD CELLARS ● **Shiraz** Clare Valley
TORBRECK ● **Woodcutters Red**
WYNNS ● **Shiraz** Coonawarra
YALUMBA O **Viognier** Y

Australia/Victoria & Tasmania

Viticulture was more important in Victoria than in either South Australia or New South Wales in the 19th century but the arrival of phylloxera triggered a decline for much of the state. In the late 1960s the first steps were taken towards a revival that has rapidly gained pace since the early 1980s. Victoria offers an arguably unequalled diversity of site and climate permutations in Australia, while much more is being made of Tasmania's cool climatic conditions. As an example of an increasing regionality, Heathcote Shiraz and Tasmanian Pinot Noir are now emerging as two potentially outstanding regional styles following a mini-explosion in quality, having previously only boasted more isolated successes. Other regions such as Henty, Gippsland or Macedon Ranges also seem set to gain wider recognition amongst consumers of quality wines.

North-East Victoria

Around the towns of **Rutherglen** and **Glenrowan** is the most significant area of Victoria viticulture to have survived its fall. Unique, intensely sweet fortified wines made from raisined Muscat and Muscadelle (sold as Tokay) grapes are often subject to long ageing in hot conditions. A classification of the Rutherglen wines has recently been introduced. Beyond a basic Rutherglen category, in ascending order, are the Classic, Grand and Rare quality levels. Robust, earthy reds are also made from Shiraz, Durif and Cabernet Sauvignon. The heat of Rutherglen is in contrast to the cooler areas to the south-east. Fine Chardonnay and Pinot Noir are made at **Beechworth**. Meanwhile, in the **Alpine Valleys** (including Ovens Valley) and **King Valley,** vineyards extend from the heat of Milawa into the lower reaches of the Australian Alps, part of the Great Dividing Range, where altitude is critical to cooler-climate viticulture in New South Wales. A wide range of grapes is grown but an unusual development is the propagation of Italian varieties.

Western & Central Victoria

One of the strengths of Victoria is the great diversity of Shiraz styles, with top-class examples from **Henty**, Grampians, Pyrenees and Bendigo, the last particularly notable for examples from the now separate region of **Heathcote**. In fact, **Bendigo** achieved fame in the 19th century for its Shiraz and this is once again a very exciting area with recent examples emerging to challenge the leading estate of Jasper Hill. **Grampians** (or Great Western as it used to be known), another survivor of Victoria's 19th century viticulture, has long been famous not only for its Shiraz (one of Australia's best comes from Mount Langhi Ghiran) but also full-flavoured sparkling wines, particularly from Seppelt Great Western. Between the two is the elevated region of **Pyrenees** where both Shiraz and Cabernet Sauvignon are made, to very high standards in the case of Dalwhinnie. In **Goulburn Valley** another pocket of Victoria's wine production has been maintained. The region is vast, but the best producers are concentrated in the south in an area not a great distance east of Heathcote. Fine Shiraz is brilliant from its leading producers, Tahbilk and Mitchelton, but Cabernet Sauvignon and Riesling, as well as Marsanne and other white and red Rhône varieties are beginning to excel. Vineyards in the **Central Victorian High (or Mountain) Country** and Strathbogie Ranges are most suited to aromatic white varieties.

Port Phillip

The leading region among those lying close to the state capital of Melbourne is the **Yarra Valley**. First developed in the 19th century, its modern revival dates from the 1960s. Within its substantial confines there exist any number of mesoclimates but it is generally cool and damp by Australian standards. The Yarra Valley provides great examples of Pinot Noir and Chardonnay but also fine

Bordeaux blends, though there can be a struggle for ripeness in cooler vintages. Shiraz is less important but of high quality from the likes of Yarra Yering. The best wines are fruit-rich but softly textured and stylishly complex. There is also fine fizz although most examples include grapes sourced from outside the region. The Port Phillip zone also includes Geelong, Sunbury and the Mornington Peninsula. **Geelong**, thanks mostly to Gary Farr of Bannockburn, has a reputation for intense, powerful Shiraz, Pinot Noir and Chardonnay. The same theme is echoed in the cool **Mornington Peninsula** whose many small producers, though focusing on Pinot Noir and Chardonnay, can produce elegant, stylish Shiraz too. In **Sunbury**, especially the higher-altitude **Macedon Ranges**, the best reds are at the margins for achieving full ripeness but in the best years the quality is super in wines such as Craiglee's Shiraz or the Virgin Hills Cabernet Sauvignon-based blend.

Gippsland

Gippsland is a vast, cool zone in the south-east of Victoria with some exceptional isolated pockets of vineyards, but its marginal climate is always likely to deter all but a mad few. Yet quality can be very high even if quantities are scarce. Try to find the Pinot Noirs of Bass Phillip or the Chardonnays and Pinots of Nicholson River and Paradise Enough.

Tasmania

Across Bass Strait in Tasmania, the cooler, wetter climate has deterred the industry giants from invasion and its modern development has only really taken off in the past decade. As well as the dominant Pipers Brook group there are now dozens of tiny holdings from which tiny quantities of increasingly fine Pinot Noir are produced by a just a few talented winemakers. Riesling and Chardonnay are also successful, the latter important (with Pinot Noir) in the island's flourishing premium sparkling wine production.

A-Z of Producers by region

Beechworth
GIACONDA

Bendigo
BALGOWNIE

Central Victorian High Country
DELATITE
TALLAROOK

Geelong
BANNOCKBURN
BY FARR
SCOTCHMANS HILL
SHADOWFAX

Gippsland
BASS PHILLIP

Grampians
BEST'S
MOUNT LANGI GHIRAN
SEPPELT GREAT WESTERN

Heathcote
HEATHCOTE WINERY
JASPER HILL

King Valley
BROWN BROTHERS

Macedon Ranges
HANGING ROCK
VIRGIN HILLS

Mornington Peninsula
DROMANA ESTATE
MAIN RIDGE
PARINGA ESTATE
STONIER

Murray Darling
LINDEMANS

Nagambie Lakes (Goulburn Valley)
MITCHELTON
TAHBILK

Pyrenees
DALWHINNIE
SUMMERFIELD
TALTARNI

Rutherglen & Glenrowan
ALL SAINTS
BAILEYS OF GLENROWAN
CAMPBELLS
CHAMBERS ROSEWOOD
MORRIS

Sunbury
CRAIGLEE

Tasmania
HOOD WINES/WELLINGTON
STEFANO LUBIANA
MOORILA ESTATE
PIPERS BROOK

Yarra Valley
COLDSTREAM HILLS
DE BORTOLI (VICTORIA)
DIAMOND VALLEY
GREEN POINT VINEYARDS / DOM. CHANDON
METIER WINES
MOUNT MARY
SEVILLE ESTATE
TARRAWARRA
YARRA BURN
YARRA YERING
YERING STATION/YARRABANK
YERINGBERG

Other
BERINGER BLASS

Some comments on vintages and when to drink

The generalised Vintage charts below cover some of the most ageworthy styles and will prove most useful when taken together with comments on style and ageing within individual producer entries. Many powerful, full-bodied red can be drunk young but an increasing number will not be at their best for at least five years. Top-quality Chardonnay and Pinot Noir are likely to show at their best only with three to six years' ageing. In terms of longer-term cellaring potential, great premium Victorian Shiraz or Cabernet-based reds can improve for at least a decade. Both the vintage ratings and when to drink assessments generally only apply to the top rated examples (three star wines or higher).

Victoria & Tasmania vintages

	Bendigo/Heathcote Shiraz	Grampians/Pyrenees Shiraz	Yarra Valley/ Mornington Pen. Pinot Noir	Tasmanian Pinot Noir
2003	★★★★/★★★★★ A	★★★★/★★★★★ A	★★★★/★★★★★ A	★★★★/★★★★★ A
2002	★★★★/★★★★★ A	★★★/★★★★ A	★★★★ A	★★★★/★★★★★ A
2001	★★★★/★★★★★ A	★★★★/★★★★★ A	★★★★ B	★★★/★★★★ B
2000	★★★★ A	★★★/★★★★ A	★★★★/★★★★★ B	★★★★ B
1999	★★★★ A	★★★★ A	★★★/★★★★ C	★★★/★★★★ C
1998	★★★★/★★★★★ B	★★★★/★★★★★ B	★★★★/★★★★★ C	★★★★/★★★★★ C
1997	★★★★/★★★★★ B	★★★★ B	★★★★/★★★★★ C	★★★★ C
1996	★★★★ B	★★★★/★★★★★ B	★★★★/★★★★★ C	
1995	★★★ C	★★★/★★★★ C	★★★/★★★★ C	
1994	★★★★ C	★★★★ C		
1993	★★★ C	★★/★★★ C		
1992	★★★/★★★★ C	★★★/★★★★ C		
1991	★★★★/★★★★★ C	★★★★/★★★★★ C		
1990	★★★★★ C	★★★★/★★★★★ C		

ALL SAINTS   Rutherglen & Glenrowan   www.allsaintswine.com.au

Owner: Peter Brown   All Saints Road, Wahgunyah VIC 3687

Peter Brown bought this high-quality producer of Rutherglen Muscat and Tokay from his family (BROWN BROTHERS) in 1999. The fortifieds already have quite a reputation while the table wines are rapidly improving. The Classic-level versions are relatively youthful and raisiny, the Grand add more richness and complexity, but Rare examples are that much more refined with terrific length of flavour. As overwhelming as these wines can be, Rare is a good place to start. Otherwise there's rich, characterful Shiraz and Durif if you're looking for something muscular and meaty. The Shiraz needs at least five years' ageing, the Durif needs 10 or more. (PW)

● **Shiraz** Carlyle★★ £D   ● **Durif** Carlyle★★ £C
O **Rutherglen Muscat** Classic★★ £C   Grand★★★ £D   Rare★★★★ £F
O **Rutherglen Tokay** Classic★★ £C   Grand★★★ £D   Rare★★★★★ £F

BAILEYS OF GLENROWAN   Glenrowan   www.beringerblass.com.au   A: BBI

Owner: Beringer Blass   Taminick Gap Road, Glenrowan VIC 3675

In acquiring Baileys in 1996, Mildara Blass (now BERINGER BLASS) added some rich, original fortified Australian Muscat and Tokay to its portfolio. Apart from these sometimes outstanding fortified wines, Baileys was known for one of Victoria's most robust and gutsy Shirazes. However, in the most recent vintages the Shiraz has taken on more refinement with finer structure, yet retaining good fruit intensity. 1904 Block and 1920 Block Shiraz are named for when the vineyards on which they are based were planted. The fortifieds are particularly rich, sweet examples, lacking the elegance or refinement of others but with plenty of power and flavour. The finest versions are Winemaker's Selection but these are made only in tiny quantities and are difficult to obtain. (PW)

● **Shiraz** 1920 Block★★ £C   1904 Block★★★ £D
● **Cabernet Sauvignon**★ £B
O **Liqueur Tokay** Founder★★★ £B   O **Liqueur Muscat** Founder★★ £B

BALGOWNIE   Bendigo   www.balgownie.com   A:Cap, WRk

Owner: Forrester family   Hermitage Road, Maiden Gully VIC 3551

After a long period of ownership by Mildara Blass (now BERINGER BLASS) Balgownie is finally showing a return to the form it originally showed under its founder Stuart Anderson. Major vineyard expansion is underway and it is to be hoped that the quality of recent releases of Shiraz and Cabernet Sauvignon in particular will be maintained. Maiden Gully is the new second label, producing fresh, fruit-driven Cabernet/Shiraz and Chardonnay. (DM)

● **Shiraz**★★★ £C   ● **Cabernet Sauvignon**★★★ £C
● **Pinot Noir**★ £C   O **Chardonnay**★★ £D

BANNOCKBURN   Geelong   A: Neg, ACh, Res, NYg

Owner: Philip Harrison   Midland Highway, Bannockburn VIC 3331

Winemaker Gary Farr's achievement is all the more remarkable given the relatively low profile of Geelong as a wine-producing region. Having established a considerable reputation by the mid-1980s he has managed to keep the quality and the profile of Bannockburn among the country's leaders. Cabernet was the fashionable variety and Pinot Noir almost unheard of in Australia when a deep, rich extracted example was first produced by Farr. Much of Farr's viticultural (including high-density planting) and winemaking (partly whole-bunch pressed) practices for Pinot Noir were modelled on

Domaine DUJAC in Burgundy. The wine's deep spice, plum and savoury, undergrowth (at times, stemmy) character has always been individual; never noted for finesse, it is complex, ageworthy and impressively structured. Serré is a version based on particularly close-planted vines. Shiraz and Chardonnay have never been far behind in quality or recognition either. Cabernet/Merlot can show a leafy, slightly unripe aspect. The new wines from Gary Farr's own vineyards (BY FARR) make for an interesting comparison. (PW)

● **Pinot Noir**★★★★ £D
● **Shiraz**★★★ £D ● **Cabernet/Merlot**★★ £C
O **Chardonnay**★★★ £D

BASS PHILLIP Gippsland   A: Bal, NYg

Owner: Phillip Jones Hunts Road, Leongatha South, VIC 3953

Phillip Jones has gone out on a limb, opting for the vast, cool expanse of Gippsland for his winemaking venture. There are other notable wine producers here but they are as remote from each other as from other regions. Leongatha is further south and east than Mornington Peninsula and not far from Wilson's promontory, the mainland's most southerly point. The downside are the variable vintage conditions, producing very ripe fruit on occasions, but just as often the vines can struggle for ripeness. From very closely spaced vineyards (at least in Australian terms) he has produced Pinot Noir of a quality that puts it among the very best in Australia. Early vintages, in the mid- to late-1980s, were made in minuscule quantities but the vineyard area has been gradually increased. The key to the wines' quality is the structure and length on the palate and the purity of the fruit. Only grapes of the requisite standard make the successive levels, from the most forward yet serious regular Pinot through more intense, complex Premium to a deep, structured Reserve that needs at least five years' age. A tiny amount of Chardonnay and Gamay are also made. The wines are very expensive, in part due to their cult status. Two slightly less expensive versions of Pinot Noir, the Crown Prince and the Village, have also recently been produced. (PW)

● **Pinot Noir**★★★ £F Premium★★★★ £G Reserve★★★★ £H

BERINGER BLASS www.beringerblass.com.au

Owned by the Australian-based brewer Fosters, Beringer Blass is one of the world's largest premium-wine groups. As well as BERINGER, WOLF BLASS and JAMIESONS RUN/MILDARA, estates and brands include BAILEYS, MOUNT IDA, St Huberts, Yarra Ridge and YELLOWGLEN from Victoria; MAGLIERI and SALTRAM (including Mamre Brook and Metala) from South Australia; ROTHBURY in New South Wales & Queensland; MATUA VALLEY in New Zealand; CHATEAU ST JEAN and CHATEAU SOUVERAIN from California North Coast; STAGS LEAP WINERY and ST CLEMENT in Napa; and MERIDIAN in California Central Coast. Australian brands Greg Norman Estates and Black Opal are also part of the group.

BEST'S Grampians www.bestswines.com   A: Cac, JNi, Fsp, FWC

Owner: Thomson family Best's Road, Great Western VIC 3377

Best's is as synonymous with the Great Western (now officially Grampians) district of Victoria for table wines as Seppelt is for sparkling wines. The family has been here since the 19th century; Viv Thomson is the current incumbent with eldest son, Ben, in charge of the vineyards. The Concongella vineyards particularly favour Shiraz, which can be very good indeed, whether the consistently deep and peppery Bin O or a very limited-release Thomson Family version. A varietal Pinot Meunier comes from vines descended from original 1860s vineyard cuttings and is savoury and complex. Recent Riesling and Chardonnay show nicely defined varietal character. Merlot, Cabernet Franc, Pinot Noir and a Late Harvest Muscat are also made. From a separate estate, St Andrews, at Lake Boga (Swan Hill) come Best's more budget-priced Victoria range, including a decent Shiraz. (PW)

- **Shiraz** Great Western★★★ £C
- **Cabernet Sauvignon** Great Western★★ £C
- **Pinot Meunier** Great Western★★ £C
- O **Chardonnay** Great Western★★ £C   O **Riesling** Great Western★ £B

BROWN BROTHERS   King Valley   www.brown-brothers.com.au   A: BBE

Owner: Brown family   Meadow Creek Road, Milawa VIC 3678

With a production of three-quarters of a million cases this is quite a family business. Aided by an assortment of different mesoclimates, there is good consistency through an extremely diverse range of varietals (including Graciano, Nebbiolo and Tarrango). The wines are soundly made and competitively priced with sensitive handling of each different variety at different quality levels. However, while the wines offer agreeable drinking only rarely do they rise above the humdrum. Most wine enthusiasts will find something more individual and expressive elsewhere. Family Reserve and Limited Release bottlings generally denote higher quality and one or two wines worthy of more serious consideration include the Noble Riesling and Shiraz/Mondeuse/Cabernet. Given the proximity to Rutherglen you might reasonably expect to find fortified wine. As well as setting ALL SAINTS back on its feet before selling it to one of their own (Peter Brown), Brown Brothers makes more than adequate examples of Liqueur Muscat and Very Old Tokay. Obtaining some of the better Limited Release wines (including Riesling and Sparkling Shiraz) requires a personal visit or sending a friend or envoy to the winery. (PW)

- **Shiraz/Mondeuse/Cabernet**★★ £C   O Noble **Riesling**★★ £C
- O **Liqueur Muscat**★★ £C   O **Very Old Tokay**★★ £C

CAMPBELLS   Rutherglen & Glenrowan   www.campbellswines.com.au   A: WSS, WVt, ACh

Owner: Campbell family   Murray Valley Highway, Rutherglen VIC 3685

As always in Rutherglen the reputation of this producer depends on the quality of the fortified wine, and here they are consistently good. Impressively flavoursome in the cheaper examples, there is marvellous complexity, intensity and refinement in the Rare level Isabella Tokay and Merchant Prince Muscat. Campbells reds, in particular The Barkly Durif, can show real intensity but are high in alcohol and, although they are sometimes good examples of a robust, gutsy style, they can also be too coarse, lacking definition and even the balance to repay cellaring. While the potential seems to exist for something better, a Limited Release Malbec needs to be more soundly made. Some white wine is also made. (PW)

- O **Rutherglen Tokay**★★★ £C   Liquid Gold★★★★ £E   Rare Isabella★★★★★ £G
- O **Rutherglen Muscat**★★ £C   Rare Merchant Prince★★★★★ £G
- **Shiraz** Bobbie Burns★ £C   **Durif** The Barkly★★ £C

CHAMBERS ROSEWOOD   Rutherglen & Glenrowan   A: L&W, WVt

Owner: Chambers family   Barkley Street, Rutherglen VIC 3685

Many of the great fortified-wine producers of North-West Victoria have their beginnings in late-Victorian times; Chambers goes as far back as 1858. It is the stocks of extremely old wines that contribute not only to the incredible concentration and intensity of the Rare versions of Rutherglen Muscat and Tokay (previously sold simply as Old Liqueur Tokay and Old Liqueur Muscat) but also their remarkable texture and extraordinary flavour complexity. The tea-leaf elegance of the Tokay contrasts with the more dried-fruits, raisiny character of the Muscat. The Special bottlings, now classified Grand, are also very fine, although at the regular, if relatively inexpensive level, there is good richness but the balance and flavours are much less inspiring. Table wines are also made. Prices below are based on a 75cl bottle, though they are sold in halves. (PW)

O **Rutherglen Muscat** ★ £D Grand★★★ £F Rare✪✪✪✪✪ £G
O **Rutherglen Tokay**★★ £D Grand★★★★ £F Rare✪✪✪✪✪ £G

COLDSTREAM HILLS   Yarra Valley   www.coldstreamhills.com.au   A: ScE, Odd

Owner: Southcorp   31 Maddens Lane, Coldstream VIC 3770
This high-profile Yarra Valley winery, founded in 1985 by wine critic James Halliday (who had previously been in partnership in the Hunter Valley winery BROKENWOOD), is now part of the SOUTHCORP portfolio of small to medium-sized wineries. An original output in the first vintage of a little under 500 cases has risen to over 50,000 cases. Vineyard holdings exceed 100 ha and further expansion is planned. Burgundy is the inspiration for both Pinot Noir and Chardonnay that are age-worthy but nevertheless emphasise attractive youthful fruit. Whole bunches are used in vinifying the Pinot Noir and cool fermentation with extensive lees contact and ageing in high grade French oak provides the approachable style of the Chardonnay. There is good Cabernet Sauvignon and Merlot now as well. Briarston is a Bordeaux-style blend (varying year by year) of Cabernet Sauvignon, Merlot, Malbec and Cabernet Franc. (DM)

● **Cabernet Sauvignon** Reserve★★★ £E   ● **Briarston**★★★ £D
● **Merlot**★★ £C   Reserve★★★ £D
● **Pinot Noir**★★ £C   Reserve★★★ £D
O **Chardonnay**★★ £C   Reserve★★★ £D

CRAIGLEE   Sunbury   www.craiglee.com.au   A:M&V, The, NYg

Owner: Patrick Carmody   Sunbury Road, Sunbury VIC 3429
Craiglee is a tiny cool-climate winery and vineyard an hour or so north of Melbourne. The emphasis here is on structured, elegant, well-crafted wines with a real capacity to age. Chardonnay is marked by a restrained melon character to its fruit, with well-judged, subtle use of oak. Like nearby VIRGIN HILLS with its Cabernet Sauvignon, the Shiraz here is at the extreme margin for achieving full ripeness. Certainly in the warmer years, it is one of the best in the state. In cooler or more variable vintages the classic pepper and spice character can be slightly overwhelmed by an intense minty/spearmint influence. (DM)

● **Shiraz**★★★ £D   O **Chardonnay**★★★ £D

DALWHINNIE   Pyrenees   www.dalwhinnie.com.au   A: J&B, BBR, P&S

Owner: David & Jenny Jones   Forest Hut Rd, Moonambel VIC 3478
This is the best winery in the Pyrenees region and one of the best both in the state and Australia. The organically tended vineyards are planted in granite soils at a higher altitude than many of their neighbours and produce wines of real structure and finesse. Rick Kinzbrunner of GIACONDA is now the consultant winemaker overseeing increasingly impressive Pinot Noir. A small amount of Eagle Series Shiraz is made from a tiny 1.2-ha vineyard. Chardonnay is restrained and lightly tropical but with real intensity and structured for medium-term cellaring. Both the Cabernet and Shiraz will improve in bottle for five, often ten years. (DM)

● **Cabernet Sauvignon** Moonambel★★★ £D   ● **Shiraz** Moonambel★★★★ £D
● **Pinot Noir**★★★ £D   O **Chardonnay** Moonambel★★★★ £D

DE BORTOLI (VICTORIA) Yarra Valley www.debortoli.com.au A: DeB

Owner: De Bortoli family Pinnacle Lane, Dixon's Creek VIC 3775

De Bortoli is well-known for its big-volume inexpensive blends and varietals from Riverina but the better wines (the sweet Noble One excepted – see De Bortoli, New South Wales) are made in and, for the most part, sourced from the Yarra Valley. The winemaking is headed by Stephen Webber whose wife Leanne De Bortoli directs operations. Stylish Chardonnay, intense, dark cherry and plum-fruited Pinot Noir, and attractive, spicy Shiraz (including very limited quantities of a denser, more complex GS Reserve) appear under the Yarra Valley label, but the wines lack the depth and expression of better examples and can also suffer from a lack of complete ripeness. The flagship Melba Barrel Select is made in small quantities and is predominantly Cabernet Sauvignon with only a little Shiraz, Merlot or Cabernet Franc included. Gulf Station wines are less expensive but also sourced from the Yarra Valley. The Shiraz and Chardonnay stand out and provide good value, though other Gulf Station varietals can sometimes be surpassed by the cheaper Windy Peak wines, which include fruit from wider sources. (PW)

De Bortoli Yarra Valley:
O **Chardonnay**★★ £C ● **Pinot Noir**★★ £C
● **Shiraz**★★ £C ● **Melba Barrel Select**★★★ £E
Gulf Station:
O **Chardonnay**★ £B ● **Shiraz**★ £B

DELATITE Central Victorian High Country www.delatitewinery.com.au A: JEF, ACh, Por

Owner: Ritchie family Stoneys Road, Mansfield VIC 3722

Mansfield in the Central High Country of Victoria is one of the state's many cool outposts to be exploited. Wines have been made from these steep slopes, with views across to the alpine retreat of Mount Buller, since 1982. The wines are lighter and exhibit cooler, more delicate flavours than the majority of Australian wines. So much so that a lack of ripeness can be a problem and the most successful varieties are those most suited to more marginal climates. There's an interesting aromatic, floral Riesling and a spicy Gewürztraminer, both of which, though light and crisp, are intense and ageworthy. Chardonnay shows some style too, though it lacks a little depth. Reds are markedly cool and minty in style and only occasionally achieve ripe tannins in the Cabernet or Cabernet-based Devil's River, a blend of Cabernet Sauvignon, Malbec and Shiraz. A number of other varietals are made including Sauvignon Blanc, Pinot Gris, Pinot Noir, Merlot and Shiraz. Some sparkling wine, Delmelza Pinot/Chardonnay, is also made. (PW)

O **Riesling**★★ £B O **Gewürztraminer** Dead Mans Hill★★ £B
O **Chardonnay**★ £C

DIAMOND VALLEY Yarra Valley www.diamondvalley.com.au A: Cac, WVt, T&W

Owner: David Lance 2130 Kinglake Road, St Andrews VIC 3761

Small winery established in 1982 producing slightly over 5,000 cases a year. While the Yarra Valley range is well-crafted with good varietal fruit, it is the Estate wines, in particular the superb Pinot Noir, which stand out. The Chardonnay is rich and lightly tropical with well judged oak, while the Estate Pinot is marked by concentrated – almost gamey – forward plum and black fruit, all underpinned by a not inconsiderable oak influence. Showy in its youth but with real structure too, it will be all the better for five years' ageing. (DM)

● **Cabernet Merlot**★★ £C Estate★★★ £D
● **Pinot Noir**★★ £C Estate★★★★ £D
O **Chardonnay**★★ £C Estate★★★ £D

DROMANA ESTATE Mornington Peninsula www.dromanaestate.com.au A: Cac

Owner: Dromana Estate Ltd   25 Harrisons Road, Dromana VIC 3936

Garry Crittenden continues to drive this small Mornington Peninsula estate, which is now expanding into the Yarra Valley as well. The premium label is Dromana Estate for wines from estate-grown fruit. The focus is on Pinot Noir and Chardonnay but also includes a somewhat leafy but increasingly ripe, spicy berry-fruited Cabernet/Merlot and a stylish, cool but ripe Shiraz. Both Chardonnay and Pinot Noir are good examples but the relatively restrained, complex Reserves offer much more. Much of the interest in this producer comes from the production of Italian varietals based on King Valley fruit. Sold under the Garry Crittenden label, all are recently much improved (particularly the 2000 vintage) and are generally attractive and well-made though only Arneis, Barbera and Dolcetto really come close to the intensity and character of good Italian examples; Nebbiolo and Sangiovese still want for finesse in both fruit and tannins. Schinus is a second label for Sauvignon Blanc, Chardonnay and Merlot of variable quality from diverse sources. (PW)

● **Pinot Noir**★ £B Reserve★★★ £D
● **Cabernet/Merlot**★ £B ● **Shiraz**★★ £B
● **Barbera** i Garry Crittenden★ £B ● **Dolcetto** i Garry Crittenden★ £B
O **Chardonnay**★ £B Reserve★★★ £D O **Arneis** i Garry Crittenden★★ £B

BY FARR Geelong A:Tan, NYg

Owner: Gary Farr   c/o Bannockburn, Midland Highway, Bannockburn VIC 3331

In 1999 Gary Farr released four new varietals from 4.8 ha of his own vineyards adjacent to BANNOCKBURN. Initially the wines were known as Bannockburn by Farr but are now simply By Farr. The wines are made at the Bannockburn winery but, coming from new clones on differing soil types and aspects, the wines are distinctly different. Shiraz, Chardonnay and Pinot Noir all show a little more elegance and refined varietal character, if not quite the weight and richness, at least not yet. Viognier is the major point of difference and seems set to show the hallmark Bannockburn weight and structure and therefore eclipse the high-alcohol but structure-deficient character of many Australian examples of this variety. It is too early to rate these wines yet but all are priced significantly higher than those from Bannnockburn. (PW)

GIACONDA Beechworth www.giaconda.com.au A: M&V, Res, NYg

Owner: Rick Kinzbrunner   McClay Rd, Beechworth VIC 3747

Production here is tiny at around a 1,000 cases. As a result the wines are extraordinarily difficult to track down. A small amount is sold in the UK with the bulk accounted for by a dedicated mailing list and more recently sold by tender over the internet. Pinot Noir and Chardonnay are Australian cool-climate classics, almost Burgundian in style with an approach to vinification that mirrors the best of the Côte d'Or. The Pinot Noir is astonishingly rich and opulent, the Chardonnay structured and immensely refined: it requires a minimum of five years' ageing to really unfurl and is regularly on the cusp of five stars. There is a new stylish Shiraz and a rich, full-on white blend of Chardonnay and Roussanne (85/15), Nantua Les Deux, and 100 per cent Roussanne, Aeolia. All of the wines will keep very well. (DM)

● **Cabernet/Merlot**★★★ £D ● **Pinot Noir**★★★★ £E
● **Shiraz** Warner Vineyard★★★★ £D
O **Chardonnay**★★★★ £E O **Nantua Les Deux**★★★ £D

GREEN POINT VINEYARDS/DOM. CHANDON   Yarra Valley   A: MHn, Vne, Amp, IVi

Owner: LVMH   Maroondah Highway, Coldstream VIC 3770
The prestigious Yarra Valley operation is one of the most important of the Moët-Hennessey foreign investments. It could probably survive on the tourists alone but, with a team led once more by Dr Tony Jordan (ex WIRRA WIRRA in South Australia), an increasing number of still and sparkling wines are made to a high standard. Still and sparkling Pinot Noir and Chardonnay are characterised by clarity, intensity and good breadth. Reserve Chardonnay adds a little depth and more lavish if sophisticated oak treatment; a Reserve Pinot Noir shows concentrated plummy fruit and a powerful structure. Of the sparkling wines the Vintage Brut is the mainstay but a little Blanc de Blancs, Blanc de Noirs and Brut Rosé are also made. All show fine texture, ripe fruit and good richness and improve with a little age. A non-vintage blend is not of the same order. Recently released is a new premium bottling Cuvée Prestige in a richer, late-disgorged (with six years on its lees) style – its first vintage is 1995. The still wines are marketed as Green Point Vineyards, the sparkling wines as part of the worldwide Chandon Estates entity (Green Point by Chandon). (PW)
O **Vintage Brut**★★★ £C   O **Vintage Blanc de Blancs**★★★ £C   O **Vintage Blanc de Noirs**★★ £C
O **Chardonnay**★★ £C Reserve★★★ £D
● **Pinot Noir**★ £C Reserve★★★ £D

HANGING ROCK   Macedon Ranges   www.hangingrock.com.au   A: TWS, AWA, IWD

Owner: John and Ann Ellis   88 Jim Road, Newham VIC 3422
Both John and Ann (née Tyrrell, daughter of the late Murray TYRRELL) are steeped in winemaking experience, having been involved with some of the country's leading producers before securing their own property in 1985. Their vineyards on the Jim Jim, an extinct volcano, are as cool as any in Australia and are planted predominantly to Pinot Noir and Chardonnay for one of Australia's top sparkling wines, Macedon Cuvée. A blend of vintages, the current release (VIII) is 60 per cent Pinot to 40 Chardonnay. Consistency and richness are maintained by drawing from a substantial resource of reserve wines for each successive release. A rich, intense Shiraz is from the warmer Heathcote region, famed for Shiraz of the quality of JASPER HILL. Production resumed in 1997, after a break of five years, from new vineyards (chiefly Athol's Paddock and Colbinabbin Estate) and has been a powerful expression of fruit and oak in every vintage since. Other wines include a cool, crisp Sauvignon Blanc from the Jim Jim vineyards and some late-harvested styles. Victoria-labelled wines come from diverse sources while Rock is an inexpensive second label. (PW)
● **Shiraz** Heathcote★★★ £C
O **Macedon Cuvée**★★★ £C
O **Sauvignon Blanc** Jim Jim★ £B

HEATHCOTE WINERY   Heathcote   www.heathcotewinery.com.au   A: HHB, WRk

Owner: Stephen Wilkins   183-185 High Street, Heathcote VIC 3523
An improving Central Victoria winery with an intriguing assortment of grape varieties. Vineyards total 25 ha either owned or under contract in a warm elevated area of 200–250 m that escapes some of the cloud cover more typical in southern Victoria but is cooler than Bendigo. The Newlan's Lane vineyard provides a Chardonnay with a mix of citrus and ripe peach fruit that is balanced and attractive with just a couple of years' age. The same vineyard also provides an attractive, gently varietal example of Viognier (Curagee), though, as with many Australian examples, it lacks real Viognier weight and definition in the mouth. Curagee is bigger and more muscular than Mail Coach Shiraz which is relatively lightly oaked with lovely texture, weight and balance. (PW)

● **Shiraz** Mail Coach★★ £B   Curagee★★ £D
O **Chardonnay**★ £B

HOOD WINES/WELLINGTON   Tasmania

Owner: Andrew & Jenny Hood   Cnr Richmond & Denholms Roads, Cambridge TAS 7170
It's surprising that Andrew Hood has time to make a little wine for himself given the number of other small wineries that benefit from his expertise. Numerous tiny estates (including Elsewhere Vineyard and Meadowbank) can boast really good Pinot Noir as well as other varieties that producers from warmer parts of the mainland can only envy. His signature style is full ripeness, good texture, delicate extraction and restrained oak in both Chardonnay and Pinot Noir. All of his own wines are sold under the Wellington label. A cool, slightly minerally Riesling is also made in an Iced version where the unfermented juice is frozen to remove some water and increase concentration. It is difficult to find these wines, but if you're in Tasmania… (PW)
● **Pinot Noir**★★★ £C
O **Chardonnay**★★★ £C   O **Riesling**★★ £C

JASPER HILL   Heathcote   A:Yap, P&S, NYg, N&P

Owner: Ron Laughton   Drummonds Lane, Heathcote VIC 3523
The production here is small at around 3,000 cases a year and the wines can be very difficult to track down but its worth the effort. Like the finest producers in the Northern Rhône, the approach is one of minimal intervention: no irrigation, minimal vineyard treatments and virtually sulphur-free reds. Yields are tiny from the sparse, granite-based soils, between one and two tons to the acre. Just one white is produced, a powerful stuctured Riesling, full of subtle citrus but minerally and toasty with three or four years' ageing. The two Shirazes are remarkable, the Georgia's Paddock slightly more opulent, both rich, concentrated and full of exotic dark berry fruit and spice, with a marvellous supple texture underpinning them. They are amongst Australia's very finest. While they will easily age for twenty years or more they can be broached with just a few years in the cellar. A Nebbiolo is also now available and looks very promising. (DM)
● **Shiraz** Georgia's Paddock★★★★★ £F   ● **Shiraz/Cabernet Franc** Emily's Paddock★★★★★ £F
O **Riesling** Georgia's Paddock★★★ £C

LINDEMANS   Murray Darling www.lindemans.com.au   A: ScE

*Owner: **Southcorp**   Edey Road, Karadoc via Mildura VIC 3496*
Lindemans' principal production complex is at Karadoc but the best wines come from the Limestone Coast, and, at least until recent times, the Hunter Valley. The Karadoc facility is one of Australia's largest and produces millions of bottles of Bin 65 Chardonnay that are made year in, year out along with other big-volume Bin wines. There are also the LEO BURING wines and a number of the finest fortified wines that can be found in Australia. Given the quantities made you might expect the Bin 65 to taste rather simple and dilute or, worse, as confected and unnatural as some of its rivals do. Yet it delivers a lot of flavour, good balance and a certain style that owes much to good fruit sources; part of the fruit is said to come from Padthaway. The red equivalent to Bin 65 is the Bin 45 Cabernet Sauvignon but it doesn't reach the same standard. Nevertheless, this, Bin 50 Shiraz and Bin 40 Merlot, although not the best, are far from being the weakest performers (*vis à vis* other big brands) in their price category. (PW)
O **Chardonnay** Bin 65★ £B

STEFANO LUBIANA Tasmania www.stefanolubiana.com A: NYg, UnC

Owner: Steve & Monique Lubiana 60 Rowbottoms Road, Granton TAS 7030
This small Tasmania operation is a veritable giant compared to some of the micro-boutique operations that make just a few hundred cases here. The 10 ha of vineyards lying above the Derwent River are part of a much larger property and produce Pinot Noir and Chardonnay of a persuasive style and refinement. The fruit in each is very pure and intense, the wines elegant and vibrant and capable of at least three or four years' age. As well as second versions of Chardonnay (Sur Lie) and Pinot Noir (Primavera), Sauvignon Blanc and Pinot Grigio are made. A non vintage Brut sparkling wine is based on Pinot Noir with a little Chardonnay. (PW)

● **Pinot Noir**★★★ £D
O **Chardonnay**★★★ £D O **Riesling**★★ £D

MAIN RIDGE Mornington Peninsula www.mre.com.au A: Cac, NYg

Owner: Nat & Rosalie White 80 William Road, Red Hill VIC 3937
Tiny but now long-established Mornington Peninsula estate dedicated to Chardonnay and Pinot Noir. Though established around the same time as STONIER and DROMANA ESTATE, Main Ridge chose to remain small and artisanal in its production. Although the wines can show some vintage variation, at best they are elegant and classy yet with plenty of drive and personality. Prices are high but not dissimilar to their neighbours'. Reserve, Half Acre is made from a vineyard with shallow topsoil. (PW)

● **Pinot Noir**★★★ £D Half Acre★★★ £D
O **Chardonnay**★★★ £D

METIER WINES Yarra Valley A: HHB, P&S

Owner: Martin Williams Healesville Road, Yarra Glen VIC 3775
Tiny boutique winery owned by Martin Williams, who also makes the wine at TALLAROOK. The Chardonnay is extremely well-crafted with subtle use of oak and lees and currently offers exceptional value. The Pinot Noir has a fine texture and undoubtedly has potential, but the fruit quality has been more variable as has its propensity to age. A tiny amount of Viognier is produced from high-altitude vineyards in the Central Victorian High Country. (DM)

● **Pinot Noir** Schoolhouse Vineyard★★ £E Tarraford Vineyard★★ £C
O **Chardonnay** Schoolhouse Vineyard★★★★ £C Tarraford Vineyard★★★★ £C

MITCHELTON Nagambie Lakes www.mitchelton.com.au A: Men, WSc, FWC

Owner: **Lion Nathan** *Mitchellstown Road, Nagambie VIC 3608*
Located on the banks of the Goulburn River, Mitchelton is part of a prestigious grouping (others are PETALUMA and KNAPPSTEIN in South Australia and STONIER) acquired in late 2001 by Australasian brewer Lion Nathan. A well-established portfolio of wines has been developed and maintained over nearly three decades by the highly respected winemaker Don Lewis. The intense floral and lime scented Blackwood Park Riesling is also made in Late Harvested and Botrytis versions. Many of the whites combine citrusy flavours with more exotic, tropical notes, together with both vigour and good acidity. The top red, Print Shiraz, can exude a class and finesse not seen in the Barossa blockbuster styles. French oak is favoured for reds and a concerted move to lower yields since the mid-90s has brought increased concentration to many of the wines. A new Vineyard Series label includes varietal Chardonnay, Viognier, Shiraz and Cabernet. Mitchelton was also one of the first to

develop red and white Rhône blends, once known as Mitchelton III but now as Airstrip white, comprising Marsanne, Roussanne and Viognier, and Crescent red from Shiraz, Mouvèdre and Grenache. Varietal Marsanne is a speciality with intense honeysuckle aromas and flavours and has even been made in a *vin de paille* version. Victoria Series or Preece-labelled varietals can sometimes prove very good value for money. Least expensive are the Thomas Mitchell wines. (PW)

● **Shiraz** Victoria Series★ £B Vineyard Series★★ £C Print★★★★ £E
● **Shiraz/Mourvèdre/Grenache** Crescent★★ £C
O **Chardonnay** Victoria Series★ £B Vineyard Series★★ £C
O **Viognier** Vineyard Series★ £C O **Marsanne/Roussanne/Viognier** Airstrip★★ £C
O **Riesling** Blackwood Park★★★ £C

MOORILLA ESTATE Tasmania www.moorilla.com.au A: ABy

Owner: Moorilla Estate Trust 655 Main Road, Berriedale TAS 7011
The impressive new Moorilla museum of antiquities appears likely to become more of a magnet for visitors than the wines. Yet this long-surviving Tasmania winery, though no longer family-owned, has been resurgent under Alain Rousseau (although he has now left). Good cool, citrusy whites include a tight, minerally, appley Riesling, sometimes also made in a rare botrytised version. A Reserve Pinot Noir of increasing ripeness and richness, but with impressive texture and complexity too, is one of a growing number of fine Tasmania Pinots – difficult as they are to acquire. Sourced from the warmer Tamar Valley, Reserve Cabernet and Reserve Cabernet/Merlot might once have tasted rather tough and unripe but in recent good vintages the wines have been ripe and concentrated. Dense, powerful Syrah also shows much promise. (PW)

● **Pinot Noir** White Label★ £B Reserve★★★ £C
● **Cabernet/Merlot** Reserve★★ £C ● **Cabernet Sauvignon** Reserve★★★ £C
O **Riesling**★★ £B O **Chardonnay** White Label★★ £C
O **Estate Brut**★★ £C

MORRIS Rutherglen & Glenrowan A: Cas

Owner: Orlando Wyndham group (Pernod Ricard) Mia Mia Road, Rutherglen VIC 3685
Although owned by Orlando since 1970, the tradition of family winemaking, producing some of Australia's excellent fortified wines, continues here – David Morris having taken over from his famous father Mick Morris in 1993. There is great age in these intelligently blended wines, particularly in the Old Premium versions of fortified Muscat and Tokay (Muscadelle). The regular Liqueur Muscat, tasting of intense rich, slightly toffeed, sweet raisins, is very typical of the style, even if it doesn't have the elegance which might tempt some palates to try another example. The Old Premium version of Muscat offers similar intensity but more complexity, while in Old Premium Tokaythereis excellent richness but arguably less elegance and less of the classic Tokay flavours of other examples. Nonetheless the quality, richness and complexity in all the Liqueur Muscat and Liqueur Tokay wines can't be disputed. Old Premium 'Amontillado' and 'Tawny Port' are also made. Red wines including Shiraz and Durif can be sound but lack refinement. (PW)

O **Liqueur Muscat**★★ £B Old Premium★★★★ £E
O **Liqueur Tokay**★★★ £B Old Premium★★★★ £E

MOUNT LANGI GHIRAN Grampians www.langi.com.au A: Lib, ACh, Res, Vne

Owner: Trevor Mast & Riquet Hess Warrak Road, Buangor, VIC 3375
Dynamic, go-ahead organic vineyard and winery operation based in the remote Grampians in

Central Victoria. The real interest here are the top reds and in particular the remarkable and stylish Shiraz, among Australia's top half-dozen examples of the variety. Made from 44-year-old vines, the 2002 includes two per cent Viognier. A richly textured Cabernet/Merlot (one third Merlot) from estate vineyards contrasts with the cool, minty Joanna Cabernet which comes from Wrattonbully fruit. Sangiovese looks set to improve as fruit from clones from ISOLE E OLENA start to come on-stream. A second Shiraz, Cliff Edge, first made in 1999, shows promise too while the reasonably-priced Billi Billi Creek, dominated by Shiraz but with around 30 per cent Grenache, has plenty of style if not the greatest depth. Whites are well fashioned including a popular fruit-driven Pinot Gris. The Four Sisters wines (produced in collaboration with Alister Purbrick of TAHBILK) are vinified to emphasise their fruit. Trevor Mast has recently established another partnership with the Rhône *négociant* M CHAPOUTIER and the Terlato Wine Group. They have planted new vineyards in the Pyrenees and the Grampians for premium Shiraz. (PW)

Mount Langhi Ghiran:
- **Shiraz★★★★★** £E Cliff Edge★★★ £C ● **Cabernet/Merlot★★★★** £D
- **Cabernet Sauvignon** Limestone Coast Joanna★★★ £C
- **Sangiovese** Nut Block★★ £C ● **Shiraz/Grenache/Cabernet** Billy Billy Creek★★ £B
- O **Riesling★★** £B O **Pinot Gris★★** £B

Four Sisters:
- **Grenache/Shiraz** McLaren Vale★ £B O **Sauvignon/Semillon** McLaren Vale★ £B

MOUNT MARY Yarra Valley   A: Bal, JAr, BBR, F&R

Owner: John Middleton 22–24 Coldstream West Road, Lilydale VIC 3140
John Middleton's Mount Mary is one of Victoria's holiest of holies, where the quality is whispered about by devotees, in complete contrast to the ballyhoo that emanates from South Australia's big guns. Quantities are small and grapes come from the estate's unirrigated vineyards. Quintet (Cabernet Sauvignon, Merlot, Cabernet Franc, Malbec and Petit Verdot) is graceful and refined with intense berry and cassis flavours, a wine that will easily keep for 20 years from a good vintage. The Pinot Noir can age for about half as long, starting out deceptively light but building on its pure fruit core with age. Two whites, a Chardonnay and Triolet (a blend of Sauvignon, Semillon and Muscadelle) show restrained fruit and oak but can age well too. (PW)

- **Quintet★★★★** £G ● **Pinot Noir★★★** £G
- O **Triolet★★★** £F O **Chardonnay★★★** £F

PARINGA ESTATE Mornington Peninsula www.paringaestate.com.au   A: Adm

Owner: Lindsay McCall 44 Paringa Rd, Red Hill South, VIC 3937
Top-notch small estate with around 4,000 cases produced annually. What is most remarkable about Paringa is not only the quality of the Chardonnay and Pinot Noir but also its Shiraz. Certainly this tends to work best in warmer years but when vintage conditions are benign the wine benefits from an unusually long ripening period. The PE label is a combination of bought-in fruit and younger Paringa vines. (DM)

- **Pinot Noir★★★** £D PE★★£C ● **Shiraz★★★★** £D
- O **Chardonnay★★★** £D PE★★ £C

PIPERS BROOK Tasmania www.pbv.com.au   A: Cap, ACh, FWC

Owner: Pipers Brook Vineyard Limited 1216 Pipers Brook Road, Pipers Brook TAS 7254
Dr Andrew Pirie founded the winery back in 1974 and it has risen to become the dominant force in

the tiny Tasmanian wine industry and includes more than 200 ha of vineyards. The majority of shares is now held by Kreglinger Australia, part of the Belgian de Moor family's Kreglinger group, who have also established a new venture in South Australia's Mount Benson region. Early 2003 saw the sudden departure of Andrew Pirie (to PARKER Coonawarra Estate) but the focus has always rightly been on cool-climate varieties, in particular Pinot Noir, Chardonnay and Riesling. The wines generally show lovely varietal fruit characters with extra nuance and richness as well as oak in the Reserve-level wines. Sparkling wine has also been a strength since the much-heralded launch of Pirie, which is arguably the best Australian sparkling wine yet made. The wines don't offer exceptional value but are priced fairly for the quality compared to other Australian examples or equivalent Burgundian quality in Pinot or Chardonnay. With the 1999 vintage a small amount of single-site Pinot Noir (The Blackwood and The Lyre from sections of the Heemskerk Vineyard) joined a Chardonnay (The Summit) made since 1997 from 2 ha. All are priced £E. Ninth Island is a separate entity drawing largely from the former Rochecombe vineyards and as well as very creditable Chardonnay and Pinot Noir there are several other varietals and a non-vintage Brut. (PW)

Pipers Brook:
● **Pinot Noir** Estate★★ £C Reserve★★★ £D
O **Chardonnay** Estate★★ £C Reserve★★★ £D
O **Riesling** Estate★★ £C **Gewürztraminer** Estate★★ £C
O **Pirie Vintage★★★★** £D

Ninth Island:
● **Pinot Noir★** £B   O **Chardonnay★** £B

SCOTCHMANS HILL   Geelong   www.scotchmanshill.com.au   A: Orb, Odd, WVt, WSc

Owner: Browne family   190 Scotchmans Road, Drysdale VIC 3222
Situated on the Bellarine Peninsula just south-east of Geelong the vineyards enjoy a cool maritime climate. Production is sizeable for the region at more than 60,000 cases but quality remains admirable, particularly considering the prices. The Pinot Noir is a strength, with ripe plum fruits, nicely handled oak and a seductive texture, while Shiraz and Cabernet/Merlot can be individual and appealing, if sometimes struggling for ripeness. The Chardonnay is restrained with just a hint of oak showing through in the background. The Sauvignon is grassy and nettley, and marked by lightly tropical cool fermentation aromas. It is best drunk as young as possible. Swan Bay is the second label mainly produced from a second property, Spray Farm. (PW)

● **Pinot Noir★★★** £C Swan Bay★ £B   ● **Cabernet/Merlot★★★** £C   ● **Shiraz★★★** £C
O **Chardonnay★★** £C   O **Sauvignon Blanc★★** £B

SEPPELT GREAT WESTERN   Grampians   www.seppelt.com.au   A: ScE

Owner: Southcorp   Moyston Road, Great Western VIC 3377
This is Seppelt's renowned sparkling-wine operation, which also includes quite a number of very good table wines, many of which are sourced from cool-climate areas where the company has significant plantings. The Drumborg varietals, which come from the cool south-west corner of Victoria, are now some of the best wines in the range. Riesling and Pinot Noir highlight the potential but even Cabernet Sauvignon, which can show a cool, leafy influence, can also be cedary and berryish in the best years. Pinot Grigio and a new Chardonnay are sourced from the same area as is much of the fruit for ripely plummy Sunday Creek Pinot Noir. Dorrien Cabernet Sauvignon, based on an old-vine parcel of a vineyard of the same name in the Barossa, is a richly textured, earthy, cedary and black-fruited wine aged in (mostly) French oak. Partalunga Chardonnay comes from vineyard holdings in the Adelaide Hills; it is only made in the best years but can show some of the distinctive regional character. Harpers Range

Cabernet and Chalambar Shiraz are blended across a number of cooler regions but increasingly show good fruit and balanced tannins. The range of sparkling wines has been consolidated but is led by a distinctive creamy, citrusy Salinger (Chardonnay, Pinot Noir and Pinot Meunier), for long one of the most consistent premium Australian sparkling wines, and Drumborg Show Sparkling Reserve, which has six years on its lees. Vintage Brut Fleur de Lys is less expensive and more overtly fruity but with some leesy influence. However most exceptional of the traditional-method sparkling wines made here is the red Great Western Show Sparkling Shiraz (which spends six years on its lees and is only available around 10 years after the vintage), arguably the most intriguing and complex example of its type. The cheaper Original version comes from South Australian fruit. Inexpensive varietals and blends are sold under the Moyston label. The best wines unfortunately are not always easy to find outside of Australia. (PW)

● **Cabernet Sauvignon** Dorrien★★★ £C Harpers Range★ £B
● **Shiraz** Great Western★★★ £C Chalambar★ £B
● **Pinot Noir** Drumborg★★ £D Sunday Creek★ £C
○ **Chardonnay** Partalunga★★★ £C ○ **Riesling** Drumborg★★ £C
○ **Salinger Vintage**★★ £C ● **Sparkling Shiraz Vintage Show**★★★ £D

SEVILLE ESTATE Yarra Valley www.sevilleestate.com.au A: Lib, Vne, NYg, WVt, ACh

Owner: Brokenwood & others Linwood Road, Seville VIC 3139
Seville Estate, founded by Dr Peter McMahon, was one of the Yarra Valley's pioneers (of the modern era) and has produced small volumes of fine varietals, particularly Shiraz, during the past 30 years. Top New South Wales producer BROKENWOOD has had a major stake since 1997 and the wines are now made by their widely respected winemaker, Iain Riggs. The vineyards are on the cooler side of the valley and accordingly suffer a little in cooler vintages. At their best however they are powerful and fruit-accented with well-integrated oak and good definition both in terms of structure and flavour. Chardonnay can improve for up to five years; reds are better with five years' or more. Small amounts of Reserve Cabernet and Shiraz (from vines more than 30 years old) have recently been produced. (PW)

● **Shiraz**★★★ £C ● **Cabernet Sauvignon**★★ £C
● **Pinot Noir**★★★ £C ○ **Chardonnay**★★ £C

SHADOWFAX Geelong www.shadowfax.com.au A: M&V, Res, WVt, NYg

Owner: Mansion group K Road, Werribee VIC 3030
Shadowfax (a name taken from Tolkien's *Lord of the Rings*) is a very new, exciting operation based in Werribee Park between Melbourne and Geelong. Sourcing small parcels of the best grapes from a number of districts, young Matt Harrop has the responsibility of producing wines to match the high standards set by the acclaimed Mansion Hotel, but has a stunning new winery in which to do so. Besides a Sauvignon Blanc/Semillon of good weight and interest, there is full but tightly structured Chardonnay (made from Geelong and Yarra Valley fruit) and vibrant, spicy, fruit-driven Shiraz from McLaren Vale. The latter two wines impress for their structure as well as the balanced use of new oak. But these are only the beginnings, as Pinot Noir from Geelong and Cabernet Sauvignon from the Yarra have been added and there's also two single-vineyard Shirazes (One Eye, Pink Cliffs) first produced from low-yielding Heathcote fruit in 2001, which will be rated with further vintages. (PW)

○ **Sauvignon Blanc/Semillon**★★ £B ○ **Chardonnay**★★★ £C
● **Shiraz** McLaren Vale★★ £C

STONIER   Mornington Peninsula   www.stoniers.com.au   A: Men, Vne, FWC

*Owner: **Lion Nathan**   2 Thompsons Lane, Merricks VIC 3916*
Established in 1977 by Brian Stonier, this operation was one of the first premium wineries to emerge from the Mornington Peninsula. The potential first highlighted by Stephen Hickinbotham has been cemented under his successor Tod Dexter since the late 1980s. Dexter's own vineyard of 7ha contributes to the Stonier resource. The recent inflow of money, first from PETALUMA and lately from Lion Nathan, might prompt talk of a sell-out but the structure and resources suggest otherwise. Of the latest releases, regular Chardonnay and Pinot Noir show lovely fruit and balance, though want for depth and structure; the Reserves however offer much more – more, indeed, than the price differential suggests. The Reserve Chardonnay is splendidly distinctive with a gently spicy, oak-influenced, lemon zest, lemon peel and nectarine character and good breadth and intensity. The Reserve Pinot Noir shows balanced oak together with good depth and ripeness. (PW)

● **Pinot Noir**★£C Reserve★★★£D
O **Chardonnay**★£B Reserve★★★ £C

SUMMERFIELD   Pyrenees   www.pyrenees.org.au/summerfield.htm   A: BBR, NYg

Owner: Summerfield family   Main Road, Moonambel, VIC 3478
This predominantly red-wine producer has been making wines since 1979, having first established vineyards in 1970. The first real leap in quality came with consultancy from Drew NOON (South Australia), the then state oenologist, in the late 1980s. Mark Summerfield, now responsible for the winemaking, has set about reducing yields but retains a measure of input from Noon. The powerful reds are richer, riper, deeper and more consistent than previously but always with a measurable dash of oak. Shiraz is the real star, particularly the Reserve (Estate in older vintages). The muscular, minty Reserve Cabernet is now beginning to benefit from the use of some French oak. Both Reserves will keep for a decade or more (PW)

● **Shiraz**★★£C ● Reserve★★★£E
● **Cabernet Sauvignon**★£C Reserve★★£D
● **Cabernet/Merlot**★★£C

TAHBILK   Nagambie Lakes   www.tahbilk.com.au   A: PLh, WVt, Fsp, The

Owner: Alister Purbrick   Tahbilk, VIC 3608
Historic winery which along with HENSCHKE has some of the oldest plantings of Shiraz anywhere in the world. One plot dates back to 1860. Production is not inconsiderable at close to 100,000 cases a year and an extensive range of wines are available at the cellar door. Vinification of the reds is very traditional: open-top wooden fermenters are used and hand plunging *(pigeage)* employed. In no small part the considerable age of the vines contributes to the structured, tannic style of the wines when young. They are very ageworthy but demand patience, up to 10 years for the reserves and 1860 Vines. Of good fruit-driven whites, the Marsanne is a regional benchmark and the largest single planting in Victoria. New and promising too are varietal Roussanne and Viognier. (DM)

● **Cabernet Sauvignon**★★£B Reserve★★★£D
● **Shiraz**★★£B Reserve★★★£D 1860 Vines★★★★£F
O **Marsanne**★★£B O **Chardonnay**★£B
O **Riesling**★★£B O **Semillon**★★£B

TALLAROOK Central Victorian High Country www.tallarook.com A: HHB

Owner: Luis Riebl Dabyminga, Ennis Road, Tallarook VIC 3659
These elevated, cooler vineyards to the north of Melbourne have both strong Aboriginal and early colonial links. The winery, while still a baby, looks an interesting bet for the future, having wisely invested in the Martin Williams MW (METIER) consultancy winemaking team. 14 ha includes a little Viognier, Marsanne, Roussanne as well as more substantial amounts of Chardonnay, Pinot Noir and Shiraz. Already intelligently-made wines include a toasty Chardonnay of good weight and a gently creamy Marsanne. Pinot Noir is bright and supple but with a rather coarse fruit character in 2000. (PW)
O Chardonnay★★ £C   O Marsanne★ £B

TALTARNI Pyrenees www.taltarni.com.au A: Lay, FSt, T&W, WRk

Owner: Red Earth Nominees RMB 4369, Taltarni Road, Moonambel VIC 3478
With139 ha this is the Pyrenees' (in Western Victoria) biggest producer. Taltarni, like CLOS DU VAL in the Napa Valley, was established in 1972 by John Goelet. For long, Dominique Portet crafted the wines here while brother Bernard continues to oversee the Clos du Val wines. By the mid-80's Taltarni was widely admired for gutsy, structured varietals that highlighted the potential of the Pyrenees. Some wines have been too tough and extracted, others have lacked balance but the best bottles have aged superbly. It appears that since Dominique's retirement (with the 1998 vintage) the reds are being gently modernised by his successor Shane Clohesy. The other great facet to Taltarni is the sparkling-wine production which reaches its zenith in Clover Hill, from a separate Tasmanian estate with 21 ha planted to Chardonnay, Pinot Noir and Pinot Meunier. A second, smaller Tassie vineyard, Lalla Gully, is likely to provide a more consistent source for Sauvignon than the estate version which, although intense and characterful in cooler years, can be rather flat and short-lived from warmer vintages. Both red and white Fiddleback are newish, second-label, fruit-accented, blended wines made from both estate and bought-in grapes. (PW)
● Shiraz★★★ £C   ● Merlot★★ £C
● Cabernet Sauvignon★★ £C
O Clover Hill★★★ £C   O Brut Taché★ £B

TARRAWARRA Yarra Valley www.tarrawarra.com.au A: CRs, May, WSc, Vts, P&S

Owner: Besen family 311 Healesville Road, Yarra Glen VIC 3775
Tarrawarra has been single-minded in its aim of producing top-quality Burgundian-modelled Chardonnay and Pinot Noir. Its success in turning out rich, structured concentrated and complex examples of both owe much to the dedication and skill of winemaker Clare Halloran. The Chardonnay is 100 per cent barrel-fermented with some use of *bâttonage*, while the Pinot Noir receives a cold, pre-fermentation maceration, open fermenters are used and around 25 per cent of the oak is new. Increasing vine age and skill in producing higher quality fruit are also important to quality. Both wines benefit from age and are best at least three to five years after the vintage. Kosher Chardonnay and Shiraz are made under the Kidron label. Owner Marc Besen is also the wealthy benefactor behind a new Tarrawarra Art Museum. (PW)
● Pinot Noir★★★ £D   O Chardonnay★★★ £C

VIRGIN HILLS Macedon Ranges www.virginhills.com.au A:Str, Vne

Owner: Michael Hope 17 Piper Street, Kyneton VIC 3444
Just one wine is made here, a blend of Cabernet Sauvignon, Shiraz and Merlot. The winery and

vineyard are now owned by Michael Hope of HOPE ESTATE in the Hunter Valley after several recent changes in ownership. Quality would look to be remaining in the top division. Vineyard practice is organic, minimal intervention is employed during vinification and the wine is virtually sulphur-free. At the limit of ripening for these varieties the wine is not produced every year. When conditions are favourable it is a magnificent elegant, cedary red; in cooler years there can be a marked green undercurrent. (DM)

● **Virgin Hills**★★★★£D

YARRA BURN   Yarra Valley   www.brlhardy.com.au   A: BRL, Sav

*Owner: **Hardy Wine Company**   Settlement Road, Yarra Junction VIC 3797*
Yarra Burn is the headquarters of BRL HARDY'S substantial Yarra Valley operations, though quantities are small. The group only took control of the winery (established in 1975) in 1995 but the wines increasingly bear the hallmarks of premium BRL Hardy examples, with a rich fruit core, balance, complexity and well-integrated oak, though a bold premium Bastard Hill bottling of the Pinot Noir is a bit overdone. The Yarra Burn sparkling wine, which includes all three Champagne grapes, is yet another fine example from the Yarra Valley, with a cool, crisp elegance missing from so many Australian sparkling wines in the past. (PW)

O **Chardonnay**★★£B Bastard Hill★★★£D
O **Yarra Burn**★★£C
● **Pinot Noir**★★£C ● **Shiraz**★★★£C

YARRA YERING   Yarra Valley   A: Adm, JNi, ACh, BBR, NYg

Owner: Dr Bailey Carrodus   Briarty Rd, Gruyere, VIC 3770
While considered at times eccentric by some of his neighbours, Bailey Carrodus produces a remarkable array of very good to exceptional wines even if on occasion the results have been variable. Many of the vines are relatively venerable, particularly for the Yarra, with some plantings now over 30 years old. Dry Red No.1 is a blend of mainly Cabernet Sauvignon with Merlot, Cabernet Franc and Malbec while Dry Red No.2 is mainly Shiraz with a little Viognier. Also extremely impressive is the Underhill Shiraz but all of the reds are very fine, concentrated and show real finesse. The Pinot Noir is in a very rich, full-on style, and the cedary Merlot is notable for its remarkable cellar-door price tag. New and more reasonably priced is Dry Red No.3. Carrodus also makes a small amount of an impressive fortified port-style wine labelled Portsorts. (DM)

● **Dry Red No.1**★★★★ £E ● **Dry Red No.2**★★★★★ £E
● **Shiraz** Underhill★★★★ £E
● **Pinot Noir**★★★★ £F ● **Merlot**★★★★ £H
O **Dry White No.1**★★★ £E O **Chardonnay**★★★★ £E

YERING STATION/YARRABANK   Yarra Valley   www.yering.com   A: Sec, Res, ACh

*Owner: Rathbone family/**Champagne Devaux**   38 Melba Highway, Yarra Glen VIC 3775*
Yering Station was the name of a historic property in the Yarra Valley established in the first half of the 19th century. Part of the original estate has been revived, including an old winery building, and the complex has become another important stop on the Yarra Valley tourist trail. A wide range of mostly varietal wines is made to a good standard, but which sometimes lack a little concentration and depth; the best wines are the pricey Reserves. Yarrabank is Yering Station's joint venture with Champagne house Devaux. The (vintage-dated) Yarrabank cuvée shows a more refined, elegant character than many top Australian sparkling wines, but also a fine, ripe, fruit intensity and stylish

complexity, and is well-priced against the competition. Yarra Edge is a label used for wines made from a separate (leased) property. (PW)

○ **Yarrabank Brut**★★★ £C
○ **Chardonnay**★ £B   Reserve★★★ £D
○ **Pinot Gris** Botrytis★★ £C   ○ **Marsanne**★ £B
● **Pinot Noir**★ £B   Reserve★★★ £D
● **Cabernet Sauvignon** Reserve★★£D   ● **Merlot**★★£C

YERINGBERG   Yarra Valley   A: JAr, WVt

Owner: Guill de Pury   Maroondah Highway, Coldstream, VIC 3770
Fascinating winery for its history as well as for its excellent wines. The vineyard shares the same site as the original Yeringberg vineyard, which was destroyed by *phylloxera*, but is much smaller in its current manifestation. The Pinot Noir is good but can lack a touch of flesh, while both the whites are subtle and restrained but possess real elegance and flair. It is the Dry Red that truly excels here, a blend of Cabernet Sauvignon, Merlot, Cabernet Franc and Malbec. Both rich and cedary, with age it acquires a level of elegance and finesse seen in few other Australian reds. (DM)

● **Pinot Noir**★★ £D   ● **Yeringberg Dry Red**★★★★ £E
○ **Marsanne/Roussanne**★★★ £C   ○ **Chardonnay**★★★ £D

OTHER WINES OF NOTE

APSLEY GORGE (Tasmania) ● **Pinot Noir** £C   ○ **Chardonnay** £C
ARTHURS CREEK ● **Cabernet Sauvignon** Yarra Valley £D   ○ **Chardonnay** Yarra Valley £C
BERRYS BRIDGE (Pyrenees) ● **Shiraz** £C   ● **Cabernet Sauvignon** £C
BINDI (Macedon Ranges) ● **Pinot Noir** Original Vineyard £E   ○ **Chardonnay** Quartz £E
BULLERS CALLIOPE (Rutherglen) ○ **Liqueur Tokay** Rare £F   ○ **Liqueur Muscat** Rare £F
CHATEAU LEAMON (Bendigo) ● **Shiraz** Reserve £D   ○ **Riesling** £B
FREYCINET (Tasmania) ● **Pinot Noir** £D   ○ **Chardonnay** £C   ○ **Riesling** £C
KARINA VINEYARD (Mornington Peninsula) ○ **Chardonnay** £C   ○ **Riesling** £B
KNIGHT GRANITE HILLS (Macedon Ranges) ● **Shiraz** £C
MOOROODUC ESTATE (Mornington Peninsula) ○ **Chardonnay** Estate £C
● **Pinot Noir** Wild Yeast £D
MOUNT IDA (Bendigo) ● **Shiraz** £C
NICHOLSON RIVER WINERY (Gippsland) ○ **Chardonnay** £E   ● **Pinot Noir** £E
OAKRIDGE ESTATE (Yarra Valley) ● **Merlot** £C   ● **Shiraz** £C   ○ **Chardonnay** Reserve £C
OSBORNS (Mornington Peninsula) ● **Pinot Noir** £C   ○ **Chardonnay** £C
PAUL OSICKA ● **Shiraz** Heathcote £B
PARADISE ENOUGH (Gippsland) ○ **Chardonnay** £C   Reserve £C   ● **Pinot Noir** £C
PASSING CLOUDS (Bendigo) ● **Angel Blend** (Cabernet Sauvignon) £C
● **Shiraz/Cabernet** Graeme's Blend £C
PLUNKETT ● **Shiraz** Strathbogie Ranges Reserve £C
DOMINIQUE PORTET ● **Shiraz** Heathcote £C   ● **Cabernet Sauvignon** Yarra Valley £C
REDBANK (Pyrenees) ● **Sally's Paddock** (Cabernet Sauvignon/Shiraz/Malbec) £D
RED HILL ESTATE (Mornington Peninsula) ○ **Chardonnay** £C   ● **Pinot Noir** £C
ROCHFORD (Macedon Ranges) ○ **Chardonnay** £C   ● **Pinot Noir** £D   ● **Cabernet/Merlot** £C
SORRENBERG (Beechworth) ○ **Chardonnay** £D   ● **Shiraz** Havelock Hill £C
SPRINGVALE (Tasmania) ○ **Chardonnay** £C   ● **Pinot Noir** £D
STANTON & KILLEEN ○ **Rutherglen Muscadelle** (Tokay) £C   ○ **Rutherglen Muscat** £C   ○ Classic £D
T'GALLANT (Mornington Peninsula) ○ **Pinot Gris** Tribute £C   ○ **Chardonnay** £C
TURRAMURRA ESTATE (Mornington Peninsula) ○ **Chardonnay** £C   ● **Pinot Noir** £C   ● **Shiraz** £C
WARRENMANG (Pyrenees) ● **Shiraz** Estate £D   ● **Grand Pyrenees** (Cabernet blend) £D

WATER WHEEL ● **Shiraz** Bendigo £B ● **Cabernet Sauvignon** Bendigo £B
WILD DUCK CREEK (Bendigo) ● **Shiraz** Springflat £E Reserve £F
YELLOWGLEN ○ **Vintage Brut** £B

Author's choice (PW)

10 diverse first-rate Victorian Shiraz
CRAIGLEE ● **Shiraz**
DALWHINNIE ● **Shiraz** Moonambel
JASPER HILL ● **Shiraz** Georgia's Paddock
MITCHELTON ● **Shiraz** Print
MOUNT LANGHI GHIRAN ● **Shiraz**
PARINGA ESTATE ● **Shiraz**
SEPPELT GREAT WESTERN ● **Show Sparkling Shiraz**
SUMMERFIELD ● **Shiraz** Reserve
TAHBILK ● **Shiraz** 1860 Vines
YARRA YERING ● **Shiraz** Underhill

6 cellarworthy classic red blends
MOUNT LANGHI GHIRAN ● **Cabernet/Merlot**
MOUNT MARY ● **Quintet**
REDBANK ● **Sally's Paddock**
VIRGIN HILLS ● **Virgin Hills**
YARRA YERING Dry Red No. 1
YERINGBERG ● **Dry Red**

6 exemplary Victorian/Tasmanian Pinot Noir
BANNOCKBURN ● **Pinot Noir** Geelong
BASS PHILLIP ● **Pinot Noir** Reserve
DIAMOND VALLEY ● **Pinot Noir** Estate
GIACONDA ● **Pinot Noir**
STEFANO LUBIANA ● **Pinot Noir** Tasmania
PIPERS BROOK ● **Pinot Noir** Reserve Tasmania

10 top whites with personality
BY FARR ○ **Viognier** Geelong
COLDSTREAM HILLS ○ **Chardonnay** Yarra Valley Reserve
DALWHINNIE ○ **Chardonnay** Moonambel
GIACONDA ○ **Nantua Les Deux**
JASPER HILL ○ **Riesling** Georgia's Paddock
METIER ○ **Chardonnay** Schoolhouse Vineyard
MITCHELTON ○ **Marsanne/Roussanne/Viognier**
PIPERS BROOK ○ **Riesling** Estate
TALTARNI ○ **Clover Hill (sparkling)**
YERINGBERG ○ **Marsanne/Roussanne**

10 undervalued wines
BALGOWNIE ● **Shiraz** Bendigo
BEST'S ● **Shiraz** Great Western
DELATITE ○ **Riesling**

DROMANA ESTATE O **Arneis** i Garry Crittenden
DROMANA ESTATE ● **Shiraz**
HEATHCOTE WINERY ● **Shiraz** Mail Coach
LINDEMAN'S O **Chardonnay** Bin 65
MITCHELTON O **Riesling** Blackwood Park
MOUNT LANGHI GHIRAN ● **Shiraz/Grenache/Cabernet** Billi Billi Creek
TAHBILK O **Marsanne**
WYNNS ● **Shiraz** Coonawarra
YALUMBA O **Viognier** Y

New South Wales not only makes a sizeable contribution to Australia's production of bulk wine but 160 km north-west of its largest city, Sydney, has a wine region of magnetic tourist attraction in the Hunter Valley. Thanks to the Great Dividing Range much potential remains and new regions will continue to make an impact if developed with quality as the foremost consideration.

Hunter Valley

New South Wales' most traditional region is not, regrettably, the state's most suited region to viticulture. The Lower **Hunter Valley** is peppered with estates lying just west of the Brokenback Range but, despite regular cloud cover, conditions are very hot and the greatest part of its rainfall usually comes as the growing season reaches its climax. Great vintages are the exception rather than the norm yet some marvellous ageworthy Shiraz and Semillon are produced, though few of the latter examples are still made in the famed long-lived, minerally, toasty-but-unoaked Semillon style of old.

Central Ranges & Southern New South Wales

Mudgee and the other regions which run down the western side of the Great Dividing Range are better protected from cyclonic deluges, making them both cooler and drier. Much of the grape production from Mudgee and **Cowra** has been dominated by the big producers and the harvest has been Hunter-bound. Mudgee produces intensely flavoured Cabernet Sauvignon, Shiraz, Chardonnay and Semillon, though few producers other than Huntington Estate and Rosemount give the region the recognition it deserves. Cowra Chardonnay has a well-established distinctive, lush, full style of its own. Gaining increasing significance are **Orange**, **Hilltops** and, from close to the border with Victoria, the chilly, elevated **Tumbarumba** region. Similarly cool and elevated, with the associated risk of frost damage, are the vineyards of the **Canberra District** lying to the north of the country's capital (but still in New South Wales itself). Despite the difficult, marginal conditions, the best reds are Cabernet/Merlot blends and Shiraz; the latter can show a wonderful cool-climate expression. The best whites are produced from Riesling and Chardonnay.

Big Rivers

Big Rivers suggests a lot of water and the vast vineyards of this zone are dependent on irrigation. The zone incorporates the commercially important bulk-producing regions of **Riverina** and, shared with Victoria on the Murray River, **Murray Darling** and **Swan Hill**. Not generally associated with fine quality, Riverina is the source of De Bortoli's Noble One from botrytis-enriched Semillon grapes.

Queensland

Producing wine in sub-tropical Queensland is fraught with difficulties. Nonetheless wine is produced from **South Burnett**, near Kingaroy, and in the **Granite Belt** around Stanthorpe, in the Great Dividing Range, where it is cooler and elevated. Despite sometimes difficult vintage conditions Shiraz can be good.

A-Z Producers by region

Canberra District
CLONAKILLA

Riverina
DE BORTOLI

Hunter Valley
ALLANDALE
BROKENWOOD
LAKE'S FOLLY
MCWILLIAM'S MOUNT PLEASANT
MEEREA PARK
ROSEMOUNT ESTATE
TYRELL'S

Mudgee
HUNTINGTON ESTATE

Some comments on vintages and when to drink

The generalised Vintage charts cover some of the most ageworthy styles and will prove most useful when taken together with comments on style and ageing within individual producer entries. Many wines can be drunk young but an increasing number will not be at their best for at least five years. Hunter Valley Semillon can take two decades in its stride while top Hunter or Mudgee Shiraz and Cabernet have similar ageing potential. Both the vintage ratings and when to drink assessments generally only apply to the top rated examples (three star wines or higher).

New South Wales vintages

	Hunter Valley Shiraz	Central Ranges Shiraz	Hunter Valley Semillon
2003	★★★★ A	★★★★/★★★★★ A	★★★★ A
2002	★★★/★★★★ A	★★★★/★★★★★ A	★★★/★★★★ A
001	★★★ A	★★★ A	★★★★ A
2000	★★★★/★★★★★ A	★★★ A	★★★★/★★★★★ A
1999	★★★★ A	★★★/★★★★ A	★★★★ A
1998	★★★★/★★★★★ A	★★★★ A	★★★★/★★★★★ B
1997	★★★ B	★★★ B	★★★/★★★★ C
1996	★★★★/★★★★★ B	★★★★ B	★★★★/★★★★★ B
1995	★★★/★★★★ C	★★★★/★★★★★ C	★★★/★★★★ C
1994	★★★/★★★★ C	★★★★ C	★★★★ C
1993	★★★/★★★★ C	★★/★★★ C	★★★/★★★★ C
1992	★★★ D	★★/★★★ C	★★★ D
1991	★★★★★ C	★★★/★★★★ C	★★★★/★★★★★ C

ALLANDALE   Hunter Valley   www.allandalewinery.com.au   A: AWA

Owner: Wally & Judith Atallah   Lovedale Road, Lovedale NSW 2321
Established in 1978, this is still a relatively small Hunter Valley operation with a reputation for
consistently full-flavoured, complex Chardonnay but also archetypal very ripe, oak-influenced Shiraz
as well as classically typed Hunter grown Verdelho and Semillon. Bill Sneddon's winemaking has
given the wines their individual stamp and impressive flavour intensity - traditional, in the best sense,
without compromise to the particular winemaking trend of the day. In addition to the fruit from 7
ha of Allandale vineyards, grapes are bought in from other Hunter growers and increasingly diverse
sources including Mudgee, Hilltops and McLaren Vale. Both Orange and Mudgee Cabernet
Sauvignon were produced in 2001. (PW)

● **Shiraz** Matthew★★★ £C   ● **Cabernet Sauvignon** Hilltops★★ £C
O **Chardonnnay★★★** £B   O **Semillon★★** £B   O **Verdelho★★** £B

BROKENWOOD   Hunter Valley   www.brokenwood.com.au **A: Lib, ACh, P&S, Res, Vne, WSc**

Owner: Brokenwood Wines   McDonalds Road, Pokolbin NSW 2320
A benchmark Lower Hunter winery, Brokenwood was established in 1970 by a number of partners
including former lawyer and wine writer James Halliday. Production has grown to a not inconsiderable
70,000 cases a year but the quality remains uniformly high. Winemaker Iain Riggs is responsible for
the direction of both the widely sourced Brokenwood wines and those of Yarra Valley winery
SEVILLE ESTATE, acquired in the late 1990s. While there is good Cabernet Sauvignon it is the
Shiraz that has earned the greatest renown. Both the Rayner (McLaren Vale) and Graveyard
(Hunter) wines are immensely rich and impressive. The latter has remarkable depth, intensity
and length, becoming very complex with the seven or eight years' age it needs to show at its best.
It is among Australia's elite in stunning years like 1998 and 2000. Another Hunter example, the
Mistress Block, has real panache. The Semillon whites are classic expressions of the grape: low in
alcohol, slow to develop, becoming immensely honeyed and very intense as they peak with eight to
ten years. The ILR version with classic length, depth and structure, is only released after five years'
ageing. There's also aromatic, lightly honeyed Verdelho from Cowra and rich and lightly tropical
Chardonnay. The premium Graveyard Chardonnay is fermented with wild yeasts, shows considerable
new oak but has real depth and intensity and adds weight and dimension with three or four years.
New is a very promising Forest Edge Vineyard Chardonnay from Orange. Relatively inexpensive
Harlequin and Cricket Pitch reds and whites are crafted to be immediately appealing and drinkable. In
the Cricket Pitch red, Cabernet Sauvignon and Merlot are the major varieties but there is better
expression in the Shiraz/Cabernet Franc-dominated Harlequin red. Cricket Pitch white is a grassy, citrusy
Sauvignon Blanc/Semillon blend with a hint of barrel-fermentation, while the Harlequin is an unoaked
blend of Chardonnay and Verdelho. The range is completed by a fine late-harvest Riesling from the Jelka
Vineyard (McLaren Vale), but you'll have to go to the cellar door to get this one. (DM & PW)

● **Shiraz★★★** £C   Rayner Vineyard★★★★ £D   Graveyard Vineyard★★★★★ £F
● **Cabernet Sauvignon★★★** £C   ● **Harlequin Red★★** £B   ● **Cricket Pitch Red★★** £B
O **Chardonnay★★★** £C   Graveyard Vineyard★★★★ £D
O **Semillon★★★** £B   ILR Reserve★★★★ £C
O **Harlequin White★** £B   O **Cricket Pitch White★★** £B   O **Verdelho★★** £B

CLONAKILLA   Canberra District   www.clonakilla.com.au   A: Lib, ACh, BBR, P&S

Owner: Kirk family   Crisps Lane, Murrumbateman NSW 2582
Tim Kirk is realising the potential first developed by his father Dr John Kirk, an Australian research

scientist of Irish descent. Clonakilla's top red, Canberra District Shiraz (also labelled Shiraz Viognier) includes around seven per cent Viognier and is now one of the best in the country distinguished particularly by its individual expression of an Australian Shiraz-based blend. The pepper, spice, floral and berry amalgam is not only distinctive but elegant and supported by a depth, weight and structure that should have at least five years' ageing. A varietal Viognier is very good too, with delightful mayblossom and ripe peach aromas, tighter, with better structure and intensity and without the excessive ripeness or alcohol of many Australian examples. Made as they are on a similarly small scale these really are wines to contrast with examples from good growers of Côte Rôtie or Condrieu. A Hilltops Shiraz, while much cheaper than the Canberra District version, is quite different, more one-dimensional without the same depth, expression or sheer style. Chardonnay, Riesling, Semillon/Sauvignon Blanc and Cabernet/Merlot are also produced. This small 6 ha property will grow but one hopes mercifully slowly. (PW)

● **Shiraz**★★★★ £E Hilltops★★ £C
O **Viognier**★★★ £D

DE BORTOLI   Riverina   www.debortoli.com.au   A: DeB

Owner: De Bortoli family   De Bortoli Road, Bilbul NSW 2680
Vast winery based in the Riverina near Griffith. Output is around three million cases a year and almost all is accounted for by bulk-market labels. The majority of the fine-wine output is accounted for at the Yarra Valley winery (see DE BORTOLI Victoria). The best of the budget wines here are released under the Sacred Hill and Vat Series labels. Quality is fairly ordinary but the Sacred Hill Semillon/ Chardonnay and Vat Series Chardonnay stand out, with decent fruit and moderate intensity. The real interest from a quality point of view is in the botrytis-influenced Semillons and now the fortified Black Noble. The latter is produced in a similar fashion to the liqueur Tokays of Rutherglen from a *solera* which is based on Semillon. As well as a rich, raisiny character the wine is finely balanced with fresh tangy acidity. The Vat Series Botrytis Semillon is a lesser version of the Noble One but displays a full, peachy, lightly honeyed character. The Rare Dry Botrytis Semillon is just that: dry and barrel-fermented but with no residual sugar. The wine is full of rich, concentrated flavours from the dessicated grapes. Last but by no means least, the Noble One is Australia's greatest sweet wine and has been for the last two decades and more. There is a weight, depth and concentration that only the very greatest Sauternes and Barsac will possibly eclipse. Very long and extremely ageworthy, the wine requires over five years in the cellar to fully show its remarkable, complex, honeyed character. (DM)

O **Semillon** Vat Series★★ £C Rare Dry★★★ £C Noble One★★★★ £E
O **Black Noble**★★★★ £D

HUNTINGTON ESTATE   Mudgee   A: JIC

Owner: Roberts family   Cassilis Road, Mudgee NSW 2850
A consistently excellent winery and still the best in Mudgee despite the emergence of ROSEMOUNT labels from the area. Production remains relatively small at around 20,000 cases a year and is spread across a wide range, some of which are only available through mail order and at the cellar door. Very good regular Cabernet/Merlot, Cabernet Sauvignon and Shiraz have been joined by Reserve bottlings of Cabernet Sauvignon and Shiraz. The reserves particularly are quite marked by their full, American-oak component but the quality of the fruit can easily absorb the wood, something that not all Australian reds aged in this type of vessel achieve. The top white is Semillon which, like many Hunter examples, sees no wood and similarly requires considerable patience – drinking this style in its youth can prove very disappointing. There is also a rich, barrel-fermented Chardonnay and a fruit-filled, early-drinking Semillon/Chardonnay. The wines represent particularly good value for money. (DM)

● **Cabernet Sauvignon**★★★ £B Reserve★★★ £C ● **Cabernet/Merlot**★★★ £B
● **Shiraz**★★★ £B Reserve★★★★ £C
O **Semillon**★★★ £B O **Chardonnay** Barrel Fermented★★ £B O **Semillon/Chardonnay**★★ £B

LAKE'S FOLLY Hunter Valley www.lakesfolly.com.au   A: Lay

Owner: Peter Fogarty   Brokes Road, Pokolbin NSW 2320
Top-quality Lower Hunter producer. Originally established in 1963 by Sydney surgeon Max Lake it was sold to Peter Fogarty in 2000. Rodney Kempe has taken on the winemaking reins, although Stephen Lake is still providing consultancy. Just two wines are made here and production is small at around 4,500 cases a year. The Chardonnay in particular was an early benchmark among high-quality Australian whites. During the mid-1990s the wines were still good but didn't reach the levels of old. They do, however, look to be back on top form now. The Red is subtle, restrained and well-structured. It has none of the exuberant, ripe, sometimes overripe, black fruits found elsewhere. The Chardonnay is rich, opulent and buttery with very well-judged oak adding a subtle, spicy, nutty character. Both are ageworthy and will evolve well over a decade, the Red often longer. (DM)
● **Lakes Folly Red**★★★ £D
O **Chardonnay**★★★★ £D

MCWILLIAM'S MOUNT PLEASANT Hunter Valley   A: McW

Owner: McWilliam's   Marrowbone Road, Pokolbin NSW2320
This is the good stuff, make no mistake. There are other good wines from this large company's other operations including increasingly good wines from Barwang in southern New South Wales but these are the gems. The Semillons, only released with four to five years' bottle age start out slowly but have marvellous toasty, citrus and herb intensity that continues to build in the bottle with many years' age. The characteristic intense toastiness is not due to oak but the inherent character that develops when these Hunter Semillons are built to last. Shiraz too is deep and individual, the particular fusion of oak, savoury, earth, leather, black cherry and licorice give an indication of the complexity but there are other nuances too here that you just won't get anywhere else. Old Paddock and Old Hill comes from two very old estate vineyards and is particularly long-lived. Intensely flavoured Chardonnay owes some of its complexity to oak but is not overwhelmed by it. Getting hold of these wines can be a problem unless you happen to live in Australia yet perhaps the most remarkable thing are the very reasonable prices. If you buy the Semillon relatively young put it away somewhere out of reach for a decade or more. (PW)
● **Shiraz** Rosehill★★ £C Maurice O'Shea★★★ £C Old Paddock & Old Hill★★★★ £D
O **Semillon** Elizabeth★★★ £B Lovedale★★★★ £D O **Chardonnay** Maurice O'Shea★★★ £C

MEEREA PARK Hunter Valley www.meereapark.com.au   A: Lib

Owner: Meerea Park Wines Pty Ltd   Lot 3, Palmers Lane, Pokolbin NSW2320
An extensive range is produced at this small to medium-sized winery with a production of around 10,000 cases a year. The first vintage was 1991 and the wines are all crafted from bought-in fruit. Quality ranges from good to very good. The tight, citrusy Chardonnay is barrel-fermented with wild yeasts and sourced from old Hunter vines. High-toast French oak is used, which can be more than apparent. Viognier shows the typically peachy fruit of the variety with a hint of spice. It is part barrel-fermented and kept on lees. Semillon is unoaked in the classic Hunter Valley style and will benefit from four or five years' cellaring. Verdelho likewise sees no oak and is fermented cool to emphasise the unusual spicy, pungent-green character of the grape. Of the reds the Cabernet/Merlot

is aged in French oak and is in a leaner style, almost leafy. The Aunts Shiraz is sound and well-made but the Alexander Munro is a serious notch up. Dense, concentrated and almost leathery with powerful, smoky, black fruit. (DM)

● **Cabernet Merlot**★★ £C ● **Shiraz** The Aunts★★ £C Alexander Munro★★★ £D
○ **Chardonnay** Alexander Munro★★ £D ○ **Semillon** Epoch★★ £B
○ **Viognier** Lindsay Hill★★ £C ○ **Verdelho** Lindsay Hill★★ £B

ROSEMOUNT ESTATE Hunter Valley www.rosemountestates.com A: ScE, Odd

Owner: Southcorp Rosemount Road, Denmman NSW 2064

This large winery is now itself a part of the huge SOUTHCORP umbrella of wine interests. There is also a facility at McLaren Vale (see ROSEMOUNT MCLAREN VALE), but the main Rosemount base is the Upper Hunter. Production is now in excess of two million cases a year and, despite this, veteran wine-maker Philip Shaw continued to maintain generally high standards throughout the extensive portfolio until his departure mid-2003. The two lower-priced ranges under the Diamond varietal and Diamond Blend dual varietal labels offer some reasonable drinking if not a great deal of excitement. The whites in particular are marked by forward, simple, tropical fruit but stand out from many of their competitors at this level. The Hill of Gold range of varietals from Mudgee show good fruit intensity and texture, particularly in good Chardonnay and ripe, black-fruited Shiraz. Also from Mudgee, the premium Blue Mountain Shiraz/Cabernet Sauvignon is among the better reds now emanating from this lesser-known region. Rich and concentrated it is aged in American oak with an almost earthy, rustic component. Well-crafted Cabernet Sauvignon, Shiraz and Merlot from the Orange Vineyard, planted at an altitude of close to 1,000 metres, show their cooler climate origins. The Shiraz particularly is classy and restrained, aged in French rather than American oak. Least of several premium Chardonnay, the Show Reserve falls a long way short of its form of a decade or more ago. The Orange vineyard version wtih its spicy citrus and ripe-fruited character is in marked contrast to the richer, more intense, complex Roxburgh wine. The latter remains one of the benchmark Australian examples of the variety, if lacking a touch of the splendour it once showed. Giants Creek Chardonnay is aged in older oak to preserve its fruit character. Show Reserve Semillon is typical of the Hunter style; with only a hint of oak, the wine is both restrained and deserves at least three or four years' ageing. (DM & PW)

● **Cabernet Sauvignon** Hill of Gold★★ £B Orange Vineyard★★★ £D
● **Shiraz** Hill of Gold★★ £B Orange Vineyard★★★ £D ● **Merlot** Orange Vineyard★★ £D
● **Shiraz/Cabernet Sauvignon** Blue Mountain★★★ £E
○ **Chardonnay** Hill of Gold★★ £B Show Reserve★★ £C Giants Creek★★ £C
○ **Chardonnay** Orange Vineyard★★★ £D Roxburgh★★★★ £F
○ **Semillon** Show Reserve★★ £C ○ **Kirri Billi** Vintage Brut★★ £D

TYRRELL'S Hunter Valley www.tyrrells.com.au A: Par, WSc

Owner: Tyrrell family Ashmans, Broke Road, Pokolbin NSW 2320

Fiercely traditional, family-owned and run winery dating back to the 1860s. The range is now very extensive and production is approaching one million cases a year. The portfolio is split into four ranges under the Long Flat, Old Winery, Individual Vineyard and Private Bin labels. Unsurprisingly it is the more expensive Vineyard and Private Bin wines which offer the greatest interest. The Long Flat Shiraz is the best of the lower-level wines, with some straightforward berry fruit and quite aggressive tannin. Of the Old Winery wines, which are sourced from vineyards in McLaren Vale as well as the Lower Hunter, the Shiraz and Semillon are good bets. The Shiraz has decent, smoky, dark berry fruit, the Semillon offers something of the Hunter style in a forward, more obviously fruit-driven style. The Lost Block Semillon by contrast is more classic, as is the Vat 1, which is released with several years' age and is one of the finest examples in the region. Of the two vineyard-designated

Chardonnays, the Shee-Oak is fermented in stainless steel and kept on fine lees, and shows well-crafted, varietal melon character. Moon Mountain is part-fermented in French oak which seems to add just an extra dimension. Dwarfing these, though, is the Vat 47– one of Australia's great Chardonnays for three decades. Rich and very concentrated, it has always shown refinement and balance. The Brokenback Shiraz takes this variety up a notch but the wine is more berry fruit-driven than dense and powerful. The Vat 9 Shiraz adds an extra dimension but the blended Vat 8 Shiraz/Cabernet has as yet disappointed. Some critical success has been achieved over the years with Pinot Noir but one would have to conclude that the Hunter climate is not propitious to successful cultivation of the variety and results have been variable. Top Shiraz and Semillon demand cellaring. (DM)

● **Shiraz** Old Winery★ £B Brokenback★★ £C Vat 9★★★ £E
O **Chardonnay** Shee-Oak★ £C Moon Mountain★★ £C Vat 47★★★★ £E
O **Semillon** Old Winery★ £B Lost Block★★ £C Vat I★★★★ £E

OTHER WINES OF NOTE

ABERCORN (Mudgee) ● Shiraz £C
ALLANMERE (Hunter) O **Chardonnay** Durham £C O **Verdelho** £B
● **Shiraz** £C ● **Cabernet Sauvignon** £C
ARROWFIELD (Hunter) ● **Shiraz** Show Reserve £C O **Chardonnay** Show Reserve £C
BIMBADGEN (Hunter) O **Chardonnay** £B ● **Shiraz** £B Signature £C
BOTOBOLAR (Mudgee) ● **Shiraz** £C O **Marsanne** £B
BRINDABELLA HILLS (Canberra District) O **Riesling** £B O **Sauvignon/Semillon** £B
DRAYTONS (Hunter) ● **Shiraz** Bin 5555 £B O **Verdelho** £B
EVANS FAMILY (Hunter) O **Chardonnay** Pinchem £C
GLENGUIN (Hunter) ● **Shiraz** £C Pokolbin Vineyard £C
HOPE ESTATE (Hunter) O **Verdelho** £B O **Chardonnay** £B O **Semillon** £B
● **Merlot** £B ● **Shiraz** £B
LINDEMANS O **Semillon** Hunter River Reserve £D
LARK HILL (Canberra District) ● **Pinot Noir** £D O **Chardonnay** £C O **Riesling** £B
MARGAN FAMILY (Hunter) O **Semillon** £B ● **Shiraz** £C ● **Cabernet Sauvignon** £C
MIRAMAR (Mudgee) ● **Cabernet Sauvignon** £C O **Chardonnay** £B
POOLE'S ROCK (Hunter) O **Chardonnay** £C
REYNOLDS (Orange) O **Chardonnay** Orange Reserve £B ● **Merlot** Orange Marble Man £C
● **Cabernet Sauvignon** Orange The Jezebal £C
ROTHBURY ESTATE (Hunter) ● **Shiraz** Brokenback £D O **Chardonnay** Brokenback £C
O **Semillon** Hunter Valley £B Brokenback £C
TEMPUS TWO (Hunter) O **Semillon** Reserve £B O **Chardonnay** Cowra £B
THISTLE HILL (Mudgee) ● **Cabernet Sauvignon** £B O **Chardonnay** £B
KEITH TULLOCH (Hunter) O **Semillon** £C ● **Merlot** £C ● **Shiraz** Kester £D
● **Forres Blend** (Cabernet Sauvignon/Petit Verdot/Merlot) £D
WINDOWRIE (Cowra) ● **Shiraz** Estate £C O **Chardonnay** Estate £C
YARRAMAN ESTATE (Hunter) ● **Chambourcin** Black Cypress £B

Author's choice (PW)

10 classic Hunter/Mudgee reds

ALLANDALE ● **Shiraz** Matthew
BROKENWOOD ● **Shiraz** Graveyard Vineyard
BROKENWOOD ● **Shiraz** Rayner Vineyard
HUNTINGTON ESTATE ● **Cabernet Sauvignon**

HUNTINGTON ESTATE ● Shiraz
LAKE'S FOLLY ● Lake's Folly red
MCWILLIAM'S MOUNT PLEASANT ● Shiraz Maurice O'Shea
MCWILLIAM'S MOUNT PLEASANT ● Shiraz Old Hill & Old Paddock
ROSEMOUNT ● Shiraz/Cabernet Mountain Blue
TYRRELL'S ● Shiraz Vat 9

10 definitive Hunter/Mudgee whites

ALLANDALE O Chardonnay
BROKENWOOD O Chardonnay Graveyard Vineyard
BROKENWOOD O Semillon ILR Reserve
HUNTINGTON ESTATE O Semillon
LAKE'S FOLLY O Chardonnay
MCWILLIAM'S MOUNT PLEASANT O Chardonnay Maurice O'Shea
MCWILLIAM'S MOUNT PLEASANT O Semillon Lovedale
ROSEMOUNT O Chardonnay Roxburgh
TYRRELL'S O Chardonnay Vat 47
TYRRELL'S O Semillon Vat 1

10 new stars

CLONAKILLA ● Shiraz Canberra District
CLONAKILLA O Viognier
HOPE ESTATE O Verdelho Hunter Valley
LARK HILL O Riesling Canberra District
MEEREA PARK O Semillon Hunter Valley Epoch
MEEREA PARK ● Shiraz Alexander Munro
ROSEMOUNT O Chardonnay Orange Vineyard
ROSEMOUNT ● Shiraz Orange Vineyard
KEITH TULLOCH O Semillon Hunter Valley
KEITH TULLOCH ● Shiraz Hunter Valley Kester

Western Australia

Australia's biggest state is virtually all desert but it does have a cool coastal skirt that runs south from the state capital, Perth, and around the south-western corner to parts kept cool and damp under the influence of the Southern Ocean. WA contributes only a tiny amount to Australia's total wine production (3 per cent) but by our reckoning accounts for more like 10 per cent of its premium wine.

Greater Perth

The **Swan District** (Swan Valley) is the historic heart of Western Australian viticulture. It is extremely hot and dry but with varieties such as Verdelho, Chenin Blanc, Chardonnay and Semillon some surprisingly good whites have been produced. Houghton dominates production and its ageworthy, big-volume 'White Burgundy' (now HWB) is the most famous and remarkable wine of the region. Reds, including Shiraz and Cabernet Sauvignon, can be characterful and well-made even if the best wines are likely to include a component from Great Southern.

South-West Australia

Nearly all of Western Australia's premium wines come from this zone and its two most important regions, Margaret River and Great Southern.

Margaret River

The **Margaret River** juts into the Indian Ocean but despite problems of wind and the ravenous local wildlife, especially the birds, its 'founding doctors' (establishing Vasse Felix, Moss Wood and Cullen in the late 60s and early 70s) were soon followed by Leeuwin Estate and others. Wines of remarkably rich, pure, deeply textured fruit from Cabernet Sauvignon and Chardonnay have been produced in the decades since and the region continues to grow apace. At its heart, the Willyabrup Valley is the most densely planted, but high quality is also achieved to the north and south. Sauvignon Blanc and Semillon (both individually and combined) and Shiraz are made to a high standard too. To the north and east of Margaret River, **Geographe** incorporates a large swathe of countryside, stretching from the coast inland. Capel Vale, located on the coastal strip, is the leading winery but inland valleys are also being developed.

Great Southern

Great Southern, as its name suggests, is an especially large region. **Frankland River** is currently the most planted of five sub-regions, and often excels with Riesling, Chardonnay, Shiraz, Cabernet Sauvignon and Cabernet Franc. Producers include the likes of Alkoomi and Frankland Estate but grapes are also sourced from here by those based outside the region such as Houghton. **Mount Barker's** potential has long been highlighted by Plantagenet, but others too make particularly fine Shiraz as well as excellent Riesling and Chardonnay. **Porongurup** lies east of Mount Barker while **Albany** and **Denmark**, which can be wetter, reach down to the coast and again scattered vineyards can provide marvellous fruit.

Other regions of the SW Australia zone

Between Great Southern and Margaret River even more far-flung vineyards are appearing in the gaps between extensive tracts of forest in three emerging areas, **Blackwood Valley**, **Manjimup** and **Pemberton**. The latter, the most exposed to the Southern Ocean, has already achieved wider recognition thanks to Picardy and Salitage. Smokier Pinot Noir it is surely not possible to find, the distinctive wines being influenced by the effects of the controlled burning of forest fires. Chardonnay, Shiraz and the Bordeaux varieties are also successful.

A-Z Producers by region

Denmark
HOWARD PARK

MOSS WOOD
PIERRO
VASSE FELIX

Frankland River
ALKOOMI
FRANKLAND ESTATE

Mount Barker
CHATSFIELD
GOUNDREY
PLANTAGENET

Geographe
CAPEL VALE

Pemberton
PICARDY

Margaret River
CAPE MENTELLE
CULLEN
EVANS AND TATE
LEEUWIN ESTATE

Swan District
HOUGHTON

Some comments on vintages and when to drink

These generalised Vintage charts cover some of the most ageworthy styles and will prove most useful when taken together with comments on style and ageing within individual producer entries. While many wines can be drunk young, top full-bodied Margaret River Cabernet demands at least five years' cellaring. Great Southern Shiraz is usually a little more approachable but can also be long-lived. Top-quality Chardonnay and Pinot Noir only show their full potential with three to five years' ageing, while exceptions like Leeuwin Estate Art Series Chardonnay can age for more than 10 years. The best Great Southern Riesling is up there with the best from the eastern states and will keep for at least five to six years. Both the vintage ratings and when to drink assessments generally only apply to the top rated examples (three star wines or higher).

Western Australian vintages

	Margaret River Cabernet	Great Southern Shiraz	Margaret River Chardonnay
2003	★★★★ A	★★★/★★★★ A	★★★/★★★★ A
2002	★★★★ A	★★★★ A	★★★★ B
2001	★★★★/★★★★★ A	★★★★/★★★★★ A	★★★★/★★★★★ C
2000	★★★★ A	★★★ B	★★★★ C
1999	★★★★/★★★★★ B	★★★ B	★★★★ C
1998	★★★ B	★★★ C	★★★ C
1997	★★★★ B	★★★★ B	★★★★/★★★★★ C
1996	★★★★/★★★★★ B	★★★★/★★★★★ C	★★★★ C
1995	★★★★/★★★★★ C	★★★★/★★★★★ C	★★★★★ C
1994	★★★★★ C	★★★★/★★★★★ C	★★★★/★★★★★ D
1993	★★★★ C	★★/★★★ C	
1992	★★★/★★★★ C	★★★★ C	
1991	★★★★/★★★★★ C	★★★/★★★★ C	

ALKOOMI Frankland River www.alkoomiwines.com.au   A: Lay, WVt, P&S

Owner: Merv Lange RMB 234, Wingebellup Road, Frankland WA 6396

This winery in remote Frankland River has now grown to a substantial size, with an output of some 80,000 cases a year. Fruit comes entirely from estate-owned vineyards and the top reds are impressive. Cabernet Sauvignon is blended with a little Malbec and is in a refined rather than weighty style. Shiraz is full of black fruit and spicy pepper; the Jarrah has real weight and depth. Equally impressive is the Blackbutt, a blend of Cabernet Sauvignon, Malbec and Merlot which is structured and needs four or five years' ageing. The top white is Wandoo, unusual in being 100 per cent Semillon from some of the oldest vines – good if pricey. Others include a fresh and zesty Sauvignon Blanc, tight and well-structured Chardonnay and a characteristically fine and complex Great Southern Riesling that becomes toasty with age. There's also two fruit-driven basics under the Southlands label: the red a blend of Cabernet Sauvignon, Shiraz and Merlot; the white Semillon, Chenin Blanc and Sauvignon Blanc. (DM)

● **Cabernet Sauvignon★★** £C ● **Blackbutt★★★** £D
● **Shiraz★★★**£C Jarrah★★★ £D
O **Chardonnay★★** £C O **Riesling★★★** £B
O **Sauvignon Blanc★** £B O **Wandoo★★★** £E

CAPE MENTELLE Margaret River www.capementelle.com.au   A: Par, JNi, ACh, N&P, P&S

Owner: LMVH Wallcliffe Road, Margaret River, WA 6285

Now owned by LMVH and absorbed some years ago by VEUVE CLICQUOT along with sister winery CLOUDY BAY in New Zealand. Cape Mentelle has always had the lower profile of the two. David Hohnen, the founder who ran operations until 2003, consistently produced very good wines. Partially oaked, the Semillon/Sauvignon Blanc is ripe, spicy even smoky with real class if sometimes wanting for a little more defintion and structure. Wallcliffe is a special selection of the same grapes from a vineyard of the same name that is vinified in American and French oak. It was rather oaky in 2000 but much more restrained in 2001. More time is needed to better discern the style being pursued. Chardonnay is rich, powerful and complex, just needing a little class for really fine. Among the reds Cabernet/Merlot comes from Trinders Vineyard and has good depth, breadth and intensity allied to a very ripe dark berry fruit character in warm vintages. Better still is Cabernet Sauvignon deserving of at least six to seven years' age. Bold and concentrated with well-judged oak, the wine shows impressive dark berry fruit complexity and length of flavour. Dark fruits and black pepper characterise the Shiraz, which gets limited new oak, both American and French. A rare Australia example of Zinfandel is a classic of the variety: full, brambly and with not inconsiderable alcohol. Available locally are Georgiana, a unoaked blend of Sauvignon Blanc, Chenin and Semillon, and Marmaduke from mostly Shiraz, Mourvèdre and Grenache. Both are intended for fruity, early drinking. A sound, small range of reds and whites under the Ironstone label is released in the UK. (PW)

● **Cabernet Sauvignon★★★★** £D ● **Cabernet/Merlot★★** £C
● **Shiraz★★★** £C ● **Zinfandel★★★** £C
O **Chardonnay★★★** £C O **Semillon/Sauvignon Blanc★★★** £C

CAPEL VALE Geographe www.capelvale.com   A: AHW, P&S

Owner: Peter Pratten Lot 5, Stirling Estate, Mallokup Road, Capel WA 6271

An extensive range of red and white is produced at this winery to the north of the Margaret River at Geographe. Production is now quite considerable for Western Australia at some 150,000 cases a year. The CV range offers good everyday drinking in both red and white. Of greater interest, though, are the Capel Vale wines, particularly two splended whites from the premium Connoisseur range,

Whispering Hill Riesling and Frederick Chardonnay. The former is steely and toasty, very well-structured and with a piercing citrus core. The Chardonnay is rich, opulent and with exotic fruit and subtly handled oak. The Riesling, particularly, will evolve well for over a decade. Of the regular Capel Vale wines, both Verdelho and Riesling are well crafted and Sauvignon Blanc/Semillon can be impressively pungent. Chardonnay is subtly oaked and with real intensity. The reds tend to elegance rather than concentration and have good fruit intensity but somehow cry out for more weight and texture. The premium Merlot, Howecroft stands out. (DM)

Capel Vale
- **Cabernet Sauvignon/Merlot** Howecroft★★ £D
- **Merlot**★★£B Howecroft★★★ £D ● **Shiraz**★ £B Kinnaird★★ £D
- **Chardonnay**★★ £C Frederick Reserve★★★£D ○ **Sauvignon Blanc/Semillon**★ £B
- **Riesling**★★ £B Whispering Hill★★★ £C ○ **Verdelho**★★ £B

CHATSFIELD Mount Barker www.chatsfield.com.au   A: Cac, DWS

Owner: Dr Ken & Joyce Lynch O'Neill Road, Mount Barker WA 6324
This impressive, small 16-ha family operation now produces around 6,000 cases per year of well-crafted and very fairly priced wines. The wine is now produced at the Porongorup winery, a partnership between Chatsfield and other local wineries. Consultant winemaking comes from JOHN WADE, responsible for the early quality of both PLANTAGENET and HOWARD PARK and now making his own wines as well. Both Gewürztraminer and Riesling are produced in a dry, structured and ageworthy style. The latter is tight, minerally when young and will age superbly. Cabernet Franc is not only unusual but one of the best in Australia. It is full of bramble and leafy character but not a bit unripe in an elegant, medium-weight style closer to the Loire Valley than St-Émilion. The Shiraz is great value – chock full of dark fruit, liquorice and black pepper. Refined, supple and long it will benefit from three or four years' ageing but could be drunk sooner. (DM)
- **Cabernet Franc**★★ £B ● **Shiraz**★★★ £C
- **Riesling**★★ £B ○ **Chardonnay**★★ £C ○ **Gewürztraminer**★★ £B

CULLEN Margaret River www.cullenwines.com.au   A: Lib, ACh, Vne

Owner: Cullen family Caves Road, Cowaramup WA 6284
Outstanding Margaret River operation with a long tradition of excellence, now producing close to 20,000 cases a year from well-established estate vineyards. Made by Vanya Cullen, the wines are marked by their finesse, superior structure and complexity, putting them in a different class to many of their neighbours. The Cabernet Sauvignon/Merlot, usually around two-thirds Cabernet Sauvignon with up to 10 per cent of Cabernet Franc is now named in honour of Di Cullen who did so much to establish the Cullen reputation. Of top classed growth (Bordeaux) quality it sets the standard for the Margaret River. Its superb fruit is highlighted by outstanding breadth, depth and structure. The 1999 perhaps just edges the 2000, with real promise in 2001 but it always deserves at least five years' ageing. Almost at the same level, Cullen Chardonnay, utilising natural yeasts and whole-bunch pressed, is a magnificently crafted white full of intense, pure citrus fruit and has unmistakable class and great length. The Sauvignon Blanc/Semillon (or sometimes Semillon/Sauvignon Blanc) is part barrel-fermented and shows lovely texture and balance. A powerful, somewhat backward new red blend, Mangan, and very good in both 2001 and 2002, is named for a vineyard owned by Vanya's brother Rick and his wife. Unusually it comes from Malbec, Petit Verdot and Merlot. Also new are Ellen Bussell red (Cabernet/Merlot) and white (Semillon/Sauvignon/Verdelho), from the first vintage the red is cool and expressive while the white has good texture. There are also two easy-drinking blended wines: Velvet Red and Classic Dry White. Both are Margaret River-sourced and fresh and fruit-driven. (PW)

● **Cabernet Sauvignon/Merlot** Diana Madeline★★★★ £E   ● **Mangan**★★★ £D   ● **Pinot Noir**★★ £D
○ **Chardonnay**★★★★ £E   ○ **Sauvignon Blanc/Semillon**★★★ £C

EVANS & TATE   Margaret River   www.evansandtate.com.au   A: AWs, P&S

Owner: Evans & Tate Ltd   Lionel's Vineyard, RSM 482 Payne Road, Jindong WA6280
This is now a very substantial operation with most of its development in the Margaret River though it was the original producer of quality Shiraz in the very hot Swan Valley. Nowadays Gnangara Shiraz is sadly no more than a simple, fruit-driven wine, one of several under the Gnangara label. Of an extensive Margaret River collection, Chardonnay is an ripe fruit-driven style lacking weight, structure and ageing potential. Sauvignon Blanc/Semillon has both grassy and riper notes but can be a bit lean while Cabernet/Merlot (labelled Barrique 61prior to the 2001 vintage) is very flavoursome with very ripe berryish fruit. Shiraz is similarly very ripe with a spicy intensity. The best wines come from the 26 ha Redbrook vineyard in the Wilyabrup Valley subregion. Chardonnay is crafted using an array of Burgundian techniques but is surprisingly restrained, recalling the quality of mid-nineties Margaret River efforts. Shiraz is spicy and intense, one of the best examples of this variety in the region. Redbrook Cabernet Sauvignon is also quite impressive and ageworthy. (PW)
● **Shiraz** ★★ £B Redbrook★★★ £D   ● **Cabernet/Merlot**★★ £B
● **Cabernet Sauvignon** Redbrook ★★★ £E
○ **Chardonnay**★ £B Redbrook★★★ £D   ○ **Sauvignon Blanc/Semillon**★★ £B

FRANKLAND ESTATE   Frankland River   www.franklandestate.com.au   A: M&V, P&S

Owner: Judi Callam & Barrie Smith   Frankland Road, Frankland WA 6396
Established in 1989 and, like ALKOOMI, based near remote Frankland in the western side of the Great Southern region. Production has increased to 15,000 cases a year and quality is good to very good. Great store is placed on managing the vineyards, including consultancy from expert Richard Smart. All the Isolation Ridge wines, comprising Chardonnay, Riesling, Cabernet Sauvignon and Shiraz, are impressive. The Riesling stands out with its tight, apple and mineral fruit. It has the structure for real ageing. Shiraz is full of black pepper and attractive, brambly fruit, the Cabernet marked by an intense, small berry-fruit character. Olmo's Reward is a blend of Cabernet Franc, Merlot, Malbec and Cabernet Sauvignon. It is sleek and stylish with ripe, dark, spicy fruit, supple and velvety tannin and good length. There are now two single-vineyard Rieslings, Cooladera and Poison Hill. (DM)
● **Cabernet Sauvignon** Isolation Ridge★★ £C   ● **Shiraz** Isolation Ridge★★★ £C
● **Olmo's Reward**★★★ £D
○ **Chardonnay** Isolation Ridge★★ £C   ○ **Riesling** Isolation Ridge★★★ £B

GOUNDREY   Mount Barker   www.goundreywines.com.au

Owner: Vincor   Langton, Muir Highway, Mount Barker WA 6324
In just a few years businessman Jack Bendat built Goundrey into a substantial and high-profile operation before selling to Vincor (owner of Canadian wineries CHATEAU DES CHARMES, MISSION HILL and SUMAC RIDGE amongst others) in 2002. There are 187 ha of estate vineyards and production now exceeds a quarter of a million cases per year. There are three main ranges produced. The Goundrey Reserves are the most exciting. The Reserve Merlot is full, plummy and approachable while the Reserve Cabernet Sauvignon is denser and more structured. Reserve Shiraz is medium-weight with some depth, though it does lack the concentration of the top examples from the region. Of the white Reserves, Riesling is well-crafted and full of green apple and and mineral notes while the Chardonnay is sound

but often marked by coarse oak. The Goundrey and Fox River ranges offer an array of simple, attractive, fruit-driven styles. However the overriding impression is that volume rather than character is the driving force here. (PW)

● **Merlot** Reserve★ £C   ● **Cabernet Sauvignon** Reserve★★ £C   ● **Shiraz** Reserve★ £C
O **Chardonnay** Reserve★ £C   O **Riesling** Reserve★★ £B

HOUGHTON   Swan District   www.houghton-wines.com.au   A: BRL, WSc

Owner: Hardy Wine Company   Dale Road, Middle Swan WA 6056
The biggest operation in Western Australia but being caught up in volume terms by both EVANS & TATE and GOUNDREY. The range is considerable, with fruit sourced throughout the vinegrowing areas of the state. The flapship is the remarkable Jack Mann red, a dense and massive blend of Cabernet Sauvignon, Shiraz and Malbec sourced from Frankland River and Mount Barker. It demands five or six years' ageing to even hint of its best. Regional wines from Frankland River, Pemberton and Margaret River are also impressive including the Frankland River Shiraz. Ratings for more of these wines will be added in the future. A premium Gladstones version of Frankland River Shiraz is also produced but difficult to find outside of Australia. Below the regional range come a mid-price Crofters range (sold only in Australia) then the more basic Line range which includes HWB, known locally in Australia as Show Reserve White Burgundy. This is one of the most successful and the most impressive of Australia's many volume brands. A variable blend but generally including Chenin Blanc, Muscadelle and Verdelho, it is almost unique among such wines in that it will age well. It certainly has a persistent and intense, ripe fruit character in its youth with depth and structure. (PW)

● **Shiraz** Frankland River★★★ £C   ● **Jack Mann**★★★★ £F
● **Cabernet Sauvignon** Margaret River★★ £C   O **HWB**★★ £B

HOWARD PARK   Denmark   www.howardparkwines.com.au   A: L&W, JNi, P&S, NYg

Owner: Jeff & Amy Burch   Scotsdale Road, Denmark WA 6333
Barely a decade ago, this substantial operation with wineries in Denmark in the Great Southern and at Margaret River was a small, high-quality label with just a Riesling and Cabernet-based red produced by JOHN WADE in small quantities while he was winemaker at PLANTAGENET. There are now well over 200 ha of estate vineyards and new planting is going on all the time. The two labels are Howard Park and Madfish. The three top wines are labelled simply Howard Park. Riesling is a superb, structured and very ageworthy example of the variety. It vies with LEEUWIN for the best example in Western Australia. The Cabernet Sauvignon/Merlot, sometimes labelled Cabernet Sauvignon, is variable both the composition (if usually including around a quarter Merlot) and source with fruit from Margaret River, Pemberton and Denmark. Dense, powerful and profound it remains one of Australia's great reds although vintages in the late 1990s are not quite as impressive as earlier ones. Chardonnay is in a restrained, tight and very structured style. Backward when young it will evolve well with age. Also under the Howard Park range are impressive region specific Shiraz and Cabernet Sauvignon. The Scotsdale pair are produced from Great Southern while the Leston wines are from Margaret River. A Madfish offers wines with immediate fruit character and appeal. The Premium Red and White have been consistent varying blends and forward, spicy, black pepper and dark-fruited Shiraz and a tropical, smoky Chardonnay have also impressed across a number of vintages. They are generally well-priced and drink well on release. (DM & PW)

Howard Park
● **Cabernet Sauvignon/Merlot**★★★★ £E
● **Cabernet Sauvignon** Scotsdale★★★ £C   Leston★★★ £C

● **Shiraz** Scotsdale★★★ £C Leston★★★ £C
O **Riesling**★★★★ £C O **Chardonnay**★★★★ £C

Madfish
● **Premium Red**★ £B ● **Shiraz**★★ £B ● **Pinot Noir**★★ £B
O **Chardonnay**★★ £B O **Premium White**★ £B

LEEUWIN ESTATE Margaret River www.leeuwinestate.com.au A: DDr, BBR, P&S

Owner: Horgan family Stevens Road, Margaret River WA 6285
One of the very best properties in the Margaret River, Leeuwin Estate has been producing excellent
Chardonnay and Riesling under the Art Series label for two decades now. Production is sizeable at
more than 60,000 cases a year but still small by comparison to some Margaret River producers. The
Art Series wines are the pinnacle. The Sauvignon Blanc is a very stylish example with an impressive
mineral structure. Riesling is very intense with mineral, lime and a marvellous toasty persistence with
four or five years' age. Chardonnay is extraordinarily rich and and powerful, yet balanced, intense
and complex; a long-lived Australian classic. The fruit and texture are such that the oak is seamlessly
integrated with three or four years' cellaring. Art Series reds include Pinot Noir and a fine Cabernet
Sauvignon which shows a complex fusion of cooler and riper fruit with excellent structure and
length. A second tier of wines, the Prelude Vineyards label includes a Classic Dry White, based on
Sauvignon Blanc, and a Chardonnay with good richness and structure but which evolves much faster
than the Art Series wine. Prelude Cabernet/Merlot has good weight and texture. Siblings, a third
label, is for everyday Sauvignon/Semillon and Shiraz. Sparkling wine from Great Southern Pinot
Noir and Chardonnay was first produced from the 1998 vintage. (PW)
● **Cabernet Sauvignon** Art Series★★★★ £E ● **Cabernet/Merlot** Prelude Vineyards★★ £C
● **Pinot Noir** Art Series★★ £D
O **Chardonnay** Art Series★★★★★ £E Prelude Vineyards★★ £C O **Riesling** Art Series★★★ £C
O **Sauvignon Blanc** Art Series★★★ £C O **Sauvignon Blanc/Semillon** Siblings★ £B

MOSS WOOD Margaret River www.mosswood.com.au A: Lay, NYg, P&S

Owner: Keith & Clare Mugford Metricup Road, Willyabrup WA 6280
Very fine, small 8-ha Margaret River estate. Bill Pannell who now runs PICARDY founded Moss
Wood in 1969 and production remains small under the Mugfords at around 6,000 cases. Semillon
has always been remarkable here and a benchmark for the region. The wine is unwooded and shows
restrained fruit in its youth. It will be all the better for five years' ageing. Chardonnay is in a full,
opulent style with smoky, spicy new oak evident in its youth. The Cabernet Sauvignon is one of the
very finest in the region – complex, powerful and structured, even dense and extracted, in contrast
to other more fruit-driven examples from the region. Rich blackberry and cassis emerges as the wine
becomes increasingly harmonious with age. In order to expand their business but retain the core
quality of the Moss Wood wines, the Mugfords purchased the 7-ha Ribbon Vale vineyard and
winery in 2000, adding a further 5,000 cases to production. Vinification takes place at Moss Wood.
The range has been reduced to just three wines; while Merlot stands out, a very good Semillon has
now been incorporated into the Semillon/Sauvignon Blanc blend. The wines thus far are reasonably
concentrated and are produced from fairly low-yielding vines but can be expected to show greater
refinement and complexity in the future following changes to their vinification. Moss Wood also
produce wines from growers' vineyards: Cabernet Sauvignon from Glenmore Vineyard in Yallingup
(northern Margaret River), and Chardonnay and Pinot Noir from the Lefroy Brook Vineyard in
Pemberton. (PW)

Moss Wood:
- **Cabernet Sauvignon★★★★** £F   Glenmore Vineyard★★★ £C
- ○ **Chardonnay★★★★** £E   Lefroy Brook Vineyard★★★ £C   ○ **Semillon★★★★** £C

Ribbon Vale:
- **Cabernet/Merlot/Malbec★★** £C   ● **Merlot★★★** £C
- ○ **Semillon/Sauvignon Blanc★★** £B

PICARDY   Pemberton   www.picardy.com.au   A: Cap, Lay, P&S

Owner: Bill Pannell   Cnr Eastbrook Road & Vasse Highway, Pemberton WA 6260
This is now established along with SALITAGE as one of the two best wineries in Pemberton. Bill Pannell established MOSS WOOD but diverted his attention to PICARDY in 1993. The Burgundy varieties and Shiraz are all successful. Cabernet Sauvignon, Merlot and Cabernet Franc are also planted, although the results are not quite as good. There can be a marked leafy note showing through in the Cabernet/Merlot. Chardonnay is in a tight and restrained style. The oak is in no way oppressive. Pinot Noir is full of dark, berry-fruit aromas which support the judicious oak treatment. Shiraz is equally impressive now. The oak here is now better integrated and there is a real intensity of dark pepper and black fruit. Elegant, long and lightly minerally. (DM)
- **Cabernet/Merlot★★** £C   ● **Merlot/Cabernet★★** £C   ● **Shiraz★★★** £C
- **Pinot Noir★★★** £C   ○ **Chardonnay★★★** £C

PIERRO   Margaret River   A: MSd, BBR

Owner: Dr Mike Peterkin   PO Box 522, Brusselton WA 6280
Pierro produces one of the finest, most complex and beguiling Chardonnays in Western Australia. The wine possesses a remarkable array of secondary flavours and is quite unlike the majority of Aussie Chardonnay. Citrus, mineral and grilled nuts overwhelm the senses and the wine is rich, buttery and very long. There is a fine, youthfully grassy, melony Semillon/Sauvignon Blanc labelled LTC; intense and with just a hint of background oak. The top wines are completed by a minty, almost eucalypty Cabernet Sauvignon/Merlot. Well-judged oak is aided by completing fermentation in barrique and the wine is rich, concentrated and cedary. A first-class example if not quite on a par with the very best in the region. Mike Peterkin also makes the wines of the 9-ha Fire Gully vineyard. Whites, including Semillon/Sauvignon and Semillon, are fresh and fruity and have the edge over the reds, a Cabernet/Merlot and a Shiraz, which want for depth and richness. (DM)

Pierro:
- ○ **Chardonnay★★★★** £E   ○ **Semillon/Sauvignon Blanc** LTC★★★ £C
- **Cabernet Sauvignon/Merlot★★★** £E   ● **Pinot Noir★★** £D

Fire Gully:
- **Cabernet/Merlot★** £C   ○ **Semillon/Sauvignon Blanc★★** £B

PLANTAGENET   Mount Barker   www.plantagenetwines.com   A: Lib, ACh

Owner: Lionel Sampson & Son   Albany Highway, Mount Barker WA 6324
Plantagenet is the top winery at Mount Barker and among the very best in the Great Southern region. Production has risen to over 50,000 cases a year yet a high standard and remarkable consistency have been maintained by winemaker Gavin Berry. The winery is also an important source of contract winemaking facilities for many small estates in the region. Wines under the Plantagenet label include a smoky Pinot Noir at the ripe strawberryish end of the spectrumfrom Great Southern and Pemberton fruit and spicy, grapefruity Chardonnay with oak and lees adding

complexity. Cabernet Sauvignon shows good richness and a certain elegance but without the extra depth or power found in the best from the Margaret River. Shiraz, on the other hand, is mightily impressive for the price, with smoky, minerally, white pepper and dark fruits character – as much Northern Rhône as Western Australia. A very perfumed, toasty, limey and well-structured Riesling is among the finest in the region, particularly with five years' age. Omrah is the second label and there is excellent intensity to an impressive Unoaked Chardonnay and good fruit in a Sauvignon Blanc which should be drunk young. Of two Omrah reds, Shiraz outshines a Cabernet/Merlot. Hazard Hill red and white are sold locally while fruit is widely sourced for similarly good value, exported Hellfire Bay Chardonnay and Shiraz/Grenache. (PW)

Plantagenet:
● **Shiraz** Mount Barker★★★★ £D   ● **Cabernet Sauvignon** Mount Barker★★★ £C   ● **Pinot Noir**★★ £C
○ **Chardonnay** Mount Barker★★★ £C   ○ **Riesling** Mount Barker★★★ £C

Omrah:
● **Shiraz**★★ £B   ● **Cabernet/Merlot**★ £B
○ **Chardonnay** Unoaked★★ £B   ○ **Sauvignon Blanc**★ £B

VASSE FELIX   Margaret River   www.vassefelix.com.au   A: Neg, L&W, Tan, P&S, Han, NYg

Owner: Holmes à Court family   Cnr Caves Road & Harmans South Road, Cowaramup WA 6284
Vasse Felix is now a sizeable Margaret River operation, producing some 125,000 cases a year. There is a large range but its reputation has been maintained over a long period by the top reds. The Cabernet/Merlot shows good plum and berry fruit while the Cabernet Sauvignon is denser and better structured. Shiraz is more subtle than many but has good intensity in the best years. The Heytesbury red is a blend of Cabernet Sauvignon, Shiraz, Merlot and Malbec. Rich and concentrated, it has an additional dimension over the other reds. Fine oak is very well-integrated, with the cassis and dark chocolatey fruit emerging after four or five years' ageing. Chardonnay is the leading white, with a fine balance of fruit and oak in the regular example but more oak, power and complexity in the Heytesbury version, though this wine can sometimes lack balance. Semillon is given a short period of oak treatment in American and French barrels. It takes on a marked toasty character and when successful this meshes well with a good fruit core though sometimes tends to excess. There is also a sparkling Brut *méthode champenoise* which is produced from all three Champagne varieties although the Pinot Meunier component is negligible. The Noble Riesling is restricted to vintages when botrytis occurs naturally and is rich and concentrated, with an intense peach and citrus character. Theatre Red and White are early-drinking red and white styles while Classic Dry White and Classic Dry Red offer a touch more depth – all are sourced throughout Western Australia. (DM)

● **Heytesbury**★★★★ £E   ● **Cabernet Sauvignon**★★★ £D   ● **Cabernet/Merlot**★★★ £C
● **Shiraz**★★★ £D   ○ **Semillon**★★ £B   ○ **Semillon/Sauvignon Blanc**★★ £B
○ **Chardonnay**★★★ £B   Heytesbury★★★ £C   ○ **Noble Riesling**★★★ £E

OTHER WINES OF NOTE

AMBERLEY ESTATE (Margaret River) ○ **Semillon** £C   ● **Shiraz** £D
ASHBROOK ESTATE (Margaret River) ○ **Semillon** £C   ● **Cabernet/Merlot** £C
BROOKLAND VALLEY (Margaret River) ○ **Semillon/Sauvignon Blanc** £B   ○ **Sauvignon Blanc** £C
● **Cabernet Sauvignon/Merlot** £C   ● **Shiraz** £B
CHESTNUT GROVE (Manjimup) ○ **Verdelho** £B   ● **Merlot** £C
CLAIRAULT (Margaret River) ○ **Semillon/Sauvignon Blanc** £B   ○ **Riesling** £B
● **Clairault Reserve** (Cabernet Sauvignon/Cabernet Franc/Merlot) £E
PAUL CONTI (Swan District) ○ **Chardonnay** Tuarts £B   ● **Shiraz** Mariginiup £C   Medici £C

DEVIL'S LAIR (Margaret River) O Chardonnay £D
DRIFTWOOD ESTATE (Margaret River) O Chardonnay £C ● Shiraz £C
FERMOY ESTATE (Margaret River) O Chardonnay £B O Semillon £B
● Cabernet Sauvignon £C ● Merlot £C
GILBERTS (Great Southern) O Riesling £B
HAYSHED HILL (Margaret River) ● Cabernet Sauvignon £C
KARRIVALE (Great Southern) O Riesling Gibraltar Rock £B ● Shiraz Gibraltar Rock £C
KARRIVIEW (Great Southern) O Chardonnay £C ● Pinot Noir £C
KILLERBY (Geographe) O Semillon £B ● Cabernet Sauvignon £C ● Shiraz £C
LEAPING LIZARD (Margaret River) O Semillon/Sauvignon Blanc £B ● Cabernet/Merlot £B
LOST LAKE (Pemberton) O Chardonnay £C ● Pinot Noir £C ● Shiraz £C
MOSS BROTHERS (Margaret River) ● Shiraz £C
MOUNT TRIO (Great Southern) O Sauvignon Blanc £B ● Cabernet/Merlot £B
OLD KENT RIVER (Great Southern) ● Pinot Noir £B ● Shiraz £C
PALANDRI (Margaret River) ● Cabernet/Merlot £B ● Shiraz £B
● Cabernet Sauvignon £B Reserve £C
PALMER WINES (Margaret River) ● Cabernet/Merlot £C ● Merlot £C
REDGATE (Margaret River) O Chardonnay £C
SALITAGE (Pemberton) O Chardonnay £C ● Pinot Noir £D
SMITHBROOK (Manjimup) O Chardonnay £C ● Cabernet Sauvignon £C
STELLA BELLA (Margaret River) O Sauvignon Blanc £B ● Sangiovese/Cabernet Sauvignon £B
SUCKFIZZLE AUGUSTA (Margaret River) O Sauvignon Blanc/Semillon £C
● Cabernet Sauvignon £C
TINGLE-WOOD (Great Southern) O Riesling Yellow Tingle £B
VOYAGER ESTATE (Margaret River) O Sauvignon Blanc/Semillon £B O Semillon £B
● Cabernet Sauvignon/Merlot £C ● Shiraz £C
JOHN WADE WINES (Great Southern) O Riesling £B O Merlot/Cabernet Franc £C
WATERSHED (Margaret River) ● Cabernet/Merlot £B ● Shiraz £B
WESTFIELD (Swan District) O Chardonnay £B O Liqueur Muscat £C
WIGNALLS (Great Southern) O Chardonnay £C ● Cabernet Sauvignon £C ● Pinot Noir £C
WILLESPIE (Margaret River) O Semillon/Sauvignon Blanc £B ● Cabernet Sauvignon £C
WOODY NOOK (Margaret River) ● Cabernet Sauvignon £C
XANADU (Margaret River) O Semillon £C O Semillon/Sauvignon Blanc £B O Chardonnay £C
● Lagan Estate Reserve (Cabernet Sauvignon/Cabernet Franc/Merlot) £D

Author's choice (PW)

10 top Margaret River reds
CAPE MENTELLE ● Cabernet Sauvignon
CULLEN ● Cabernet Sauvignon/Merlot Diana Madeline
CULLEN ● Mangan
HOWARD PARK ● Cabernet Sauvignon Leston
LEEUWIN ESTATE ● Cabernet Sauvignon Art Series
MOSS WOOD ● Cabernet Sauvignon
PIERRO ● Cabernet Sauvignon/Merlot
XANADU ● Lagan Estate Reserve
VASSE FELIX ● Cabernet Sauvignon
VASSE FELIX ● Heytesbury

10 distinguished WA whites
CAPE MENTELLE O Semillon/Sauvignon Blanc Margaret River
CAPEL VALE O Riesling Whispering Hill
CULLEN O Chardonnay Margaret River
CULLEN O Sauvignon Blanc/Semillon Margaret River

HOWARD PARK O Chardonnay
HOWARD PARK O Riesling
LEEUWIN ESTATE O Chardonnay Arts Series
LEEUWIN ESTATE O Riesling Arts Series
MOSS WOOD O Chardonnay Margaret River
PIERRO O Chardonnay Margaret River

10 Great Southern red stars

ALKOOMI ● Shiraz Frankland River Jarrah
CHATSFIELD ● Shiraz Mount Barker
FRANKLAND ESTATE ● Olmo's Reward
HOUGHTON ● Jack Mann
HOUGHTON ● Shiraz Frankland River
HOWARD PARK ● Cabernet Sauvignon/Merlot
PICARDY ● Pinot Noir Pemberton
PICARDY ● Shiraz Pemberton
PLANTAGENET ● Shiraz Mount Barker
SALITAGE ● Pinot Noir Pemberton

10 excellent value for money wines

ALKOOMI O Riesling Frankland River
CAPE MENTELLE ● Cabernet/Merlot Trinders
CAPEL VALE O Verdelho
CULLEN ● Ellen Bussell Red Margaret River
HOUGHTON'S O HWB
PALANDRI ● Cabernet/Merlot Margaret River
PLANTAGENET OMRAH O Chardonnay Unoaked
PLANTAGENET OMRAH ● Shiraz
STELLA BELLA O Sauvignon Blanc Margaret River
WATERSHED ● Shiraz Margaret River

New Zealand

New Zealand's image is primarily built around intense, vibrant, fruit-driven whites for immediate consumption. It is also an industry of technical wines, made in the winery on a scientific basis. Fifteen years ago, against a background of so much poorly made wine in Europe, it seemed that they, together with the Californians and Australians, were the only ones getting it right. But now Europe is being revitalised on the basis of better health in the vineyard, in areas it has had centuries to define and redefine. The clearest direction for New Zealand has come from well-educated, widely travelled, outward-looking winemakers such as John Buck (Te Mata), Michael Brajkovich (Kumeu River), Kim Goldwater (Goldwater Estate) and, more recently, Steve Smith (Craggy Range). All have had an influence way beyond their own small wineries. Wines of better structure and greater longevity are now on the increase from both new and existing vineyard areas.

The Regions

Despite rapid expansion in the 1990s, New Zealand's production (two-thirds white) is set to remain small in world terms, currently about one-tenth of that of Bordeaux. With a generally cool climate the significance of what grape variety/varieties to plant and where took on greater significance than in warmer, easier climes. Twenty years ago Müller-Thurgau dominated the vineyard area; 10 years later Sauvignon Blanc took on a significance way beyond the area planted to it and in the last decade Chardonnay has been the vine planted in greatest numbers, with Pinot Noir coming up on the rails. Along the way Cabernet Sauvignon has found its place (in Hawkes Bay and on Waiheke Island) and Merlot has been more than a mere flirtation. Gradually the industry has moved southwards through Gisborne and Hawkes Bay before confirming Marlborough as its leading region. Many regions or pockets within regions have taken on their own identity based on a grape variety or two.

New Zealand's first vineyard was planted in the far north of New Zealand in the the Bay of Islands but its early history was centred around **Auckland**, the country's largest city. Despite the city's often warm, humid conditions, some favourable mesoclimates are to be found in **Kumeu** and **Huapai** (to the west), where producers have been successful with Chardonnay as well as Merlot and Cabernet Sauvignon. Other vineyard pockets on the fringes of a sea of suburbia include Matakana, Cleveden and Mangere but it is offshore in the Hauraki Gulf on **Waiheke Island**, where conditions are generally warmer and drier, that Merlot and Cabernet have been most successful, a fact highlighted and confirmed in many vintages since Stonyridge's first in 1987. There are now more than 30 wineries on the island.

In the eastern central part of the North Island are its two most productive regions. While **Gisborne** often struggles with rain and humidity during the growing season, the drier **Hawkes Bay** has become the country's leading area for blends based on the classic Bordeaux varieties. Malbec, Merlot and Cabernet Franc as well as Cabernet Sauvignon make an important contribution to the region'a reds. An unprecedented number of fine, fully ripe examples emerged with the 1998 vintage as the ranks of good producers swelled. The best reds have an intense berryish fruit, balanced oak, acidity and ripe tannins. The **Gimblett Gravels**, free-draining gravels centred on an old river bed, are being promoted by a consortium of producers as a geographically-defined 'appellation'. Many leading producers now also make some stylish but ripe Syrah, while Zinfandel is also gaining a foothold. For whites, as well as the ubiquitous Chardonnay, good Gewürztraminer is being produced.

A long way south of Hawkes Bay is the **Wairarapa** region, which lies within the political boundaries of the country's capital, Wellington. Though the extent of its most promising viticultural land, the terraces around the small town of **Martinborough**, is extremely limited, other favoured pockets of viticulture could yet emerge from a region that benefits, like other protected eastern regions, from a relatively low autumnal rainfall. The best early examples of New Zealand Pinot Noir came from here though they remain few in number. Some potential has also been shown for Chardonnay, Riesling and lately Pinot Gris.

Marlborough, New Zealand's most important viticultural area, is at the north-eastern tip of the South Island. Like Hawkes Bay it is favoured both climatically, often with fine weather late into the growing season, and geologically, thanks to mostly free-draining soils. Yet most of the major decisions about where and what to plant were made on a purely commercial basis. That is, where the land was cheapest and the grape most prolific. Montana's development of Marlborough in the 1970s was intended as a cheap source of Müller-Thurgau but some Sauvignon was planted as well and it has never looked back. Marlborough's most important grapes are Sauvignon Blanc, source of nearly all of the country's top examples, Chardonnay and Pinot Noir. The range and intensity of flavour can be most impressive, even if adding more depth and structure has so far been limited to a few top producers. Of growing importance is Pinot Gris, while Riesling, both in dry and sweeter styles, has been successful. **Nelson**, slightly cooler and wetter than Marlborough, perseveres with a similar grape mix but site selection is more critical as is the dedication required from producers such as Neudorf.

The vineyards of **Canterbury** lie to the west of Christchurch, the South Island's largest city, and are well-protected from the worst weather from the west by the Southern Alps. The most promising sub-region, **Waipara**, though usually afforded long fine autumns, requires further protection from north-westerly winds in the form of windbreaks. Although the soils are calcareous and well-drained, there seems only just sufficient heat to fully ripen Pinot Noir, Chardonnay and Riesling – the most successful varieties in the region as a whole. Pegasus Bay and Waipara West are the two most important estates to emerge.

In **Central Otago** conditions are like nowhere else in the country. There is even a continental-type climate influence with long hot days and cool nights during the growing season. Interestingly this is also the one part of the country where the rock types are much older geologically and hillsides are favoured for frost protection. Pinot Noir is emerging as the most important variety, though the potential for fine Riesling, Chardonnay, Pinot Gris and Gewürztraminer is already proven too.

A- Z Producers by region

Auckland
MONTANA
VILLA MARIA

Kumeu, Auckland
KUMEU RIVER

Waikeke Island, Auckland
GOLDWATER ESTATE
STONYRIDGE

Gisborne
MILLTON
MONTANA

Hawkes Bay
ALPHA DOMUS
CRAGGY RANGE
MONTANA/CHURCH ROAD
STONECROFT
TE MATA
UNISON
VILLA MARIA

Martinborough/Wairarapa
ATA RANGI
BORTHWICK

DRY RIVER
MARTINBOROUGH VINEYARD

Marlborough
CLOUDY BAY
FROMM
GROVE MILL
HUNTER'S
ISABEL ESTATE
MONTANA/BRANCOTT ESTATE
SERESIN
VAVASOUR
VILLA MARIA
WITHER HILLS

Nelson
NEUDORF

Waipara/Canterbury
MOUNTFORD
PEGASUS BAY

Central Otago
FELTON ROAD
MT DIFFICULTY
MOUNT EDWARD

Vintage Summary

With a few exceptions, New Zealand whites don't have a good reputation for ageing and many Chardonnays that are attractive with one or two years age are falling apart with three or more. Even the very best Marlborough Sauvignon won't improve the way a top Sancerre or Pouilly-Fumé can. In fact the majority need to be consumed within the first year after the vintage. The few exceptions have been noted in the producer entries. Riesling and sweet wines will generally keep a little longer.

Reds do have a growing reputation for keeping but don't seem to develop and mature in the same way European wines do. But they do keep and the fruit holds up well. Those based on Cabernet Sauvignon, as might be expected, show the greatest longevity and come, in the main, from Waiheke or Hawkes Bay. Top examples now usually need five years' ageing but can keep for ten from an excellent vintage. The best recent Waiheke vintages include 2000, 99, 98, 94, 93, 91 and 90, while 97 and 96 aren't bad. In Hawkes Bay the best reds are likely to come from 2000, 98, 97, 95, 94 or 91 but 99 and 96 are by no means poor from a good producer. Of the mushrooming number of fine Pinot Noir, three to six years' age is likely to be the window of optimum drinking but some of the newer or more extracted styles might need five years or more. Martinborough had a run of fine vintages for Pinot Noir between 1996 and 2001, while Marlborough or Central Otago should yield a good Pinot (if from a good producer) from any vintage since 1998. The 2003 vintage in New Zealand was small and difficult after the bumper crop of 2002, with the best results expected from Central Otago.

ALPHA DOMUS   Hawkes Bay   www.alphadomus.co.nz   A: McK, NYg

Owner: Ham family   1829 Maraekakaho Road, RD 1, Hastings
Alpha Domus was established in 1991 and has only been making wines since 1995, yet it has produced some of the best reds from Hawkes Bay in recent top vintages. Grapes are sourced exclusively from 20 ha of vineyard planted to Sauvignon Blanc, Semillon and Chardonnay, plus Merlot, Cabernet Sauvigon, Cabernet Franc and some Malbec. The Navigator, based on Merlot (around 60 per cent) but complemented by the Cabernets and five per cent Malbec, is ripe and composed with good concentration – as, too, is a regular Merlot/Cabernet Sauvignon. AD is the premium label. The Aviator (Cabernet Sauvignon with some Merlot, Malbec and Cabernet Franc) is very impressive in its ripeness, intensity and concentration and better balanced than previously. AD Chardonnay is slightly over-worked but richly textured, while an unoaked Chardonnay is tangy and peachy if wanting for more expression. Semillon appears in a regular, very ripe style as well as a rich botrytised version, AD Noble Selection. Newer to the range is a ripe and berryish Pinot Noir. (PW)
- **The Navigator★★★** £D   ● **AD The Aviator★★★** £E
- **Merlot/Cabernet Sauvignon★★** £C   ● **Pinot Noir★★** £C
- O **Chardonnay** Unoaked★★ £B AD★★★ £C   O Semillon★★ £B

ATA RANGI   Martinborough   www.atarangi.co.nz   A: Lib, MHv, WSc, Kwi

Owner: C Paton & P Pattie, O Masters & A Paton   Puruatanga Road, PO Box 43, Martinborough
From an original 5 ha site, brother and sister Clive and Alison Paton and their partners have built an enviable reputation centred on Pinot Noir. They now draw upon 33 ha of vineyards (mostly owned but some are contracted grapes from neighbouring families), the majority on the Martinborough Terrace. Yields are low, the vine age now averages around 20 years and the quality of the fruit shows in the wines. Clive Paton and Oliver Masters forge New Zealand's most consistently fine Pinot Noir, though there are of course rivals for the out-and-out best example in a given vintage, including FELTON ROAD, FROMM, VILLA MARIA and the well-established DRY RIVER. The wine has a depth and structure that requires a little patience but brings a richness and complexity with three to five years' age, by which time many other New Zealand examples have fallen apart. The quality of the spicy, cedary, berryish Célèbre (Cabernet/Syrah/Merlot) is more vintage-dependent but usually offers good depth and richness in a cool style. Craighall, the premium Chardonnay, is produced from a vineyard adjacent to the winery; a second, Petrie, comes from a 4.5-ha vineyard at East Taratahi to the north of Martinborough. Pinot Gris with intense quince-like fruit is one of the most promising Antipodean examples. Some Sauvignon is made along with a botrytised Riesling (when conditions permit), while a varietal Syrah is a new addition. (PW)
- **Pinot Noir★★★★** £E   ● **Célèbre★★★** £C
- O **Chardonnay** Craighall★★★ £C Petrie★★ £B   O **Pinot Gris** Lismore★★ £C

BORTHWICK   Wairarapa   www.borthwick.co.nz   A: JAr

Owner: Borthwick family   Dakins Road, R D 7, Wairarapa
Borthwick's 27 ha of vineyards, like those to the south in Martinborough are planted on free-draining river terraces. Though only established in 1996, Borthwick has pioneered viticulture in the Dakins Road area. Roseworthy trained and widely experienced Paddy Borthwick has similarly placed his faith in Pinot Noir. Though the vines are still very young, the wine already shows impressive ripeness, breadth and complexity. Riesling too is promising; intense and pungent if not yet with the structure to stand long ageing. Other wines, all estate-sourced, include varietal Sauvignon Blanc and Chardonnay and reds from Merlot, Cabernet/Merlot and Sangiovese. Limited tastings preclude rating all the wines

but suggest this will be a producer to follow. (PW)

O **Riesling**★★ £B   ● **Pinot Noir**★★★ £B

CLOUDY BAY   Marlborough   www.cloudybay.co.nz   A: CBy, Par, VCq, NYg, Rae

Owner: LVMH   PO Box 376, Jacksons Road, Blenheim
Established in 1985 by David Hohnen of CAPE MENTELLE (Western Australia), Cloudy Bay is probably New Zealand's best-known winery internationally and produces its most famous Sauvignon Blanc. Both Cape Mentelle and Cloudy Bay are now under the umbrella of French luxury goods giant LVMH yet despite ever bigger volumes and changing vineyard sources (there are now 60 ha of vineyards supplemented by bought-in grapes), the Sauvignon remains one of Marlborough's best. The stylish aromas and range of fruit flavours (nettles, blackcurrant leaf and tropical notes) are complemented by a structure that provides an uncharacteristic ability (in the region) to age for at least a year or two – but there's not quite the concentration or intensity of one or two others. Te Koko is a barrel-fermented and aged version with an oak-given complexity yet the nettly fruit is not overwhelmed and it shows considerable style and finesse. It's very good with two or three years' age and promises to keep for longer. Chardonnay has long been made to a high standard though can be a bit overdone in flavour and structure, lacking expression and finesse, while Pinot Noir shows increasing character and intensity if not yet the texture or dimension of the best New Zealand examples. Another highly acclaimed wine is Pelorus, both a creamy, soft fruit-centred and bread dough example with lots of immediate appeal (if no more), and the vintage-dated version, tighter and more intense with better structure and further ageing potential after its release. (PW)

O **Sauvignon Blanc**★★★ £C Te Koko★★★ £D   O **Chardonnay**★★ £C
O **Pelorus** Non-Vintage★★ £C Vintage★★★ £D   ● **Pinot Noir**★★ £D

CRAGGY RANGE   Hawkes Bay   www.craggyrange.com   A: Cap, ACh, NYg

Owner: Peabody family & Steve Smith   253 Waimarama Road, Havelock North, Hawkes Bay
New Zealand's most dynamic winery early in the new century. Named for the Craggy Range in Hawkes Bay's Tukituki Valley, a stunning new winery complex has been built to process grapes from a patchwork of outstanding vineyard sites split between Hawkes Bay, Martinborough and Marlborough. Direction comes from viticultural expert Steve Smith, who established a reputation while providing high-quality fruit for VILLA MARIA. The first varietals were all concentrated, well-structured with an extra intensity and definition not seen in most New Zealand wines. These include two Marlborough Sauvignon Blanc: a nettly Avery Vineyard example and a slightly minerally, smoky, classy Old Renwick. Also sourced from Marlborough is an excellent intense and vibrant Riesling from 25 year-old vines in the Rapaura Vineyard (and made in a rich botrytised style in 2000). Ripe berryish Merlot and intense nectarine and citrus Chardonnay have been sourced from the Seven Poplars vineyard in Hawkes Bay, and lately from Gimblett Gravels too. A series of 'Prestige' wines is being established from vineyards in the Gimblett Gravels. The quality of all the wines is very exciting and they will be rated with further tastings. They are Les Beaux Cailloux (Chardonnay), The Quarry (mostly Cabernet Sauvignon with some Merlot and a little Cabernet Franc), Sophia (Merlot-based but complemented by Cabernet Franc and Malbec) and Le Sol (Syrah). Newish Martinborough varietals include Te Muna Sauvignon Blanc and Martin's Road Pinot Noir. (PW)

O **Sauvignon Blanc** Avery Vineyard★★★ £B Old Renwick★★★★ £C
O **Chardonnay** Seven Poplars★★★ £C   O **Riesling** Rapaura Vineyard★★★ £C
● **Merlot** Seven Poplars★★ £C

DRY RIVER Martinborough
A: J&B,NYg, Rae

Owner: Julian Robertson & Oliver family trust Puruatanga Road, Martinborough

A small estate that acquired an enviable cult following due to the unstinting devotion by Dr Neil McCallum to producing the highest quality fruit from around 10 ha of prime Martinborough vineyards. Dry River has arguably the best record in the country of producing high-quality ageworthy reds and whites. Despite wide acclaim and the evident complexity, depth and richness of texture in the wines, including the best Gewürztraminer, Riesling and Pinot Gris in the country, relatively few seem to have been inspired to reach the same levels. Under new (American) ownership from 2003 (the same as for TE AWA FARM), it remains to be seen how much the estate will expand and what future direction quality will take. In the meantime, despite a lack of cleanliness in some 1998 and 99 wines, don't hesitate to try the wines if the opportunity arises. To date the wines have been mostly sold in New Zealand through an exclusive mailing list but a little is exported. A little Syrah is also made. (PW)

● **Pinot Noir★★★** £E O **Pinot Gris★★★** £D
O **Riesling** Craighall★★★ £D O **Gewürztraminer★★★** £D O **Chardonnay★★★** £D

FELTON ROAD Central Otago www.feltonroad.com
A: Wso, BBR, ACh, Rae

Owner: Nigel Greening Bannockburn, RD 2, Central Otago

Every now and then a very talented winemaker comes to the fore with unprecedented results in a given region, such as the likes of Didier DAGUENEAU in Pouilly Fumé, Alvaro PALACIOS in Priorat or Helen Turley (MARCASSIN) in Sonoma. Blair Walter is such a one. Yet with Pinot-mad Englishman Nigel Greening taking over Stewart Elm's inspired creation in 2000 and Gareth King in the vineyard, this is very much a team effort. The estate comprises 14 ha with an additional 8 ha at Cornish Point as well as leased vineyards (The Sluicings and Drystone). Pinot Noir shows a richness and complexity that most other New Zealand examples have only hinted at – a quality of fruit effortlessly expressed. While there are a number of other promising efforts in Central Otago, the single-vineyard Block 3 and Block 5, in particular, set the standard for the region. Chardonnay and Riesling too are very good including a rare and excellent unoaked Chardonnay. As well as another good Pinot Noir, a Pinot Gris is produced from Cornish Point but the first effort seems a little overdone. Demand has pushed prices up, particularly for the Pinots, but whites remain affordable. Single-vineyard Block 1 Riesling (made in a rich medium-dry Spätlese style) was produced from 2001 and Block 2 Chardonnay from 2002. (PW)

● **Pinot Noir** Block 3★★★★ £D Block 5★★★★ £D
● **Pinot Noir★★** £C Cornish Point★★ £C
O **Chardonnay★★** £C Barrel Fermented★★★ £C O **Riesling★★** £C Dry★★★ £C

FROMM Marlborough www.frommwineries.com
A: L&W, NYg

Owner: George & Ruth Fromm Godfrey Road, RD 2, Blenheim

Fromm is not one winery but two. One is in Malans in Switzerland, the other in Marlborough. Marlborough's Fromm Vineyard is planted almost exclusively to red grapes with a strong leaning towards Pinot Noir (as are the Swiss vineyards). Grapes are also sourced from the William Hoare Vineyard and the Bamfield Vineyard (both in the Brancott Valley), which provide more Pinot Noir as well as other grapes, including Chardonnay and Riesling for the white wines. A separate bottling of Pinot Noir is produced from the gently undulating 15-ha Clayvin Vineyard, owned jointly with UK wine merchant Lay & Wheeler. It was produced again in 2000 after a break of four years due to replanting. The wines are made by George (Georg) Fromm and Hätsch Kalberer and the philosophy is one of low yields, fully ripe grapes and minimal intervention in the winemaking to give as natural an expression of the wines as possible. They show good character and flavour intensity particularly in the Reserve Syrah and Pinot Noir. A Reserve Merlot includes a little Cabernet Franc and Malbec. Small quantities of Gewürztraminer and Sauvignon Blanc are produced as well as a Malbec/Merlot blend since 1999. (PW)

La Strada

● **Pinot Noir★** £C Fromm Vineyard★★ £D ● **Syrah** Reserve★★ £C
○ **Riesling★★** £B ○ **Chardonnay★** £C Reserve★★ £C

GOLDWATER ESTATE Waiheke Island, Auckland www.goldwaterwine.com A: Hal

Owner: Kim & Jeanette Goldwater 18 Causeway Road, Putiki Bay, Waiheke Island
Kim Goldwater pioneered quality wine production on Waiheke Island in Auckland's Hauraki Gulf in 1978 and has long produced a powerful, structured Cabernet Sauvignon/Merlot with good balance, ripeness and concentration in the best years. The wine keeps well and with age impresses more for its elegance and complexity than for concentration but has very good depth and dimension. It deserves to be drunk with a minimum of five years' age. Though more pricey, at least as impressive is the Waiheke Island Merlot from the Esslin Vineyard, with rich plum and berry fruit and spicy oak. A little of a premium Chardonnay is also produced from the Zell Vineyard. As well as the 10 ha of vineyards on Waiheke, a further 35 ha in Marlborough are contracted under a long-term lease. Dog Point Sauvignon Blanc usually shows good aromatic Marlborough Sauvignon character while Roseland Chardonnay shows good structure and some restraint with attractive citrus flavours and well-integrated oak. A new vineyard has been recently planted in the Gimblett Gravels district of Hawkes Bay. (PW)

● **Cabernet Sauvigon/Merlot★★★** £E ● **Merlot** Esslin★★★ £F
○ **Chardonnay** Roseland★★ £B Zell★★★ £B ○ **Sauvignon Blanc** Dog Point★★ £B

GROVE MILL Marlborough www.grovemill.co.nz A: CRs, Odd, Kwi

*Owner: **The New Zealand Wine Company Ltd** Waihopai Valley Road, Marlborough*
Grove Mill has grown rapidly since being established in 1988. While many of the grapes are supplied under contract, a series of vineyards have been either leased or bought outright to increase the amount under the winery's direct control. Since the first vintage the wines made by David Pearce have delivered consistently ripe fruit and are characterised by their almost overwhelming fruit intensity and concentration. In the Sauvignon this is slightly at the expense of greater expression and complexity. A partially barrique-fermented and oak-aged Chardonnay, like several of the better examples in the region, can be a touch overdone, not lacking for weight or structure but somewhat dominated by secondary, winemaking-given characters (including the oak) at the expense of a clearer expression of the fruit. A Pinot Gris displays less varietal expression than some but nonetheless shows good richness and balanced acidity while Pinot Noir can show an overripe character. Sanctuary, named for a wetland project that has been developed at the Waihopai Valley vineyard, is a second label that includes Chardonnay, Riesling and Sauvignon Blanc. A second Pinot Gris is made under the Frog Haven label. (PW)

Grove Mill
○ **Sauvignon Blanc★★★** £B ○ **Riesling★★** £B
○ **Chardonnay★★** £B ○ **Pinot Gris★★** £B ● **Pinot Noir★** £C

HUNTER'S Marlborough www.hunters.co.nz A: Lay, WSc, NYg, Kwi

Owner: Jane Hunter Rapaura Road, Blenheim
Jane Hunter remains one of the best known personalities in the New Zealand wine industry, having

produced some of Marlborough's best wines for a decade and a half. The wines, made by Gary Duke, show a harmony, a charm and a gentler character when compared with some of Marlborough's brasher efforts. Sauvignon Blanc in two versions has always been the focus of production. If the regular unoaked version doesn't show quite the structure or intensity of some of the newer top examples, there is a very fine ripe fruit depth, good concentration and the wine is consistently long and stylish. The Winemakers Selection (previously 'Oak-aged') version has always shown a rare deft touch when integrating a gently oak-given structure and creaminess with a ripe tropical fruit intensity. The perfumed raspberry, cherryish Pinot Noir is also a good expression of its fruit if missing the intensity or concentration of others. The sparkling wine is also most attractive, well-structured, not hugely complex but with a fresh ripe fruit intensity to it. A little Merlot is also made. (PW)

O **Sauvignon Blanc**★★★ £B Winemakers Selection★★★ £C
O **Riesling**★★ £B   O **Gewürztraminer**★ £B   O **Chardonnay**★★ £C
O **Miru Miru** Brut Vintage★★ £C   ● **Pinot Noir**★★ £C

ISABEL ESTATE   Marlborough   www.isabelestate.com   A: M&V, NYg, Kwi

Owner: Michael & Robyn Tiller   72 Hawkesbury Road, Renwick, Marlborough

The finest privately owned estate in Marlborough produces five outstanding varietals from more than 50 ha of its own well-established vineyards. For many years the grapes had been sold to others and production under the Isabel label only commenced in 1994 but almost immediately it became the source of, arguably, New Zealand's finest (certainly one of the top three or four) Sauvignon Blancs. If less established than CLOUDY BAY it has been more consistent over recent vintages. Early vintages showed unprecendented structure and concentration but since 1999 there has been greater expression and refinement including a hint of mineral and smokiness. This means that without compromising its structure it doesn't need to be drunk within a year of the vintage, unlike so many examples. The wines come only from estate vineyards planted at around twice the average density, accounting at least in part for the extra intensity and concentration in the wines. Pinot Noir impresses with vivid plum, cherry and raspberry flavours and a savoury complexity, with a promising texture and breadth in the most recent vintages that suggest it will soon compete with the very best New World examples. Chardonnay has been exciting but not consistently so: at its best it is intense without becoming syrupy with good dimension and depth. A bright crunchy Riesling shows typical Isabel fruit intensity including limey, citrus and stone fruit flavours. The Pinot Gris with an attractive pear and quince fruit is one of a growing number of good New Zealand examples. (PW)

O **Sauvignon Blanc**★★★★ £C   O **Pinot Gris**★★ £C
O **Chardonnay**★★ £C   O **Riesling**★★ £C   ● **Pinot Noir**★★★ £D

KUMEU RIVER   Kumeu, Auckland   www.kumeuriver.co.nz   A: Box, Far, WSc

Owner: Brajkovich family   550 Highway 16, Kumeu, Auckland

Michael Brajkovich is one of New Zealand's most important winemakers. Although the family vineyards are in the now less than fashionable Kumeu district, west of Auckland, his intelligent, non-conformist approach showed it was possible to make better wines by rejecting some of the rigid, purely technical doctrines of winemaking that dominated styles in the late 1980s. Instead he adapted to a New Zealand context the best from established wine cultures and has made arguably the country's best Chardonnay for more than a decade. The use of indigenous yeasts, hand picking of the grapes and whole-bunch pressing are now practised by others. Both the Kumeu River Chardonnay and Maté's Vineyard (an original vineyard replanted in 1990) are barrel-fermented and aged, and put through a full malolactic fermentation. The resulting wines are richly textured, complex with well-integrated oak characters and are also atypically ageworthy for New Zealand Chardonnay; they are usually best with three to five years' age but often keep for longer. Of the two, the Maté's version can show just a little more refinement and persistence. Melba is a ripe, characterful blend of Merlot, Malbec and Cabernet Franc. In recent vintages both a promising Pinot Noir and a rich yet floral Pinot Gris have been made. Exceptional vintage conditions allowed a varietal Merlot to be made in 2000. The Brajkovich Signature Series is an inexpensive second label. All the wines are now bottled under Stelvin caps. (PW)

O **Chardonnay**★★★★ £C   Maté's Vineyard★★★★ £D
O **Pinot Gris**★★ £C   ● Melba★★ £C

MARTINBOROUGH VINEYARD   www.martinborough-vineyard.co.nz   **A: Adm, NYg, ACh**

Owner: Duncan Milne & partners   Princess Street, Martinborough
Martinborough Vineyards built an international reputation following the recruitment of Larry McKenna as full-time winemaker. From his first vintage in 1986 he set about making Pinot Noir and Chardonnay from fully ripe grapes of the highest possible quality. His success brought acclaim for the region as a whole; its free-draining soil and particularly dry mesoclimate had been recommended in a scientific study and this originally led to the company's establishment by Duncan Milne. Despite a tendency to over-extraction in the Reserve in the mid-1990s, the underlying fruit quality of the Pinot Noir has generally been very good, developing impressive texture and a stylish complexity with three to four years' age or more. Other wines, if not quite of the same order, have been ripe and full-flavoured. A bold oaky Chardonnay has wanted for more refinement as well as depth yet has good complexity and will usually improve for at least three or four years, while Riesling is full and intensely flavoured. In 2003 some of the Riesling was late-picked and partially botrytised for a richer, off-dry style called Manu. Larry McKenna left to develop his own project in 1999 (Escarpment Vineyard) and current releases from winemaker Claire Mulholland show a gentler touch but the usual flavour complexity. Pinot Gris, unusual in being partly barrel-fermented, and Sauvignon Blanc (Pirinoa Block) are also made. New is a second Pinot Noir, Te Tera. (PW)

● **Pinot Noir**★★★ £D   Reserve★★★ £E
O **Chardonnay**★★ £C   O **Riesling** Jackson Block★★ £B

MILLTON   Gisborne   www.millton.co.nz   A: Vcs

Owner: James & Annie Millton   Papatu Road, Manutuke, Gisborne
New Zealand's leading proponent of biodynamics is also the leading winery in the Gisborne region, where most of the vineyards are in the hands of the big producers. Endeavouring to produce 'natural' wines, they have succeeded admirably in making whites of good fruit richness and intensity. The warm but humid Gisborne autumns favour the production of botrytis and the wines are often characterised by the extra intensity and flavours this brings. From 20 ha (across the Riverpoint, Opou, Te Arai and Naboths vineyard sites) there has been real success with three varieties in particular: Chenin Blanc, Riesling and Chardonnay. Chenin Blanc has been the country's best since the late 80s and the Riesling has rarely been surpassed, but there is a purity and intensity to the fruit in all three wines. More recently, under a Growers Series label, Viognier from the Tietjen vineyard and a Gewürztraminer have been made. Late-harvested 'Special Bunch Selection' versions of Riesling and Gewürztraminer are also produced as is some red, including a Merlot/Cabernet. (PW)

O **Riesling** Opou Vineyard★★★ £B   O **Chardonnay** Opou Vineyard★★ £B
O **Chenin Blanc** Te Arai Vineyard★★★ £B

MONTANA   Gisborne, Marlborough & Auckland   www.montanawines.com   A: Mon, Odd

*Owner: **Allied-Domecq**   171 Pilkington Road, Auckland 1130*

Montana is far and away New Zealand's largest producer, responsible for well over half of the country's total output. Its recent acquisition of Corbans (2000) has further swollen its already extensive vineyard holdings in the three largest wine-producing regions: Gisborne, Hawkes Bay and Marlborough. The expansion of a small Corbans vineyard in Waipara (which provided fine Amberley Riesling) to Pinot Noir and more Riesling is a new departure. The Montana volume comes from brands like Timara, Azure Bay and the regular Montana varietals, which include consistently drinkable Chardonnay and Sauvignon Blanc with good varietal character. There are no silly prices here and the Reserves and, more especially, the Estate-labelled wines can add more sophistication, structure and concentration. In Marlborough, the impressive Brancott Winery is the command centre of more than 1,400 ha of vineyards including the Brancott Estate, in its own valley on the south-eastern side of the Wairau Valley, and also major new plantings in the Awatere Valley. In collaboration with DEUTZ (the Champagne house), some of New Zealand's best sparkling wines have also been made in Marlborough. By contrast, the Church Road winery in Hawkes Bay is a (relatively small) separate entity whose red wines have been developed under guidance from Bordeaux *négociant* Cordier. As well as regular and Reserve bottlings, small-volume, experimental Cuve Series wines can be bought locally. Church Road's winemaker, Tony Prichard, also fashions Montana's flagship red, Tom, named after the legendary pioneer of Cabernet Sauvignon in Hawkes Bay, Tom McDonald. Made from Merlot, Cabernet Sauvignon and Cabernet Franc, less than 10,000 bottles were produced in the first three vintages (95, 96 and 98). Two other premium wines are Virtu, a barrique-fermented and aged botrytised sweet wine from Semillon, and a new non-vintage deluxe *cuvée* of Lindauer called Grandeur. Leading Corbans wines that continue to be produced include the well-established Stoneleigh varietals and premium Cottage Block Marlborough Sauvignon Blanc and Chardonnay. (PW)

Gisborne
O **Chardonnay** Gisborne Reserve★ £B Ormond Estate★★ 'O' £C
O **Gewürztraminer** Gisborne Reserve★ £B Patuthai Estate 'P'★★ £C

Montana Brancott Winery
O **Sauvignon Blanc** Brancott Estate 'B'★★ £C
O **Chardonnay** Reserve★ £B Renwick Estate 'R'★★ £C
● **Pinot Noir** Reserve★ £B ● **Cabernet Sauvignon** Fairhall Estate 'F'★ £C
O **Lindauer** Special Reserve★ £B Grandeur★★ £C
O **Deutz** Marlborough Cuvée Non-Vintage★★ £C
O **Deutz** Marlborough Blanc de Blancs Vintage★★ £C

Church Road
O **Chardonnay**★ £B Reserve★★ £C
● **Cabernet/Merlot** Reserve★★ £C ● Tom★★★ £F

Corbans (Marlborough)
O **Sauvignon Blanc** Cottage Block★★ £C
O **Chardonnay** Private Bin★ £B Cottage Block★★ £C

MT DIFFICULTY   Central Otago   www.mtdiffculty.co.nz   A: BFs, Vne, NYg, Kwi

Owner: Mt Difficulty partnership   Felton Road, Bannockburn, Cromwell, Central Otago

One of the most promising of a new wave of wineries in Central Otago, established as recently as 1998. The wines are now made in its own modern winemaking facility by Matt Dicey. The four partners, including Matt's father, Robin Dicey, own between them some 40 ha of vineyard, giving scope for single-vineyard interpretations as well as blended examples. Pinot Noir is the star wine, a

2001 adding more weight and density than previously seen, but Chardonnay and Sauvignon Blanc show attractive fruit if less convincing structure and depth. Riesling is made in different versions, varying both in origin and the degree of sweetness and will be rated in the future. (PW)

● **Pinot Noir★★★** £D

MOUNT EDWARD   Central Otago   A: BFs, BBR, Vne, WSc, Kwi

Owner: Alan Brady   34 Coalpit Road, Gibbston, Queenstown, Central Otago
This very small Central Otago winery is a virtual one-man operation. Having founded the nearby Gibbston Valley Alan Brady has considerable experience of the particular pecularities of this part of the region. As well as making an increasingly good Pinot Noir there is a small quantity of Riesling planted. Sourced from quite well-established vines the Pinot has a very attractive, ripe, yet sappy quality that adds richness with a little age. Successive recent vintages also show increasing weight and depth. Quantities are likely to remain small but this is one of the classier examples of Central Otago Pinot Noir. (PW)

● **Pinot Noir★★** £E

MOUNTFORD   Waipara, Canterbury   www.mountfordvineyard.co.nz A: M&V, Han, The, NYg

Owner: Michael & Buffy Eaton   434 Omini Road, Waipara, North Canterbury
Mountford's owners are among those who have put their faith in Waipara's limestone-rich soils. They are aided in their quest to make one of New Zealand's best Pinot Noirs by employing specialist vine-yard and winemaking expertise. They must also surely be one of few to employ a blind winemaker in C P Lin. There is an extra class and complexity to the Pinot Noir that suggest that the Eatons have got it right where others in Waipara are still struggling. First impressions of a Chardonnay made in a full-bodied, concentrated, oak-influenced style suggests that this too could be something special. (PW)

● **Pinot Noir★★★** £E

NEUDORF   Nelson   www.neudorf.co.nz   A: RsW, WSc

Owner: Tim & Judy Finn   Neudorf Road, RD 2, Upper Moutere, Nelson
Neudorf stood for fine quality in the Nelson region when neighbouring Marlborough was a fraction of the size it is now. Yet while Marlborough has expanded rapidly, quality in Nelson has been advanced by Neudorf and just a few others dedicated to maximising the quality of the fruit in their vineyards. Moderately high densities and relatively low yields play a part in producing wines with good concentration but which aren't overworked in the winery. Nonetheless even the Finns have resorted to producing a Sauvignon Blanc from Marlborough as well as one from local Moutere fruit. A rich, complex Moutere Chardonnay has been successful too and is a good deal better than most Marlborough examples. Sometimes showing a botrytis influence there is good depth though it could still use a little more refinement. A second Chardonnay is more widely sourced, while a perfumed Moutere Riesling with floral and mineral aromas has been consistently good. Wine made from grapes sourced from new vineyards at Brightwater is beginning to supplement the existing range. A little Pinot Gris has been made in both Marlborough and Nelson versions. (PW)

O **Chardonnay** Moutere★★ £D   O **Riesling** Moutere★★ £B
O **Sauvignon Blanc** Marlborough★★ £B   ● **Pinot Noir** Moutere★ £B

PEGASUS BAY   Waipara, Canterbury   www.pegasusbay.com   A: MHv, WSc, BBR, Kwi

Owner: Donaldson family   Stockgrove Road, Amberley, RD 2, North Canterbury

Pegasus Bay is Waipara's and Canterbury's leading winery. This is very much a family operation and one of Ivan Donaldson's sons, Matthew, has forged a very successful winemaking duo with his partner Lynette Hudson, who he recently married. Both are trained winemakers. Matthew's reds include an increasingly good plummy, fleshy Pinot Noir capable of a little age. Prima Donna is a superior selection made only in the best vintages. A Cabernet/Merlot is also produced though this is more variable in quality. Maestro is another special selection. All the reds are bottled unfiltered. The whites, made by Lynette are arguably more consistent and include good richly textured examples of Chardonnay and Sauvignon/Semillon as well as a fruit-rich Riesling, especially good in a late-harvested, botrytis-affected version, Aria. There is also an occasional botrytised version of Chardonnay, Finale. (PW)

O Riesling★★ £B Aria★★★ £B   O Sauvignon Blanc/Semillon★★ £C
O Chardonnay★★ £B   ● Pinot Noir★★ £C

SERESIN   Marlborough   www.seresin.co.nz   A: JAr

Owner: Michael Seresin   Bedford Road, Blenheim

Style and image play a bigger part than usual in the projection of this rather sophisticated Marlborough winery established by film producer Michael Seresin in 1992. Releases from the late 1990s showed some very attractive forward fruit and reasonable depth but tended to fall away a little with a lack of persistence on the finish. If anything some of the most recent releases have been even weaker but with Brian Bicknell (who did much to establish quality at ERRÁZURIZ in the mid-1990s) as winemaker there's a real possibility that the great care taken over image and presentation will be at least equalled by the wines. New vineyard purchases (Tatou Block and Raupo Creek) will add substantially to the existing 'Seresin Estate' block of 44.5 ha of vineyards. Small amounts of a Malbec and 'Cabernets' (Cabernet Sauvignon/Cabernet Franc) have also been made. Olive oil production is taken seriously too. Prices match the presentation. (PW)

O Chardonnay★ £C Reserve★★ £C   O Riesling★ £C   O Pinot Gris★ £C
O Sauvignon Blanc★ £C   ● Pinot Noir★★ £D

STONECROFT   Hawkes Bay   www.stonecroft.co.nz   A: L&S, NYg, Rae

Owner: Alan Limmer   Mere Road, RD 5, Hastings

Stonecroft, the project of soil scientist Dr Alan Limmer, earned a reputation for rich, characterful examples of Syrah and Gewürztraminer that helped to broaden the interest (among New Zealand producers) in varieties other than the mainstream Chardonnay, Sauvignon Blanc, etc. All the Stonecroft wines, from the small, sheltered and particularly warm 10 ha of vineyards, are bold and richly textured, with concentrated fruit. Syrah, Gewürztraminer and Chardonnay are now the focus of production. The latter is bold and powerful, with a depth and substance missing from most New Zealand Chardonnay if not yet showing the refinement or elegance that should be possible here. Syrah, with a refined mineral, blackcurrant, plum character and a hint of white pepper, is the real star. Structured but with the rich fruit on the finish that is common to all these wines, it is best drunk with five years' age or more. None was produced in 2000 as the fruit wasn't considered of sufficient quality. Ruhanui, based on Cabernet Sauvignon but with significant amounts of Merlot and Syrah (20 and 15 per cent respectively in the 2000), shows ripe stylish fruit but its days may be numbered. A good, if unusual, spicy, tropical-fruit Sauvignon has already been discontinued (last vintage 2001). (PW)

● Syrah★★★ £D ● Ruhanui★★ £B
○ Chardonnay★★★ £C ○ Gewürztraminer★★★ £C

STONYRIDGE Waiheke Island, Auckland www.stonyridge.co.nz A: MHv, Kwi

Owner: Stephen White   80 Onetangi Road, Waiheke Island
Stephen White's small north-facing vineyard is managed along organic lines and produces what is deservedly the most famous wine from Waiheke Island. The stated aim is to produce the best Bordeaux-style red in the world. Nonetheless it is very much a lifestyle orientated project with pleasures of the sun and the sea woven into its otherwise serious pursuit. Made since 1987, Larose Cabernets is a blend of predominantly Cabernet Sauvignon with lesser amounts of Merlot, Cabernet Franc, Malbec and Petit Verdot. Aided by naturally low fertility, the fruit quality owes much to meticulous vineyard care resulting in yields typically around 25 hl/ha. The grapes are then transformed into a rich but harmonious blend of new oak and intense berry fruit with impressive ripeness, depth and balance. The fruit intensity holds up well with age though there is perhaps not quite the mellowed evolution in the structure that would be seen in a northern hemisphere red of similar quality. Optimum drinking therefore is probably between three and six years of age, though they will keep for much longer. As well as developing a Grenache/Syrah/Mourvèdre blend, a second wine, Airfields, and a little varietal Merlot and Chardonnay (Row 10) have also been produced. (PW)
● Larose Cabernets★★★★ £F

TE MATA Hawkes Bay www.temata.hb.co.nz A: JEF, NYg, Kwi

Owner: Buck & Morris families   Te Mata Road, Havelock North
John Buck revived Te Mata in late 1978 (vines were first planted here in 1892) and almost immediately established it as one of the best producers in the country. That wasn't so difficult then but despite the greatly increased competition Te Mata has lost none of its lustre. There has always been a coherence to the estate's direction that has proved an inspiration to other would-be New Zealand winemakers. Production has reached 25,000 cases but the range has not expanded greatly and the quality and image of the wines has been at least maintained. The wines, made by Peter Cowley since 1994, impress for their style, harmony and elegance yet don't lack for fruit or intensity. One wine, Coleraine, symbolises the estate; its ability to age with some grace and an appreciable mellowing of its structure is almost unique in the country. There can be a trace of greenness in cooler years but with five years' age or more it is nearly always distinguished by soft, caressing blackcurrant, cherry and berry fruit and a long richly textured finish. Both it and Awatea, though labelled Cabernet/Merlot, include Cabernet Franc as well as Cabernet Sauvignon in the blend. Syrah hasn't yet the texture of a top example of the variety but shows a stylish cool pepper and raspberry fruit intensity. Barrique-fermented and aged Elston Chardonnay has long been one of New Zealand's best while the barrel-fermented Cape Crest Sauvignon Blanc is a rare good example from Hawkes Bay. (PW)
● Cabernet/Merlot★ £B Awatea★★ £C Coleraine★★★★ £D
● Syrah Bullnose★★ £C
○ Chardonnay Elston★★★ £C
○ Sauvignon Blanc Cape Crest★ £C Castle Hill★ £C

UNISON Hawkes Bay www.unisonvineyard.co.nz A: MHv, N&P

Owner: Bruce & Anna-Barbara Helliwell   2163 Highway 50, RD 5, Hastings
Unison has been dedicated to the production of a top-quality blended red in the Gimblett Gravels of Hawkes Bay since 1993. Two versions are produced, Unison and Unison Selection, based on a 6-ha

high-density, low-yielding vineyard planted to Merlot, Syrah and Cabernet Sauvignon. The composition of each wine varies according to the success of each variety in a given year. Unison has a moderately long maceration time (16–18 days in 2000) and spends a year in oak but only a third of it in barriques. Though there is not always a significant step-up in quality the Selection is based on the very best fruit and undergoes a longer maceration (three weeks) and spends 12 months exclusively in barriques (new and second use) before further ageing in large oak. Though occasionally struggling for ripeness, both add more breadth, depth and complexity over some of the more overtly fruit-driven Hawkes Bay reds. Both wines typically need at least five years' age to show at their best. (PW)

● **Unison** Gimblett Gravels★★★ £C   ● **Unison Selection** Gimblett Gravels★★★ £D

VAVASOUR   Marlborough   www.vavasour.com   A: Orb

Owner: Vavasour family   Redwood Pass Road, Lower Dashwood, Marlborough

Vavasour is an excellent producer located away from the main hub of Marlborough viticulture. Vavasour's vineyards are a little south and east in the Awatere Valley, where there has recently been extensive planting by other producers and where it is claimed to be drier without the high water table common to much of the plantings in the Wairau Valley. Vavasour's Glenn Thomas makes two ranges of wines from 30 ha of estate vineyards as well as grapes bought in under contract. Two excellent Sauvignon Blanc are produced under the Vavasour label. Both show a minerally, ripe fruit intensity and a structure and depth that puts them among the very best Marlborough examples. 'Single Vineyard' Sauvignon from a plot on the 'home' Awatere vineyards is fermented and aged in used French barriques and shows a restrained oak influence but needs at least two or three years' ageing to reach its best. The regular Vavasour example consistently shows good vigour and distinctive mineral, slightly smoky aromas which seem to owe something to the wine's Awatere origins. This minerally Awatere quality can also be glimpsed in a tight but creamy Vavasour Chardonnay and a relatively light but fresh, aromatic Riesling that has a little residual sweetness. Pinot Noir, sourced from relatively young Awatere vines and Wairau fruit, shows good potential. Dashwood varietals are by no means a poor second (as can often be the case with a second label) and include an excellent zingy, nettly Sauvignon Blanc and an attractive gently oaked Chardonnay as well as a Cabernet Sauvignon and a Pinot Noir. (PW)

Vavasour
O **Sauvignon Blanc**★★★ £B Single Vineyard★★★ £C
O **Chardonnay**★★★ £B   O **Riesling**★★★ £B
● **Pinot Noir**★ £C
Dashwood
O **Sauvignon Blanc**★★ £B   O **Chardonnay**★★ £B

VILLA MARIA   Auckland & Marlborough   www.villamaria.co.nz   A: HMA, Odd, WSc

Owner: George Fistonich   Mangere, Auckland / Cnr Paynters & New Renwick Road, Blenheim

The formidable Villa Maria group, with impressive wineries in both Auckland and Marlborough, also includes the independently run Hawkes Bay estates of Esk Valley and Vidal Estate. Most enviable is the company's record of combining quality, quantity and consistency. Most impressive are the Reserve-level wines. Chardonnay can impress for its fruit intensity and improves with a little age but superior are the Reserve Sauvignon Blancs – among Marlborough's best in a succession of good vintages since 1999. Villa Maria is now trying to do the same for Pinot Noir in the new Reserve and Lloyd Vineyard releases. Deeply coloured, intense and with a lot of extract, there is a concentration and fruit character that shows real potential. Fine Reserve reds (based on Merlot and Cabernet Sauvignon) from Hawkes Bay have been made for more than a decade both from Villa Maria and

Vidal Estate and show lots of ripe plum, berry and blackcurrant fruit intensity, if not quite the depth to match. Esk Valley wines are made by Gordon Russell and the outstanding wine is The Terraces, a blend of Malbec, Merlot and Cabernet Franc. Made only in top vintages, it is a rich, intense and powerful Hawkes Bay red and the group's finest wine (recent vintages are 2000, 98 and 95). Esk Valley Reserve Merlot/Cabernet Sauvignon/Malbec can also be very good if slightly more variable in quality. Villa Maria Cellar Selection can provide good varietal fruit but the whites need to be drunk young. Even the Private Bin whites can be very drinkable and despite a sometimes monotone Sauvignon Blanc, there's an adequate citrusy, peachy Chardonnay and a relatively simple but intense Riesling. New Pinots are expensive but prices are otherwise reasonable. (PW)

Villa Maria
- ● **Merlot/Cabernet Sauvignon** Gimblett Gravels Reserve★★★ £C
- ● **Pinot Noir** Cellar Selection★ £C   Reserve★★★ £D   Single Vineyard Lloyd★★★ £E
- ○ **Sauvignon Blanc** Cellar Selection★ £B   Reserve Wairau River★★ £C   Reserve Clifford Bay★★★ £C
- ○ **Chardonnay** Cellar Selection★ £B   Reserve★★ £B

Esk Valley
- ● **The Terraces★★★★** £F   ● **Merlot/Cabernet Sauvignon /Malbec** Gimblett Gravels Reserve★★★ £D
- ○ **Chardonnay** Reserve★★ £C

Vidal Estate
- ● **Merlot/Cabernet Sauvignon** Gimblett Gravels Reserve★★ £C   ○ **Chardonnay** Reserve★★ £C

WITHER HILLS   Marlborough   www.witherhills.co.nz   A: CHk, Odd, WSc, Kwi

*Owner: **Lion Nathan**   114 New Renwick Road, RD 2, Blenheim*
Brent Marris, the experienced winemaker who set up the Wither Hills operation, and his father John, viticulturalist and grape grower, combined their vineyard resources and expertise prior to being bought out in 2002. Holdings run to 300 ha but for the moment just three wines are made: Sauvignon Blanc, Chardonnay and Pinot Noir. The Sauvignon shows plenty of ripe gooseberry fruit if lacking the structure of the best examples. The Chardonnay is better, with nicely integrated oak and a lovely ripe peach and melon intensity within a tight structure which promises to develop well, just missing an extra dimension for a higher rating. The Pinot Noir, with full, spicy, ripe cherry and berry fruit flavours and depth, shows good expression that puts it among the better Marlborough examples. Like the Sauvignon Blanc, the Chardonnay and Pinot Noir can be drunk soon after they are released but both should also improve for three or four years. (PW)
- ○ **Sauvignon Blanc★** £B   ○ **Chardonnay★★** £B
- ● **Pinot Noir★★** £C

OTHER WINES OF NOTE

Please note that 'Cabernets' indicates that both Cabernet Sauvignon and Cabernet Franc are included in a blend.

ALANA ESTATE ● **Pinot Noir** Martinborough £C
BABICH ● **Syrah** Winemaker's Reserve £B   ● **Cabernet Sauvignon** The Patriarch £D
○ **Chardonnay** Irongate £C
BENFIELD & DELAMERE (Martinborough) ● **Merlot/Cabernet** £D
BLACK RIDGE (Central Otago) ● **Pinot Noir** £D   ○ **Gewürztraminer** £C
CARRICK (Central Otago) ● **Pinot Noir** £D   ○ **Sauvignon Blanc** £C
CELLIER LE BRUN ○ **Marlborough Brut Non-Vintage** £C   ○ **Marlborough Blanc de Blancs** £D
CHARD FARM (Central Otago) ○ **Riesling** £B   ○ **Chardonnay** Judge & Jury £C
● **Pinot Noir** Finla Mor £C

CLIFFORD BAY ESTATE O Sauvignon Blanc Marlborough £B

COLLARDS O Chenin Blanc Hawkes Bay £B   O Sauvignon Blanc Rothesay £C

O Riesling Queen Charlotte Marlborough £B   O Chardonnay Rothesay £C

KIM CRAWFORD O Sauvignon Blanc Marlborough £B   O Riesling Marlborough Dry £B

O Pinot Gris Marlborough £B   O Chardonnay Tietjen Gisborne £C Pia £E   O Rory Brut Vintage £C

● Merlot Te Awanga Hawkes Bay £C   ● Tane (Merlot/Cabernet Franc) £E

● Pinot Noir Anderson Vineyard Marlborough £D

DELEGAT'S O Chardonnay Reserve Hawkes Bay £B

FAIRHALL DOWNS O Sauvignon Blanc Marlborough £B

FORREST ESTATE O Sauvignon Blanc Marlborough £B

GIBBSTON VALLEY (Central Otago) O Chardonnay Reserve £C   ● Pinot Noir Reserve £D

GIESEN O Sauvignon Blanc Marlborough £B   O Chardonnay Reserve Canterbury £C

● Pinot Noir Reserve £C

GOLDRIDGE ESTATE ● Cabernet Sauvignon/Merlot Matakana Premium Reserve £B

GREENHOUGH (Nelson) O Riesling £B   O Chardonnay £C   ● Pinot Noir Hope Vineyard £D

HATTON ESTATE (Hawkes Bay) ● Tahi Gimblett Gravels (Cabernets/Merlot) £E

HERZOG ● Montepulciano Secret of Marlborough £E

JACKSON ESTATE O Sauvignon Blanc Marlborough £B

LAWSON'S DRY HILLS (Marlborough) O Sauvignon Blanc £B   O Gewürztraminer £B

O Riesling £B   O Chardonnay £B

MATAKANA ESTATE ● Moko (Cabernets/Malbec/Merlot) £C   O Pinot Gris £C

MATARIKI (Hawkes Bay) ● Quintology Gimblett Gravels (Cabernets/Merlot/Syrah/Malbec) £D

● Syrah Gimblett Gravels Reserve £D   O Sauvignon Blanc Reserve £B

MATUA VALLEY O Chardonnay Judd Estate Gisborne £C Ararimu Hawkes Bay £D

O Sauvignon Blanc Shingle Peak Marlborough £B Reserve £C

● Merlot/Cabernet Sauvignon Ararimu Hawkes Bay £D

MILLS REEF (Hawkes Bay) O Sauvignon Blanc Reserve £B   ● Cabernet/Merlot Elspeth £C

MORTON ESTATE (Hawkes Bay) O Chardonnay Black Label £C   ● Pinot Noir Black Label £C

● Merlot/Cabernet Black Label £D   O Sauvignon Blanc Stone Creek Marlborough £B

LE GRYS/MUD HOUSE (Marlborough) O Sauvignon Blanc £B

NAUTILUS O Sauvignon Blanc Marlborough £B

NGATARAWA (Hawkes Bay) ● Merlot/Cabernet Sauvignon Alwyn Reserve £D

O Chardonnay Alwyn Reserve £D   O Riesling Noble Harvest Alwyn Reserve £E

NOBILO O Sauvignon Blanc Marlborough £B Icon Series £B

OLSSENS OF BANNOCKBURN (Central Otago) ● Pinot Noir £D Jackson Barry £E

O Riesling £B

PALLISER ESTATE (Martinborough) O Sauvignon Blanc £B

C J PASK (Hawkes Bay) ● Cabernet/Merlot £B   ● Merlot Reserve £C   ● Syrah Reserve £C

● Cabernet Sauvignon Reserve £C

PROVIDENCE ● Cabernet/Merlot £F

RED METAL (Hawkes Bay) ● Merlot/Cabernet Franc Basket Press £D   ● The Merlot £F

RIPPON VINEYARD (Central Otago) ● Pinot Noir £D   O Riesling £C   O Chardonnay £C

SAINT CLAIR (Marlborough) O Sauvignon Blanc £B   O Chardonnay Omaka Reserve £C

● Merlot Rapaura Reserve £C

ALLAN SCOTT (Marlborough) O Chardonnay £B   O Riesling £B   O Sauvignon Blanc £B

SEIFRIED ESTATE/REDWOOD VALLEY (Nelson) O Riesling Dry £B

O Sauvignon Blanc £B   O Gewürztraminer £B

SILENI (Hawkes Bay) O Semillon £C   O Chardonnay £C   ● Merlot/Cabernets £C

SQUAWKING MAGPIE (Hawkes Bay) ● Cabernet/Merlot Gimblett Gravels £D

STAETE LANDT (Marlborough) O Sauvignon Blanc £B   O Pinot Gris £C   O Chardonnay £C

TE AWA FARM (Hawkes Bay) ● Boundary Gimblett Gravels (Merlot/Cabernets) £D

TE MOTU VINEYARD (Waiheke Island) ● Cabernet Sauvignon/Merlot £E

TORLESSE (Waipara) ● Pinot Noir Torlesse Selection £C

TRINITY HILL (Hawkes Bay) ● Cabernet/Merlot Gimblett Road £D   ● Syrah Gimblett Road £E

VALLI (Central Otago) ● Pinot Noir Bald Hills £D Colleen's Vineyard £D

VOSS ESTATE (Martinborough) O **Riesling** £B O **Chardonnay** Reserve £C ● **Pinot Noir** £D
WAIPARA WEST ● **Pinot Noir** Waipara £C ● **Ram Paddock Red** (Cabernets/Merlot) £B
O **Sauvignon Blanc** Waipara £C
WHITEHAVEN/MANSION HOUSE BAY (Marlborough) O **Sauvignon Blanc** £B ● **Pinot Noir** £C

Author's choice (PW)

10 top Cabernet or Merlot based reds
ALPHA DOMUS ● **AD The Aviator** Hawkes Bay
CRAGGY RANGE ● **Sophia** Gimblett Gravels
ESK VALLEY ● **The Terraces** Hawkes Bay
GOLDWATER ESTATE ● **Cabernet Sauvignon/Merlot** Waiheke Island
MATARIKI ● **Quintology** Gimblett Gravels
RED METAL ● **The Merlot** Hawkes Bay
STONYRIDGE ● **Larose Cabernets** Waiheke Island
TE MATA ● **Coleraine** Hawkes Bay
TE MOTU VINEYARD ● **Cabernet Sauvignon/Merlot** Waiheke Island
UNISON ● **Selection** Gimblett Gravels

10 leading Pinot Noir or Syrah
ATA RANGI ● **Pinot Noir** Martinborough
BORTHWICK ● **Pinot Noir** Wairarapa
FELTON ROAD ● **Pinot Noir** Central Otago Block 3
FROMM ● **La Strada Pinot Noir** Marlborough Fromm Vineyard
MARTINBOROUGH VINEYARD ● **Pinot Noir** Martinborough
MOUNT DIFFICULTY ● **Pinot Noir** Central Otago
MOUNTFORD ● **Pinot Noir** Waipara
STONECROFT ● **Syrah** Hawkes Bay
TE MATA ● **Syrah** Hawkes Bay Bullnose
VILLA MARIA ● **Pinot Noir** Marlborough Reserve

10 arresting Sauvignon Blanc
CLOUDY BAY O **Sauvignon Blanc** Marlborough
CRAGGY RANGE O **Sauvignon Blanc** Marlborough Old Renwick
GROVE MILL O **Sauvignon Blanc** Marlborough
HUNTER'S O **Sauvignon Blanc** Marlborough
ISABEL ESTATE O **Sauvignon Blanc** Marlborough
MONTANA O **Sauvignon Blanc** Marlborough Brancott Estate 'B'
NEUDORF O **Sauvignon Blanc** Marlborough
PALLISER ESTATE O **Sauvignon Blanc** Martinborough
VAVASOUR O **Sauvignon Blanc** Marlborough Single Vineyard
VILLA MARIA O **Sauvignon Blanc** Marlborough Reserve Clifford Bay

10 diverse high quality whites
ATA RANGI O **Pinot Gris** Martinborough Lismore
ATA RANGI O **Chardonnay** Martinborough Craighall
CRAGGY RANGE O **Les Beaux Cailloux Chardonnay** Gimblett Gravels
DRY RIVER O **Pinot Gris** Martinborough
FELTON ROAD O **Riesling** Central Otago Dry
KUMEU RIVER O **Chardonnay** Kumeu
MILLTON O **Chenin Blanc** Gisborne Te Arai Vineyard
PEGASUS BAY O **Chardonnay** Waipara
STONECROFT O **Gewürztraminer** Hawkes Bay
TE MATA O **Chardonnay** Hawkes Bay Elston

Dramatic and positive change in South Africa has seen an increased involvement in the wine industry by all ethnic groups and much work and research have gone into improving the quality of the nation's vineyards. There is no doubting that wine quality at the upper end of the market here is good and improving, but the shortage of dynamic and truly exciting new producers remains depressing when comparing the country with its competitors. Although an increasing number of reds approaching world class are now being made, South Africa still wants for more reds of indisputable class and complexity. There has been a recent trend towards micro-production garage-style wines but it remains to be seen how many of these will stand the test of time.

The Regions

The principle focus of quality wine production in South Africa is centred around **Stellenbosch** WO. The region is one of the most attractive to visit anywhere in the world with towering mountains rising seemingly out of the ocean. Stellenbosch itself is not only home to some of the largest wine companies in the country but also to some of its most impressive. There is a wide variation of mesoclimates within the WO with maritime breezes and the Simonsberg and Helderberg mountains playing a role in tempering conditions. In the coolest areas Sauvignon Blanc and Chardonnay (including some impressive barrel-fermented examples) are both successful, as is the occasional Riesling. Chenin Blanc tends to be much in the local style with some residual sugar. Stellenbosch reds are among the best in the country. Pinotage can be particularly striking in the warm vineyards to the north-east of Stellenbosch. Decent Bordeaux-style reds abound and a number of wineries are producing excellent results with Shiraz. Merlot can be good but also a touch vegetal. Although the wines are less rustic than of old and with much of the virus infection once prevalent now removed, a marked minty note found in a number of reds can be overpowering.

To the north of Stellenbosch is the second-largest region, **Paarl**. The area is warm and reds including some very successful Shiraz and Merlot are produced. There are also a number of cooler mesoclimates where the odd decent Sauvignon Blanc and Semillon are made, as well as Chardonnay and some fine Pinot Noir. White Rhône varieties are also increasingly widely planted. To the immediate east is **Franschhoek**. The valley here gets cooler as you move east and up to higher altitudes. Again, very good Shiraz and Cabernet Sauvignon are produced as well as earlier-ripening whites and Pinot Noir. To the east of Stellenbosch is the cool **Durbanville** region and then south of Cape Town **Constantia** is home to a small number of good producers. The climate is cool and moderated by both Indian and Atlantic Ocean breezes and whites are more successful than the reds. Some way to the east of Stellenbosch are the regions of **Worcester** and **Robertson**. The latter has some potential for good whites grown in limestone soils.

The vast, semi-desert and arid expanse of the **Klein Karoo**, several hundred kilometres inland, sees the production of some reasonable fortified styles but is too hot to produce fine table wines. **Swartland** just to the north-west of Paarl appears to have real potential. Hillside vineyards planted on well-drained granite soils are the source of good Pinotage, Shiraz and Merlot.

Vintages

The top Cape reds will develop and keep well, the best up to a decade. The majority should be approached sooner. Whites generally need drinking as soon after release as possible although the odd barrel-fermented Chardonnay will develop in the short term. 2003 promises to be a very good year for the Cape. 2002 Cabernet Sauvignon was very promising, with more variable Merlot. Good earlier years to consider for premium reds are 2001, 2000, 1998, 1997, 1995 and 1994.

BEYERSKLOOF   Stellenbosch   heidi@beyerskloof.co.za   A: RSo

Owner: Beyers Truter/Krige family   PO Box 107, Koelenhof 7605

Beyers Truter owns this property in partnership with the Krige family, which own KANONKOP where Truter is also the winemaker with Simon Halliday. He makes a stylish and vibrant Pinotage in a lighter style than that at Kanonkop and a dense and burly Cabernet Sauvignon. This is in a rich chocolatey style with abundant evidence of new oak. It will be better with five years' cellaring. Newly added are a fruity rosé and a well-priced red blend Synergy. This comprises Merlot, Pinotage and Cabernet Sauvignon and is sourced from a number of sites around Stellenbosch. It is ripe, plummy and forward with a spicy hint of oak and can be enjoyed with a couple of years' ageing. (DM)

● **Pinotage** Stellenbosch★ £B   ● **Synergy** Stellenbosch★★ £B
● **Cabernet Sauvignon** Stellenbosch★★★★ £D

BOEKENHOUTSKLOOF   Franschhoek   boeken@mweb.co.za   A: Orb

Owner: Boekenhoutskloof Investments (Pty) Ltd   PO Box 433, Franschoek 7690

This farm is located on the higher and cooler slopes of Franschhoek and is producing some of the most stylish wines in the Cape. Syrah is produced from bought-in fruit but is intense, refined and full of black, spicy fruit. It displays the weight and texture of good Hermitage. The Cabernet Sauvignon is in a dense and cedary style with supple, velvety tannin. It will benefit from at least four or five years' ageing. The premium range is completed by a pure and subtly oaked Semillon. Structured and worth cellaring this is of a different order to most South African examples. A full, brambly and spicy Rhône style blend, the Chocolate Box, is sourced from Franschoek fruit and comprises Syrah, Grenache and some very old vine Cinsault. It is only available in the UK. There is also a range of attractively fruity and characterful varietal wines under the Porcupine Ridge label, which are sourced from Coastal Region fruit. Most recently added was simple but attractive, fruit-driven Wolftrap, a blend comprising Pinotage, Cabernet Sauvignon, Mourvèdre and Cinsault. (DM)

Boekenhoutskloof
● **Cabernet Sauvignon** Estate Franschhoek★★★★★ £E
● **Shiraz** Estate Franschhoek★★★★ £E
O **Semillon** Estate Franschhoek★★★ £C

Porcupine Ridge
● **Cabernet Sauvignon**Porcupine Ridge★★ £B   ● **Syrah** Porcupine Ridge★★ £B
O **Sauvignon Blanc** Porcupine Ridge★ £B

BOUCHARD FINLAYSON   Walker Bay   bf.overstrand.co.za   A: Bib

Owner: Peter Finlayson/Paul Bouchard   Kleine Hemel en Aarde, PO Box 303, Hermanus 7200

Peter Finlayson was originally the winemaker at neighbouring HAMILTON RUSSELL before establishing his own operation in partnership with Paul Bouchard of the Bouchard family, former owners of BOUCHARD PÈRE ET FILS. There are close to 16 ha of vineyard, dominated by Pinot Noir. The style differs from Hamilton Russell: the wine is more extracted, given a period of post-fermentation maceration that makes it denser, but it could do with just a touch more elegance. It will develop nicely with two or three years. A barrel selection Tête de Cuvée is also produced. There are two Chardonnays, Kaaimansgat from the Overberg WO and the opulent, homegrown Missionvale bottling. There is also a clean, zesty Sauvignon Blanc as well as a simple clean-fruited blend of Kerner, Gewürztraminer, Riesling, Sauvignon Blanc and Chardonnay labelled Blanc de Mer. Chardonnay will stand a little ageing, Sauvignon should be drunk young. The most recent addition is Hannibal, an unusual red blend of Sangiovese, Nebbiolo and Pinot Noir. It will be interesting to see how the Italian varieties compare with examples from California and Australia. (DM)

● **Pinot Noir** Galpin Peak Walker Bay★★★ £D
O **Chardonnay** Kaaimansgat Overberg★★ £C Missionvale Walker Bay★★ £C
O **Sauvignon Blanc** Walker Bay★ £B

FAIRVIEW ESTATE   Paarl   www.fairview.co.za   A: CHk, WSc

Owner: Charles Back   PO Box 583, Suider Paarl 7624
Charles Back makes an extensive range at his Paarl farm, with much of the focus centred on Rhône
styles. He makes the humorously-named red and white Goats do Roam, which are well crafted if very
simple Rhône blends. These have been supplemented by Goat Roti, which despite its name actually
blends Shiraz with Grenache, Carignan and Viognier. Of more significance are the Red Seal Range
Cyril Back Shiraz and Primo Pinotage. The latter is produced from low-yielding old bush vines and
avoids some of the more excessive bubble-gum, acetate aromas the variety can display. A Beacon
Block Shiraz is also now produced from younger vines, as is a Solitude Shiraz, aged in a combination
of French and American oak. Among the regular Fairview labels is a honeyed, peachy Viognier and
a good, unusual, weighty blend of Zinfandel and Cinsault. Chardonnay shows marked oak and is in
a very ripe tropical style. Drink the whites young; the reds are very approachable early but will stand
limited ageing. Charles Back also owns the SPICE ROUTE COMPANY at Swartland. (DM)

● **Shiraz** Cyril Back Paarl★★ £B   ● **Zinfandel/Cinsault** Paarl★ £B
O **Chardonnay** Coastal Region★ £B   O **Viognier** Paarl★★ £B

GLEN CARLOU   Paarl   glencarl@mweb.co.za   A: AWs, NYg

Owner: Finlayson family/Donald Hess   PO Box 23, Klapmuts 7625
The Finlaysons produce particularly impressive Chardonnay, quite different from and more stylish
than most examples from the Cape. They have some 107 ha of vineyards in the foothills of the
Simonsberg Mountains, which they own in partnership with Donald Hess of the HESS
COLLECTION in California. There are no overtly rich or tropical notes in either of the two
Chardonnays. The regular bottling is tight, minerally and restrained, the Reserve is concentrated,
with citrus, cheesy lees notes and toasty oak all entering the equation. Both are structured and capable
of three or four years' bottle-development. The Pinot Noir and Grand Classique Bordeaux blend are
good and ripe but lack the flair of the Chardonnays. Shiraz and Zinfandel are also now produced. (DM)

● **Grand Classique** Paarl★★ £C   ● **Pinot Noir** Paarl★ £C
O **Chardonnay** Paarl★★ £B Reserve Paarl★★★ £C

GRANGEHURST   Stellenbosch   www.grangehurst.co.za   A: Bib

Owner: Jeremy Walker   PO Box 206, Stellenbosch 7599
Jeremy Walker produces a small hand-crafted range of red wines from his 15 ha of vineyards. They are
stylish, concentrated and among the better examples produced in the Cape. The Pinotage is
impressively ripe and full-bodied with plenty of spicy, dark berry fruit. Nikela is an unusual blend
which, as well as those usual suspects Cabernet Sauvignon and Merlot, contains a sizeable dollop of
Pinotage. Good and reasonably concentrated it has a vibrant dark-berry fruit character with a hint of
menthol in the background. The top wine is the Cabernet Sauvignon/Merlot which is structured and
in need of three or four years' cellaring. Future plans include a move towards Rhône varieties. (DM)

● **Cabernet Sauvignon/Merlot** Stellenbosch★★★ £C   ● **Nikela** Stellenbosch★★ £B
● **Pinotage** Stellenbosch★★ £B

HAMILTON RUSSELL VINEYARDS   Walker Bay   hrv@hermanus.co.za   A: Hal, WSc

Owner: Hamilton Russell family   Hemel-en-Arde Valley, PO Box 158, 7200 Hermanus
The original and most impressive producer of both Pinot Noir and Chardonnay in the cool and visually stunning Walker Bay. The wines have much improved over the last decade, with better clones planted and a concerted effort to isolate the very best aspects of the vineyards for each variety. No artificial fertilizers are used in the stony, clay soils and cover crops are planted to optimise fruit riepening. Chardonnay is refined but has attractive, lightly tropical notes and real intensity with a pure, almost European mineral undercurrent. Pinot Noir is rich and full of dark berry fruit, with just a hint of hung meat emerging. Chardonnay as well as Pinot Noir is consistently on the cusp of four stars. A second label, Southern Right, is for Sauvignon Blanc and Pinotage sourced from the Western Cape. (DM)
● **Pinot Noir** Walker Bay★★★★ £D
O **Chardonnay** Walker Bay★★★ £D

KANONKOP   Stellenbosch   www.kanonkop.co.za   A: RSo

Owner: Krige family   PO Box 19, Elsenburg 7607
This is arguably the best Pinotage producer in South Africa. An extensive holding of old bush vines is a major contributing factor and winemaker Beyers Truter has a formidable track record with the variety. His wines are always powerful, chunky and with firm but not aggressive tannins. The regular bottling and the Bouwland Reserve are both impressive, the Auction Reserve even more so. Very good Cabernet Sauvignon is also produced here; the Paul Sauer label has an extra dimension and is blended with Cabernet Franc and Merlot. Both are rich, cedary and ageworthy with a refinement of fruit rarely encountered in the Cape. Kadette is a cheerful soft and plummy blend of Pinotage, Cabernet Sauvignon and Merlot. (DM)
● **Cabernet Sauvignon** Stellenbosch★★★ £D   ● **Paul Sauer** Stellenbosch★★★★ £D
● **Pinotage** Stellenbosch★★★ £C

MEERLUST   Stellenbosch   www.meerlust.co.za   A: MMD, Tan

Owner: Hannes Myburgh   PO Box 15, Faure 7131
Historic old wine farm first established in 1693 and located just to the south of Stellenbosch in a relatively cool mesoclimate. Reds, produced from the Bordeaux varieties, and rich and toasty Chardonnay are among the very best of their kind in the Cape. Vineyard holdings are not small: there is a total of nearly 400 ha under vine and Viognier has also been planted in cool False Bay. Merlot is very good and the Cabernet/Merlot/Cabernet Franc Rubicon blend is rich, concentrated and marked by cedar and exotic dark fruits, with not a hint of the baked and jammy flavours often found among its peers. Pinot Noir is good – ripe enough and oaky but it fails to reach the same heights. (DM)
● **Merlot** Stellenbosch★★ £C   ● **Pinot Noir** Reserve Stellenbosch★★ £C
● **Rubicon** Stellenbosch★★★ £D
O **Chardonnay** Stellenbosch★★★ £C

MEINERT   Stellenbosch   meinert@netactive.co.za   A: RsW

Owner: Martin Meinert   PO Box 7221, Stellenbosch 7599
Martin Meinert was the winemaker at VERGELEGEN before André van Rensburg. He established his own label in 1997 in the Devon Valley and produces around 4,000 cases a year solely from the

Bordeaux varieties. The Merlot is reasonably rich, concentrated and plummy with firm tannins providing the structure for ageing over the next five years or so. The Cabernet/Merlot is tight and backward in its youth, quite a lean style that needs cellaring to put on weight but should become more refined and harmonious with some age. Meinert is now focusing fully on Cabernet Sauvignon from the Devon Valley area, which replaces the Cabernet/Merlot blend. (DM)

● **Cabernet Sauvignon/Merlot** Stellenbosch★★ £C   ● **Merlot** Stellenbosch★★ £C

NICO VAN DER MERWE   Stellenbosch   wilhelmshof@xsinet.co.za

Owner: Nico van der Merwe/Robert Alexander   PO Box 12200, Stellenbosch 7613
Nico van der Merwe is the winemaker at SAXENBERG and CHÂTEAU CAPION in France's Languedoc region. Under his own label he produces a very fine blend of Shiraz and Cabernet Sauvignon. Production is small at around 500 cases a year. The Shiraz component is sourced from 27 year old vines grown in granite soils, the Cabernet from 11 year old vines. The vineyards are carefully managed with summer pruning to keep yields low and irrigation is avoided. Nico plans to source fruit in the future from his own vineyards towards Walker Bay. Vinification is modern with both hand plunging and pumping over the cap during fermentation and the wine is kept on its skins for a further two weeks. Malolactic is in barrel and 50 per cent new oak used for ageing. The result is a dense, classically minty style of Cape red but with real depth and concentration. The wine will drink well young but evolve over a decade or more. (DM)

● **Mas Nicolas** Stellenbosch★★★★ £D

MORGENHOF   Stellenbosch   www.morgenhof.com   A: McK

Owner: Anne Cointreau-Huchon   PO Box 365, Stellenbosch 7599
Medium-sized, French-owned estate with a production of around 25,000 cases a year. An extensive range includes sparkling and fortified wines. Chardonnay is in an oaky style with marked buttery malolactic character, Sauvignon Blanc is typically zesty and fresh, and there is a barrel-fermented Chenin Blanc with that charcteristic hint of residual sugar so typically employed in the vinification of the variety here. Reds include Merlot, Malbec/Merlot and Pinotage but most impressive are the Cabernet Sauvignon and Première Selection. This latter wine is a blend of Cabernet Sauvignon, Merlot and Cabernet Franc. It is sweet and moderately rich while the Cabernet is firm, structured and with a characteristic Cape mintiness. Both will stand a little age. Merlot and Cabernet Sauvignon Reserve labels have both been introduced with the 1998 vintage and look promising. (DM)

● **Cabernet Sauvignon** Stellenbosch★★ £C   ● **Première Selection** Stellenbosch★ £C
● **Pinotage** Stellenbosch★ £C
O **Chardonnay** Stellenbosch★★ £B

MULDERBOSCH   Stellenbosch   www.mulderbosch.co.za   A: JAr

*Owner: **Hydro Holdings**   PO Box 548, Stellenbosch 7599*
Produces one of the best piercing varietal Sauvignon Blancs. This is surprising because the meso-climate of the vineyard here is reasonably hot. The key is tightly controlled yields and harvesting ripe but not over ripe grapes. Subtly oaked Chardonnay, now in Barrel Fermented and regular bottlings and a Barrel Fermented Sauvignon Blanc are also good but without the piercing intensity of the regular Sauvignon, which is cool-fermented in tank. A Chenin Blanc, Steen-op-Hout, sees a touch of oak and there is a red blend, Faithful Hound, comprising the Bordeaux varieties Merlot, Cabernets Sauvignon and Franc and a touch of Malbec. The latter will improve with three or four years' cellaring but can show a slightly green, angular character. (DM)

● **Faithful Hound** Stellenbosch★★ £C
O **Chardonnay** Barrel Fermented Stellenbosch★★★ £C
O **Sauvignon Blanc** Stellenbosch★★ £B Barrel Fermented Stellenbosch★★ £C

RUSTENBERG Stellenbosch www.rustenberg.co.za   A: Men, L&S

Owner: Barlow family   PO Box 33, Stellenbosch 7599
Considerable investment has been put into this farm in recent years and the winery is now gravity
fed, with some good results. There are three Brampton-label wines sourced from Stellenbosch; a
straightforward Sauvignon Blanc with simple gooseberry fruit, a Cabernet/Merlot with soft, forward,
red-berry fruit and an Old Vines red blend of Merlot and Cabernet. Of greater substance are the
Rustenberg wines. Two Chardonnays are produced with intense citrus notes and well-judged oak, as
well as the Rustenberg John X Merriman and Peter Barlow reds. The former, a Bordeaux blend with
a high proportion of Merlot, shows sweet berry fruit and spicy oak. Peter Barlow is a more structured
and ageworthy varietal Cabernet Sauvignon. Shiraz and Viognier are to be added to the range. (DM)
● **Cabernet Sauvignon Peter Barlow** Stellenbosch★★★ £D ● **John X Merriman** Stellenbosch★★ £C
O **Chardonnay** Stellenbosch★★ £B Five Soldiers Stellenbosch★★★ £C

SADIE FAMILY WINES Swartland sadiefamily@mail.com   A: RsW, NYg

Owner: Eben Sadie   PO Box 1019, Malmesbury 7299
Eben Sadie, the original winemaker at SPICE ROUTE, formed his own tiny winery Sadie Family in
the late 1990s. At present just one wine is made here, a very fine red Columella, an almost varietal
Syrah with just a tiny proportion of Mourvedre. It is a wine of remarkable dark, spicy complexity;
rich, almost exotic, with a supple texture and great intensity. Inevitably it is made from very low
yields, from seven leased vineyard parcels around Swartland, half of which are populated with old
bush vines. Eben controls all the viticultural aspects. There is no irrigation and he prefers to control
vine growth through crop thinning. The must gets a cold soak prior to fermentation and maceration
often lasts longer than five weeks. The wine is basket-pressed and aged in oak for close to two years
while fining and filtration are avoided. A tiny amount (just over 100 cases) of a white Palladius, a
blend of Viognier, Chardonnay, Chenin Blanc and Grenache Blanc was first made with the 2002 vintage. Eben is also involved in a new project in Priorat in Spain, producing barely 150 cases of a
Carignan and Grenache blend called Dits del Terra. Immediately approachable, Columella will
develop very well for a decade or more. (DM)
● **Columella** Swartland★★★★★ £E

SAXENBURG Stellenbosch www.saxenburg.co.za   A: Fie

Owner: Buhrer family   PO Box 171, Kulls River 7580
Swiss-owned farm, which also owns Domaine CAPION in France's Languedoc region. There are over
90 ha of vineyards supplemented by bought-in fruit to cover requirements. The Standard, Reserve
and Estate ranges provide decent fruit-driven reds and whites but it is the Private Collection Label
that particularly stands out. A cap classique sparkler a Chardonnay and Sauvignon Blanc are
produced and can be impressive with good varietal fruit and stylishly handled oak in the
Chardonnay. The Private Collection reds comprise a warm and plummy Merlot with rich, vanilla
oak; a tightly structured Cabernet Sauvignon marked by notes of cassis and cedar; and impressive
Shiraz, which is full of dark black fruit and Rhône-like licorice and black pepper. Shiraz Select is
richer and fuller with very fine, ripe and supply textured tannins, long and harmonious. Both
Shirazes stand out among South African reds. (DM)

● **Cabernet Sauvignon** Private Collection Stellenbosch★★★ £C
● **Merlot** Private Collection Stellenbosch★★ £C
● **Shiraz** Private Collection Stellenbosch★★★ £C Select Stellenbosch★★★★ £D
● **Pinotage** Private Collection Stellenbosch★★ £C
O **Chardonnay** Private Collection Stellenbosch★★ £C
O **Sauvignon Blanc** Private Collection Stellenbosch★★ £B

SPICE ROUTE COMPANY Swartland   A: Eno

Owner: Charles Back   PO Box 645, Malmesbury 7300
Now wholly owned by Charles Back of FAIRVIEW the wines at this warm-climate Swartland property
have been good to sometimes very good in recent vintages. There is a regular Cabernet/Merlot blend,
along with sound fruity Sauvignon Blanc and Chenin Blanc. Shiraz, Pinotage and Viognier have
been added more recently. All are released under the standard label. As well as these, a simple fruit
driven Sauvignon Blanc and a Cabernet/Merlot are released under the third-tier Andrew's Hope
label. The Flagship range of red varietals, though, are a real step up. The Syrah is full of dark
blackberry and spice, round and supple; the Merlot is softer and with marked plum and sweet oak.
The Pinotage is loaded with dark black, very ripe fruit and is marked by firm tannin, the structure
sometimes threatening to overwhelm the wine. All will develop well in the medium-term. (DM)
● **Merlot** Swartland★★★ £C   ● **Pinotage** Swartland★★★ £C   ● **Syrah** Swartland★★★ £C

SPRINGFIELD Robertson www.springfieldestate.com   A: Bib

Owner: Bruwer family   PO Box 770, Robertson 6705
The best property in the warm Robertson area is producing decent fresh, grassy Sauvignon Blanc Life
from Stone and some good to very good Chardonnay with close-to-organic practices. Cabernet
Sauvignon has been less impressive – quite lean with a marked leafy component behind its fruit. A
Méthode Ancienne bottling has now been added which is fermented from wild yeasts and aged on lees
after malolactic in barrel. It is bottled without filtration. Chardonnay is tight and citrusy with well-
judged oak and a rich, buttery component provided by malolactic fermentation. Of additional weight
and substance is the very good special bottling of Chardonnay Méthode Ancienne, produced only in
the best years. Wild yeasts are again used to vinify both Chardonnays and filtration is avoided. (DM)
O **Chardonnay** Wild Yeast Robertson★★ £B Méthode Ancienne Robertson★★★ £C
O **Sauvignon Blanc** Life from Stone Robertson★ £B

STELLENZICHT Stellenbosch www.stellenzicht.co.za   A: Hal

*Owner: **Lusan Holdings (Pty) Ltd**   PO Box 104, 7604 Vlottenburg*
A quite extensive range is produced at this Stellenbosch farm by winemaker Guy Webber, who took
over from André van Rensburg after he moved to VERGELEGEN. A regular range of varietals under
the Hill and Dale label offers decent value and both red and white varietals appear under the Golden
Triangle label. Sauvignon Blanc is fresh and zesty and there is some nutty, toasty Chardonnay but
best of the whites is a restrained well crafted Semillon Reserve. Pinotage is ripe and brambly with a
hint of that acetate character frequent in the variety. The flagship Syrah is very classy stuff: structured
and impressive with well-judged oak, it will develop well with three or four years' ageing. A premium
Stellenzicht Bordeaux blend bottling has now been added. (DM)
● **Cabernet Sauvignon** Stellenbosch★ £B   ● **Stellenzicht** Stellenbosch★★ £C
● **Syrah** Stellenbosch★★★ £C   ● **Pinotage** Stellenbosch★★ £B
O **Sauvignon Blanc** Stellenbosch★ £B   O **Chardonnay** Stellenbosch★★ £B
O **Semillon** Reserve Stellenbosch★★★ £C

THELEMA Stellenbosch www.thelema.co.za   A: Eno, NYg

Owner: Gyles Webb   PO Box 2234, 7599 Stellenbosch
Gyles Webb is generally accepted as one of the best viticulturalists and winemakers in the Cape. The family's vineyard and winery are located at altitude on the slopes of the Simonsberg and this contributes to the quality of the fruit. The vineyards are well managed and controlled yields are nevertheless reasonably productive. There's good Chardonnay and Cabernet Sauvignon as well as steely, minerally Riesling. Merlot can be less impressive but is reasonably concentrated and ripely plummy. Sauvignon is piercing and full of lightly tropical, green fruits. It should be consumed as soon as it is released. Reserves of Merlot and Cabernet Sauvignon are a step up from the regular examples. Shiraz and Pinotage in as yet very small quantities have now been added to the range. (DM)

● **Cabernet Sauvignon** Stellenbosch★★ £C   Reserve★★★ £D   ● **Merlot** Stellenbosch★★ £C
○ **Chardonnay** Stellenbosch★★ £C   ○ **Sauvignon Blanc** Stellenbosch★★ £B
○ **Riesling** Stellenbosch★★ £B

VEENWOUDEN Paarl   A: Sec, NYg

Owner: Deon van der Walt   PO Box 7086, North Paarl 7623
The reputation of this property is based on three wines, all of which have their roots in Bordeaux. Production is now around 6,000 cases and Merlot in particular has been outstanding among Cape examples: supple, rich and with a real mineral hint of its terroir. The Classic, a typical Bordeaux blend, is also impressive. Similar in style, the Vivat Bacchus has a touch of Malbec and is more open and approachable. There is minimal interference in the cellar and fine-quality French oak is used throughout, some of it new. The range has now been marginally expanded to include a Shiraz and a tiny amount of Chardonnay Special Reserve. (DM)

● **Merlot** Paarl★★★ £C   ● **Vivat Bacchus** Paarl★★ £C   ● **Classic** Paarl★★★ £C

VERGELEN Stellenbosch www.vergelegen.co.za   A: NYg, WSc

Owner: Anglo American Farms Ltd   PO Box 17, Somerset West
This historic wine farm dates back to 1700 and is located on hillside vineyards south of Stellenbosch. The winery was designed by French architects but you feel it is more like a new-wave Napa Valley operation than anything else. Gravity plays an important role in cellar-handling operations. André van Rensburg took on the winemaking mantle here after Martin MEINERT moved on to produce his own label. There is a straightforward blended white from Chenin Blanc, Muscat, Sauvignon Blanc, Chardonnay and Semillon, finished with a hint of residual sugar. Varietal Sauvignon Blanc and Chardonnay are both impressive, particularly the Reserves, which have real structure and grip. Merlot is ripe and vibrant and contains eight per cent Cabernet Sauvignon. Cabernet Sauvignon has a hint of Merlot and Cabernet Franc, while the Vergelegen Red is one of the best reds yet from the Cape. Shiraz has now been added to the range and is impressively refined and stylish. A white Bordeaux style blend is new to the range and promises much. (DM)

● **Cabernet Sauvignon** Stellenbosch★★★ £C   ● **Merlot** Stellenbosch★★ £C
● **Shiraz** Stellenbosch★★★ £C   ● **Vergelegen** Stellenbosch★★★★ £D
○ **Chardonnay** Stellenbosch★★ £B   Reserve Stellenbosch★★★ £C
○ **Sauvignon Blanc** Stellenbosch★★ £B   Reserve Stellenbosch★★ £C

WARWICK ESTATE Stellenbosch www.warwickwine.co.za A:RsW,WSc

Owner: Norma Ratcliffe PO Box 2 Elsenburg 7607

The Bordeaux red varieties are the most significant plantings on this medium-sized farm neighbouring KANONKOP. Like its neighbour there are also old Pinotage bush vines planted and these produce one of the better brambly, concentrated examples of the variety. Some of the harvest is regularly sold off and the balance results in some very good Cabernet Sauvignon and Cabernet Franc and the stylish, structured blend Trilogy, produced from Cabernet Sauvignon, Merlot and Cabernet Franc. A lighter red blend of Cabernet Sauvignon, Merlot and some Pinotage, Three Cape Ladies, can be enjoyed young. The range is completed by a leesy Chardonnay of reasonable depth and a recently added Sauvignon Blanc, Professor Black. (DM)

● **Cabernet Franc** Stellenbosch★★ £C   ● **Cabernet Sauvignon** Stellenbosch★★★ £C
● **Merlot** Stellenbosch★★ £C   ● **Pinotage** Old Bush Vines Stellenbosch★★ £C
● **Three Cape Ladies** Stellenbosch★★ £C   ● **Trilogy** Stellenbosch★★ £C
○ **Chardonnay** Stellenbosch★ £B

OTHER WINES OF NOTE

AGUSTA WINES ● **Cabernet Sauvignon** Count Agusta Franschoek £C
ASHANTI ● **Cabernet Sauvignon** Paarl £C   ● **Pinotage** Paarl £C
BACKSBERG ● **Klein Babylonstoren** Paarl £B
GRAHAM BECK ○ **Blanc de Blancs** Vintage Robertson £C
BELLINGHAM ● **Cabernet Franc** Spitz Coastal Region £C   ● **Pinotage** Spitz Coastal Region £C
BERGKELDER ○ **Pongrácz** Non Vintage Stellenbosch £C
BOPLAAS ● **Cape Vintage Reserve Fortified Red** Calitzdorp £C
BOSCHENDAL ● **Shiraz** Paarl £C   ○ **Chardonnay** Reserve Paarl £B
BUITENVERWACHTING ● **Christine** Constantia £C   ○ **Chardonnay** Constantia £B
BWC WINES ● **Shiraz** Paarl £C
CABRIÈRE ESTATE ○ **Pierre Jourdan Blanc de Blancs** Non-Vintage Franschoek £C
PAUL CLUVER ○ **Weisser Riesling** Elgin £B
CONDÉ ● **Cabernet Sauvignon** Stellenbosch £E
CONSTANTIA UITSIG ○ **Chardonnay Reserve** Constantia £C
CORDOBA ● **Cabernet Sauvignon** Stellenbosch £B
DARLING CELLARS ● **Cabernet Sauvignon** Groenekloof £B
DELHEIM ● **Shiraz Vera Cruz Estate** Simonsberg-Stellenbosch £C
DE TOREN ● **Fusion V** Stellenbosch £D
DE TRAFFORD ● **Cabernet Sauvignon** Stellenbosch £C   ● **Merlot** Stellenbosch £C
DIEMERSFONTEINE ● **Pinotage** Stellenbosch £B   ● **Shiraz** Stellenbosch £B
EIKENDAL ○ **Chardonnay** Stellenbosch £B
NEIL ELLIS ● **Shiraz** Stellenbosch £B   ○ **Sauvignon Blanc** Groenekloof £B
FLAGSTONE ● **Cabernet Sauvignon** The Music Room £C
GROOT CONSTANTIA ○ **Chardonnay** Reserve Constantia £B
GROOT POST ○ **Chardonnay** Swartland £B   ● **Merlot** Swartland £C
JACK AND KNOX WINECRAFT ○ **Semillon** Greenhill Wellington £B
● **Cabernet Sauvignon** The Estoril £C   ● **Shiraz** The Outsider Swartland £C
JORDAN ● **Cobblers Hill** Stellenbosch £C   ○ **Chardonnay** Stellenbosch £B
KAAPZICHT ● **Estate Red** Stellenbosch £D   ● **Steytler Vision** Stellenbosch £D
KLEIN CONSTANTIA ○ **Sauvignon Blanc** Constantia £B   ○ **Vin de Constance** Constantia £E
LA MOTTE ● **Shiraz** Franschoek £C   ● **Millenium** Franschoek £C
LAIBACH ● **Cabernet/Merlot** Stellenbosch £B   ○ **Chardonnay** Stellenbosch £B
L'AVENIR ● **Pinotage** Stellenbosch £B
LE BONHEUR ● **Cabernet Sauvignon** Stellenbosch £C

LE RICHE ● Cabernet Sauvignon Reserve Stellenbosch £C
LONGRIDGE ○ Chardonnay Stellenbosch £B
MONT DU TOIT● Mont du Toit Wellington £D   ● Le Sommet Wellington £F
MURATIE ESTATE ● Shiraz £B
NEDERBURG ○ Edelkeur Noble Late Harvest Auction Reserve Paarl £E
NEETHLINGSHOF ○ Noble Late Harvest Stellenbosch £C
OVERGAAUW ● Tria Corda Stellenbosch £C
PLAISIR DE MERLE ● Cabernet Sauvignon Paarl £C
RAATS FAMILY WINES ○ Original Chenin Blanc Stellenbosch £E   ● Cabernet Franc Stellenbosch £C
RIDGEBACK ● Shiraz Paarl £D
ROOIBERG ● Pinotage Robertson £B
RUST EN VREDE ● Estate Red Stellenbosch £C
SIMONSIG ● Tiara Stellenbosch £C   ● Pinotage Redhill Stellenbosch £C
SIYABONGA ● Pinotage Wellington £C
STARK ● Cabernet Sauvignon Stellenbosch £C
STEENBERG ○ Sauvignon Blanc Reserve Constantia £C   ○ Semillon Constantia £C
UITERWYK ● Pinotage Top of the Hill Stellenbosch £B
VILLIERA ● Cru Monro Paarl £B   ○ Sauvignon Blanc Traditional Bush Vine Paarl £B
WATERFORD ● Cabernet Sauvignon Stellenbosch £C   ○ Sauvignon Blanc Stellenbosch £B
ZONDERNAAM ○ Sauvignon Blanc Stellenbosch £B

Author's choice (DM)

A selection of emerging Cape new classics
BEYERSKLOOF ● Cabernet Sauvignon Stellenbosch
BOEKENHOUTSKLOOF ● Cabernet Sauvignon Estate Franschhoek
GLEN CARLOU ● Chardonnay Reserve Paarl
HAMILTON RUSSELL VINEYARDS ● Pinot Noir Walker Bay
KANONKOP ● Paul Sauer Stellenbosch
NICO VAN DER MERWE ● Mas Nicolas Stellenbosch
RUSTENBERG ● Cabernet Sauvignon Peter Barlow Stellenbosch
SADIE FAMILY WINES ● Columella Swartland
SAXENBURG ● Shiraz Select Stellenbosch
SPICE ROUTE COMPANY ● Syrah Swartland
THELEMA ● Cabernet Sauvignon Reserve Stellenbosch
VERGELEGEN ● Vergelegen Stellenbosch

Six benchmark Pinotage
GRANGEHURST ● Pinotage Stellenbosch
KANONKOP ● Pinotage Stellenbosch
SAXENBURG ● Pinotage Private Collection Stellenbosch
SPICE ROUTE COMPANY ● Pinotage Swartland
STELLENZICHT ● Pinotage Stellenbosch
WARWICK ● Pinotage Old Bush Vines Stellenbosch

Aglianico Late ripening, southern Italy red grape of real importance and considerable potential. Ageworthy with a noble structure, its smoky, minerally, berry-fruited character gains greater complexity and refined texture with keeping. The best wines come from Campania (Taurasi and various IGTs) and to some extent Basilicata (Aglianico del Vulture) and Puglia but don't expect greatness from the increasing amounts of inexpensive Aglianico now appearing from the same regions.

Albariño Galicia's (north-west Spain) great white hope, Albarino is often compared to Viognier. It not only shares some of Viognier's perfume and succulent peachiness but also the wide disparity in quality levels. Try only a top rated example from a good producer where yields low and the wine-making expert. As Alvarinho, Portugal's best examples (sold as varietal Vinho Verdes) don't yet match the best from its northern neighbour.

Alicante Bouschet Characterful red-fleshed crossing (that claims Grenache as a parent) once heavily planted in southern France. Though more often used as a blending grape decent varietal examples are made in Portugal's Alentejo, Central Italy (especially Tuscany or Emilia) and California.

Arneis Piedmont's leading white grape for dry whites is starting to make an impression in California and Australia. Light, dry but rather enticing perfumed examples generally need to be drunk very young; lightly oaked versions will keep a little longer but aren't necessarily superior.

Baga The grape of Portugal's Bairrada region. Potentially a bruiser but when fully ripe from modest yielding vines it produces wines of great character if not seductive charm. Its distinctive earth, coffee, plum and berry fruit character is allied to depth and richness with age. In decline in the neighbouring Dão region where it is less suited.

Barbera Marvellous Piedmont grape which comes in any number of styles and quality levels. The greatest acclaim comes for rich, modern oaked-aged versions but some unoaked versions can also be stunning. There are many good examples as both Barbera d'Alba and Barbera d'Asti and occasionally convincing versions from Emilia. Simple, supple, fruity, quaffing Barbera can be good too. Once important in California, this is where the next best examples can be found; Australia also makes adequate versions while potential also exists in Argentina.

Bical One of the best native Portuguese varieties for dry whites though that's not saying much. Good body, aroma and acidity are possible if rarely achieved. Luis Pato's single vineyard Vinha Formal seems likely to realise the limits of what is possible. Also made sparkling.

Blaufränkisch Important red variety in Austria's Burgenland where it is often blended with other varieties to moderate its relatively high acidity and tannin. Of minor importance in Washington State and Germany where it is known as Lemberger. One and the same as Hungary's Kékfrankos.

Bobal Widely planted red variety in central Spain capable, it would seem, of producing concentrated smoky, black-fruited reds. It is early days but some powerful reds, rich in fruit and extract, from unirrigated, low-yielding old vine fruit are starting to emerge (see Mustiguillo).

Bonarda In Italy what is called Bonarda is most important in Oltrepò Pavese and Colli Piacentini (as Croatina). In the latter, it can be blend with Barbera for a characterful red, Gutturnio. Argentina's Bonarda is not related but from old vines complex, aromatic, supple reds can be produced.

Brachetto Unusual Piedmontese variety that has obtained DOCG status in Brachetto d'Acqui. Often it is medium-dry and either *frizzante* or fully sparkling but with a wonderful, grapey perfume and flavour if drunk young and fresh from a producer like Braida.

Cabernet Franc Parent variety of the more famous Cabernet Sauvignon it is more successful in cooler soils. Only in the Anjou and Touraine in the Loire Valley does it thrive as a varietal as despite its importance on Bordeaux's Right Bank it is almost invariably blended with Merlot and some Cabernet Sauvignon. Its importance as a component in Bordeaux style blends both at home and around the world is undeniable. Though it can emulate the flavours of its off-spring, it can miss its extra richness and depth and also show more of a raspberry-like fruit and a more leafy, herbal or even floral, component.

Cabernet Sauvignon   Grown almost everywhere, a grape of forceful and easily recognisable personality, it is much more fussy in showing at its best. Though capable of great richness, depth and structure, a lack of full ripeness in both fruit and tannin tends to detract from so many examples. A long growing season and well-drained soils are two prerequisites to producing the greatest elegance and classic telltale blackcurrant but also black cherry or blackberry flavours that mesh so well with new French oak. Though Cabernet Sauvignon dominates blends, the majority of top examples many do include a percentage of complementary varietals such as Merlot or Cabernet Franc which complement it in both flavour and structure. Many countries have identified at least one region where it really excels with the greatest riches from the Médoc, Napa Valley, Tuscany, Coonawarra and Margaret River. A significant number of world class examples have also come from Washington State, New Zealand, Chile, Argentina as well as a few from Spain and South Africa.

Canaiolo   Chiefly Tuscan variety and used to complement Sangiovese but discarded by many in favour of Merlot or Cabernet Sauvignon for their Chianti Classico. A mini revival is underway as some producers seek to produce reds of more individual character.

Cannonau   Sardinian version of Grenache, for long produced as an inexpensive quaffing red, Cannonau di Sardegna. One of two committed growers are beginning to realize its true potential. Rare good fortified versions are also made from late-harvested or dried grapes.

Carignan   Infamous red grape of the Languedoc-Roussillon still widely planted and often very high- yielding resulting in dilute, astringent wine. However from low yields and fully ripe fruit its a different beast. Deeply coloured, robust but characterful reds are possible not only in the Midi but also occasionally in Spain (as Cariñena), Sardinia (as Carignano) and California (as Carignane).

Carmenère   Old Bordeaux variety of increasing importance in Chile where much of it continues to be sold as Merlot. As they are often planted in a field blend together the disparity in ripening times further compromises the quality of fruit from high-yielding vines. Once isolated and made from well-established low-yielding vines it has excellent potential with a characterful wild berry and spice character. Also thought to be confused with other grapes in regions where plantings were established from Bordeaux cuttings in the 19th century.

Castelão   Portuguese grape also still widely known as Periquita, extensively grown in the southern regions but most successful in the Palmela DOC in the Terras do Sado region.

Chardonnay   Ironically the only significant wine regions where this grape is not grown are found in France. The great white grape of Burgundy has a great affinity for oak and can produce whites of marvellous texture, depth and richness but will also render a wonderful expression of its origins where yields are low. High quality grapes allied to winemaking sophistication is essential – too many examples, wherever they are made, show a clumsy winemaking fingerprint (excessive leesy, skin contact or oak flavours) or inferior fruit (under-ripe, over-ripe) or are simply unclean, acidified or lacking balance. Chardonnay forms a part of almost all top quality sparkling wines, especially Champagne. When varietal and sparkling it is known as Blanc de Blancs. Rich botrytised versions are unusual but have been made to a high standard in the Mâconnais, Austria and New Zealand.

Chasselas   Relatively neutral white grape also known as Fendant in Switzerland where it assumes greater importance and produces whites of higher quality than anywhere else in the world. The best examples reflect something of the specific *terroirs* with good structure and minerality in Dézaley and Calamin. From the opposite, southern shore of Lac Léman in Savoie come the best French examples (including Crépy). Rare decent examples are also made in the Loire (Pouilly-sur-Loire) and Alsace.

Chenin Blanc   High quality white grape of Touraine and Anjou in the Loire Valley. Outstanding long-lived wines ranging from dry to sweet are made and owe much to the grape's high acidity. Apple and citrus flavours within a firm, demanding texture are usually complemented by floral, honey and mineral characters with quince, peach even apricot in sweeter styles. Despite there being more extensive plantings in California and South Africa, good examples from outside the Loire remain few.

Washington State and New Zealand also provide one or two. Also an important base for some good quality sparkling wines.

Ciliegiolo   Difficult central Italian variety, not least, to pronounce. One of several natives (also see Colorino, Canaiolo) being revived by committed growers seeking more authentic Tuscan reds than those that rely in part or whole on foreign varieties. One or two varietal examples from old vine fruit show a captivating wild cherry character.

Cinsaut/Cinsault   Characterful Rhône variety where taken seriously. Can add perfume and complexity both to southern Rhône blends and wines from the Languedoc and Corsica, especially when yields are low.

Colorino   Deep coloured red grape of Central Italy and Tuscany, once used to beef up Chianti made by the *governo* technique. Mostly used along with Canaiolo to complement Sangiovese but very occasionally contributes significantly to reds of tremendous character, depth and richness, from isolated locations where the vines are of high quality.

Cortese   Piedmont grape of moderate quality best known for the mostly undistinguished Gavi. A handful of producers have improved both concentration and character of their wines through lower yields; the subtle use of oak can also help. Other examples such as those from the Monferrato hills can be attractively fruity if rarely showing much depth or refinement.

Corvina   Leading red variety in Italy's Veneto for Valpolicella, Amarone and Recioto della Valpolicella. Though only giving moderate colour and tannin its thickish skins help it to resist rot during the drying process or *appassimento*. The related Corvinone can bring more colour, concentration and structure to a blend.

Dolcetto   Piedmont grape capable of wonderful fruit intensity yet lively acidity and moderate tannin. Most of the best examples with a mineral or herbal streak to black cherry or black plum fruit, are unoaked and mean't to be drunk with between one and three years' age but there are ageworthy exceptions, especially those from old low-yielding vines whether in the Dogliani or Alba zones. Known as Ormeasco in Liguria.

Encruzado   Portuguese variety starting to show considerable quality in the Dão region. Subtly oaked it can show good depth, a gentle texture and a refined, perfumed, slightly exotic fruit character.

Erbaluce   Little seen Piedmont white of pronounced acidity but with attractive fruit when fully ripe and dry as Erbaluce di Caluso. Caluso Passito, from dried grapes is potentially better quality while a little sparkling wine is also made.

Falanghina   Another potential star grape from southern Italy set to rival Fiano and Greco. Though still not widely seen the number of good examples, showing impressive texture and flavour with a couple of years' age, is on the increase.

Fiano   Perfumed and flavoursome white grape from Campania from which increasing amounts of spicy, dry whites with fullish peachy, slightly nutty fruit are made. Late-harvested versions and those from botrytis affected grapes have also been successfully made.

Freisa   Characterful, perfumed Piedmont grape often made *frizzante* (lightly sparkling), sometimes with a little residual sugar. A handful of dry versions are excellent where its predisposition to astringency on the finish has been mastered.

Gaglioppo   Late-ripening southern Italian red variety of chief importance in Calabria. The colour can develop quite quickly and the tannin and alcohol levels can be high. From moderate yields, wines can show impressive depth and develop a rich, chocolaty, savoury complexity.

Gamay   The grape of the Beaujolais region and well-suited to its granitic soils. Examples range from the dilute and insipid to the impressively deep and fruity. Most but not all of it is produced by semi-carbonic maceration producing a supple texture but partly compromising its cherry fruit perfume and flavour. Plantings extend into the Mâconnais to the north where it performs poorly; mercifully, some at least, is being replaced by Chardonnay. The only really significant other area where the true Gamay grape is planted is in Touraine in the Loire Valley.

Garganega   The 'good' grape of Soave capable of producing intense, sleek whites when yields are low. Even more impressive when made from late-harvested or dried grapes (for Recioto di Soave).

Garnacha   see Grenache

Gewürztraminer / Traminer   Both of these names are used to describe a remarkably aromatic distinctive grape variety that has produced good examples from around the world. This versatile grapy white is redolent in scents from the floral and musky to rose petal, lychee and spices. Styles range from the light and fresh to rich, oily textured wines and from dry to off-dry through late-harvested to sweet, botrytised wines. Weaker efforts lack definition and a certain coarseness, particularly on the finish, is only avoided in top quality examples. The greatest range of styles and highest quality comes from Alsace which is followed by Italy's Alto Adige and Germany. Though fewer in number the best new world examples arguably come from New Zealand but there is good quality too in Australia, California, Oregon and Canada and in Chile's Casablanca Valley.

Grauburgunder   see Pinot Gris

Graciano   Mostly a minor component in Rioja this is a variety of limited planting that nonetheless adds character and complexity to Tempranillo dominated blends. Rare varietal examples highlight its intriguing perfume and suggest it has further potential.

Greco   Or more specifically Greco di Tufo (to distinguish it from other similar names) does come originally from Greece and does well on the volcanic soils in Campania's Avellino hills in southern Italy. At its best it is attractively scented with citrus, peachy fruit and a firm texture and slightly nutty finish.

Grenache   Leading grape variety in the southern Rhône where it forms the backbone wines from the leading appellations, including Châteauneuf-du-Pape and Gigondas. Quality and style vary enormously but is capable of great longevity when produced from low-yielding fruit. Grenache also forms a component of many of Languedoc-Roussillon's reds including Banyuls and Collioure near the border with Spain. As Garnacha it is the base for some of Spain's top reds in the small but dynamic region of Priorat but is also the leading variety in several other appellations in the north-east of the country. It is also a significant component in many reds from Navarra and Rioja. In Sardinia, it goes under the name of Cannonau. In Australia some of the best vines were uprooted before its quality potential was reassessed. It is now part of, often high quality, fashionable blends that usually include Shiraz and Mourvèdre.

Grenache Blanc   Previously undistinguished grape particularly important in southern Rhône and Languedoc whites. Low yields and better winemaking have given it much more personality and it is sometimes made varietally.

Grüner Veltliner   From terraces above the Danube in the Wachau region in Lower Austria, this relatively unknown grape can produce remarkably good full-bodied whites. Neighbouring regions of Kremstal, Kamptal and Traisental can also produce peppery, citrus, yellow plum flavoured wines that become gently honeyed and increasingly complex with age. Its tendency to high alcohol needs to be balanced by good acidity and fruit richness. More everyday examples can be dilute and lack charm.

Jaen   Important component in red Dão blends and capable of good fruit intensity if relatively modest structure. Its smoky, spicy, berryish fruit has occasionally been fully expressed in one or two varietal examples. Probably the same grape as the Spain's Mencía.

Lagrein   Grape found in Trentino-Alto Adige (North-East Italy) and fast becoming the most important red variety in the region. Both supple, fruity everyday reds and deep coloured, concentrated, often oak-aged, reds full of bramble, dark plum and cherry fruit, are being made in increasing numbers. It has the fruit intensity of other native North-East reds but more moderate tannin and acidity levels that suggest it has potential elsewhere too.

Malbec   Essentially another of Bordeaux's rejects, the peppery, black-fruited Malbec has found favour as the major constituent of Cahors in South-West France but has become even more strongly associated with Argentina. The latter examples tend to be softer and more approachable but can want for structure but there is high quality from both sources. Good quality is also obtained from a limited amount of old vine plantings in South Australia while it is on the increase in Chile and performs well in New Zealand. It is of minor importance in the Loire Valley where it is known as Cot.

Malvasia   This name covers a great many closely related varieties from Italy, Spain and Portugal. In North-East Italy Malvasia Istriana can be a characterful dry white. In Tuscany dried Malvasia grapes bring more quality when added to Trebbiano for Vin Santo while in Lazio Malvasia can rescue the whites of the Colli Albani, such as Frascati, from blandness. In the south it turns sweet when made from *passito* grapes on the volcanic island of Lipari. In Spain it can add substance to some white Rioja while in Portugal's Douro Malvasia grapes could end up in White Port or as a dry white. As Malvasia Fina one or two good varietal white Dão are made while on Madeira it is the grape responsible for the richest, sweetish style of Madeira, Malmsey.

Malvasia Nera   A black version of Malvasia of considerable importance in Puglia but also found elsewhere in Italy, mostly in the south but also in Tuscany. Aromatic, its distinctive black plum fruit adds character to reds usually based on either Negroamaro, Primitivo or Sangiovese.

Marsanne   At its best this is an intensely flavoured white with succulent peach and apricot fruit and often a tell-tale honeysuckle character. It is particularly important in northern Rhône whites, sometimes in partnership with Roussanne. It is also produced in Hermitage as *Vin de Paille*. It crops up again in blends in Côtes du Rhône whites (but not white Châteauneuf-du-Pape), Languedoc-Roussillon and even in Provence. It is grown too in Switzerland's Valais (as Ermitage) and makes a rare appearance (or two) in Italy. Its use in California is likely to increase while the best examples in Australia come from the Goulburn Valley in Victoria.

Melon de Bourgogne   The grape responsible for the many bland dry whites of Muscadet. The best examples however can be both refreshing and flavoursome, usually owed, at least in part, to ageing *sur lie*.

Merlot   There are very few significant wine producing countries where there isn't at least some Merlot, even Switzerland and Canada have plenty of it. Its home though is in Bordeaux and it can range from a few per cent to almost varietal (as in Château Pétrus). Much Merlot is lean, weedy and under-ripe. In fact few Merlot-dominated wines in fact come close to those of Bordeaux's Right Bank. Although good ripe, lush reds have been produced from Australia, New Zealand, Chile, Argentina, South Africa, California, Washington State and Italy, very few of these combine that richness with the classic berry plumminess and fruitcake, spice, fig or clove character that make it so enticing. Tuscany and California do it most often but in Chile (where it is mixed up with Carmenère) and elsewhere, great examples are the exception.

Mondeuse   Characterful French grape from Savoie. High in acidity but capable of intense beetroot, plum and cherry flavours and an attractive floral scent. Though a localised variety, one producer (Cottanera) has planted it at altitude in Sicily. It may be one and the same as Fruili's Refosco.

Montepulciano   Gutsy peppery red variety that dominates the adriatic seaboard in central Italy. Most examples are fruity with good extract and colour; a mere handful develop the breadth, refinement and complexity of which it is also capable.

Mourvèdre   High quality grape found in southern France at the very limits of ripening. It is most important incarnation is as powerful, tannic and ageworthy Bandol but some in Châteauneuf-du-Pape use it for blending as do producers in the Languedoc-Roussillon. In Spain (as Monastrell) it has been rather neglected in terms of producing high quality but a handful of producers in Jumilla and elsewhere are starting to realize its potential there. In Australia and California it is sometimes called Mataro but in both places it can also excel both varietally and in blends.

Muscadet   see Melon de Bourgogne

Muscat There is a whole family of Muscat grapes and it comes in many guises however there three principal grapes: Muscat Blanc à Petits Grains, Muscat of Alexandria and Muscat Ottonel. It can be dry, medium-dry or sweet – whether from dried grapes or fortified or a combination of the two. It is also made sparkling. What all the best examples have in common is the intense, heady grapiness – that taste of the grape itself. Only occasionally is it a wine for ageing. Alsace makes it both dry and intensely sweet, in southern France there are the *Vins Doux Naturel* of Beaumes de Venises and Rivesaltes (amongst others). In Germany (called Muskateller) it ranges from dry to sweet and Austria's best examples are also sweet. Spain makes light sweet versions of Moscatel while Portugal has the sweet fortified Moscatel de Setúbal. In Italy there's Asti or the better Moscato d'Asti and there's also yellow and pink forms of it (Moscato Giallo and Moscato Rosa) in the North-East – usually made off-dry. Off-shore from Sicily the grapes Zibibbo are dried for raisiny, apricotty Passito di Pantelleria. In Greece, Samos Muscat is produced. In North-East Victoria the intense raisiny Rutherglen Muscat is produced while in the US dry, medium-dry and sweet examples are produced by a few (but including Black Muscat and Orange Muscat). From South Africa comes the famed rich, sweet Vin de Constance. In fact there seemly no end to it.

Nebbiolo The classic variety of Piedmont that remains almost exclusively the source of high quality examples of the grape. Capable of exquisite aroma and flavour its youthful austerity and tannin, while less formidable than in the past, can still present a challenge to some palates. Its dark raspberry, cherry or blackberry fruit, herb and floral aromas take on increasing complexity with age and the best examples give a wonderful expression of their *terroir*. Oak needs to be used with care in order not to overwhelm its unique perfumes and flavour. Lighter, fragrant but fruity examples of the grape can be a bit hit and miss, often being produced from less good sites. The only source of Nebbiolo-based wines in any significant quantity outside Piedmont is as Valtellina Superiore in Lombardy where it is called Chiavennasca.

Negroamaro For long the basis of many of the often rustic, raisiny reds from Puglia's Salento peninsula in southern Italy including Salice Salentino. Its dark, bitter flavours are not to everyone's taste but are sometimes toned down by other varieties such as Malvasia Nera. Subject to better wine-making it has recently shown much greater potential including some exciting varietal examples.

Nerello Mascalese Once seen only as a high-yielding blending variety, it is now emerging as a complementary grape to the increasingly highly-regarded Nero d'Avola. From its origins on volcanic soils around the slopes of Mount Etna, it can show good perfume and texture. It also often blended with the related Nerello Cappuccio.

Nero d'Avola Widely planted in Sicily and currently seen as the island's best native red variety. It produces rich, intense, deep-coloured reds with a peppery black-fruited character and adding more depth and complexity with age. Is said to be related to Syrah.

Petit Verdot Sometimes an important minor component in Bordeaux, especially the Médoc but increasingly too in similar blends made in other regions where Cabernet Sauvignon is successful. Late ripening, it can show more than hint of violet in aroma as well as intense blackberry fruit. Varietal examples are rare.

Petite Sirah The name given to Durif in California which produces powerful, robust tannic varietal wines with dense spicy, brambly fruit. Also used to add complexity to some leading examples of Zinfandel.

Picolit White grape in Friuli (North-East Italy) from which are produced stylish, moderately sweet whites with dried peach, pear and floral characters. Its individuality and elegance are often dismissed by those expecting something richer and more powerful.

Piedirosso A grape variety probably used by the Romans and undergoing something of a revival in Campania's current rebirth. It has good acidity and a dark wild fruit character but is mostly used in blends, often complementing Aglianico.

Pignolo   Previously obscure Friulian variety capable of showing an impressive black-fruited richness and the vibrant acidity typical of reds from native varieties in North-East Italy.

Pinot Bianco   see Pinot Blanc

Pinot Blanc   Variety most associated with Alsace and Italy's Alto Adige and Friuli. In Alsace old low yielding vines give it good character though is often blended with the delightfully scented Auxerrois which can make the better wine. It is also the basis of most Crémant d'Alsace. The Italians take it as seriously as anyone and produce some fine (both oaked and unoaked) whites with a cream and walnuts character. German examples can show good intensity but can be spoilt by a lack of balance or too much oak. Decent examples have also been produced in California, Oregon and Canada.

Pinot Grigio   see Pinot Gris

Pinot Gris   Excellent white grape most associated with Alsace where it produces distinctively flavoured whites of intense spice, pear and quince flavours. Late-harvested it takes on an almost exotic, honeyed richness and nobly-rotted *Sélection des Grains Nobles* can be superb. In Germany as Grauburgunder or Ruländer good examples are made in warmer regions. Beyond simple Italian Pinot Grigio, there are some fine concentrated, delicately creamy examples from Friuli and Alto Adige. Oregon has made something of a speciality of it to complement its Pinot Noir while despite its proven potential in New Zealand it has only recently captured the imagination of a wider number of wine producers. Good examples are also made in Victoria and Canada.

Pinot Meunier   Very important component in most Champagne blends if rarely used for anything else. Early ripening and as a wine, early developing, it complements both Chardonnay and Pinot Noir. While ignored by many New World producers of premium sparkling wines, some do have significant plantings of the variety.

Pinot Noir   Success with Pinot Noir beyond Burgundy has been slow coming but there are now many regions in the world at least emulating the fabulous flavour complexity if not the structure and supreme texture of the top Burgundies. Flavours include cherry, raspberry, strawberry but can also include sappy, undergrowth characters or become more gamey in response to both origin and wine making. The expressions of *terroir* and differing winemaking interpretations in Burgundy are almost endless. Outside of Burgundy those regions or countries emerging with the greatest potential for Pinot Noir are California, Oregon, New Zealand, Tasmania but also cool parts of Victoria, South Australia and Western Australia. Success in Italy, Germany, Austria, Chile and South Africa is considerably more limited yet further potential exists. Pinot Noir is also very important as a component of most of the world's best sparkling wines.

Pinotage   Characterful yet tainted South African variety due to its tendency to produce unattractive paint-like aromas (isoamyl acetate). A crossing of Cinsaut and Pinot Noir, from old bush vines in particular it can produce deep, concentrated reds with spicy, plum and berry fruit flavours uncompromised by any volatile esters. The occasional adequate example is produced in New Zealand.

Primitivo   DNA fingerprinted as one and the same as Zinfandel, though debate continues about where in Europe they originated from. As Primitivo it is increasingly important in southern Italy, particularly in Puglia where old *alberello*-trained vines produce robust, characterful reds with moderate ageing potential.

Refosco   Somewhat derided grape, occasionally encountered outside its native Friuli in North-East Italy. Poorer examples are characterised by harsh tannins and high acidity but more care in the vineyard is resulting in high quality fruit with a brambly character. Produced both as part of a blend and varietally, good examples are on the increase. It may be related to Mondeuse.

Ribolla   Ribolla Gialla, as it is often called, produces characterful herb-scented dry whites in its native Friuli in North-East Italy.

Rieslaner   High quality late-ripening crossing of Riesling and Silvaner. Tiny amounts of outstanding sweet wines are produced in Germany's Pfalz and Baden regions when the grapes are fully ripe.

Riesling   This outstanding white grape has an almost infinite number of expressions. Styles vary from bone dry to intensely sweet, from low alcohol to powerful and full-bodied. Its impressive range of flavours including apple, citrus, peach and apricot, are complemented by a minerality that subtle differences of place or *terroir* bring. It is nearly almost made varietally and aged in stainless steel or large old wood. Obtaining full ripeness and the right balance between sugar and acidity is crucial to quality. The most delicate, exquisite Riesling comes from Germany though there are many different expressions there while Alsace provides the fullest, most powerful examples. Austria's Wachau is closer to this style than Germany but with purity and minerality of its own. Australia also produces high quality Riesling, showing different expressions from Western Australia to the Clare, Eden Valley and Tasmania. The considerable potential for Riesling in New Zealand has yet to be fully realised. Good examples also come from the US; as much in Washington State and the Fingers Lakes region of New York State as California or Oregon. Some examples of Canadian Icewine are based on Riesling.

Roussanne   High quality white grape that is difficult to grow. Roussanne's impressive texture and depth can be seen in wines from both the northern and southern Rhône, sometimes on its own but other times complementing Marsanne. It is also favoured by some of the leading quality producers in Languedoc-Roussillon and Provence, if mostly in blends. Outside France, California and Australia have a few high quality whites based, at least partly, on Roussanne.

Sagrantino   Central Italian variety localized at Montefalco in Umbria. Potentially rich in extract, tannin and with high acidity its true potential as an outstanding dry red has been realized by a single producer (Caprai) but others make increasingly good examples. Rarer are good sweet *passito* versions, from dried grapes.

Sangiovese   The leading variety in Italy and the grape that dominates production in Tuscany. All the classic Tuscan appellations are based on it and the improvement in quality is on-going as the revolution in winemaking is being followed by one in the vineyard. Styles range from the light and fruity to oaky, powerful and tannic but the best are pure, refined and individual. It is made to a very high standard both varietally and in blends with Cabernet Sauvignon and Merlot yet some of the most distinctive expressions include a small percentage of minor native varieties such as Canaiolo or Colorino. The most important area for its production outside Tuscany is Romagna but it also plays an important role in Umbria. Good if not great examples have been produced in California – both varietally or in blends with Cabernet or other varieties. One or two adequate examples are made in Australia though most are little more than attractive everyday reds.

St-Laurent   Pinot Noir like Austrian grape held in high regard locally. Only the very best examples, however show a texture and complexity that suggests top Pinot Noir or Burgundy.

Sauvignon Blanc   Aromatic white grape capable of a wide range of expression and quality. The most structured and ageworthy examples come from France whether the classic mineral-laced wines of Sancerre and Pouilly-Fumé (now richer and riper than previously) or the more oak-influenced, peachy examples from Bordeaux (some blended with Sémillon) that will age for more than a decade. The most overt fruit expression is seen in examples from Marlborough in New Zealand but most of these need to be drunk within a year of the vintage. Bright gooseberryish Sauvignon for immediate drinking is also made in Chile's Casablanca Valley and good vibrant, nettly Sauvignon Blanc from South Africa is on the increase. Some of the best Australian examples of Sauvignon Blanc have very ripe gooseberry fruit with a hint of tropical flavours; it is also sometimes blended with Sémillon. California offers both fresh, more herbaceous examples and riper ,melon and fig versions capable of some age. North-East Italy provides high quality Sauvignon with good structure but more restraint. Reasonable examples come from Spain and Austria too though the latter are usually best when unoaked. Sauvignon Blanc is also important in combination with Sémillon for Bordeaux's sweet wines.

Scheurebe   German crossing that can produce intensely flavoured whites from Spätlese levels and higher. Balance and ripeness are essential to rich and succulent wines with a piercing blackcurrant, grapefruit or peach character.

Schioppettino Native of Italy's Friuli, this obscure grape with high acidity but a spicy, wild berry fruit intensity, has recently been treated seriously by one or two dedicated producers.

Sémillon Great Sémillon comes from either of two sources: France or Australia. In Bordeaux Sémillon is made both dry, in usually oak-aged blends with Sauvignon Blanc (as it is in Bergerac), or sweet where it is typically the dominant component in all its great sweet wines. Botrytis enrichment is the key to the power, flavour richness and complexity of the best long-lived Sauternes and Barsac. Lesser appellations can also make attractive sweet wines and some good examples come from neighbouring Monbazillac. The classic Australian Sémillon comes from the Hunter Valley. Though increasing rare, unoaked wines become remarkably toasty and honeyed with a decades' age or more. Oaked-aged examples are made to give more immediate pleasure; those from the Margaret River are usually combined with Sauvignon Blanc. Relatively few rich, sweet Australian examples are also made. New Zealand and South Africa have had some success with dry examples of the grape.

Seyval Blanc Decent quality hybrid grape that manages to get ripe in the coolest of winemaking countries. Can show good weight and an attractively herbal, appley, citrusy freshness. The best examples come from England, Canada and the eastern US.

Shiraz Australian name for the French grape Syrah but also favoured by some South African producers. Australia produces a galaxy of styles from the powerful, American-oaked blockbuster to more elegant, more Rhône-like expressions aged in French oak. Every region produces a different stamp whether Hunter Valley, Clare, Barossa, Eden Valley, McLaren Vale, Grampians, Heathcote, Great Southern or one of many other exciting areas to which is added the interpretation and quality achieved by individual producers. Sparkling Shiraz is an Australian speciality and not as frightening as it sounds though a tannic finish can mar some flavousome examples. South Africa also has an increasing number of high quality examples. Also see Syrah.

Silvaner/Sylvaner The majority of good Silvaner comes from Germany's Franken region while that given the French spelling, Sylvaner, comes from Alsace. A relatively neutral grape it can take on real richness and and a smoky, spicy flavour in the latter (especially when produced from old vines) while the German examples can show more of a minerally, nuanced subtlety – an intriguing earthy, appley character. Occasional good examples are produced in most other German regions but also in Italy's Alto Adige and (as Johannisberg) in Switzerland's Valais.

Syrah The home of Syrah is in the northern Rhône where a range of appellations give the most classic expression to one of the most exciting red grapes in the world. Those showing the most aromatic, smoky, white pepper and herbs expression come from Côte Rôtie (where they often include a little Viognier); broader, more powerful, minerally versions come from the hill of Hermitage. Many good examples also come from the surrounding appellations of Crozes-Hermitage, Cornas and Saint-Joseph. Syrah is also made varietally in the southern Rhône but more often is used to complement Grenache. As well as being important in Provence many of the best wines from the Languedoc-Roussillon are either based on it or include a significant percentage. Some very good varietal Syrah also comes from Italy where it is also added in small amounts to an increasing number of reds. Spain and Portugal also have good quality interpretations of the grape but Australia apart (also see Shiraz) the best Syrah outside of France comes from the US, primarily California but also Washington State. A few good examples of Syrah come from Chile and Argentina.

Tannat Vine from France's basque country, most important in Madiran where its powerful tannins need to be softened. Also an important component in other reds from this south-west corner of France – such as Irouléguy. Widely grown too in Uruguay but its few decent quality examples have yet to show real consistency.

Teroldego Extremely localised red grape grown on the gravelly soils of the Campo Rotaliano in Italy's Trentino region. From low yields it produces an impressive smoky, minerally black-fruited red capable of long ageing. Seems certain to have potential elsewhere.

Tempranillo Spain's leading red grape and a first class one though that has not always been apparent going by the quality from the most famous appellation based on it – Rioja. The grapes need to be concentrated and retain acidity, something more often achieved in Ribera del Duero (as Tinto Fino) where the best powerful blackberry and black plum reds are among Spain's very best. Tempranillo is also important in many other appellations including Toro (as Tinta de Toro) and Costers del Segre (as Ull de Llebre) — both varietally or as blends. As Tinta Roriz it is extremely important both in the production of Port but also as a component in Douro where its splendid aromatic complexity is sometimes fully realised. It is also important both varietally and in blends in several other Portuguese regions where there has recently been a massive increase in planting. In Alentejo in southern Portugal (as Aragonês) it is usually combined with Trincadeira and can develop into deep, savoury reds with age. Tempranillo also has potential in Australia and Argentina.

Tinta Roriz/Aragonês   see Tempranillo

Tocai Friulano   Found in North-East Italy, this grape produces refined dry whites with herb, citrus and nectarine character. It is difficult to believe but it is said to be related to the poor quality Sauvignonasse (Sauvignon Vert) variety still widely grown in Chile and for long passed off as Sauvignon Blanc.

Touriga Franca   The backbone of much Port and usually blended with Tinta Roriz and Touriga Nacional amongst others. Also important in table wines from the Douro. It has even been made varietally but a profusion of such examples seems unlikely as it lacks the definition and distinction of Touriga Nacional and the potential stylish complexity of Tinta Roriz.

Touriga Nacional   The most fashionable grape in Portugal's Douro. Increasingly made varietally both in the Douro and most other Portuguese regions. An integral part of most Port blends but often in much smaller percentages than is generally perceived. It is characterised by its deep colour, floral even violet aromas and dark damson plum, mulberry or blackberry fruit and a dash of pepper. Though capable of producing deep, fleshy varietal reds it is usually better complemented by Tinta Roriz, Touriga Franca and other grapes (as it is when made as port).

Trincadeira   Important southern Portuguese grape. It doesn't like rain and needs to be fully ripe – its spicy, blackberry character forms a vital part of most Alentejo red blends.

Verdicchio   Leading variety in Italy's Marche region on the Adriatic coast. Made both oaked and unoaked it can produce moderately ageworthy whites of good texture and depth if only moderate flavour.

Vermentino   Lemony, herb-scented Italian variety that shows at its best on the Tuscan coast and in the north of Sardinia. The best are extremely stylish and a delight to drink young if only rarely showing more depth or weight.

Vernaccia   Refers to any number of different unrelated grapes in Italy. The Vernaccia of San Gimignano is dry, with some character and style in the best examples.

Verduzzo   Verduzzo Friulano, widely grown in North-East Italy, can be made into a refined sweet wine when late-harvested or from dried grapes. One small zone, Ramandolo, has recently been granted DOCG status.

Vespaiolo   Named for the *vespe* (wasps) drawn to its sweet grapes in the autumn, this white grape is responsible for the late-harvested and passito style sweet whites of one famous producer (Maculan) in Italy's Veneto. It also produces attractive dry whites.

Viognier   There is no other Viognier quite like the best Condrieu (in the northern Rhône). From this small appellation the wine is opulent, lush and superbly aromatic – rich in apricot and peach with floral, blossom, honeysuckle and spice. Most are dry and best drunk young though a few age quite well, especially when they have acquired an enhanced structure from delicate oak treatment. One or two examples are made from late-harvested grapes. Viognier has become increasingly important in the southern Rhône, Languedoc-Roussillon and Provence, sometimes made varietally but as often injecting some perfume and fruit into a blend. There's a little in Italy, Austria and Greece. In California and Australia there are a fair number of good examples but only handful of these have the concentration and balance to suffice as a substitute for Condrieu.

Weissburgunder see Pinot Blanc

Welschriesling White grape with a poor reputation due the nasty whites produced from it in central and eastern Europe. However in Austria's Burgenland it is an important component in many of the best sweet whites. Known as Riesling Italico in North-East Italy.

Zinfandel The grape California made its own. From a rich resource of old free-standing vines, rich, powerful and concentrated wines are produced – most typically full of peppery, blackberry fruit and sometimes a riper raisiny, pruny character. Great examples come from Dry Creek, Russian River, Sonoma Valley, even Napa but also the Sierra Foothills and the Central Coast. It also grown successfully in Arizona and Washington State and there's also a little Zinfandel in New Zealand, Australia, Chile and South Africa. Also see Primitivo.

Zweigelt Austrian grape produced from a crossing of St. Laurent and Blaufränkisch. Widely planted, most examples are rather ordinary but as well as one or two decent varietal examples, it also contributes to some leading blended Austrian reds.

Glossary

A

AC Appellation Controlée is the top category of French wine regulations and guarantees origin, grape varieties and style.

Acidification Addition of acid to must or wine if the wine has either naturally low acidity or is from a particularly warm grown climate. Usually in the form of tartaric acid.

Alberello Free standing bush vines, common in southern Italy.

Assemblage This is the final blend of a wine prior to its bottling. Many fine wines are assembled from different components after ageing. This process will determine the final selection for wines such as those from top Bordeaux Châteaux.

Autolysis Enzymatic process in sparkling wine whereby dead yeast cells add increased flavour to wine. The longer the period the richer and more complex the characteristic becomes. Sparkling wines with less than 18 months on their yeast sediment will have little or no autolysis character.

B

Bâtonnage Stirring of a wines fine lees to provide additional flavour and texture. Commonplace among top white Burgundies and other premium barrel fermented whites and also now lesser whites as well. Lees also need stirring to provide limited aeration and to avoid the development of off smelling sulphides.

Barriques The most well-known barrel type of 225 litre capacity. The Burgundian Pièce is fractionally larger with thicker staves than the classic Bordeaux barrique.

Biodynamic Method of organic farming that seeks to promote the natural balance of the land. This includes both soil and plants. Natural treatments are used to protect the vineyard and applications carried out in line with lunar and planetary activity. Many first class wine producers now farm biodynamically.

Bocksbeutel Squat, flattened flask-shaped bottle used in Germany's Franken region.

Botte/Botti Large wooden vessels used for ageing wines in Italy. There will be no oak influence on flavour and the containers are often of substantial size. Foudres in France provide similar conditions.

Botrytis Botrytis or Botrytis Cinerea is a fungal infection of the vine which is particularly harmful to red grapes. In certain unique conditions though it provides for the development of Noble Rot in areas such as Sauternes, the Mosel and the Loire Valleys Coteaux du Layon. In late warm harvests with early morning humidity and sunny days the grapes will dehydrate concentrating their sugar and flavour. Wines produced from such grapes have a uniquely intense, peachy character.

Botrytised Wine produced from grapes effected by noble rot.

C

Canopy Management Vineyard management techniques designed to improve yield and quality as well as minimizing risk of vine disease. Utilises a number of trellising/training systems to better expose the vines foliage and fruit to sunlight, resulting in improved photosynthesis and grape ripening.

Carbonic maceration Method used prior to conventional fermentation of red wine whereby colour rather than tannin is extracted. This occurs during a limited fermentation which takes place within grapes kept in anaerobic conditions. The berries will gradually split and fermentation will proceed as normal. Red winemaking particularly of Pinot Noir but also other varieties may involve using whole uncrushed grape bunches and partial carbonic maceration will occur. Greater colour and flavour complexity can be achieved. The flavours are forward and vibrant often resembling bubble gum and can have a hint of green pepper from the grape stems. The process has long been used in Beaujolais but increasingly elsewhere.

Canteiro Term that refers to the supports given to casks of Madeira where they are stored to be heated solely by natural means (without recourse to estufagem) -refers to this system of ageing generally.

Cépage French term for grape variety.

Cépage ameliorateurs This means an improving variety. The term has been widely used in Languedoc-Roussillon where there have been increasing amounts of Syrah, Grenache and Mourvedre planted in addition to the widely distributed Carignan.

Champagne method Method for the production of sparkling wine originating in Champagne. A secondary fermentation takes place in bottle and the wine is left on the resulting yeast lees. The finest sparkling wine is all made in this way.

Chaptalisation The addition of sugar to grape must to increase its alcoholic strength. If added during fermentation has the added effect of prolonging the process. Some winemakers feel this can add complexity.

Clonal Selection see Clones

Clones Vines reproduced by taking cuttings of original plants. Vines reproduced by clonal selection Vines reproduced by taking cuttings of original plants. Vines reproduced by clonal selection provide for uniformity of yield and flavour but wines produced from whole vineyards of the same clone can lack complexity. Many fine winegrowers instead use mass selection (see Sélection Massale) establishing vineyards from a range of original vinecuttings.

Cold maceration Period prior to fermentation where crushed red grapes are kept in solution with the juice at a cool temperature to extract both colour and primary fruit flavours.

Cold soaking See Cold maceration

Commerciante Italian Broker or Merchant

Cork taint See TCA

Coulure Incomplete fruit set after flowering caused by cool or wet conditions. Some fruit loss can be positive to quality.

Cru Classé (CC) Classification of Bordeaux wines. Those from the Médoc (from 1er to 5ème Cru Classé/ first to fifth growth) and Barsac/Sauternes (1er or 2ème Cru Classé/ first and second growths) are covered by a famous classification of 1855. Graves (1959) and Saint-Émilion (Grand Cru Classé or Premier Grand Cru Classé) are also classified, the latter is now subject to revision every ten years (the last in 1996).

Cryo-Extraction Process used during sweet wine production where a must is frozen in order to concentrate the wine. Used in particular in Sauternes in poorer vintages with low botrytis levels. (also see Must Concentration).

Cuvaison This is the period during red wine vinification where the grape skins and other solid matter are kept in solution in the grape juice and then finished wine. This may include a period cold maceration to extract more colour, followed by fermentation and in some cases continued contact post-fermentation to round the wines tannins and provide greater harmony.

Cuve French term for a wine vat or tank. Can be used for fermentation or storage/ageing and is made from wood, stainless steel or concrete.

D

Débourbage Period where white grape juice or wine is left in order for solid matter to settle. Lighter aromatic and fruity whites will require all solids settling whereas a top white Burgundy or Chardonnay is more likely to be vinified from only partially settled must. Straightforward commercial whites may also be fined and even filtered as well prior to fermentation.

Demi-muid A wooden barrel of, generally 600 litre capacity. Although sometimes used to refer to smaller sizes they are always considerably larger than a barrique. (also see Tonneaux)

De-stemmed Most wine must is crushed and de-stemmed prior to fermentation. Some whites however, particularly Chardonnay may be whole bunch pressed and reds may include whole bunches added to the fermentation vat. Wine produced by carbonic maceration will also retain its stems. Traditionally made reds may also be vinified with some of their stems in order to add additional tannin and structure. In the case of the latter aggressive green tannins can be extracted if the stems as well as the grapes are not fully ripe.

DO Denominación de Origen is Spain's main regulatory category which defines both origin and methods of production. It is not however it the highest – Priorat and Rioja have DOC status.

DOC The Italian Denominazione di Origine Controllata is the main category for that country's protection of wine names and styles. Regulations cover origin, grape varieties and both the type and length of ageing permitted. Many have been revised or at least modified in response to progress to higher quality but there is much debate as to how best protect tradition while accomodating those committed to higher quality. There are well over 300 and many of these include sub-categories. While some DOCs boast numerous quality wines, others fail to deliver even a single premium wine. Also see DOCG. In Portugal Denominação de Origem Controlada is the highest regulated category recently extended to include broad regional areas (with sub-zones) to make for easier identification as Portuguese wines increase in popularity.

DOCG The top level of Italian wine appellations, Denominazione di Origine Controllata e Garantita includes a guarantee of origin and stipulates grape varieties but like the French AC it does not ensure top quality.

Dosage Sparkling wine produced from the Champagne method will be topped up after disgorging with a mix of wine and sugar and this dosage determines the style and sweetness of the final wine.

E

Einzellage Individual vineyard site usually preceded by a village name on a label. While providing better definition of a wines origins than a grosslage name there is no classification system that differentiates the best sites from inferior ones. However a classification system is currently being promoted (see Grosses Gewächs).

Élévage The handling of wine from fermentation to bottling.

En Primeur Sale of wine while still in barrel. Commonplace now in Bordeaux and becoming so in Burgundy and other regions.

Enology The science of winemaking.

Enologist A winemaker.

Erste Lage The term used in the Mosel for the first-rate vineyard sites that equate to Grosses Gewächs.

Erstes Gewächs The top tier of the VDP sponsored classification system of top vineyard sites as used in the Rheingau (also see Grosses Gewächs)

Estufagem The process of heating wine (in hot stores or estufa) in the production of Madeira, simulating the sea voyages across the tropics that gave rise to the style.

Extraction Process where tannins, colour and other matter is extracted during Maceration. (also see Cuvaison).

F

Field blend Wine produced from vineyards planted to a mix of grape varieties. The practice is increasingly rare.

Filtration The removal of solid particles by means of a filter prior to bottling. While it saves the time required for a natural settling it may also rob a wine of flavour and character. Where the wine is healthy both filtration and fining (see below) have proved to be unnecessary.

Fining Process used to clarify grape juice or wine by removing the smallest (soluble) microscopic particles which attach themselves to the fining agents added. Great care should be used to avoid stripping the must or wine of flavour.

Flor The thin yeast film found on dry Fino and Manzanilla sherries after fermentation. It is unstable and dissolves when exposed to high alcohol. Amontillado sherries will have started life as Finos but will have been unable to sustain their Flor cover. The salty taste it provides is unique.

Foudres French term for large wooden vats used to age wine in.

G

GI Geographical Indications is the slowly evolving Australian delimitation of its wine regions and is split into four levels. The broadest is the political boundary of 'state' (for example, South Australia), followed by 'zones' (Mount Lofty Ranges) which split the state into smaller parts and give some coherency to a group of often already well-established 'regions' (Adelaide Hills, Clare Valley). More definition within both established or new regions is made possible by the granting of subregions (Lenswood and Piccadilly in the Adelaide Hills).

Grand cru French wine classification. In Burgundy and Alsace this refers to specific vineyard sites. In Champagne to villages with vineyards of the best potential. For Bordeaux see Cru Classé.

Grand Vin Refers to a producers top wine. Commonly used in Bordeaux.

Green harvesting Crop thinning by cutting down the number of grape bunches in order to promote ripening and reduce yields. There will be a greater impact on yield and fruit quality if this is done after veraison (when the berries change colour). Popular among some growers, others maintain a well balanced vineyard with sufficient winter pruning produces the best results.

Grosses Gewächs German system of classification being promoted by the VDP, a consortium of leading estates. The term Grosses Gewächs is used in regions other than the Mosel (see Erste Lage) and Rheingau (see Erstes Gewächs).

Grosslage Broad grouping of vineyards in Germany, often permits the inclusion of grapes from inferior plots in a blend.

Guyot Old and very well established French vine training system. One or two fruiting canes are trained along wires with the new seasons shoots trained above on a second wire.

H

Hybrid Vine variety produced by crossing two different vine species. This is often an American vine crossed with a European vinifera vine. A crossing is produced by two varieties of the same species.

IGT Indicazione Geografica Tipica is the Italian equivalent of the French Vins de Pays

I

Inox French for stainless steel. In wine terms generally refers to fermenting and ageing in stainless steel vessels.

Irrigation Only very selectively permitted in the EU, irrigation is widely practiced in much of the new world where there is insufficient rainfall during the vines growing season. If practiced with restraint it can aid ripening and improve both yield and quality. Most effective is drip irrigation which directly feeds the vines roots. Sprinklers and flood irrigation are much less effective.

L

Lees The sediment left after fermentation, including the dead yeast cells. White wine will often be racked off the gross lees but some sediment will remain which is known as the fine lees. This is important in providing additional flavour and texture as well as acting as an anti-oxidant during early barrel maturation. Lees stirring (see Bâtonnage) is regularly practiced at the same time. An increasing number of top quality reds are also now being aged on lees, some with micro-oxygenation.

Lieu-dit A specific vineyard or climat which has no official classification but identified on a label when that site has been bottled separately from other village-level wine. Regularly found on Alsace and Burgundy labels.

M

Maceration The period during which flavour, colour, tannins and other components are leeched from the grape skins before, during and after fermentation. Temperature plays an important role with primary fruit aromas and colour extracted at cooler temperatures whereas more tannin is released with heat. The cap of grape skins formed during fermentation needs to be kept in solution with the fermenting must and various methods are used which also aid extraction (see Pigeage). Pre-fermentation maceration (see Cold maceration) is regularly practiced as well as extended post fermentation maceration which helps to polymerise the wines tannins, making them rounder and softer in texture. Some skin contact prior to fermentation is also practiced by a number of producers of white wines (see Macération Pelliculaire).

Macération carbonique See Carbonic Maceration

Macération pelliculaire French expression meaning skin contact. In effect it refers to the period of just a few hours where white wine must is macerated with its skins prior to fermentation. Semillon and Sauvignon Blanc in Bordeaux and Chenin Blanc in the Loire as well as more aromatic varieties like Muscat have all successfully been vinified using this technique. Excessive skin contact will result in coarseness and very early oxidation.

Malolactic fermentation Chemical process whereby malic acid is transferred into softer lactic acid. All red wine is put through malolactic but for whites it depends on the variety and style. For aromatic varieties such as Sauvignon Blanc and Riesling the process is avoided. For cool climate top quality Chardonnay it will add weight and texture. It may often be blocked with warmer grown Chardonnay to preserve acidity. Top reds including Cabernet Sauvignon and similarly structured and tannic blends are increasingly having the malolactic conducted in new oak. The wines are lusher and more softly textured, particularly in their youth but long term development remains a questionmark.

Mass Selection See Sélection Massale.

Meritage Term used in the United States to describe a Bordeaux style blend either red or white.

Mesoclimate The localised climate found generally within a vineyard or small specific area and responsible for particular characteristics found in the resulting wines. Often incorrectly referred to as a microclimate. The latter is in fact the very specific climate of the vine canopy.

Méthode Traditionelle See Traditional Method

Metodo Classico See Traditional Method

Micro-oxygenation Cellar operation devised by Patrick Ducournau in Madiran to assist in softening the often aggressively tannic wines produced from the local Tannat. Now increasingly practiced around the globe, small quantities of oxygen are regularly pumped into the ageing wine avoiding the need to rack the wine from one container to another, minimising handling and providing better balanced, finer tannins.

Millerandage Irregular fruit development after flowering caused by cool weather. Yield is reduced because some berries are smaller. Quality though is likely to improve. This characteristic of smaller and larger berries in the same grape bunch is often referred to as hen and chickens.

Moelleux French term meaning medium-sweet.

Monopole French for a solely owned vineyard site, particularly relevant in Burgundy.

Mousseux French for sparkling.

Must Grape juice.

Must concentration Any of a series of techniques for removing water from grape juice in order to make more concentrated wine. As well as evaporation under vacuum, freeze concentration (see Cyro-Extraction), which simulates eiswein/icewine production, can be used to remove water. Reverse Osmosis is a sophisticated process that allows the water content in finished wine to be reduced.

N

Négociant French term for a wine merchant. They may buy grapes as well as finished wine and also have their own vineyards and properties. While there has been a trend in Burgundy and other areas to more wines being Domaine-bottled an increasing number of small producers are also now acting as négociants as well.

Négociant-manipulant In Champagne, a merchant who also makes wine. Includes all the great Champagne houses.

Noble Rot See Botrytis.

O

Oenologue French term for an enologist.

Organic An increasing number of winegrowers around the world are now producing wines without recourse to chemical treatments in the vineyard and with a minimum of chemical additives during vinification. (also see Biodynamic).

Oxidation Exposure of must or wine to air. Controlled oxidation is important in the maturation of wine before bottling and can add complexity to fortified wines aiding the production of rancio character. Oxidation of grape juice is also popular in producing barrel fermented white wine particularly premium Chardonnay. Reduction is the opposite of oxidation.

P

Passerillage Grapes that are late-harvested and have dried and become partially raisined concentrating their sugar but are not effected by noble rot.

Passito Italian for wine made from dried grapes.

Phenolics Compounds found in grapes and extracted during vinification. These include tannins, flavour compounds and anthocyanins (responsible for the colour in red wines). See also Cuvaison, Extraction and Maceration.

Phylloxera Vine aphid which was the great scourge of the worlds vineyards in the 19th century. It can be resisted by planting vinifera varieties on resistant American species rootstocks.

Pigeage Method of plunging down the cap produced during red wine fermentation. This can be done by hand plunging with a number of devices or even by foot. A number of specialist automatic machine driven methods have also been developed. Particularly common and successful among the latter is the Rotofermenter. Pigeage can be gentler and less aggressively extractive than remontage or pumping the must back over itself.

Propagated Meaning reproduced. In viticultural terms this most commonly refers to vegetative propagation using cuttings taken from other vines.

Q

Quinta Portuguese term which refers to either a wine estate or a single vineyard.

R

Racked Winery procedure where must or wine is pumped or transferred under gravity from one container to another. This is both to remove the wine from solids but also to provide adequate aeration during maturation.

Rancio Maderised character with burnt, toffee like aromas produced in the development of aged fortified wines through a combination of controlled oxidation and exposure to heat. Banyuls, Maury and Rivesaltes in the Roussillon as well as the fortified Muscats and Tokays of Rutherglen all show classic rancio character.

Récemment dégorgé French term meaning recently disgorged. This can either relate specifically to the actual disgorging of a Champagne method sparkling wine from its bottle sediment but also to the style of wine. These tend to have spent an extended period on there yeast lees. The quintessential example of this style is Bollinger RD.

Reduced This is the opposite of oxidised. Excessive reduction can result in the development foul smelling sulphides during cask ageing and so wines need to be exposed to controlled aeration during this phase, this can be achieved by either racking or more recently the use of micro-oxygenation.

Reductive Refers to wines that are in a reduced state.

Ried Term used in Austria to denote a specific vineyard site.

Residual Sugar There is always a small portion of unfermentable sugar in wine even those that are technically classified as dry. It is commonplace in some whites particularly straightforward fruit driven styles to purposely leave a hint of residual sugar. More serious wines from cooler regions like Alsace and the Mosel may well be completed with some sugar left naturally. Late harvested wines are deliberately left on the vine to accumulate sufficient sugar to ensure considerable sweetness after vinification. (also see Botrytis)

Ripasso Term registered by Valpolicella producer Masi. Used to refer to an enrichment of the already the fermented wine by passing it over the skins of Amarone, adding alcohol, texture and character. Variations exist – see Introduction to North-East, Central & Southern Italy.

Rootstock The plant formed from the root system of the vine to which the scion (fruiting part) is grafted. Most vinifera vines (the european species to which most quality grape varieties belong) are grafted on to rootstocks of American vines (or hybrids of them) due to its resistance to phylloxera.

Roseworthy Famous winemaking college in South Australia whose graduates have had an impact both in Australasia and around the globe.

S

Saignée Running off some free run juice prior to fermentation in order to increase the ratio of skins and solids in the must and therefore flavour and tannin. Regularly practiced in the production of top quality Pinot Noir.

Sélection Massale Mass Selection – the propagation of new plants from existing vines rather than the use of a single clone. Typically only the best vines are used in order to enhance the overall quality within a plot.

Solera A system of fractional blending used in Jerez in the production of sherry to provide consistency and enrichment. It is also used in some extent in other fortified production such as Rutherglen or Madeira. The name is derived from the bottom rung of a series of barrels containing the oldest wine. Only a small part of the wine is drawn from this bottom level at one time. Successive levels are then replenished by younger wines from the level above.

Stelvin/Stelvin Cap Closure used instead of cork to avoid any possible contamination of the wine by TCA, oxidation or other potential spoilage from external sources.

T

TCA Chemical compound, its full name is 2,4,6-trichloroanisole, responsible for most of the off flavours in wine caused by contaminated corks. Chlorine reacts with the cork to produce the contamination and the aroma can be picked up in minute quantities. Cork taint remains a major problem in spoilt wine and alternative methods of closure are on the increase. The chemical or variants of it can also be found elsewhere and has been a cause of contamination in some wine cellars.

Terra Rossa Reddish coloured loam over a limestone base, most famously associated with Coonawarra in South Australia but also found in other wine regions.

Terroir French concept which considers the unique physical environment of a site or vineyard. Also refers to the character in a wine that is derived from its origins rather than the grape variety.

Tonneaux A bordeaux barrel size of 900 litres but can often be used to refer to considerably smaller vessels. What is referred to in Italy as tonneaux can vary from double-sized barriques to that of demi-muid.

Traditional method The classic method of Champagne production (see Champagne method) as it is referred to in other regions for sparkling wines made in this way. Known as méthode traditionelle or méthode classique in other parts of France, as metodo classico in Italy.

Triage Selective sorting of grapes prior to fermentation order to remove inferior quality fruit.

Tris Multiple passages through a vineyard to selectively pick late harvested or botrytis effected grapes. In order to produce great wines it may be necessary to make many such passes. In Bordeaux Tri also refers to the sorting of grapes generally after harvest. This selection process is vital in all wineries to ensure top quality wines.

U

Unfiltered See filtration

Unirrigated See Irrigation

V

Vatting Period where wine is macerated and fermented prior to ageing. See also Cuvaison.

VDP Verband Deutsches Prädikatsweinguter - a consortium of Germany's leading estates (currently with 200 members) founded in 1910. To qualify estates must have vineyards of recognised quality and achieve higher standards than that required by German wine law. The VDP is also behind a three tier classification model for German wines (see Grosses Gewächs). Members use the VDP 'eagle' on their capsules or labels.

Vendange vert See Green Harvesting

Versteigerungswein Auction wines, specifically those set aside by German producers for sale at the annual VDP auction.

Vin Doux Naturels French term for fortified wines. These are sweet, achieved by adding fortifying spirit part way through fermentation in much the same way as is practiced in producing Port.

Vin De Paille Rare type of dry white wine produced from dried and concentrated grapes. Traditional laid out on straw mats after harvesting.

Vin de Pays French category of regional identification for wines that fall outside either the boundaries or regulations of an AC.

Vin Jaune Jura wine made from Savagnin grapes aged in old casks under a voile (a film of yeast not unlike Flor that covers Fino sherry) that results in a distinctive oxidised nutty character.

Vinho Regional Portuguese category of wine regulation that offers the most flexibility in terms of origin and grape variety.

Vignoble A vineyard or close grouping of vineyards.

Vignaiolo Italian term for a vine-grower.

Volatile Acidity The volatile acids in wine are those that are unstable and chief among these is acetic acid. Excessive exposure of a wine with high volatile acidity to air will encourage a bacterial reaction that causes off volatile aromas (similar to nail varnish) and will eventually convert wine to vinegar.

Y

Yield The size of crop yielded from a vineyard. Yield is fundamental to wine quality. In general the smaller the yield the greater the wine quality. There are though many additional influences. If yield is reduced too much then the vines balance and equilibrium will be disturbed and quality will suffer. Increasingly yields are measured per vine rather than per acre or hectare because of the variable conditions within a vineyard and the density of planting. Older vines are naturally less productive and when their crop is reduced the resulting grapes can be of exceptional quality. In all cases the yield of a vine should be sufficiently restricted in order to achieve complete physiological ripeness.

Buying guide

A code is provided in most A-Z producer entries and these can be found listed alphabetically on the pages that follow. In the first instance these are intended to give the most direct link with that producer in the UK and the code will indicate the agent or direct importer of the wines. In some instances the code refers to an agent who sells only to the trade or acts purely as a producers representative in the UK but most of these should still be able to suggest retail stockists of a given wine. With this new 2004 edition we have also added, where possible, one or two retailers who are regular stockists of these wines. In a few cases where we have found there to be no UK agent or retailer we have suggested a broker who has traded some vintages of the wine. Where there is no code at all we hope that producers inclusion will prompt someone in the UK to sell these wines. We have already been able to fill in some of the gaps between our first and second editions. Many of these codes refer to a leading independent merchant/retailer who sell much of the best or most interesting wine in this country – often very competitively priced against the bigger, better known brands. While we haven't profiled individual merchants, a glance through the agent codes within any regional section is likely to give a good idea as to which ones have a particular strength there.

There are no codes given in Bordeaux as most wine from the leading châteaux is sold through a Bordeaux broker (*courtier*) or agent and then to retailers and merchants in different countries. While the system is elaborate it is not so difficult to obtain many of the wines. Both independent UK merchants, such as one of 'The Bunch' (a group of six leading merchants - Adm, Tan, JAr, C&B, L&W, Yap) and leading broker/shippers (such as Farr Vintners) are the best place to start. These contacts also provide the opportunity to buy wine en primeur or ex-cellars. This requires paying for the cost of the wine before it is shipped with the additional costs (freight, VAT and duty) paid on its arrival in the UK. Purchasing wine in this way was once seen as an investment opportunity for would be speculators, but it is now increasingly important as the only means of obtaining the best, not only from Bordeaux but also from Burgundy, the Rhône, or some Vintage Port. It also usually means that the wine hasn't changed hands several times already. Leading merchants will also prove useful when buying older vintages as will auction houses and brokers (additional contacts have been provided at the end of the list of codes).

Supermarkets account for the bulk of wine sold in the UK. However their ranges tend to be dominated by the ubiquitous big volume brands – much of it outside of the scope of this book. The small production of many high quality estates remains outside their reach whether as part of a deliberate decision on the part of the producer or due to logistical reasons. Nonetheless the best supermarkets include those producers who combine quality and quantity. In addition there is an increasing trend toward the inclusion of a selection of fine wines of more limited availability in their flagship stores or through an on-line facility. Though supermarkets have not been included as agents or leading stockists, a search on their internet sites can be used as a quick check for availability. There are also an increasing number of Internet-only retailers whose search engines provide a further aid to tracking down a hard to find wine.

It is also worth noting that a growing number of producers now sell their wine direct via a mailing list or over the internet. Such is the demand for their wines there is no need for them to use an agent and the cost saving is effectively passed on to the wine drinker. This applies particularly to leading new world producers who often have oversubscribed lists composed entirely of consumers in their local market – yet some choose to retain a small percentage of their production for export via a foreign merchant. Individual producers websites are worth checking for information about buying their wines.

3DW – 3D Wines Ltd
1-2 North End, Swineshead, Lincolnshire PE20 3LR
Tel 01205 820745
Fax 01205 821042
info@3dwines.com
www.3dwines.com

A&B – A & B Vintners
Little Tawsden, Spout Lane,
Brenchley, Kent TN12 7AS
Tel 01892 724977
Fax 01892 722673
info@abvintners.co.uk
www.abvintners.co.uk

ABy – Anthony Byrne
Ramsey Business Park, Stocking Fen Road,
Ramsey, Cambridgeshire, PE26 2UR
tel 01487 814555
fax 01487 814962
admin@abfw.co.Uk
www.abfw.co.uk

ACh – Andrew Chapman Fine Wines
14 Haywards Road, Abingdon, Oxon, OX14 4LB
tel 01235 550707
fax 0870 136 6335
info@surf4wine.co.uk
www.surf4wine.co.uk

Adm – Adnams
Sole Bay Brewery, Southwold, Suffolk, IP18 6JW
tel 01502 727222
fax 01502 727223
wines@adnams.co.uk
www.adnams.co.uk

ADo – Allied Domecq Wine UK
Argentum, 2 Queen Caroline Street,
London, W6 9DX
tel 020 8323 8196
fax 020 8323 8313
www.allieddomecqplc.com

AHW – AH Wines
Back Street, West Camel, Yeovil,
Somerset, BA22 7QB
tel 01935 850166
fax 01935 851264

AlF – Alfie Fiandaca
Unit 4, Westpoint Trading Estate,
Alliance Road, London W3 0RA
tel 01935 850166
fax 01935 851264

All – Alliance Wine Co
7 Beechfield Road, Willowyard Estate,
Beith, KA15 1LN
tel 01505 506060
fax 01505 506066
sales@alliancewine.co.uk
www.alliancewine.co.uk

Alo – Alouette Wines
Prenton Way, North Cheshire Trading Estate,
Prenton, Wirral, CH43 3DU
tel 0151 6089900
fax 0151 608 8844
info@alouettewines.co.uk
www.alouettewines.co.uk

Alv – Alivini
Units 2 & 3, 199 Eade Road, London, N4 1DN
tel 020 8880 2526
fax 020 8880 2708
enquiries@alivini.com

Amp – Amps Fine Wines
6 Market Place, Oundle, Peterborough PE8 4BQ
Tel 01832 273502
Fax 01832 273611
info@ampsfinewines.co.uk
www.ampsfinewines.co.uk

Anl – Anglo International Wine Shippers
Chantarella House, 25 New Road,
Esher, Surrey, KT10 9PG
tel 01372 469841
fax 01372 469816

ARe – Arthur Rackham Emporia
216 London Road, Burpham, Guildford GU4 7JS
Tel 0870 870 1110
Fax 0870 870 1120
cellars@ar-emporia.com
www.ar-emporia.com

Ast – Astrum Wine Cellars
6 Thornsett Road, Earlsfield, London, SW18 4EN
Tel 020 8870 5252
Fax 020 8870 2244
sales@astrumwinecellars.com
www.astrumwinecellars.com

AVn – Allez Vins!
PO Box 1019, Long Itchington, Southam,
Warks, CV47 9ZU
tel 01926 811969
fax 01926 811969
www.allezvins.co.uk

AWA – Australian Wine Agencies
21 Southlea Road, Datchet, Slough,
Berkshire, SL3 9BY
tel 01753 544546
fax 01753 591369
info@australian–wine.co.uk
www.austwineagencies.com

AWs – Australian Wineries
28 Recreation Ground Road, Stamford,
Lincolnshire, PE91EW
tel 01780 755810
fax 01780 766063
admin@australianwineries.co.uk
www.australianwineries.co.uk

Bal – Ballantynes of Cowbridge
3 Westgate, Cowbridge, Glamorgan, CF71 7AQ
tel 01446 774840
fax 01446 775253
ballantynes@btinternet.co.uk
www.ballantynes.co.uk

Bac – Bacchus Fine Wines
Warrington House Farm Barn,
Bucks MK46 4HN
Tel 01234 711140
Fax 01234 711199
wine@bacchus.co.uk
www.bacchus.co.uk

BBE – Brown Brothers Europe
River View Lodge, Ray Mead Road,
Maidenhead, Berkshire SL6 8NJ
tel 01628 776446
fax 01628 776136
info@brownbrotherswines.co.uk
www.brown–brothers.co.au

BBl – Beringer Blass UK
Regal House, 70 London Road,
Twickenham, TW1 3QS
Tel 020 8843 8411
Fax 020 8843 8422
info@beringerblass.co.uk
www.beringerblass.com

BBR – Berry Bros & Rudd
3 St James Street, London, SW1A 1EG
Tel 020 7396 9600
Fax 020 7396 9611
orders@bbr.com
www.bbr.com

BcV – Bricco Vini
Little Acre, Hall Lane, Cotes Heath,
Staffordshire ST21 6RT
Tel 01782 791798
Fax 01782 791787
ceretto@awwines.co.uk

Bel – Bella Wines Limited
Beaufort House, 28 Lisburn Road,
Newmarket, Suffolk, CB8 8HS
Tel 01638 604899
Fax 01638 604901
sales@bellawines.co.uk
www.bellawines.co.uk

Ben – Bennetts
High Street, Chipping Campden,
Gloucestershire, GL55 6AG
Tel 01386 840392
Fax 01386 840974
enquiries@bennettsfinewines.com
www.bennettsfinewines.com

BFs – Bonhote Foster
The Mews, Broadagte House, Steeple,
Bumpstead, Suffolk, CB9 7DG
Tel 01440 730779
Fax 01440 730789
acf@bonhotefoster.co.uk
www.pinotpeople.co.uk

BGL – Bottle Green Ltd
19 New Street, Horsforth, Leeds, LS18 4BH
Tel 0113 2054500
Fax 0113 2054501
info@bottlegreen.com
www.bottlegreen.com

Bib – Bibendum
113 Regents Park Road, London, NW1 8UR
Tel 020 7449 4100
Fax 020 7722 7354
sales@bibendum-wine.co.uk
www.bibendum-wine.co.uk

Bir – Birchwood Agencies
Birchwood House, Victoria Road,
Dartford, DA1 5AJ
Tel 01322 627500
Fax 01322 627488
info@birchwoodagencies.co.uk

Blx – Bordeaux Index
6th Floor, 159 - 173 St John's Street,
London, EC1V 4QJ
Tel 020 7253 2110
Fax 020 7490 1955
sales@bordeauxindex.com
www.bordeauxindex.com

Box – Boxford Wine Co
Spring Cottage, Butchers Lane, Boxford,
Sudbury, Suffolk, C010 5EA
Tel 01787 210187
Fax 01787 211391
boxfordwine@cs.com

BRL – BRL Hardy Europe
Hardy House, 140 High Street, Esher,
Surrey, KT10 9QJ
Tel 01372 473000
Fax 01372 473100
www.brlhardy.com.au

BRW – Big Red Wine Company
41 Dartmouth Road, London, NW2 4ET
Tel 020 8208 0192
Fax 020 8208 0192
sales@bigredwine.co,uk
www.bigredwine.co.uk

B-S – Billecart-Salmon UK
Thornton House, Thornton Road,
London, SW19 4NG
Tel 020 8405 6345
Fax 020 8405 6346
info@billecart-salmon.co.uk
www.billecart-salmon.co.uk

BSh – Burgundy Shuttle
168 Ifield Road, London, SW10 9AF
Tel 020 7341 4053
Fax 020 7244 0618
mail@burgundyshuttle.ltd.uk
www.burgundyshuttle.co.uk

But – Butler's Wine Cellar
247 Queen's Park Road, Brighton,
East Sussex BN2 2XJ
Tel 01273 698724
Fax 01273 622761
henry@butlers-winecellar.co.uk
www.butlers-winecellar.co.uk

BWC – Berkmann Wine Cellars
10/12 Brewery Road, London, N7 9NH
Tel 020 7609 4711
Fax 020 7607 0018
info@berkmann.co.uk
www.berkmann.co.uk

C&B – Corney & Barrow
12 Helmet Row, London, EC1V 3TD
Tel 020 7539 3200
Fax 020 7608 1373
wine@corbar.co.uk
www.corneyandbarrow.com

C&C – Champagnes & Châteaux
21 Abbeville Mews, 88 Clapham Park Road,
London, SW4 7BX
Tel 020 7498 4488
Fax 020 7498 4499
info@champagnesandchateaux.co.uk
www.champagnesandchateaux.co.uk

C&O – C & O Wines
14 Roscoe Park Estate, Park Road,
Timperley, WA14 5QH
Tel 0161 976 3696
Fax 0161 962 4542

C&R – Classic & Rare
The Famous Old Brewery, Springfield Road,
Crawley, West Sussex RH10 6AL
Tel 01293 525111
sales@classicrarewines.com
www.classicrarewines.com

Cac – Cachet Wine
Red Duster House, 101 York Street, Hull,
East Yorkshire, HU2 0QX
Tel 01482 581792
Fax 01482 587042

Cam – Cambridge Wine Merchants
2 Mill Road, Cambridge CB1 2AD
Tel 01223 568991
Fax 01223 568992
info@cambridgewine.com
www.cambridgewine.com

Cap – Capricorn
Brook House, 4 Northenden Road, Gately,
Cheshire, SK8 4DN
Tel 0161 908 1360
Fax 0161 908 1365
sales@capricornwines.co.uk
www.capricornwines.co.uk

Car – Carringtons
Angel House, Angel Street,
Manchester, M4 1BQ
Tel 0161 832 5646
Fax 0161 832 5626
carringtons@winebeerandspirits.co.uk

Cas – Castang Wine Shippers
8 Cardwen Farm Estate, Pelyent,
Cornwall, PL13 2LH
Tel 01503 220359
Fax 01503 220650
sales@castang-wines.co.uk
www.castang-wines.co.uk

Cav – Cavavin/Le Bon Vin
340 Brightside Lane, Sheffield S9 2SP
Tel 0114 256 0090
Fax 0114 256 0092
cavavin@lebonvin.co.uk
www.lebonvin.co.uk

CBg – Charles Blagden
135 Avenue Joseph Lioter,
84740 Velleron, France
Tel 0033 4 90 20 07 07
Fax 0033 4 90 20 05 77
blagwin@aol.com

CBy – Cloudy Bay
15 St George Street, London, W1S 1FH
Tel 020 7408 7430
Fax 020 7408 7457
www.cloudybay.co.nz

CCC – Cave Cru Classé
Unit 13 Leathermarket, Weston Street,
London, SE1 3ER
Tel 020 7378 8579
Fax 020 7378 8544
enquiries@ccc.co.uk
www.cave-cru-classe.com

Cco – Champagne Company
26 Astwood Mews, London, SW7 4DE
Tel 020 7373 5578
Fax 020 7373 4777
ukchampagne@aol.com
www.champagnecompany.co.uk

CdP –Les Caves de Pyrene
Pew Corner, Old Portsmouth Road, Arlington,
Guildford, Surrey, GU3 1LP
Tel 01483 538820
Fax 01483 455068
orders@lescaves.co.uk
www.lescaves.co.uk

Che – Cheviot UK / WM Morton
137 Shawbridge Street, Glasgow G43 1QQ
Tel 0141 649 9881
Fax 0141 649 7074

CHk – Charles Hawkins
Hall Gardens, 56 High Street East,
Uppingham, Rutland, LE15 9HG
Tel 01572 823030
Fax 01572 823040
www.charleshawkins-wines.com

Cht– Charterhouse Wine Co Ltd
82 Goding Street, London, SE11 5AW
Tel 020 7587 1302
Fax 020 7587 0982

ChV – Château Vintners
121 Beaufort Street, London, SW3 6BS
Tel 020 7376 8828
Fax 020 7376 8818
chateauvintners@yahoo.co.uk

Cib – Ciborio
Ciborio House, 74 Long Drive, Greenford,
Middlesex, UB6 8XH
Tel 020 8578 4388
Fax 020 8575 2758
www.ciborio.com

CKr – Christopher Keiller Fine Wine
Tel 01209 215706
Fax 01209 215706
ghost@gladys.demon.co.uk
www.gladys.demon.co.uk/finewineservices.html

Col - Colombier Vins Fins
Colombier House, Ryder Close,
Cadley Hill Industrial Estate,
Swadlincote, Derbyshire, DE11 9EU
Tel 01283 552552
Fax 01283 550675

Con – Connolly's Wine Merchants
Arch 13, 220 Livery Street, Birmingham, B3 1EU
Tel 0121 236 9269
Fax 0121 233 2339
sales@connollyswine.co.uk
www.connollyswine.co.uk

CPp – Christopher Piper Wines
1 Silver Street, Ottery St Mary,
Devon, EX11 1DB
Tel 01404 814139
Fax 01404 812100
sales@christopherpiperwines.co.uk

CRs – Chalié Richards
2 Grove House, Foundry Lane, Horsham,
West Sussex, RH13 5PL
Tel 01403 250500
Fax 01403 250123
admin@chalie-richards.co.uk

CTy – Charles Taylor / Montrachet Fine Wine
59 Kennington Road, London, SE1 7PZ
Tel 020 7928 1990
Fax 020 7928 3415
www.montrachetwine.com

CWF – CWF Ltd (Continental Wine & Food)
Trafalgar Mills, Leeds Road, Huddersfield HD2 1YY
Tel 01484 538333
Fax 01484 544734

CyT – Concha y Toro UK
MWB Business Exchange, John Eccles House,
Robert Robinson Avenue, Oxford OX4 4GP
Tel 01865 338013
Fax 01865 338100
enquiries@conchaytoro.cl
www.conchaytoro.com

D&D – D & D Wines
Adams Court, Adams Hill, Knutsford,
Cheshire, WA16 6BA
Tel 01565 650952
Fax 01565 755295
ddwi@ddwinesint.com

D&F – D & F Wines
Centre House, St Leonards Road,
London, NW10 6ST
Tel 020 8838 4399
Fax 020 8838 4500
inquiry@dandfwines.fsnet.co.uk
www.interreach.com/d&f

Dan – Danmar International
Unit 4, Beta Way, Thorpe Industrial Park,
Egham, Surrey TW20 8RS
Tel 01784 477812
Fax 01784 477813
sales@danmarinternational.co.uk
www.danmarinternational.co.uk

DAy – Dreyfus Ashby & Co
143a High Street, Tonbridge, Kent, TN9 1DH
Tel 01732 361639
Fax 01732 367834
office@dreyfusashby.co.uk

DDr – Domaine Direct
6-9 Cynthia Street, London, N1 9JF
Tel 020 7837 1142
Fax 020 7837 8605
mail@domainedirect.co.uk
www.domainedirect.co.uk

DeB – De Bortoli Wines UK
Minchington Farm, Farnham,
Blandford Forum, DT11 8DE
Tel 01725 516467
Fax 01725 516403
debortoli@talk21.com
www.debortoli.com.au

Dec – Decorum Vintners
Unit 12, Grand Union Centre,
West Row, London W10 5AS
Tel 020 8969 6581
Fax 020 8960 7693
admin@decvin.com
www.decvin.com

Dis – Discover Wine
PO Box 104, Stevenage,
Hertfordshire SG1 3EG
Tel 0870 3300267
Fax 0870 3307910
www.discover-wine.co.uk

DLW – Daniel Lambert Wine Agencies
8 Rhodfas Ceirios, Pen-y-Fai, Bridgend CF31 4GG
Tel 01656 661010
Fax 01656 668088
dwlawine@aol.com
www.dwla.co.uk

DWS – Direct Wine Shipments (NI)
5/7 Corporation Square, Belfast, BT1 3AJ
Tel 028 9050 8000
Fax 028 9050 8002
enquiry@directwine.co.uk
www.directwine.co.uk

E&T – Elliot & Tatham
The Wheatsheaf Inn, West End, Northleach,
Gloucestershire, GL54 3EZ
Tel 01451 861688
Fax 01451 861037

Ear – Earle Wines
Applegarth, Wormald Green, Harrogate,
North Yorkshire, HG3 3PS
Tel 01765 677296
Fax 01765 677839
www.earlewines.com

EGe – Ernst Gorge
73 High Street, Dorchester-on-Thames,
Oxon OX14 3LF
Tel 01865 341817
Fax 01865 343184

Ehr – Ehrmanns
29 Corsica Street, London, N5 1JT
Tel 020 7418 1800
Fax 020 7359 7788
ehrmanns@ehrmanns.co.uk
www.ehrmanns.com

EJG – E & J Gallo
Swan House, Cowley Business Park,
Uxbridge UB8 2AD
Tel 01895 818003
Fax 01895 818043

Eno – Enotria
4-8 Chandos Park Estate, Chandos Road,
London, NW10 6NF
Tel 020 8961 4411
Fax 020 8961 8773
marketing@enotria.co.uk

EoR – Ellis of Richmond
Unit 1, Richmond House, The Links,
Popham Close, Hanworth, Middlesex, TW13 6JE
Tel 020 8744 5550
Fax 020 8744 5581
www.ellisofrichmond.co.uk

Eur – Eurowines
93 Bollo Lane, Chiswick, London, W4 5LU
Tel 020 8747 2100
Fax 020 8994 8054
enquiries@eurowines.co.uk
www.eurowines.co.uk

Eve – Evertons
Main Road, Ombersley, Droitwich, WR9 0EU
Tel 01905 620144
Fax 01905 621073
sales@evertons.com

EWG – EWGA
(European Wine Growers Associates)
Challan Hall, Silverdale, Lancashire LA5 0UH
Tel 01524 701723
Fax 01524 701189

ExC – Ex Cellar
20 Craddocks Parade, Ashtead KT21 1QJ
Tel 01372 813937
Fax 01372 813937
simon@excellar.co.uk

F&R – Fine & Rare Wines Ltd
Pall Mall Deposit, 124-128 Barlby Road,
North Kensington, London W10 6BL
Tel 020 8960 1995
Fax 020 8960 1911
wine@frw.co.uk
www.frw.co.uk

Fal – Falcon Vintners
74 Warren Street, London W1T 5PF
Tel 020 7388 7055
Fax 020 7388 9546
info@falconvintners.co.uk

Far – Farr Vintners
19 Sussex Street, Pimlico, London, SW1V 4RR
Tel 020 7821 2000
Fax 020 7821 2020
sales@farr-vintners.com
www.farr-vintners.com

FCA – Fraser Crameri Associates
The Stable, Cottenden View, Stonegate,
Wadhurst, East Sussex TN5 7DX
Tel 01580 200304
Fax 01580 200308
fraser@frasercrameri.com
www.frasercrameri.com

FDB – First Drinks Brands
Imperial House, Imperial Way,
Southampton SO15 0RB
Tel 023 8031 2000
Fax 023 8031 1111
contact@first-drinks-brands.co.uk

FEM – F & E May Ltd
Viaduct House, 16 Warner Street,
London EC1R 5HA
Tel 020 7843 1600
Fax 020 7843 1601
sales@fandemay.com
www.fandemay.com

FFW – Food & Fine Wine
760 Eccleshall Road, Sheffield S11 8TB
Tel 01142 668747
Fax 0870 8912376
www.foodandfinewine.com

Fie – Fields Wine Merchants
3 Pickering Place, London, SW1A 1EA
Tel 020 7589 5753
Fax 020 759 6179
fields@bbr.com
www.fieldswine.com

Fin – The Fine Wine Company Ltd
145 North High Street, Musselburgh EH21 6AN
Tel 0870 7606205
Fax 0870 7606215
mail@thefinewinecompany.co.uk
www.thefinewinecompany.co.uk

Fol – Folio Wines
The Silver Cellars, Weymouth Avenue,
Dorchester, DT1 1QD
Tel 01305 751300
Fax 01305 751302
www.foliowines.com

For – Forth Wines
Crawford Place, Milnathort,
Kinross-Shire, KY13 9XF
Tel 01577 866001
Fax 01577 866020
enquiries@forthwines.com
www.forthwines.com

Frt – Freixenet UK
Freixenet House, 23 Wellington Business Park,
Dukes Ride, Crowthorne, Berkshire, RG45 6LS
Tel 01344 758500
Fax 01344 758510
enquiries@freixenet.co.uk
www.freixenet.co.uk

Frw – Friarwood
26 New Kings Road, Fulham,
London, SW6 4ST
Tel 020 7736 2628
Fax 020 7731 0411
sales@friarwood.com
www.friarwood.com

FSA – see SsG

Fsp – Flagship Wines Ltd
39 Rowan Close, St Albans AL4 0ST
Tel 01727 841968
Fax 01727 841968
info@flagshipwines.co.uk
www.directwineline.com

FSt – Frank Stainton Wines
3 Berry's Yard, Finkle Street, Kendal,
Cumbria, LA9 4AB
Tel 01539 731886
Fax 01539 730396
admin@stainton-wines.co.uk
www.stainton-wines.co.uk

FWC – Fareham Wine Cellar
55 High Street, Fareham, Hampshire PO16 7BG
Tel 01329 822733
Fax 01329 282355
dominic@farehamwinecellar.co.uk
www.farehamwinecellar.co.uk

FWW – FWW Wines UK Ltd
15 South Ealing Road, London W5 4QT
Tel 020 8567 1589
Fax 020 8567 1594
sales@fww.demon.co.uk

G&C – Growers & Château
Oak House, 271 Kingston Road,
Leatherhead, Surrey, KT22 7PJ
Tel 01372 374239
Fax 01372 377610
info@winesite.net
www.winesite.net

Gal – Gallery Wines
The Gomshall Gallery, 56 Station Road,
Gomshall, Surrey GU5 9LB
Tel 01483 203795
Fax 01483 203282

Gau – Gauntleys
4 High Street, Exchange Arcade,
Nottingham, NG1 2ET
Tel 0115 911 0555
Fax 0115 911 0557
rhone@gauntleywine.com
www.gauntleywine.com

GBa – Georges Barbier
267 Lee High Road, London, SE12 8RU
Tel 020 8852 5801
Fax 020 8463 0398
georgesbarbier@f2s.com

GBr – G Bravo & Son Ltd
28 Shaftesbury Ave, London WC2H 8EG
Tel 020 7836 4693
Fax 020 7836 5657

Gel – Gelston Castle Fine Wines
5 Courtyard Cott, Castle Douglas,
Kirkcudbrightshire, DG7 1QE
Tel 01556 503012

GFy – Folly Wines
Chestnut Road, London Road, Chalford,
Gloucestershire, GL6 8NR
Tel 01453 731509
Fax 01453 731134
info@follywines.co.uk
www.follywines.co.uk

Goe – Goedhuis & Co
6 Rudolf Place, Miles Street,
London, SW8 1RP
Tel 020 7793 7900
Fax 020 7793 7170
enquiries@goedhuis.com
www.goedhuis.com

GrD – Growers Direct
2 Station Road, Swavesey,
Cambridge, CB4 5QJ
Tel 01954 230176
Fax 01954 231822

Gun – Gunson Fine Wines
Haysbridge Farm, Brickhouse Lane,
South Godstone, RH9 8JW
Tel 01342 843974
Fax 01342 843955
gunsonfinewines@aol.com

GVF – Grand Vins de France
Carrayol Arch, 8 Church Crescent,
London, N10 3ND
Tel 020 8442 1088
Fax 020 8444 4288
www.grandvins.co.uk

GWW – Great Western Wine
The Wine Warehouse, Wells Road,
Bath, Somerset, BA2 3AP
Tel 01225 322800
Fax 01225 442139
post@greatwesternwine.co.uk
www.greatwesternwine.co.uk

H&B – Hall Batson
28 Whiffler Road, Norwich, NR3 2AZ
Tel 01603 415115
Fax 01603 484096
info@hallbatson.co.uk
www.hallbatson.co.uk

Hal – Hallgarten
Dallow Road, Luton, Bedfordshire, LU11UR
Tel 01582 722538
Fax 01582 723240
sales@hallgarten.co,uk
www.hallgarten.co.uk

Han – Handford Fine Wine
12 Portland Road, Holland Park,
London W11 4LE
Tel 020 7221 9614
Fax 020 7221 9613
www.handford.net

Har – Harris Fine Wine
4 Albion Way, Kelvin Industrial Estate,
East Kilbride, G75 0YN
Tel 01355 571157
Fax 01355 571158

Has – Haslemere Cellar
16 West Street, Haslemere,
Surrey, GU27 2AB
Tel 01428 645081
Fax 01428 645108
info@haslemerecellar.co.uk
www.haslemerecellar.co.uk

Hay – Hayward Bros Ltd
44 Willow Walk, London SE1 5SF
Tel 020 7237 0576
Fax 020 7237 6212
wine@haybrowine.co.uk
www.haybrowine.co.uk

HBJ – Hayman Barwell Jones Ltd
24 Fore Street, Ipswich, Suffolk, IP4 1JU
Tel 01473 232322
Fax 01473 280381
www.hbjwines.co.uk

HHB – H & H Bancroft
1 China Wharf, Mill Street, London, SE1 2BQ
Tel 020 7232 5450
Fax 020 7232 5451
sales@handhbancroft.co.uk
www.handhbancroft.co.uk

HHC – Haynes, Hanson & Clark
25 Eccleston Street, London, SW1W 9NP
Tel 020 7259 0102
Fax 020 7259 0103
london@hhandc.co.uk

Hil – Hill International Wines (UK)
Stonehouse Farm, Ashby Road, Woodville,
Swadlincote, Derbys DE11 7BP
Tel 01283 217703
Fax 01283 550309

His – Hispa Merchants Ltd
Warwick House Business Centre,
181-183 Warwick Road, London, W14 8PU
Tel 020 7370 4449
Fax 020 7370 5086
sales@hispamerchants.com
www.hispamerchants.com

HMA – Hatch Mansfield Agencies
New Bank House, 1 Brockenhurst Road,
Ascot, Berks, SL5 9DJ
Tel 01344 871800
Fax 01344 871871
sales@hatch.co.uk
www.hatchmansfield.co.uk

HRp – Howard Ripley
25 Dingwall Crescent, London, SW18 3AZ
Tel 020 8877 3065
Fax 020 8877 0029
info@howardripley.com
www.howardripley.com

HSA – HS Wine Agencies
76 Impington Lane, Impington,
Cambridge CB4 9NJ
Tel 01223 234604
Fax 01223 234604
hswineagencies@ntlworld.com

HWC – HWCG
Threm Hall, Start Hill,
Bishop's Stortford, Hertfordshire, CM22 7TD
Tel 01279 873500
Fax 01279 873501
wine@hwcg.co.uk
www.hwcg.co.uk

IGH – Ian G Howe
35 Appletongate, Newark,
Nottinghamshire, NG24 1JR
Tel 01636 704366
Fax 01636 610502
howe@chablis-burgundy.co.uk
www.chablis-burgundy.co.uk

Itv / IWS – Italvini / International Wine Services
Punch Bowl Park, Cherry Tree Lane,
Hemel Hempstead, HP2 7EU
Tel 01442 206800
Fax 01442 206888
iws@intwine.co.uk
www.wine-info.co.uk

IVi – I Vini
No. 6 Hayes House, 6-8 Dyer Street,
Cirencester, Gloucestershire GL7 2PF
Tel 01285 655595
Fax 01285 650684
enquiries@ivini.co.uk
www.ivini.co.uk

IVV – In Vino Veritas
3 Wessex Court, Main Road,
Shuttington, Staffs, B79 0DS
Tel 01827 899449
Fax 01827 899936
webmaster@ivvltd.com
www.ivvltd.com

IWD – Interwine Ltd
The Office Suite, Inn on the Green,
The Old Cricket Common, Cookham Dean, SL6
9NZ
Tel 01628 473920
Fax 01628 478660
info@interwinedirect.com
www.interwinedirect.com

J&B – Justerini & Brooks
61 St James Street, London, SW1A 1LZ
Tel 020 7484 6400
Fax 020 7484 6499

JAr – John Armit
5 Royalty Studios, 105 Lancaster Road,
London, W11 1QF
Tel 020 7908 0600
Fax 020 7908 0601
info@armit.co.uk
www.armit.co.uk

Jas – Jascots Wine Merchants Ltd
The Observatory, Pinnacle House,
260 Old Oak Common Lane, London NW10 6DX
Tel 020 8965 2000
Fax 020 8965 9500
ben@jascots.co.uk
www.jascots.co.uk

JBa – Julian Baker
Pound House, Bures Road, Wissington,
Nayland, Colchester, CO6 4LU
Tel 01206 262538
Fax 01206 263574

JEF – John E Fells
Fells House, Prince Edwards Street,
Berkhamstead, HP4 3EZ
Tel 01442 870900
Fax 01442 878555
info@fells.co.uk
www.fells.co.uk

JIC – Just In Case
Symes Corner, Bank Street, Bishops Waltham,
Hampshire SO32 1AN
Tel 01489 892969
Fax 01489 892969

JNi – James Nicholson
27a Killyleagh Street, Crossgar,
County Down, BT30 9DQ
Tel 028 4483 0091
Fax 028 4483 0028
info@jnwine.com
www.jnwine.com

JNV – Jackson Nugent Vintners
30 Homefields Road,
London, SW19 4QF
Tel 020 8947 9722
Fax 020 8944 1048
www.jnv.co.uk

JTD – JT Davies & Son
7 Aberdeen Road, Croydon, CR0 1EQ
Tel 020 8681 3222
Fax 020 8681 5931
postbox@jtdavies.co.uk
www.jtdavies.co.uk

KJn – Kendall Jackson UK
Lamb House, Church Street,
Chiswick, London, W4 2PD
Tel 020 8747 2840
Fax 020 8987 6160
kjsales@kjmail.com

**Kwi – Kiwi Wine / The Brilliants Wine
Merchants Ltd**
62c Salcott Road, London SW11 6DE
Tel 0870 0433944
Fax 0870 0433945
nicholas@kiwiwines.net
www.kiwiwines.net

L&S – Lea & Sandeman
170 Fulham Road, Chelsea,
London, SW10 9PR
Tel 020 7244 0522
Fax 020 7244 0533
info@leaandsandeman.co.uk
www.londonfinewine.co.uk

L&T – Lane & Tatham
12 Market Place, Devizes SN10 1HT
Tel 01380 720123
Fax 01380 720111
wines@lanetat.demon.co.uk

L&W – Lay & Wheeler
Gosbecks Park, 117 Gosbecks Road,
Colchester, Essex, CO2 9JT
Tel 0845 330 1855
Fax 01206 560002
sales@laywheeler.com
www.laywheeler.com

LaC – La Caneva
Business Design Centre,
52 Upper Street, London, N1 0QH
Tel 020 7354 3738
Fax 020 7354 1015
mail@lacaneva.com
www.lacaneva.com

Las – L'Assemblage
Pallant Court, West Pallant, Chichester,
West Sussex PO19 1TG
Tel 01243 537775
Fax 01243 538644
sales@lassemblage.co.uk
www.lassemblage.co.uk

Lay – Jeroboams / Laytons
8-12 Brook Street, London W1Y 2BH
Tel 020 7259 6716
Fax 020 7495 3314
sales@jeroboams.co.uk
www.jeroboams.co.uk

Lib – Liberty Wines
Unit A53, The Food Market,
New Covent Garden, London, SW8 5EE
Tel 020 7720 5350
Fax 020 7720 6158
info@libertywine.co.uk
www.libertywine.co.uk

LLt –Louis Latour UK
7a Grafton Street, London, W1S 4EH
Tel 020 7409 7276
Fax 020 7409 7092
enquiries@louislatour.co.uk
www.louislatour.com

LoW – For the Love of Wine
4 Beaver Close, Buckingham,
Buckinghamshire, MK18 7EA
Tel 01280 822500
Fax 01280 823833
www.i-love-wine.co.uk

L-P – Laurent Perrier UK
66-68 Chapel Street, Marlow,
Buckinghamshire, SL7 1DE
Tel 01628 475404
Fax 01628 471891
enquiries@laurent-perrier.co.uk
www.laurent-perrier.co.uk

Lwt – Laithwaites / Direct Wines Ltd
New Aquitaine House, Exeter Way,
Theale, Reading, Berkshire RG7 4PL
Tel 0870 444 8383
Fax 0870 444 8182
www.laithwaites.co.uk

LyS – Laymont & Shaw
The Old Chapel, Millpool, Truro,
Cornwall, TR1 1EX
Tel 01872 270545
Fax 01872 223005
info@laymont-shaw.co.uk
www.laymont-shaw.co.uk

M&V – Morris & Verdin
Unit 2, Bankside Industrial Estate,
Sumner Street, London, SE1 9JZ
Tel 020 7921 5300
Fax 020 7921 5333
info@m-v.co.uk
www.morris-verdin.co.uk

Maj – Majestic Wine Warehouses
Majestic House, Otterspool Way,
Watford, WD25 8WW
Tel 01923 298226
Fax 01923 819105
info@majestic.co.uk
www.majestic.co.uk

Mar – Martinez Wines
35 The Grove, Ilkley,
West Yorkshire, LS29 9NJ
Tel 01943 603241
Fax 01274 742439
editor@martinez.co.uk
www.martinez.co.uk

Max – Maxxium
Maxxium House, Castle Business Park,
Stirling, FK9 4RT
Tel 01786 430500
Fax 01786 430600

May – Mayfair Cellars
203 Seagrove Road, Fulham,
London, SW6 1ST
Tel 020 7386 7999
Fax 020 7386 0202
sales@mayfaircellars.co.uk
www.mayfaircellars.co.uk

MCD – Marne & Champagne Diffusion
18 Bolton Street, London, W1J 8BJ
Tel 020 7499 0070
Fax 020 7408 0841
sales@mcduk.com

McK – McKinley Vintners
14 Kennington Road, London, SE1 7BL
Tel 020 7928 7300
Fax 020 7928 4447
info@mckinleyvintners.co.uk

MCl – Matthew Clark
Whitchurch Lane, Whitchurch,
Bristol, BS14 0JZ
Tel 01275 836100
Fax 01275 836726
www.mclark.co.uk

McW – McWilliam's Wines
Swan House, Cowley Business Park, Cowley Road,
Uxbridge, Middlesex UB8 2AD
Tel 01895 813444
Fax 01895 818048

MCW – Morgan Classic Wines
Crown House, 4 Market Lane, Lewes,
East Sussex, 7BN 2NT
Tel 01273 487000
Fax 01273 487700
sales@morganclassics.com
www.morganclassicwines.com

Men – Mentzendorff
8th Floor, Prince Consort House,
27-29 Albert Embankment, London, SE1 7TJ
Tel 020 7840 3600
Fax 020 7840 3601
www.mentzendorff.co.uk

Mer – Meridian
Brook House, 4 Northenden Road,
Gatley, Cheshire, SK8 4DN
Tel 0161 908 1350
Fax 0161 908 1355
www.meridianwines.co.uk

Mgi – Mille Gusti
17 Roseberry Gardens, London, W13 0HD
Tel 020 8997 3932
Fax 020 8566 8480
millegusti@hotmail.com

MHn – Moët Hennessey UK
13 Grosvenor Crescent, London, SW1X 7EE
Tel 020 7235 9411
Fax 020 7235 6937

**MHv – Margaret Harvey /
Fine Wines of New Zealand**
PO Box 476, London NW5 2NZ
Tel 020 7482 0093
Fax 020 7267 8400
margaret.harvey@btinternet.com
www.fwnz.co.uk

Mis – Mistral Wines
5 Junction Mews, Sale Place, London, W2 1PN
Tel 020 7262 5437
Fax 020 7402 7957
info@mistralwines.co.uk

MMD – Maison Marques & Domaines
Burleigh House, 17-19 Worple Way,
Richmond, Surrey, TWO10 6AG
Tel 020 8332 2223
Fax 020 8334 5900
maison@mmdltd.co.uk

Mon – Montana Wines / Allied Domecq UK
Argentum, 2 Queen Caroline Street,
London W6 9DX
Tel 020 8323 8196
Fax 020 8323 8313
www.montanawines.co.nz

Mor – Moreno Wines
26 Macroom Road, Maida Vale, London W9 3HY
Tel 020 8960 7161
Fax 020 8960 7165
sales@moreno-wines.co.uk

MPe – Michael Peace MW
24 Drayson Mews, London W8 4LY
Tel 020 7937 9345
Fax 020 7937 7884
michaelpeace@btinternet.com

MSd – Milton Sandford
The Old Chalk Mine, Warren Row Road,
Knowl Hill, Berskhire, RG10 8QS
Tel 01628 829449
Fax 01628 829424
sales@milton-sandford.demon.co.uk

MtC – Morgenrot-Chevaliers
Olde Forge, Bent Street Estate, Kearsley,
Bolton, BL4 9DH
Tel 01204 573093
Fax 01204 861609
sales@morgenrot.co.uk
www.morgenrot-chevaliers.co.uk

MVs – Merchant Vintners
Red Duster House, York Street, Hull,
East Yorkshire, HU2 0QX
Tel 01482 329443
Fax 01482 213616

N&P – Nickolls & Perks
37 High Street, Stourbridge,
West Midlands, DY8 1TA
Tel 01384 394518
Fax 01384 440786
sales@nickollsandperks.co.uk
www.nickollsandperks.co.uk

Neg – Negociants UK
Davenport House, Bowers Way,
Harpenden, Herts, AL5 4EW
Tel 01582 462859
Fax 01582 462867
neguk@negociants.com

Nid – Nidderdale Fine Wines
2a High Street, Pateley Bridge,
North Yorkshire HG3 5AW
Tel 01423 711703
info@southaustralianwines.com
www.southaustralianwines.com

NoG – Noble Grape
21-27 Brandon Terrace, Edinburgh, EH3 5DZ
Tel 0131 556 3133
Fax 0131 556 8766
info@thenoble-grape.co.uk
www.thenoble-grape.co.uk

NWW – New World Wines
519 Old York Road, Wandsworth,
London, SW18 1TF
Tel 020 8877 3555
Fax 020 8877 1476
info@newworldwines.co.uk
www.newworldwines.co.uk

NYg – Noel Young Wines
56 High Street, Trumpington,
Cambridgshire, CB2 2LS
Tel 01223 844744
Fax 01223 844736
admin@nywines.co.uk
www.nywines.co.uk

Oak – Oakley Wine Agencies
PO Box 3234, Earls Colne,
Colchester, CO6 2SU
Tel 01787 220070
Fax 01787 224734
oakleywine@btconnect.com

Oas – Oastwell
Beechurst, Lingfield, Surrey, RH7 6NZ
Tel 01342 832069
Fax 01342 832385

Ock – Ockse Wines
67 Ashburnham Grove, London SE10 8UJ
Tel 020 8691 2846
Fax 020 8691 2841
office@ocksewines.net
www.ocksewines.net

Odd – Oddbins
31-33 Weir Road, London, SW19 8UG
Tel 0800 328 2323
Fax 0800 328 3848
customer.services@oddbinsmail.com
www.oddbins.com

O-F – Oldacre-Field
York House, 6 Hazel Road, Altrincham,
Cheshire, WA14 1HL
Tel 0161 928 4898
Fax 0161 929 7064

Orb – Orbital Wines
Elkington Lodge, Welford,
Northants, NN6 6HA
Tel 01858 570600
Fax 01858 570601
www.orbitalwines.co.uk

OWL – O W Loeb
3 Archie Street, London SE1 3JT
Tel 020 7234 0385
Fax 020 7357 0440
finewine@owloeb.com
www.owloeb.com

P&S – Philglas & Swiggot
21 Northcote Road, London SW11 1NG
Tel 020 7924 4494
Fax 020 7924 4736
contact@philglas-swiggot.co.uk
www.philglas-swiggot.co.uk

Par – Paragon Vintners
Regent Gate, 21 Dartmouth Street,
London, SW1H 9BP
Tel 020 7887 1800
Fax 020 7887 1810
welcome@paragonvintners.co.uk

Pat – Patriarche Wine Agencies
7 Rickett Street, Fulham, London, SW6 1RU
Tel 020 7381 4016
Fax 020 7381 2023
sales@patriarchewines.com

PaV – Passione Vino
15 Derinton Road, London SW17 8JA
Tel 020 8672 1941
Fax 020 8672 7132
info@passionevino.co.uk
www.passionevino.co.uk

PBW – Paul Boutinot Wines
Brook House, 4 Northenden Road,
Gatley, Cheshire, SK8 4DN
Tel 0161 908 1370
Fax 0161 908 1375
www.paul-boutinot.co.uk

PDn – Pimlico Dozen / Vintage Cellars
33 Churton Street, London, SW1V 2LT
Tel 020 7630 6254
Fax 020 7233 7536
vintagecellars@winecellarsales.co.uk
www.winecellarsales.co.uk

PFx – Percy Fox & Co
Templefields House, River Way,
Harlow, Essex, CM20 2EA
Tel 01279 633542
Fax 01279 633780
percyfoxmarketing@guinnessudv.com

PLB – Private Liquor Brands
Dorset House, 64 High Street,
East Grinstead, RH19 3DE
Tel 01342 318282
Fax 01342 314023
general@plb.co.uk
www.plb.co.uk

PLh – Peter Lehmann Wines UK
Godmersham Park, Godmersham,
Canterbury, Kent, CT4 7DT
Tel 01227 731353
Fax 01227 738538
admin@lehmannwines.com
www.peterlehmannwines.com.au

Pol – Pol Roger Ltd
Shelton House, 4 Conningsby Street,
Hereford, HR1 2DY
Tel 01432 262800
Fax 01432 262806
wineshops@polroger.co.uk
www.polroger.co.uk

Por – Portland Wine
152a Ashley Road, Hale, Altrincham, Cheshire
Tel 0161 928 0357
Fax 0161 905 1291
portwineco@aol.com
www.portlandwine.co.uk

POs – Peter Osborne & Co
Watcombe Manor Farm, Ingham Lane,
Watlington, Oxfordshire, OX9 5EJ
Tel 01491 612311
Fax 01491 613322
info@peterosbornewine.co.uk
www.peterosbornewine.co.uk

PRc – Pernod Ricard UK
8-10 Lampton Road, Hounslow,
Middlesex, TW3 1JL
Tel 020 8538 4000
Fax 020 8538 4488
general@pernodricard-uk.com

PVF – Producteurs et Vignerons de France
Toad Hall, Wilbury Road, Hove,
East Sussex, BN3 3JJ
Tel 01273 730277
Fax 01273 328691
vdf@pavilion.co.uk
www.pavilion.co.uk

PWa – Peter Watkins Wine

2 Manor Road, Pitsford, Northampton, NN2 9AR
Tel 01604 882370
Fax 01604 889465
sales@peterwatkinswine.co.uk
www.peterwatkinswine.co.uk

PWy – Peter Wylie Fine Wines

Plymtree Manor, Plymtree,
Cullompton, Devon EX15 2LE
Tel 01884 277555
Fax 01884 277557
peter@wylie-fine-wines.demon.co.uk
www.wyliefinewines.co.uk

Rae – Raeburn Fine Wines

The Vaults, 4 Giles Street, Leith,
Edinburgh, EH6 6DJ
Tel 0131 343 1159
Fax 0131 332 5166
sales@raeburnfinewines.com
www.raeburnfinewines.com

Rec – Recount Wines

44 Lower Sloane Street,
London, SW1W 8BP
Tel 020 7730 6377
Fax 020 7730 6377

Ren – Renvic Wines

2 School Cottages, Abington Pigotts,
Nr Royston, Herts SG8 0SQ
Tel 01763 852470
Fax 01763 852470

Res – La Réserve / Mark Reynier Fine Wines

56 Walton Street, Knightsbridge,
London, SW3 1RB
Tel 020 7589 2020
Fax 020 7581 0250
realwine@la-reserve.co.uk
www.la-reserve.co.uk

Rev – Revelstoke Wine Co

213 Putney Bridge Road, London SW15 2NY
Tel 020 8875 0077
Fax 020 8875 0477
info@revelstoke.co.uk
www.revelstoke.co.uk

RGr – Richard Granger Fine Wine

West Jesmond Station, Lyndhurst Avenue,
Newcastle NE2 3HH
Tel 0191 281 5000
Fax 0191 281 8141
sales@richardgrangerwines.co.uk
www.richardgrangerwines.co.uk

RHW – Roger Harris Wines

Loke Farm, Weston Longville,
Norfolk, NR9 5LG
Tel 01603 880171
Fax 01603 880291
sales@rogerharriswines.co.uk
www.beaujolaisonline.co.uk

RMi – Robert Mondavi UK

Tel 01491 826475
Fax 01491 839778
graham.adlard@robertmondavi.com

RRl – Robert Rolls

36-37 Charterhouse Square,
London EC1M 6EA
Tel 020 7606 1166
Fax 020 7606 1144
mail@rollswine.com
www.rollswine.com

RSJ – RSJ Wine

115 Wootton Street, London SE1 8LY
Tel 020 7633 0881
Fax 020 7401 2455
www.rsj.uk.com

RSo – Raisin Social

Tripod House, 105-107 Lansdowne Road,
Croydon, CR0 2BN
Tel 020 8686 8500
Fax 020 8681 7939
info@raisin-social.com
www.raisin-social.com

RsW – Richards Walford

Hales Lodge, Pickworth,
Nr Stamford, Lincolnshire, PE9 4DJ
Tel 01780 460451
Fax 01780 460276

RTo – Royal Tokay UK

41 St James's Place, London SW1A 1NS
Tel 020 7495 3010
Fax 020 7493 3973
sales@royal-tokaji.com

Rui – Ruinart UK
13 Grovesnor Crescent,
London, SW1X 7EE
Tel 020 7416 0592
Fax 020 7416 0593
www.ruinart.com

RWs – Reid Wines
The Mill, Marsh Lane, Hallatrow,
Bristol, BS39 6EB
Tel 01761 452645
Fax 01761 452642

RyR – Raymond Reynolds
Station Road, Furness Vale,
High Peak, SK23 7SW
Tel 01663 742230
Fax 01663 742233
info@raymondreynolds.co.uk
www.winesfromportugal.com

Sav – Savage Selection
The Ox House, Market Place, Northleach,
Gloucestershire, GL54 3EG
Tel 01451 860896
Fax 01451 860996
wine@savageselection.co.uk
www.savageselection.co.uk

ScE – Southcorp Europe
Grange House, 15 Church Street,
Twickenham, TW1 3NL
Tel 020 8917 4600
Fax 020 8917 4646

SCh – Sommeliers Choice
9 Dagnall Park, South Norwood,
London SE25 5PW
Tel 020 8689 9643
Fax 020 8689 9643
sommelierschoice@aol.com

Sec – Seckford Wine Agencies
Dock Lane, Melton, Ipswich, Suffolk, IP12 1PE
Tel 01394 446622
Fax 01394 446633
sales@seckfordwines.co.uk
www.seckfordwines.co.uk

SFW – Stokes Fine Wines
41 Trewint Street, London, SW18 4HB
Tel 020 8944 5979
Fax 020 8944 5935
sales@stokesfinewines.com

SsG – Stevens Garnier
47 West Way, Botley, Oxford, OX2 0JF
Tel 01865 263300
Fax 01865 791594
info@stevensgarnier.co.uk
www.stevensgarnier.co.uk

Str – Stratford's Wine Agencies
High Street, Cookham on Thames,
Berkshire, SL6 9SQ
Tel 01628 810606
Fax 01628 810605
sales@stratfordwine.co.uk
www.stratfordwine.co.uk

SVS – Stone, Vine & Sun
No.13 Humphrey Farms, Hazeley Road,
Twyford, Winchester SO21 1QA
Tel 0845 061 4604
Fax 01962 717545
sales@stonevine.co.uk
www.stonevine.co.uk

SWB – Southern Vintners
The Yarn Store, Dogley Mills, Penistone Road,
Fenay Bridge, Huddersfield HD8 0LE
Tel 01484 608898
Fax 01484 609495
info@southernvintners.com

Swg – Swig
188 Sutton Court Road, London W4 3HR
Tel 08000 272 272
Fax 020 8995 7069
imbibe@swig.co.uk
www.swig.co.uk

T&W – T & W Wines
51 Kings Street, Thetford, Norfolk, IP24 2AU
Tel 01842 765646
Fax 01842 766407
contact@tw-wines.co.uk
www.tw-wines.co.uk

Tan – Tanners Wine Merchants
26 Wyle Cop, Shrewsbury, Shropshire, SY11XD
Tel 01743 234500
Fax 01743 234501
sales@tanners-wines.co.uk
www.tanners-wines.co.uk

The – Theatre of Wine
75 Trafalgar Road, Greenwich, London SE10 9TS
Tel 020 8858 6363
Fax 020 8305 1936
daniel@theatreofwine.com
www.theatreofwine.com

THt – Thorman Hunt
4 Pratt Walk, Lambeth, London, SE11 6AR
Tel 020 7735 6511
Fax 020 7735 9779
info@thormanhunt.co.uk

TPt – Terry Platt
Council Street West, Llandudno, LL30 1ED
Tel 01492 874099
Fax 01492 874722
plattwines@clara.co.uk

Tur – Turville Valley Wines
The Firs, Potter Row, Great Missenden,
Buckinghamshire, HP16 9LT
Tel 01494 868818
Fax 01494 868832
info@turville-valley-wines.com
www.turville-valley-wines.com

TWS – Thierry's Wine Services
Horsefair House, The Horsefair, Romsey,
Hampshire, SO51 8EZ
Tel 01794 507100
Fax 01794 516856
info@thierrys.co.uk
www.thierrys.co.uk

UnC – Uncorked
Exchange Arcade, Broadgate, London EC2M 3WA
Tel 020 7638 5998
Fax 020 7638 6028
drink@uncorked.co.uk
www.uncorked.co.uk

V&C – Valvona & Crolla
19 Elm Road, Edinburgh EH7 4AA
Tel 0131 556 6066
Fax 0131 556 1668
wine@valvonacrolla.co.uk
www.valvonacrolla.co.uk

VCq – Veuve Clicquot
Third Floor, 15 St George's Street,
London, W1S 1FH
Tel 020 7408 7430
Fax 020 7408 7457
yellow@veuve-clicquot.co.uk
www.veuveclicquot.fr

Vcs – Vinceremos Organic Wines
74 Kirkgate, Leeds LS2 7DJ
Tel 0113 244 0002
Fax 0113 288 4566
webinfo@vinceremos.co.uk
www.vinceremos.co.uk

VDu – Van Duuren Wines Ltd
3 Framfield Road, Hanwell, London W7 1NG
Tel 020 8567 4428
Fax 020 8567 4428
svanduuren@aol.com

Ver - Veritaus & Co
The Old Stables, Wiggins Yard, Bridge Street,
Godalming, Surrey, GU7 1HW
Tel 0870 7704112
Fax 0870 7704113
info@veritaus.com
www.veritaus.com

Vex - Vinexcel Ltd
29 Rowan Drive, Cheadle Hulme SK8 7DU
Tel 0161 485 4592
Fax 0161 485 1791

Vic - Vickery Wines
Unit 2 Home Farm, Luton Hoo Estate, Luton,
Bedfordshire, LU1 3TD
Tel 01582 456180
Fax 01582 456716
islay@vickerywines.co.uk
www.vickerywines.co.uk

Vig - La Vigneronne
Fax 0033 4 90 47 13 21
lavigneronne.france@wanadoo.fr
Also try: **Han**

Vim – Vinum
1 Barrow Walk, Brentford, Middlesex TW8 0RA
Tel 020 8847 4699
Fax 020 8847 4771
vinum@vinum.co.uk
www.vinum.co.uk

Vin – Vineyard Cellars
Denford Manor Farm, Lower Denford,
Hungerford, Berkshire, RG17 0UN
Tel 01488 681313
Fax 01488 681411
jameshocking@vineyardcellars.com
www.vineyardcellars.com

ViV – Vitis Vinifera
33 Godfrey Way, Great Dunmow, Essex, CM6 2AY
Tel 01371 873383
Fax 01371 873383

Vne - Villeneuve Wines Ltd
1 Venlaw Court, Peebles EH45 8AE
Tel 01721 722500
Fax 01721 729922
wines@villeneuvewines.com
www.villeneuvewines.com

Vni – Vinites UK
37 Montholme Road, London SW11 6HX
Tel 020 7924 4974
Fax 020 7228 6109

Vns – Vinoceros
Stanley Way, Cardrew, Redruth,
Cornwall, TR15 1SP
Tel 01209 314711
Fax 01209 314712
enquiries@vinoceros.com
www.vinoceros.com

VOC – Val d'Orbieu-Cordier Group
73 Moore Park Road, London, SW6 2HH
Tel 020 7736 3350
Fax 020 7731 3695

VRt – Vintage Roots
Farley Farms, Bridge Farm, Reading Road,
Arborfield, Berkshire RG2 9HT
Tel 0118 976 1999
Fax 0118 976 1998
info@vintageroots.co.uk
www.vintageroots.co.uk

VsV / VTr – Vine Trail
266 Hotwell Road, Hotwells, Bristol, BS8 4NG
Tel 0117 921 1770
Fax 0117 921 1772
enquiries@vinetrail.co.uk
www.vinetrail.co.uk

Vts – Veritas Wines
103 Cherry Hinton Road, Cambridge CB1 7BS
Tel 01223 212500
info@veritaswines.co.uk
www.veritaswines.co.uk

VWs – Vinifera Wines
Units 2&3, 199 Eade Road, London N4 1DN
Tel 020 8880 2526
Fax 020 8442 8215
vinifera@alvini.com
www.alivini.com

Wat – Waterloo Wine Co.
6 Vine Yard, London, SE1 1QL
Tel 020 7403 7967
Fax 020 7357 6976
sales@waterloowine.co.uk
www.waterloowine.co.uk

Wav – Waverley Vintners
PO Box 22, Crieff Road, Perth, PH1 2SL
Tel 01738 472000
Fax 01738 630338
contactus@waverley-group.co.uk
www.waverley-group.co.uk

WBn – Wine Barn
2 Stable Cottages, Church Barns, East Stratton,
Winchester, Hampshire SO21 3XA
Tel 01962 774102
Fax 01962 774102
info@thewinebarn.co.uk
www.thewinebarn.co.uk

WEx – Winexcel
5 Avebury Close, Horsham,
West Sussex RH12 5JY

Wgg – Wigglesworth Wine
Pipe House, Vines Cross, East Sussex, TN21 9EH
Tel 01435 813740
Fax 01435 813866
william@wigglesworth.co.uk
www.wigglesworth.co.uk

WGW - WG White
Caspian House, 650 River Gardens,
Feltham TW14 0RB
Tel 020 8831 1400
Fax 020 8893 2535
sales@wgwhite.co.uk
www.wgwhite.co.uk

WhW – Whittaker Wines
35 Chatsworth Road, High Lane, Bredbury
Cheshire, SK6 8DA
Tel 020 8878 2302
Fax 020 8876 5580
sales@whittakerwines.com
www.whittakerwines.com

Win – The Winery
4 Clifton Road, Maida Vale, London, W9 1SS
Tel 020 7286 6475
Fax 020 7286 2733

Wit – Withers Agencies
1 South Street, Lewes, East Sussex, BN7 2BT
Tel 01273 477132
Fax 01273 476612

WRk – Wine Raks
21 Springfield Road, Aberdeen AB15 7RJ
Tel 01224 311460
Fax 01224 312186
enq@wineraks.com
www.wineraks.com

WSc – The Wine Society
Gunnels Wood Road, Stevenage, SG1 2BG
Tel 01483 741177
Fax 01483 741392
memberservices@thewinesociety.com
www.thewinesociety.com

WSe – Wineservice
Semper Fidelis Mews, Wire Mill Lane,
Lingfield, Surrey RH7 6HJ
Tel 01342 837333
Fax 01342 837444
sales@wineservice.co.uk

WSo – Winesource
393 Ham Green , Holt, Trowbridge,
Wiltshire, BA14 6PX
Tel 01225 783007
Fax 01225 783152
winesource@saqnet.co.uk

WSS – Siegel Wine Agencies
Regent House, 123 High Street, Odiham,
Hampshire, RG29 1LA
Tel 01256 701101
Fax 01256 701518
wine@walter-siegel.co.uk
www.walter-siegel.co.uk

Wtr – Winetraders
3 TBAC Business Centre, Avenue Four,
Station Lane, Witney, Oxfordshire OX28 4BN
Tel 01993 848777
Fax 01993 848778
winetraders@winetraders.org.uk
www.winetraders.org.uk

WTs – The Wine Treasury
69 - 71 Broadway, London, SW8 1SQ
Tel 020 7793 9999
Fax 020 7796 8080
quality@winetreasury.com
www.winetreasury.com

WVt – The Wine Vault
Tel 01622 687768
sales@winevault.co.uk
www.winevault.co.uk

WWs – Western Wines
1 Hawksworth Road, Central Park, Telford,
Shropshire, TF2 9TU
Tel 01952 235700
Fax 01952 235711
manager@western-wines.com
www.western-wines.com

Yap – Yapp Brothers
The Old Brewery, Mere, Wiltshire, BA12 6DY
Tel 01747 860423
Fax 01747 860929
sales@yapp.co.uk
www.yapp.co.uk

Yng – Young and Company
The Ram Brewery, Wandsworth, London,
SW18 4JD
Tel 020 8875 7000
Fax 020 8875 7197
winedirect@youngs.co.uk
www.youngswinedirect.co.uk

Other wine traders of note

Bonhams
65-69 Lots Road, London SW10 0RN
Tel 020 7393 3900
Fax 020 7393 3906
wine@bonhams.com
www.bonhams.com

Christie's
8 King Street, St James's, London SW1Y 6QT
Tel 020 7839 9060
Fax 020 7839 1611
thudson@christies.com
www.christies.com

Sotheby's
34/35 New Bond Street, London W1A 2AA
Tel 020 7293 6423
Fax 020 7293 5961
wine.london@sothebys.com
www.sothebys.com

Uvine (Universal Wine Exchange)
Swan Court, 9 Tanner Street, London SE1 3LE
Tel 020 7089 2200
Fax 020 7089 2211
enquiries@uvine.com
www.uvine.com

Wilkinson Vintners
Unit 1 Bickerton House, Bickerton Road,
London N19 5JT
Tel 020 7272 1982
Fax 020 7263 2643
wilkinson@finewine.co.uk

Index

This producer index is ordered according to the name by which an estate is most commonly referred. There is priority to surnames but otherwise they appear as they are written. 'Domaine' is ignored but 'Château', 'Castello', 'Quinta' etc are respected as is the definite article when implicitly part of the name (eg Il Poggione appears under 'I'). The only exception is in Bordeaux where 'Château' is also ignored and the name of the château or estate takes precedent.

A

A, Domaine de l' **45**

Aalto **434**

Abadía Retuerta **434**

Abbaye de Tholomies **273**

Abbaye Sylva Plana **273**

Abbazia Santa Anastasia **414**

Abbona, Anna Maria **291**

Abbona, M & E **291**

Abbotts Wines **272**

Abercorn **689**

Abotia, Domaine **283**

Abreu **547**

Abrigo, Giovanni **323**

Abrigo, Orlando **323**

Acacia **547**

Accademia dei Racemi **414**

Accordini, Stefano **394**

Accornero & Figli, G **323**

Acham-Magnin **504**

Achaval-Ferrer **609**

Achs, Paul **518**

Adam, Jean-Baptiste **163**

Adams, Tim **624**

Adanti **408**

Adelaida Cellars **588**

Adelsheim **601**

Adine, Christian **88**

Aéria, Domaine d' **243**

Agassac, Château d' **19**

Agrapart **176**

Agriverde **408**

Agro de Bazán **434**

Aguilas, Pierre **194**

Aguirre **617**

Agusta Wines **727**

Ahlgren **588**

Aigle, Domaine de l' **272**

Aiguelière, Domaine de l' **272**

Aiguilhe, Château d' **46**

Aires Hautes, Domaine des **272**

Aladame, Stéphane **138**

Alana Estate **717**

Alante Vineyards **589**

Alario, Claudio **291**

Alary Daniel et Denis **221**

Alban **577**

Albet I Noya **448**

Albrecht, Domaine Lucien **155**

Alderbrook **541**

Aldinger **504**

Alemany I Corrio **448**

Alessandria, Gianfranco **291**

Alfieri, Marchesi **324**

Alión, Bodegas y Viñedos **447**

Alkoomi **693**

All Saints **664**

Allaines, Francois d' **138**

Allandale **685**

Allanmere **689**

Allegrini **378**

Allemand, Thierry **205**

Alliet, Philippe **183**

Allimant-Laugner **163**

Almaviva **609**

Almeida Garrett **473**

Almondo, Giovanni **323**

Alpha Domus **705**

Alquier, Jean-Michel **251**

Alta Vista **609**

Altamura **571**

Altare, Elio **292**

Altesino **334**

Altos de Medrano **617**

Alvear **448**

Alves de Sousa, Domingos **458**

Alysses, Domaine des **272**

Alzinger, Leo **518**

Amadieu, Domaine des **222**

Amberley Estate **699**

Ambra, Fattoria **370**

Ambroise, Bertrand **88**

Ameillaud, Domaine de l' **243**

Amido, Domaine **222**

Amiot, Domaine Guy et Fils **89**

Amiot-Servelle **90**

Amirault, Yannick **183**

Amity Vineyards **593**

Amouriers, Domaines des **222**

Ampeau, Robert **138**

Ancien **541**

Ancienne Cure, Domaine de L' **283**

Anderson, S **547**

Andersons Conn Valley **571**

Andrew Murray Vyrds **577**

Andrew Will **593**

Angélus, Chateau **46**

Angerville, Marquis d' **90**

Anges, Domaines des **243**

Angludet, Chateau d' **19**

Annie's Lane **624**

Anselmi **378**

Antaño **448**

Antichi Vigneti di Cantalupo **292**

Antinori **334**

Antiyal **617**

Antonnelli **408**

Antonopoulos **523**

Antugnac, Domaine d' **272**

Anubìs **609**

Apaltagua **617**

Apex **601**

Apollonio **427**

Apsley Gorge **680**

Araldica Vini Piemontesi **292**

Araujo **547**

Arcadian **588**

Arche, Château d' **19**

Archery Summit **593**

Arena, Antoine **272**

Aresti **617**

Argiano **335**

Argiolas **415**

Argüeso, Herederos de **448**

Argyle **593**

Arietta **548**

Arizu, Leoncio **617**

Arjolle, Domaine de L' **272**

Arlaud, Hervé et Cyprien **138**

Arlot, Domaine de l' **90**

Armailhac, Chateau d' **19**

Armand, Comte **91**

Arnoux, Domaine Robert **91**

Arnoux, Père et Fils **138**

Arretxia, Domaine **283**

Arrosée, Chateau l' **46**

Arrowfield **689**

Arrowood **527**

Arroyo, Ismael **435**

Artadi **435**

Artesa **571**

Arthurs Creek **680**

Ascheri **293**

Ashanti **727**

Ashbrook Estate **699**

Ashton Hills **624**

Ata Rangi **705**

Atalon **548**

Atlas Peak **571**

Au Bon Climat **577**

Aubuisières, Domaine des **183**

Aupilhac, Domaine d' **272**

Aurelles, Domaine des **272**

Ausone, Chateau **46**

Australian Domaine Wines **657**

Autard, Domaine Paul **243**

Auther, Domaine **163**

Auvenay, Domaine d' **91**

Auvigue **151**

Avignonesi **335**

Ayala **176**

Azelia **293**

Azienda Agricola Lohsa **360**

B

Babcock Vineyards **578**

Babich **716**

Bablut, Domaine de **194**

Bachelet, Denis **92**

Bachelet-Ramonet **138**

Bacio Divino **548**

Backsberg **727**

Badia a Coltibuono **370**

Badia di Morrona **370**

Bagnolo, Tenuta di **371**

Baileys of Glenrowan **664**

Balbo, Susana **613**

Balestard-La-Tonnelle, Château **62**

Balgownie **664**

Balland, Domaine **194**

Balland-Chapuis **194**

Balnaves **625**

Balthazar, Domaine **205**

Banfi **336**

Bannister **541**

Bannockburn **664**

Banti, Erik **336**

Bara, Paul **167**

Barat, Domaine **88**

Barbadillo **446**

Barbeito **458**

Barberani **408**

Barbi, Fattoria dei **370**

Barbour **571**

Barde-Haut, Château **62**

Barge, Gilles **205**

Baricci **370**

Barjac, Guy de **220**

Barletta Bros **657**

Barnard Griffin **601**

Barnaut, Edmond **167**

Barnett Vineyards **571**

Barolo, Marchesi di **324**

Barone Ricasoli **361**

Barossa Valley Estate **625**

Barrabaque, Château **62**

Barral, Domaine Léon **272**

Barratt Wines **625**

Barraud, Daniel et Martine **142**

Barreda, Juan de la **448**

Barrot, Domaine Lucien **223**

Barry, Brian **657**

Barry, Jim **626**

Barthod, Ghislaine **92**

Basciano, Fattoria di **336**

Basignani **604**

Basilisco **427**

Bass Phillip **665**

Bassermann-Jordan **487**

Bastanich **394**

Bastian **504**

Bastor-Lamontagne, Château **19**

Batailley, Château **20**

Batasiolo **323**

Baudana, Luigi **294**

Baudouin, Patrick **183**

Baudry, Bernard **184**

Baudry, Domaine J &C **194**

Bauduc, Château **62**

Baumard, Domaine des **184**

Bava **295**

Béates, Domaine de **251**

Beaulieu Vineyard **548**

Beaulieu, Château **52**

Beaumont des Crayères **176**

Beauregard, Château **47**

Beaurenard, Domaine de **223**

Beau-Séjour Bécot, Château **47**

Beauséjour, Château **47**

Beau-Soleil, Château **62**

Beaux Frères **594**

Bechtold, Jean-Pierre **163**

Beck, Graham **727**

Becker, Domaine Jean **155**

Becker, J B **504**

Bedell **604**

Behrens and Hitchcock **527**

Bel Air La Royère, Château **63**

Bel Air Marquis d'Aligre, Château **20**

Bel-Air, Château **43**

Belgrave, Château **20**

Belguardo, Tenute **342**

Belisario **408**

Bell Wine Cellars **571**

Belland, Roger **92**

Bellavista **294**

Belle Vue, Château **43**

Belle, Albert **205**

Bellefont-Belcier, Château **63**

Bellegarde, Domaine **283**

Bellevue, Château **63**

Bellingham **727**

Bellivière, Domaine de **194**

Belondrade y Lurton **448**

Belvedere **541**

Ben Marco **613**

Benanti **415**

Benessere **571**

Benfield & Delamere **717**

Benotto, Carlo **323**

Benziger **527**

Bercher, Weingut **487**

Bergaglio, Nicola **323**

Bergdolt **504**

Bergé, Domaine Bertrand **272**

Bergkelder **727**

Beringer **549**

Beringer Blass **665**

Berliquet, Château **63**

Bernadotte, Château **43**

Bernard, Les Domaines **243**

Bernardins, Domaines des **243**

Bernardus **578**

Bernhard-Riebel, Domaine **163**

Berrod, René **151**

Berrys Bridge **680**

Bersan, Domaine **88**

Bersano **323**

Baerta, Guido **323**

Bertagna, Domaine **138**

Bertani **394**

Bertelli **295**

Bertheau, Pierre **138**

Berthet-Rayne, Domaine **243**

Berthoumieu, Domaine **278**

Berti, Stefano **400**

Bessin, Jean-Claude **78**

Best's **665**

Bethany **626**

Bethel Heights **601**

Beychevelle, Château **20**

Beyer, Lucien **155**

Beyerskloof **720**

Biale, Robert **549**

Bianchi **617**

Biffar, Josef **487**

Biguet, Domaine de **220**

Bilbainas, Bodegas **448**

Billard-Gonnet **138**

Billaud-Simon **78**

Billecart-Salmon **167**

Bindella **370**

Bindi **680**

Binomio **408**

Biondi-Santi **337**

Birchwood Estate **657**

Bisci **408**

Bisquertt **617**

Biston-Brillette, Chateau 43
Bitouzet-Prieur, Vincent 138
Bize, Domaine Simon et Fils 93
Black Ridge 716
Blackjack Ranch 588
Blain-Gagnard 93
Blanck, Domaine Paul 156
Blandy's 465
Blankiet Estate 571
Blass, Wolf 626
Bleasdale 657
Blin, H 174
Blockheadia Ringnosii 550
Blue Mountain 604
Boas Quintas 477
Boasso Gabutti, Franco 323
Boccadigabbia 400
Boeger 541
Boekenhoutskloof 720
Boesch, Léon 163
Bogle Vineyards 541
Boglietti, Enzo 295
Bogoni, Carlo 394
Boillot et Fils, Domaine Jean 94
Boillot et fils, Lucien 94
Boillot, Jean-Marc 94
Bois Dauphin 243
Bois de Boursan 223
Bois Guillaume, Domaine du 139
Boisseyt-Chol, Domaine 220
Boissonet, Domaine Frederic 220
Bollinger 167
Bon Pasteur, Chateau le 48
Bonalgue, Chateau 63
Bongiovanni 295
Bonhomme, Andre 142
Bonneau du Martray, Domaine 95
Bonneau, Henri 223
Bonnefond, Domaine 206
Bonnet, Alexandre 177
Bonnet, Château 48

Bonny Doon 579
Bonserine, Domaine de 206
Boplaas 727
Borges, H M 477
Borgo del Tiglio 378
Borgo Salcetino 370
Borgo San Daniele 379
Borgo Scopeto: 339
Borie de Maurel, Domaine 272
Borie La Vitarèle, Domaine 251
Boroli, S & E 323
Borsao 448
Borthwick 705
Boscarelli 337
Boschendal 727
Boschis, Francesco 323
Bosco, Ca' del 297
Bosquets des Papes 217
Bosquets, Domaine des 243
Botobolar 689
Botromagno 427
Bott-Geyl, Domaine 156
Bouchard Finlayson 720
Bouchard Père, et fils 95
Bouchard, Pascal 88
Bouchassy, Domaine 243
Bouchon, Viñedos Julio 617
Boudin, A & F 80
Bouissière, Domaine de la 243
Bouley, Jean-Marc 138
Bourgeois, Domaine Henri 184
Bourgeon, René 138
Bourillon-Dorléans, Domaine 185
Bouvet-Ladubay 194
Bouvier, Domaine René 139
Bouzereau Et Fils, Michel 96
Bovard, Domaine Louis 511
Bovio 323
Bowen Estate 627
Boxler, Albert 156
Boyd-Cantenac, Chateau 21

Boyer-Martenot **96**

Braida **296**

Brana, Domaine **283**

Branaire, Château **21**

Brand's of Coonawarra **627**

Brane-Cantenac, Château **21**

Breaky Bottom **523**

Brelière, Jean-Claude **139**

Bremerton **657**

Bressy Masson, Domaine **243**

Bretón, Bodegas **448**

Breton, Domaine **194**

Breuer, Georg **487**

Brewer Clifton **579**

Brezza, Giacomo **323**

Bricco Maiolica **296**

Bricco Mondalino **323**

Brick House **601**

Briday, Domaine Michel **139**

Brigaldara **394**

Briggs, August **541**

Bright Brothers **477**

Brindabella Hills **689**

Brintet, Domaine **96**

BRL Hardy **634**

Broadley Vineyards **601**

Brocard, Jean-Marc **79**

Broglia - La Meirano **323**

Brokenwood **685**

Brookland Valley **699**

Brovia **297**

Brown Brothers **666**

Brown, Chateau **43**

Bru-Baché, Domaine **283**

Bruce, David **588**

Brûlesécaille, Château **63**

Brumont, Alain **278**

Brun Despagne, Château **63**

Brun, Jean-Paul **152**

Bruna **323**

Bründlmayer **511**

Bruno, Domaine Paul **617**

Brunori, Mario & Giorgio **408**

Brusset, Domaine **224**

Bryant Family **550**

Bucci **408**

Buehler Vineyards **571**

Buhl, Reichstrat Von **488**

Buisserons, Domaine des **243**

Buitenverwachting **727**

Bullers Calliope **680**

Bunan, Domaines **272**

Buonamico, Fattoria del **338**

Burgaud, Bernard **205**

Burgaud, Jean-Marc **151**

Burge Family **628**

Burge, Grant **627**

Burgess Cellars **571**

Burguet, Alain **97**

Buring, Leo **657**

Bürklin-wolf **488**

Burmester **477**

Burn, Ernest **157**

Burrier, Joseph **151**

Burrowing Owl **604**

Bussia Soprana **297**

Bussola, Tommaso **379**

Buxy, Cave des Vigneron de **139**

BWC Wines **727**

By Farr **669**

Byington **588**

Byron **588**

C

C.A.R.M.I.M. **477**

Ca del Solo **579**

Ca' Rossa **323**

Ca' Dei Frati **379**

Ca' Marcanda **370**

Ca' Viola **298**

Cabasse, Domaine **243**

Cabotte, Domaine La **244**

Cabreo, Tenute del 347

Cabrière Estate 728

Cabrol, Domaine de 272

Cabutto 323

Cadence 601

Cadet Bon, Château 63

Cafaro 550

Caggiano, Antonio 415

Cailbourdin, Alain 185

Caillot, Domaine 139

Caillou, Château 21

Cain Cellars 550

Cakebread Cellars 551

Calatrasi 427

Caldaro, Viticoltori 394

Caldwell 571

Cálem 477

Calera 580

Caliterra 617

Callaghan Vineyards 605

Calon-Ségur, Château 21

Calot, Domaine F et J 143

Cambria 580

Camensac, Château 22

Cameron 600

Campbells 666

Campillo 448

Campo Viejo 448

Camus-Bruchon, Lucien 139

Can Feixes 448

Can Ràfols Dels Caus 448

Candido 427

Canepa 617

Canepa Cellars 541

Canet-Valette, Domaine 252

Canoe Ridge Vineyard 594

Canon, Château (Pomerol) 63

Canon, Château (Saint-Émilion) 48

Canon-de-Brem, Château 48

Canon-la-Gaffelière, Château 48

Canon-Moueix, Château 63

Cantelauze, Château 63

Cantele 427

Cantemerle, Château 22

Cantenac-Brown, Château 22

Cantina Colli Amerini 408

Cap de Mourlin, Château 63

Capaccia, Podere 370

Caparzo, Tenuta 338

Cape Mentelle 693

Capel Vale 693

Capezzana 339

Capiaux, Sean 541

Capichera, Tenute di 427

Capion, Domaine 272

Capmartin, Domaine 283

Cappellano 323

Caprai, Arnaldo 400

Caracciolo, Tenuta 408

Carbonnieux, Château 22

Cardinale 551

Carignan, Château 63

Carillon et Fils, Louis 97

Carlisle 541

Carmen 610

Carmenet 541

Carmes Haut-Brion, Château les 23

Carmignani, G. Fuso 370

Carneros Creek 571

Carobbio 370

Carparelli 427

Carpineto 370

Carré-Courbin, Domaine 139

Carretta, Tenuta 323

Carrick 716

Carriere, JK 601

Carsin, Château 49

Cartlidge and Browne 571

Casa Agricola Rui Madeira 477

Casa Castillo 436

Casa de la Ermita 448

Casa de Saima 477

Casa Emma 370

Casa Ferreirinha 462

Casa Lapostolle 611

Casa Santos Lima 477

Casa Silva 611

Casal Branco 477

Casale Bevagna 414

Casale-Falchini 370

Casaloste 339

Casanova di Neri 340

Cascabel 628

Cascina Castlèt 323

Cascina Chicco 298

Cascina Fonda 323

Cascina Garitina 323

Cascina La Ghersa 323

Cascina Monreale 323

Casenove, Domaine de 252

Casòn Hirschprunn 385

Cassagne Haut-Canon, Château 63

Cassan, Domaine de 243

Castel del Paolis 408

Castelgiocondo, Tenuta di 348

Castell del Remei 437

Castell'sches Domänenamt 504

Castellani & Figli, Michele 394

Castellare di Castellina 340

Castellari Bergaglio 323

Castello dei Rampolla 342

Castello del Terriccio 340

Castello del Trebbio 370

Castello della Paneretta 341

Castello della Sala 401

Castello di Ama 341

Castello di Argiano 372

Castello di Bossi 370

Castello di Brolio 361

Castello di Cacchiano 370

Castello di Farnetella 370

Castello di Fonterutoli 341

Castello di Meleto 370

Castello di Monsanto 343

Castello di Montepò 337

Castello di Poppiano 342

Castello di Querceto 370

Castello di Sesti 372

Castello Vicchiomaggio 344

Castello, Cantina del 394

Castelluccio 401

Castelmaure, Caves de 272

Castera, Domaine 283

Castiglioni, Castiglioni 348

Castorani, Podere 402

Castoro Cellars 588

Cataldi Madonna 408

Catena 610

Catena Zapata 610

Cathiard, Sylvain 97

Caudrina 299

Cauhapé, Domaine 279

Causse-Marines, Domaine de 283

Cavalleri 323

Cavalotto 299

Cave Coopérative de Fleurie 151

Cave de Cairanne 224

Cave de Cleebourg 163

Cave de Cocument 283

Cave des Clairmonts 220

Cave Spring Cellars 604

Caves Aliança 458

Caves du Mont Tauch 274

Caymus 551

Cayron, Domaine du 224

Cayuse 605

Cazenove, Charles de 177

Cazes, Domaine 252

Céago 541

Cecchi 370

CedarCreek 604

Celler de Cantonella 448

Celler de Capçanes 436

Celler del Pont 448

Cellier des Templiers **253**

Cellier Le Brun **716**

Cennatoio **370**

Centolani **370**

Cerbaiona **370**

Ceretto **300**

Cérons, Château de **63**

Certan-de-May, Château **49**

Cesani **370**

Cesconi **379**

Ceuso **416**

Château d'Acqueria **243**

Château de l'Amarine **272**

Château d'Ampuis **207**

Château d'Aydie **279**

Château Barréjat **280**

Château Bas **272**

Château Baudare **283**

Château de Beaucastel **225**

Château Beaulieu **280**

Château Belingard **283**

Château de Bellet **253**

Château Bellevue-La-Forêt **283**

Château Bonhomme **272**

Château Bouscassé **278**

Château Cabrières **243**

Château de Caladroy **272**

Château Calisanne **272**

Château Camplazens **272**

Château Campuget **272**

Château Caapitoul **253**

Château Cascadais **272**

Château Cazal-Viel **272**

Château du Cèdre **280**

Château de Cazeneuve **253**

Château de la Chaize **151**

Château de Chamirey **132**

Chateau des Charmes **604**

Château. de Combebelle **272**

Château de Coulaine **194**

Château Coupe Roses **272**

Château d'Epiré **185**

Château d'Esclans **272**

Château des Estanilles **254**

Château de Fesles **185**

Château. Flaugergues **272**

Château de Fonsalette **226**

Château. Fontségugne **243**

Château. Fortia **243**

Château Fuissé **143**

Château. Gaillard **195**

Château. Gaudrelle **195**

Château de la Genaiserie **193**

Château Gléon Montanie **272**

Château de Gourgazaud **272**

Château de Grand Moulas **243**

Château. Grand Moulin **272**

Château Grande-Cassagne **272**

Château Grès Saint-Paul **254**

Château Grézan **272**

Château Grillet **207**

Château de la Guimonière **186**

Château du Hureau **186**

Château des Jacques **144**

Château de Jau **273**

Château de Jonquières **255**

Château Kefraya **523**

Château l'Euzière **254**

Château l'Évangile **51**

Château La Baronne **272**

Château La Bastide **272**

Château La Canorgue **243**

Château Lafitte-Teston **283**

Château la Gardine **226**

Château Lagrezette **280**

Château La Moulière **283**

Château Lamartine **283**

Château La Nerthe **226**

Château La Roque **273**

Château La Sauvageonne **272**

Château de Lascaux **272**

Château de Lastours **272**

Château La Tuilerie **272**
Château La Varière **195**
Château La Voulte Gasparet **257**
Chateau Leamon **680**
Château Le Roc **283**
Château Le Thou **272**
Château Les Miadoux **283**
Château Les Rigalets **283**
Château Les Palais **272**
Château. de La Liquière **272**
Château de La Maltroye **140**
Château Mansenoble **272**
Château Maris **272**
Château Masburel **283**
Château Mas Neuf **255**
Château Maucoil **243**
Château Megyer **523**
Château de Mercey **132**
Chateau Montelena **552**
Château Montlys **220**
Château de Montmirail **243**
Château de Montpezat **272**
Château Montus **279**
Château du Moulin-à-Vent **152**
Château Mont-Redon **226**
Château Mourgues du Grès **255**
Chateau Musar **523**
Château de La Négly **272**
Château de Nouvelles **273**
Ch. d'Or et de Gueules **256**
Château D'Oupia **273**
Château Pajzos **523**
Château Pech-Celeyran **273**
Château Pech-Latt **273**
Château Pesqué **227**
Château Peyros **283**
Château de Pibarnon **256**
Château Pierre-Bise **187**
Château Plaisance **283**
Château Planères **273**
Chateau Potelle **552**

Château Pradeaux **256**
Château Puech-Haut **273**
Château de la Ragotière **195**
Château Rayas **227**
Château Real Martin **273**
Château Redortier **227**
Château de Ripaille **283**
Château Roche Redonne **273**
Château Romanin **273**
Château des Rontets **144**
Château de Roquefort **273**
Château. des Roques **243**
Château de Rouanne **243**
Château de la Roulerie **186**
Château Roumanières **273**
Château Routas **256**
Château du Rozay **220**
Château de Rully **132**
Château Saint-Auriol **273**
Château Saint-Cosme **227**
Château Saint-Estève d'Uchaux **228**
Chateau St Jean **528**
Château Saint-Roch **243**
Château Sainte-Eulalie **273**
Château de Sainte-Louande **195**
Chateau Ste Michelle **594**
Château. des Sarrins **273**
Château de la Saule **139**
Château de Segries **243**
Château Signac **243**
Château Simone **257**
Château de Soucherie **195**
Chateau Souverain **541**
Château Theulet **283**
Château Thivin **144**
Château de Tigné **195**
Château Tirecul-la-Gravière **281**
Château de Tiregand **283**
Château Tour des Gendres **281**
Château. des Tours **228**
Château de Tracy **187**

Château. du Trignon **243**
Château Val Joanis **243**
Château de Valcombe **237**
Château Vannières **257**
Château de La Verrerie **243**
Château Veyran **273**
Château Viella **281**
Château Vignelaure **273**
Château de Villeneuve **187**
Château Villerambert-Julien **273**
Château Virgile **273**
Chablisienne, La **79**
Chain Of Ponds **628**
Chalk Hill Winery **527**
Chalone **580**
Chambers Rosewood **666**
Champ des Treilles, Château du **63**
Champalou, Didier **185**
Champet, Joel **220**
Champy, Maison **98**
Chanabas, Domaine de **243**
Chandon de Briailles **98**
Chandon, Domaine **670**
Chanrion, Nicole **151**
Chanson, Pere et Fils **139**
Chante Perdrix **243**
Chantegrive, Chateau de **23**
Chantemerle, Domaine de **80**
Chapel Down **523**
Chapel Hill **629**
Chapelle Lenclos **280**
Chapoutier Australia **629**
Chapoutier, M **206**
Chappellet **551**
Charavin, Didier **243**
Charbaut, Guy **177**
Charbonnière, Domaine de la **225**
Chard Farm **716**
Chardonnay, Domaine du **88**
Charlemagne, Guy **177**
Charlopin, Philippe **99**

Charmail, Chateau **23**
Charpentier, Jacky **177**
Charrière, Domaine de la **190**
Chartron & Trebuchet **139**
Charvet, Gerard **151**
Charvin, Gerard **225**
Chasse-Spleen, Chateau **23**
Chatelain, Jean-Claude **185**
Chatenay, Laurent **195**
Chatenoy, Domaine de **195**
Chatsfield **694**
Chaume-Arnaud, Domaine **228**
Chauvenet, Jean **139**
Chauvenet-Chopin, Hubert **139**
Chauvin, Chateau **49**
Chave, Domaine Yann **208**
Chave, Jean-Louis **208**
Chavy et Fils, Gerard **99**
Chehalem **595**
Chêne, Domaine du **208**
Chênes, Domaine des **258**
Cherchi, Giovanni **417**
Chereau-Carre **195**
Chestnut Grove **699**
Cheval Blanc, Château **49**
Chevalier, Domaine de **24**
Chevillon, Robert **100**
Cheysson, Domaine Emile **151**
Chèze, Domaine Louis **208**
Chiappini, Giovanni **370**
Chiarlo, Michele **300**
Chidaine, Francois **195**
Chignard, Michel **151**
Chimney Rock **571**
Chionetti, Quinto **300**
Chivite **448**
Chofflet-Valdenaire **139**
Chorey, Domaine du Château de **100**
Christmann **489**
Christoffel, Joh. Jos **504**
Christopher Creek **541**

Church Road **711**

Churchill **459**

Ciacci Piccolomini D'Aragona **344**

Cigliuti, Fratelli **300**

Cima **370**

Cimicky, Charles **629**

Cims de Porrera **437**

Cinelli Colombini, Donatella **370**

Cissac, Château **24**

Citadelle, Domaine de la **243**

Citran, Château **43**

Clair, Bruno **100**

Clair, Denis et Françoise **139**

Clairault **699**

Clape, Auguste **209**

Clarendon Hills **630**

Clarke, Château **24**

Classic Mclaren **657**

Clavel, Domaine **258**

Clavelier, Bruno **101**

Clelia Romano **427**

Clerc-Milon, Chateau **24**

Clerico, Domenico **301**

Clifford Bay Estate **717**

Climens, Château **25**

Cline Cellars **552**

Clinet, Château **50**

Clonakilla **685**

Clos d'Agon **448**

Clos de l'Anhel **273**

Clos Bagatelle **273**

Clos Baudoin **195**

Clos du Bois **528**

Clos de la Briderie **195**

Clos du Caillou **229**

Clos des Cazaux **229**

Clos Centeilles **258**

Clos du Clocher **63**

Clos de la Coulée de Serrant **187**

Clos des Fées, Domaine du **258**

Clos du Fief, Domaine du **152**

Clos Figueras **448**

Clos Floridène **25**

Clos Fourtet **53**

Clos Haut-Peyraguey, Chateau **25**

Clos i Terasses **437**

Clos des Jacobins, Château **63**

Clos du Jaugeyron **43**

Clos du Joncuas **243**

Clos la Coutale **283**

Clos LaChance **580**

Clos Lapeyre **282**

Clos l'Église **50**

Clos Marie **273**

Clos du Mont Olivet **229**

Clos Mogador **438**

Clos Naudin, Domaine du **188**

Clos de l'Oratoire **57**

Clos de l'Oratoire des Papes **243**

Clos Pegase **571**

Clos Petite Bellane **230**

Clos Puy Arnaud **59**

Clos del Rey **273**

Clos de la Roilette / Coudert **144**

Clos Rougeard **188**

Clos Sainte-Magdeleine **273**

Clos Saint-Landelin, Domaine du **160**

Clos Saint-Michel **243**

Clos Salomon **139**

Clos de los Siete **611**

Clos de Tart **101**

Clos Thou **283**

Clos Triguedina **282**

Clos Uroulat **282**

Clos du Val **571**

Clos de Varenne **186**

Closel, Domaine du **188**

Clos Roche Blanche **195**

Clotte, Chateau la **50**

Cloudy Bay **706**

Clovallon, Domaine de **272**

Clusel Roch **209**

Cluver, Paul **727**

Coche-Bizouard, Domaine Alain **139**

Coche-Dury, Jean-Francois **102**

Cockburn **459**

Coderche, Jorge **618**

Codorniu **448**

Coffaro, David **541**

Cognard, Max **195**

Cogno, Elvio **301**

Cohn, B R **541**

Col d'Orcia **345**

Cold Heaven **581**

Coldstream Hills **667**

Colgin Cellars **554**

Colin, Domaine Marc et Fils **102**

Colin-Deléger, Michel et Fils **102**

Colinot, Anita et Jean-Pierre **80**

Colla, Poderi **323**

Collards **717**

Collelungo **370**

Collemattone **370**

Collesorbo **370**

Collet, Domaine Jean et fils **88**

Colli di Lapio **427**

Collier, Domaine du **195**

Colombaio di Cencio **345**

Colombier, Domaine du **209**

Colombo, Domaine Jean-Luc **210**

Colonge, Andre **151**

Colonial Wine Company **657**

Colosi, Cantine **427**

Colpetrone **408**

Colterenzio **380**

Columbia Crest **595**

Columbia Winery **595**

Combe-Blanche, Domaine de la **273**

Combier, Domaine **210**

Commanderie de Peyrassol **273**

Concannon **588**

Concha y Toro **612**

Concièrgerie, Domaine de la **88**

Condé **727**

Confiance, Ma **63**

Confuron , Domaine Jean-Jacques **103**

Confuron-Cotétidot, Domaine Jack **103**

Conn Creek **571**

Cono SUR **612**

Conseillante, Chateau la **50**

Constantia Uitsig **727**

Conterno, Aldo **301**

Conterno, Giacomo **301**

Conterno, Paolo **323**

Conterno-Fantino **302**

Conti, Leone **408**

Conti, Paul **699**

Contini, Attilio **427**

Contino **438**

Contrada Castelletta **408**

Contratto **302**

Contucci **370**

Cooper Mountain Vineyards **601**

Coppo, Luigi & Figli **302**

Corbans (Marlborough) **711**

Corbillères, Domaine de **195**

Cordero di Montezemolo **303**

Cordier, Domaine Père et Fils **145**

Cordoba **727**

Corey Creek **604**

Coriançon, Domaine des **243**

Corino, Giovanni **303**

Coriole **630**

Corison **553**

Corne-Loup, Domaine du **244**

Cornerstone Cellars **571**

Coroncino **402**

Correggia, Matteo **303**

Corsin **145**

Corte Sant'Alda **380**

Corteforte **394**

Cortes de Cima **459**

Cortese, Guiseppe **323**

Cos **427**

Cos d'Estournel, Château **25**

Cos Labory, Château **26**

Cosentino **571**

Cossart Gordon **465**

Costanti **346**

Costantini, Piero **408**

Costers del Siurana **438**

Cotat, Pascal/Francis **188**

Cote Monpezat, Château **63**

Coteaux des Travers, Domaine **230**

Cottanera **417**

Cotturi **541**

Coufran, Château **43**

Couhins-Lurton, Château **26**

Couly-Dutheil **195**

Courbis, Domaine **210**

Courcel, Domaine de **104**

Couroulu, Domaine du **244**

Coursodon, Domaine Pierre **211**

Courtade, Domaine de la **259**

Courteillac, Domaine de **63**

Courtilles, Domaine de **273**

Cousiño Macul **617**

Couspaude, Château la **51**

Coutet, Château **26**

Crabtree **631**

Craggy Range **706**

Craig, Robert **553**

Craiglee **667**

Crampilh, Domaine du **284**

Craneford **657**

Crawford, Kim **717**

Crianza Castilla la Vieja,Bodegas de **436**

Crios **613**

Cristia, Domaine de **244**

Cristiano Van Zeller **463**

Cristom **596**

Crochet, Lucien **189**

Croft **460**

Croix Canon, La **63**

Croix de Labrie **63**

Croix Senaillet, Domaine de la **151**

Croix-de-Gay, Château la **51**

Cronin **589**

Cros de la Mure **230**

Cros, Château du **63**

Crown Estates **523**

Crozes, Domaine de la Voute des **151**

Cru Barréjats **43**

Crusius **504**

Cuadrado, Hermanos **437**

Cuilleron, Domaine Olivier **244**

Cuilleron, Yves **211**

Cullen **694**

Culombu, Domaine **272**

Cusona **370**

Cusumano **416**

Cuvaison **553**

CVNE **448**

D

D'Angelo **418**

Dagueneau, Didier **189**

Dagueneau, Jean-Claude **195**

Dal Forno, Romano **381**

Dalem, Château **63**

D'Alessandro, Luigi **346**

Dalla Valle **554**

Dalwhinnie **667**

Damijan **394**

Damilano **323**

Damoy, Domaine Pierre **104**

Dampt, Daniel **80**

Dancer, Vincent **139**

Dão Sul **467**

D'Arenberg **631**

Darioush **554**

Dark Star **589**

Darling Cellars **727**

Darviot-Perrin **104**

Dashwood **715**

Dassault, Château **63**

Daubrée, Martin **220**

Dauphine, Château de la **63**

Dauvissat, Rene et Vincent **80**

Dauzac, Château **26**

Davalos, Raul **617**

Davis Bynum **541**

Daysse, Domaine de la **244**

De Angelis, Tenuta **408**

De Bartoli, Marco **418**

De Batté, Walter **323**

De Bortoli **686**

De Bortoli (Victoria) **668**

De Bortoli Yarra Valley **668**

De Castellane **177**

De Conciliis **427**

de Cruzeau, Château **43**

De Sousa **177**

De Toren **727**

De Trafford **727**

De Venoge **177**

Decugnano dei Barbi **408**

Defaix, Daniel-Etienne **81**

Dehlinger **528**

Dei **346**

Deiss, Marcel **157**

Del Cerro **370**

Del Dotto **571**

Delaforce **460**

Delamotte **177**

Delaporte, Vincent **195**

Delas Frères **211**

Delatite **668**

Delaunay, Domaine **195**

Delbeck **177**

Delegat's **717**

Delesvaux, Philippe **189**

Delétang, Olivier **190**

Delgado Zuleta **448**

Delheim **727**

Delille Cellars **596**

De Loach **541**

Deltetto **323**

Denbies **521**

Denois, Jean-Louis **273**

Desmirail, Château **43**

Destieux, Château **63**

Desvignes, Domaine Louis-Claude **145**

Déthune, Paul **177**

Dettori **418**

Deurre, Domaine de **230**

Deutz **168**

Deux Roches, Domaine des **145**

Devevey, Jean-Yves **139**

Devil's Lair **700**

Dézat, Andre **195**

Dezi **408**

DFJ Vinhos **477**

Di Majo Norante **402**

Diamond Creek **554**

Diamond Valley **668**

Diconne, Jean-Pierre **139**

Diefenhard **504**

Diemersfonteine **727**

Diffonty et Fils **244**

Digioia-Royer **139**

Diochon, Domaine **151**

Dipoli, Peter **394**

Dirler-Cadé, Domaine **163**

Disznókö **521**

Doisy-Daëne, Château **26**

Doisy-Védrines, Château **27**

Domaine Carneros **554**

Domaine Chandon **555**

Domaine Santa Barbara **589**

Domaine Ste Michelle **596**

Domäne Wachau **513**

Domdechant Werner'sches **489**

Domecq, Pedro **439**

Domingos Soares Franco **463**

Dominio de Pingus **438**

Dominio de Valdepusa **441**

Dominio del Plata **612**

Dominique, Château La **51**

Dominus Estate **555**

Donnafugata **419**

Dönnhoff **489**

Dopff & Irion **163**

Dopff au Moulin **163**

Doquet-Jeanmaire **177**

Dorices, Domaine des **195**

Dorigo, Girolamo **381**

Dover Canyon **589**

Dow **460**

Dr Pauly-Bergweiler **500**

Drappier **177**

Draytons **689**

Drei Donà - La Palazza **402**

Driftwood Estate **700**

Drius, Sergio & Mauro **394**

Droin, Jean-Paul **81**

Dromana Estate **669**

Drouhin, Domaine **596**

Drouhin, Joseph **82, 105**

Drouin, Corinne et Thierry **151**

Drouin, Jean-Michel **151**

Druet, Pierre-Jacques **190**

Dry Creek Vineyards **529**

Dry River **707**

Duband, David **139**

Duboeuf, George **146**

Dubost, Domaine **151**

Duc de Magenta **115**

Duca di Salaparuta **427**

Duclaux, Domaine **244**

Duclaux, Edmond et David **220**

Ducru-Beaucaillou **27**

Dugat, Claude **105**

Dugat-Py, Bernard **106**

Duhart-Milon, Château **27**

Dujac, Domaine **106**

Dumaine, Olivier **220**

Dumangin, Jacky **177**

Dumazet, Pierre **212**

Dumien-Surette, Domaine **220**

Dumol **541**

Dunham Cellars **601**

Duplessis, Gerard **82**

Durand, Eric et Joel **212**

Durrand-Perron, Domaine **284**

Durban, Domaine **231**

Dureil-Janthial, Domaine Vincent **107**

Durup et Fils, Jean **82**

Dutschke **631**

Duval-Leroy **177**

Duxoup Wine Works **541**

E

Easton **588**

Eberle Winery **589**

Ecard, Maurice et Fils **139**

Echeverria **617**

Écu, Domaine de l' **195**

Edmeades **529**

Edmunds St John **581**

Edna Valley **581**

Edwards & Chaffey **632**

Edwards, Luis Felipe **618**

Edwards, Merry **541**

Église-Clinet, Chateau l' **51**

Egly-Ouriet **168**

Ehler's Grove **571**

Eikendal **727**

Einaudi, Luigi **304**

El Molino **571**

El Principal **613**

Elderton **632**

Élise, Domaine d' **88**

Elk Cove **601**

Ellis, Neil **727**

Elyse **571**

Emrich-Schönleber **490**

Enate **448**

Enclos, Domaine de L' **235**

Engel, Domaine Rene **107**

Ente, Arnaud 107

Ermitage du Pic Saint Loup 273

Errázuriz 612

Erste & Neue – Prima & Nuova 394

Esk Valley 716

Esmonin, Frederic 107

Esmonin, Sylvie 108

Espiers, Domaine des 231

Esporão 461

Estancia 589

Estézargues, Cave d' 244

Etchart 617

Etoile, L' 274

Etude 571

Etxegaraya, Domaine 284

Eugénio de Almeida, Fundacao 477

Europvin Falset 448

Evans & Tate 695

Evans Family 686

Evharis Estate 521

Excellence de Bois Pertuis 52

Eymael, Robert 498

Eyrie Vineyard 601

Eyrins, Château des 43

F

Fabre Montmayou 617

Facchin, Christian 220

Failla Jordan 541

Fairhall Downs 717

Fairview Estate 721

Faiveley, Domaine 108

Faizeau, Château 63

Falasco 395

Falesco 403

Falfas, Château 63

Fall Creek 604

Fantino, Alessandro & Gian Natale 323

Fargues, Château de 43

Far Niente 556

Fassati 371

Faugères, Château 52

Faurie, Bernard 212

Faury, Philippe 220

Fauterie, Domaine de 212

Fayolle, Cave 220

Fazi Battaglia 408

Feiler-Artinger 511

Felline 414

Felluga, Livio 381

Felluga, Marco 390

Felsina, Fattoria di 347

Felton Road 707

Feotto dello Jato 427

Feraud-Brunel 231

Fermoy Estate 700

Fernández, Alejandro 439

Ferrand, Domaine de 244

Ferrando 323

Ferrara, Benito 427

Ferrari 394

Ferrari Carano 541

Ferraton, Domaine Michel 220

Ferreira 461

Ferrer-Ribière 273

Ferret, Domaine J A 146

Ferrière 27

Fessy, Henry 147

Fetzer Vineyards 530

Feudi di San Gregorio 419

Feudo Principi di Butera 427

Fèvre, William 83

Feytit-Clinet, Château 63

Fichet, Jean-Philippe 109

Fiddlehead Cellars 589

Fieuzal, Château de 27

Fife 571

Figeac, Château 52

Filhot, Château 43

Filiputti & D'Isanto 371

Filiputti, Walter 382

Filliatreau 195

Finca Allende **434**

Finca El Retiro **617**

Finca Flichman **617**

Fire Gully **698**

Firestone **589**

Firriato **427**

Fisher **541**

Flacher, Gilles **220**

Flagstone **727**

Fleur-Cardinale, Château **63**

Fleur-Pétrus, Château la **52**

Flora Springs **556**

Florio, Cantine **427**

Flowers **542**

Fog, Adrian **542**

Fogarty, Thomas **589**

Foillard, Jean **147**

Fojo **462**

Foley Estate **589**

Folie à Deux **571**

Folonari, Tenute di Ambrogio e Giovanni **347**

Fombrauge, Château **53**

Fonbadet, Château **43**

Fondrèche, Domaine de **232**

Fonroque, Château **63**

Fonseca **462**

Fonseca, José Maria da **463**

Font Caude, Domaine **259**

Font de Michelle **232**

Font Sane, Domaine de **232**

Fontaine-Gagnard, Richard **109**

Fontana Candida **408**

Fontanabianca **323**

Fontanafredda **304**

Fontanel, Domaine **259**

Fontedicto **273**

Fontenil, Château **53**

Fontenille, Domaine de **244**

Fontodi **347**

Foppiano **530**

Foradori **382**

Força-Real **273**

Forest, Michel **151**

Forey, Domaine Père et Fils **139**

Forges, Domaine des **190**

Forman **571**

Forrest Estate **717**

Forteto della Luja **304**

Fossacolle **371**

Fourgeray de Beauclair **139**

Four Sisters **674**

Fournier, Domaine **195**

Fourrier, Domaine **109**

Fowler, Ralph **632**

Fox Creek **633**

Fox Run **604**

Foxen **589**

Franc Mayne, Château de **63**

Francs, Château de **63**

Frank, Dr. Konstantin **604**

Frankland Estate **695**

Franus, Peter **557**

Freemark Abbey **571**

Freie Weingärtner Wachau **512**

Freixenet **448**

Frejau, Domaine Lou **244**

Frescobaldi, Marchesi de' **348**

Frescobaldi/Mondavi **348**

Freycinet **680**

Frick **530**

Frick, Pierre **163**

Fritz Winery **530**

Frog's Leap **557**

Fromm **707**

Fuentes, Cellers J M, **439**

Fuligni **349**

Fürst, Rudolf **505**

G

Gachon, Domaine **220**

Gadais, Domaine **195**

Gaffelière, Château la **53**

Gagliole **349**

Gagnard, Jean-Noël **110**

Gaia Estate **523**

Gaillard, Pierre **213**

Gainey **581**

Gaja **304**

Galah **657**

Galardi **420**

Galet des Papes **244**

Gallet, Henri **220**

Gallino, Filippo **305**

Gallo of Sonoma **531**

Gallois, Dominique **139**

Galluccio **604**

Gallura, Cantina **427**

Gangloff, Domaine Yves **213**

Gantenbein **518**

Garaudet, Paul **139**

Garde, Château la **43**

Gardet **177**

Gardies, Domaine **260**

Garetto, Tenuta **323**

Garofoli **403**

Gary Farrell **529**

Gasse, Vincent **220**

Gastaldi **323**

Gatinois **177**

Gauby, Domaine **260**

Gaunoux, Jean-Michel **139**

Gaussen, Jean-Pierre **273**

Gavoty **273**

Gay, Château le **63**

Gay-Coperet, Domaine **151**

Gazin, Château **54**

Geantet-Pansiot **110**

Gehringer Brothers **604**

Gehrs, Daniel **589**

Génot-Boulanger **139**

Geoffrey, Domaine Alain **88**

Geoffroy, René **177**

Gerbeaux, Domaine des **151**

Gerin, Jean-Michel **213**

Germain, Domaine Henri et Fils **110**

Germano, Ettore **305**

Geyser Peak **531**

Ghisolfi, Attilio **306**

Ghizzano, Tenuta di **349**

Giaconda **669**

Giacosa, Bruno **306**

Giacosa, Fratelli **323**

Gialdi **518**

Gibbston Valley **717**

Giesen **717**

Gigou, Joël **190**

Gilberts **700**

Gilette, Château **43**

Gillardi **324**

Gimonnet, Pierre et Fils **168**

Gineste, Domaine de **284**

Ginglinger, Paul **163**

Gini **394**

Girard **571**

Girard, Jean-Jacques **139**

Girardin, Vincent **111**

Giraud, Henri **177**

Girault, Pierre **195**

Giroud, Camille **139**

Gisborne **711**

Giscours, Château **43**

Gitton, Domaine **195**

Glaetzer **657**

Glen Carlou **721**

Glenara **657**

Glenguin **689**

Gloria, Château **28**

Goisot, Ghislaine et Jean-Hugues **83**

Goldridge Estate **717**

Goldwater Estate **708**

Gonon, Domaine **220**

González Byass **440**

Gosset **169**

Göttelmann, Weingut **490**

Gouges, Domaine Henri 111
Gould Campbell 476
Goulet, Georges 177
Goundrey 695
Gourt de Mautens 233
Goutorbe, Henri 177
Gracia 63
Gracia (Chile) 614
Graham 464
Graillot, Alain 214
Gramenon, Domaine 233
Gramp, Tim 657
Grand Bourjassot, Domaine 244
Grand Crès, Domaine du 273
Grand Devers, Domaine des 244
Grand Recosind 448
Grand Renouil, Château 63
Grand Tinel, Domaine de 233
Grand Veneur, Domaine 244
Grand-Mayne, Château 54
Grand-Pontet, Château 54
Grand-Puy-Ducasse, Château 43
Grand-Puy-Lacoste, Château 28
Grands Chênes, Château les 44
Grange des Pères, Domaine de la 260
Grangehurst 721
Grangeneuve, Domaine de 244
Granger, Pascal 151
Granja Fillaboa 448
Grans-Fassian 491
Grapillon d'Or, Domaine 234
Grasso, Elio 306
Grasso, Fratelli 324
Grasso, Silvio 307
Gratien & Meyer 195
Gratien, Alfred 169
Grattamacco 349
Grave, Château la 63
Gravner, Josko 395
Gray Monk 604
Grecaux 273

Green, Patricia 597
Green and Red Vineyard 558
Green Point Vineyards 670
Greenhough 717
Greenock Creek 633
Greenwood Ridge Vineyards 542
Gresser, A & F 163
Greysac, Château 44
Grgich Hills 558
Grimaldi, Giacomo 324
Gripa, Domaine Bernard 220
Grippat, Jean-Louis 214
Grivault, Albert 140
Grivot, Domaine Jean 112
Groffier, Robert 112
Groot Constantia 727
Gros, A F 112
Gros, Anne 113
Gros, Frère et Soeur 139
Gros, Michel 113
Gros Noré, Domaine du 261
Gross, Alois 518
Grosse Pierre, Domaine de la 152
Grosset 633
Grossot, Jean-Pierre 83
Groth 571
Grove Mill 708
Gruaud-Larose, Château 28
Guado al Tasso 335
Gualdo del Re 350
Guelbenzu 448
Guenoc 542
Guerrieri Rizzardi 395
Guffens-Heynen, Domaine 147
Guicciardini Strozzi 370
Guigal, E 214
Guillemot-Michel, Pierette et Marc 151
Guindon, Domaine 195
Guiraud, Château 28
Gulf Station 668
Gunderloch 491

Gundlach-Bundschu **542**

Gutiérrez de la Vega **448**

Guyon, Domaine Antonin **113**

Guyot, Domaine Jean-Claude **195**

H

Haag, Weingut Fritz **491**

Haan **657**

Haart, Reinhold **492**

Haas, Franz **383**

Hacienda Monasterio **448**

Hain,Kurt **504**

Hamelin, Thierry **88**

Hamilton **634**

Hamilton Russell Vineyards **722**

Hamilton's Ewell **657**

Handley **542**

Hanging Rock **670**

Hanna **542**

Hanzell **531**

Hardegg, Graf **518**

Hardy, Geoff **658**

Hardys **635**

Harlan Estate **558**

Hartford **532**

Hartford Court **532**

Hartford Family Winery **532**

Hartwell Vineyards **571**

Haselgrove **635**

Hatton Estate **717**

Hauner **427**

Haut-Bages-Libéral, Château **44**

Haut-Bailly, Château **29**

Haut-Batailley, Château **29**

Haut-Bergeron, Château **44**

Haut-Bergey, Château **44**

Haut-Bertinerie, Château **63**

Haut-Brion, Château **29**

Haut-Carles, Château **63**

Haut-Chaigneau, Château **63**

Haut-Corbin, Château **63**

Hauteborne, Domaine de la **195**

Haut-Gardère, Château **44**

Haut-Marbuzet, Château **29**

Haut-Tropchaud, Château **63**

Havens **559**

Hawthorne Mountain **604**

Hayshed Hill **700**

Haywood **542**

Heathcote Winery **670**

Heddesdorff, Freiherr Von **504**

Hedges Cellars **601**

Heger, Dr **504**

Heggies **656**

Heidsieck, Charles **169**

Heinrich **517**

Heitz Cellars **559**

Heller Estate **589**

Hendry **571**

Henriot **169**

Henriques & Henriques **458**

Henry **273**

Henry Estate **601**

Henry of Pelham **604**

Henrys Drive **635**

Henschke **636**

Herdade dos Coelheiros **477**

Herdade Grande **477**

Heresztyn **140**

Heritage Wines **658**

Héritier **274**

Héritiers Comtes Lafon, Domaine des **151**

Hermitage, Domaine de L' **273**

Herzog **717**

Hess Collection **559**

Hessen, Prinz von **492**

Heyl zu Herrnsheim, Freiherr **492**

Heymann-Löwenstein **493**

Hidalgo **440**

Hidden Cellars **542**

Hiedler **518**

Hilberg - Pasquero **324**

Hillebrand **604**
Hillstowe **636**
Hirsch **513**
Hirtzberger, Franz **512**
Hobbs, Paul **532**
Hoff, Stephen **657**
Hofstätter **383**
Hohler **324**
Hollick **637**
Hommage de Malesan **63**
Hood Wines **671**
Hope Estate **689**
Hop Kiln **542**
Hortus, Domaine de l' **261**
Hosanna, Château **63**
Houghton **696**
Hövel, Von **504**
Howard Park **696**
Howell Mountain Vineyard **571**
Hudelot-Noëllat **114**
Huet L'Echansonne **191**
Hugel et Fils **158**
Humbert Frères **140**
Hunter's **708**
Huntington Estate **686**

I

I Balzini **371**
I Feudi di Romans **395**
I Giusti & Zanza **371**
I Paglieri - Roagna **324**
Icardi **307**
Ijalba **441**
Il Borro **371**
Il Bruscello **371**
Il Carnasciale **371**
Il Carpino **383**
Il Greppone Mazzi **362**
Il Macchione **371**
Il Palazzino **350**
Il Paradiso **372**

Il Podere dell' Olivos **582**
Il Poggione **351**
Ilarria, Domaine **284**
Illuminati **408**
Imesch Vins **518**
Inama **384**
Incognito **651**
Ingoldby **657**
Inniskillin **604**
Inniskillin Okanagan **604**
Intesi, Cantine **408**
Iron Horse Vineyards **532**
Irvine **657**
Isabel Estate **709**
Isabella **324**
Isole e Olena **350**
Issan, Château d' **30**

J

J Wine Company **542**
J P Vinhos **464**
Jaboulet Ainé, Paul **214**
Jack and Knox Winecraft **727**
Jackson Estate **717**
Jackson-Triggs **604**
Jacob, Domaine Lucien **138**
Jacquart **177**
Jacquart, A **177**
Jacqueson, Henri et Paul **114**
Jacquesson **170**
Jade Mountain **560**
Jadot, Louis **115**
Jaffurs Cellars **589**
Jamek, Josef **518**
Jamesport **604**
Jamet, Domaine **215**
Jamiesons Run **637**
Janasse, Domaine de la **234**
Janin, Domaine Paul et Eric **148**
Janodet, Jacky **151**
Jarvis **571**

Jasmin, Domaine **215**
Jasper Hill **671**
Javillier, Patrick **115**
Jayer-Gilles, Domaine **140**
J C Cellars **589**
Jeanneret **657**
Jeannin-Naltet, Domaine **140**
Jenke **657**
Jermann, Vinnaioli **384**
Jobard, Francois **116**
Jobard, Rémi **116**
Joblot, Domaine **140**
Joguet, Domaine Charles **195**
Johannishof, Weingut **504**
John, Stephen **657**
Johner, Karl-Heinz **504**
Joly, Domaine Virgile **273**
Joncier, Domaine du **244**
Jones Family **571**
Jones, Trevor **638**
Jonqueyres, Château les **63**
Jordan **727**
Jordan, J **542**
Josmeyer **163**
Jost, Weingut Toni **493**
Jouard, Vincent et François **140**
Judd's Hill **571**
Juge, Domaine Marcel **220**
Juillot, Domaine Émile **140**
Juillot, Domaine Michel **116**
Juliusspital **493**
Jung, Domaine Roger **163**
Juris **517**
Jurtschitsch Sonnhof **513**
Justices, Château les **44**
Justin **582**

K
Kaapzicht **727**
Kangarilla Road **657**
Kanonkop **722**

Kante, Edi **394**
Karina Vineyard **680**
Karlsmühle **494**
Karly **589**
Karrivale **700**
Karriview **700**
Karthäuserhof, Weingut. **494**
Katnook Estate **638**
Keenan, Robert **571**
Kendall-Jackson **533**
Kennedy, Kathryn **582**
Kenwood Vineyards **542**
Kerpen, Heribert **504**
Kesseler, August **504**
Kesselstatt, Von **494**
Kientzler, André **158**
Kilikanoon **638**
Killerby **700**
King Estate **597**
Kirkland Ranch **571**
Kirwan, Château **30**
Kistler **533**
Klein Constantia **727**
Knappstein **639**
Knappstein Lenswood **639**
Knight Granite Hills **680**
Knipser **505**
Knoll, Emmerich **514**
Koehler-Ruprecht **505**
Kollwentz-Römerhof **513**
Kongsgaard **560**
Konzelmann **604**
Koves-Newlan **571**
Kracher **514**
Kreydenweiss, Marc **158**
Krug **170**
Kruger-Rumpf **505**
Kuentz-Bas **163**
Kühn, Peter Jakob **495**
Kumeu River **709**
Kunde Estate **542**
Künstler, Franz **496**

L

L'Avenir **727**

L'Ecole No **41 597**

La Agricola **617**

La Arboleda **618**

La Barbatella **307**

La Bastide Blanche, Domaine **261**

La Berta **408**

La Bienfaisance, Château **47**

La Braccesca **334**

La Brancaia **352**

La Cappucina **392**

La Carraia **408**

La Castellada **395**

La Cerbaiola **363**

La Ciarliana **371**

La Comandina **371**

La Corte **420**

La Crema **534**

La Croix de Peyrolie **54**

La Ferme Blanche **273**

La Fiorita Lamborghini **404**

La Fleur du Boùard **63**

La Fourmone, Domaine **244**

La Fuga, Tenuta **347**

La Galantin **273**

La Garance, Domaine de **273**

La Garrigue, Domaine **232**

La Gerla **371**

La Giustiniana **308**

La Grange de Quatre Sous **273**

La Jasse Castel **273**

La Jota **562**

La Lagune, Château **31**

La Massa **352**

La Monacesca **404**

La Mondotte **55**

La Morandina **324**

La Motte **727**

La Navette, Domaine **244**

La Palazzola **408**

La Poderina **371**

La Préceptorie de Centernach **273**

La Rampa di Fugnano **371**

La Regola **371**

La Rocalière, Domaine **244**

La Roquette, Domaine **234**

La Rosa **618**

La Sansonina **394**

La Scolca **308**

La Selva **371**

La Serénité **32**

La Sirena **571**

La Soufrandière, Domaine **149**

La Soufrandise, Domaine **151**

La Soumade, Domaine **236**

La Spinetta **308**

La Strada **708**

La Suffrène **273**

La Tapada **448**

La Terrasse d'Elise **273**

La Tosa **408**

La Tour-Carnet, Château **44**

La Tour Vieille, Domaine **262**

La Tour-Boisée **274**

La Valentina **408**

La Viola **409**

La Volta, Tenuta **323**

Labastide Saint-Dominique, Domaine **244**

Labégorce-Zédé, Château **44**

Labet, Domaine **284**

Labranche-Laffont, Domaine **284**

Lackner-Tinnacher **518**

Lacroix-Vanel, Domaine **273**

Ladoucette, De **195**

Laetitia **584**

Lafarge, Michel **117**

Lafaurie-Peyraguey, Château **30**

Lafite-Rothschild, Château **30**

Lafleur, Château **55**

Lafleur-Gazin, Château **63**

Lafon, Château **44**

Lafon, Domaine des Comtes **117**

Lafond-Roc-Epine, Domaine **234**

Lafon-Rochet, Château **31**

Lafran-Veyrolles **261**

Lageder, Alois **385**

Lagrange, Château **31**

Lagrange, Château **63**

Laibach **727**

Laible, Andreas **496**

Lail Vineyards **561**

Lake Breeze **639**

Lake's Folly **687**

Lallement **177**

Lamarche, François **118**

Lambardi, Maurizio **352**

Lambert Bridge **542**

Lambourne Family **571**

Lambrays, Domaine des **118**

Lambruschi, Ottaviano **324**

Lame Delisle Boucard, Domaine **195**

Lamoreaux Landing **604**

Lamothe, Chateau **44**

Lamothe-Guignard, Chateau **31**

Lamy, Hubert et Olivier **118**

Lamy-Pillot, René **140**

Lanari **409**

Lancaster Estate **542**

Landmann, Seppi **163**

Lanciola **352**

Landmark **534**

Lanessan, Château **31**

Lang, Helmut **518**

Langlois-Château **195**

Langoa-Barton, Château **32**

Langwerth von Simmern **505**

Lano, Gianluigi **324**

Lanson **170**

Lapeyre, Domaine Luc **273**

Lapierre, Hubert **151**

Lapierre, Marcel **151**

Laporte, Domaine **273**

Larcis-Ducasse, Château **63**

Lark Hill **689**

Larmande, Château **63**

Larmandier-Bernier **170**

Laroche, Domaine **84**

Laroche, Michel **618**

Larredya, Domaine **284**

Larrivet Haut-Brion, Château **32**

Larue, Domaine **140**

Lascombes, Château **44**

Lassarat, Domaine Roger **148**

Latour Saint-Martin **195**

Latour, Château **32**

Latour, Louis **119**

Latour-à-Pomerol, Château **55**

Latour-Giraud **119**

Latour-Martillac, Château **33**

Laulan, Domaine de **284**

Laurel Glen **534**

Laurent, Dominique **119**

Laurent-Perrier **171**

Lavacchio **371**

Laville Haut-Brion, Château **33**

Lavoro & Salute **425**

Lawson's Dry Hills **718**

Lazy Creek **542**

Le Boncie, Podere **371**

Le Bonheur **727**

Le Calcinaie **371**

Le Calvane **371**

Le Casalte **371**

Le Cinciole **371**

Le Clos de Caveau, Domaine **244**

Le Corti **353**

Le Dôme **55**

Le Filigare **353**

Le Fonti, Fattoria **353**

Le Fonti, Azienda Agricola **371**

Le Gallais **499**

Le Grys **717**

Le Macchiole **353**

Le Pupille **354**

Le Querce, Tenute **420**

Le Ragose **395**

Le Riche **728**

Le Salette **385**

Le Terrazze **404**

Le Trame **371**

Le Vieux Donjon **244**

Le Vigne di San Pietro **395**

Lea, Domaine **262**

Leacocks **465**

Leaping Lizard **700**

Leasingham **640**

Lebreton, J Y **195**

Leccia, Domaine **273**

Lechenaut, Domaine **140**

Leclerc Briant **177**

Leconfield **640**

Leda Viñas Viejas **441**

Leeuwin Estate **697**

Leflaive, Domaine **121**

Leflaive, Olivier **120**

Legland, Bernard **84**

Legoeuil, Domaine Catherine **244**

Legrand, René-Noel **195**

Legras **177**

Lehmann, Peter **640**

Leitz, Weingut Josef **496**

Lemencier, Jacques **220**

Lengs & Cooter **657**

Leonardo da Vinci, Cantine **371**

Leone de Castris **427**

Leonetti Cellars **598**

Leopardi Dittajuti **409**

Léoville-Barton, Château **33**

Léoville-las-Cases, Château **34**

Léoville-Poyferré, Château **34**

Leroy, Domaine **121**

Les Aphillanthes, Domaine **235**

Les Cailloux **235**

Les Clefs d'Or, Domaines **244**

Les Creisses, Domaine **262**

Les Crêtes **324**

Les Goubert, Domaine **236**

Les Grands Bois, Domaines **244**

Les Hautes Cances, Domaines **244**

Les Pallières **236**

Les Verdots **284**

Lesec Selections, Patrick **235**

Levet, Bernard **220**

Lewelling **571**

Lewis Cellars **561**

Liards, Domaine des **195**

Librandi **421**

Lichtlé, François **163**

Lignier, Hubert **122**

Lilbert **177**

Lilian-Ladouys, Château **44**

Limerick Lane **542**

Lindemans (Coonawarra & Padthaway) **641**

Lindemans (Murray Darling) **671**

Lindemans (Hunter Valley) **689**

Lingenfelder **505**

Lionnet, Domaine Jean **220**

Liot, Château **44**

Liparita **571**

Lis Neris **395**

Lisini **355**

Littorai **542**

Livernano **355**

Livingston Moffett **561**

Livon **395**

Lockwood **589**

Lodola Nuova **362**

Loewen, Weingut Carl **505**

Loimer **515**

Lokoya **562**

Long Vineyards **571**

Long-Depaquit **84**

Longoria **589**

Longridge **728**

Longue Toque, Domaine **244**

Loosen, Dr **497**
López de Heredia/Viña Tondonia **448**
Loredan Gasparini **395**
Lorenzon **395**
Lorenzon, Domaine **140**
Los Vascos **618**
Lost Lake **700**
Loubens, Château **63**
Louvière, Château la **34**
Löwenstein, Furst **505**
Lubiana, Stefano **672**
Luca **610**
Lucangeli Aymerich di Laconi **409**
Lumière **521**
Lumpp, François **122**
Luna **562**
Luneau, Pierre **195**
Lungarotti **409**
Lurton, Bodega **617**
Lusco do Miño **448**
Lustau, Emilio **441**
Lynch-Bages, Château **34**
Lynch-Moussas, Château **34**
Lynmar Winery **534**
Lyonnat, Château du **63**

M

Ma Vérité **36**
Macle, Domaine Jean **284**
MacCrostie **571**
McCray Ridge **542**
McCrea Cellars **601**
McDowell **542**
McKinlay **601**
McLean's Farm **657**
McWilliam's Mount Pleasant **687**
Maculan **386**
Madeira Wine Company **465**
Mader, Jean-Luc **163**
Madfish **697**
Madone, Domaine de la **151**

Madonia, Giovanna **407**
Maffini, Luigi **427**
Magaña **448**
Magdelaine, Château **56**
Maglieri **641**
Magnien, Domaine Michel et Fils **122**
Magnien, Jean-Paul **140**
Magnin, Domaine Louis **284**
Magpie Estate **657**
Mailly Grand Cru **177**
Main Ridge **672**
Maîtres Vigneronnes de Saint-Tropez **274**
Majella **642**
Malandes, Domaine des **85**
Malartic-Lagravière, Château **35**
Malescot-Saint-Exupéry, Château **35**
Malle, Château de **35**
Malvirà **309**
Manarine, Domaine La **237**
Manciat, Jean **151**
Manciat-Poncet **151**
Mancini, Fattoria **404**
Mann, Domaine Albert **159**
Mansion House Bay **718**
Mantellassi **371**
Manzone, Giovanni **309**
MAPA **618**
Mapema **619**
Marbuzet, Château **44**
Marcadet, Alain **195**
Marcarini **310**
Marcassin **535**
Marcevol, Domaine **274**
Marchand, Jean-Philippe **140**
Marchesi di Grésy **310**
Marchesi Pancrazi **371**
Marcoux, Domaine de **236**
Marengo, Mario **324**
Marfée, Domaine de la **262**
Margaine **177**
Margan Family **689**

Margaux, Château **36**

Margerand, Jean-Pierre **151**

Marietta Cellars **542**

Marimar Torres **535**

Marion **395**

Marionnet, Henry **195**

Markham Vineyards **572**

Maroslavac-Leger **140**

Marqués de Cáceres **448**

Marqués de Griñón **441**

Marqués de Murrieta **442**

Marqués de Riscal **442**

Marqués de Vargas **448**

Marquis-de-Terme, Château **44**

Marronniers, Domaine des **84**

Marsau, Château **64**

Marsiliana, Tenuta **353**

Martinborough Vineyard **710**

Martinelli **535**

Martinetti, Franco M **310**

Martínez **477**

Martínez Bujanda **448**

Martini, Lorenz **387**

Martini, Louis M **571**

Martray, Laurent **151**

Mas Amiel **263**

Mas Blanc, Domaine du **263**

Mas Bruguière **263**

Mas Carlot, Domaine du **274**

Mas Champart **264**

Mas Crémat **274**

Mas d'En Gil **448**

Mas d'Espanet **265**

Mas de Boislauzon **244**

Mas de Daumas Gassac **265**

Mas de Fournel **274**

Mas de Gourgonnier **274**

Mas de Guiot **274**

Mas de l'Ecriture **274**

Mas de la Dame **264**

Mas de Libian **244**

Mas de Martin **274**

Mas de Mortiès **266**

Mas des Bressades **274**

Mas des Chimères **274**

Mas Foulaquier **274**

Mas Granier **274**

Mas Haut-Buis **265**

Mas Igneus **449**

Mas Jullien **265**

Mas Martinet **442**

Mas Mouries **266**

Mascarello, Bartolo **311**

Mascarello, Giuseppe & Figli **311**

Masciarelli **409**

Masi **386**

Maso Besler **388**

Mason Cellars **572**

Masseria Li Veli **427**

Masseria Pepe **414**

Massi di Mandorlaia **342**

Massia Vecchia **371**

Masson-Blondelet **195**

Mastroberardino **421**

Mastrojanni **355**

Matakana Estate **717**

Matanzas Creek **536**

Matariki **717**

Matarromera **448**

Materne-Haegelin, Domaine **163**

Mathieu, Domaine **244**

Mathieu, Serge **171**

Matrot, Domaine **123**

Matthews Cellars **601**

Matua Valley **717**

Maucaillou, Château **44**

Maume, Bertrand **140**

Mauro **443**

Maurodos **443**

Maximin Grünhaus **497**

Maxwell **643**

Mayacamus **572**

Mayo Family 542

Meerea Park 687

Meerlust 722

Meinert 722

Melini 371

Melka 572

Mellot, Alphonse 191

Melton, Charles 642

Méo-Camuzet 123

Mer Soleil Winery 583

Meridian Vineyards 589

Merino, Miguel 448

Merkelbach, Alfred 505

Merlin 148

Merlin Cherrier, Domaine 195

Merlini 371

Merrill, Geoff 643

Merryvale 572

Merwe, Nico Van Der 723

Métaireau, Louis 195

Metier Wines 672

Métrat, Domaine Bernard 151

Meulenhof 505

Meyer-Fonné 164

Meyer-Näkel 505

Meyney, Château 44

Miani 395

Michael, Peter 536

Michel, Robert 220

Michelot, Alain 140

Michel-Schlumberger 542

Mikulski, François 123

Mildara 637

Millbrook 604

Mille-Roses, Château 44

Millot, Jean-Marc 140

Mills Reef 717

Miner Family Vineyards 562

Minuto - Cascina Luisin, Luigi 324

Miramar 689

Mission Haut-Brion, Château la 36

Mission Hill 604

Mitchell 644

Mitchelton 672

Mittnacht-Klack, Domaine 164

Moccagatta 311

Moët et Chandon 171

Moines, Domaine aux 195

Molettieri, Salvatore 427

Molino, Mauro 311

Molitor, Markus 498

Mollet, Florian 195

Ornella Molon Traverso 388

Monardière, Domaine de la 244

Monbousquet, Château 56

Monbrison, Château 44

Mönchhof 498

Monchiero Carbone 325

Moncuit, Pierre 172

Mondavi, Robert 563

Mongiron, Château 64

Monnaie, Domaine de la 195

Mont d'Or, Domaine du 518

Montalcino, Cantina di 371

Montana 711

Montana Brancott Winery 711

Montaribaldi 324

Mont du Toit 728

Monte Bernardi 355

Monte Rossa 324

Montebaco, Bodegas 448

Montecalvi 371

Monteillet, Domaine du 215

Montepeloso 356

Montes 614

Montevertine 356

Montevetrano 422

Montgilet, Domaine de 195

MontGras 618

Monti 324

Monti, Antonio & Elio 405

Monticello 441, 572

Montille, Hubert de **124**

Montirius, Domaine **244**

Montpertuis, Domaine de **237**

Montrose, Château **36**

Montvac, Domaine de **244**

Montviel, Château **64**

Moon Mountain Vineyard **536**

Moorilla Estate **673**

Moorooduc Estate **680**

Moraga **589**

Mordorée, Domaine de la **237**

Moreau, Domaine Bernard et Fils **140**

Moreau, Louis, Domaine **85**

Morel, Albert **151**

Morey Blanc **125**

Morey, Bernard **124**

Morey, Domaine Marc **124**

Morey, Pierre **125**

Morey-Coffinet, Domaine Michel **140**

Morgan Winery **583**

Morgante **422**

Morgassi Superiore **324**

Morgenhof **723**

Moris Farms **356**

Moroder **409**

Morot, Domaine Albert **125**

Morris **673**

Mortet, Denis **126**

Mortet, Thierry **140**

Morton Estate **717**

Mosbacher, Georg **498**

Moschioni **395**

Mosnier, Sylvain **88**

Moss Brothers **700**

Moss Wood **698**

Mossio, Fratelli **324**

Mouchão, Herdade Do **477**

Moulin de Ciffre **266**

Moulin de la Gardette **237**

Moulin Haut-Laroque, Château **56**

Moulin Pey-Labrie, Château **56**

Moulin Rouge, Château du **44**

Moulin Saint-Georges, Château **56**

Moulin, Domaine du **244**

Moulinier, Guy **274**

Mt Difficulty **711**

Mount Eden Vineyards **583**

Mount Edward **712**

Mount Horrocks **643**

Mount Ida **680**

Mount Langhi Ghiran **673**

Mount Mary **674**

Mount Trio **700**

Mount Veeder Winery **572**

Mountadam **644**

Mountford **712**

Mouton, Domaine **220**

Mouton, Gérard **140**

Mouton-Rothschild, Château **37**

Mud House **717**

Mueller, Robert **536**

Muga **443**

Mugneret, Dr Georges **126**

Mugneret, Gérard **140**

Mugneret-Gibourg **126**

Mugnier, Jacques-Frédéric **128**

Mulderbosch **723**

Müller, Egon **499**

Müller-Catoir **499**

Mumm Napa **563**

Mumm, G H **172**

Murana, Salvatore **422**

Muratie Estate **728**

Muré, René **159**

Muri-Gries **395**

Murinais, Domaine du **216**

Murphy-Goode **541**

Murrieta's Well **589**

Mustiguillo **443**

Muzard et Fils, Domaine Lucien **140**

N

Nada, Fiorenzo **312**

Naddef, Philippe **140**

Nairac, Château **37**

Nalle Winery **541**

Nalys, Domaine de **244**

Nardi, Silvio **371**

Natter, Domaine Henry **191**

Nautilus **717**

Navarro Vineyards **541**

Nederburg **728**

Neethlingshof **728**

Negri, Nino **312**

Negro & Figli, Angelo **312**

Neirano, Tenute **324**

Nepenthe **644**

Neudorf **712**

Neumayer **514**

Neveu, Roger **195**

Newlan **572**

Newton **563**

Neyers **572**

Ngatarawa **717**

Nichols Winery **589**

Nicholson River Winery **680**

Nicolas Feuillatte **177**

Niebaum-Coppola Estate **563**

Niedermayr, Josef **387**

Niellon, Michel **128**

Niepoort **465**

Niero-Pinchon, Domaine **216**

Nieto Senetiner **614**

Nigl **515**

Nikolaihof **516**

Ninth Island **675**

Nittardi **371**

Nittnaus, Anita & Hans **518**

Nobilo **717**

Noblet, Gilles **151**

Noon **658**

Norman **589**

Norton, Bodega **617**

Nottola **371**

Nova **572**

Nozzole, Tenuta di **347**

Nyetimber **522**

O

Oakford **572**

Oasi degli Angeli **405**

Oberto, Andrea **313**

Oddero, Fratelli **313**

Odfjell Vineyards **615**

Odoardi **427**

Ogereau, Domaine **192**

Ogier, Domaine Michel **216**

Ojai **584**

Old Kent River **700**

Oliveira, Perreira D' **477**

Oliveto **371**

Olivier, Château **44**

Olssens of Bannockburn **717**

Omrah **699**

Opitz, Willi **518**

Optima **542**

Opus One **564**

Oratoire Saint-Martin, Domaine de l' **238**

Oremus **522**

Orenga de Gaffory **274**

Orlando **645**

Ormes-de-Pez, Château les **44**

Ormes-Sorbet, Château les **44**

Ornellaia, Tenuta dell' **357**

Orsat, Caves **518**

Orsolani **313**

Osborne **448**

Osborns **680**

Osicka, Paul **680**

Ostertag **160**

Otazu **448**

Ott, Domaine **274**

Ouches, Domaine des **192**

Overgaauw **728**

P

Pabiot, Domaine Jean **195**

Pacenti, Siro **357**

Pacific Echo **537**

Paço de Teixeró **469**

Pago de Carraovejas **448**

Pahlmeyer **564**

Paillard, Bruno **172**

Paitin **314**

Palacio, Bodegas **448**

Palacios Remondo **444**

Palacios, Alvaro **444**

Palari **422**

Palazzo Vecchio **371**

Palazzone **409**

Palladino **324**

Pallister Estate **717**

Palmer (Champagne) **177**

Palmer (Long Island) **604**

Palmer Wines (Margaret River) **700**

Palmer, Château **37**

Paloma **572**

Panizzi **371**

Panther Creek **598**

Panzanello **371**

Paola di Mauro **408**

Paoletti **572**

Papapietro Perry **536**

Pape-Clément, Château **37**

Paracombe **658**

Paradigm **564**

Paradise Enough **680**

Paradiso, Fattoria **409**

Paraiso Springs **589**

Parent, Domaine Jean et Annick **140**

Parent, François **112**

Paret, Alain **220**

Paringa Estate **674**

Paris, Vincent **220**

Parize, Domaine Père et Fils **140**

Parker Coonwarra Estate **645**

Parker, Fess **589**

Parusso, Armando **314**

Pascal, Domaine Jean et Fils **140**

Pask, C J **717**

Passing Clouds **680**

Passion de Prieuré Malesan **57**

Passot, Alain **152**

Paternoster **423**

Pato, Louis **466**

Patz and Hall **565**

Paulett **658**

Paulinshof, Weingut **505**

Pauly-Bergweiler, Dr **499**

Paumanok **604**

Pavelot, Jean-Marc **127**

Pavie, Château **57**

Pavie-Decesse, Château **57**

Pavie-Macquin, Château **58**

Pavillon-Mercurol, Domaine **220**

Pazode Señorans **448**

Peachy Canyon Winery **584**

Pecchenino, Fratelli **314**

Pecorari, Pierpaolo **395**

Pecota Robert **572**

Pegasus Bay **713**

Pegaü, Domaine du **238**

Pegos Claros **473**

Peju **572**

Pélaquié, Domaine **244**

Pelissero **315**

Pellé, Henry **192**

Pellegrini **604**

Peller Estates **604**

Penfolds **645**

Penin, Château **62**

Penley Estate **646**

Penner-Ash **598**

Pepi **572**

Pepper Bridge Winery **598**

Perdrix, Domaine des **132**

Père Caboche, Domaine **244**

Père Pape, Domaine du 244
Pérez Pascuas 444
Pernot, Domaine Paul et Fils 128
Perret, Domaine André 216
Perrier, Joseph 173
Perrières 267
Perrier-Jouët 173
Perrin, Domaine 238
Perrin, Roger 244
Perrone, Elio 324
Perrot-Minot 128
Pertaringa 658
Pertimali 358
Pertinace, Vignaioli Elvio 325
Pervini 414
Pesquier, Domaine 244
Petaluma 647
Petit Val, Domaine du 196
Petits Quarts, Domaine des 196
Petit-Village, Château 58
Petra 372
Petroio, Fattoria di 372
Petrolo 358
Pétrus, Château 58
Pewsey Vale 656
Peyrabon, Château 44
Peyre Rose, Domaine de 267
Pez, Château de 44
Pezzi King 542
Pfaffenheim 164
Pfaffl 518
Pfeffingen, Weingut 505
Phélan-Ségur, Château 44
Phelps, Joseph 565
Philipponnat 173
Piaggia 372
Pian delle Vigne 334
Piancornello 372
Piaugier, Domaine de 238
Picardy 698
Piccinini 274

Pichler, F-X 516
Pichler, Rudi 518
Pichon, Christophe 220
Pichon, Philippe 220
Pichon-Longueville, Château 38
Pichon-Longueville-Lalande, Château 38
Pichot, Domaine 196
Picq, Gilbert & Ses Fils 86
Pierazzuoli, Enrico 372
Pieri, Agostina 372
Pieropan 387
Pierro 698
Piétri-Géraud 274
Pieve del Vescovo 405
Pieve Santa Restituta 358
Pikes 647
Pillitteri Estates 604
Pillot, Fernand & Laurent 140
Pillot, Jean et Fils 128
Pillot, Paul 141
Pin Beausoleil, Château le 64
Pin, Château le 58
Pinard, Vincent 192
Pine Ridge 565
Pineraie, Domaine 284
Pinon, Domaine 196
Pinson, Domaine Louis 86
Pintas 467
Pio Cesare 315
Piper-Heidsieck 174
Pipers Brook 674
Pira 324
Pira, E & Figli 315
Pira, Luigi 316
Pirineos 449
Piron, Dominique 152
Pirramimma 658
Pithon, Domaine Olivier 274
Pithon, Jo 196
Pittnauer 518
Pivot, Jean-Charles 152

Plageoles, Domaine **284**

Plaisir de Merle **728**

Planeta **423**

Plantagenet **698**

Plumpjack **566**

Plunkett **680**

Poças **477**

Pochon, Domaine Étienne **217**

Pöckl, Josef **518**

Poggerino **358**

Poggio al Sole **359**

Poggio Antico **372**

Poggio Bertaio **409**

Poggio di Sotto **372**

Poggio Gagliardo **372**

Poggio San Polo **372**

Poggio Scalette **359**

Poggiolungo **372**

Poggiopiano **360**

Pointe, Château La **64**

Pojer & Sandri **387**

Pol Roger **174**

Poliziano **360**

Polz, Erich & Walter **518**

Pommery **174**

Pommier, Denis **86**

Ponsot, Domaine **129**

Pontet-Canet, Château **38**

Ponzi **599**

Poole's Rock **689**

Porcupine Ridge **720**

Portet, Dominique **680**

Potel, Nicolas **129**

Potel-Aviron **152**

Potensac, Château **39**

Poudéroux, Domaine **274**

Poujeaux, Château **39**

Prà **395**

Prager, Weingut **516**

Pratesi **372**

Prats & Symington **476**

Pressac, Château **64**

Pretterebner **518**

Prevostini, Mamete **324**

Pride Mountain **572**

Prieler **518**

Prieur, Domaine Paul **196**

Prieuré de Saint-Jean-de-Bébian **267**

Prieuré-Lichine, Château **39**

Primo Estate **648**

Primo Palatum **283**

Principiano, Ferdinando **316**

Producteurs Plaimont **284**

Produttori del Barbaresco **293**

Prose, Domaine de la **274**

Providence **717**

Prudhon, Henri **141**

Prüm, Joh. Jos **500**

Prüm, S A **505**

Prunier, Michel **141**

Prunotto **316**

Puffeney, Domaine Jacques **284**

Puiatti **395**

Punset **324**

Punters Corner **658**

Puygueraud, Château **59**

Pycnantha Hill **658**

Q

Quady **584**

Quails' Gate **604**

Quarles Harris **476**

Quénard, André et Michel **284**

Querbach **505**

Quercia al Poggio **372**

Querciabella **360**

Quilceda Creek Vintners **599**

Quinault l'Enclos, Château **59**

Quinta da Cortezia **467**

Quinta da Gaivosa **458**

Quinta da Lagoalva **477**

Quinta da Ponte Pedrinho **473**

Quinta da Portela da Vilariça **471**
Quinta da Terrugem **459**
Quinta da Viçosa **473**
Quinta das Bágeiras **477**
Quinta das Maias **473**
Quinta de Abrigada **477**
Quinta de Baixo **478**
Quinta de Cabriz **467**
Quinta de Chocapalha **478**
Quinta de Foz de Arouce **473**
Quinta de la Rosa **468**
Quinta de Paços **478**
Quinta de Pancas **478**
Quinta de Pellada **478**
Quinta de Roriz **468**
Quinta de Vimioso **473**
Quinta do Basileiro **468**
Quinta do Carmo **478**
Quinta do Côtto **469**
Quinta do Crasto **469**
Quinta do Encontro **468**
Quinta do Infantado **469**
Quinta do Mouro **478**
Quinta do Noval **470**
Quinta do Portal **470**
Quinta do Vale da Raposa **458**
Quinta do Vale Doña Maria **471**
Quinta do Vale Meão **471**
Quinta do Vallado **471**
Quinta do Vesuvio **472**
Quinta dos Carvalhais **474**
Quinta dos Roques **472**
Quintarelli **388**
Quintessa **566**
Quivira **542**
Qupé **584**

R

Raats Family Wines **728**
Rabasse-Charavin, Domaine **239**
Rabaud-Promis, Château **39**

Rabiega, Domaine **267**
Raccaro, Dario **395**
Race, Laurence et Denis **87**
Rafanelli, A **537**
Ragot, Domaine **141**
Rahoul, Château **44**
Raifault, Domaine **196**
Raïmat **449**
Rainoldi, Aldo **317**
Ramage-la-Batisse, Château **44**
Rame, Château la **64**
Ramey **566**
Ramonet **130**
Ramos, João Portugal **473**
Ramos Pinto **473**
Random Ridge **542**
Rapet, Domaine Père et Fils **130**
Raquillet, François **141**
Rasmussen, Kent **572**
Raspail-Ay, Domaine **239**
Ratti, Renato **317**
Rauzan Despagne, Château **64**
Rauzan-Gassies, Château **44**
Rauzan-Ségla, Château **39**
Ravanès **274**
Raveneau, Domaine François **87**
Ravenswood **537**
Ravenswood Lane **648**
Raymond **572**
Raymond-Lafon, Château **40**
Rayne-Vigneau, Château de **40**
RBJ Vintners **658**
Real Companhia Velha **474**
Rebholz, Ökonomierat **500**
Rectorie, Domaine de la **268**
Red Hill Estate **680**
Red Metal **717**
Redbank **680**
Redde, Domaine Michel **196**
Redgate **700**
Redwood Valley **717**

Reif Estate **605**

Reignac, Château **59**

Reinert, Johann Peter **505**

Reininger **601**

Relagnes, Domaine des **244**

Réméjeanne, Domaine **239**

Remelluri **445**

Remillier, Jean-Paul **220**

Remirez de Ganuza **449**

Remizières, Domaine des **217**

Remoriquet, Henri et Gilles **141**

René, Domaine Roy **188**

Renjarde, Domaine de **233**

Renou, René **196**

Renwood **585**

Respide-Médeville, Château **44**

Ress, Balthasar **505**

Revello, Fratelli **317**

Reverdy, Pascal et Nicholas **196**

Reverie **572**

Rex Hill **599**

Reyes, Teófilo **449**

Reynella **649**

Reynolds **689**

Reynon, Château **60**

Ribbon Vale **698**

Ribeauvillé **164**

Ricchino **324**

Ricci Curbastro **324**

Richard, Hervé **220**

Richaud, Marcel **240**

Richeaume, Domaine **268**

Richmond Grove **658**

Richou, Domaine **196**

Richter, Max Ferd. **500**

Riddoch **638**

Ridge Vineyards **585**

Ridgeback **728**

Ridgeview **523**

Riecine **361**

Rieflé, Domaine **164**

Rieussec, Château **40**

Riffault, Claude **196**

Rijckaert, Domaine **148**

Rimbert, Domaine **268**

Rinaldi, Guiseppe **324**

Rioja Alta **445**

Riojanas, Bodegas **449**

Rion, Domaine et Fils **131**

Rion, Patrice & Michèle **131**

Rippon Vineyard **717**

Riseccoli **372**

Rivera **427**

Rivière, Château de la **60**

Roally, Domaine de **151**

Robert, Alain **177**

Robert-Denogent, Domaine **149**

Robin, Gilles **220**

Roblet-Monnot **141**

Roc D'Anglade **274**

Roc de Cambes, Château **60**

Rocca delle Macìe **372**

Rocca di Castagnoli **372**

Rocca di Montegrossi **362**

Rocca, Albino **318**

Rocca, Bruno **318**

Rocche Costamagna **324**

Rocche dei Manzoni **318**

Roccolo Grassi **388**

Rochemorin, Château de **44**

Rocher Bellevue Figeac, Château **64**

Rocher, Domaine Eric **220**

Rocher, Dominique **240**

Roches Bleues, Domaine les **152**

Roches Neuves, Domaine des **193**

Rochford **680**

Rochioli, J **538**

Rockford **649**

Rocking Horse **572**

Roda **445**

Rodet, Antonin **131**

Rodriguez, Telmo **449**

Roederer Estate **538**
Roederer, Louis **174**
Roger, Jean-Max **196**
Rol Valentin, Chateau **64**
Rolet, Domaine **284**
Rollan-de-By, Château **40**
Rolly-Gassmann **160**
Romanée-Conti, Domaine de la **132**
Romate, Sanchez **449**
Rombauer **572**
Romer-du-Hayot, Château **44**
Roncée, Domaine du **196**
Ronchi di Manzano **389**
Ronco del Gelso **389**
Ronco del Gnemiz **395**
Ronco delle Betulle **395**
Rooiberg **728**
Ros, Domaine Elian da **284**
Rosa del Golfo **427**
Rosemount (McLaren Vale) **649**
Rosemount Estate **688**
Rosenblum Cellars **585**
Rosiers, Domaine des **151**
Ross, Stephen **589**
Rostaing, René **217**
Rothbury Estate **689**
Rotllán I Torra **449**
Roty, Joseph **141**
Rouge Garance, Domaine **244**
Rouget, Château **64**
Rouget, Emmanuel **132**
Roulot, Domaine **133**
Roumier, Domaine **133**
Rousseau, Domaine Armand **133**
Rouvinez **518**
Roxan, Casa Vinicola **409**
Royal Tokaji Wine Company **523**
Royer-Girardin, Domaine Aleth le **140**
Rubino, Tenute **428**
Rudd Estate **572**
Ruffino, Tenementi **362**

Ruinart **175**
Russiz Superiore **389**
Rust en Vrede **728**
Rustenberg **724**
Rutini, Felipe **617**
Rutz Cellars **542**
Rymill **650**

S

Sablonnettes, Domaine des **196**
Sabon, Roger **240**
Saddleback Cellars **572**
Sadie Family Wines **724**
Saint-Clair **717**
St Clement **572**
Saint-Désirat, Cave Co-operative de **220**
Saint-Amant, Domaine **244**
Saint-André de Figuière **274**
Saint-Andrieu, Domaine **274**
Saint-Antoine **274**
Saint-Augustin **522**
Saint-Benoît, Domaine **244**
Sainte-Anne, Domaine **241**
St Francis Vineyards **539**
Saint-Gayan, Domaine **244**
St Hallett **650**
St Innocent **601**
Saint-Luc, Domaine de **244**
Saint-Martin La Garrigue **274**
Saint-Pierre, Château **41**
Saint-Roch, Domaine **244**
Saint-Sifferein, Domaine des **245**
St Supéry **572**
Saint-Vincent, Domaine **196**
St. Urbans-Hof **501**
Saintsbury **566**
Saladini Pilastri **409**
Salentein, Bodegas **617**
Sales, Château de **64**
Salicutti, Podere **372**
Salitage **700**

Salomon, Undhof **518**

Salon **175**

Saltram **650**

Salviano **409**

Salvioni **363**

Salwey, Weingut **505**

Samos Co-operative **523**

San Fabiano Calcinaia **363**

San Felice **363**

San Fereolo **319**

San Filippo - Fanti **364**

San Filippo - Rosi **372**

San Francesco, Fattoria **428**

San Gervasio **364**

San Giusto a Rentennano **364**

San Guido, Tenuta **365**

San Leonardo **390**

San Michele Appiano, Produttori **390**

San Patrignano **406**

San Romano **324**

Sandeman **474**

Sandrone, Luciano **318**

Sanford Winery **586**

Sang des Cailloux **241**

Sansonnet, Château **64**

Sansonnière, Domaine de la **193**

Sant' Agata, Cantine **324**

Sant' Antonio, Tenuta **395**

Sant' Evasio, Cantine **324**

Santa Barbara **409**

Santa Barbara Winery **589**

Santa Carolina **618**

Santa Cruz Mountains Vineyard **589**

Santa Duc, Domaine **241**

Santa Rita **615**

Santadi **424**

Santé, Bernard **152**

Enrico Santini **365**

São João, Caves **478**

Saracco **319**

Sarda-Malet **274**

Sarrazin, Domaine Michel et Fils **141**

Sartarelli **406**

Sassetti, Livio **358**

Sassicaia **365**

Satta, Michele **365**

Saucelito Canyon **589**

Sauer, Horst **501**

Saumaize, Jacques et Natalie **151**

Saumaize-Michelin **149**

Sausal **537**

Sautereau, Domaine **196**

Sauzet, Étienne **134**

Savary, Francine et Olivier **88**

Saxenburg **724**

Scagliola **324**

Scala Dei **449**

Scarzello e Figli, Giorgio **324**

Scavino, Paolo **319**

Schaefer, Willi **502**

Schaetzel, Domaine Martin **164**

Schäfer-Fröhlich **505**

Scharzhof **499**

Scherer, André **164**

Scherrer Vineyard **542**

Schiopetto **391**

Schistes, Domaine des **269**

Schleret, Domaine Charles **164**

Schloss Gobelsburg **517**

Schloss Johannisberg **505**

Schloss Lieser, Weingut **503**

Schlosss Reinhartshausen **505**

Schloss Saarstein **505**

Schloss Schönborn **502**

Schloss Vollrads **505**

Schlossgut Diel **502**

Schlumberger, Domaines **164**

Schmitt's Kinder **505**

Schoffit, Domaine **161**

Schramsberg **567**

Schubert, Von **497**

Schueller, Gérard **164**

Scopetone **372**
Scotchmans Hill **675**
Scott, Allan **717**
Screaming Eagle **567**
Scrimaglio, F & M **324**
Seavey **572**
Sebaste, Mauro **324**
Sebaste, Sylla **324**
Sebastopol **542**
Secondé, François **175**
Seghesio **538**
Seghesio, Aldo & Riccardo **320**
Segonzac, Château **64**
Seguela, Domaine **269**
Seguin, Château **64**
Seifried Estate **717**
Selbach-Oster **503**
Selene **572**
Sella & Mosca **424**
Selosse, Jacques **176**
Selvapiana, Fattoria **366**
Seña **615**
Senard, Comte **134**
Señorío de San Vicente **449**
Seppelt **661**
Seppelt Great Western **675**
Sequoia Grove **572**
Sérafin, Christian **135**
Serafini & Vidotto **395**
Serègo Alighieri **386**
Serene, Domaine **600**
Seresin **713**
Sergue, Château **64**
Serraiola **372**
Serres Mazard **274**
Sertolis Salis **324**
Servin, Domaine **88**
Sette Ponti **366**
Settesoli **428**
Sebastiani **542**
Seven Hills **601**

Sevenhill Cellars **658**
Seville Estate **676**
Shadowfax **676**
Shafer **567**
Shaw & Smith **651**
Showket **572**
Sidónio de Sousa **475**
Siduri **539**
Sierra Vista **589**
Sieur d'Arques **269**
Sigalas-Rabaud, Château **42**
Signorello **572**
Sileni **717**
Silices de Quincy **193**
Silvan Ridge **601**
Silver Oak Cellars **568**
Silverado Vineyards **572**
Simi **542**
Simonsig **728**
Sine Qua Non **589**
Sineann **601**
Sinfarosa **414**
Sinskey, Robert **572**
Siran, Château **44**
Siyabonga **728**
Skalli-Fortant de France **274**
Skewis **542**
Skillogalee **658**
Smith Haut Lafitte, Château **41**
Smith W H **539**
Smith Woodhouse **475**
Smithbrook **700**
Snowden **572**
Sociando-Mallet, Château **42**
Sogrape **475**
Sokol Blosser **601**
Soldera **366**
Solitude **542**
Solitude, Domaine de la **244**
Sonoma-Cutrer **539**
Sorbaiano **372**

Sorg, Bruno 164
Sorin 274
Sorrel, Mark 217
Sorrenberg 680
Sottimano 320
Soulez, Pierre 196
Soulez, Yves 193
Southcorp 652
Soutiran-Pelletier 177
Spadafora 428
Sparr, Pierre 164
Specogna 395
Speri 395
Spice Route Company 725
Spoletoducale 409
Sportoletti 406
Spottswoode 568
Spring Mountain Vineyard 572
Spring Vale 680
Springfield 725
Staete Landt 717
Stag's Leap Wine Cellars 568
Staglin Family 568
Stanton & Killeen 680
Stark 728
Stavedog Lane 648
Steele 540
Steenberg 728
Stein, Weingut am 505
Stella Bella 700
Stellenzicht 725
Step Road 658
Stephan, Jean-Michel 220
Stephens, D R 572
Sterling Vineyards 572
Stonecroft 713
Stonehaven 658
Stonestreet 540
Stoney Ridge 605
Stonier 677
Stony Hill 569

Stonyridge 714
Storybook Mountain Vineyard 569
Stringy Brae 658
Stuhlmuller 542
Suau, Château 44
Suavia 395
Suckfizzle Augusta 700
Suduiraut, Château 42
Sumac Ridge 605
Summerfield 677
Summers Ranch 572
Suremain, Domaine de 141
Suremain, H et Y de 141
Suveraia 372
Swan, Joseph 542
Swanson 569
Symington 476
Szepsy, Istvan 522

T
Tablas Creek 586
Taburno, Cantina del 428
Tahblik 677
Taille aux Loups 194
Taillefer, Château 64
Tain l'Hermitage, Cave de 218
Taittinger 176
Talbot, Château 42
Talbott, Robert 586
Talenti 367
Taliano, Michele 325
Tallarook 678
Talley Vineyards 587
Talmard, Domaine Gérald et Philibert 151
Talmard, Domaine Paul et Mallory 151
Taltarni 678
Taluau, Joël 196
Tamarack Cellars 601
Tamellini 395
Tanner, Lane 587
Tarapacá 618

Tardieu-Laurent 241

Tardy, Jean 141

Tarius 542

Tarlant 177

Tarrawarra 678

Tarsus 449

Tasca d'Almerita 424

Tatachilla 652

Taurino, Cosimo 425

Tavignano 409

Tayac, Château 64

Taylor's 476

Taylors/Wakefield Cellars 658

Te Awa Farm 717

Te Mata 714

Te Motu Vineyard 717

Tedeschi 391

Telaro 425

Tement, Manfred 518

Tempé, Marc 164

Tempier, Domaine 270

Temple Bruer 658

Tempus Two 689

Tenaglia, Tenuta La 309

Tenuta di Trinoro 367

Tercic, Matijaz 391

Terlano, Cantina 392

Terme, Domaine du 245

Termeno, Cantina Produttori 395

Terra Gens 409

Terrabianca 372

Terraces, The 572

Terranoble 618

Terras Gauda 446

Terrazas de Los Andes, Bodega 617

Terre Cortesi Moncaro 409

Terre da Vino 325

Terre degli Svevi 428

Terre del Sillabo 372

Terre Inconnue, Domaine 270

Terre Rosse, Cascina delle 325

Terre Rosse, Vigneto delle 409

Terre Rouge, Domaine de la 587

Terrebrune, Domaine de 270

Terredora di Paolo 428

Terres Dorées, Domaine des 152

Tertre, Château du 44

Tertre-Dugay, Château 64

Tertre-Rôteboeuf, Château 60

Teruzzi e Puthod 372

Tesch 505

Testarossa 588

Testut, Philippe 88

Tête, Michel 152

Teyssier, Château 60

Teyssonières, Domaine les 245

T'Gallant 680

Thackrey, Sean 588

Thanisch, Dr. H 505

Thanisch, Erben 505

Thelema 726

Thévenet, Jean 150

Thibault, Domaine 196

Thibert, Domaine Père et Fils 150

Thiers, Jean-Louis 220

Thieuley, Château 61

Thistle Hill 689

Thomas, Domaine Charles 135

Three Choirs 523

Tiefenbrunner 395

Tikal 610

Tinel, Domaine Annick 196

Tingle-wood 700

Tinhof 518

Titus 572

Togni, Philip 570

Tollot-Beaut 136

Toques et Clochers 269

Torbreck 652

Torii Mor 601

Torino, Michel 616

Torlesse 717

Tormaresca 426
Toro Albalá 449
Torraccia 274
Torre de Oña, Bodega 445
Torre Quarto 428
Torreón de Paredes 618
Torres 446
Torres, Miguel 618
Torrevento 428
Tour Blanche, Château la 42
Tour de Mirambeau, Château 64
Tour du Bon, Domaine de la 271
Tour du Haut-Moulin, Château 44
Tour Figeac, Château la 64
Tour Haut-Brion, Château la 42
Tour-Haut-Caussan, Château 44
Tour-Du-Pin-Figeac, Château la 64
Tourelles, Domaine les 245
Trabucchi 395
Trapadis, Domaine du 242
Trapet, Domaine Père et Fils 136
Trapiche 617
Trappolini 408
Travaglini, Giancarlo 325
Tre Monti 409
Tremblay, Gérard 88
Trentadue 542
Trerose 372
Trevallon, Domaine de 271
Tria 542
Triacca 320
Tribut, Domaine Laurent 88
Triebaumer, Ernst 518
Triennes 274
Trimbach 161
Trinity Hill 717
Troplong-Mondot, Château 61
Trotanoy, Château 61
Trottevieille, Chateau 64
Truchard 572
Tua Rita 367

Tualatin 601
Tulloch, Keith 689
Tunnel, Domaine du 218
Turckheim 164
Turkey Flat 653
Turley Cellars 570
Turnbull 572
Turramurra Estate 680
Tyrrell's 688

U

Uberti 325
Uccelliera, Fattoria 372
Uiterwyk 728
Umani Ronchi 407
Umathum 518
Unger, Dr 518
Unison 714
Usseglio, Domaine Raymond 245
Usseglio, Pierre 242

V

Vacheron, Domaine 194
Vajra, G D 320
Val d'Orbieu 271
Val di Suga 372
Valandraud, Château de 62
Valdespino 454
Valdicava 368
Valdipiatta 372
Valdivieso 616
Valentini 407
Valette, Domaine 150
Valgiano, Tenuta di 368
Vall Llach, Celler 447
Vallarom 395
Valle dell' Acate 428
Valley Vineyards 523
Valli 717
Vallone 426
Vallouit, Domaine de 220
Valpantena, Cantina 395

Valpiculata **449**

Valpolicella, Cantina Sociale **396**

Valtellina, Fattoria **368**

Vannucci, Mauro **372**

Vaquer **274**

Varaldo, Rino **325**

Varramista, Fattoria **372**

Vasse Felix **699**

Vatan, Domaine André **196**

Vauroux, Domaine de **87**

Vavasour **715**

Vecchie Terre di Montefili **369**

Veenwouden **726**

Vega Sicilia, Bodegas **447**

Veglio, Mauro **321**

Velenosi, Ercole **409**

Velich **517**

Ventura, Jane **449**

Veramonte **618**

Verda, Domaine **245**

Verdignan, Château **44**

Vergelen **726**

Verget **136**

Veritas **653**

Vérité **540**

Vermentino, Cantina Sociale **428**

Vernay, Daniel **221**

Vernay, Domaine Georges **218**

Verquière, Domaine de **245**

Verrière, Domaine de la **245**

Verset, Noël **221**

Vesselle **177**

Vessigaud, Domaine **151**

Veuve Clicquot **176**

Viader **570**

Vial-Magnères **274**

Viberti, Eraldo **325**

Vidal Estate **715**

Vidal-Fleury **221**

Vie di Romans **392**

Vieille Cure, Château la **62**

Vieille-Julienne, Domaine de la **242**

Vietti **321**

Vieux Château Gaubert **44**

Vieux Château-Landon **44**

Vieux-Château-Certan **62**

Vieux Robin, Château **44**

Vieux-Télégraphe, Domaine du **242**

Vigil **589**

Vignalta **392**

Vigna Rionda – Massolino **322**

Vigna Runc **384**

Vignamaggio **372**

Vigneau-Chevreau, Domaine **196**

Viking **658**

Villa Arceno **372**

Villa Bel Air, Château **43**

Villa Cafaggio **369**

Villa Maria **715**

Villa Matilde **428**

Villa Monte Rico **373**

Villa Monteleone **396**

Villa Pillo **369**

Villa Poggio Salvi **337**

Villa Russiz **393**

Villa Sant' Anna **373**

Villa Simone **408**

Villa Sparina **325**

Villaine, Aubert et Pamela, de **137**

Villamagna **400**

Villard Estate **618**

Villard, François **219**

Villars, Château **64**

Villemaurine, Château **64**

Villeneuve, Domaine de **245**

Villiera **728**

Vilmart **177**

Viña Bajoz **449**

Viña Casablanca **616**

Viña Leyda **618**

Viña Pérezcruz **618**

Viña Quebrada de Macul **618**

Viña San Pedro **618**
Viña Solorca **449**
Viñas del Vero **449**
Vincent **135**
Vine Cliff **572**
Vineland **605**
Vineyard **29 572**
Vinha d'Ervideira **478**
Vinicola del Priorat **449**
Viniterra **617**
Vino Noceto **589**
Vins de Vienne, Les **219**
Vionery, Domaine Georges **152**
Virgin Hills **678**
Vissoux, Domaine du **152**
Vistalba, Domaine **617**
Vistorta **396**
Viticoltori Associati del Vulture **428**
Viu Manent **618**
Vocoret, Domaine **88**
Voerzio, Gianni **322**
Voerzio, Roberto **322**
Voge, Alain **219**
Vogüé, Domaine Comte George de **137**
Voillot, Joseph **141**
Von Strasser **572**
Voss Estate **718**
Vougeraie, Domaine de la **138**
Voyager Estate **700**

W

Wade Wines, John **700**
Wagner, Dr Heinz **504**
Waipara West **718**
Wakefield Cellars **658**
Walch, Elena **396**
Walla Walla Vintners **601**
Wandanna **373**
Waninga **658**
Warre **476**
Warrenmang **680**

Warwick Estate **727**
Water Wheel **681**
Waterford **728**
Watershed **700**
Weaver, Geoff **653**
Wegeler Erben, Geheimrat J **505**
Wehrheim, Dr **505**
Weil, Robert **503**
Weinbach, Domaine **162**
Weinert **617**
Wellington (Tasmania) **671**
Wellington Vineyards (California) **542**
Wendouree **654**
Westfield **700**
Whitcraft **589**
White Rock **572**
Whitehall Lane **572**
Whitehaven **718**
Wiemar, Hermann J **604**
Wignalls **700**
Wild Duck Creek **681**
Wild Horse Winery **589**
WillaKenzie Estate **601**
Willamette Valley Vineyard **601**
Willespie **700**
Williams & Humbert **449**
Williams Selyem **541**
Willows Vineyard **658**
Wilson Vineyard **658**
Windowrie **689**
Wirra Wirra **654**
Wirsching, Hans **506**
Wither Hills **716**
Wittmann, Weingut **504**
Wöhrwatg **506**
Wolf, J L **506**
Woodstock **655**
Woodward Canyon **600**
Woody Nook **700**
Wright, Ken **600**
Wynns **655**

X

Xanadu **700**

Y

Yacochuya **617**

Yalumba **656**

Yamhill Valley Vineyards **601**

Yarra Burn **679**

Yarra Yering **679**

Yarrabank **679**

Yarraman Estate **689**

Yellowglen **681**

Yering Station **679**

Yeringberg **680**

Yon Figeac, Château **64**

Yquem, Château d' **43**

Z

Zaca Mesa **589**

Zaccagnini & C. **408**

Zaccagnini, Ciccio **408**

Zamò, Le Vigne di **393**

ZD Wines **572**

Zecca, Conti **426**

Zema Estate **657**

Zenato **394**

Zerbina **407**

Zilliken **506**

Zinck, Paul **164**

Zind-Humbrecht **162**

Zondernaam **728**

Zuani **396**

Zündel, Christian **518**